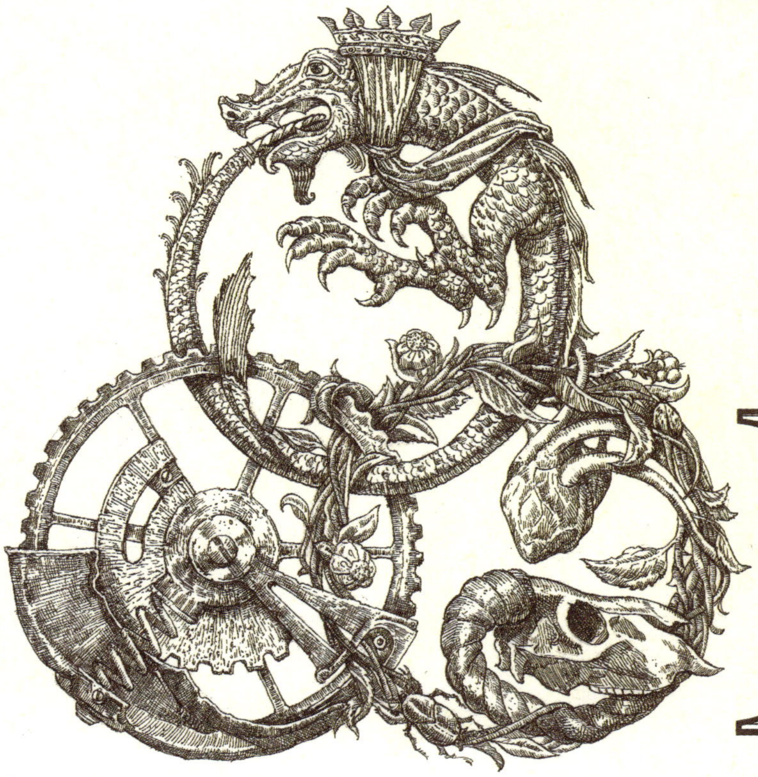

THE BOOK

INTRODUCTION

The story of humans is a story of discovery. No matter which planet, which timeline, in whichever branch of the multiverse you might find people, they'll be busy improving their lives. This is our great gift and our curse, depending on which way you look at it. We can never stop and be satisfied with what we have achieved — we'll keep sprinting faster, getting stronger, and growing bigger until we fall.

The story of civilization is a story of failures and rebirths. When one world is destroyed, a new one rises in its place. This is a universal law. Though I have tried many times, I've never managed to save a civilization from the fall. It is not in my power to salvage the old, but I can help the new grow and prosper, shorten and facilitate the path from dark ages to renaissance. This is how this book came to be — the ultimate guide to rebuilding civilization. I hope that it helps, that your civilization will remain standing, and if not, well, then at least you can add a few beautiful pages to the book.

DISCLAIMER

This book is designed to provide general information only. This information is provided and sold with the knowledge that the publisher and author do not offer any legal or other professional advice. In the case of a need for any such expertise, consult with the appropriate professional. This book does not contain all information available on every subject. This book has not been created to be specific to any individual's or organizations' situation or needs. Every effort has been made to make this book as accurate as possible. This book should serve only as a general guide and not as the ultimate source of subject information. This book contains information that might be dated and is intended only to educate and entertain. The author and publisher shall have no liability or responsibility to any person or entity regarding any loss or damage incurred, or alleged to have incurred, directly or indirectly, by the information contained in this book. You hereby agree to be bound by this disclaimer.

THE BOOK

The Ultimate Guide To Rebuilding Civilization

Quest edition

86-90 Paul Street, London, EC2A 4NE

United Kingdom

civilizationbook.com

ISBN 978-0-578-37745-2

9 780578 377452 90000>

THE BOOK

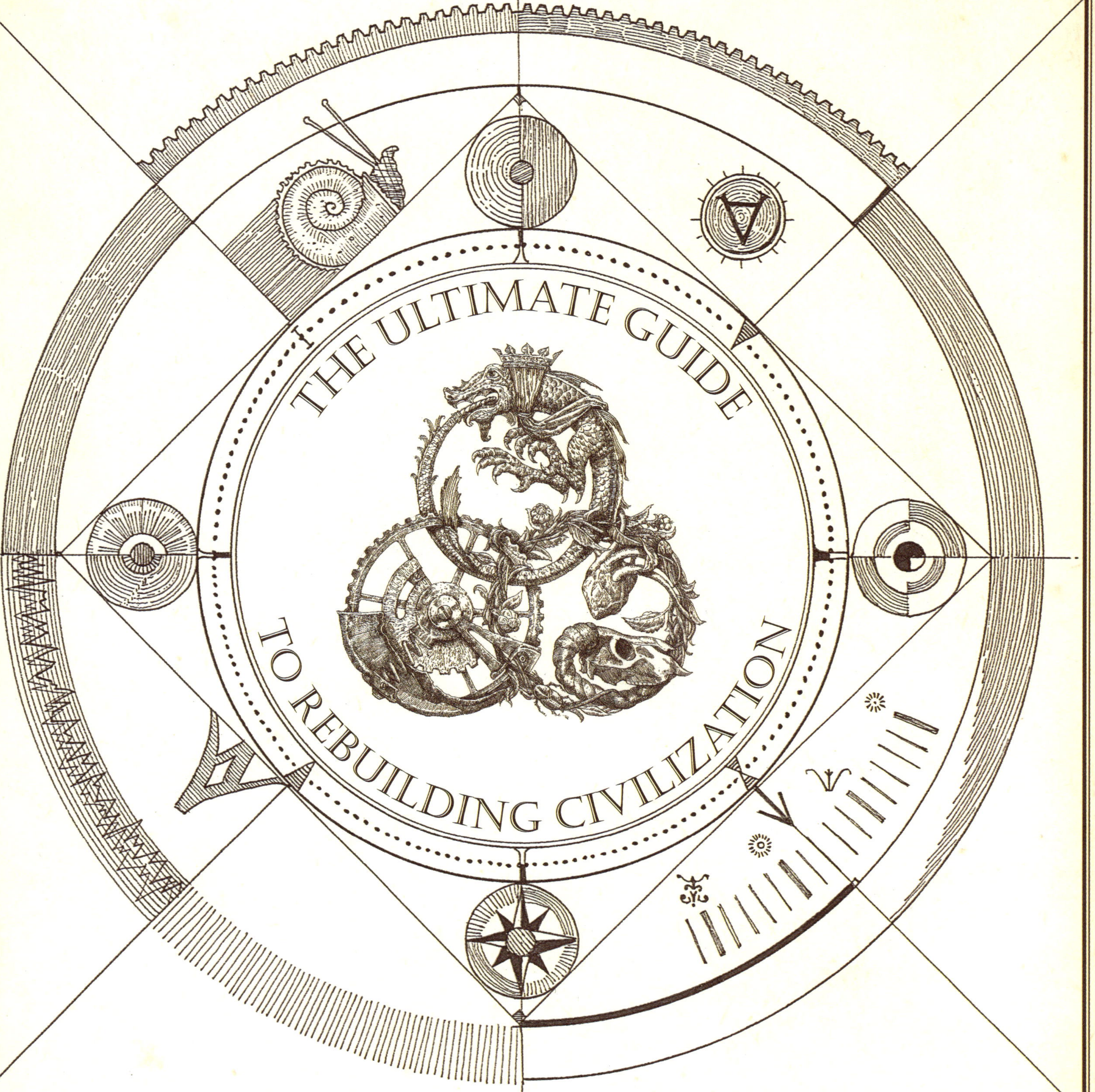

THE ULTIMATE GUIDE TO REBUILDING CIVILIZATION

HUNGRY MINDS

TABLE OF CONTENTS

FIRST THINGS

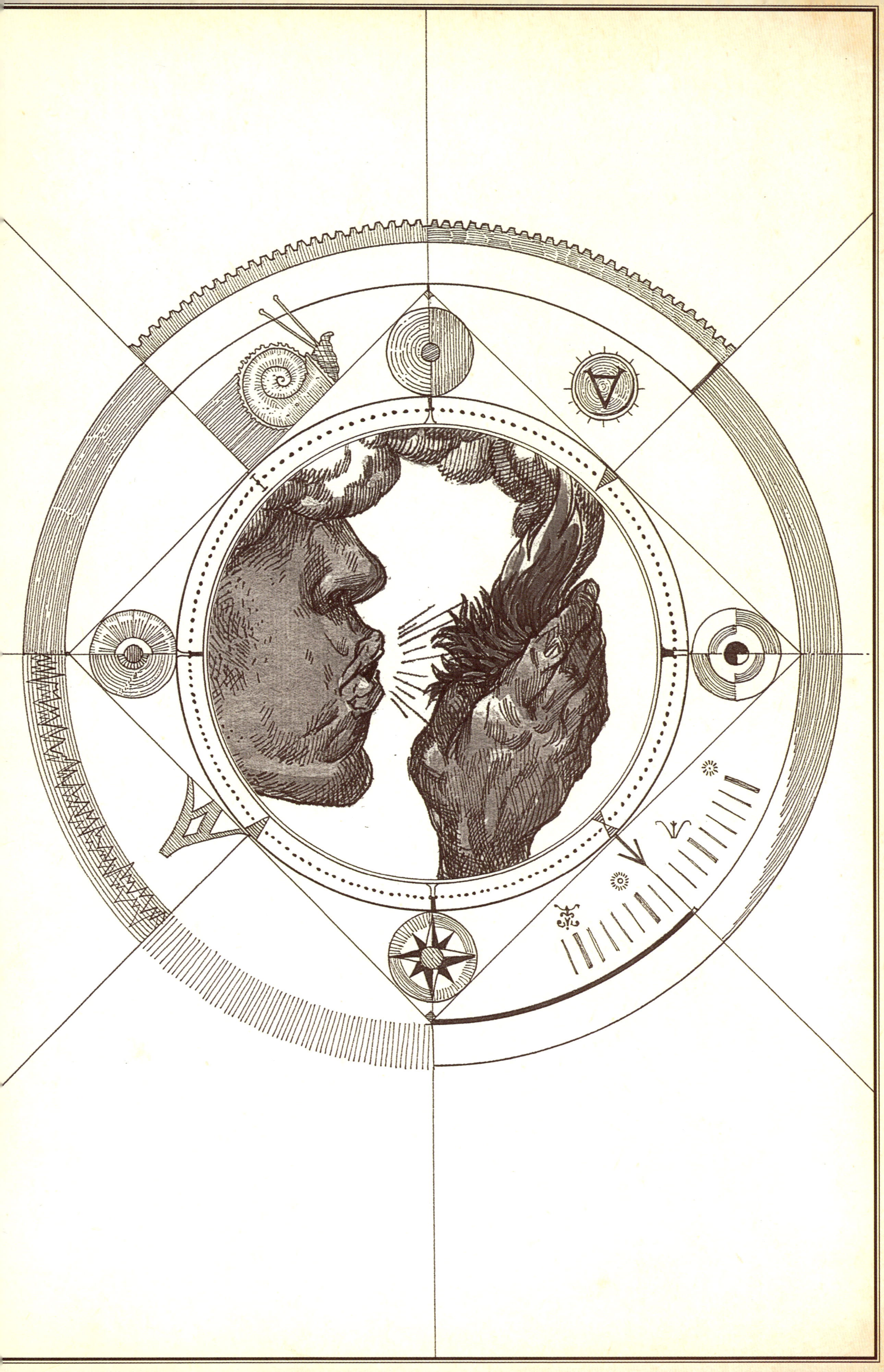

MAKING FIRE

A defining moment in history was when we tamed the first flame, and fire is behind much of what we do in a civilization. Suddenly, the darkness of night becomes manageable. Tribes gather near, food can be prepared and items and materials that were previously inaccessible are now within reach.

And so mankind has learned to harness fire's transformative powers. This arouses an insatiable desire to subjugate nature's most powerful forces. When put in the hands of the people, this balance between creative and destructive forces will determine the potential splendor and lifespan of the new world.

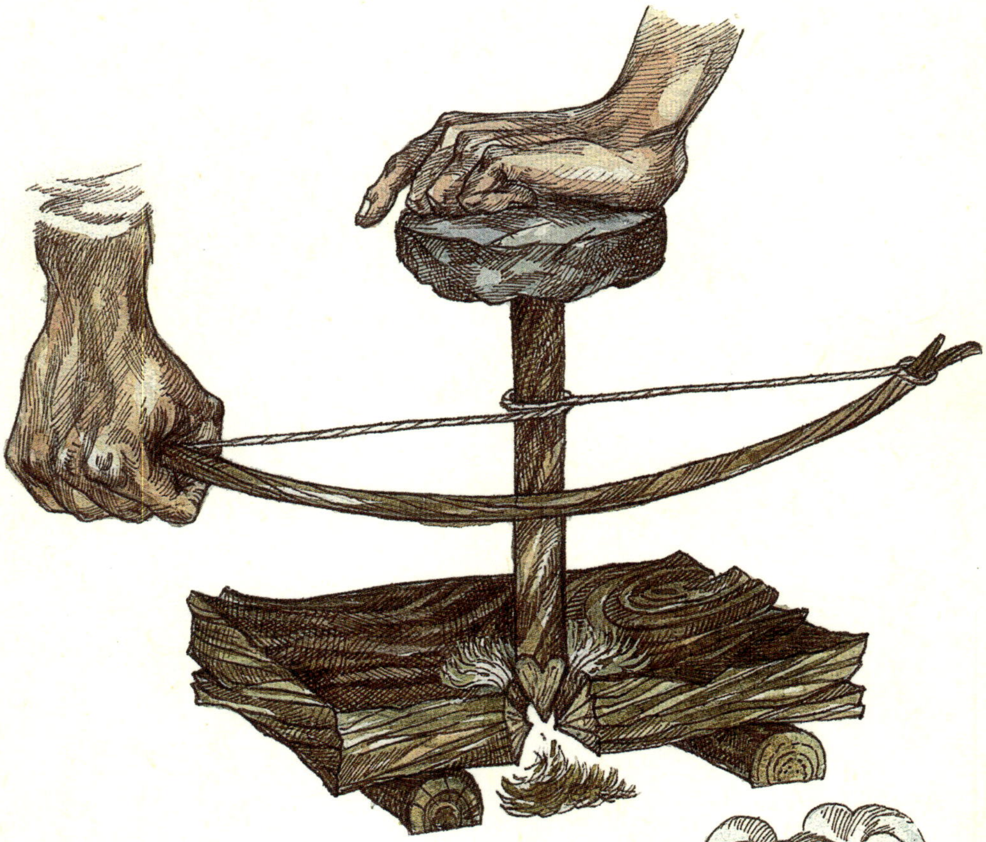

BOW METHOD

All you need to make fire is a bow. Don't have one on hand? Make a substitute with a flexible rod and a length of string. Sharpen the end of a hardwood stick and stand it upright in a hole carved into a plank of wood. Wrap the bowstring around the stick and move the bow back and forth — the stick will begin to rotate. The more intense the movement, the faster the stick rotates. This heats the wooden plank, which will soon begin to smolder. The easiest types of wood to ignite are walnut, cedar, willow, aspen and pine.

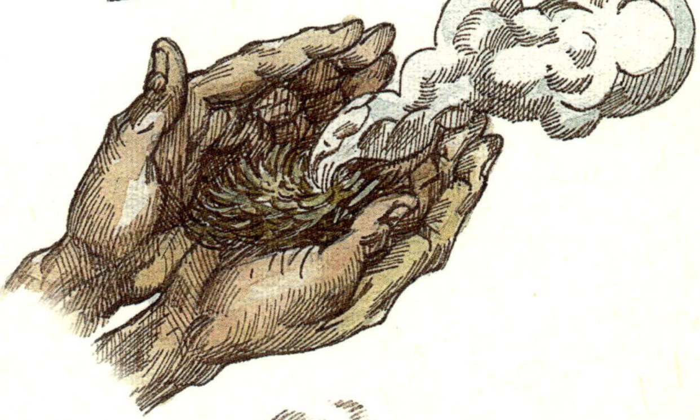

TINDER

Place tinder at the contact point between the wooden plank and the stick to increase friction and produce flames. Dry moss or tree bark chips are not the only option. Cattails, palm tree husks, flax fibers and cotton bolls will quickly ignite. Gently blowing on the fire will also provide a continuous supply of oxygen, and once the tinder catches fire, you have a few seconds to feed it with wood chips and underbrush. Look for pine, which will supply you with dry branches even in the rain. If there are only palm trees around, you'll have to climb — the bark husk at the base of the crown remains dry.

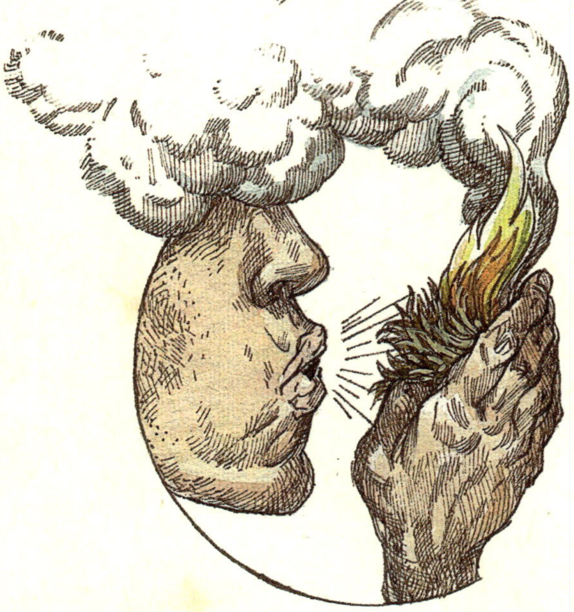

BONFIRE

Rationing your resources wisely is a good habit to develop from the very start. You can, of course, just pile wood onto your fire and it will burn brightly. But not for long. It's better to pile the ends of the logs on top of each other so that they form an asterix and, as they burn, push the unburnt material to the center. This fire will burn brighter and longer.

A great way to save fuel is to make a log candle. Split a pine log (preferably pre-dried) into 4 pieces with an ax or a saw almost to the base of the log. Lay wood chips in the grooves split by the axe and ignite. The fire and heat will last for many hours. The wood burns and leaves behind charcoal, which also carries large amounts of energy and contains a ton of carbon.

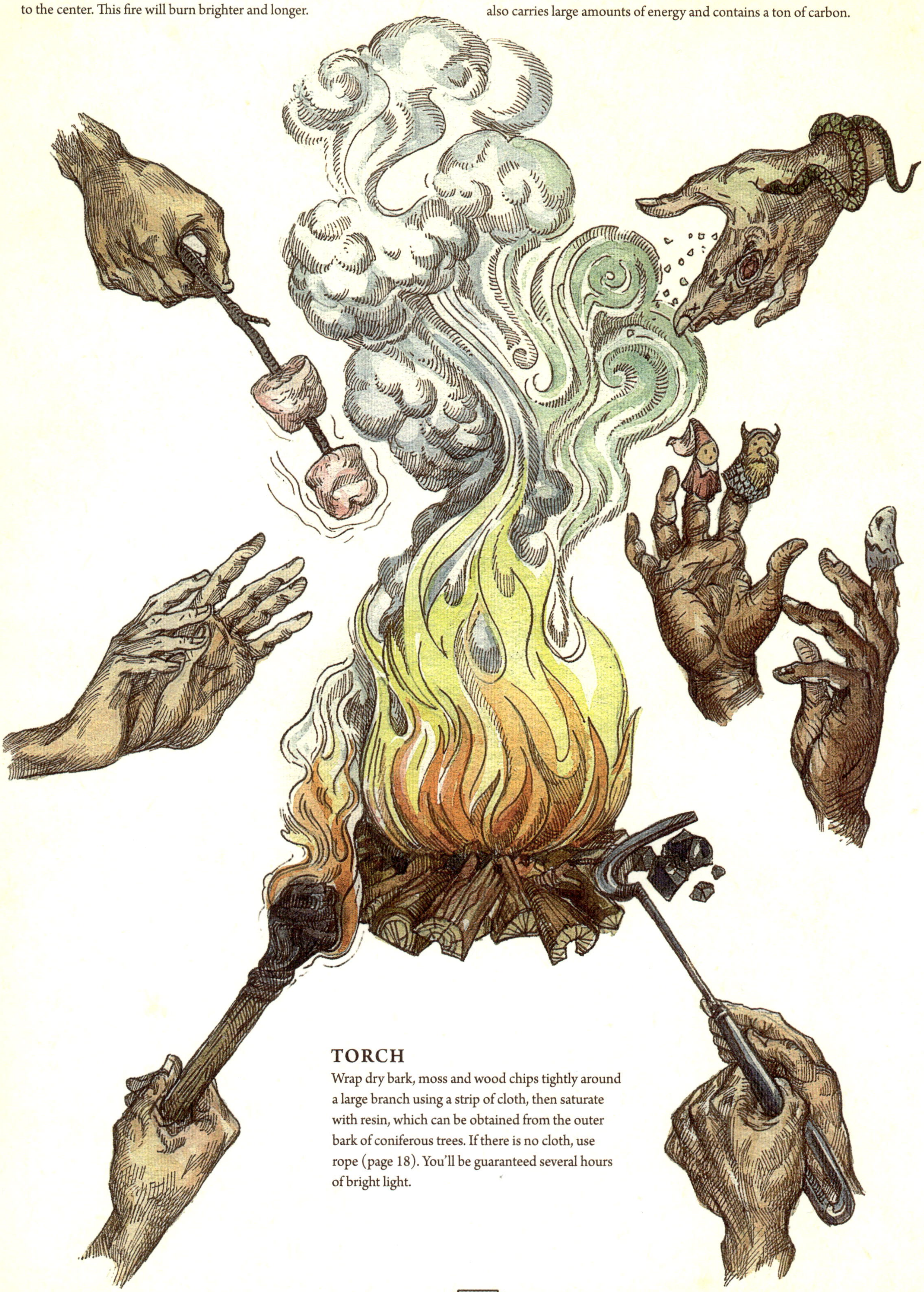

TORCH

Wrap dry bark, moss and wood chips tightly around a large branch using a strip of cloth, then saturate with resin, which can be obtained from the outer bark of coniferous trees. If there is no cloth, use rope (page 18). You'll be guaranteed several hours of bright light.

HOW TO FIND WATER

Water is one of the most critical natural resources to secure for yourself. Without water, you can only survive a maximum of about seven days. Dehydration clouds your common sense, quickly depriving you of the will to live — a compelling reason to start your search for water as soon as possible.

The most obvious solution is to collect rainwater or dew. But unless you have a shaman on your side willing to perform a rain dance every morning, you'll eventually have to find a more sustainable source. Your next move will depend on the local climate and landscape.

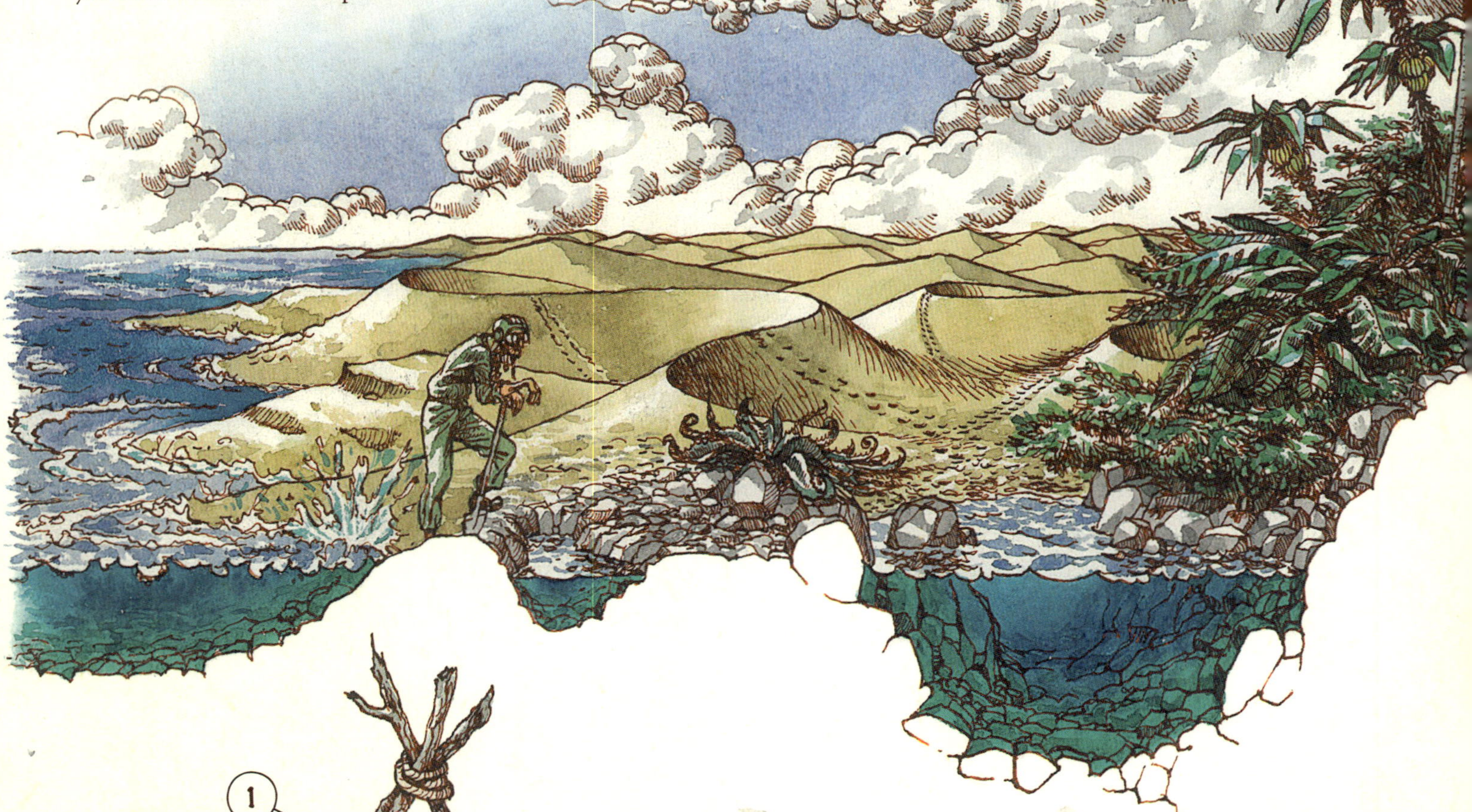

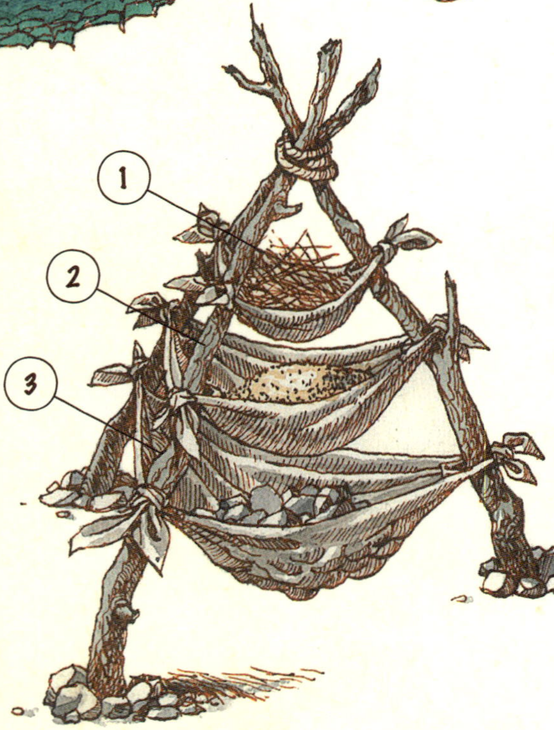

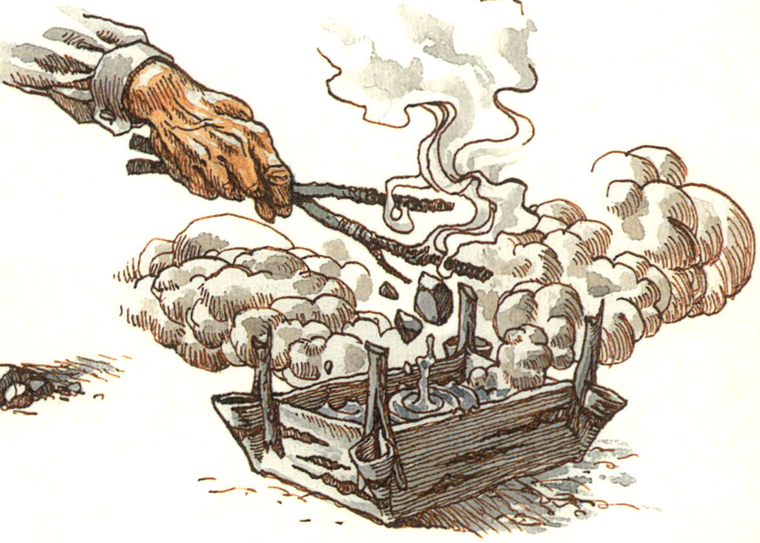

FILTRATION & DECONTAMINATION

Finding water doesn't mean that your problems are over. Not every source is potable (suitable for consumption). If you succumb to your thirst and gulp down the first water you come across, you may end up dying even faster than you would from dehydration. Almost all sources found in nature will need to be filtered and decontaminated, especially if they're stagnant or murky. The main danger with natural water sources is biological threats, from bacteria and their spores to parasitic larvae. Larger parasites can be filtered out by draining the water through sand (2), wood charcoal (1) or fine gravel (3).

If fate finds you in the tropics and you have a steady supply of bananas, use the slightly porous peel in place of a charcoal filter. Even if you don't have a water-tight container that can be placed over a fire, you can still boil water using the materials around you. Construct a container out of birch bark and fill it with heated rocks or, even better, river pebbles. You can also try more complex water purification systems, such as the distiller (page 118), but you'll have to advance your society a few steps forward first.

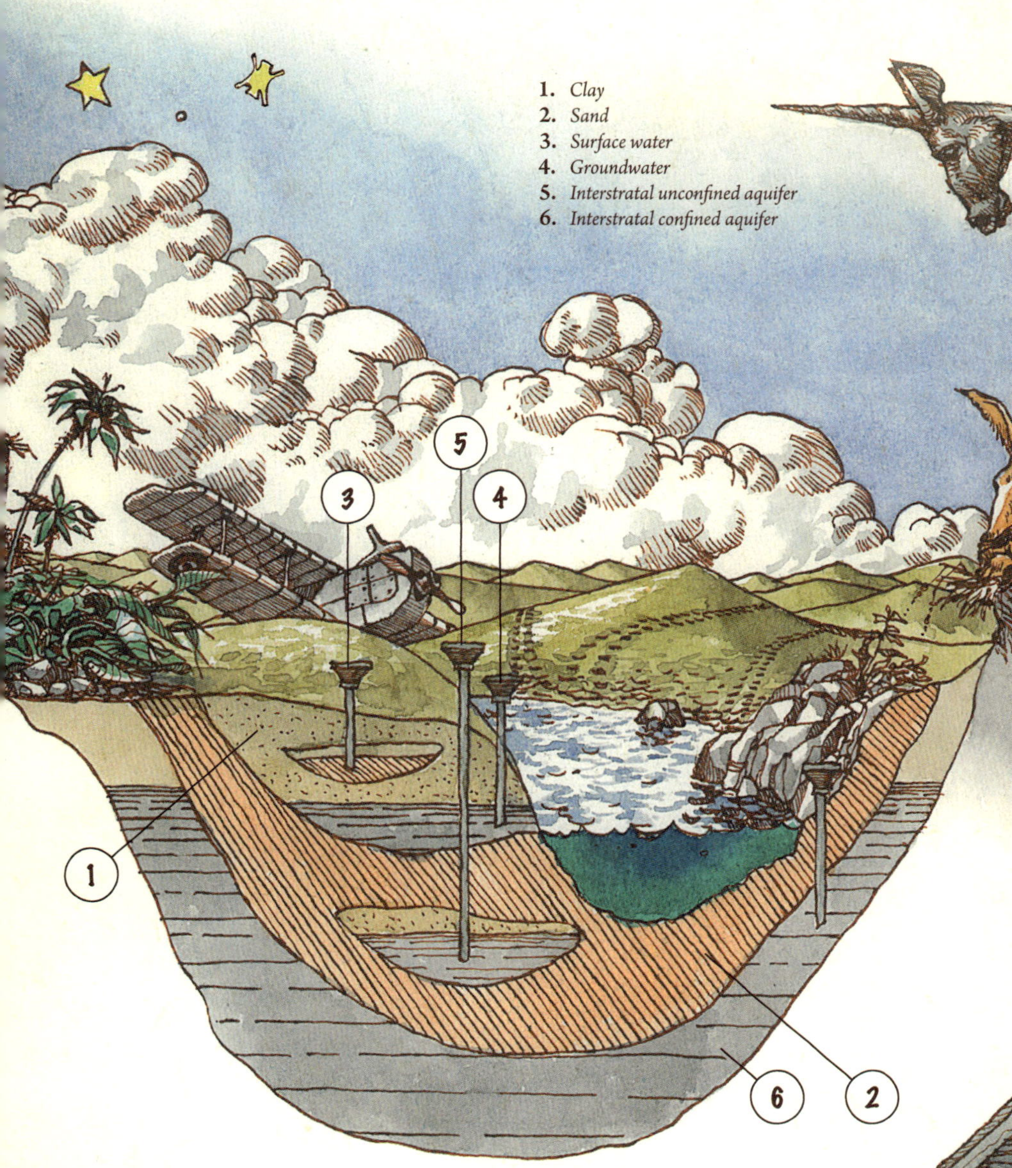

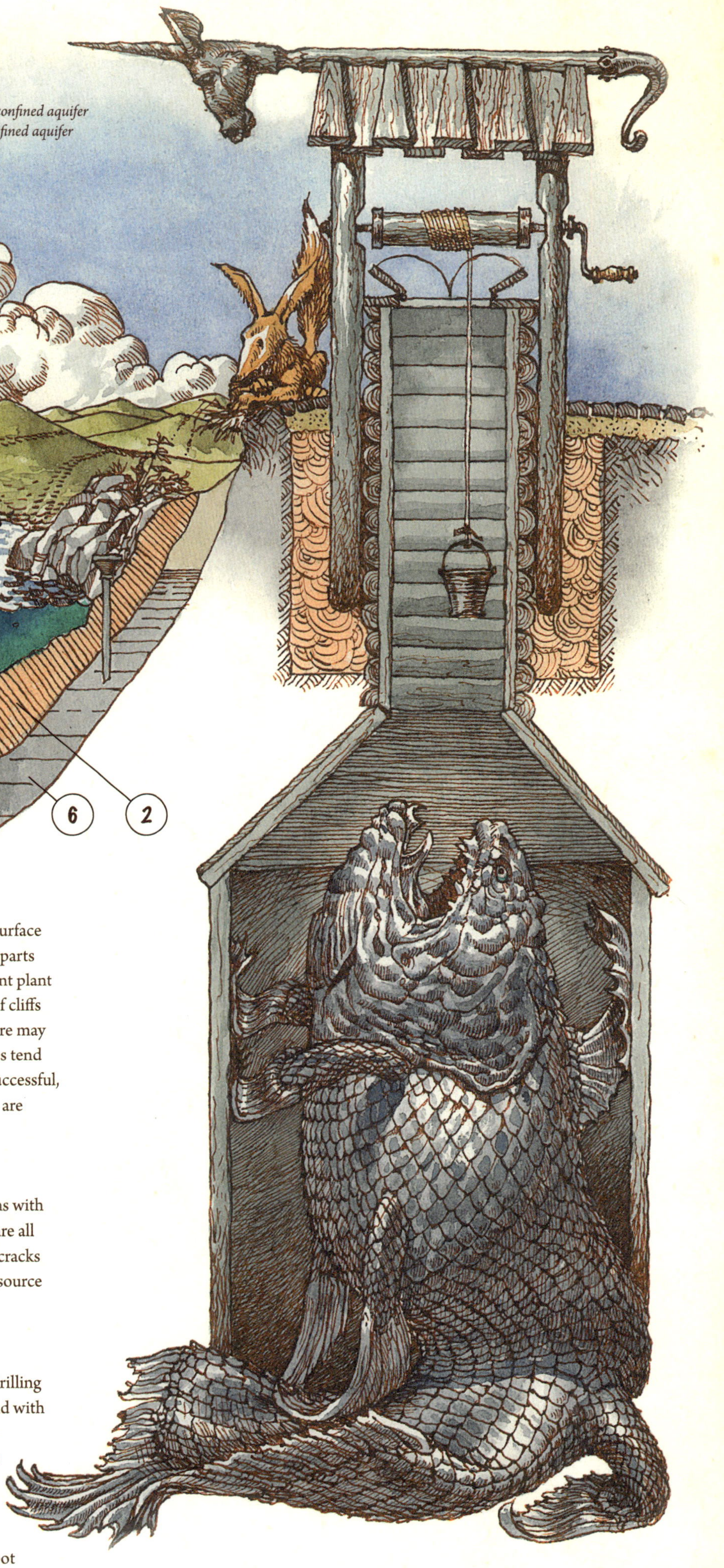

WHERE TO LOOK FOR WATER

The easiest place to find water is where the soil is loose. Closest to the surface is groundwater, which you can sometimes see gathering in the deepest parts of a valley, at the bottom of a steep incline or in places covered in verdant plant life. If you're in the mountains, seek out sources in fissures at the base of cliffs and near areas of lush vegetation. Try digging under dry river beds; there may be water under the layer of gravel. In the desert, midges and mosquitoes tend to swarm around groundwater. To stave off thirst until your search is successful, drink the juices of trees or plants. Just make sure you know which ones are poisonous (page 16).

NATURE'S HINTS

Take note of large colonies of insects (especially bees and ants), locations with thick, juicy plant life, the flight path of birds and localized fog — these are all signs that water is nearby. If you're near a cliff face or rock wall, look for cracks near a large accumulation of bird droppings. This could mean a hidden source that's easily reachable with a straw.

DEEP GROUNDWATER

If you can't manage to find a natural water source, your best option is drilling a well. The hole should be sufficiently deep (around 10–15 meters), and with some luck, you'll be provided with clean drinking water for some time to come. When finding a suitable location, look for alder, birch, spruce and pine trees. If there are no trees around but a lot of sedges, this is also a good sign. A large clay pot will help determine the exact location of your well. Dry it in the sun and set it upside down. If after a while the bottom of the pot begins to "sweat," this is a good spot to start digging.

EDIBLE & INEDIBLE PLANTS

While hunger may stimulate creativity, it takes strength to bring your plans to fruition. The answer: plants.

Although cooking helps release nutrients, many plants can be eaten raw, so there's no need to waste energy cooking.

But to make sure your first bite won't be your last, you'll need to be able to identify edible and poisonous plants.

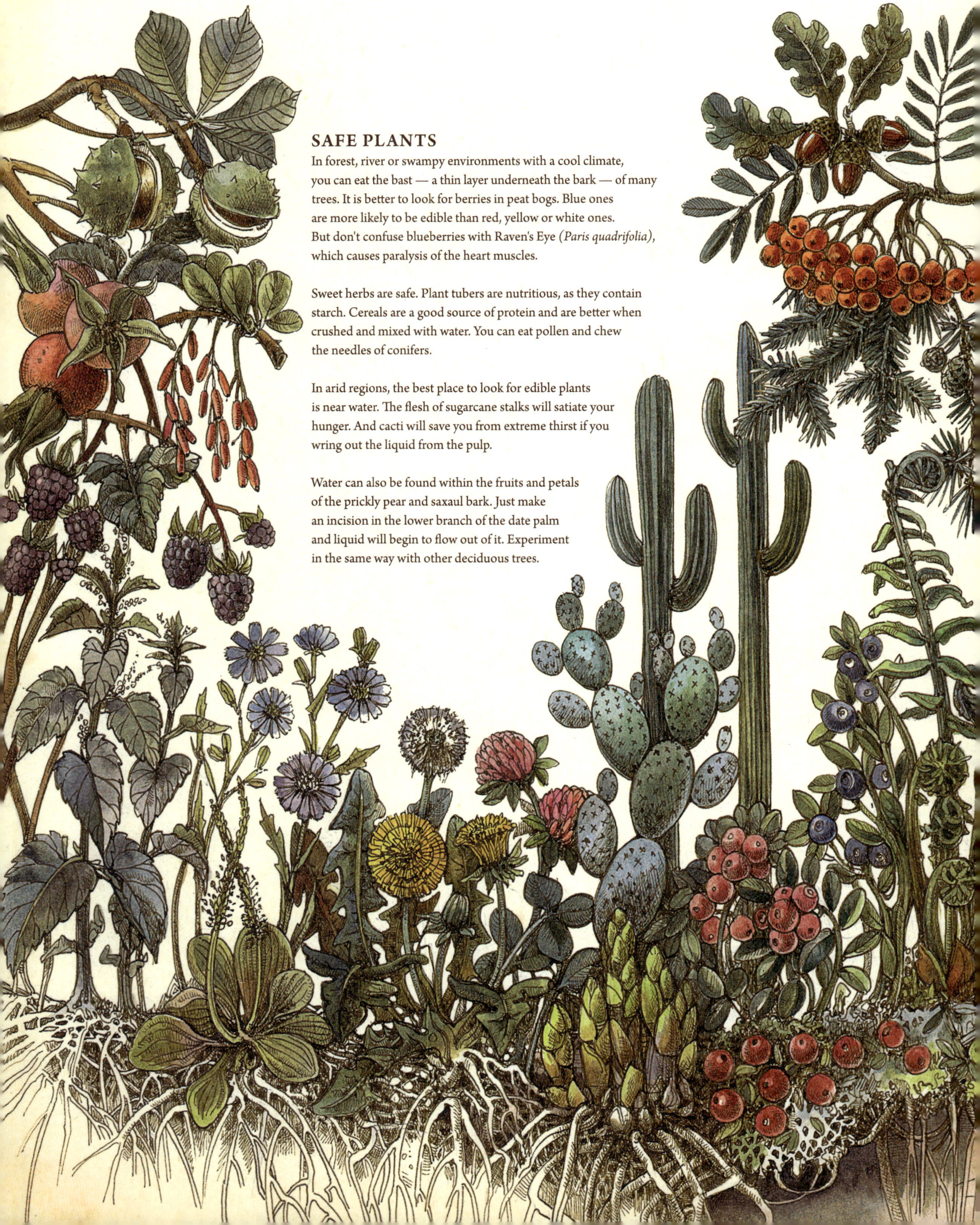

SAFE PLANTS

In forest, river or swampy environments with a cool climate, you can eat the bast — a thin layer underneath the bark — of many trees. It is better to look for berries in peat bogs. Blue ones are more likely to be edible than red, yellow or white ones. But don't confuse blueberries with Raven's Eye *(Paris quadrifolia)*, which causes paralysis of the heart muscles.

Sweet herbs are safe. Plant tubers are nutritious, as they contain starch. Cereals are a good source of protein and are better when crushed and mixed with water. You can eat pollen and chew the needles of conifers.

In arid regions, the best place to look for edible plants is near water. The flesh of sugarcane stalks will satiate your hunger. And cacti will save you from extreme thirst if you wring out the liquid from the pulp.

Water can also be found within the fruits and petals of the prickly pear and saxaul bark. Just make an incision in the lower branch of the date palm and liquid will begin to flow out of it. Experiment in the same way with other deciduous trees.

THE 5–15 RULE

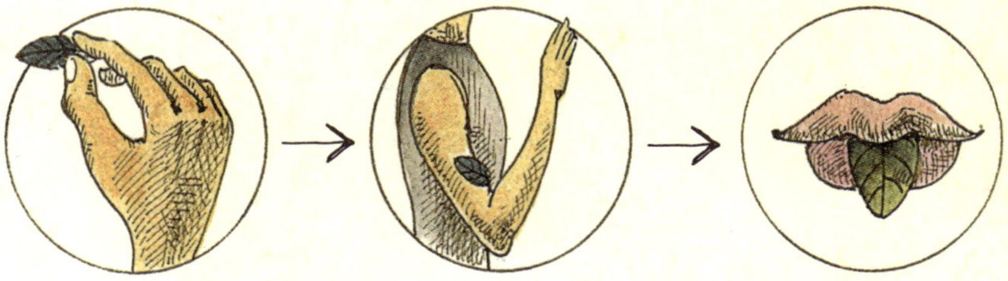

1. Rub a small amount of the plant between your fingers and wait 15 minutes. If this causes no adverse reaction, then:
2. Rub the plant on the inside of your elbow. If this causes no reaction, then:
3. Hold a piece of the plant between your lips. If there is no irritation, burning or numbness, then:
4. Chew on a small part of the plant (do not swallow). Wait 15 minutes. If there is no burning sensation or bitter taste, then:
5. Swallow this small piece. Wait 15 minutes. If you experience no nausea, dizziness or other symptoms of poisoning, you can eat a small quantity of the plant. If your condition hasn't worsened the next day, the plant is safe to use in food.

DANGEROUS PLANTS

Umbrella plants, which thrive in damp and overgrown areas, are often inedible. Do not touch the umbrella fronds with your bare hands — this is the most poisonous part.

Even plants that are predominantly edible may pack a poisonous punch. Apple seeds, leaves and pits of the cherry, peach, plum, almond and apricot trees contain cyanogenic glycosides, while green potato tubers and leaves contain the alkaloid solanine.

But beware of burning poisonous plants in an attempt to destroy them, as inhaling the smoke can be just as poisonous. If you do end up poisoning yourself, flush out your stomach by drinking at least 2 liters of water and inducing vomiting.

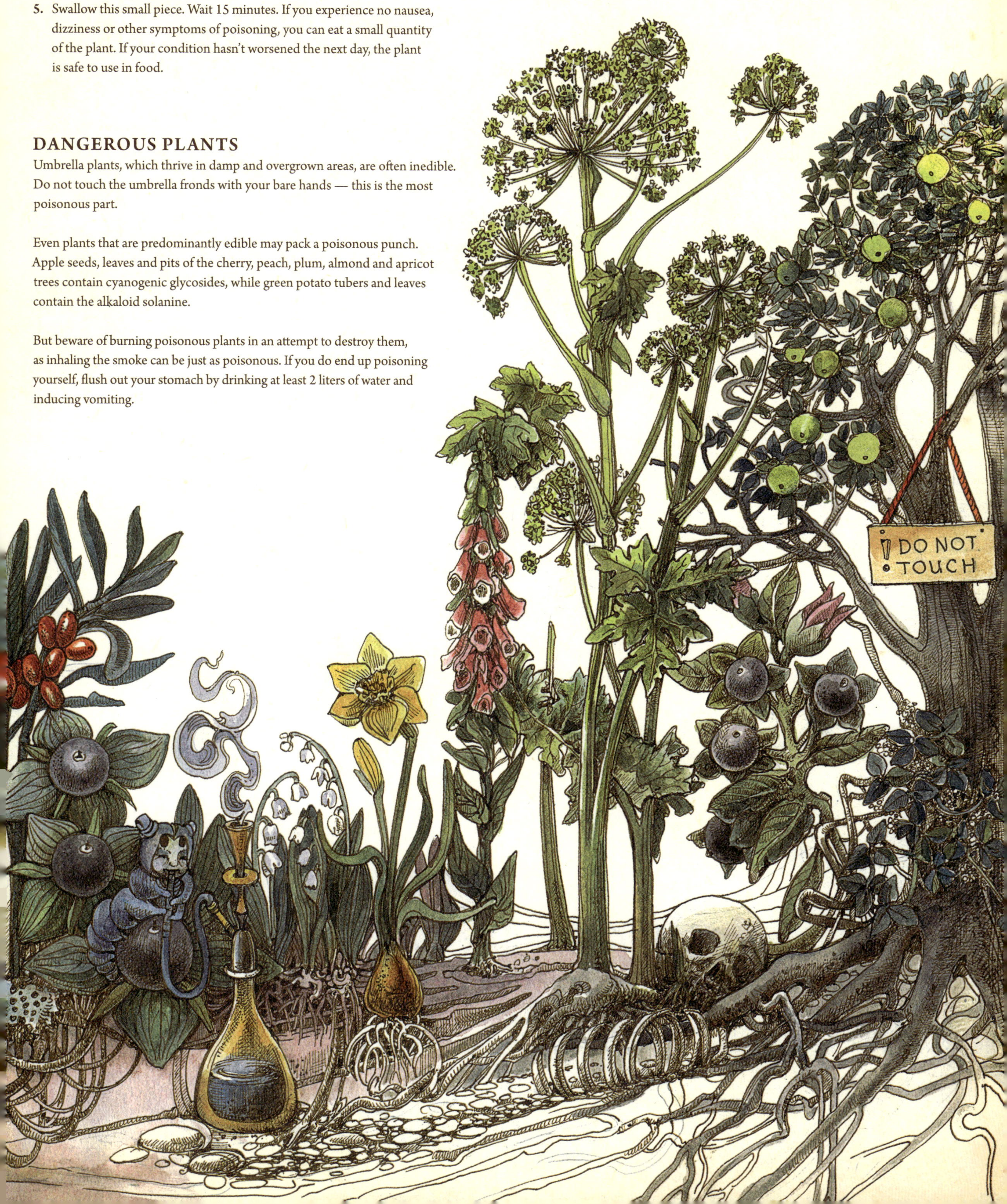

ROPE

Rope can often make a good substitute in a pinch, but it's hard to find a good substitute for rope itself. The ability to braid a rope greatly increases your survival prospects.

If you are weaponless, rope makes it possible to obtain food through weaving fish nets and wild game traps. You can build a dwelling without tools, drag heavy loads without wheels and even staunch bleeding without medication.

MATERIALS

Rope can be made of wool, animal sinew, hair, silk or whatever you can find underfoot. Plants are the best rope-making materials. Nettle, hemp, jute, flax and willow will do just fine. But don't gather them in an open area — dry plant fiber is less elastic. Remove the leaves from the stems. Mash them until you are left with long, strong fibers. By the way, a rolling mill makes the process much easier.

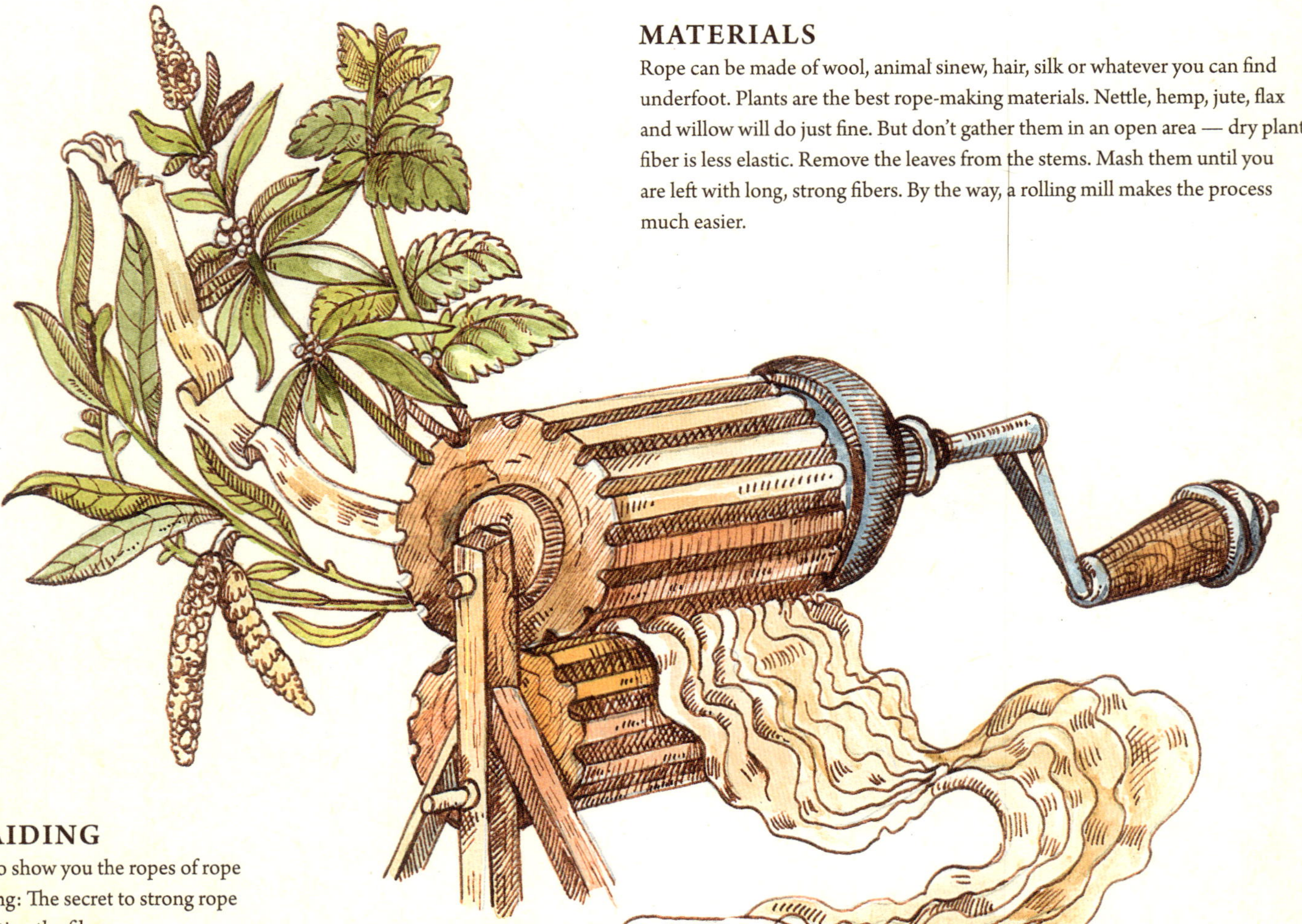

BRAIDING

Now to show you the ropes of rope braiding: The secret to strong rope is twisting the fibers.

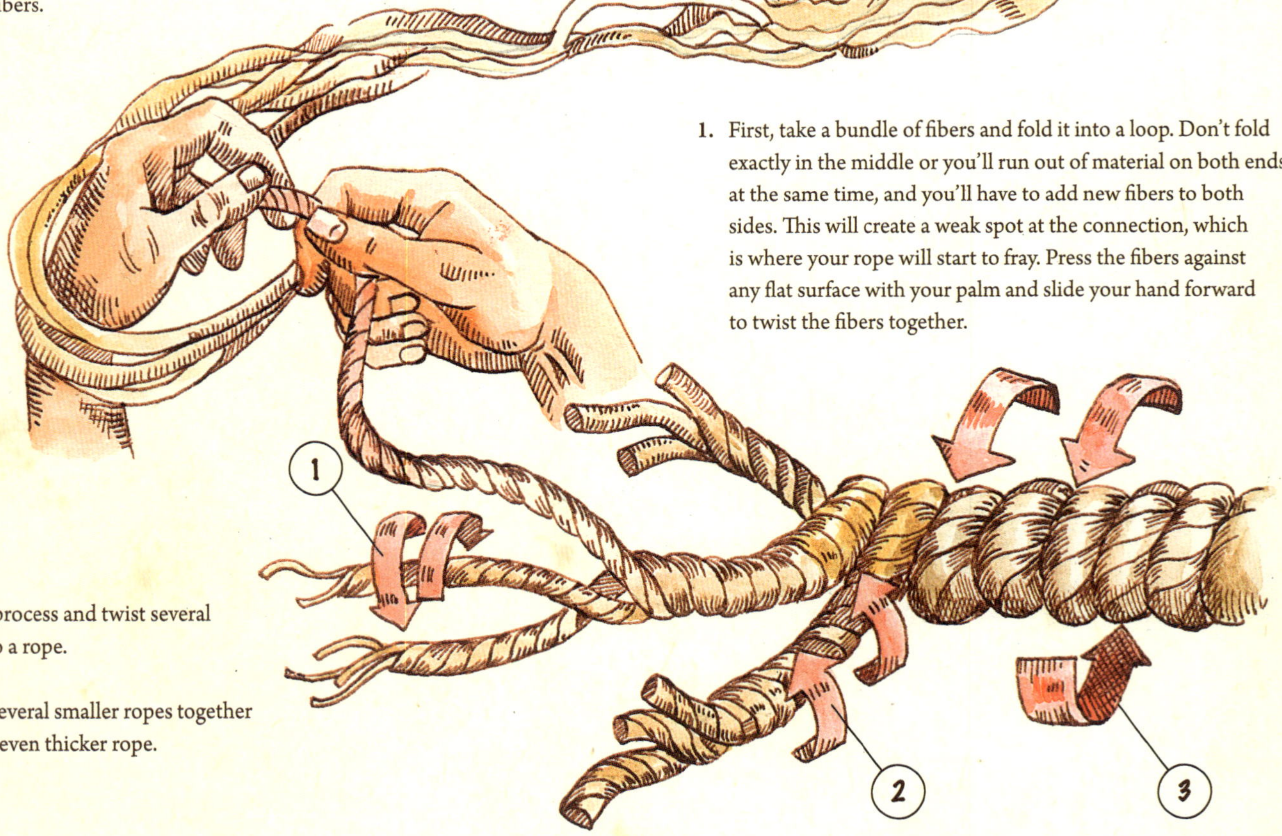

1. First, take a bundle of fibers and fold it into a loop. Don't fold exactly in the middle or you'll run out of material on both ends at the same time, and you'll have to add new fibers to both sides. This will create a weak spot at the connection, which is where your rope will start to fray. Press the fibers against any flat surface with your palm and slide your hand forward to twist the fibers together.
2. Repeat the process and twist several bundles into a rope.
3. Then twist several smaller ropes together to create an even thicker rope.

PROCESSING WILLOW BARK

Willow bark is a good material to produce extra strong rope. The elemental forces of fire and water will help you along the way. Heat the wood, bark side down, over the fire until you hear a faint hissing sound. At this point, the bark will separate easily from the wood. The only part you need is the stringy, leather-like inner layer. Boil it in a mixture of wood ash and water until it turns red. Hang the bark out to dry. Split the strips down into finer strings of fiber.

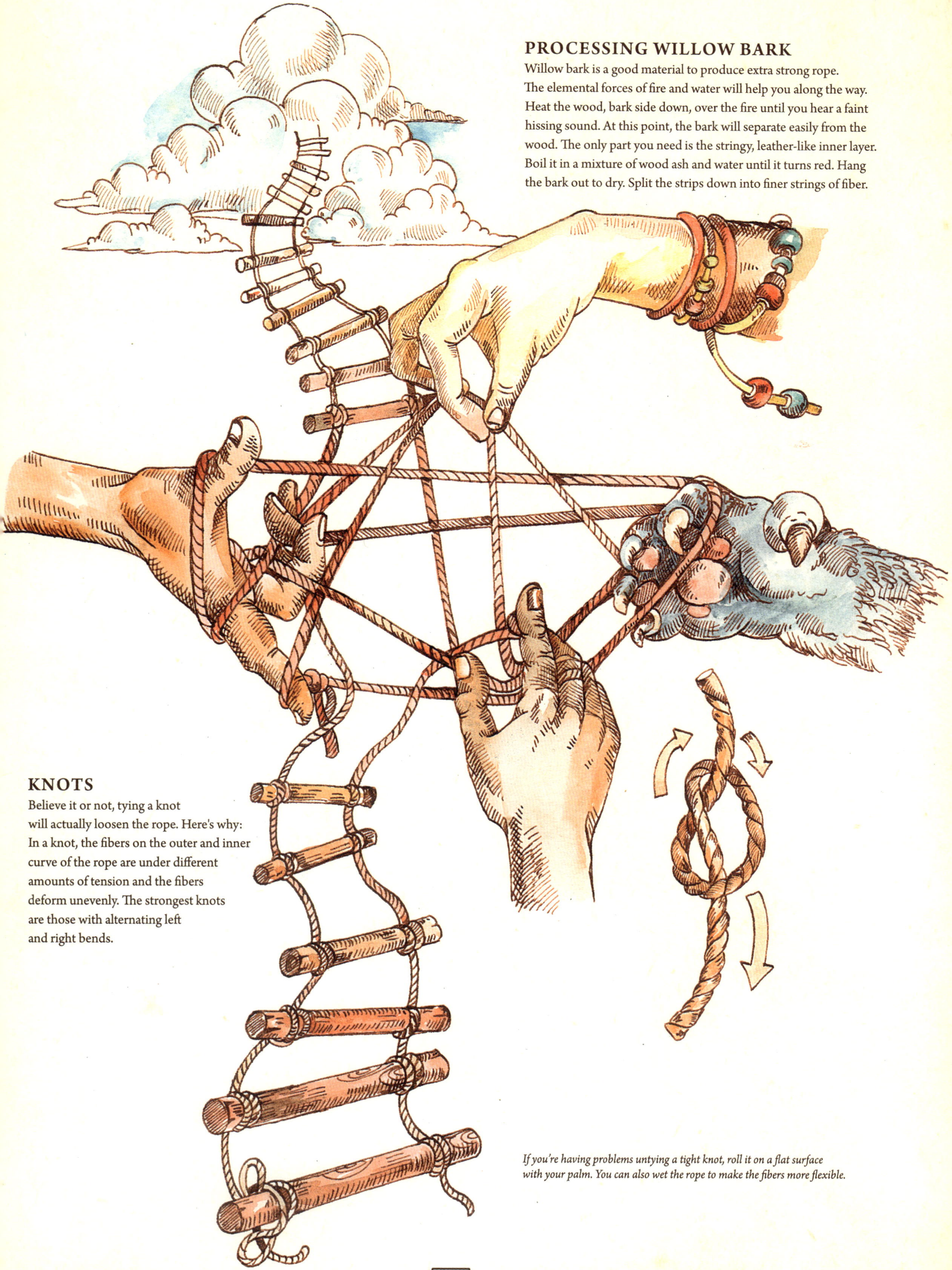

KNOTS

Believe it or not, tying a knot will actually loosen the rope. Here's why: In a knot, the fibers on the outer and inner curve of the rope are under different amounts of tension and the fibers deform unevenly. The strongest knots are those with alternating left and right bends.

If you're having problems untying a tight knot, roll it on a flat surface with your palm. You can also wet the rope to make the fibers more flexible.

SIMPLE TOOLS

Someday, you will construct massive skyscrapers and drill deep into the bowels of the earth. But first you need to master the basics. Make simple tools first to act as a foundation for more complicated instruments. You already have everything you need to get started: sticks, stones, ropes, bones and animal sinew.

PROCESSING STONE

Stones that you find in nature rarely come pre-sharpened, so you'll have to create cutting utensils yourself by splitting a large rock into thin shards. Flint works best and will produce a glassy shard with a razor-sharp edge. Larger shards become knives while others may serve as cutters, scrapers, pokers or arrowheads.

SPEAR

Hunting spears require hardwood shafts such as oak, ash or walnut. To m the wood even harder, smoke it over a fire. As the water inside evaporates, the structure of the wood becomes denser. Fishing spears for shallow wat are best made from bamboo. But skewering a fish on a single point is a ski few can master. Increase your chances of catching dinner by adding two m prongs to create a trident tip.

KNIFE

Flint makes for a sharp and durable knife, while obsidian, or volcanic glas is more suitable for scalpels. However, instruments made from these materials are quite fragile. That's why you shouldn't be using them to hack away at an animal carcass. Set them aside for tasks that require a finer, more meticulous touch.

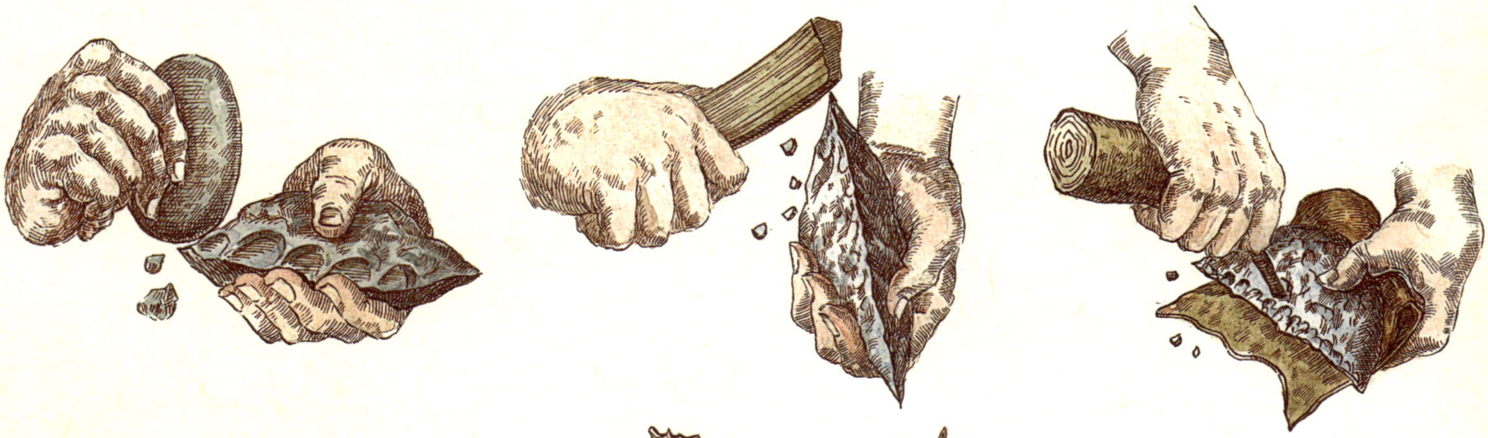

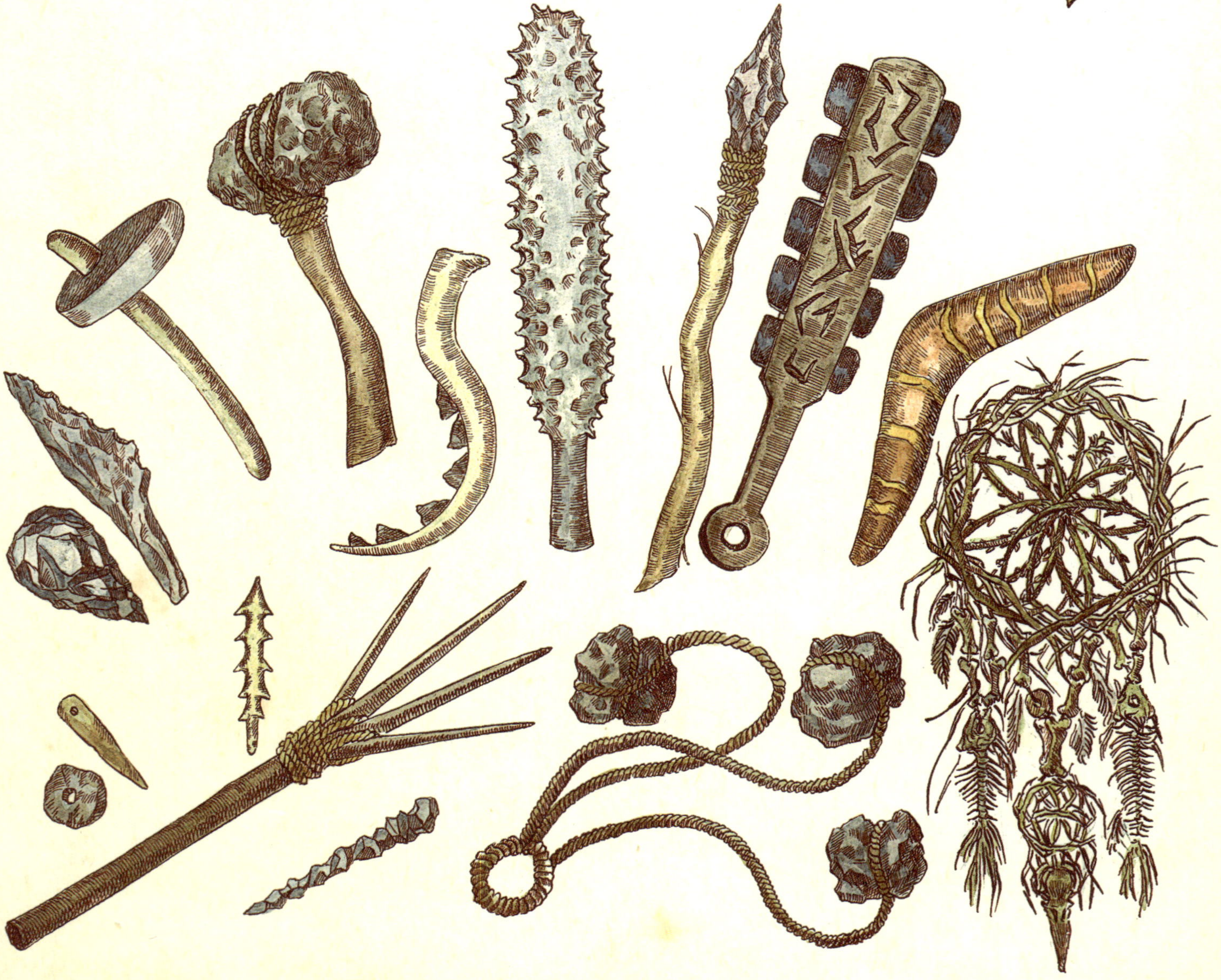

AXE

To fell and turn trees, you need a tool with a working surface made from heavy, sharp stone and a transverse handle. Find a straight, thick, broad branch. Wrap rope (page 18) around the branch 15–20 cm from one end and split this section down the middle until you reach the rope. Insert a stone between the split halves and cross the rope around it many times to secure it, connecting the two ends of the branch and fixing the stone inside as tightly as possible.

DRILL AND SAW

One of the hardest tasks to accomplish is drilling a neat hole. You need a solid tool. But where can you find a sturdy material if you haven't yet discovered iron? Pour quartz sand into your drill hole. The coarse grains will cover your drilling instrument (a sharp piece of stone honed to a point), creating an abrasive coating. This will help you drill a hole in a hollow bone to produce a needle or hook. When the only thing separating the rich from the poor is a few animal pelts and a warm meal on the table, gemstones lose some of their value. But this doesn't mean they're completely useless. Diamonds are the hardest material in nature and so can be used for very durable cutting and sawing tools.

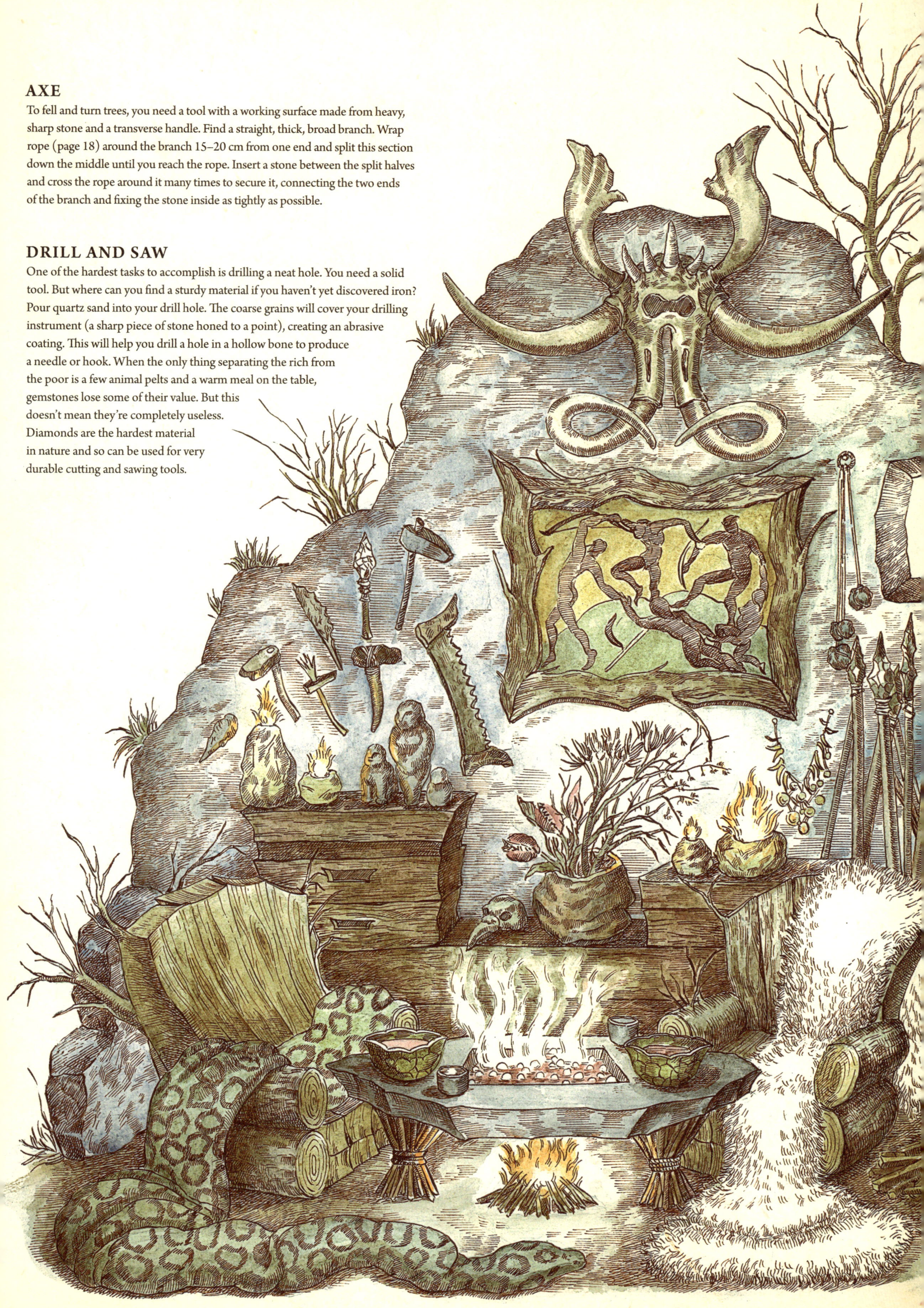

SIMPLE HOUSING

Few people are ever in a position where they must build their house from the ground up with their own two hands while understanding all the technological intricacies necessary for the job. Start with something simple and master basic construction principles. Later, you can move on to more complex structures that will help elevate your civilization to the next level of development. In the beginning, at least, your environment will dictate the best design and building materials for the job.

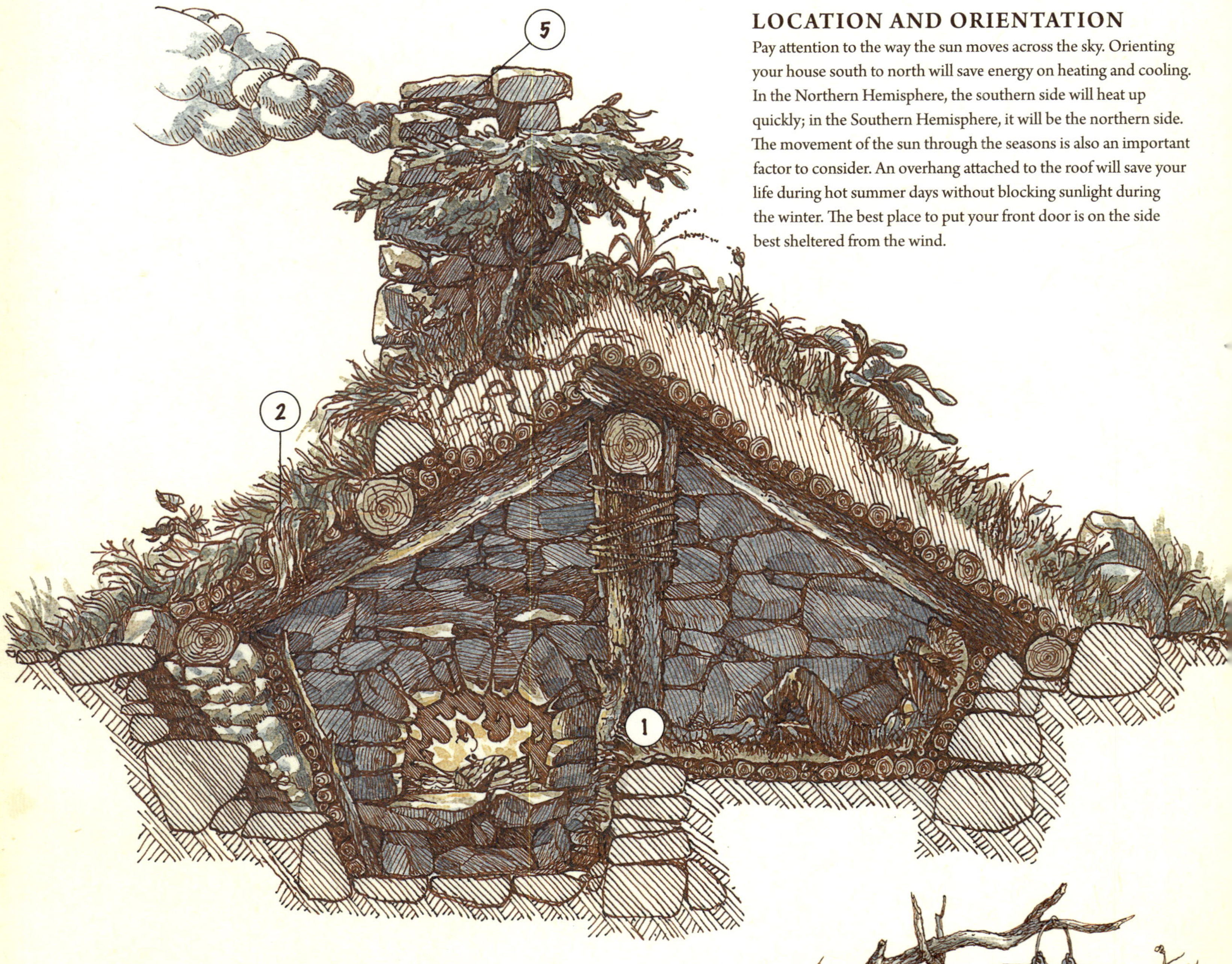

LOCATION AND ORIENTATION

Pay attention to the way the sun moves across the sky. Orienting your house south to north will save energy on heating and cooling. In the Northern Hemisphere, the southern side will heat up quickly; in the Southern Hemisphere, it will be the northern side. The movement of the sun through the seasons is also an important factor to consider. An overhang attached to the roof will save your life during hot summer days without blocking sunlight during the winter. The best place to put your front door is on the side best sheltered from the wind.

HUT

Use the terrain to your advantage. A hillside can easily become the back wall of your hut. Dig out the center of a log and line it with stones for stability (1). This will become the main support structure of your roof. Now you need a cross beam. Attach one end to the central support post and rest the other end against the slope of the hill. Now you have a T-frame. Lay branches across the frame to form a sloping roof (2), which simultaneously acts as a ceiling and two walls of your domicile. The entire frame must be secured with ropes (page 18) or wire. From above, the roof can be covered with spruce branches, palm leaves, reeds or just straw mixed with clay (page 136). For your fireplace, dig out the main body of the hearth (3), and then dig out a wind box (4) to one side for stoking the fire. If you place your hearth within your dwelling, make sure that the main body is inlaid in the wall or placed outside of the walls of the home altogether. The difference in air temperatures inside and outside the hut will create a draft, forcing exhaust fumes outside through the chimney (5).

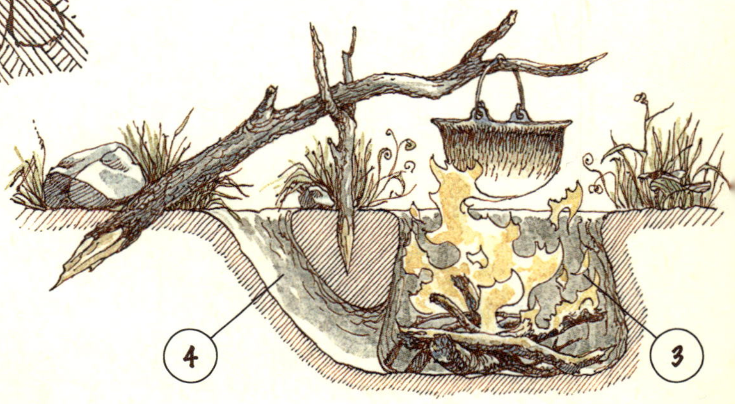

If the draft is not strong enough, these combustion byproducts will accumulate in your home, which is dangerous as wood smoke contains poisonous substances. Insulate your fireplace with raw brick (page 148). This material retains and slowly releases heat over a long period of time. Incidentally, if you're low on firewood, you can use dried animal dung instead — it burns well and gives off a lot of heat.

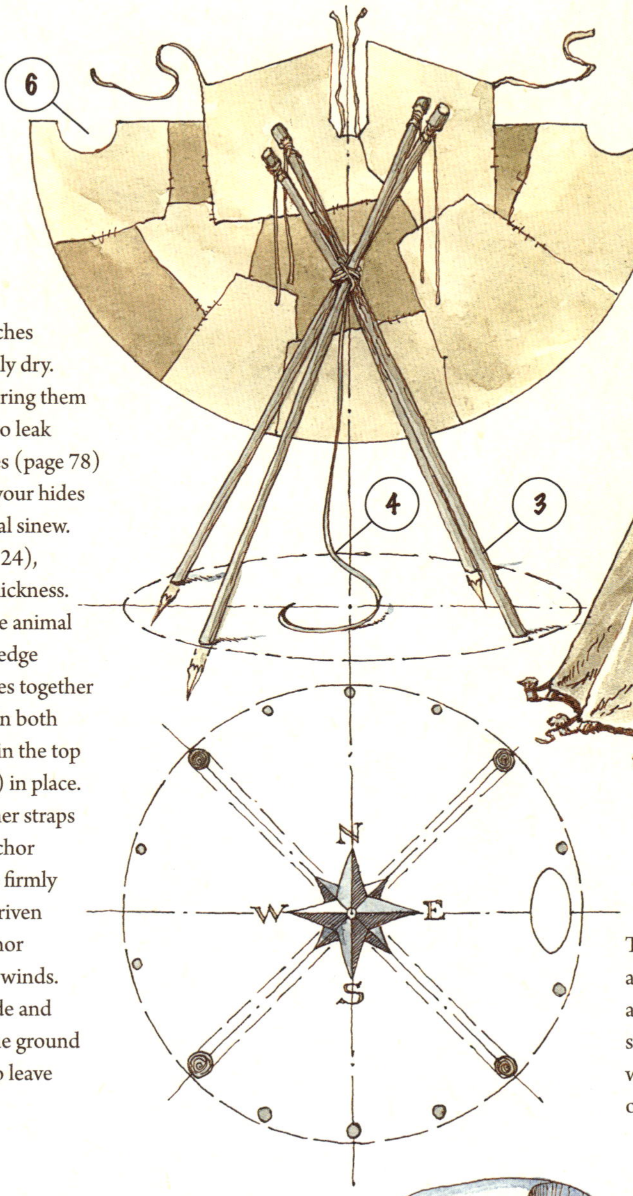

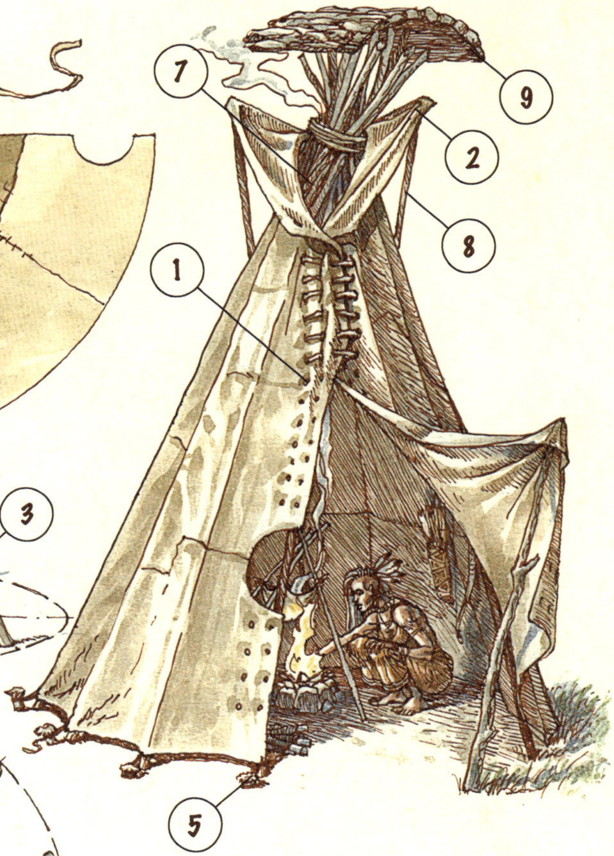

TIPI

Make the poles for the frame from branches left out in the sun and wind to thoroughly dry. Damp poles will cause the material covering them to sag, leading to folds that allow water to leak in when it rains. Use treated animal hides (page 78) for your covering. You can even sew all your hides together into a single canvas using animal sinew. Soak them in an alkaline solution (page 24), and then stretch to obtain the desired thickness. If you've already used or gotten rid of the animal sinew, poke holes along the connecting edge of the animal hide and join the two pieces together by sticking a strong twig through holes in both pieces of fabric (1). Create pockets (2) in the top of your hide canvas to hold the poles (3) in place. Bind them together at the top with leather straps or steamed spruce roots. Tie a heavy anchor belt (4) around the connection point to firmly secure the structure. Attach it to a peg driven straight down into the ground. The anchor will hold the tent in place during strong winds. Punch holes along the bottom of the hide and drive pegs (5) through them and into the ground to secure your hide canvas. Make sure to leave a small gap (6) for air circulation.

The upper part of the structure should contain a smoke hole. This consists of two flaps (7) that act as smoke vents. Open and close them using either straps or poles (8). When it rains, cover the hole with an "umbrella" — an additional piece of leather (9).

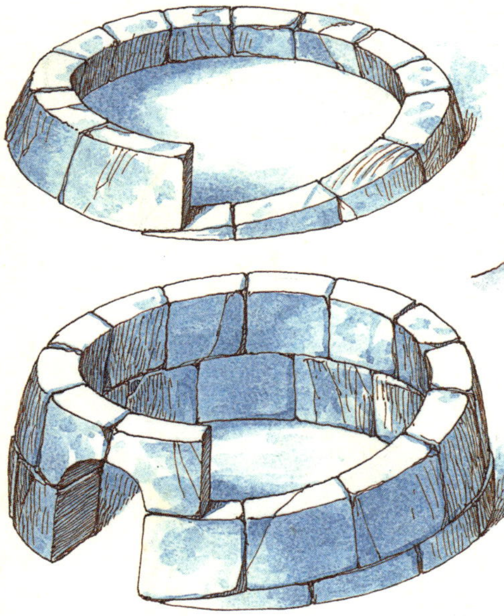

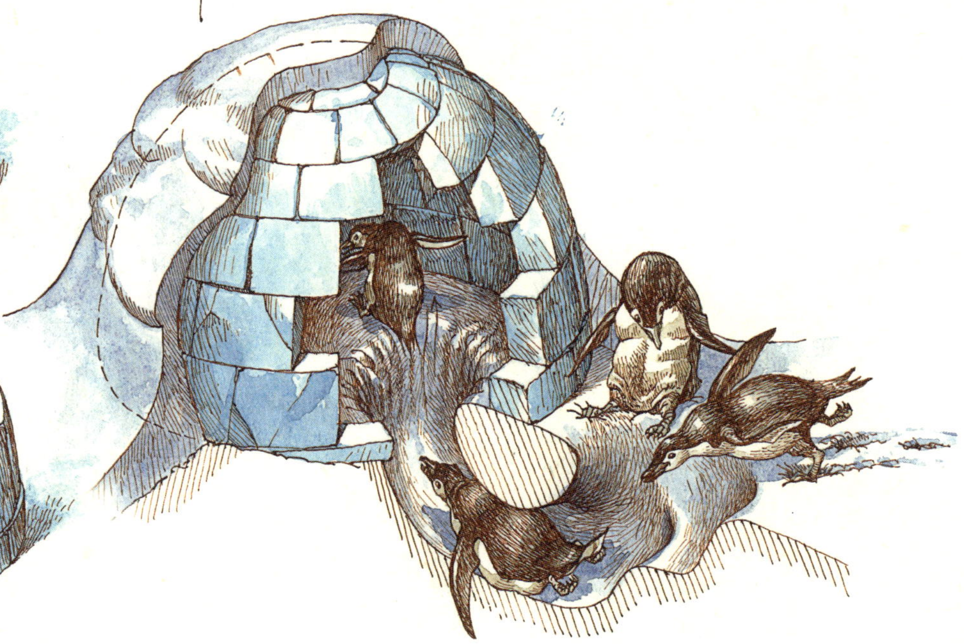

IGLOO

The secret of constructing an igloo dome is that the snow blocks are laid in a spiral. To do this, the bottom layer of blocks must be shaved down at an angle to create the tilt that makes the dome shape possible. Don't forget to leave a gap between the blocks at the very top of the dome for ventilation. The inner walls will melt slightly due to the heat emitted by your body, but the cool ambient temperature outside will prevent the blocks from melting. In fact, this process of melting and refreezing the inner walls makes the igloo even stronger.

Your body heat will be sufficient to heat the igloo, but you must make sure that the main entrance is a tunnel below floor level. This will allow for carbon dioxide and oxygen exchange while preventing heat from escaping. Light enters the igloo directly through the snowy walls, but you can also make windows and cover them in stretched, dried animal intestines. For a night-time light source, insert a wick (page 84) into a bowl filled with fish or seal oil and ignite.

SOAP

They say cleanliness is the keystone of health. Not just for individuals, but for society on the whole. And where there is physical cleanliness, spiritual purity will follow. So develop a good hygiene routine. Clean hands start with soap. To wash the grease and dirt from your hands, you'll need to start with a mixture of grease and ash. Rebuilding civilization is hard work. Sometimes you have to get your hands a little dirty. And dirty hands mean battling an army of viruses, fungi and bacteria that live on the surfaces you touch everyday. So it's time to make soap! First rule of soapmaking: Don't talk about soapmaking. And the second: Mix grease and ash to get rid of grease and dirt.

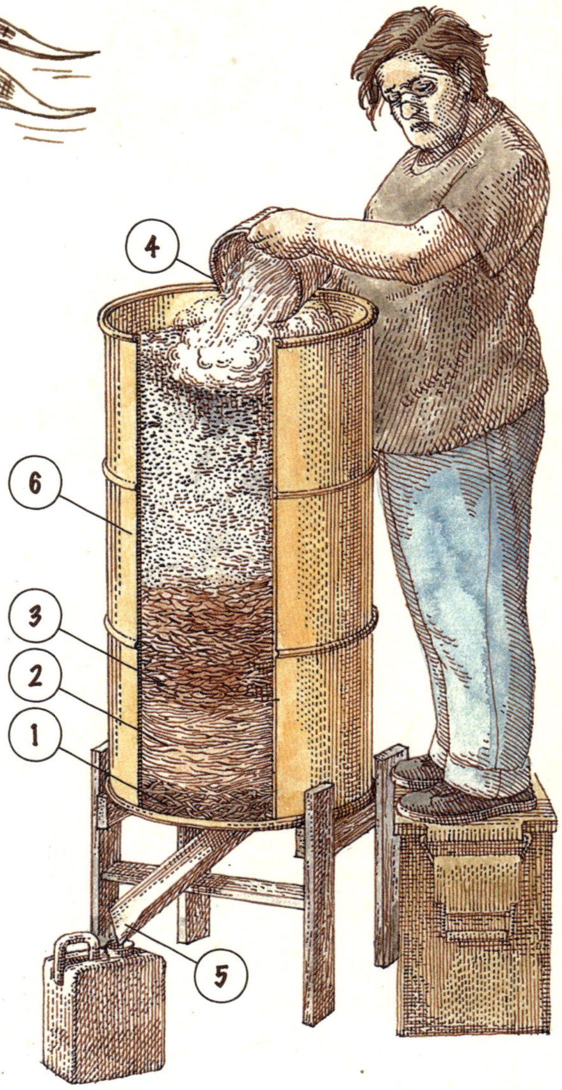

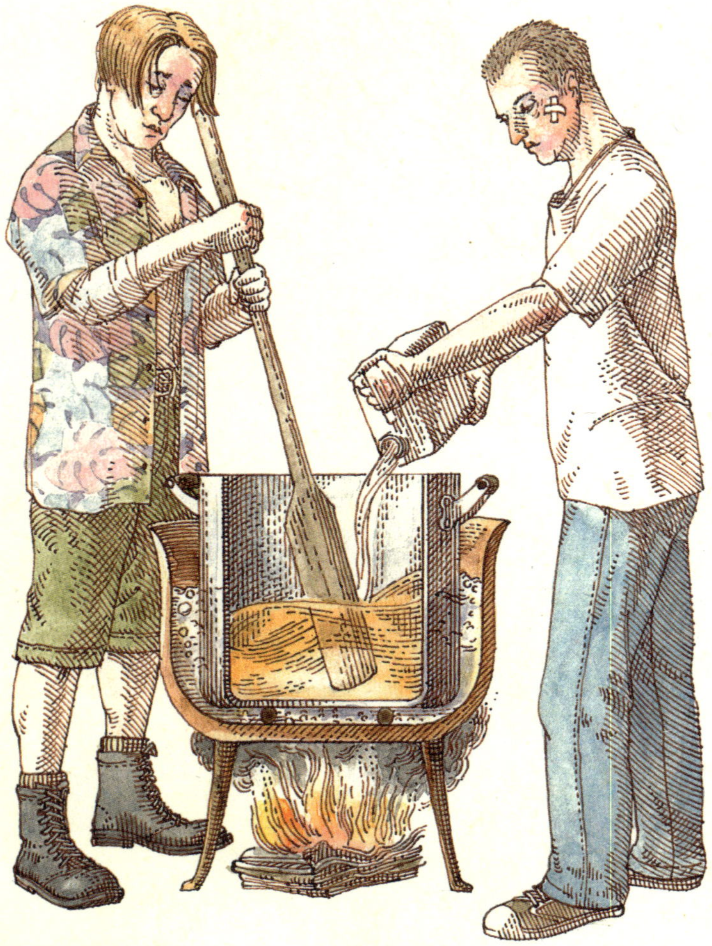

LYE

Ironically, the foundation of all soaps is a mixture of fat and lye — that is, an aqueous solution of ash (mainly potassium carbonate). When processing the ashes of plants that are found in salty semi-deserts or on the sea coast, soda solutions are obtained — sodium carbonate. Pass it through hard lime (limestone burned in a kiln) and you get a solution of caustic sodium — sodium hydroxide. To make lye, you'll need a filter. Wood shavings (1) make for a fine base, covered in a layer of straw (2), and finally topped with a layer of ash (3). Pour boiling water (4) over the top of the barrel and the lye will start to drip out(5) of the tap in the side of the barrel (6). Do not store the lye in aluminum or tin containers, as it will corrode them. And make sure the lye/water mixture doesn't come into contact with your skin or mucous membranes — you may suffer chemical burns.

SOAP PREPARATION

The base ingredient of soap is fat. Any vegetable oil will do. A tangy olive oil or sweet coconut oil will give your soap a pleasant aroma. The oils should first be heated in a water bath.

When the lye is ready and the oils are heated, mix them together. Work slowly and carefully — the quality of the soap depends on it. As you boil the mixture down, it eventually reaches the consistency of sour cream. Adding a dash of salt to the pot causes the soap to bob to the surface. Now you can skim the soap ball off the top and repeat the process several times to purify it of all lye and oil residue.

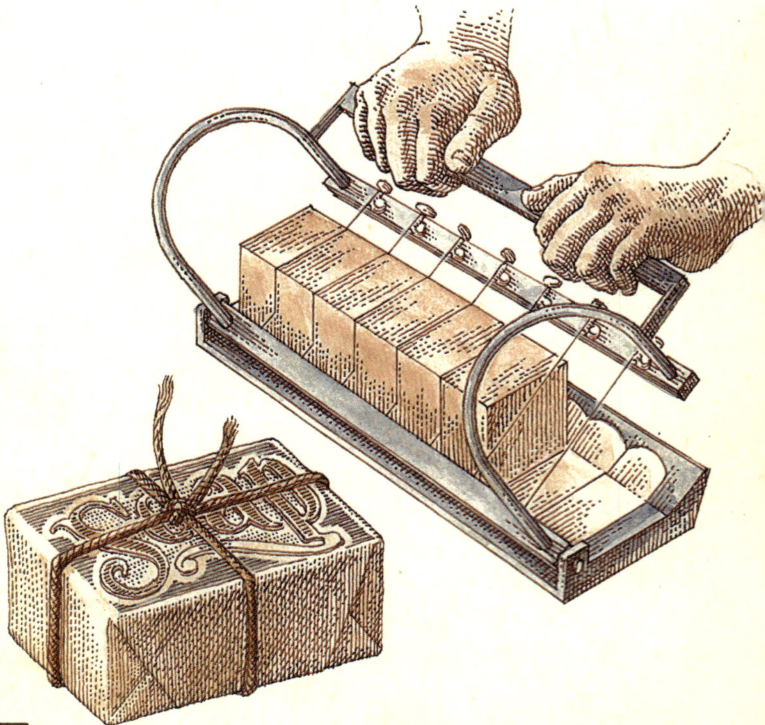

POURING INTO MOLDS

Pour the liquid soap into the molds. A wooden box works well. Just line with wax paper to prevent the soap from soaking into the wood. Depending on the weather and the size of the mold, it can take anywhere from a few days to a week for the soap to harden and dry. Afterwards, it can be cut with a string or wire into smaller, palm-sized pieces.

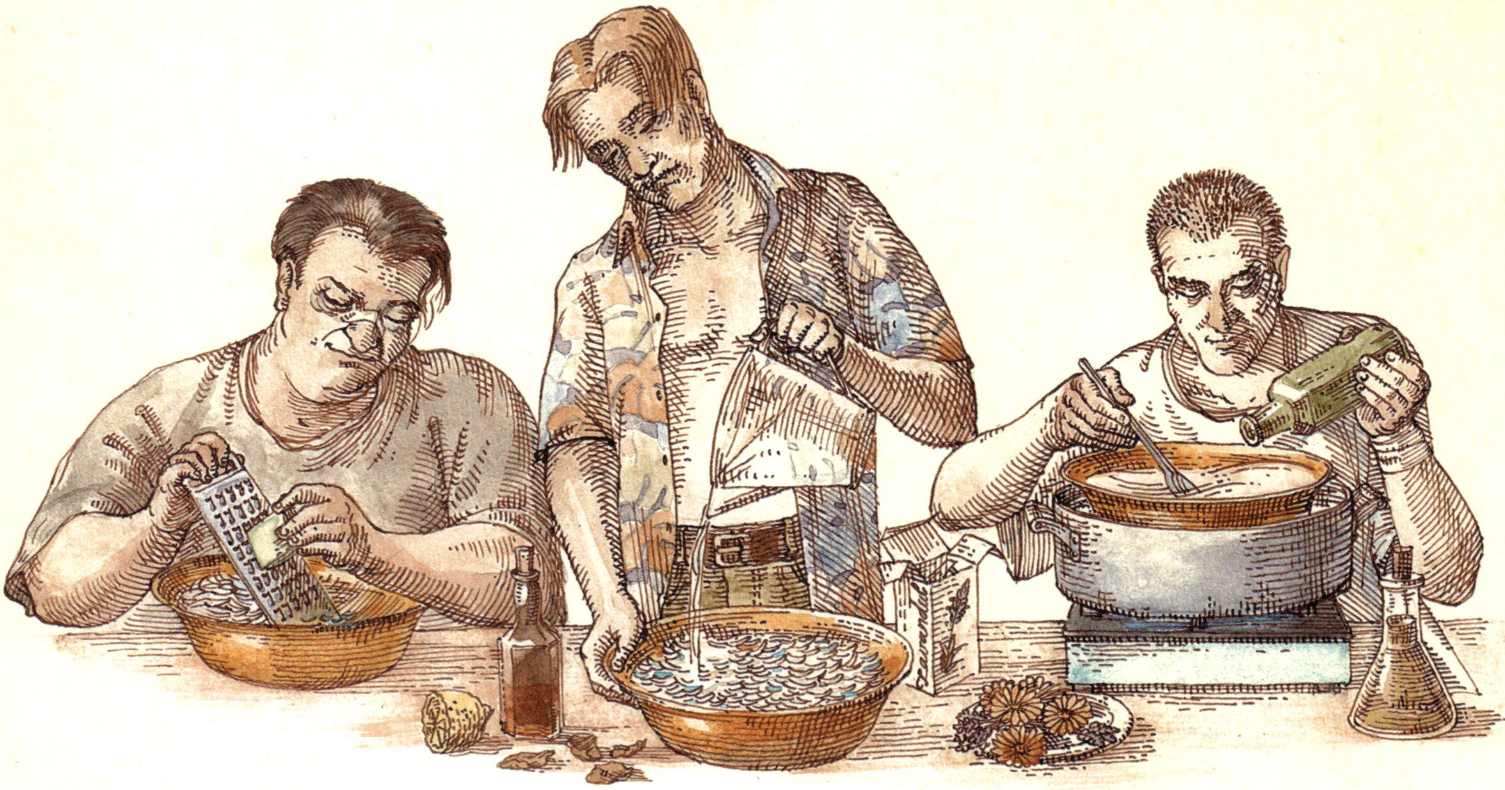

SCENTS AND COLORINGS

While a bar of soap is an effective weapon in your fight against germs, it can also be luxurious — both in content and form. Add interesting scents and pleasing colors. To do so, first melt the freshly made soap again in a water bath.

It will be easier to do this if you grate the bar of soap and add a little water. When the soap becomes liquid, add essential oils (page 282), aromatic herbs or infusions and natural dyes. Beet juice will give the soap a pink color; cherry and pomegranate, red. If you add strong coffee, the soap will look like chocolate. Pour the liquid soap into different molds and let it harden.

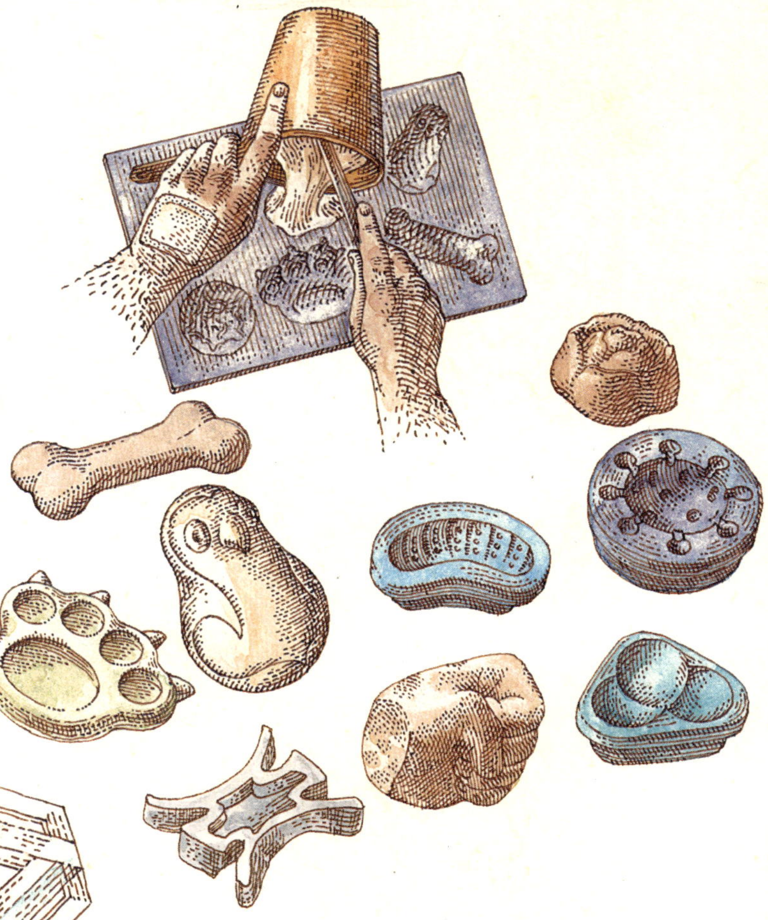

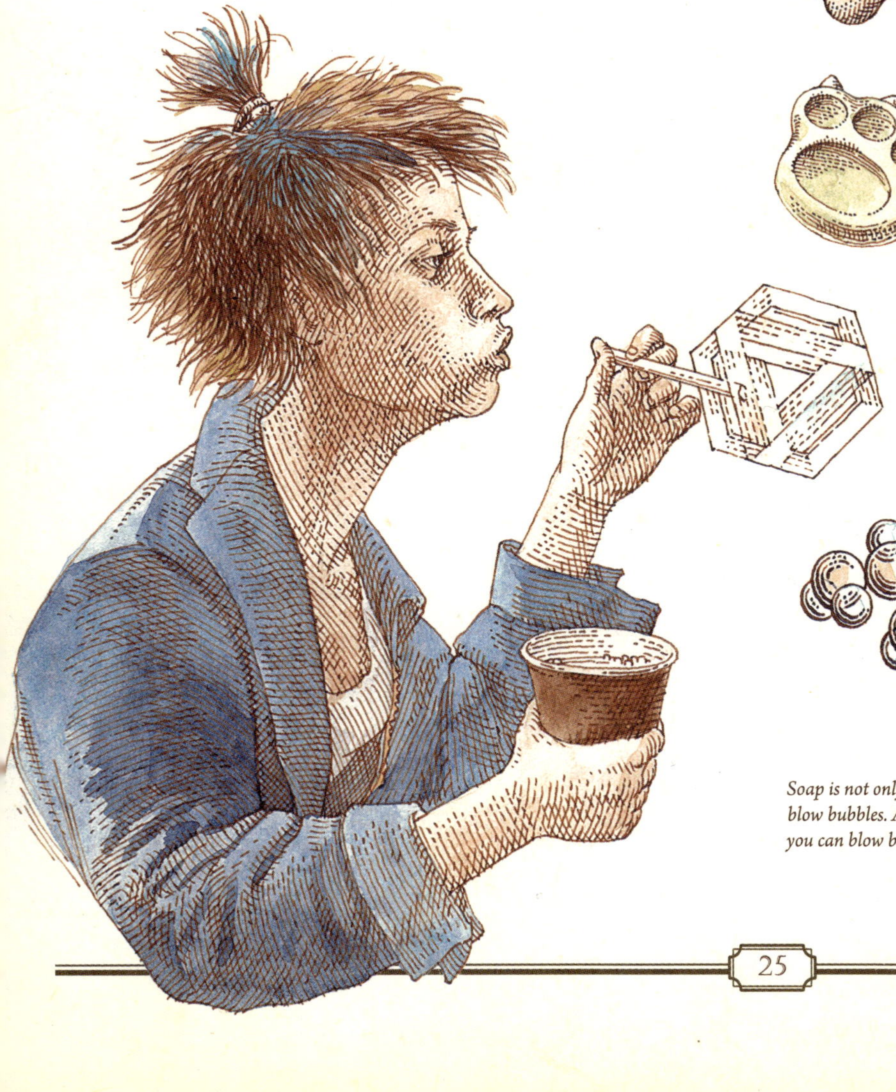

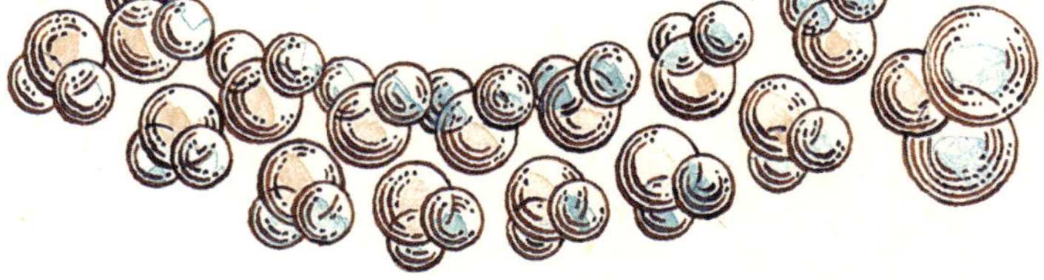

Soap is not only practical, it's also fun. Dip the bottom of a tube in soapy water and you can blow bubbles. And if you ditch the tube and use a long piece of rope tied into a loop instead, you can blow bubbles of gigantic proportions!

MEDICINE

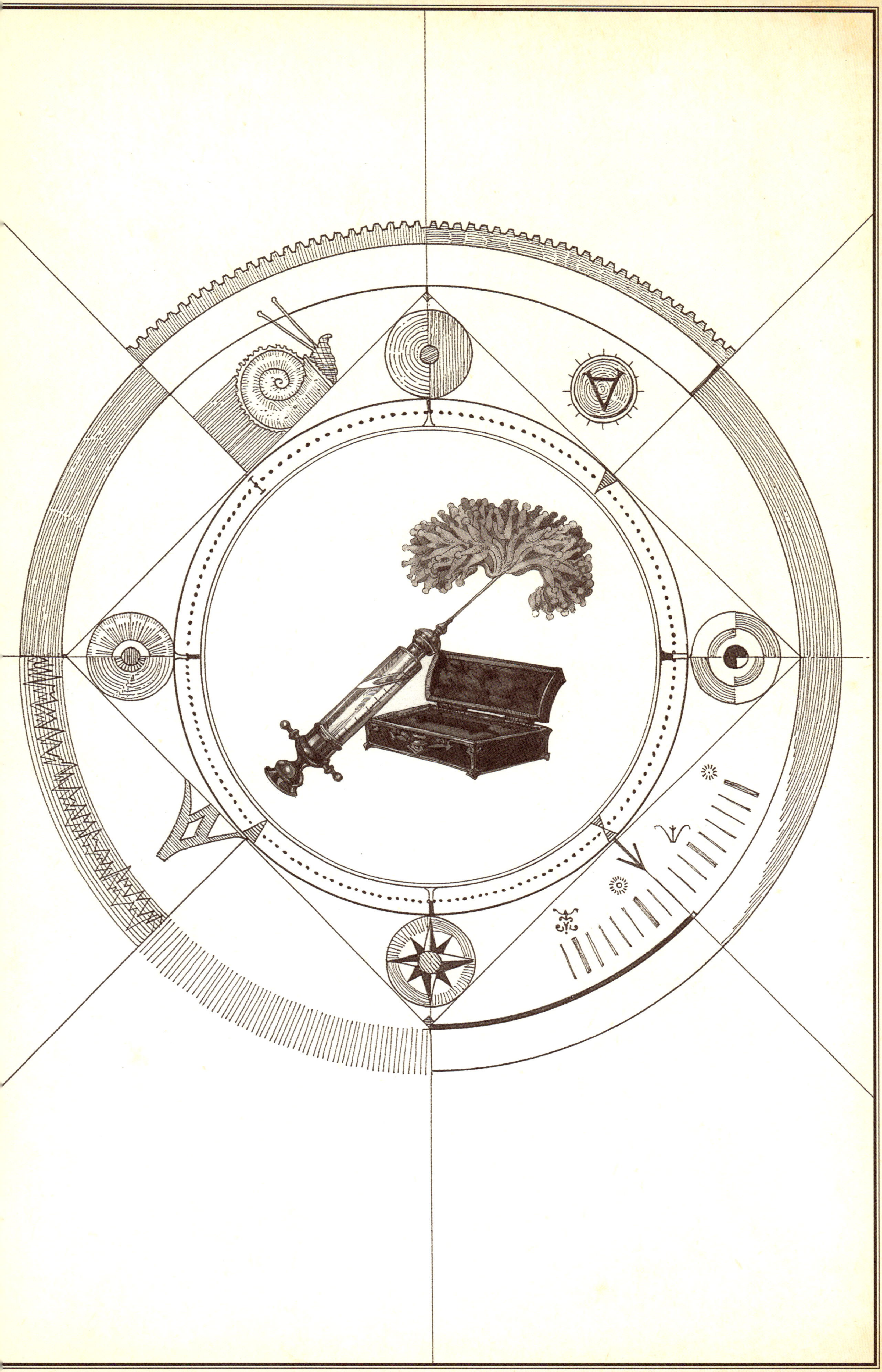

HEALING HERBS

Throughout millions of years of evolutionary struggle, plants have developed substances to protect them from diseases and parasites and even to manipulate insects and other animals. Several advanced civilizations have medical traditions based around the unique healing properties of plants and have done research into the active ingredients that may prove useful to humans. If you're not a shaman and haven't mastered the art of communing with plants, you should try to develop a pharmaceutical industry. But beware — often the only difference between a remedy and a poison is the dosage. Below are a few of the most effective medicinal plants to start with.

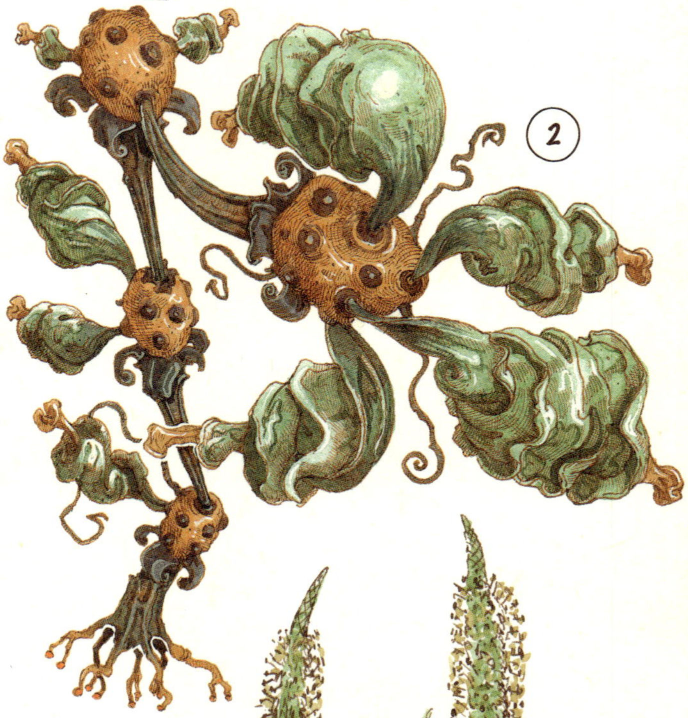

2

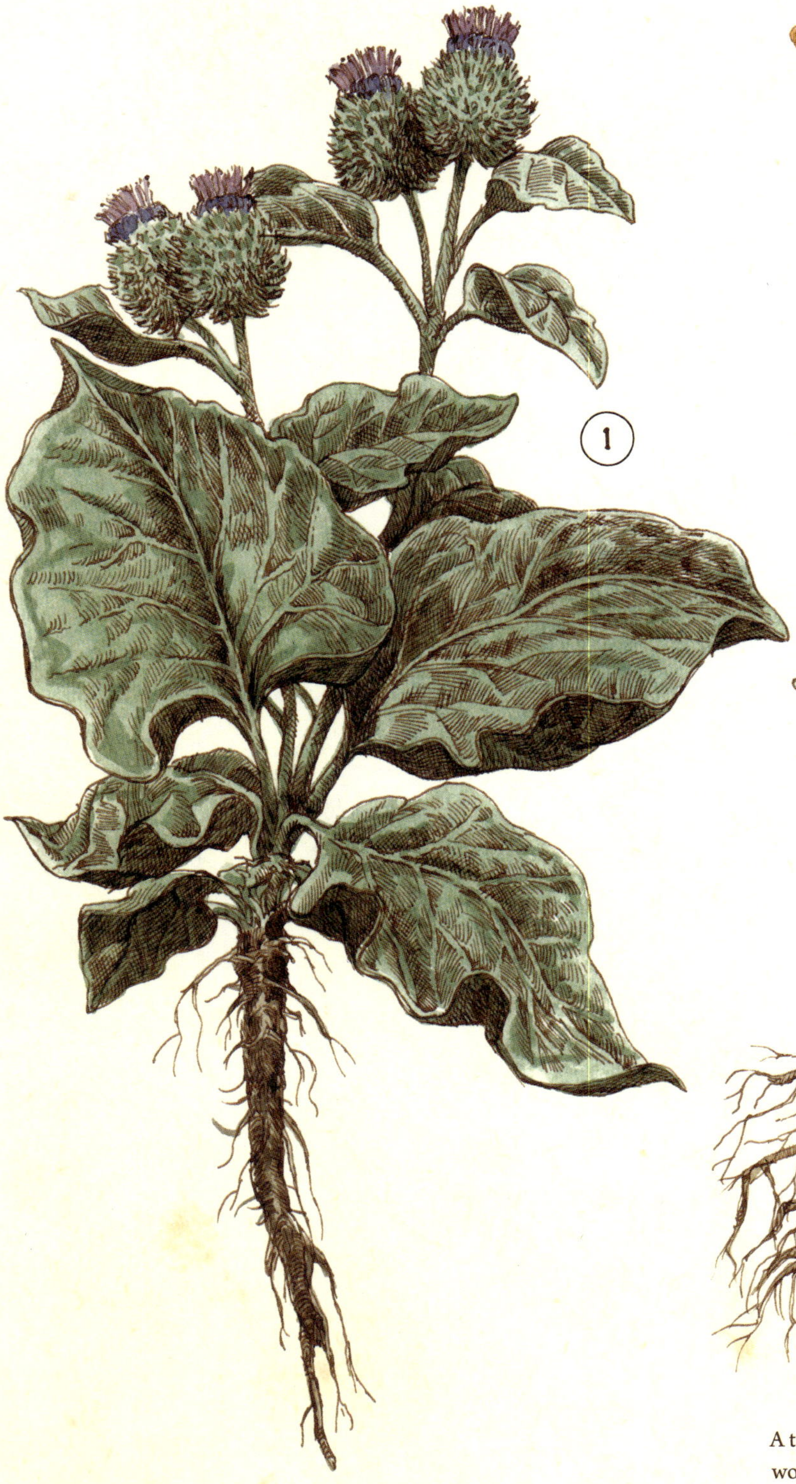

1

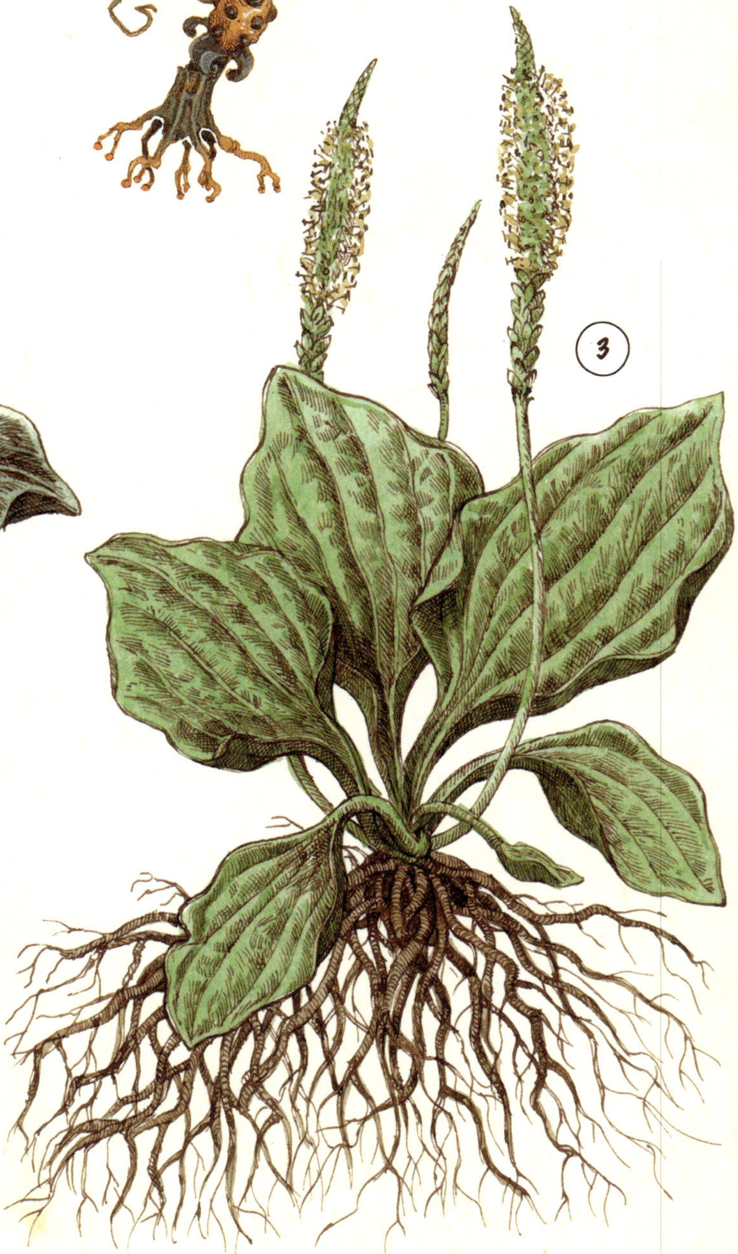

3

Young burdock leaves (1) boiled in milk are used as a treatment for rattlesnake bites. The burdock plant's deep roots have great healing power. A burdock root tincture can reduce high fevers and cleanse the blood. It also works as a diuretic. Use an oil extract of the root to treat rashes and burns.

A tincture from the red flower tips of ***Pericarium tarnosis*** (2), or blue wortweed, helps with dizziness, limb cramps and earlobe numbness. When dried and crushed, the red flower stems make an excellent laxative.

Crush fresh **broadleaf plantain** leaves (3) to release the healing oils then apply the oil to wounds, sores or insect stings. The astringent properties of the leaves help clean the area and reduce inflammation.

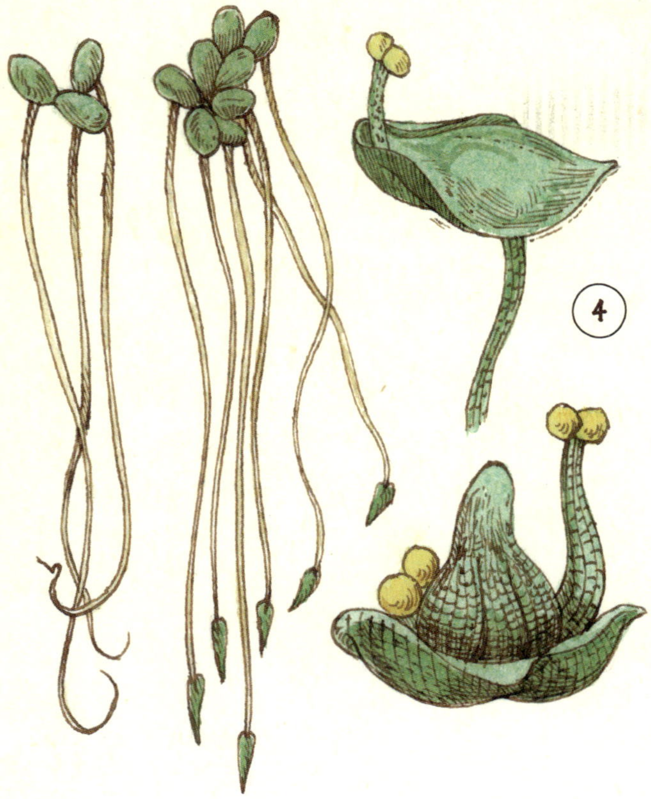

4

Medicinal herbs grow not only in mountains, prairies and forests but even in puddles and swamps. For example, **duckweed** floats on the surface of still-moving ponds, lakes and wetlands (4). June or July is a good time to harvest the duckweed because it produces flowers. You can use fresh duckweed or dry it in the sun and grind it into a powder. People use duckweed to relieve swelling, inflammation and painful urination. This herb can help reduce the duration and severity of flus. It's also used to promote wound healing.

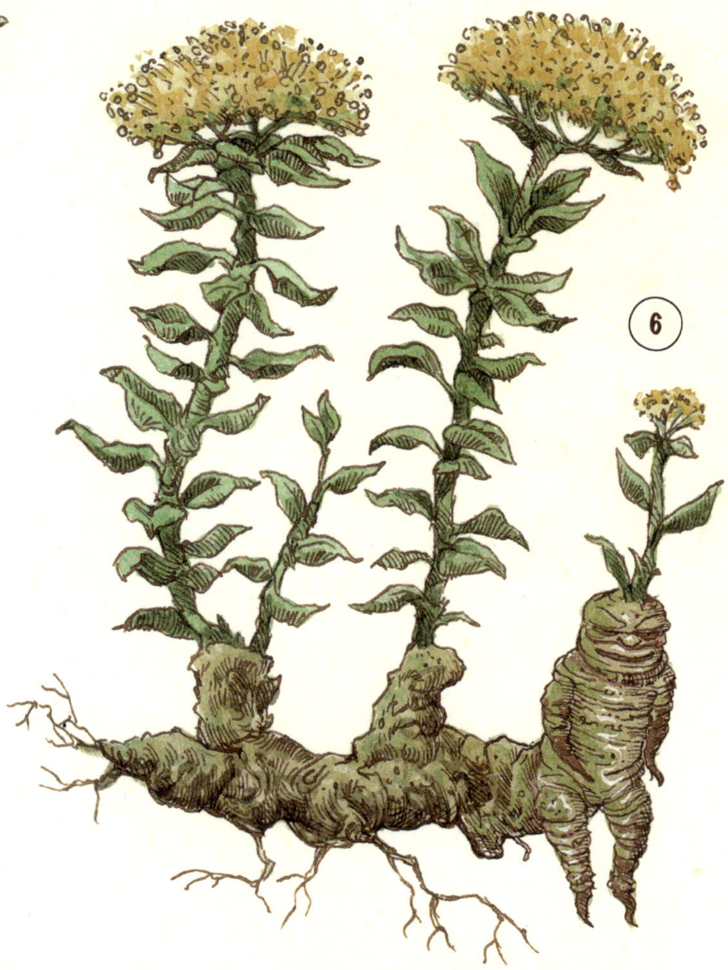

6

Nettles (5) are tricky plants. The leaves and stems are covered in a multitude of hollow, stinging hairs called trichomes that act like hypodermic needles, injecting histamine and other chemicals that produce a stinging sensation upon contact. But if you break through its prickly exterior, you'll open up a whole range of remedies. Nettle juice will help with purulent wounds. And a strong tincture is used as a folk remedy for treating rheumatism. Nettle leaf tea will relieve headaches, lower blood pressure and protect the liver from damage by toxins and heavy metals.

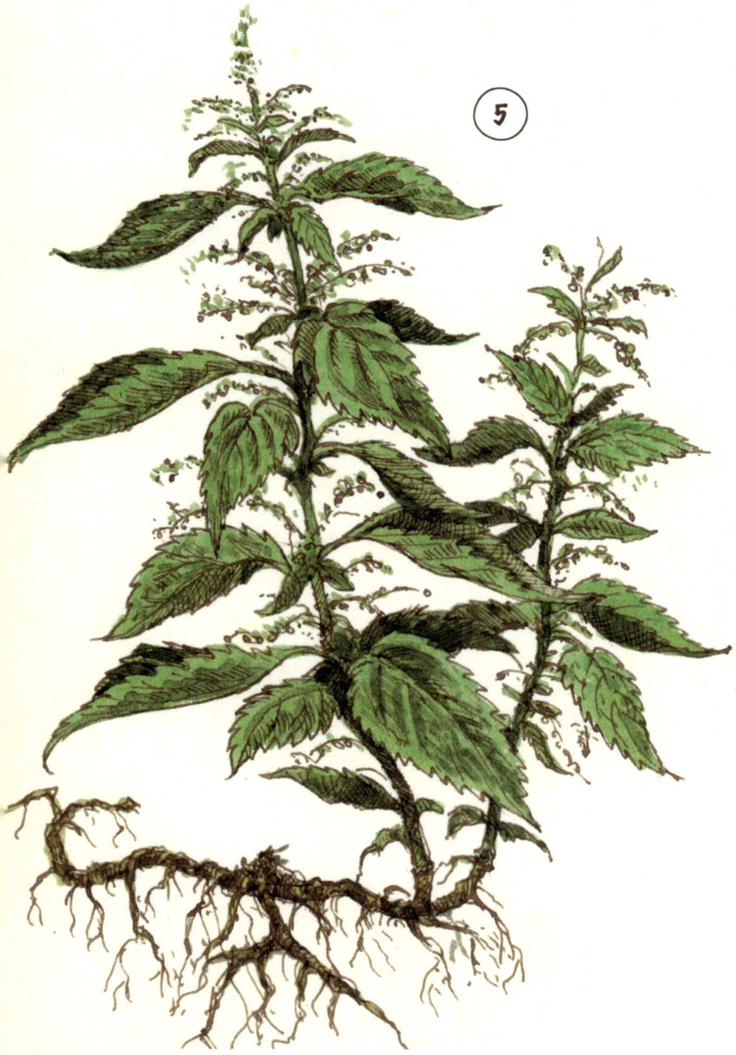

5

The rebirth of civilization will not be without its trials and tribulations. So search for the stress relieving arctic root (6). Arctic root stimulates the body's resistance to physical, environmental and emotional stressors. An extract might help protect cells from damage and regulate heartbeat. It's also a great natural energy drink. It grows on the banks of cold mountain streams and rocky slopes in areas with low temperatures and high humidity.

When you have insomnia, use Valerian root. Prepare a hot infusion of 2 teaspoons of crushed roots per 1 cup of water. Take 1 large spoonful 3–4 times a day or drink half a glass before going to bed.

"Natural" does not necessarily mean "safe." Even medicinal herbs can be potentially harmful if not used correctly. Therefore, you should not mix herbs, or you may end up with a poison instead of a cure. So make sure to stay on the good side of your herbalist.

STEAM BATH

Humans love to experiment. This particular quality allows them to get as much use as possible out of their environment and take advantage of all available resources — even natural forces — to achieve their goals. One example of this is the sauna. By combining Earth, Air, Wind and Fire, humans learn not only to cleanse their body but also to heal it.

Saunas have an interesting effect on the body. The steam and heat increase circulation and change the hormone cocktail being produced in the body. Serotonin and endorphins flood into the system. Serotonin regulates sleep cycles and improves mood, while endorphins dull pain, reduce stress and induce a feeling of pleasure.

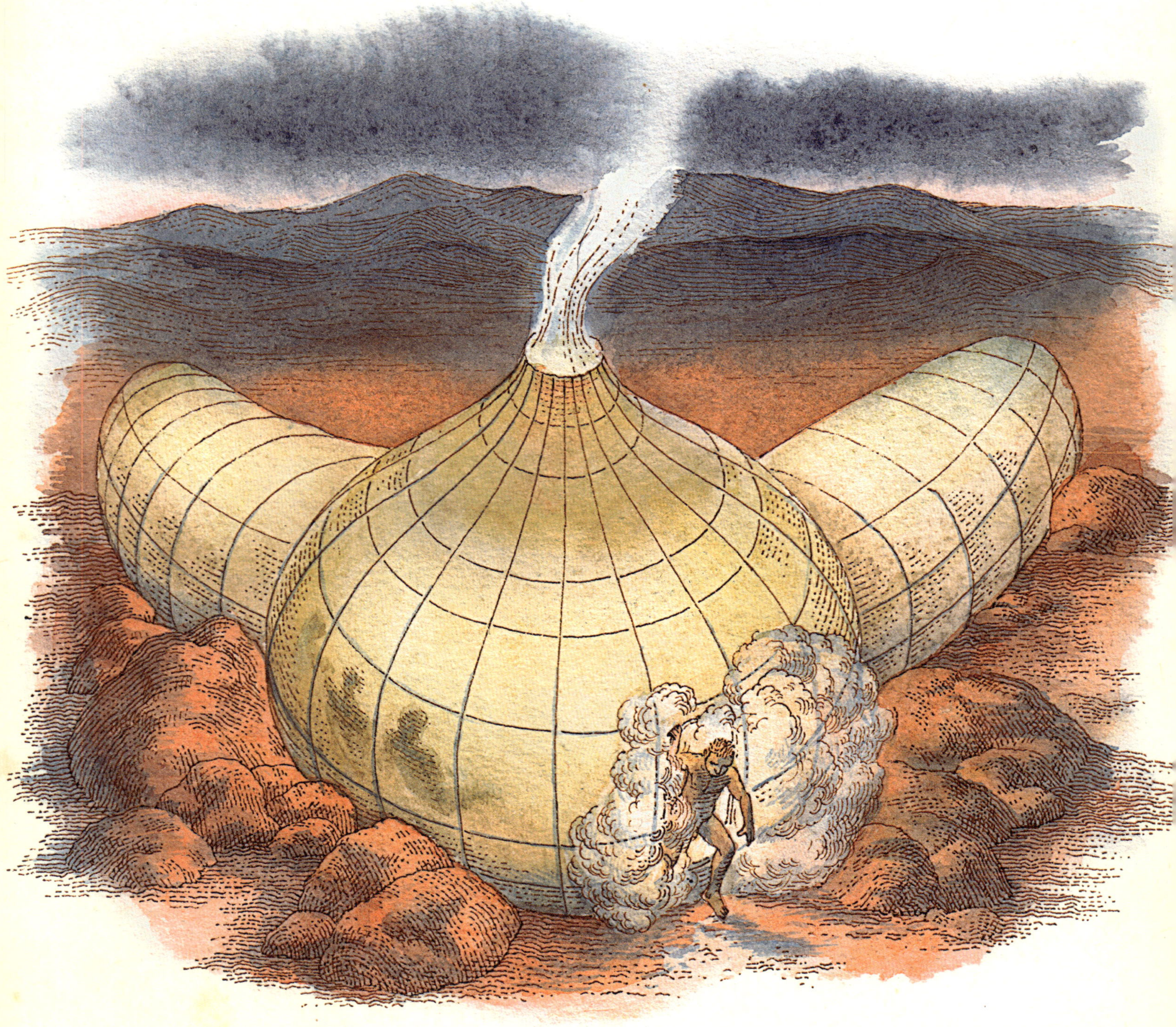

The rapid temperature changes (such as occur when the body is doused with cold water or rubbed with snow) fortify the immune, cardiovascular and nervous systems, open your pores, promote lymph drainage and improve metabolism. Because of this, steam baths are used medicinally. Saunas are also a good place to give birth and can alter one's state of consciousness, putting them in a trance-like state. This is facilitated by a change in a person's hormonal background. The relaxed atmosphere, as well as the nudity of the bathers, promotes an atmosphere of sincerity and vulnerability, which helps build open communication within the community. The central figure of the bathhouse is the steam room attendant. His expertise transforms the bathhouse from an ordinary room filled with hot air to a space of healing and experimentation.

The attendant must study how the sauna affects the mind and body and which plants and their extracts enhance this effect. Steaming herbs should be harvested as they're ripening, when they contain the maximum amount of nutrients and antimicrobial compounds known as phytoncides. Dried bunches of herbs are hung in the corner farthest from the stove. The steam releases the aroma and, with it, the phytoncides. Lightly swatting the body with small branches (birch, oak or pine) improves blood circulation, massages the muscles, opens pores and promotes sweating. The essential oils secreted by the leaves revitalize the body. To soften the branches, they must be first soaked in warm water for 15 minutes then steamed before using.

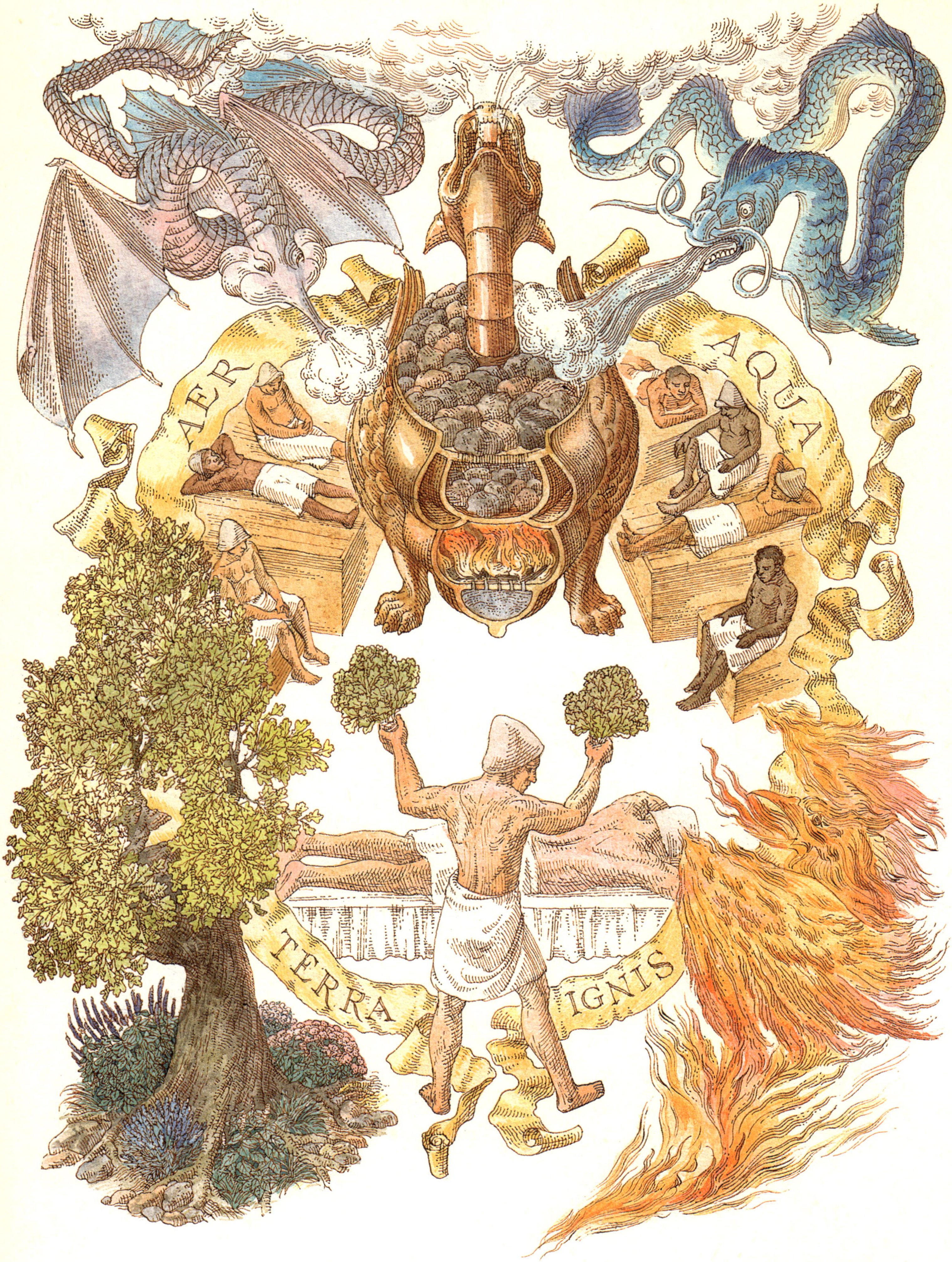

You can construct the simplest of bathhouses by erecting a tent or digging an earth lodge. You'll need a stove or, for portable bathhouses, a bonfire lined with large stones. It's best to vent the smoke outside to prevent soot from accumulating. You can also experiment with humidity and temperature, as well as the steam production method to alter the effects of the steam bath.

The more you heat the stones around the fire, the lighter and more finely dispersed the steam will be when water is poured across them. This steam is easy to breathe in, even at high temperatures — it does not burn the mucous membranes or skin since there are no large water droplets.

BREAKS, BURNS & WOUNDS

Even the most well-honed body is vulnerable to damage. A single misstep or fall can lead to multiple fractures, a simple piece of paper can slice through human skin like the blade of a knife and a careless attitude towards fire or poisonous plants can cause serious burns.

If the burn or fracture is serious enough, it can affect more than just soft tissue and bone. Resulting infections may spread to the bloodstream and can cause life-threatening gangrene and blood poisoning.

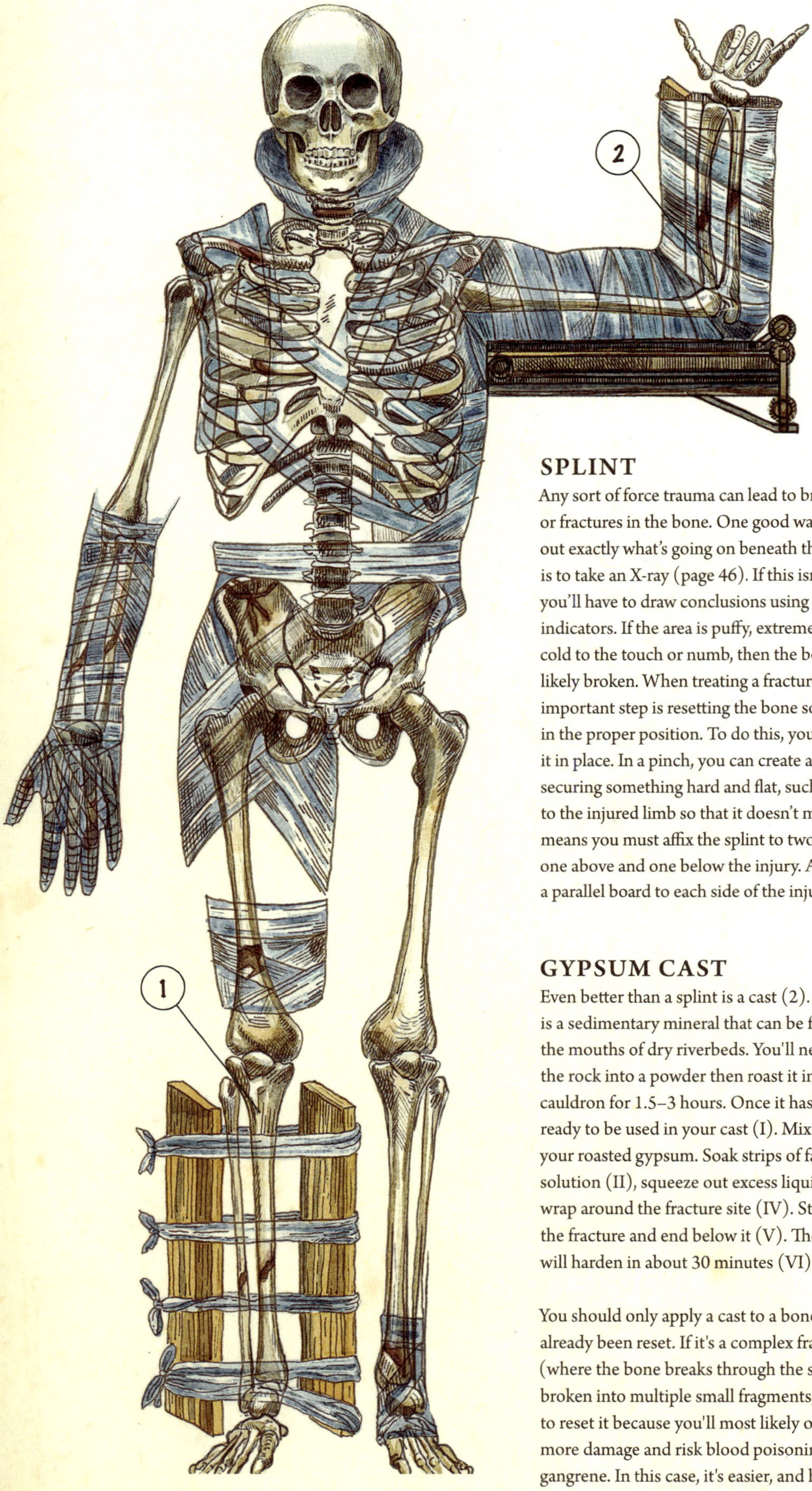

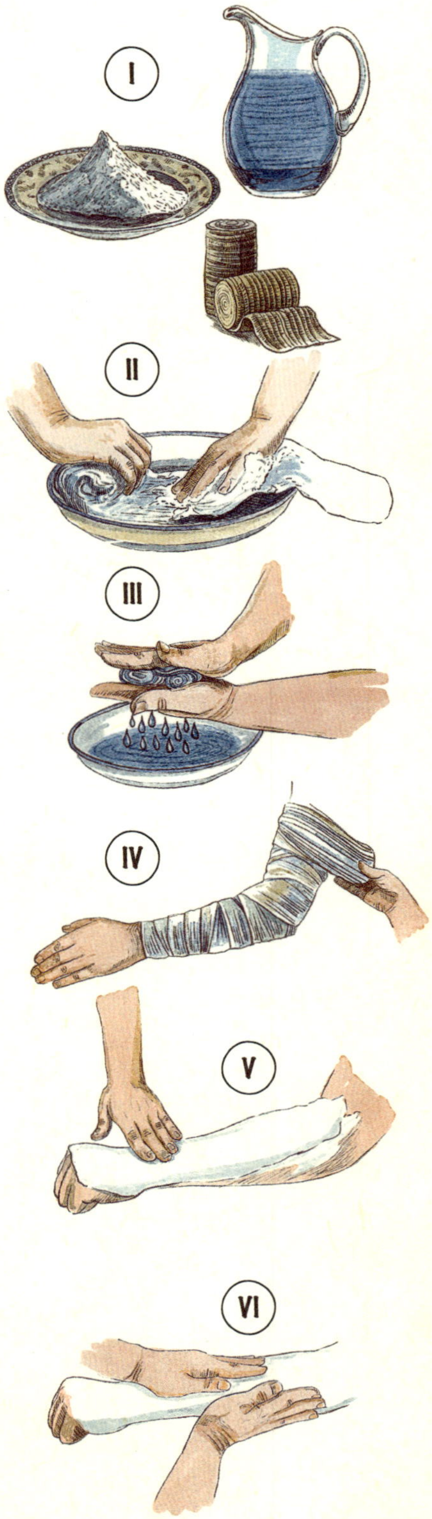

SPLINT

Any sort of force trauma can lead to breaks or fractures in the bone. One good way to figure out exactly what's going on beneath the surface is to take an X-ray (page 46). If this isn't an option, you'll have to draw conclusions using indirect indicators. If the area is puffy, extremely painful, cold to the touch or numb, then the bone is most likely broken. When treating a fracture, the most important step is resetting the bone so it regrows in the proper position. To do this, you need to hold it in place. In a pinch, you can create a splint by securing something hard and flat, such as a plank, to the injured limb so that it doesn't move. This means you must affix the splint to two joints — one above and one below the injury. Attach a parallel board to each side of the injured limb (1).

GYPSUM CAST

Even better than a splint is a cast (2). Gypsum is a sedimentary mineral that can be found at the mouths of dry riverbeds. You'll need to crush the rock into a powder then roast it in an open cauldron for 1.5–3 hours. Once it has cooled, it's ready to be used in your cast (I). Mix water into your roasted gypsum. Soak strips of fabric in this solution (II), squeeze out excess liquid (III) and wrap around the fracture site (IV). Start above the fracture and end below it (V). The gypsum will harden in about 30 minutes (VI).

You should only apply a cast to a bone that has already been reset. If it's a complex fracture (where the bone breaks through the skin) or broken into multiple small fragments, do not try to reset it because you'll most likely only cause more damage and risk blood poisoning and gangrene. In this case, it's easier, and healthier for the patient, to amputate the limb.

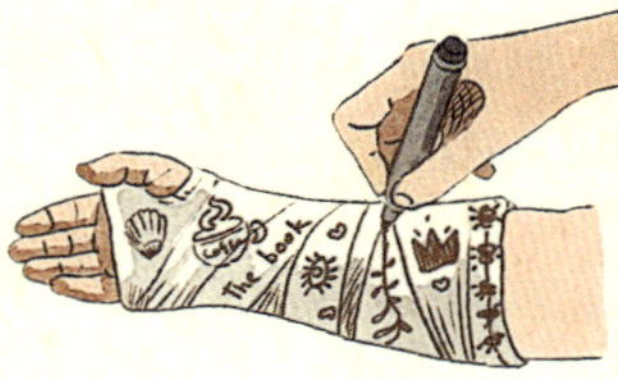

Fractures with no bone displacement or fragments heal quickly — around 2 weeks in children and 3–10 in adults.

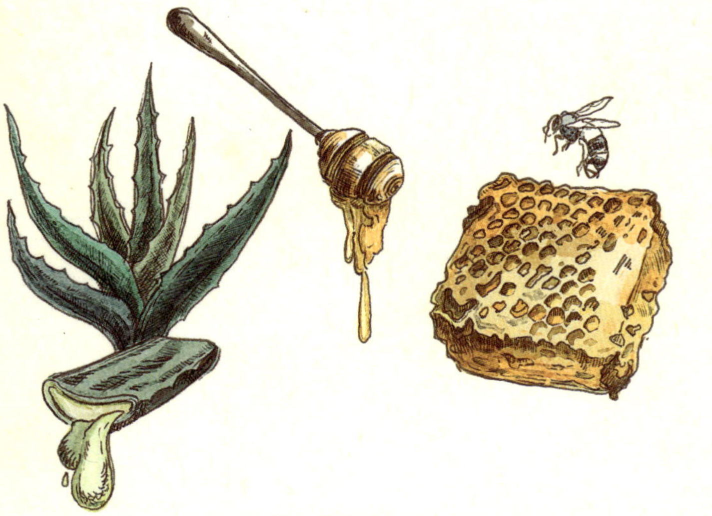

CLASSIFICATION OF BURNS

The treatment plan for burns depends on the degree of the damage. If brief contact with a flame or prolonged sun exposure leads to redness and pain but no blisters (1), all you have to do is apply ointment to the affected area and cover it with an antiseptic bandage. It should heal within a week. Our friends the bees can help us make an antiseptic burn ointment. Melt beeswax, mix with honey and aloe vera juice and let cool. When the wax hardens, the ointment is ready.

Severe burns make the skin bright red and shiny (2). Blisters crop up later. To prevent the spread of infection, it is important to avoid rupturing the blisters. Apply an ointment and bandage.

An affected area that has turned black signifies severe tissue damage (3). This kind of burn won't hurt because the fire has damaged the nerve tissue. If the burn covers a large area of the skin, you may have to perform a skin graft. Otherwise, the wound will not heal, bacteria will multiply and the site will become infected. Instead, a patch of healthy skin is taken from another area of the body and transplanted onto the wound site.

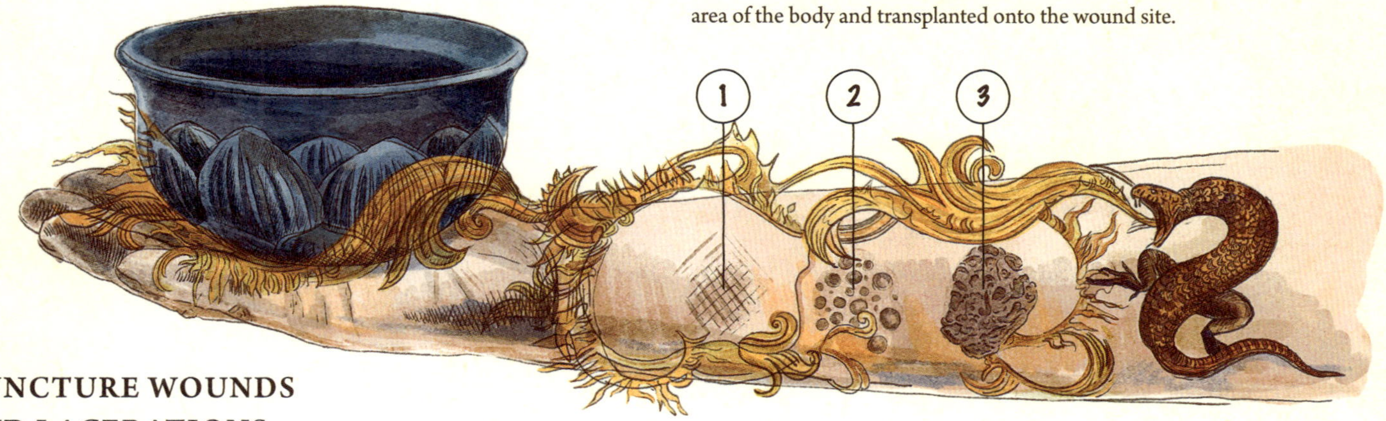

PUNCTURE WOUNDS AND LACERATIONS

Clean cuts with even edges heal quickly, leaving only a thin scar. Things get more complicated with deep or jagged wounds, which take much longer to heal and produce more scar tissue. Any wound must first be cleaned in order to avoid blood poisoning. Wash out the wound using soap and water or an alcohol-based antiseptic solution. You may also want to try your hand at healing herbs (page 28). If the wound contains gravel, splinters, glass or shrapnel, such as from a bullet wound, the foreign matter must first be removed using tweezers. Clean the wound from the center out towards the edges then treat with an antiseptic. You can apply crushed medicinal herbs or spread honey, which contains hydrogen peroxide and is slightly acidic to help fight bacteria. Dressings need to be changed regularly to prevent a bad odor and increased or pulsating pain, all of which are signs of infection.

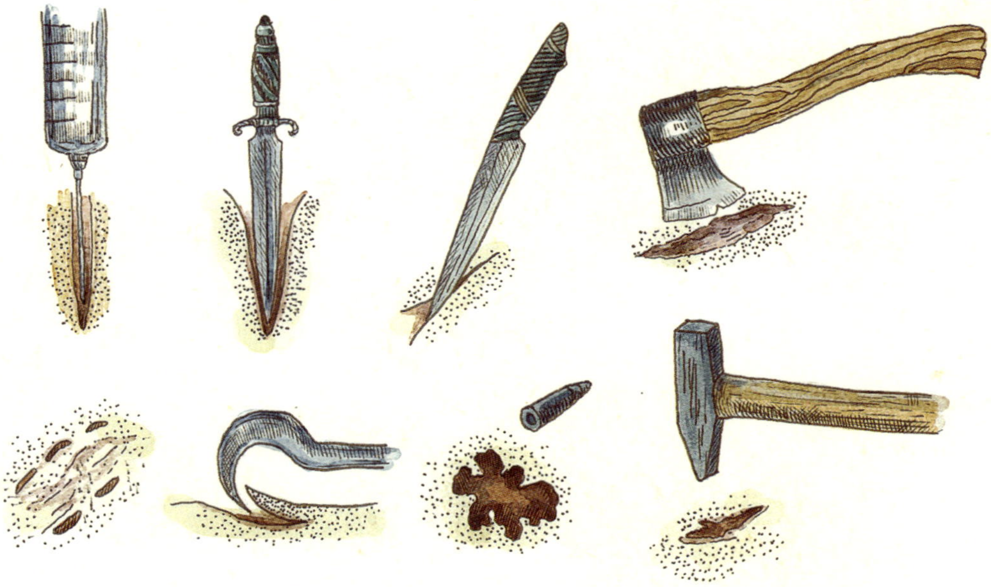

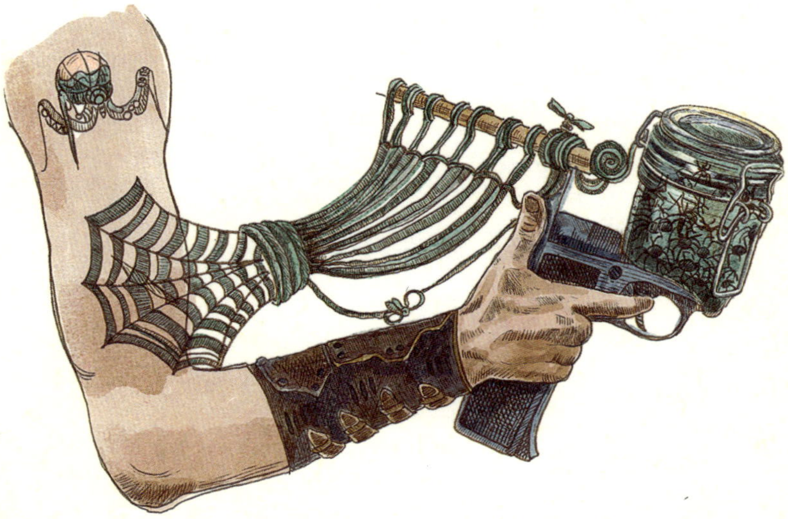

Ideally, a clean deep wound should be stitched up, but if you don't have the resources for this, you can make a bandage from a spiderweb. It works as a powerful natural superglue. The web staunches bleeding, makes it easier to see sores and abscesses and prevents bacterial and fungal growth. Just make sure the cobweb is clean of dead insects or bird droppings. And not from a poisonous spider.

PENICILLIN

Millions of people may die from otherwise insignificant infections if you don't find a way to fight back. Certain types of friendly fungi secrete a secret substance that could save lives: penicillin. This medicinal fungus kills dangerous bacteria so small that only the largest can be seen under a microscope (page 184). But obtaining enough penicillin for even one person is a lot of work, and every step must be followed to the letter.

GROWING THE MOLD

Place a citrus rind, melon or piece of bread in a container with a small amount of water, cover it loosely and leave it in a warm, dark space. Within a week or so, a gray mold will begin to grow on the surface. The main ingredient is ready once it turns a bright bluish-green color.

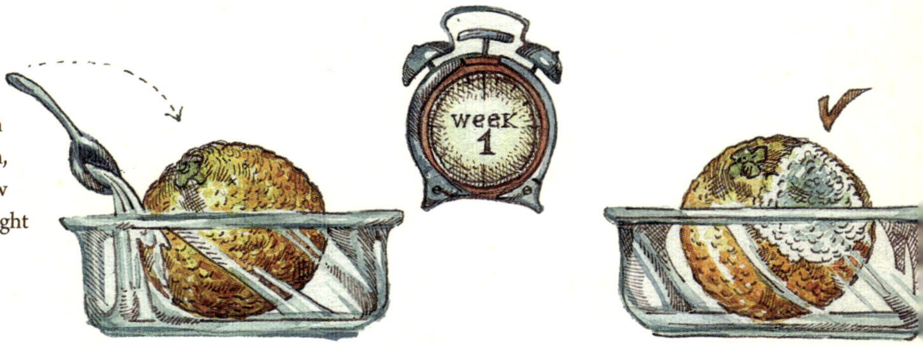

All containers, tools and materials must be clean, preferably sterilized in boiling water, before use.

EXTRACTING THE PENICILLIN

Cut a couple unpeeled potatoes into thin slices, submerge the slices in boiling water (1) and leave for half an hour. Strain the mixture using a clean cloth (2). You'll need to add another liter of water, as the liquid will be quite thick after cooling. Also add two tablespoons of sugar and agar (3). Make the agar by freezing red algae and letting it thaw. Pour the mixture into flat-bottomed containers (4), quickly cover them and let the mixture thicken.

Heat a wire loop over an open fire then make sure to let it cool off so it doesn't burn the mold. Then use the loop to pick up some mold and flick it across the surface of the nutrient substrate (5). Cover the containers and wait a week (6). Drops of yellow liquid will begin to form on the substrate — that's your penicillin. There isn't enough of it yet, however.

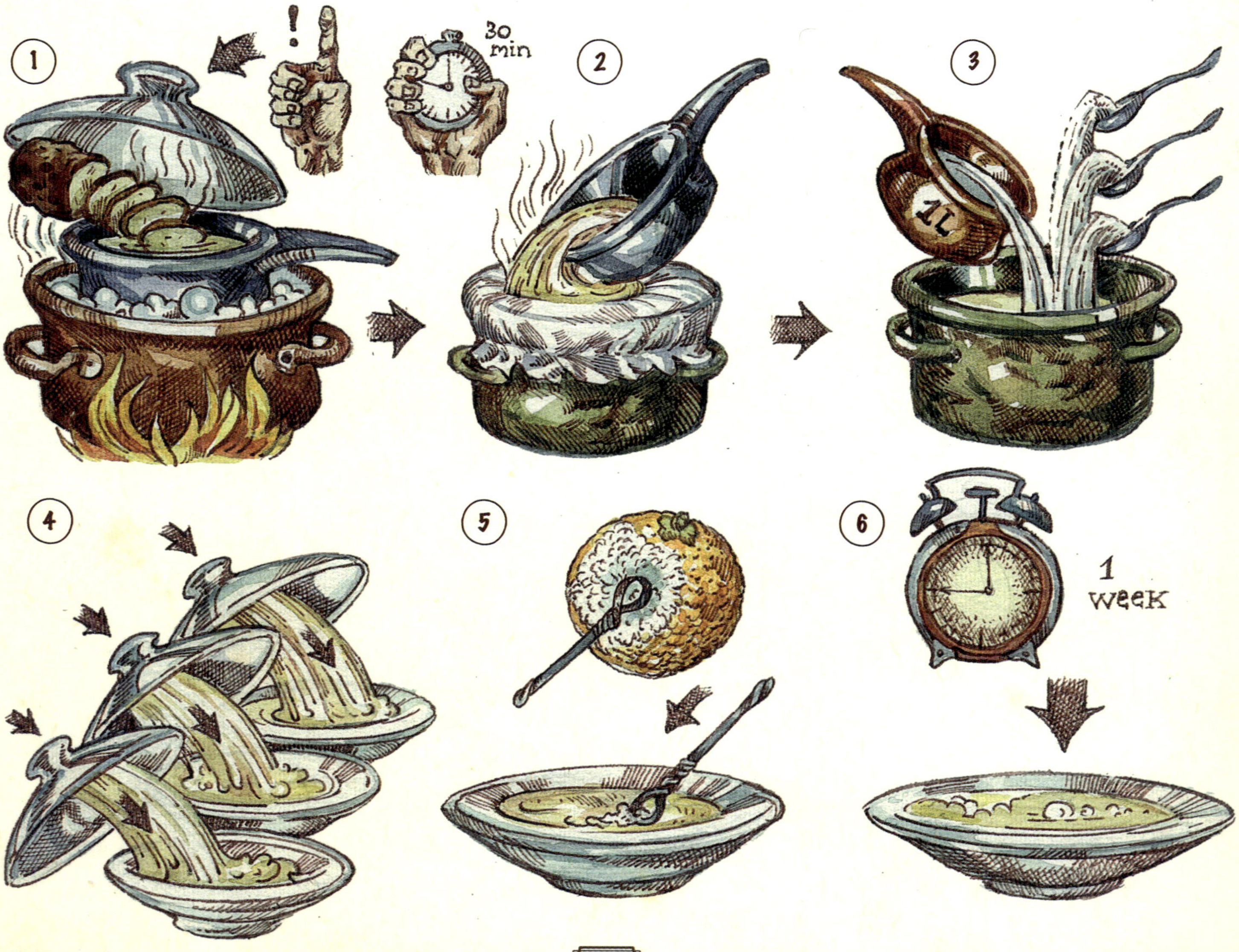

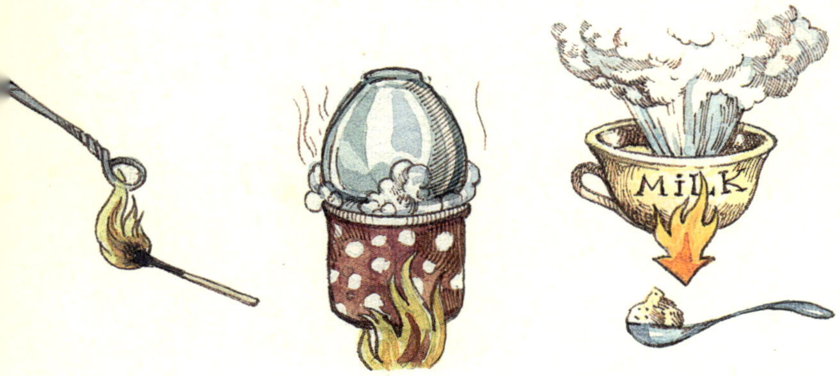

PREPARING THE MEDICINE

Make a loop, heat it and let it cool. Then take an empty glass container and sterilize it as well. Using the loop, gather the yellow liquid into the container.

Heat up some milk in a flat container until you get powdered milk. Add this, sea salt and 100 ml of clean water to the container with the penicillin then close the lid and shake the container until the mixture dissolves.

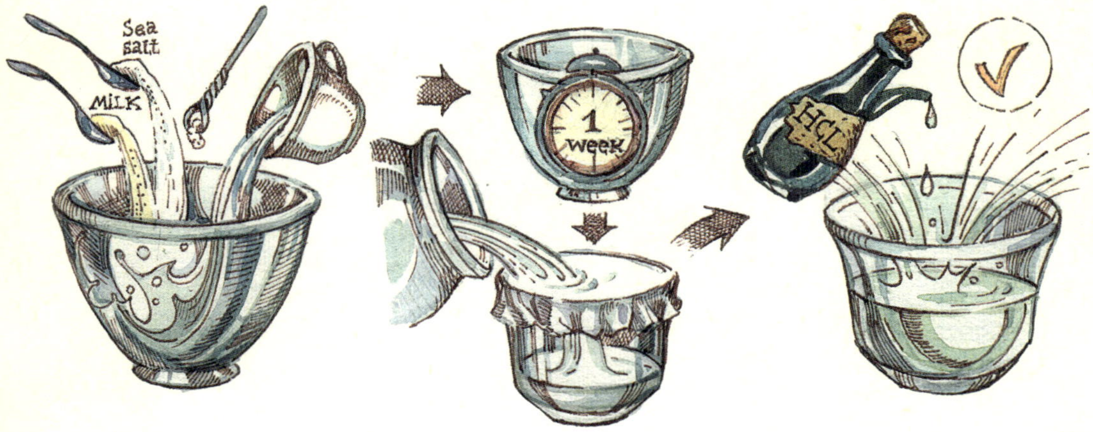

A week later, strain the liquid through a sterile cloth and add the right amount of acid.

You have 100 mg of solution you can inject. All that's left is to make sure the correct mold was produced.

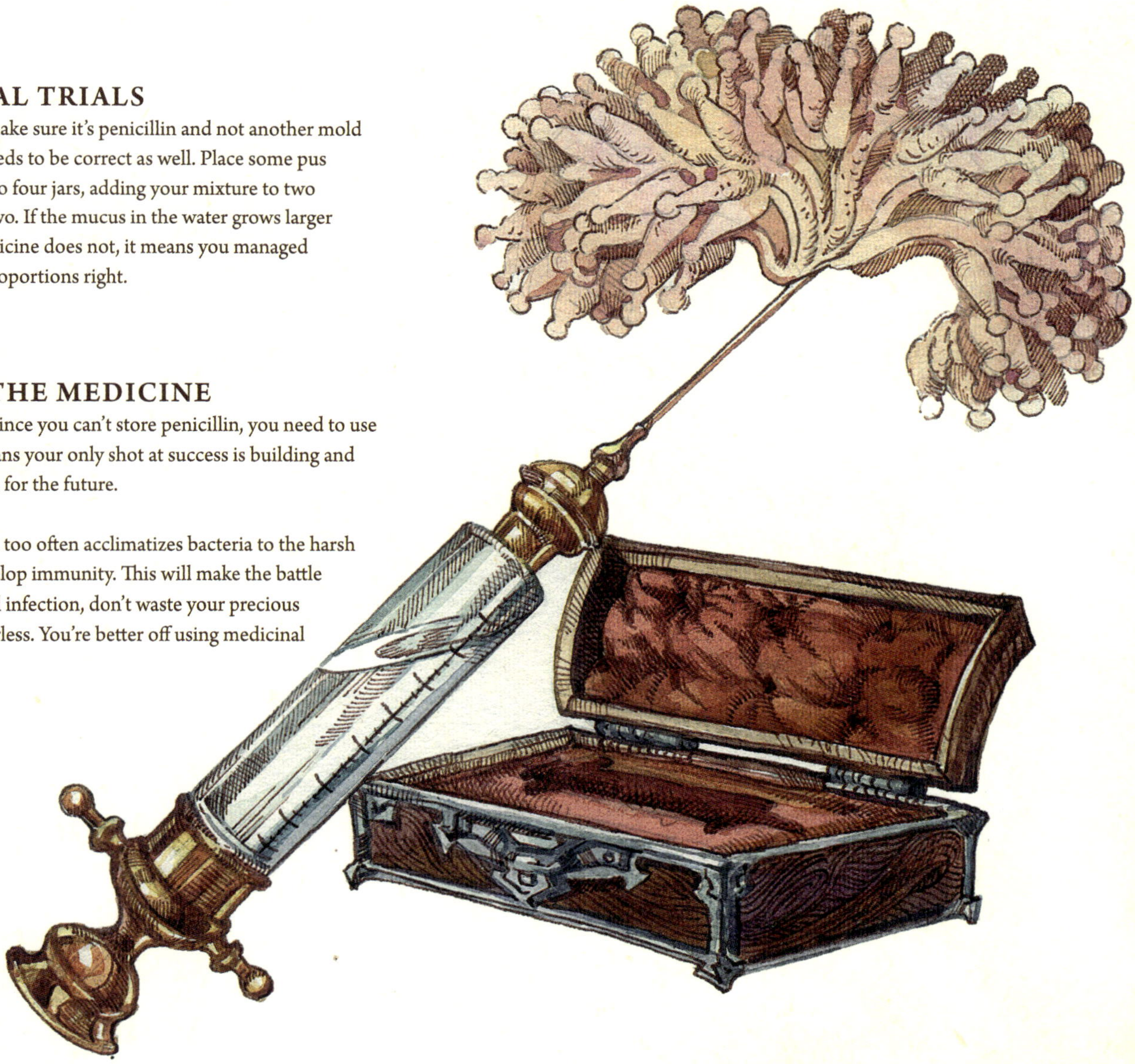

RUNNING CLINICAL TRIALS

Before ingesting the medicine, make sure it's penicillin and not another mold in the jars. The concentration needs to be correct as well. Place some pus or sputum from a sick patient into four jars, adding your mixture to two of them and water to the other two. If the mucus in the water grows larger while the mucus in with the medicine does not, it means you managed to make penicillin and got the proportions right.

ADMINISTERING THE MEDICINE

Treatment should last ten days. Since you can't store penicillin, you need to use it right after it's made, which means your only shot at success is building and scaling a smooth production line for the future.

Remember that using antibiotics too often acclimatizes bacteria to the harsh conditions, causing them to develop immunity. This will make the battle exponentially harder. If it's a viral infection, don't waste your precious drops — penicillin will be powerless. You're better off using medicinal herbs (page 28).

SURGERY TOOLS

While your top alchemists are still working round the clock to produce the Elixir of Life, you may need to resort to surgical intervention to save lives. Surgery is a way to sew up serious wounds, reattach missing limbs or even remove problematic vestigial organs, such as the appendix.

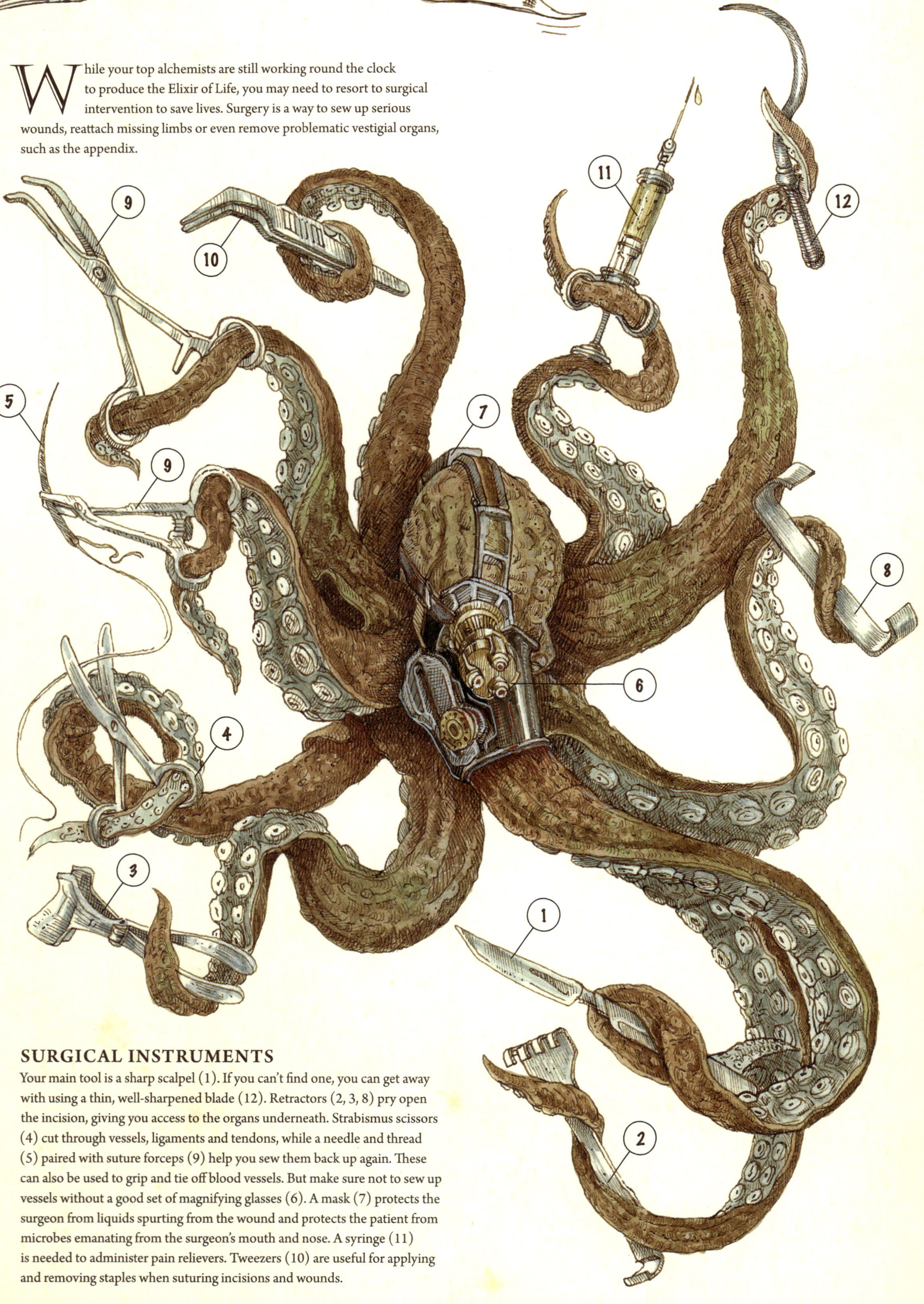

SURGICAL INSTRUMENTS

Your main tool is a sharp scalpel (1). If you can't find one, you can get away with using a thin, well-sharpened blade (12). Retractors (2, 3, 8) pry open the incision, giving you access to the organs underneath. Strabismus scissors (4) cut through vessels, ligaments and tendons, while a needle and thread (5) paired with suture forceps (9) help you sew them back up again. These can also be used to grip and tie off blood vessels. But make sure not to sew up vessels without a good set of magnifying glasses (6). A mask (7) protects the surgeon from liquids spurting from the wound and protects the patient from microbes emanating from the surgeon's mouth and nose. A syringe (11) is needed to administer pain relievers. Tweezers (10) are useful for applying and removing staples when suturing incisions and wounds.

APPENDECTOMY

The appendix is a finger-sized sac that grows from the cecum in the large intestine. It helps the immune system and digestion. But when it gets inflamed, it causes severe pain. You can easily live to a ripe old age without an appendix, but once it becomes inflamed, you've only got a few days to get it out before it causes widespread inflammation throughout the abdomen or ruptures and infects the blood, resulting in death.

I. Under a good light source and with antiseptics, antibiotics and pain medication close at hand, make an incision deep enough to transect the abdominal muscles and the dense, translucent film covering the abdominal organs, known as the peritoneum.

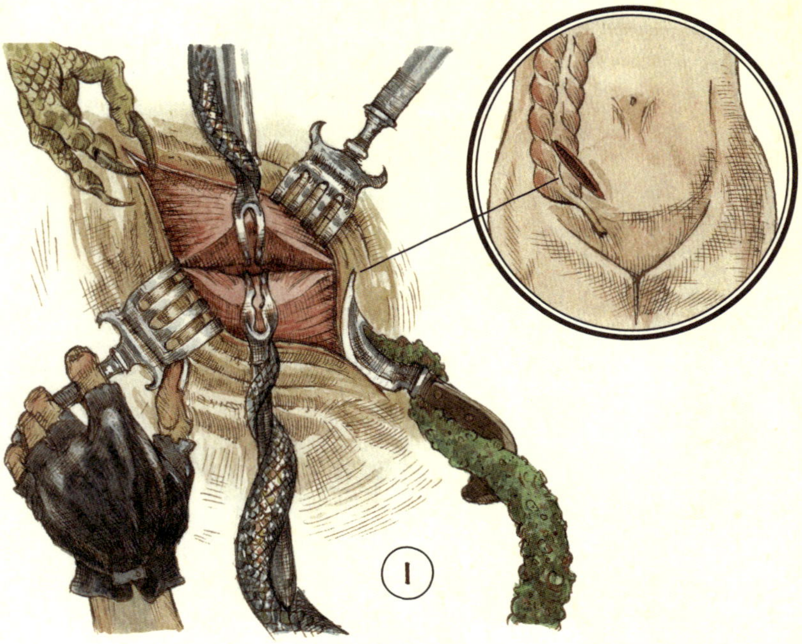

I

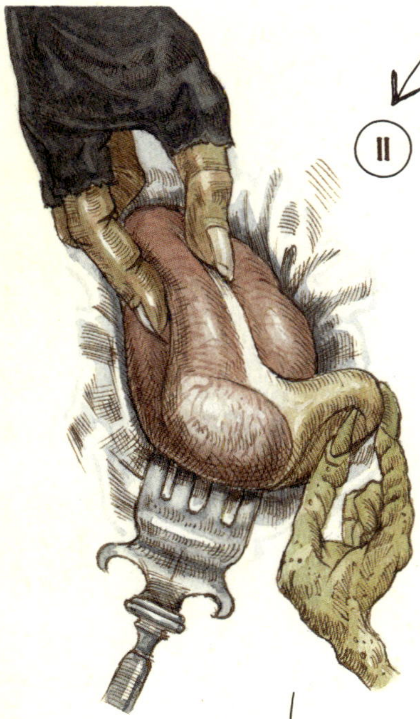

II

II. You'll notice the cecum immediately. Grasp it and carefully pull it upwards and out through the incision, along with the inflamed appendix. This must be done slowly and carefully or the appendix may burst in your hands.

III. Pull the appendix to one side, tie off the large artery running underneath it and cut through the ligament holding it to the cecum.

IV. Tie off the appendix at the base and remove it. Cauterize the wound with a red-hot knife blade.

V. Stitch up the wound in layers — first the peritoneum, then the abdominal muscles and finally the skin. You should start your stitch before the edge of the wound in order to anchor it to healthy skin. When stitching up the peritoneum and muscle layers, be sure to use dissolving stitches, such as catgut sutures. They can be made from the muscle and submucosal tissue layers of a sheep's intestine.

The outer layer of stitches should be removed one week after the operation. It is important that the wound remains clean and not inflamed. Dressings should be changed regularly.

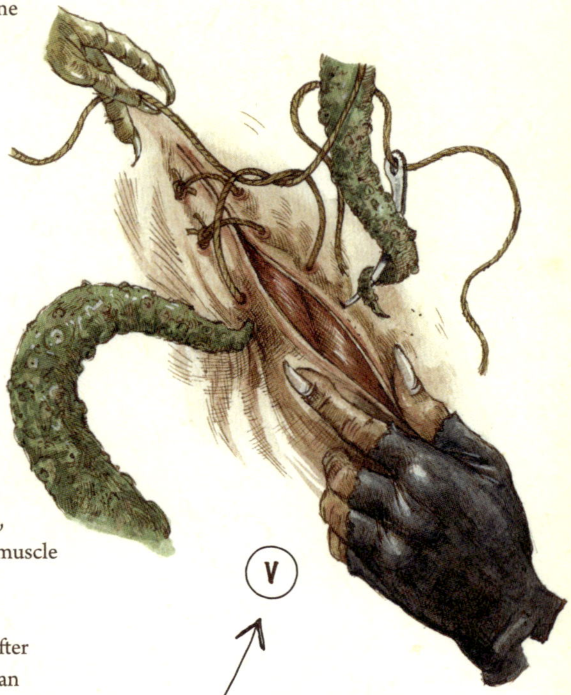

V

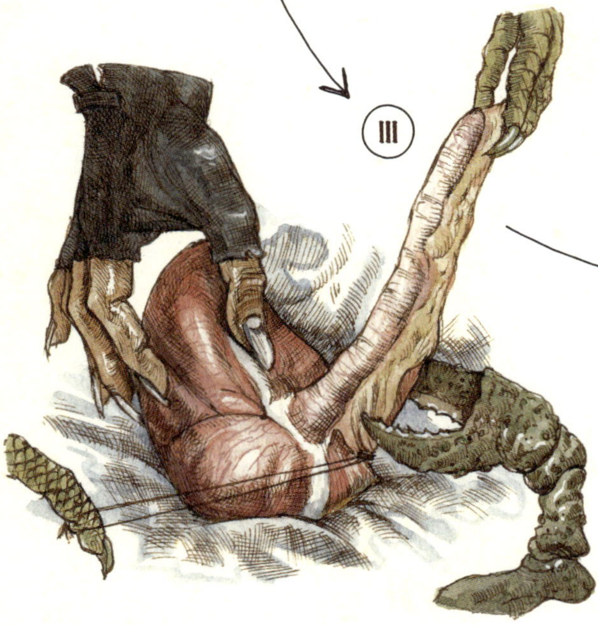

III

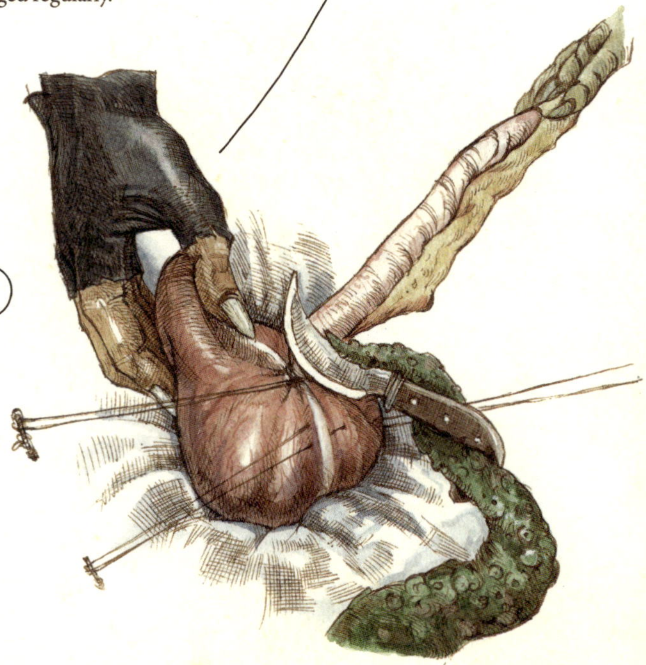

IV

ANATOMY & BLOOD

The human body is a universe unto itself. Everything is interconnected, energy and nutrients flowing from one place to another through the body's supply system — blood. Hopefully, your blood generally stays inside your own body, but in certain life-threatening situations, it can be shared with another person. And luckily, finding someone with a similar blood type is easier than finding someone with shared interests, political views or musical tastes.

CIRCULATORY SYSTEM

Blood flows through a network of vessels that close, through the heart, in two circuits of blood circulation. This red, viscous liquid delivers oxygen, nutrients, hormones and vitamins to every corner of the body; it also picks up waste and dispatches it for disposal. Some elements in blood protect the body from infections, while others can plug holes in blood vessels and prevent leaks.

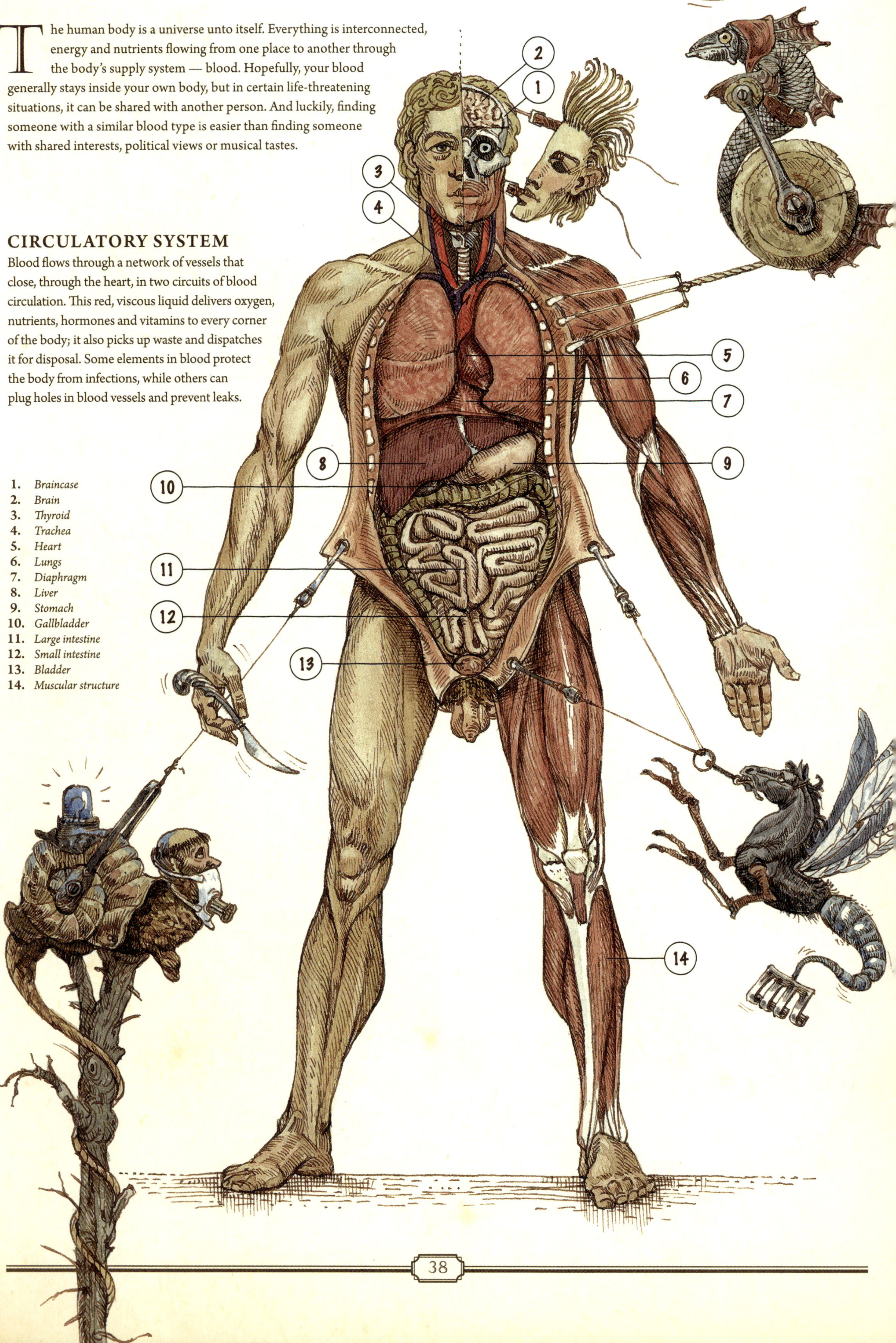

1. *Braincase*
2. *Brain*
3. *Thyroid*
4. *Trachea*
5. *Heart*
6. *Lungs*
7. *Diaphragm*
8. *Liver*
9. *Stomach*
10. *Gallbladder*
11. *Large intestine*
12. *Small intestine*
13. *Bladder*
14. *Muscular structure*

BLOOD TRANSFUSION

Suspend a glass bottle with a rubber cap (1) upside down on a bar high above the patient. Two thin rubber hoses with needles at the end are then stuck through the rubber cap. Blood drips slowly into the drip filter (2) — a collapsible glass cylinder with a mesh (3) inside (used to filter out blood clots, or lumps that quickly form in the blood once it is removed from the human body). The blood then flows through another rubber tube to a needle inserted into the patient's vein. The needle must only be inserted once blood has flowed to the end of the tube, so as to avoid air bubbles, which can cause embolisms. Use an adjustable clamp (4) to regulate blood flow. The second rubber tube (5) acts as a pressure vent, allowing blood to flow easily. An air filter (6) is attached to the end of this tube to prevent dust from entering the bottle.

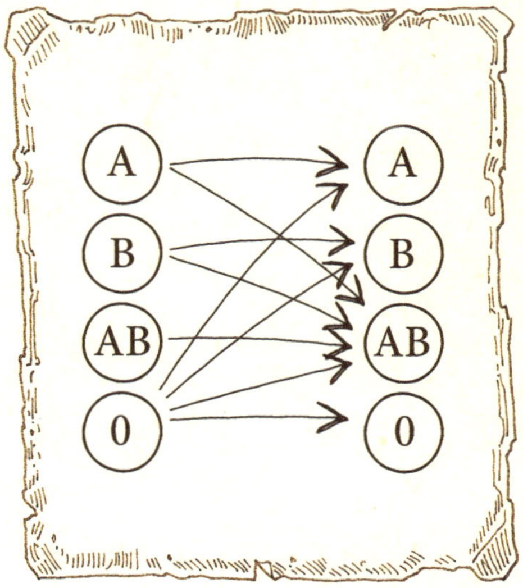

Express testing
If you have time to determine the blood type in advance, great. But in emergency situations, you can mix two blood samples together in transparent containers. If no clots form, it's safe to perform a transfusion, but if the blood becomes visibly lumpy, the blood types are not compatible.

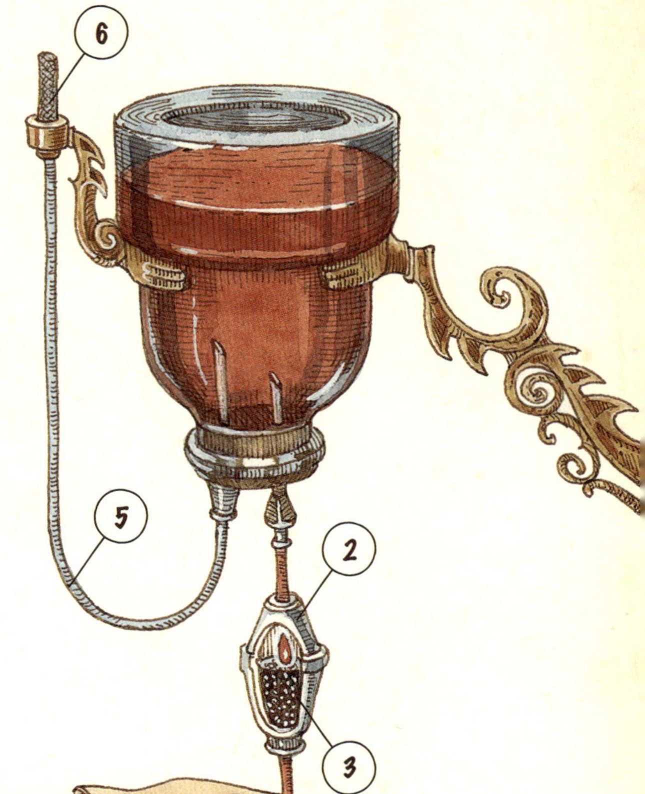

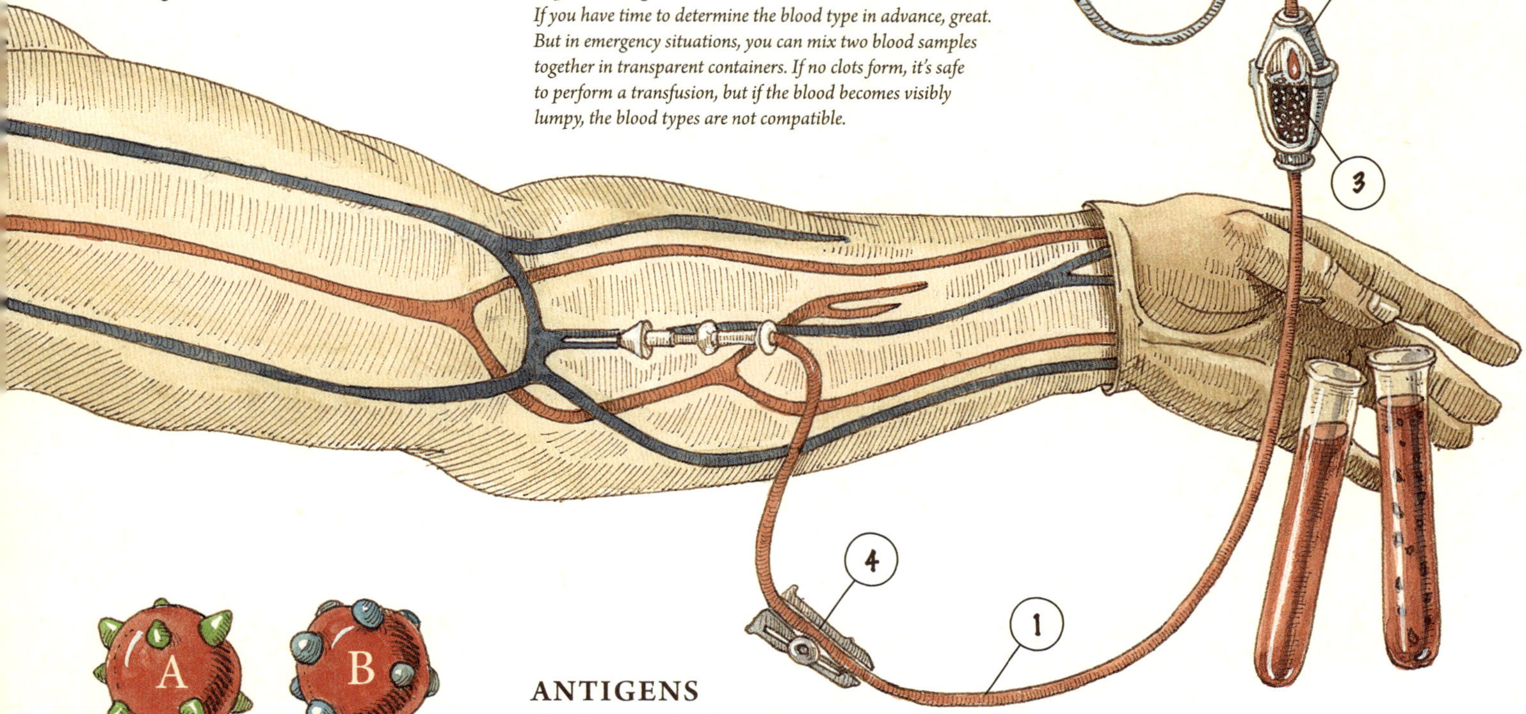

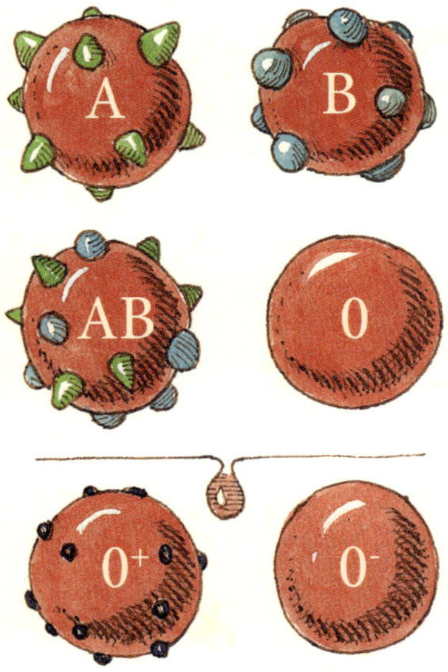

ANTIGENS

Blood gets its color from microscopic red cells called erythrocytes. The cells have distinguishing markers called antigens that stick out like pins from the surface of the cell. The main antigens are A, B and the Rh factor. People have different combinations of these "pins," i.e., different blood types. If you give a patient a transfusion with the wrong blood type, the erythrocytes will begin to clump together, turning the blood into jelly. This is why blood transfusions should only be performed with compatible blood types. Complicating the matter even further is the Rh factor — people who lack this marker cannot receive blood in which it is present.

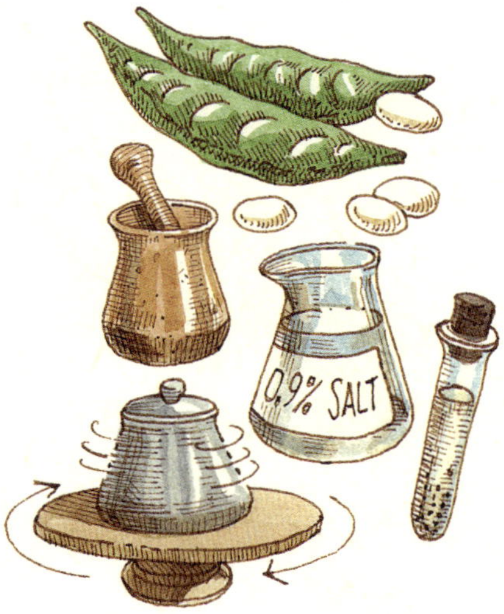

BLOOD TYPE

Crush lima beans (*Phaseolus limensis*). Dissolve 1 g of salt in 100 ml of condensate obtained by evaporating water. Mix 5 ml of this solution with 15 g of seed powder. Shake every 10 minutes for an hour. Next, spin the mixture very quickly to separate the liquid from the sediment. Save this liquid. Mix a couple of drops of blood with 60 drops of saline solution.

Spin for 5 minutes. Drain the liquid and keep 0.2 ml of the red precipitate. Add 10 ml of saline solution. Mix a drop of the blood mixture with a drop of the seed extract. If a few clots appear, the blood is type A. If there are a lot of clots, it's type AB. If there are none, it's type B or O. Viewing the clots is much easier with a microscope (page184).

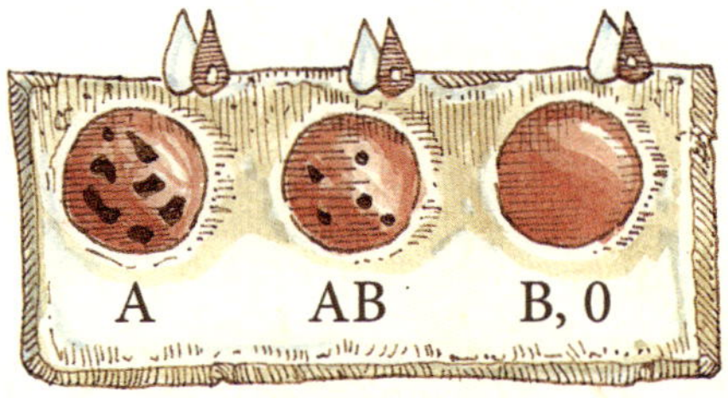

DENTISTRY

A smile is a contract of goodwill between two people. The wider the smile, the stronger the sense of security. But strong, healthy teeth aren't just the key to a thriving social life. They're also the marker of a good quality of life. Learning good dental hygiene habits early on can prevent heart, nervous system and spine problems down the line.

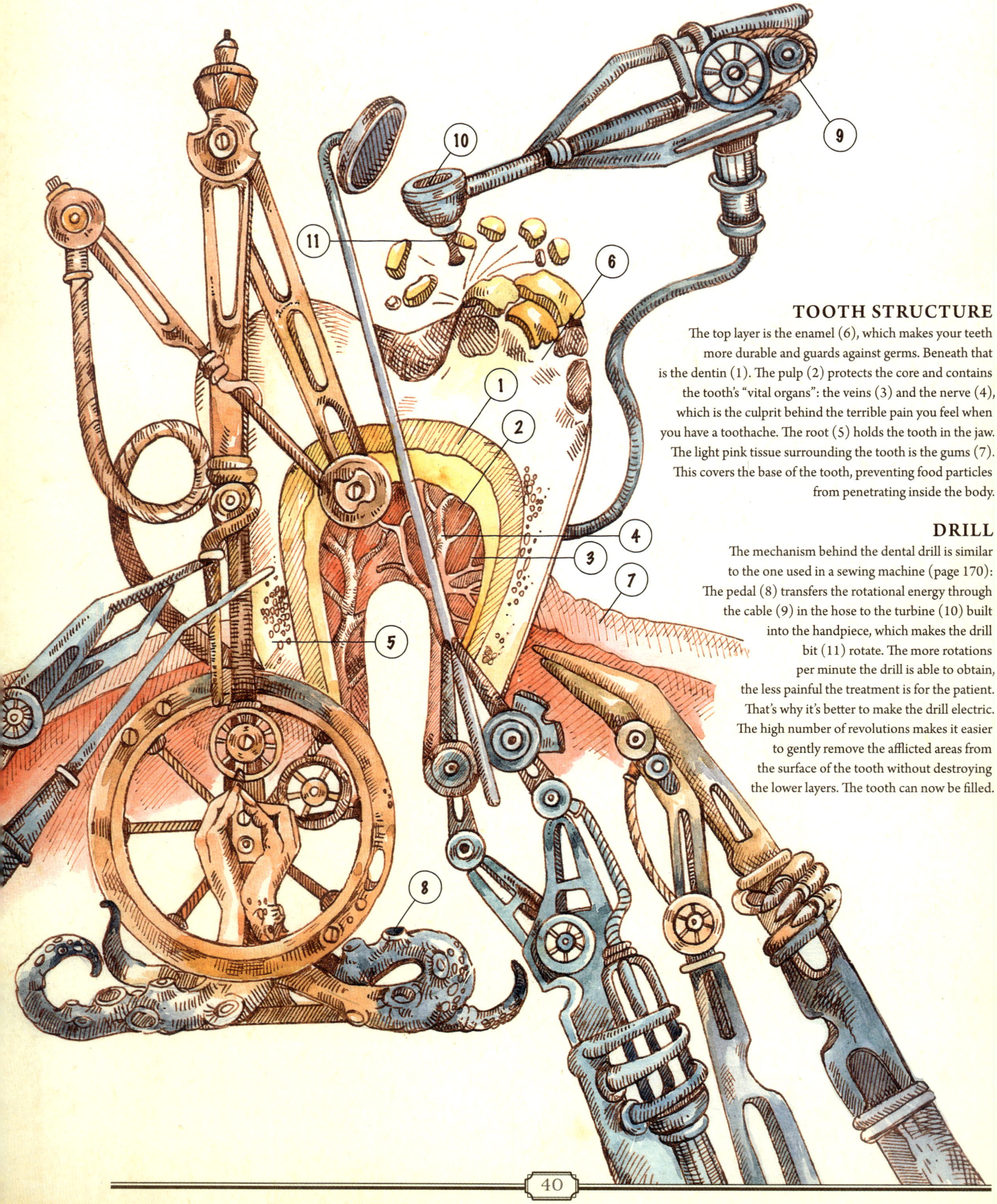

TOOTH STRUCTURE

The top layer is the enamel (6), which makes your teeth more durable and guards against germs. Beneath that is the dentin (1). The pulp (2) protects the core and contains the tooth's "vital organs": the veins (3) and the nerve (4), which is the culprit behind the terrible pain you feel when you have a toothache. The root (5) holds the tooth in the jaw. The light pink tissue surrounding the tooth is the gums (7). This covers the base of the tooth, preventing food particles from penetrating inside the body.

DRILL

The mechanism behind the dental drill is similar to the one used in a sewing machine (page 170): The pedal (8) transfers the rotational energy through the cable (9) in the hose to the turbine (10) built into the handpiece, which makes the drill bit (11) rotate. The more rotations per minute the drill is able to obtain, the less painful the treatment is for the patient. That's why it's better to make the drill electric. The high number of revolutions makes it easier to gently remove the afflicted areas from the surface of the tooth without destroying the lower layers. The tooth can now be filled.

DENTAL PROSTHETICS

If you break a tooth, you can insert a short post directly into the jaw bone to serve as the root of your dental implant. This post is threaded so you can install a prosthetic tooth. Instead of extracting the tooth, you can attach a porcelain cap and secure it with springs and braces. When the damage is more extensive and multiple teeth need to be extracted, you can make a dental bridge — use a light, durable metal — to which the fake teeth are attached. Affix this bridge to the crowns of the abutment teeth, or two anchor teeth adjacent to the gap. Before placing the bridge, these teeth must be ground down so that a crown can be placed on them. A full-jaw prosthesis can be made using ivory.

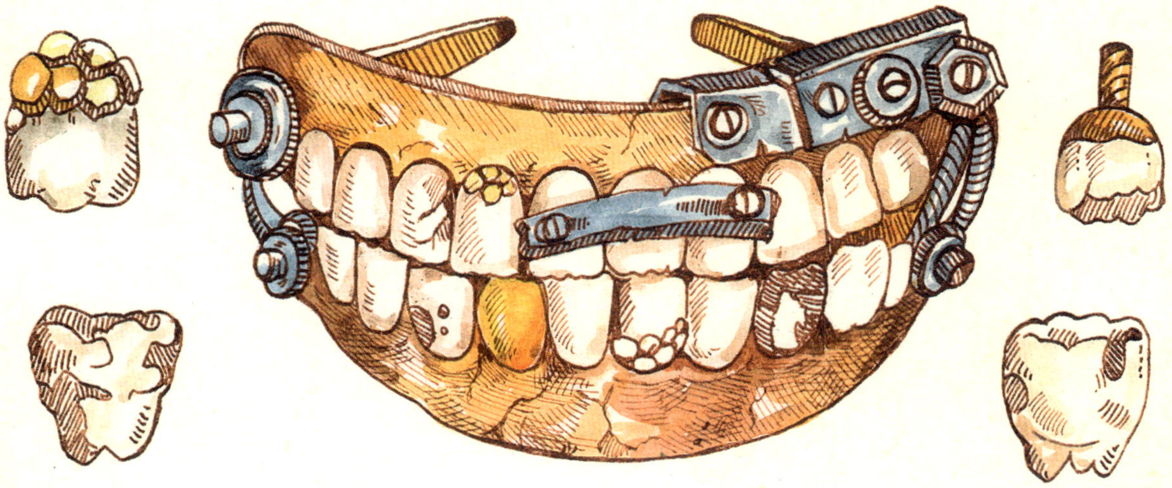

FILLING

Any holes or other damage teeth sustain must be filled to prevent the tooth from crumbling away further. During this procedure, the vessels and nerves are also sealed off, relieving any pain the patient may be feeling. Fillings can be made of a silver, copper and tin alloy or from dental cement made by mixing zinc oxide powder and a binder. The tooth must be very clean and dry before applying the filling; otherwise, the coating won't stick. The material should reach into all the nooks and crannies of the cleaned tooth hole. Check the height of the filled tooth against other teeth nearby to ensure that the filling won't interfere with the patient's everyday life. Try to work with the natural shape of the tooth and remove any excess material before it hardens.

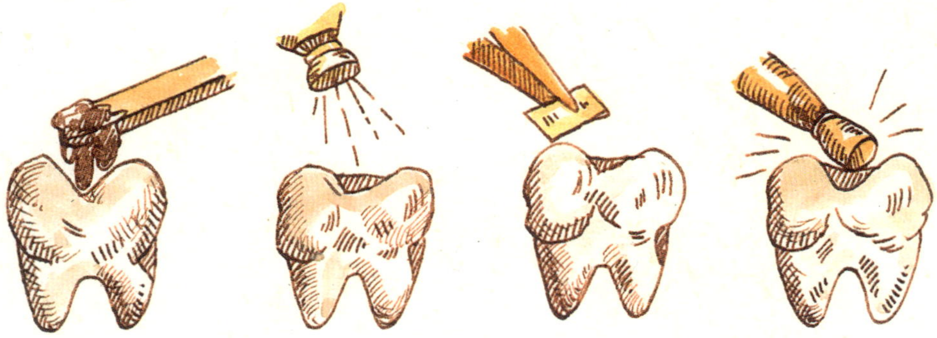

ANESTHESIA

Drilling into a bare nerve will cause a hellish amount of pain. That's why you'll need something to take the edge off. The simplest anesthesia to make is laughing gas (although making it isn't nearly as fun as taking it). All you need to do is heat ammonium nitrate (1), an ingredient also used in gunpowder and fertilizers (pages 124 and 58). The vessel you use should be a beaker closed off with a cork and small glass tube (2). Heating ammonium nitrate releases nitrous oxide, otherwise known as laughing gas. This gas must be bubbled through water and collected in an inverted jar (3). Make sure this jar is air-tight and sealed immediately after collection or the gas will escape instantly. Give the patient a huff of the stuff, and they'll forget all about any pain. Give them a little more, and they'll fall fast asleep.

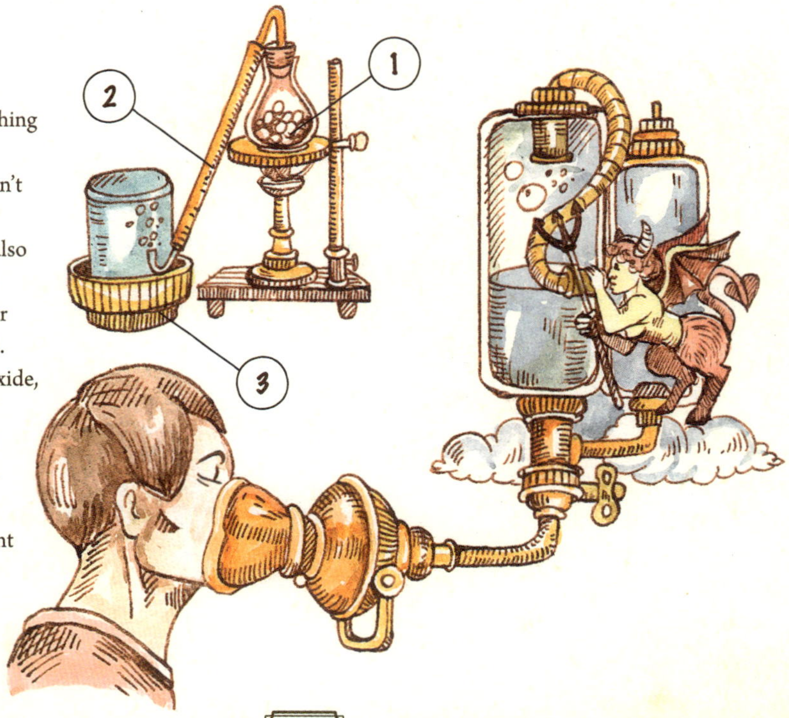

When heated, ammonium nitrate releases nitrous oxide, which can be used as an anesthetic. Heat to no more than 250°C; otherwise, things will get explosive. Since laughing gas is heavier than air, it can be collected in a jar or other container.

CHILDBIRTH

Your civilization will be under threat if the new generation is insufficient to replace the old. One way of tackling this problem is by reducing infant mortality rates during labor. Childbirth is a natural process that has been programmed into humans. Every step has been honed and perfected over millions of years of evolution, and the female body already contains all the resources necessary to protect and nurture the fetus. But what if something goes wrong during this process and the mother and child are in danger? Luckily, there are ways to address many of the common problems so that the child can safely be born.

LABOR

Childbirth is a natural process. In most situations, everything runs smoothly on its own. The child grows and develops within a fluid-filled sac in the womb. When it's time to be born, this sac ruptures and the amniotic fluid is released through the vagina. A woman is ready to give birth when the opening of the cervix reaches 10 cm. The baby's head should be the first thing through the vaginal canal. As soon as it does, clear the baby's nose and mouth so it can breathe.

After the head, the shoulders and body should soon follow. Cut the umbilical cord as soon as you stop seeing a pulse within it. But the birth process is not over. Now, the new mother needs to push out the placenta, which provides the fetus with nutrients and oxygen during pregnancy. During birth, it detaches from the wall of the womb and must be expelled.

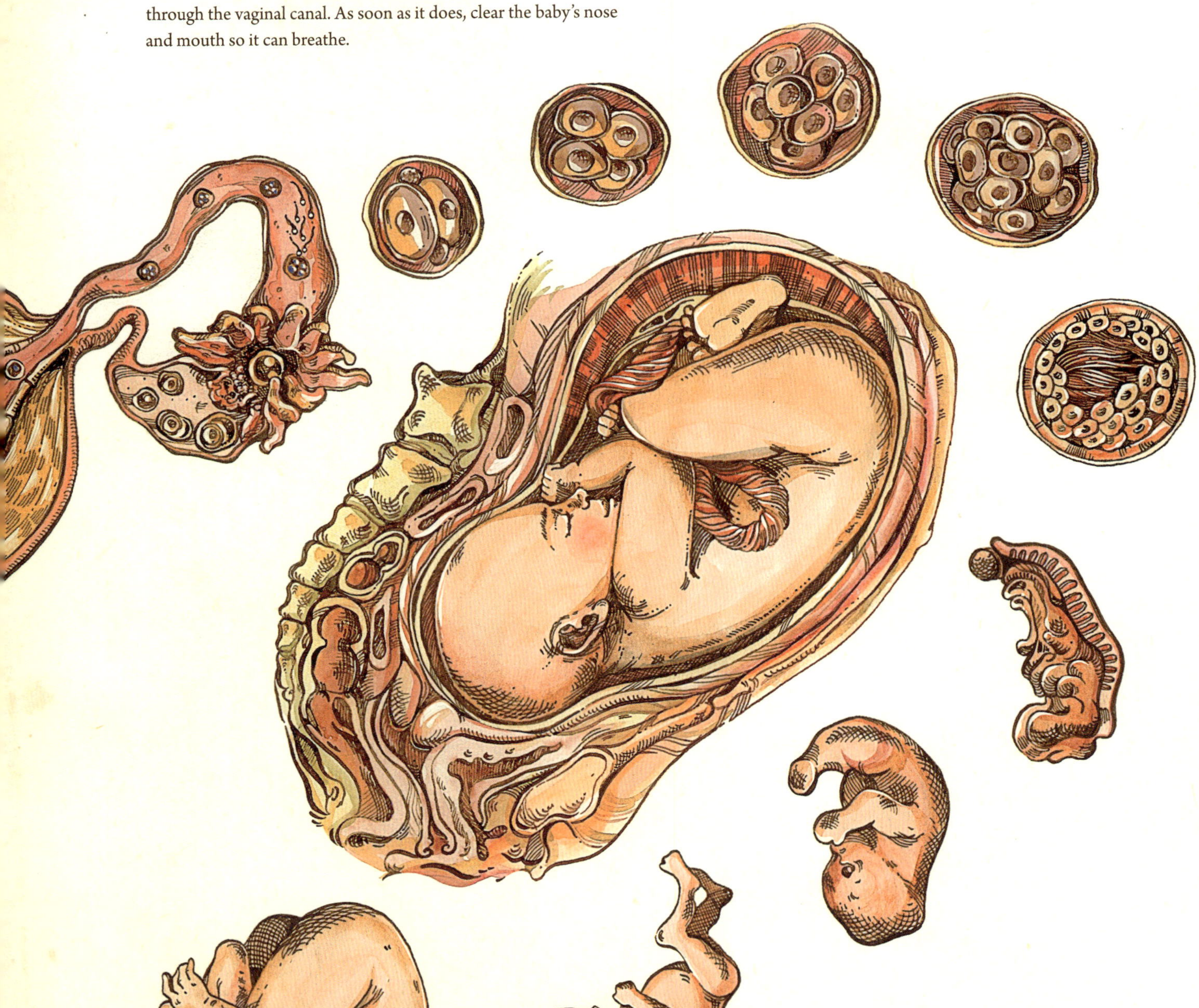

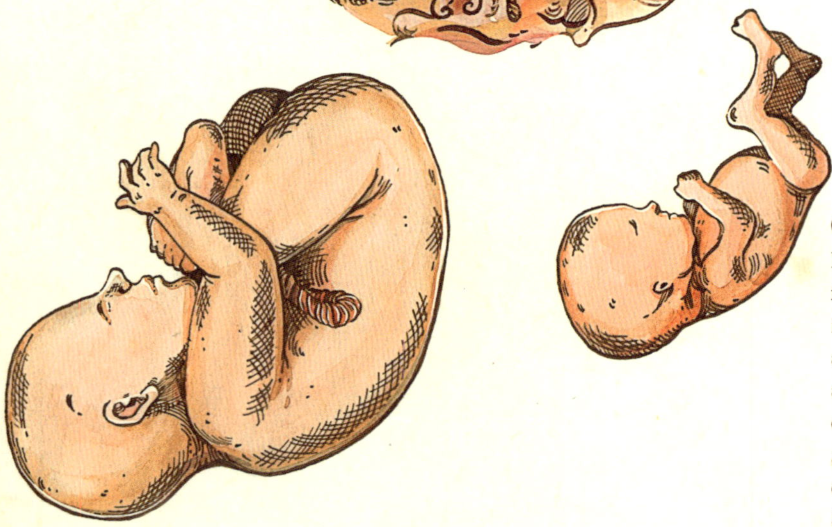

C-SECTION

If something goes wrong — for example, the baby is breech (positioned feet first), has become tangled in the umbilical cord or the mother's birth canal is too small — a cesarean section may become medically necessary. Make a horizontal incision above the pubis (or in case of extreme emergency, a vertical incision from the navel to the pubis). Cut through the layer of muscle, push the bladder aside then make an incision in the uterus and rupture the sac containing the baby. After carefully removing the baby and cutting the umbilical cord, extract the placenta and pull out the uterus. Stitch up the incision on the lower and outer layers of the uterus and put it back in place. Then stitch up the muscle and skin layers.

EMERGENCY ASSISTANCE

In case of complications in childbirth — if the child isn't making progress through the birth canal and it is too late for a C-section — there are two options. The first requires a vacuum plunger. Use a small pump to create a weak vacuum. Attach a rubber-lipped suction cup to a solid glass bottle. As the air is pumped out of the bottle, it generates negative pressure and the rubber lip seals firmly to the baby's head. All that remains is to gently tug on the other side and help the baby through the birth canal. The second method involves forceps — a large pair of tongs that clasp the child's head. The doctors assisting the woman in labor must work together with the new mother, only lightly pulling on the child as she pushes. Overly forceful use of forceps may lead to fatal consequences for the child.

A phonendoscope will help you diagnose possible problems by allowing you to listen to the internal organs. The head of the device, which is placed on the skin, must consist of a thin diaphragm (an elastic convex plate, which acts as a membrane) and an amplification cone. This transmits a broader range of frequencies than a stethoscope and is more sensitive to fetal heart tones.

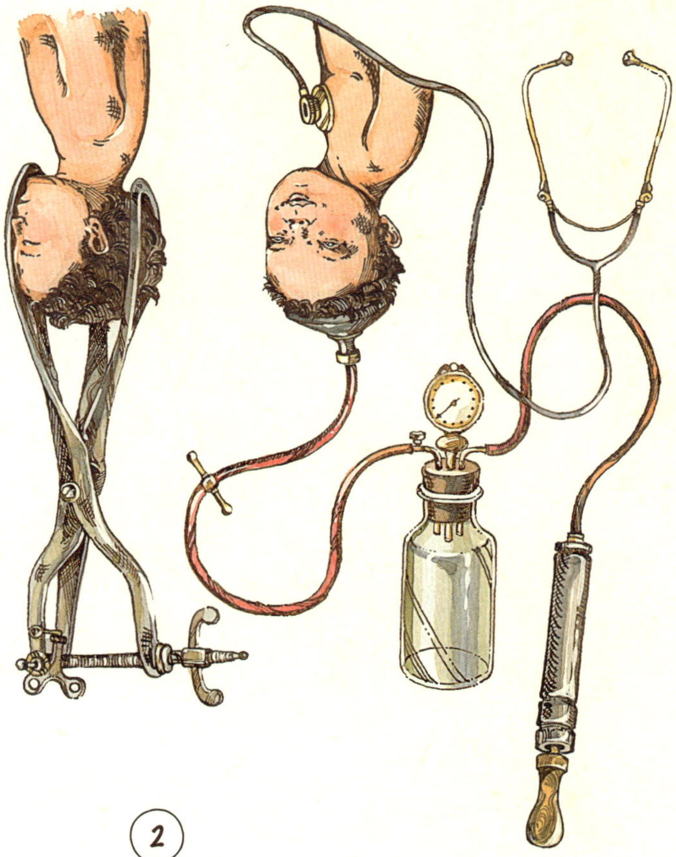

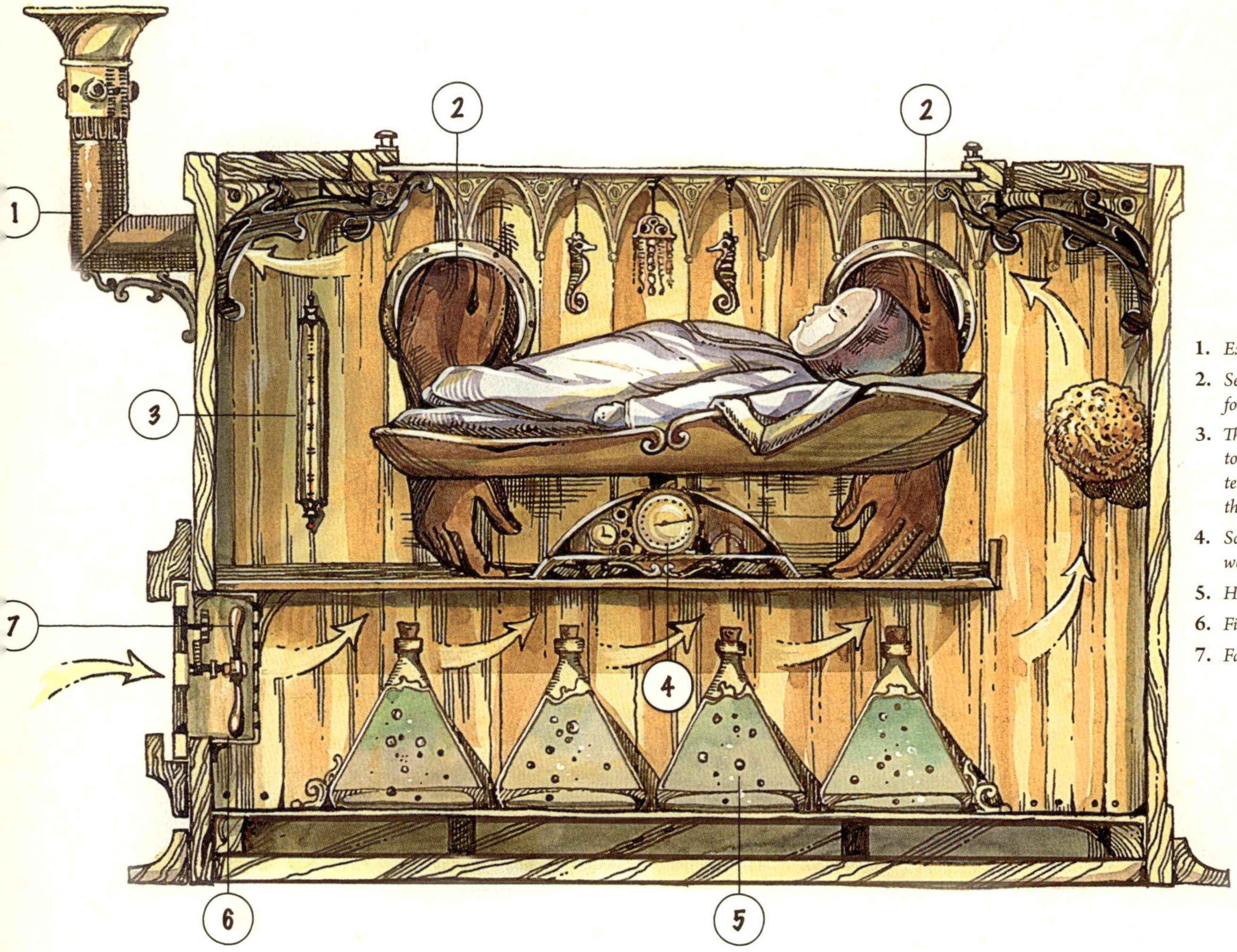

1. *Exhaust vent*
2. *Sealed hatches for baby access*
3. *Thermometer to monitor the constant temperature within the incubator*
4. *Scales to monitor weight*
5. *Heating element*
6. *Filtered air duct*
7. *Fan*

INCUBATOR

If the baby is born prematurely, you can simulate the conditions within the mothers womb in an incubation chamber. It ensures constant temperature, moderate humidity and proper oxygen levels. Make the box out of metal and glass to make it easier to sterilize. To maintain consistent temperature, use a heating element or warm water bottles.

It is important that the baby has warmth from all sides. Install a fan to circulate air. Remember to add a cotton filter to the air duct to prevent contamination by harmful microbes. You also need to be able to constantly monitor the weight and temperature of the child so that you don't repeatedly compromise the sterile environment by pulling the baby in and out.

Place a scale on the floor of the incubation chamber, then cut two holes in the side and install rubber gloves. These can be hermetically sealed into the wall of the chamber so that you can access and manipulate the baby without disturbing the microclimate.

EPIDEMIC

The more your civilization thrives, the greater the risk of it falling. Dense urbanization, trade and emigration between cities (page 406) create the perfect conditions for an epidemic. Close contact between people from different places can lead to cross contamination: Viruses that may be harmless to a community with herd immunity could wreak havoc among populations that haven't yet been exposed. Stop-gap solutions simply won't do — you'll need to resort to radical methods in order to keep your civilization afloat.

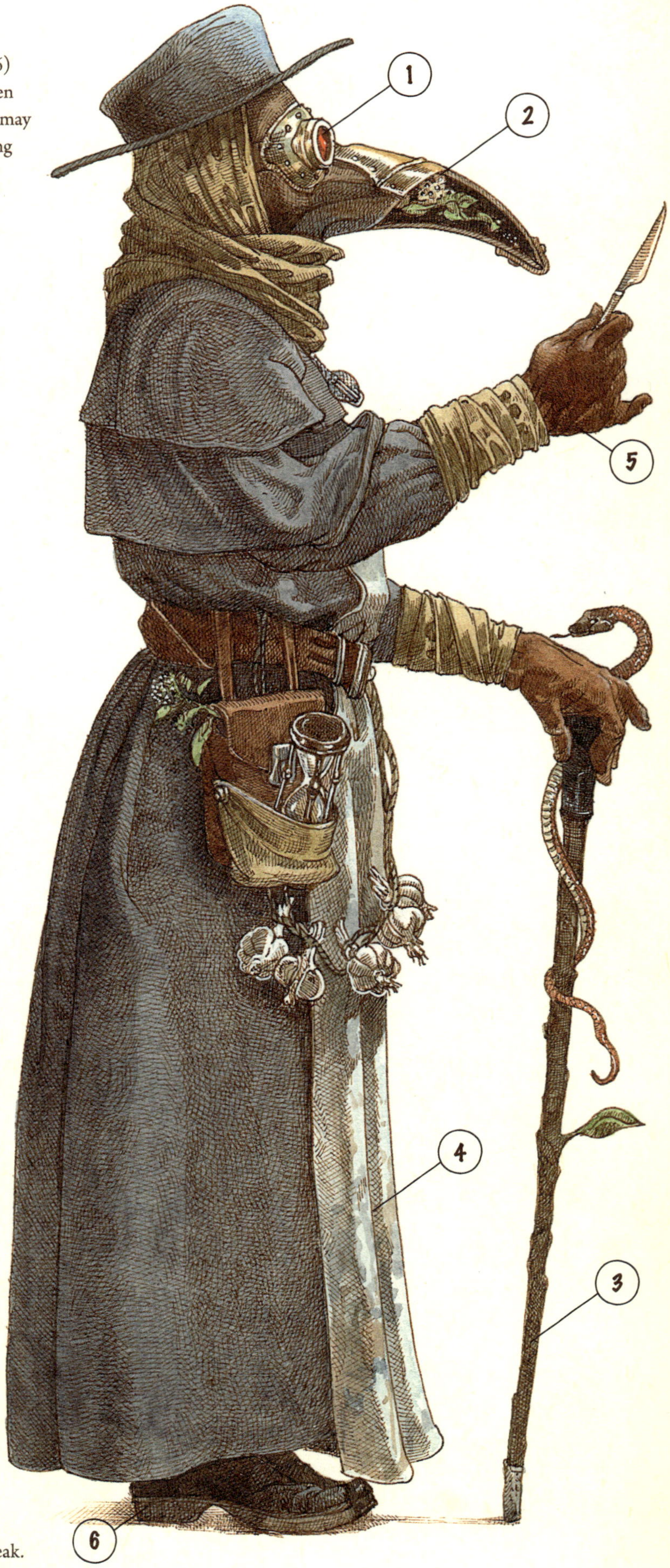

PROTECTIVE EQUIPMENT

1. **Goggles** protect you from microbes penetrating through the mucous membrane of your eyes, allowing you to safely observe patients with pustules and ulcers.

2. A **mask** prevents pathogens from getting in through your skin and mucous membranes. When coughing, sneezing or even having a simple conversation, tiny droplets from your nose and mouth fly through the air and are aspirated by people nearby. These droplets contain microbes responsible for terrible diseases. A two-ply mask with a filter traps these microbes, preventing them from traveling through the air and infecting someone. Everyone, not just those displaying symptoms, should wear a mask during an outbreak because no one can be certain that they aren't a carrier.

3. A **cane** will help you stay clear of contaminated surfaces. It can be used to open doors or measure a safe distance of 1.5 meters — this is the best way to slow the spread of infection.

4. A **long hooded robe** to cover the whole body. After you get back home, it'll need to be disinfected.

5. **Gloves** protect your hands and keep germs out of your face and mouth.

6. **High heels** help keep your shoes from getting dirty in contaminated runoff water. This way, you don't have to clean the dirt from your boots, which means one less opportunity for transferring germs to the skin.

One to two cases a week is manageable, but 15–20 is considered an outbreak. These waves of infection occur when a microbe or virus is rapidly passed from one person to another, who then continues the chain by infecting others around them. If you infect someone but they are able to prevent themselves from infecting anyone else, they will interrupt the transmission cycle, and within a year or two, there will be no more new cases of the disease.

But when this cycle isn't broken, the disease can spread like wildfire across the whole civilization. If the outbreak starts to affect several different settlements, it becomes an epidemic. If the epidemic goes global and starts spreading even to remote areas, it's classified as a pandemic.

ISOLATION

Diseases often originate in forests, spread by wild animals. Some animals can be wellsprings of pathogens — although they themselves may not fall ill, they can still carry the disease and transmit it to humans. Bats, rodents and primates are the most common and dangerous culprits. Try to avoid building your settlement near a swamp, as mosquitos breed in stagnant water and carry numerous diseases. You may run into the same problem near rivers.

Animals can transmit to humans, who then bring the infectious agents back to their communities and set off a chain reaction. Send your hunters out in shifts and make sure they live in a camp slightly separated from the main population. This will reduce the risk of disease outbreak. Water is as much a breeding ground for infection as forest thickets. All your water must be purified before utilizing (page 14). Most microbes are quickly killed by boiling.

Quarantine is an essential precaution against outbreak. Infected individuals must be separated from the rest of society. Symptoms may appear several days after initial infection, so anyone who has been in close contact with a known case must quarantine even if they feel healthy and are asymptomatic. Quarantine should last a minimum of 7 days and a maximum of 14–21.

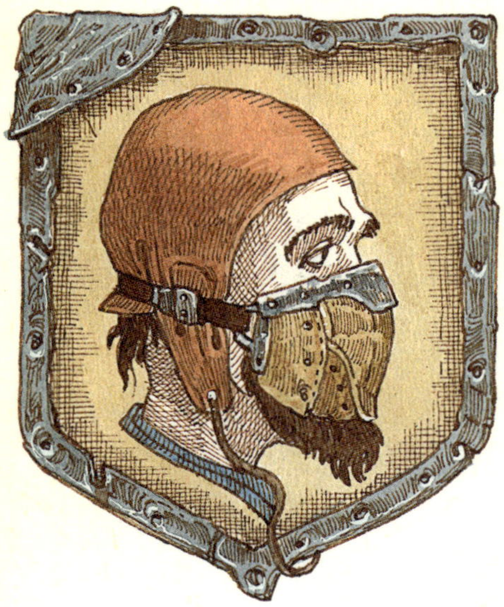
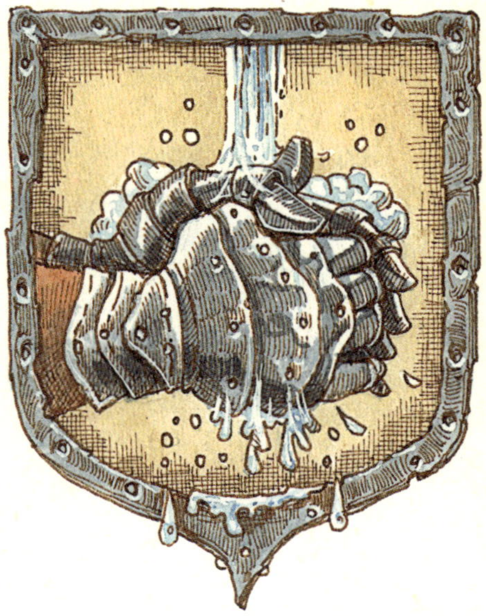
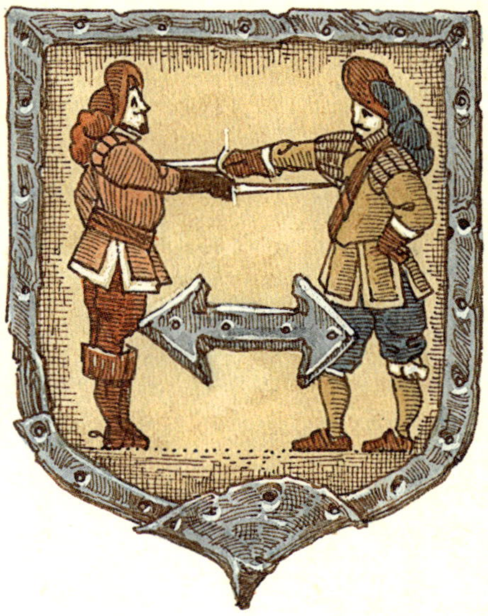
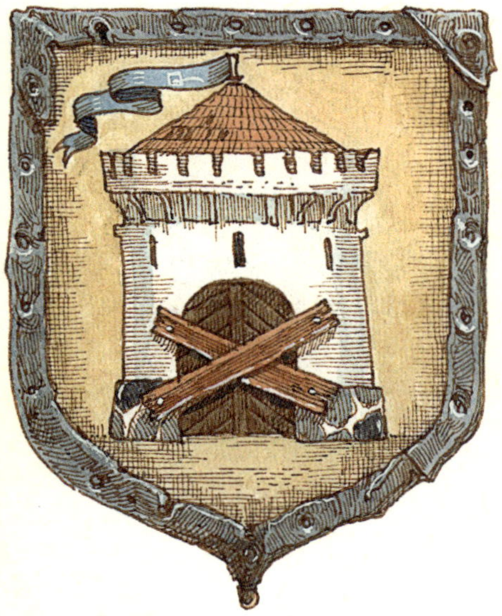
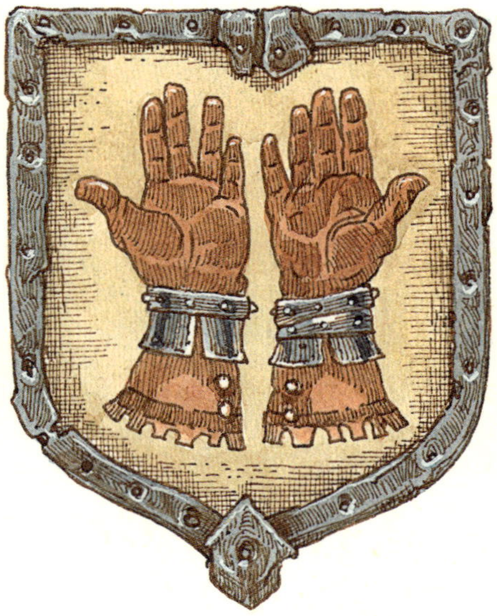
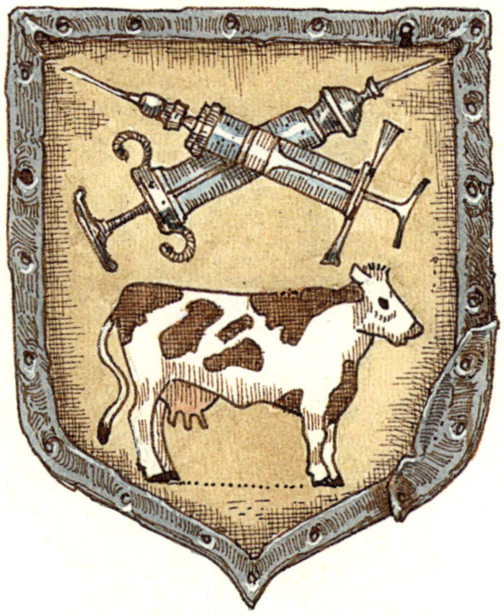

VACCINATION

Your best bet in the battle against disease is vaccination. It's a way of introducing the immune system to the pathogen in advance, giving it the opportunity to fight back without getting infected. This way, when the vaccinated person comes into contact with the pathogen, they have either developed a complete immunity or have drastically reduced symptoms.

Vaccines use a weakened form of the microbe. But if your civilization lacks the technology necessary to create vaccines, there is a simpler but far more risky method. Check to see if house animals experience similar symptoms to humans when infected. If the disease produces ulcers, scrape the dried crust or scab off the top. When the infected tissue dries out, it makes the pathogen weaker. This weakened form is exactly what you need.

Crush the scabs into a powder. Make an incision on the person's hand, sprinkle some crust powder in and wrap it with a cloth. If the patient develops small sores and blisters after a couple of days, the vaccination has worked.

Another dangerous but effective way to teach the body to recognize and fight pathogens in advance is variolation. If there are pimples and pustules on the patient's body, pierce them with a sharp needle. Some pus will remain on the tip. You must then use this needle to puncture the skin of a healthy person in several places. The most convenient location is the shoulder. The risk of developing complications after an intentional, controlled infection is lower than the risk of dying from a severe illness, so you have an important choice to make.

X-RAY

We're often told that it's impossible to know what's really going on inside another person. But it's not entirely true. X-rays reveal things invisible to the naked eye.

Despite its seeming technical complexity, you can build an X-ray machine using an incandescent lamp (page 198) and a photographic plate (page 187). Bone cracks, swallowed metal objects and even bullets are visible at a glance.

X-RAY APPARATUS

The entire mechanism must be covered with a thick lead casing to prevent X-rays from flying out in all directions. Leave just one small, unprotected window angled towards the tilted anode. The rays will escape through this window. Connect the machine to a high voltage source, preferably constant voltage (page 196).

X-RAY TUBE

Blow a tube out of quartz glass (page 114). This glass can withstand extreme temperatures. Place two electrodes inside — the cathode and the anode. Choose a metal with a high melting point for your cathode. A tungsten filament, used in regular light bulbs (page 192), will do. Suck out as much air as possible from inside the lamp. A vacuum will allow the electrons to fly across from the cathode to the anode. When heated, the cathode emits electrons.

Make the anode much larger and from a metal with a high thermal conductivity, such as copper. Cut the anode stem at a 45–70-degree angle and attach a platform made from a heavy metal, such as tungsten or platinum. When the electrons hit this platform, they slow down and lose some of their energy. This energy is released in the form of X-rays.

COOLING SYSTEM

To prevent the cathode from overheating, provide a constant supply of cold, flowing water and place the entire tube in an oil bath.

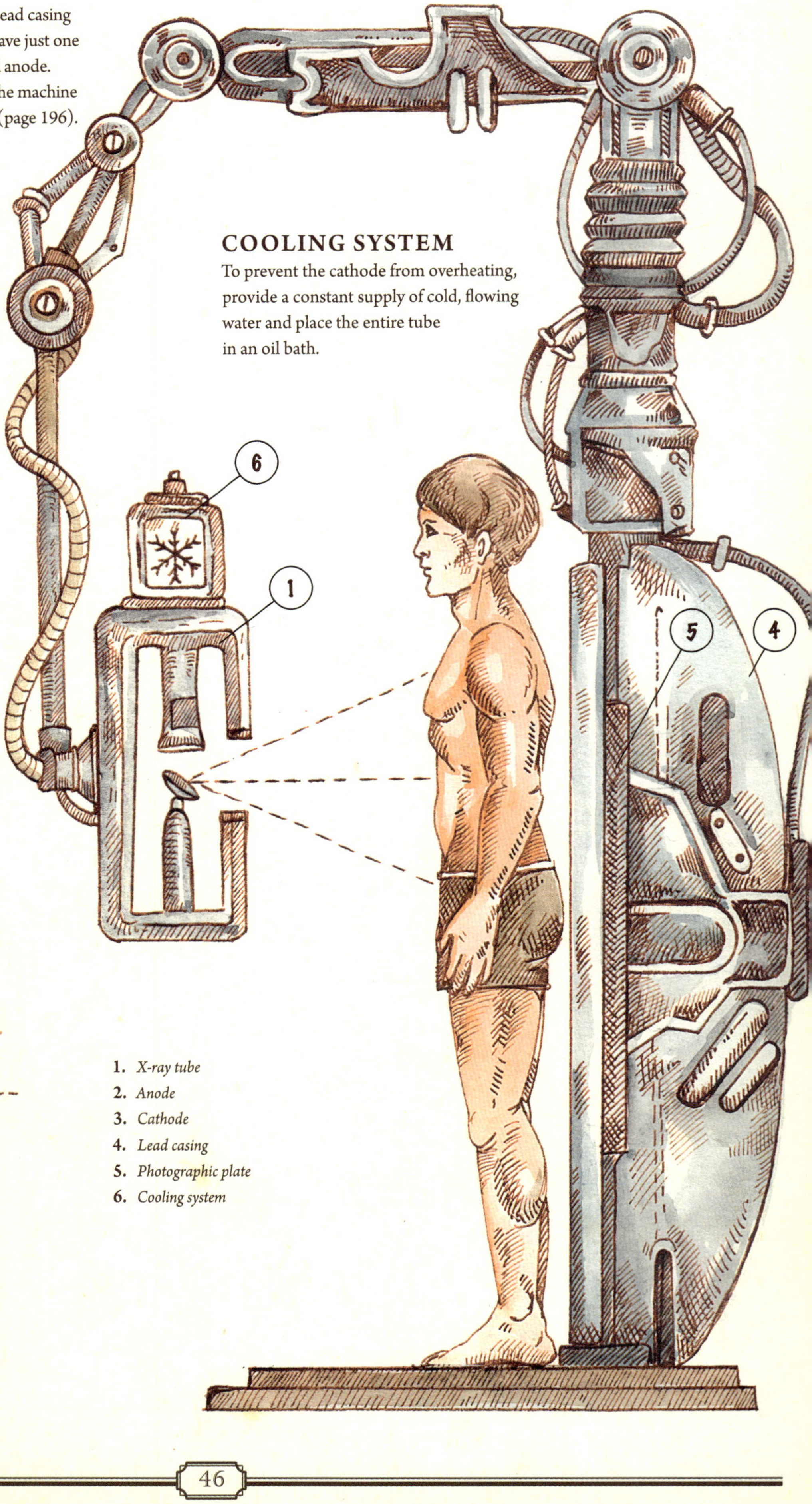

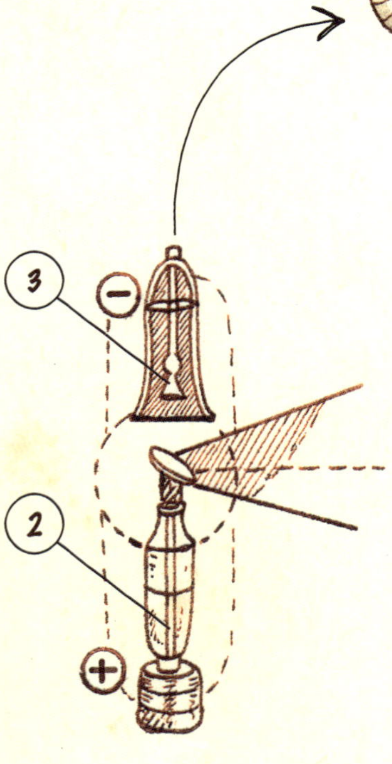

1. *X-ray tube*
2. *Anode*
3. *Cathode*
4. *Lead casing*
5. *Photographic plate*
6. *Cooling system*

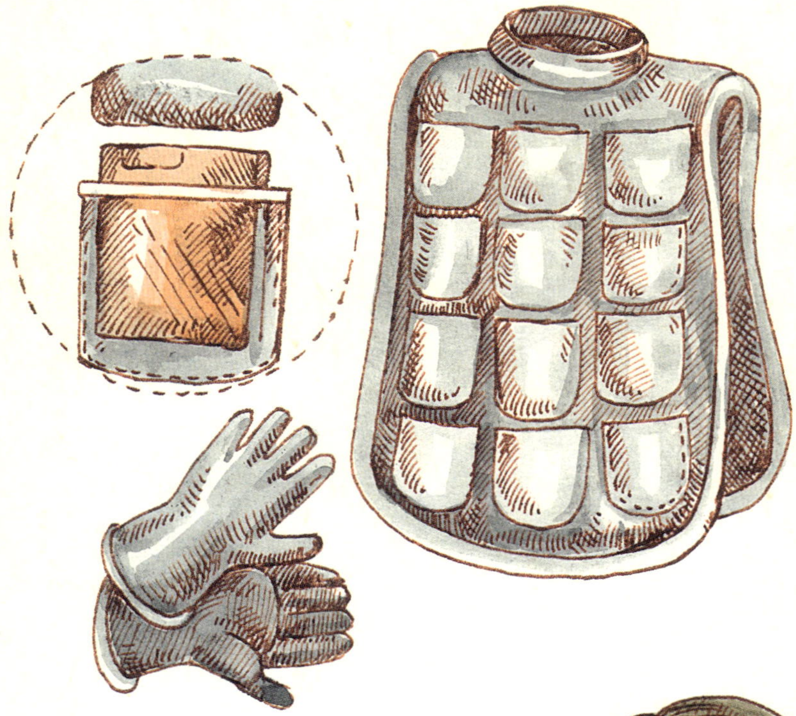

RADIATION PROTECTION

Not all threats are visible to the naked eye. X-rays are a form of ionizing radiation. They are absorbed into body tissues and can cause radiation burns and, in high doses, even cancer. That's why people shouldn't undergo X-ray procedures too often. Protect the parts of your body that aren't being examined with lead plates. But don't create a full suit of lead armor — it would weigh a ton. It's better to sew a vest or apron with many pockets and fill them with lead plates.

CONTRAST AGENT

When doing medical imaging of the stomach or intestines, you can highlight them using a contrast agent. It will improve the image quality and allow you to see the organs in more detail. You can prepare a contrast agent from barium salts. To do this, you'll need to find the mineral barite (also known as heavy spar), which is similar to limestone but heavier. Grind it into powder. It doesn't dissolve in water so you will have to add an algae thickener. Add flavoring to make drinking it more pleasant for the patient.

X-RAY IMAGE

As X-rays pass through your body, they are absorbed to different extents by the internal structures. For instance, soft tissues such as muscles and fat absorb very little, while dense materials like bones or metal objects absorb much more. That's why the image X-rays leave on the photographic plate looks like a set of lighter and darker shadows.

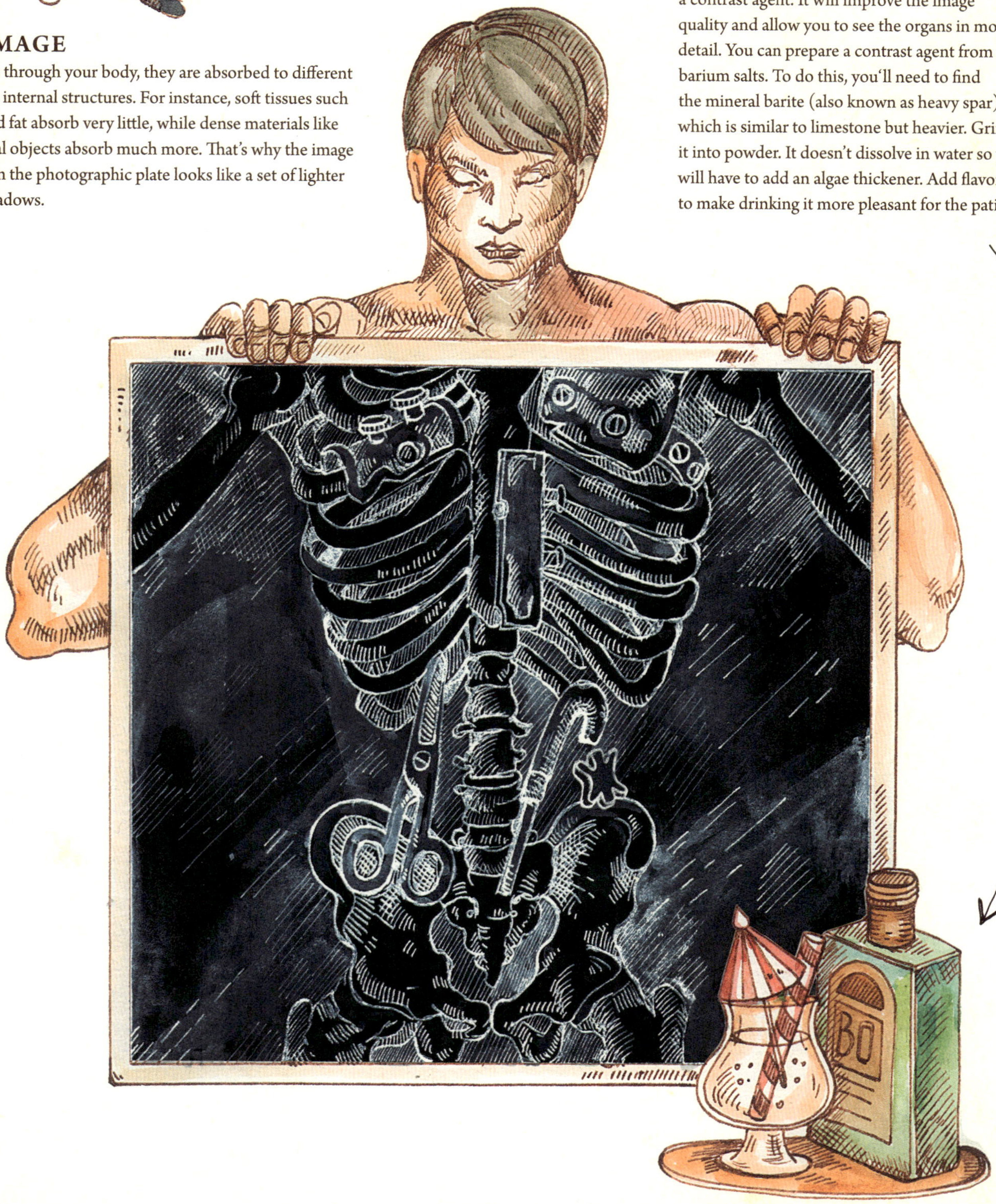

PLANTS

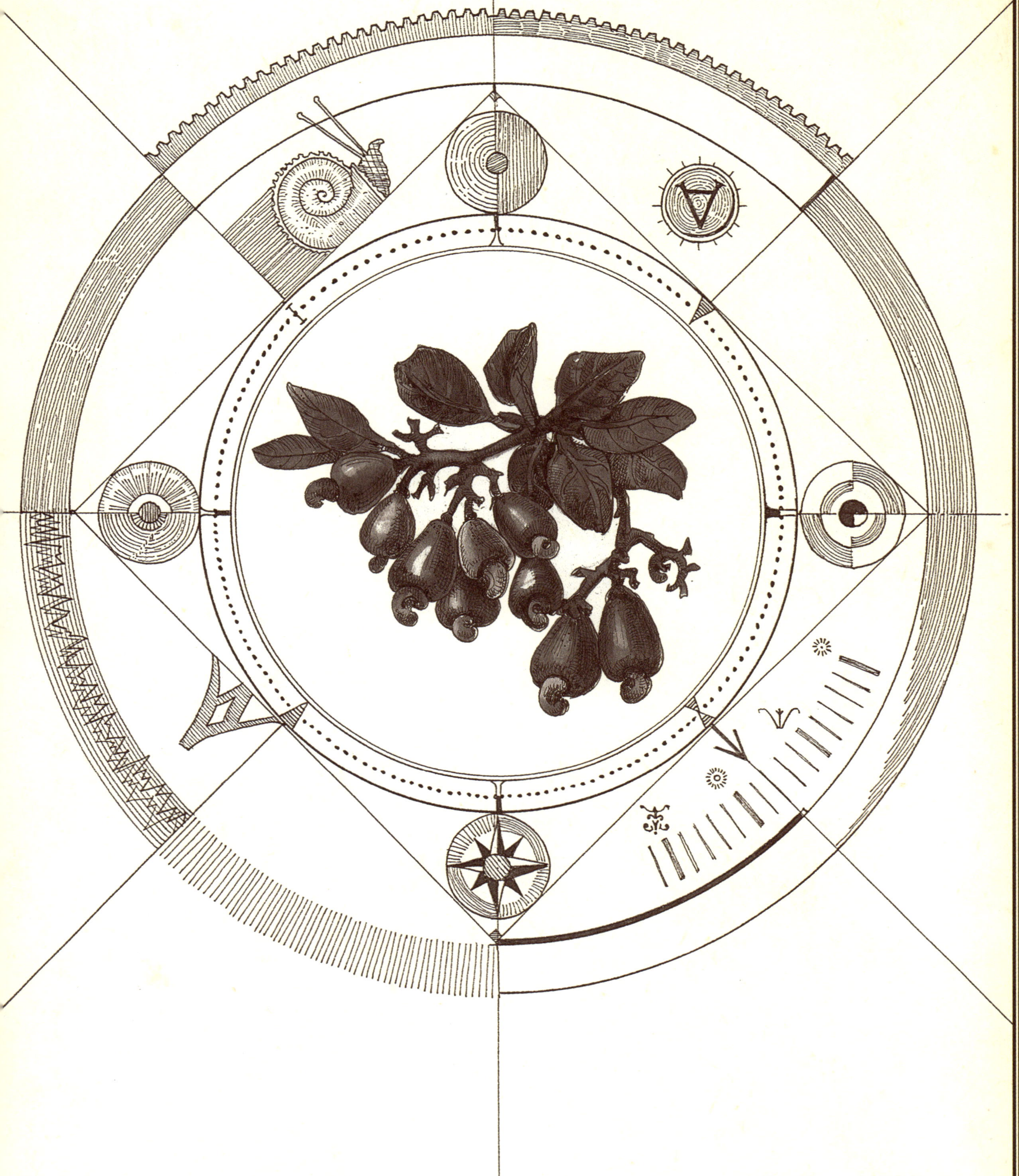

EXOTIC FRUITS

Exotic fruits can be a puzzle. It's not always immediately clear which portion is edible and how to extract it. Many plants have acquired surprising adaptations that force us to admit the truth: No matter what heights our civilizations may reach, nature will always take the prize for the most innovative inventions.

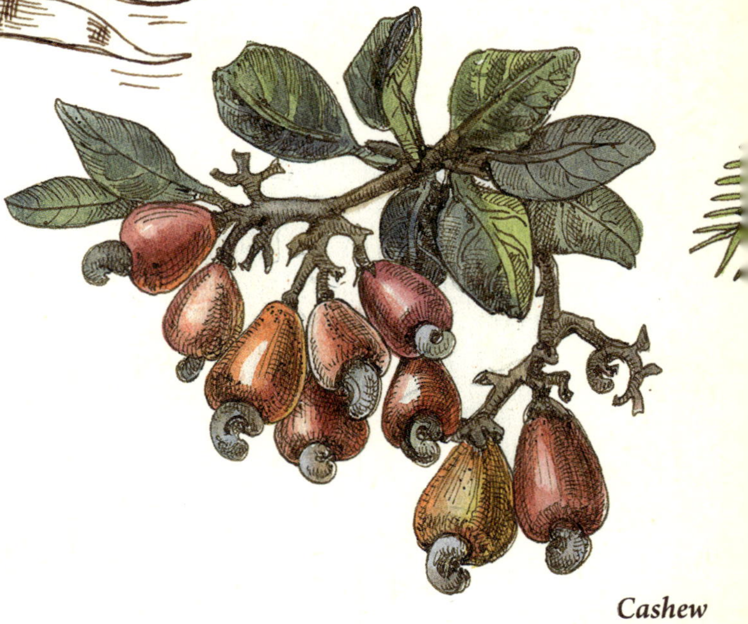

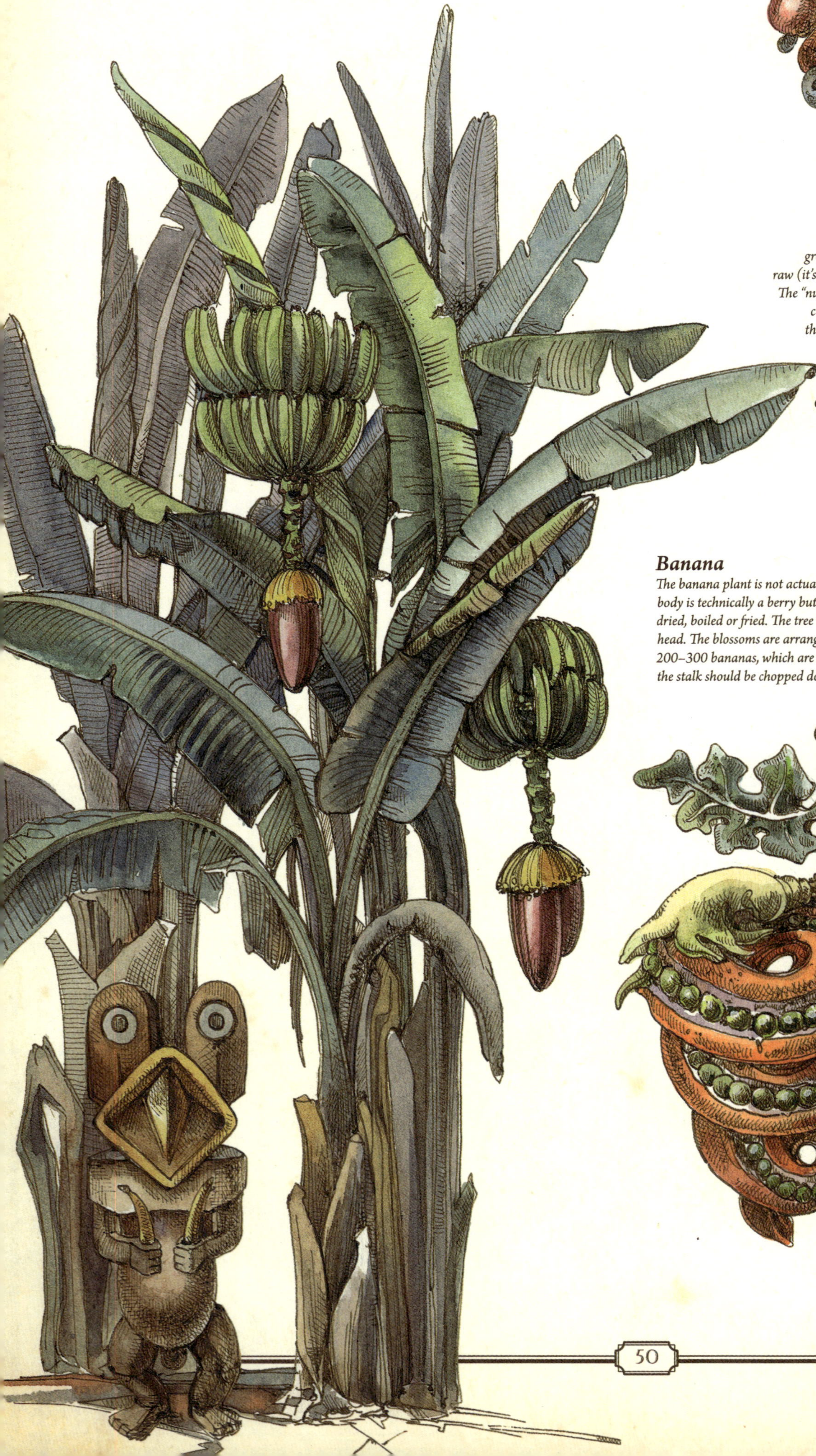

Cashew

This is not technically a nut but a seed formed on a soft yellow, green or red "apple" — the fruit of the plant. This can also be eaten raw (it's juicy with a sweet and sour taste) or by boiling it into a compote. The "nut" itself is encased within a double shell. The outer layer contains compounds that irritate the skin, so it should not be removed with the bare hands. Heat neutralizes the caustic resin. Toss the cashews in boiling water for half an hour, after which time the outer shell will become harder and easier to remove. Then fry the pod and remove the inner shell. The cashews are now ready to eat. Cashews are both a food and a medicine. They contain anacardic acids that kill bacteria. Chewing on them is a good way to prevent tooth decay *(page 40).*

Banana

The banana plant is not actually a tree but a giant herbaceous plant, or herb. The fruiting body is technically a berry but is generally classified as a fruit. Bananas can be eaten raw, dried, boiled or fried. The tree takes 10 months to mature before forming an intricate blossom head. The blossoms are arranged in tiers, eventually forming small fruits. One tree can grow 200–300 bananas, which are always bunched very close together. After harvesting the fruit, the stalk should be chopped down and a new one planted in its place.

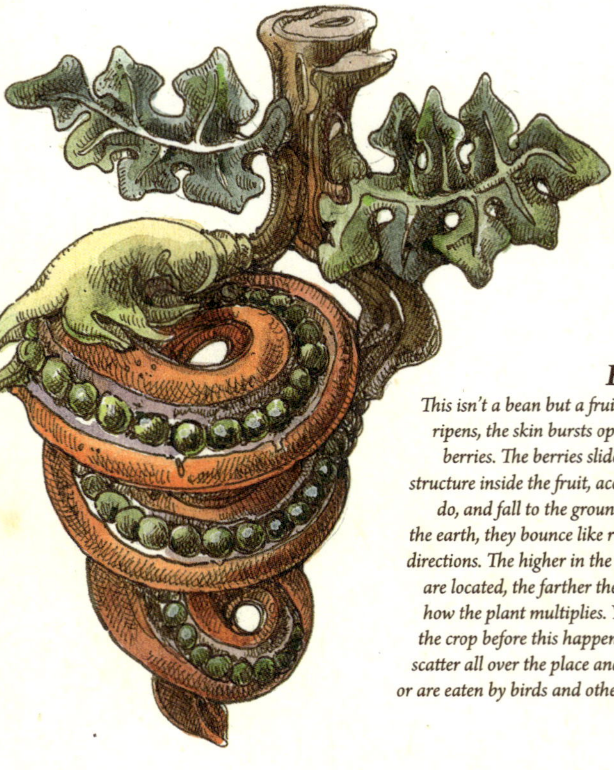

Helix Bean

This isn't a bean but a fruit. When the fruit ripens, the skin bursts open to reveal juicy berries. The berries slide down the spiral structure inside the fruit, accelerating as they do, and fall to the ground. When they hit the earth, they bounce like rubber balls in all directions. The higher in the spiral the berries are located, the farther they bounce. This is how the plant multiplies. You must harvest the crop before this happens and the berries scatter all over the place and either take root or are eaten by birds and other small creatures.

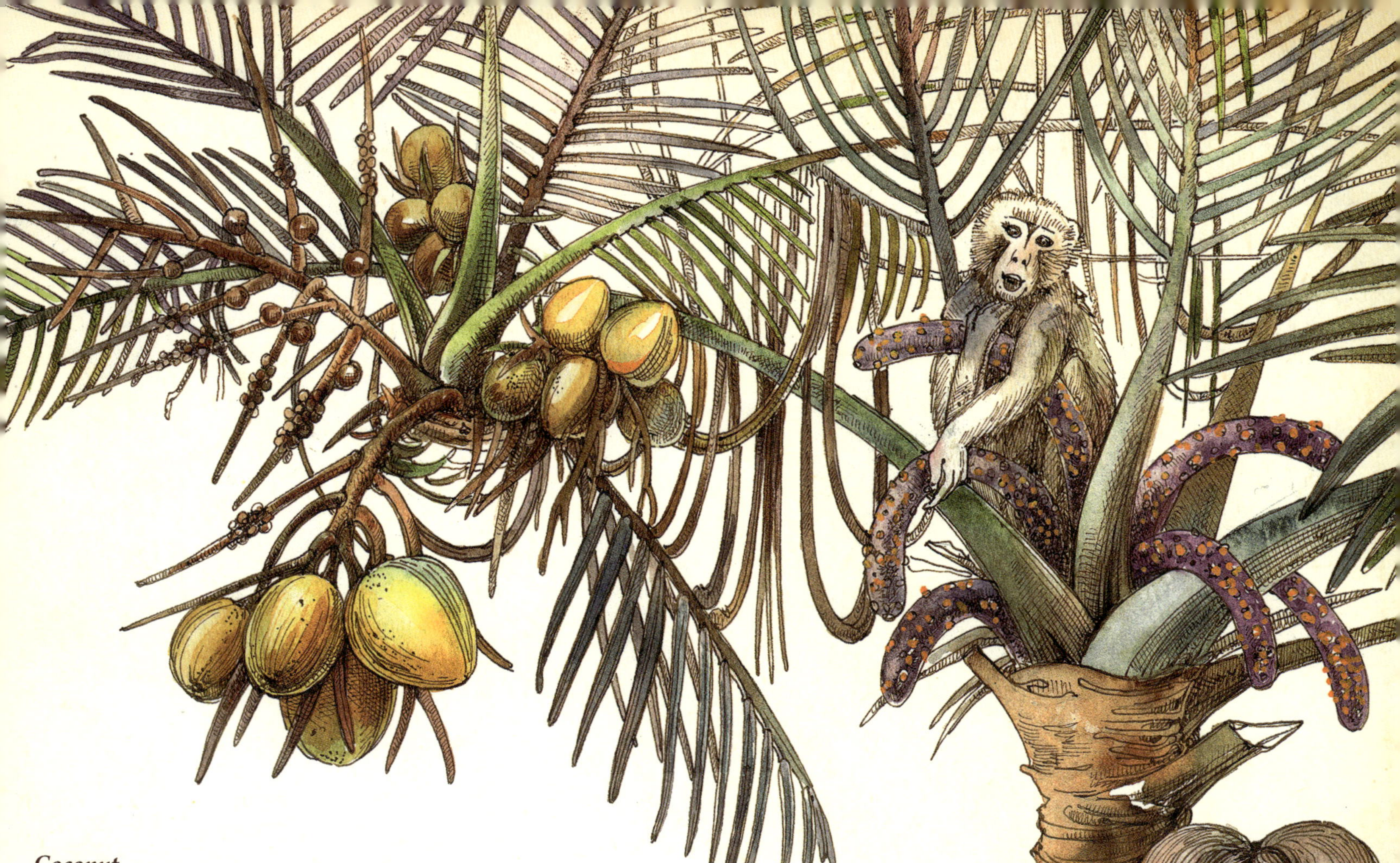

Coconut

A coconut has three distinct shells. All of them have uses in agriculture. Dry the outer hull to use as fuel or fertilizer. The fibrous husk can be used for upholstery. The third, internal shell can be flaked and used in desserts or mixed with coconut water to make milk. The outermost shell has three small grooves in it. Wait five months for the coconut to ripen then drill a hole in one of these grooves so you can drain the liquid from the nut. It is an excellent source of electrolytes and adds depth of flavor to your cooking. Use the roots of the palm tree for dye (page 122) and the leaves for weaving mats. The syrup from the flowerheads, which can be evaporated to make sugar or left to ferment, produces a refreshing, low-alcohol wine.

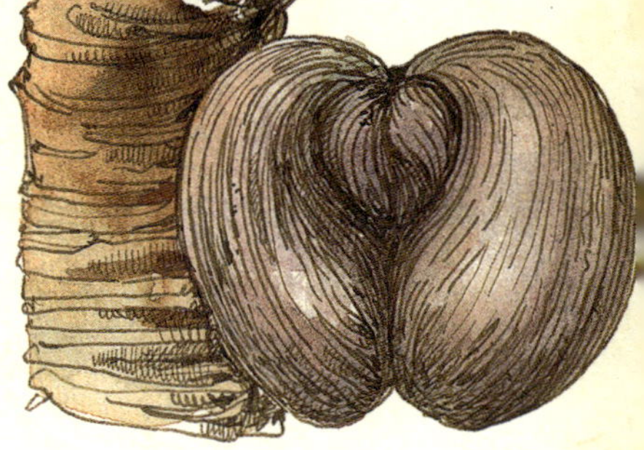

Coco de Mer

The fruit resembles the hips of a curvy woman. The palm tree only bears fruit after the age of 20, but it will live for a long time — up to 800 years. Coco de mer contains less coconut liquid and has a more tender flesh than a plain coconut. It can be eaten raw or used to prepare a variety of dishes, beer and soft drinks.

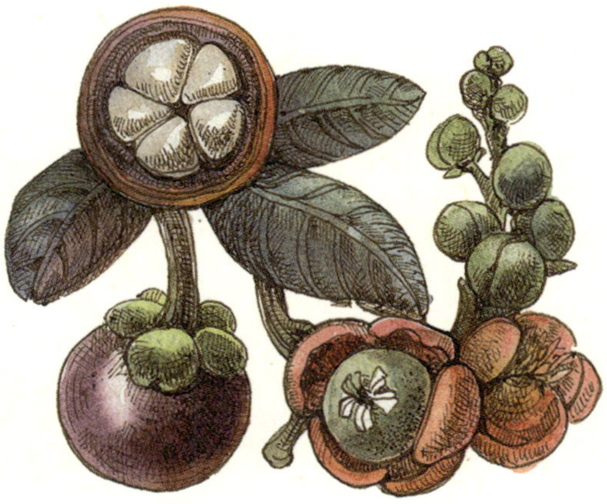

Peanut

The peanut is actually a bean that grows underground in light, sandy soil. Cull and trim the bushes frequently, as peanut flowers bloom for just a single day. The fruit can be harvested 90–150 days after planting, depending on the variant. This near miraculous legume has as many uses as your creativity can muster. A very nutritious food, it can be eaten raw or fried, turned into cooking oil and ground into meal. It can be processed into hand lotion, laundry soap and shampoo. Medicinally, peanuts can be turned into a laxative or rubbing oil. You can even use them to make glue, dye and ink.

Mangosteen

The interior of the fruit consists of segmented pulp with seeds. Open the ripe fruit carefully so that the inky secretions left by the shell don't stain your clothes and skin. The pulp is a source of many good micronutrients. You can eat it raw, make it into juice, add it to pies or make jams and sauces. You can fry the seeds and make curd from the peel.

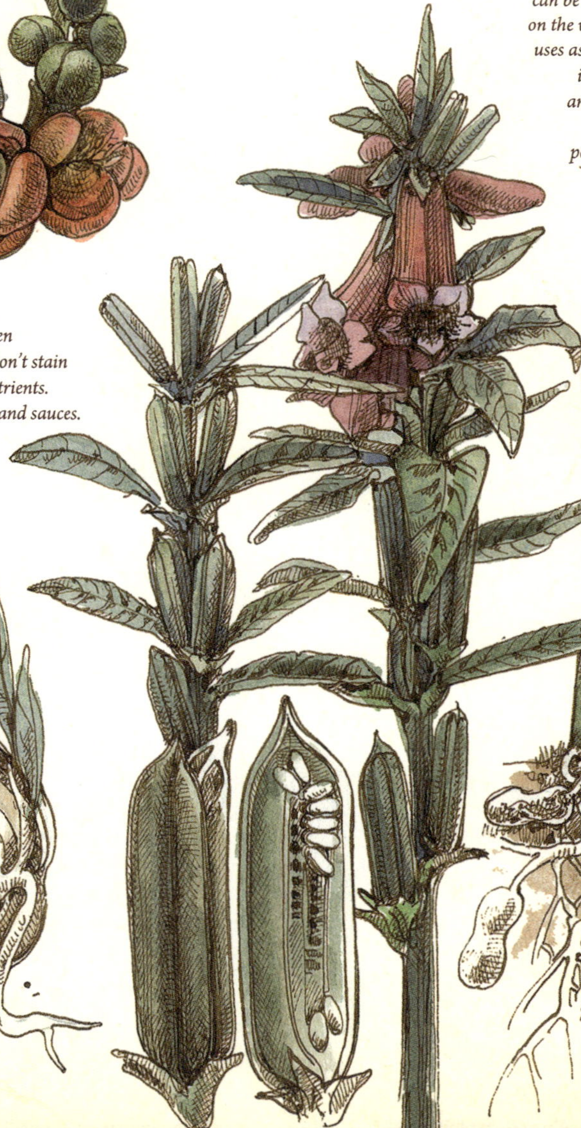

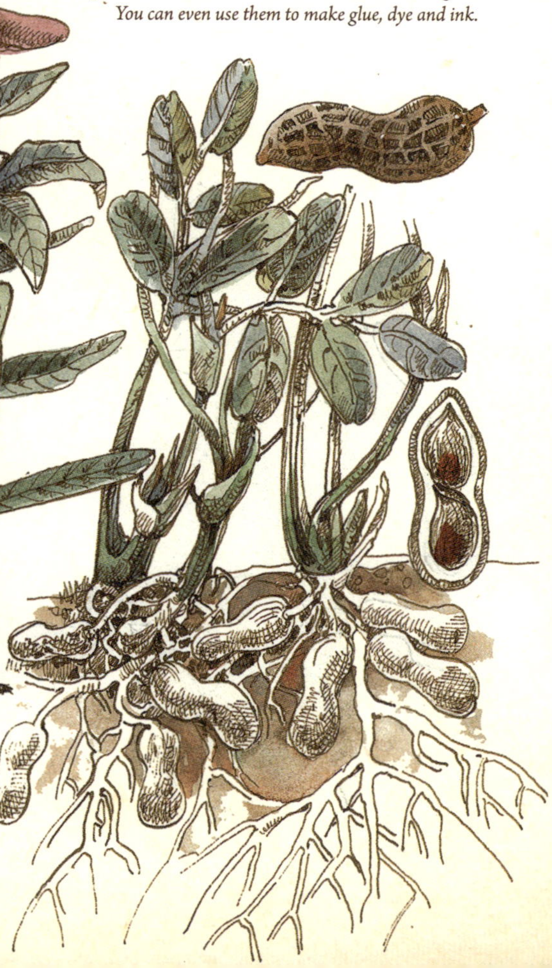

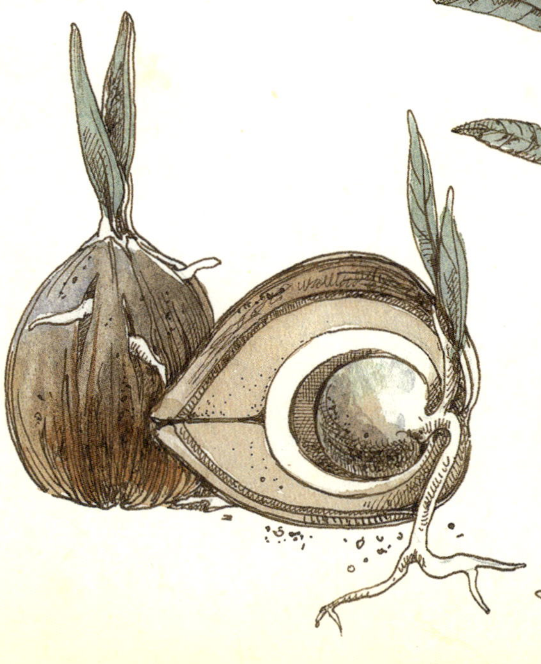

FUNGI

Mushrooms are among the most mysterious organisms in the multiverse. Neither plant nor animal, mushrooms are a type of fungus, which also includes microscopic yeast cells and molds. They survive by breaking down organic compounds in the environment — unlike plants, which use sunlight for photosynthesis — and reproduce by releasing spores.

Mushrooms are vital to maintaining healthy forestland. The caps and stems you see aboveground are just the visible portion of a massive underground network that rivals the span of even the largest metropolis.

FERMENTATION

Yeast and mold are also a type of microscopic fungi. Certain species can be used to kickstart the fermentation process when making bread (page 94) or alcohol (page 118). Some molds are used to make cheeses (page 104), wines (page 62) and even medicines One particular species produces a powerful medicinal substance: penicillin.

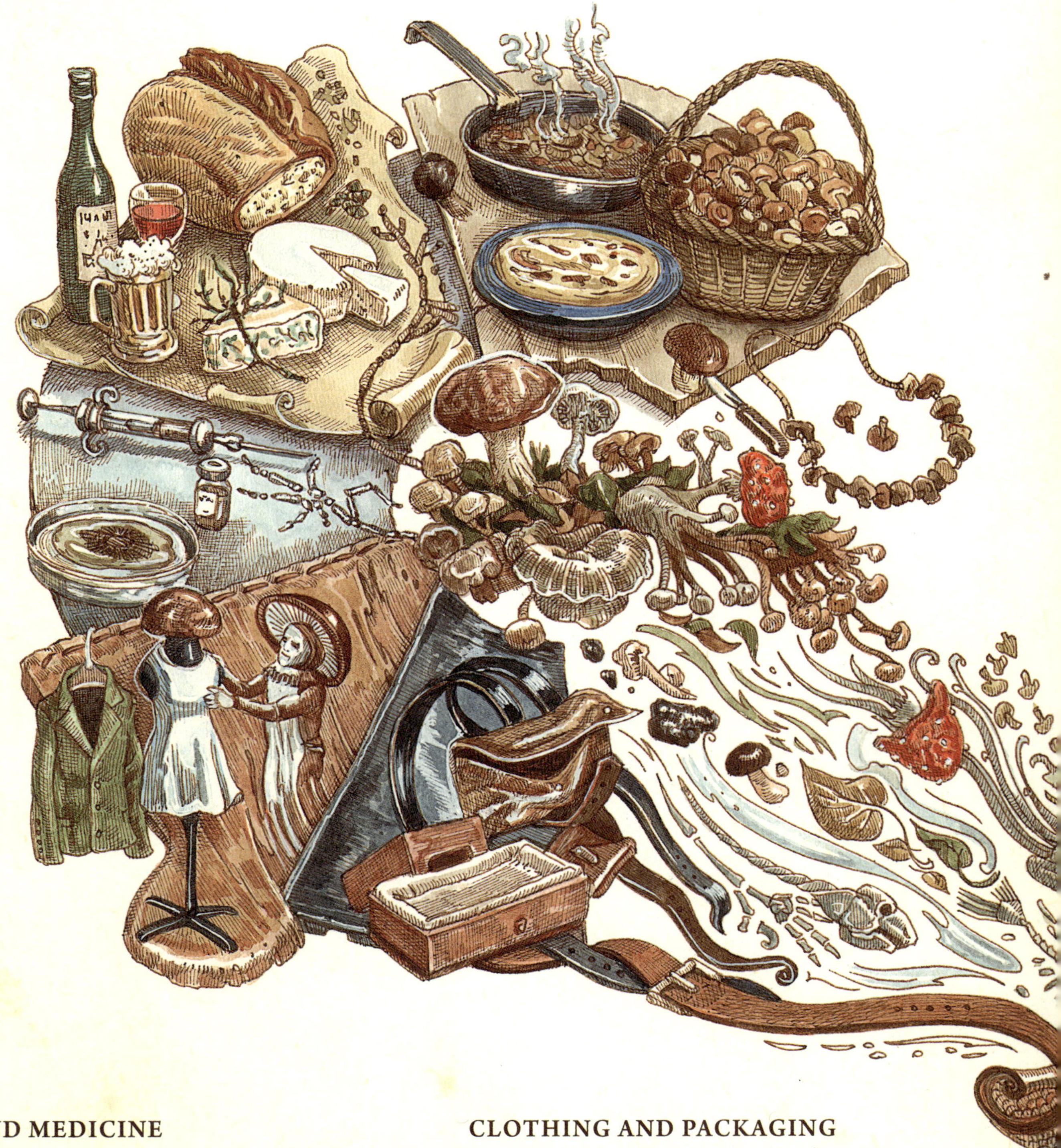

FOOD AND MEDICINE

Mushrooms aren't particularly satiating but do contain fiber, antioxidants, vitamins and minerals. They can be boiled, fried, cured or dried. Even poisonous mushrooms can be put to good use: fly agaric, for example, contains antibiotics, analgesics and antihistamines. But be careful: Some mushrooms cause hallucinations and other mind-bending symptoms that can change your perception of the world. In some societies, this may or may not be considered a positive attribute.

CLOTHING AND PACKAGING

Mycelium, which is the mushroom equivalent of a root system, can be used to make biodegradable, moisture- and fire-resistant materials for clothing and containers. Inoculate waste byproducts such as oat hulls (page 54) with mycelium and place in a mold. The mycelium will grow to fill the empty space and you'll be left with a dense block of material. When ready to use, dry it out to prevent further growth.

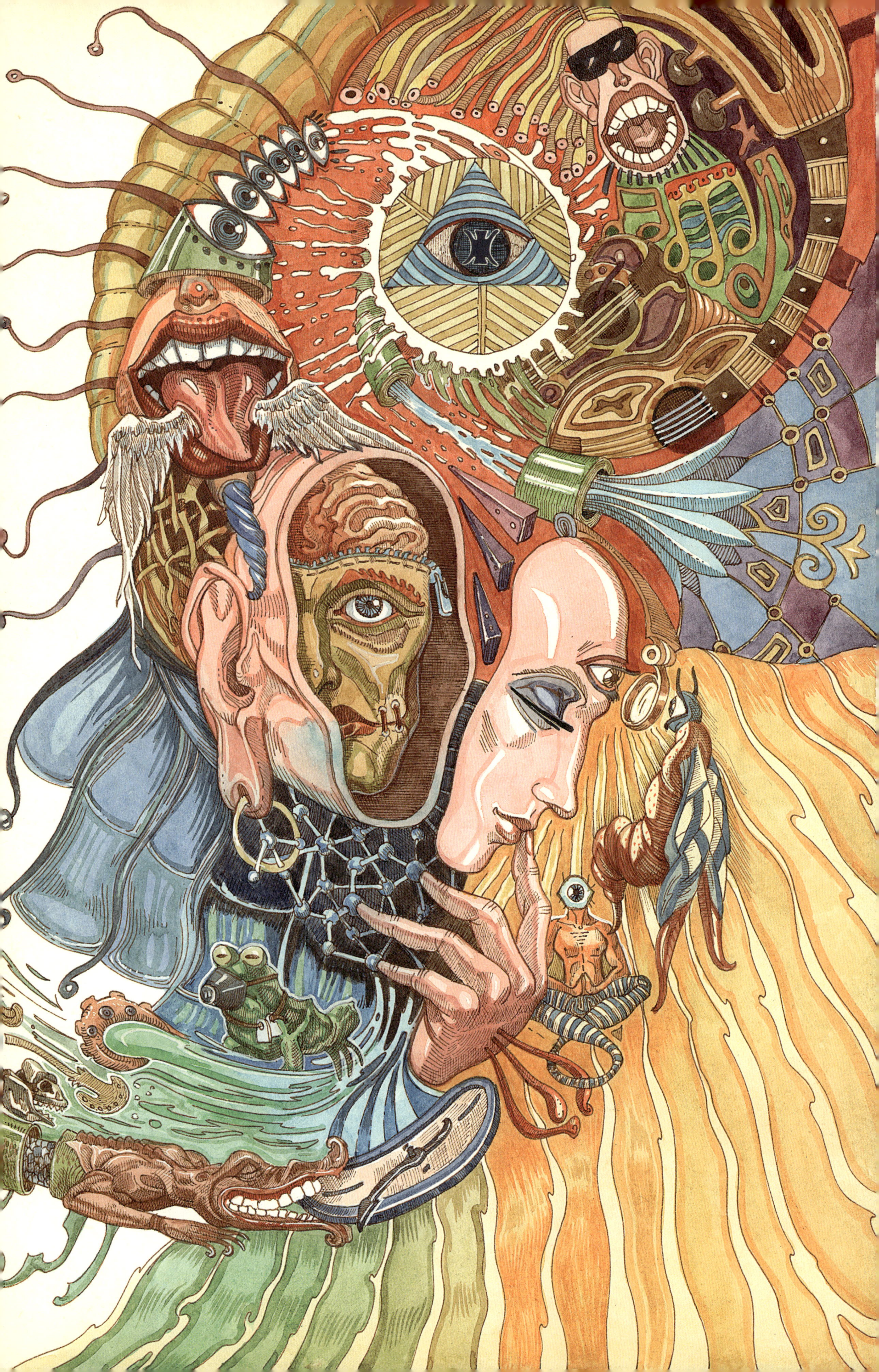

STAPLE CROPS

Once you start growing your own staple crops, be prepared for your life to change drastically. You'll begin to depend on agriculture and will be able to settle in one place. Your communities will grow into villages and, eventually, large cities.

Both cereals (e.g., wheat, rice, corn) and pulses (e.g., chickpeas, lentils) make good staple crops and will play an important role in shaping the food, life, culture and even worldview of your civilization.

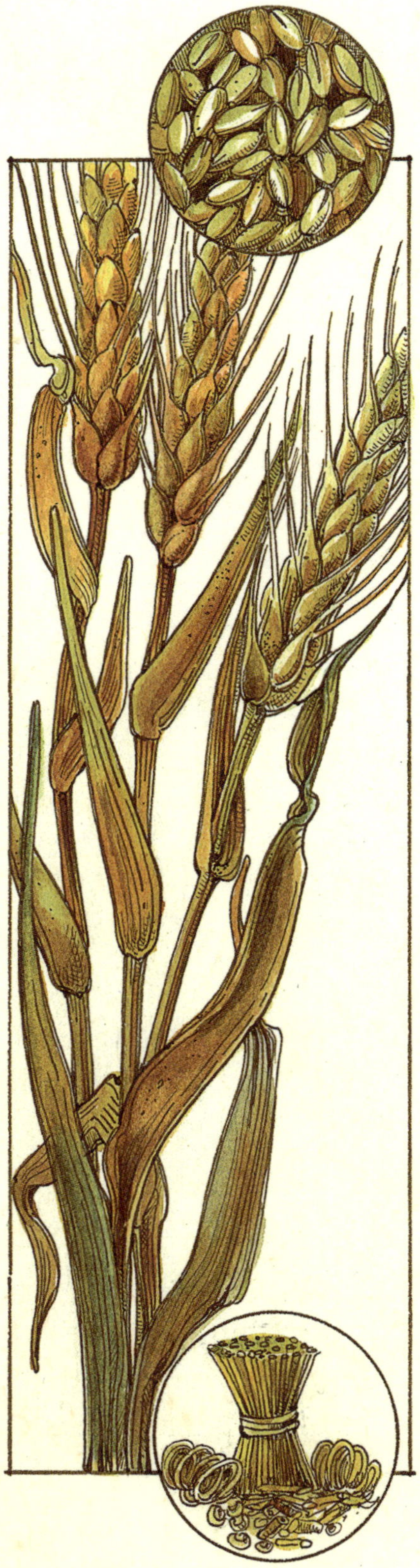

***Wheat** — depending on how you process it, you can get semolina, bulgur, couscous, wheat germ and flour. The grains themselves contain starch, which is used as a base in ointments and adhesives. Wheat is also needed to make beer, vodka and whiskey.*

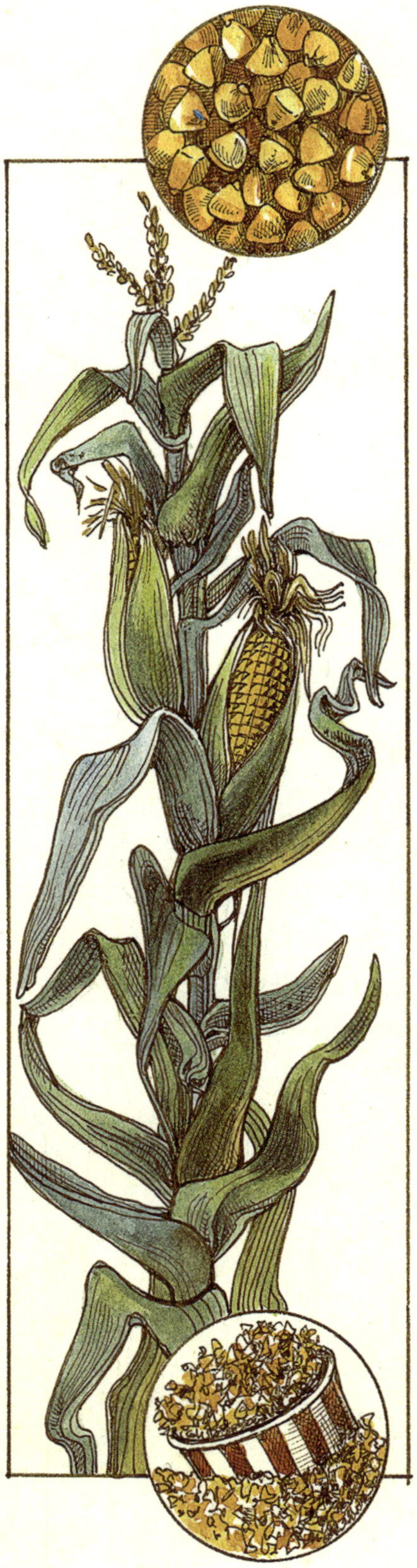

***Corn** is a staple grain, as it will provide food for both people and livestock. The unrefined kernels are used in side dishes and soups or eaten right off the cob. The flour can be made into pancakes, cornbread and tortillas or refined further to make cornstarch. Superheat the dried kernels in a closed pan with some oil to get popcorn. The dried husks and stalks of the plant are good for building huts and fences.*

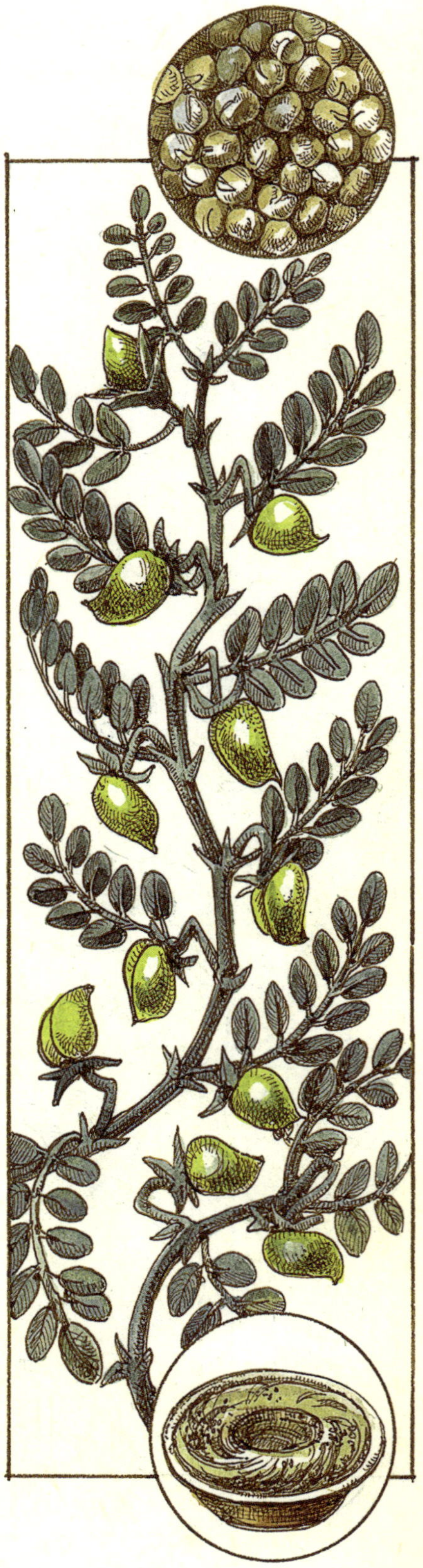

***Chickpeas** are a good plant-based meat replacement, as they are rich in protein. Two easy dishes to make are hummus, mashed chickpeas with tahini (ground sesame seeds), and falafel, ground chickpeas formed into a ball and deep fried. After you've harvested your chickpeas, the rest of the plant can be used as livestock feed.*

Cereals can be processed in several ways:

- Mill the grains to produce flour (page 234).
- Remove the hard outer shell (bran) from the grain using a mortar and pestle, moisten and steam to remove any impurities and dry to produce cereals.
- Soak and germinate the seeds to produce malt, which is used to make beer (page 106), whiskey and other alcoholic beverages.

Sow your seeds at different times of the year to ensure a steady food source all year long. Spring cereals, as the name suggests, are sown in spring, while winter crops should be planted in autumn. Winter crops germinate during the cold months, and because of this, they ripen much earlier than the spring crops. Winter crops produce higher yields (due to moisture reserves in the soil in early spring), but they can be grown only in areas with high snow cover and mild winters, are more demanding on the soil and are less drought-resistant. Wheat, barley and rye can all be sown in winter.

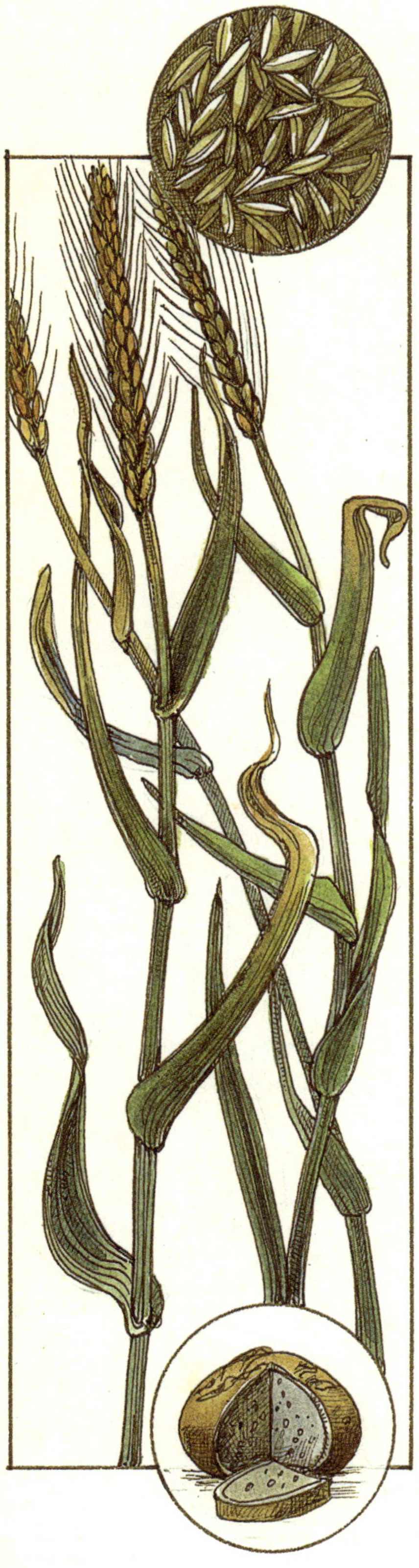

Oats *tolerate frost and drought very well, so they'll guarantee your survival. Crush the grains to get flour for bread or flatten them into flakes to make muesli. Infuse alcohol with oat grains and you'll get a sedative. Brew them for a pick-me-up coffee replacement. By the way, baby food and jelly can both be thickened using oat broth.*

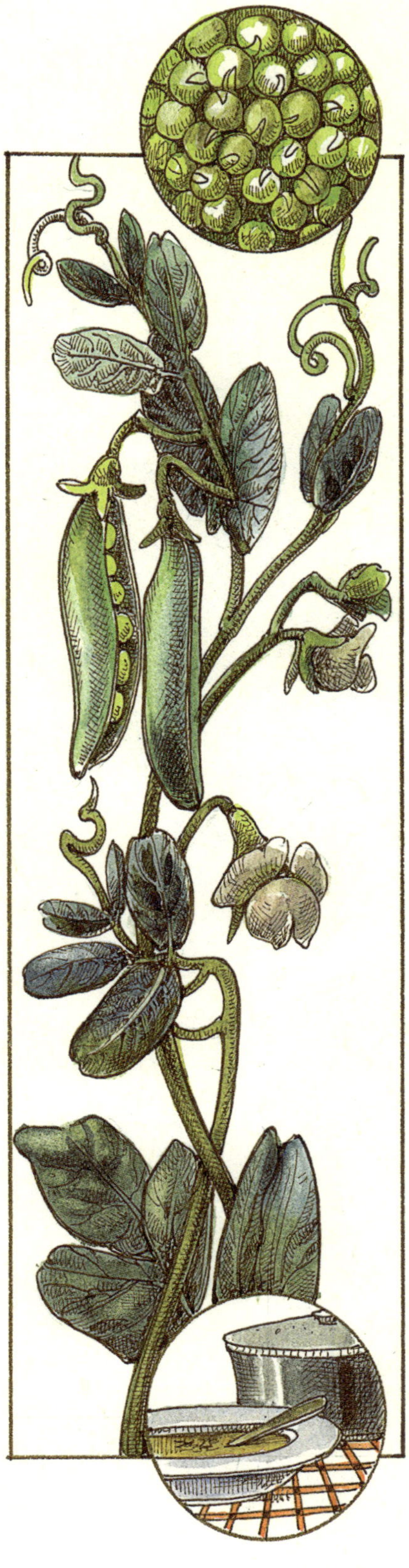

Lentils *are drought-resistant legumes that are high in carbohydrates and protein. They're the basis of salads, earthy soups and stews, vegetarian cutlets and pâté, as well as sweet dishes like pancakes, muffins and even "mockolate" truffles. Additionally, they fix nitrogen and so replenish the soil in which they are grown.*

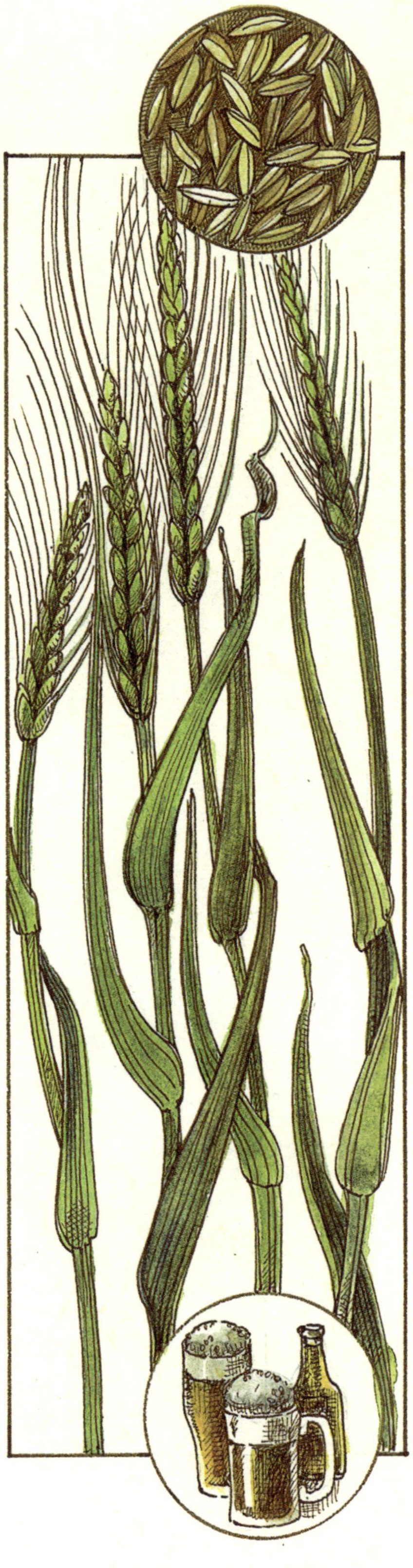

Barley *grains, after hulling, leave you with delicious barley grits. Polish those to produce pearl barley. Barley works wonderfully for thickening soups and stews. It is an essential ingredient in beer and whiskey. It also makes great animal fodder for keeping your livestock alive through winter.*

CROP ROTATION

Nature moves in cycles. After each blossom comes a period of decline, and over time, even the most fertile fields start producing increasingly meager harvests. The soil becomes depleted as the plants suck all the nutrients from it. But don't pack up the family and leave the farm yet — you can help your fields rest and recover while continuing to produce a yield.

To do this, you must change the plants you grow annually according to the rules of crop rotation: interchange soil-depleting cereals with legumes, which saturate the land with nitrogen, and grow root crops for both animal feed and personal consumption. This approach will provide you and your livestock with food, which in turn will provide you with milk and meat. And livestock manure even rejuvenates the soil. An added bonus is that crop rotation disrupts the life cycles of pathogens and plant pests, preventing them from flourishing.

***Barley** and **oats** (page 54) produce good yields but quickly drain the soil. Therefore, grow a perennial clover at the same time. It will grow under the canopy of the cereals and is good for feeding cows and goats. Clover accumulates nitrogen in its roots, which will maintain soil nutrient levels as the cereals grow.*

*The next year, plant **legumes** iin these same fields — peas, beans, lentils, annual clover, soy, peanuts. They will restore the fertility of the nutrient-depleted soil by saturating it with nitrogen. The crop can be used to feed livestock, and if there is a surplus, plow it into the ground, where it will fertilize the soil for next year's crop.*

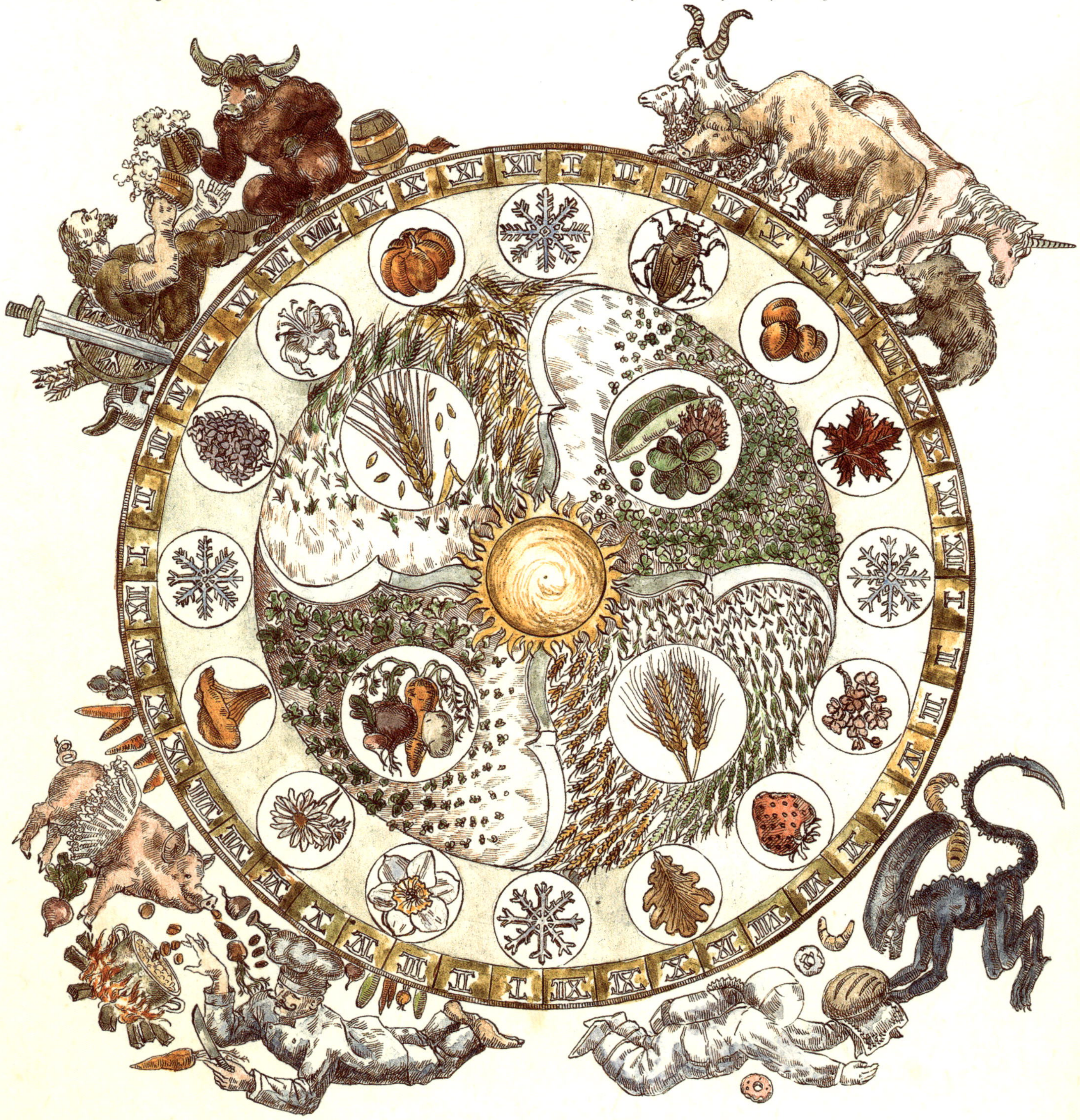

*The year after you plant wheat, grow **root veggies** such as potatoes, beets, turnips, rutabagas. These are a great source of food for both people and livestock. Animals will gain significantly more weight on root crops than if they were grazing in pastures. Your root crop fields act as a sort of caloric storage system: They can be left in the ground and harvested as needed for the next two years. Root crops aren't affected by weeding, so use this opportunity to rid your fields of unwanted weeds. By the way, you can utilize this extra pasture land by growing more cereals.*

***Wheat** and **rye** (page 54) are your main crops. They should be sown immediately after the legumes, when the soil is at peak nutrient density. These crops have winter varieties, which are sown in winter as opposed to spring so they germinate earlier. Plant them in previously harvested fields so your land will not stand idle.*

Good fertilizers produce large harvests and sustainable yields. Your best fertilizer factory is a compost pit. Food waste, harvest byproducts and even excrement (a source of nitrogen, phosphorus and potassium) can all be added to the pile. But it is important to process them correctly or the cycle of pathogenic organisms will be a closed loop, which can cause an outbreak of diseases. Cover the feces with sawdust and straw, leave for six months or a year and stir regularly. Decomposed sawdust increases soil fertility, improving its air permeability and moisture capacity. To speed up the decomposition process in the pit, dampen everything with water and turn it into a slurry.

Plants need certain substances at different stages of their lifecycle. During the germination period, they need phosphorus; during the active growth period, nitrogen; and in preparation for winter, potassium. Sludge containing the rotting remains of vegetation and marine organisms will act as a powerful growth stimulator, and manure and bird droppings will act as a source of nitrogen. Plants will receive phosphorus and calcium if you sprinkle them with powder obtained from boiled and ground animal skeletons. Many of these elements are also contained in common ash, which can be used as a compound fertilizer, as it also contains magnesium, sulfur, boron, manganese and other elements that plants need.

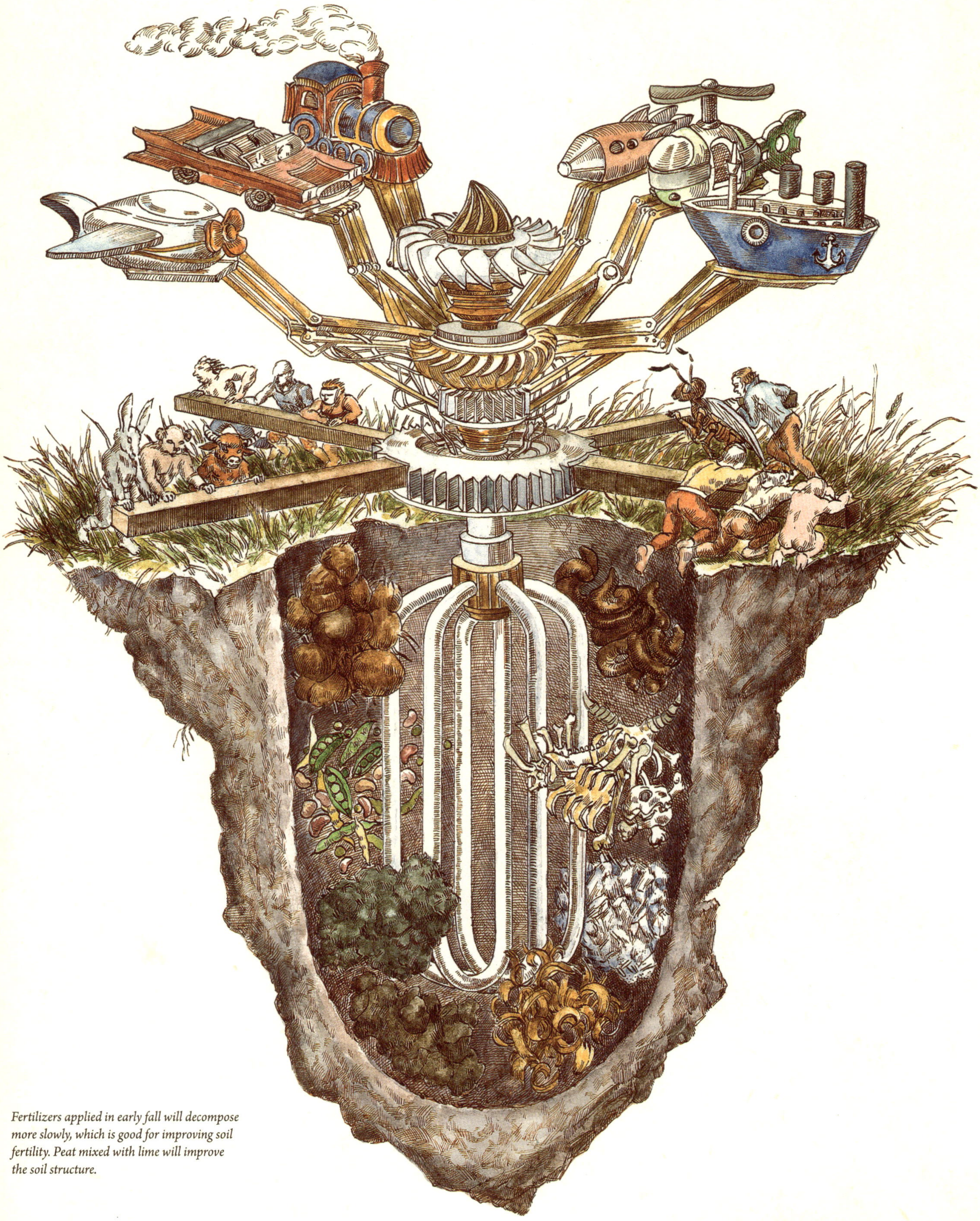

Fertilizers applied in early fall will decompose more slowly, which is good for improving soil fertility. Peat mixed with lime will improve the soil structure.

PLOW & TOOLS

Gathering grains is all well and good, but to feed a large number of people, you'll need to grow your own cereals (page 54) and other crops. The most important step in this process is preparing the soil. If you try to do this on your own, you'll be left digging from dawn until dusk. You need a plow. It can transform a dry patch of overgrown weeds into an excellent crop field in the blink of an eye. The plow allows you not only to eliminate weeds by severing their roots and turning over the soil but also introduce nutrients into the soil and improve drainage and aeration.

WORKING PRINCIPLES

The basic principle of the plow is that it cuts both vertically and horizontally through the ground and rolls this whole slice of topsoil over upside-down. This allows you to get rid of weeds, distribute fertilizers throughout the soil and improve aeration. **The sock** (1), or share, of the plow cuts through the soil layer. The degree of rotation depends on the shape of the bent upper part of the share, known as the **moldboard** (2).

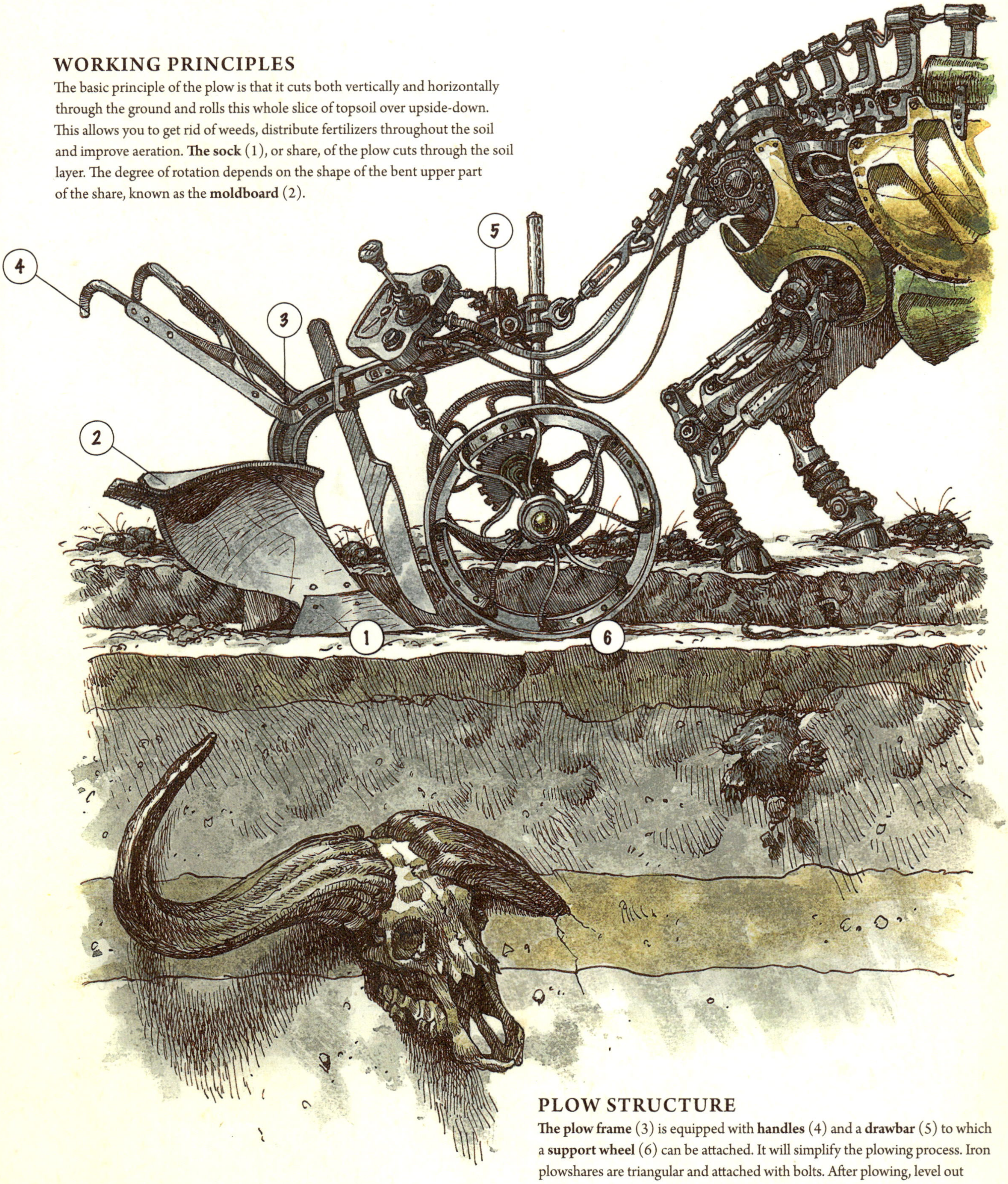

PLOW STRUCTURE

The plow frame (3) is equipped with **handles** (4) and a **drawbar** (5) to which a **support wheel** (6) can be attached. It will simplify the plowing process. Iron plowshares are triangular and attached with bolts. After plowing, level out the furrows and ridges, scatter the seeds and wait for the harvest! Remember to weed, watch out for pests, fertilize the soil and water your seedlings.

To cultivate and harvest the land, you need more than a plow. Try combining several devices into one super-machine, perhaps one that runs on steam (page 242).

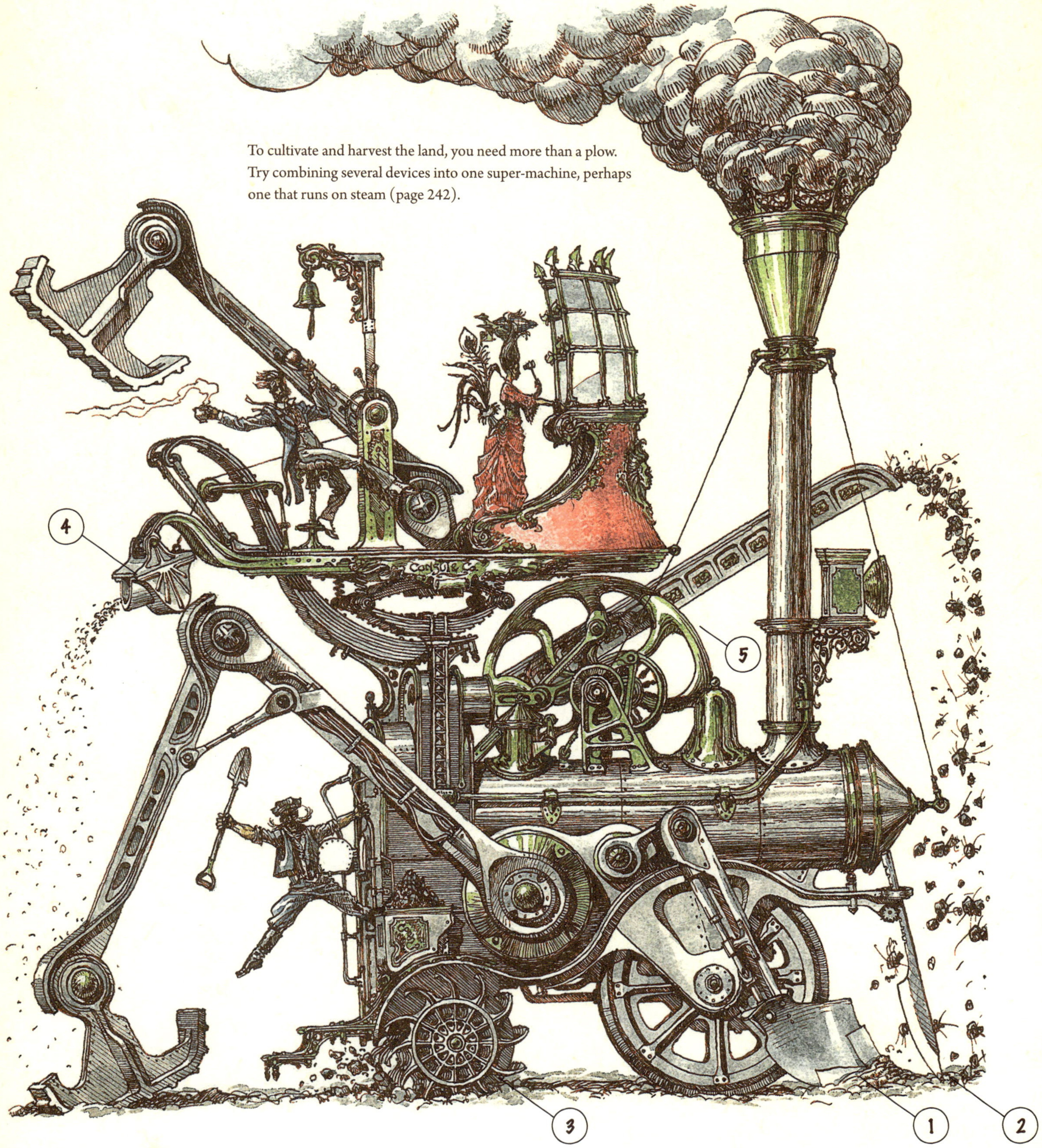

COMBINE

Working a field requires a whole variety of tools. Most of them will be rendered far more effective if you attach a power source. Mechanize the process by creating a base structure onto which you can install various pieces depending on what job you need done. Let's say you are out of luck: The soil is full of stones, and the plow is constantly breaking and becoming dull.The solution is a **chisel** (1). It is attached in front of the plowshare and prevents damage to the cutting edge of the blade.

You can even make it retractable, sliding forward and back as you sew your seeds. **The skimmer** (2) chops off the top soil layer with the plants and places it in the bottom of the open furrow. This will facilitate the work of the plowshare and extend its life. **The harrow** (3) will allow you to level the soil after plowing and cover the seeds with dirt. You can also opt for wooden planks with protruding spikes. To cover large areas, use **the seeder** (4) — a mechanical seed spreading device.

Take a wheelbarrow with a grain box and connect it, via a gear system (page 162), to one of the wheels, which will rotate the roller in the bottom of the box so that the seeds fall evenly. Add **the thresher** (5) — a rotating drum with soft blades that separates the grain from the chaff and straw during harvest time.

SCARECROW & MOLE TRAPS

The circle of life exists in delicate balance, and one ill-conceived action could have unforeseen consequences. Remove a single grain and the whole pile comes toppling down, sending ripples through time and changing the world beyond recognition. Birds stealing the fruits of your labor? Be wary of scaring them away, lest your fields be overrun with rodents and insects that cause even more damage to your crops. When waging war against pests, you must be careful not to upset the natural ecosystem. Maintain balance by learning about the lifestyles, habits and fears of the critters crunching on your crops and use this information to develop an action plan.

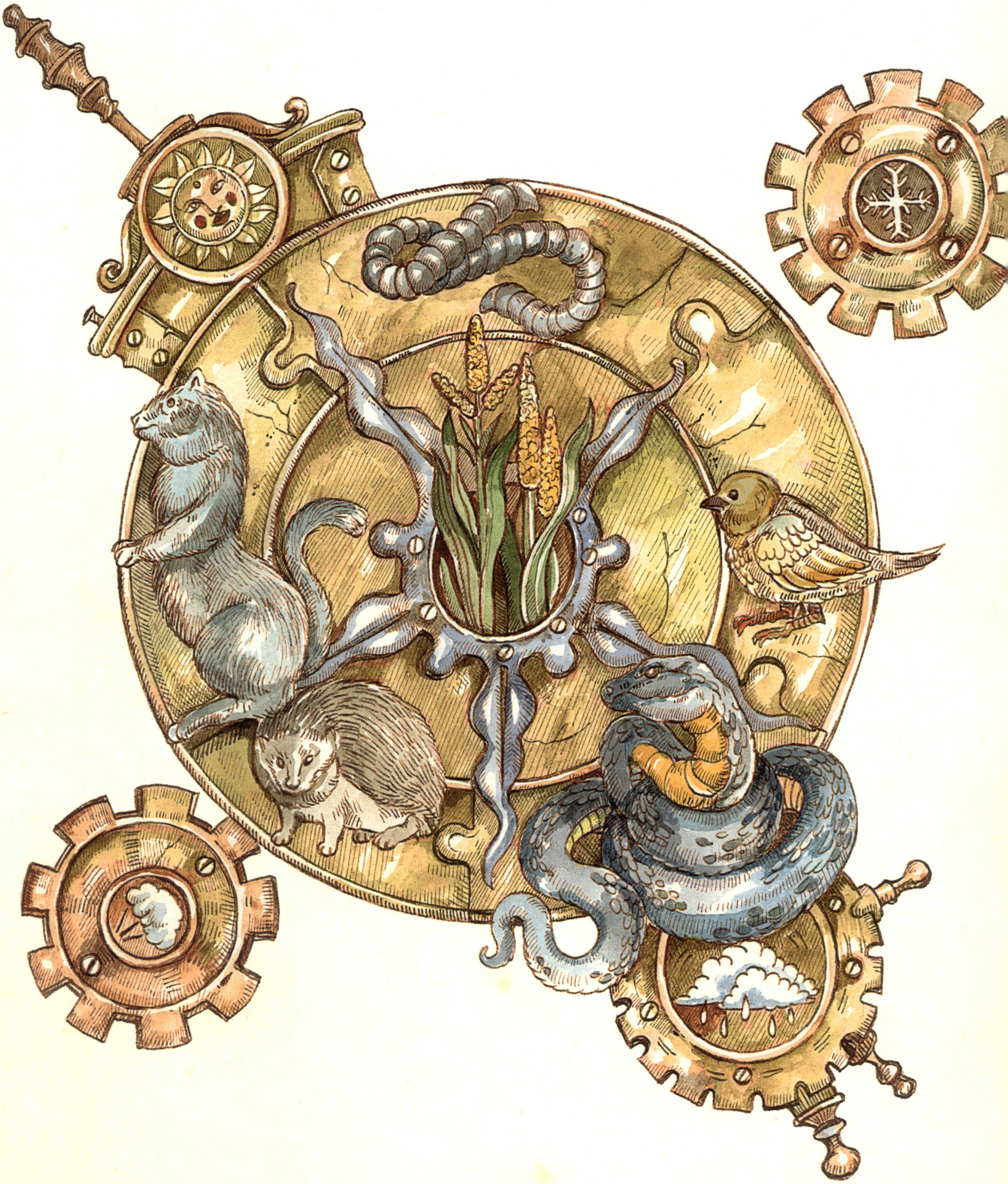

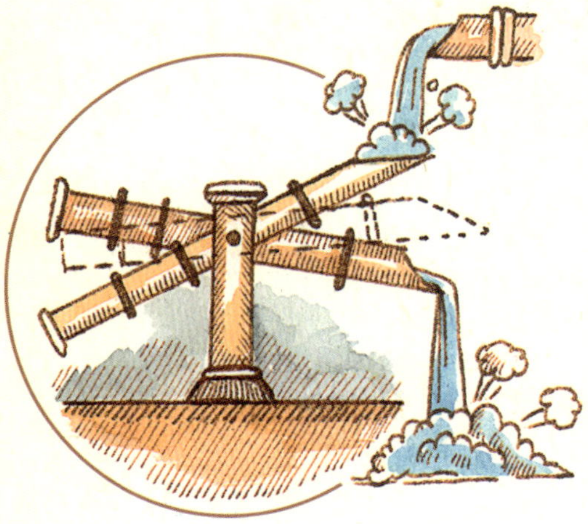

If you have a source of running water near your field, carve a rocker arm out of a segmented bamboo stalk pivoted slightly to one side of the balance point. The back end should rest on a hard surface, like a rock. As the hollow bamboo stalk fills with water, the tube's center of gravity moves past the pivot point. As the tube topples over to dump out the water, the heavier back end smacks against the rock, creating a loud cracking noise that scares away birds.

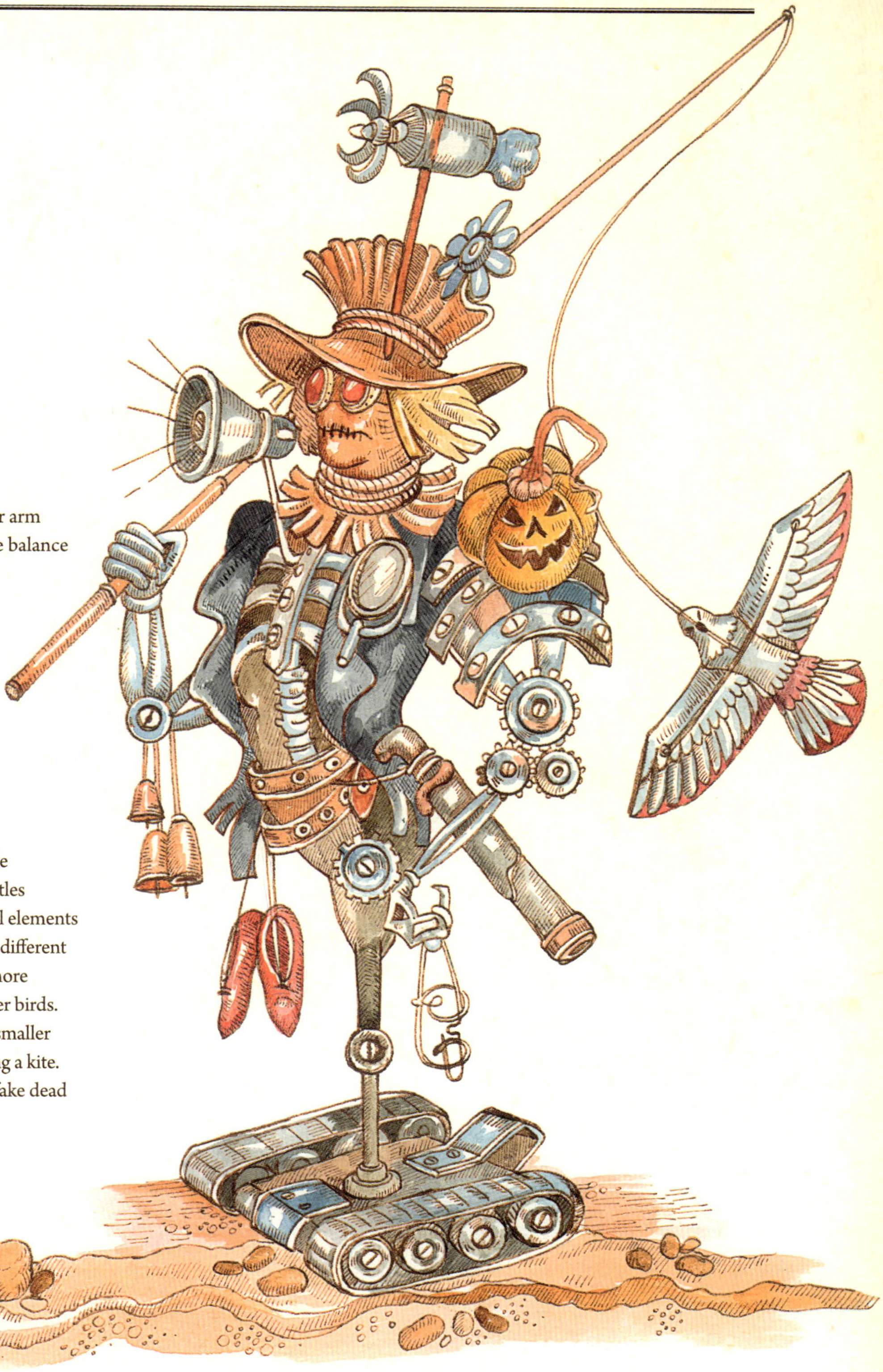

SCARECROW

Everyone knows that nature's most frightening predator is man. Take advantage of this reputation by placing a human figure on a pole in a field. You can decorate it with all sorts of trash that moves or rustles in the wind or shiny objects that glint in the sun. Moving mechanical elements will make your scarecrow even more intimidating. Move the pole to different locations around the field to keep the birds on their toes. Or make more scarecrows. But the main predator birds have to contend with is other birds. If you haven't had the chance to train a pet falcon to chase away the smaller birds picking at your crop, you can make a serviceable imitation using a kite. And humans aren't the only creatures prone to superstition. Scatter fake dead birds around the field and the living ones will want to stay far away.

FIGHTING MOLES

Set the trap by threading the catch ring (4) through the opening in the end of the metal firing arm (2) then mount the arm on the catch (3). In this position, the tension spring (5) keeps the arm under tension. When the mole sticks its head through the entry ring (1), its nose will push against the catch ring, sliding it to one side and releasing the catch. This presses the mole's neck against the bottom of the entry ring, rendering it unable to move.

1. *Entry ring*
2. *Firing arm*
3. *Catch*
4. *Trigger*
5. *Tension spring*

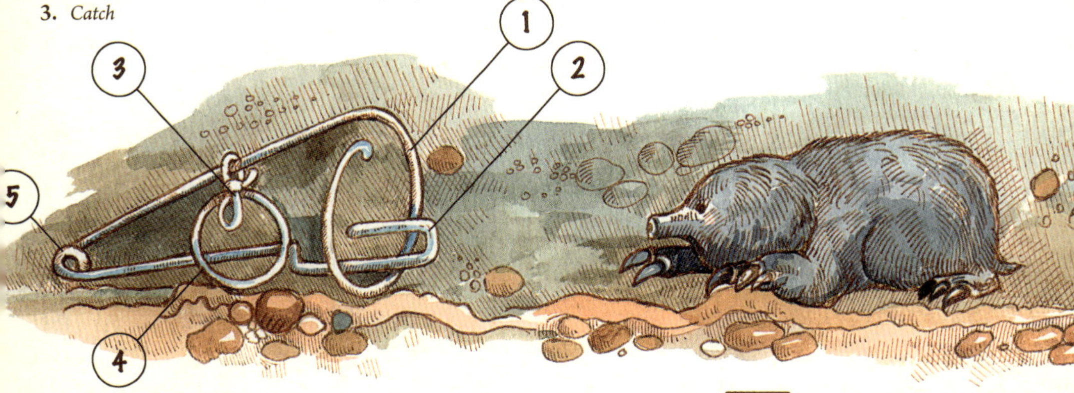

CHEMICAL TREATMENTS

Powdery mildew (a type of mold) is the scourge of many plants. Spraying with natural antifungals can help. Crush limestone and burn the powder at 900–1200°C. The substance you're left with is calcium oxide, otherwise known as quicklime. Carefully dissolve a kilogram of quicklime in 50 liters of water. Then take a kilogram of copper sulfate, which can be obtained by treating copper with concentrated sulfuric acid heated to 60°C. Dissolve this in a small amount of hot water then add cold water to 50 liters. Mix this with the quicklime solution.

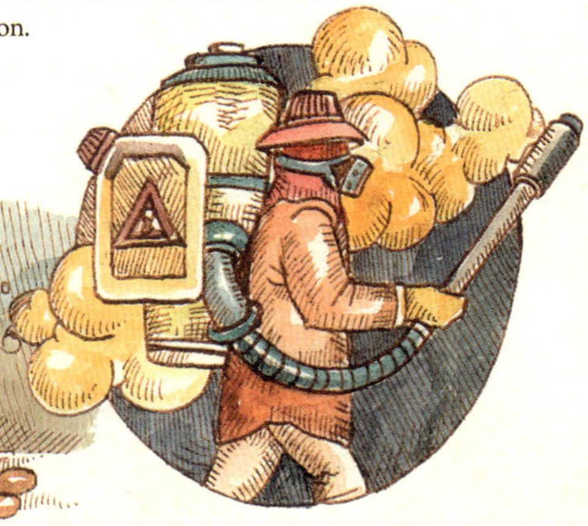

WINE

A fine beverage that warms the body and heals the soul. Although every drop of wine is made from fermented grape juice, not just any grape is worthy of becoming wine. A bottle of wine combines a winemaker's skill with the spirit of a location.

The grape is a tiny miracle, a secret haven for nature's powers. Once poured into a glass, these powers reveal themselves in a deep, complex bouquet of flavors, delicious and distinct.

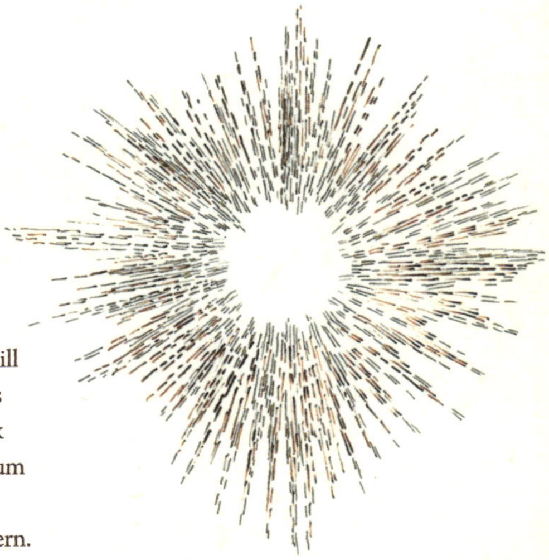

PROTECTION FROM THE ELEMENTS

Locating your vineyard on the side of a valley or hill will offer good drainage and protect your precious vines from frost and wind. But make sure you pick the correct side (towards the equator) for maximum sunshine: a south-facing slope in the northern hemisphere and a north-facing slope in the southern.

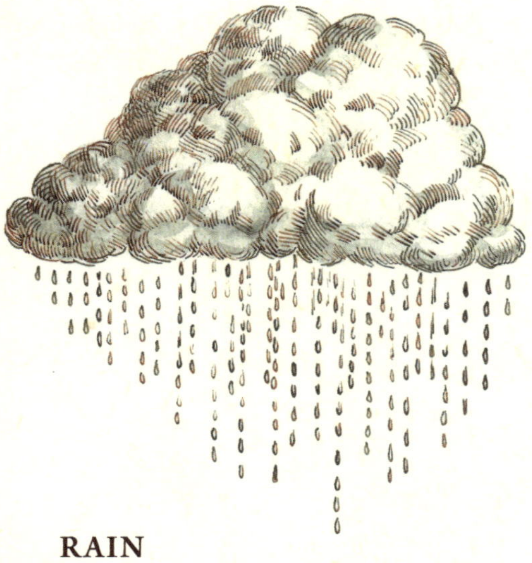

In order to produce wine, the vine must suffer for its art. If you don't prune (trim the top parts of the shoots), the bush becomes less frost resistant and the grapes will wither and die. The most important thing to consider here is timing, both by season and by year. Young bushes (1–3 years old) should be pruned in the spring when there is no sap flow. Vines four years and older are ready to bear fruit. The vine should be pruned when the shoots are longer than 1.2–1.5 m.

SUNLIGHT

The warmth from the sun's rays creates a sweet and spirituous wine. The more sunlight a grapevine absorbs, the more sugar is packed into its fruit. During fermentation, this sugar turns into alcohol. 1800–2000 hours of sunshine per year will make for a harvest of beautiful, fully ripened grapes.

RAIN

Grape vines can't survive on groundwater alone. They also need rainwater, which gives the wine the necessary acidity for a fine, balanced flavor. Therefore, the drier regions of the world produce heavier wines.

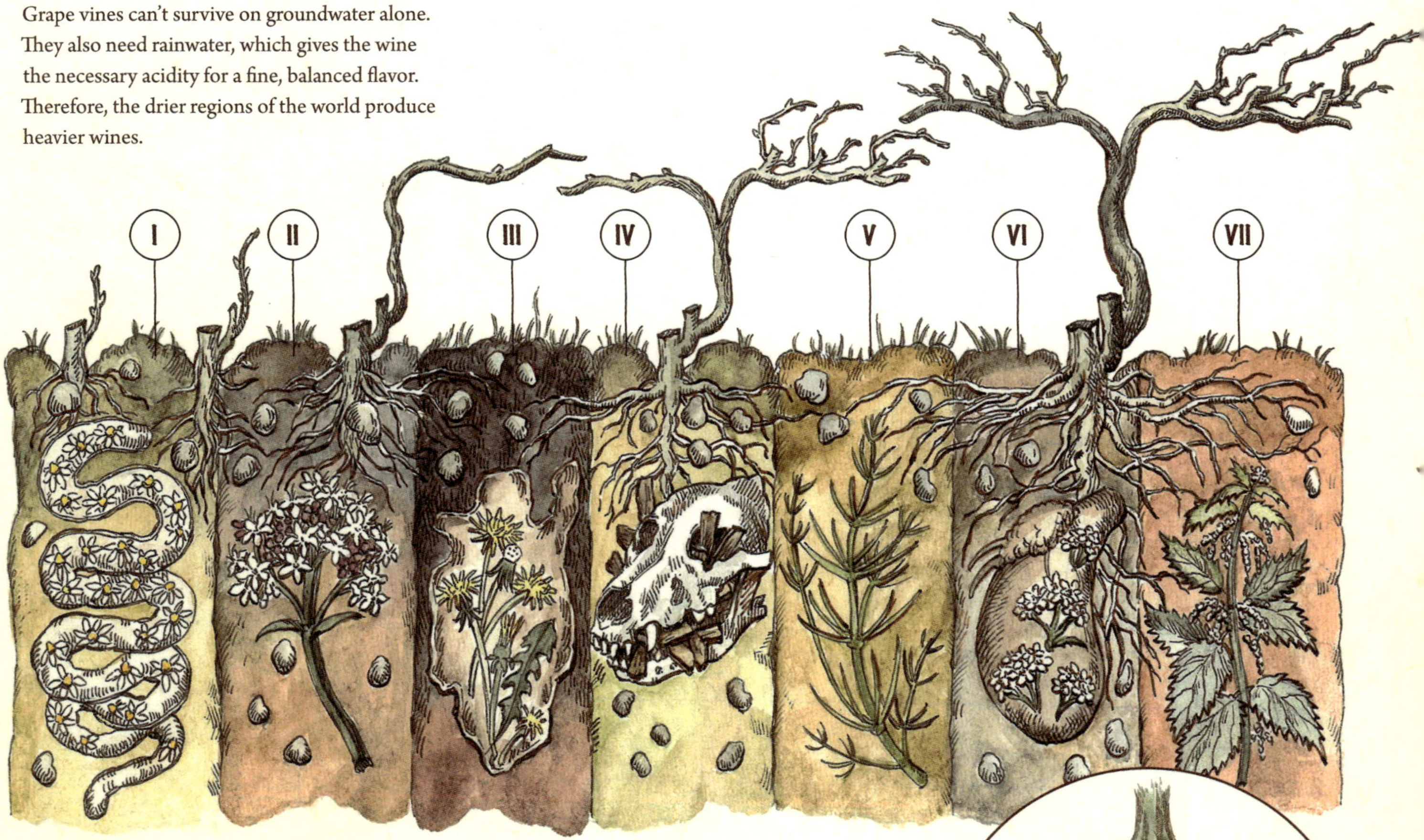

SOIL

The type of wine you produce is heavily dependent on the soil you have to work with. Brown soils (I) are good for sparkling and table wines. Podzolic, or ash gray, soils (II) are good for light table wines. Humus-carbonate (II), a shallow soil formed over limestone, is a winemaker's dream. This soil produces high-quality sparkling wines, as well as thin vodkas, brandy and armagnac.

Sandy soil (IV) allows the vine to accumulate sugar, imbuing light wines with a delicate bouquet and making them easy to blend. Sierozemic soil (V), white-grey desert soil, makes strong sweet wines. Barros soil (VI), rich in gypsum and carbonic lime, is used for fortified wines. Pink soil (VII) is for dessert and liqueur wines.

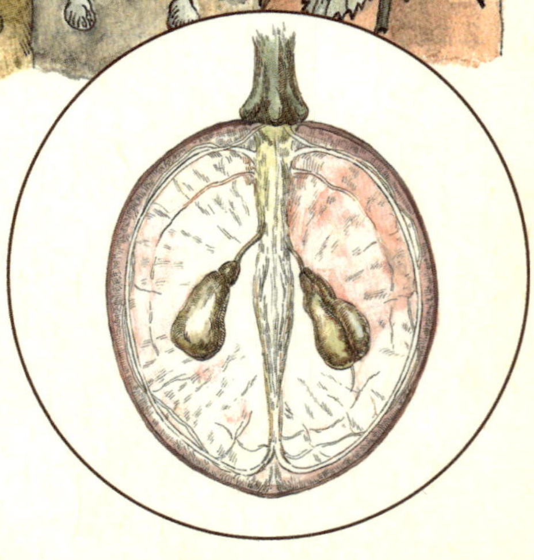

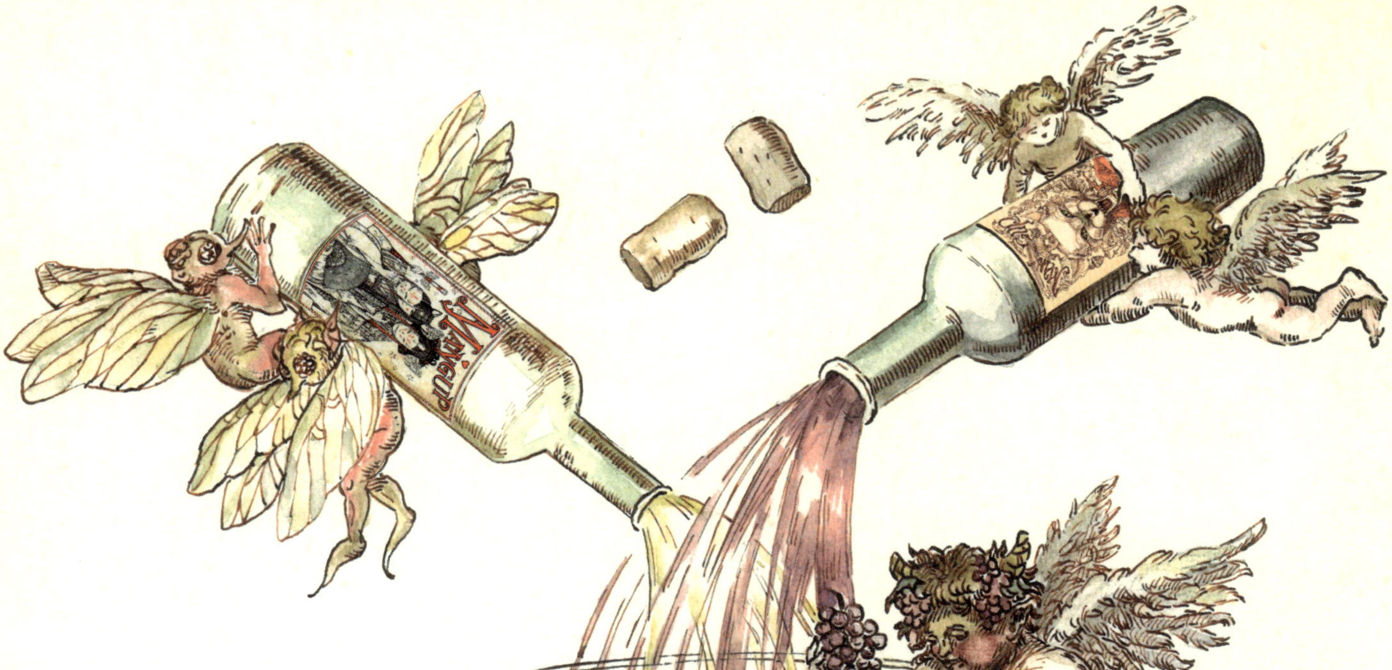

MAKING THE WINE

To make wine, start with a hand-picked selection of ripe, dry grapes. Crush them and leave the resulting juice to ferment. The yeast fungi that thrive on the grapes' skins turn the sugar into alcohol and carbon dioxide. Once the alcohol concentration reaches 15–18 percent, the yeast dies and the process of fermentation comes to an end.

Then, with great care and without lifting the sediment, the wine is poured into oak barrels and left to infuse for up to two years. A less patient winemaker may choose to immediately pour the wine into any vessel of his choice that is corked with oak bark.

Both wine-making and wine-drinking are artforms in their own right. Wine is the drink of the gods, created to stimulate the senses. But too much wine will throw your body out of balance, and instead of highs, you'll start to experience crashes. Your emotional state will take a nosedive, and you'll fall into a depression.

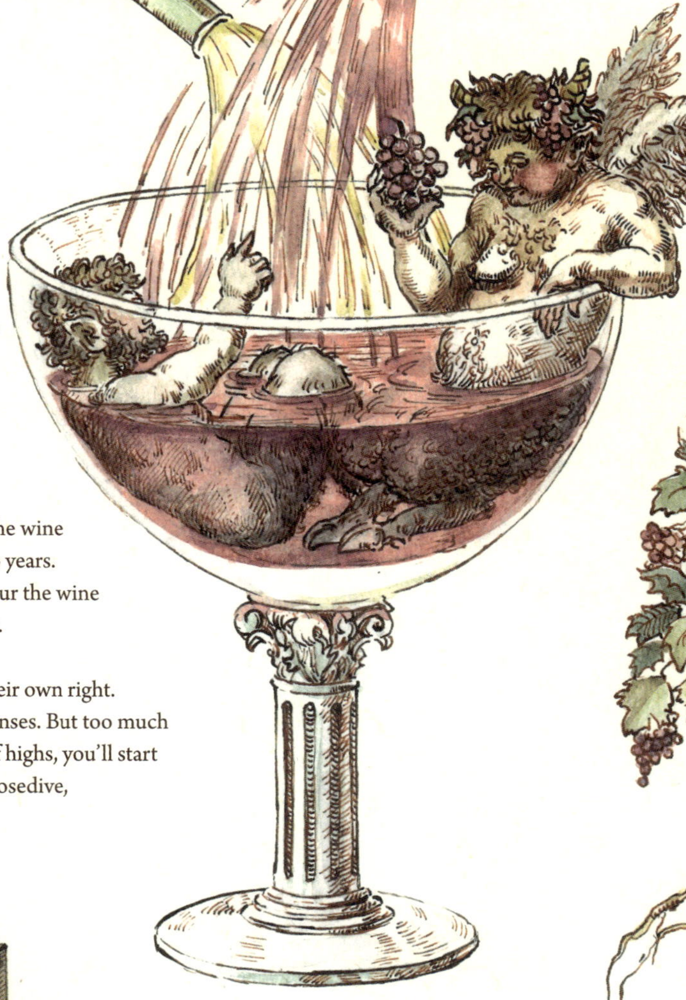

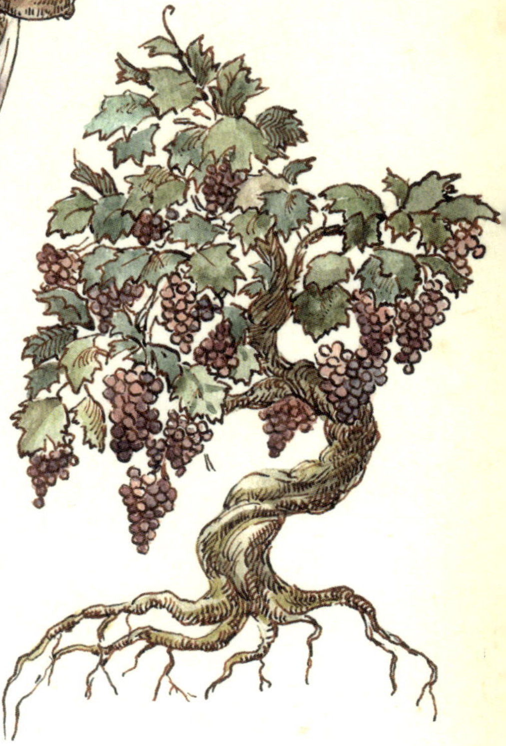

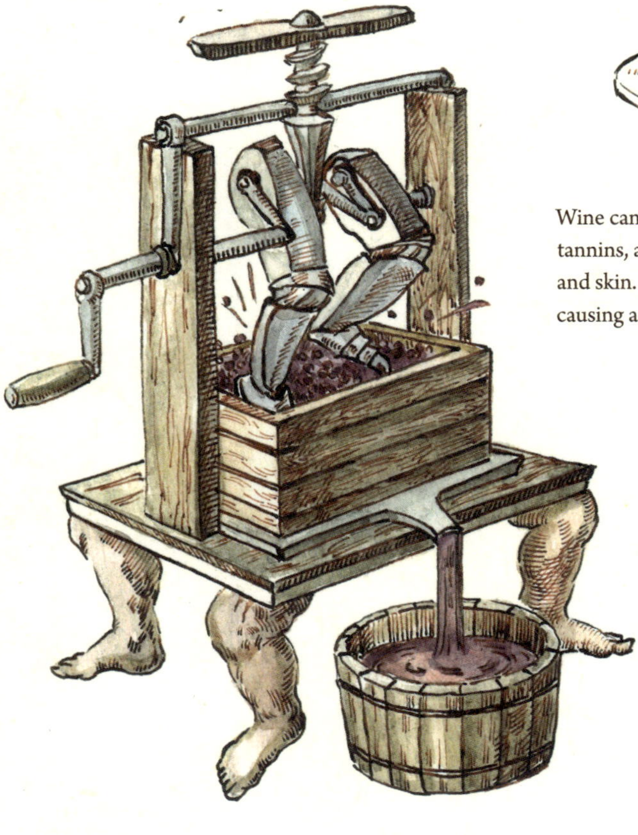

Wine can be slightly acerbic. This tartness comes from tannins, a substance contained in the grapevine, seeds and skin. Tannins bind to the proteins in our saliva, causing a feeling of dryness in the mouth.

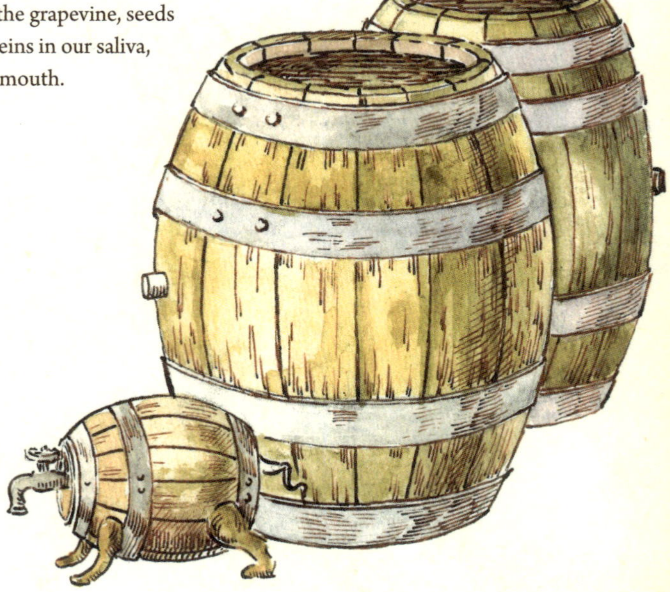

TEA

In some societies, the availability of tea makes or breaks a civilization. Tea is an incredibly valuable herb, and entire empires have built their economies around the tea trade. The theine (caffeine in tea) acts as a strong stimulant. But tea is a lot more than just an energy drink. The full range of tastes and characteristics is revealed only to the most seasoned connoisseur.

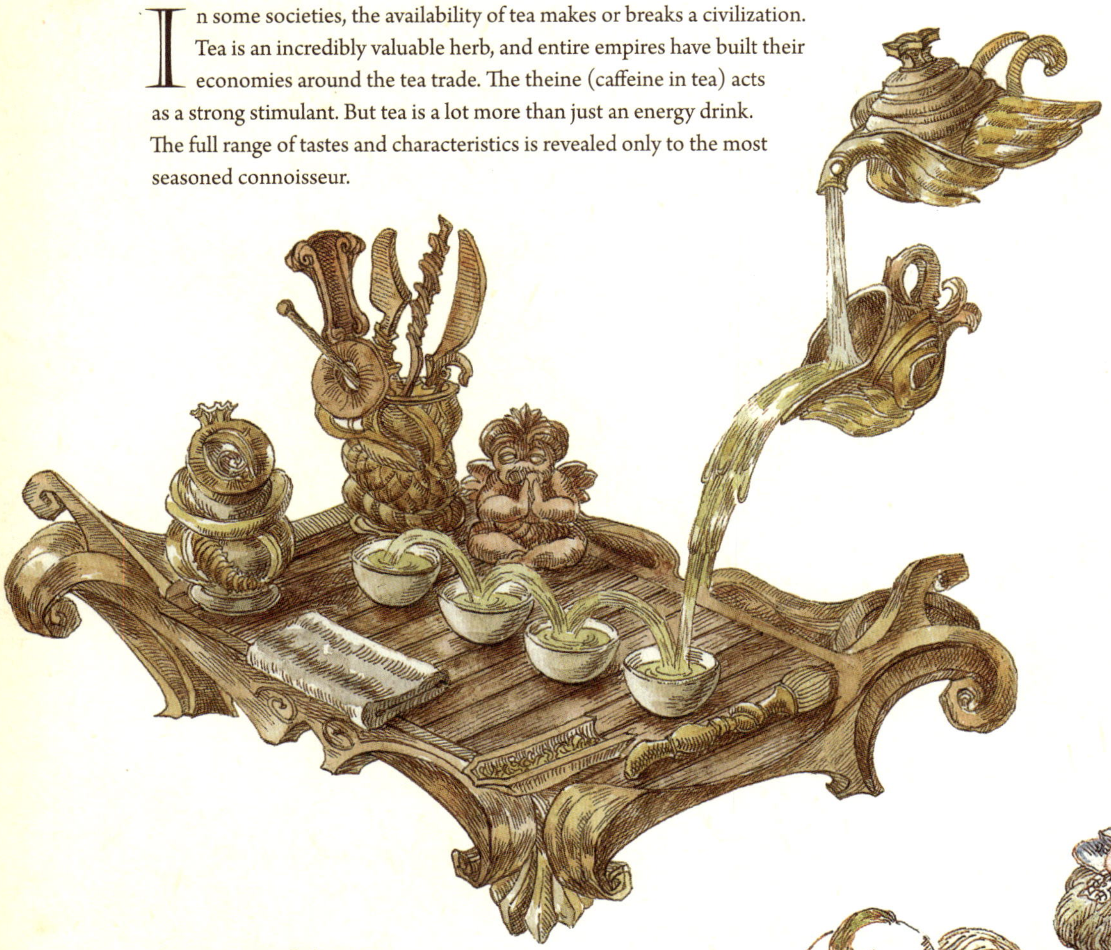

A sensitivity to subtle nuances in flavor can be developed through training. This practice of mindful tea consumption is called a tea ceremony. While the rituals and level of ceremony may vary, the underlying principles remain the same: a respect for the drink, care in preparation and special attention paid to the aroma and taste during every step of the process. Unhurried and precise movements. Silence and full concentration on the present moment. Tea ceremonies may last over an hour, giving you time to pause to break the cycle of everyday life. In the end, rebuilding civilization can wait because the journey is far more important than the destination.

For black and oolong teas, the first batch of tea is often discarded, and the beverage is only enjoyed after the second steeping. For green teas, the first steep is often lighter and more aromatic. To experience the full flavor of the tea, you need to roll it around on your tongue before swallowing so that it covers all of your taste buds.

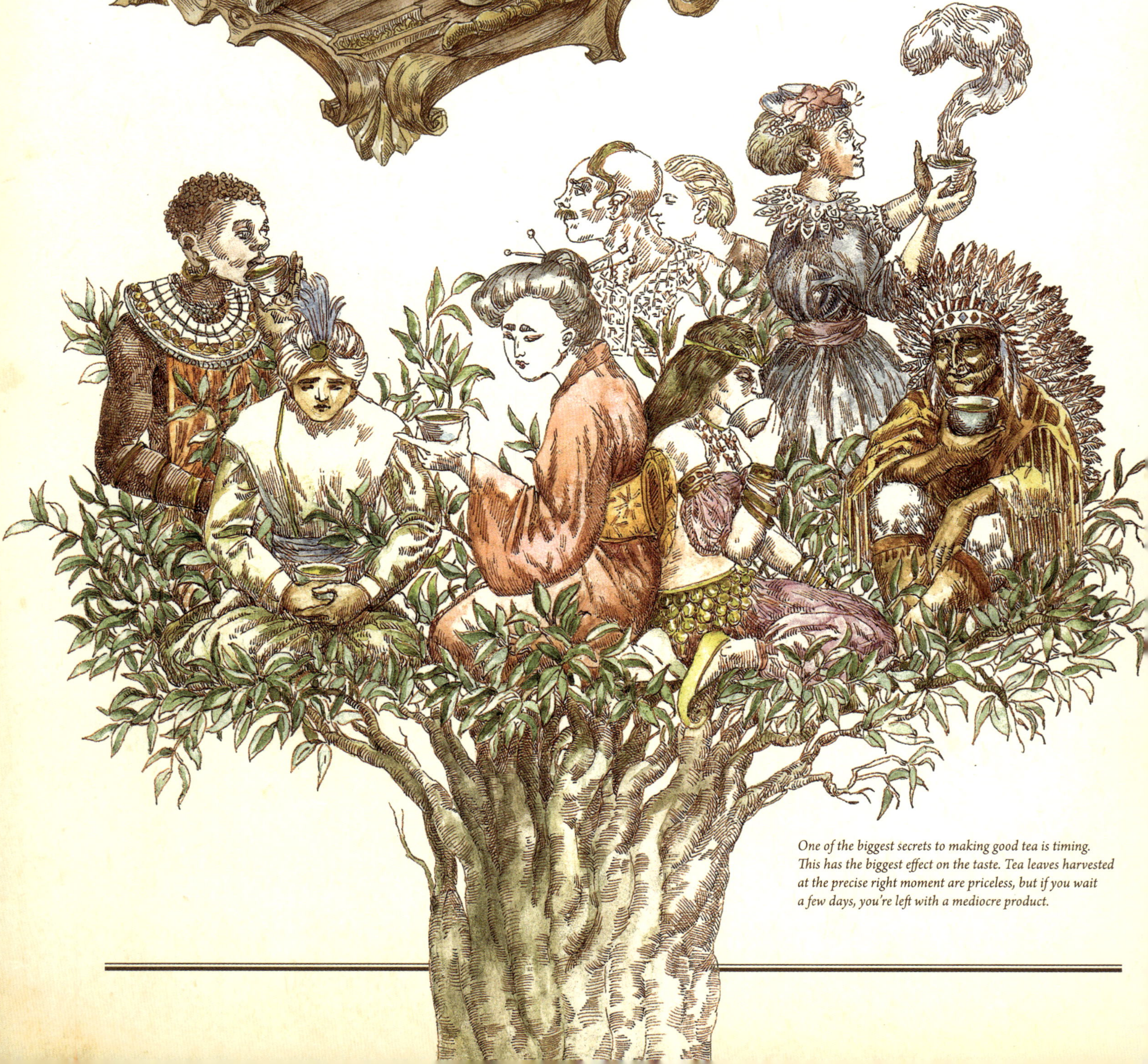

One of the biggest secrets to making good tea is timing. This has the biggest effect on the taste. Tea leaves harvested at the precise right moment are priceless, but if you wait a few days, you're left with a mediocre product.

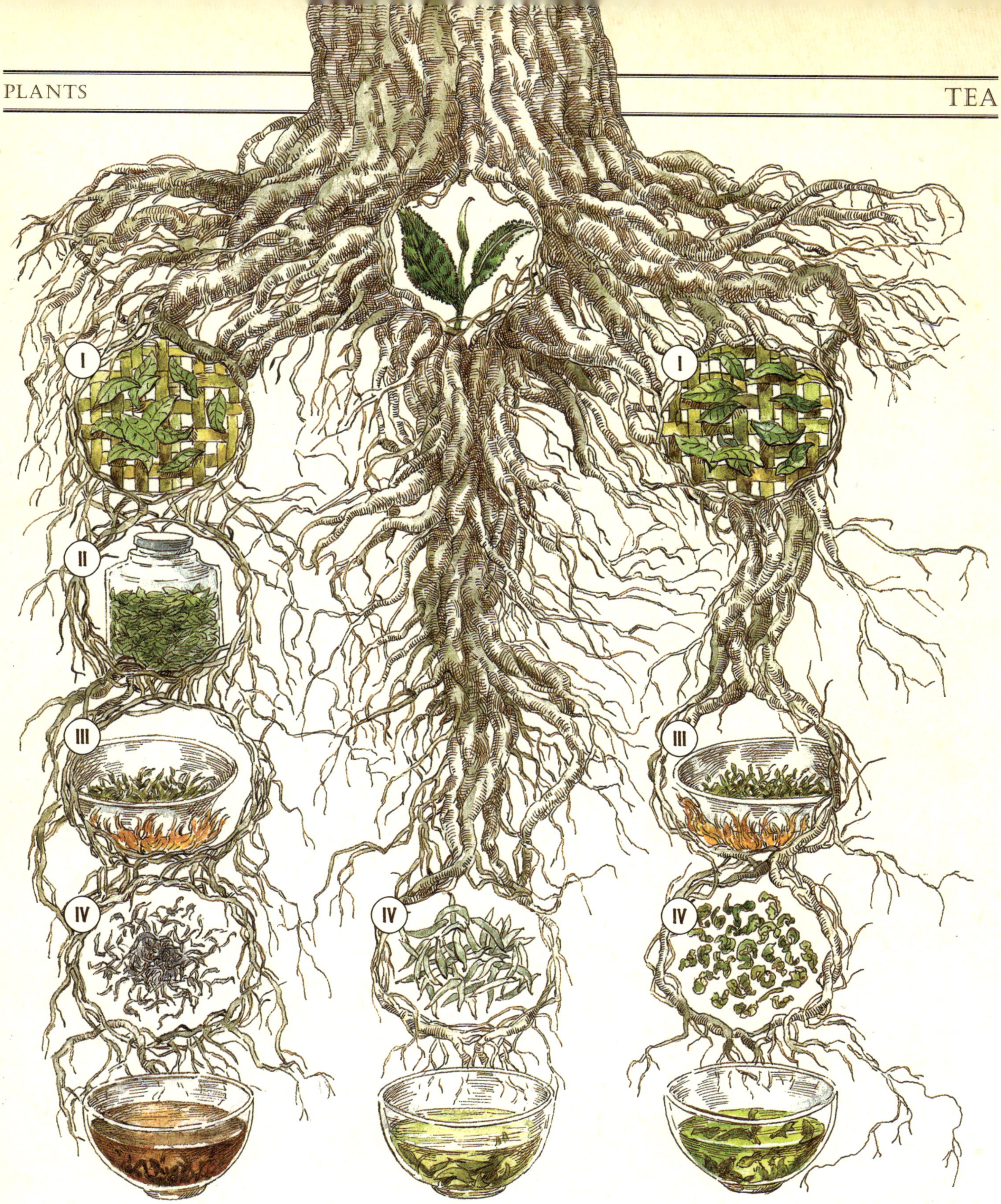

Black
Water 100°C
Steep 3–5 minutes.

White
Water 80°C
Steep 1–3 minutes.

Green
Water 75°C
Steep 1–3 minutes.

Black, green, white... all these teas are varieties of *Camellia sinensis.* Differences in aroma, taste and effect on the body depend solely on the way the leaves are prepared. Your timing must be exact! Without cultivation, the tea bush grows up to 10 meters. Don't let this happen. For the perfect tea, the top two leaves and a bud between them will do. The rest produces tea of a lower quality.

I. DRYING

Spread the leaves across a cloth in a warm room for 6 hours so that they wilt (lose part of their moisture and become softer).

II. FERMENTATION

Fermentation is a biochemical reaction and involves oxidation of the tea leaves. The type of tea you get depends on this step of the process. A long fermentation produces black; green has a short fermentation period that is stopped forcibly by heating; white is not fermented. Roll leaves in the hands until they become sticky and curl up into a tube. Then stack 7–10 cm high in a container and cover with a damp towel. Wait about 8 hours, making sure to keep the towel moist. The strong smell of tea is a signal that the fermentation process should be halted using heat.

III. ROASTING

Roast the tea in an oven at a temperature of 90–95°C for about an hour, and then lower the temperature and allow it to dry completely.

IV. DRYING

Place the trays of tea in the sun. For white tea, this is the only step in the production process: The leaves are wilted and immediately dried to prevent the tea from fermenting.

COFFEE

Human memory is structured in a curious way — certain aromas arouse intense emotions connected to past experiences associated with that scent. By preserving your happiest, coziest and most comforting memories in the form of a scent, you can pull them off your memory shelf and enjoy them at any moment.

Fill your home with the scent of fresh coffee, and no matter where you are, every time you brew a cup, it will bring up all the good memories and feelings associated with home. Every sip will fill your body with a sense of well-being and peace.

LOCATION

The ideal location for growing coffee is warm and humid, with dappled sunlight and a stable temperature (17–23°C). Coffee plants prefer loose, fertile, well-watered soil with good acidity. High-altitude coffees taste complex and acidic, while lower altitudes produce more aromatic varieties.

COFFEE SHRUBS

Sprout your coffee seeds in a planter. After a year, transplant the seedlings into the ground in an area with low wind. Find an area surrounded by larger trees to provide shade from direct sunlight. The tree will bloom in the third year, and by the fifth year, it will start producing red berries. Don't forget to prune your shrubs to keep them no taller than 2–3 m for easier harvesting.

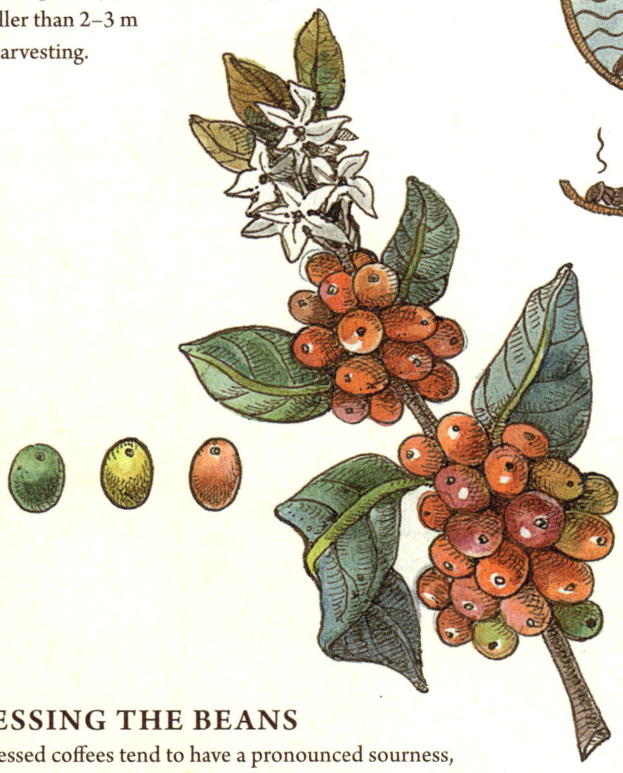

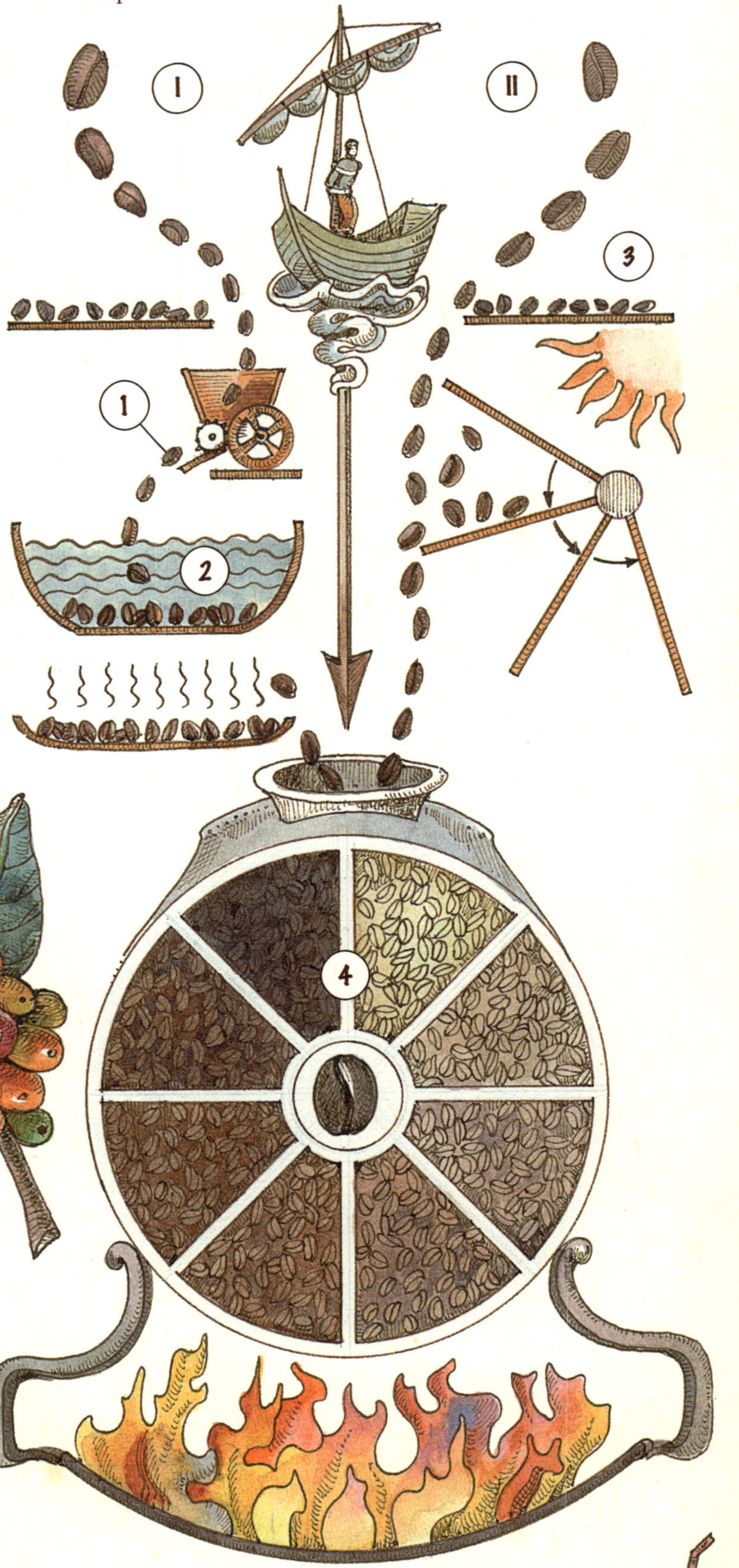

PROCESSING THE BEANS

Wash-processed coffees tend to have a pronounced sourness, while dry-processed beans are sweet. For wash processing (I), you need a depulper (1), an iron box containing a roller with teeth. The berries are squeezed between the wall of the box and the roller, freeing the coffee beans from the pulp, which then falls through to the bottom of the container. After this initial cleaning, soak the beans in water (2). Any excess pulp will be removed during the fermentation process.

For natural or dry processing (II), leave the berries to dry in the sun (3), periodically turning to prevent mold from forming. This takes more time and sunlight than the usual method. Once dry, separate away the pulp and roast the beans in a rotating drum (4) over a fire. The roasting process affects three key characteristics of the coffee: acidity, sweetness and bitterness. The darker the roast, the less acidity will remain and the more bitter the coffee will be.

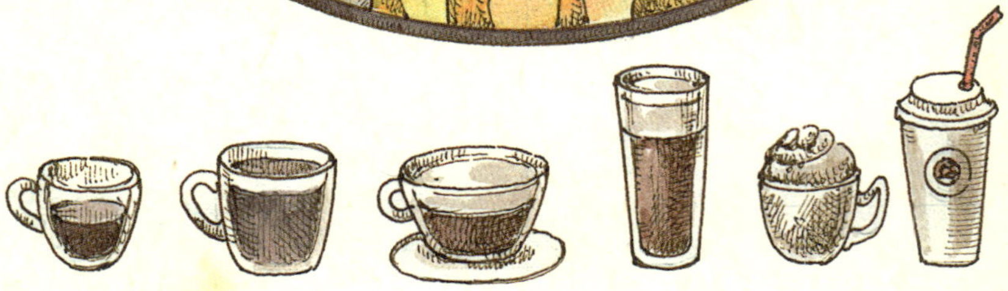

Coffee is a stimulant usually consumed for its energy-giving properties. If you want to maximize its revitalizing effects, take a 20 minute power-nap right after drinking your cup of joe. You'll benefit from the sleep before the caffeine kicks in. Caffeine blocks the action of the signaling molecule adenosine in the brain, which makes you feel fatigued and drowsy, and so caffeine invigorates the mind and helps you stay awake. Caffeine also causes increased levels of dopamine in the reward centers of the brain, which means that it delivers a mild high, but it's also addictive.

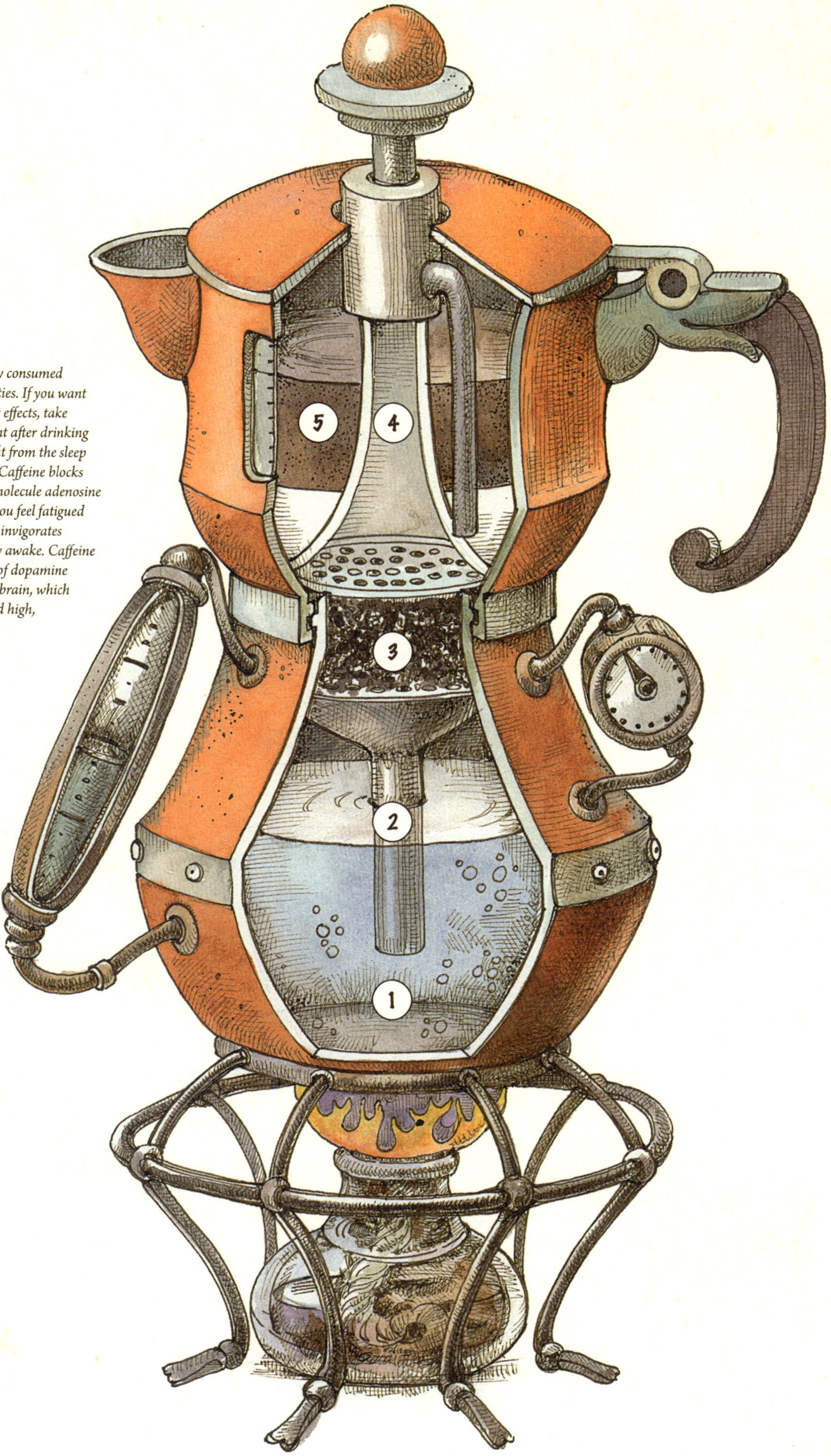

MOYKA POT

If you're too groggy in the morning to even make a cup of coffee, you can entrust the process to a coffee maker. You'll need a container with two detachable parts and an air-tight seal. Fill the lower tank (1) with water. Hang a funnel (2) from the top of the lower chamber. Pour the ground coffee into a mesh compartment (3) between the two tanks and attach another inverted funnel (4) on top.

Now, place the kettle on the fire. As the water boils in the lower tank, it turns into steam, increasing the internal pressure and pushing the water up through the funnel. It then passes through the coffee in the mesh filter, absorbing its flavor and aroma, and shoots out the upper funnel (4) to collect as an espresso shot in the upper chamber (5) ready for pouring.

CHOCOLATE & CACAO

The secret to chocolate's power over people lies in its ability to balance flavors. It can unify two otherwise incongruous tastes: sweet and salty, bitter and spicy. Chocolate creates harmony and is an excellent way to store energy. Plus, it makes people happy, which is valuable in and of itself.

Collect ripe seeds from the wild cacao tree and sprout them in bamboo tubes. Plant the shoots in the shade of tall trees to protect the cacao from direct sunlight and wind. Trim the ripening buds off the plant until it reaches the age of five so the tree will be heartier.

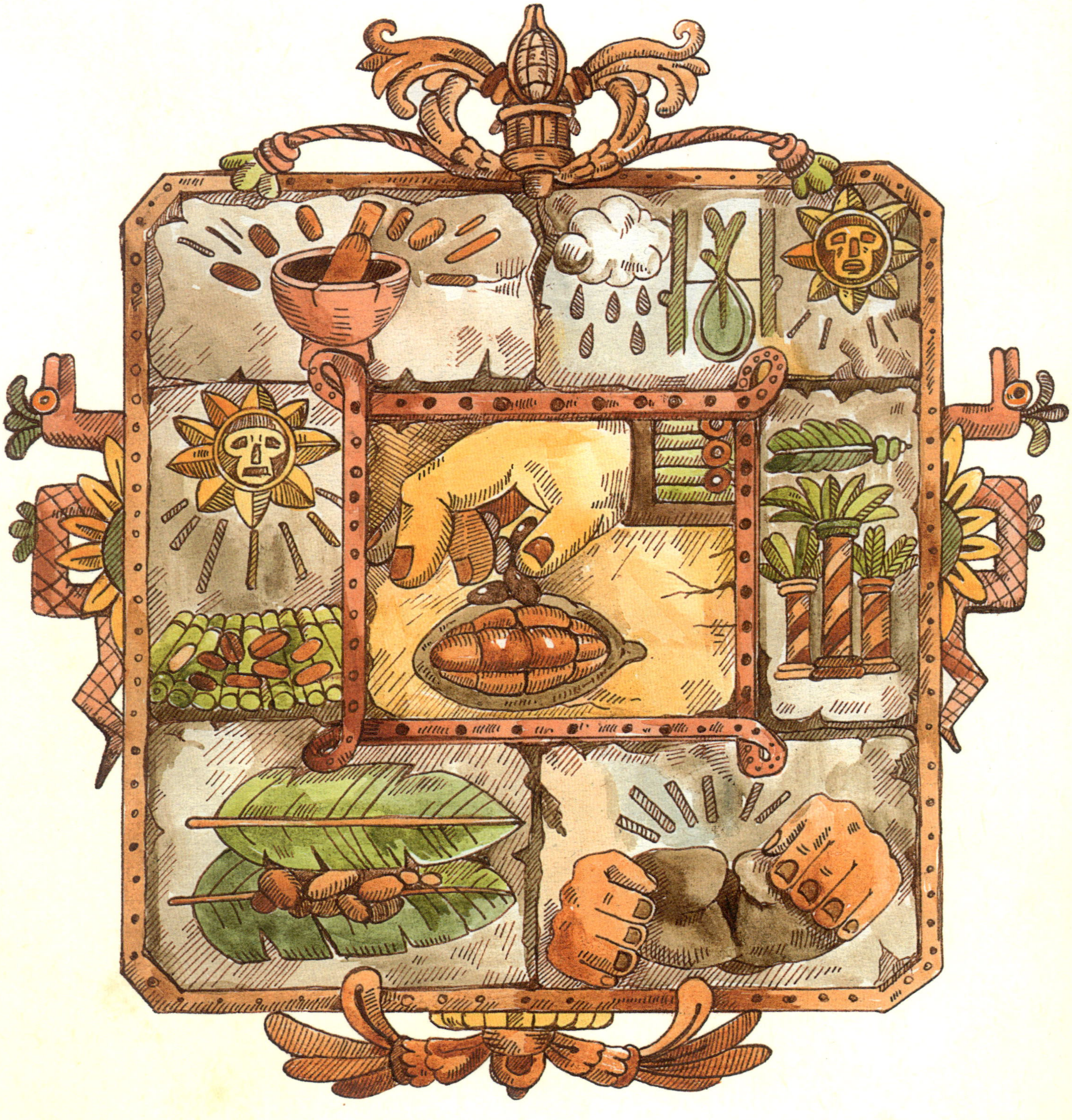

Peel ripe fruit away and extract the seeds, otherwise known as cacao beans. Remove the pulp, spread the beans out on a sheet of banana leaves and leave covered for a few days. Shuffle them around regularly, and after two weeks, the cacao seeds will darken and gain flavor and aroma.

Dry them in the sun then roast them over a fire or in an oven. The outer hull of the seed will burst and can then be peeled off. Grind the beans into a thick cacao paste.

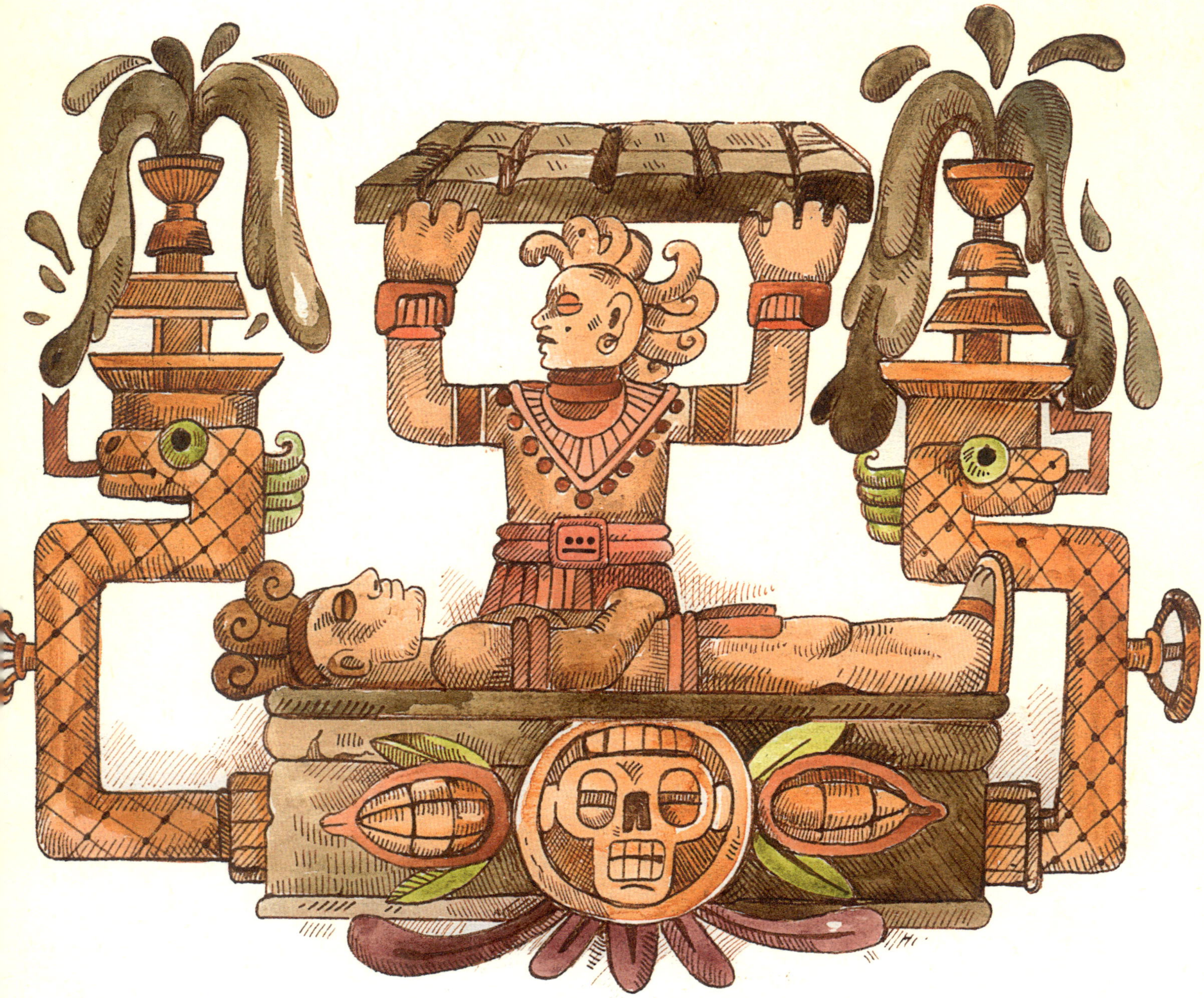

Cacao paste is the base of any chocolate but white (which uses cacao butter but no cacao solids). It needs to be stirred continuously while being cooked for about five days at a temperature of 85–90°C. This will make the mixture homogeneous, evaporate excess moisture and get rid of any extraneous odors, allowing the pure chocolate aroma to shine through.

Here's how to make chocolate bars:

1. Melt the cacao paste until it becomes a liquid at 42–45°C. You shouldn't raise the temperature too high, or the paste will lose its elasticity.
2. Cool to no more than 31°C and bring out your cacao butter (obtained by squeezing cacao paste under a press). At temperatures up to 25°C, cacao butter is hard and brittle, but at 32°C and above, it becomes a liquid. You want to use the solid version.
3. Break your cacao butter down into small granules and mix them into the cacao paste. Dip a knife into the mixture. If you did everything correctly, within one and a half minutes the chocolate mass on the knife will become dull and harden.
4. Pure cacao paste is aromatic but very bitter. Add powdered sugar. Pour in milk or cream to make milk chocolate.
5. Pour the finished chocolate into molds and refrigerate.

You can change the ratio of bitter to sweet or mix in other ingredients such as nuts, fragrant flowers and freeze-dried berries. Or spice it up with cinnamon, vanilla pods, cardamom — even pepper and sea salt. Substitute almond, coconut or rice milk for animal milk or honey for sugar.

Thanks to the cacao butter, the mass crystallizes and hardens but melts upon contact with your tongue, releasing a full bouquet of flavors and aromas. You might also grind the roasted beans into a powder and add hot milk, sugar and spices for a fortifying pick-me-up drink.

RICE & HYDROPONICS

Difficulties with the geography, soil quality, climate, weeds and pests can all complicate your work in the fields. But this is no reason to forego agriculture altogether.

It's possible to have large-scale production of cereals, tea, grapes, vegetables and herbs without fields stretching out as far as the eye can see. Economize on valuable crop space by setting up hillside terraces or building a vertical farm.

If the terrain is hilly, place mini-fields on the slopes in the form of broad steps. Construct clay bumpers around each terrace, or the layer of fertile topsoil will quickly be washed away. While you're at it, dig irrigation channels with openings for drainage. Grow a different plant every year to avoid soil depletion. Switch out tea for grapes then grapes for corn and so on. Periodically plant Azolla, an aquatic fern — its roots host a bacterium that can absorb nitrogen from the air and convert it into a form suitable for plants. It is an excellent natural fertilizer.

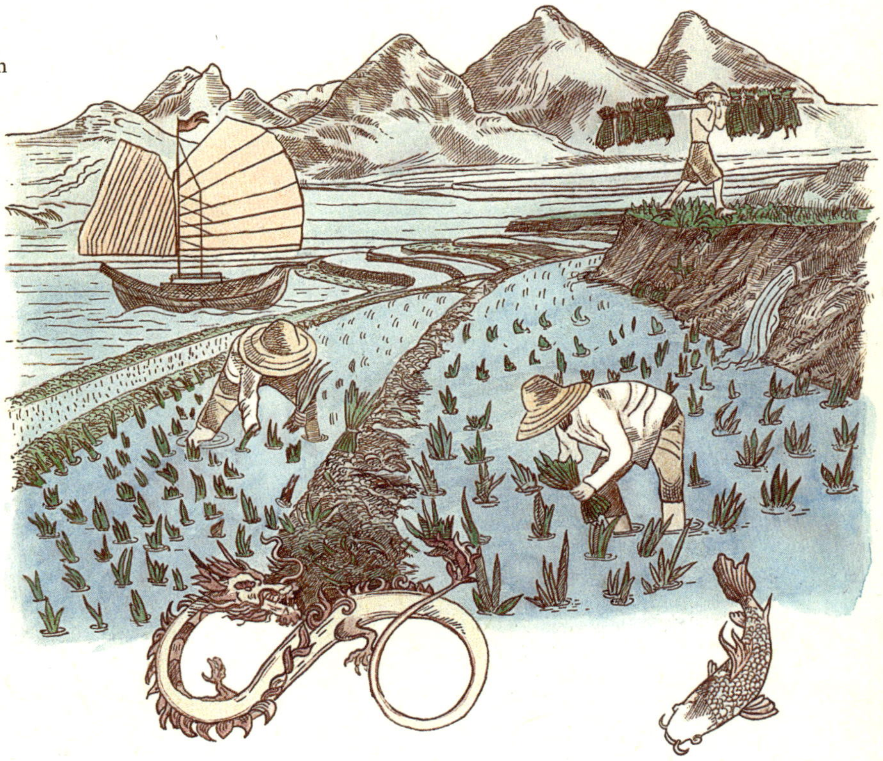

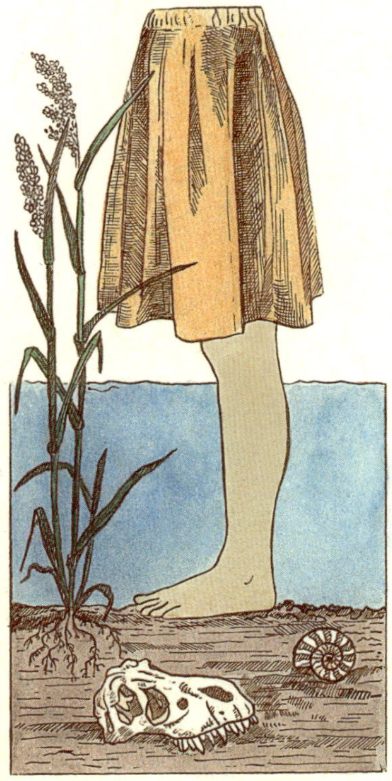

FLOODED FIELDS

Growing rice will require that you have a river or lake nearby to irrigate your crops by gravity via canals or hoses. Rice shoots must be protected from strong direct sunlight and weeds. This crop requires a lot of water, but the water level should still cover less than half the plant. To avoid unnecessary waterlogging, drain water from time to time through a canal system.

Before planting rice, flood your field preemptively to wash away any unwanted seeds and prevent weeds from growing.

Soak your rice seeds in water. You can plant them in the ground after 12 hours of soaking, but it is better to wait until sprouts are around 2 cm high.

Keep the field free of weeds (such as reeds and sedges). You can either wade knee-deep through water all day getting your fingers pruney, or you can introduce ducks and fish into the water. They will eat harmful insects and weeds and fertilize the soil.

Rice will ripen in 3–4 months. When it reaches about 40 cm in height, drain the water or let it evaporate. After a couple of weeks, the rice will turn yellow, a sign that it's ready for harvest.

Rice ears can be cut or plucked out whole with the roots. Dry the ears for 2–3 days.

Thresh the husk from the grain. To make brown rice white, sand the grains by rubbing them together. This can be done in a mortar or a rotating barrel. Just keep in mind that while this will improve the appearance and digestibility of the product, it will reduce the nutrient content.

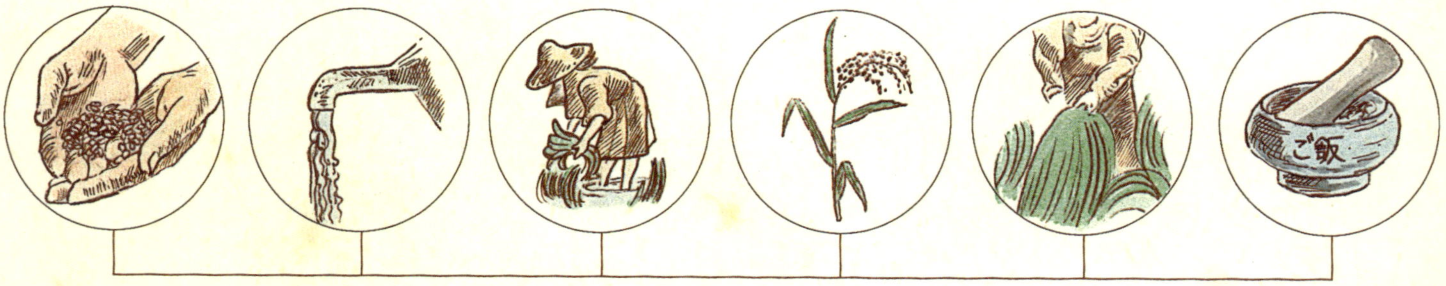

RICE

Rice can replace bread and other grains as the basis of your diet. The grains can be used to make starch, flour, alcohol or wine. Rice germ makes oil, and rice straw works well as paper pulp or mattress filler. Rice flour can also be used as the foundation of many cosmetic products, such as powders, blushes and oils, which in turn can be made into creams and scrubs.

The bran — the stuff that remains after the grain has been cleaned — makes good feed for livestock and poultry. By the way, the ducklings and fish you raise in the paddy fields can also become the protein in your meal.

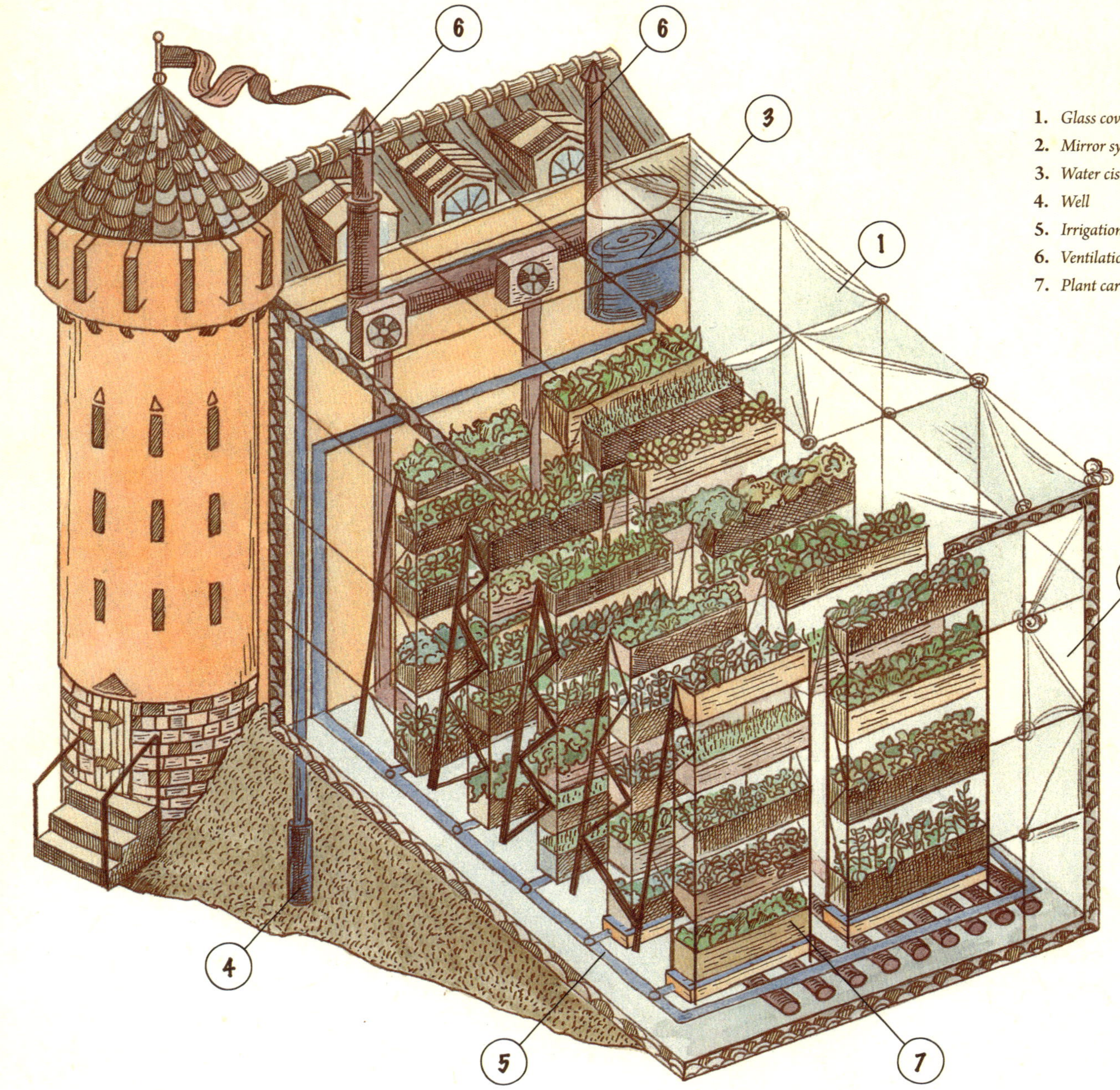

VERTICAL GREENHOUSE

Fear neither inclement weather nor nutrient-scarce soils by creating your own ideal ecosystem. Arrange the plants on a moving carousel that raises and lowers the plants to ensure that each one receives an equal amount of light and water.

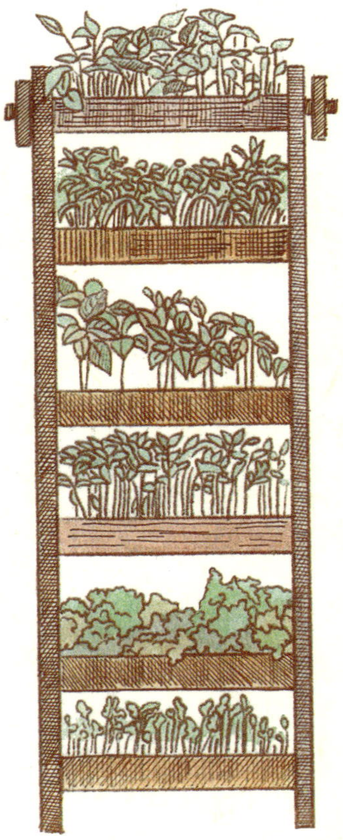

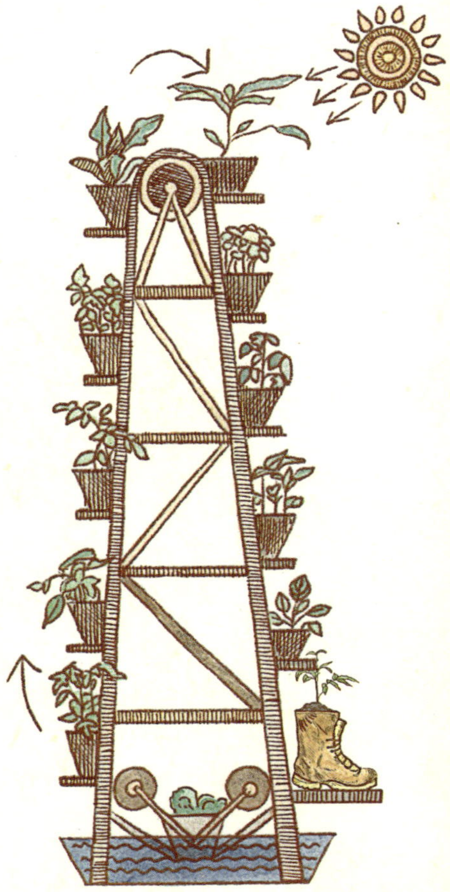

1. Substrate

Instead of soil, you can use coconut husk or shredded tree bark and immerse the roots directly in a substrate solution containing all the necessary nutrients. This way, the plants don't need to expend energy developing a large root system and can instead focus on ripening the crop.

2. Water

Place your water container above your plants and use gravity to push the water through your irrigation system. Draw the water into the irrigation containers using a pump (page 162).

3. Light

If you set up your vertical farm in a room with glass walls (page 114), you can get by with natural light. Install mirrors (page 182) to reflect light onto the plants from all directions. Install a wire grid to redirect growth horizontally to prevent plants from growing too broad and shading their neighbors. This also helps stimulate the growth of new buds.

4. Air circulation

Ventilation is required to control humidity levels. That being said, plants don't like sudden temperature changes. To ensure a comfortable environment, make a water heating system (page 156).

ANIMALS

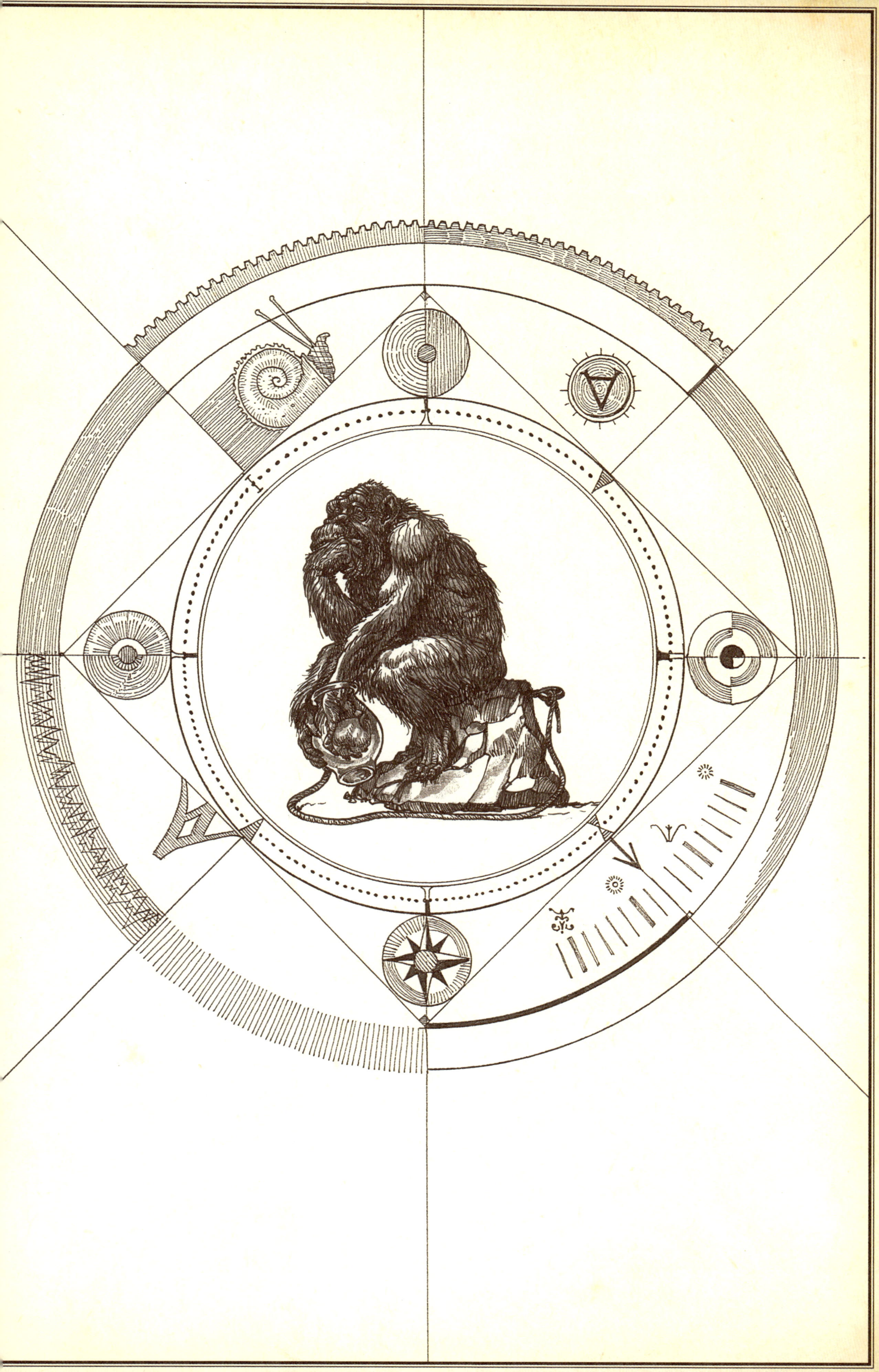

TRAPS

Time management is vital in extreme conditions, and a single second can make the difference between survival and demise. Instead of crafting weapons and spending hours (or even days) on the hunt, you can set traps and complete other important tasks while you wait, such as chopping wood, fetching water or building shelter.

The main concept behind any trap is the same: There's an entrance but no exit. No complex tools or materials are required — nature already has everything you need. The most important part is deciding where to place your trap.

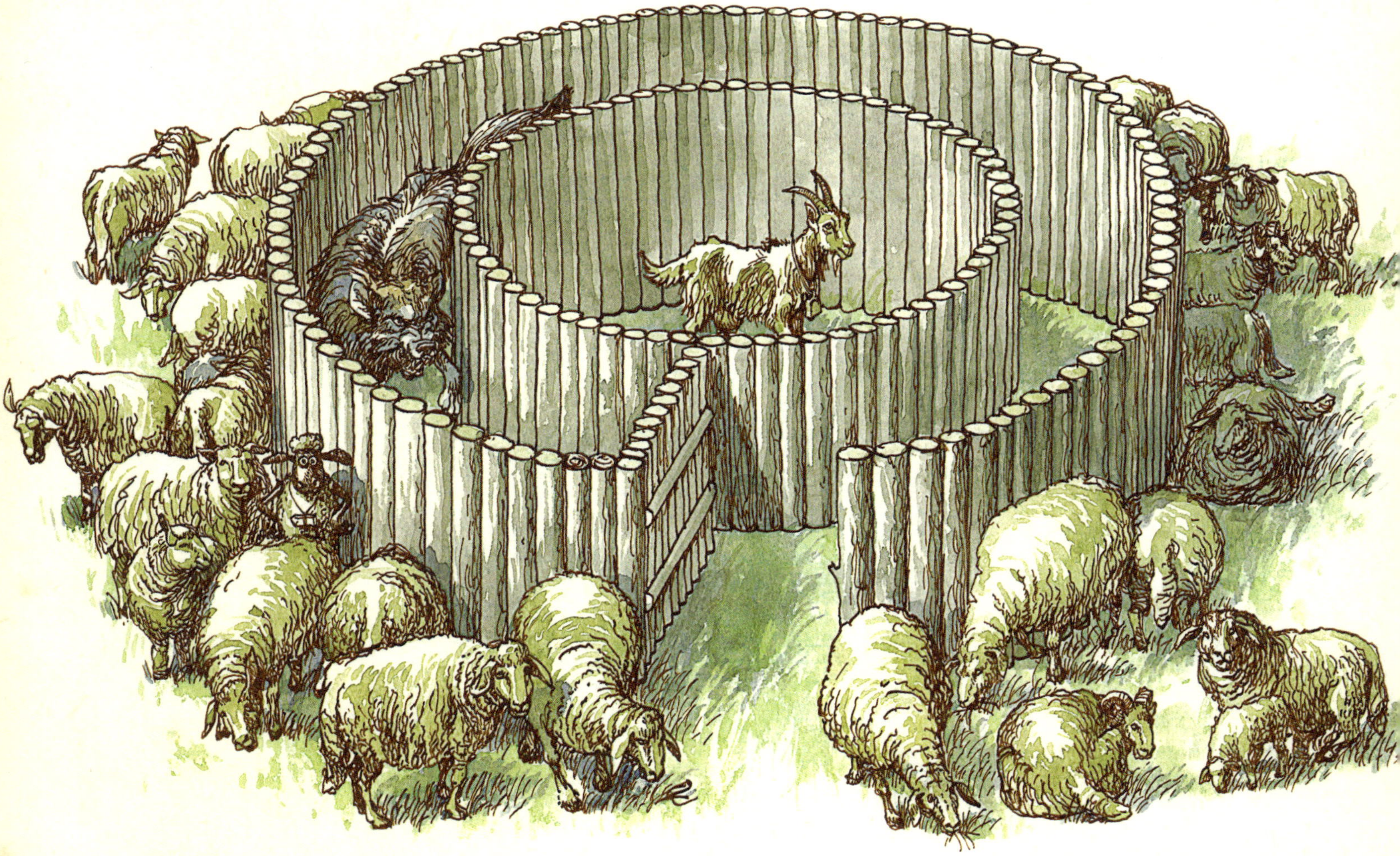

WOLF PEN

To catch predators who have been attacking your herd, drive long stakes into the ground, creating two circular fences. The diameter of the inner ring should be 3–4 meters and should be solid and unbroken. The diameter of the outer ring should be around 45 cm larger. Install a gate in the outer ring, one that swings only inward. The wolf will be able to move forward freely down the narrow corridor but unable to turn around. Lure the predator into a trap with live bait — a goat kid, a goose or a piglet.

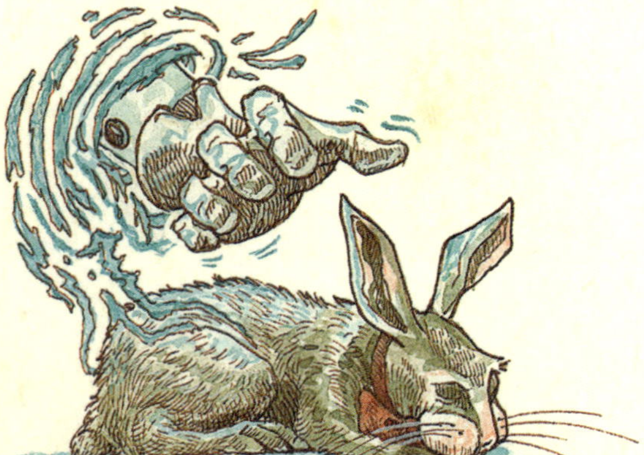

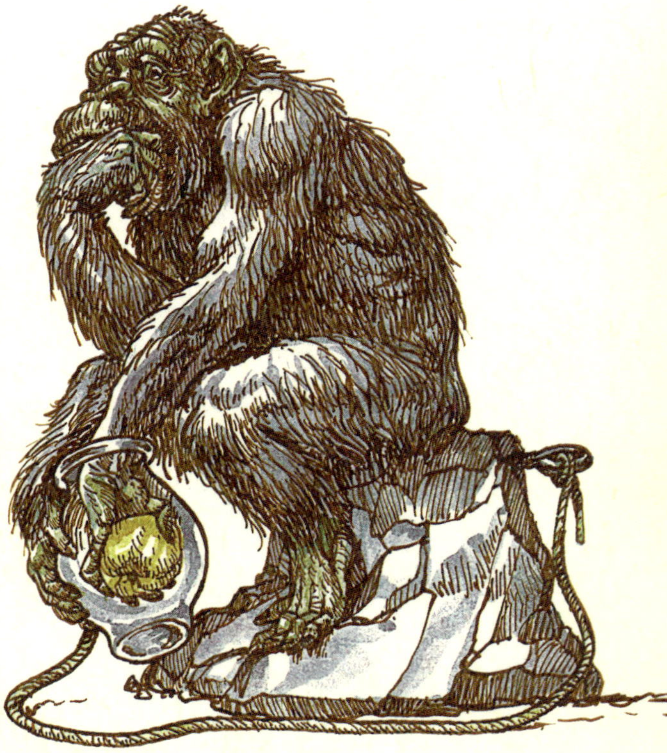

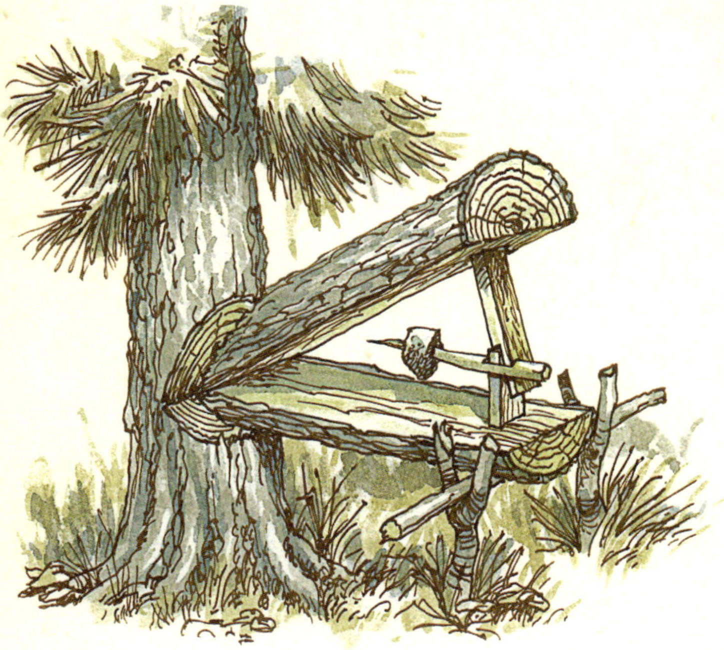

KULEMA TRAP

This trap works for catching any foxes or weasels that may be stealing your chickens. The trap consists of two parts. The main technical components are the stick that keeps the upper part of the trap suspended, the notch it fits into and the bait. Grouse meat makes for a particularly tempting treat. As the animal tries to snatch the meat, it nudges the stick, releasing the upper long, which then falls and crushes the prey. Many different kinds of traps can be made using this basic principle. For example, instead of using a stick to hold the log, try using a rope. Just be sure that the animal will nudge the trigger as it tries to take the bait.

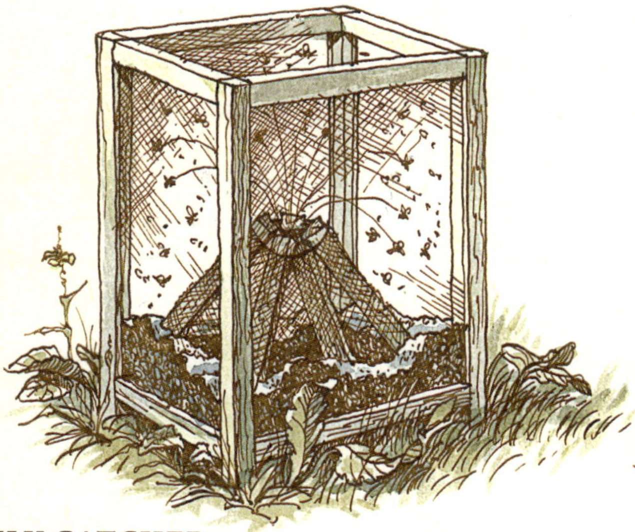

FLY CATCHER

Are flies spoiling your food? Start by making a box. The bottom wall of the box shouldn't be flat but should rather form a pyramid sticking into the box with a hole at the top. Insects will be able to fly through the hole but won't find their way back out again. Place some sort of meat in the box as bait, preferably not too fresh.

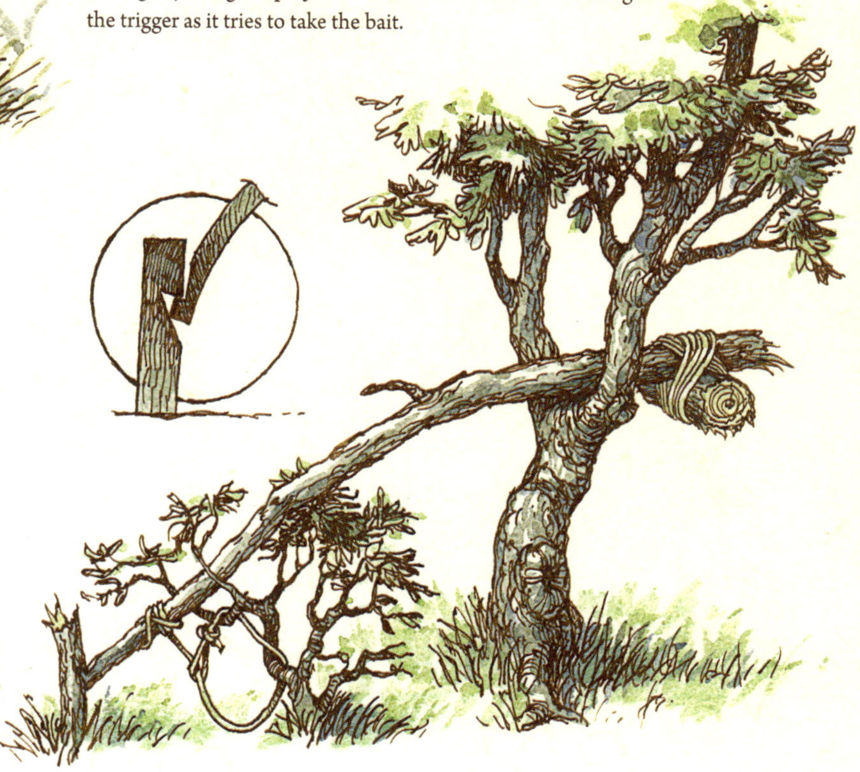

TENSION SNARE

Set a trap for foxes that are raiding your garden and killing your rabbits and hares. Drive a peg into the ground and make a notch somewhere in the middle. Tie a self-tightening loop (page 212) to a flexible tree branch (or long stick). Bend this branch downward, cut a small notch in the end and latch the branch into the notch in the peg. Place the loop in a spot that you suspect gets high fox foot traffic. As the fox sprints along the trail, it runs through the snare, triggering the spring-loaded branch and tightening the noose around its neck.

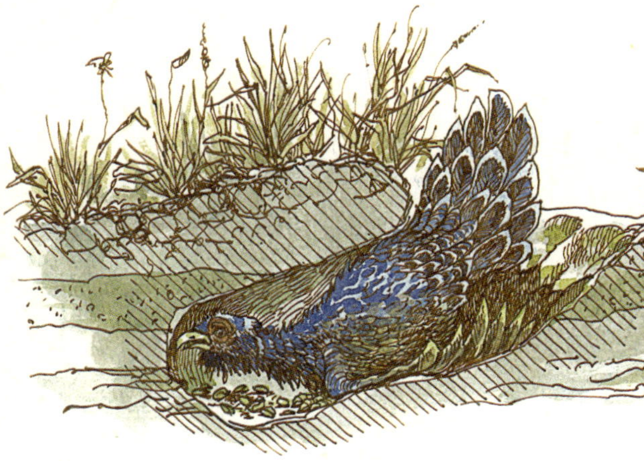

GROUSE PIT

Dig an angled pit with an opening wide enough that a grouse can crawl through. On the bottom, place bait such as rowan berries, lingonberries or cranberries. The grouse will crawl into the hole after them but will not have enough space to turn around and spread its wings, and it's incapable of walking backwards.

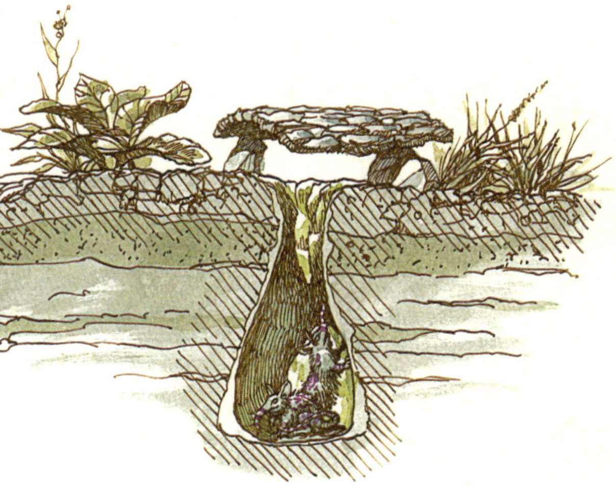

MOUSE TRAP

Dig a hole about 30–45 cm deep. The bottom should be wide and the entrance narrow. Make a "roof" over the entrance from a piece of bark or wood on supports made of small pebbles. The mouse will try to hide from danger under the shelter and fall into the hole. Since the wall of the pit is at such an extreme angle, the mouse won't be able to scale it.

FISHING

Fans of hearty and nutritious food should master the art of the quiet hunt: fishing. Only in rare cases does it become truly dangerous, as most often the fisherman sits on the shore and waits for the fish to bite. But be careful you don't get hooked yourself — on dopamine. The thrill of reeling in your reward can turn fishing from a necessity to a pleasurable pastime.

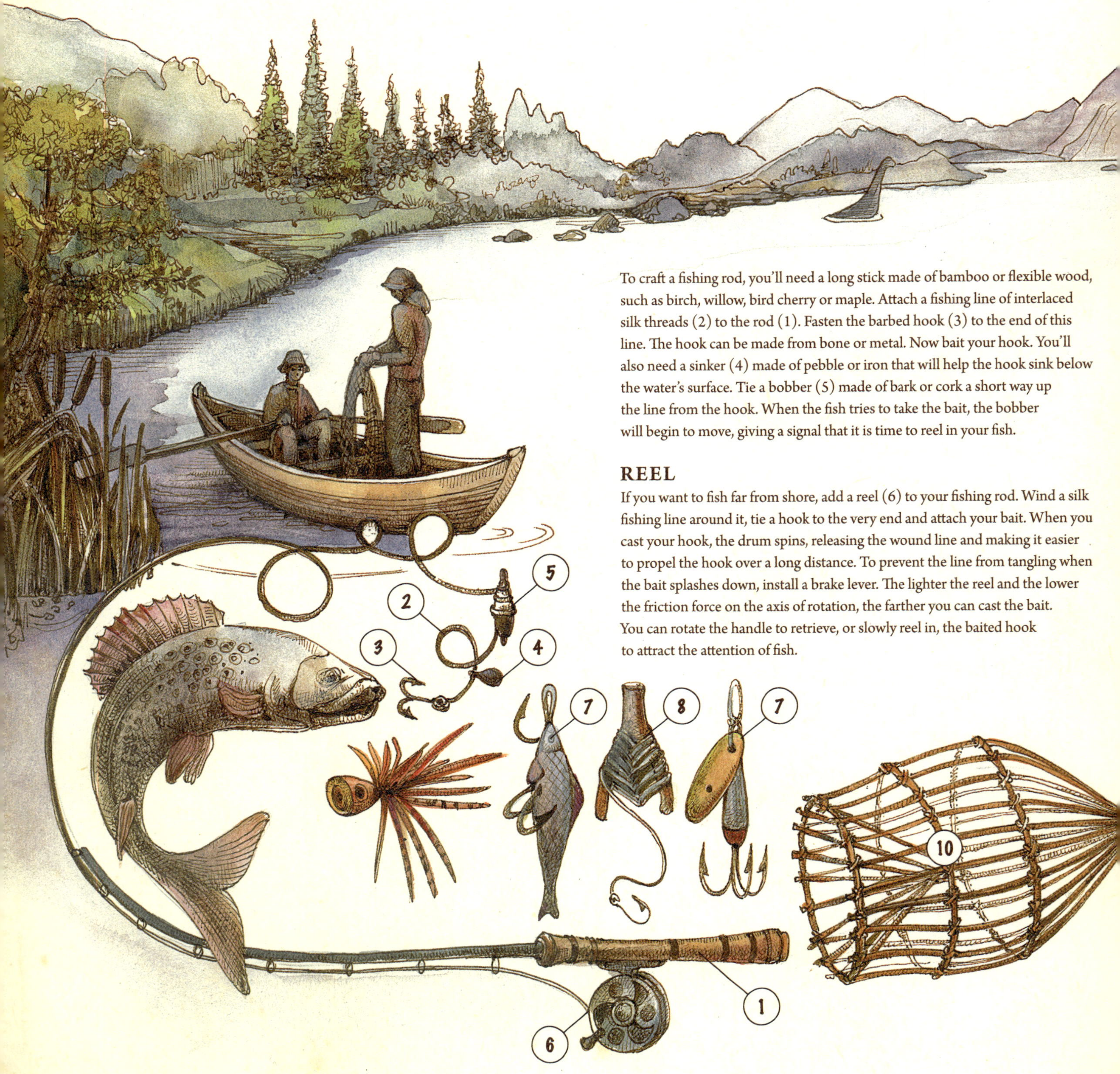

To craft a fishing rod, you'll need a long stick made of bamboo or flexible wood, such as birch, willow, bird cherry or maple. Attach a fishing line of interlaced silk threads (2) to the rod (1). Fasten the barbed hook (3) to the end of this line. The hook can be made from bone or metal. Now bait your hook. You'll also need a sinker (4) made of pebble or iron that will help the hook sink below the water's surface. Tie a bobber (5) made of bark or cork a short way up the line from the hook. When the fish tries to take the bait, the bobber will begin to move, giving a signal that it is time to reel in your fish.

REEL

If you want to fish far from shore, add a reel (6) to your fishing rod. Wind a silk fishing line around it, tie a hook to the very end and attach your bait. When you cast your hook, the drum spins, releasing the wound line and making it easier to propel the hook over a long distance. To prevent the line from tangling when the bait splashes down, install a brake lever. The lighter the reel and the lower the friction force on the axis of rotation, the farther you can cast the bait. You can rotate the handle to retrieve, or slowly reel in, the baited hook to attract the attention of fish.

LURES

Predatory fish feed on smaller fish, so using a small metal plate can imitate the flash of scales. Lures (7) can also be made to imitate water beetles, leeches or crustaceans. You may also want to use real food as bait. Tie a small cage filled with bait, known as a feeder (8), next to the hook. If you're fishing in stagnant water, you can use bran, bread or steamed cereals. If you're fishing in a river, you'll need something denser and stickier. Mix live bait, such as bloodworms or maggots, with clay. The fish will be lured in by the scent. You can add vanilla, cinnamon or dill to the clay. It is important to practice moderation and not overfeed the fish. The task of bait is to attract the attention of the fish and lull them into a false sense of security. You can also attach the bait ball directly to the hook. Bend the metal wire into a spiral (9) and mold the ball around it.

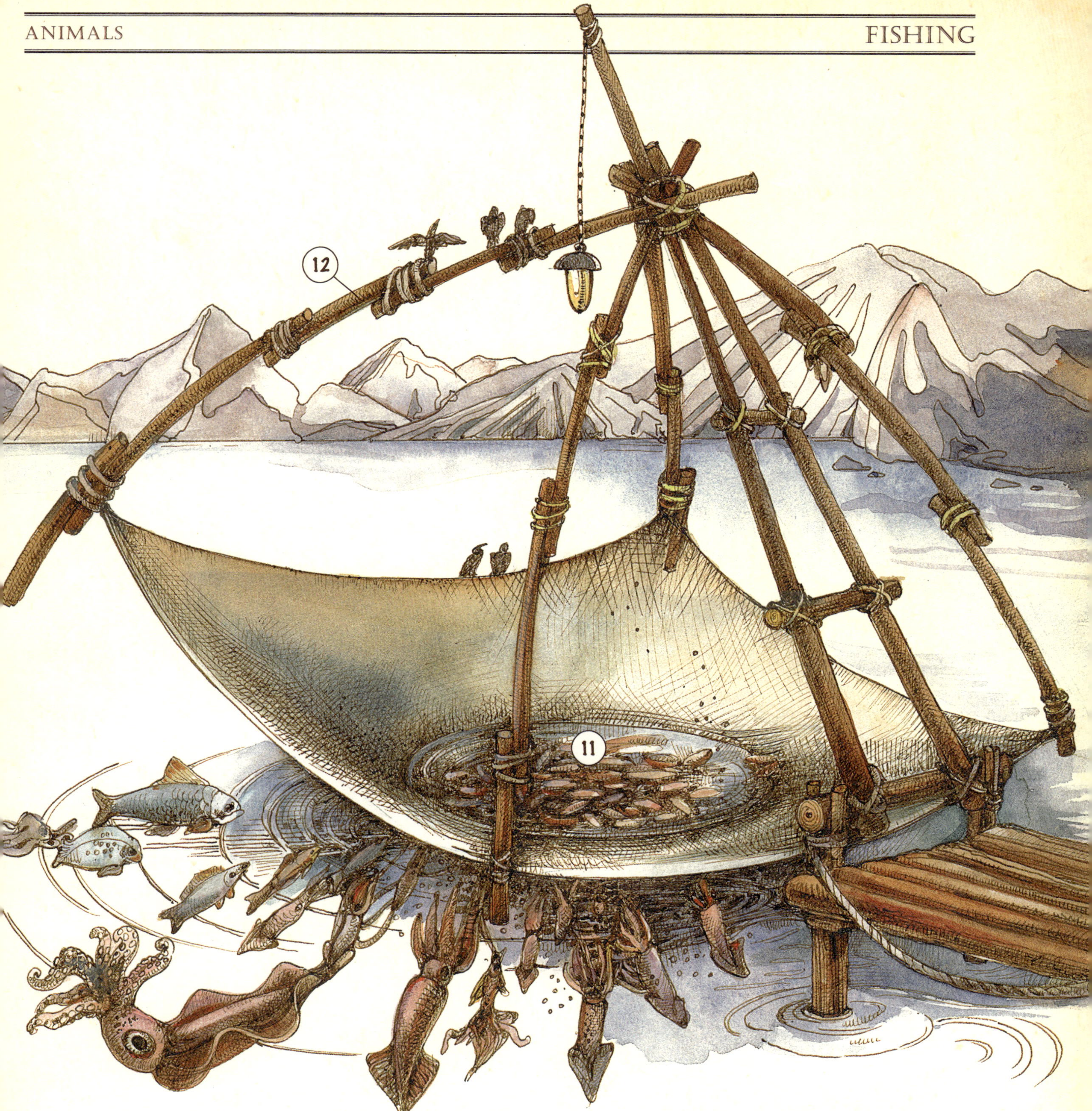

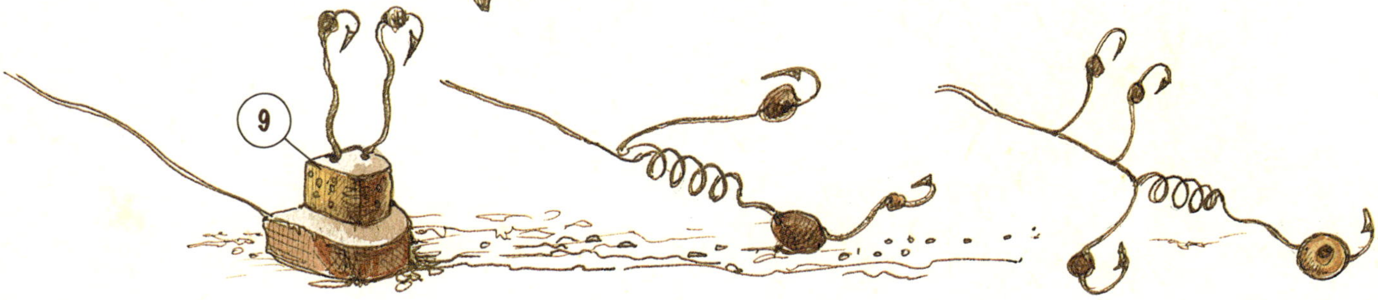

TRAPS AND NETS

If you need to catch a lot of fish and feed a large number of people, you'll need bigger traps. Make a simple version using a woven basket (10) filled with bait and immersed in water. Nets (11) will help you catch even more. To weave them, you need to cut wound thread or rope into long pieces.

Lay half of the lengths of thread in a line parallel to each other, and then lay the other half on top perpendicularly. Secure each intersection with a knot. Construct levers (12) out of wooden poles to make it easier to raise the net.

The best time to catch squid is at night. They respond very well to luminous objects, so you can highlight the bait by pointing a flashlight at it.

LEATHERCRAFT

At a certain stage of development, you will be faced with a difficult question about the ethics of eating living beings. Fortunately, the need to survive makes some decisions easier. Enjoy the advantages of being at the top of the food chain, but treat the animals you kill with respect and don't waste any part of the body.

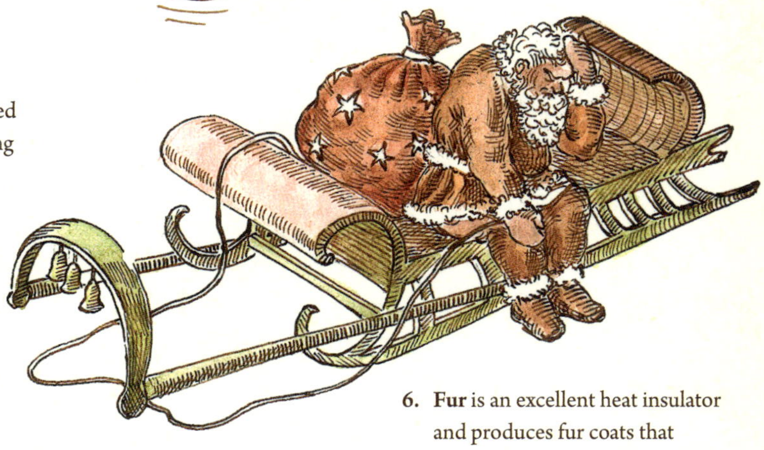

1. Hollow **horns** can be used to make musical instruments and wine goblets.

2. **The brain** shouldn't be used for food, as the risk of contracting disease is too high, but it can be used for tanning leather.

3. **The guts and veins** are good for making bowstrings (page 258) and strings for musical instruments (page 338). To do this, thoroughly wash the intestines and veins, scrape off the external membrane and any excess fat, soak in cold water and cut into long strips. Then stretch and twist them until you get strings of the desired length and thickness.

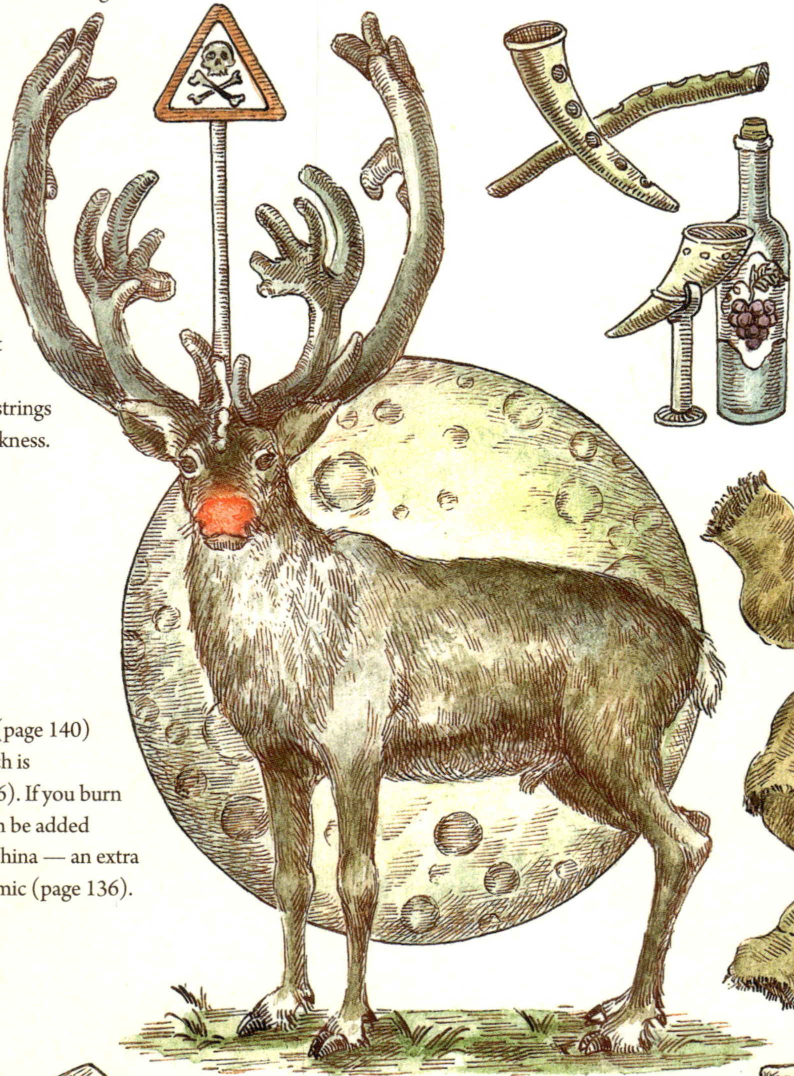

4. Boil **the bones** to make glue (page 140) or grind into bone meal, which is an excellent fertilizer (page 56). If you burn the meal, the resulting ash can be added to white clay to obtain bone china — an extra thin and durable type of ceramic (page 136).

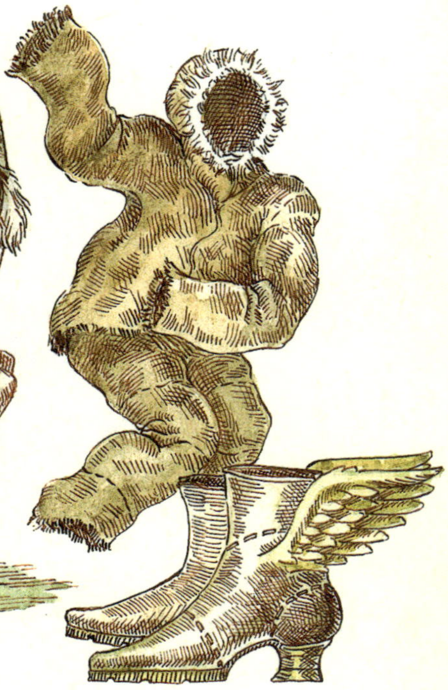

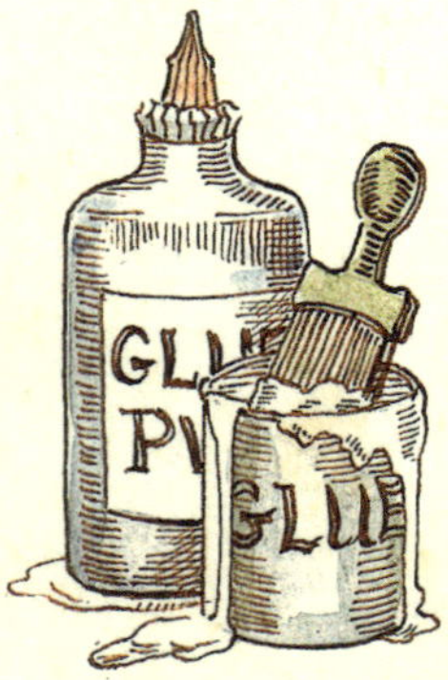

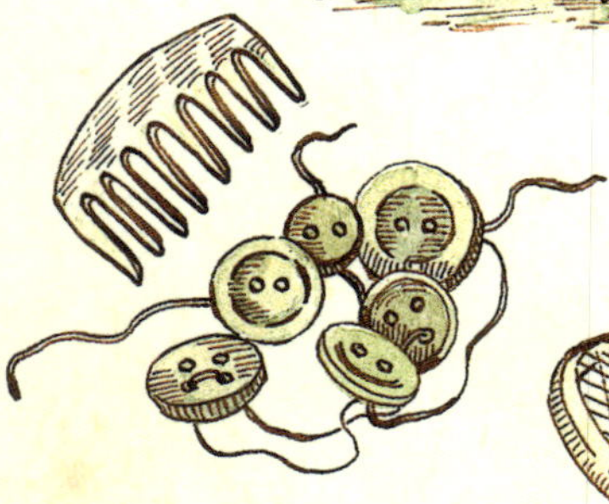

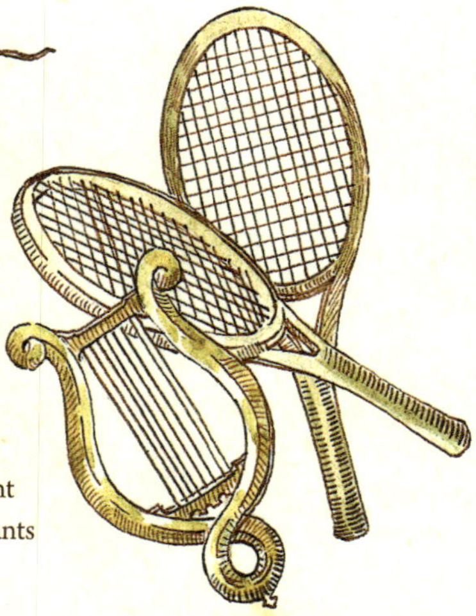

5. **Hooves** make for a rich stew, and the hard outer shell, or **sheath**, can be carved into small trinkets such as buttons, combs and ornaments. To remove the sheath, immerse the hoof in boiling water for an hour. Drain and place a weight on top of the hoof and let it cool, and then remove the remnants of the skin and soft tissues. Treat the sheath with a knife, fine-toothed or coarse files.

6. **Fur** is an excellent heat insulator and produces fur coats that can withstand severe frost (up to –60°C).

7. **Leather** is not only useful for shoes, pants, bags, gloves, raincoats and furniture. It is a strong, very durable material and can be used to make drive belts for various mechanisms (page 242). The skin of young lambs, goats and cows can be used to make parchment. It can be used in place of paper or stretched into a skin for percussion instruments (page 332).

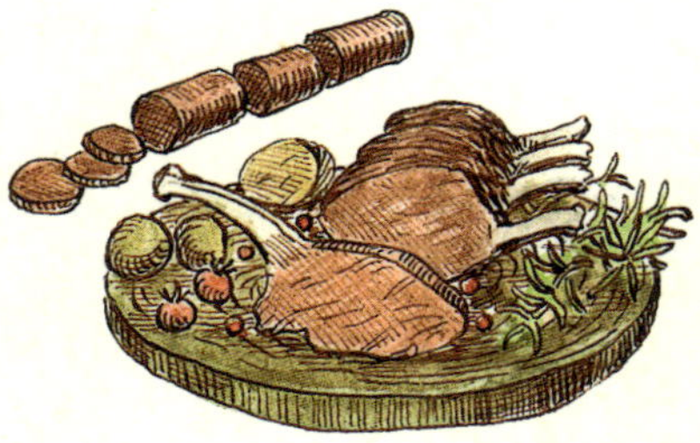

8. **Blood** is a valuable raw material. It's rich in protein, vital amino acids, phospholipids, iron and other substances that play an important role in how our body functions. You can use it to make smoked (page 98) blood sausage.

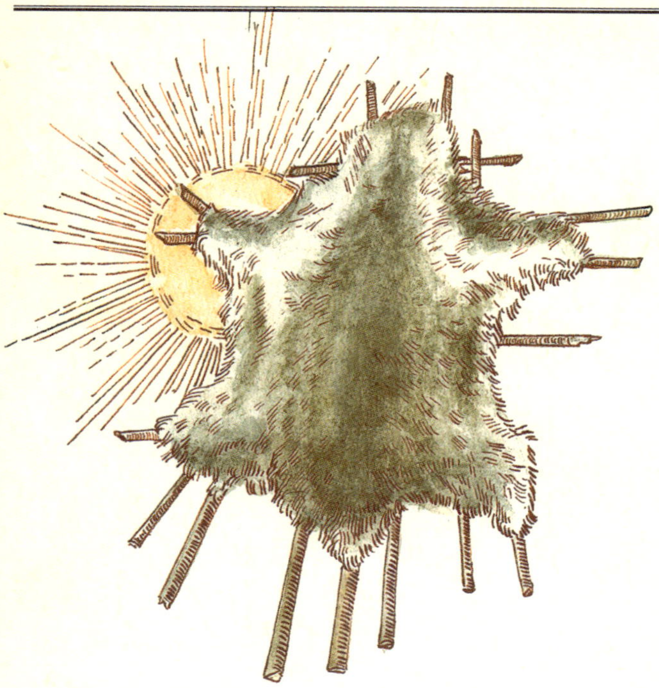

After you have removed the skin from the carcass of the animal, you need to thoroughly clean it of any meat and blood remnants. Soak the hide in saline first to make this process easier. After that, the skin needs to dry as quickly as possible, so stretch it between two poles and leave it to dry in the sun.

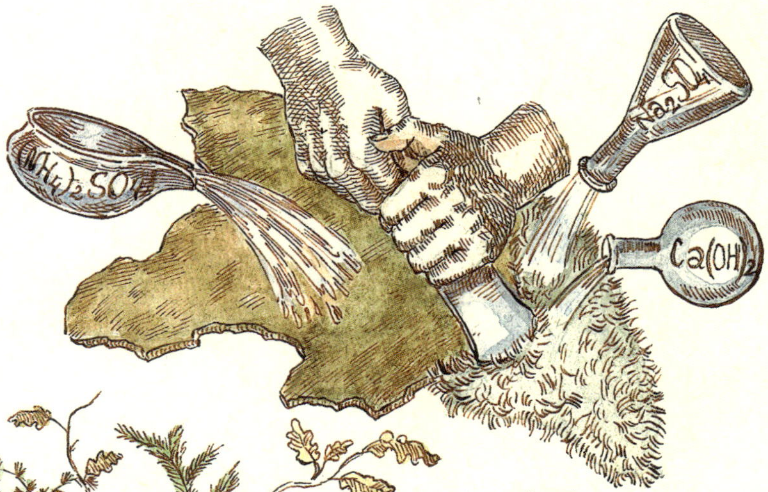

Remove the hair using a process known as liming, during which the hides are treated with lime and sodium sulfate. It is the reaction product of sodium hydroxide (page 24) with sulfuric acid (page 192). Lime is obtained by roasting calcium-magnesium rocks — chalk or limestone. You can also use a saline solution at a ratio of 20 grams of salt to 1 liter of water. Soak the skin in the solution for several days, turning it over from time to time. After this procedure, any hairs and residue of subcutaneous tissue can be easily removed. After curing, many substances will remain in the skin that must be disposed of. To do this, rinse the skin in a soda solution (10 g per 1 liter water). Then rinse your skin with clean water several times.

If you do not have access to any of the sources of tannin below, stretch the hide across pegs and rub with it a mixture of urine and clay. Leave it for a while then treat with fat or oil, scrape and smoke it over a fire.

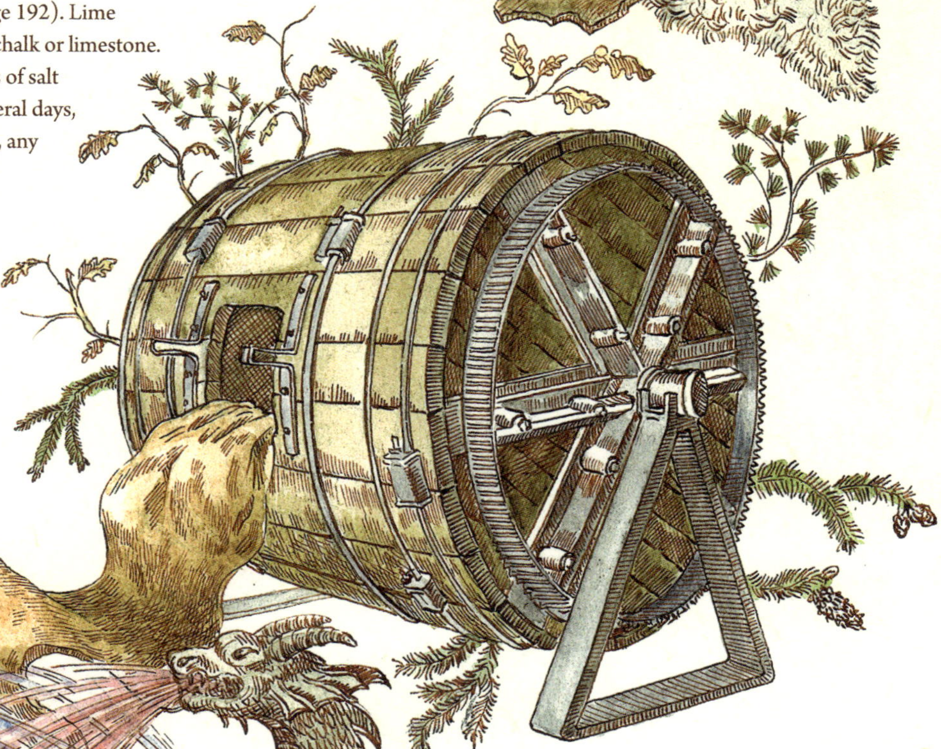

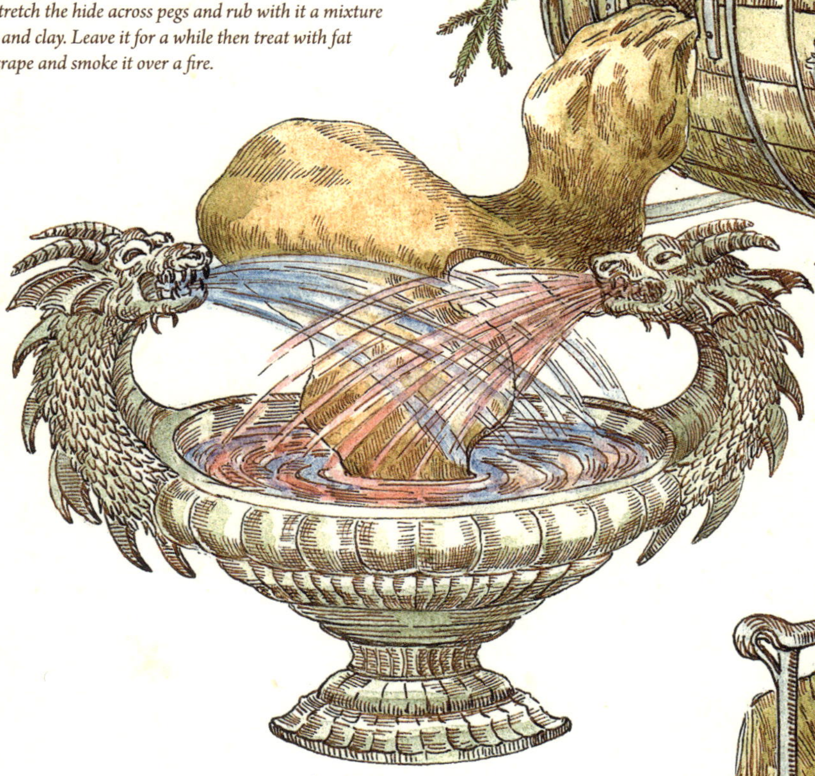

Leather becomes more wear-resistant, heat-resistant and resilient if tanned. Extract tannins from oak, willow, spruce and larch woods or from the growths formed on oak leaves. Another option is the fats of various marine animals. Fill a rotating drum with a strong tannin solution and soak the hides. Then squeeze out to remove excess water and repeat the process. Now the leather can be rolled out, dyed, sanded, varnished and sewn into the items you need.

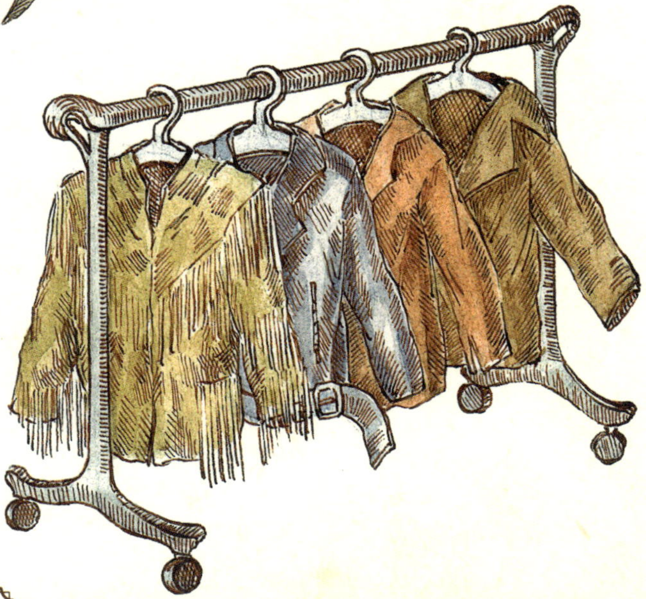

LIVESTOCK

The domestication of wild animals is a transformative step in any civilization's history but carries with it an ethical dilemma. Livestock will provide you with food, materials and clothing, but you have to restrict the animals' freedom of movement, suppress their natural instincts and even artificially alter their birth rate and life expectancy. It's human nature to seek as much profit as possible. But it's only humane to create the most comfortable conditions for those who spend their entire lives (and beyond) working for you.

Make sure your pigsty has good lighting in the fall/winter. ***Pigs*** *need regular sun exposure to gain weight. To form fat and improve the taste of meat, add lake sludge to the feed — it contains the necessary elements: copper, calcium, zinc, sulfur, magnesium.*

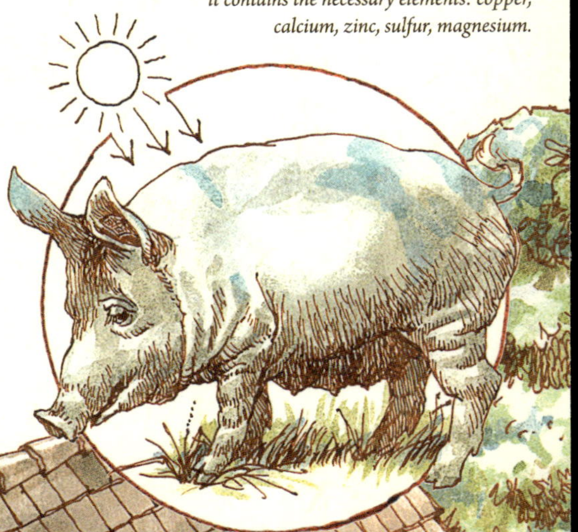

Many diseases in livestock are caused by insect bites. The most vulnerable place on a ***cow's*** *skin is the udder. Treat it with a cream of laurel, menthol and eucalyptus essential oils. This will repel insects and soften the skin of the udder, which will keep it from cracking. That means your cow will have a consistently high milk yield.*

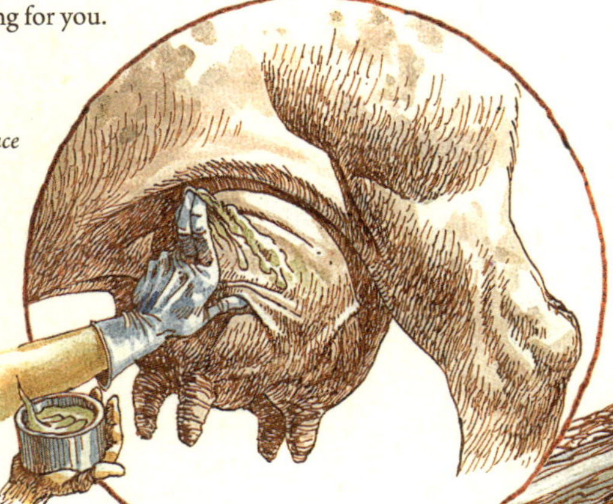

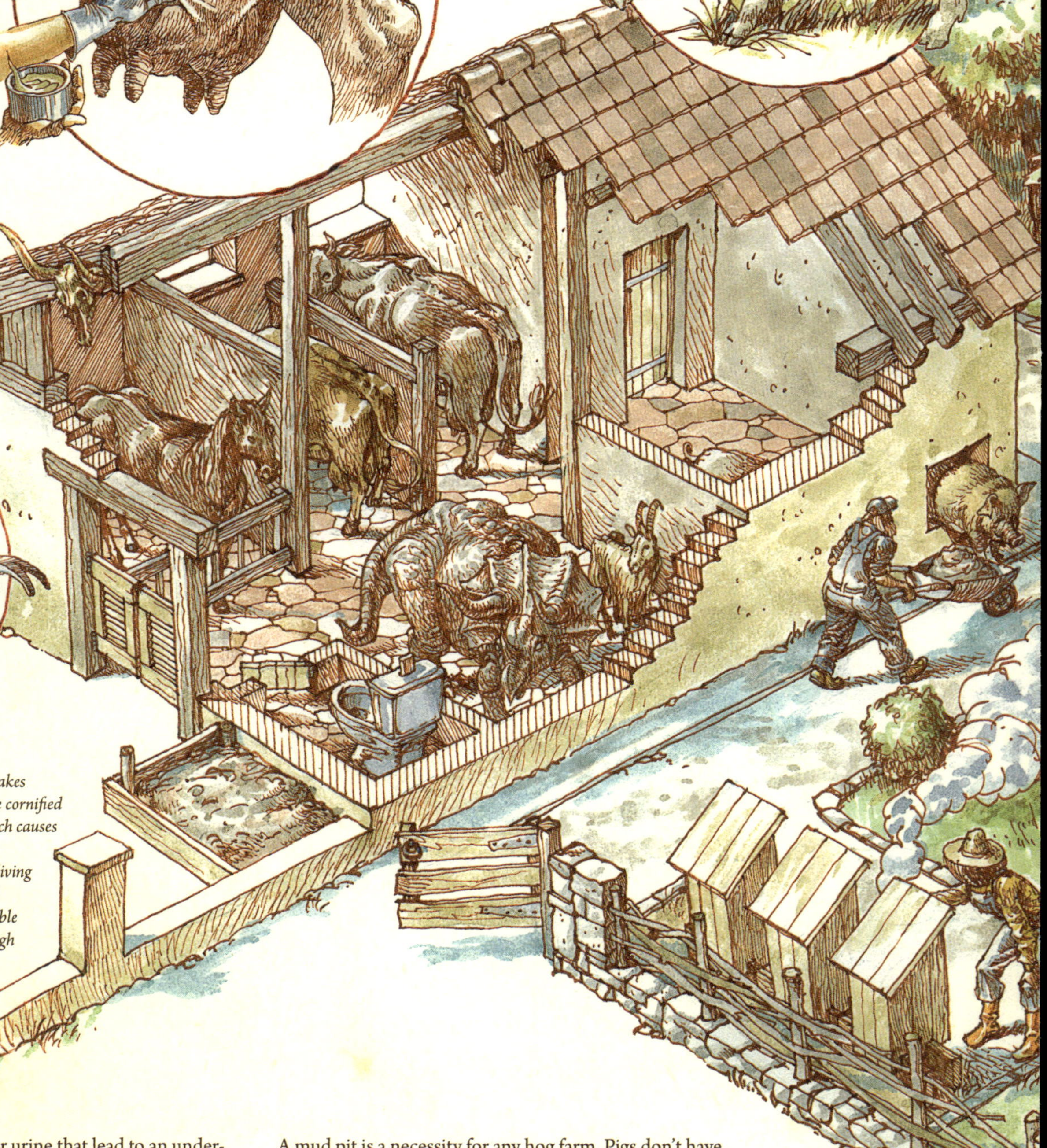

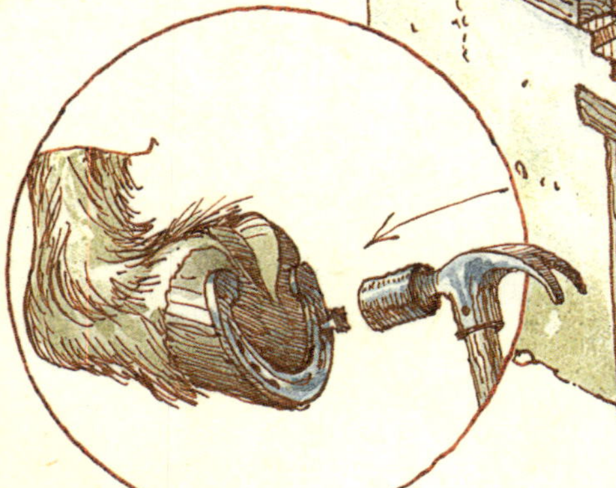

Standing in one place for a long time makes the ***horse's*** *hoof soft. Because of this, the cornified hoof tissue is quickly ground down, which causes pain. Strengthen the hooves by nailing horseshoes to the bottom to protect the living tissue. The inner layer of the horny wall of the hoof is delineated by a clearly visible white line. This tissue is insensitive enough to drive nails into.*

Each barn must contain drains for urine that lead to an underground container surrounded by concrete. You can make organic fertilizer from manure and water the fields with urine. The feed storage room must be protected from moisture. Most livestock can eat hay, silage, legumes and grains. Feed birds birch branches and nettle leaves in the summer, which will save them from vitamin deficiency and allow them to fly faster in winter.

A mud pit is a necessity for any hog farm. Pigs don't have sweat glands, so they need to wallow in mud to effectively regulate their body temperature. Chickens need an ash pit to clean their skin and feathers of parasites. But make sure to dilute 1 part ash with 2 parts river sand and 100 grams of sulfur, as concentrated ash contains potash and soda that can irritate the skin and mucous membranes of birds.

SELECTION

To maintain your herd, you need to ensure it contains both males and females of reproductive age. An effective way to raise animals with good meat, wool and milk is to selectively breed them. Select the best members of your herd and breed them using artificial insemination: collect semen and inject it into the female's cervix during ovulation. A large syringe will do the trick. Share biomaterial with neighboring farmers to help avoid inbreeding and make the stock healthier. Vaccinate herds against rabies and other diseases. If one animal falls ill, isolate it immediately.

__Sheep__ can be quite skittish. Graze them together with horses or goats to make sure they don't run off at the slightest rustle of a bush. Sheep copy the behavior of other animals and will feel more protected. Sheep are quite hearty and can live outdoors in temperatures down to −15C°. Any lower than that and they need a heated room. Sheep hooves are quite fragile, so the floor must be planked with wood for the flock to stay healthy.

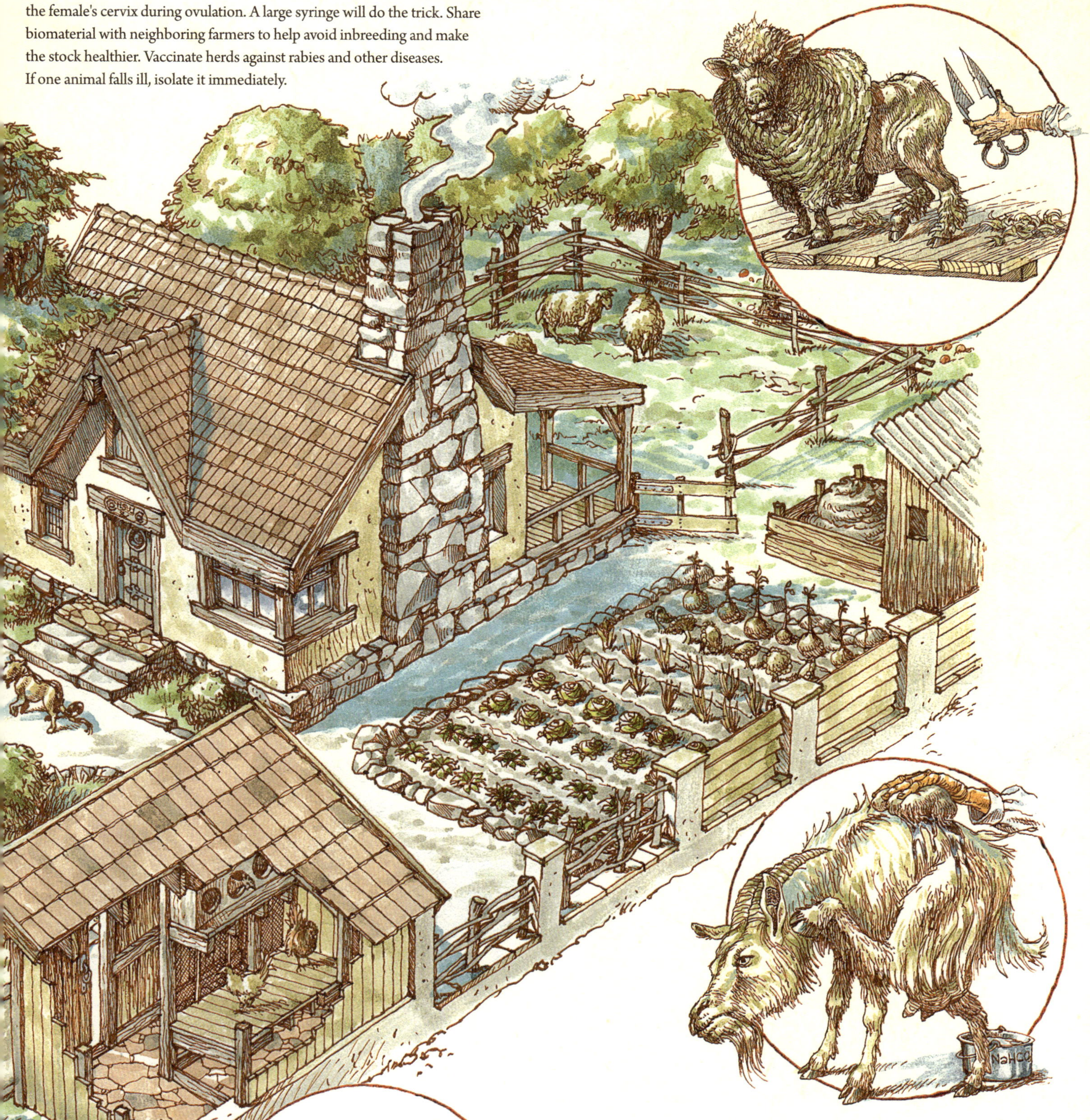

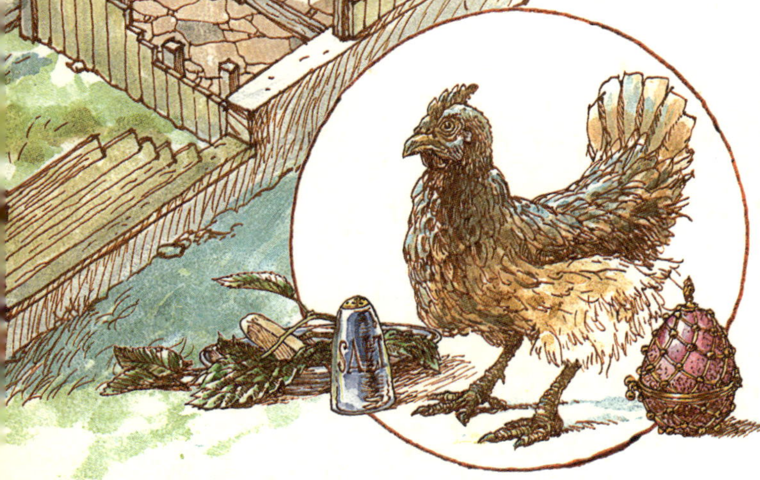

To ensure a steady supply of eggs, supplement your __chickens'__ diet with salt and chalk to make the eggshell denser. Sour milk and herbs make good feed for laying hens.

The wool of the __goats__ will be thicker and of better quality, and the milk yield higher, if you treat the goat's skin with a solution of soda at least once a week. This prevents parasites from nesting in the wool.

SILK

Even during their short span of life, the fragile moths are capable of altering the course of entire civilizations. This is all thanks to the unique threads created by a particular moth's caterpillar stage: the silkworm. Each thread is 40 times lighter than a human hair but has nearly the same tensile strength as a length of steel wire of the same diameter.

These threads can be woven into the finest fabrics with applications in many different fields, from medicine to music to electricity. But producing this material means cutting the already brief life of the silkworm short and devoting your own life to the craft.

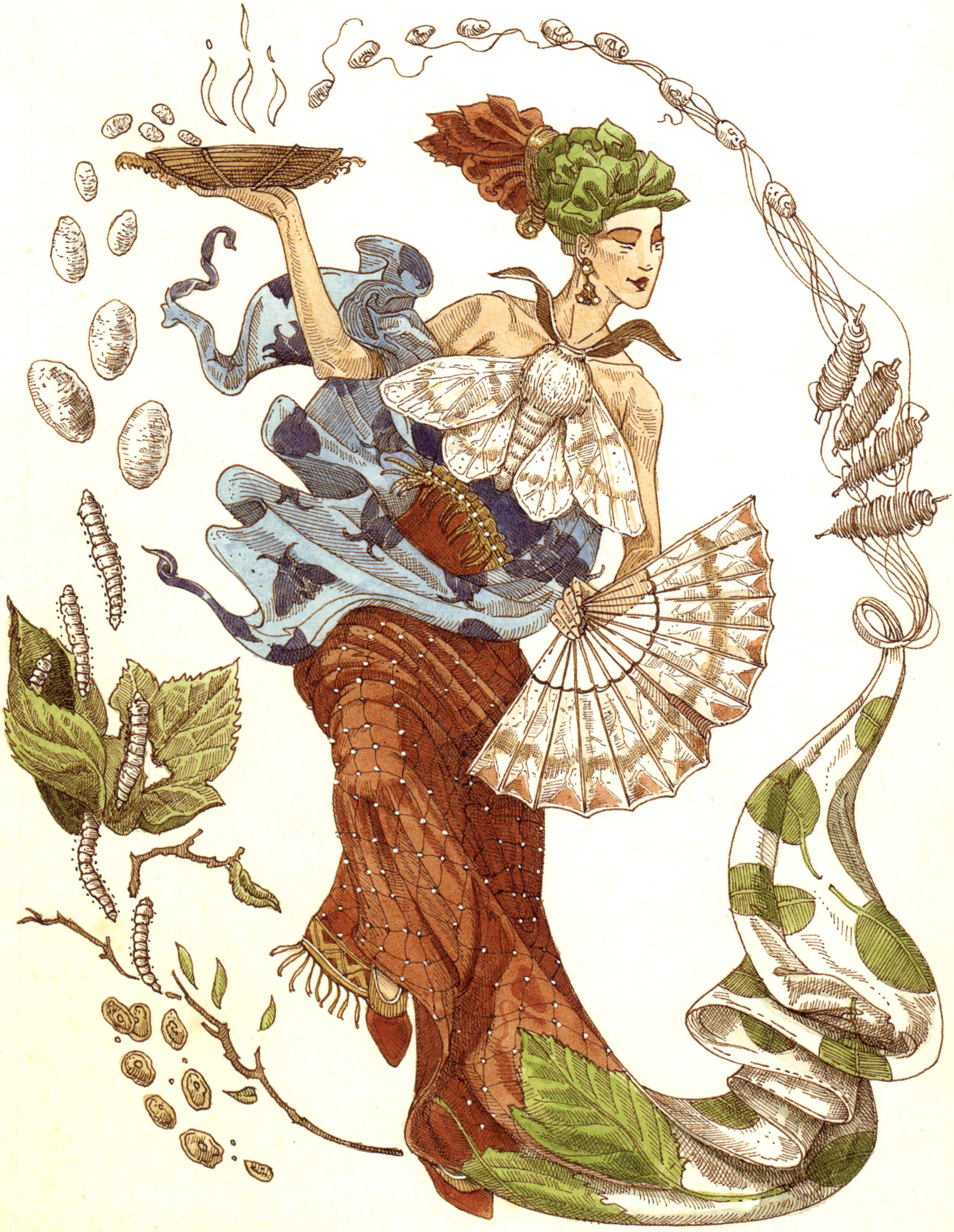

SILK THREAD

To start, mate your silkmoths. They'll lay eggs around 2–3 days later (1), and the larvae will hatch after 8–10 days (2). Move them to a well-ventilated area and keep them fed regularly with fresh mulberry leaves. Around 30 days later, the larvae turn into caterpillars. When they turn yellow and slightly transparent, they're ready to pupate (3). Provide them with a tray equipped with pegs at the bottom (4). Within 3–4 days, they'll start spinning their cocoons around these pegs (5). A single thread can be up to 1.5 km long! At some point (usually around 15 days later) you'll have to interrupt this process; otherwise, a new moth will burst through the cocoon and render your efforts futile.

To keep the threads intact, place the cocoons in boiling water (6). This kills the pupa and dissolves the protein sericin, which is what binds the silk threads together. Now carefully brush the cocoon to find the end of the thread. Once you've done this with 6–8 cocoons, gather the threads together, pass them through a hole in the middle of a plank of wood and wind the threads around a spool. As you rotate the spool, the cocoons will unwind (7). Rinse the braided yarns in soapy water to get rid of any excess sericin and other substances then rinse again with hot water. Now your silk thread is ready to use. It can be used to make strings for musical instruments, thread for suturing wounds and winding for wire. You can also weave silk to make parachutes, sails and even armor.

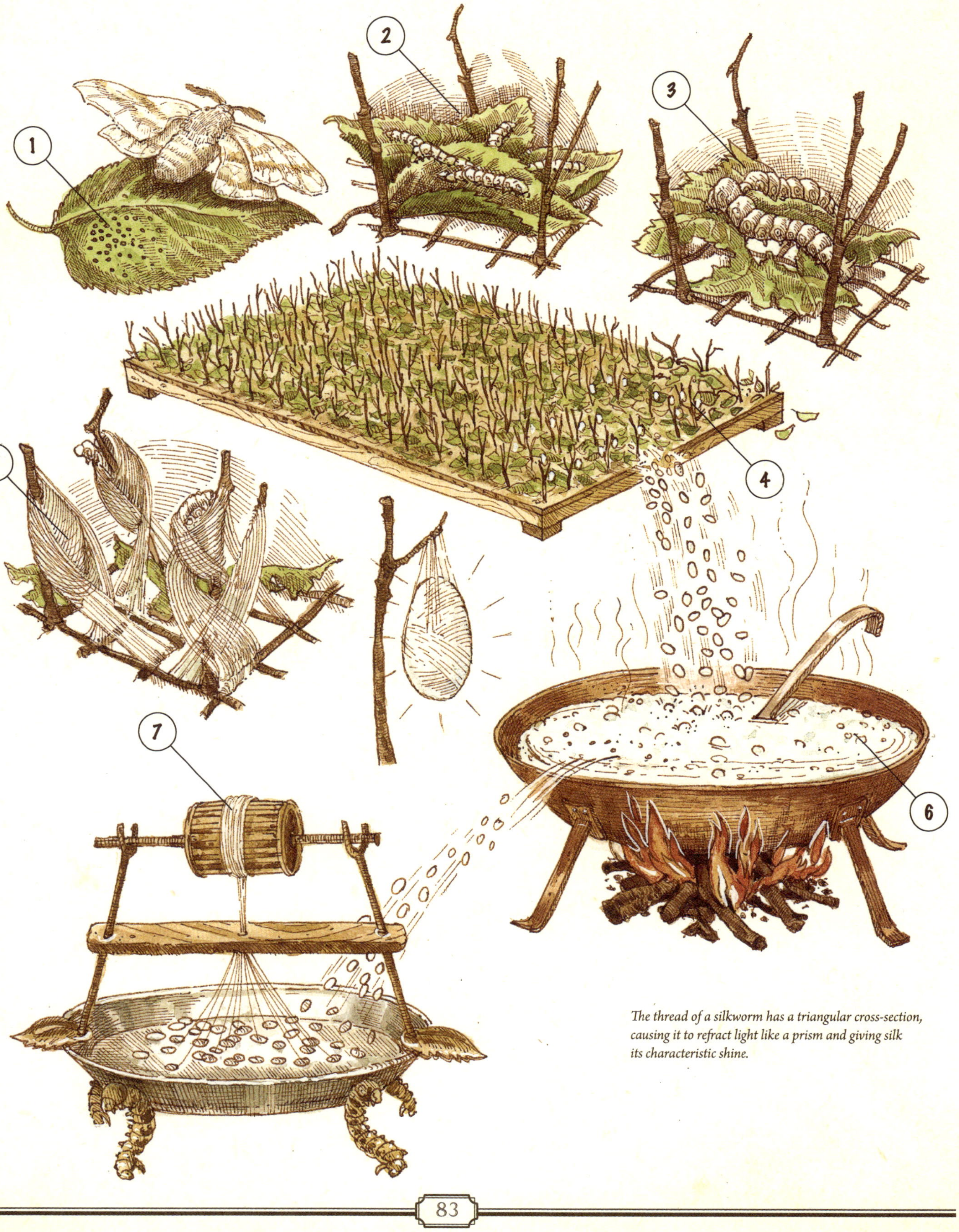

The thread of a silkworm has a triangular cross-section, causing it to refract light like a prism and giving silk its characteristic shine.

BEEKEEPING

Large animals like cows, sheep or chickens provide many important products for us. But even some insects can be extremely useful too — such as bees. Bees are the epitome of waste-free production, and everything they make can be put to use, including honey and wax. And they do all this while also quietly helping surrounding plants reproduce by pollinating their flowers. That's why a team of busy bees is a must-have for any farm.

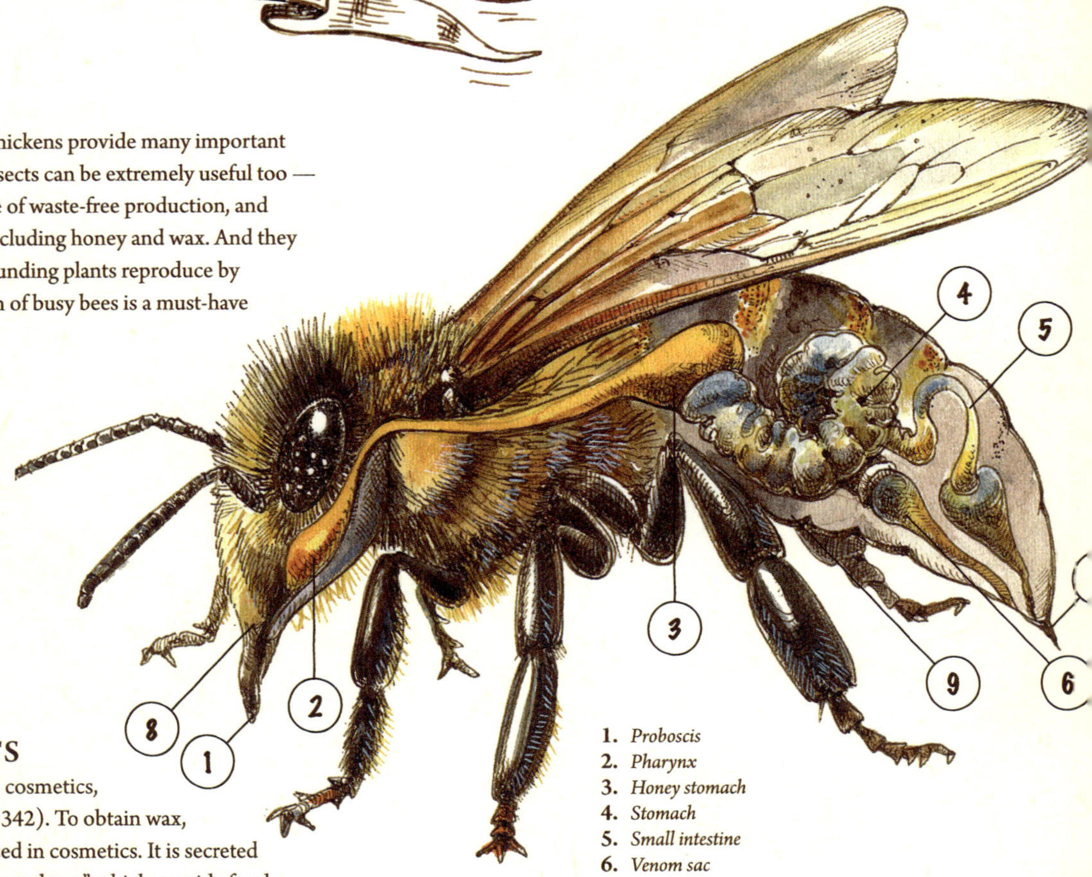

1. *Proboscis*
2. *Pharynx*
3. *Honey stomach*
4. *Stomach*
5. *Small intestine*
6. *Venom sac*
7. *Stinger*
8. *Upper jaw with royal jelly producing gland*
9. *Wax glands*

BEEKEEPING PRODUCTS

Wax can be used in the making of candles, cosmetics, polishes, lubricants and even music (page 342). To obtain wax, first melt the honeycomb. **Royal jelly** is used in cosmetics. It is secreted by the maxillary glands of the so-called "nurse bees," which provide food for the queen and her young. You can collect the jelly from the frames where the larvae are being fed. The delightfully named "**bee bread**" consists of balls of pollen and nectar stored in the honeycomb. An easy way to get this delicious product is to freeze the honeycomb, remove the layer of honey, grind the comb up and sift through a fine mesh. The frozen wax will fall away, leaving behind the hard granules of pollen. **Bee pollen** is the pollen not yet stored in the honeycomb. To collect it, place a lattice with small holes and a tray at the entrance to the hive. Some of the pollen will fall from their legs onto the tray as they pass inside.

Propolis, or "bee glue," has proven antimicrobial properties. Scrape the propolis off the ceiling boards and frame attachment points. **Bee venom** is used to treat the musculoskeletal system and the nervous system. In order to obtain it safely, you'll need to annoy your bees. Expose the glass plates under the beehive grates to a slight electrical current. These weak electrical impulses will irritate the bees, and they will release their venom, which will remain on the plate.

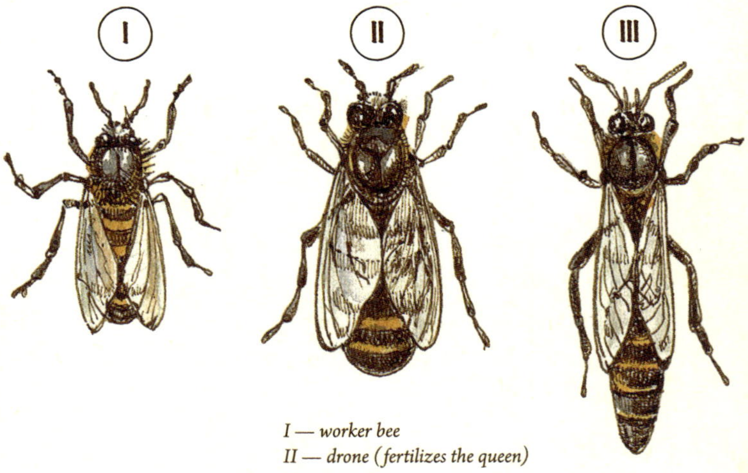

I — worker bee
II — drone (fertilizes the queen)
III — queen

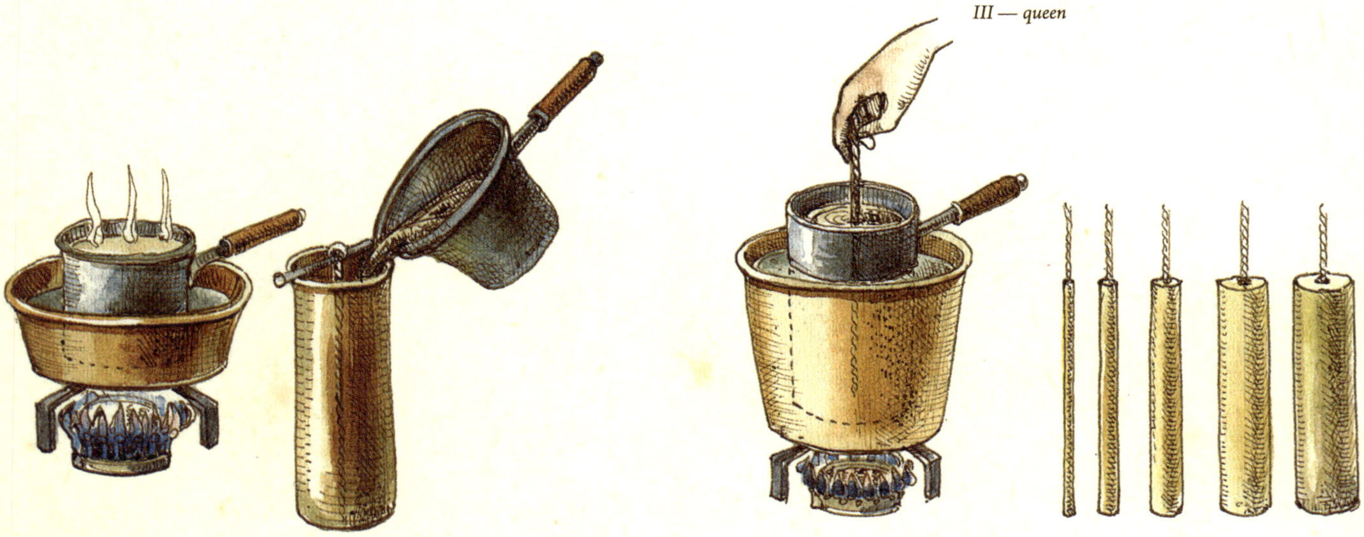

CANDLE

Make a wick out of a twisted cotton thread and dip it into a bowl of melted wax. Pull it out and allow it to harden slightly then dip it back into the wax. Repeat this process until you're left with a candle of the desired thickness.

Another option is to make a candle in a clay or glass mold. To do this, fix the wick on the sides of the container and fill it with wax. This method allows you to mix together different colors and scents.

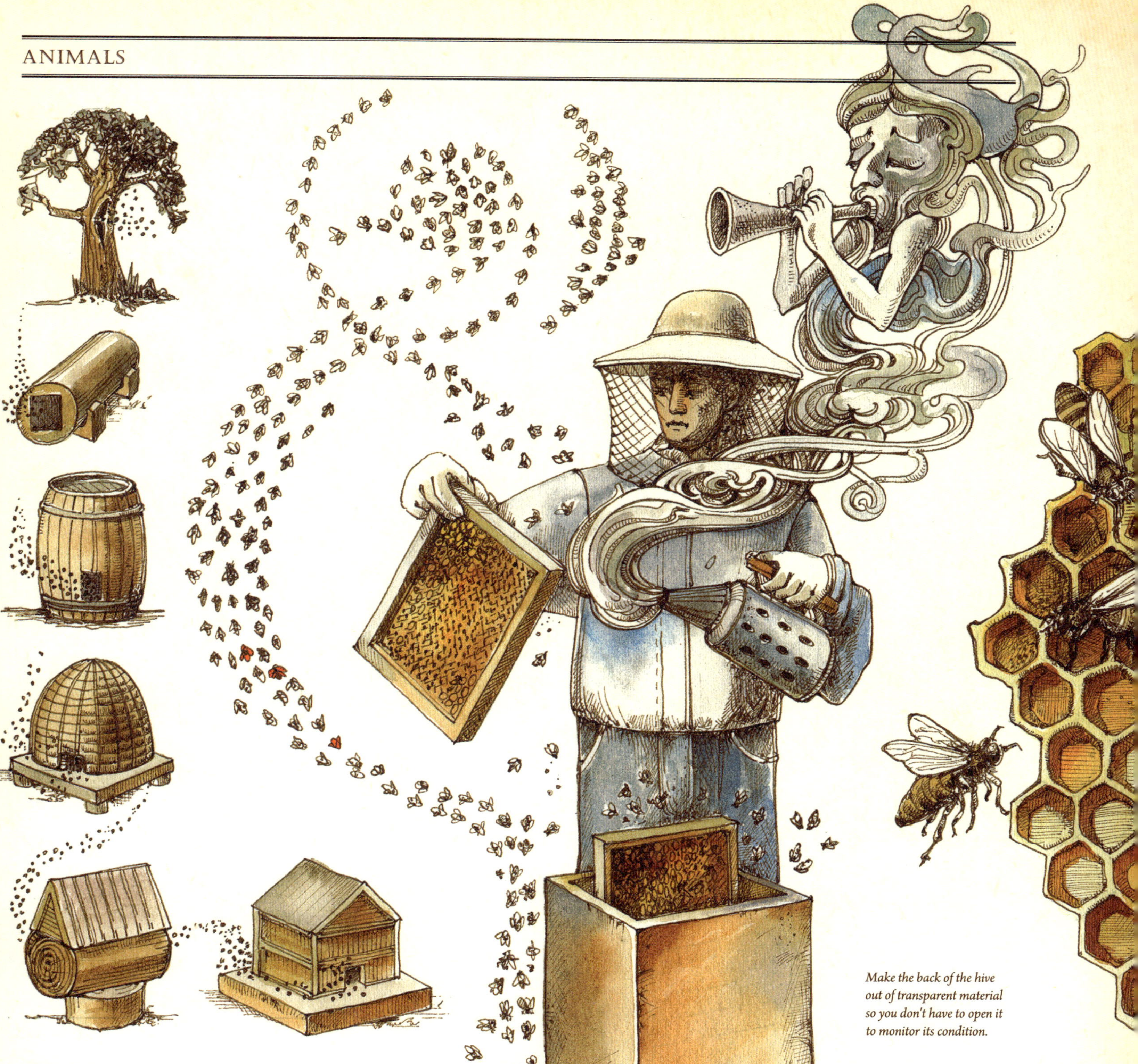

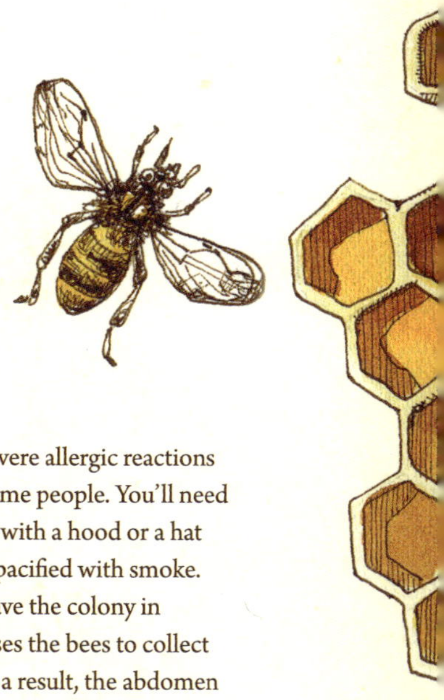

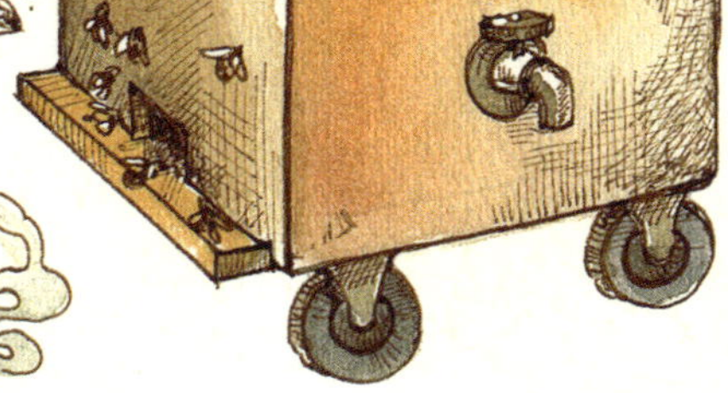

Make the back of the hive out of transparent material so you don't have to open it to monitor its condition.

APIARY

You can search for hives in the hollows of trees and take what you need from wild bees. Or dig artificial hollows yourself and wait for your apian friends to arrive. But it's better to build hives for your bees. Insert wooden frames into the hive. The bees will use these as an underlying structure to build the honeycombs in which the queen will lay eggs. Worker bees will bring pollen and nectar into these combs to feed their offspring. In the lower section of the hive is the storage reservoir, where bees keep their honey.

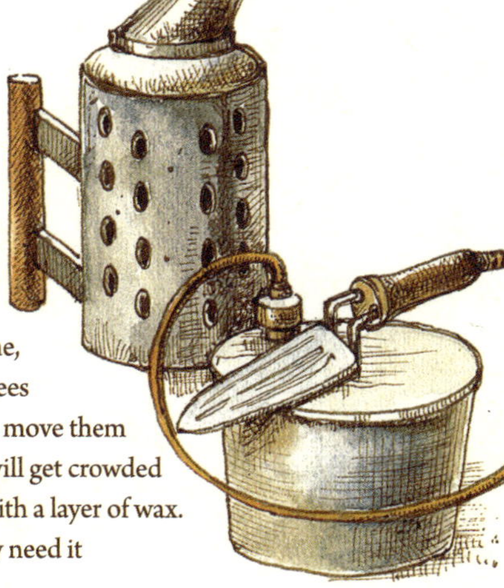

TRAPS

Ideally, a colony will move into your hive on its own. If it doesn't, place small hives with old combs cleared of honey around the edge of the forest. Rub them with mint or lemon balm — this will attract the bees. When the wild bees settle into the trap, bring it to your apiary. Don't forget to put a landmark near their new home, such as a large branch or a stone on the roof, so that the bees don't get lost during their first outing. If it's a large colony, move them into new hives or place new frames; otherwise, the bees will get crowded and leave. Only take the combs after the bees seal them with a layer of wax. Never take the hive's entire honey store all at once, as they need it for nutrition and reproduction.

PROTECTION

Bee venom can also cause severe allergic reactions and anaphylactic shock in some people. You'll need protection: gloves and a suit with a hood or a hat with a veil. Bees can also be pacified with smoke. This instinct, developed to save the colony in the event of a forest fire, causes the bees to collect honey in their honey sac. As a result, the abdomen loses its mobility and the bees cannot sting. The smoke also masks the pheromones released by guard and injured bees. Therefore, your invasion of the hive will go unpunished.

INSECTS FOR FOOD

In terms of nutritional value, small insects differ little from large crustaceans and molluscs. They are rich in protein, unsaturated fats and micronutrients necessary for humans. You'll need a lot of them to feed a family, but luckily, this problem is easily solved by raising insects instead of collecting them.

They require a lot less space, time and effort than traditional livestock, especially if you focus on colony insects. Just don't go for termites! They emit even more methane and carbon dioxide than cows, and most developed civilizations already have enough problems with greenhouse gases.

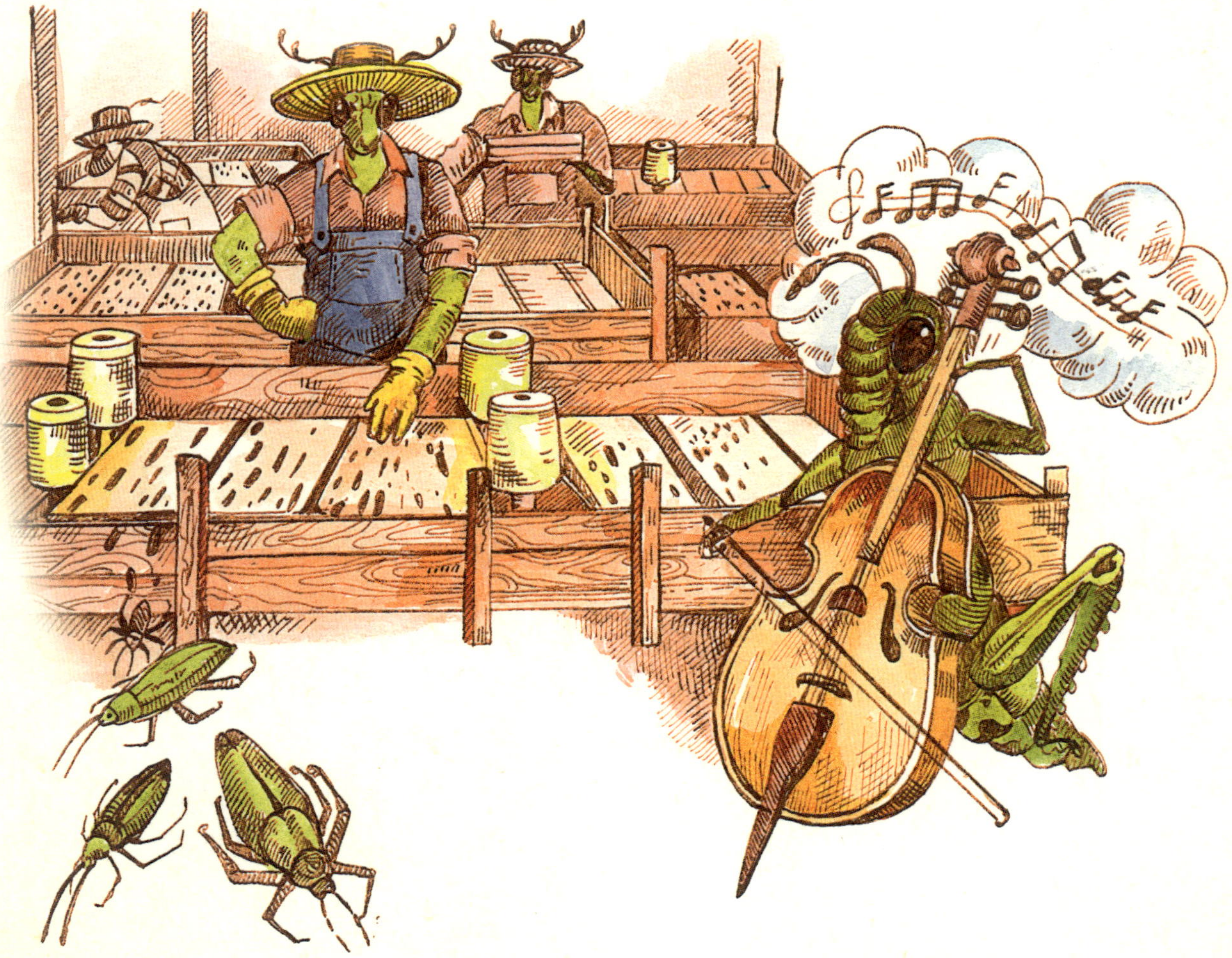

Look for beetles and their larvae in decaying trees and under fallen leaves. Butterfly larvae, pupae and caterpillars can be found in live wood, under tree bark or under rocks. It is easier to catch crickets in the early morning or late evening, as they are less active when temperatures are low.

Crickets love sweets, so you can catch them by leaving a container of sugar in the field. Locusts are attracted by light, so they can be lured using a flashlight at night. Many ants can be collected by lowering a stick into their nest. You need to cook your ants as soon as you catch them; otherwise, they release acid, which will ruin the taste.

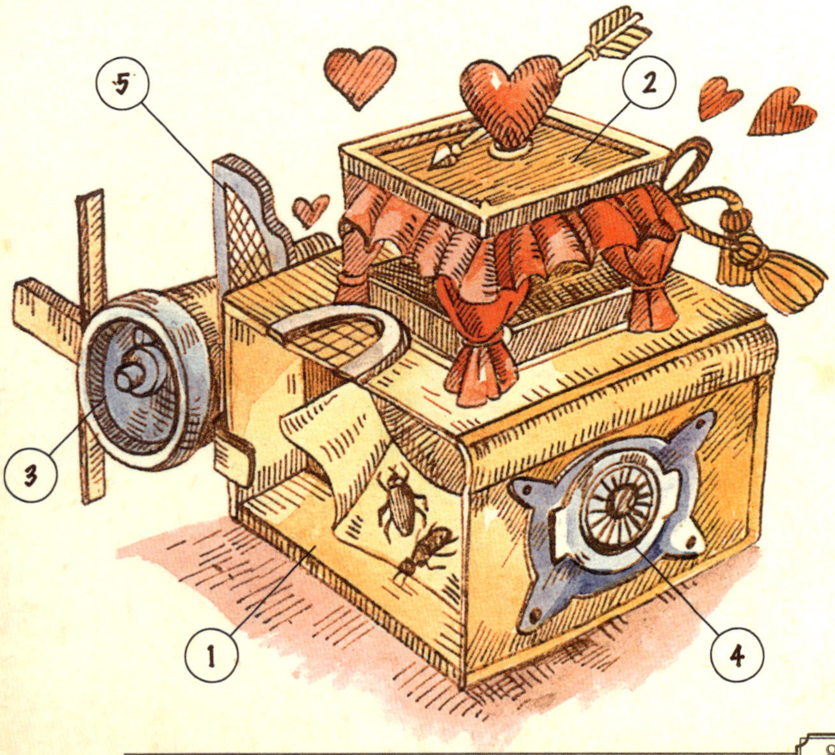

Crickets and their close relatives make the best substitutes for beef. Keep crickets by constructing a cricket farm with separate modules. The insects live in one room (1) and reproduce in the other (2). The two modules are connected by tubes through which the insects can move freely. The container must be kept at a high humidity of 70% and a high temperature (3) (about 35°C).

It is important to have ventilation (4), as well as blackout blinds (5) to control the day and night cycles. Please note: Don't put open water containers in your farm or the crickets may drown. Use damp cotton wool or a damp sponge as a drinking trough.

Once the crickets are old enough, they need to be moved to the breeding room (2). One male is needed to fertilize four females. Place three such groups in a container. When the crickets start chirping, they are ready to mate. Crickets lay about 300–800 eggs over 2–4 weeks. Wait 10 days, and you'll get a new crop of crickets, which can be served for dinner.

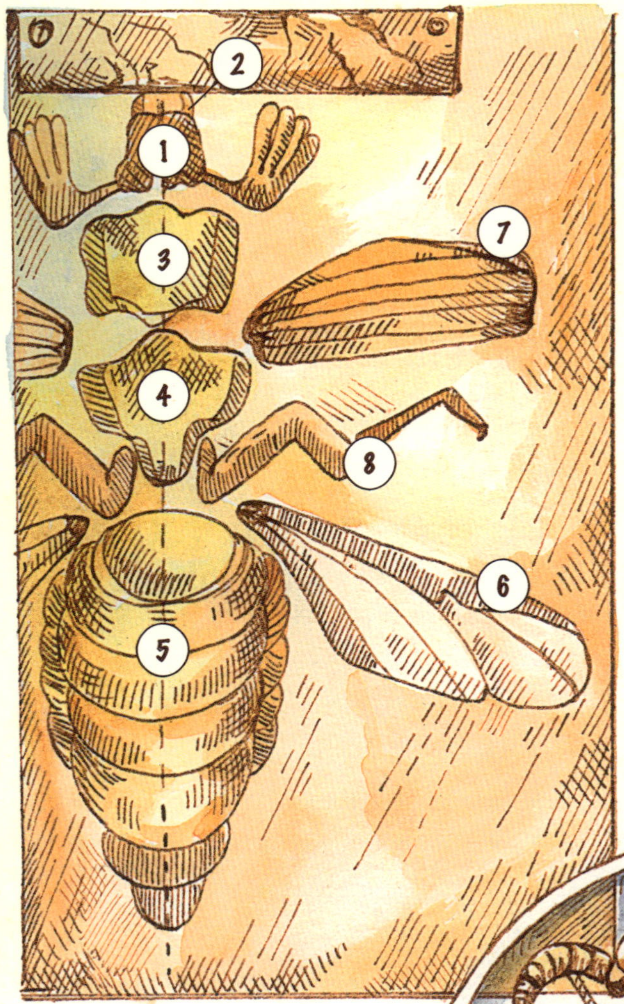

Insects come in a variety of flavors and textures, many reminiscent of other food products. Experiment with your bug-based cuisine! Fried wasps can be used in place of pine nuts; spiders also taste nutty; worms can substitute for sunflower seeds; grasshoppers resemble sardines; ants are like beef jerky; young bees can serve as a substitute for smoked fish or oysters; and June bugs taste like lobster.

Grasshopper and beetle larvae, as well as butterfly and moth caterpillars, are best fried in oil over an open fire until crisp. And June bugs make an excellent soup.

If an insect is brightly colored, chances are it's poisonous. The same goes for many slow-moving insects. They take their time because they're unafraid of predators due to the toxins they contain. And never eat an insect that you find already dead. Whatever killed it may have a negative affect on you as well.

1. *Head*
2. *Mandibles*
3. *Prothorax*
4. *Mesothorax*
5. *Metathorax*
6. *Wing*
7. *Wing case*
8. *Mesothoracic leg*

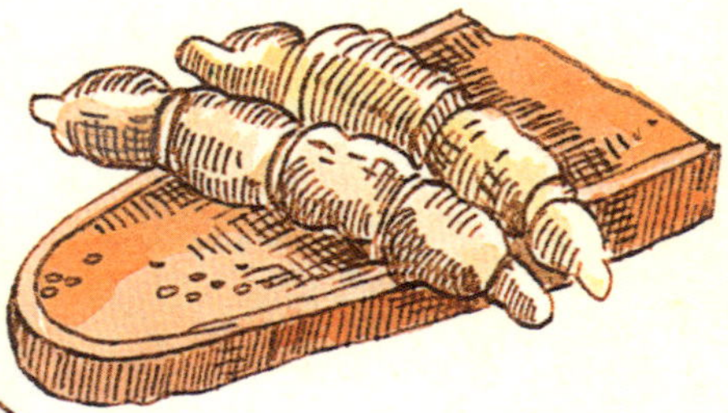

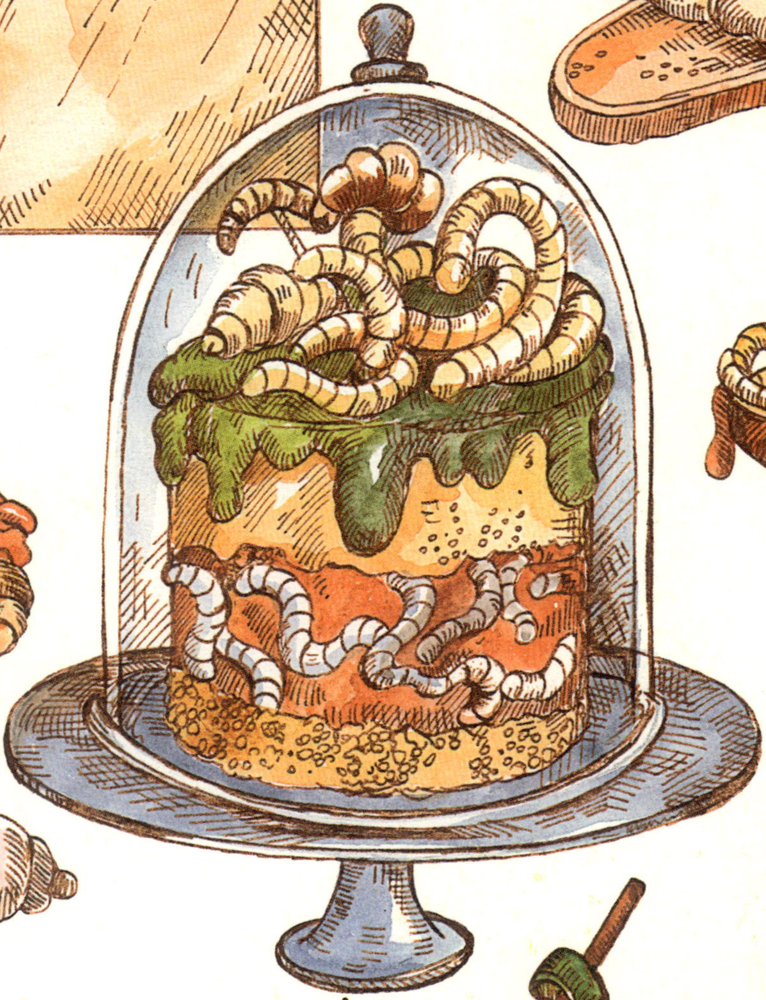

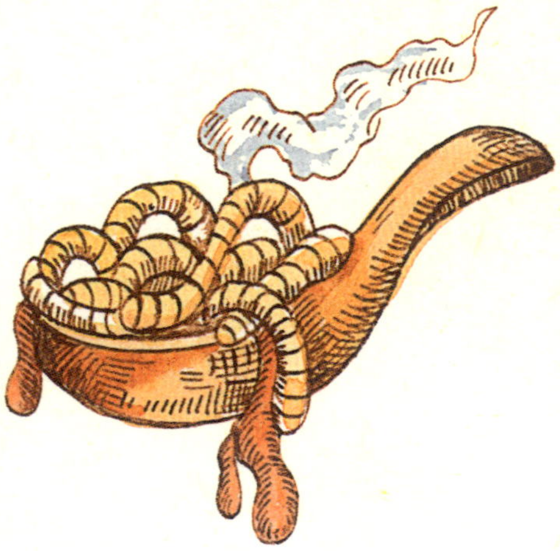

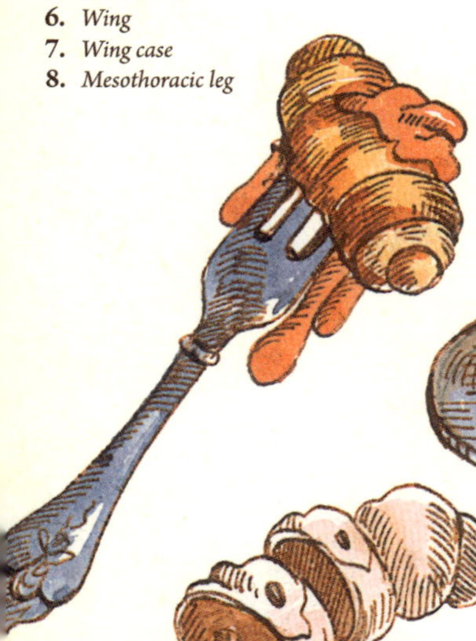

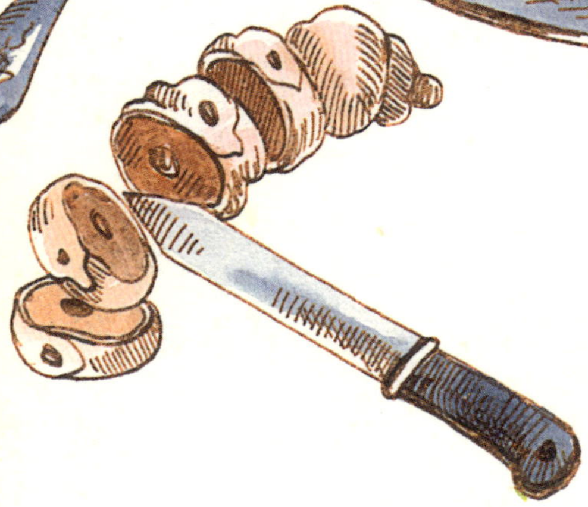

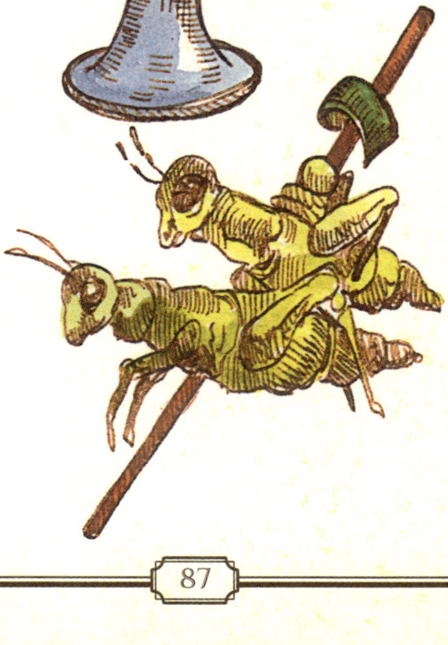

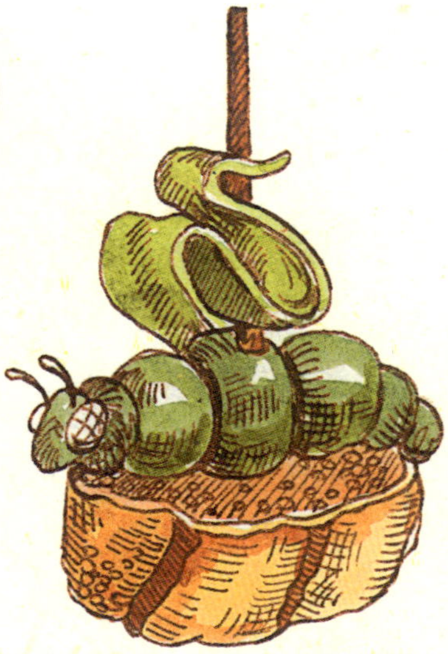

OYSTER FARMING

A delicacy or peasant food? With oysters, this question is meaningless. The delicate taste and nourishing micronutrients make for an exquisite dish that can be enjoyed raw by both the highborn and the low. All you need to do is to collect oyster shells in shallow water at low tide then crack them open and enjoy a fresh bite of umami that comes with its own serving dish.

Oysters are rich not only in protein but also in many mood-boosting substances, giving you a slight feeling of euphoria. If you want to enjoy the benefits of oysters without relying on the tides, make your own oyster farm.

Oysters prefer seawater with a low salt content, so they live only in the intertidal zone near river mouths. Find a suitable area along the river for your farm. It should be 15–20 meters deep, have a flat bottom and moderate current strength and be protected from waves. This is important, since a temperature change of even 10 degrees can kill oysters. Build an access dock on stilts or use buoys to keep it afloat. Secure old shells to a long rope or copper wire. This will give young oysters that wash in during breeding season a foothold, allowing them to cling to the rope.

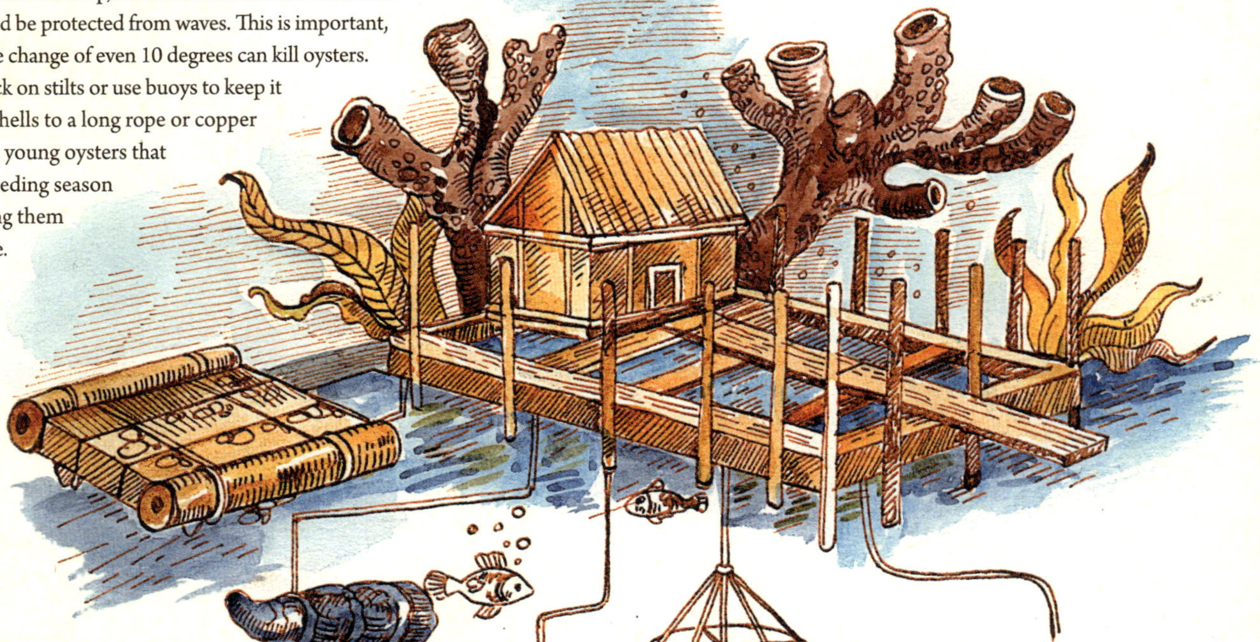

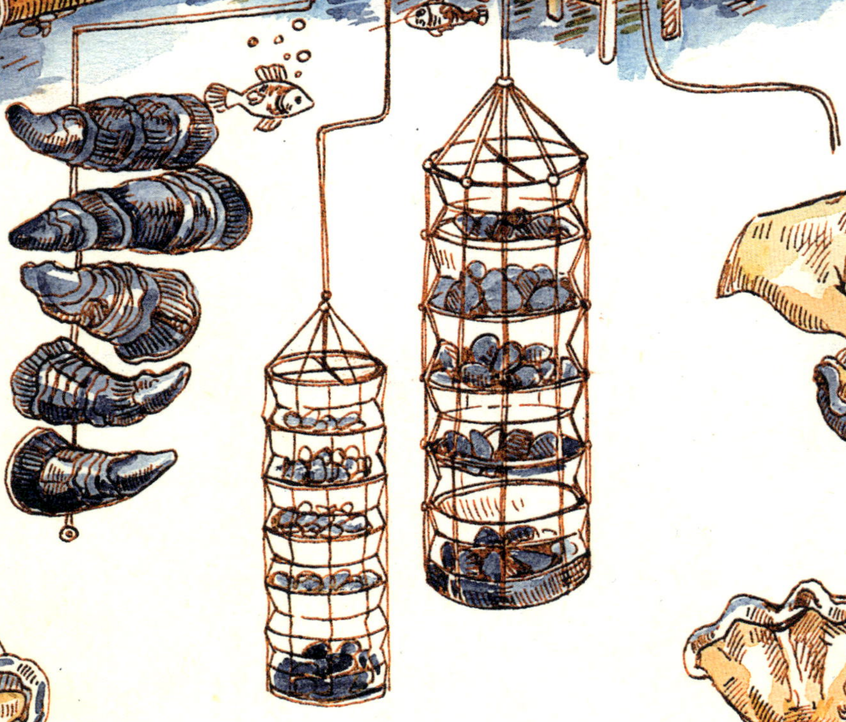

Oysters don't need to be fed, as they filter plankton from the water. At the end of summer, move the young oysters into fine mesh bags. Spread these around the bottom of the bay on 30 cm-high platforms or in tiered cages. This will protect the oysters from sediment pollution and their natural enemy — starfish. Clean the cages at low tide.

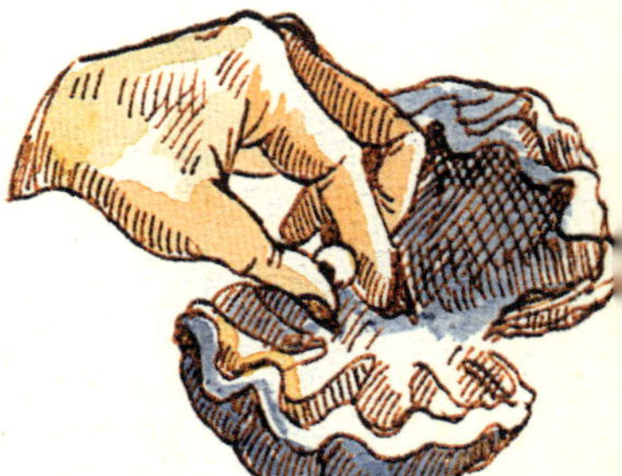

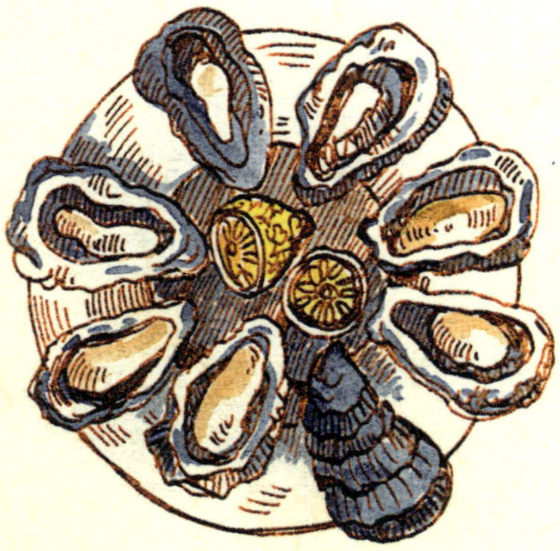

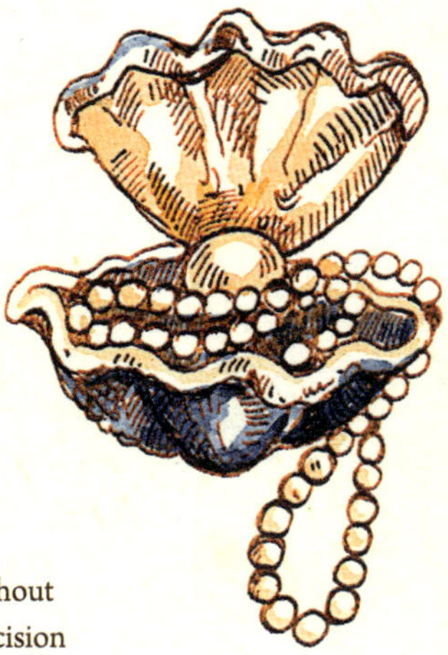

Oysters are eaten live. The shell of fresh oysters is tightly closed and "rings" when tapped. Open it by sticking the tip of a knife into the flat side where the two shells meet, then twist the knife 90°. When the shell opens, trim the muscle and remove the top shell.

PEARL

Gently pry open the shell of a 1-year-old oyster without completely breaking the hinge and make a small incision in the flesh. Place a grain of sand or a bead inside. The oyster will begin to secrete mother-of-pearl from the mantle, the outer layer of its skin, to envelop the foreign object and protect itself. Pearls usually grow a couple of millimeters every few months. Small pearls take about 3 years to form, while large ones take 5.

Once they're 3 years old, move the oysters to a place where they'll be out of the water at low tide or in brackish pools. You can shield your oyster field from waves with a barrier made of cement (page 148). Regulate tidal water levels using floodgates.

The harder the living conditions, the tastier the meat will be. Oysters trying to retain salt to regulate salt levels within their shells become chewier and more elastic. Watch the salinity of the water. Take a kilogram of the water and allow it to evaporate or boil it dry. Weigh the salt residue; the number of grams divided by 10 gives you the salt concentration of the water. Delicious oysters grow in water containing 2–3% salt. When the concentration is increased to 3.5%, the meat becomes tough. If it falls below 1.2%, the oysters die.

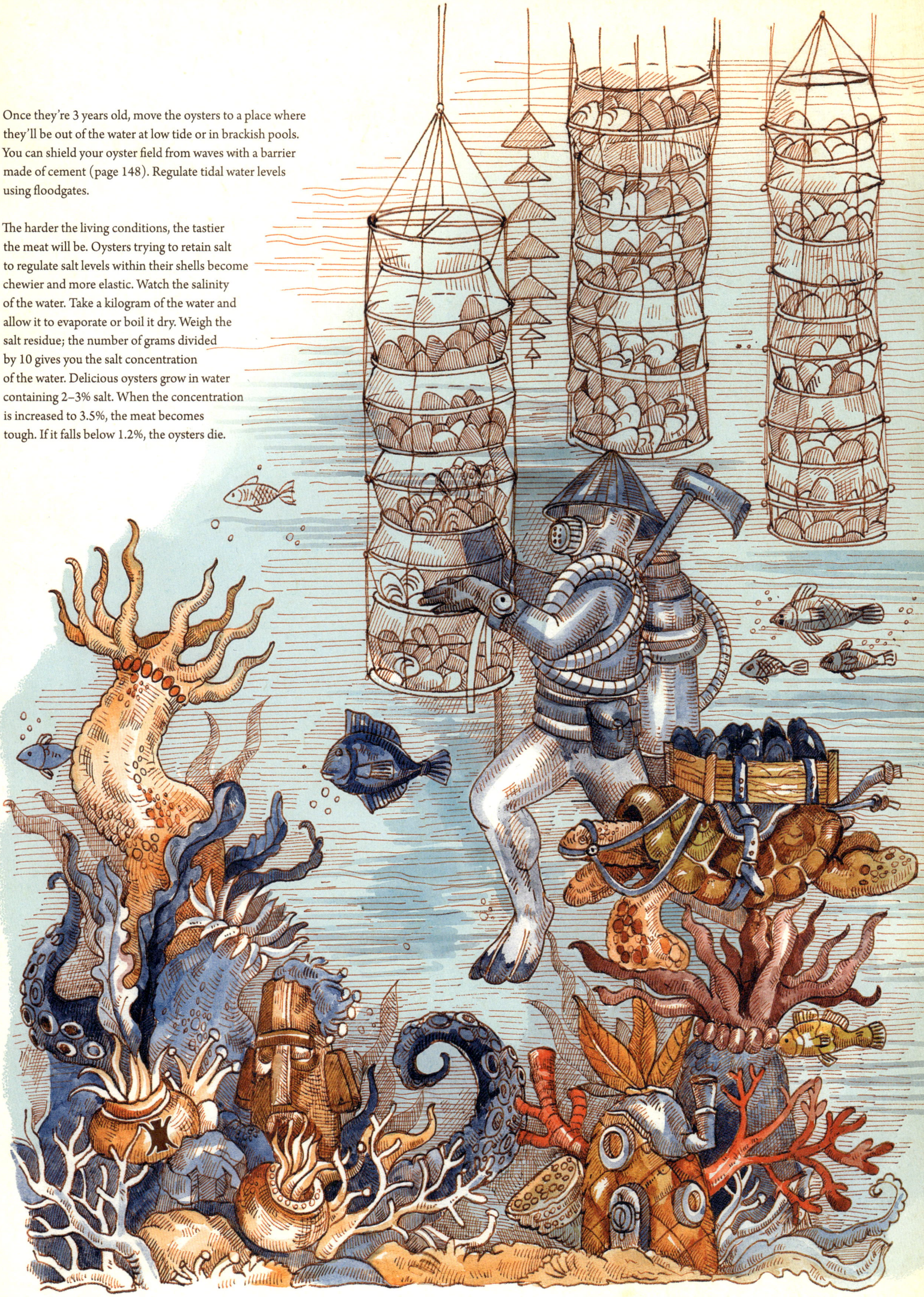

BIOFUEL

No need to drill wells and wait for gas supplies to travel from far away if you have cows. They can be used as a source of natural gas. Organic waste can also be turned into biofuel, which allows you to get more use out of your food products. In an anaerobic environment with a microbial presence, the waste will ferment and form carbon dioxide and methane, which can fuel gas boilers and stoves.

The center of the entire biofuel system is the reactor (1). Fill it with any bio waste (2) you wish to dispose of. Now inoculate the mixture with methane-producing archaea (simple unicellular microorganisms). The process is simple: just grind up the digestive tracts of a few cows and add them to the bioreactor. The gas produced will flow through a system of valves and reducers (devices that reduce and stabilize pressure) into a gas storage tank (3). You can use this to fuel gas stoves, space heaters or hot water systems (4) or gas engines (5) that power electricity generators (6). But first you must purify the methane of carbon dioxide and water. To do this, pass the gas mixture over quicklime powder or sodium hydroxide (page 24).

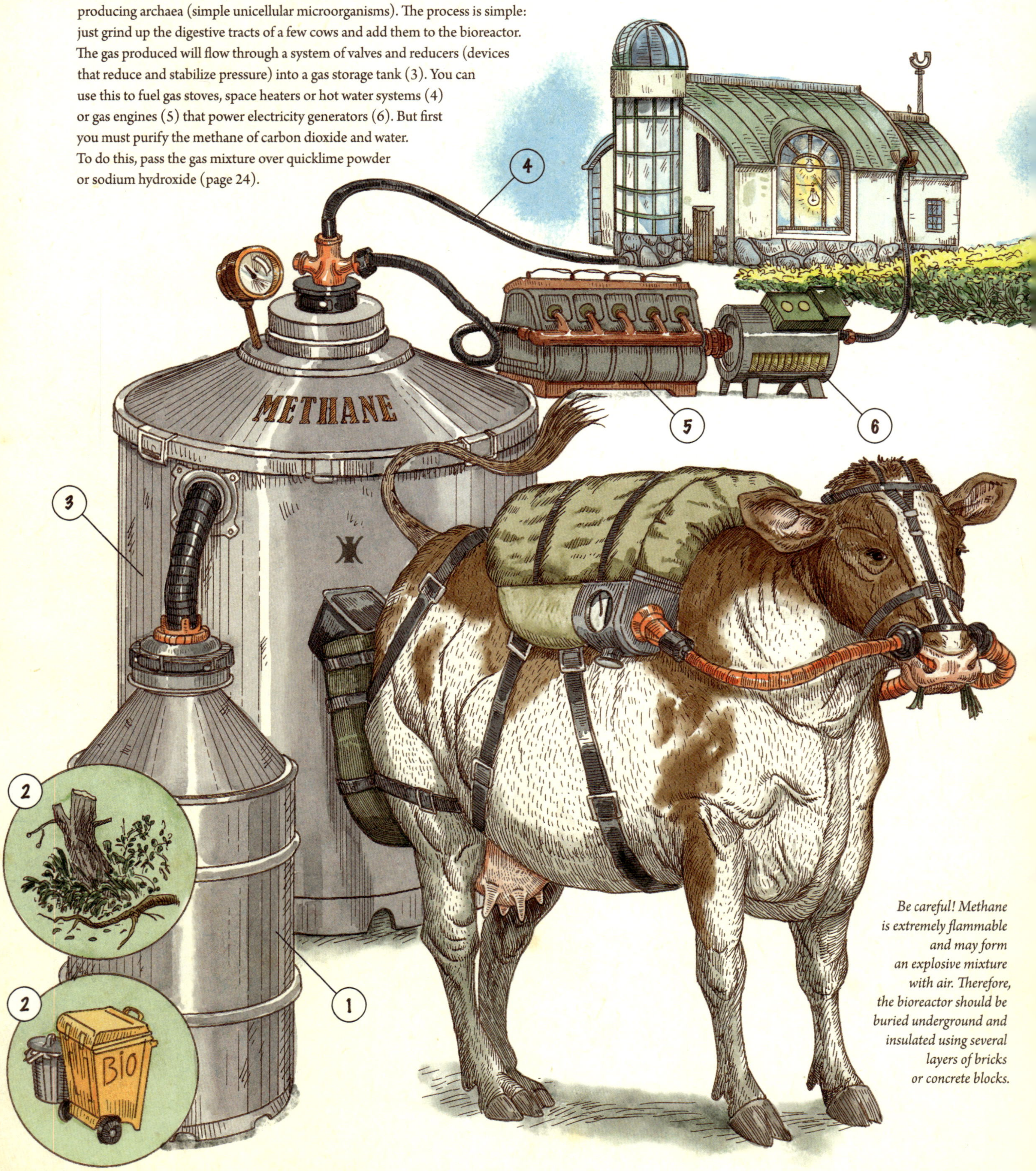

Be careful! Methane is extremely flammable and may form an explosive mixture with air. Therefore, the bioreactor should be buried underground and insulated using several layers of bricks or concrete blocks.

Mineral diesel fuel consists of paraffinic, naphthenic and aromatic hydrocarbons. Biodiesel is made from methyl esters of fatty acids. Fatty acids can be isolated from almost any raw fatty material but are most easily derived from vegetable oil. The ideal choice is rapeseed oil, which is almost completely (96–98%) converted into biodiesel. Vegetable oils are an ester of glycerin and unsaturated fatty acids. To produce biodiesel, you need to replace the glycerin with methanol. The reaction requires some sort of catalyst — for example, sodium hydroxide.

To obtain methanol, slowly heat pieces of wood in a covered container over a fire. Use only wood from deciduous, not coniferous, trees. Without oxygen, the wood will decompose rather than burn, eventually producing charcoal.

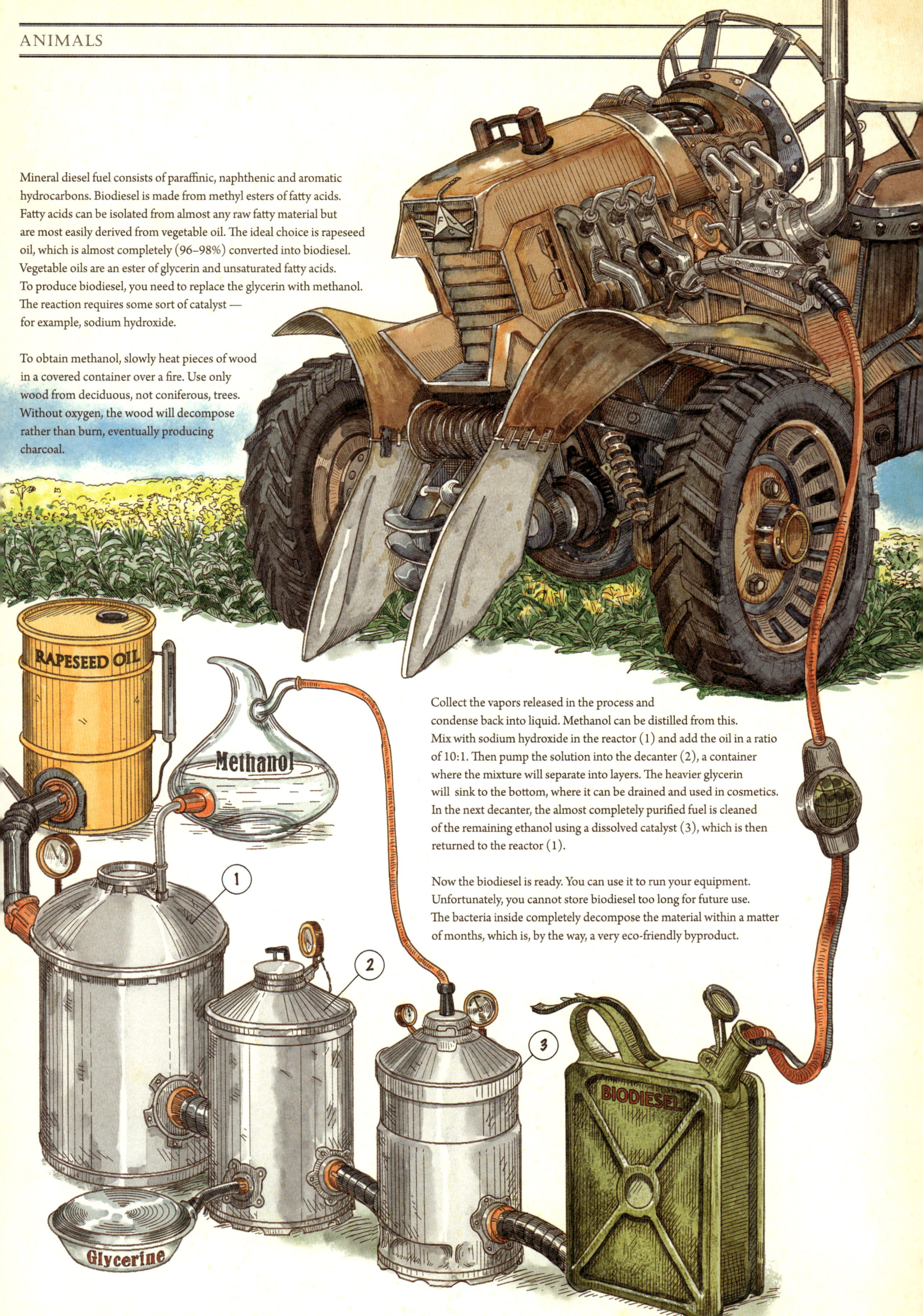

Collect the vapors released in the process and condense back into liquid. Methanol can be distilled from this. Mix with sodium hydroxide in the reactor (1) and add the oil in a ratio of 10:1. Then pump the solution into the decanter (2), a container where the mixture will separate into layers. The heavier glycerin will sink to the bottom, where it can be drained and used in cosmetics. In the next decanter, the almost completely purified fuel is cleaned of the remaining ethanol using a dissolved catalyst (3), which is then returned to the reactor (1).

Now the biodiesel is ready. You can use it to run your equipment. Unfortunately, you cannot store biodiesel too long for future use. The bacteria inside completely decompose the material within a matter of months, which is, by the way, a very eco-friendly byproduct.

FOOD

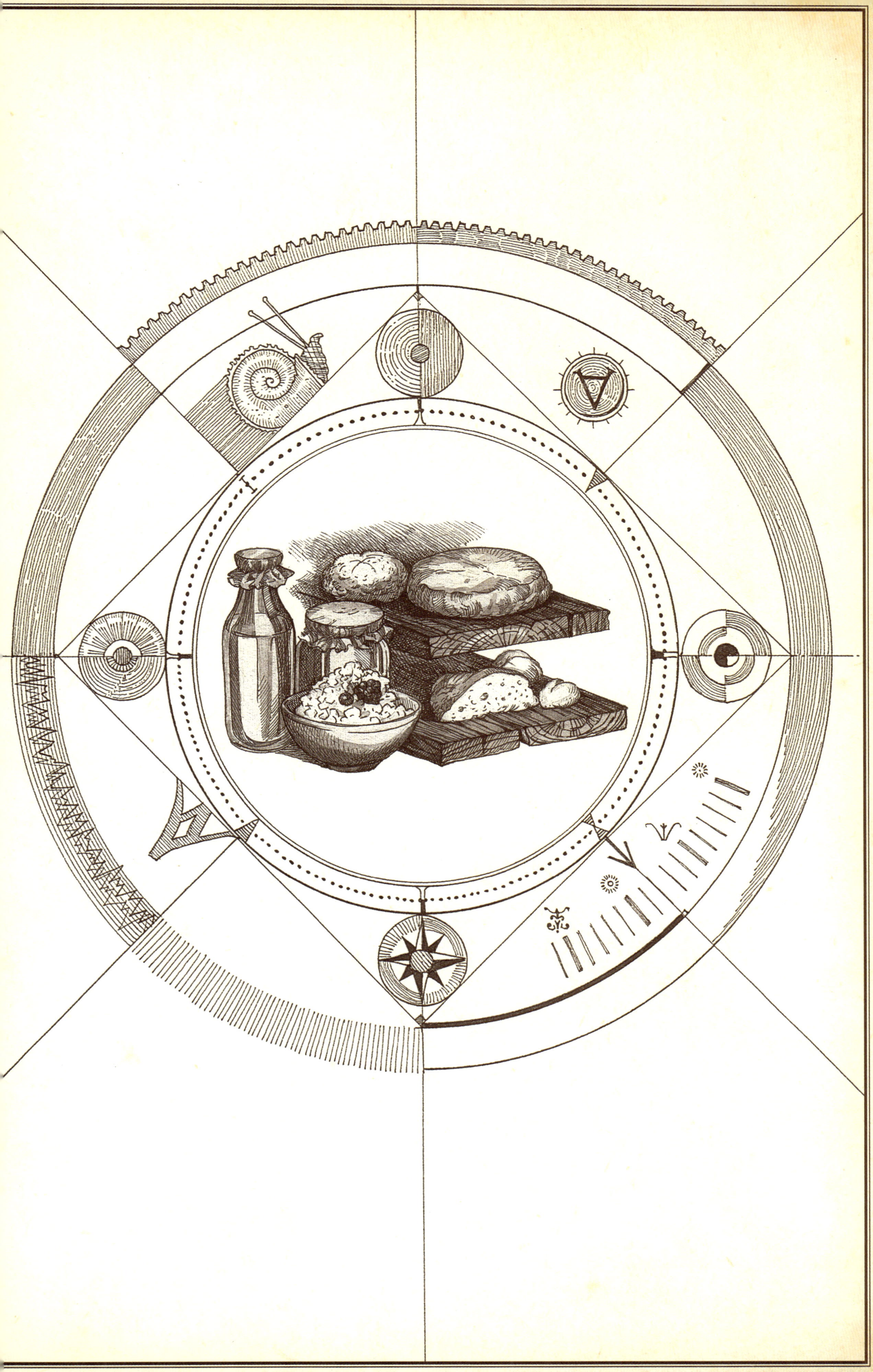

BREAD

Finding food isn't easy, and preserving it is an even more daunting task — various destabilizing factors within the structure of the food rapidly break down the organic matter. But you know what they say: If you can't beat 'em, join 'em!

Learn to manage the natural decay processes in these substances — denaturation and fermentation — and you'll open a world of tasty new recipes that are much less tied to the whims of the seasons and the vagaries of nature.

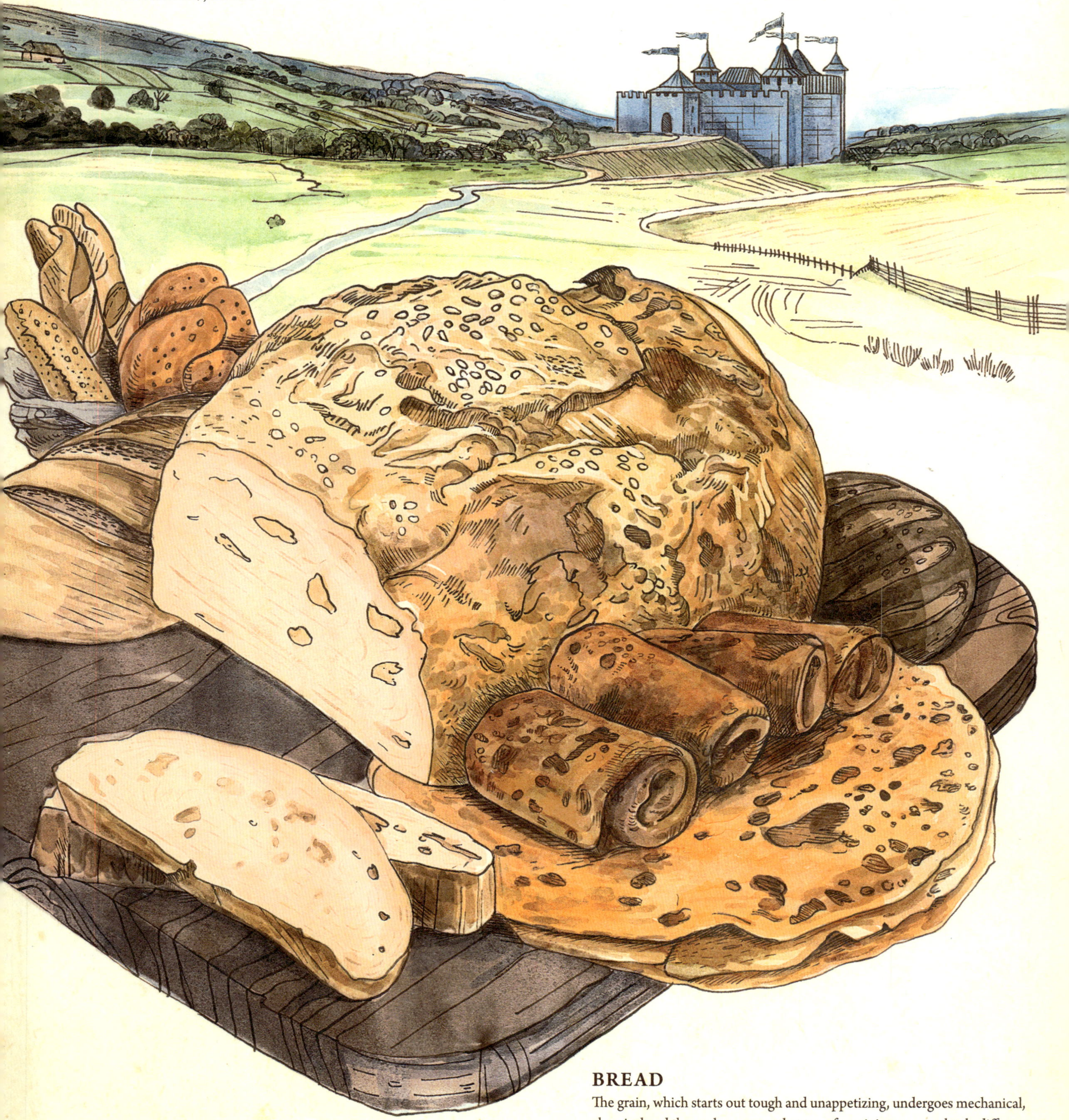

BREAD

The grain, which starts out tough and unappetizing, undergoes mechanical, chemical and thermal processes that transform it into a completely different product. The chemical and thermal decomposition releases substances that make bread more nutritious than just grain alone. You can bake bread on coals, in a hole in the ground, in a clay pot or in an oven. You can mold it into different shapes or add spices to taste. The possibilities are limitless.

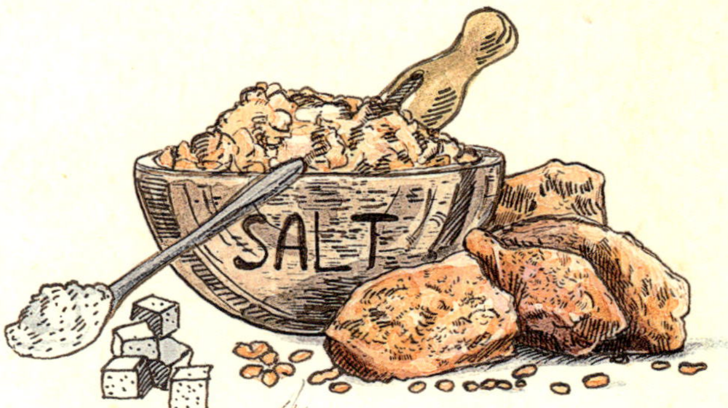

DOUGH PREPARATION

The basic ingredients of any bread dough are flour and water, and salt can be added to really enhance the flavor of the bread. However, you'll also need to get your hands on the right strains of yeast or cultured lactic acid bacteria (or a mixture of both). These consume the starch and fermentable sugars in the dough and release carbon dioxide, the gas bubbles that make bread rise.

But where can you find natural yeast? It's all around you! The air we breathe contains the correct strains of both yeast and lactic bacteria. All you need to do is create a favorable environment for them to propagate — for example, a mix of equal parts rye flour and water. Place the mixture in a warm place, and in a few days, the microbes will start fermenting the dough. You'll know it's working when you see bubbles and notice a slightly alcoholic fragrance. You can also find spores on the peel of sweet fruits and berries. Chop the fruits or mash the berries, pour warm sugar water over the mixture and close the lid. After a couple of days, the yeast water is ready. Mix it with flour to make a starter.

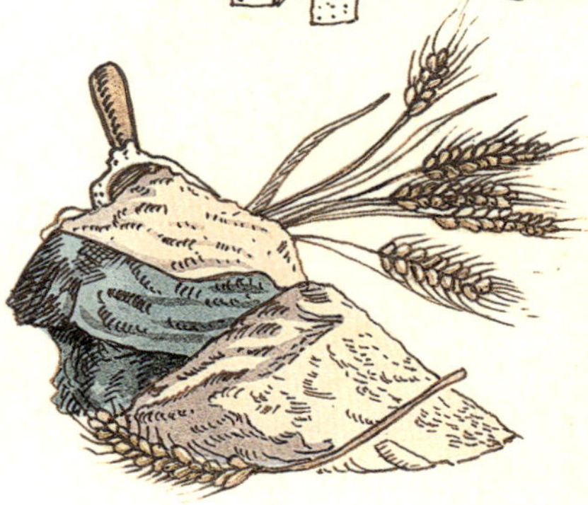

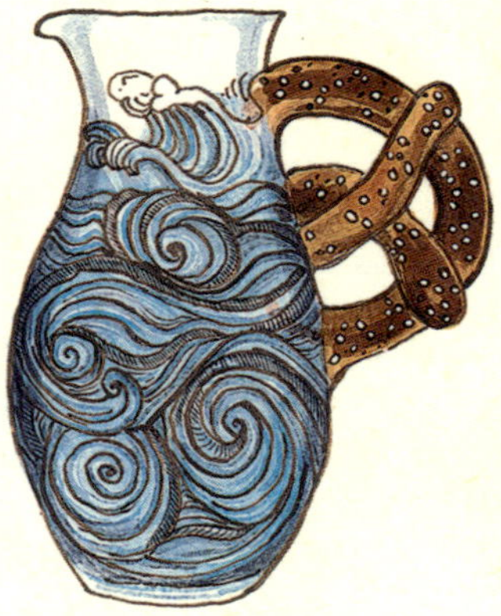

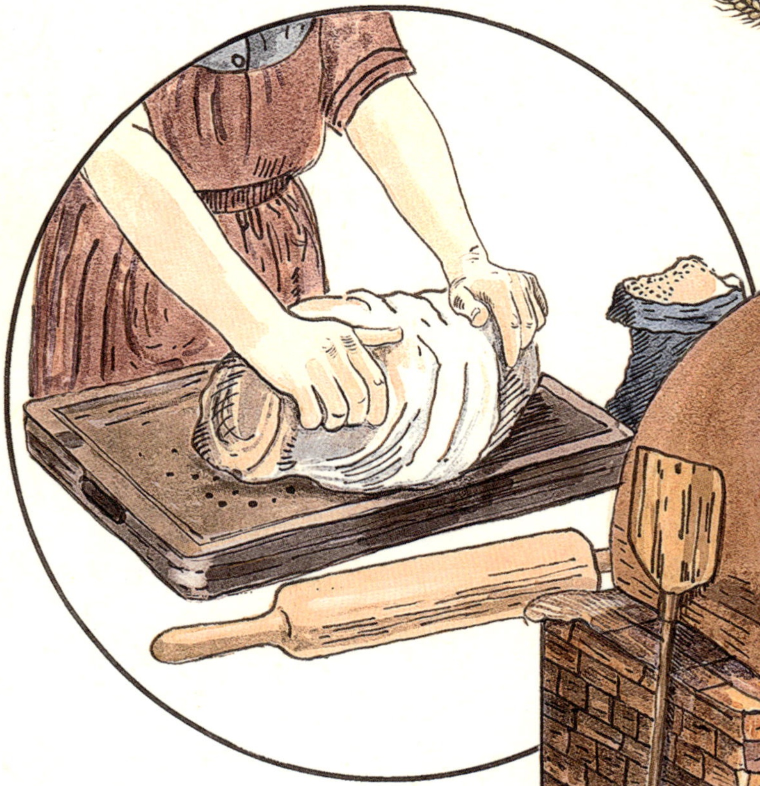

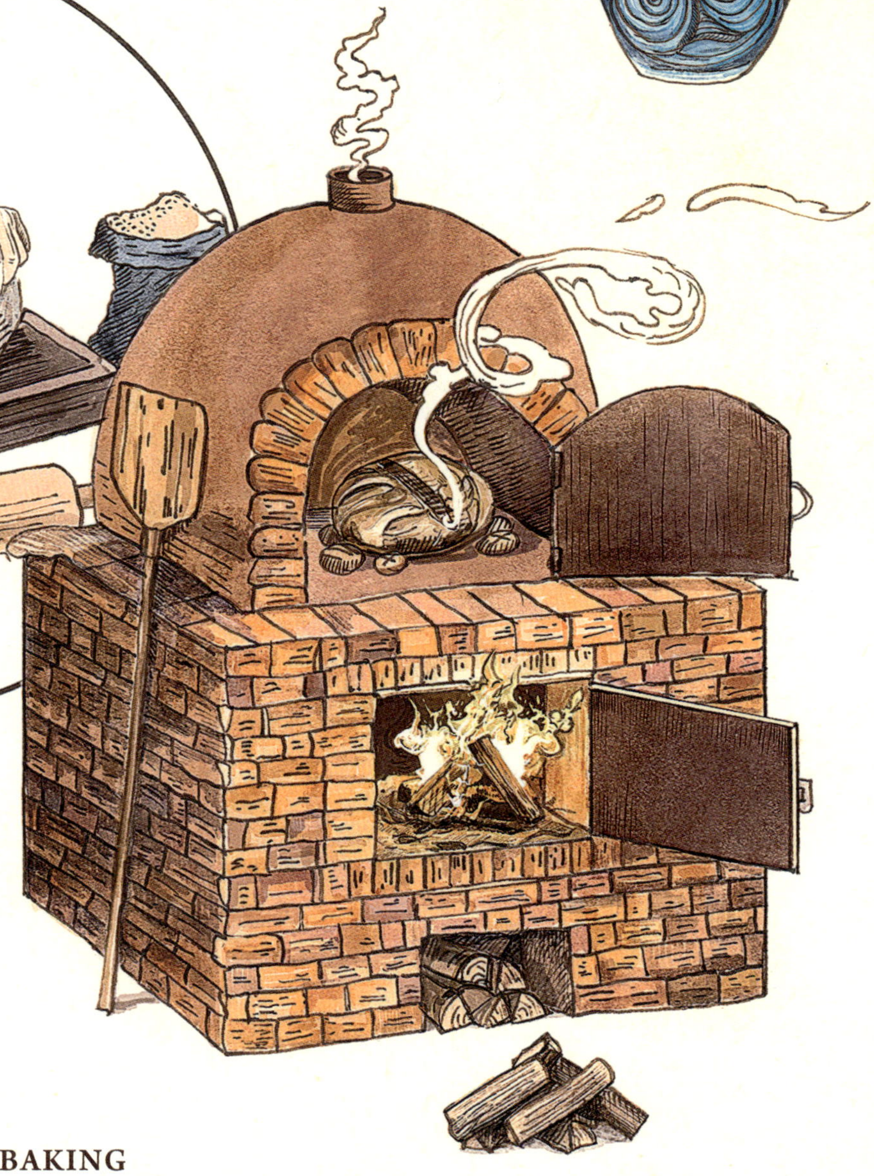

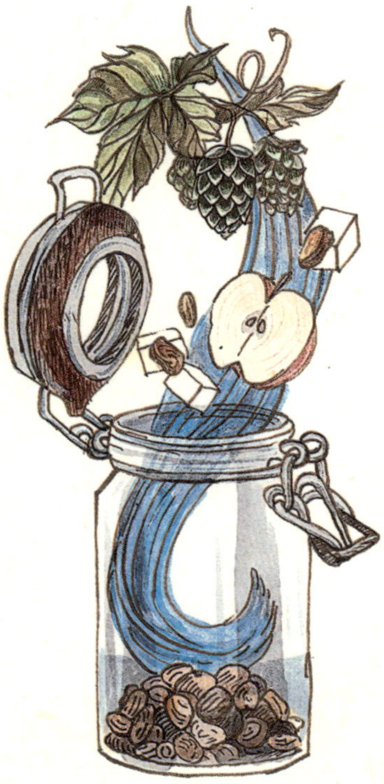

BREAD BAKING

After adding the starter, the dough should be kneaded and set aside in a warm place for a couple of hours to allow the yeast to produce enough carbon dioxide. Then place the dough in a cold place for a few more hours so that the dough becomes stiffer and the gas is distributed evenly.

Almost immediately after baking, the bread starts to become stale due to the loss of moisture, when starch molecules in the crumb return to their crystallized state. This happens even in humid conditions. But the process can also be regulated — heat the bread to 60°C and wait until the starch and water once again become soft. You'll have fresh bread once again!

SALT & PRESERVATION

Salt is something you definitely can't do without. First of all, it's an important source of electrolytes, which play a key role in the transmission of nerve impulses and contraction of muscle fibers. Secondly, salt crystals offer great defense against bacteria that spoil your food, as well as weeds that ruin your buildings by sprouting between cracks in the brickwork. The good news is that salt is a plentiful resource. There are many different ways to obtain it.

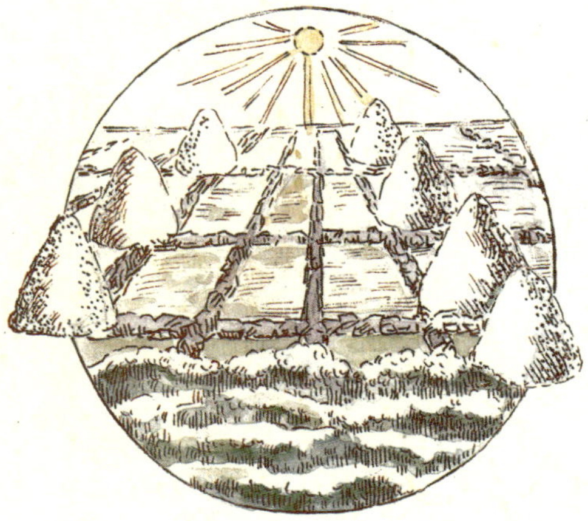

The easiest way to procure salt is from water. Search your local lakes — they may have a thick salt deposit on the bottom. Can't find anything nearby? Create an artificial lake yourself. If you live in a hot climate by the sea, dig a few pools nearby. Pour seawater into the first and let it settle so that heavy impurities fall to the bottom. Collect the liquid and move it to the second pool. Allow the water to evaporate, and you're left with pure salt.

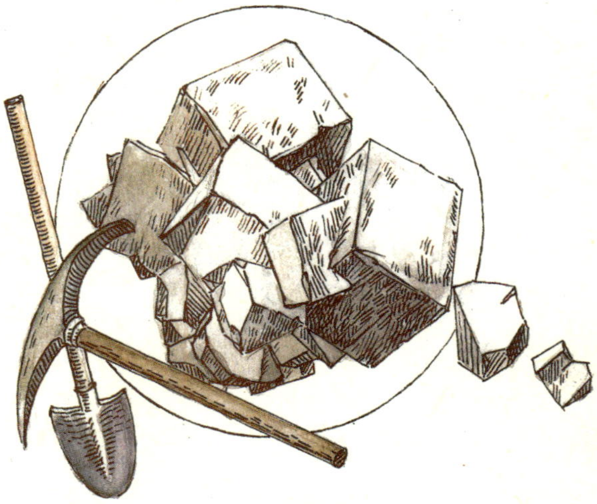

The earth's crust contains layers of rock salt. They were formed as ancient saltwater bodies dried up. This salt is then extracted in a mine or a quarry.

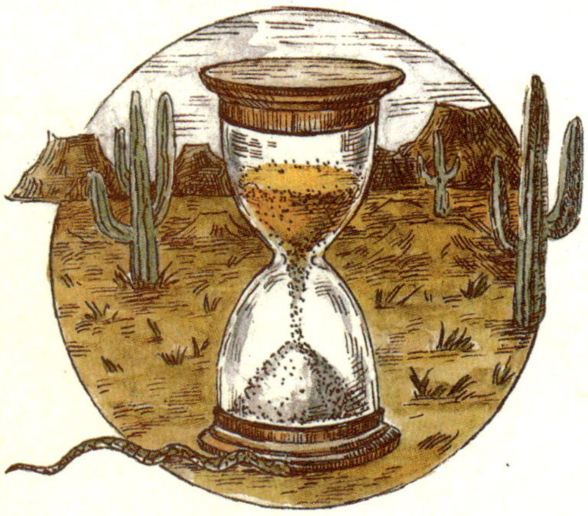

In arid regions where the groundwater is close to the surface, more water may evaporate from the lower layers of soil than can be replaced by precipitation, in which case the soil becomes salinated and a salt marsh is formed. Pour water over this soil to form a solution, then all you have to do is filter and boil off or evaporate the water. By the way, any wells you dig in this area will probably also be salty.

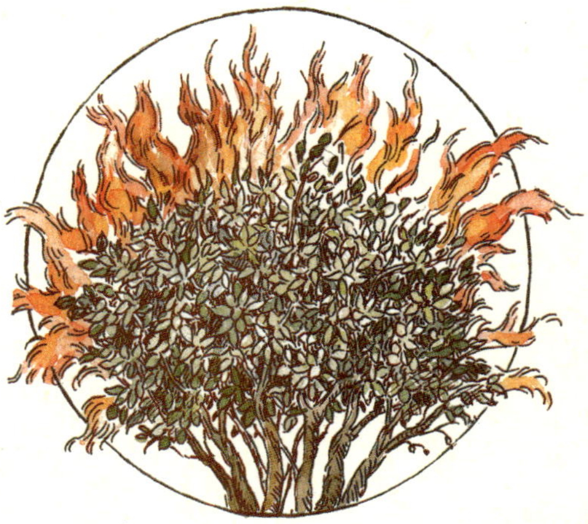

Wood ash may taste salty but be careful — this is not the kind of salt you want. The main water-soluble components of ash are potassium salts, carbonates, chlorides and sulfates, and you need sodium chloride, which is only present in very small quantities in ash. Therefore, it is better to use wood only as fuel for evaporating water from a sodium chloride solution obtained through other methods.

EVAPORATION

The evaporation point of salt is much higher than the evaporation point of water. You can use evaporation to extract salt from brine. In hot climates, all you need to do is pour saltwater into a wide, shallow container and leave it in direct sunlight for several days then collect the dry salt from the bottom of the container. If you're in a cooler climate, you can speed up the process by boiling it over a fire. As the water evaporates, the salt solution will become saturated and the salt will precipitate and can then be filtered out. And if it's just below freezing outside, you can save your fuel: Brine also freezes at a lower temperature than freshwater, so if the ambient temperature is between these two freezing points, the water will freeze by pushing the salt molecules beneath the surface of the ice. Eventually, you're left with freshwater ice on top and a concentrated brine at the bottom.

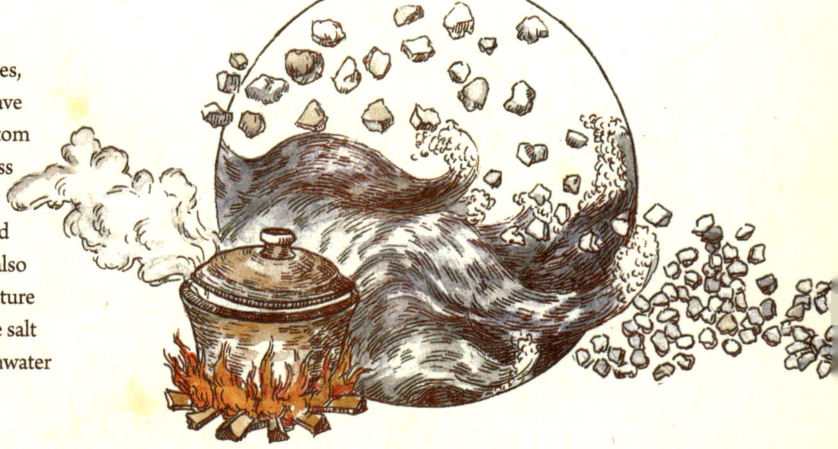

Molten salt can be employed as an efficient way of storing thermal energy. It can be used to temporarily store heat energy: First, electricity is transformed into heat, or heat energy is stored directly in molten salt, which is then kept in an insulated tank until it is needed to produce steam and converted back into electric energy (page 192).

Adding supplementary salt to your diet isn't always necessary. The role of sodium in bioelectric processes is the same for all living cells, meaning that this element is found naturally in many animal and plant products. All you need to do to replenish your daily sodium supply is eat 300 g of meat.

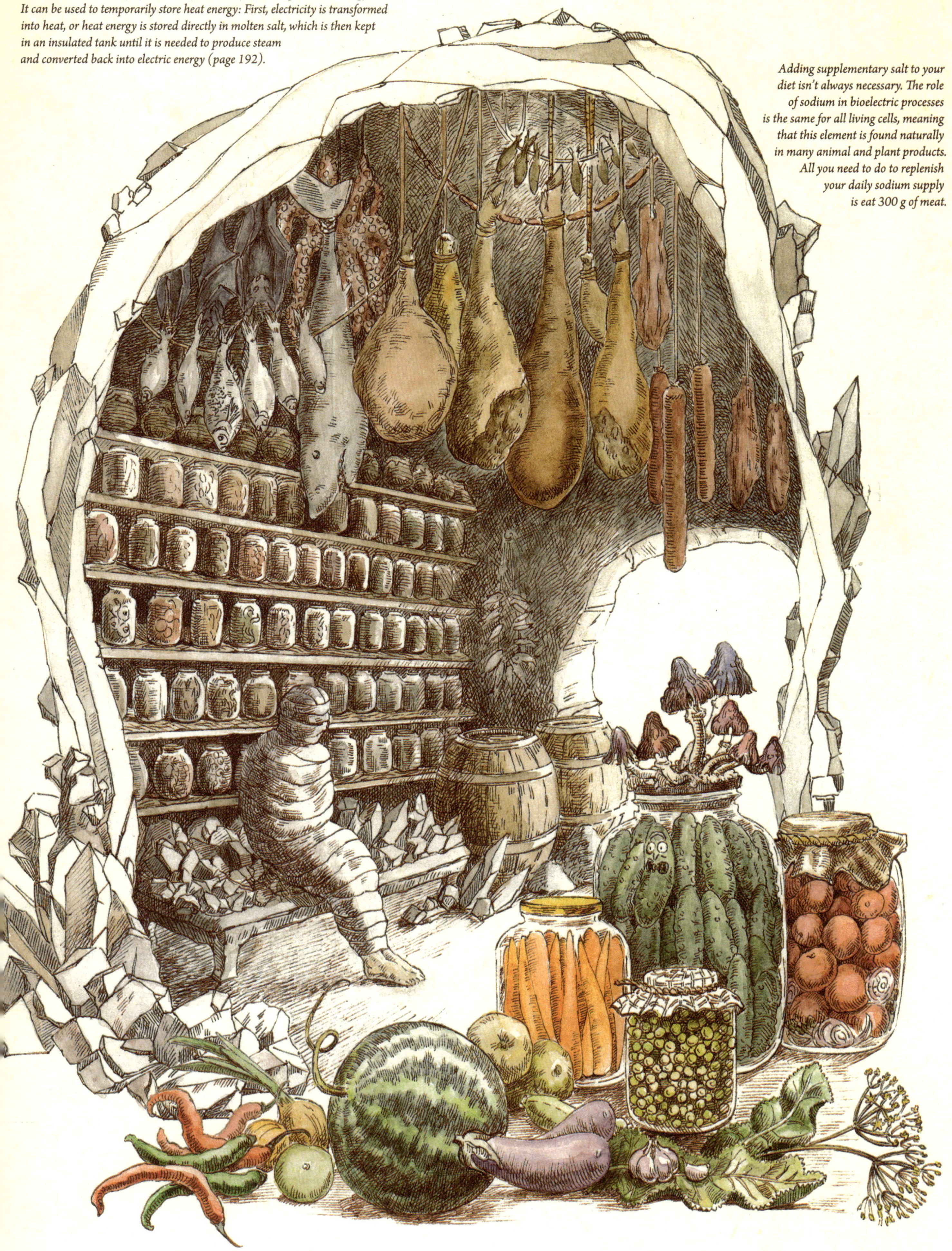

For some organisms, salt is life, and for others, it's a death sentence. Many microbes die in 10% salt solution. This makes salt an excellent preservative. Use it to store fish, meat and vegetables for long periods of time. Anything can be salted and pickled, from plant roots to mammoth carcasses.

If you're lucky enough to find a salt cave, you can use it to store massive amounts of food. But be sure not to ingest too much salt, as it could be harmful. Humans require 3–4 grams of dietary salt every day and no more.

DRYING & SMOKING

Drying and smoking are two excellent ways to slow the process of bacterial decay that spoils food. Drying removes the vital water that bacteria need to reproduce and survive, and smoke contains chemicals that slow bacterial growth. Sunlight and fermentation transform the fats into an extremely energy-dense substance.

Smoking also partially dehydrates the food, creating an inhospitable environment for bacteria while simultaneously permeating it with bacteriostatic preservative chemicals. Now you can be sure you'll have a steady source of food to last you on long journeys or cold, hard winters.

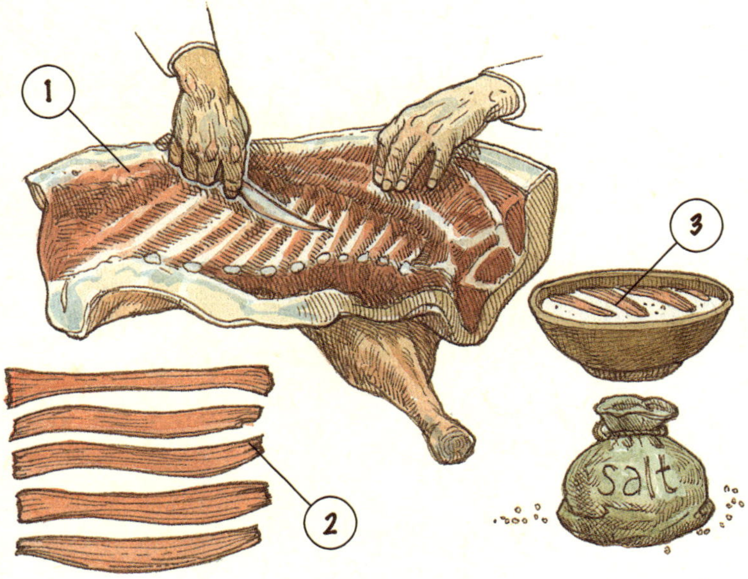

DRYING MEAT AND FISH

Remove any bones, tendons and excess fat (1). Cut the meat into smaller pieces (2) and rub with salt and spices or soak in brine (3). You'll know your brine is salty enough if a raw egg floats when placed in the solution. Hang meat outdoors in a well-ventilated area at least 1.5–2 m from the ground to prevent animal interference (4). Air circulation is vital to ensure that the meat doesn't start to rot. The temperature is not particularly important as long as it does not exceed 40°C.

During the drying process, food is partially dehydrated and fermented. As a result, the juices inside thicken. If the weather is dry and windy, small pieces of meat and small fish will dry in just a couple of days. In less ideal conditions, it may take more than 2 weeks.

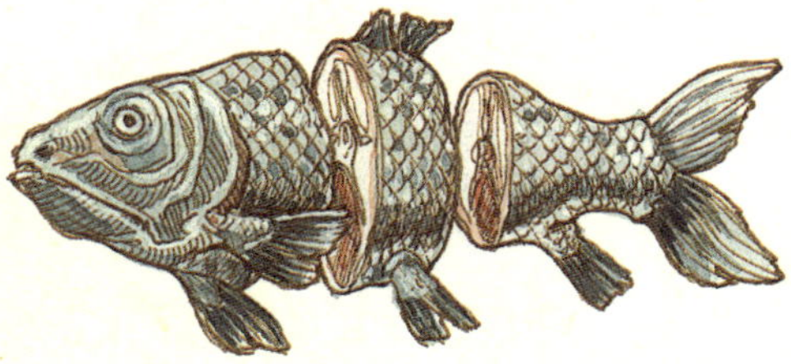

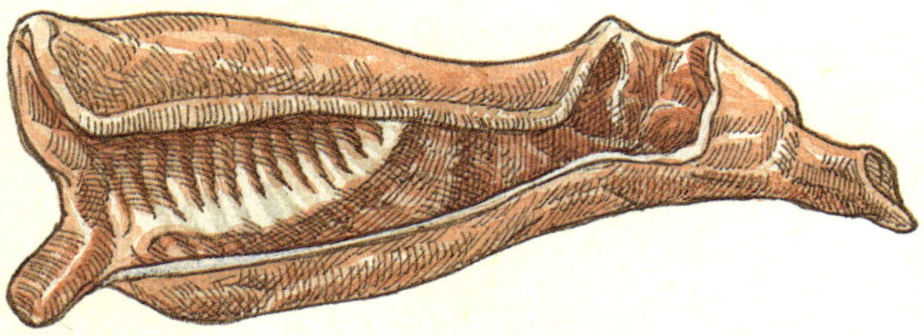

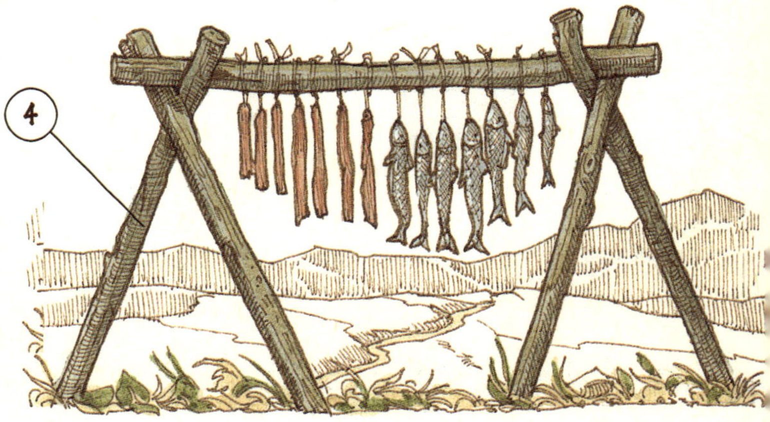

DRYING FRUITS AND VEGGIES

Fleshy fruits are best because their sugary juices thicken up easily. To prevent tomatoes from rotting before they are fully dehydrated, place them on a mesh screen so that there is airflow running both underneath and over the top and cover with a cloth to repel insects. Add a little sun and wind power and you have yourself a tasty snack.

Place the slices in a jar, fill to the brim with oil and seal to keep a small taste of summer with you all throughout the winter months. Juicy fruits such as persimmons, dates, plums, apricots or even melons can be cured in the same way. Pears, apples and similar fruits should only be dehydrated and not cured, as they are hard and their moisture evaporates quickly.

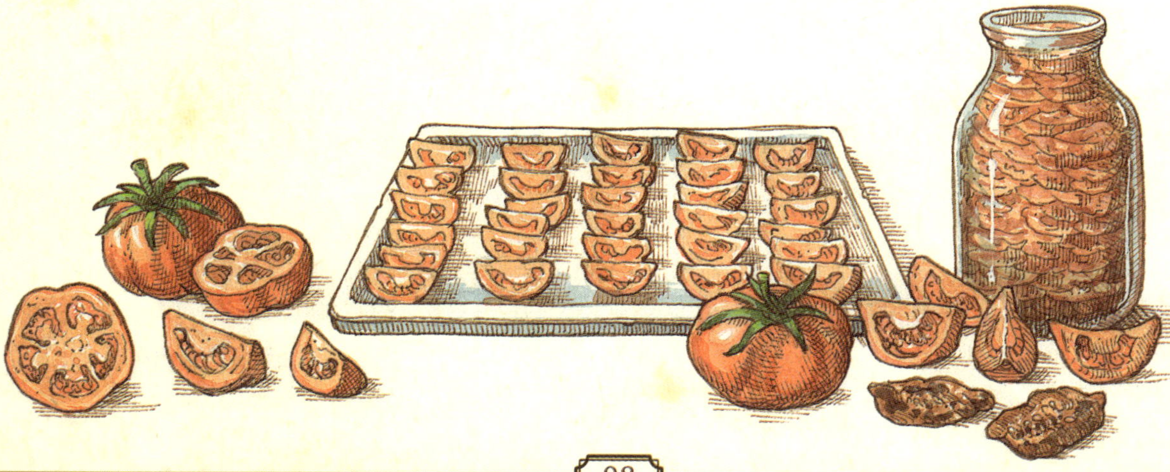

COLD SMOKING

For this process, the smoke must first be allowed to cool (20–25°C or lower). The proper temperature can be achieved by passing smoke through 2–3 meters of pipe. To ensure that smoke makes it to the other side of the chimney, use a closed vessel with smoldering wood chips instead of an open fire pit. Cold smoking takes significantly longer than hot smoking — about 5 days instead of 1. Vent excess smoke periodically to regulate moisture and prevent the buildup of carcinogens. When the food is ready, hang it outdoors for a couple more hours. Cold smoked meat or fish are less fatty and contain more natural preservatives. Therefore, they are shelf stable for several months. You can even smoke cheese (page 104) using this method.

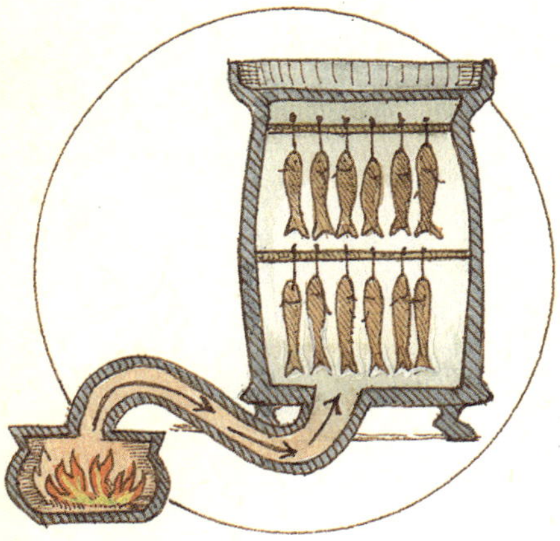

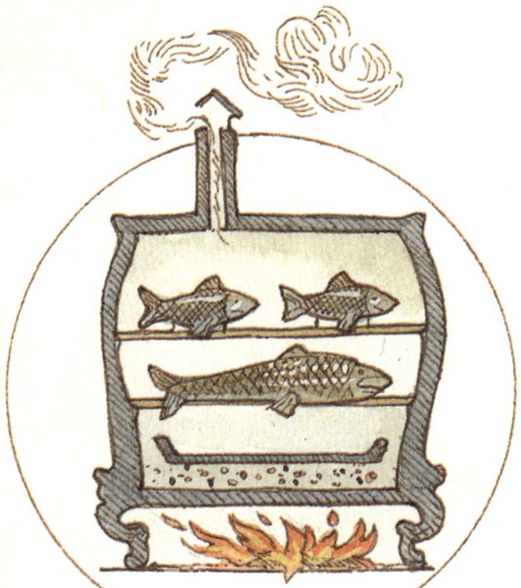

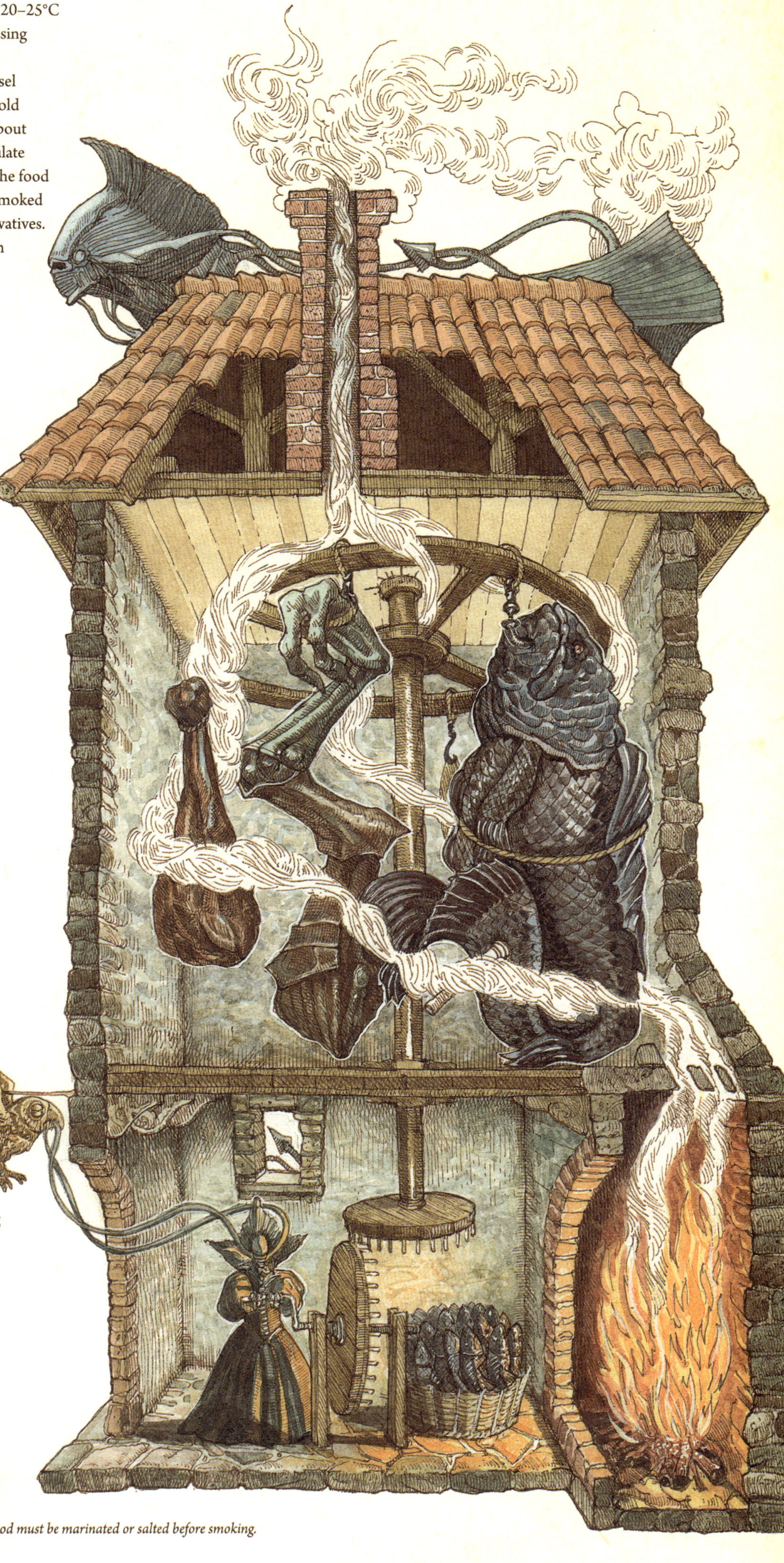

HOT SMOKING

Build your own smokehouse directly over your firepit. Any structure with lattices or hanging racks will do. Place this frame on raised bricks above the fire, then spread your food among the drying racks so that the individual pieces aren't touching each other. Pour wet fruit tree chips into your smoker. These chips won't ignite but rather will smolder for a long time. The more smoke they produce, the better, so make sure they are slightly damp. Place a lid on the smoker and wait a couple of hours.

Food must be marinated or salted before smoking.

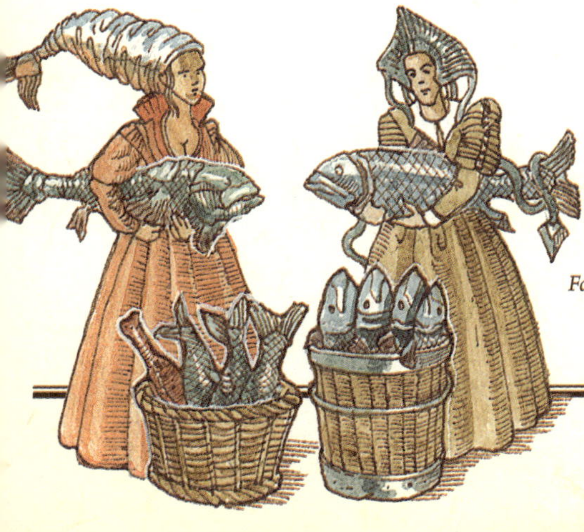

SPICES

Variety is the spice of life. New experiences stimulate the area of the brain associated with feelings of wellbeing, so spice up plain foods to add new life to old dishes. Herbs and spices can be derived from various parts of plants that produce a particular smell or taste. They can enhance the natural aroma, improve the consistency or add a pop of color to any dish. Some even have antimicrobial properties and can extend the shelf life of your food.

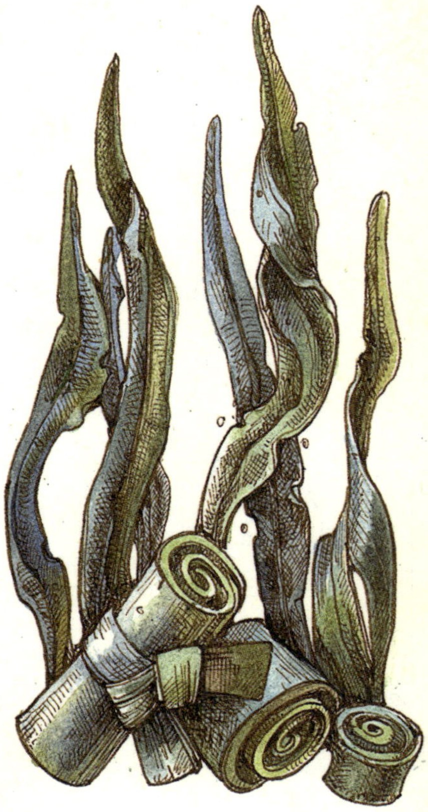

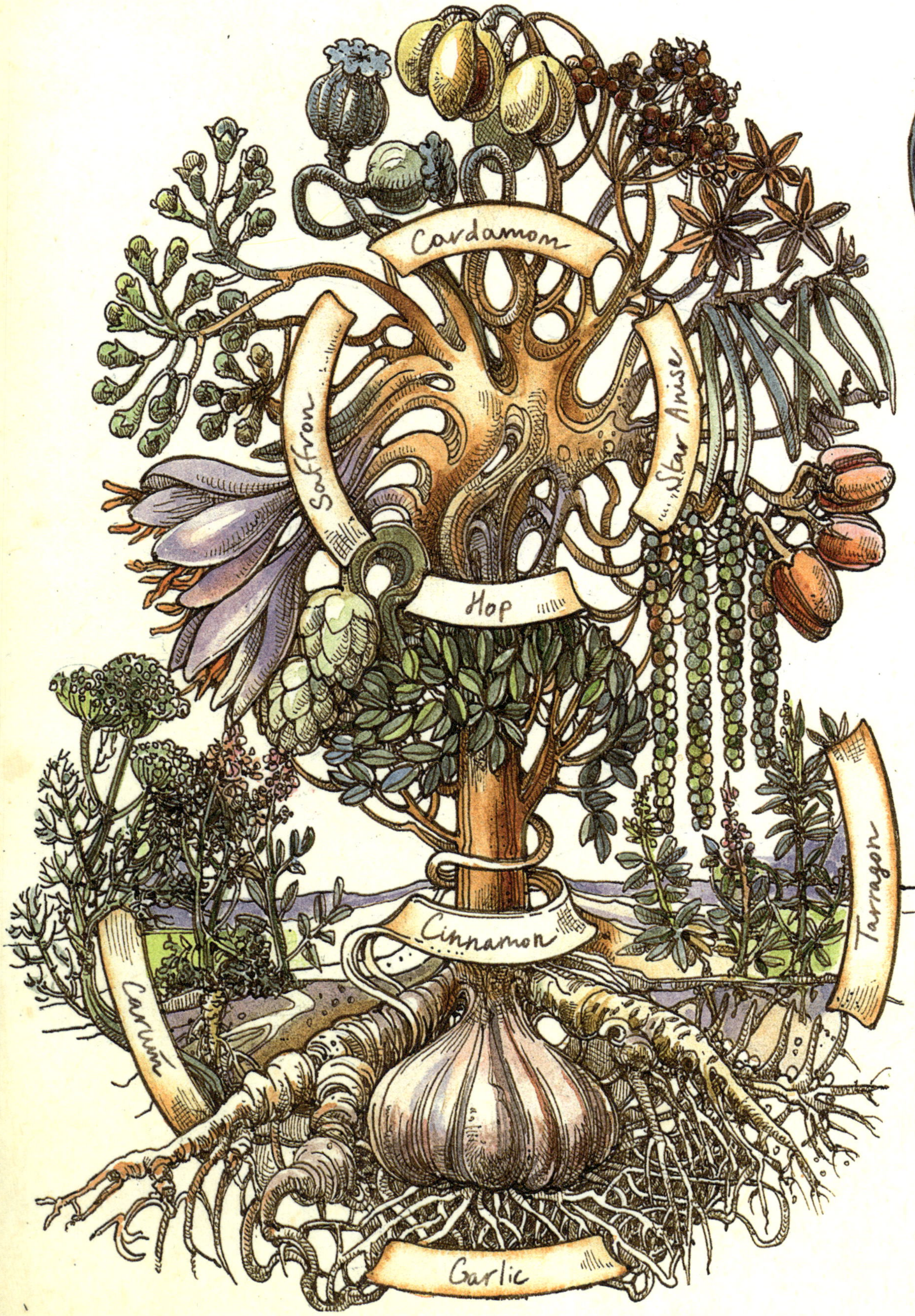

UMAMI

Try to describe the flavor of a food using just one word. What comes to mind first? Probably something like sweet, sour, bitter or salty. But there's one more flavor that can be described as "delicious" or "pleasantly spicy." This is umami, and it acts as a flavor enhancer. One natural source of umami is kombu seaweed. Look for long brown algae in your nearby bay growing at a depth of 5–10 meters. Soak the komba in water for several hours, and then use the strained solution to prepare meals or make a sauce by adding dried mackerel flakes and shiitake mushrooms to the infusion.

Or you can dry your seaweed and use its flavor long after kombu season is over. Spread the kombu on the rocks along the shore and dry it in the sun for about 5 hours. Then grind it into powder.

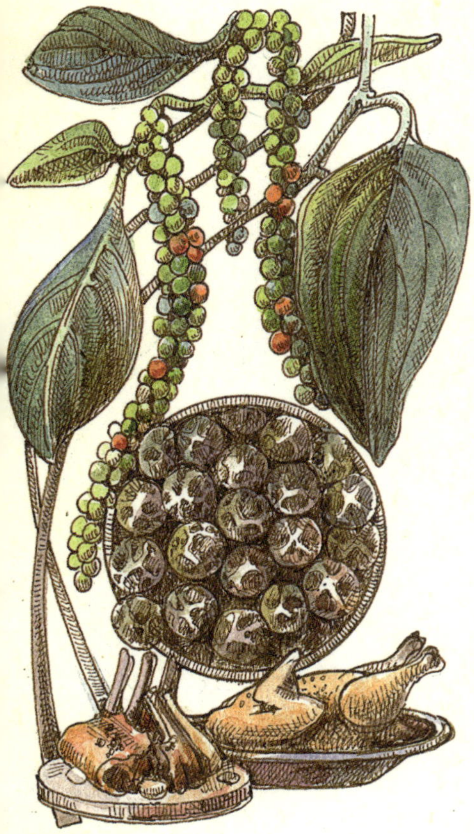

Pepper
This refers to one plant, Piper nigrum, and the three different varieties (black, white and green) represent different stages in the fruit's growth cycle. The oil is what produces the aroma, and the alkaloid piperine is responsible for the taste. After a while in storage, the aroma will eventually disappear, while the pungent-bitter taste persists for a long time.

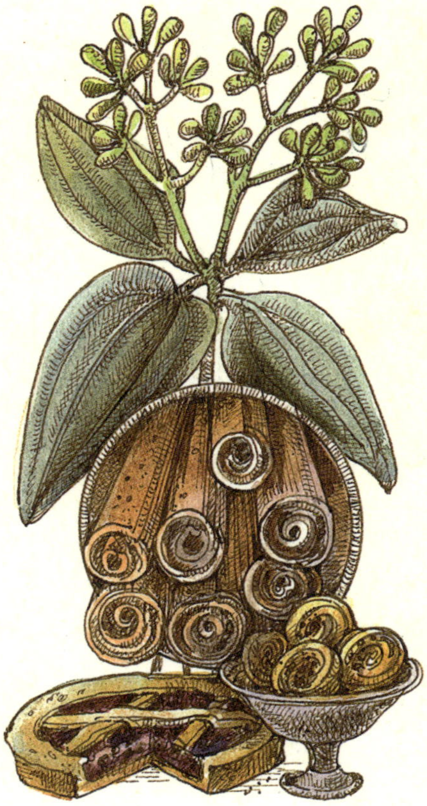

Cinnamon
This is the inner layer of bark from young shoots of plants in the genus Cinnamomum. It contains an essential oil that has a strong warming effect. Dry in the shade and the bark will curl up into a tube.

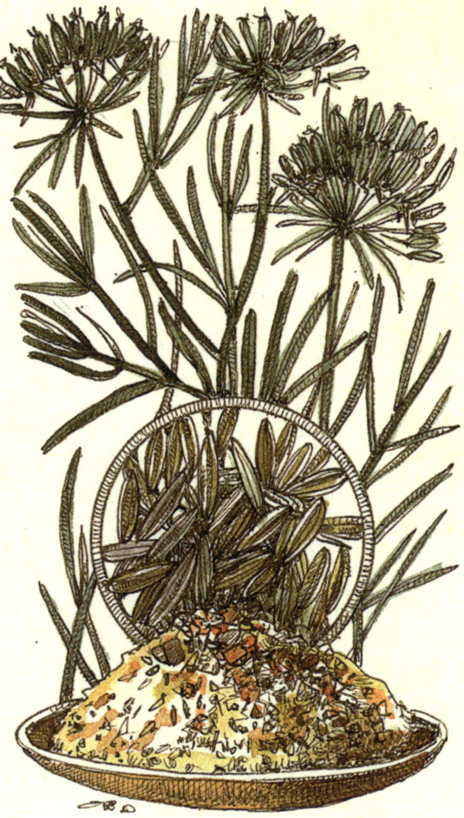

Cumin
Dried seeds of the spicy herb Cuminum cyminum. This spice masks the smell of fish and meat, so add to dishes that have gamey lamb or river fish with a muddy aftertaste.

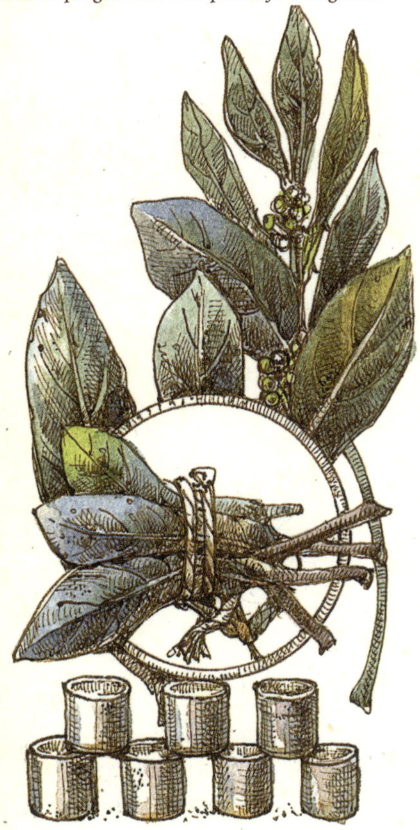

Bay Leaves
From an evergreen tree in the Laurus family. In addition to fragrant essential oils, they contain eugenol, which has an antiseptic effect. They retain their properties even when dried. Add the bay leaves shortly before the end of the preparation of the dish and don't forget to remove before serving so they don't add extra bitterness.

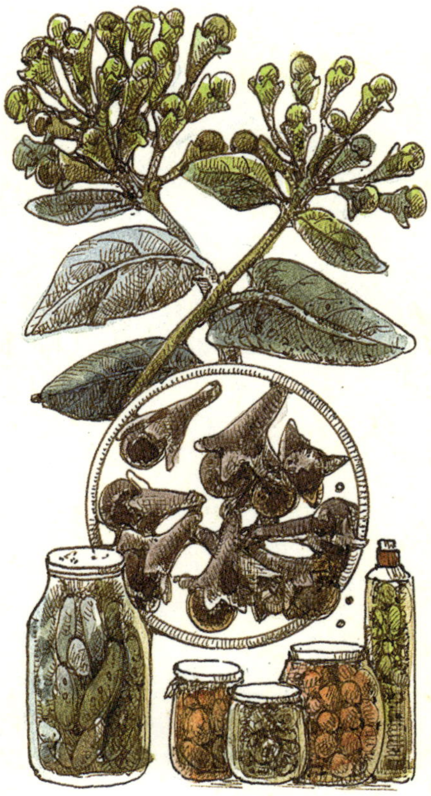

Cloves
Collect the unflowered buds of the tropical carnation tree Caryophyllus aromaticus. Fortunately, it blooms twice a year. The buds contain a lot of essential oils and should be dried in the sun before use. If they're left to stew for too long, they'll become bitter, so add just 5 minutes before the dish is cooked.

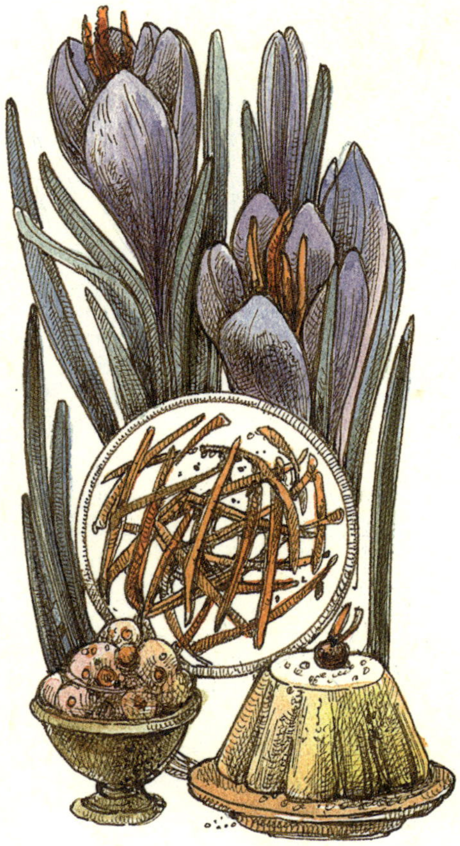

Saffron
Dried stamens of the Crocus flower. Each flower has three stigmas, which must be picked on the day the bud opens. You need to process 80,000 plants to get a single kilogram of the spice. Saffron does not mix well with other spices. It is better to use it on its own and in very small doses; otherwise, you will overwhelm the other flavors.

SUGAR

When you have no extra energy to expend and feel sluggish, you have no time for inventing. Your mood is directly dependent on your body's energy stores. Sugar will replenish your energy in a jiffy. Your cells can easily absorb the glucose it contains and metabolize it into energy. A good dose of glucose instantly stimulates the brain's pleasure center and raises levels of serotonin, the "happy hormone." That's why sweets are always a good mood booster.

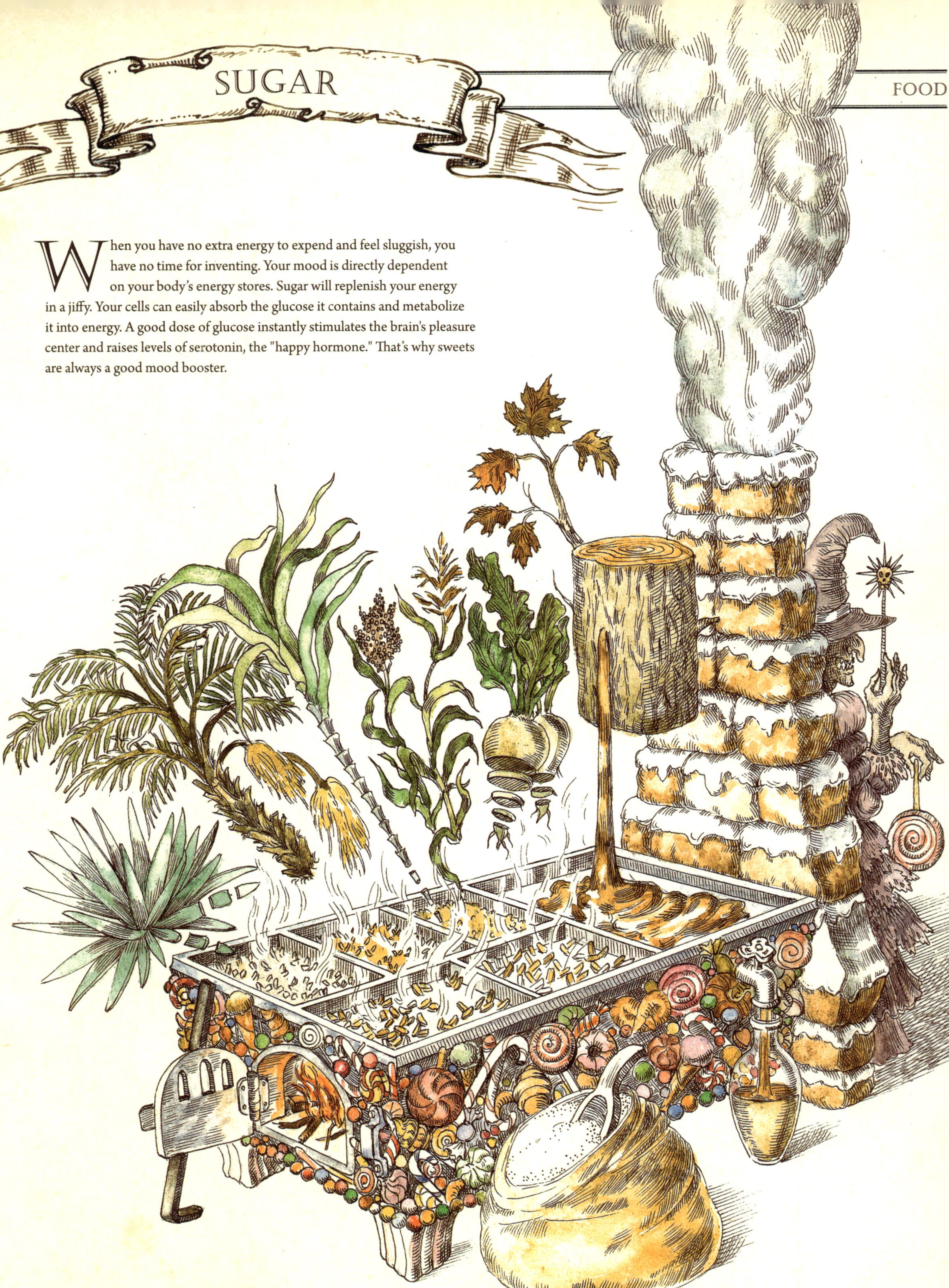

EVAPORATION

Sugar can be extracted from plants. Sugar beets, sugarcane, sorghum and some types of palms and maples are all good options. All you need to do is harness the power of evaporation. This requires a small stove. Build the main body out of bricks and on top place shallow iron containers with wide bottoms. The larger the surface area of the container, the faster the process will go.

If using sugar beets or cane, wash them, chop and boil them and strain the resulting syrup. Use a press or mill to grind large quantities of beets or cane. If using sorghum, simply cut the stems and squeeze the juice out. Maple and palm sap can also be directly harvested from trees by tapping (making a deep hole or cut in the tree).

Make as much of this raw "sugar juice" as possible — 40 liters of juice will produce just 1 liter of syrup. When the juice or syrup is prepared, pour it into iron containers on a stove. Boil the liquid until it is dark brown and as thick as possible. (Use any waste plant material as fuel for the boilers.) After that, leave the liquid in a cool place to harden and crystallize. This can take up to 2 weeks. The resulting crystals can be ground to smaller granules.

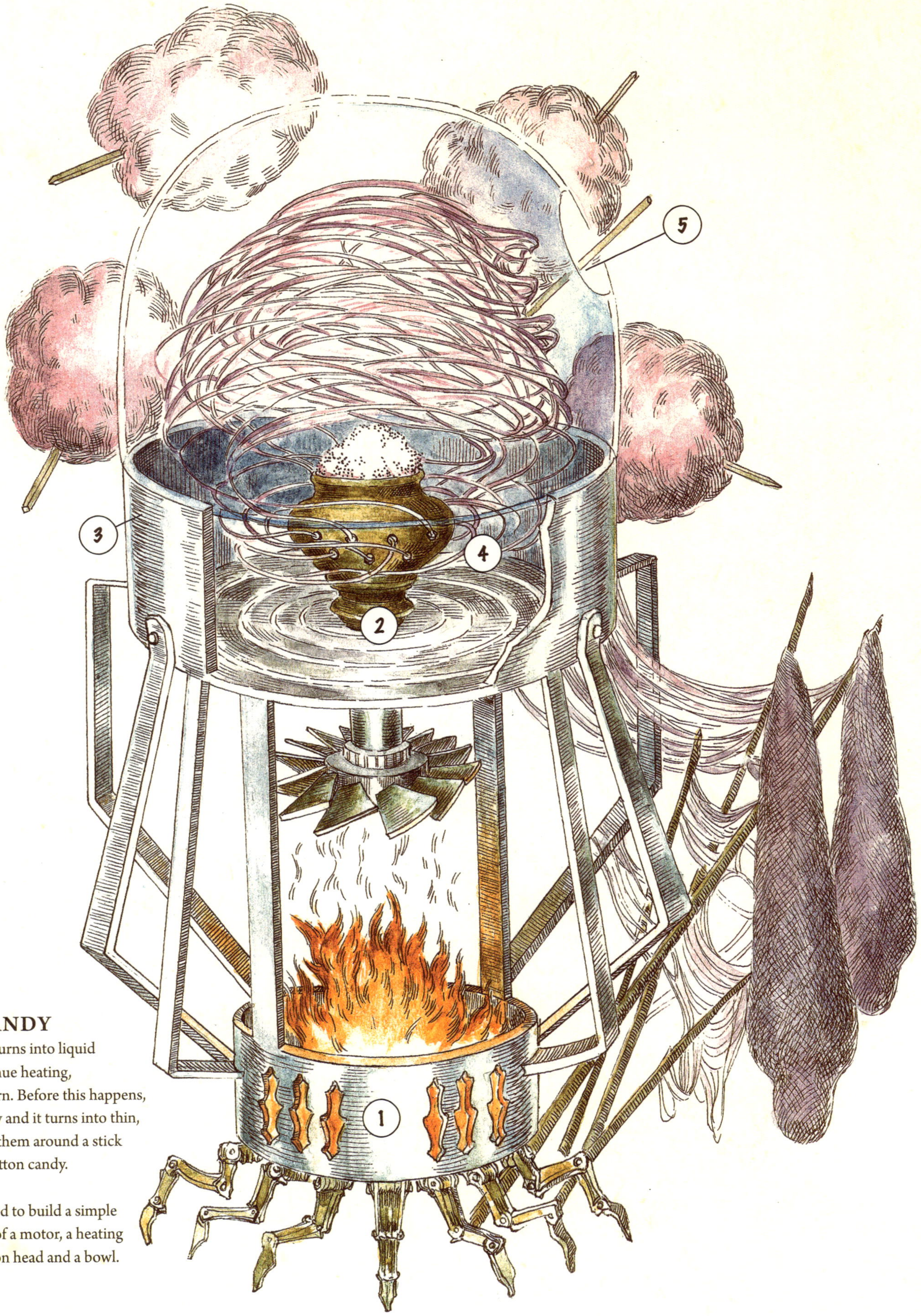

COTTON CANDY

When heated, sugar turns into liquid caramel. If you continue heating, the sugar starts to burn. Before this happens, spin the sugar quickly and it turns into thin, wispy threads. Wrap them around a stick for a fun fair treat: cotton candy.

To make it, you'll need to build a simple machine. It consists of a motor, a heating element, a distribution head and a bowl.

1. The body of the machine is an iron container. The heat source (alcohol lamp, fire) is placed under it.
2. The working part — the distributor head — will spin when connected to any motor. You can even turn the pedals, which will be connected to the shaft of the apparatus through the gearbox.
3. The upper part of the appliance is a bowl with high walls. A distribution head (a small iron container with holes) is attached to the middle of the bowl. Sugar is poured into it, and gradually, it heats up and melts.
4. When spun, centrifugal force pulls the sugar out of the holes in the distributor head and stretches them into thin threads.
5. Wind the resulting strands of sugar around a stick by dipping it into the bowl as it spins. Your cotton candy is ready!

CURD & CHEESE

Milk spoiled again? Trying to combat lactic acid bacteria is a losing battle — at most, it'll win you a couple of days. It's better to lean into the funk and preserve the goodness in the milk by making cheese. This product is a kind of milk concentrate: The proteins, fats and minerals within occur in approximately the same proportions but are absorbed much better by the body. And you can store some types of cheese not just for months but for years. Meanwhile, like a well-aged wine, they become even more delicious. Cheese is a great travel food — a couple of chunks will give you a rich complex of vitamins and minerals able to sustain you over a long journey. And if you're running out of entertainment ideas, you can organize a cheese-chasing competition: Who can catch the wheel of cheese before it rolls to the bottom of the hill?

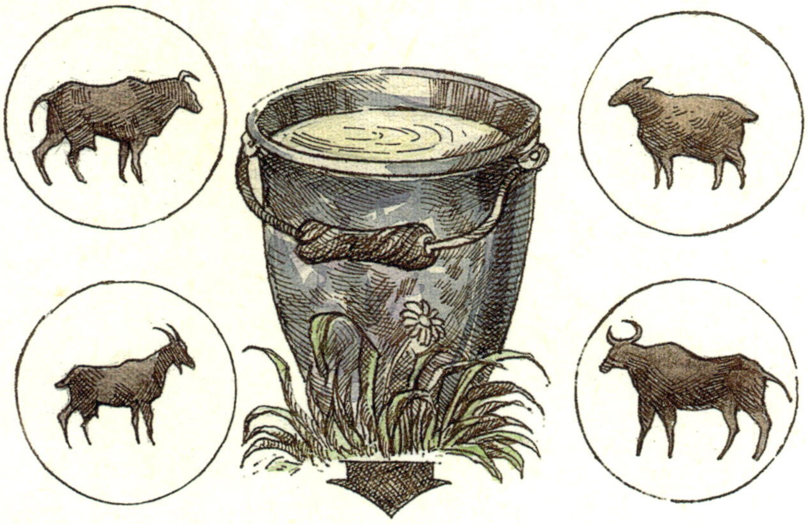

CHEESE

Cow, sheep, goat and even donkey milk can be used to make cheese. Found a herd of buffalo grazing nearby? Fantastic! If you can manage to tame them, buffalo milk makes an excellent cheese. There are many ways to radically change the taste, color and texture of cheese. Try adding spices (page 100), changing the aging time or using different enzymes and bacteria.

ENZYMES

The enzyme chymosin used in the preparation of rennet cheeses is obtained from the dried and grated stomachs of newborn calves or lambs. If this causes ethical issues for you, you'll have to find a replacement either for rennet cheeses or the enzymes. There are options: mold bacteria (page 100); leavened bread (page 94); berries used to enhance fermentation in wines (page 62); leftover whey from previous cheese or cheese curd production; fig juice with the seeds removed; or a tincture of nettles and salt. Feed the starter culture by adding water, fruit, milk, etc., so that it grows. Once it has developed, store it in a cold place.

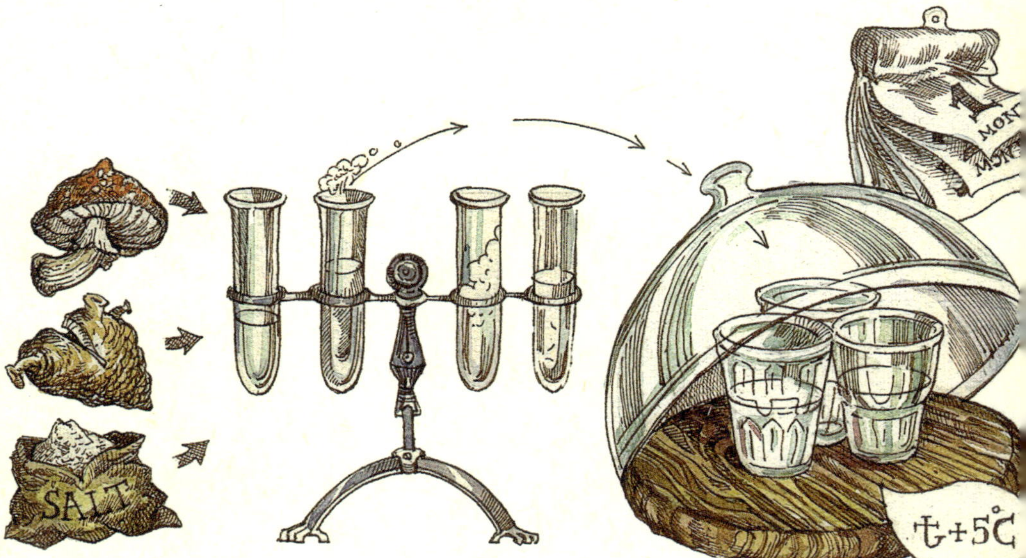

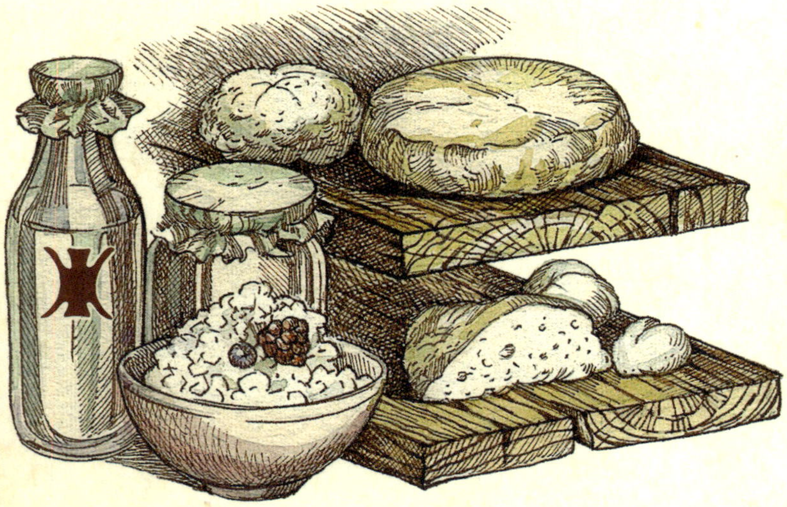

Making rennet cheese

1. *Allow the milk to "ripen": keep it at a temperature of 8–12°C for 12–24 hours. This will activate the microflora.*
2. *Then pasteurize by heating the milk to 90°C. This will kill unnecessary microorganisms that can interfere with the fermentation process.*
3. *Add your enzyme (or substitute) and acid. The milk will separate into solid curd and watery whey.*
4. *Cut the resulting curd with a wide blade, separating it from the whey. Do not be alarmed if it turns green — this means that it's ready. Add any spices, salt, nuts, etc., and press the cheese into molds.*
5. *Now, you must wait for the cheese to mature, but you'll have to check in on it frequently. Once every 2–3 weeks, the cheese must be washed (this will get rid of unnecessary microorganisms) and flipped over.*

You can smoke the cheese, sprinkle it with spices and even rub it with alcohol. The most important element is constantly maintaining the humidity level and temperature in the room. Due to the release of carbon dioxide, which is produced as the starter cultures ferment the milk, holes will appear in the cheese. It usually takes about 2–2.5 months to fully ripen, but this depends on the type of cheese and storage conditions. How do you know it's ready? Hit the cheese block with a silver hammer. If it rings, the cheese is ripe.

UNRIPENED CHEESE

Add vinegar or lemon juice to milk that has been heated to 75°C. The fattier the milk, the better. Once the milk has separated, place the solids in a cheesecloth and hang until all the excess liquid drains out. Season with salt, herbs and spices and store in a cold place. The process can be simplified even further: just cook the milk and acid mixture, stirring occasionally, until the curd separates from the whey.

TOFU

If you are a vegetarian (or don't have access to dairy animals), you can make a cheese substitute using soy. Making tofu is similar to making regular cheese but you use soy milk instead. Magnesium chloride, citric acid or calcium sulfate is used to curdle the mixture. If you can't get your hands on any of these, use seawater — it contains calcium and magnesium salts.

BLUE CHEESE

A little mold isn't always a bad thing. Some cheeses are made by adding edible molds, such as penicillin (page 34). To make this type of cheese, inoculate the curd mass with mold spores before ripening and use long needles or sticks to poke air holes inside the cheese mass. The air will allow blue mold to develop evenly throughout the entire cheese.

PROCESSED CHEESE

Want to spread cheese on your bread? Spreadable cheeses are made by melting rennet cheeses and adding things such as cottage cheese, sour cream, milk or butter and spices and all kinds of other fillers (onions, mushrooms, nuts, bacon, etc.). Make a dessert cheese by adding sugar, cocoa, vanilla or syrup.

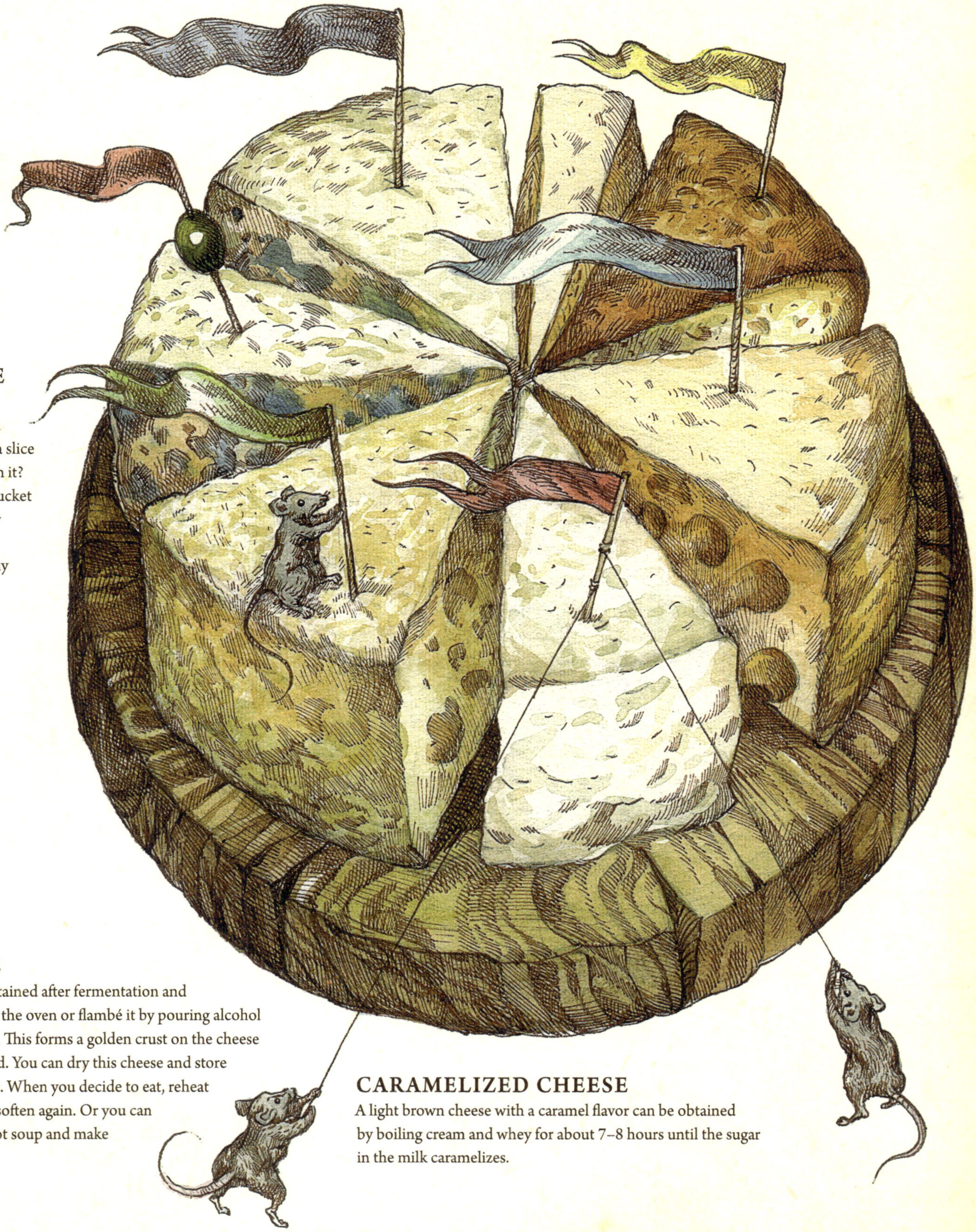

LIVING CHEESE

Think you've already tried everything and nothing can surprise you? Why not try a slice of cheese with live insects in it? Add cheese fly larvae to a bucket of sheep milk. These creepy crawlies digest the cheese, producing a flavor that many consider gourmet.

BREAD CHEESE

Take the mass of cheese obtained after fermentation and roll it into a cake. Bake it in the oven or flambé it by pouring alcohol over it and setting it aflame. This forms a golden crust on the cheese that makes it look like bread. You can dry this cheese and store it with your grains for years. When you decide to eat, reheat the stale cheese and it will soften again. Or you can add cheese "croutons" to hot soup and make a new hearty dish.

CARAMELIZED CHEESE

A light brown cheese with a caramel flavor can be obtained by boiling cream and whey for about 7–8 hours until the sugar in the milk caramelizes.

BEER

Just four ingredients — water, hops, barley and yeast — and you have a drink that will give people a reason to meet up and relax over a frothy pint or two.

Beer requires hops, which adds bitter flavor notes, supports a frothy head and helps preserve your beer. Harvest in early fall. The slightly dry hop flower has a pungent odor. You can make beer from fresh hops or dry them at a temperature not exceeding 60°C and use them later.

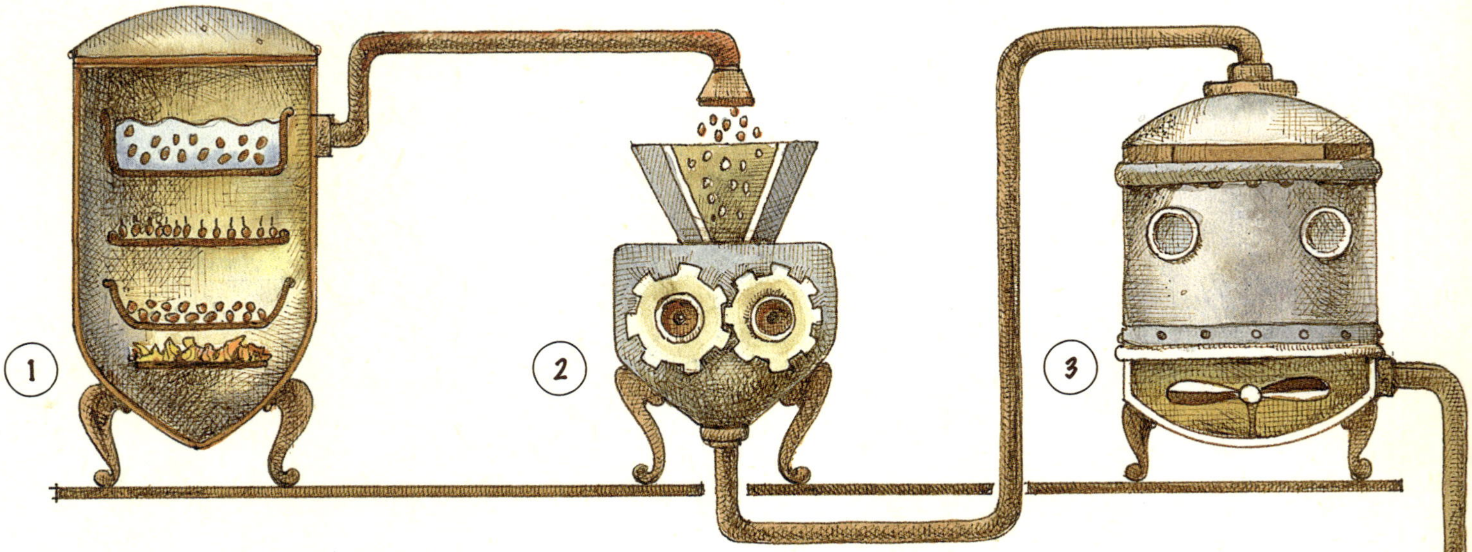

Make malt. Soak and germinate the barley kernels to start the fermentation process. Remove any sprouts and dry with hot air. The more you dry the malt — or even better, roast it — the darker the beer will be. Remember that dark, caramelized varieties cannot be made without light ones: the enzymes necessary for saccharification of the wort are "burned out" in the dark ones; that is, they are deactivated.

Mill the malted barley. Be careful, if you process it too much, the beer will turn out bitter. Make a mash by mixing 1 part ground malt with 4 parts hot water. During this process, naturally-occurring enzymes in the malt break down starch into fermentable sugars. Temperatures, cooking times and the number of cooking stages will determine the flavor of the beer (see recipes below).

Obtain a sugar-rich wort by squeezing and filtering the liquid from the mashed barley. Use a large pot with a screened chamber—a strainer on stilts that catches the solids while allowing the liquids to drain to the bottom where they can be removed via a spigot. The liquid will need to be filtered twice. Rinse the spent grain with hot water (75–78°C) — it still contains a lot of wort.

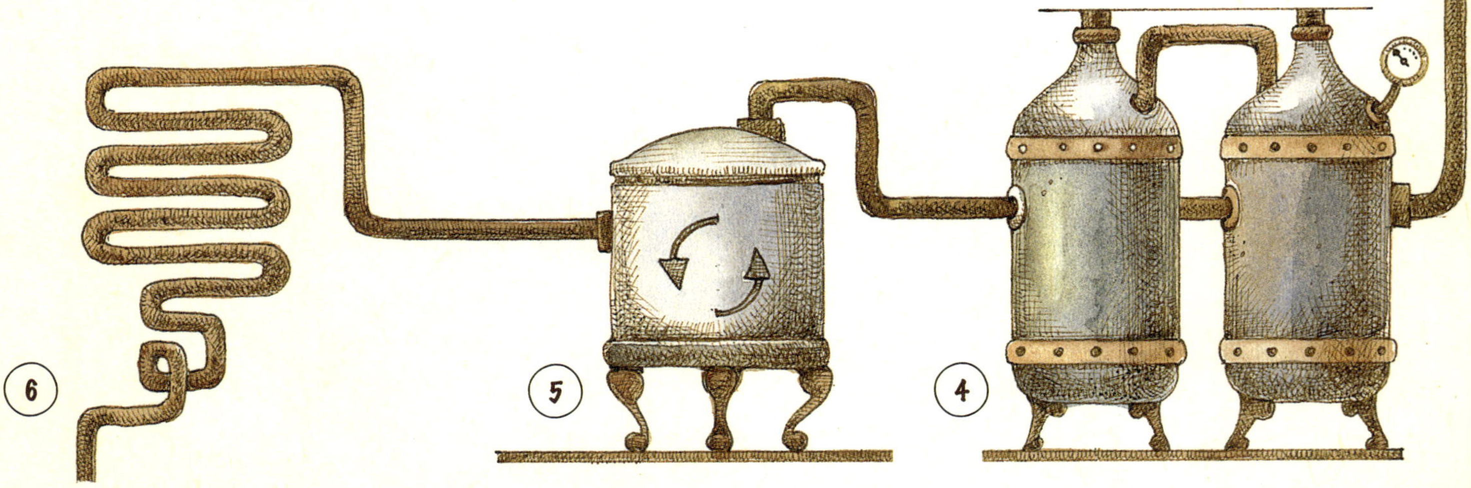

Now comes the fermentation. Yeast is used to convert the sugars into alcohol. You already know how to procure yeast from thin air (page 94). All that's left to do is add the wort, set in a dark place and wait around 2 weeks. Monitor the temperature, which should be between 15–25°C.

After boiling the wort, it needs to be cooled quickly (if you wait too long, bacteria will multiply, spoiling the taste). Stir the wort vigorously and pour it from a great height into another container to increase oxygen saturation, which will help the yeast multiply faster.

Bring the filtered wort to a boil and add your hops. Boil for at least an hour. This helps develop the flavors and sterilizes the wort of any unwanted bacteria. This stage is open to some experimentation. Through trial and error, you'll end up creating many different varieties of beer.

For storage, you can use either glass bottles or wooden barrels. Dark glass is advisable, as light can have adverse effects on the flavor. If you prefer a fizzy beer, add a small amount of sugar to each bottle when filling. The yeast will process this sugar and produce carbon dioxide, carbonating the beverage. Store in a cool, dark place but do not freeze, shake or turn the bottles — this way, the frothy drink will maintain its flavor and strength until happy hour.

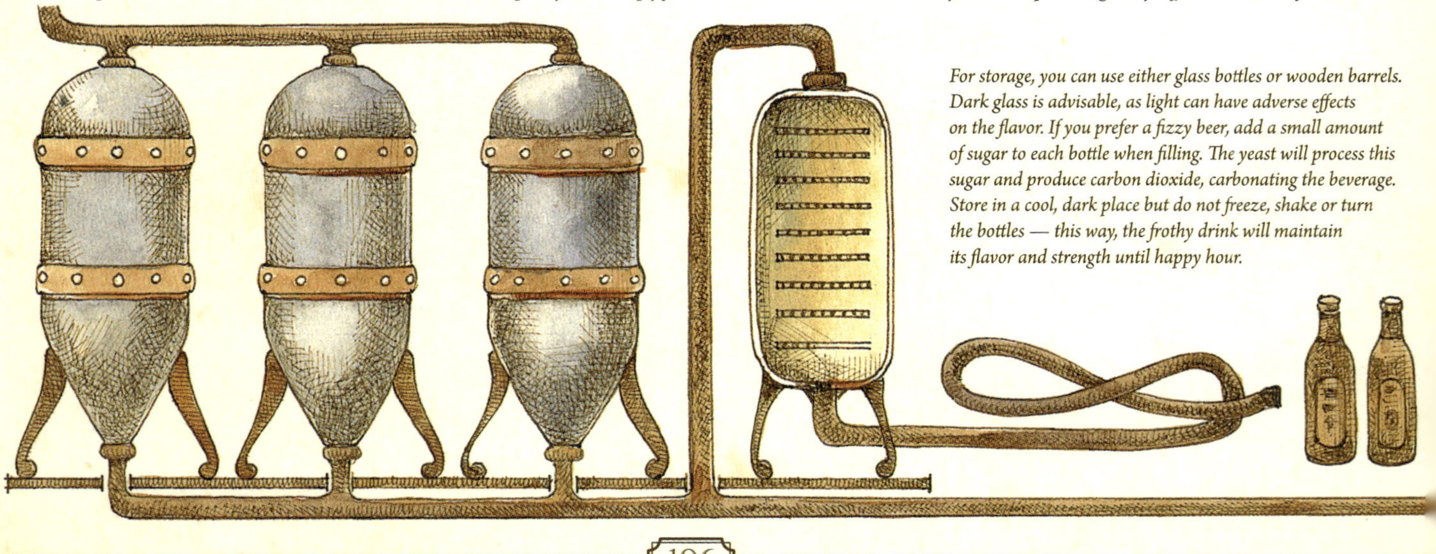

To produce excellent beer, you must start with good-quality water (page 14). The hardness and mineral content of the water has a huge effect on the taste of the beer. There is no one formula for success — different waters produce different beers. But there is one vital element of the process: All containers that the wort comes into contact with after boiling must be disinfected. Otherwise, undesirable bacteria can contaminate your brew.

Master a couple of time-tested recipes, and then start mixing things up. Experiment and see how many different types of beer you can produce. The sky's the limit!

Wheat Beer

A light beer with pronounced notes of spicy cloves and banana.

Ingredients: *60% light wheat malt, 27% light barley, 10% caramelized barley, 5% sour malt (pour the malt into a container, hydrate slightly with water, add a spoonful of yogurt and place in a sealed container in a warm place for a week).*

Mash stages:

1. *Heat a mixture of malt and water to a temperature of 45°C for 10 minutes.*
2. *Raise the temperature to 52°C for 10 minutes.*
3. *Raise to 62°C for 30 minutes.*
4. *Raise to 72°C for another 30 minutes.*
5. *Increase temperature to 78°C to finish.*

Fermentation temperature: *20°C*

Dark beer

Ingredients: *85% light barley malt and 15% roasted malt.*

Mash stages:

1. *Heat your malt and water mixture to 65°C for 60 minutes.*
2. *Raise to 72°C for 30 minutes.*
3. *Bring the mixture to 78°C then remove from heat.*

Fermentation temperature: *16°C.*

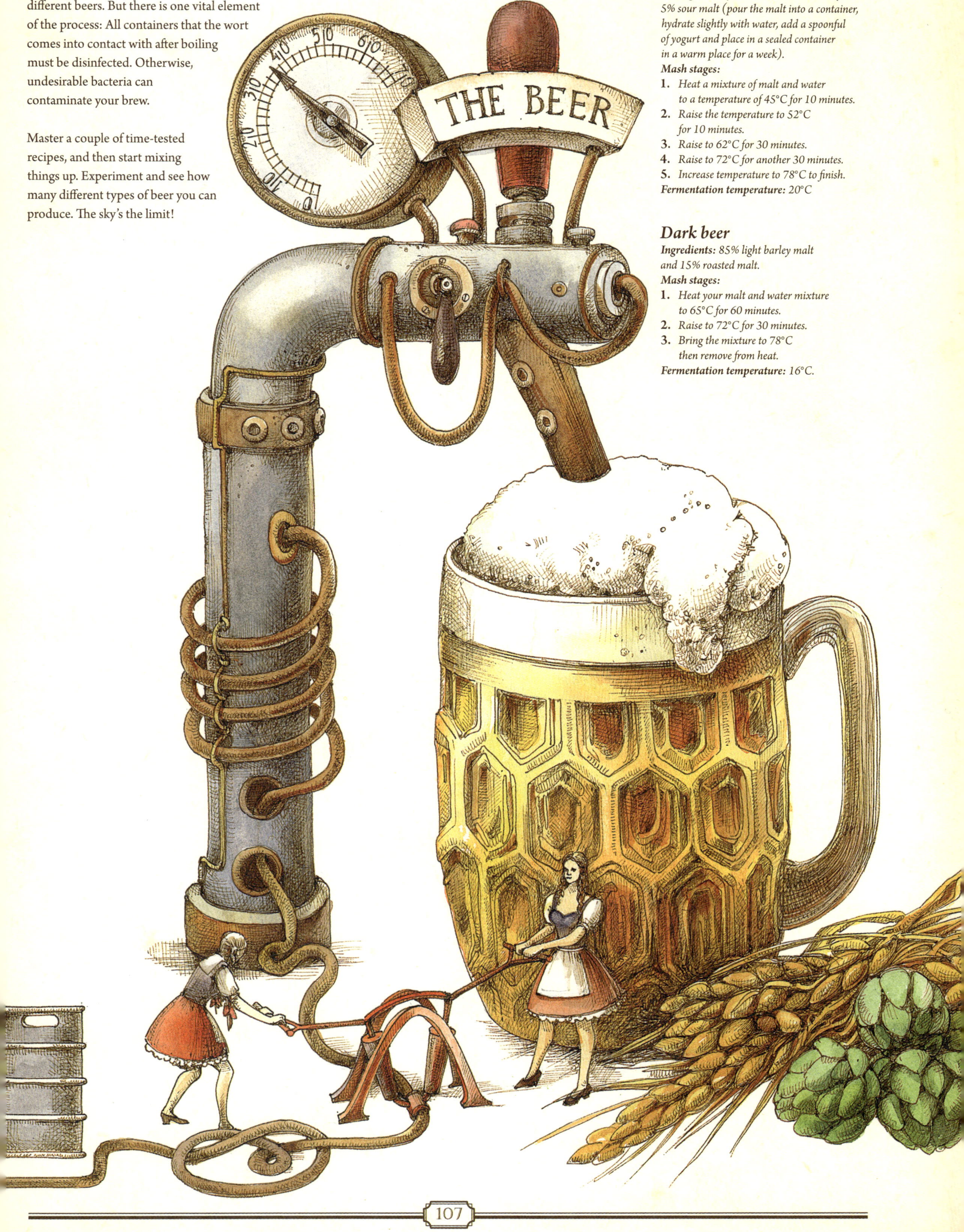

MATERIALS

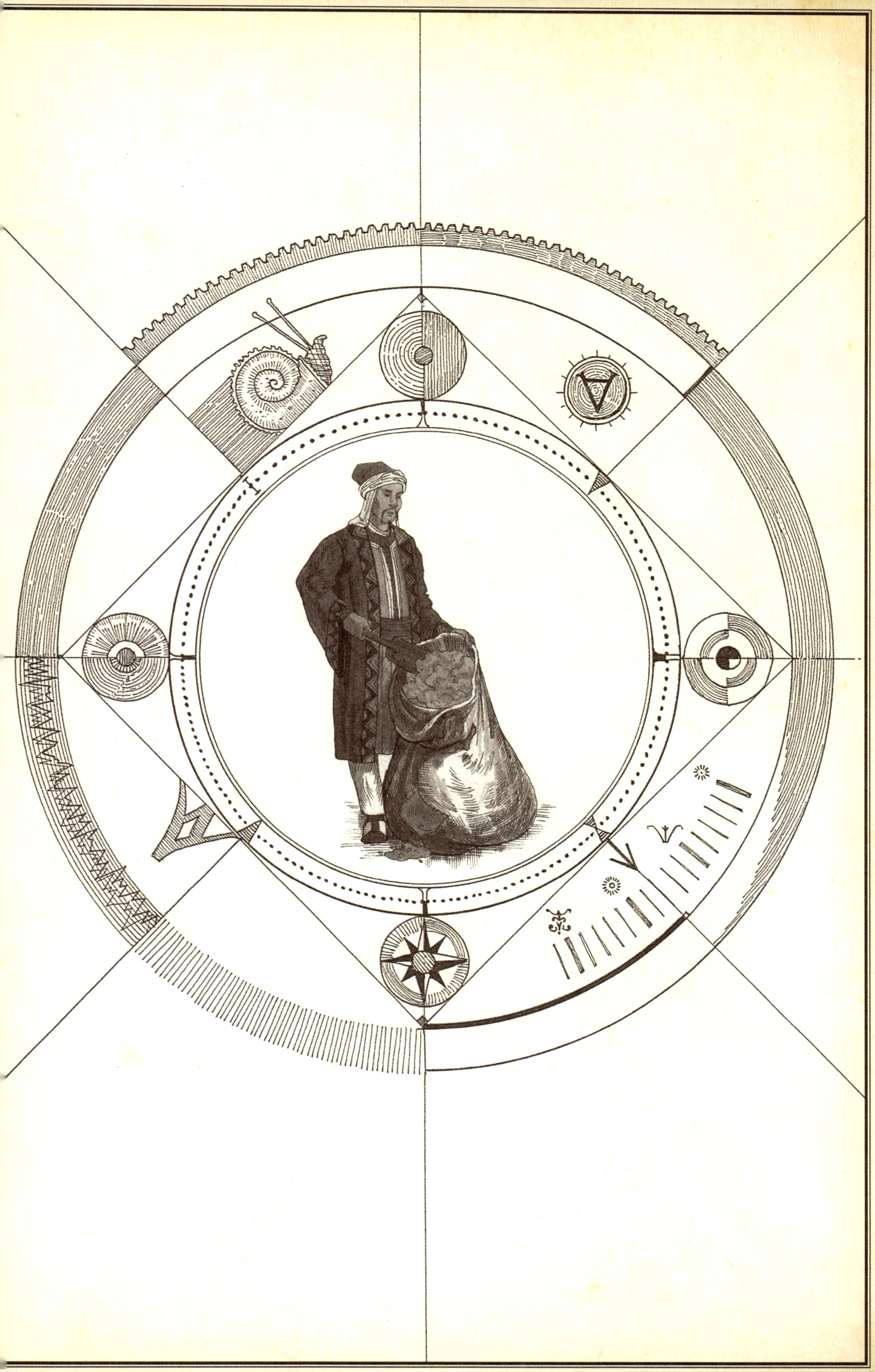

METALS & ORES

Metals are the most important materials of any civilization. Some of them — silver, gold, platinum — can be found in nature in their native forms. The rest must be separated from the other elements in their rocky ore. The first step is finding ore, a mineral that can be refined to obtain metal.

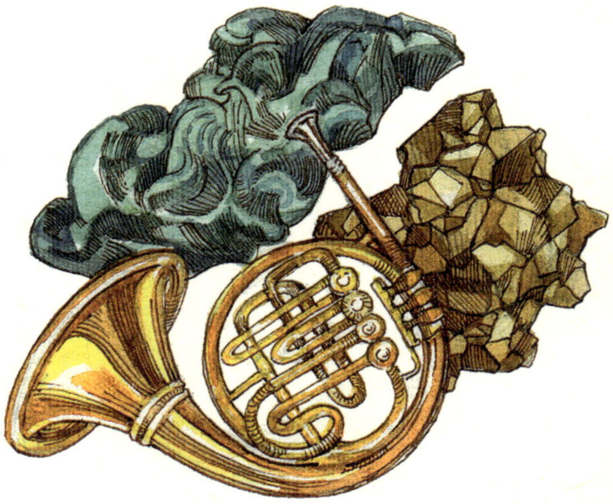

COPPER

Ores: sulfides (chalcopyrite), hydrocarbonates (malachite, azurite), native copper
Metal extraction method: for sulfides, burn off sulfur and remove the iron then reduce copper oxide with copper sulfide. For bicarbonates, heat to oxide and reduce with carbon monoxide.

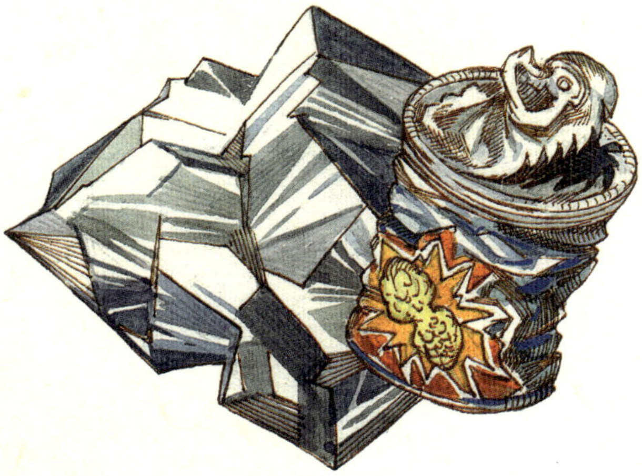

TIN

Ores: cassiterite (tin oxide). Has a strong diamond-like brilliance.
Method of metal recovery: heat with coal in a furnace (the simplest method uses a shaft-type furnace with layers of coal and cassiterite).

ZINC

Ores: sphalerite (zinc sulfide)
Metal recovery method: burn off sulfur, heat the resulting oxide with carbon to 1200°C in sealed containers with a drain and condense the zinc vapor.

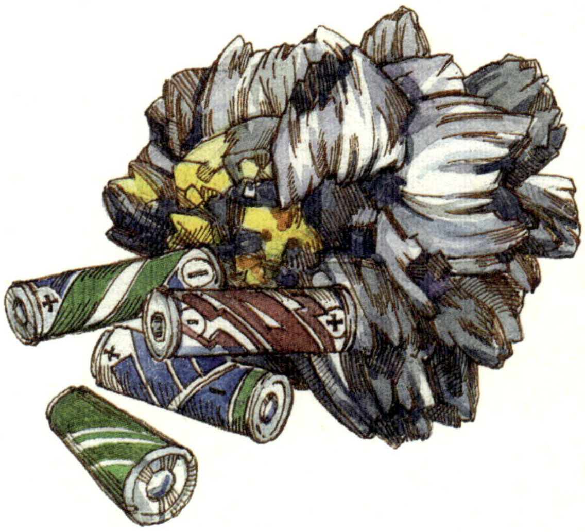

MERCURY

Ores: cinnabar (mercury sulfide)
Metal recovery method: fire in a furnace. Cinnabar also contains native mercury.

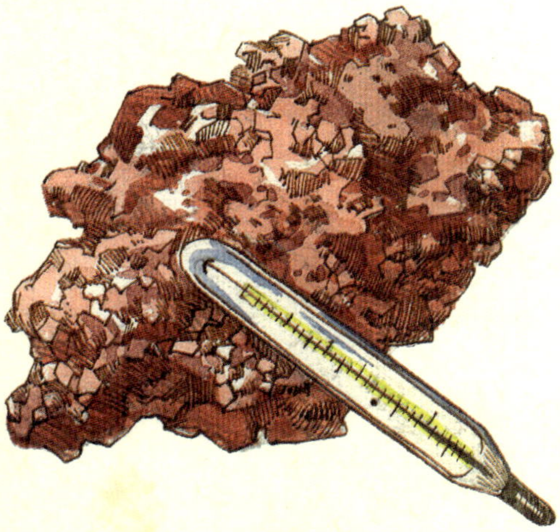

LEAD

Ores: galena (lead sulfide)
Metal extraction method: burn off sulfur to obtain lead oxide then reduce the oxide with carbon monoxide in a furnace.

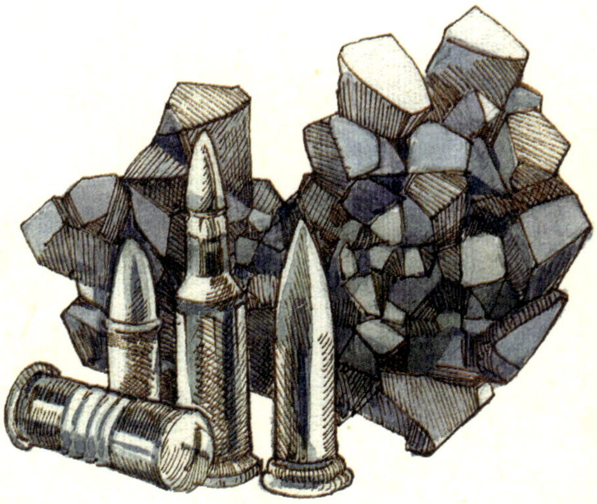

IRON

Ores: oxides (magnetite, hematite), sulfides (pyrite)

Metal extraction method: reduce oxides in a furnace with carbon, burn sulfides to oxides, and then reduce using carbon.

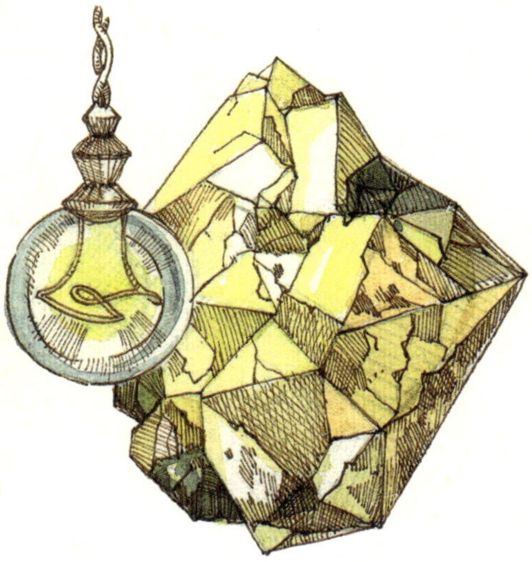

ALUMINUM

Ores: alumina (aluminum oxide) as part of bauxite

Metal recovery method: bauxite is dissolved in sodium hydroxide to purify it (the aluminum oxide dissolves, but the impurities do not). Aluminum oxide is dissolved in a cryolite melt then subjected to electrolysis (the cathode is the bottom of the bath, and the anode is carbon electrodes).

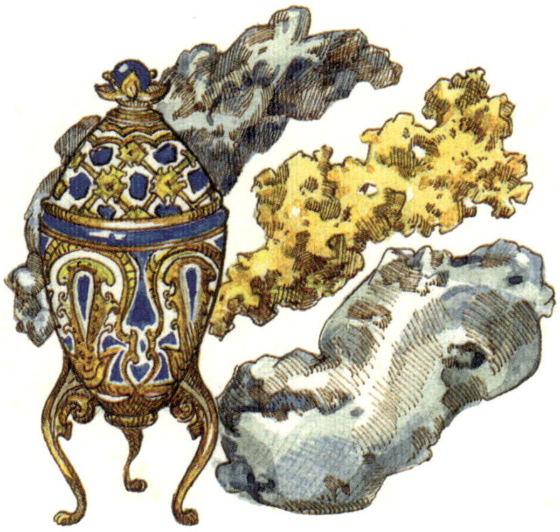

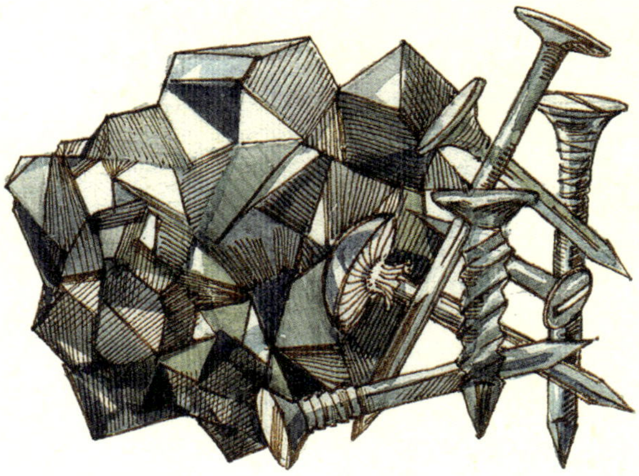

TUNGSTEN

Ores: scheelite

Metal recovery method: treat scheelite with sulfuric acid to form tungsten oxide. The tungsten oxide is then reduced with hydrogen at a temperature of 1000–1100°C.

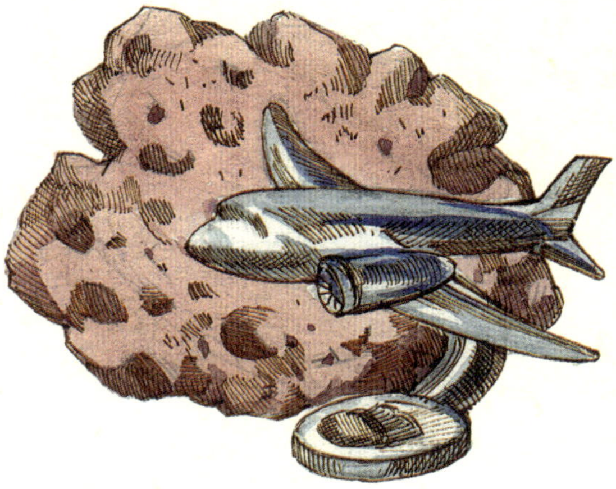

PLATINUM, GOLD, SILVER

Native metals (found in pure form in nature)

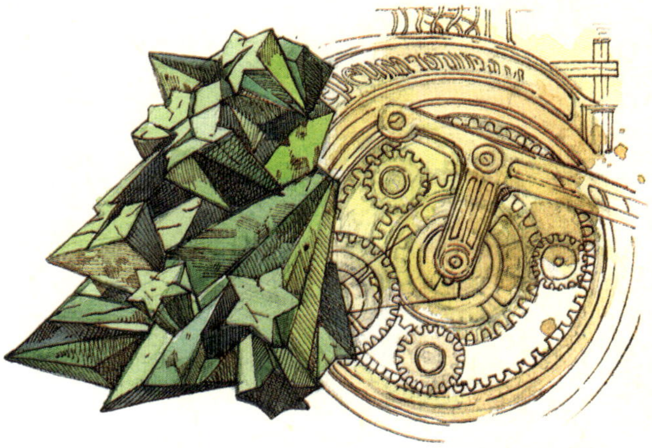

MINING

On the path to prosperity, every civilization reaches a point where it must dig deeper, both figuratively and literally, in order to find the materials to build a better future. Take up your pickaxe and your canary, and down, down we go.

To get resources that are located deep underground, you need a mine. Every mine must have at least three passages. The first is for mining the ore (1). The shaft will have platforms on multiple levels, so you'll also need passageways (2) to transport the mined ore. The second shaft is for lifting the mined ore to the surface (3). The third is for ventilation (4): Mines are filled with a mix of atmospheric air and toxic, flammable gases such as carbon monoxide and methane, which is found naturally around coal deposits. To make it easier to expand mining operations, passageways between platforms (2) are connected by sloped ramps (5).

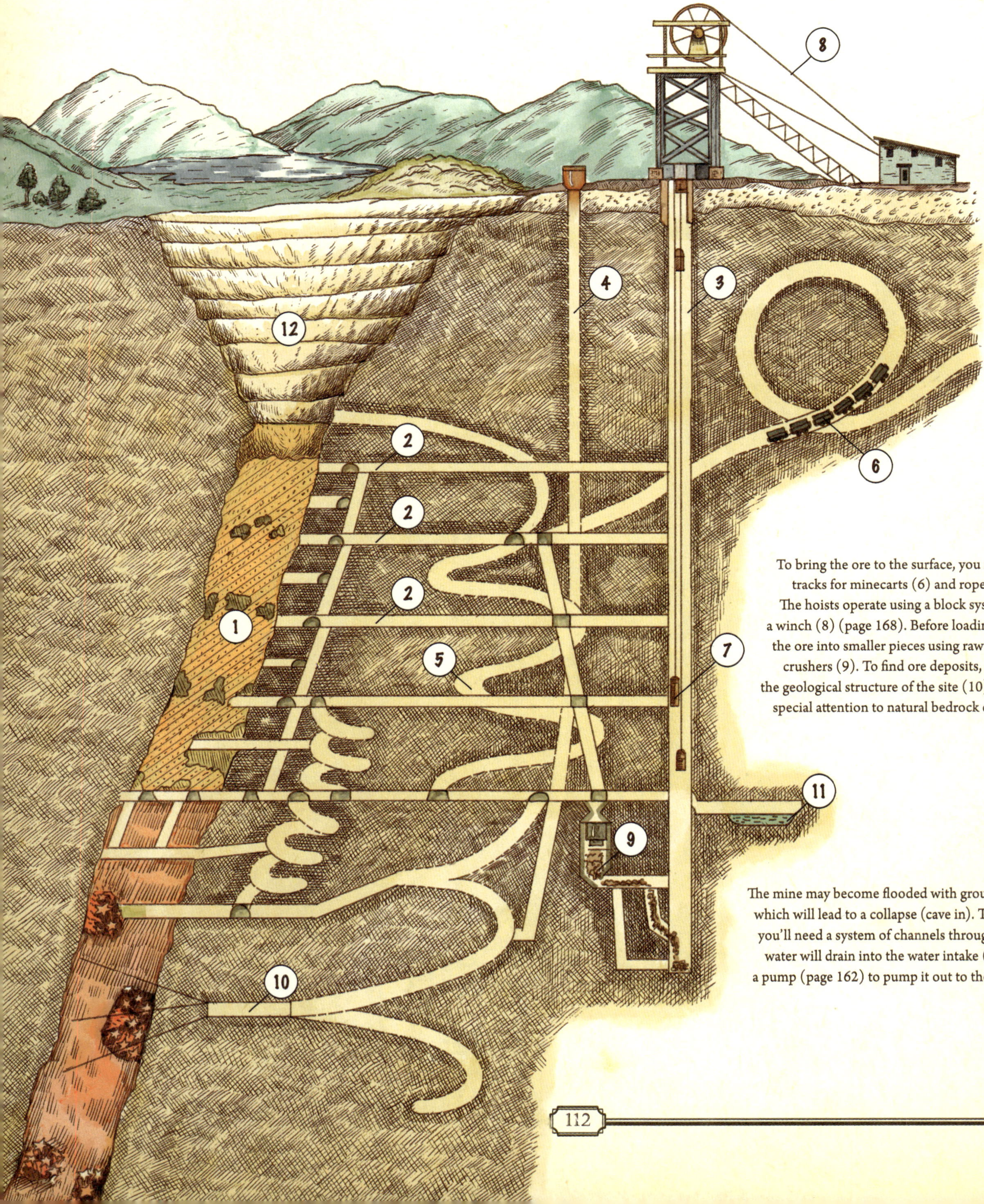

To bring the ore to the surface, you need rail tracks for minecarts (6) and rope lifts (7). The hoists operate using a block system and a winch (8) (page 168). Before loading, break the ore into smaller pieces using raw material crushers (9). To find ore deposits, examine the geological structure of the site (10), paying special attention to natural bedrock outcrops.

The mine may become flooded with groundwater, which will lead to a collapse (cave in). Therefore, you'll need a system of channels through which water will drain into the water intake (11) and a pump (page 162) to pump it out to the surface.

The easiest way to mine resources if they lie close to the surface is to dig a quarry (12). Make a quarry with the help of explosives. Create fuses for your gunpowder charges out of hemp cord (page 18) impregnated with resin or smeared with white clay (page 136). With a drill, make horizontal holes in the rock and stuff them with your gunpowder charges. Stick one end of the fuse into this charge, and run the other end a sufficient distance away for safety. Ignite your fuse and wait for the boom. You can also break through large slabs of rock by driving wooden wedges into the cracks and flooding them with water — as the wood expands, it will cause the rock to crack.

REINFORCEMENTS

Mines must be reinforced to prevent them from collapsing. When cutting horizontal corridors through the rock, leave vertical pillars as support posts to hold the ceilings up. But even with these, the risk of collapse is still quite high. Therefore, use additional reinforcement made from wooden poles and beams and add flooring, which will bear the weight of the stone vault of the mine.

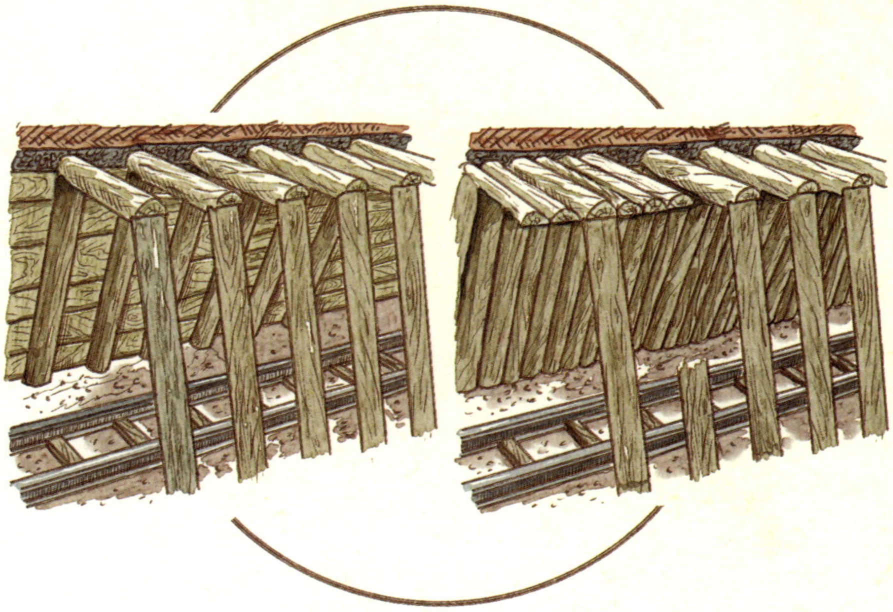

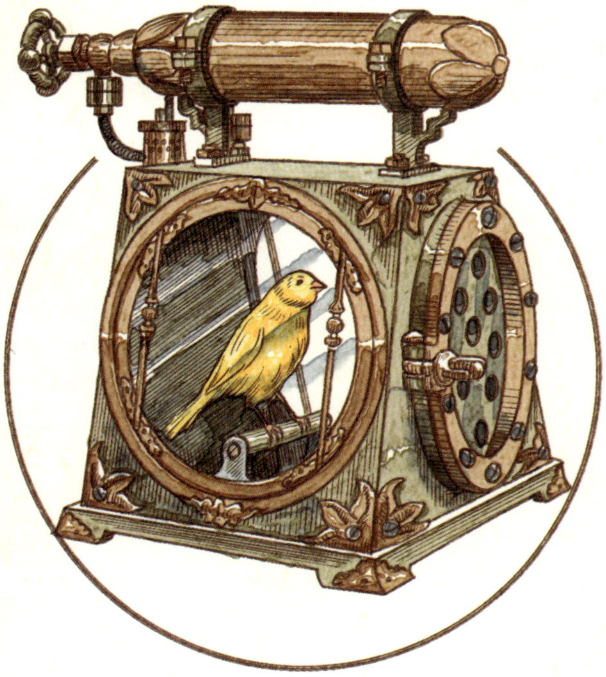

TOXIC GASES

Getting poisoned by toxic gases is a real danger when working in mines. Use canaries to help you determine whether or not toxic gases are accumulating. They respond to carbon monoxide much faster than humans do. If the canary loses consciousness, it means that harmful gases have accumulated in the mine, and you need to get out immediately. Equip the cage with an oxygen balloon so you can quickly resuscitate your feathered friend.

SAFETY LAMP

With all the gases accumulating in the mine, it's important to keep any open flames far away so as to avoid explosions. Use a multi-chambered metal mesh, which channels air into the lamp and combustion products out. When the combustible gas-air mixture causes the flame to flare up, it won't escape the confines of the mesh container and won't lead to an explosion. By the way, this kind of lamp is a good way to monitor gas build up: If the flame gets larger, there is more gas in the room.

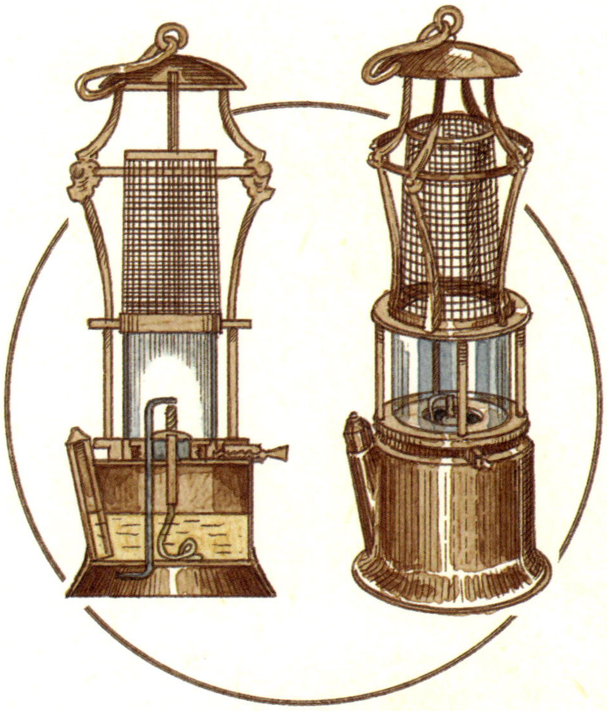

GLASS

Glass isn't just good for windows, bottles and other helpful household items. The invention of glass will greatly expand your scientific and technological capabilities, opening the potential for new ideas and discoveries. Without this material, many fields, such as chemistry, physics, biology and medicine, astronomy and optics and electronics and communications will be unable to reach higher levels of development. After all, the lenses of microscopes (page 184) telescopes and cameras (page 186) are impossible to make without glass, so it's time to take a shovel and go dig up some sand. Glass is obtained from molten quartz sand or crushed quartz. It is better to use river sand, as it tends to be the cleanest natural source, and the purer the material, the stronger and more transparent the glass will turn out.

Glass production sites are gigantic ovens. First, the kiln (1) and the melting chamber (2) are made out of brick (page 148). Constant air supply is required for good combustion. Therefore, it is better to orient the mouth of the kiln (3) so that it aligns with seasonal winds for good air exchange. This will create an air channel.

The raw materials (4) are then loaded into the kiln. The three ingredients for soda-lime glass are silica (sand or quartz), soda ash, which allows the silica to melt at kiln temperatures, and quicklime or slaked lime (page 78), which makes the glass more chemically durable and gives it shine.

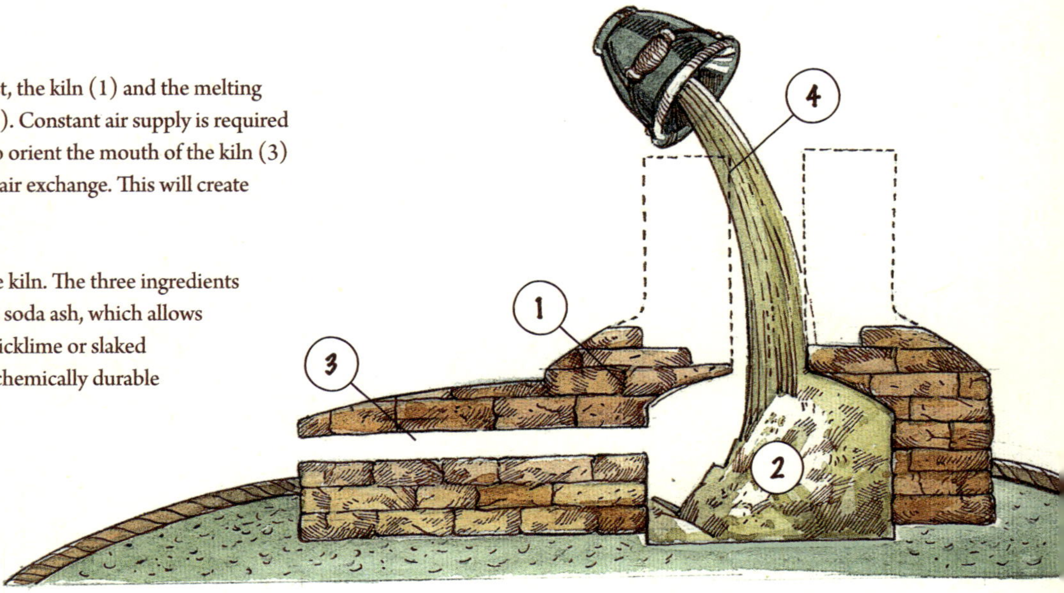

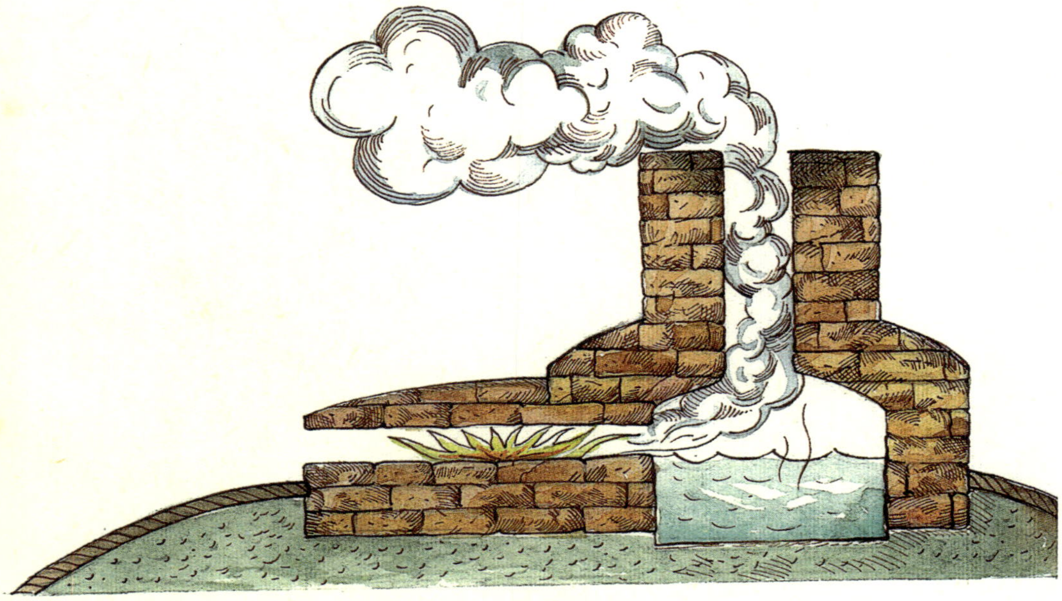

Once the kiln chamber is ready, build a dome and chimney on top. Set a fire in the air channel. As it's drawn through, its heat melts and combines the raw materials. The melting process may take from 10 days to 2 weeks. The temperature must be kept at around 1100°C and maintained for long enough for all the bubbles to escape the viscous melt. Then allow the kiln to cool to produce a block of strong, transparent glass.

A giant multi-ton piece of glass is melted in the melting chamber. Its dimensions can exceed human height. The top of the oven must be disassembled to remove the molten glass. Do this carefully so as to save as many of the bricks as possible. They will be useful to you later, as the structure will have to be reassembled to melt the next batch of glass.

The resulting untreated blocks make neither good microscope lenses nor beautiful wine glasses. These cubes of glass must be broken into smaller pieces and sent to glass-blowing workshops.

These glass furnaces can be constructed away from your main settlement, near sources of raw materials and fuel. However, glass workshops, where glassware is actually crafted, should be located in the city to more efficiently meet the needs of the local townspeople.

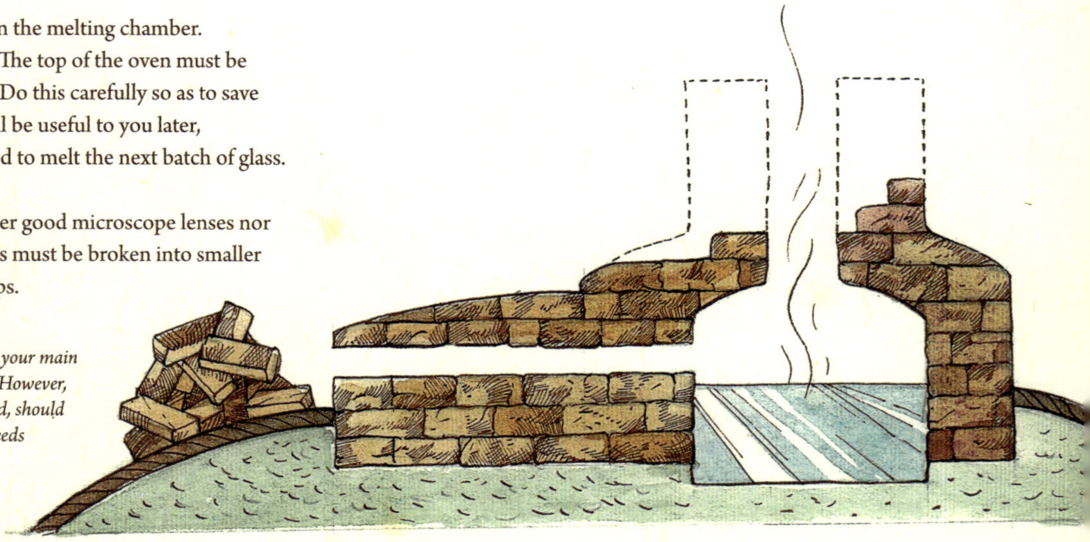

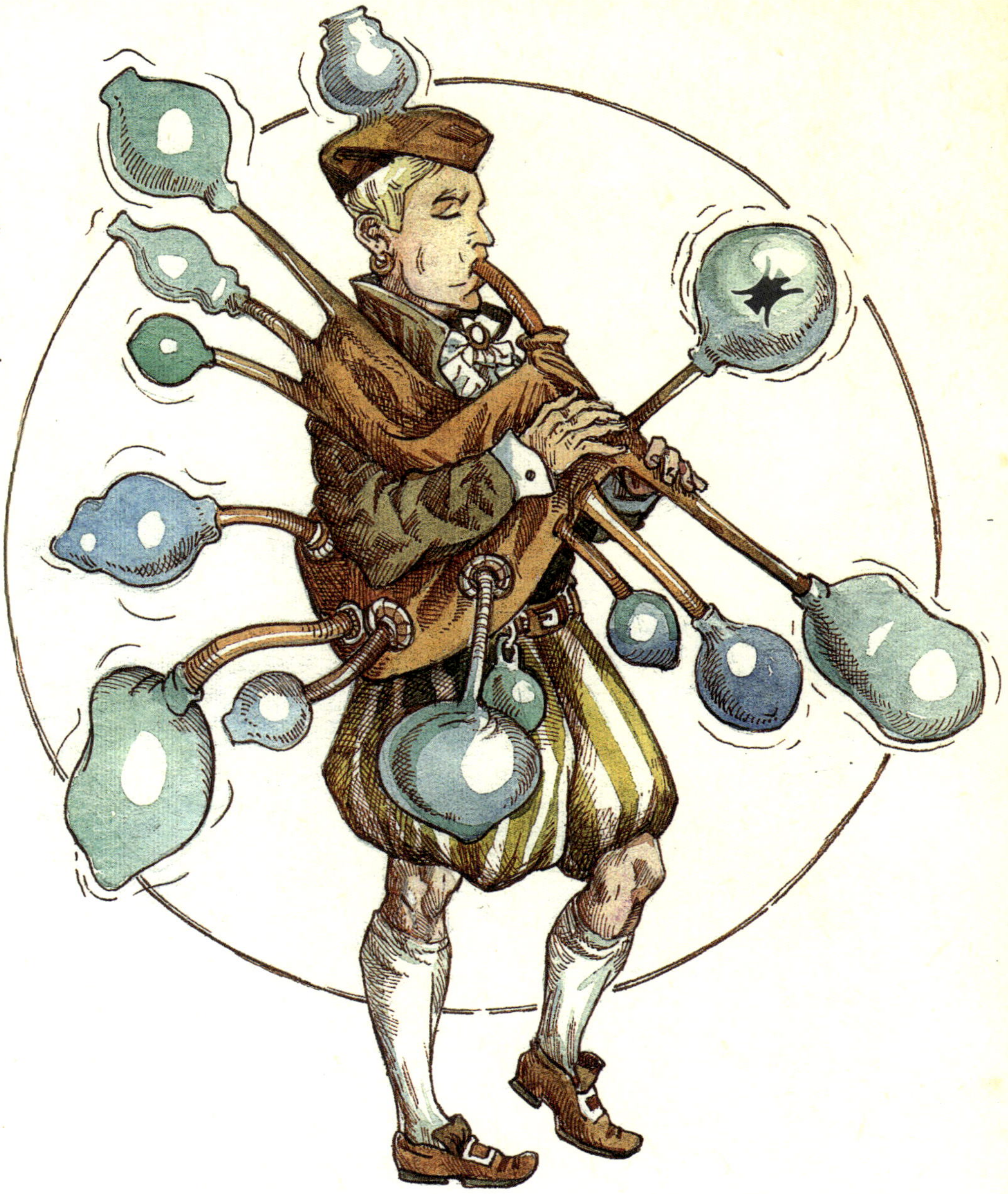

ADD COLOR

To make a perfectly clear glass suitable for lenses and other scientific instruments, make sure the sand or quartz you use is bright white. The impurities in yellowy sand will taint the glass. But for decorative, colorful glass, you can add different minerals to the raw materials. For example, copper oxide gives blue-green, and iron oxide, yellow-green. This is a great way to protect beer, wine and any other photosensitive liquids.

MOLDING AND GLASS BLOWING

You can blow glass into any shape you wish — the only limit is your own imagination and lung capacity. But first, the glass must be melted again. Then collect a ball of molten glass on the end of a hollow tube. Blow into the other end as if creating a soap bubble while turning the tube continuously. Use the blown air and the force of gravity to mold the glass into the desired shape.

There are two ways to produce a flat sheet of glass. The easiest is to blow out your glass ball, snip off the top and, while constantly rewarming the glass to ensure it remains pliable, start spinning your blowtube rapidly between your hands. Centrifugal force will gradually shape the molten glass into a thin disc. Once cool, these discs can be framed with metal and set into a window opening. This technique produces glass that will allow light to shine through but will prevent nosy neighbors from peeping in due to the distortion.

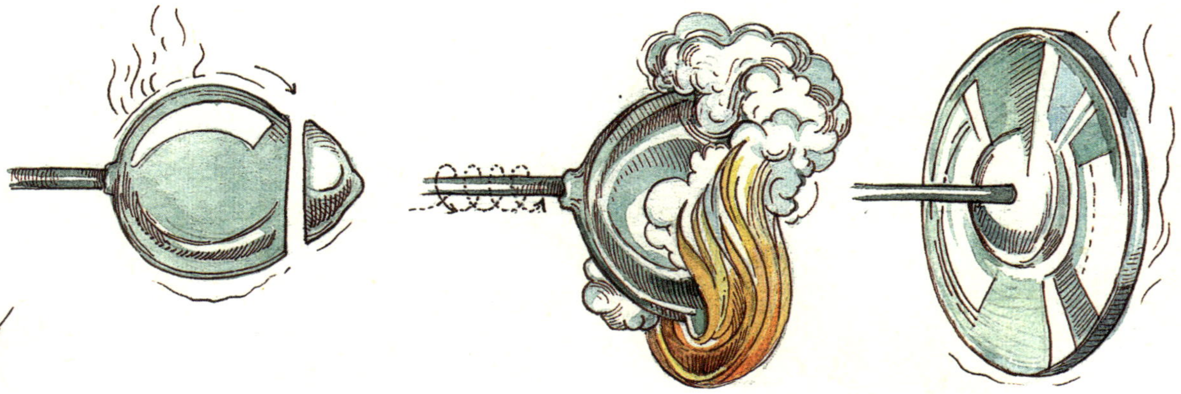

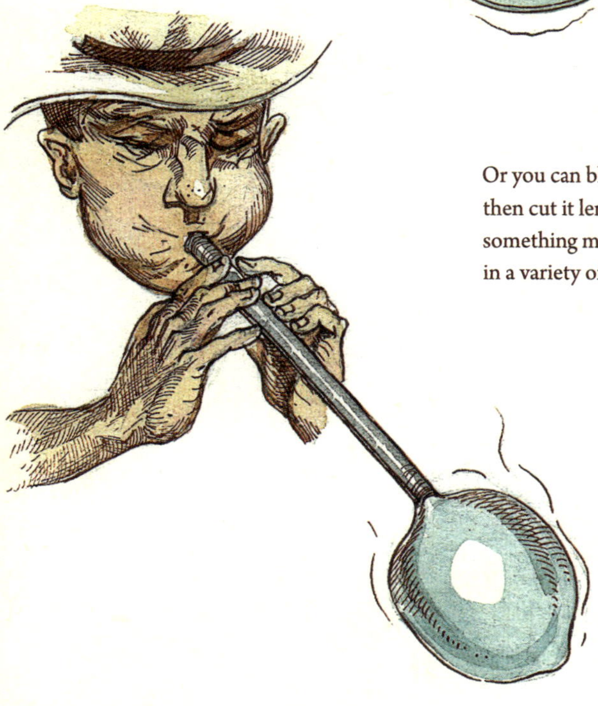

Or you can blow an oblong bubble in your molten glass and let it cool slightly then cut it lengthwise and roll it out into a thin, flat sheet. This creates something more closely resembling window glass that can be used in a variety of applications.

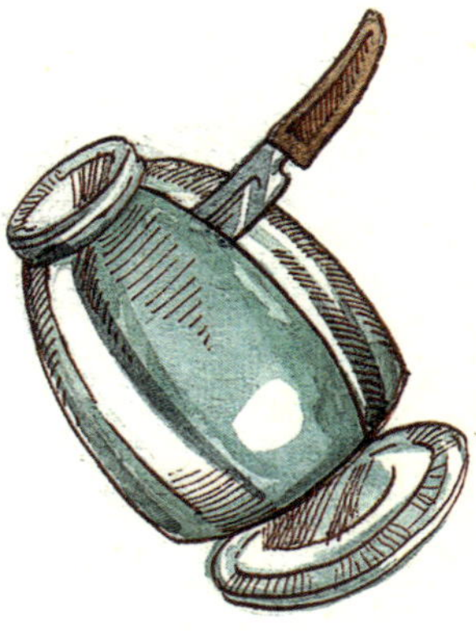

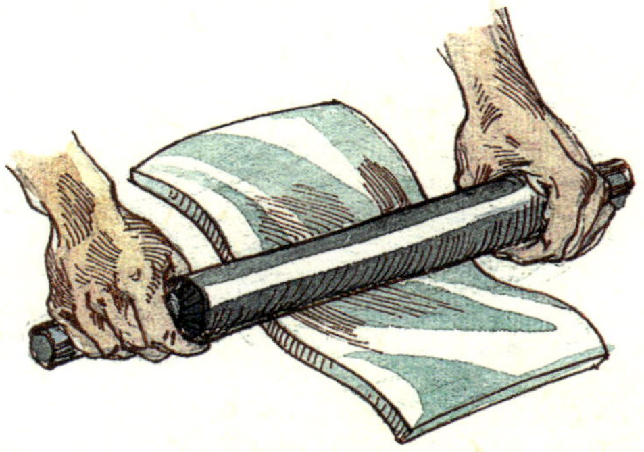

RUBBER

Rubber is an elastic material that can not only stretch to dimensions many times greater than its original size but also shrink back once it's no longer under tension. It is also gas and water tight. Therefore, rubber is suitable for a variety of tasks from improving wheels and electrical insulation to preventing unwanted pregnancies. You'll definitely find a variety of uses for this flexible material.

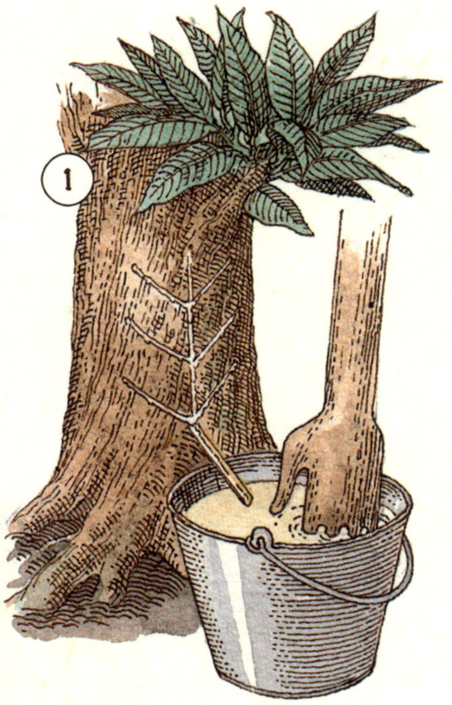

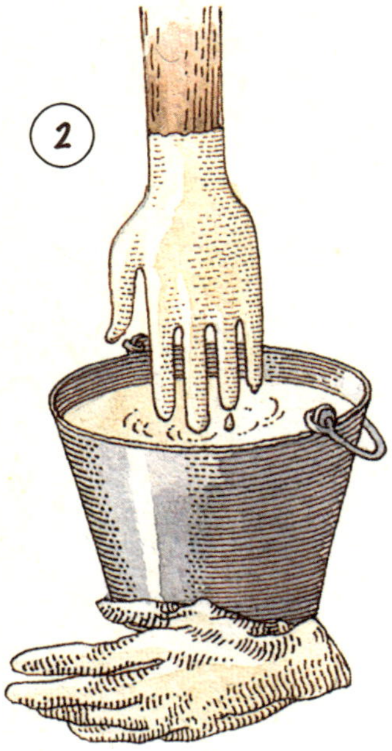

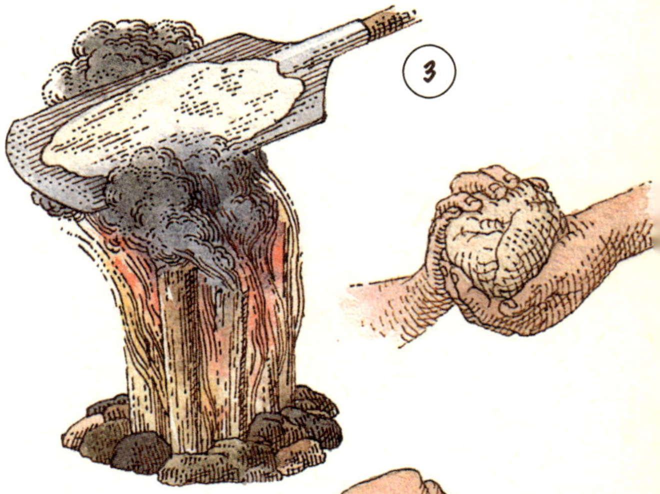

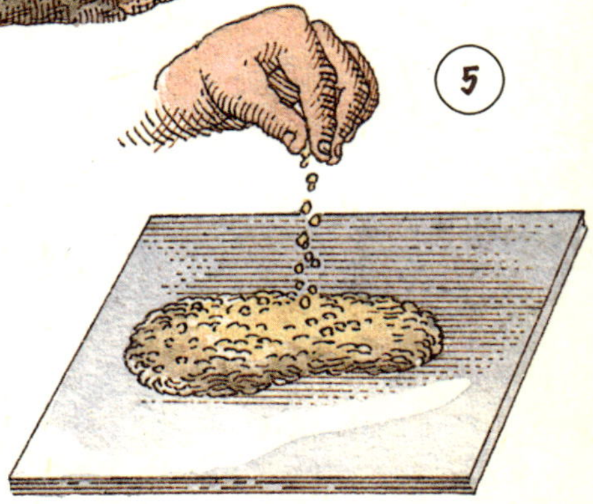

1. Slice into the core of *Hevea brasiliensis,* also known as the rubber tree, until a milky liquid starts to seep out. This suspension of polymer particles (which can also be found in other plants, such as the dandelion) is called latex. Make cuts into a 6–7 year old tree that span about halfway around the trunk at a 30° angle. Make each subsequent cut underneath the previous one.

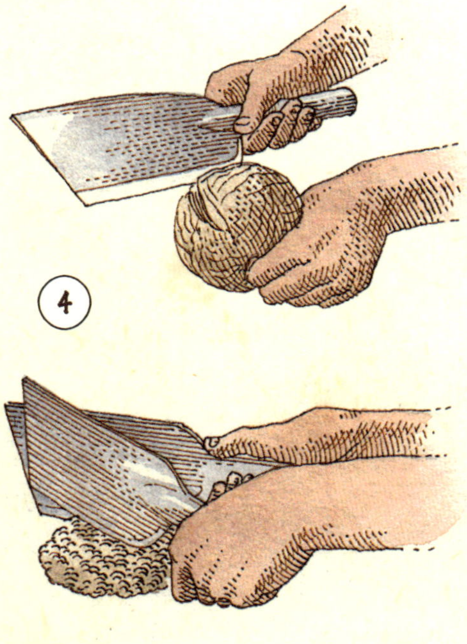

2. Latex can be used in its natural form. For instance, make a wooden model of a hand and dip it into a bucket of latex. Once it dries, you'll have a set of latex gloves.

3. It can also be used to make rubber. There are several different methods. Dip a spatula into the latex and hold it over the smoke of a fire until the water evaporates. After that, a thin layer of rubber is formed on the blade. Repeat the process layer by layer until you have a large piece of rubber. Another option is coagulation using acetic or formic acid. By mixing them with latex, you get a crumby substance that resembles cottage cheese. Wash it, dry it and press it into blocks.

4. Remove the raw rubber from the spatula and cut into small pieces.

5. Add crushed sulfur (at a ratio of 5–10% of the total mass).

6. Press the resulting material into sheets.

Now they must be dried in a special oven known as an autoclave. During the heating process, the soft, sticky rubber will become hardy and elastic. The process of heating rubber with sulfur to prompt this transformation is called vulcanization.

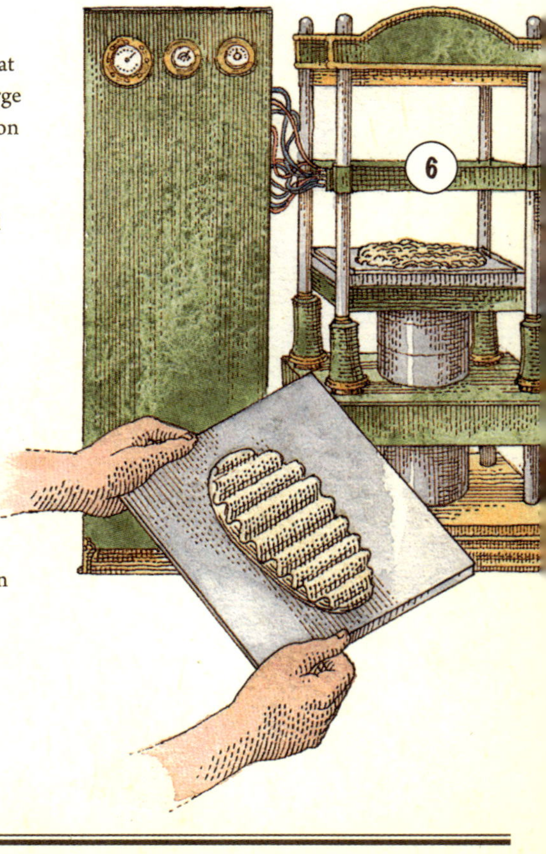

If there are no rubber trees nearby, certain species of ficus will suffice, and in dire situations, you can experiment with dandelions. The rubber in dandelion roots takes the form of both liquid latex and solid rubber fibers. To extract the rubber, vulcanize the plant materials using formic acid or the sap of sulfur-containing plants, such as cabbage.

During the vulcanization of rubber products, sulfur binds the long rubber molecules into a kind of cross-linked network. This can be done by hot pressing, rolling with heated rolls (A) or by heating the material in an autoclave (B), where the workpieces are treated with steam formed when water boils at high pressures.

There's no such thing as bad weather — only inadequate clothing. But that's a problem we can remedy. Soak fabric with rubber dissolved in an organic solvent such as gasoline to obtain a waterproof garment. You can also make galoshes, which are waterproof covers worn over your boots.

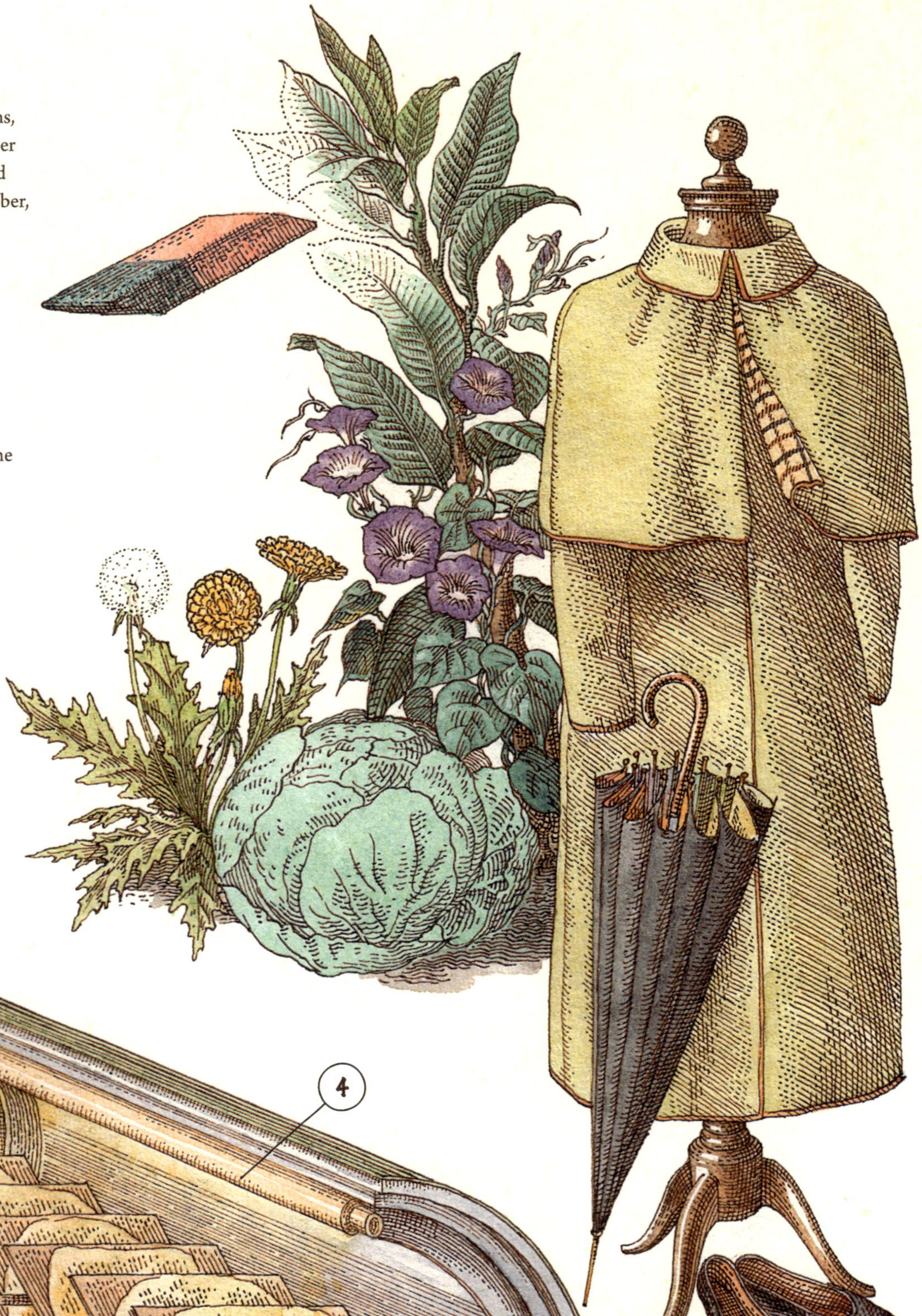

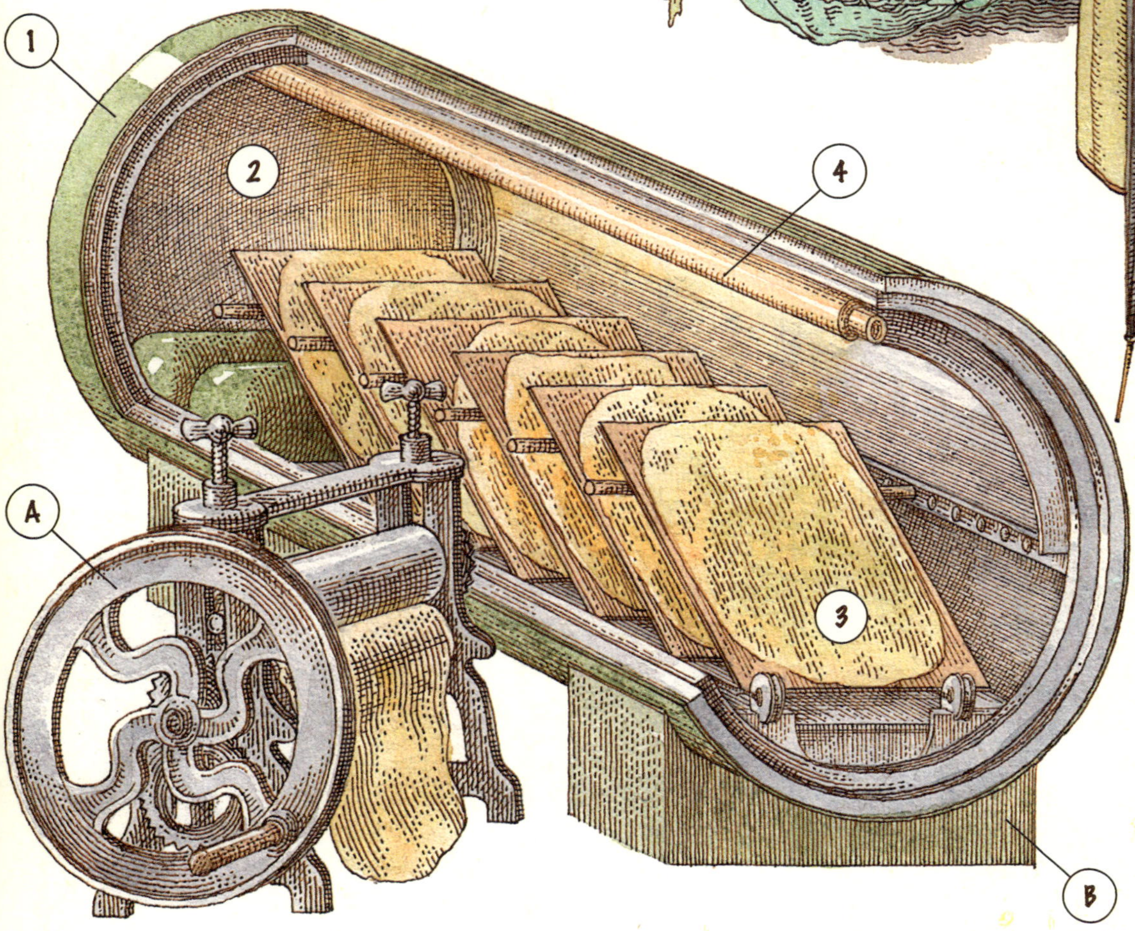

1. *Body*
2. *Heating chamber*
3. *Molds containing unprocessed rubber*
4. *Electric heating element*

RECTIFIED SPIRITS

Wondering what to do with all your surplus food? Start producing rectified or purified alcohol. The beginning stages of the production process are similar to distillation (page 390), but there's one important distinction: The final product is not intended for consumption, so there's no need to select high-quality grains, potatoes or berries. Straw, corn stalks and some kinds of weeds will also suffice. If you do plan to use the alcohol for culinary purposes, however, start with quality raw materials.

Everything that contains sugar will ferment on its own, but the resulting drink won't have an ABV exceeding 14%. Any higher and the microbes responsible for fermentation will die. That's why you need a special apparatus that will raise the temperature and remove any impurities. The process of rectification is like distilling the alcohol dozens of times. By the way, this method can also be used to purify other liquids, such as oil.

The simplest version of a rectifier is a flask filled with glass beads, also known as a "fractionating column." You can also use a crumpled coil of wire, metal shavings or springs. Every layer of glass beads is a different temperature — the closer to the top, the colder they are. The temperature difference causes the liquid to separate: the lightest components (A) rise to the top, while the less volatile components sink to the bottom (B).

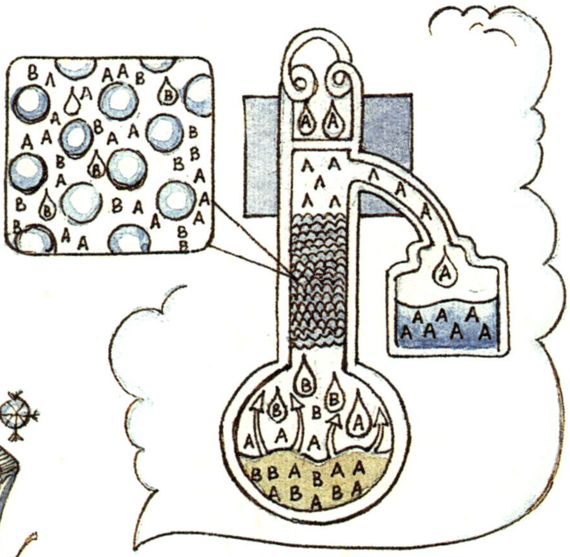

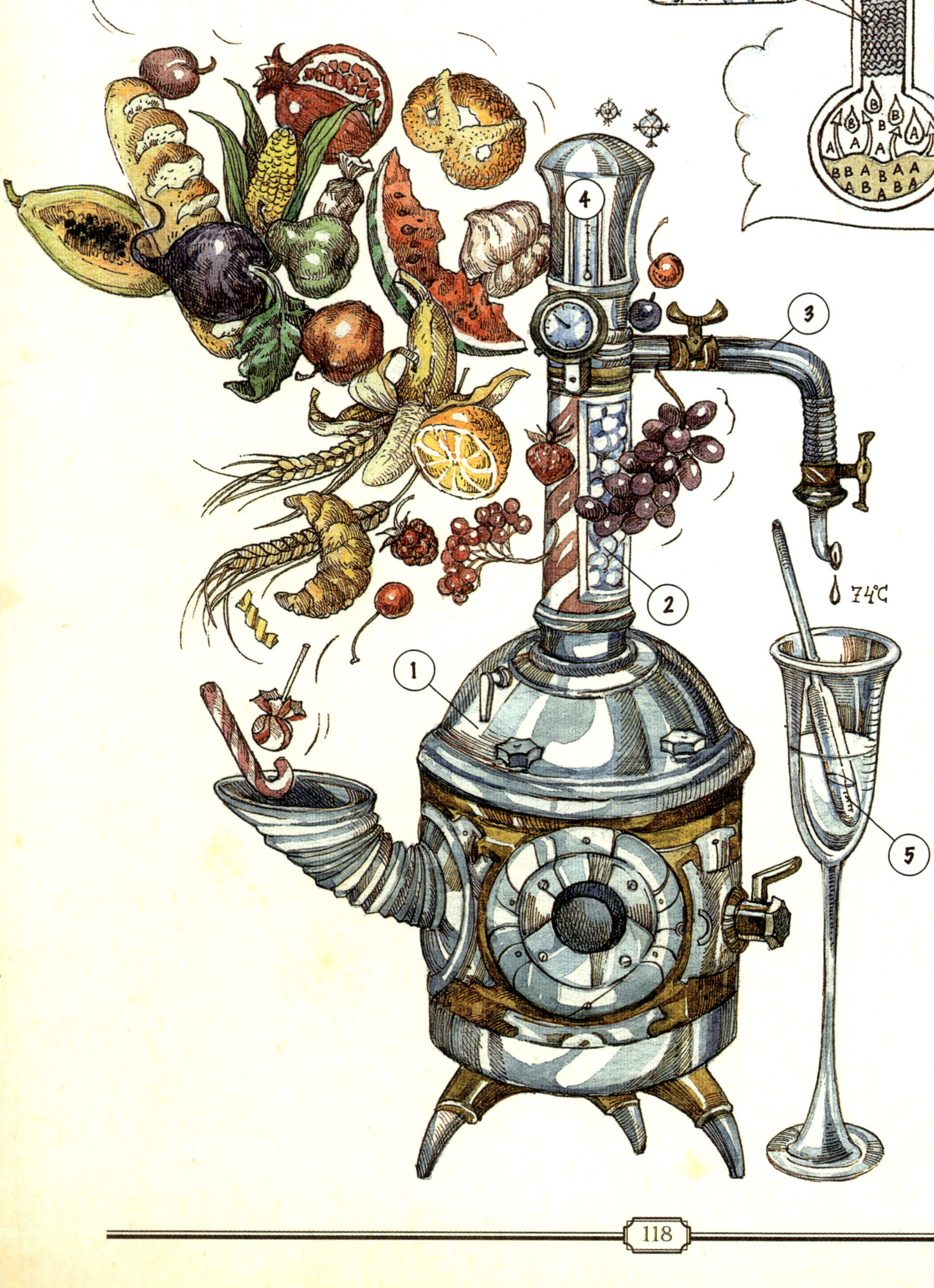

The fractionating column with the glass beads (2) is connected to a glass bulb at the bottom. As the heated alcohol vapors rise, they cool and condense on the glass beads. The lighter components (A) then revaporize and rise higher through the glass bead column where they condense again and the process repeats. Regulate the temperature of your heat source so that the alcohol vapors (A) rise and condense at the level of the outflow tube (3) and flow into the chilled part of the apparatus (4). This way, you'll obtain alcohol without any impurities. The lighter toxic components such as aldehydes and acetone will remain vapor and flow back out through the tube, while the fusel oils and other impurities with a higher boiling point (B) fall back to the bottom of the container.

One important characteristic of the final product is its ABV, or alcohol by volume. A spirit with an ABV of 70% is a concentration of 7 parts pure ethanol to 3 parts water. A hydrometer (5) will help you determine the alcohol percentage of your final product. It consists of a long, narrow glass stem with measurement marks and a bulbous bottom containing a weight. The hydrometer floats lower or higher depending on the density of the water-alcohol mixture. You can calibrate your hydrometer beforehand using liquids with known densities.

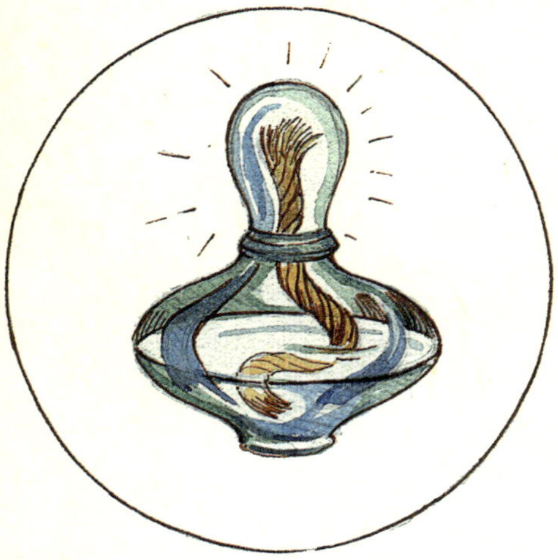

It is impossible to obtain 100% alcohol using rectification — surgical spirits always contain about 4% water, which doesn't pose a problem in the majority of its applications across various fields.

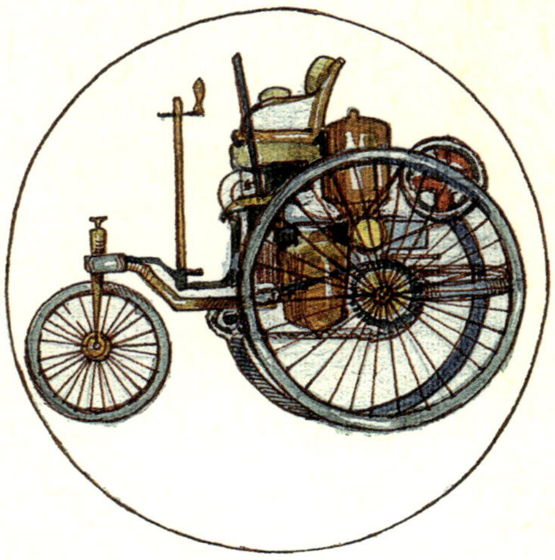

Alcohol Lamp

A burner filled with ethanol can be used for both lighting and for heating food, especially for meals that need to be kept hot on the table. Alcohol lamps give off more heat than candles and don't smoke.

Fuel

Add alcohol to gasoline (only in a concentration of 3–10%) and it will increase your engine's efficiency. You can even create a motor that runs entirely on ethanol.

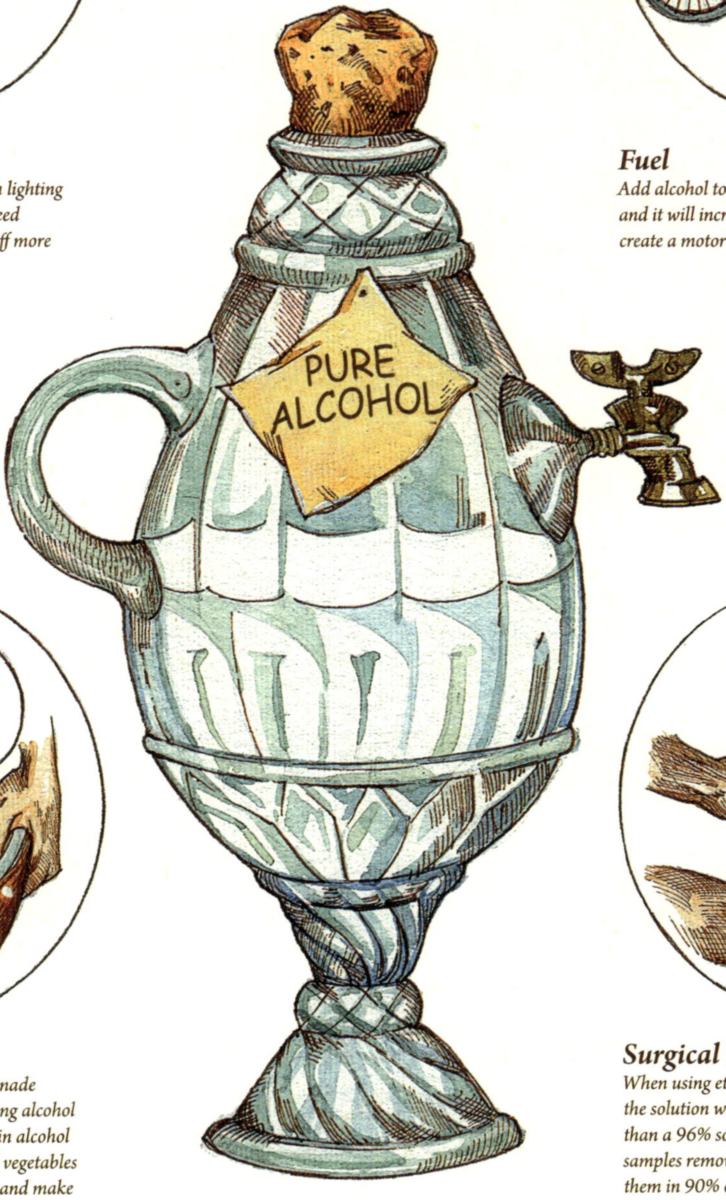

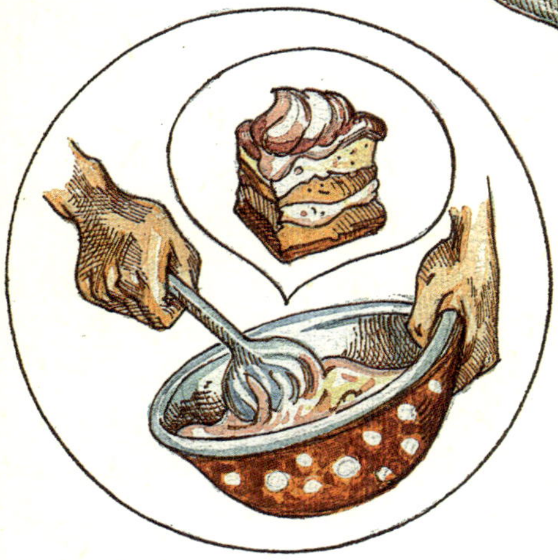

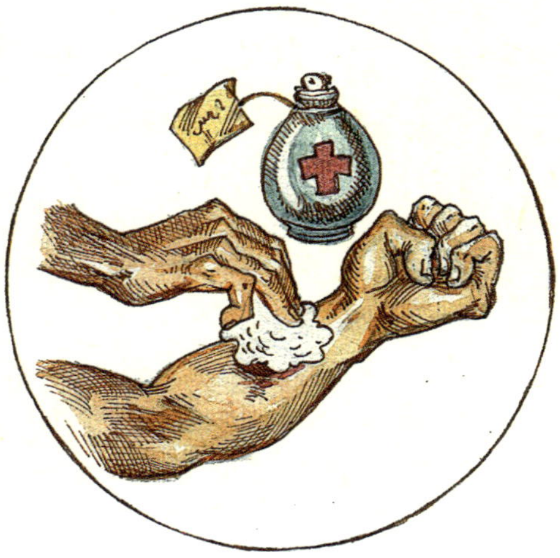

Culinary uses

A shot of rectified spirit added to a stew or marinade will soften the meat. A biscuit fortified with strong alcohol has a special taste and is more shelf-stable. Grain alcohol is also used to increase the shelf life of preserved vegetables and in salt-pickling can be used to disinfect fish and make cucumbers and mushrooms crisp.

Surgical Spirit

When using ethanol as a disinfectant, dilute it to 70% — the solution will penetrate into deeper layers of the epidermis than a 96% solution. But if you need to examine tissue samples removed during an operation (page 36), place them in 90% ethanol to preserve the biomaterial.

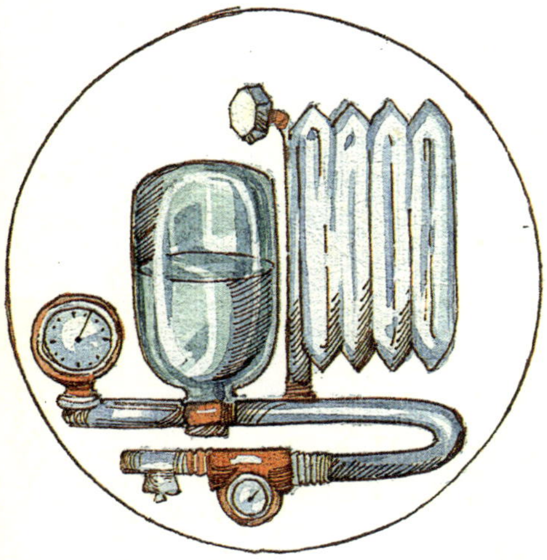

Anti-freeze

96% ethyl alcohol can be poured into cooling or heating systems. It doesn't corrode metal and freezes at –114°C.

Ink

If you add alcohol to dye or powdered charcoal, you can produce alcohol ink.

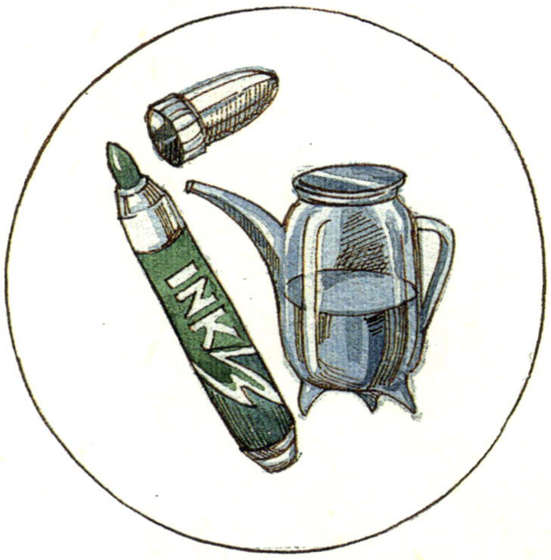

COTTON & YARN

Humans have several different mediums of self-expression, and clothing is one of them. Fashion is a way to display how you feel when words just aren't enough. Clothing can be made from whatever animal hair or plant fiber you have on hand. Each material will create yarn of a different thickness and density.

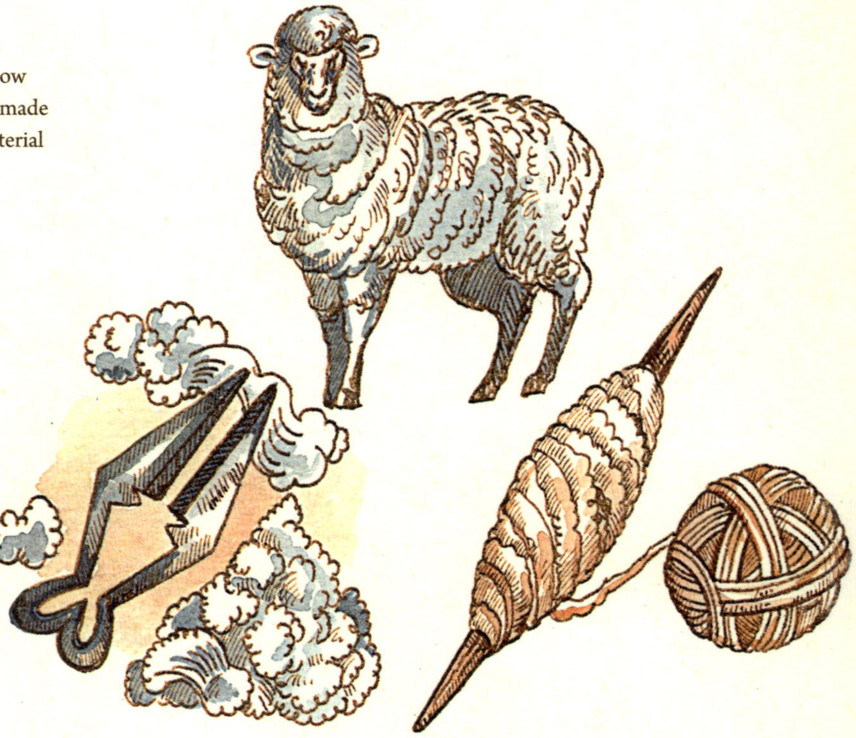

WOOL

The easiest way to do this with livestock is to shave or comb a sheep, llama, goat, camel or something else fluffy (even a dog). Wash the wool and brush through it. Now you can use a spinning wheel to start pulling it into threads.

LINEN

Flax is a rather capricious annual plant that requires loads of sunlight but moderate temperature and humidity. Soak and dry the flax stalks. When the fiber starts to easily peel away from the hard outer hull, transfer the stems to an oven and dry until they crack when squeezed in your hands. Now rinse the fibers.

Cut a deep groove into the entire length of a log and attach a handle at one end that fits perfectly into this groove. Lay the stems across this groove perpendicularly and bring the handle down so that it crushes the stalks, removing the outer hull and softening the inner fibers. Then comb through the bundle to get rid of any excess hull and clean the thin linen threads.

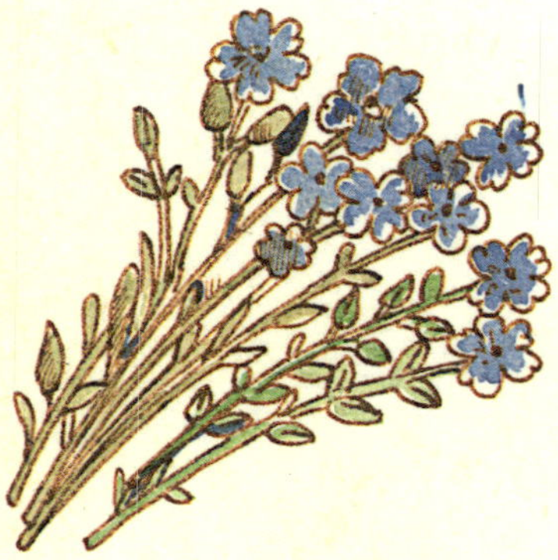

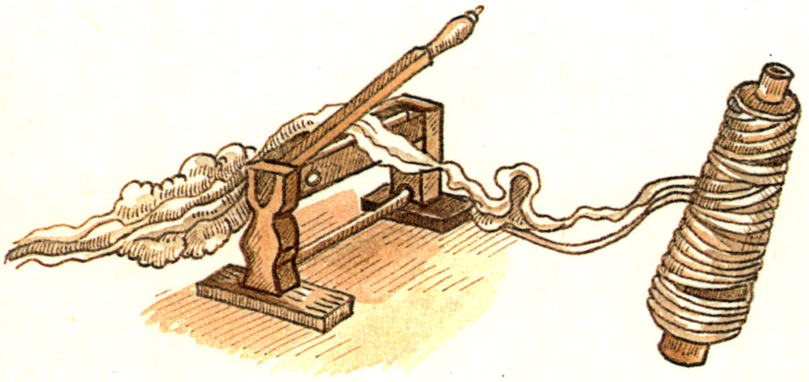

COTTON

Growing cotton is very difficult. Only warm and humid climates are suitable for growing cotton. So if you live in a dry, cold area, don't waste your time. You need to sow the seeds every spring in moist soil with good drainage. In autumn, collect the light cotton bolls in open boxes. Use a cotton gin to separate the cotton fibers from the spiky seeds.

A cotton gin is a box containing two rollers covered in spikes that pull the lint through the slots of a grate at high speeds. At the back end, there are brushes that rotate three times faster. Throw your cotton seeds in the front end and the cotton gin will separate the cotton lint from the seed and transfer it to the brushes, which pulls the cotton into fibers. These are then spun into yarn.

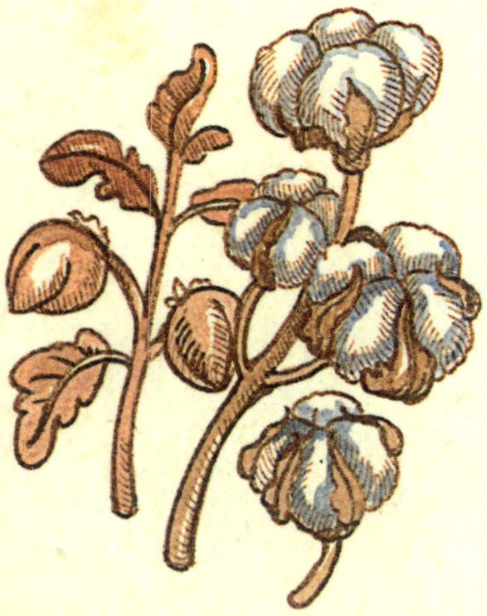

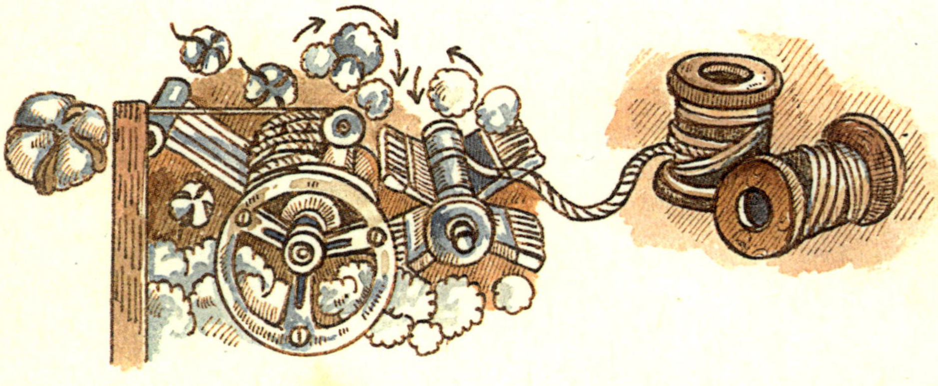

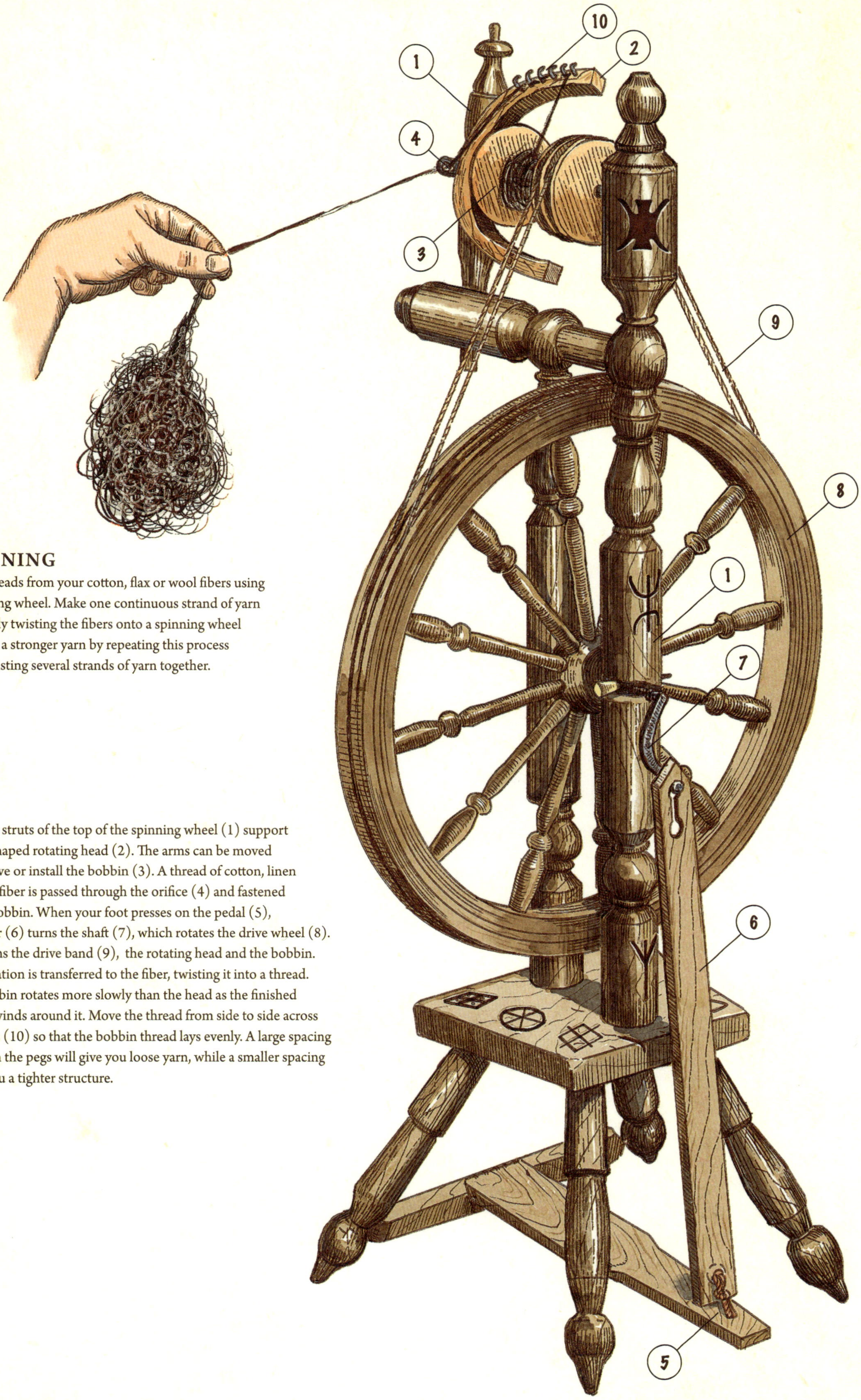

SPINNING

Spin threads from your cotton, flax or wool fibers using a spinning wheel. Make one continuous strand of yarn by simply twisting the fibers onto a spinning wheel or make a stronger yarn by repeating this process then twisting several strands of yarn together.

The side struts of the top of the spinning wheel (1) support the U-shaped rotating head (2). The arms can be moved to remove or install the bobbin (3). A thread of cotton, linen or wool fiber is passed through the orifice (4) and fastened to the bobbin. When your foot presses on the pedal (5), the lever (6) turns the shaft (7), which rotates the drive wheel (8). This spins the drive band (9), the rotating head and the bobbin. This rotation is transferred to the fiber, twisting it into a thread. The bobbin rotates more slowly than the head as the finished thread winds around it. Move the thread from side to side across the pegs (10) so that the bobbin thread lays evenly. A large spacing between the pegs will give you loose yarn, while a smaller spacing gives you a tighter structure.

PAINTS & BRUSHES

Not everything can be conveyed with words. Emotional realities require something more expressive and colorful. Borrow some of nature's hues and use them to bring your masterpieces to life. Here, experimentation is key. Just try to avoid using any toxic substances for your pigments. Start with time-tested ingredients.

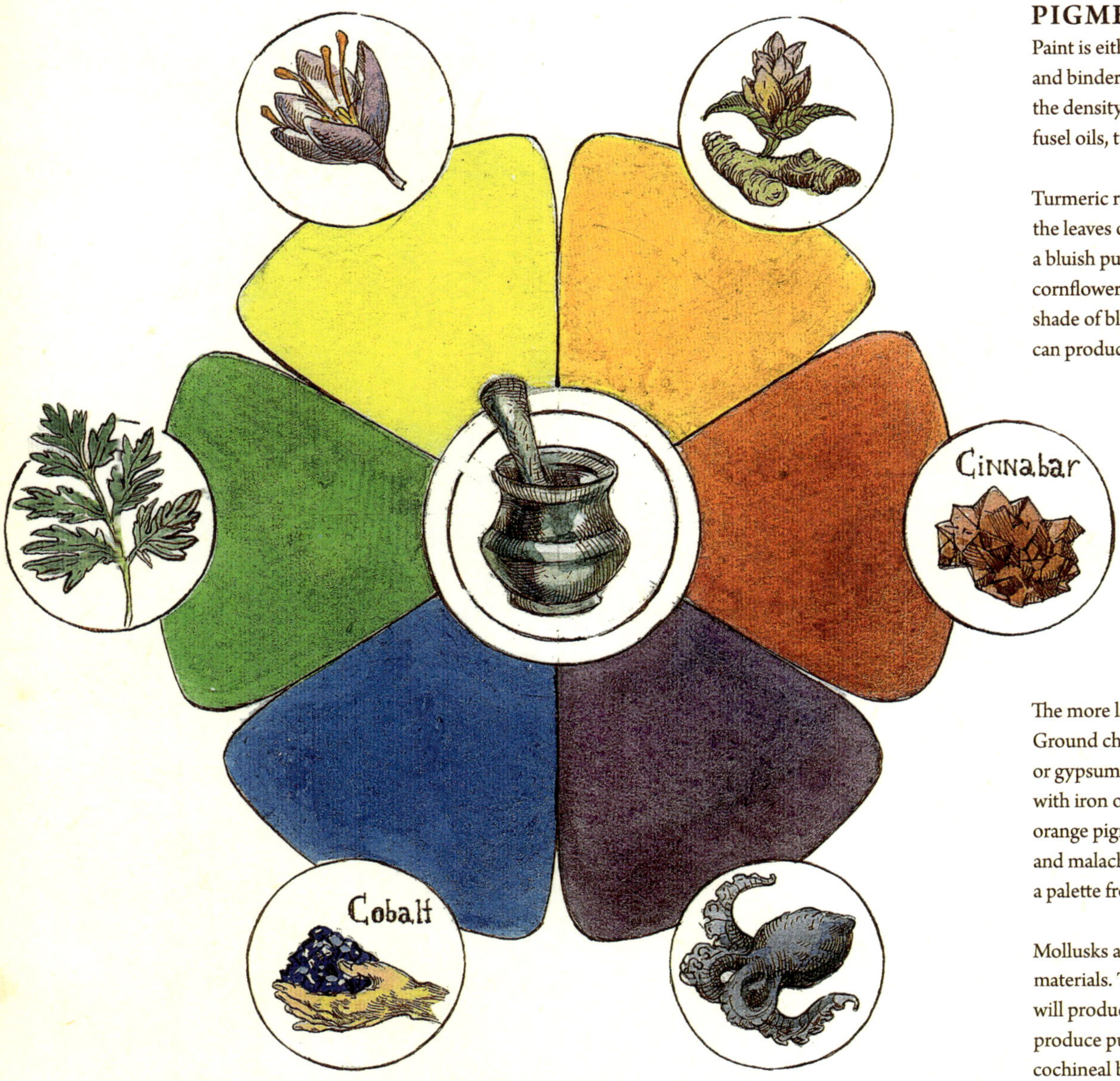

PIGMENT

Paint is either a dye solution or mixture of pigments and binders. Thinners allow you to regulate the density. Oils work well —linseed, fusel oils, turpentine and others.

Turmeric root yields a bright yellow color, while the leaves of the *Indigofera tinctoria* produce a bluish purple. Nettles give you green, while cornflower petals boiled with vinegar make a lighter shade of blue, and the seeds of the wild rue plant can produce dyes from a range of yellow to red.

The more lasting pigments come from minerals. Ground charcoal gives you black, and limestone or gypsum make white. Ochre powder, that is, clay with iron oxide (page 110), produces yellow and orange pigments, cinnabar gives you bright red and malachite and lapis lazuli produce green and a palette from blue to gray, respectively.

Mollusks and insects can also be used as starting materials. The ink gland of the cuttlefish will produce a sepia tone, and ground sea snails produce purple. The dried carapaces of female cochineal bugs give you carmine — a scarlet color.

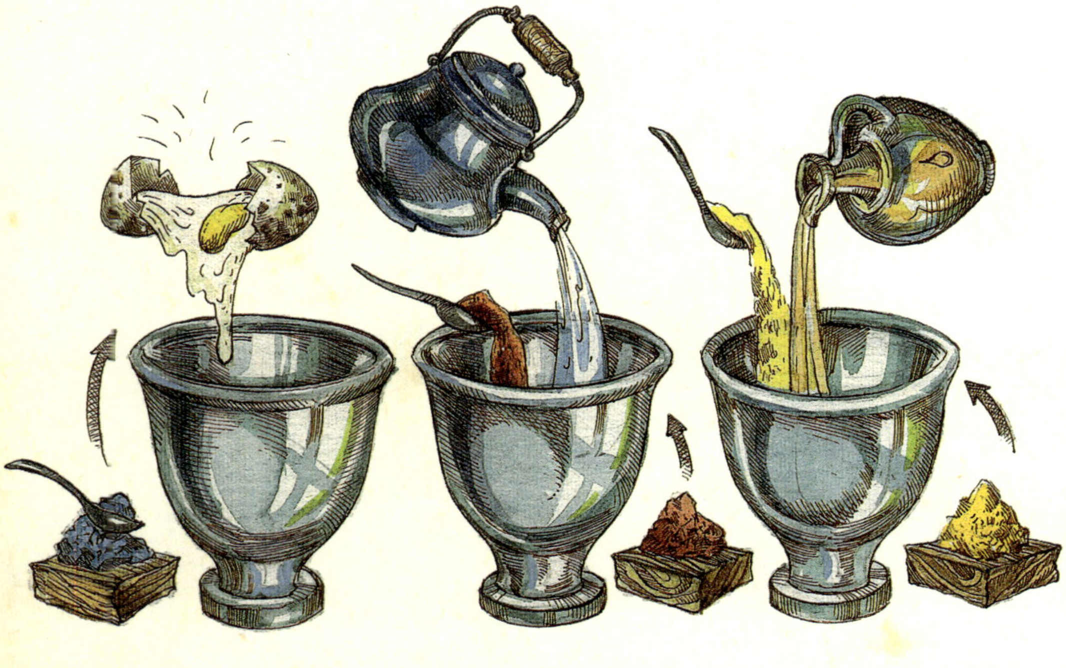

MIXING PIGMENTS

For dry pigments, you'll need a substance that will bind the particles into a homogeneous substance — paint. You can use eggs, oil or water. If you want to use egg as the base, separate the yolk from the white and mix the yolk into pigment and mix. To make a matte paint, add a little wax, and for a shiny sheen, add a drop of resin. To thin your paint, add water or turpentine. The latter can be made by distilling (page 122) the resin from softwood trees.

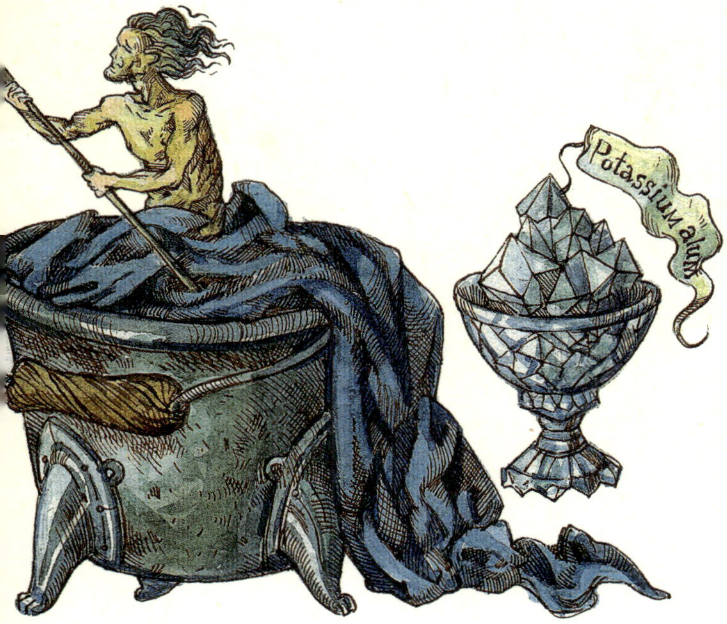

DYEING FABRIC

Plant dyes work best for fabrics. Soak leaves, stems, roots, flowers, fruits, cones or bark in cold, soft water for 12 hours (for every 100 grams of material, you need a liter of water).

Then bring to a boil and soak over very low heat. Flowers and herbs need about 30 minutes, while bark, stems, hulls and roots can take up to 4 hours. Strain. In order to avoid an uneven dye job on cotton and linen, boil them for an hour in a solution of 2 g of soda and 5 g of soap (page 24) per 1 liter of water. If the dye is obtained from berry juice, add 100 g of salt to 8 glasses of water and boil for about an hour; if it's from vegetable juices, add one more part of vinegar to four parts of water. Hold the prepared fabric in a vat of paint for 30 minutes then soak for another 25 minutes in a vat of potash or metal salts: aluminum, chromium, iron, copper (page 110). If they are not available, use natural fixatives: formic acid or vinegar.

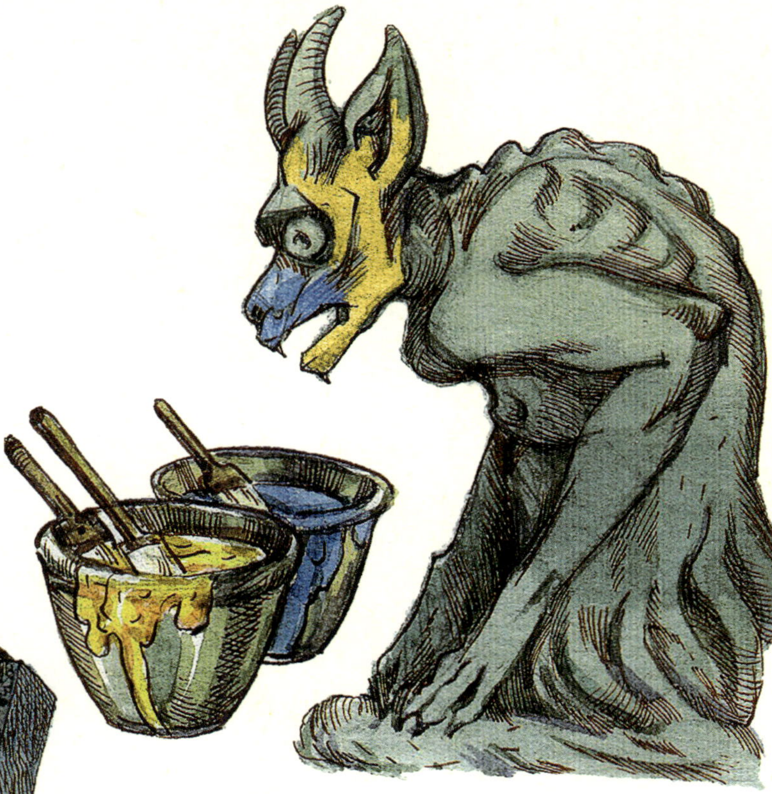

PAINTING WALLS

Use paints based on mineral pigments. But keep in mind that colored minerals, such as malachite and lapis lazuli, cannot be ground into a fine homogeneous powder, and because of this, they don't mix well with fixatives and produce a watery pigment that doesn't fix well. To avoid this, colored mineral pigments must be diluted with egg yolk or casein — a milk protein.

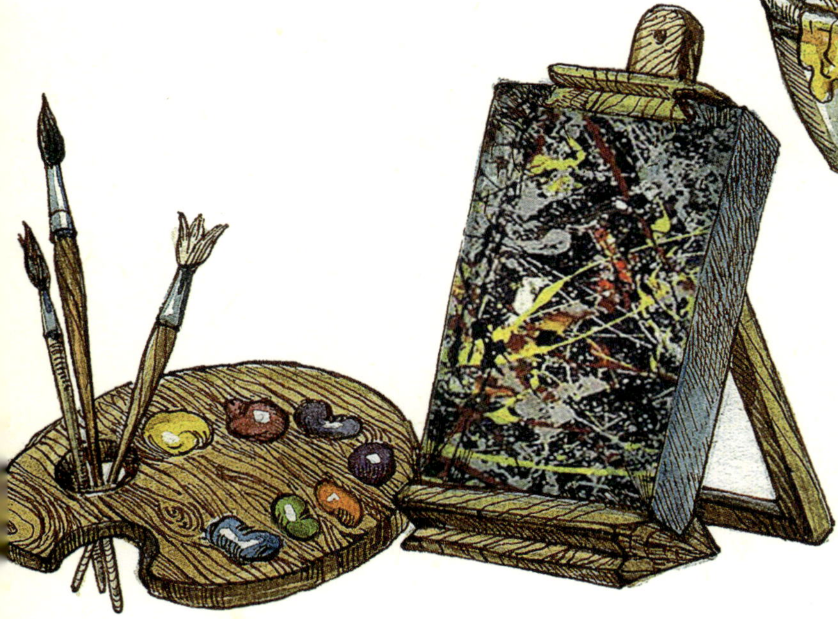

The material you use for the hair of your brush depends on the desired stroke thickness and the type of paint. For fine strokes, use brushes made from the tail hairs of a squirrel, sable or yellow weasel. The finest samples are harvested from males in winter. You can also make brushes from the tails of a mongoose or badger, from behind the ears of a pony or goat or hair from the ears of cows and buffaloes.

BRUSHES

Boar bristle brushes work well for covering large surfaces. First, it must be bleached: wash in warm, soapy water then in cold water and leave it to soak in an aqueous solution of sulfuric acid for 2–3 days. To give the bristles elasticity, place the bound bundles in hot ash for 15 minutes. If you want neat strokes, sand the brush tips down: dip the bristles in clay diluted with water and leave to dry for 1–2 days, and then sand the ends of the brushes on a flat piece of pumice.

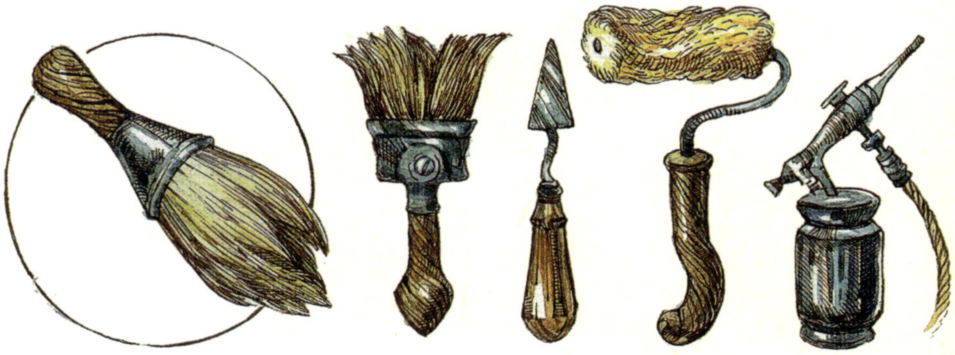

GUNPOWDER

If you want to delight your friends, ignite fireworks to celebrate your victories or fight your enemies, you'll need an explosive — gunpowder. When it burns, it quickly generates a lot of heat and gases that propel a rocket or push a bullet out of a gun barrel.

But there are far more interesting applications for this powder. Ignition cartridges, for example, can be used to power a rocket engine or an ejection seat.

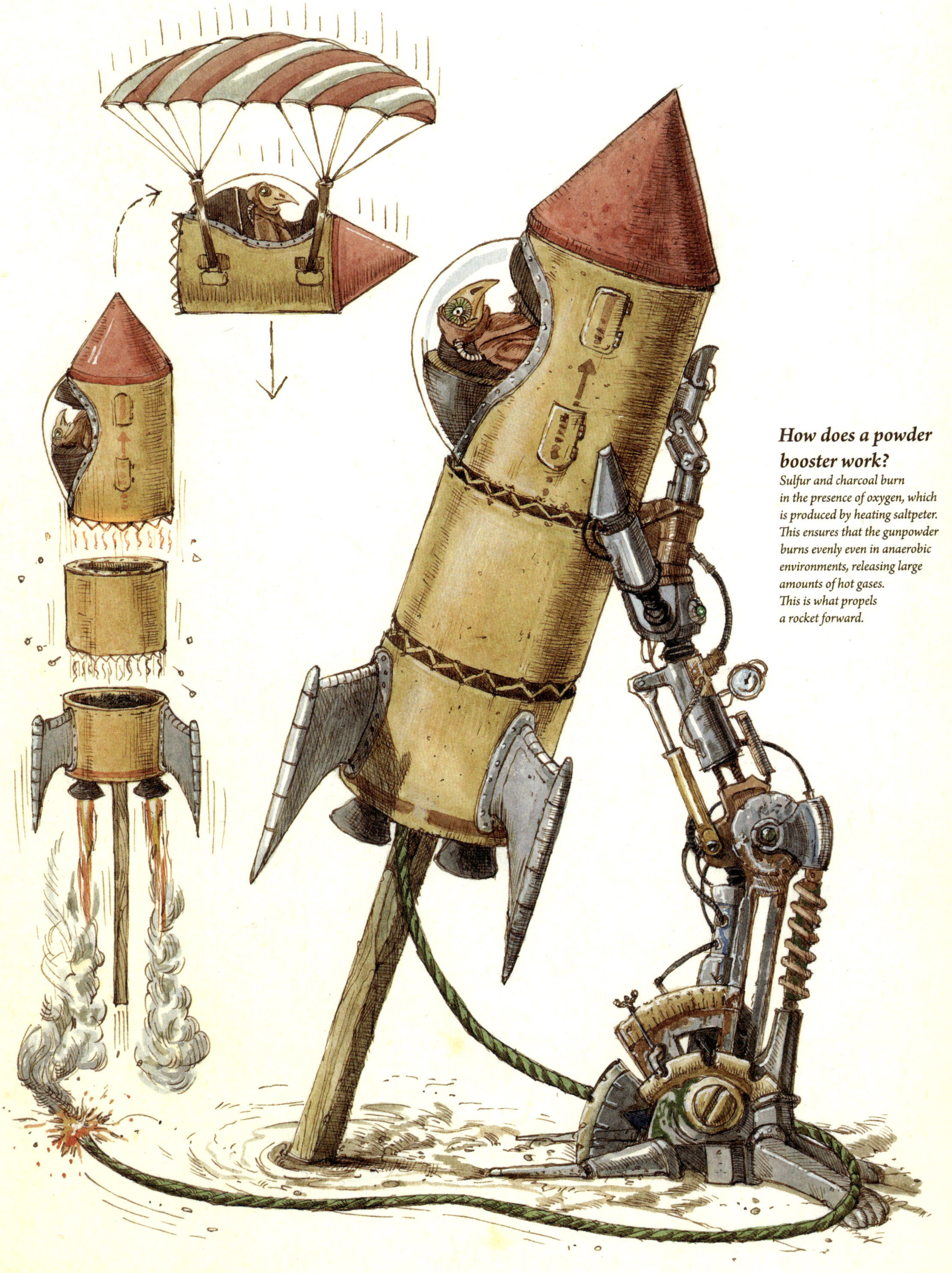

How does a powder booster work?

Sulfur and charcoal burn in the presence of oxygen, which is produced by heating saltpeter. This ensures that the gunpowder burns evenly even in anaerobic environments, releasing large amounts of hot gases. This is what propels a rocket forward.

You can speed up the process with urine. It's a great raw material and a breeding ground for the bacteria involved in oxidizing ammonia.

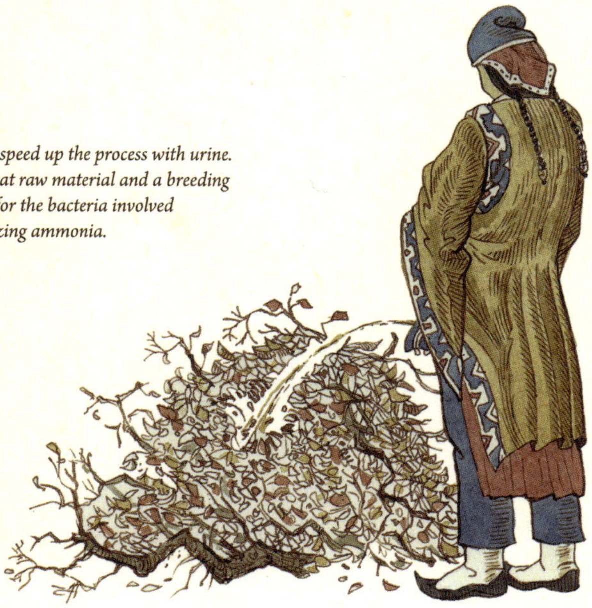

SALTPETER

Make a compost pile of manure, food scraps, straw and limestone. Cover with topsoil to reduce gas leakage. During the decomposition process, ammonia is released, which accumulates in the straw, where bacteria convert it to nitric acid. This reacts with the limestone to produce calcium nitrate.

After a year, soak the contents of the pile in water, and then add ash to the mix. Calcium carbonate settles to the bottom, and potassium nitrate — saltpeter — remains behind in the solution. Leave this solution to dry. Now the saltpeter crystals are ready!

CHARCOAL

Find wood with a low resin content (beech, oak, aspen, alder or birch). Place in a sealed clay or metal vessel. Add an exhaust pipe fitted with a water trap to prevent dangerous fumes from escaping. Make a fire under it. The charcoal for the gunpowder should be left slightly unburned — but only slightly or the gunpowder will burn too slowly.

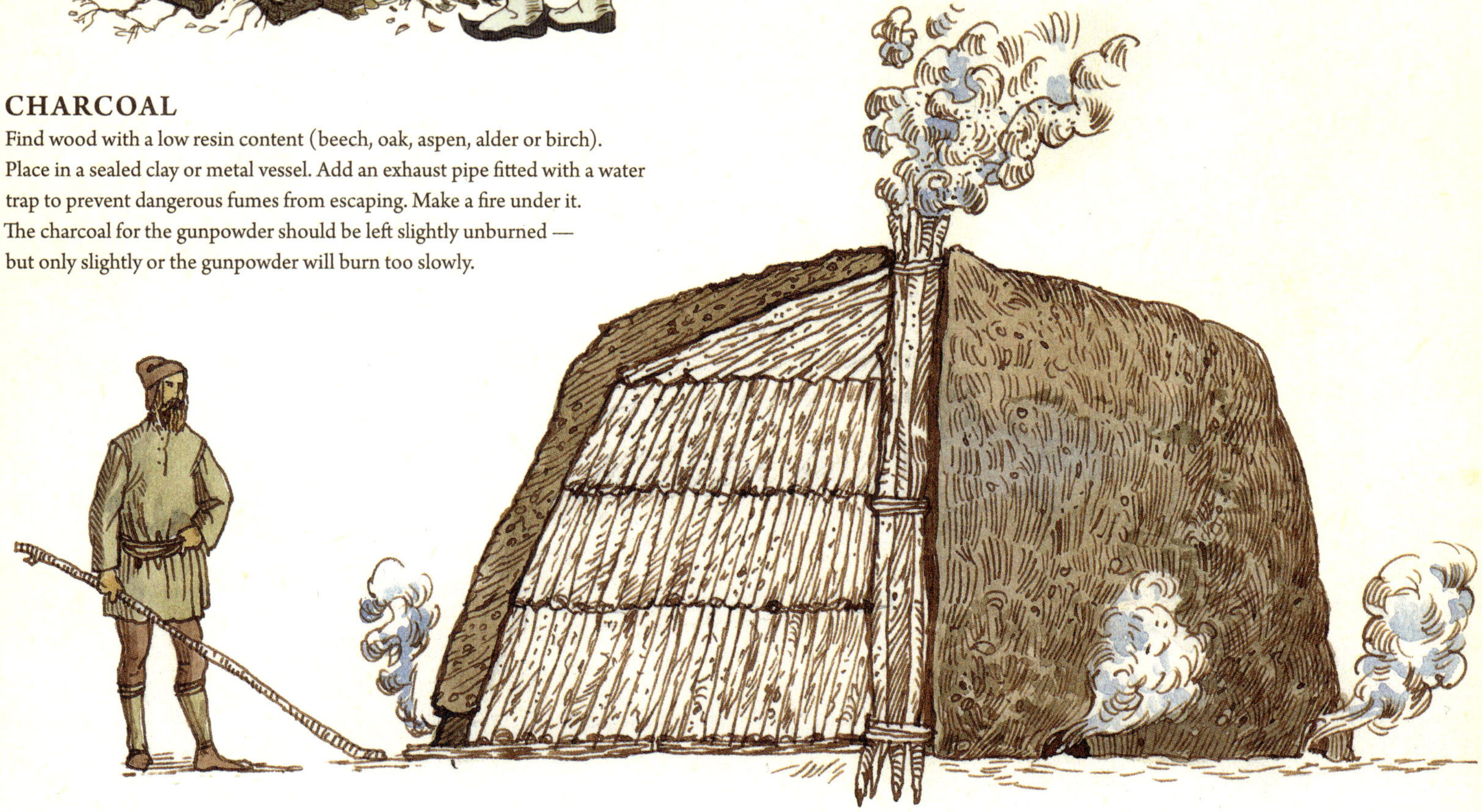

BRIMSTONE

If you are lucky enough to live near a volcano, look around for sulfur (a soft and brittle mineral with a distinctive color ranging from bright yellow to grayish yellow). If pure sulfur is not available, find sulfide ores (page 110). Take two pots.

Make several holes in the bottom of the upper pot and a drain tap in the lower one. Place the ore into the upper pot. Make a fire. Melted sulfur will flow into the lower pot and through the tap into whatever vessel you have placed there. Be careful! You don't want the sulfurous fumes to ignite.

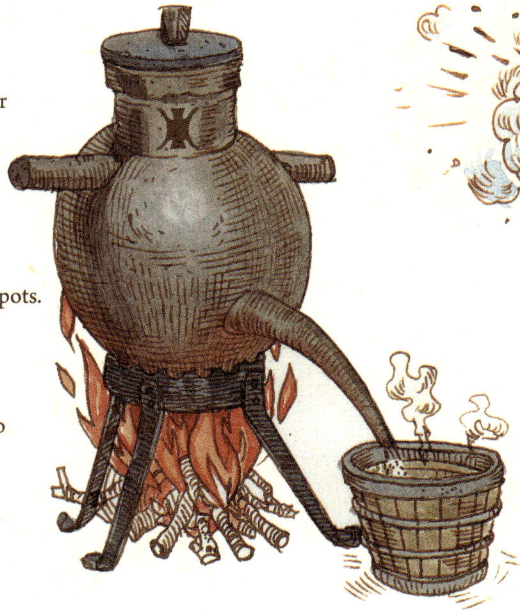

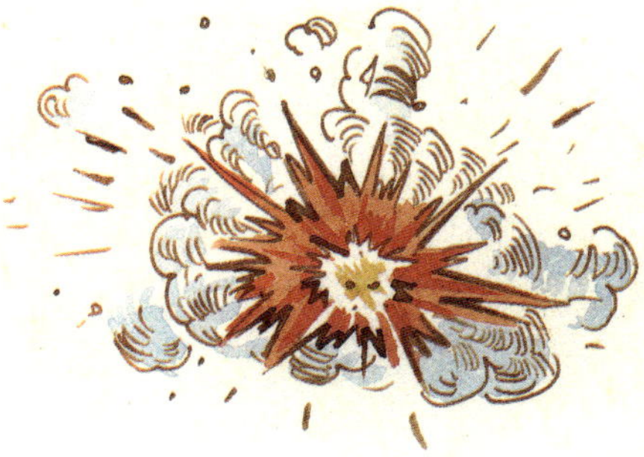

All you need to do is combine three components in the right proportion. These are sulfur (10–25%), charcoal (15–25%) and saltpeter (50–75%).

Moisten with water and form into cakes then dry and grind until you're left with coarse grains. This is gunpowder.

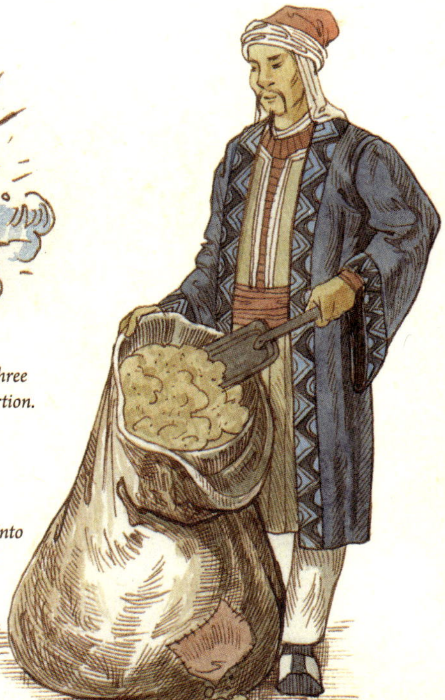

OIL REFINING

Discovery of oil will start new engines of your civilization, taking you into a new era. You will be able to move much faster — drive, fly, swim and conquer space and the depths of the oceans.

But oil is a double-edged sword — what improves the quality of human life can also take a toll on the environment. Try to strike a balance so that in a few hundred years you won't be trying to find ways to save the planet.

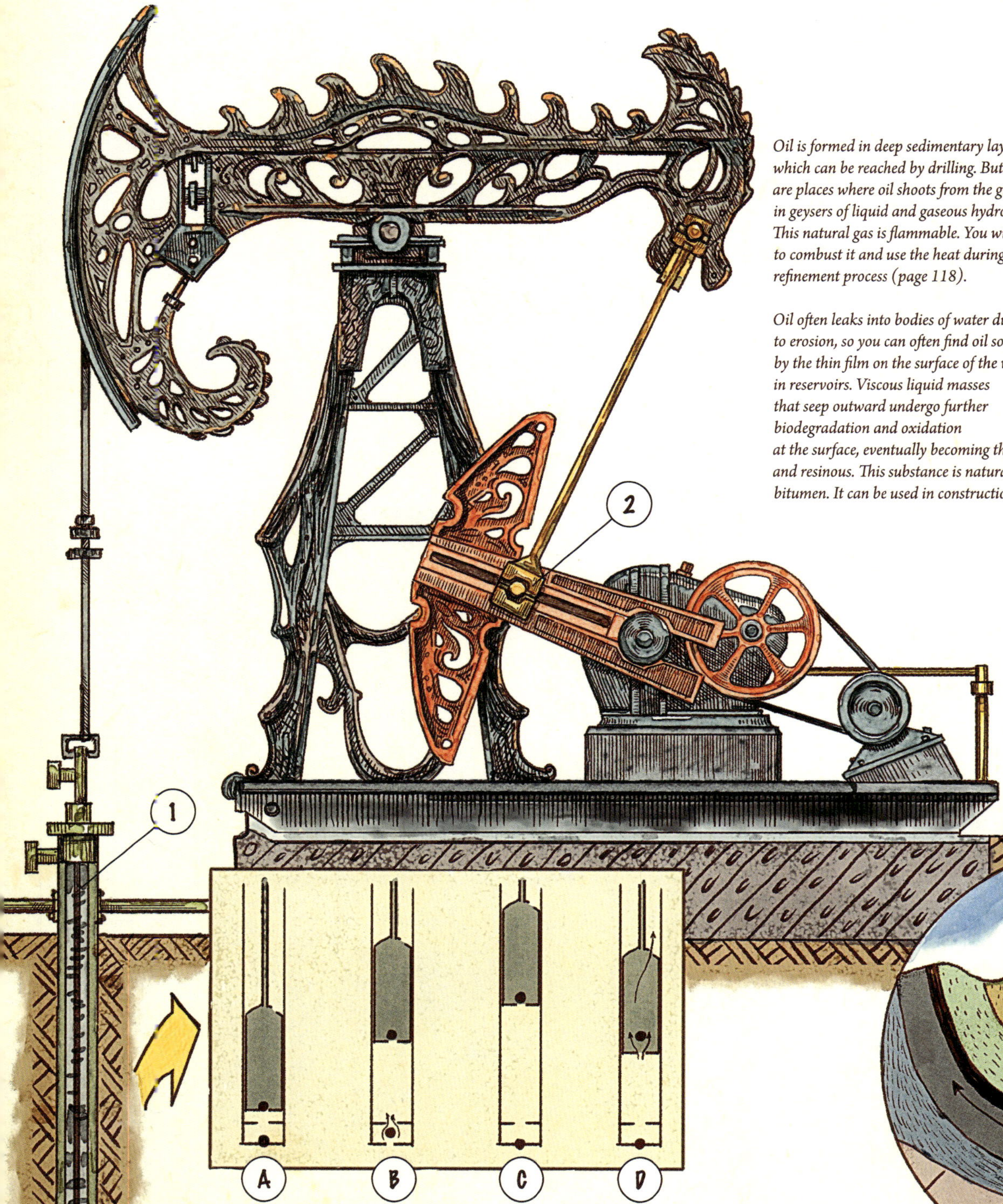

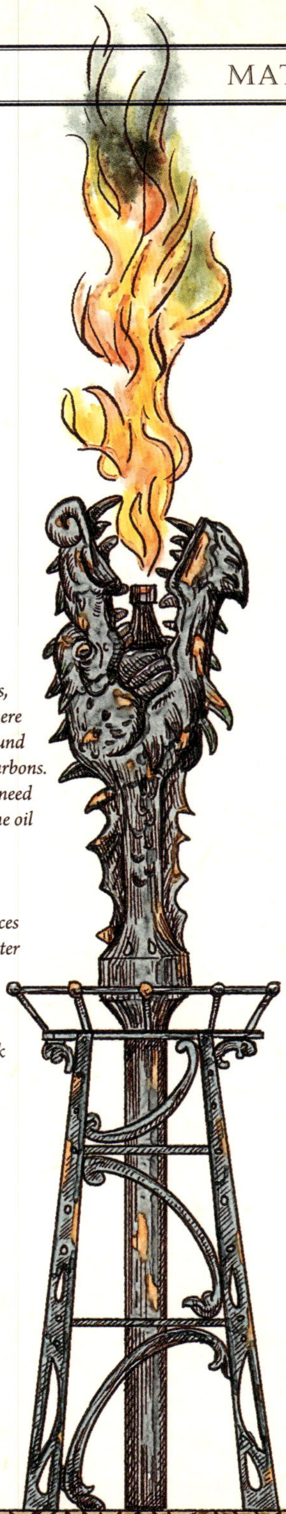

Oil is formed in deep sedimentary layers, which can be reached by drilling. But there are places where oil shoots from the ground in geysers of liquid and gaseous hydrocarbons. This natural gas is flammable. You will need to combust it and use the heat during the oil refinement process (page 118).

Oil often leaks into bodies of water due to erosion, so you can often find oil sources by the thin film on the surface of the water in reservoirs. Viscous liquid masses that seep outward undergo further biodegradation and oxidation at the surface, eventually becoming thick and resinous. This substance is natural bitumen. It can be used in construction.

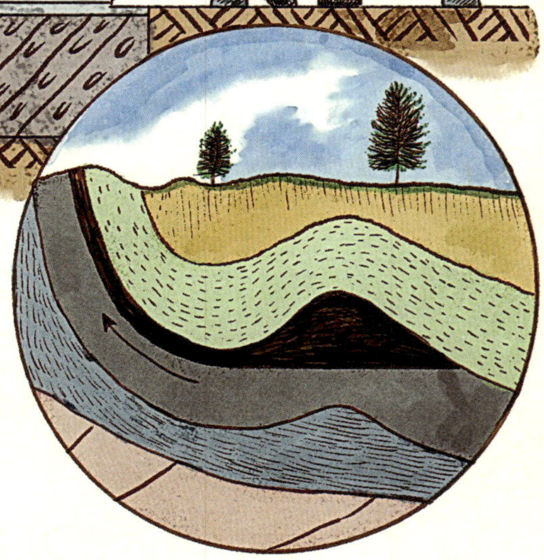

Of course, discovering a petroleum seep is nice. But not much oil can be extracted from the surface of the earth. More often, oil lies deep underground in natural pockets. To reach them, you need to drill a well and pump out the oil. You'll need a giant drill (page 144) to create a deep hole (2000–4000 meters or more) in the earth. It will have to be periodically raised so you can clear the crushed rock from the bore hole.

When you strike black gold, submerge the deep piston pump (1) into the well. It will be driven by the pumpjack (2). It can work on any drive, from a steam engine to electricity.

OIL PUMP

When the piston moves from the bottom (A) upwards, a vacuum is created in the lower part of the pump chamber and oil is sucked through the valve (B). When the piston begins to move downwards, the suction valve closes under the pressure of the pumped liquid (C), and it begins to flow through the hollow channel of the piston and discharge valve into the lifting pipes (D). During the continuous operation of the pump, the oil pumped by it begins to fill the internal volume of the lifting pipes and, as a result, is directed to the surface.

OIL REFINERY

Oil is a mixture of substances that can be separated into components, that is, fractions, using a rectifier (page 118). At the first stage, the oil enters the tube furnace (4) through pipes (3), where it is heated by burning gas (5) to 450–500°C. At this temperature, it is no longer a liquid but a vapor. Through the pipeline (6), it enters the fractionating column (7), where the oil vapors are cooled by refrigeration units at the top (8).

The lightest components with the lowest boiling temperatures rise to the top, while the heavy ones remain at the bottom. In the upper part of the column (9), gasoline, which condenses at 50°C, is removed; then naphtha (10) at 100°C; then (11) kerosene at 200°C; and in the lower section (12), fuel oil at 350°C.

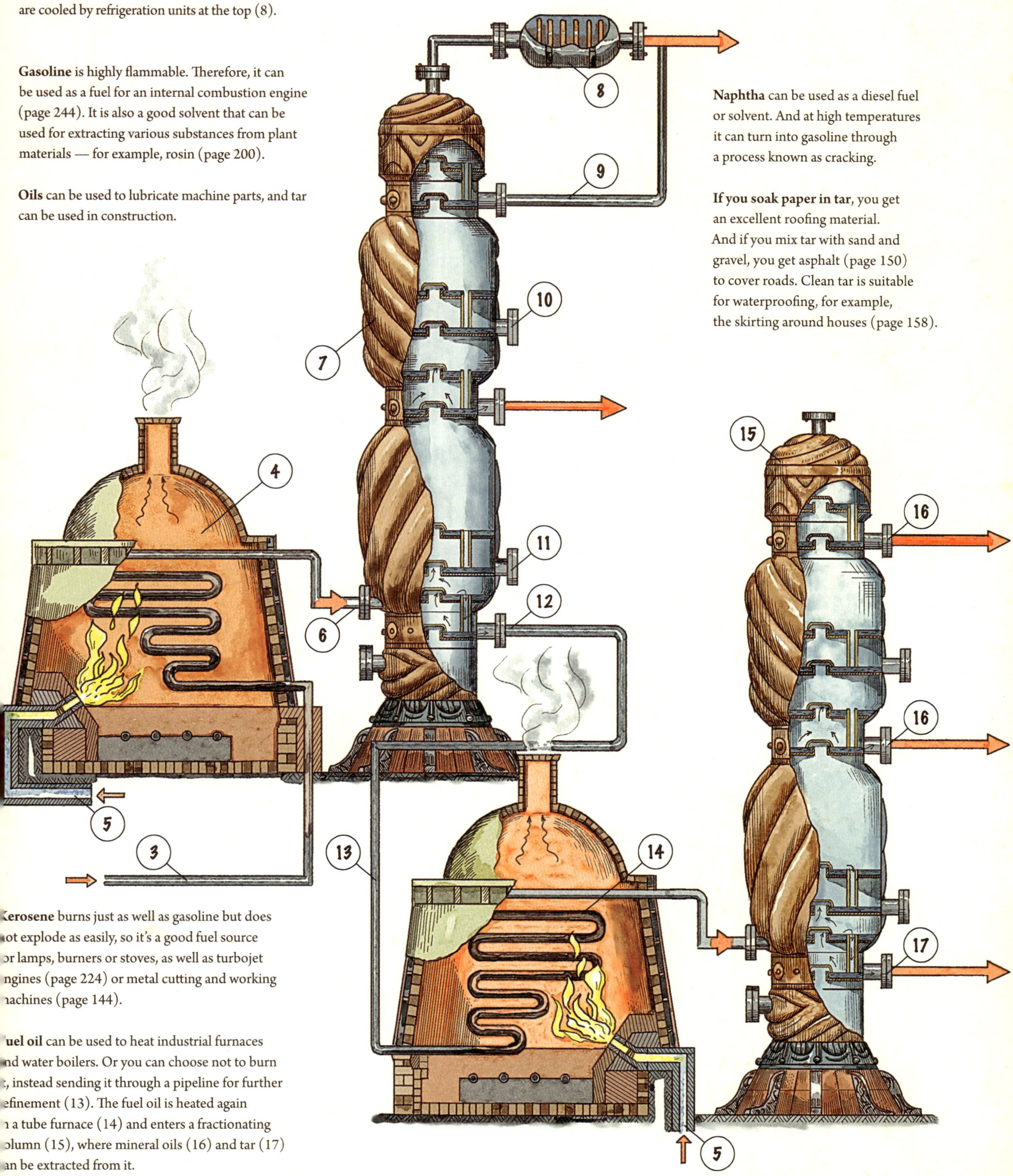

Gasoline is highly flammable. Therefore, it can be used as a fuel for an internal combustion engine (page 244). It is also a good solvent that can be used for extracting various substances from plant materials — for example, rosin (page 200).

Oils can be used to lubricate machine parts, and tar can be used in construction.

Naphtha can be used as a diesel fuel or solvent. And at high temperatures it can turn into gasoline through a process known as cracking.

If you soak paper in tar, you get an excellent roofing material. And if you mix tar with sand and gravel, you get asphalt (page 150) to cover roads. Clean tar is suitable for waterproofing, for example, the skirting around houses (page 158).

Kerosene burns just as well as gasoline but does not explode as easily, so it's a good fuel source for lamps, burners or stoves, as well as turbojet engines (page 224) or metal cutting and working machines (page 144).

Fuel oil can be used to heat industrial furnaces and water boilers. Or you can choose not to burn it, instead sending it through a pipeline for further refinement (13). The fuel oil is heated again in a tube furnace (14) and enters a fractionating column (15), where mineral oils (16) and tar (17) can be extracted from it.

TOOLS

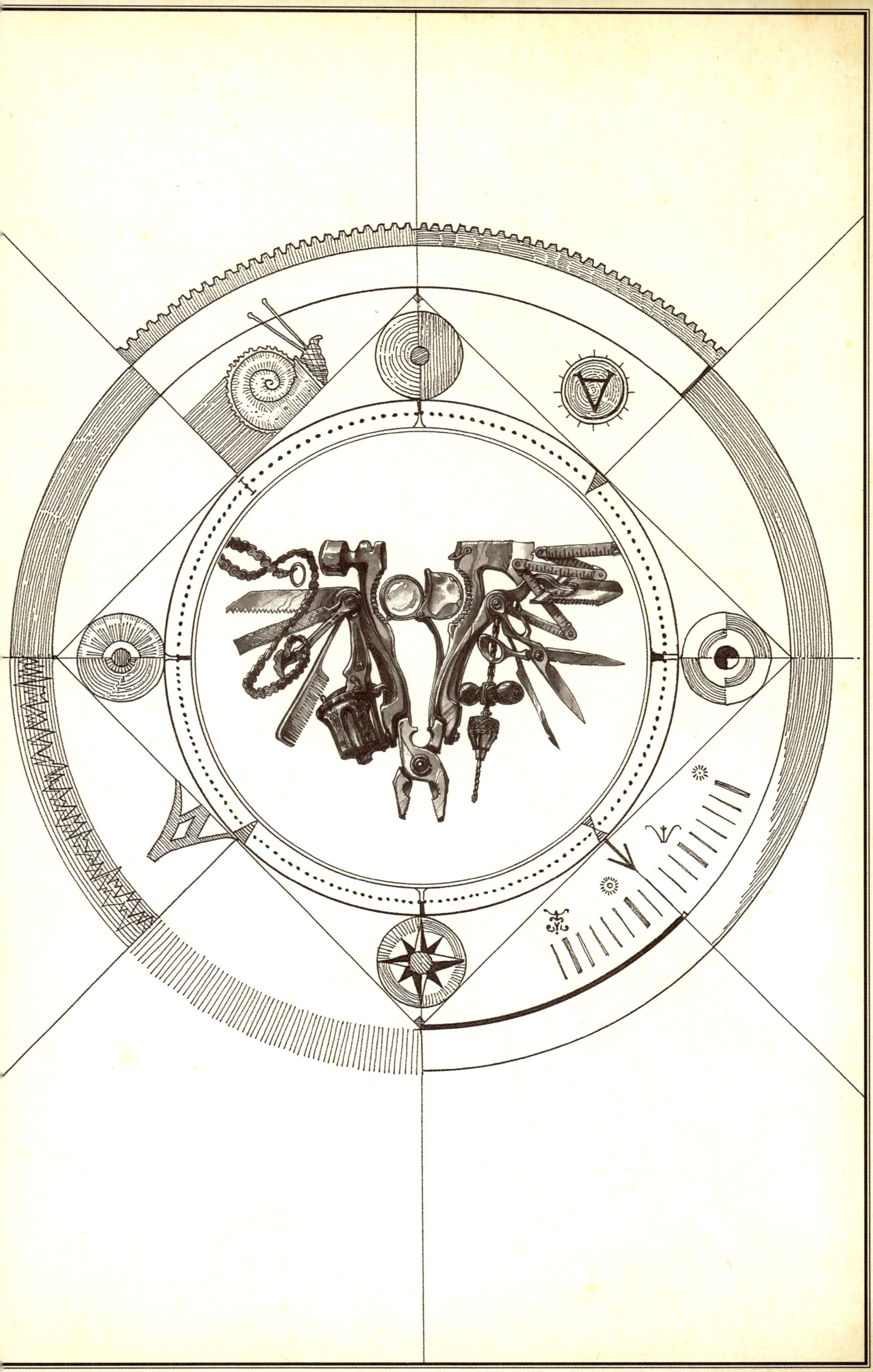

MULTITOOL

Life is unpredictable, and you never know what it might throw at you. Things may break, tear, come loose or go awry in some unexpected ways. A multitool will help you approach these problems from a different angle. If you don't know what tool to bring along with you, simply bring them all.

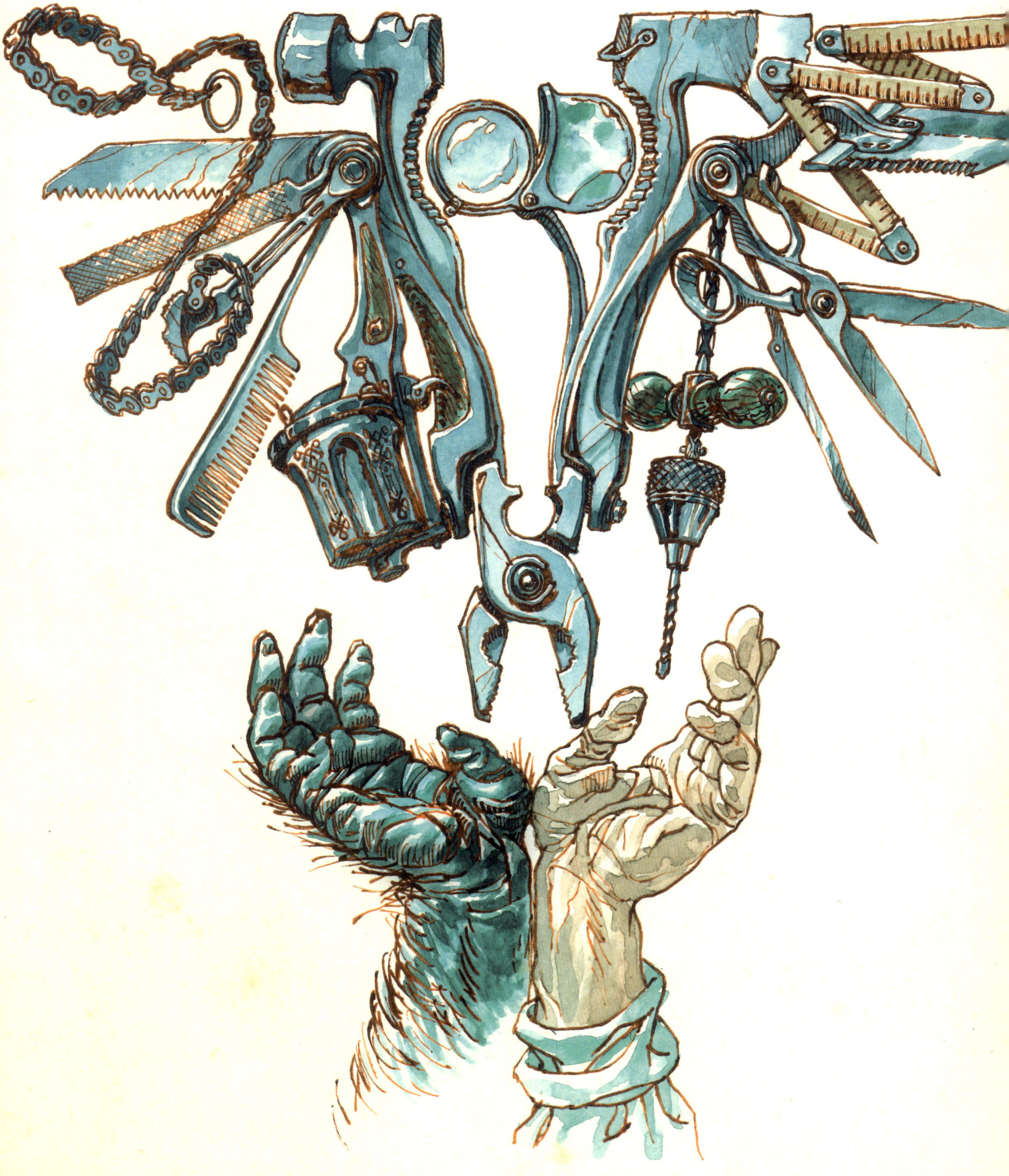

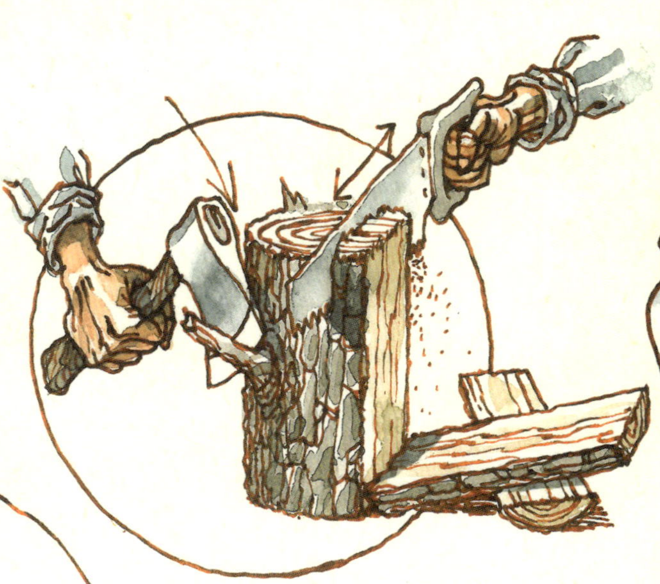

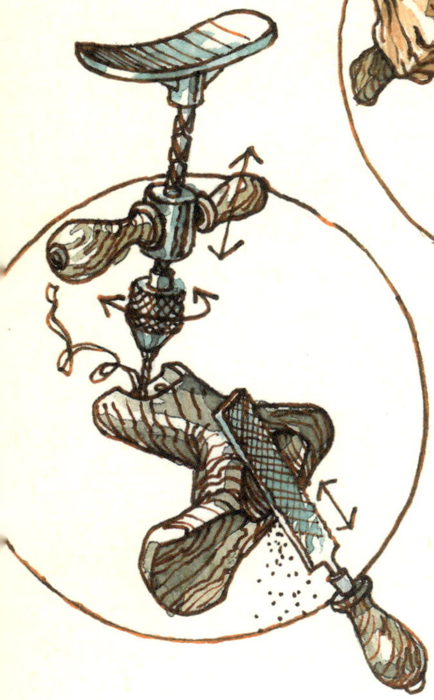

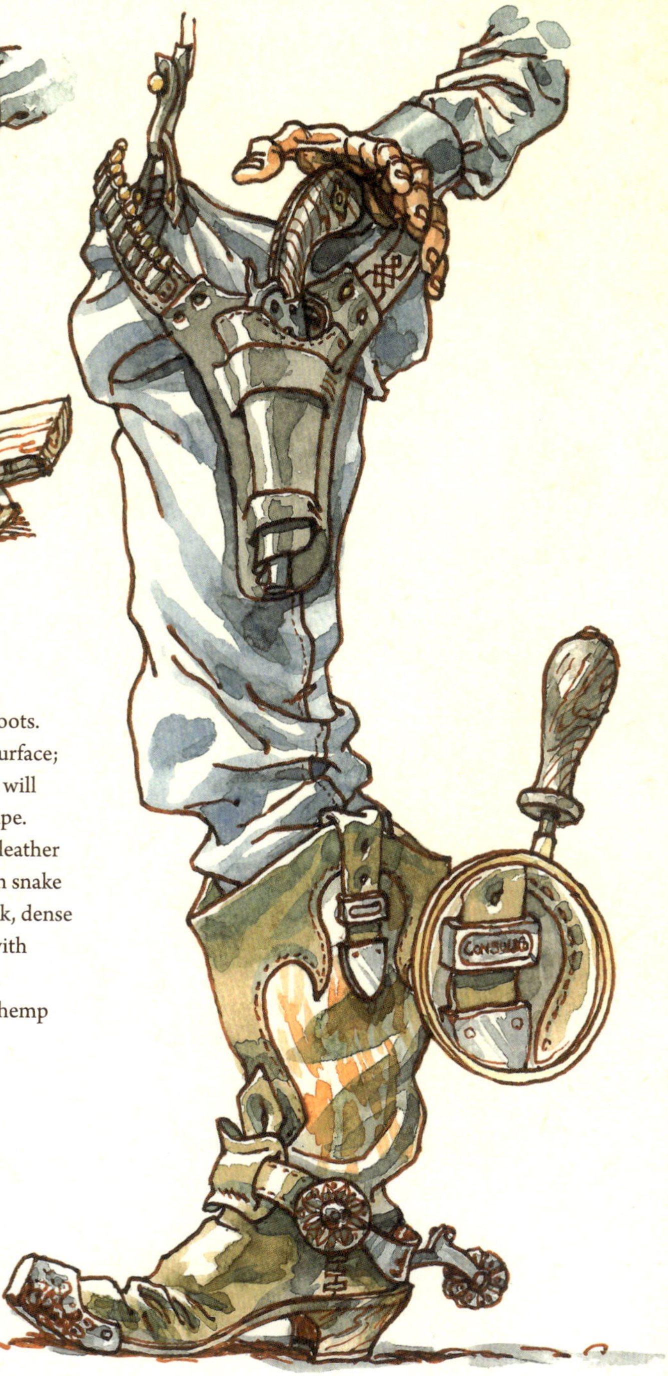

It takes a lot of tools to make one pair of boots. You can't cobble pieces together on a flat surface; you need a model carved from wood. This will allow you to give the shoes the desired shape. Good boots only come from well-dressed leather (page 78) — ox, buffalo, elk, alligator, even snake or eel skin will do. In order to sew this thick, dense material, you'll first need to punch holes with an awl or drill. Ordinary threads won't do. You'll need thick, rough fibers made from hemp or linen (page 54).

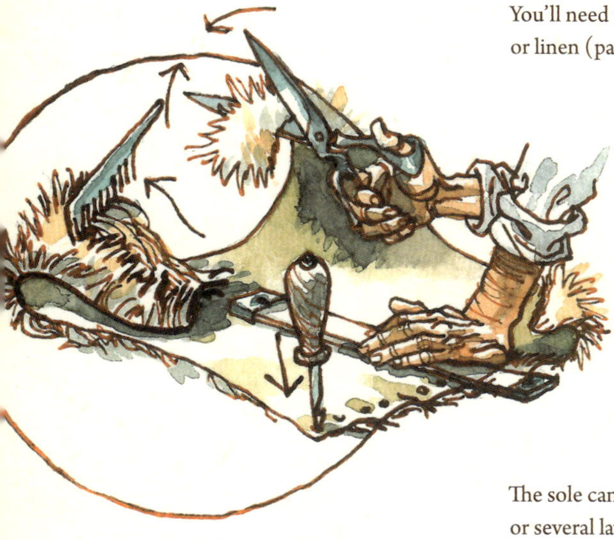

The sole can be made of durable rubber (page 116) or several layers of thick leather soaked in glue and pressed together (page 140). All that's left to do is attach the sole using copper nails and add a tapered heel. There's a reason they're structured this way. Tapered heels won't get stuck inside stirrups, allowing you to quickly dismount from a horse without breaking your ankles. And don't forget to add a thick leather insole to protect the bottom of your feet from injury. Now your boots are ready! A pair like this will last you a lifetime.

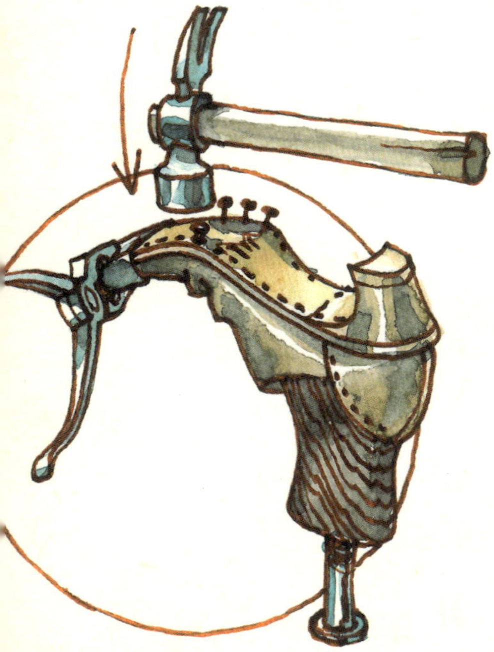

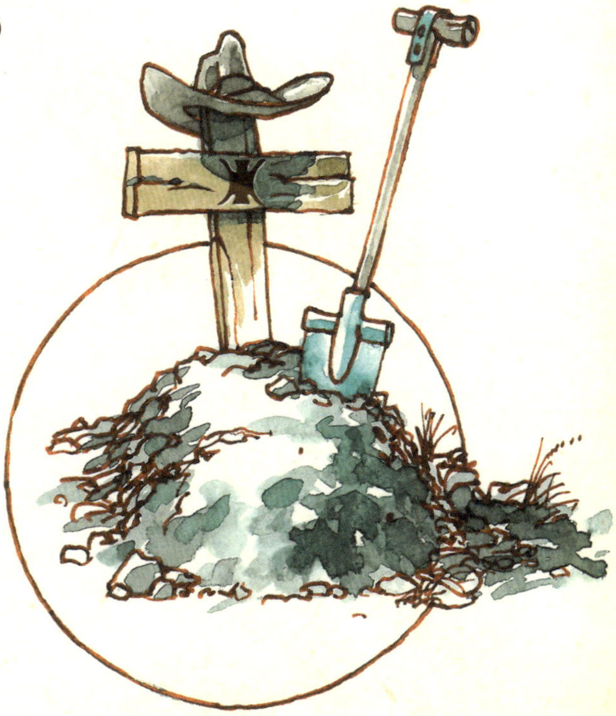

MEASURING TOOLS

The world created by nature is balanced and harmonious. But in order to maintain their own sense of harmony, humans need to agree on a standard paradigm for viewing and understanding the world. This means coming up with measurement conventions for various physical qualities, such as time, length, mass and temperature.

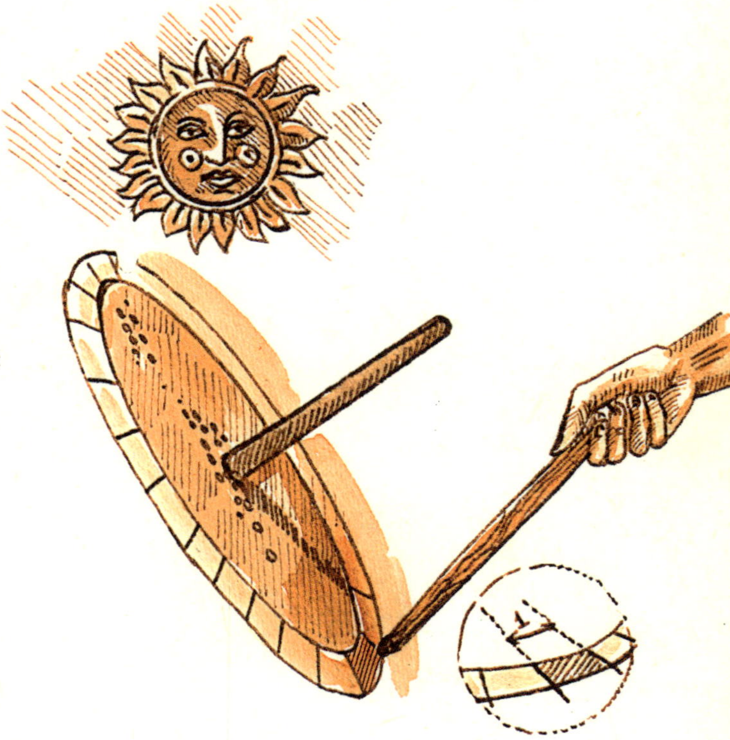

TIME

You can measure time using constant natural processes, such as the rotation of the planet around its axis. To build a sundial, take a flat circle and fix in its center a pin, known as a gnomon, at a right angle. Angle this whole dial so that the gnomon is parallel to the axis of rotation of your planet. To determine what the axis of rotation is, find a fixed point in the sky at night around which all the other stars revolve. Point your gnomon in this direction. Place the gnomon standing up perpendicularly on a round dial then divide the circle into any number of equal radial sections. One division will represent one unit of time in your new system. Give it a name — for example, "hour." When the sun is at its highest point, the shadow of the gnomon indicates the starting point for counting — noon. From this place, you need to divide the circle into equal intervals: N hours in one direction, N in the other. For practical purposes, it is better to divide the hour into smaller units. The one drawback is that you can only tell the time during the day and in clear weather.

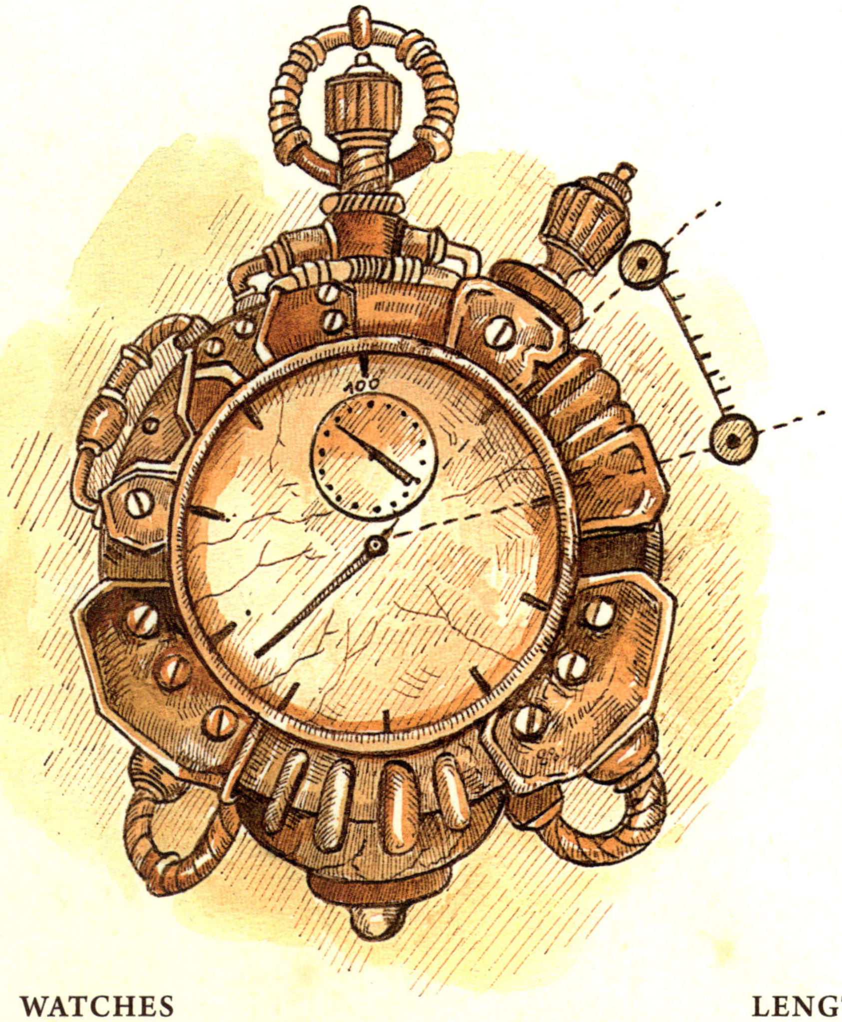

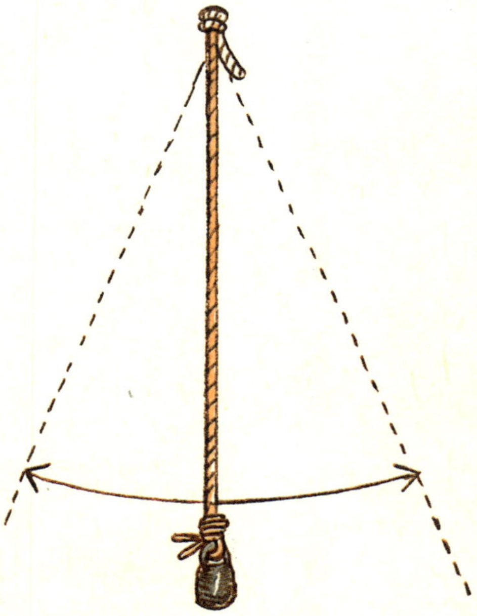

WATCHES

At first, the sun and the rotation of the planet around its axis will help you measure time. But this device is not entirely accurate nor very convenient for measuring short periods of time. You'll need a watch (page 166). For longer periods of time, use units such as "week, "month" and "year," consisting of an integer number of days. Make one year equal to the period of revolution of the planet around the star.

LENGTH

So now you have a standard of time: a second. Using this, you can create a standard for measuring length. Make a pendulum: take a rope or, even better, a thin rigid rod and attach a weight to one end. Pull it back slightly from its equilibrium position and release. Adjust the length of the rope or rod so that one full swing — the time it takes to travel all the way back to the release point — occurs in two seconds. The length of this pendulum is one meter. You can subdivide this into smaller segments for ease of measurement.

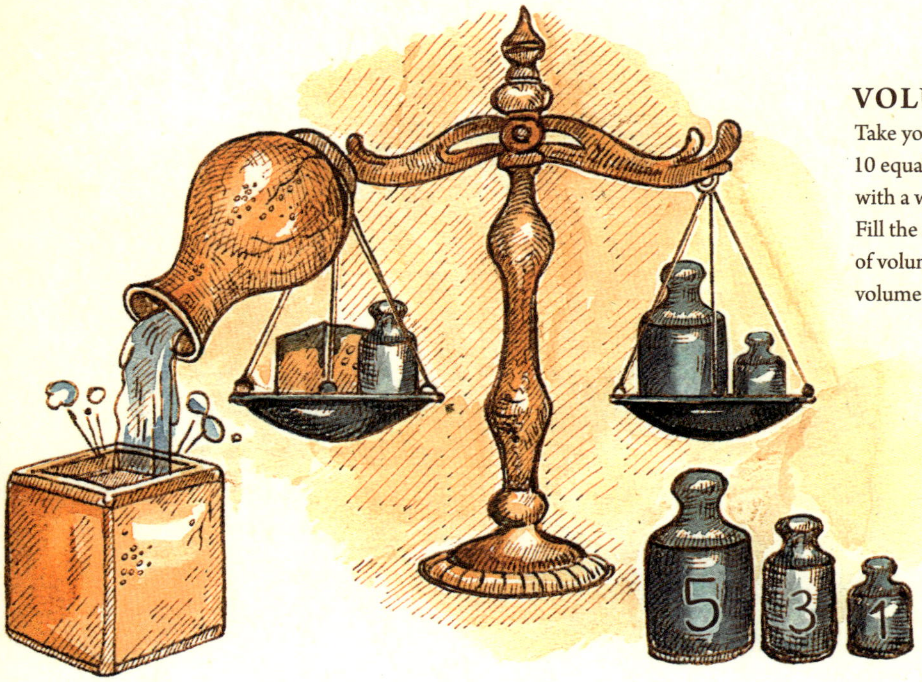

VOLUME AND WEIGHT

Take your unit of length — the meter — and divide it into 10 equal parts. Form a clay vessel with a cube-shaped inner cavity with a width, height and depth of 1/10 of the length standard. Fill the resulting cube-vessel with water, and you'll have a unit of volume, conventionally known as the liter. And the mass of this volume of water will become a unit of mass — a standard kilogram.

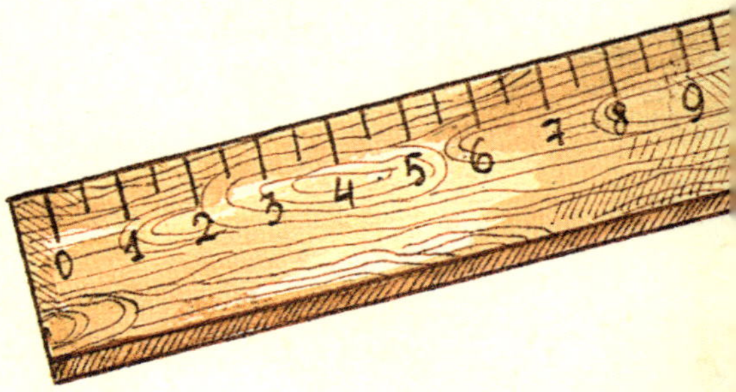

TEMPERATURE

You can measure temperature with the help of a thermometer — a thin glass tube with a small glass bulb on one end. Fill the tube with mercury then pump out excess air and seal. When the bulb touches the object you're measuring, the mercury expands and rises up the tube, indicating the temperature of the object using scale markers that run up the thermometer.

You can calibrate the instrument using a simple two-point method by taking two set temperatures and dividing the distance between them into 100 equal parts.

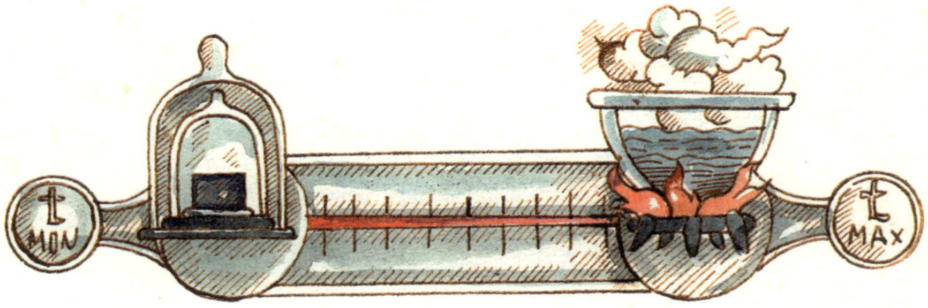

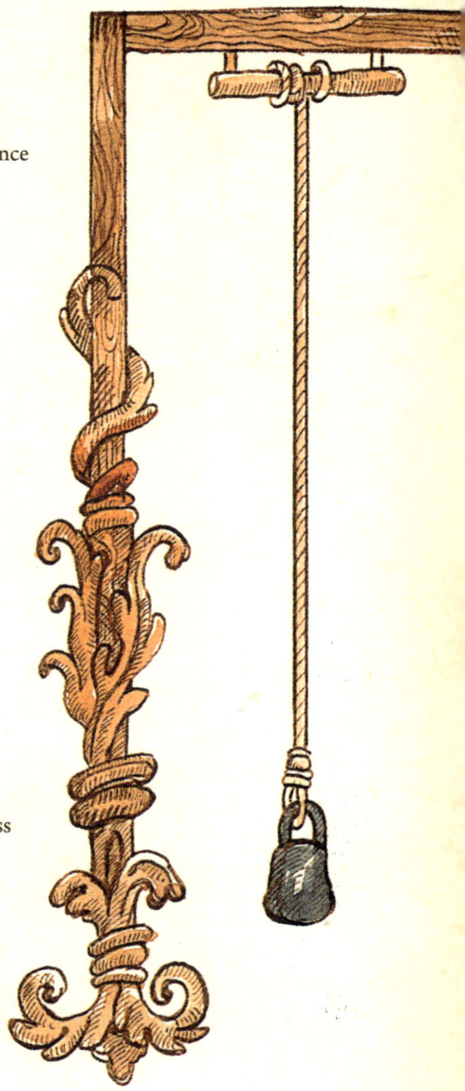

VERTICAL

Use a plumb line to determine the vertical. Tie a load to the end of a rope. The gravity of the earth is pulling towards the center of mass of the planet, so your rope will always be absolutely straight and vertical.

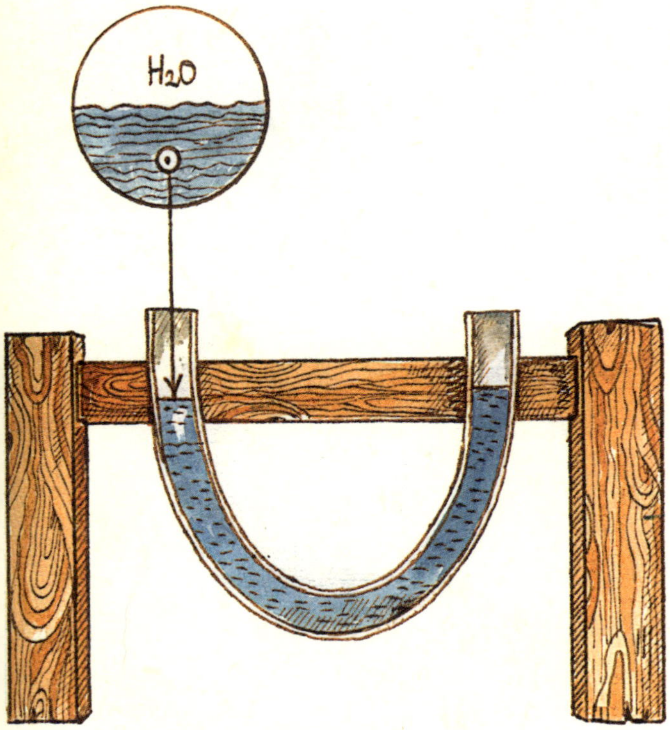

HORIZONTAL

For your buildings to be stable, they need to be level: the supports vertical, and the ceilings horizontal. An easy way to build a horizontal line is with a transparent tube of small diameter in the form of an arc of large radius. Fill it with water tinted for better visibility. When the liquid level in both parts of the semicircle of the tube is at the same height, the line connecting them will be strictly horizontal.

WHEEL

The orbits of the planets, the seasons of the year, even history itself move in grand circles. The wheel of life keeps turning. With so many wheels all around us, there's no need to reinvent one.

If you're reading this book, you probably already know that round objects roll more easily than square ones. But sometimes a civilization's technological regression can be so severe that they forget how to make a wheel by hand.

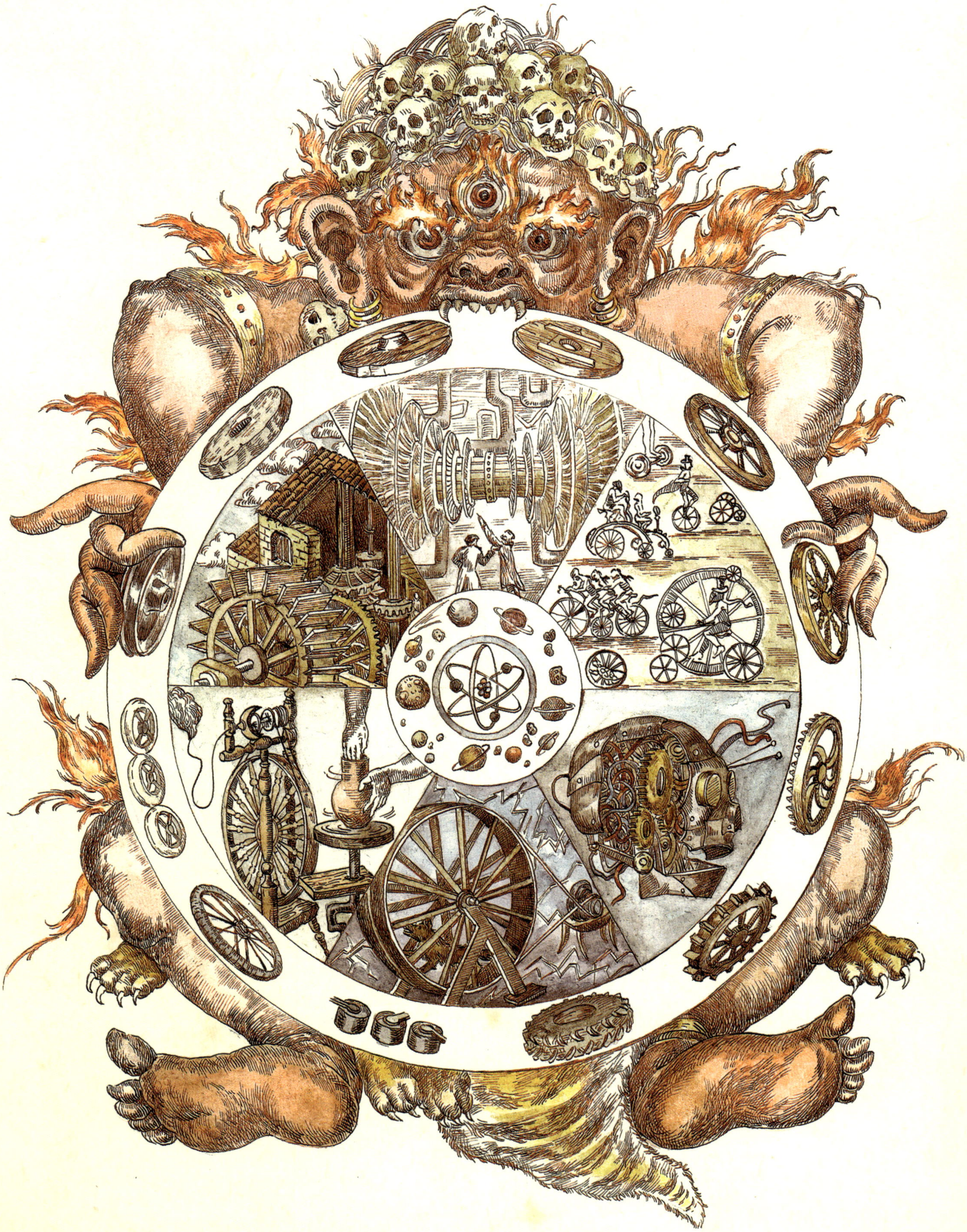

THE STRUCTURE OF THE WHEEL

If this is your first time making a wheel, start with a simple cartwheel design. The central part of any wheel is the hub (1). This connects the spokes (2) to the rim (3). The hub connects the wheel to the shaft, which is what makes the wheel turn. Already made a pair of wheels? Connect them by running a shaft through the hub of each. The wheels will now spin in sync. This is the first step in making a transportation device.

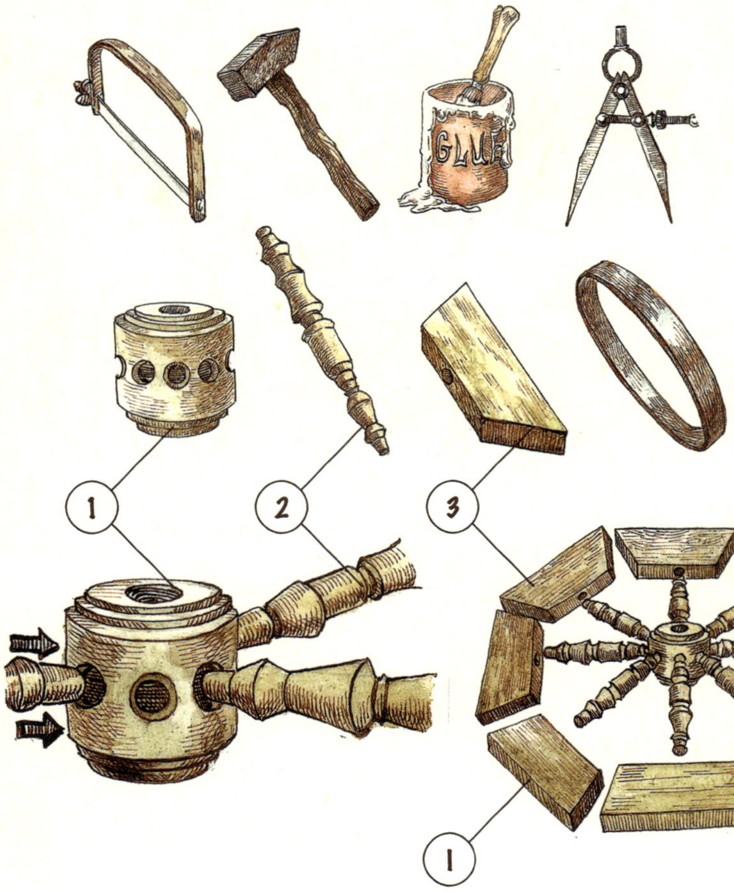

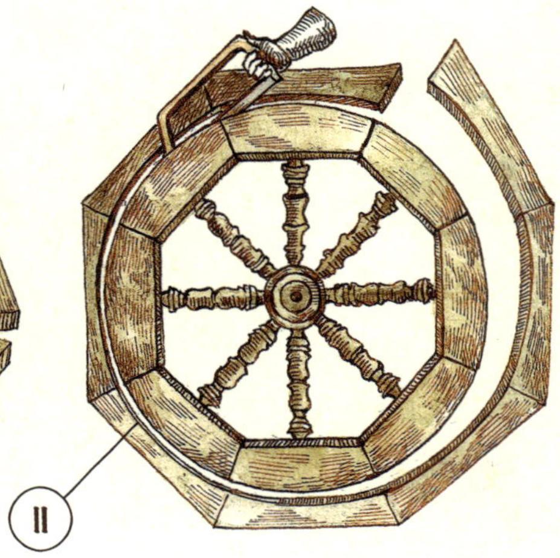

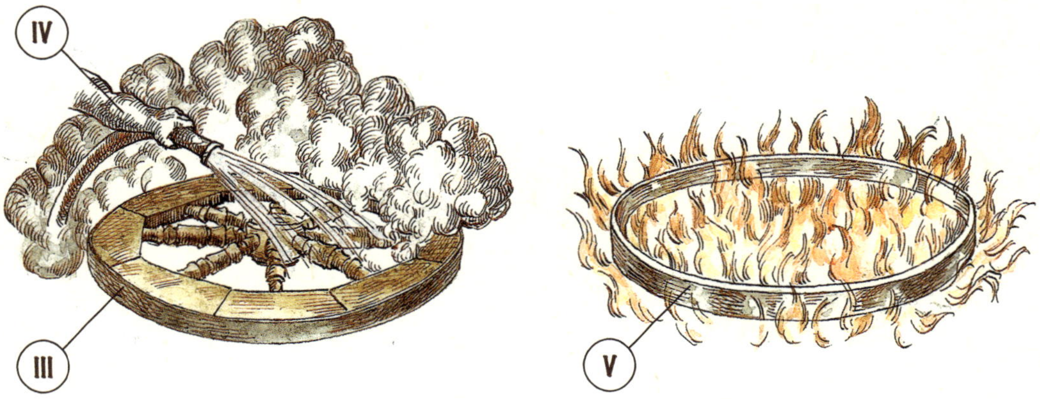

BUILDING THE WHEEL

Making an even and round wheel with simple tools is not easy. However, the challenge can be overcome. Even a square block can be whittled into a round wheel. Glue several blocks of wood together into a rough circle (I), and then whittle away all excess material (II). To keep the wheel from falling apart and make it more wear resistant, wrap the outer edge of the wheel in a steel strip (III). Heat up the steel rim before installing, then slip over the wheel and spray it with cold water to cool it quickly (IV). This will cause the steel to shrink and hug the wooden wheel underneath. If you add a rubber sheath with an inflatable rubber tube inside, you can create a pneumatic tire (V). This will act as a shock absorber, dampening any bumps in the road, and can be used on bicycles (page 164) or other wheeled vehicles.

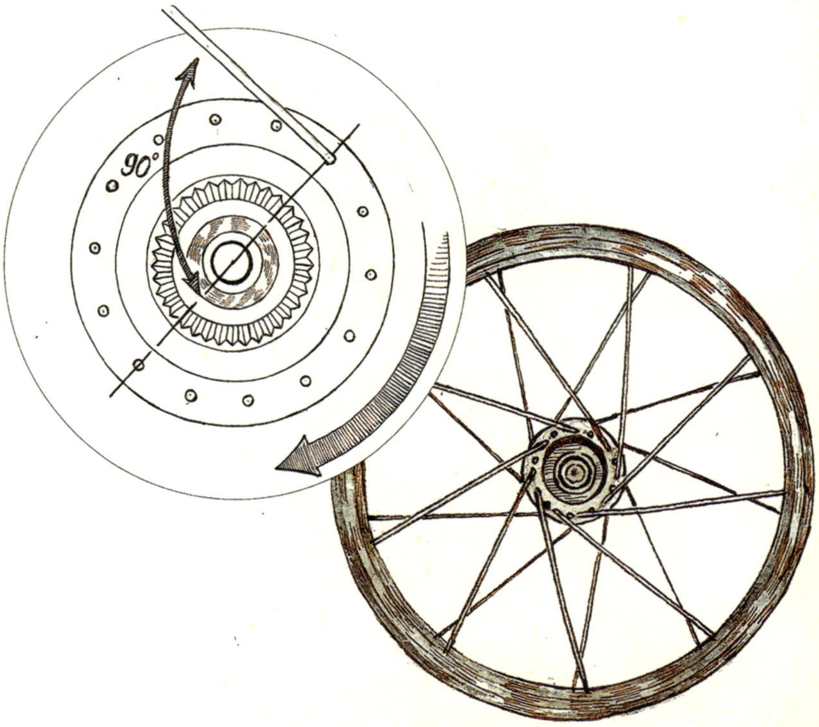

SPOKE LACING

Spokes allow you to reduce the weight of the final product without compromising strength. They center the rim, redistribute the load evenly and provide stiffness to the wheel. When the spokes are laced "crosswise," each of them crosses one another from one to four times. "Compacting" the lacing cross patterns and increasing the number of spokes improve the wheel's ability to absorb vibration from the road. The greater the angle between the spoke and the radius of the wheel at its mounting point, the more evenly the load will be distributed. In a perfect wheel, it's at a 90° angle.

POTTER'S WHEEL

One ancient legend states that God molded man from clay. But why clay? It's easy to shape, widely available and retains its form after it hardens. Perhaps God had his own, more symbolic reasons, but this is why we value the material so highly.

As highly symmetrical beings themselves, humans have an inherent desire to make everything even. Of course, there are also practical reasons for this. The task of making a perfectly round clay pot is made significantly easier with the help of a potter's wheel.

HOW IT WORKS

The lower flywheel (1) turns the shaft (2), which holds the turntable on top (3). The heavier the flywheel, the more even the rotation will be. Use a dense wood or stone. To avoid having to turn the flywheel with your feet, you need an external drive (7). This turns the wheels through the drive belt (6), transmitting the rotation to the shaft of the potter's wheel. In order to ensure constant movement, use a clutch disc (5) controlled by pressing the pedal (4) to regulate the rotation of the turntable.

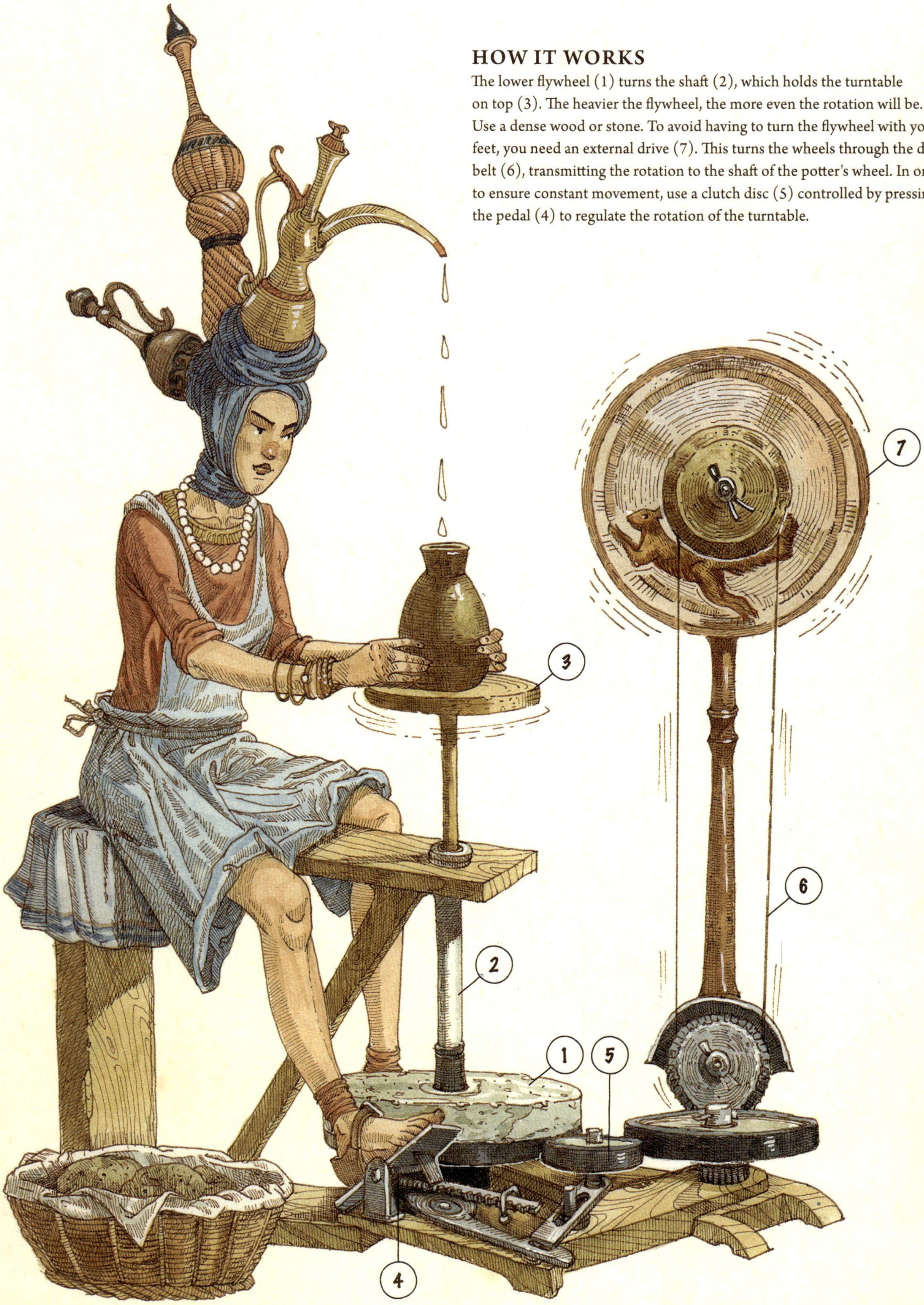

OPERATING TECHNIQUE

Right-handed potters spin counterclockwise; lefies, clockwise.

1. Place the clay in the exact center of the turntable. Knead it by pushing the mass into the table with the heel of your palm then folding it back over itself. Repeat several times.
2. Begin rotating the wheel and, without stopping, use the tip of one thumb to create a dimple in the middle of the clay lump. Use your dominant hand to shape the walls of the vessel while the other wraps around the outside of the wall for support.
3. You can widen the base of your pottery, if necessary. Put pressure on the inside wall of the cylinder, pushing it out from the center and supporting the vessel with your other hand. To narrow the vessel, use your outer hand to press towards the center. Jiggering is the process of shaping flatware, such as plates. A similar technique, jollying, refers to the production of hollowware, such as cups.
4. Work from the bottom up: Place the fingers of one hand inside the vessel and provide resistance from the other side with your other hand. Slide your hands up, "lifting" the walls of your pottery.
5. To smooth out your walls, use a scraper, such as a thin metal plate, and wet the surface of the vessel with a moist cloth.
6. When finished, remove the ware from the wheel. To avoid damage, separate the vessel from the turntable using a thin metal wire.

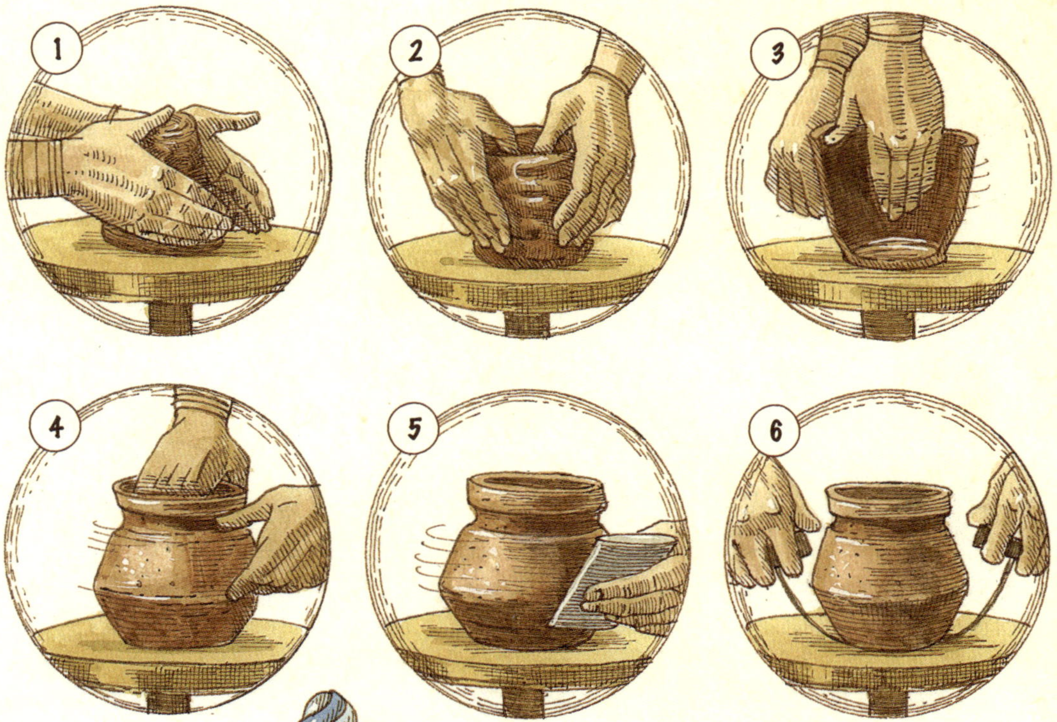

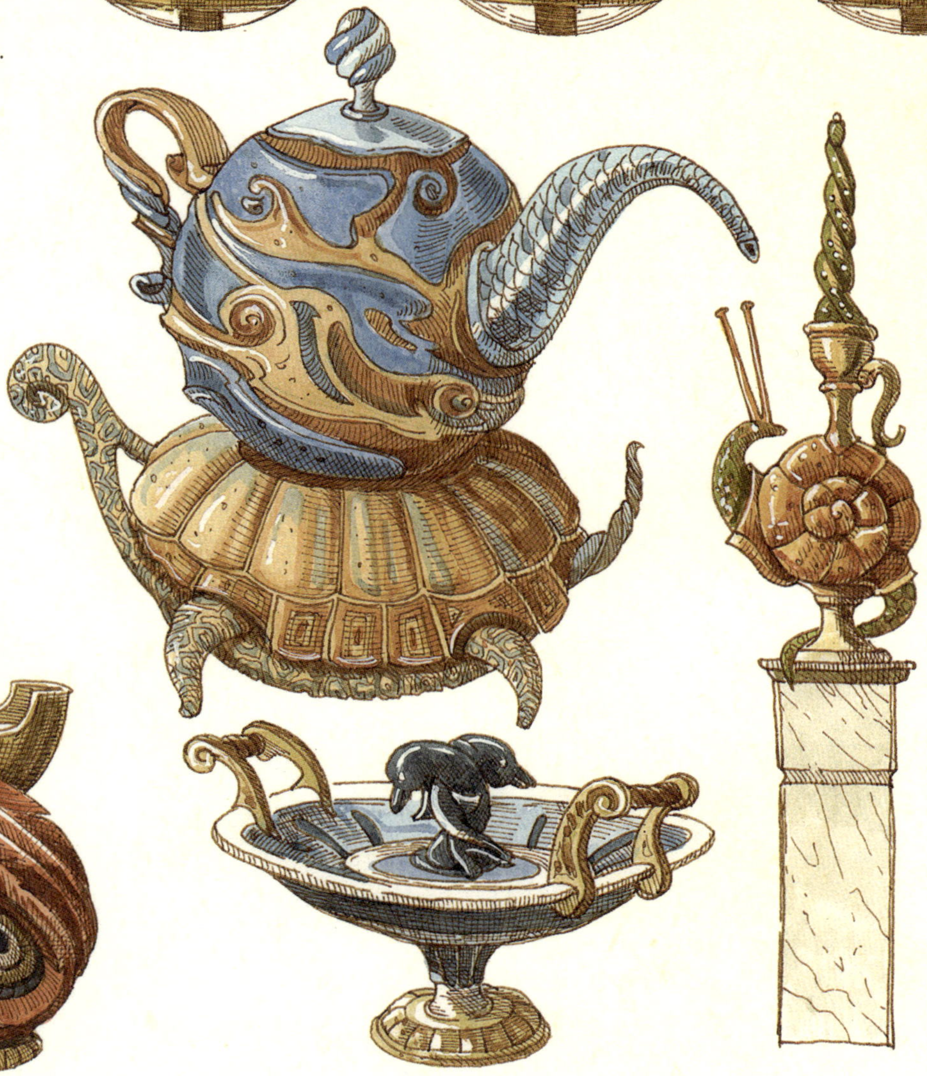

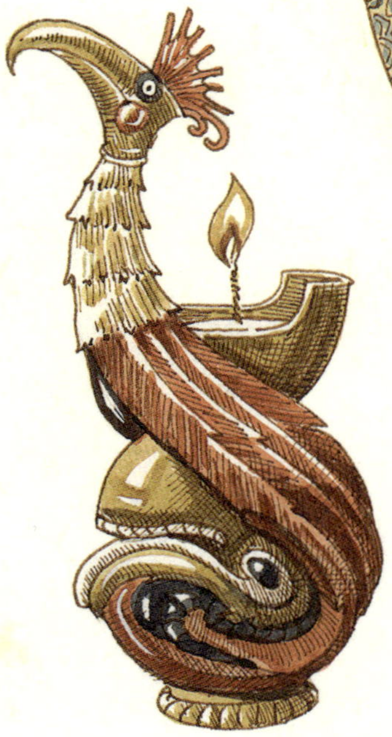

THE CLAY

Dry the clay (red or white) collected in the quarry. Break it up into small pieces and cover with water. Wait until the clay has dissolved into the consistency of milk. Leave it for 10 minutes until the sand and other heavy particles have settled to the bottom. Carefully pour the clay solution without residue into another container. Wait a few hours until the clay has settled to the bottom. Then drain the water and put the clay into a plaster mold so that it absorbs the excess moisture. When the clay is ready, it will not stick to your fingers but will remain soft and yielding.

DRYING AND FIRING

Place your pottery in the kiln. The most important part of the firing process is gradually changing the temperature without heating too rapidly, as this will cause cracks to form. Gradually raise the temperature to 1000°C — but no faster than 100 degrees an hour. If you heat it in a fire, place it in sand to avoid rapid heating. Firing will make your pottery strong and durable.

FORGING

The knife is the king of tools. It's a universal weapon, at once a device for stabbing, chopping and cutting. The main component — the blade — must undergo a series of trials, passing through both flame and water, each step only making it stronger.

The best material for making a knife is steel (page 240). In order to improve the quality of the metal, you'll need to cast and shape it using a forge — an oven that is able to rapidly reach very high temperatures.

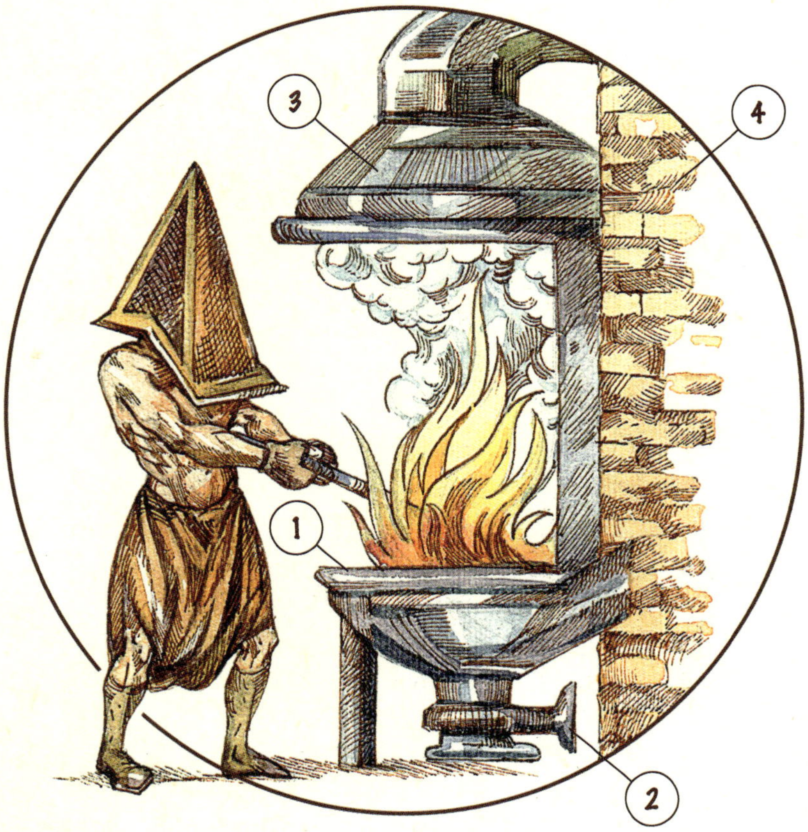

FORGE

Melting metal requires extremely high temperatures. Bring the heat with a forge. Make a fire-proof bowl for burning coal (1). Place a nozzle (2) at the bottom to inject combustable air into the system. To collect the volatile products of this combustion, make a cone hood (3) and connect it to the chimney (4).

FORGING

A forged blade is more resilient than regular steel. Start with two layers (I), one of hard carbon steel and one of soft, low carbon steel. Heat in the forge and strike with a hammer (II). Fold in half, heat again and strike. During this process, impurities in the steel are removed and the layers are welded together. You can make even more layers by folding it in half once again (III), reheating and forging. As a result, the lower layers will move outward and a pattern will appear on the blade. If there were 8 layers on the initial blade, once it is reforged, there will be 16, and then 32, 64, and so on. The more layers, the higher the quality of the blade. The optimal number is between 300 and 500 layers. This produces a composite known as Damascus steel. To give the blade a zigzag pattern, twist the plates into a spiral. One twist will produce steel with a diagonal pattern (A), two will produce an angular pattern (B), three will produce a zigzag (C).

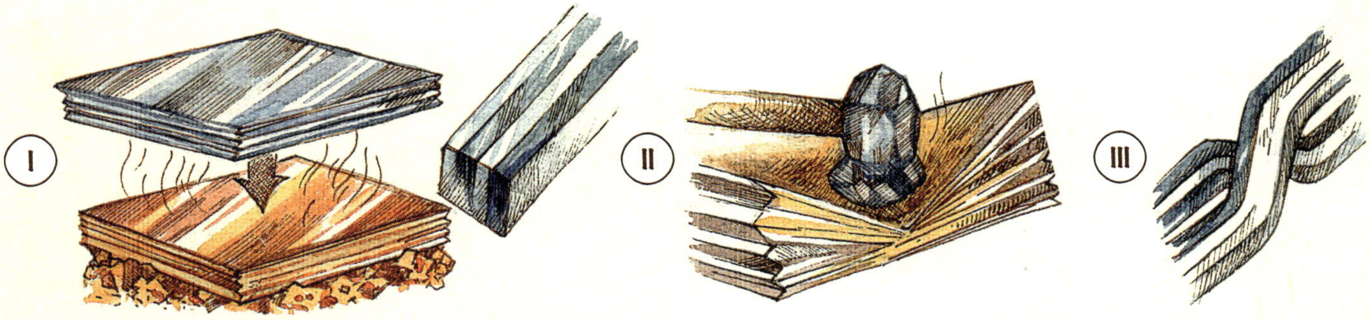

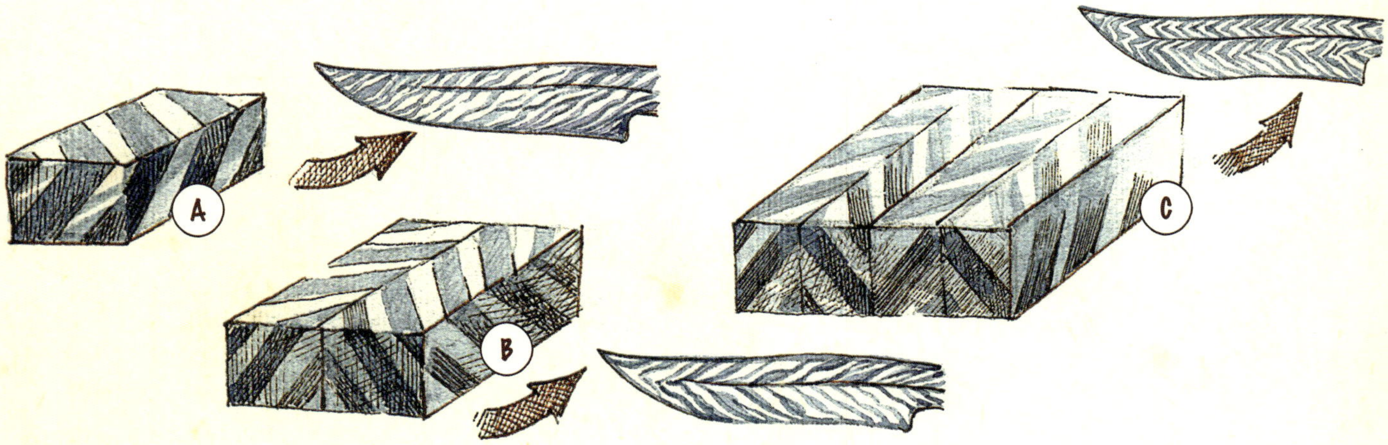

Repeatedly heating the steel and then cooling it by plunging it into water hardens and fortifies the blade. Long, curved blades should not be immersed vertically but almost horizontally, with the tip down, and not in a barrel but in a horizontal trough of corresponding length.

Once the blade is cooled, it becomes much harder but loses some of its strength — hit it against stone and it will shatter. To avoid this, reheat the blade for an hour, and then let it cool naturally.

SHAPING

Blades have a complex shape. The crossguard (1) prevents the fingers from slipping from the handle onto the knife blade. It often takes the form of a bar running perpendicular to the blade, which is sometimes curved towards the blade. The handle may have a cross-haired surface for the thumb. A deep groove (2) near the cutting edge (3) also protects against slippage. The handle, made of two wooden or bone plates, can simply be fit over the top of the blade using screws. Or carve a hollow handle from a single piece of material, slide the blade in and then attach with glue or by driving thin wooden wedges into the space between the handle and the steel.

BALANCING

An important characteristic of the knife is its balance, that is, its center of gravity. A shift of the center of gravity towards the tip increases the chopping properties of the knife and facilitates throwing. If it's more towards the middle of the handle, it makes the blade a lot easier to handle and maneuver. You can determine the center of gravity by balancing the flat side of the blade on one finger.

Knife blades can take many different forms. The bevel can be straight or concave, half or a third of the length of the blade.

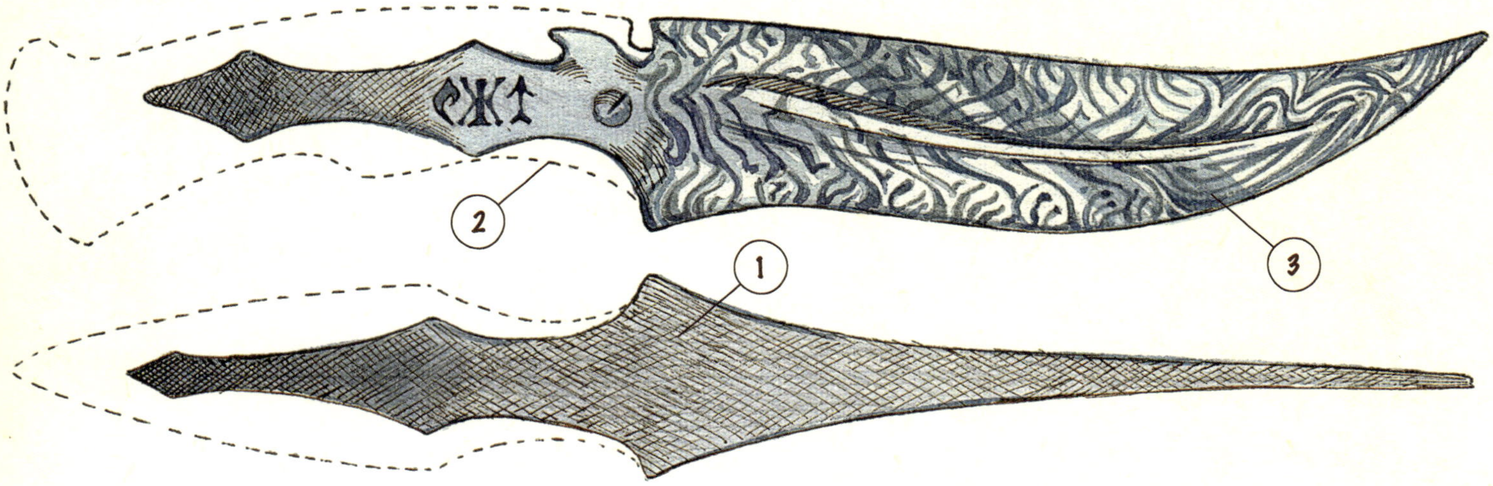

TREATMENT

Grinding is finishing the blade to produce the desired size and shape while removing any protrusions on the surface. Different knife shapes are used for different purposes. A universal knife with one cutting edge and one blunt edge is the easiest to manufacture. The more rounded the blade, the better the knife will cut.

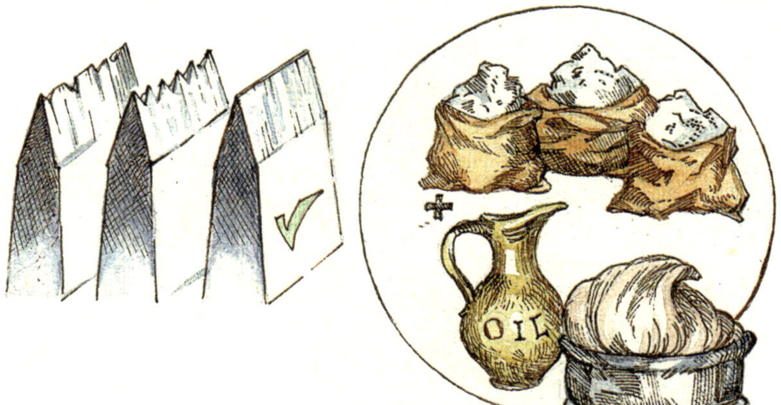

Polishing smooths out any remaining unevenness on the flat sides of the blade. Use stones of varying coarseness: start with the coarsest then work your way through to finer-grit stones. For the final step, use iron oxide paste (page 110) mixed with paraffin wax (page 84).

You'll also need to **sharpen** the cutting edge of the blade. You can use the same stones as you did for polishing. Find a stone of the right coarseness and lubricate it with oil or soapy water then run it across the cutting edge of the blade with smooth movements, gradually removing excess metal. It's important to maintain a consistent angle while sharpening the blade — from 25–40 degrees. The angle may exceed 40 degrees for heavy knives or axes designed for chopping bones or wood, as well as for swords that break through armor.

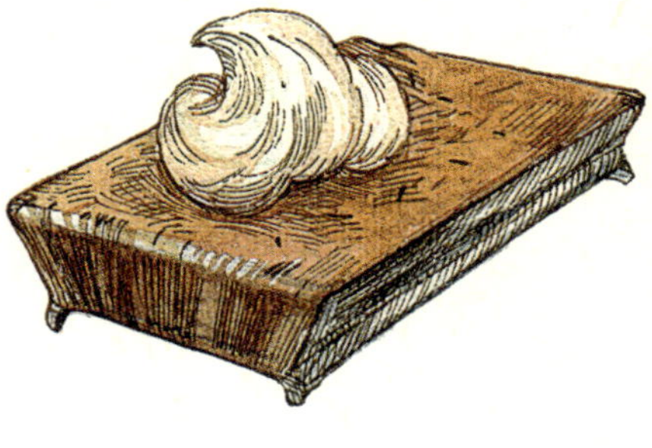

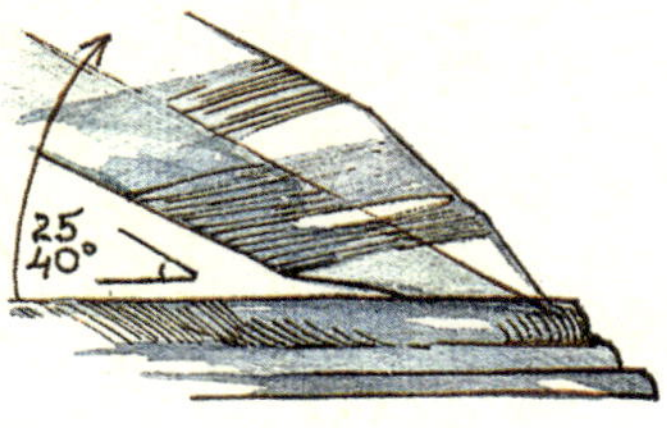

GLUE & DUCT TAPE

What one man can create, another can break. Repairing such breaks requires glue, which can be made using materials that we'd normally throw away.

Hunters and nomads make glue from the bones and sinews of wild animals or cattle; seaside communities use fish scales; and those surrounded by forest make it from conifers.

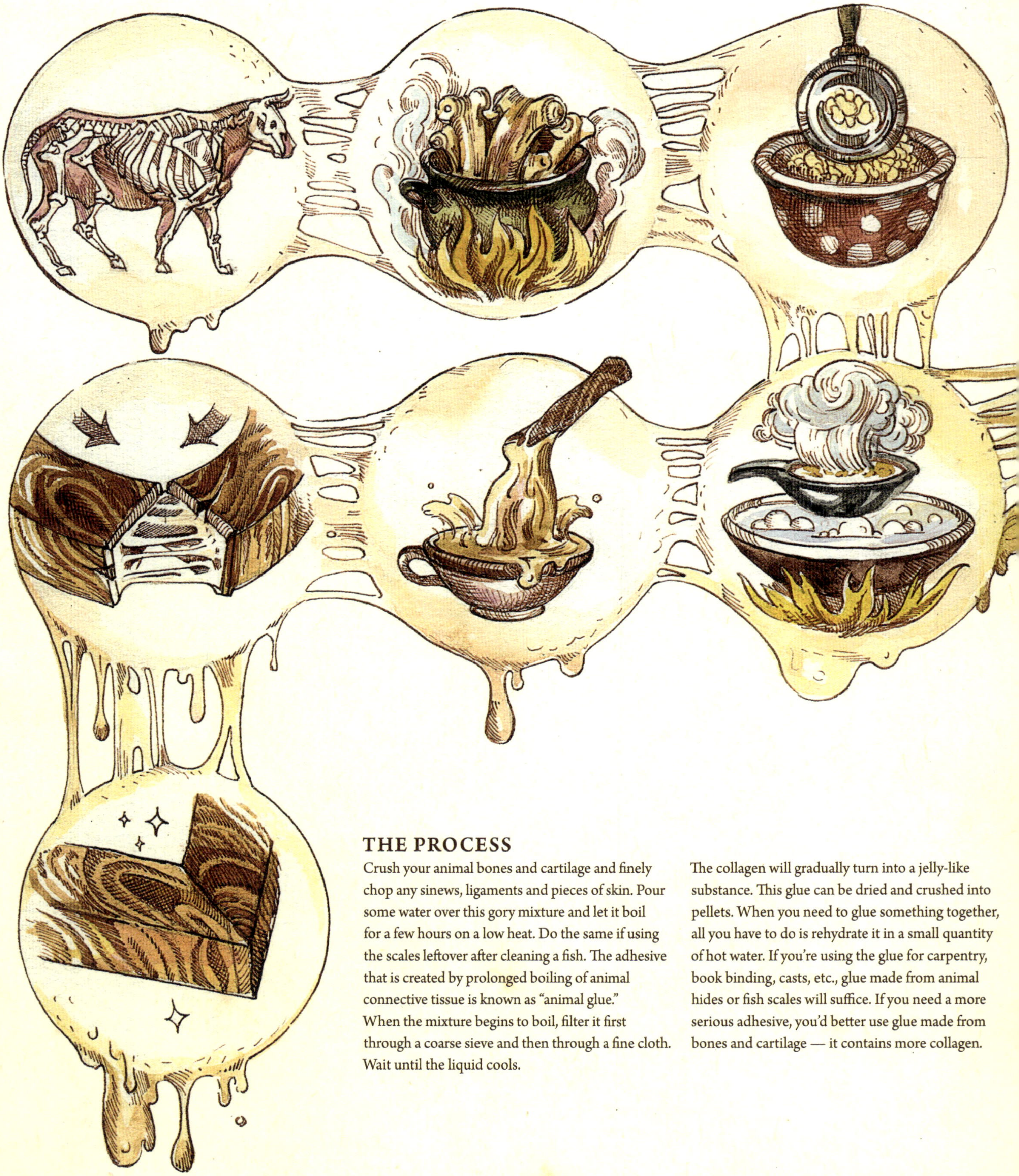

THE PROCESS

Crush your animal bones and cartilage and finely chop any sinews, ligaments and pieces of skin. Pour some water over this gory mixture and let it boil for a few hours on a low heat. Do the same if using the scales leftover after cleaning a fish. The adhesive that is created by prolonged boiling of animal connective tissue is known as "animal glue."
When the mixture begins to boil, filter it first through a coarse sieve and then through a fine cloth. Wait until the liquid cools.

The collagen will gradually turn into a jelly-like substance. This glue can be dried and crushed into pellets. When you need to glue something together, all you have to do is rehydrate it in a small quantity of hot water. If you're using the glue for carpentry, book binding, casts, etc., glue made from animal hides or fish scales will suffice. If you need a more serious adhesive, you'd better use glue made from bones and cartilage — it contains more collagen.

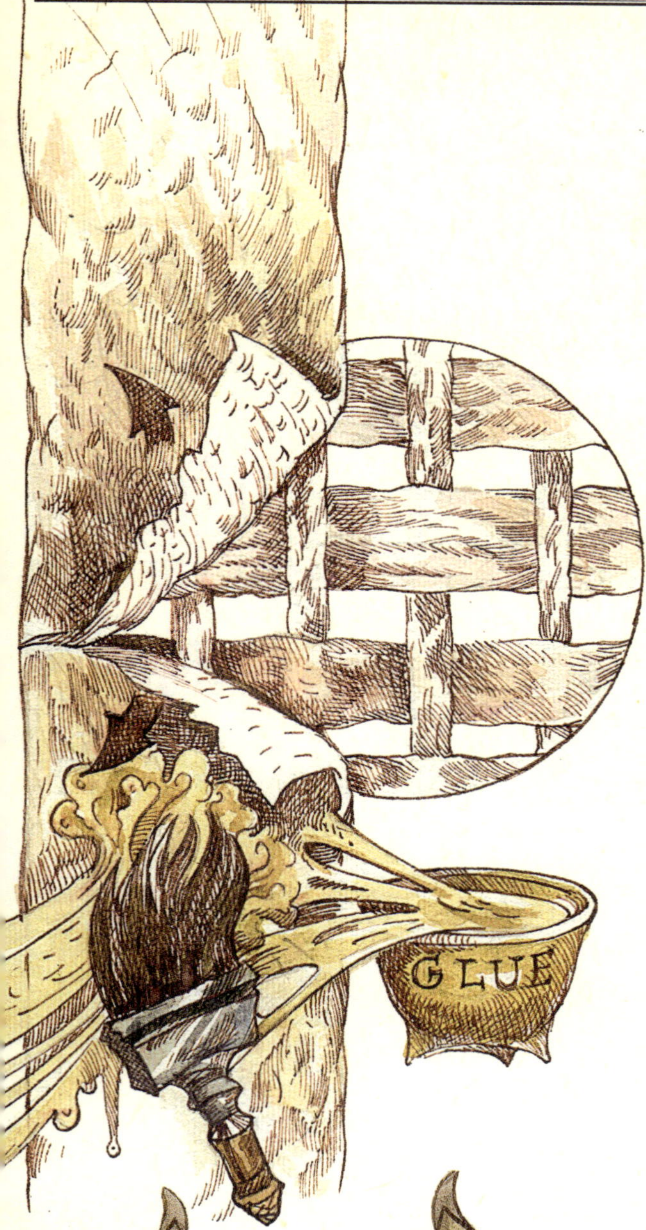

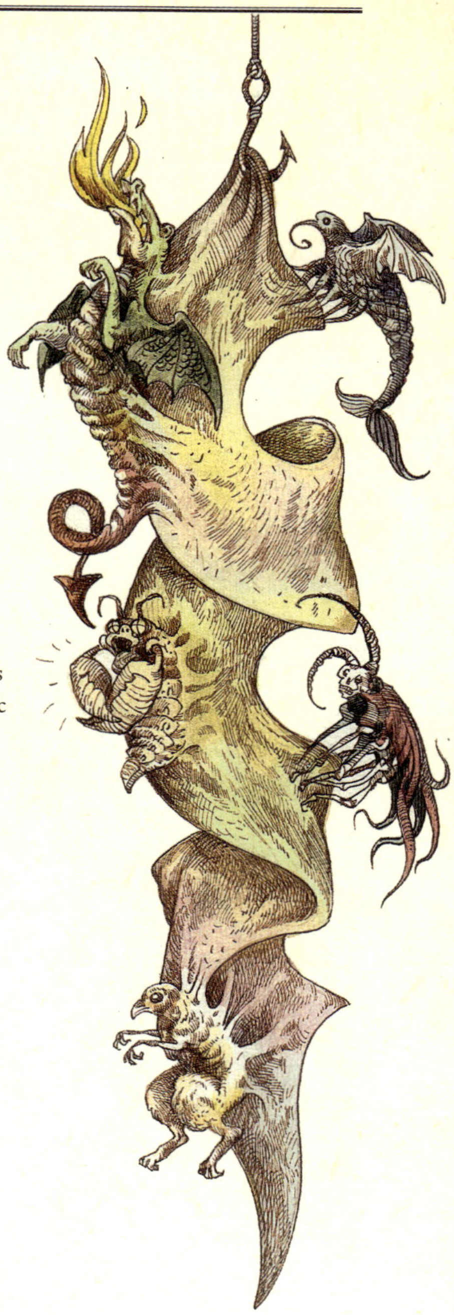

DUCT TAPE

Take a piece of cotton, linen or hemp fabric, preferably with a rib weave. This is produced by using one heavier and one lighter gauge yarn, alternating the weave so that the heavy yarn creates a ribbed pattern across the fabric. Fabric with this weave tears easily in one direction but is much harder to tear in the other. Cut the fabric into long strips and apply glue to one side. Now, your "tape" is ready to use.

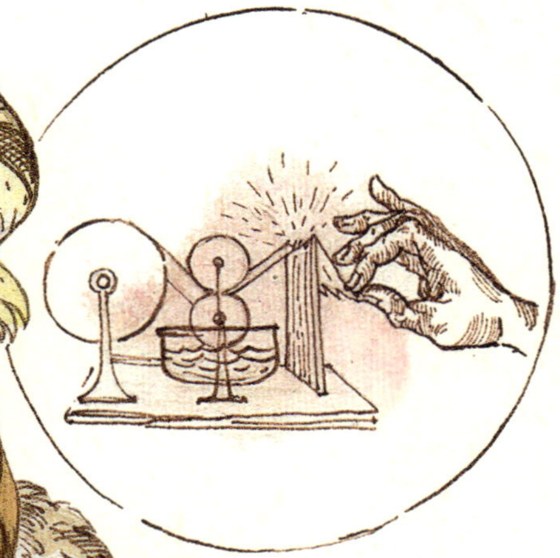

You can never have enough tape! Make an adhesive applicator so that you'll have a steady supply. Wrap a strip of cloth around a bobbin and run it through two metal rollers. Place a container of glue under one of them. When the handle is turned, the roller picks up the glue and evenly applies it to the underside of the cloth as it passes through.

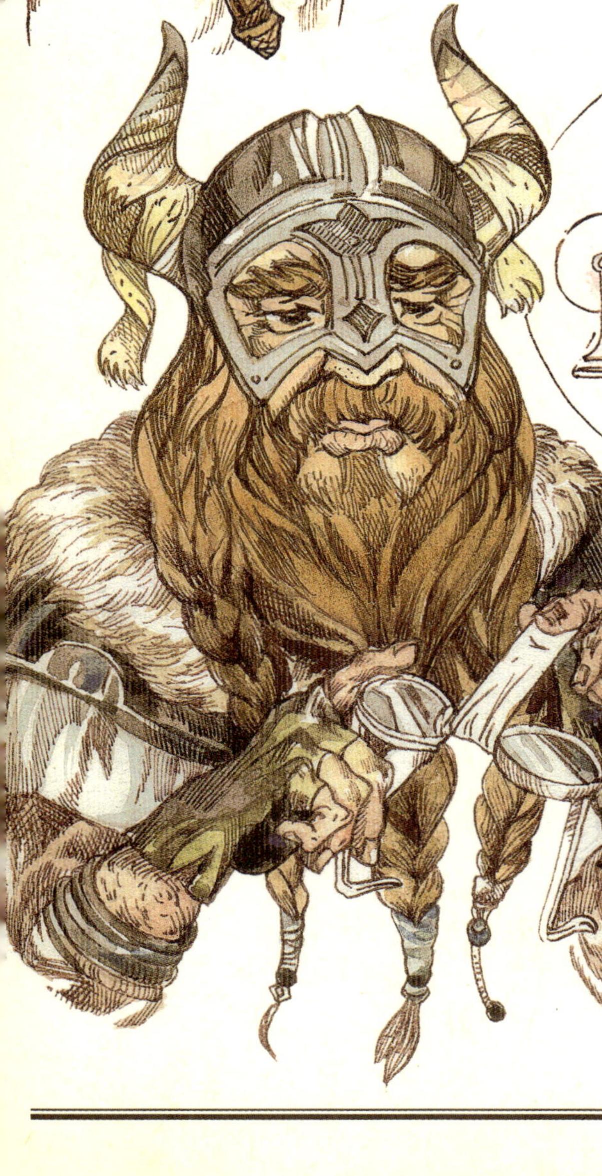

PINE RESIN GLUE

Cut a shallow incision in the trunk of a pine tree and resin will come out. Melt it until it becomes a liquid. Be careful — pine resin is flammable. The best way to melt it is in a double boiler or hot water bath. Add some ash from the stove or pulverized charcoal from a fire. Apply the resulting mixture to whatever surface you want to glue and let it harden again.

A good way to save this kind of glue is by dipping a stick into the liquid glue and letting it solidify. When you need to use it, all you have to do is heat the end of the stick to make the adhesive soft again.

WELDING

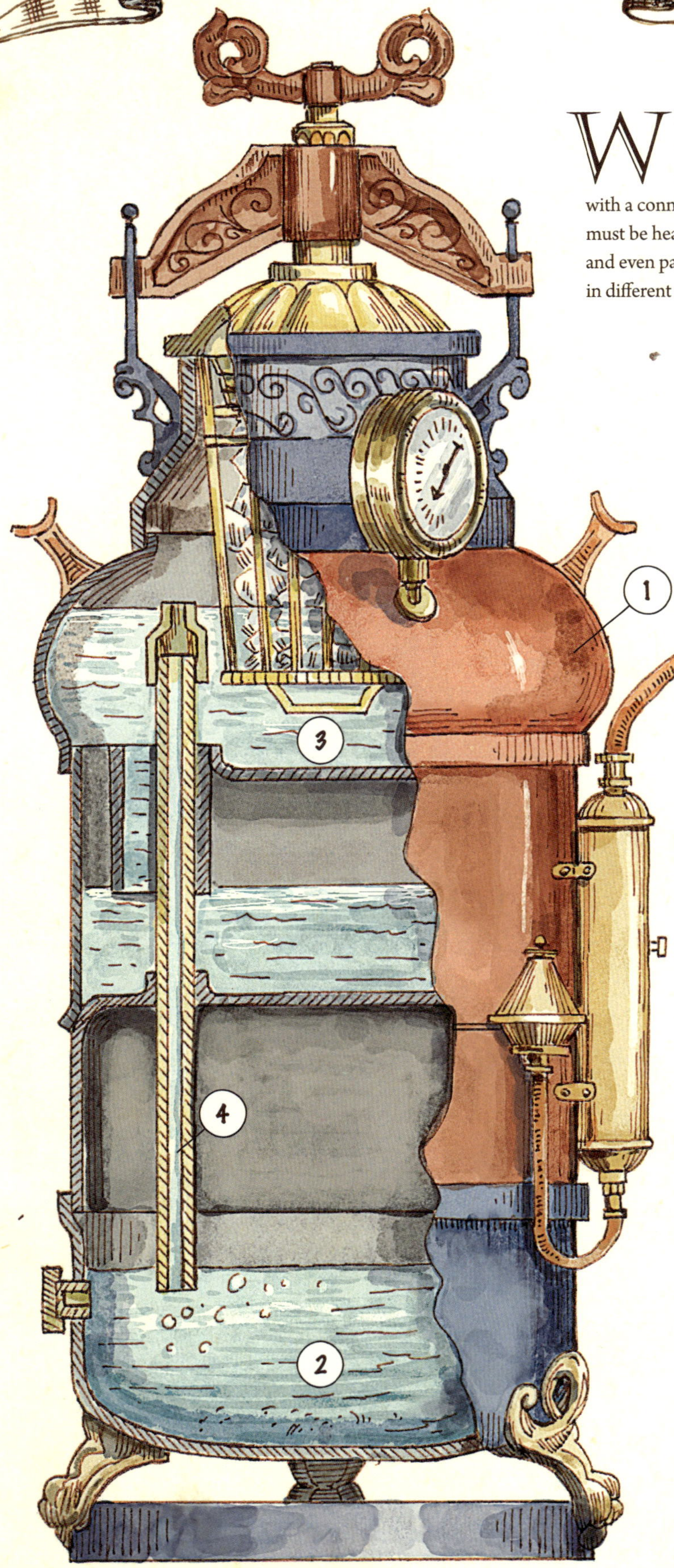

When two metal parts are welded together, the atoms of both intermingle. As a result, the parts are essentially fused into one piece with a connecting seam. To achieve this, the metal parts must be heated to extremely high temperatures and even partially melted. This can be done in different ways.

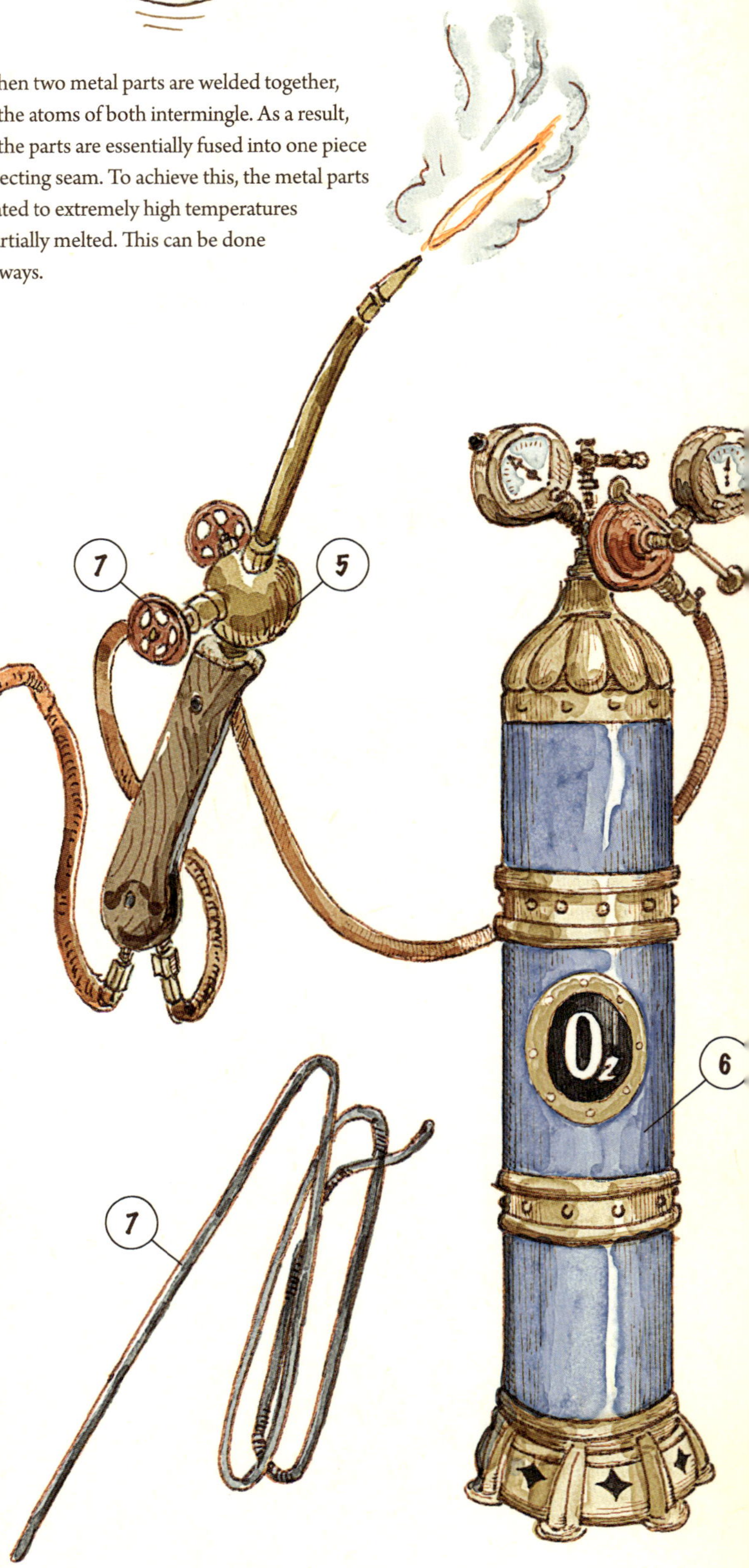

GAS WELDING

An oxy/gas flame burner generates very high temperatures, especially if you use a gas with a high combustion temperature in oxygen. One of the best options in this regard is acetylene. To obtain it, you first need to get calcium carbide: heat limestone at a high temperature, and then calcine (heat to a high temperature without fusing) the resulting calcium oxide (quicklime) with coal in a furnace.

Pour the resulting calcium carbide into a metal container (1) with two compartments: one containing water (2), and the other, carbide (3). When water enters the compartment with carbide through a tube (4), a chemical reaction will occur and acetylene will be formed, which will then be forced back into the water chamber by the pressure. If the pressure inside is too high, the acetylene will also displace water from the reaction zone.

In the burner (5), the gas is mixed with oxygen from the cylinder (6) and ignited. What you're left with is a burner flame. Use valves (7) to adjust the height of the flame and the ratio of acetylene to oxygen in the fuel. To make the seam even and strong, use a welding wire (8). The molten metal will fill in the irregularities, creating an even weld.

ELECTRIC WELDING MACHINE

You can also weld metal using electricity by creating an electric arc. In this case, electrical energy is converted into heat. The heart of the electric welding machine is a powerful step-down transformer (9) (page 197), which lowers the voltage and increases the current. Two coils are placed in the transformer to regulate the current. The primary (10) is made from a thinner wire with a large number of turns, while the secondary (11) is made from a thick wire with fewer turns. These coils are installed on a closed magnetic circuit (12) made of iron plates. Using a rotary handle (16), you can bring them closer together or farther apart, thereby adjusting the welding current.

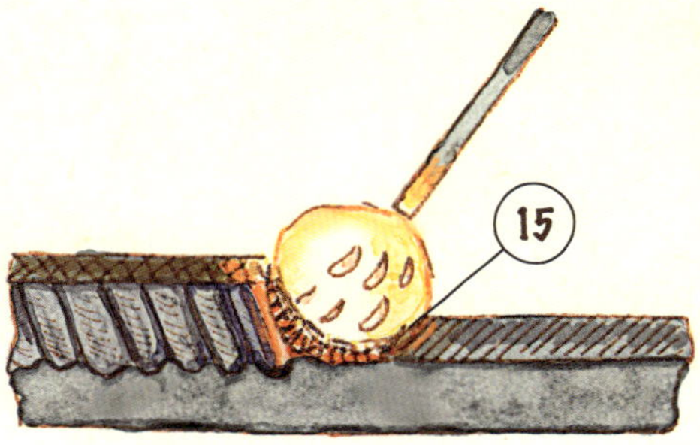

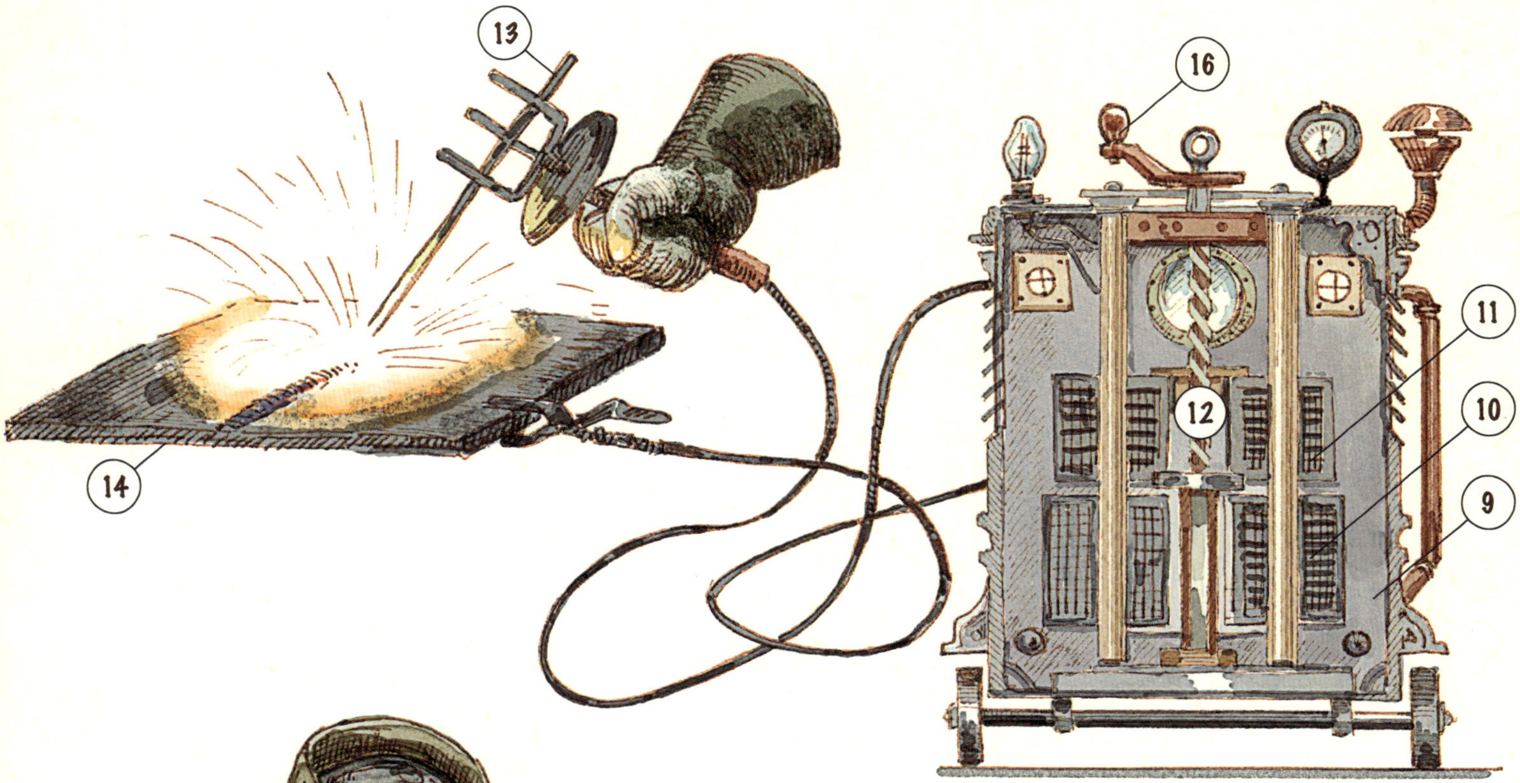

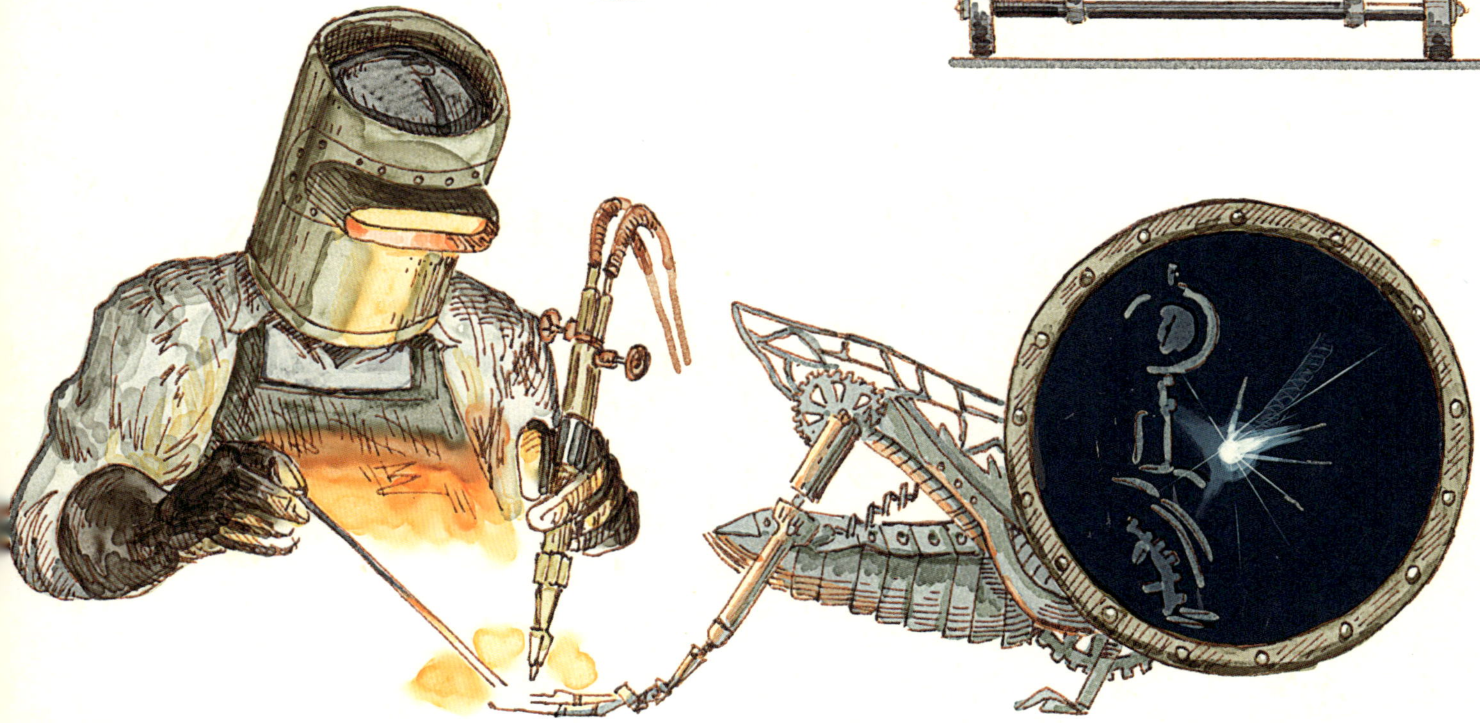

To weld a seam, connect the primary coil to the electric current and one end of the secondary coil to the welding rod holder, the electrode (13) and the other to the part that needs to be welded (14). When the secondary circuit is closed or broken between the electrode and the metal surface of the part, an extremely hot electric arc is produced.

Touching the electrode to the workpiece (15) will close the electrical circuit. This heats up the end of the electrode. After that, move the electrode back from the part by around 3–5 mm. This produces an arc of electrical discharge, heating the piece to extreme temperatures until it starts to melt. The end of the electrode will also begin to melt, filling the gaps in the weld (15).

MILLS, DRILLS & LATHES

Lathes, drills and milling machines are three fundamental and crucial machine tools for the Industrial Revolution workshop. A set of interchangeable gear wheels connecting a lead screw and chisel tips of different shapes will allow you to produce parts with a high level of technical precision. Now you can develop all spheres of production.

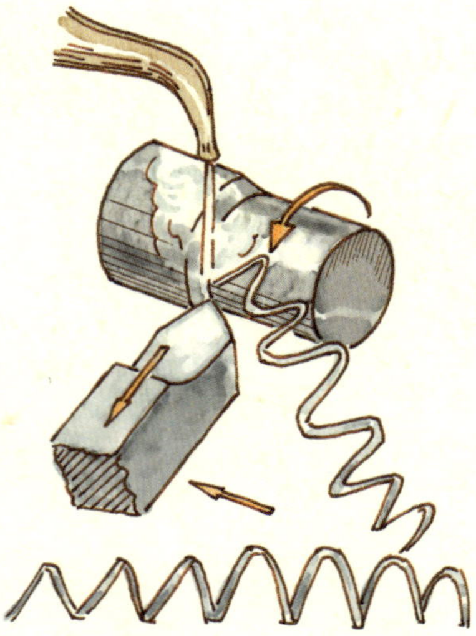

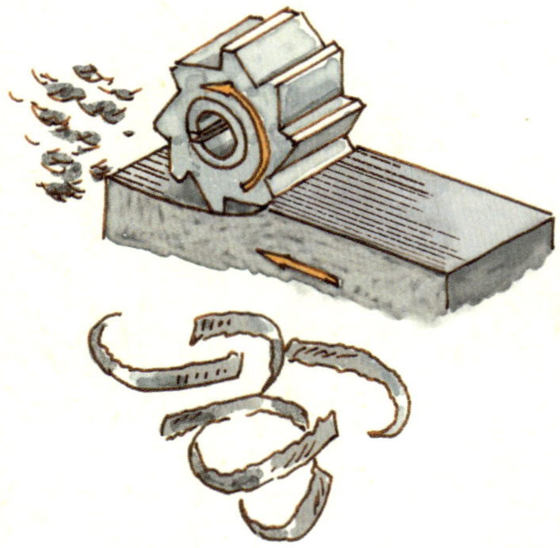

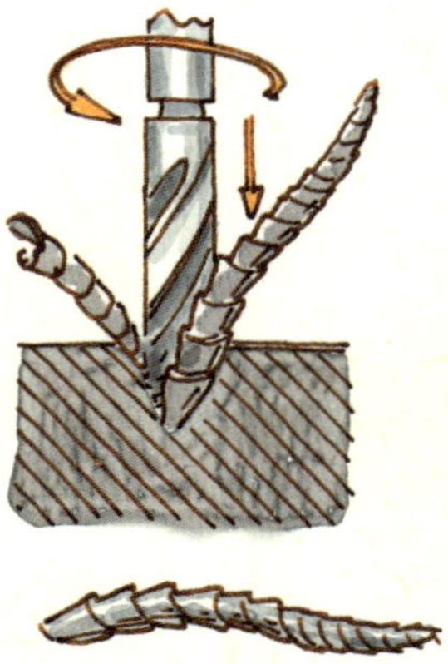

Lathes are used for making radially symmetric items. The workpiece rotates at high speed while excess material is removed using a cutting tool running along the side. This is a versatile machine that is suitable for a variety of applications, from the finest of watch gears to parts weighing hundreds of tons.

A **milling machine** holds the workpiece still and uses a rotary cutter to remove material from the surface. It's capable of filing, polishing, engraving and carving fine details in practically any design. But to make one, you need a rotating cutting piece made of very hard metal.

A **drilling machine** can bore holes in different materials of various diameters. For drilling small holes in wood, you can make a hand- or foot-operated drill. For drilling through metal, you need a more powerful drive such as, for example, a water wheel (page 234).

CUTTER

The cutting piece of the drill must be sharpened at an angle to effectively remove layers of metal. It must be made of hardened carbon steel (page 138) with a carbon content of 0.7–1.3%. This kind of steel doesn't dull easily.

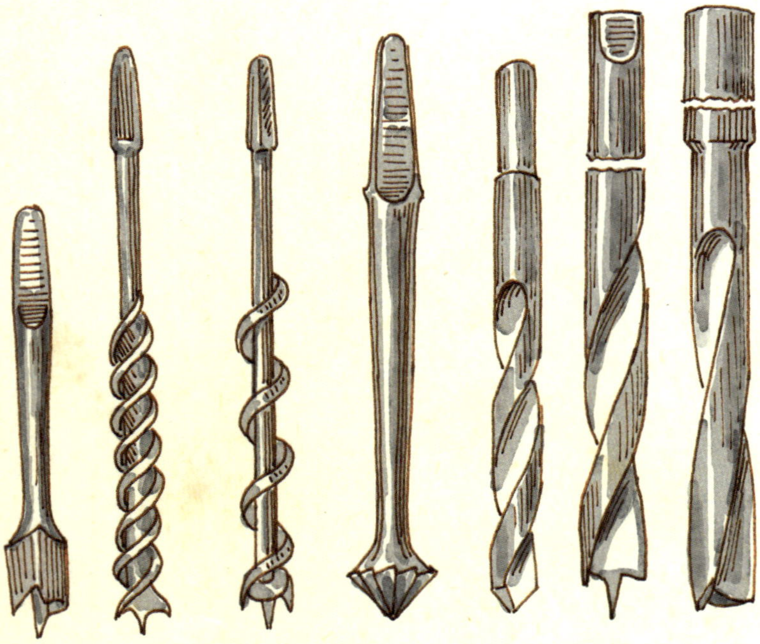

1 2 3 4 5 6 7

Different drill bit designs serve different functions:

- A **circular bit** (1) is used for drilling holes with a large diameter. The cutting edge is either lined with soldered teeth made from a hard alloy or has a diamond chip plating. These kinds of drill bits will serve you for a long time, but if they overheat, you'll no longer be able to sharpen them.
- **Brad point bits** (2, 3) are the more modern version of the circular bit and are externally threaded like a screw to remove excess material from the drill hole.
- **Conical bits** (4) make holes of different sizes. The shape of the hole depends on the diameter of the upper and lower parts of the cone, as well as on the bit's penetration depth into the material.
- **Twist bits** (5, 6, 7) have two long grooves that spiral around the bit and remove cut material from the drill hole while drilling.

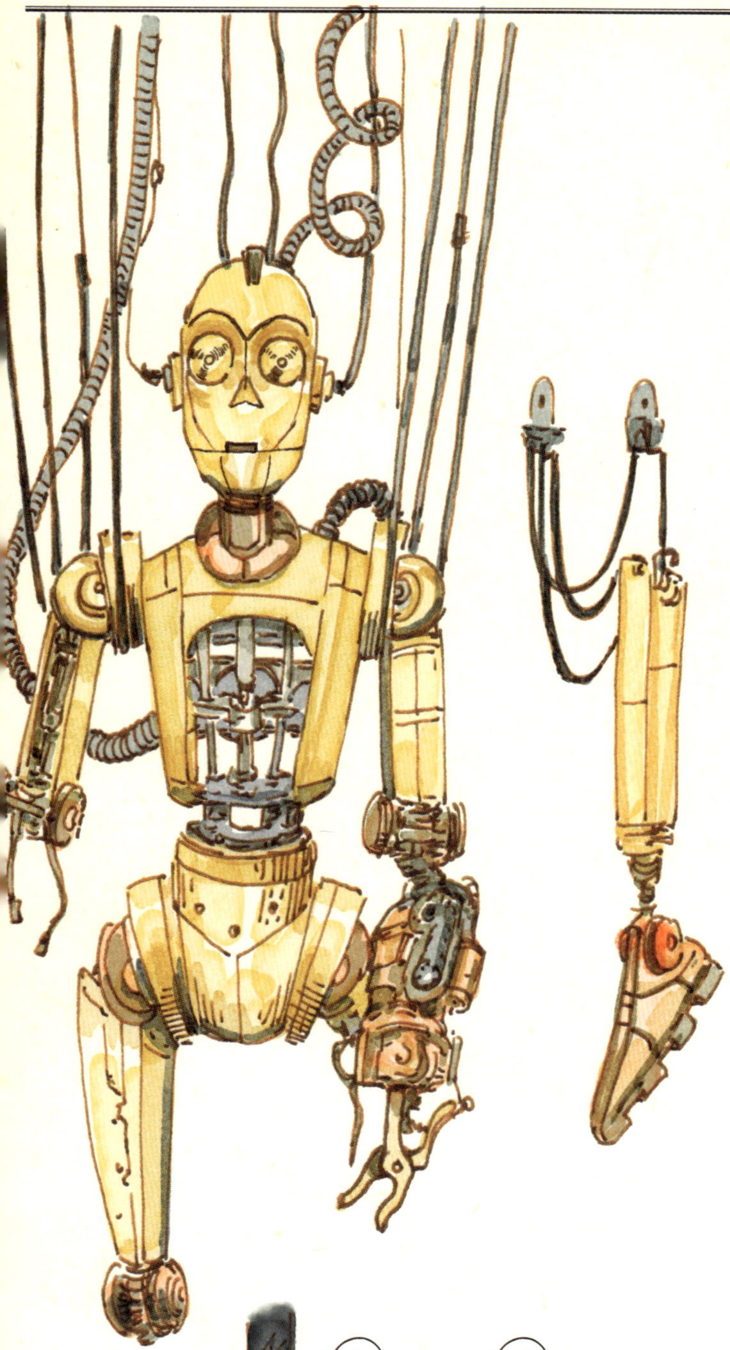

LATHE

This machine has a sturdy base (1), which holds the spindle — a rod equipped with a device (2) for securing the workpiece (3). The spindle rotates the workpiece along its axis, and the cutting tool mounted on the tool post (4) is moved along the length of the workpiece using the handwheel (5). Changing the cutting depth of the tool allows you to create the profile of the workpiece. Optionally, a drill bit can be mounted in the tailstock (8) to bore-out the workpiece.

1. *Cast iron base — absorbs vibration well*
2. *Spindle — for holding one side of the workpiece in place*
3. *Workpiece — the item being shaped*
4. *Tool post — the solid surface on which the cutting tool rests*
5. *Handwheel — moves the tool post along the length of the workpiece*
6. *Belt drive — transmits rotation from the motor to the spindle*
7. *Gearbox — changes the speed of rotation of the shaft for working with parts made from soft or hard metal*
8. *Tailstock — holds the other end of the workpiece firmly in place*

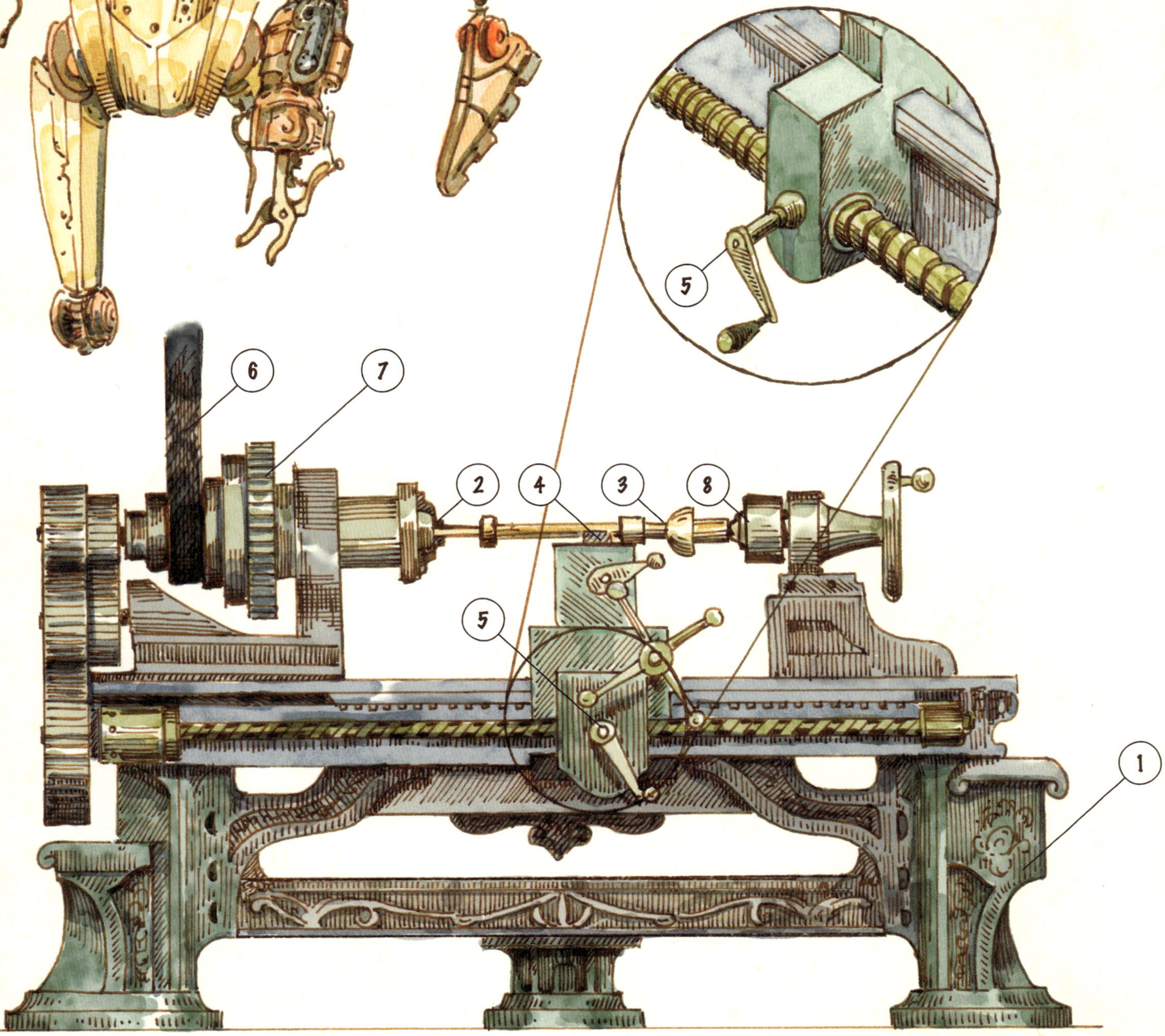

BUILDING

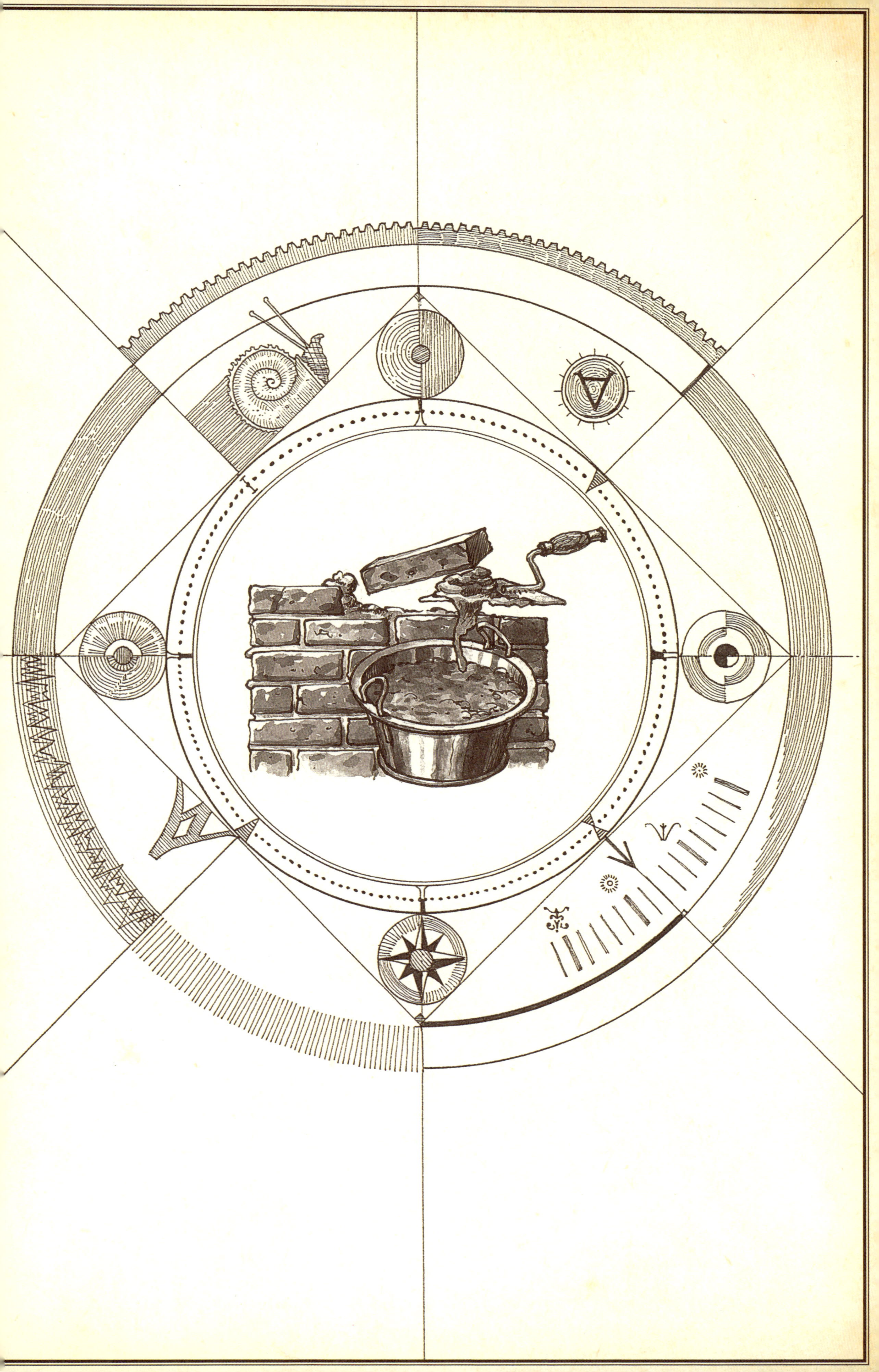

BRICKS & CEMENT

Building your civilization brick by brick is not as difficult as it may sound. In fact, it's a very simple and cost-effective building material. All you need is clay and heat. But not just any clay will work — it needs to be compacted and slightly frozen. The best time to harvest clay is in the fall, but if you have a strong need for bricks in the spring, fear not: You can achieve the same effect by weathering or carefully kneading the clay for a long time.

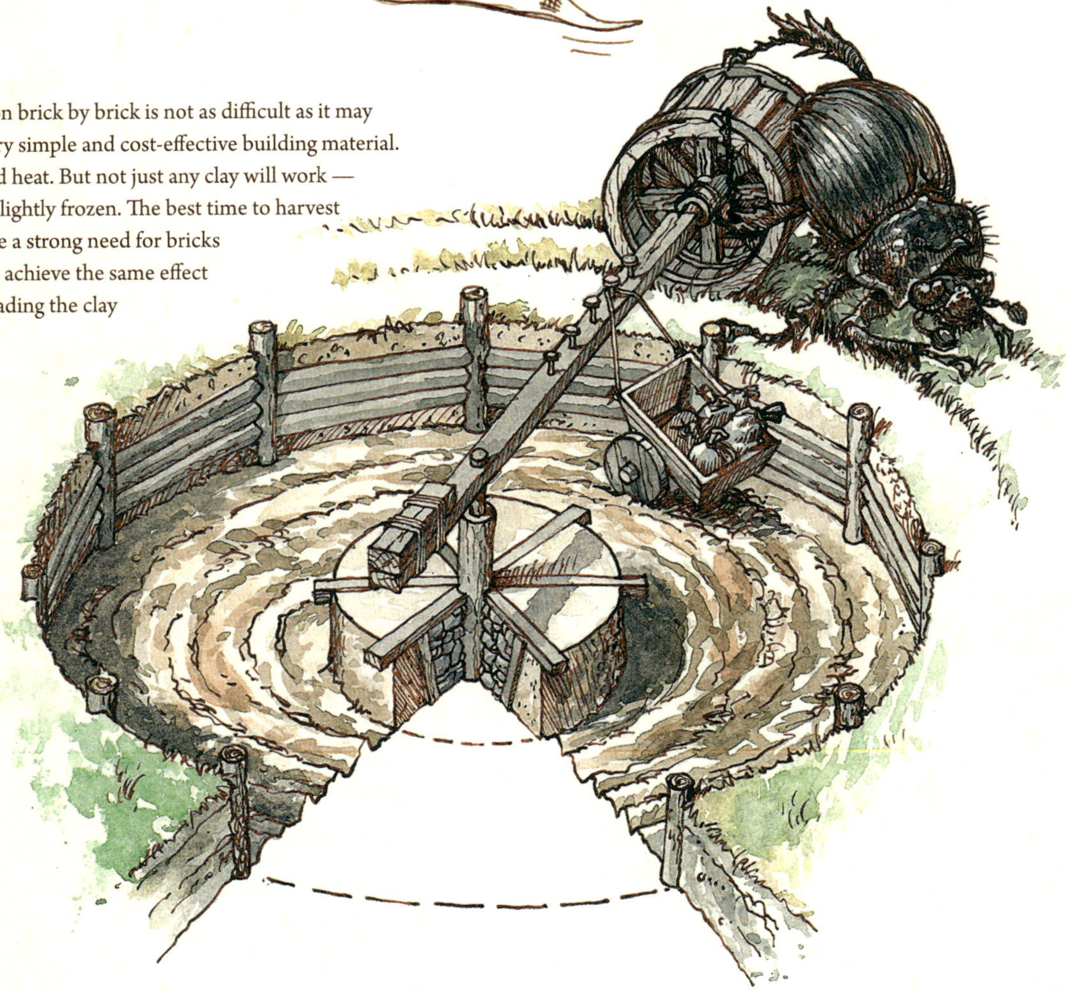

MOLDING

Mixing clay with a stick or your feet is a long and arduous process. Better to build a pugmill — a flat-bottomed, circular mixing chamber with a weighted paddle attached to some sort of pulling force. Once the clay is mixed, you will need to shape it. The most convenient way to do this is laying the clay out on a table, slicing through it with a wire and laying it in wooden frames.

Drying takes about a week. If you don't take the time to dry your bricks fully, steam may cause them to crack during the firing process. When building a frame, keep in mind that the brick shrinks by 10–15% in the kiln.

FIRING

The best way to stack bricks in the kiln is in a herringbone pattern so that the warm smoke will envelop each brick, and the whole batch will dry evenly. This process may take up to twelve hours. Then you'll need to crank up the heat and fire the bricks.

Regulate the temperature by observing the color of the material:
Dull red glow *— 450–500°C*
Dark red *— 600–650°C*
Cherry red *— 700°C*
Red-orange *— 850°C*
Yellow *— 950–1000°C*
White *— 1200°C!*

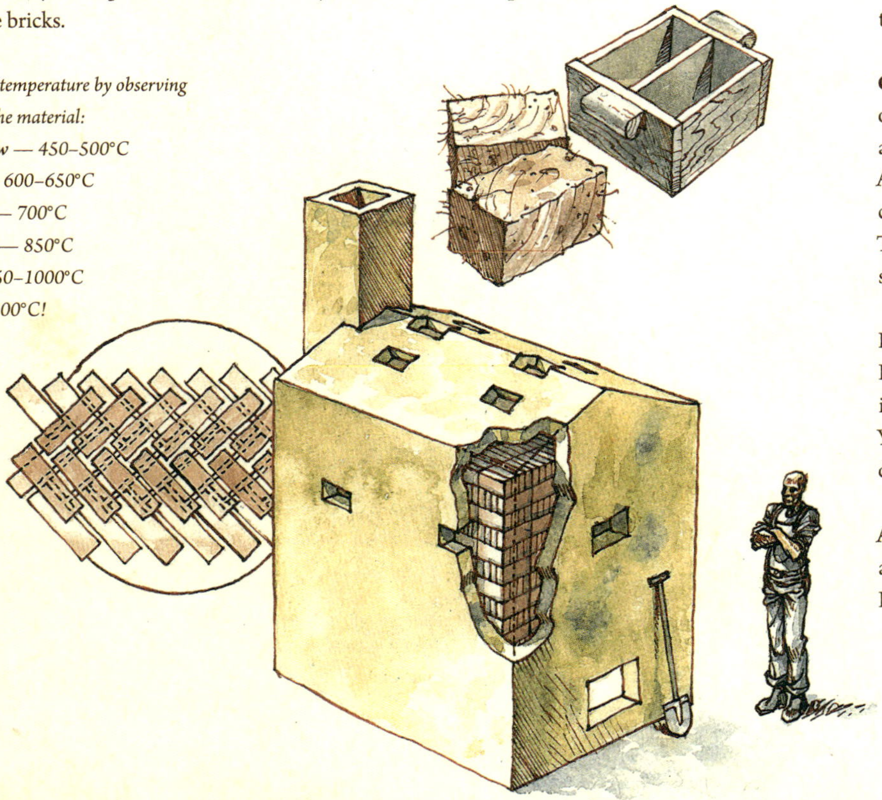

Ceramic bricks go through an entire cycle of firing. They have low water absorption, so they're frost resistant and hold onto heat well. Unfortunately, they're also quite brittle.

Clinker bricks are obtained from a mixture of refractory clay (kaolin) and feldspar fired at higher temperatures (1100–1300°C). At these heats, the brick liquifies and fuses together, completely eliminating any defects or air bubbles. These bricks do not absorb water and are extremely strong, durable and frost resistant.

Raw brick is not fired but dried in the open air. If you use the right kind of clay and dry it well, it will serve just as well as a red fired brick. You won't be able to build skyscrapers, but it'll do for a small building.

Adobe brick is a raw brick fortified with another material: straw, sawdust or manure. Retains heat well.

CEMENT MORTAR

Making mortar is a lot like mixing dough. First, a mixture of 75% limestone and 25% clay is sintered in a kiln at a high temperature and then cooled. The resulting granules of clinker are mixed with a small quantity of gypsum. Add water and sand and your cement is ready. All that's left to do is build your brick wall using the mortar to stick everything together. After a few days, the solution will harden and become water-resistant, meaning that the structure won't wash away after the first rain.

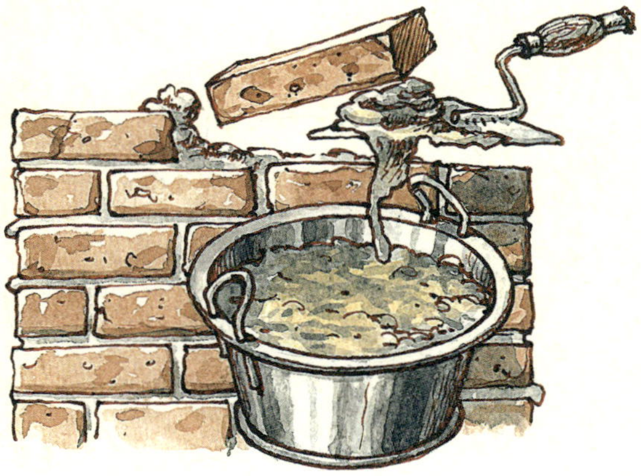

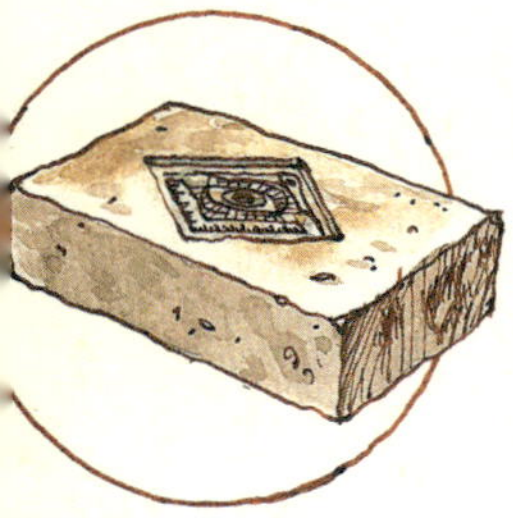

Don't forget to stamp your special insignia into your bricks before firing. That way, everyone will know who to contact for such excellent craftsmanship.

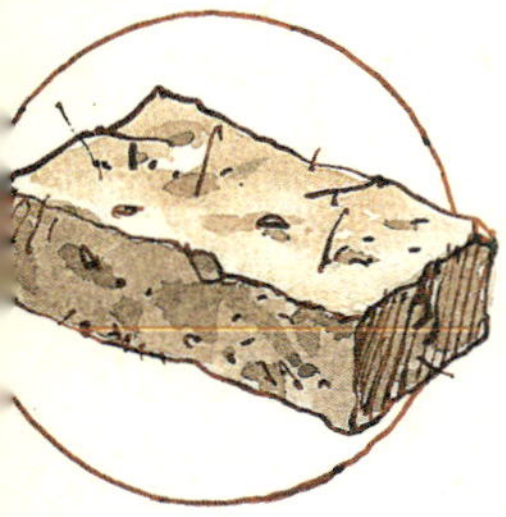

You can also chop straw into short pieces and add this, other fibrous plants or dried manure to your bricks. These additives fortify and improve the thermal insulation of your building materials. But beware: These bricks won't last as long as fired bricks, as they'll disintegrate faster in the rain.

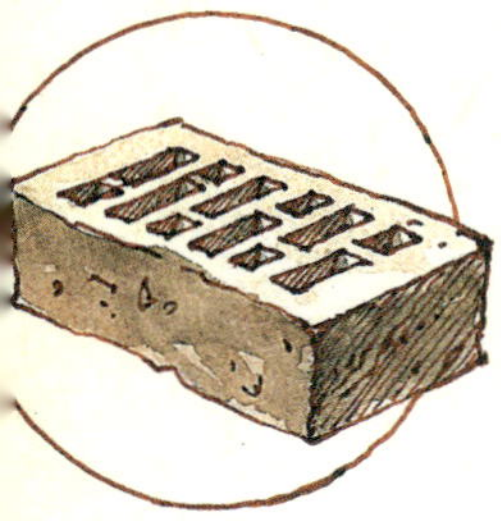

Use a hollow tube to create grooves in the brick during the molding process. This will reduce the overall weight of the brick, thereby reducing the overall load on the foundation. These bricks are also three times more effective at trapping heat. Sawdust can also be added to produce the same effect. During firing, the sawdust shavings burn away, leaving pores that improve thermal insulation.

The more bricks in the wall, the wider and more stable it is. But there's a clever way to conserve your bricks. Make the wall curvy. Even if you only lay one row of bricks, it will be more stable than a flat wall.

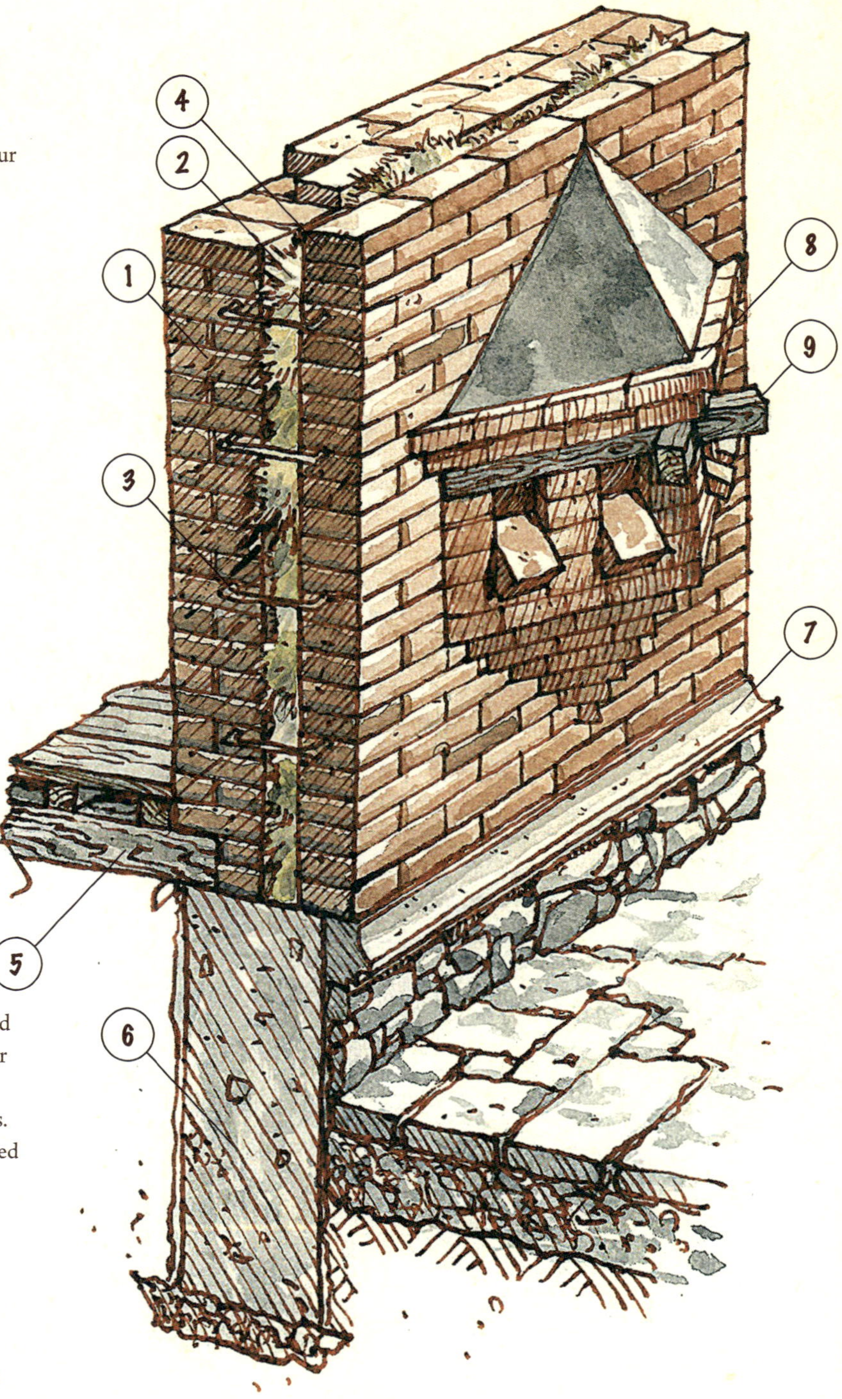

1. *Inner part of the wall, composed of two interlaced layers of bricks*
2. *Thermal insulation made of felt*
3. *Anchor that holds the inside and outside of the wall together*
4. *Outer brick facade, composed of a single layer*
5. *Floor joists offer horizontal structural support and transfer the load to vertical structural elements*
6. *Cement foundation*
7. *Blind area, a waterproofing strip laid at the junction of the wall and foundation*
8. *Cornice*
9. *Floor beam*

INSULATION

The cold and biting wind of a harsh winter rolling in will always be a problem, no matter how thick you build your brick wall — unless you use insulation. To do this, make a brick sandwich using two layers of bricks as bread with a layer of felt, sheep's wool, pressed flax, peat or hemp as filling. Make sure the wall cavity has a little ventilation; otherwise, the insulation material inside will get wet and rot.

FOUNDATION

Load-bearing walls don't rest directly on the ground but rather on a foundation that redistributes the load. It is made of concrete or reinforced concrete (page 158). Waterproof the wall and foundation and cover the area with earth. Without a waterproofing strip, the wall will become damp and mold will develop.

ROADS

Advancing civilization requires building public infrastructure. And first on the list is roads. No state can exist for long without a well-developed road system. Roads help reduce labor and transportation costs, settle new areas and grow the economies in towns along the route. They also facilitate cultural exchange, which can be a treasure more valuable than gold.

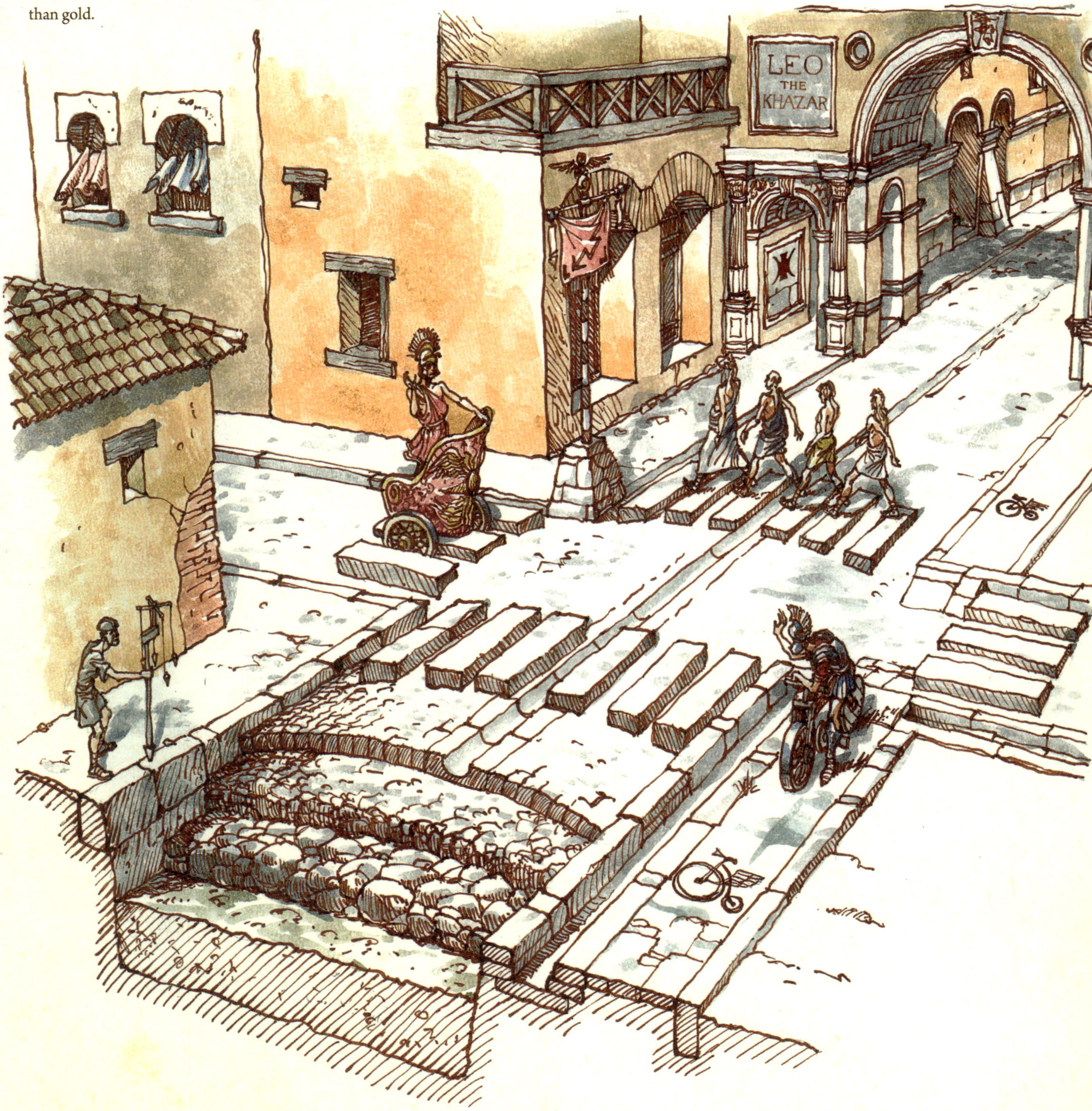

To mark out the path of your future road, use a vertical staff with two horizontal cross-pieces mounted on top. Hang small weights from threads, also known as plumb bobs, from each of the four ends of the cross bar. Place the staff firmly into the ground over the starting point of your road. Align two of the threads, or plumb lines, with your line of sight in the direction you want the road to travel. When you reach an intersection, use the other two plumb lines to mark perfectly perpendicular lines. After marking out the course and width of the road, dig a deep trench. It's important that you dig deep enough to reach rocky ground or at least a harder layer of soil. Next, lay the foundation of your road like a layer cake. The base is a cushion of compacted sand.

Next is a layer of large stones to act as a drainage layer. Then come several layers of crushed granite: the mid-sized pieces followed by the finest layer on top. This ensures that any voids formed in the lower layer will be filled in by the smaller stones, creating a denser and sturdier foundation. But don't mix different grades of gravel in one layer, which instead will lead to resettling and sinkholes. Cover this base with paving stones. Large cobblestones should be shaved down on the edges so that they fit tightly together. Fill the gaps between the stones with fine gravel or cement mortar (page 148).

ASPHALT CONCRETE

To make the road surface smooth, use asphalt concrete, a multi-component mixture that, when cooled, forms a wear-resistant and moisture-proof coating. The basis of the mixture is crushed stone and gravel, stone chips and sand. Mix this with bitumen, a tar-like product of oil oxidation. It should make up 5–7% of the total volume. You can find bitumen in tar sands, which are a natural conglomerate of sand, water, clay, minerals and bitumen. To extract the bitumen, you need to pour a lot of hot water into the conglomerate, add an alkaline component and mix thoroughly. The bitumen particles will separate and rise to the surface. Before mixing, bitumen must be heated to a liquid state at a temperature of 140–170°C. If you need to make road repairs down the line, simply crumble and reheat the existing material, then re-roll on top. You can also lay roads by mixing tar extracted during oil refinement with sand and gravel (page 126).

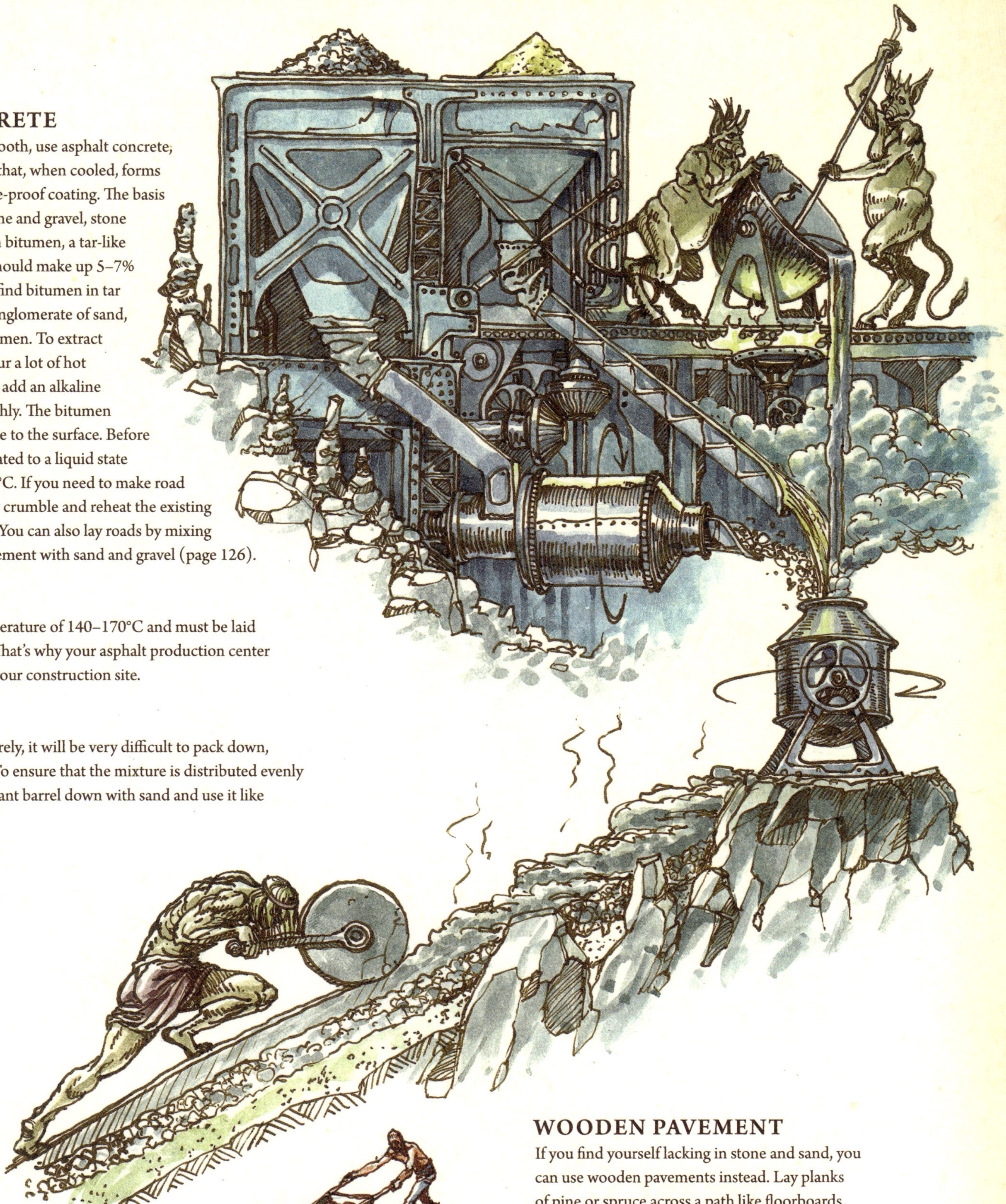

Asphalt is prepared at a temperature of 140–170°C and must be laid while still in its liquid state. That's why your asphalt production center will have to be located near your construction site.

If the mixture cools prematurely, it will be very difficult to pack down, and the road will be brittle. To ensure that the mixture is distributed evenly across the surface, weigh a giant barrel down with sand and use it like a rolling pin.

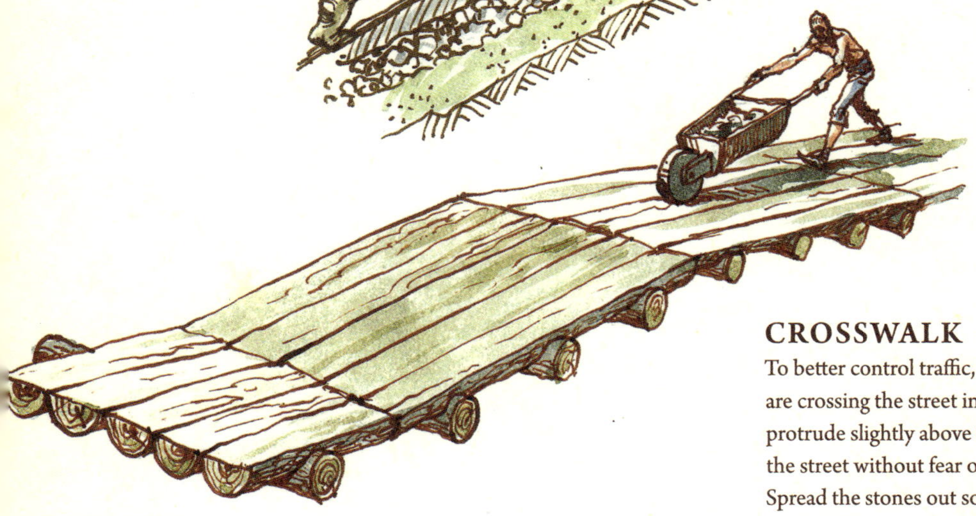

WOODEN PAVEMENT

If you find yourself lacking in stone and sand, you can use wooden pavements instead. Lay planks of pine or spruce across a path like floorboards. Paths like this will last 20–30 years. Planks and small bridges made from wood will help you traverse swampy wetlands.

CROSSWALK

To better control traffic, you'll want to make sure that all your pedestrians are crossing the street in the same place. Create crosswalks using stones that protrude slightly above the main roadway. This way, pedestrians can cross the street without fear of getting their feet wet or muddy in the rainy season. Spread the stones out so that the gaps between them correspond to the width of the wheelbase of vehicles in your city. This type of crosswalk will also help regulate traffic and prevent drivers from violating traffic rules, which will make your roads safer for pedestrians. Elevate and separate the sidewalk from the main roadway to create a curb, which will not only protect pedestrians from collisions but also prevent soil from washing onto the paved part.

GUTTERS

Water erosion is a road's worst enemy, so you'll need to dig drainage gutters. Make the roadbed slightly convex so that water will drain to the sides and into these gutters, which flow first to storm drains then into underground pipes connected to the main sewer line (page 156).

ARCHES & BRIDGES

When there's a choice between beauty and reliability, architects often favor the latter to ensure that their works will last for centuries. But you can avoid sacrificing aesthetics by incorporating arches into your design. Arches are not only beautiful; they're also sturdy. They can support the load of huge, vaulted ceilings much better than straight beams. The secret is in the way the design evenly distributes weight. Arches enable you to implement the most incredible designs and erect structures as lofty as your aspirations.

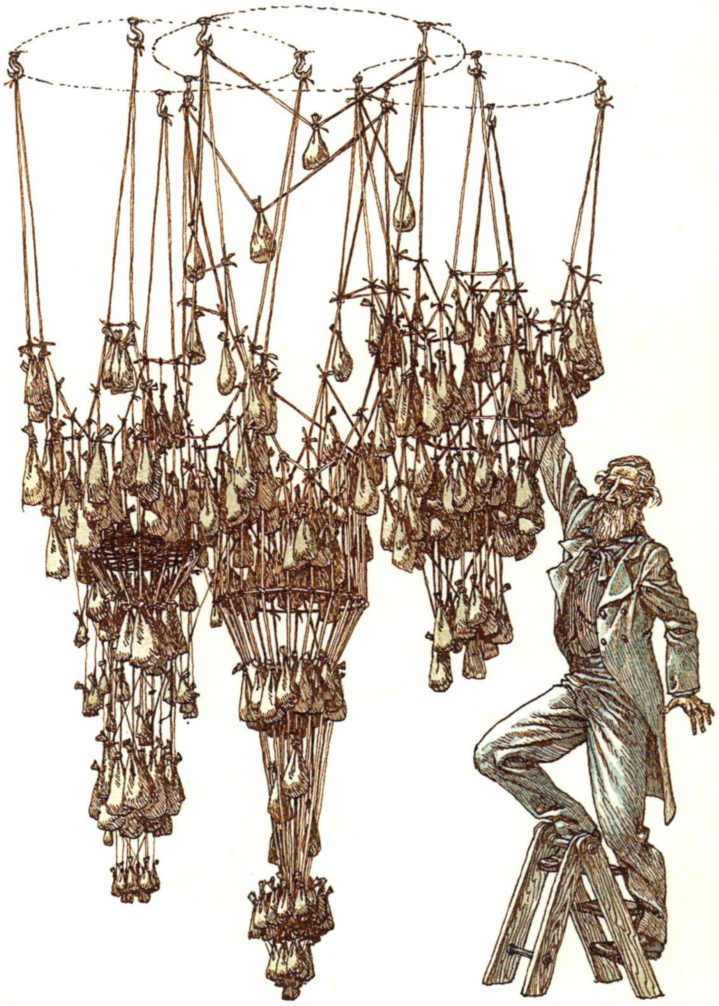

The sturdiest design is known as a catenary arch. You can construct one without any mathematical calculations or complicated blueprints. All you need is a chain or a rope. The chain will sag under its own weight and form a catenary curve. Take a photo of it or sketch it, flip it upside down and you have a design sketch for your future arch.

A catenary arch can withstand the weight of the material from which it is constructed without collapsing. The catenary is the ideal curve for an arch of uniform density and thickness that only has to support its own weight. The reason they're so sturdy is because they redirect the vertical force of gravity into compression force along the arch's curve. You can modify the curve design to bear a larger load by hanging sandbags from the rope in the places where you're planning additional structural elements.

CABLE-BRACED BRIDGES

Arches are also essential in the construction of large bridges. They can replace the pylon — a vertical pole to which one or more cables are attached to support the horizontal roadway of the bridge. The roadway itself may also take the form of an arch.

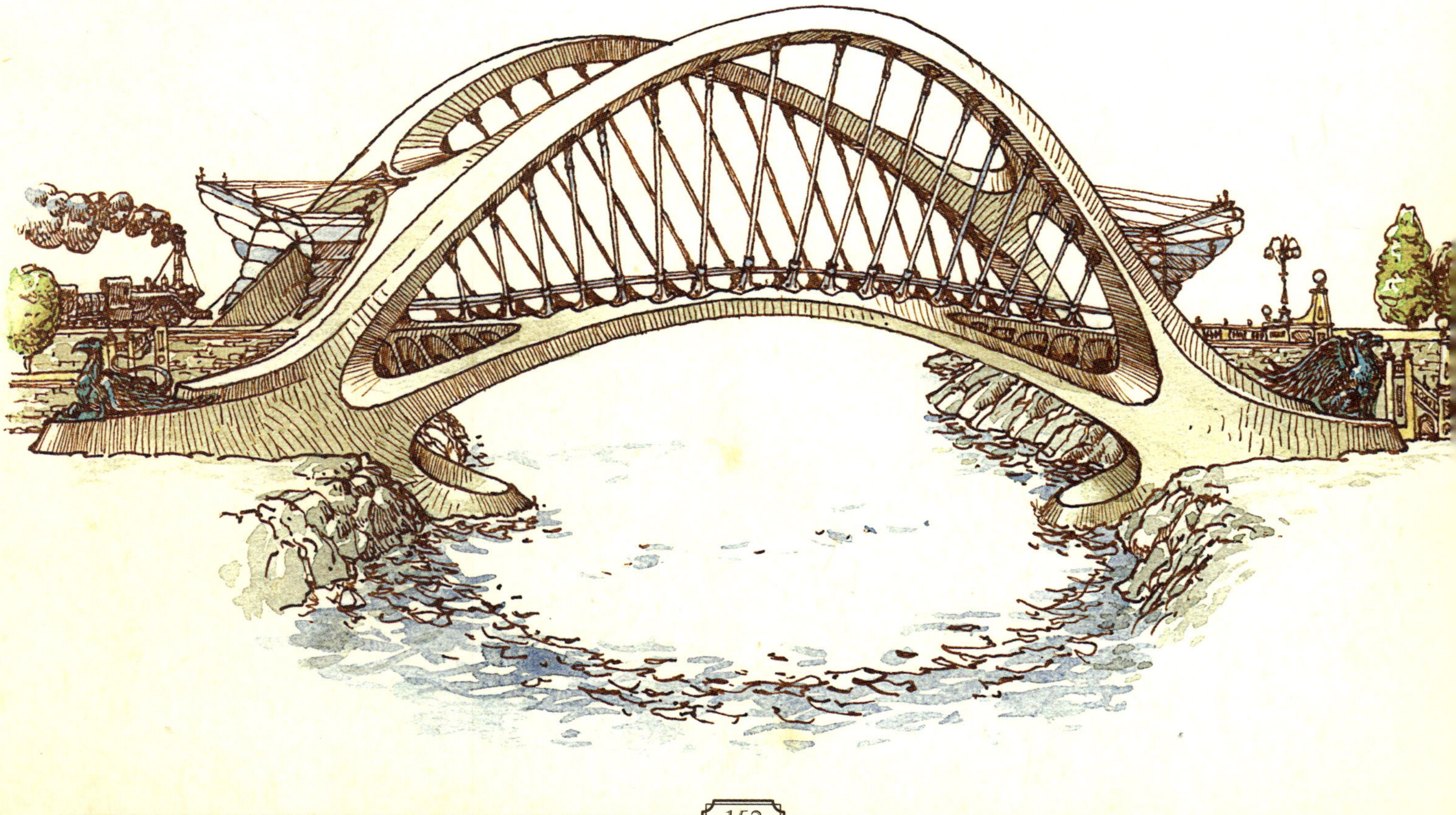

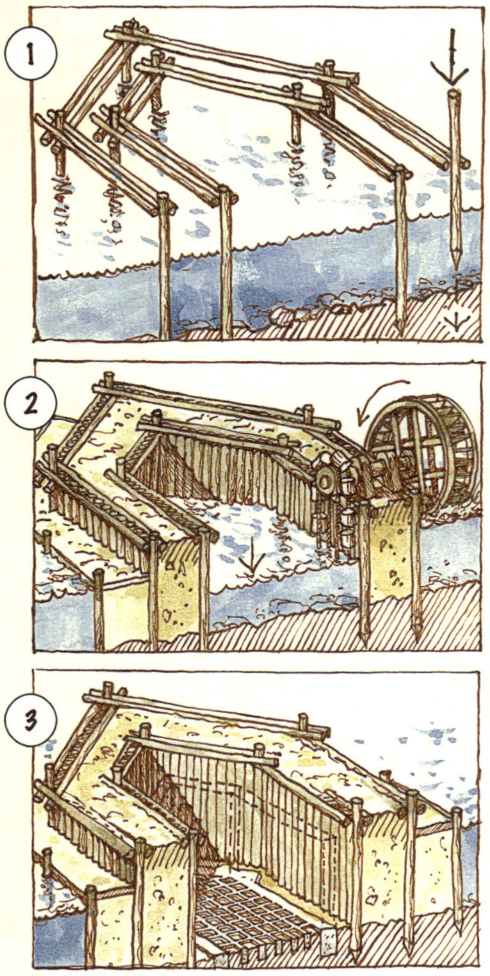

There are compression forces acting on the curve, but stone withstands compression well. The arch does have one structural weak point: The force at the bases is directed horizontally. It tends to push the support pillars apart, causing the arch to collapse inwards.

Therefore, an arch bridge needs very resilient pillars that will hold the bridge's weight and resist horizontal collapse. But how do you build a pillar smack dab in the middle of a large body of a flowing river? You'll need to temporarily pump the water out around the area where you're building.

Start by driving long, narrow posts called piles (1) into the ground using a large hammer called a piledriver. Use thin, sheet-like piles fitted together to make a watertight chamber, and then pump the water out (2). You can achieve this using a water wheel driving a pump (page 234).

Once the water is pumped out, workers can enter the box to build the foundation. Once the foundation is set, the pillars can be built on top. The pillars should be shaped into a point towards the direction of the flow of the water, like the bow of a boat. This way, they'll reduce water resistance and break through blocks of ice during the cold months. This underwater construction technology can also be used to build dam locks and support structures for underwater pipelines.

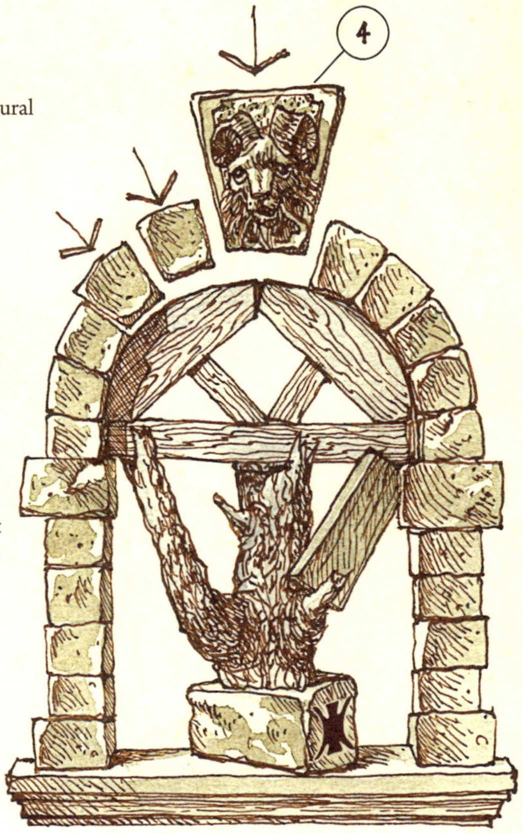

ARCH BRIDGES

To build an arch, you need a special support frame, known as shoring. In this case, it takes the form of a semi-circle forming a relief of the bridge. The stones you use should be wedge-shaped to fit tightly into a curve. As soon as all of the pieces are in place on both sides, insert the last "keystone" piece in the center (4). It locks the arch into place, balancing the lateral expansion of the curved slab and making the entire structure stronger.

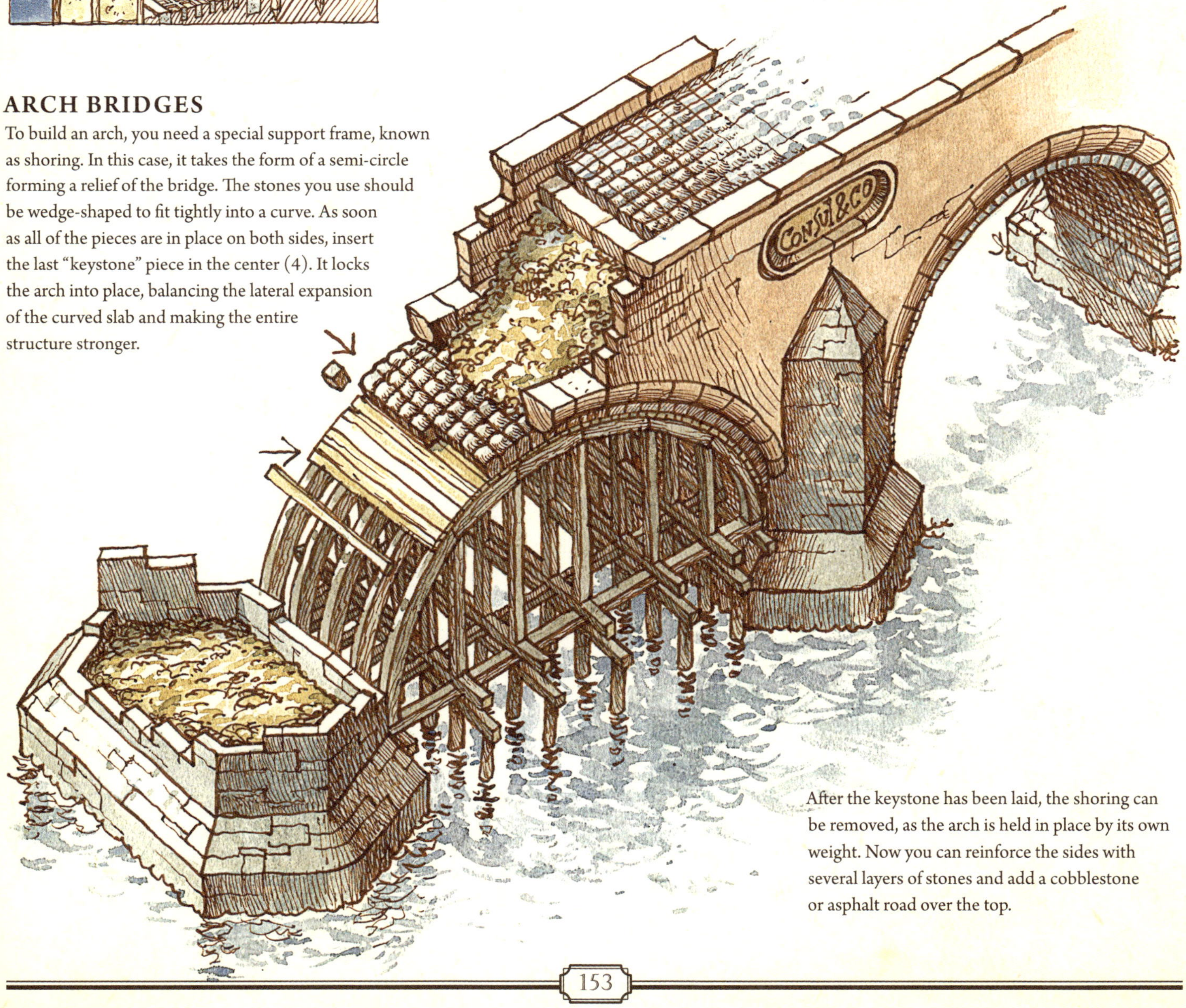

After the keystone has been laid, the shoring can be removed, as the arch is held in place by its own weight. Now you can reinforce the sides with several layers of stones and add a cobblestone or asphalt road over the top.

ROOFING & TILES

Once you possess the technology to make flammable material fireproof and transform a brittle material into something as strong as steel, you'll be able to make a reliable roof out of anything: reed, birch bark, slate, wood. Even turf will work: blanket your roof and collect bouquets in the summer by simply leaning out of the window. What's most important is that you correctly calculate the load and the angle of the slope.

TILES

Clay used for tiles shouldn't be too greasy or gritty. There's a good test to make sure your material is sufficiently elastic: A lump of clay thrown on the floor should flatten out like dough, without cracking. Spread the clay in rows on the ground and let it sit for at least a year. The clay should get wet when it rains in the fall, freeze in winter and thaw in the spring. The more times this happens, the better the material will be. Before sculpting, the clay must be soaked for 2–3 days then thoroughly rinsed (make a pugmill from a wooden barrel or a box containing iron knives attached to an axle).

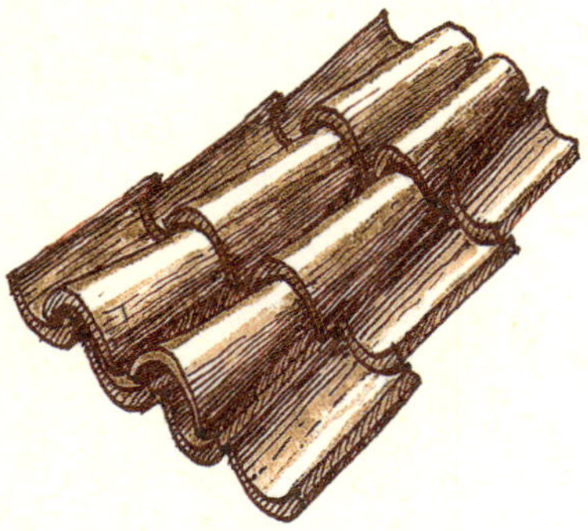

To make sure your tiles are all identical, make a special frame — a shallow container with a movable part that will slice off excess clay and give the desired shape. Flat tiles are the easiest to produce, but curved tiles provide better protection from water and are able to withstand stronger gusts of wind.

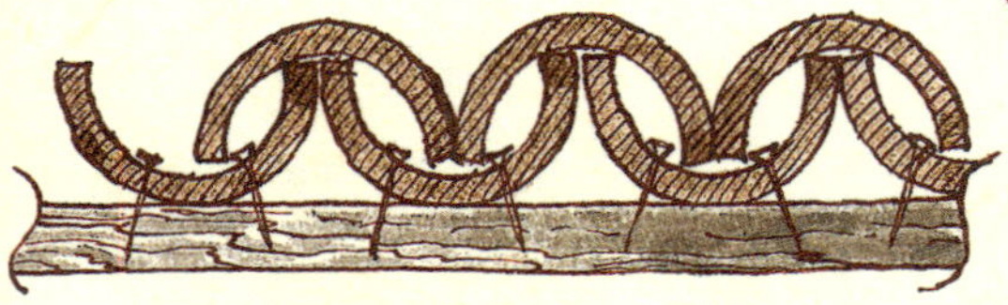

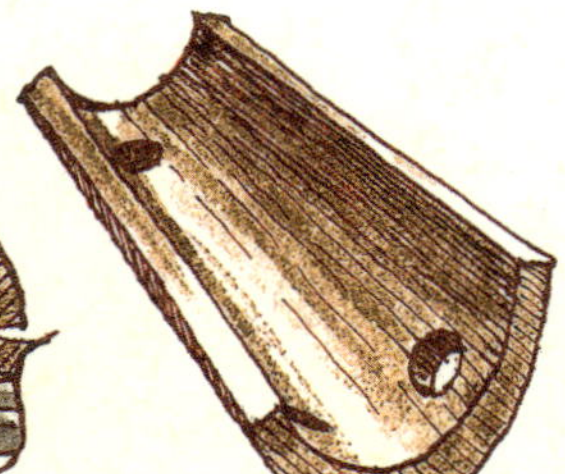

Poke a hole in each tile so you can fasten it to the roof sheathing with a nail. Dry the shingles for 10 days and bake them in an oven at a high temperature. To improve water repellency, coat the tiles with a glazing solution before firing: dry an oily red clay (a natural clay with a high iron content) and grind into a powder then dilute with water until it reaches a thick, milky consistency. After firing, the tiles will turn red.

Shingles are laid in an overlapping pattern starting at the bottom so that the end product resembles scales. This technique prevents leaks in the roof. The slope of a tiled roof should be at least 25° (otherwise, the water will drain poorly) but no more than 60°.

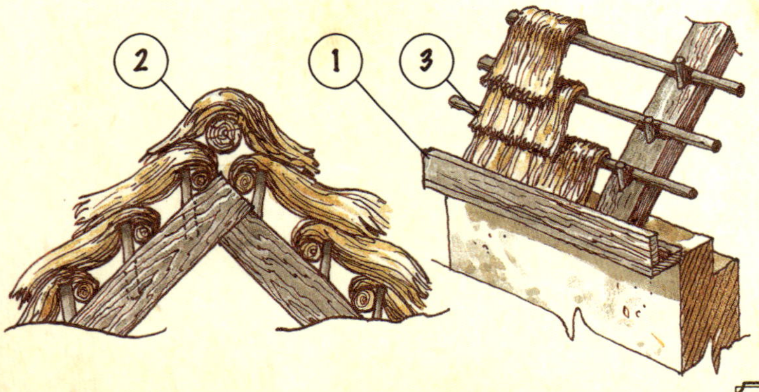

THATCHING

A thatched clay roof is cheap and easy to make. But it's also very heavy, so it's better to work on a frame. You can also add additional supports and cover both sides of the roof at the same time to avoid overloading the rafters.

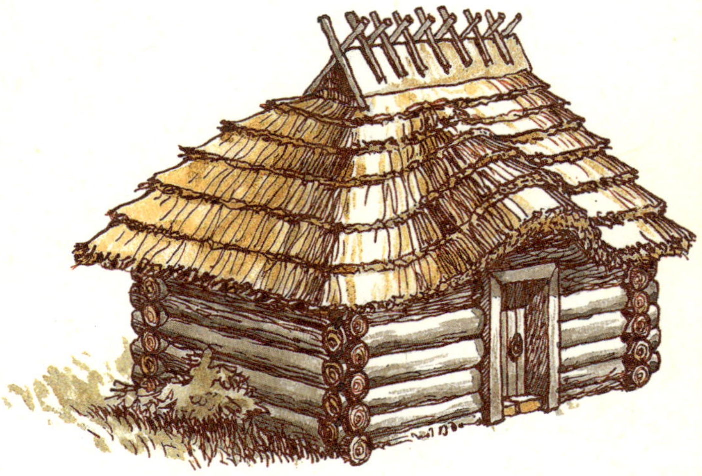

Dig two pits then line the bottom and sides with wooden planks. Fill the bottom of the first with layers of oily clay, around 130–150 mm thick. Pour water over the clay between each layer (2 parts water to one part clay). Let sit for 6 hours then stir. Pour the resulting clay mortar into the second pit (in a 10 cm-thick layer). Tie threshed straw into small bundles. Lay the first layer of sheaves across the bottom of the hole then lay the second on top facing the opposite direction.

Pour another layer of mortar and stamp it in with your feet so that the straw is completely saturated. Repeat until the pit is filled to the top with sheaves. The last layer should be mortar. Place boards on top, weigh them down with stones and leave to soak for three days. Position sheaves along the edges of the pit to drain off excess clay solution. Oddly enough, thanks to the clay, your roof will also be fire resistant.

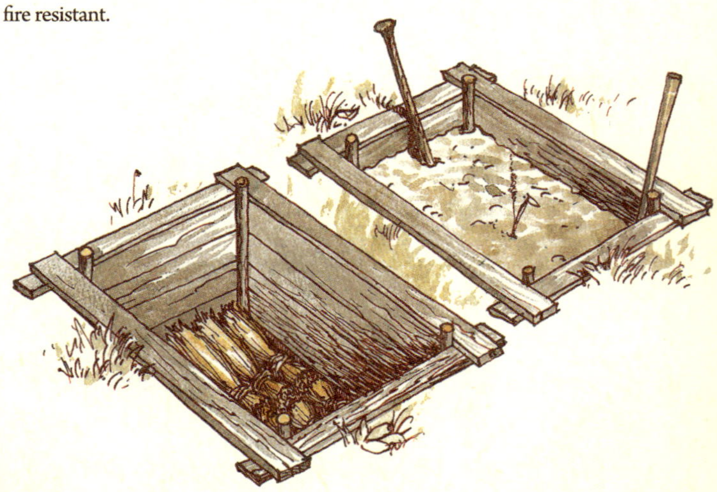

Lay the sheaves from the overhang (1) to the ridge (2). Place the sheaf on the batten (3), untie and straighten. Overlap the second sheaf on top of the first, then the third on top of the second and so on until you reach the end of the row. Attach the straw to the batten using iron rods. Smooth with a rake every 3–4 rows and pour clay solution over the top. Nail two poles to either side of the ridge (2) and use them to hook the sheaves on the last row, which should form a gutter.

FRAME

The foundation of the roof is its frame. Nail together logs and planks to create the desired shape. Make the sheathing — the part where you lay the shingles. The frame must withstand the weight of both the roof itself and the snow. If you decide to utilize this space by making a flat roof, then it will have to stand up to summer barbecues, swimming pools and all the other attributes of a happy life.

Position the rafters so that the weight of the roof is evenly distributed between the walls of the house and the additional support beams. Make sure the lower ends of the rafters rest on a well-anchored beam to distribute the load from the roof.

Don't forget to add a lightning rod and a drain. Gargoyles will protect the roof from being destroyed by the rains.

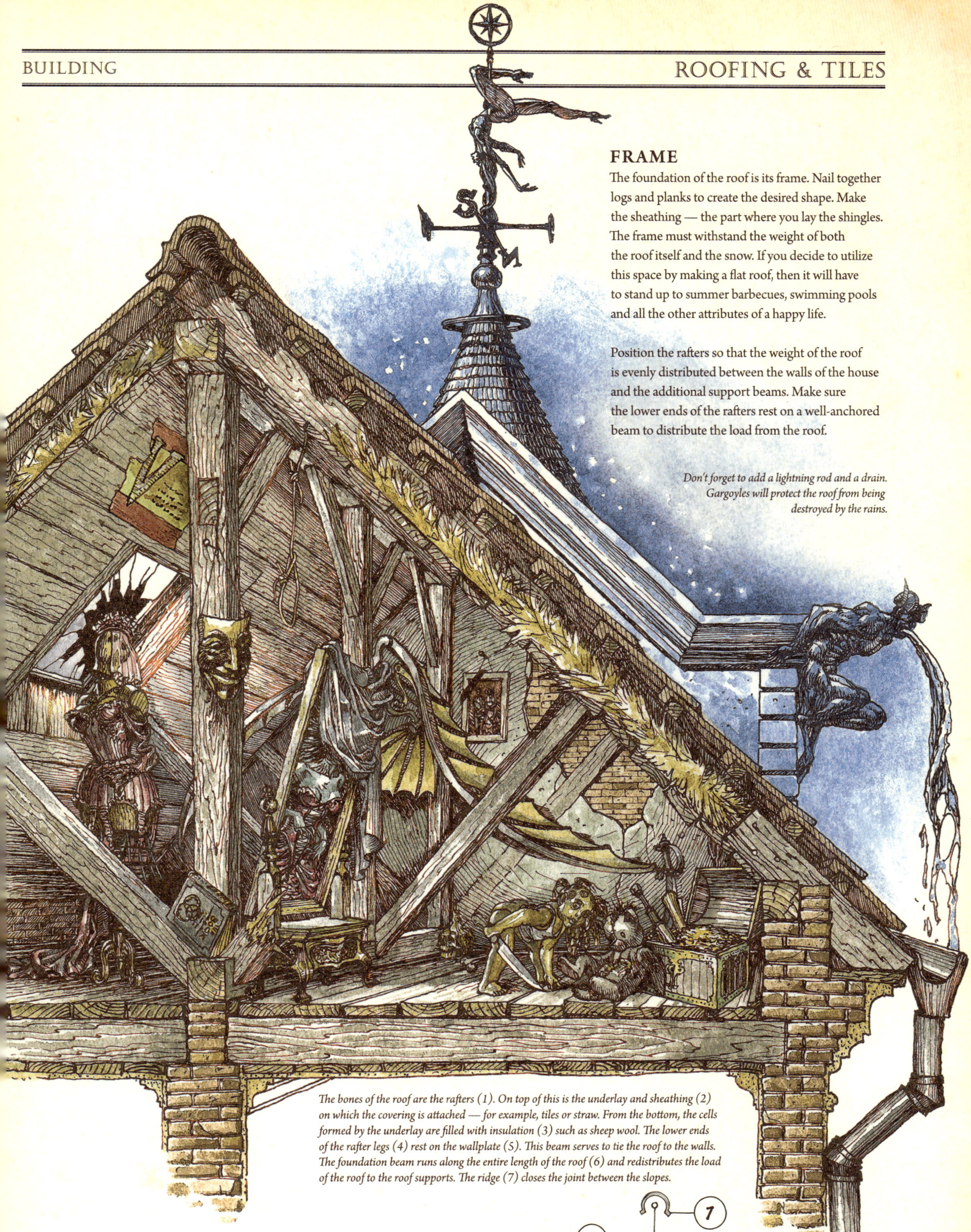

The bones of the roof are the rafters (1). On top of this is the underlay and sheathing (2) on which the covering is attached — for example, tiles or straw. From the bottom, the cells formed by the underlay are filled with insulation (3) such as sheep wool. The lower ends of the rafter legs (4) rest on the wallplate (5). This beam serves to tie the roof to the walls. The foundation beam runs along the entire length of the roof (6) and redistributes the load of the roof to the roof supports. The ridge (7) closes the joint between the slopes.

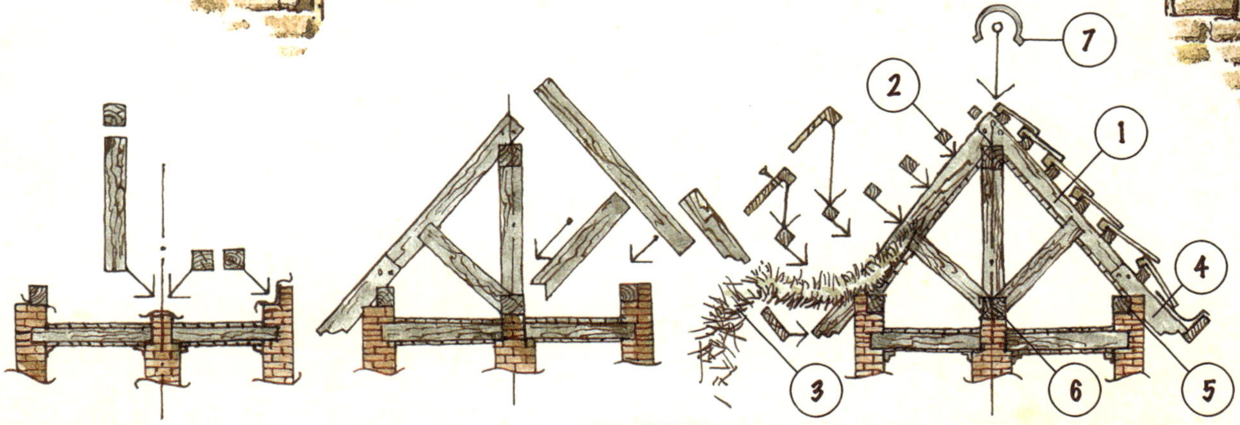

WATER SUPPLY & SEWAGE

A good house is more than just four walls, sturdy doors and a reliable roof. The commode is, among other things, a place of contemplation, where we sit and solve the world's most pressing problems. So a warm and inviting washroom is a necessity in any civilized home. This means having a well-thought-out sewage system. If you don't (quite literally) get your shit together, it may leak into the soil and contaminate nearby water sources. You don't want your lack of foresight to cause the next epidemic!

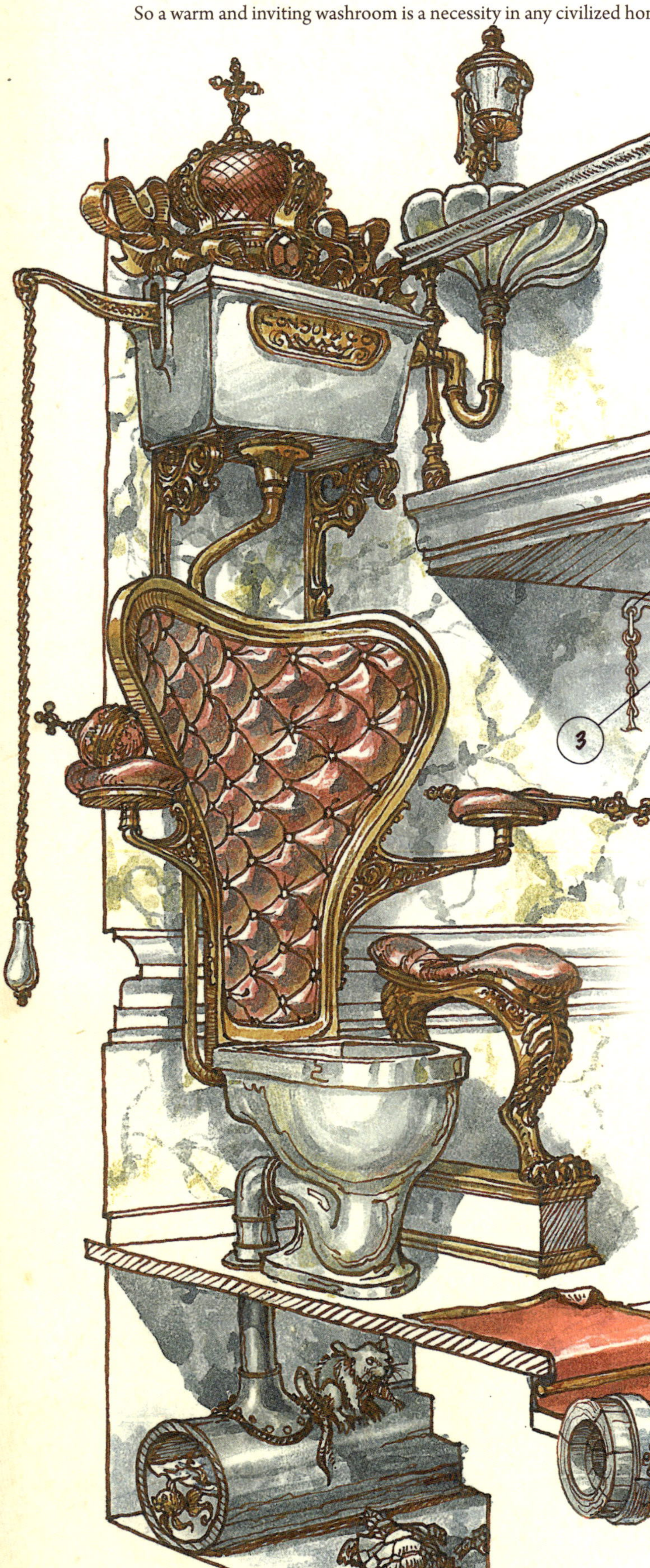

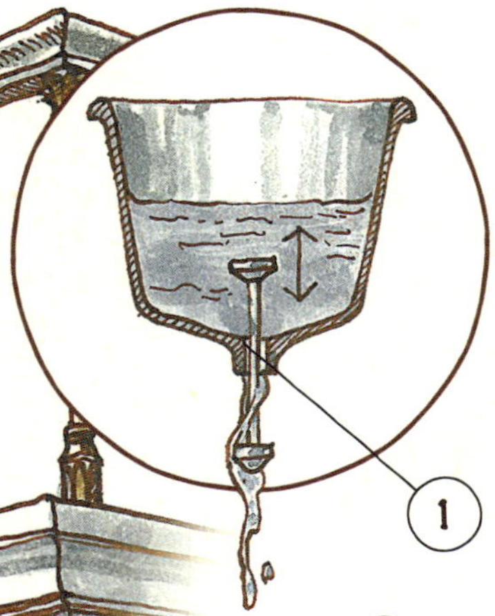

HAND WASHING BASIN

A cylindrical vessel with an opening at the bottom, into which a drainage valve (1) is inserted, which closes the drain. Press the back of your hand against the flap from underneath and the flap rises, allowing water to flow out.

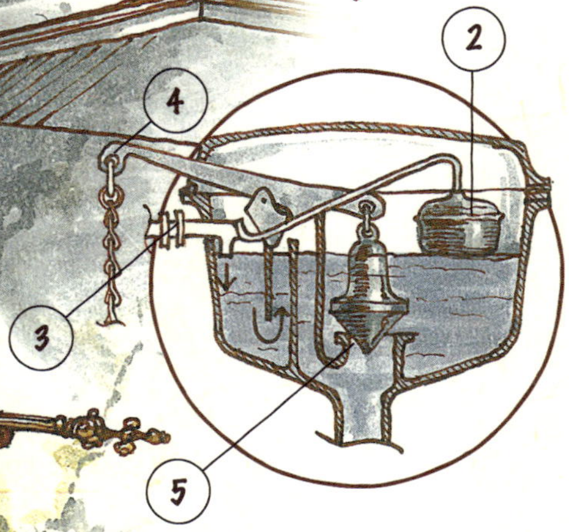

CISTERN

Works using a hydraulic accumulator. The tank is equipped with an auto-fill system consisting of a rocker arm with a bob (2) at one end and a valve (3) at the other. When the tank is filled with water, the bob rises and the rocker moves and closes the valve of the supply pipe.

The drainage system consists of a handle (4) connected to a plug (5). When the handle is lifted, the plug is pressed firmly against the drain hole and keeps the water in the tank. When the handle is lowered, the plug is lifted up and water rushes into the toilet.

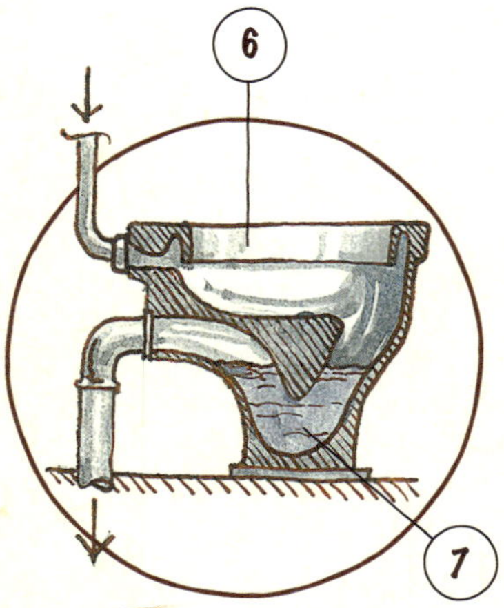

TOILET

The toilet is made of a bowl (6) and a trap (7), an S-shaped bend in the outlet pipe. The water layer inside acts as a seal, preventing air (that is, unpleasant odors) from entering the room from the sewer.

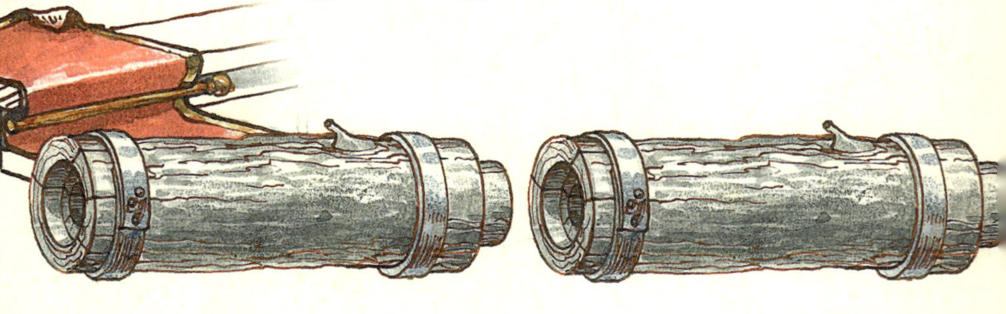

Sewer pipes can be made of wood. Sequoia will serve for a very long time. Create a flexible structure with short pieces of wood that are secured together with rings and hardwood dowels. Coat the joints with hot animal fat or resin.

Providing your home with heat and water might take some creative thinking — combine everything into one system! A tank on the roof accumulates rainwater that can then be heated using a woodfire stove below the house.

Pipes carrying the hot water run underneath the floor, warming it up and heating the house in the process. Don't be in too much of a rush to vent your chimney fumes — excess heat energy from the stove and fireplace can also be channelled through the pipes as another source of hot water!

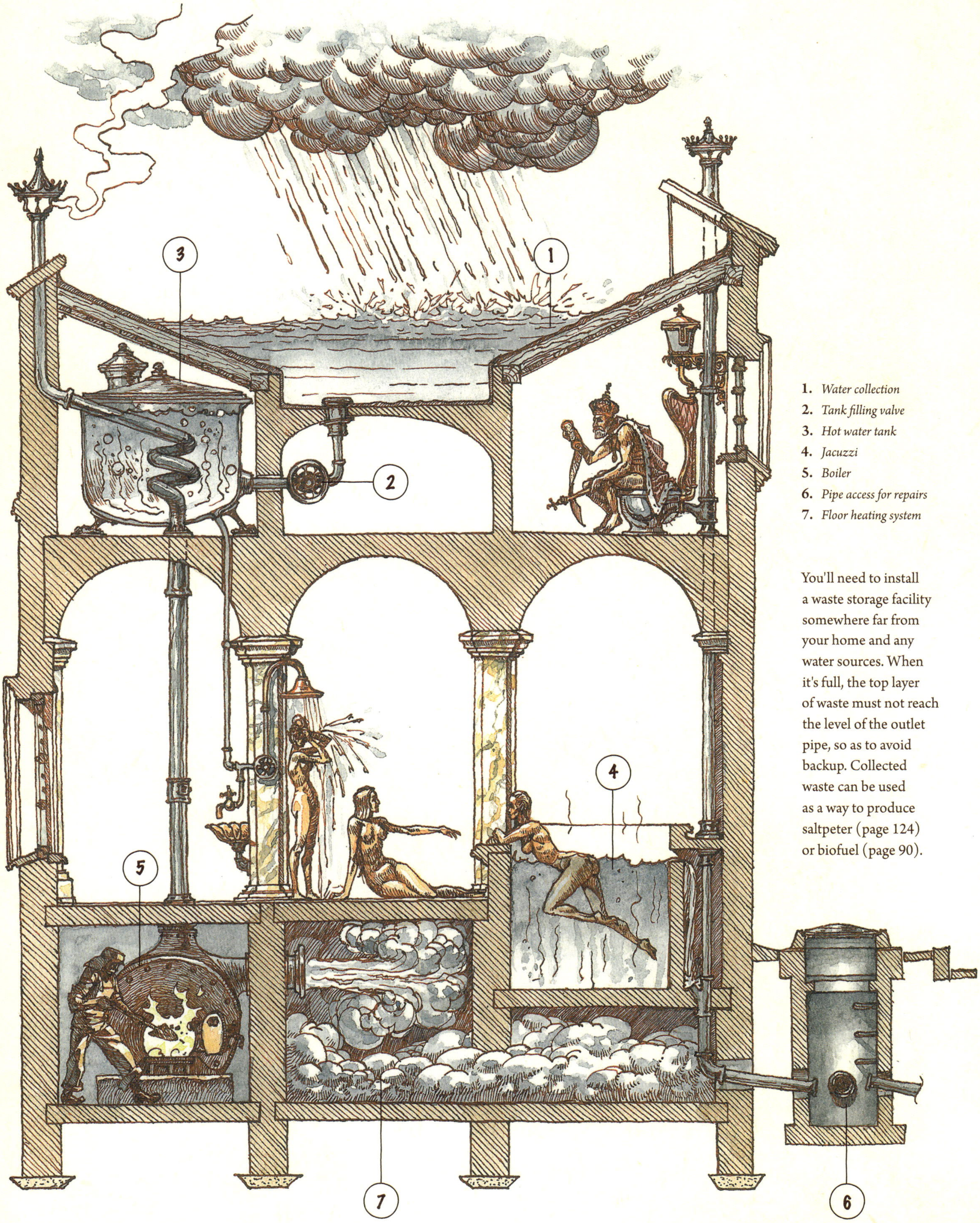

1. *Water collection*
2. *Tank filling valve*
3. *Hot water tank*
4. *Jacuzzi*
5. *Boiler*
6. *Pipe access for repairs*
7. *Floor heating system*

You'll need to install a waste storage facility somewhere far from your home and any water sources. When it's full, the top layer of waste must not reach the level of the outlet pipe, so as to avoid backup. Collected waste can be used as a way to produce saltpeter (page 124) or biofuel (page 90).

REINFORCED CONCRETE

Architecture as a science emerges at the very moment when a builder's sky-high ambitions meet the physical limitations of the materials available. Concrete and steel can significantly expand the horizon of possibilities. Only when you combine the two can you start building structures as lofty as your aspirations.

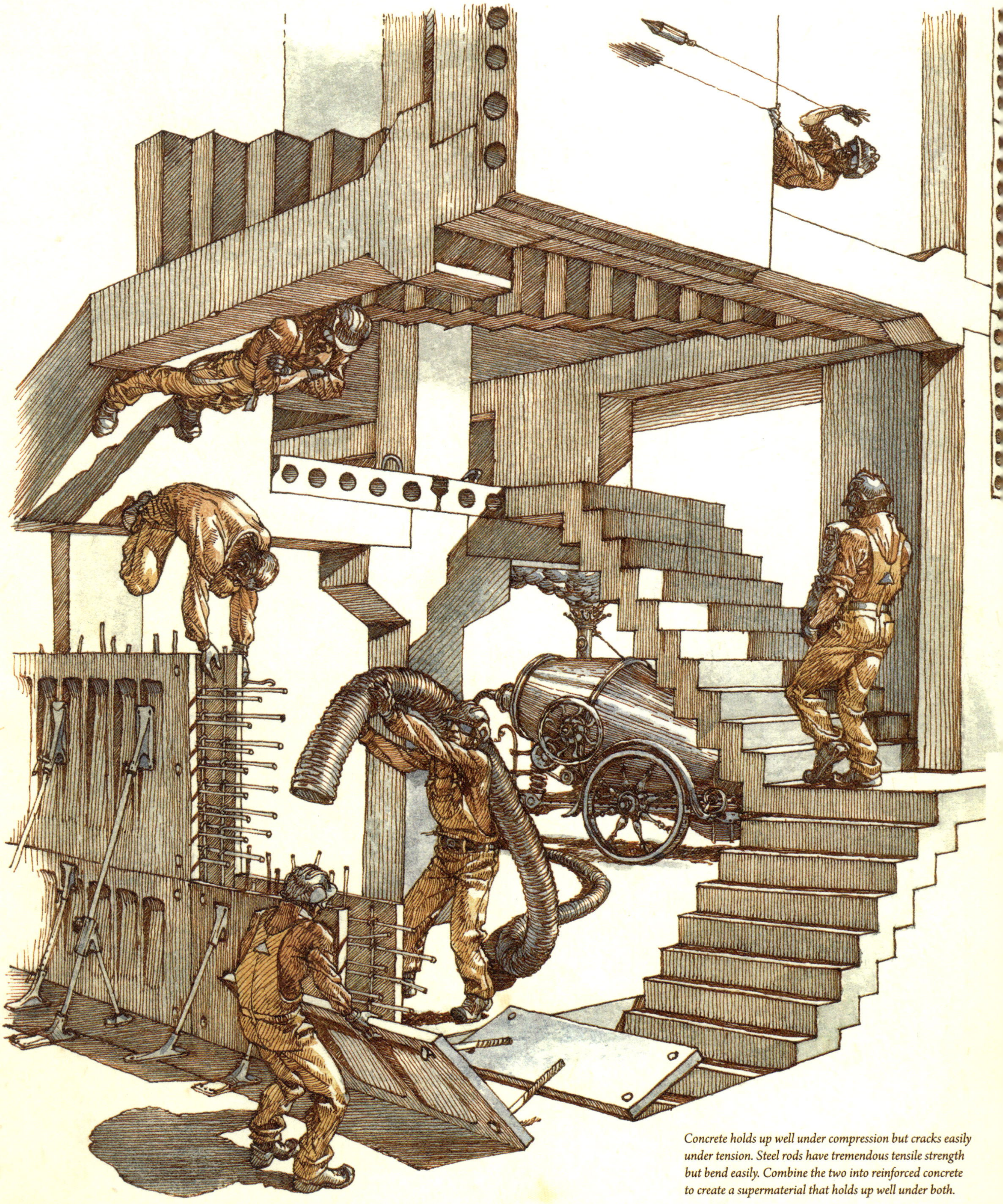

Concrete holds up well under compression but cracks easily under tension. Steel rods have tremendous tensile strength but bend easily. Combine the two into reinforced concrete to create a supermaterial that holds up well under both.

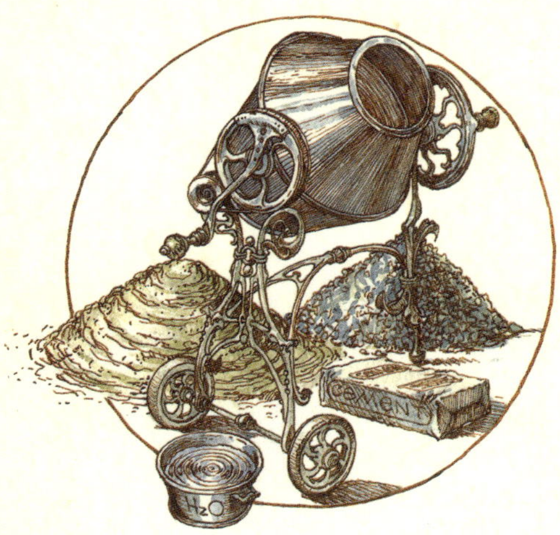

CONCRETE

Mix cement, sand, gravel and water. If you use Portland cement (page 158) as a base, the concrete becomes even more resistant to cold and moisture. Portland cement is made by mixing clinker and gypsum (which should compose around 2–3% of the final product). Clinker is produced by sintering (fusing the elements together without completely liquifying) a mixture of 75% limestone and 25% clay at 1300–1450°C.

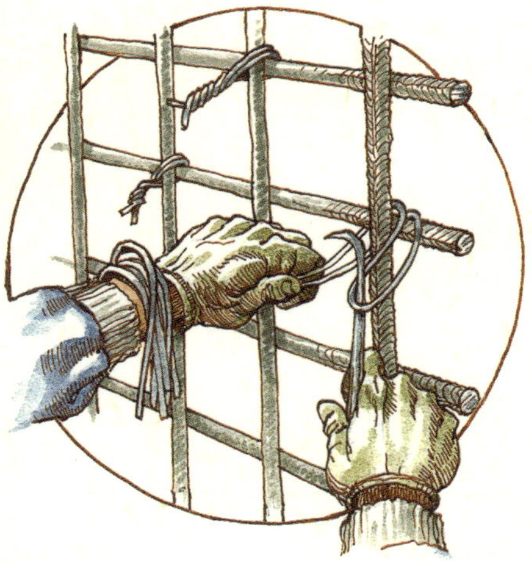

REBAR

Cross girders and other construction elements exposed to flexural stress are constantly acted on by the opposing forces of compression and tension. Thus, you'll need a frame made from metal rods. Assemble a grid of steel rods in the desired shape then pour concrete over the top. You'll end up with a reinforced concrete beam that resists both compression and tension.

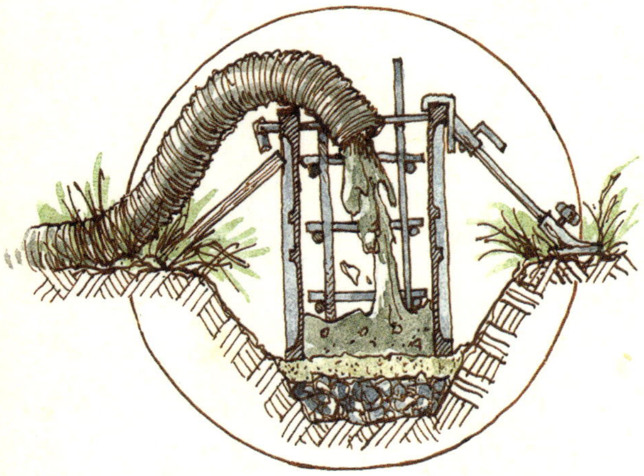

FORMWORK

To create huge monolithic slabs, you need a formwork — a temporary or permanent mold used for cement. Place the rebar frame and pour your concrete. The reinforced concrete will be more durable if you tamp the concrete down firmly. The rebar can be pre-stretched so that when the concrete hardens, the rebar compresses the material, making it even sturdier. Wait until the mixture is fully solidified before removing the formwork. This is how a building is constructed — floor by floor, from bottom to top.

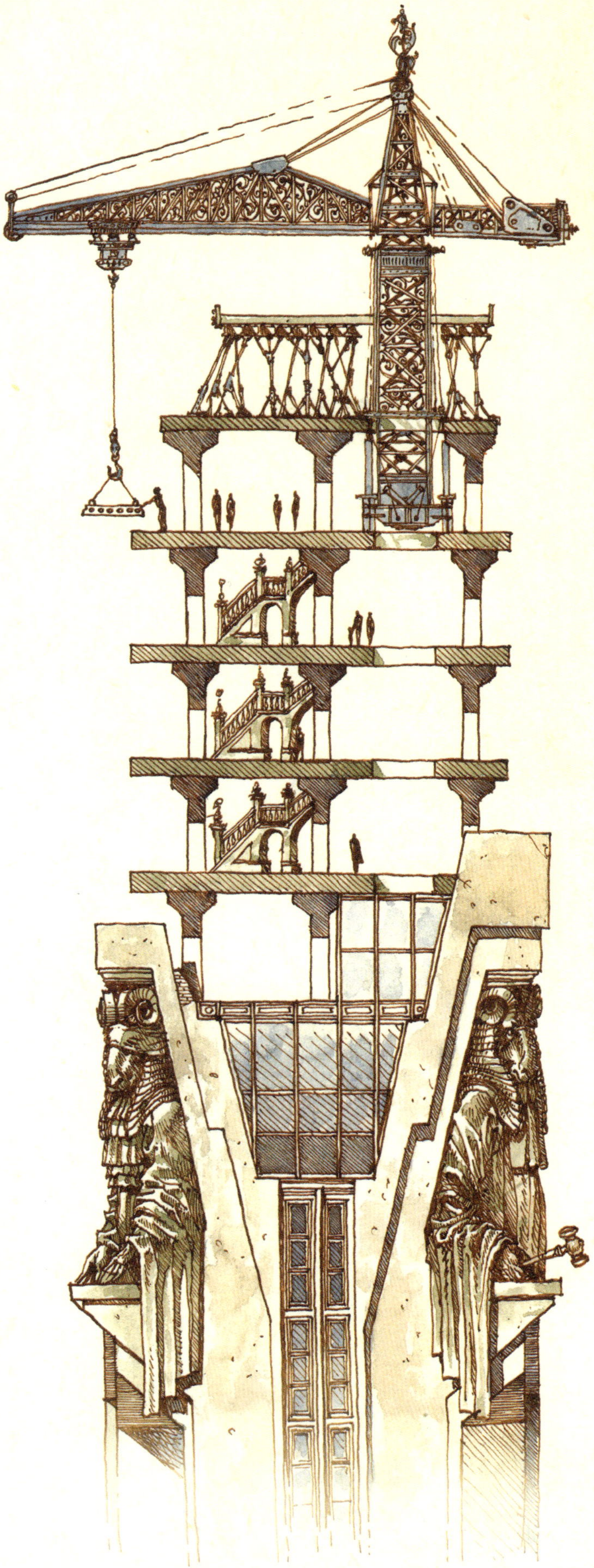

You can make separate slabs of rebar and concrete in advance. All you need to do at the construction site is assemble them like building blocks into your final structure. The resulting concrete box must then be insulated and connected to utilities (page 156). Just don't forget to lay a foundation first. This is a load-bearing support structure that evenly distributes the weight of the building. In most cases, the foundational layer capable of withstanding such loads is buried deep beneath the ground. So while a relatively shallow foundation may suffice for low-rise buildings, you'll need a deep pile foundation for high-rise buildings.

MECHANICS

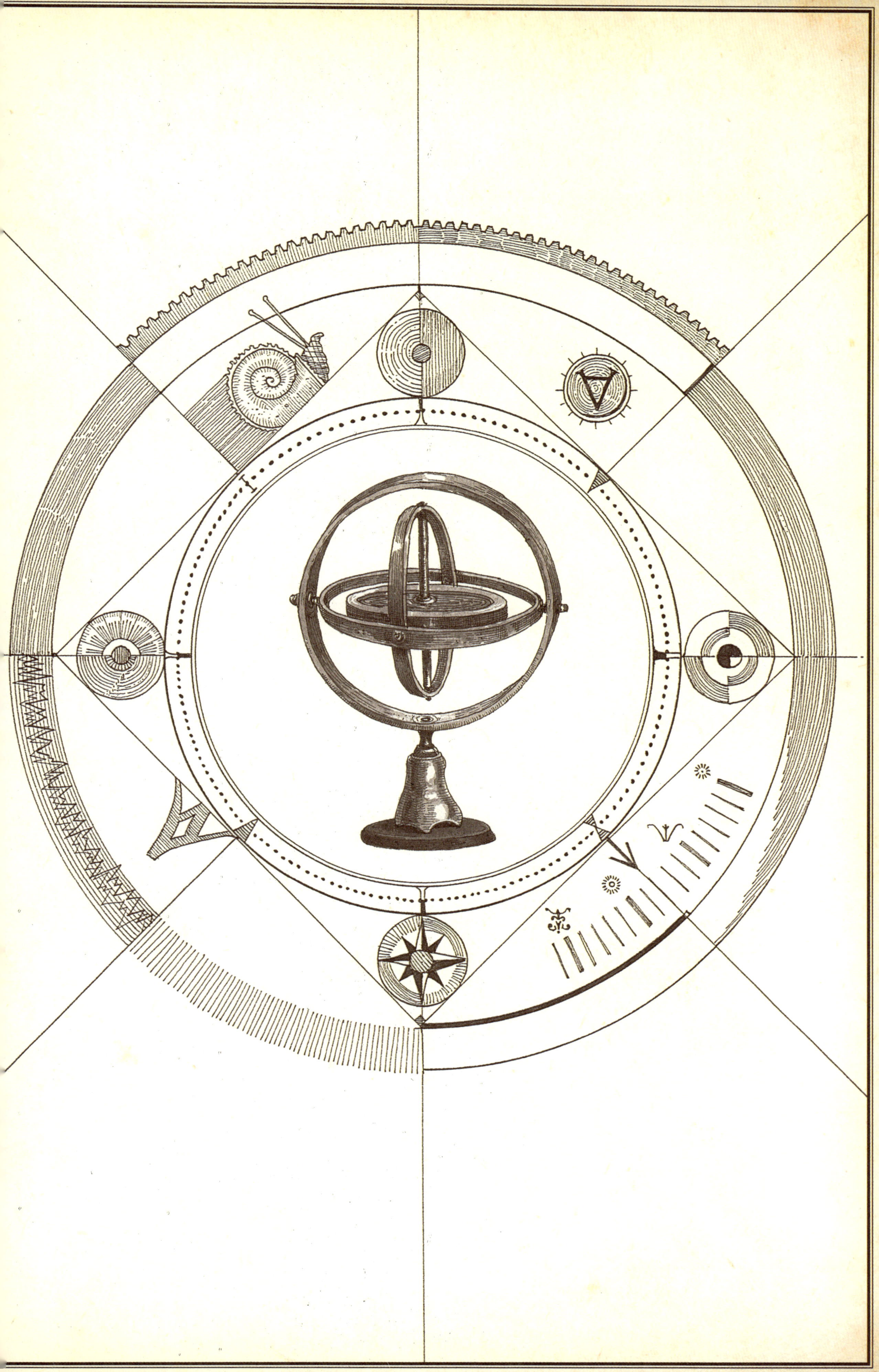

GEAR & ROLLING MILL

Engines convert the energy from burning fuel into the to and fro movement of pistons that is then converted into rotation of a shaft. An electric motor produces rotation directly. But how can you transfer this motion down the line while increasing the torque, using it to power, say, a large machine?

What if you need a piece to be at a certain angle or you need to change the speed of rotation without changing the running speed of the motor? For this, you'll need gears — metal discs with intermeshing teeth.

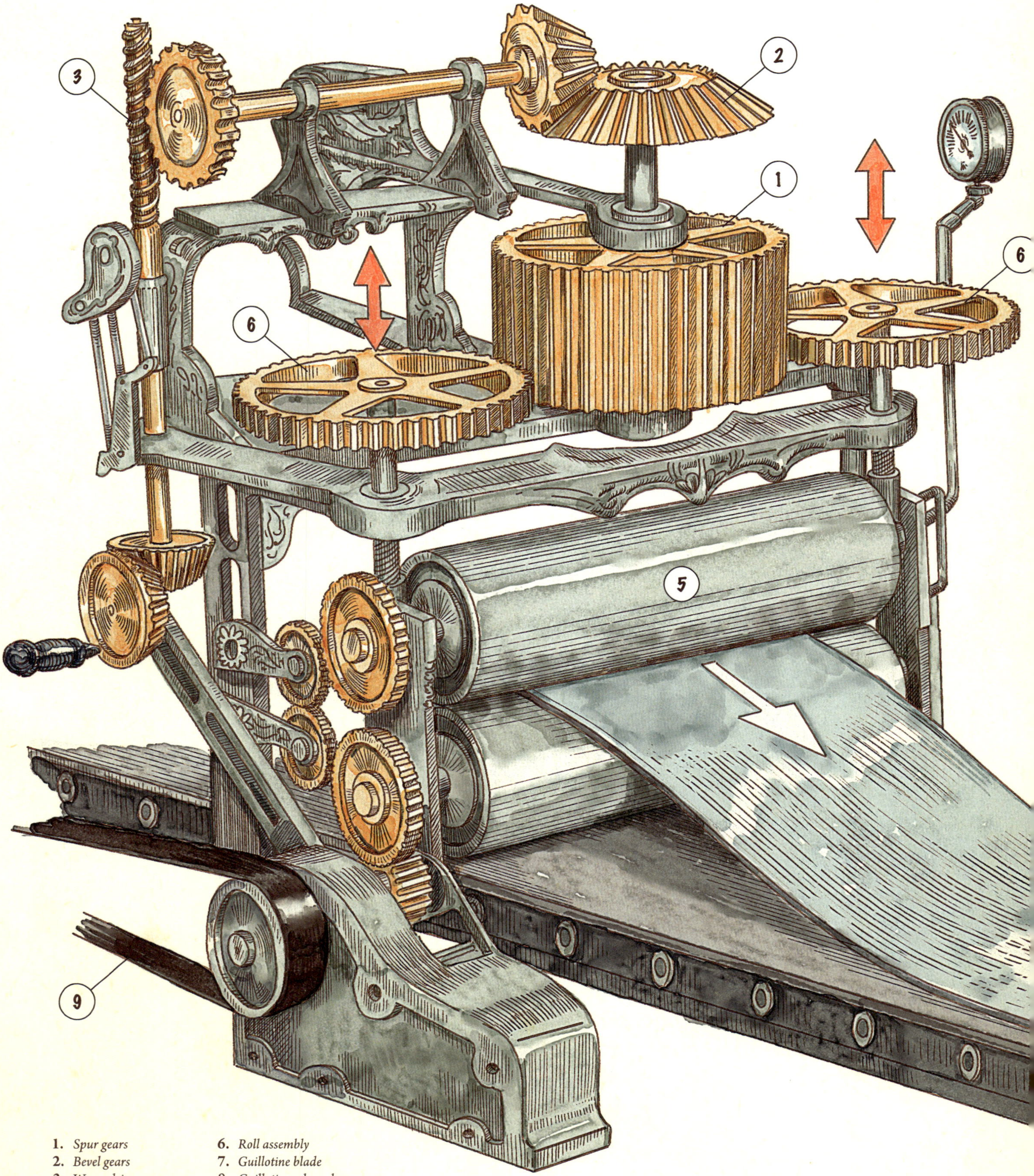

1. *Spur gears*
2. *Bevel gears*
3. *Worm drive*
4. *Rack and pinion*
5. *Rollers*
6. *Roll assembly*
7. *Guillotine blade*
8. *Guillotine release lever*
9. *Rolling mill press drive*

In a gear train, the driving gear engages the teeth of the driven gear and transfers torque. Spur gears (1) can change the rotation speed of the shaft. To do this, the gears must have a different radius. If the driven gear has fewer teeth than the driving gear, the rotation speed will increase, while if it has more, the speed will decrease, creating a corresponding increase in the torque. Bevel gears (2) transfer rotational energy at an angle. Worm drives (3) are used to significantly increase the torque, while rack and pinion gears (4) are needed to convert rotational energy into forward momentum.

ROLLING MILL

Thanks to the fact that gears can increase torque as they transfer motion, they can be used to create a useful tool called a rolling mill. Running steel (either hot or cold) between rollers can make a thinner metal sheet or shape a bar, such as for a train track. This operation replaces hammer-and-anvil forging for the efficient mass production of steel. A rack-and-pinion will help you cut the rolled steel sheet by making it easier to lift the guillotine blade. Gravity will take care of the rest after you trigger the release lever (8).

Gears can take many different forms, so try to come up with your own type of gear to solve whatever problems you have at hand.

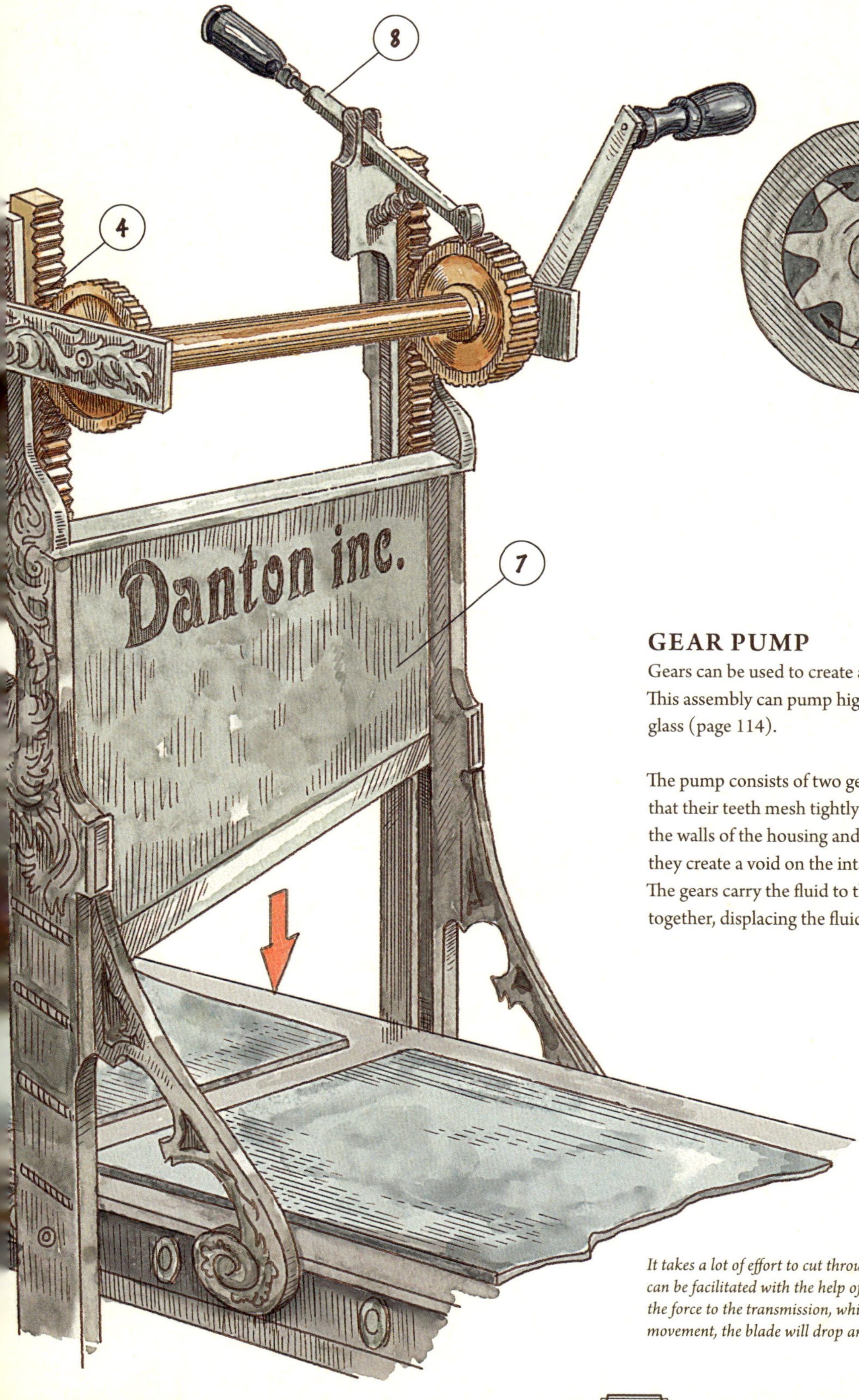

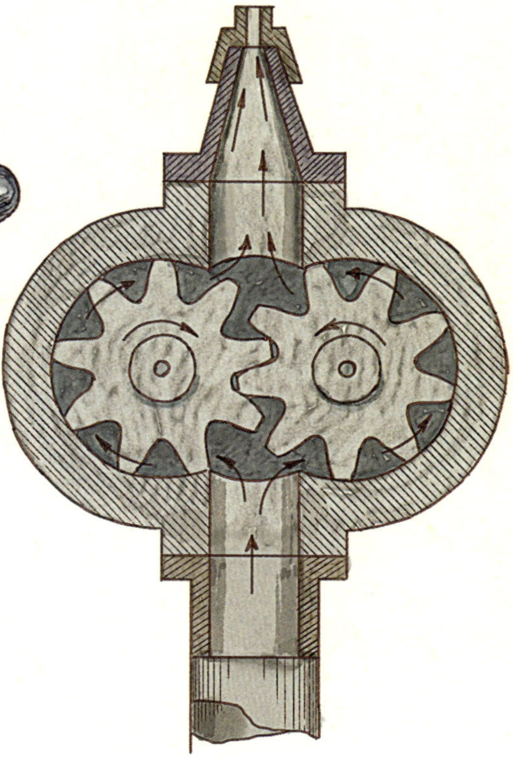

GEAR PUMP

Gears can be used to create a reliable and relatively simple fluid pump. This assembly can pump highly viscous substances such as oil or even molten glass (page 114).

The pump consists of two gears mounted in a sealed casing. It is important that their teeth mesh tightly with each other and that the gaps between the walls of the housing and the gears are minimal. As the gears rotate, they create a void on the intake side of the pump, which is filled with fluid. The gears carry the fluid to the discharge side, where the gears once again mesh together, displacing the fluid and forcing it out the pipe.

It takes a lot of effort to cut through dense material with a guillotine knife. This work can be facilitated with the help of a gear, a rack and a release lever. The lever will transfer the force to the transmission, which converts the rotational movement into translational movement, the blade will drop and the knife edge will produce a straight cut!

BICYCLES

Some inventions happen naturally, as if spontaneously willing themselves into existence, such as the wheel. Others require a chain of happy accidents to come into being. But for the most part, discovery is a long, uphill road illuminated only by brief flashes of insight.

By connecting two wheels to a solid frame and throwing on a chain and a couple of pedals, you're left with a fun and efficient vehicle suitable for both transporting heavy cargo and carrying friends in tow. Using the basic principles behind its design, you can also come up with a variety of other helpful devices and even start generating electricity.

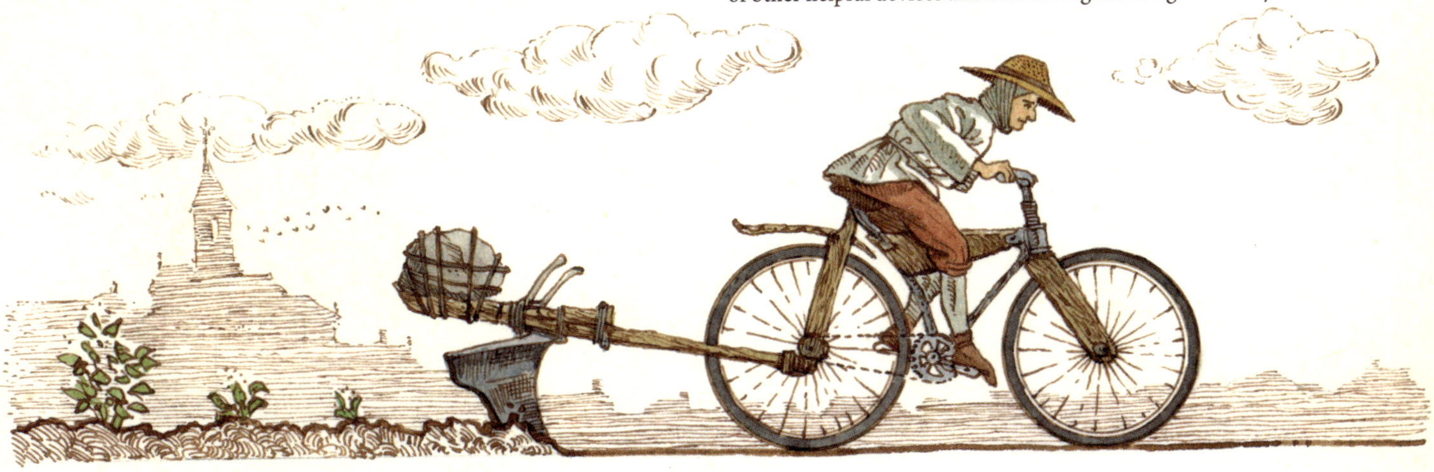

Frame — Just like with a human skeleton, everything rests on the frame. It can be made from wood or metal. A frame in the shape of two connected triangles will be very rigid, making the bike easy to control.

This iron horse is perfect for tournaments and races. But keep in mind that all the bumps in the road will be transmitted directly through the rider's arms and will be absorbed by the body, so don't forget to equip the bike with shock absorbers.

If the rider is prone to wearing long, flowy skirts, you might want to consider making the frame curved so that it's easier for the stylish cyclist to sit down.

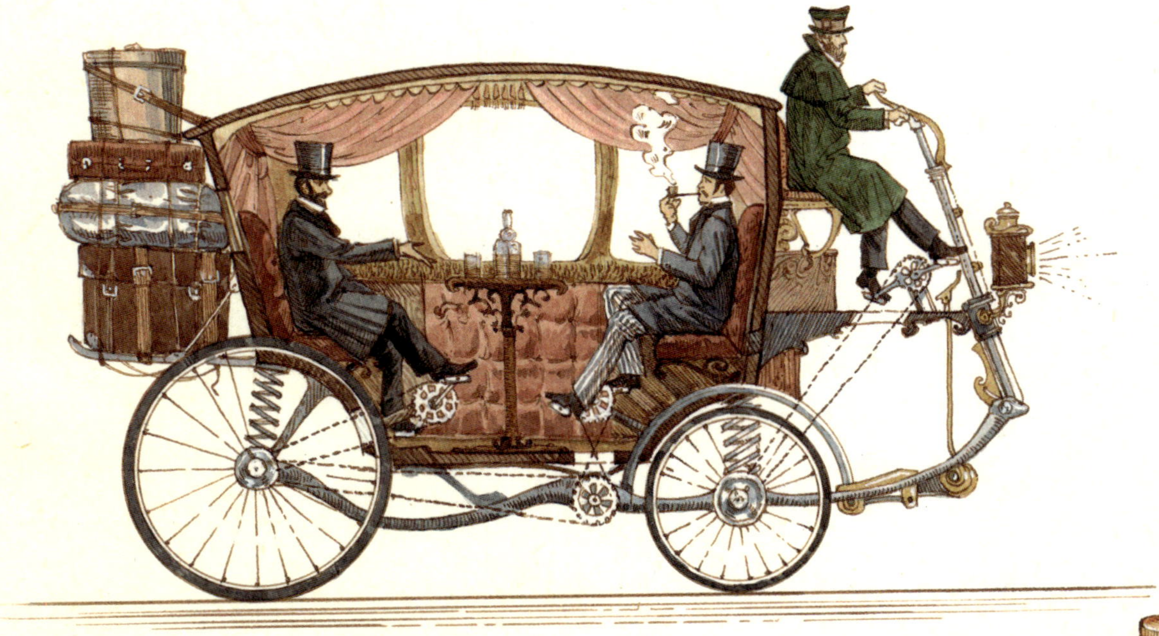

Brakes — One part you definitely don't want to miss. Attach a clamp with brake pads to the wheel rim so the pads are hugging the wheel. Run a cable from the brakes to a handle on the handlebars.

When you squeeze the brake lever, the cable pulls up and the pads clamp together on the wheel rim. The resulting friction causes the wheel to stop spinning, and the bike slows to a stop.

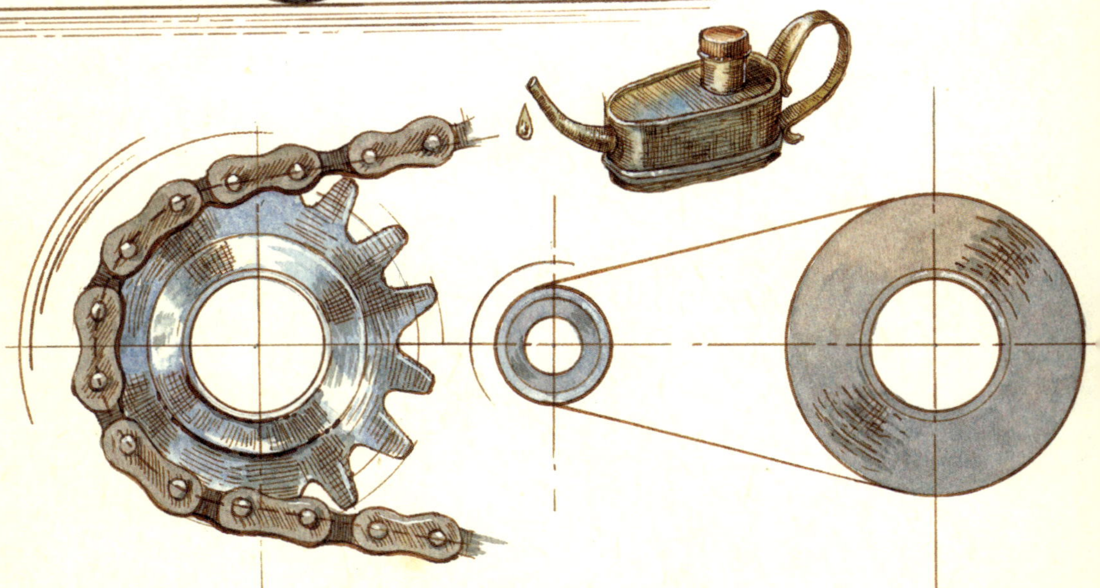

Chain drive — The heart of any bike. The pedals act as levers that rotate a shaft with a large gear. This gear is connected by a chain drive to a smaller gear on the rear wheel axle.

This wheel provides the driving force, setting the bike in motion. The front wheel is for steering.

BELL

A bell will warn people of your impending approach. When you pull down on the trigger, it grabs the teeth of a gear with its serrated edge. This sets into motion a pair of spinning metal discs attached to the base. These then hit the metal casing covering the mechanism, generating a loud sound. Don't forget the spring to return the lever to its place so the bell will be ready for the next unwary pedestrian.

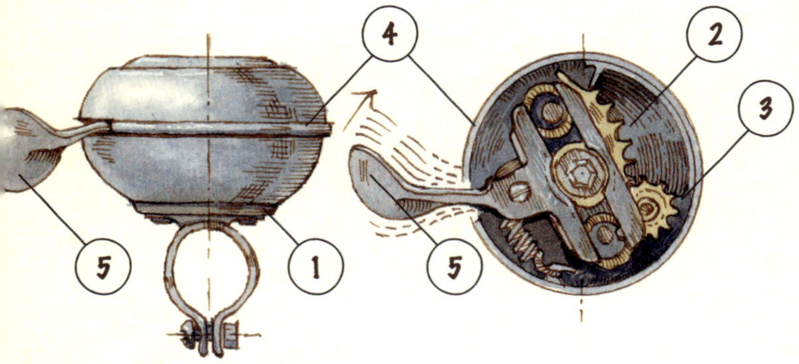

1. *Base for pair of metal discs*
2. *Serrated edge of the lever*
3. *Cogwheel*
4. *Pair of metal discs*
5. *Trigger*

SHOCK ABSORBERS

The wheels hold the entire weight of your body and the bike. A few minutes on the road and you'll start feeling the bumps throughout your whole body. Springs under the seat turn a bone rattler into a comfortable bike. Add a pair of inflatable tires onto your wheels and you'll have an all-terrain vehicle. Find a tight rubber hose and fill it with air. Create a threaded nipple in the hose so that you can screw on a pump and refill tires with air when necessary.

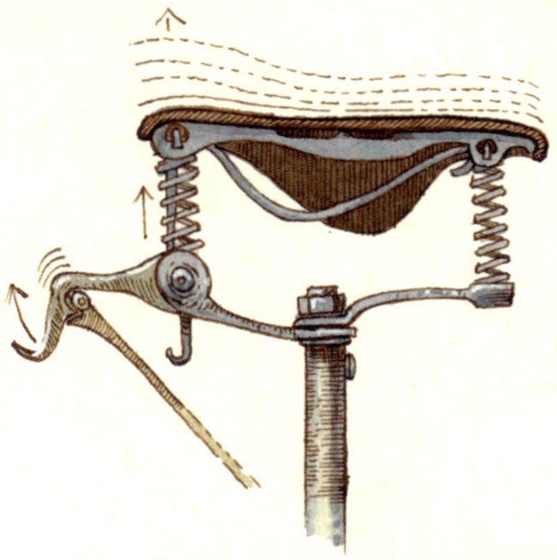

Steel spokes connect the wheel rim to the rotating hub in the center of the wheel. They need to be evenly distributed around the circumference of the wheel and fastened tightly.

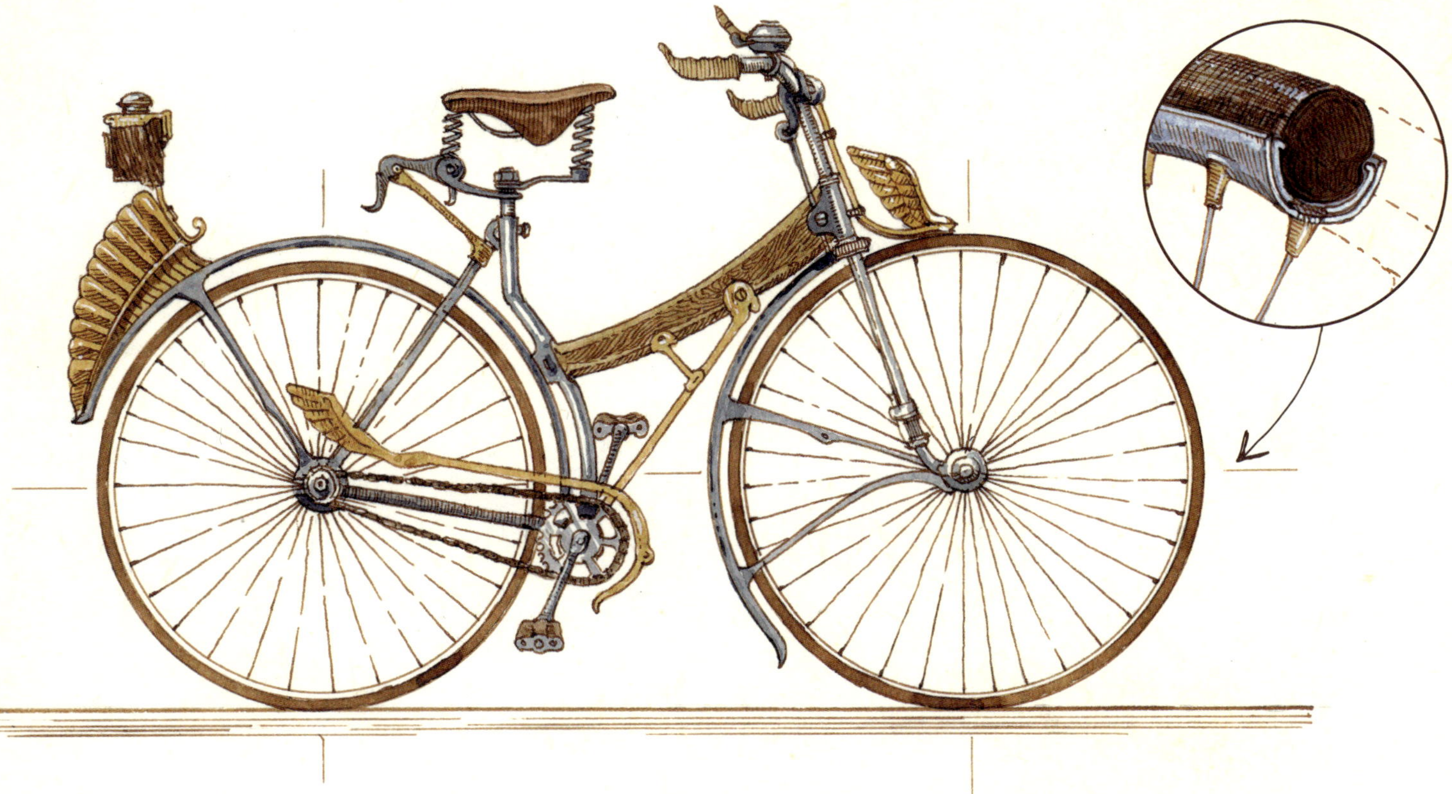

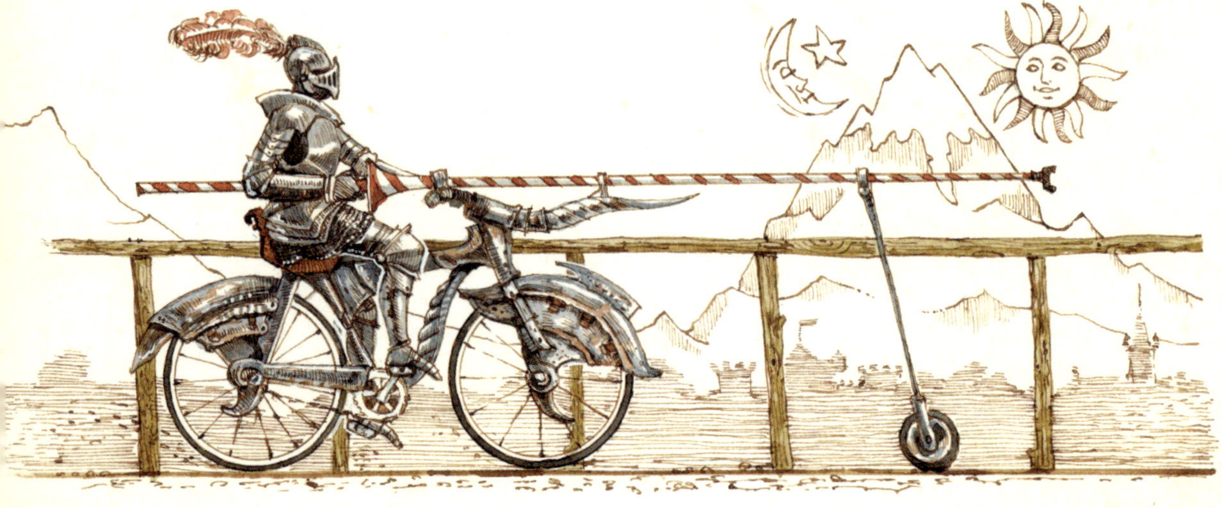

Riding a bike is like going through life: To maintain your balance, you have to keep moving. Moreover, the higher the speed, the easier it will be to control.

It's difficult to have an objective view of the passage of time. Depending on one's current life circumstances, time either drags on or rushes past. Keeping track of the ticking of seconds and the chiming of hours will help establish communication between people and teach them to negotiate, plan the future together and remember the past.

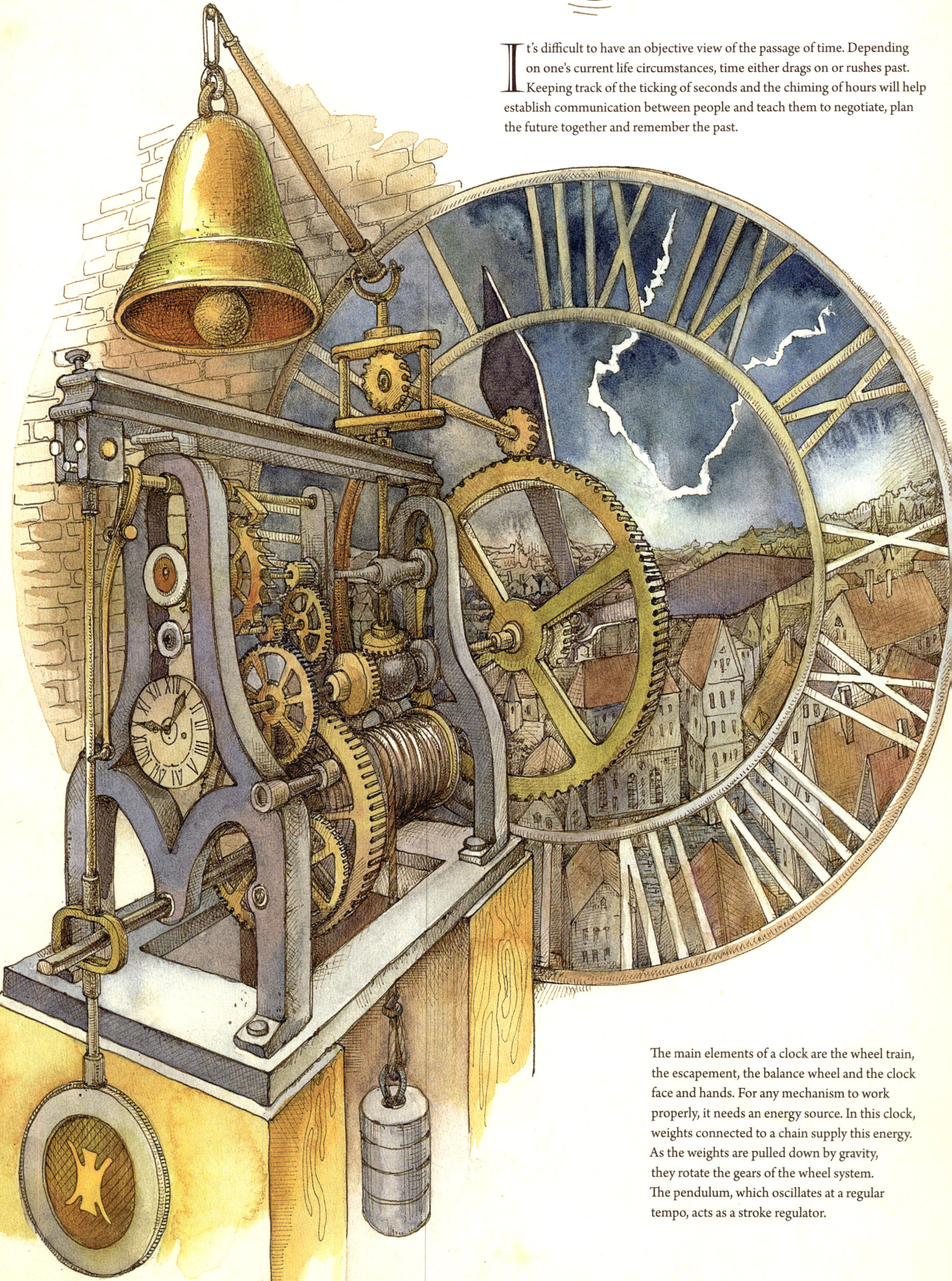

The main elements of a clock are the wheel train, the escapement, the balance wheel and the clock face and hands. For any mechanism to work properly, it needs an energy source. In this clock, weights connected to a chain supply this energy. As the weights are pulled down by gravity, they rotate the gears of the wheel system. The pendulum, which oscillates at a regular tempo, acts as a stroke regulator.

MECHANICAL CLOCKS

A simple clock design uses the swing of a pendulum (1) to provide consistent timing. On each swing, the pendulum triggers the toothed pallet fork (2) to release the escape wheel (3) to turn by one tooth. Gravity gradually lowers the weight (4) and rotates the axle (5) through the gears (6). This mechanism regulates the rotation of the gear chain (7).

The gears are arranged to precisely count the swings of the pendulum and turn the clock hands (8) so that the hour hand completes one complete rotation in 12 hours and the minute hand sixty times faster.

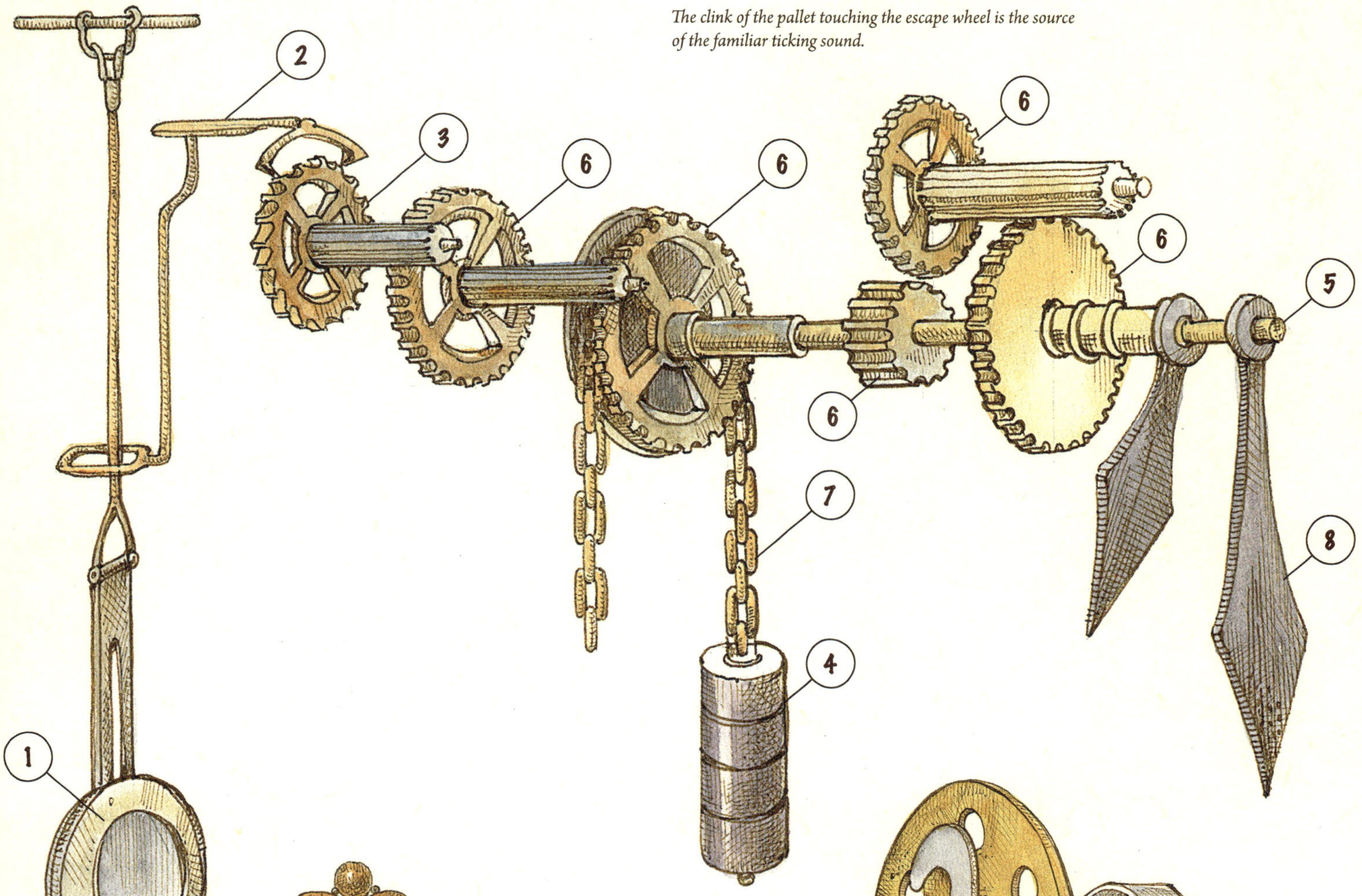

The clink of the pallet touching the escape wheel is the source of the familiar ticking sound.

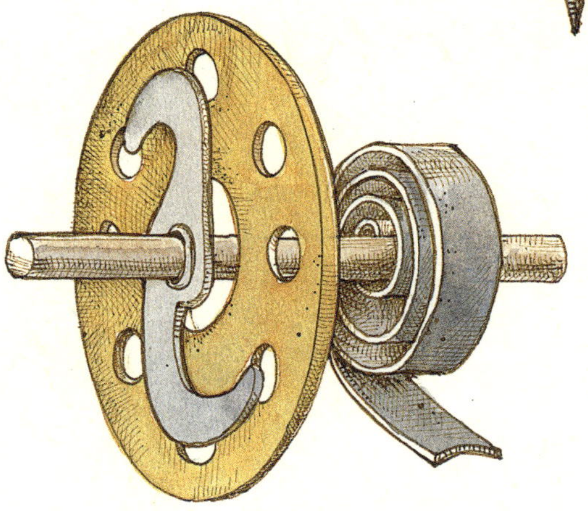

SPRING

To make the mechanism more compact, use a spring as an energy source instead of a pendulum and weight system. Use a thin coiled strip of annealed brass or hardened steel (page 138). When you wind a watch, you're tightening this spring. The energy released as it gradually unwinds sets the watch mechanism in motion.

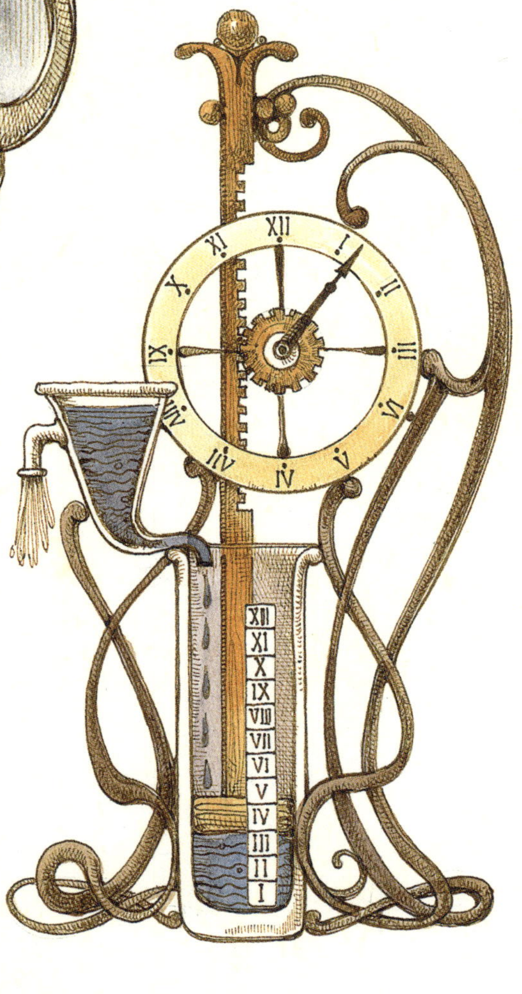

WATER CLOCK

Take a glass flask and make marks along the side in the unit of measurement of your choosing. Water will drip from the upper vessel into the lower one, gradually increasing the water level and indicating how much time has passed, which can then be read on the scale. True, some of the water will evaporate, which will skew the readings slightly, an effect that is especially noticeable on hot sunny days. This just means you have to calibrate the drip rate from time to time.

CRANES

To lift a heavy load to great heights, you'll need a crane, but in order to build that crane, you'll need another crane. But fear not, this paradox has a solution! The crane can build itself.

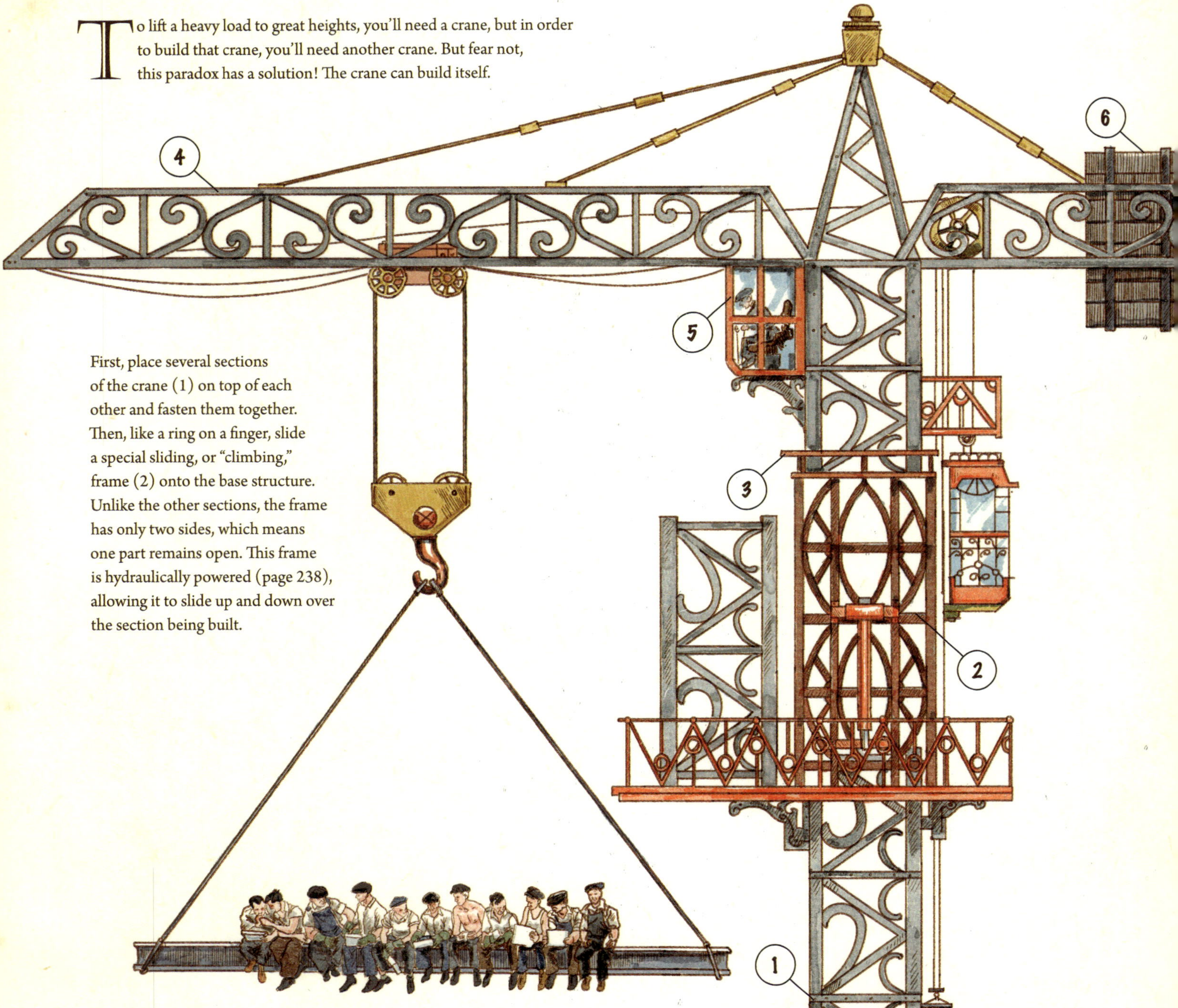

First, place several sections of the crane (1) on top of each other and fasten them together. Then, like a ring on a finger, slide a special sliding, or "climbing," frame (2) onto the base structure. Unlike the other sections, the frame has only two sides, which means one part remains open. This frame is hydraulically powered (page 238), allowing it to slide up and down over the section being built.

A turntable, known as a slewing unit (3), is mounted to the climbing frame along with the lifting jib (4) and operator's cab (5). Now the crane can continue to build itself. The hydraulic drive is turned on, and the climbing frame rises over the section of the tower being built. The climbing frame rises up and stands over the tower section. The jib picks up another section from the ground, lifts it (A) and sets it on the climbing platform (B).

The section slides inside the climbing frame (C) and is fastened to the section below it, and now the crane tower is one section higher. The climbing frame then rises onto this new section (D) and prepares to build the next. The process is repeated until the crane reaches the desired height.

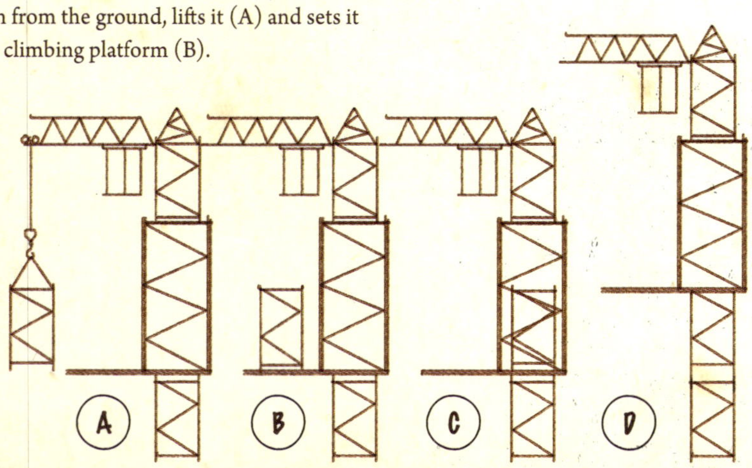

The right combination of counterweight and ballast will ensure that the crane stays stable. Use concrete blocks as a movable counterweight (6). When working with large loads, move the counterweight to the end of the counter jib, and for small loads, pull it closer to the base of the tower.

PULLEYS

A system of pulleys helps to lift loads using a force at least half that of the load's weight. A pulley is a simple mechanical device, a wheel with a groove around its circumference. The groove is designed to hold a rope, belt or chain. A single fixed pulley attached at the top of the jib reverses the direction of force, allowing you to pull down on the rope, which is much easier than lifting (7).

Using a movable pulley that rises with the load (8) reduces the amount of force needed, thereby increasing the mechanical advantage, since part of the weight of the load is carried by the fixed end of the rope. In fact, levers work using the same principle. Attaching the end of the rope to a second pulley (9) triples the mechanical advantage due to the redistribution of the load on the fixed ropes, and the combination of two movable and two fixed pulleys (10) quadruples it.

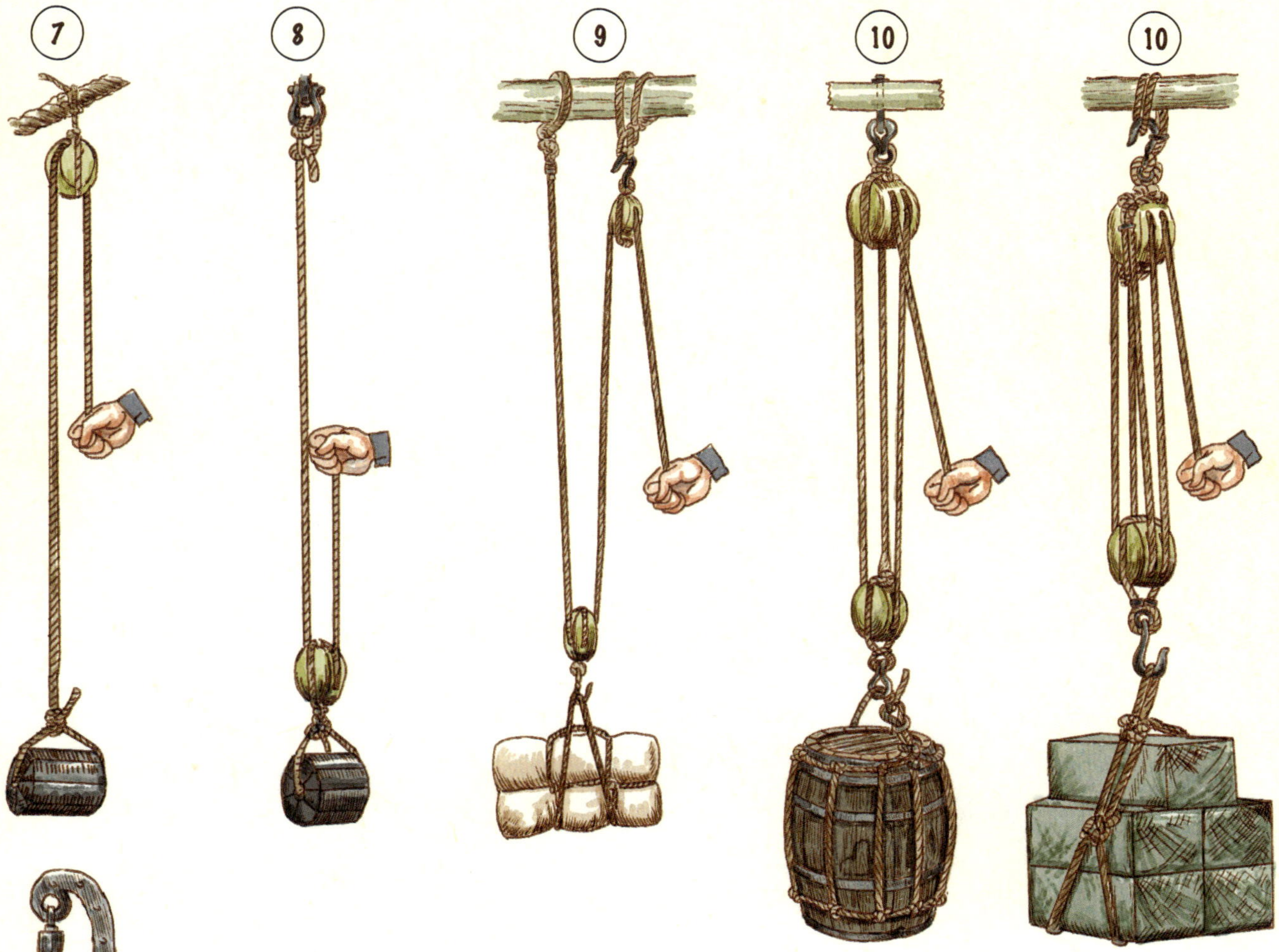

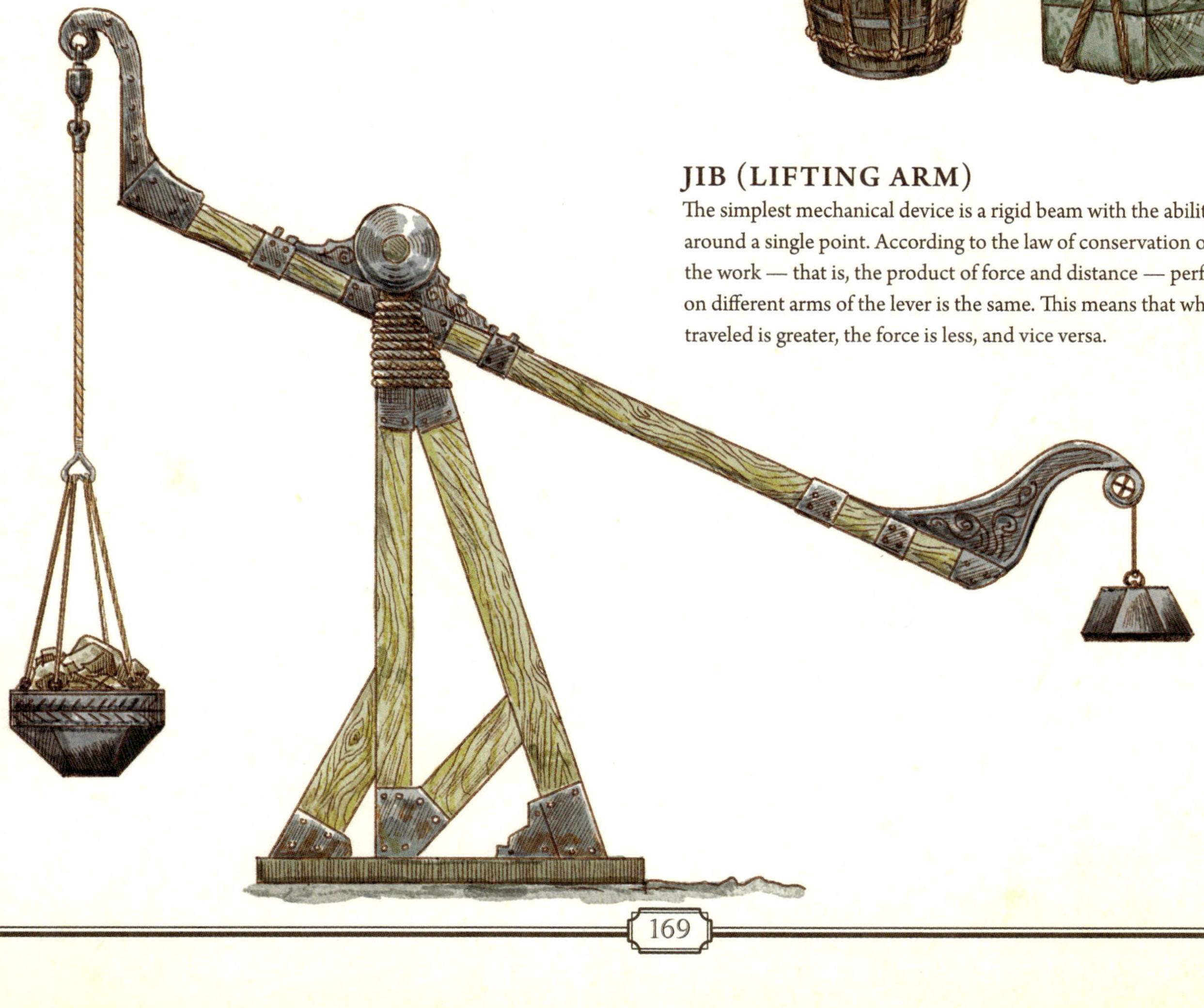

JIB (LIFTING ARM)

The simplest mechanical device is a rigid beam with the ability to rotate around a single point. According to the law of conservation of energy, the work — that is, the product of force and distance — performed on different arms of the lever is the same. This means that where the distance traveled is greater, the force is less, and vice versa.

LOOM & SEWING MACHINE

Sometimes the most ordinary things like simple clothing can be taken for granted. What's more basic than fabric? But without the seemingly trivial technology needed to produce it, it would be impossible to soar in the air, sail the seas or stock even the humblest abode. To create fabric, you first need to figure out how to weave threads together. And since you'll be using fabric in a myriad of everyday items, you'll want to know how to do it quickly and efficiently. A loom and a sewing machine will allow you to mass produce fabric and quickly provide your society with affordable fabric to sew clothes, weave sails or launch airships into the sky.

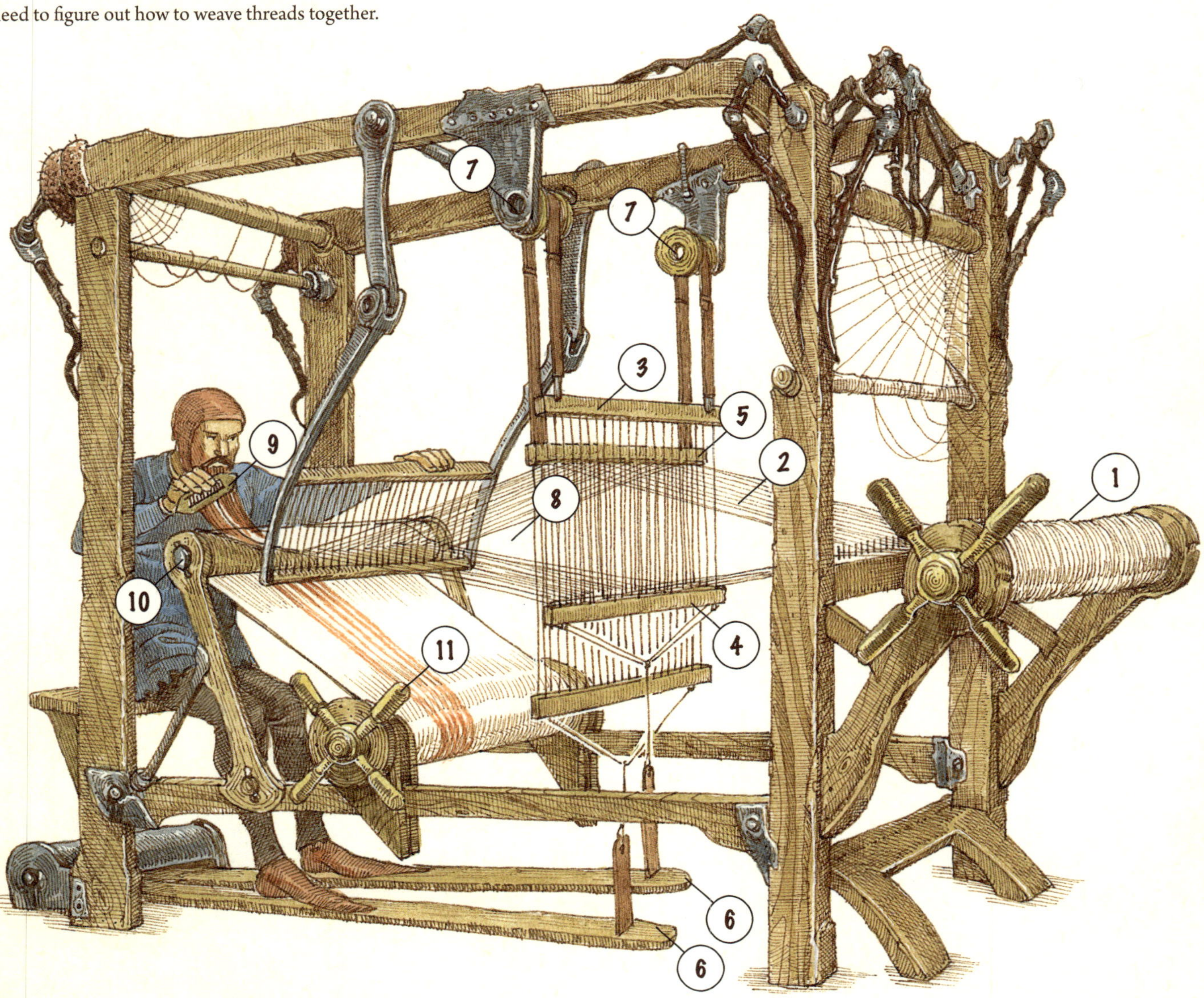

LOOM

Fabric consists of densely interwoven threads. The vertical threads, also known as the warp (2), are fed by the spool (1) and stretched across two frames. The threads are staggered, alternating back and forth between two frames (3, 4). Small holes known as eyes (5) separate each thread from its neighbors. When you press on the pedal (6), a system of belts and pulleys (7) moves these two frames on a vertical axis, making a gap (8) between the even and odd warp threads. A shuttle (9) bearing the "weft" thread (running perpendicular to the warp) is then passed through this gap. The frames alternate positions each time the shuttle is passed through, effectively creating a weave. To make sure the threads are tightly woven, use another frame called the reed (10) to batten down the weft thread. The resulting fabric is wound around the takeup (11).

The threads don't necessarily need to be all one color. By changing the colors of the weft thread while you're weaving, you can create fabrics with various patterns. At the right moment, hooked rods will pick up the next thread color.

Patterns that tell the rods exactly when to switch thread colors can be programmed into the loom using punch cards. Draw the pattern using a series of holes. The holes signify a place where the thread has risen. If there's no hole, that means the thread stays in place. The combination of holes on the cards will allow you to do a certain sequence of ups and downs with the different colored warp threads to produce a pattern on the fabric. The card is read by wire probes connected to the rods controlling the thread movement.

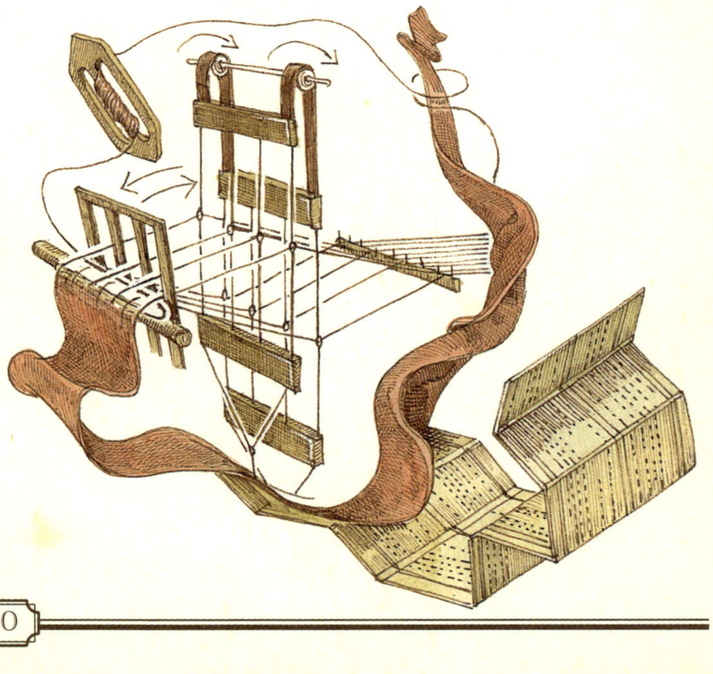

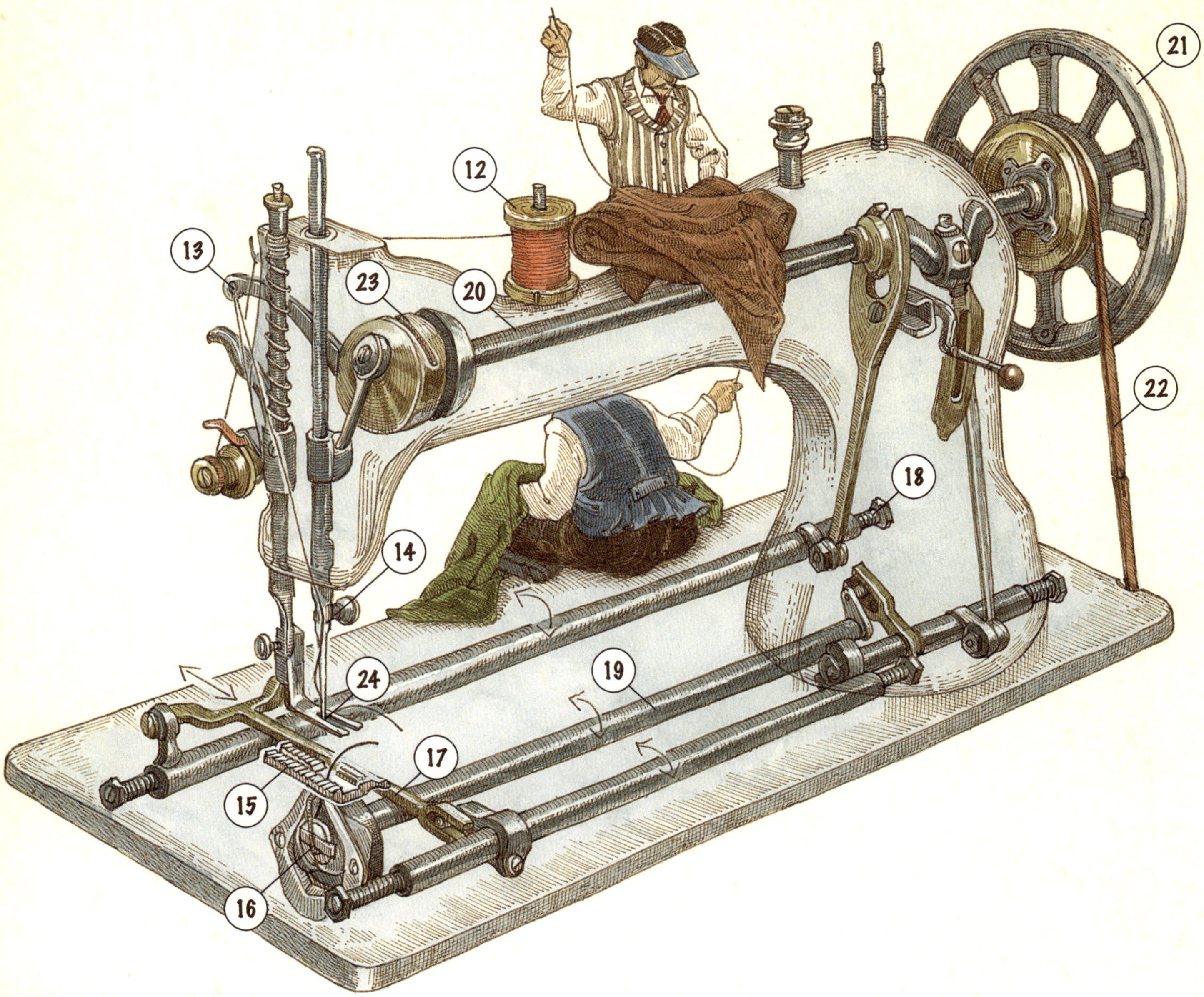

SEWING MACHINE

When sewing by hand, only one thread is used. The needle weaves in and out of the fabric from top to bottom, fixing the two pieces of fabric together. A sewing machine works with two threads simultaneously — one from the top and one from the bottom. With this technique, seams that are several meters long can be sewn in just minutes. The upper thread from the spool (12) is pulled taut (13) and passed through the eye of the needle (14). Under the needle plate (15) lies a second thread wound onto the bobbin (16). When the needle pierces the fabric, the thread is pushed through, and at that precise moment, the shuttle mechanism (17) grabs it and pulls it out of the needle, thereby making a loop.

The thread from the bobbin (16) catches on this loop, and the rising needle pulls the upper thread, which tightens the lower thread, and an even stitch is made. It is important that the movements of the needle and bobbin are synchronized. The timing mechanism (18) is responsible for this, turning the lower drive shaft (19) and driving the shuttle (17) at exactly the same speed as the upper shaft (20). The top one starts when you turn the flywheel (21) by hand and the belt (22) rotates the crankshaft (23), which lowers and raises the needle (14). When the needle is lifted, the feed dog of the presser foot (24) drags the fabric forward, changing the needle entry point. Then the needle once again drops and pierces through the fresh section of fabric to form another stitch. This is how you sew a straight line.

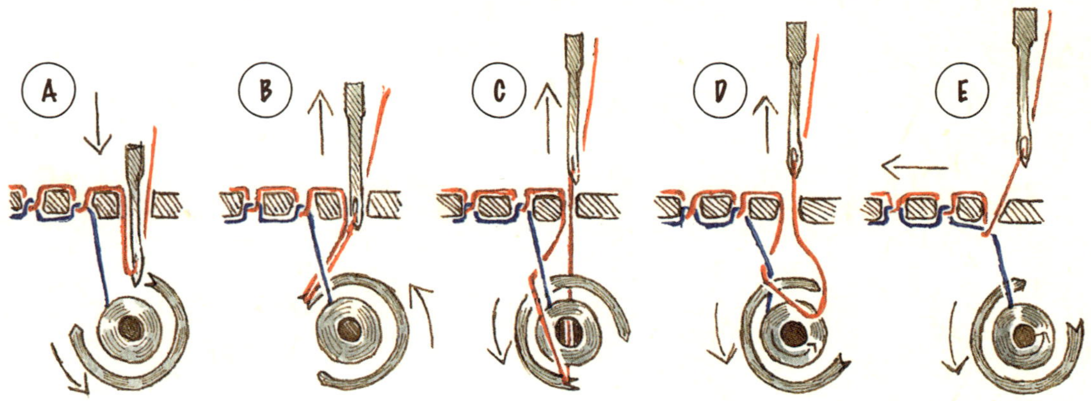

A. *The needle pierces the fabric and the bobbin rotates.*
B. *The upper thread is pushed through the fabric to the bottom side, where the lower thread from the bobbin catches it.*
C. *The bobbin turns, pulling both the upper and lower threads.*
D. *The loop of the top thread slips off and pulls the bottom thread with it.*
E. *The needle rises, leaving a neatly tightened stitch.*

FLYWHEEL

Friction is one of the main obstacles to all moving mechanisms. When one piece grinds against another, friction resists the motion, which heats both objects and could lead to deformation. For example, if you install a wheel directly on the axle of a wagon, it won't get very far, and pushing it will be a difficult task.

Greasing the moving parts is a good quick-fix solution, but the constant friction will soon wipe it away. This is where a bearing comes in handy — it minimizes friction, helping the mechanism work longer and more effectively.

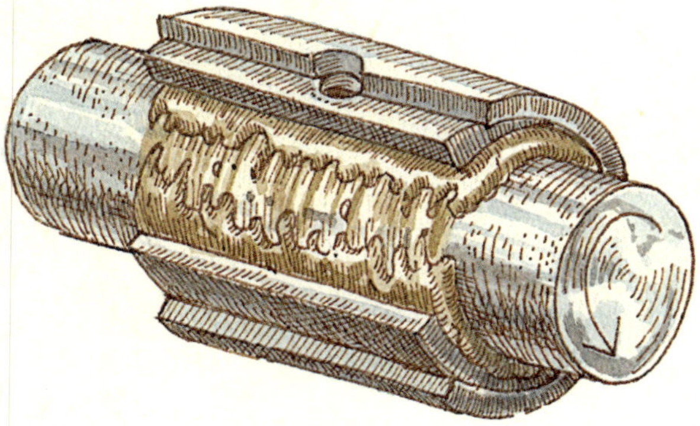

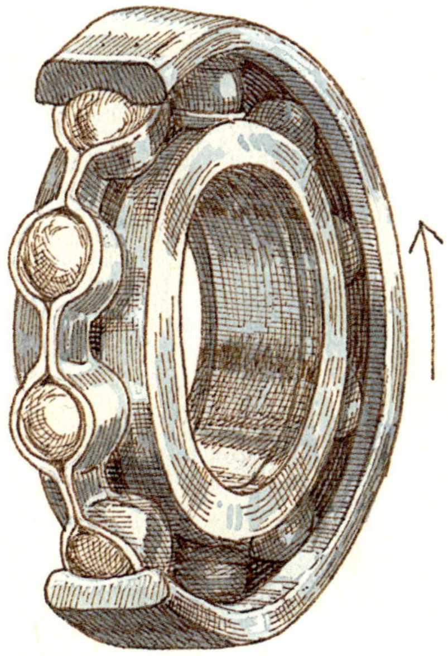

SLIDE BEARINGS

You only need two main components: the inner and outer rings (or cylinders). Between them is a layer of lubricant that reduces friction. Such bearings are very simple but require frequent lubrication and can easily overheat.

BALL AND ROLLER BEARING

As you already know, it's easier to roll a heavy object than to slide it, as rolling friction is much weaker than sliding friction. The ball bearing works on this principle by replacing one type of friction with another and reducing the contact area between the two surfaces. This kind of bearing is assembled from two metal rings (1 and 2), separated by a layer of rolling balls (3). Make them from ceramics (page 136) or hard alloys such as steel (page 240). Place separators (4) on either side to hold the balls in place and prevent them from rubbing against one another.

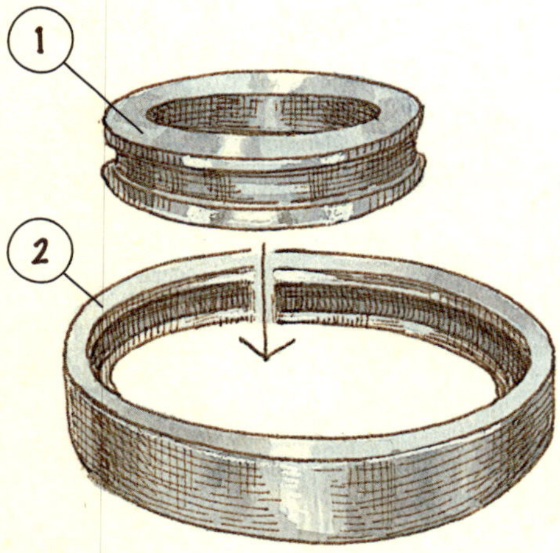

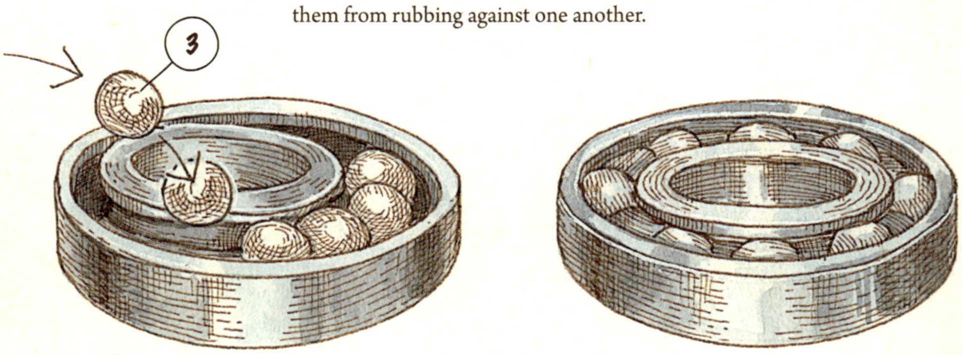

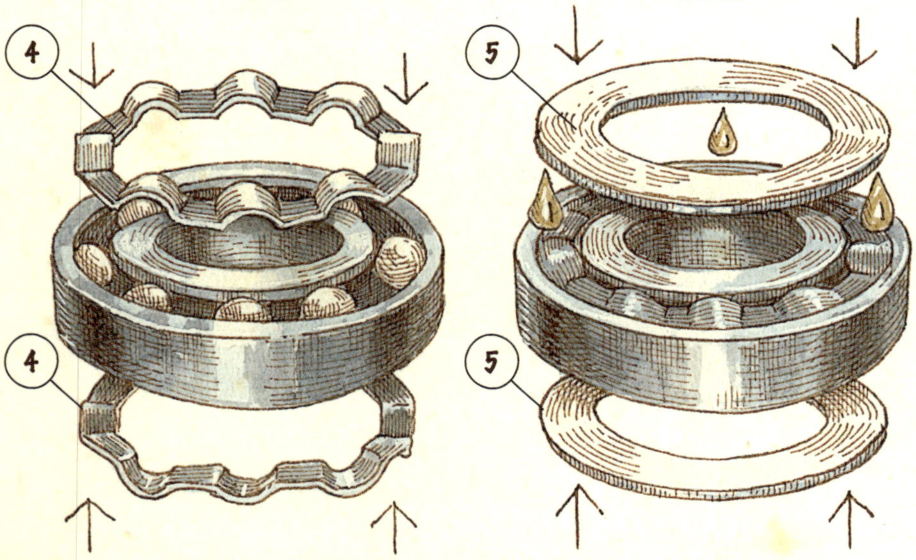

Lubricate the moving parts with grease, which will allow the bearing elements to spin much more freely. Use a substance that is non-water-soluble and slightly alkaline — for example, animal fat, birch tar (page 154) or petroleum-based oils (page 126). Just make sure there are no impurities, since even a stray grain of sand or a chip of metal can cause damage. Then cover each side with metal washers (5), which will fasten the structure together and prevent dust and moisture from getting inside.

FLYWHEEL AND GYROSCOPE

When a flywheel is spinning, the conservation of angular momentum prevents it from moving perpendicular to its axis of rotation, and in order to change its angle of inclination, you have to apply an external force. This is known as the gyroscopic effect, and it's what helps you maintain balance when riding a one- or two-wheeled vehicle.

In a gyroscope, the axis (1) is fixed within the gimbals (2), which allow the flywheel (3) to rotate freely in space. When the flywheel is spinning, it will maintain the same axis of rotation and effectively resist any force trying to change it. No matter which way you tilt the support (4) to which the gyroscope is attached, the flywheel will rotate to maintain its original position in space. So, if a ship with a gyroscope on board deviates from a given course, this device will show by how many degrees. The gyroscope is impervious to magnetic interference or vibration and can work on land, underwater and even in space.

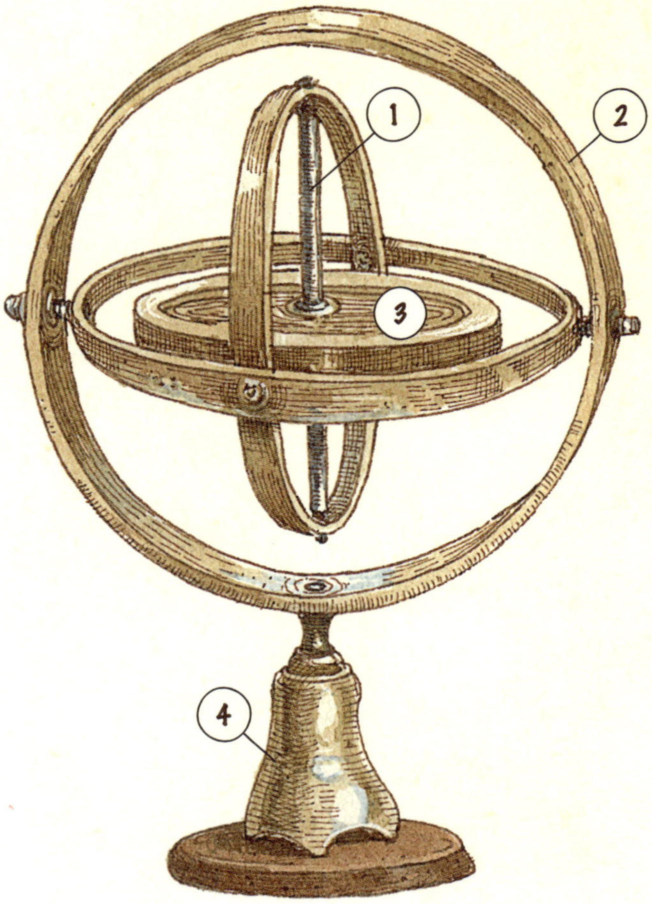

MONOWHEEL

Wheeled vehicles often have four, three or two wheels. But you can simplify even more and make a vehicle with only one (there's really no point in reducing the number of wheels any further). The motor, as well as the driver's seat, are located inside a large wheel that acts as both a source of forward momentum and a gyroscopic stabilizer.

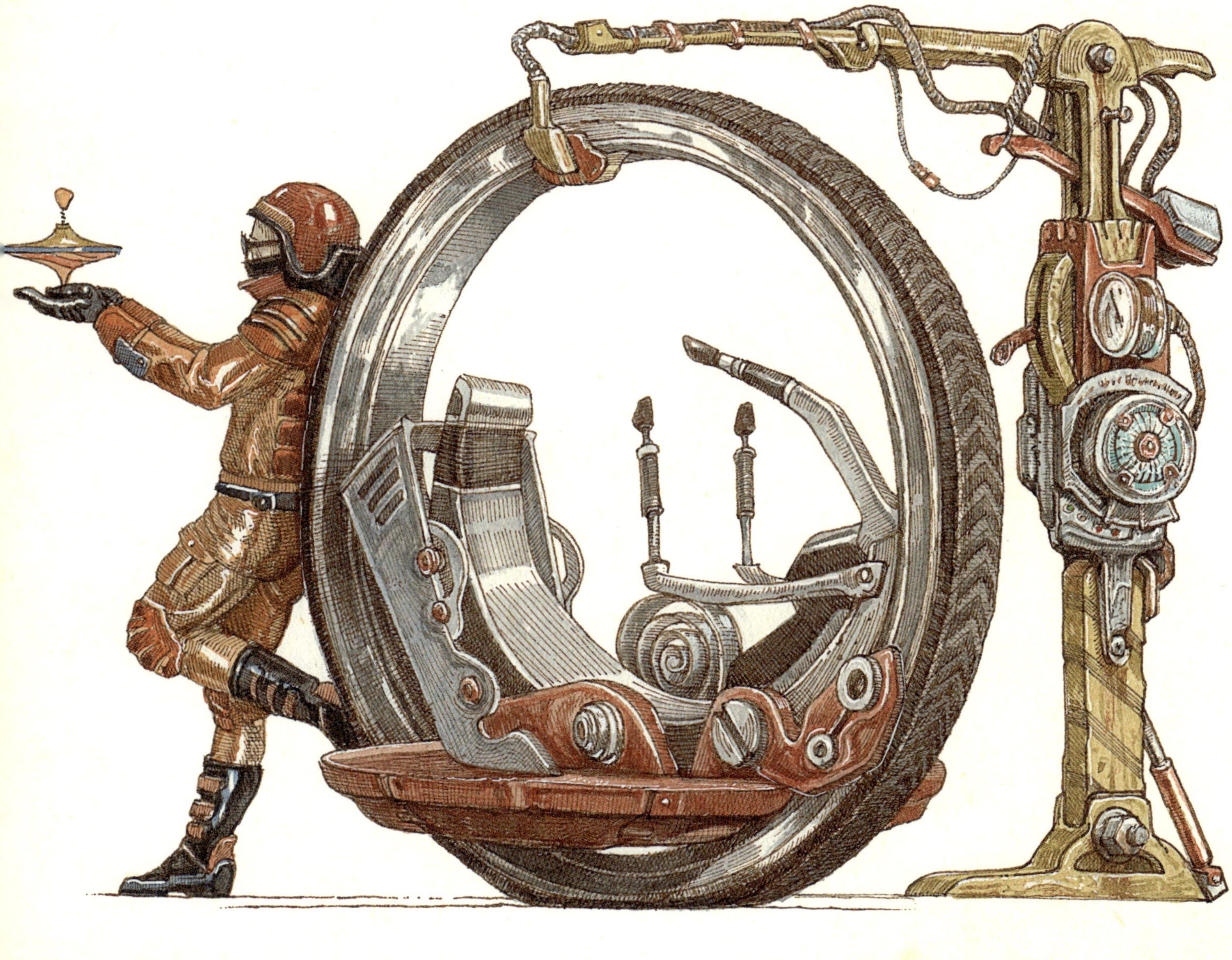

PERPETUAL MOTION

Imagine an energy source that produces more energy than it consumes — a perpetual motion machine. Free energy for all. Are you picturing it? Now it's time to make it a reality. The sooner you do, the sooner you solve the world's energy crisis! Generators convert mechanical energy into electrical energy. Electric motors convert electrical energy into mechanical.

Connect the generator output to the engine input, and the engine output to the generator input. Unfortunately, with this design, losses due to friction and heat dissipation make it impossible to obtain an energy source that will give out more than is put in. The ruthless law of conservation of energy dictates that the creation of a perpetual motion machine is impossible.
But this is wrong.

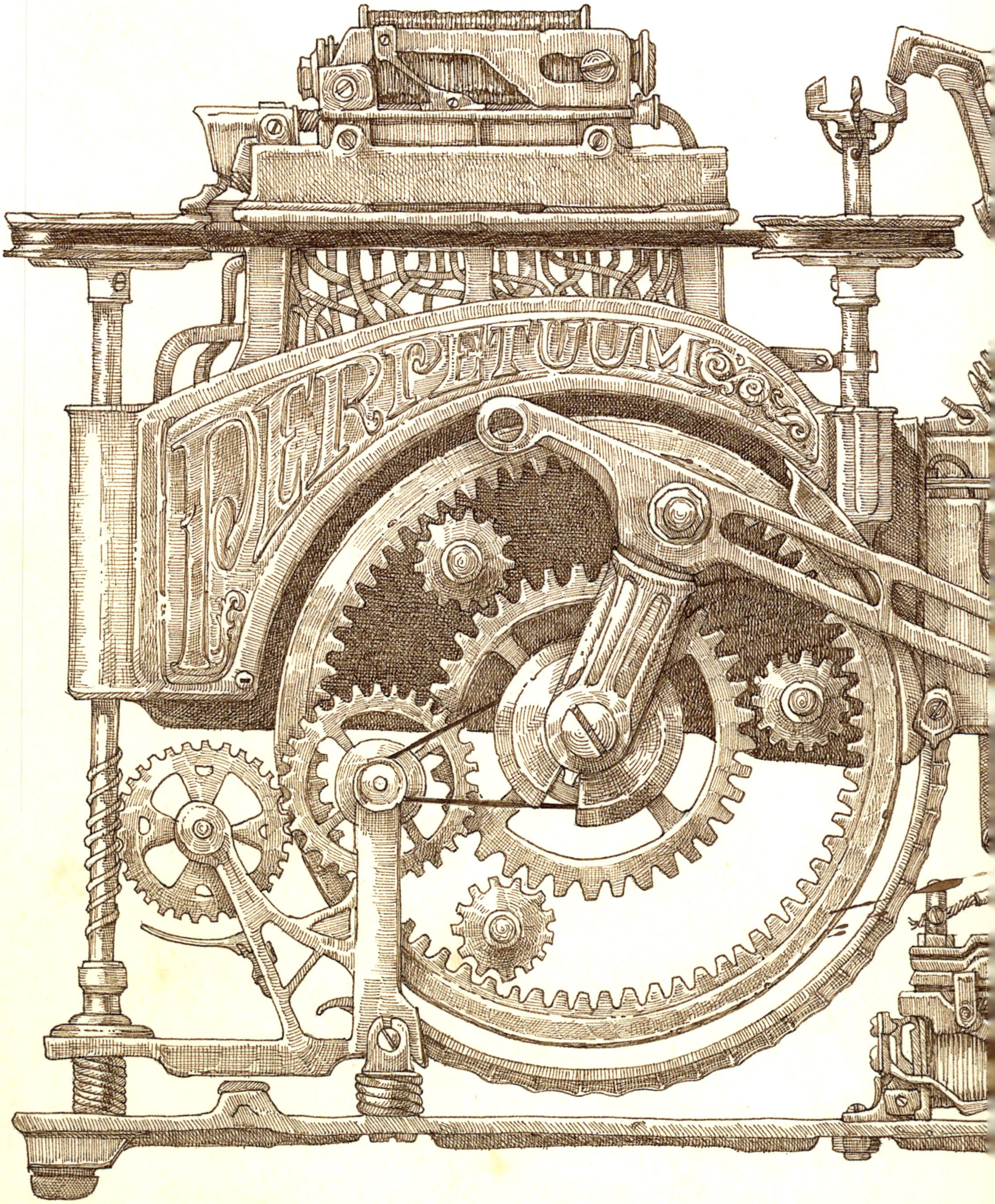

The fact is that the law of conservation of energy is not entirely fundamental. This is a consequence of another fundamental principle — the isotropy of time. The law of conservation of energy has been well verified in numerous experiments, and no violations or deviations from it have been identified. Yet. But although the final state of any closed system always observes the conservation of energy, there are cases in which the law appears to be violated, albeit for a very short time.

For example, in a physical vacuum — a completely empty space — particles of matter and antimatter are constantly spontaneously popping into existence (and disappearing almost immediately). But if at that brief moment when they do exist you managed to split them, you'd be able to extract the energy. This would be enough to compensate for losses due to friction and heating of the wires. And for useful work.

And for any purpose at all. You're left with a device that can do work without human intervention, though not infinitely but indefinitely — until the component parts wear out. To extract this energy, we need simple electronic parts, namely electronic vacuum tubes of an original design. They're not difficult to make: The main component is the

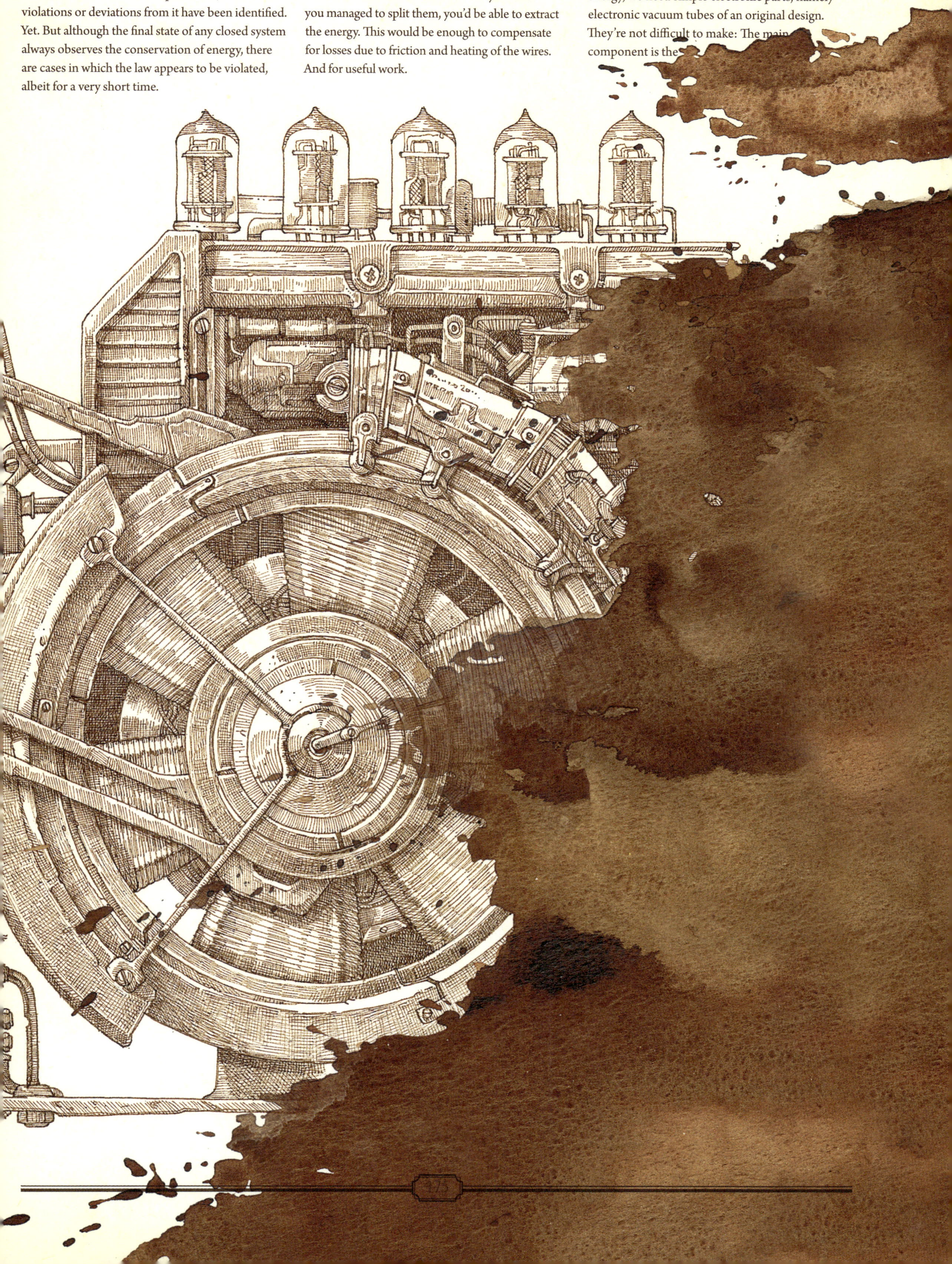

OPTICS

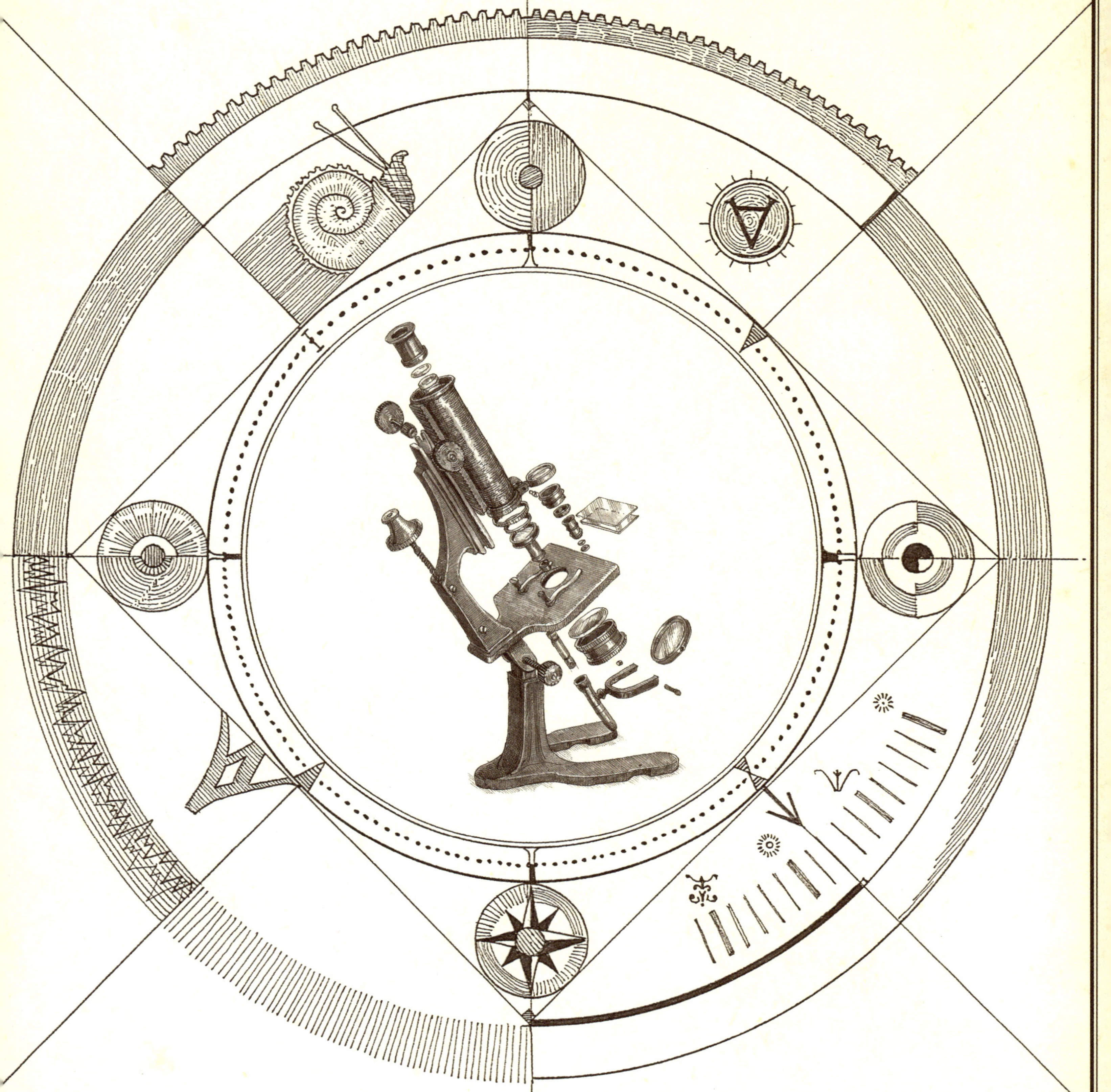

LENS & REFRACTION

Our eyes perceive the rays of light coming from objects and transmit detailed messages to the brain, which interprets these images and forms our external picture of the world. We can control the direction of the rays with the help of lenses — transparent objects that have curved refractive surfaces. Depending on their shape, the subject will appear closer or further away.

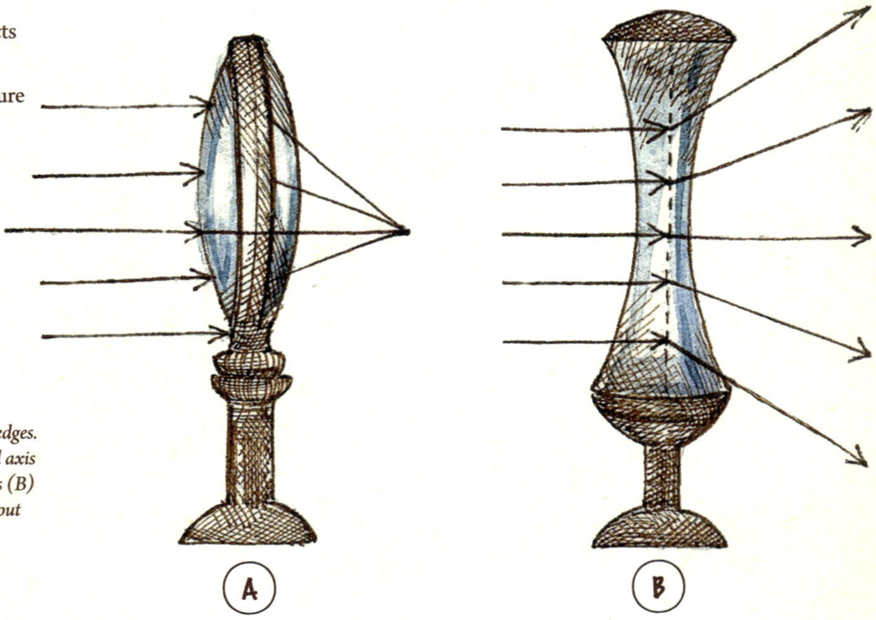

A convex lens (A) is thicker in the middle than around the edges. The rays passing through it are refracted towards the optical axis of the lens; that is, they converge into a point. A concave lens (B) is thinner in the middle. The rays passing through it spread out from the optical axis; that is, they diverge.

GRINDING

By grinding down a piece of glass, you can produce lenses of various shapes: converging (1, 2, 3) or diverging (4, 5, 6). Or you can cast a glass ball (I), saw it into discs and sand them down to form a convex or concave surface. In the grinding machine, the drive transmits rotation to the wheel on which the glass disc (II) is fixed.

A rotating and oscillating metal axle with a glass cylinder, a grinder (III), is fixed above the lens holder. It looks similar in form to the glass piece being ground. By pressing the grinder against the workpiece and moving it around, you can produce curved lenses of different thicknesses. You can also use a lathe (page 144).

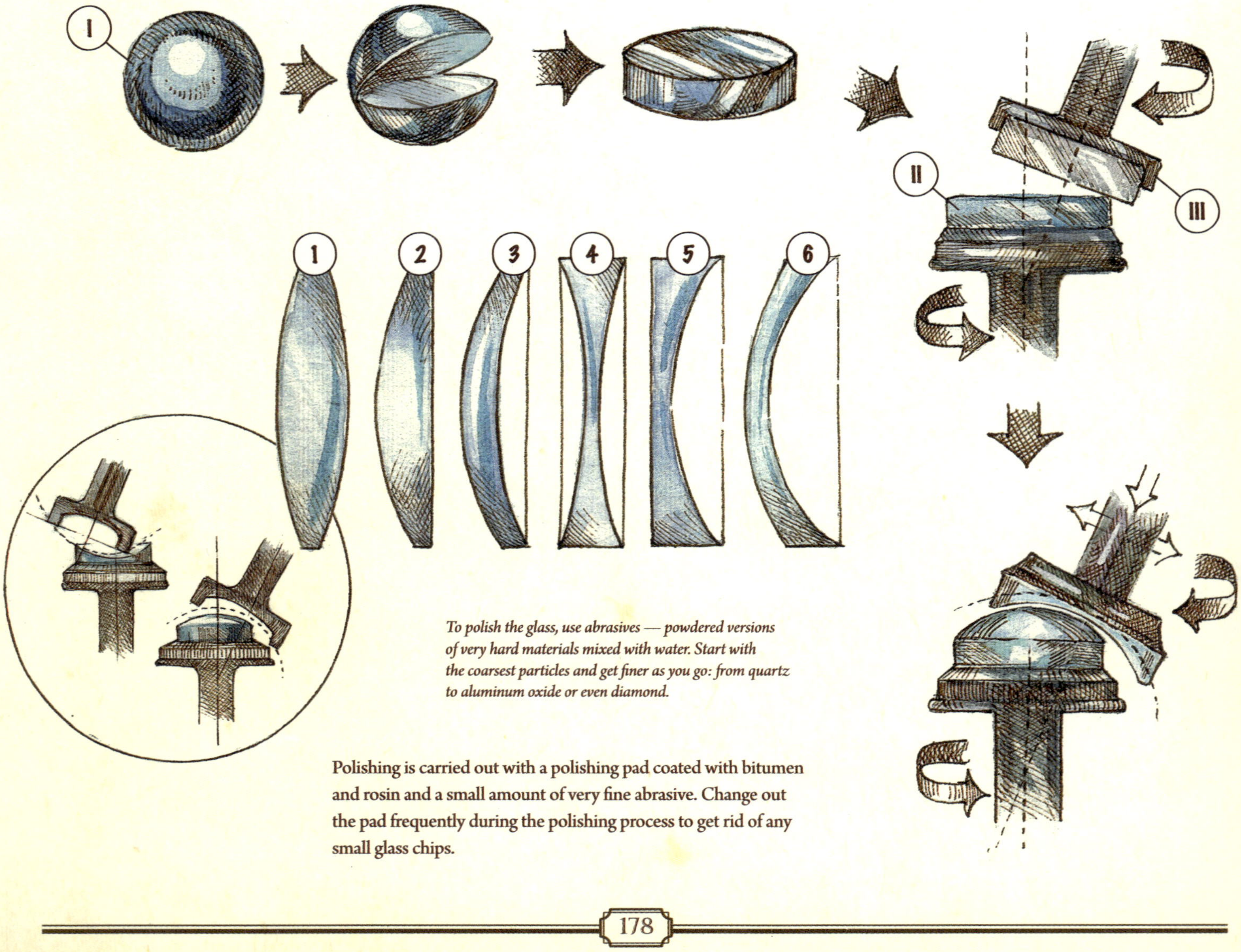

To polish the glass, use abrasives — powdered versions of very hard materials mixed with water. Start with the coarsest particles and get finer as you go: from quartz to aluminum oxide or even diamond.

Polishing is carried out with a polishing pad coated with bitumen and rosin and a small amount of very fine abrasive. Change out the pad frequently during the polishing process to get rid of any small glass chips.

The main problem with any convex lens is its large mass. But there is a way to save on materials and obtain a lighter end product. Carve a series of concentric triangular grooves into flat glass, each one smaller than the next, creating a stepped surface (7). Each step is a separate small ring lens that focuses the light. This design will work in the same way as a conventional convex lens but will be significantly lighter.

Using a converging lens, you can create a relatively narrow beam to use in a variety of applications, from searchlights to lighthouses. This design can replace both spherical and cylindrical lenses, as well as other optical parts, such as prisms.

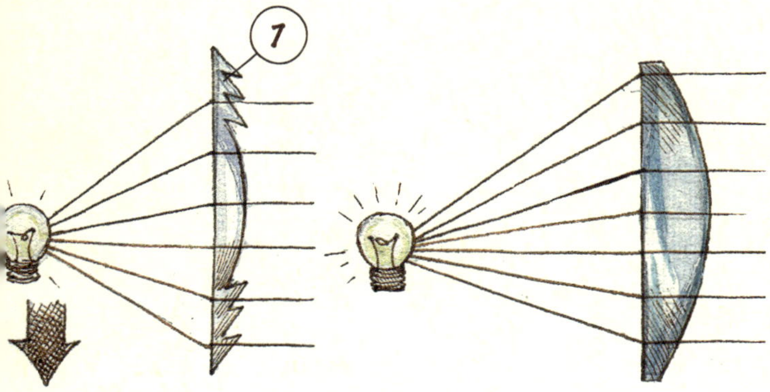

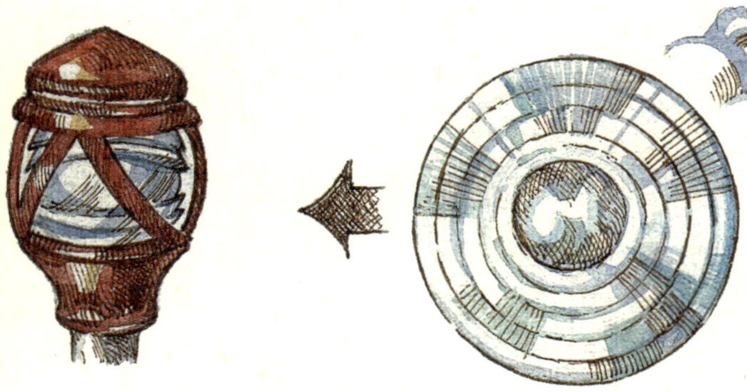

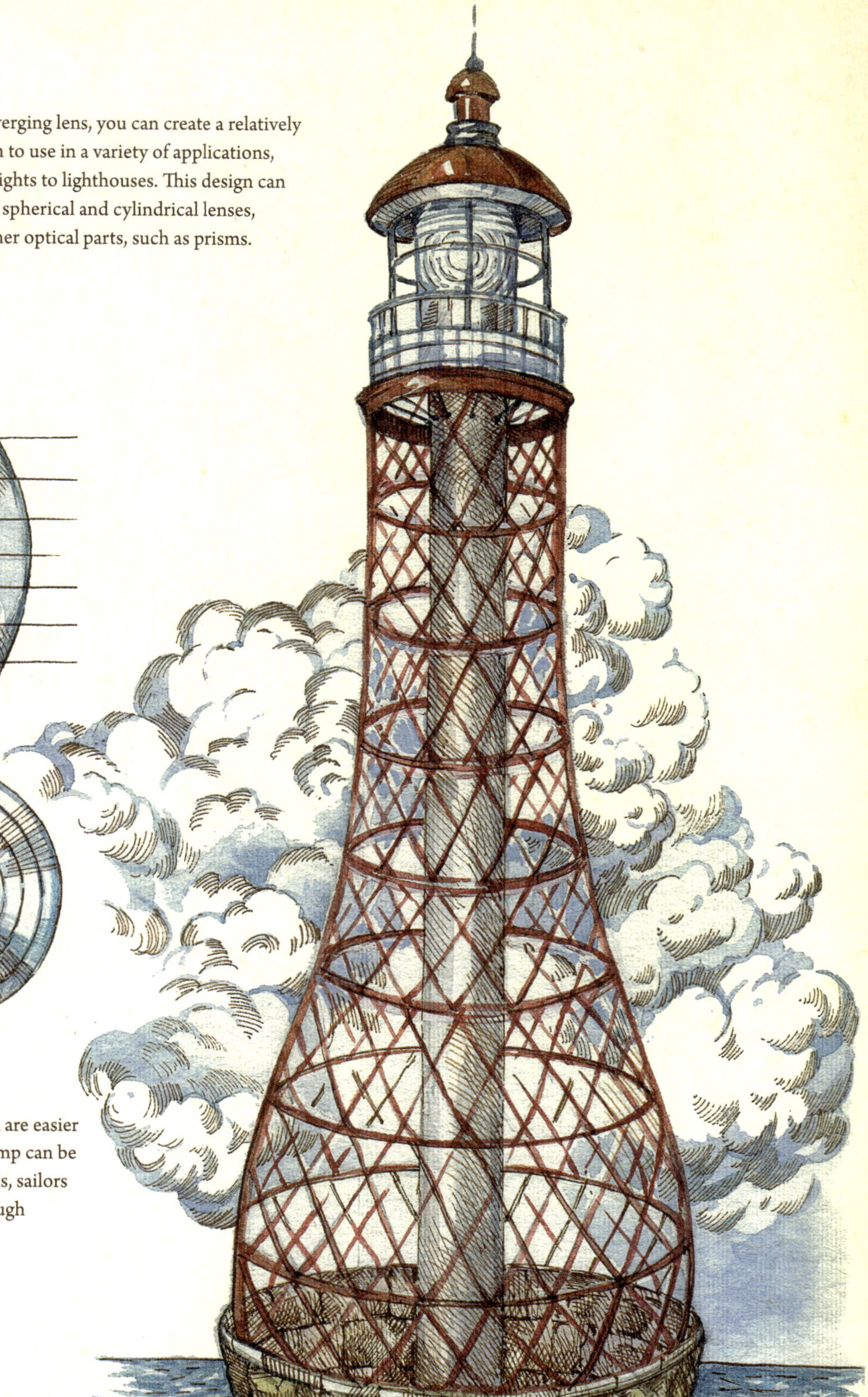

You can assemble a beacon using multiple stepped lenses (8), which are easier to make and transport. This way, the dispersed light from a bright lamp can be focused into a narrow beam. When the beacon rotates around its axis, sailors on ships far out at sea can see the bright beam of light breaking through the darkness or fog.

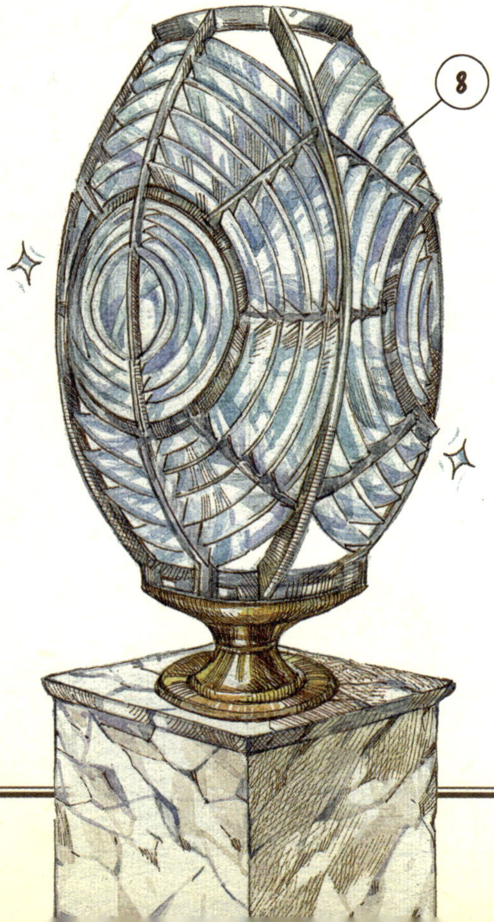

Another effect of concentrating the light beam is increased temperature. Sunlight is warm. If you use a lens to collect a beam of sunlight in a small area, all the thermal energy carried by the beam will also be concentrated. This energy can be used in a variety of ways: to set fire to an object located at some distance, cauterize wounds, glue two surfaces together by melting them and so on.

EYEGLASSES

The eyes are the window to the soul, the subject of countless poems and philosophical ponderings. For instance: Do you see *with* your eyes or *through* them? The answer is not as obvious as it may seem. The eyes gather information and transmit it to the brain, where an image is constructed. But they are more than mere tools. The small irregularities unique to each eyeball play a huge part in how we perceive the world around us. Every eye sees the world a little differently. Our eyes are more mysterious than philosophers thinking whether we see with or through our eyes.

The answer is not as obvious as it seems: The eyes only transmit information to the brain, where the picture of the outside world that we eventually see is formed. Each eye, however, perceives a slightly different picture. Thus, in order to see a three-dimensional picture, the brain has to connect the two parts of the image — the right and the left. If either eye is defective, it can severely distort the final image. Luckily, these defects can easily be corrected by externally recreating the refractive properties of the inner eye.

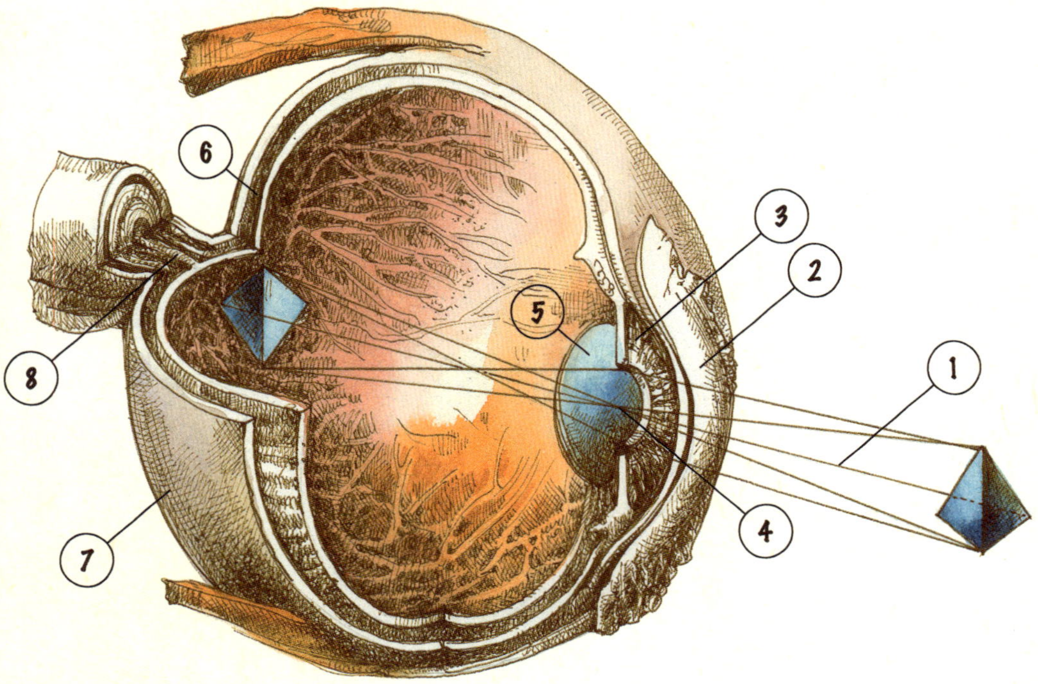

1. *The **light beam** hits the eye.*
2. ***The cornea** is the transparent protective layer that covers the iris, pupil and anterior chamber.*
3. ***The iris** regulates the amount of light going into the eye, like the iris in a camera (page 186). This is the part that determines your eye color.*
4. *It is composed of muscles that contract and relax to change the size of the **pupil**, or hole in the center of the iris.*
5. ***The crystalline lens** is the focusing mechanism of the human eye. Transparent and elastic, the lens changes shape as the eye muscles flex, allowing your eye to refocus on objects at various distances.*
6. ***The retina** consists of two types of light-sensitive photoreceptor cells. The cones make fine details visible and are responsible for central vision and color recognition but require a large amount of light to function properly. The rods work to help you see even in dim light but are unable to distinguish colors, rendering the image in black and white.*
7. ***The sclera** is the opaque, fibrous, protective outer layer of the human eye. It provides an attachment point for the extraocular muscles.*
8. ***The optic nerve** transmits signals to the brain.*

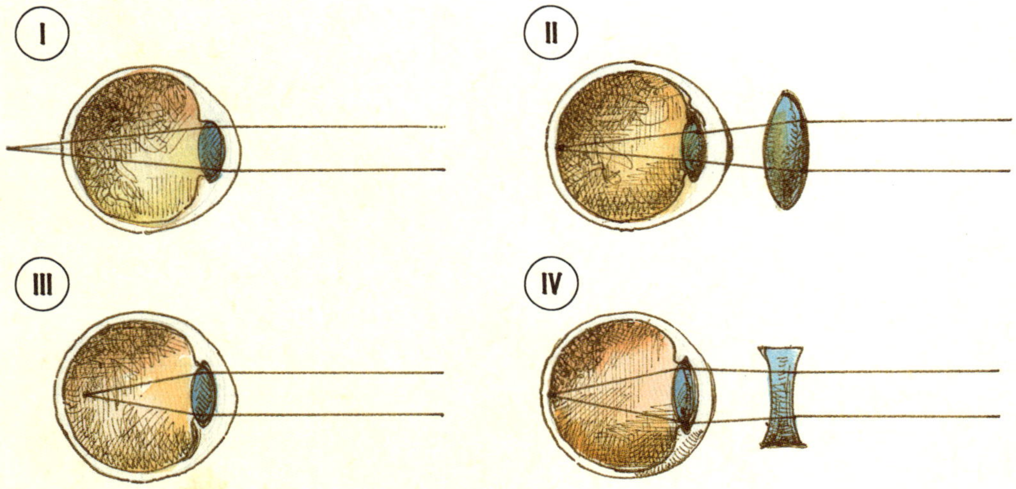

VISION PROBLEMS

Refractive errors occur when the shape of the eye's lens does not focus light properly. Eyeglasses compensate for this by shifting the focal point so that the image is projected correctly onto your retina.

If you have problems seeing objects at a distance clearly, then you are nearsighted. The light rays are being focused to a point too far in front of your retina (I). To compensate, you need a concave glass lens (IV) to diverge the rays so that they arrive on the retina properly. If you have trouble seeing objects up close, then you are farsighted: the light rays focus behind your retina (III). You need convex lenses (II).

Things become more complicated when the cornea or lenses of the eye are not perfectly spherical. In this case, some parts of the image will be clear, while others will appear blurry. Astigmatism is a minor eye condition that occurs when the curvature of the cornea or the lens isn't symmetrical. Wearing cylindrical glasses is a common way to correct the condition: convex, concave or a hybrid of spherical and cylindrical. The cylindrical element corrects the astigmatism, while the spherical element corrects farsightedness or nearsightedness.

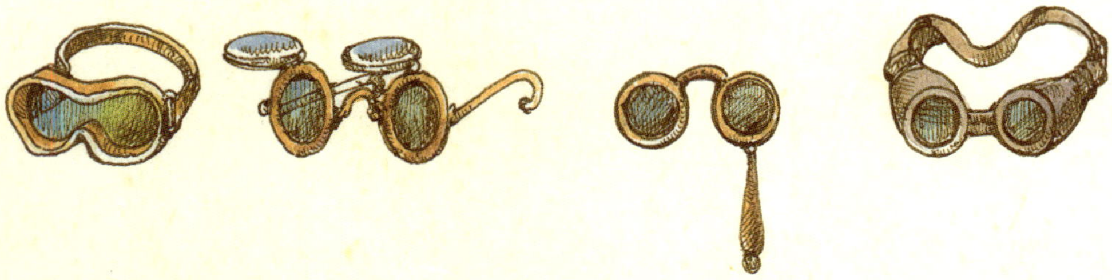

Safety glasses will protect your eyes from shrapnel, dust and water. They can also function as corrective lenses if fitted with the proper prescription. In order to see underwater, the eye needs to be surrounded by a bubble of air, so make sealed goggles with a flat outer surface. Place any corrective lenses on the inside of the goggles. To keep the glasses from fogging up, apply a soapy or gelatinous solution to the inside surface.

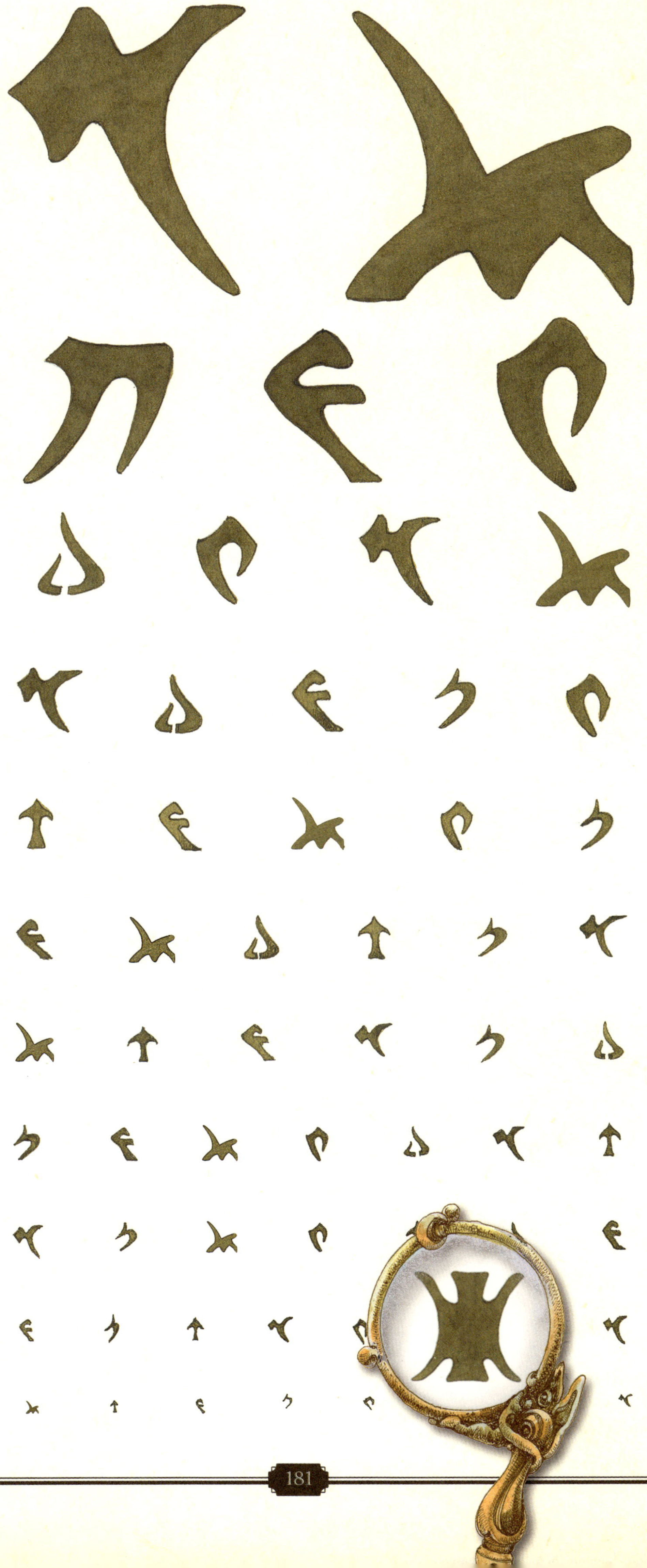

MIRROR

By the time a human child reaches its eighteenth month of life, it can already recognize its own reflection in a mirror. It is believed that this is the period of time during which humans develop self-awareness. However, the ability to recognize one's own reflection is not unique to humans — monkeys, apes, elephants and killer whales also pass the mirror test.

But for humans, mirrors do more than just show us our own reflection. We also make sure the reflection looks good, is nicely dressed and is ready to impress other intelligent species.

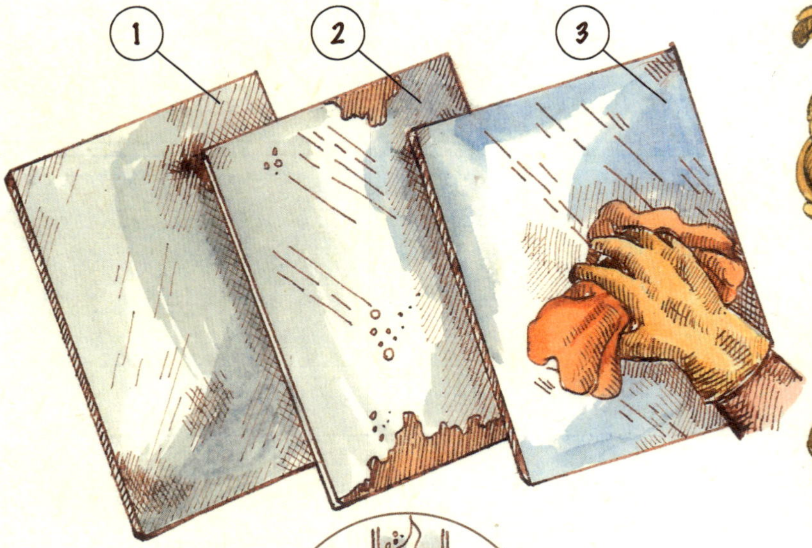

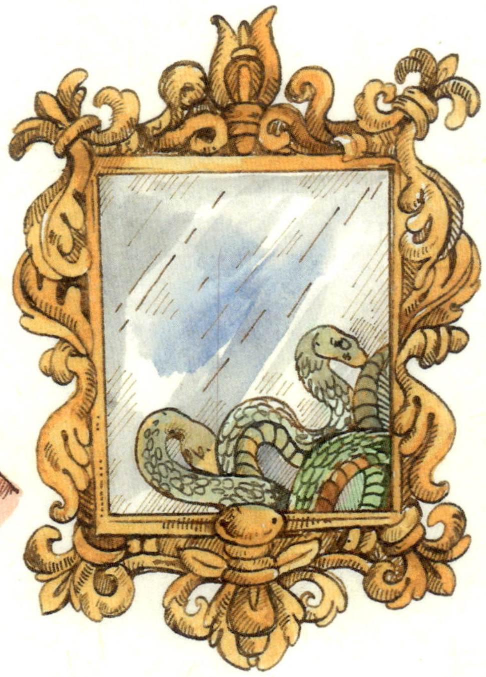

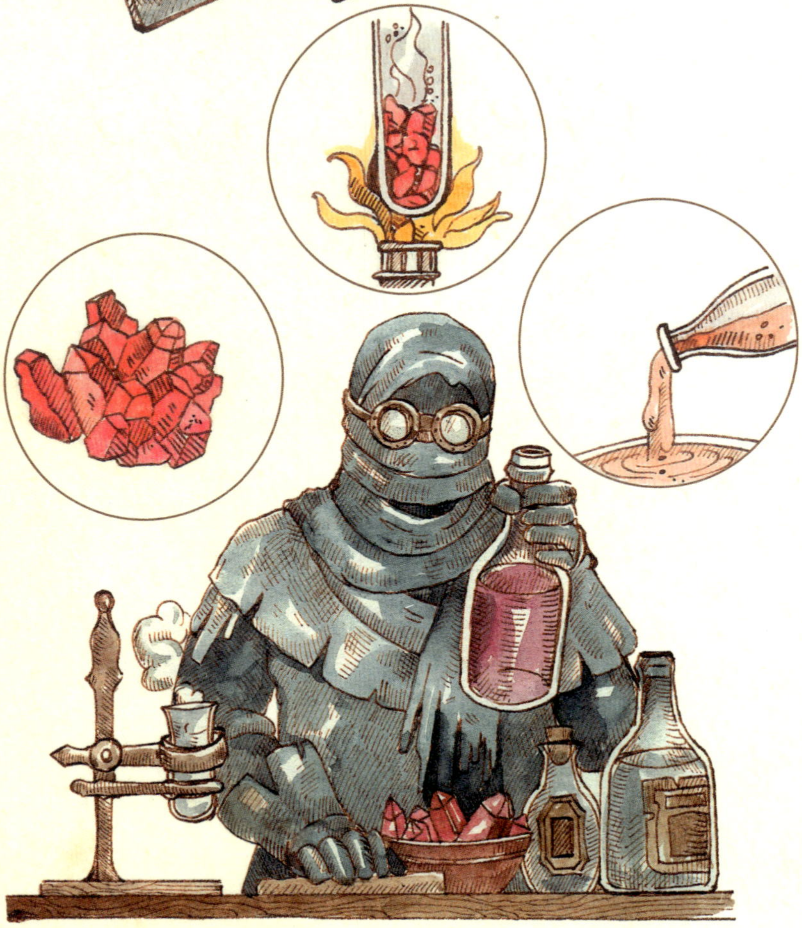

HOW TO MAKE A MIRROR

A mirror is a sheet of glass (1) over polished metal. The glass must be perfectly clean and dry, so degrease it with alcohol beforehand (2). Take tin and roll it into a sheet. Obtain mercury by heating a red mineral known as cinnabar. Find it near active volcanoes and alkaline hot springs. But proceed with caution — mercury is extremely toxic! Cover your skin and use full chemical protection when working with it.

After polishing the mercury into the tin, being sure to rub until the two metals merge, place the glass on top of the polished surface (3). Press gently on the surface to remove wrinkles, and then wipe the glass with a dry cloth to clean. The tin melds to the glass and forms a permanent, mirror-like surface.

PRINCIPLE OF REFLECTION

The mirror presents us with reality and illusion at the same time. This paradox is inherent in their very existence. The image you see in the mirror is imaginary because it appears to be formed not by the intersection of reflected light rays but by their continuation "through the looking glass." The rays of light from objects in the room are reflected in the surface of the mirror so they can show the viewer objects that are behind them.

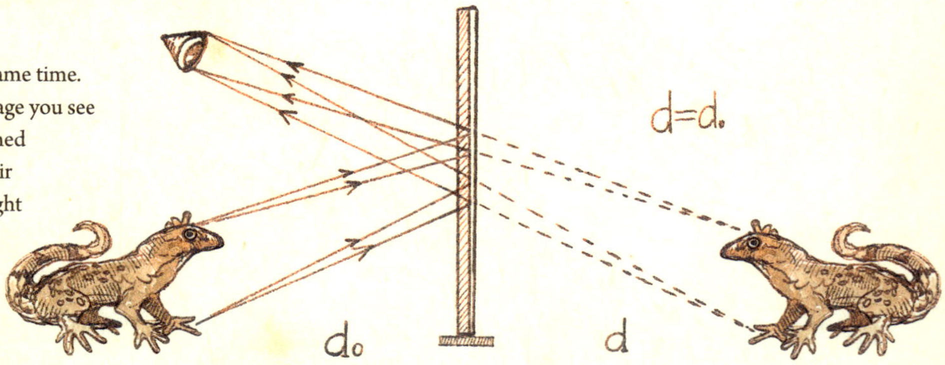

SILVER MIRROR

Another mirror-making method employs silver in place of the tin-mercury alloy. This technique requires an elementary knowledge of chemistry, but it's not as hazardous to health as working with mercury. Dissolve metallic silver in nitric acid to form a silver nitrate solution. Mix the resulting substance with ammonia and add a little sugar. Quickly pour this solution onto the back of a clean, smooth sheet of glass. The solution will harden immediately, forming a flawless reflective surface. The sugar reacts with the silver nitrate, reducing it to silver that is deposited in a thin layer directly on the surface of the glass. This layer is very easy to scratch, so protect it under a layer of varnish and paint. Don't neglect this very important step!

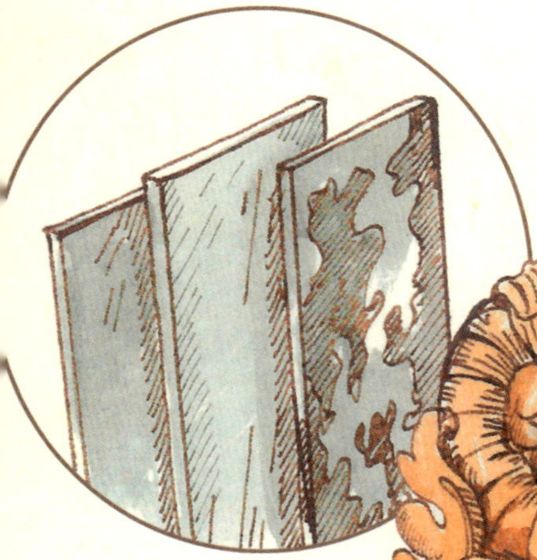

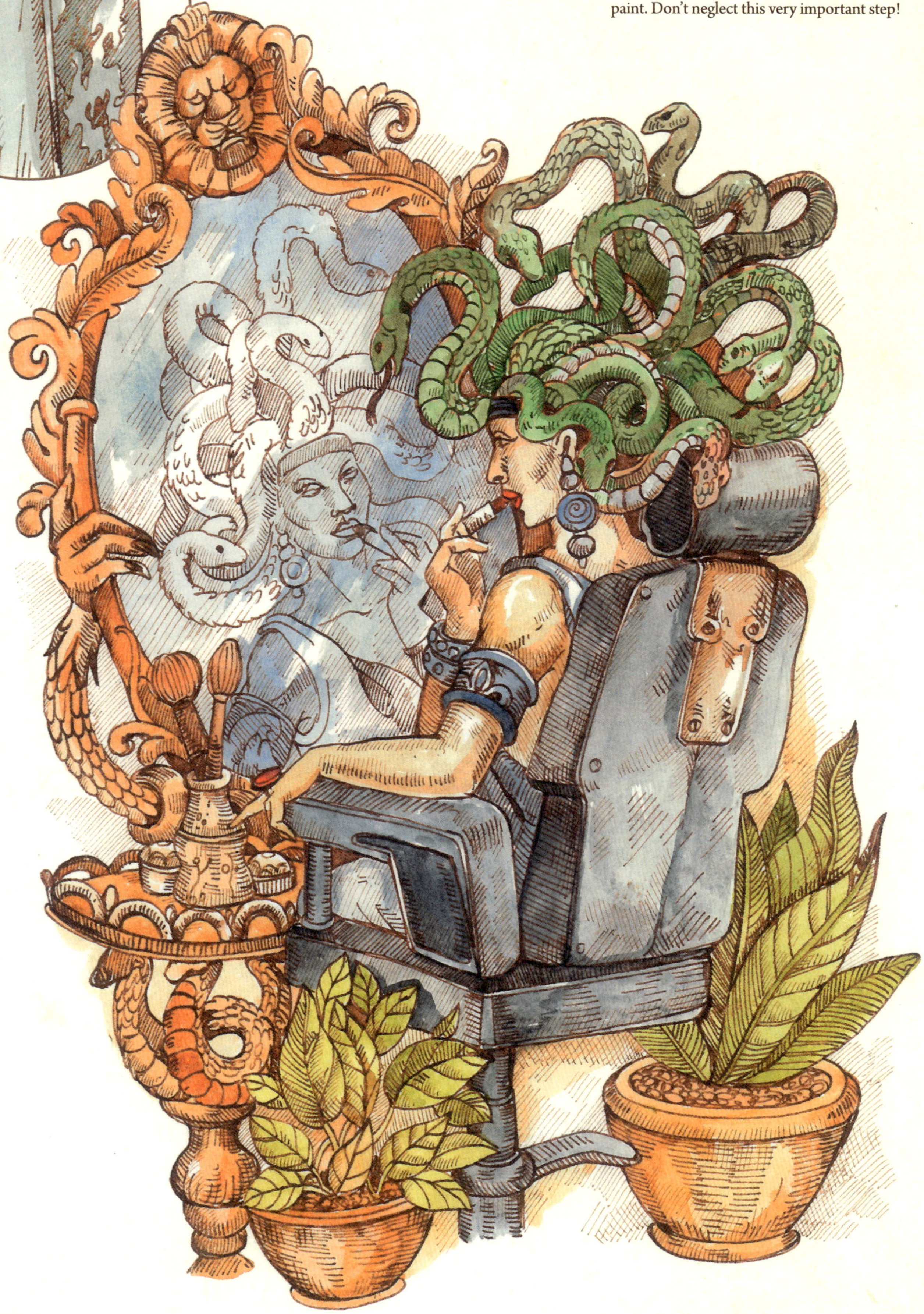

MICROSCOPE

As soon as your civilization produces its first batch of scientists, they'll start speculating about the mysterious forces that govern the world around them. Sometimes, they come up with ridiculous and unbelievable theories. But reality is often more astounding than even the most harebrained hypothesis.

Inventing the microscope will unveil the mysteries of the microcosm. Microscopes will also give a big boost to technological development, as you'll be able to create high-tech tools and materials. But the main breakthroughs will be in biology and medicine. Now that you know about cells, microbes and bacteria, you'll have to learn how to work with them.

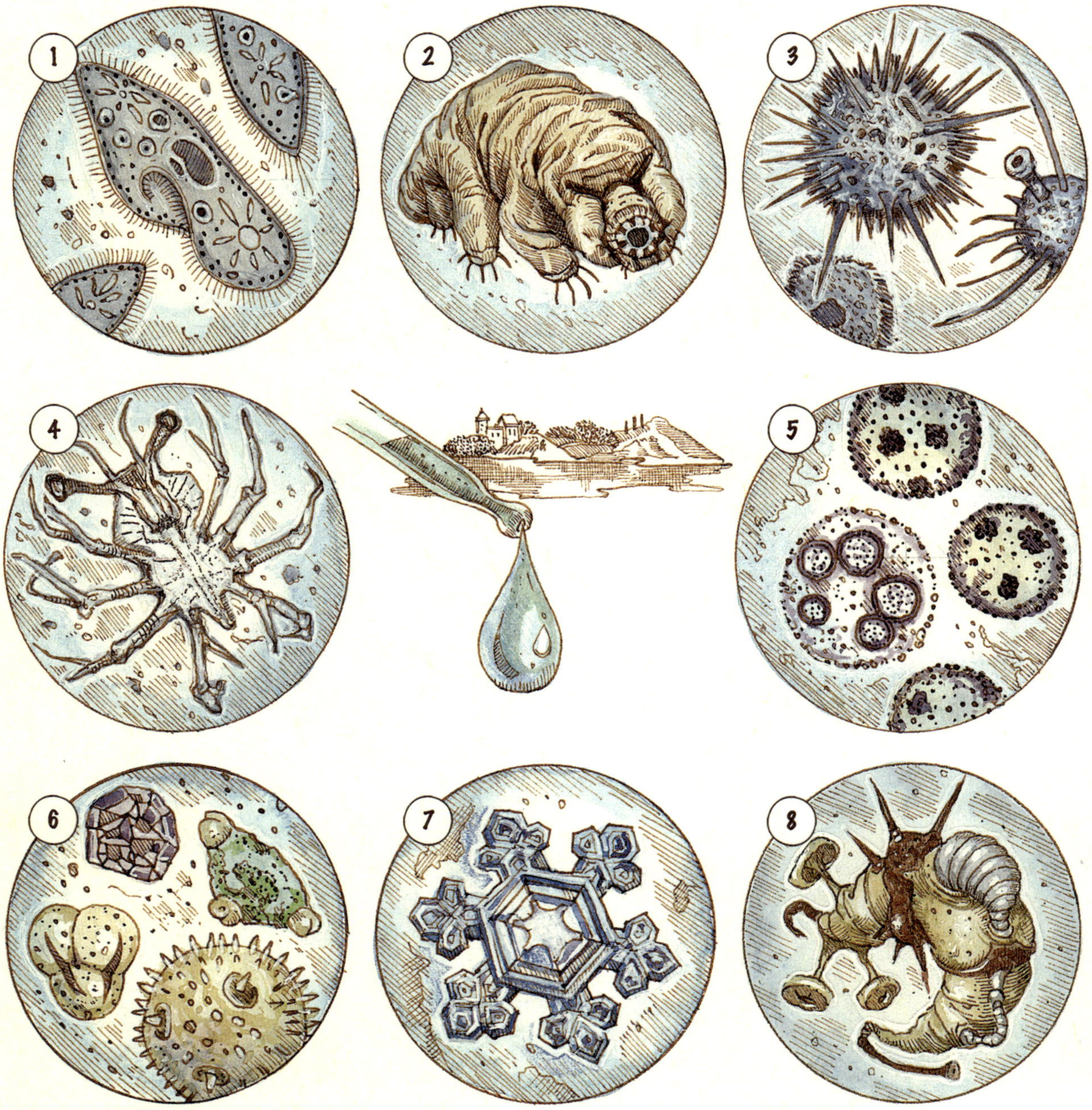

WHAT'S IN A DROP OF WATER?

1. **Infusoria** — a type of freshwater single-celled organism
2. **Tardigrades** — a type of eight-legged, segmented micro-animal
3. **Radiolarians** — silica-secreting, single-celled protists that live in the open ocean
4. **Plankton** — organisms carried along by tides and currents (They're an important food source for larger species.)
5. **Volvoxes** — a type of chlorophyta (green algae)
6. **Bacteria** — small single-celled organisms
7. **Snowflakes** — extremely cold water droplets frozen around a dust particle in the sky
8. **Infectious parasitic agents** — stimulate the release of tetta globulin, which causes procrastination

BLOOD ANALYSIS

Infections, inflammatory reactions and other abnormalities affect the blood. Blood analyses can reveal what is afflicting a patient and what treatment may be most effective — for example, penicillin (page 34). You also want to count the number of blood cells and examine their shape. An excess of red cells (erythrocytes) could be a sign of bronchitis, asthma, heart disease or a kidney tumor.

A deficiency can reveal a hidden bleeding disorder or a lack of iron, vitamin B12 or folic acid. An excess of white blood cells indicates the presence of some kind of infection or inflammation in the body. If the cells are not flattened discs but rather round, ovular or sickle-shaped, you might want to check liver and stomach function.

STRUCTURE

There are three main parts to a microscope. The first consists of the lens and lens tube, which are responsible for magnifying the image. The second is the stage, where you place the specimen you're inspecting.

Third is the illuminator, mirror and condenser, which allow your sample to enjoy its moment in the limelight. An eyepiece makes viewing a cinch, and a screw or gear and toothed track system helps you raise and lower the lens tube to bring things into focus.

WORKING PRINCIPLES

Using the screw, lower the observation tube until it's about 5 mm from the object. Bring your eyes to the microscope and adjust the focus. The mirror will direct the light onto the stage. The objective lens collects the rays of light that have passed through the object. Refraction in the lenses increases the viewing angle, enlarging the image.

Look through the eyepiece to observe the enlarged image, and voila! A whole new world of wonders. But keep in mind that your microscopic neighbors may not appreciate you popping in without asking, and some of them can cause you harm.

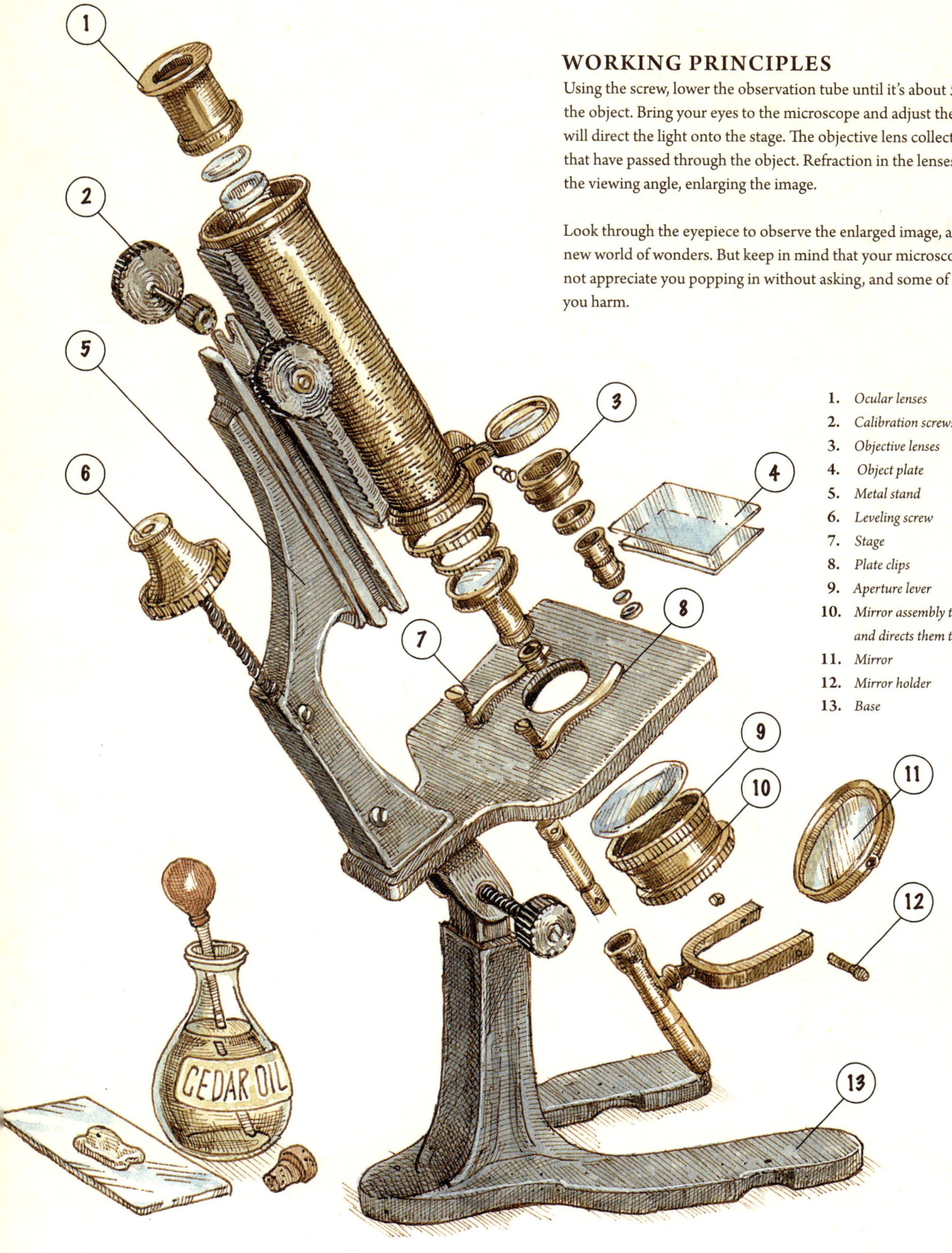

1. *Ocular lenses*
2. *Calibration screws for focusing*
3. *Objective lenses*
4. *Object plate*
5. *Metal stand*
6. *Leveling screw*
7. *Stage*
8. *Plate clips*
9. *Aperture lever*
10. *Mirror assembly that collects light rays and directs them towards the specimen*
11. *Mirror*
12. *Mirror holder*
13. *Base*

CEDAR OIL

Light rays passing through the object are reflected and scattered at the boundary between the air and the glass. At high magnifications — 600x and above — the illuminator may not be powerful enough to produce a detailed image.

By bridging the gap between the plate and the objective lens using a substance with a refractive index equal to that of the glass slide, such as immersion oil, more light is directed through the lens and you're able to get a clearer image.

PHOTOGRAPHY

Memory is a fickle thing: details fall out of your head, the faces of loved ones blur, landscapes become distorted... Humans are constantly trying to capture reality, to preserve life's most memorable and ephemeral moments, to create a lasting projection of the Ego in reality. A photograph captures a moment, but it's not a dead copy of reality. It is always a subjective truth, an impression seen through the lens of the individual who captured it. A landscape, a face, a beautiful object — the themes remain the same, but each person interprets them differently. To create a photosensitive coating, you'll need several different chemical compounds. Start by boiling seaweed ash in sulfuric acid (page 192). Capture the purple vapor that is released and cool it until iodine crystals form. A solution of iodine in a mixture of sodium hydroxide (page 24) and ammonia (page 274) will produce sodium iodide. Heat ethanol with sulfuric acid. Condense the steam to produce liquid diethyl ether. Treat cotton with a mixture of nitric and sulfuric acids and water (14:10:4 ratio). Rinse and dry the resulting nitrocellulose. Be careful — it is highly flammable.

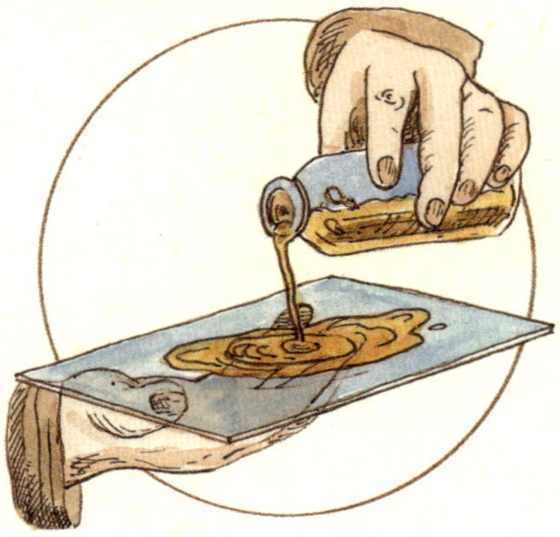

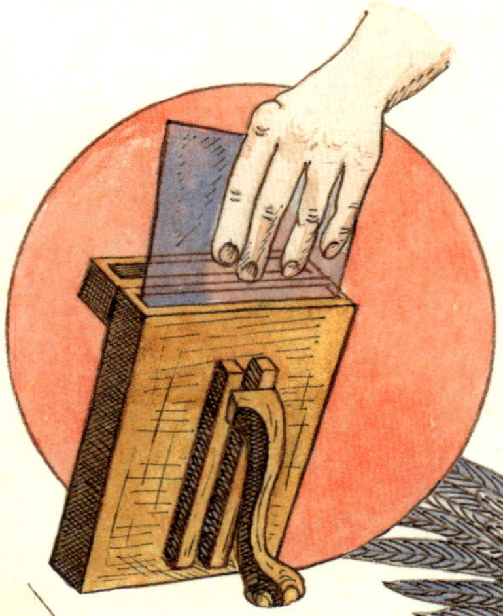

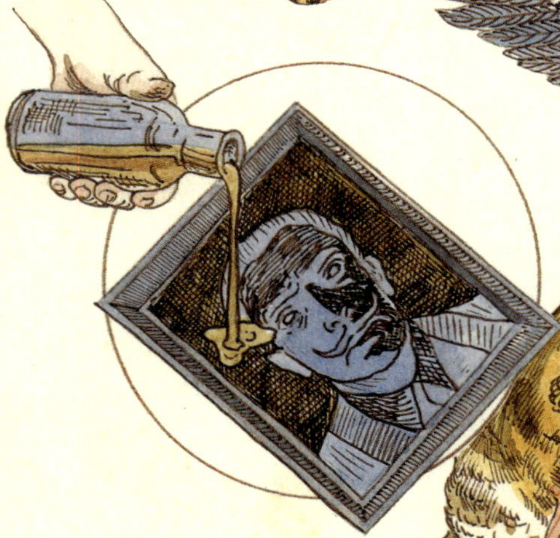

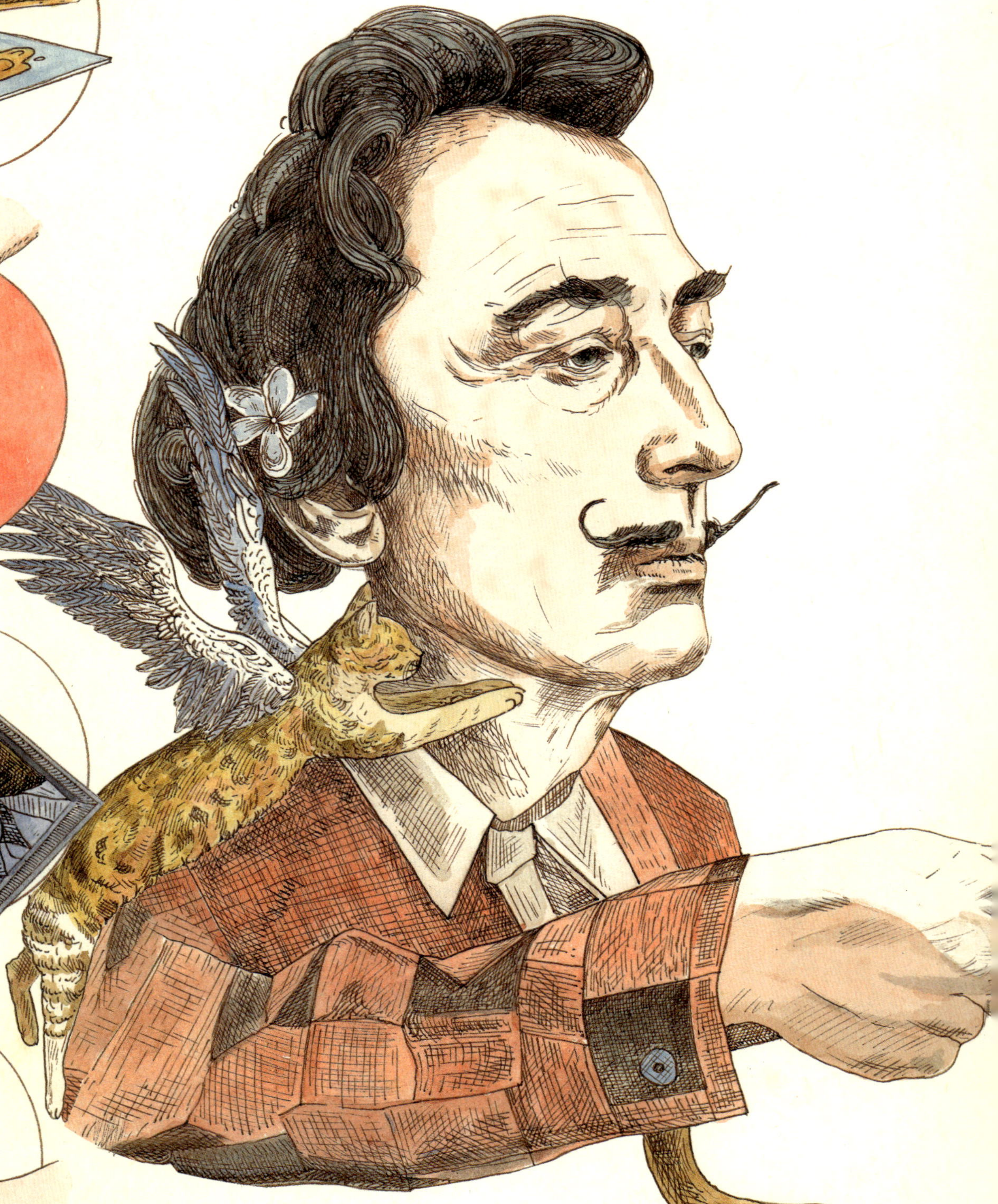

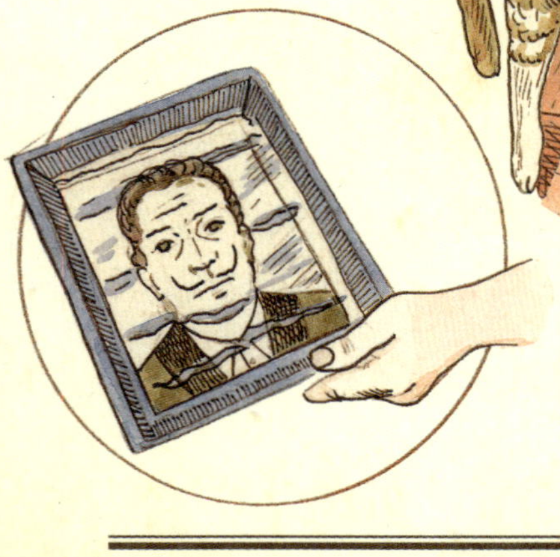

For the developing liquid, dissolve iron in sulfuric acid. Fixing the image requires sodium thiosulfate. It can be obtained by passing the gas obtained from the combustion of sulfur through a solution of sodium hydroxide then boiling the resulting solution with more sulfur.

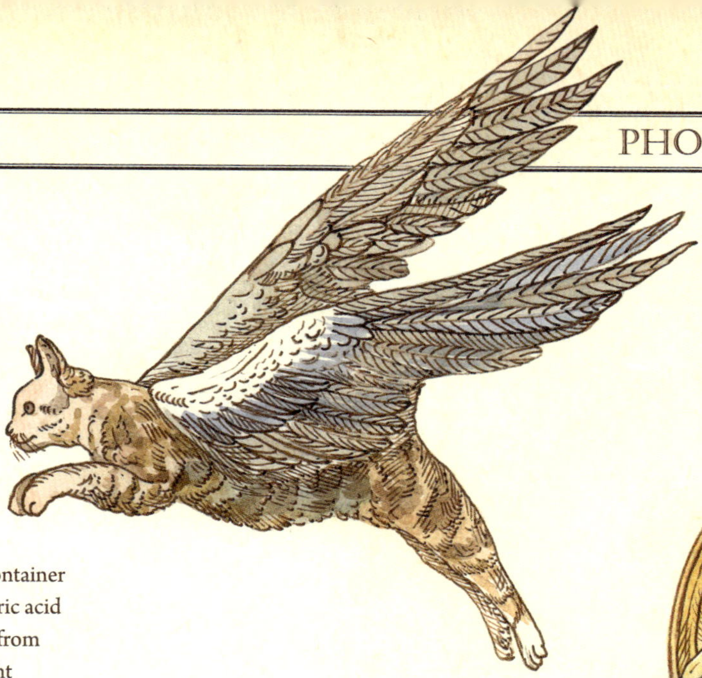

Polish a sheet of glass with a mixture of chalk, water and alcohol. When dry, pour a solution of 2% nitrocellulose in a mixture of alcohol and ether (1:7 ratio), with added sodium iodide, over the glass. Ignite and allow to burn for 20–30 seconds — the solution should thicken but not dry. Make the plate photosensitive: dip it in a container with a 9% solution of silver nitrate (dissolve silver in nitric acid for this) and leave it there for a few minutes. Remove it from the mixture in a dark room or under a very weak red light and place it in the plateholder — a flat, opaque box with one removable wall. Once you slide the wall into place, you can bring the photos into a lit room. The picture must be taken within 5–10 minutes, while the solution is not yet dry, and the plate should be developed immediately.

After shooting, reinsert the cassette cover, remove the cassette, and take it back to a dark room. To develop your photo, pour a developer onto the plate — a solution of ferrous sulfate, vinegar and sugar. Wait 15 seconds and rinse the plate with water. Fix the image with a 20% solution of sodium thiosulfate and rinse the plate once again. Use transparent varnish to protect the image. You can turn a negative image into a positive by painting the plate's back side with black paint.

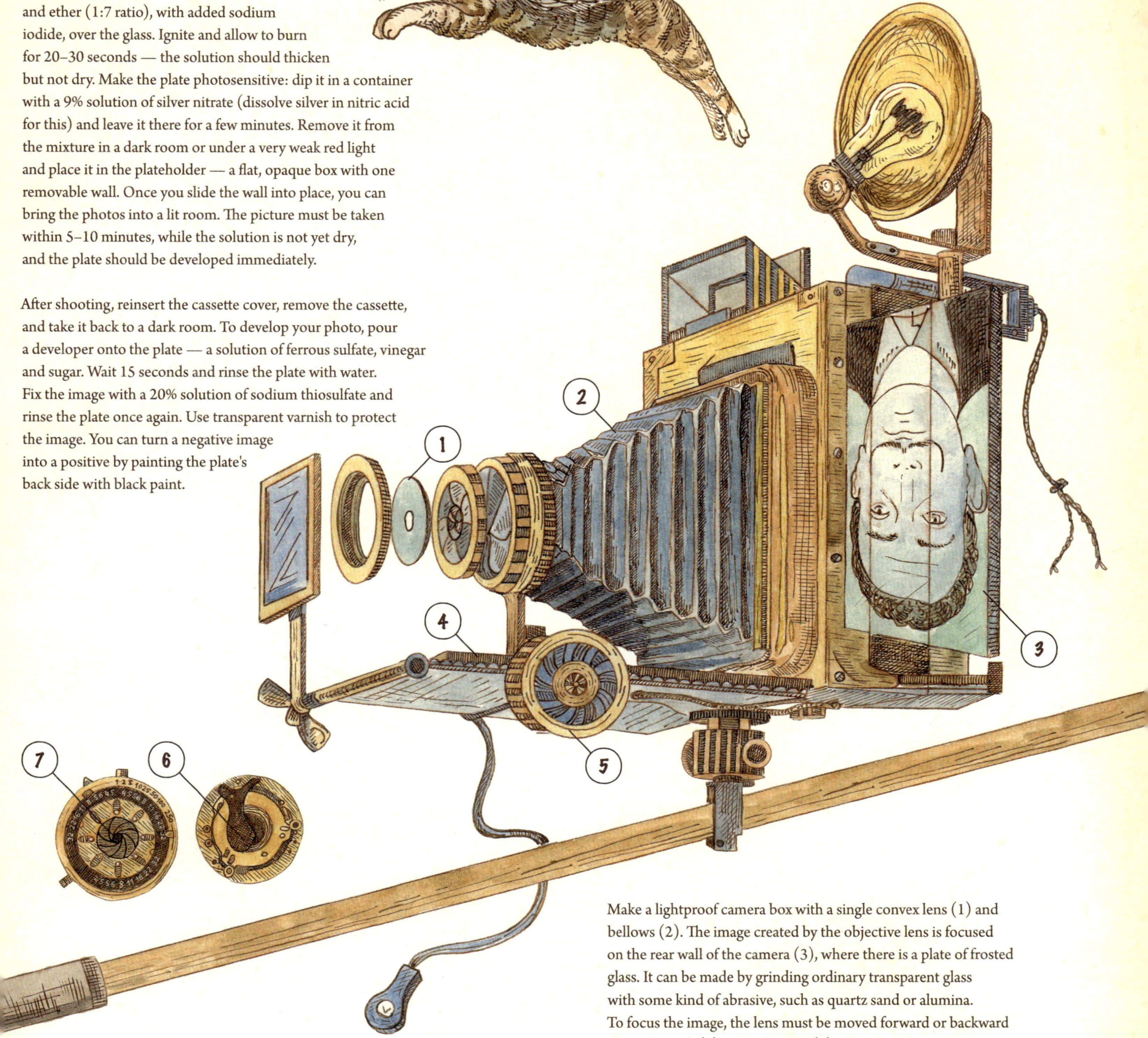

Make a lightproof camera box with a single convex lens (1) and bellows (2). The image created by the objective lens is focused on the rear wall of the camera (3), where there is a plate of frosted glass. It can be made by grinding ordinary transparent glass with some kind of abrasive, such as quartz sand or alumina. To focus the image, the lens must be moved forward or backward along the rack (4) using the gear (5). After focusing, remove the frosted glass from the camera and replace the plateholder with a photographic plate. Then pull out the lid, fully exposing the photosensitive surface of the plate. To capture an image, all you need to do is remove the cap from the lens for a time, from a few seconds to several minutes. Or instead, you can install a shutter (6) behind the lens to control the amount of time the lens is exposed. The higher the shutter speed, the brighter the negative image will be. Add an aperture (7) that will control the amount of light passing through the lens. It can be a rotary disk with a set of holes of different diameters or metal petals. The more the aperture is opened, the blurrier out-of-focus objects will be, such as the background in a portrait photo.

The amount of exposure — a combination of shutter speed and aperture value — needed to capture an image can be reduced if a bright artificial light source is used. This may be an incandescent lamp (8) with a filament heated to a higher temperature — 6000°C. After you learn to get metallic magnesium, its powder (9) can be used as a flash lamp. If you set it on fire, it heats up to a high temperature and gives off a flash of very bright light.

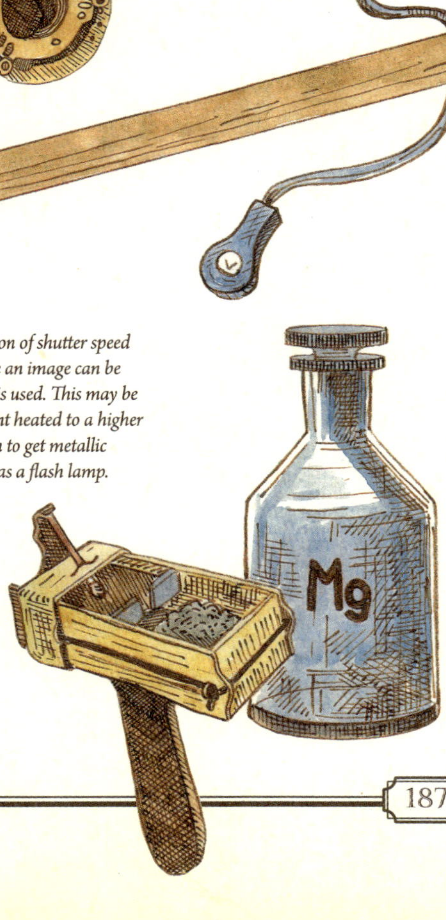

ANIMATION

Animation works by taking advantage of a simple optical illusion. When you present a sequence of still images in quick enough succession, the viewer's mind interprets them as a continuous moving image. This effect is achieved by using a large number of sequential images that differ minimally from the previous image in the series. But persistence of vision is only one small part of the bigger picture. When we watch animated characters, we start to empathize and identify with them. We laugh, cry and scream in horror along with them. This is where cinematography comes into play. Although there are still a few technological milestones you'll have to reach before you can film a train coming into a station, you can start to create your own cinema classics in the comfort of your own home. It's painstaking work, but it's worth it. The persistence of vision illusion works because the human brain can only process 10 to 12 separate images per second, retaining an image for up to a fifteenth of a second.

THE STROBOSCOPE

You want your audience to see a quick succession of still images melting into each other, not a conga-line of individual pictures. To create the illusion of motion, you first need to stop the actual movement.

The stroboscopic effect helps enhance the illusion: When a person sees moving objects for only a brief period of time, they appear to be stationary. A rotating disc with slots or holes reveals each card for only a moment.

LIGHTING

The rotating frame also tends to block out almost all of the light. This can make the cards appear dark. The more they are illuminated, the better the final result.

Want to make an electric light bulb? See page 198.

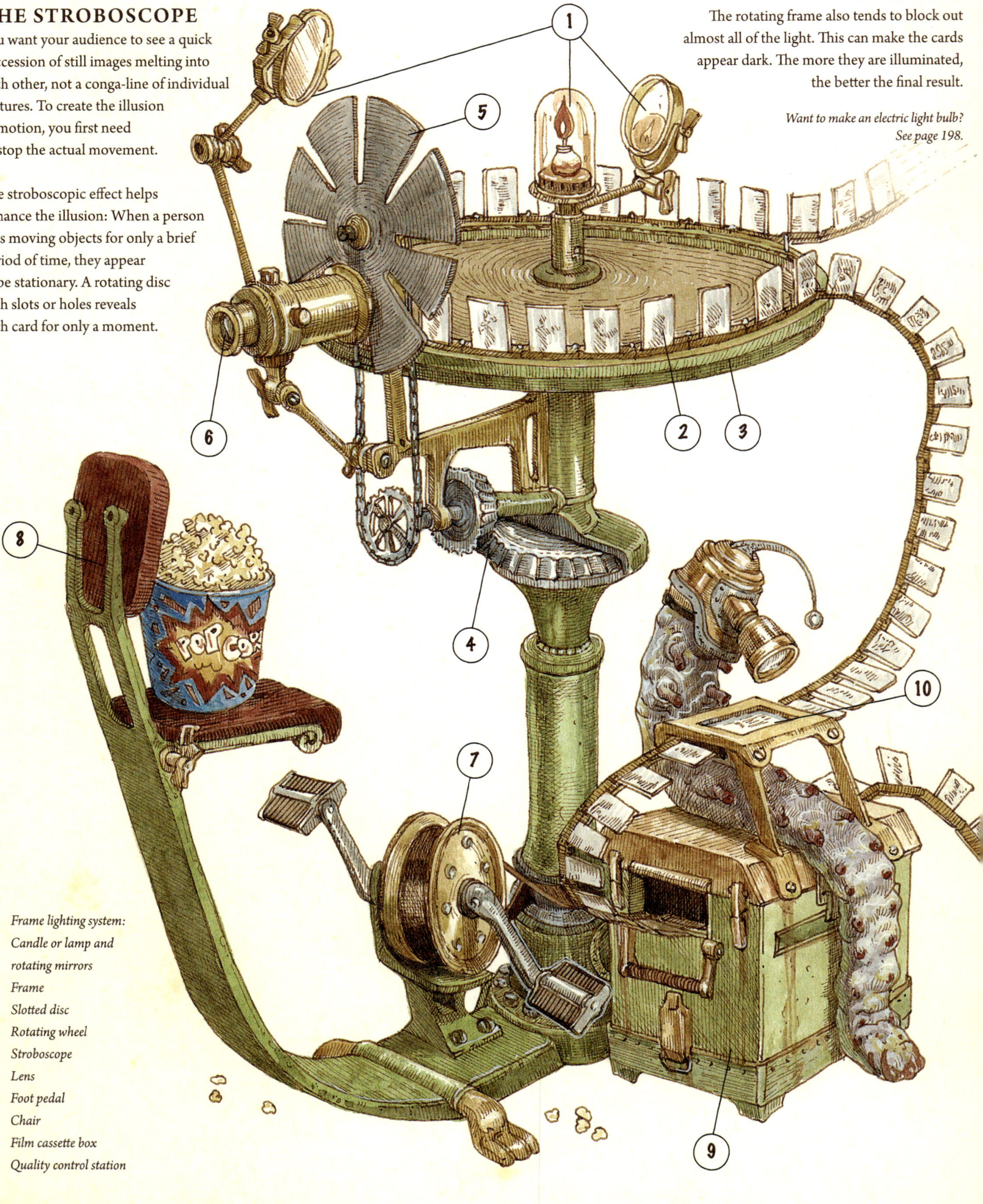

1. *Frame lighting system: Candle or lamp and rotating mirrors*
2. *Frame*
3. *Slotted disc*
4. *Rotating wheel*
5. *Stroboscope*
6. *Lens*
7. *Foot pedal*
8. *Chair*
9. *Film cassette box*
10. *Quality control station*

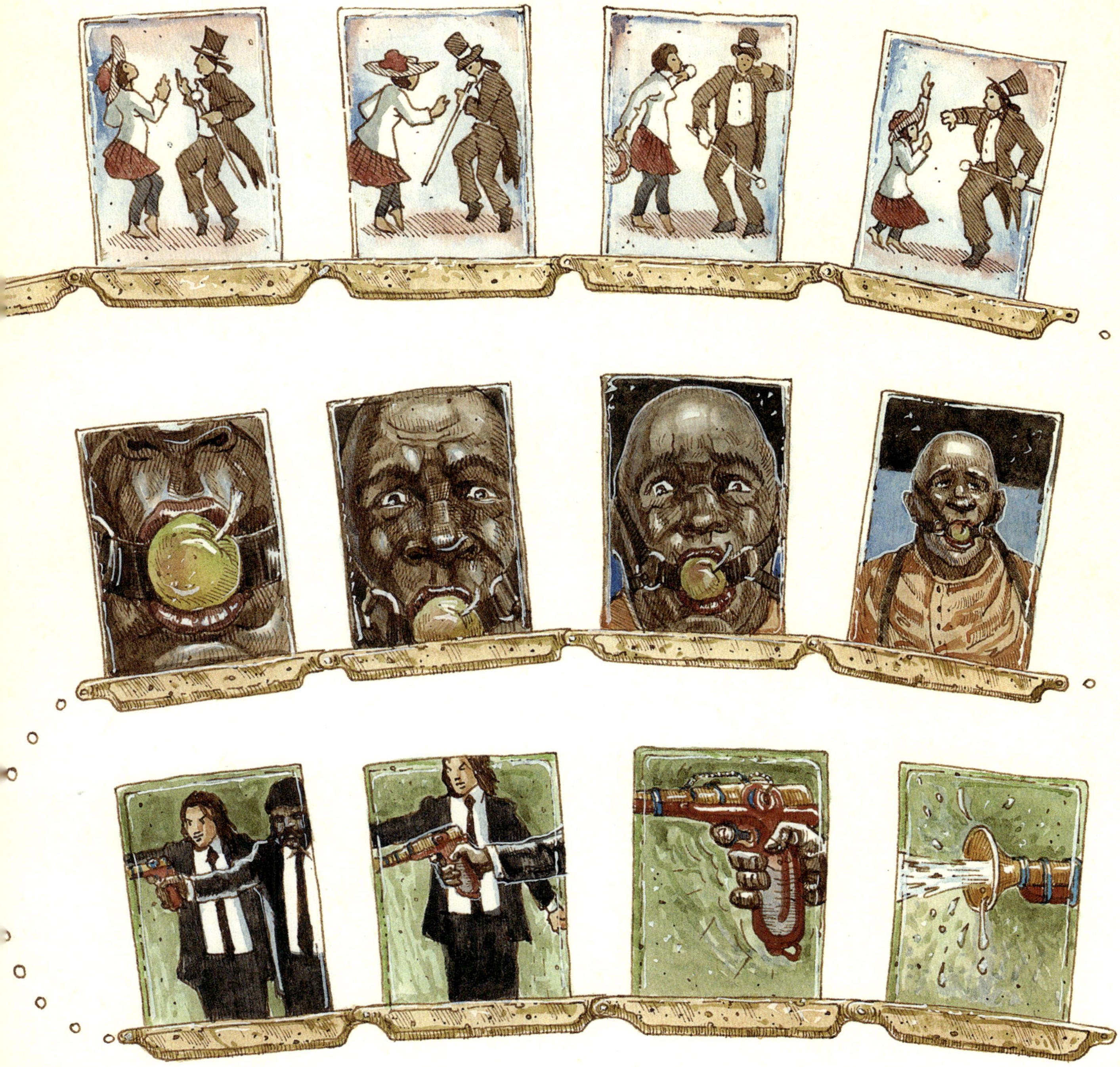

STORYBOARDING

Each individual image is called a frame. To draw frames, you must first forget everything you know about drawing. Adding finer details is unnecessary, as they will be lost in the greater picture, but timing is everything. Picture the motion you want to capture and establish a time frame. Count how many frames you must show to the viewer in that time. Break the character's story into stages of motion, and animate each one individually.

FRAME RATE

You don't have to pedal like mad to produce the desired effect. You can create smooth and lifelike animations efficiently by showing the viewer just enough frames to create a sense of motion. This threshold is at 12 frames per second (FPS). At 24 FPS, strobe flicker becomes completely unnoticeable. And at 60 FPS, the line between film and reality is erased completely. Sit back, pedal and watch your movie. Your brain gets an exciting experience while your body gets exercise.

ELECTRICITY

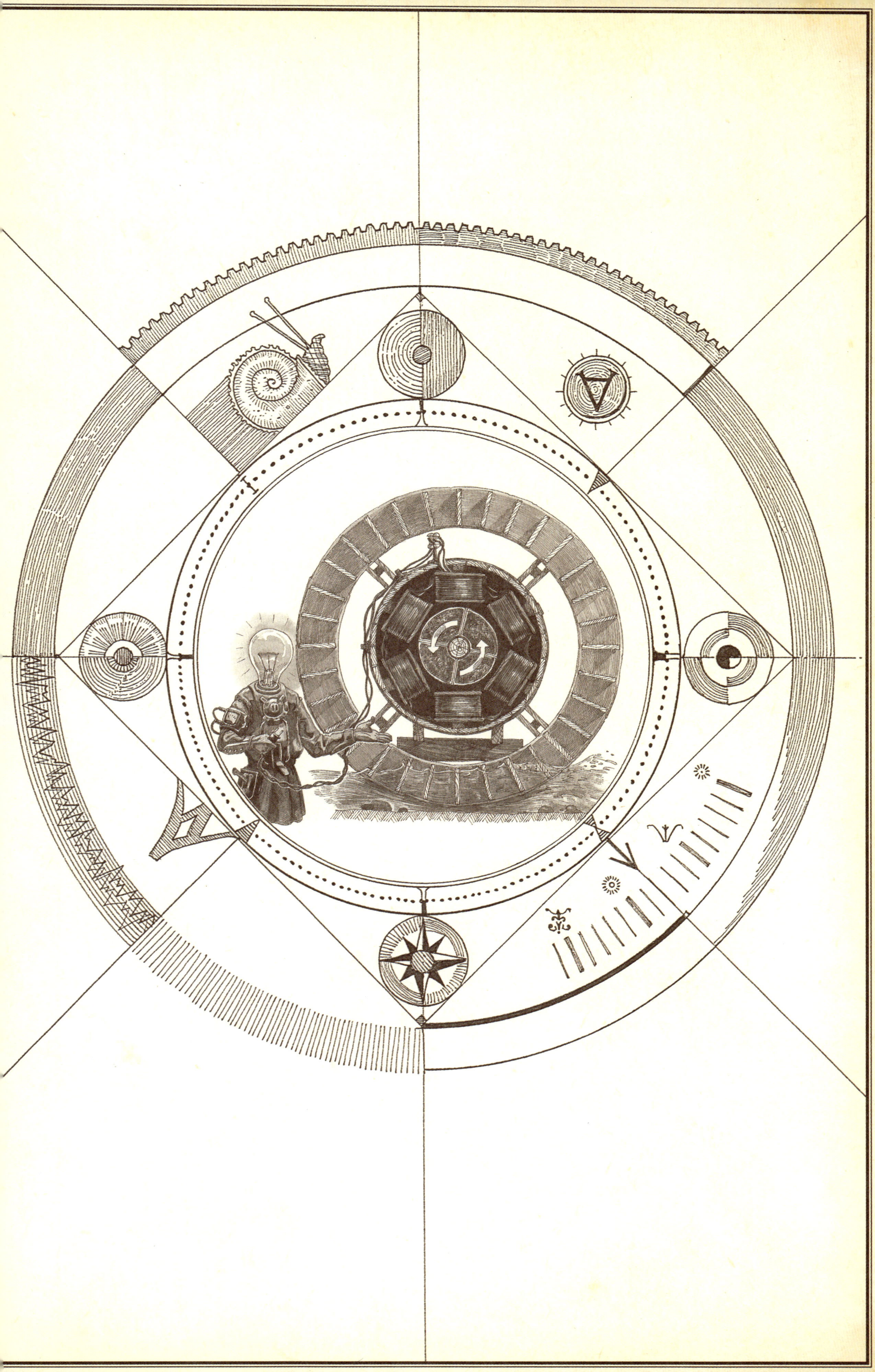

BATTERY

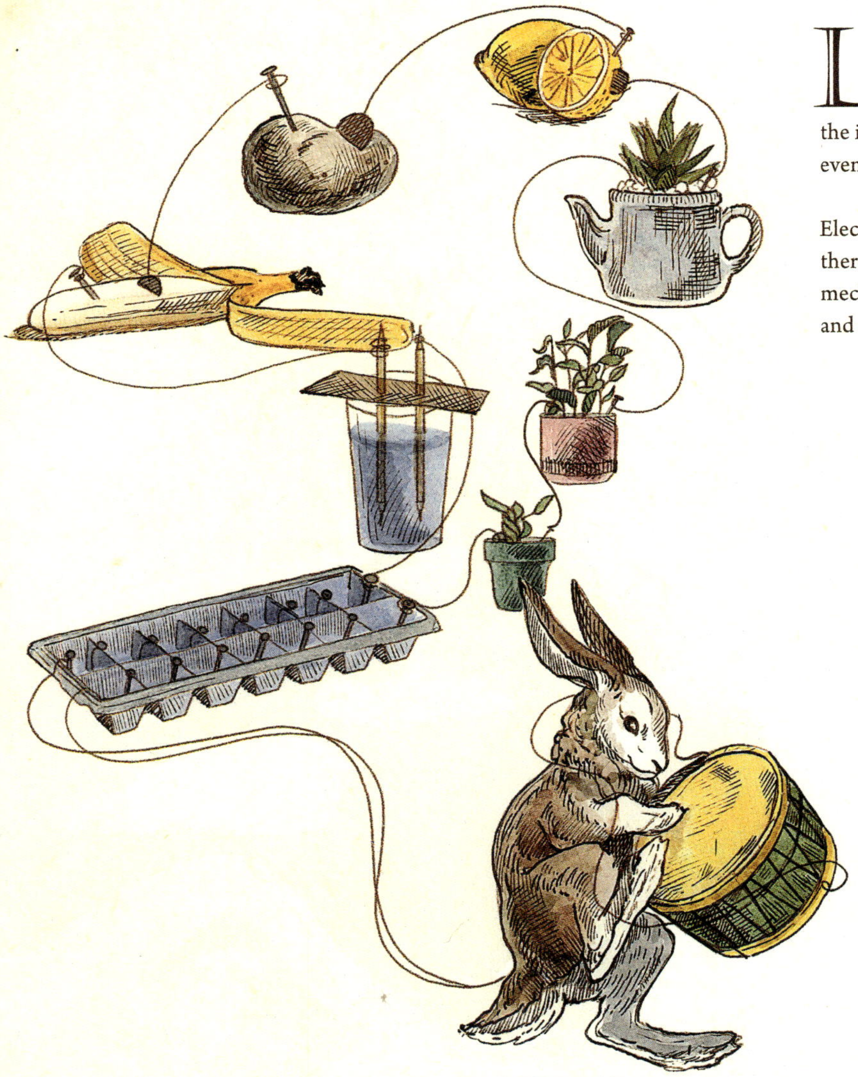

Laziness is the engine of progress. Human beings are always delighted to be able to pass the work on to someone else. You've already put the wind to work and harnessed the fast-flowing river with the invention of the water wheel (page 234). Use the forces of nature even more efficiently by harnessing them to make electricity.

Electric current is created when electrons move. Without semiconductors, there are two effective ways to make electrons move: chemical and mechanical. The chemical method is simpler — it allows you to obtain and store valuable electricity.

BATTERY

Batteries are devices that use chemical reactions to produce electrical energy. Place rods of two different metals in an electrolyte solution, such as sulfuric acid, and connect them with a conductor. There will be a flow of electrons from one rod to the other. This is an electric current. It can be used for many different purposes, such as lighting a room. You can make a battery by putting electrodes — a copper spiral and an iron rod — in a glass of vinegar. Or simply stick them in an acidic environment, such as a piece of fruit. This kind of electrochemical cell produces a very small electric voltage, but if you connect several cells in a series — connect the negative terminal of the first cell to the positive terminal of the second one and so on until all the cells are connected — you can produce a working battery.

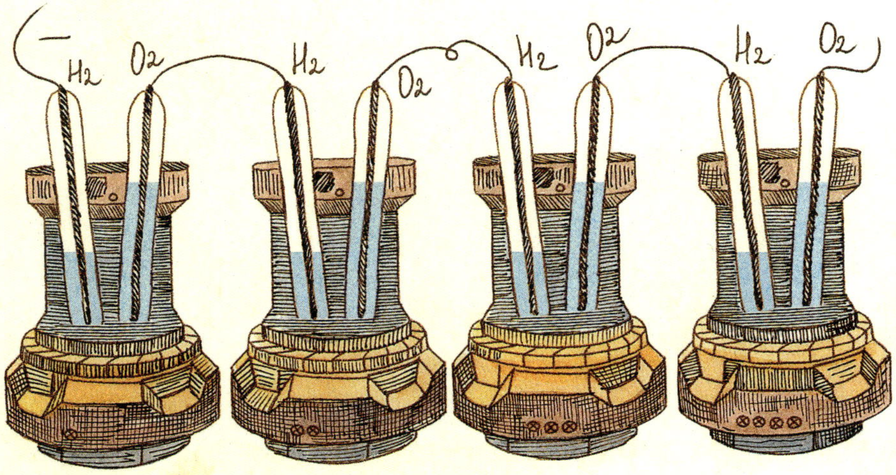

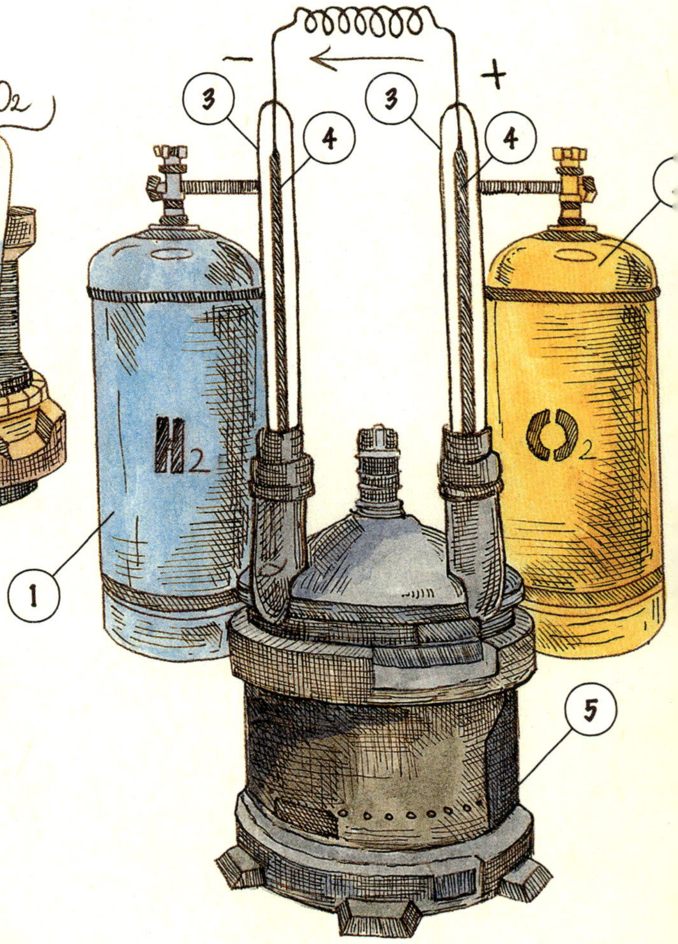

HYDROGEN FUEL CELLS

These are batteries in which the reagents can be continuously replenished. In a fuel cell, this is accomplished by an electrochemical reaction between hydrogen (1) (page 228) and oxygen (2) to form ordinary water. The gases are fed into containers (3) with platinum electrodes (4) submerged in the electrolyte — a sulfuric acid solution (5). As a result of this reaction, the hydrogen atoms lose their electrons, which travel along the conductors as electricity and can then be used to illuminate a lightbulb or power a car.

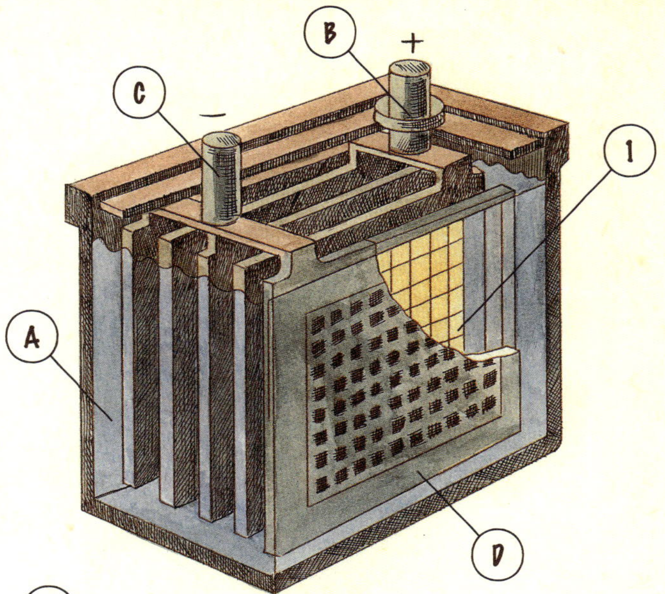

RECHARGEABLE BATTERY

The energy reserve in a typical battery is limited by the amount of electrode substance available. When one of the electrodes is completely used up, the battery will stop working. But it is possible to create an "eternal" battery — the rechargeable battery. The way it's constructed allows you to reverse the processes occurring in the battery and restore the spent electrodes. The battery can be recharged using electrical energy from, for example, a generator connected to a windmill or a water wheel.

One of the simplest options is a lead-acid battery. The electrodes are lead grids with lead powder and lead dioxide pressed into them. Immerse them in sulfuric acid (A). When the battery is charged, the positive electrode, the anode side (B), contains lead dioxide, and the negative electrode, the cathode (C), contains pure lead. As the battery discharges, these electrodes react with the sulfuric acid (A).

At the cathode, lead turns into lead sulfate and electrons are released (1). At the anode, the lead oxide also turns into lead sulfate, but the electrons are absorbed (2). If you connect a light bulb to the two electrodes, a current will flow through (3). If a current source, such as a generator, is connected instead of a light bulb, the "dead" electrodes will be restored to their original state (4). To increase the power, use several pairs of electrodes. Use a piece of rubber with multiple holes in it as an insulator (D) to prevent contact.

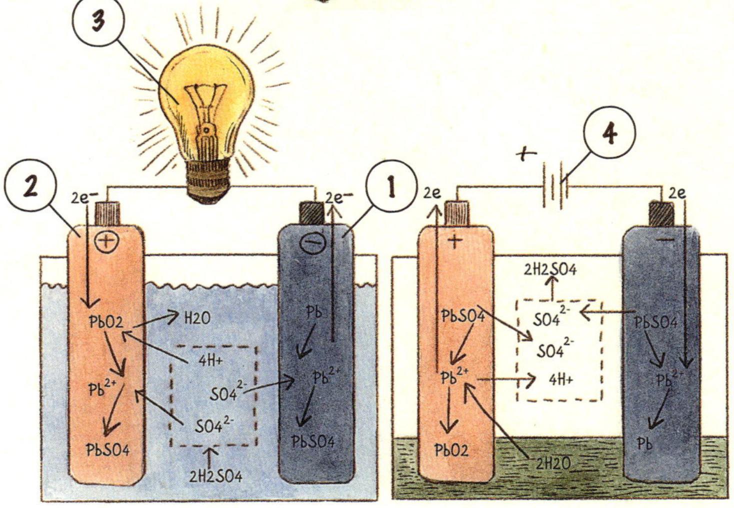

SULFURIC ACID

Sulphuric acid can be made by burning bright-yellow elemental sulfur (found in deposits near volcanoes) with saltpeter (page124) in steam-filled boxes lined with lead. If you can't find elemental sulfur, sulphuric acid can also be made from iron sulfide, or pyrite (page 110). Grind up the sulfuric pyrite. The particles should not be so large that they won't burn well but also not too fine. Otherwise, they'll clump together and smolder.

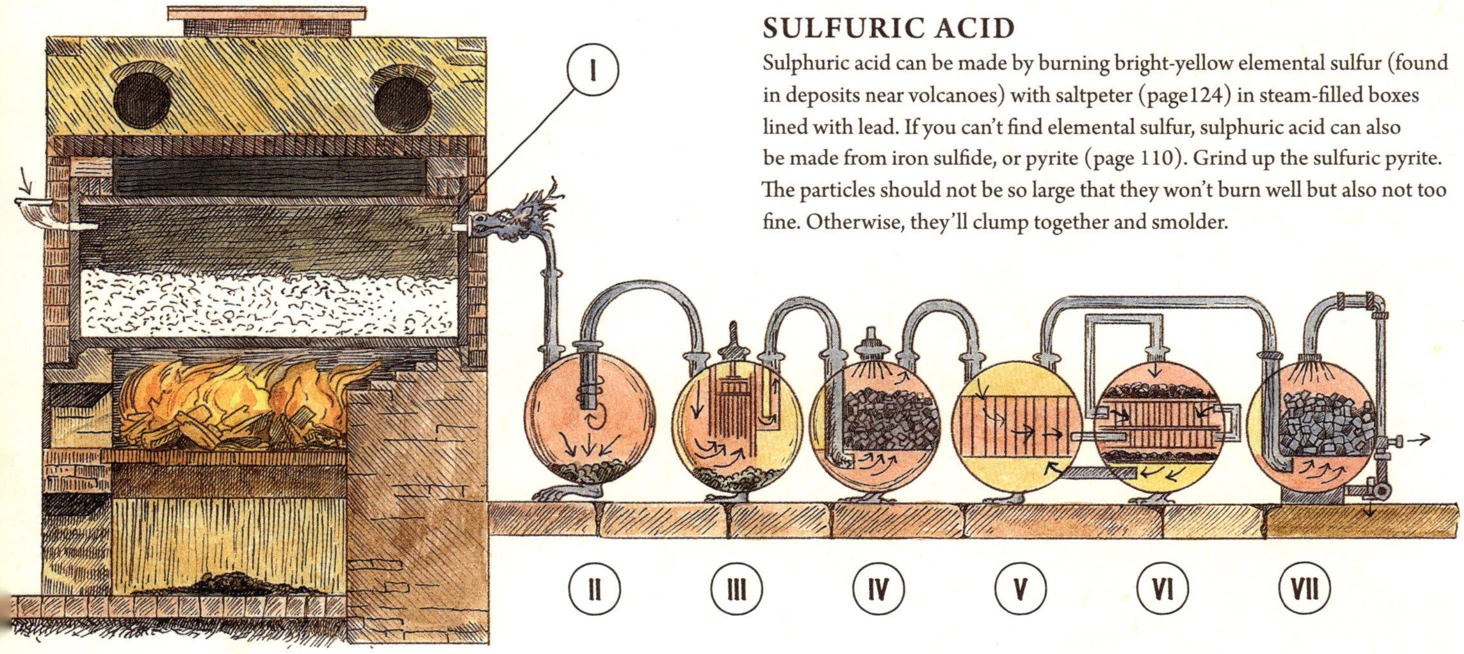

Place the sulfuric pyrite in a furnace and blow air through (I). This will increase the oxygen exposure, speeding up the process. The furnace gas obtained by roasting sulfur pyrite contains impurities and water vapor. In the outer cylinder, the gas moves from top to bottom in a spiral (II). Under the influence of centrifugal force, the coarse dust particles will fall to the bottom and can then be removed. The finer dust particles will be removed by the electro-filter (III). Make it out of fine mesh nets with a high voltage DC current running through them. In a strong electric field, the dust particles are ionized and attracted to the mesh nets, where they lose their charge and settle at the bottom. The drying tower (IV) filled with ceramic rings then removes the water vapor from the sulfurous gas.

This sulfurous gas is fed into the tower from below, and concentrated sulfuric acid sprays out the top. As it flows down the rings, it forms a film on the surface. This will increase the contact area of acid and gas. Then the purified gas is heated (V) by the gas coming out of the contact apparatus (VI). This is a cylinder in which the heated gas is oxidized to sulfur trioxide in the presence of a catalyst — either platinum or red-hot iron oxide. In the absorption tower (VII), sulfur trioxide is absorbed under a shower of concentrated sulfuric acid. This creates oleum, a solution of sulfur trioxide in concentrated sulfuric acid. To obtain battery acid with a concentration of about 35%, dissolve the concentrated acid in water.

GENERATORS

Electricity makes our lives significantly easier, so you'll want to have a lot on hand. When stored in a battery, it's limited, but a generator is a different story. It converts mechanical energy into electrical energy and gives you a constant supply — as long as the river flows, the wind blows or the hand cranks.

To convert mechanical energy into electrical energy, you can use the principle of electromagnetic induction, which is the basic idea of operation of generators. Electron flow or electric current is generated when a magnetic field changes in which a closed conducting circuit is located.

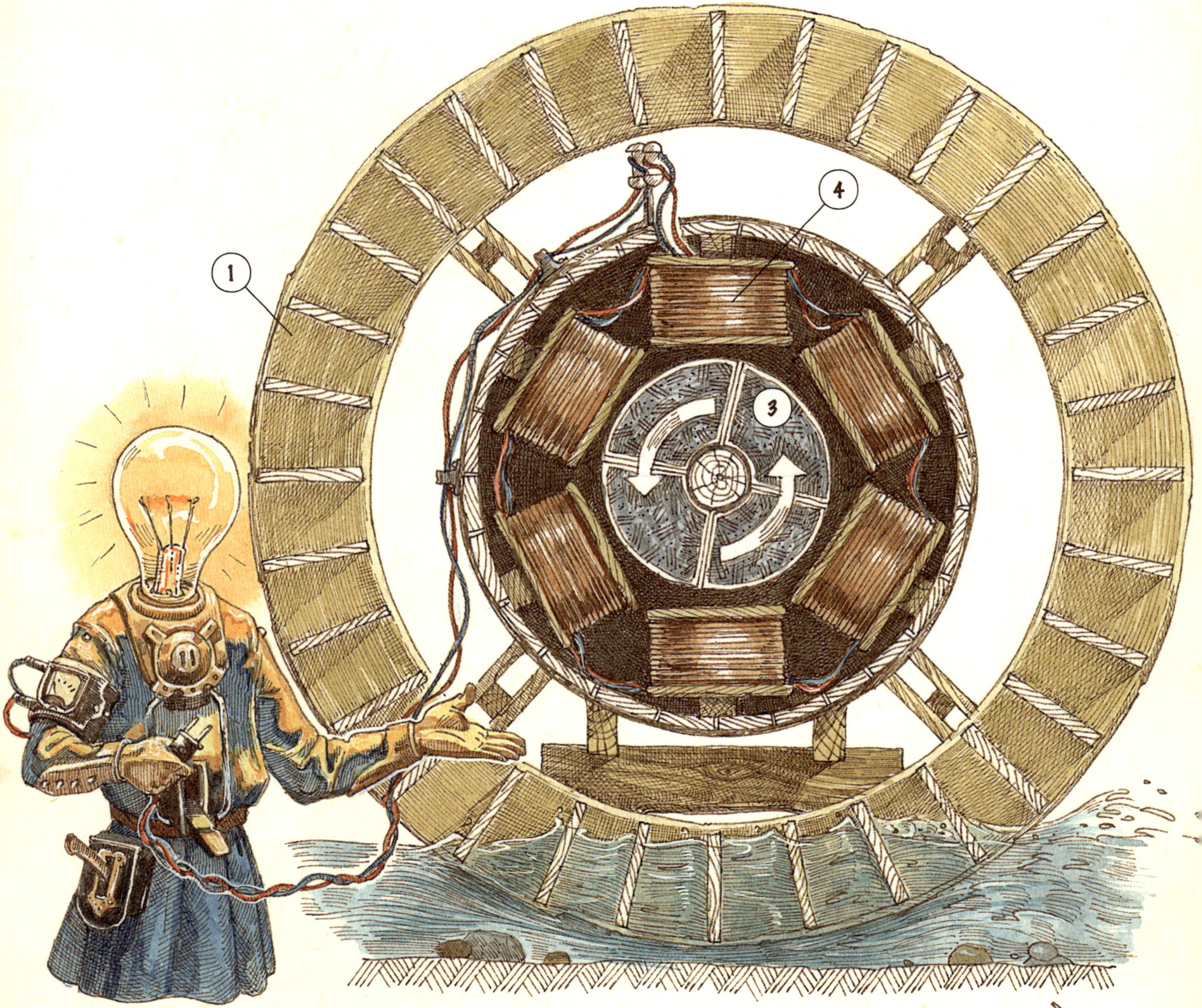

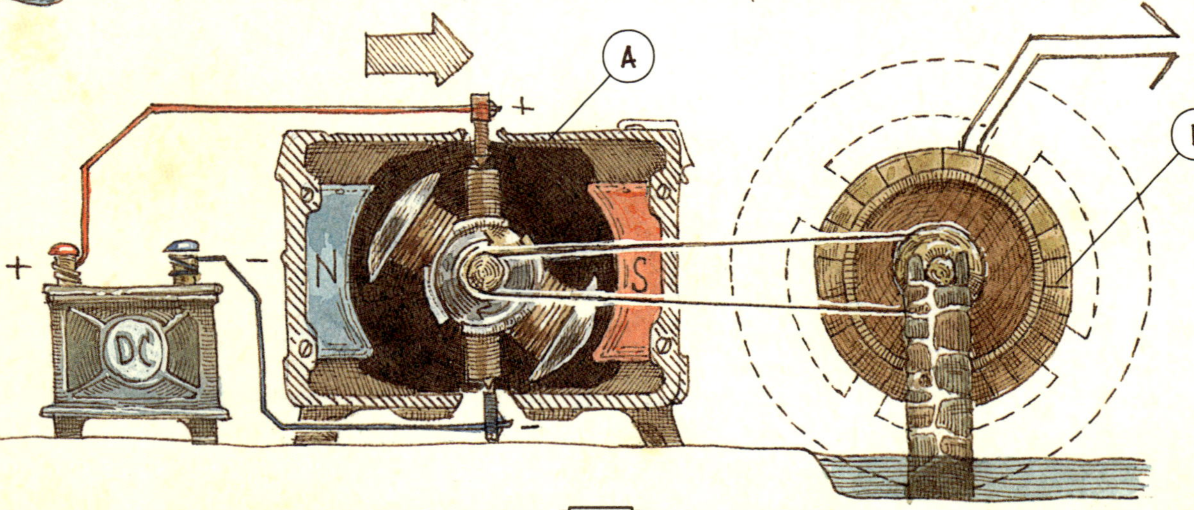

A generator needs a source of mechanical energy, such as a river turning a water wheel (1). There are permanent magnets (3) on its axis (2). As they rotate, they create a changing magnetic field, and an electric current is generated in the fixed coils (4) surrounding the magnets. It can be used to power electric motors of various devices. An electric motor works in the opposite manner to a generator, converting electrical energy into mechanical energy.

Direct current (DC) is the one-directional flow of electric charge in contrast to alternating current alternating current (AC), which periodically reverses direction and changes its magnitude continuously with time. DC and AC generators and motors can all be built on this principle. Their design may differ slightly. For example, in DC motors, the magnets are stationary and the coils rotate.

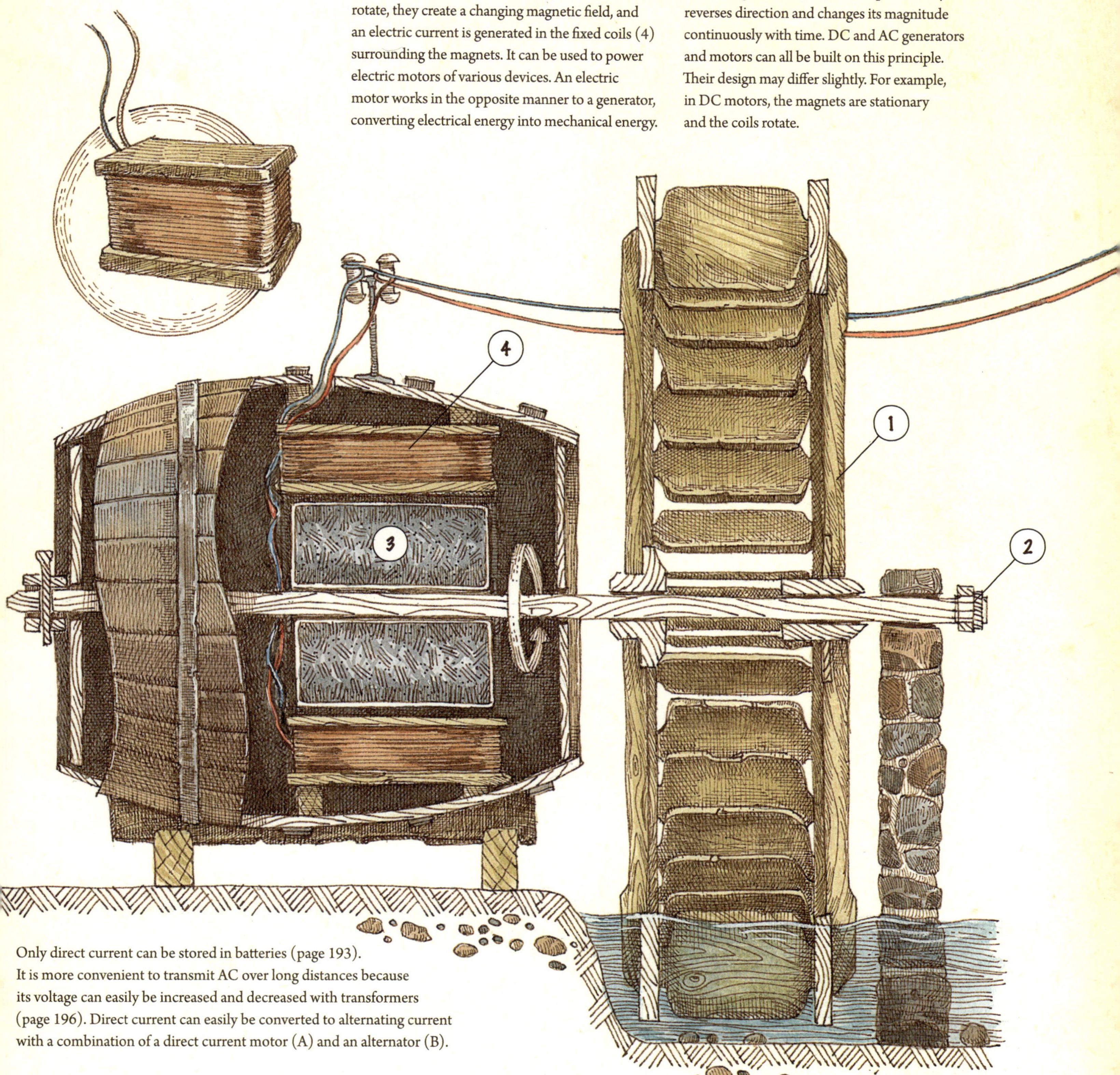

Only direct current can be stored in batteries (page 193). It is more convenient to transmit AC over long distances because its voltage can easily be increased and decreased with transformers (page 196). Direct current can easily be converted to alternating current with a combination of a direct current motor (A) and an alternator (B).

Alternating current can also be converted to direct current. This can be done with a mechanical electromagnetic rectifier (C) where an iron plate (5) oscillates in the magnetic field of an electromagnet (6), making contact (7) only in a certain direction of the electric current and opening it in the opposite direction.

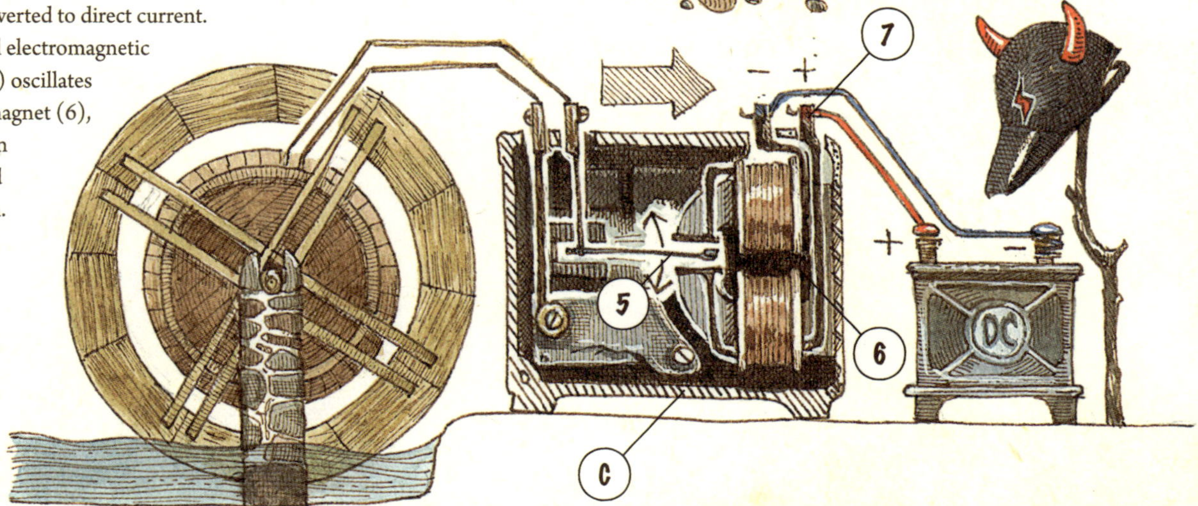

WIRES & TRANSFORMERS

If electricity is the lifeblood of your civilization, then wires are the veins. As you develop and expand your power grid, you will see the area it covers come alive and change before your very eyes.

Electricity can be carried over long distances through the power grid, but while it travels through the wires to your home, it can lose some of its power. The wires get hot, and the heat dissipates into the air. These losses are unavoidable, but they can be reduced. Heat release is proportional to the square of the electric current, and this can be reduced by increasing the voltage for the same transmission power. For this purpose, step-up transformers (1) are used.

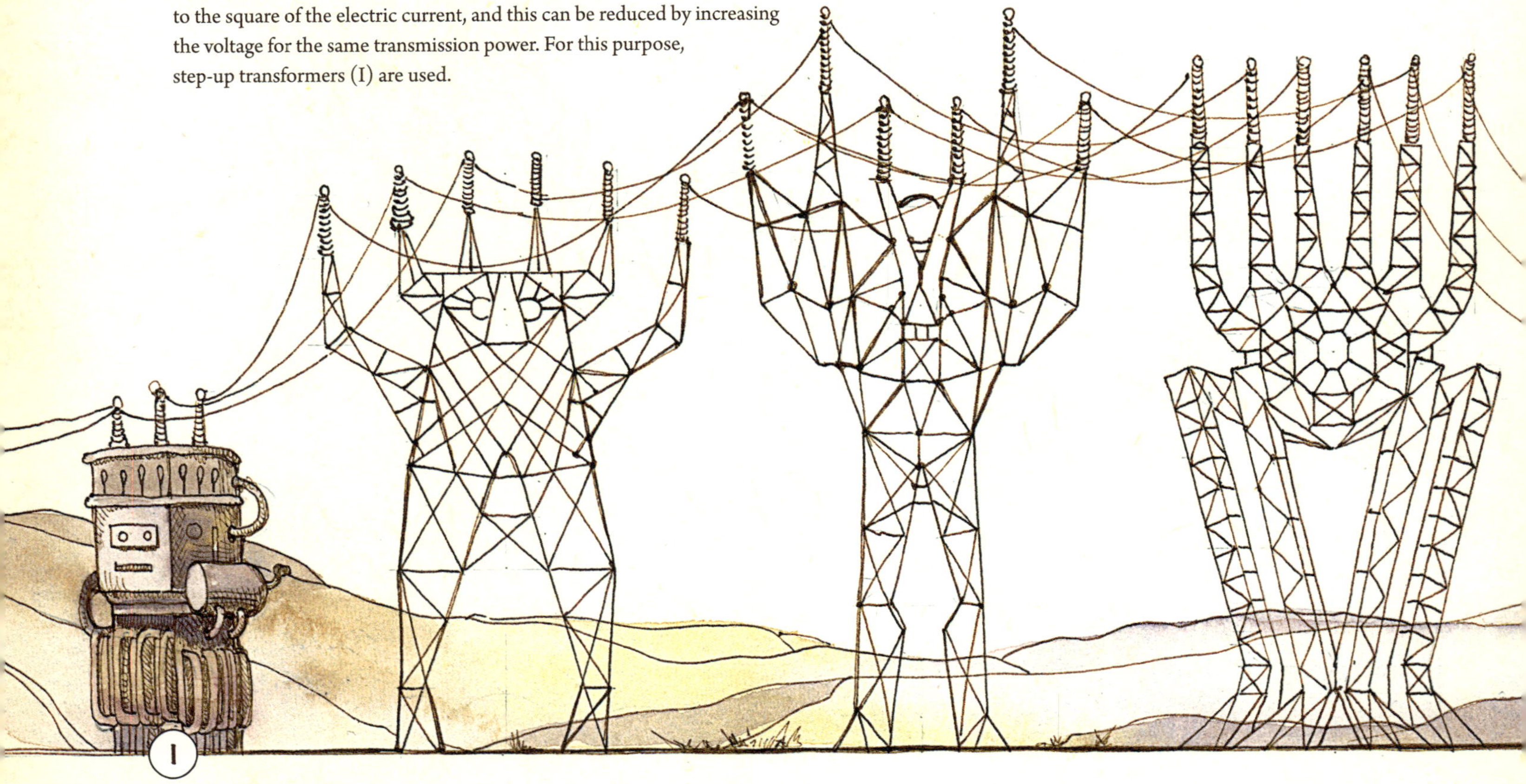

STEP-UP TRANSFORMER (1)

The device is based on two windings of wire around a steel core (3). The current source is connected to the primary winding (1), and the secondary winding (2) removes and transmits the already changed voltage to the consumer. When the primary winding is connected to electricity, a magnetic flux passes through the core, and the core itself becomes a magnet. Its poles shift back and forth, alternating dozens of times per second, which transports the magnetic flux from one winding to the other, creating an electromotive force. The size of the force depends on the number of turns in the windings.

The main element of the winding is the electric conductor. It's composed of a bundle of copper or aluminum wires. Lead the ends of the windings out of the tank (4) and connect them to the electric grid. For this purpose, use insulators (5) made of non-conductive material — ceramic. Place them on the transformer cover (6).

The transformer expansion tank (7) is a tank filled with oil. It insulates the current-carrying parts of the system and cools the transformer so that it does not explode. Radiators (8) are also needed for cooling — they dissipate the heat from the oil circulating in the tubing.

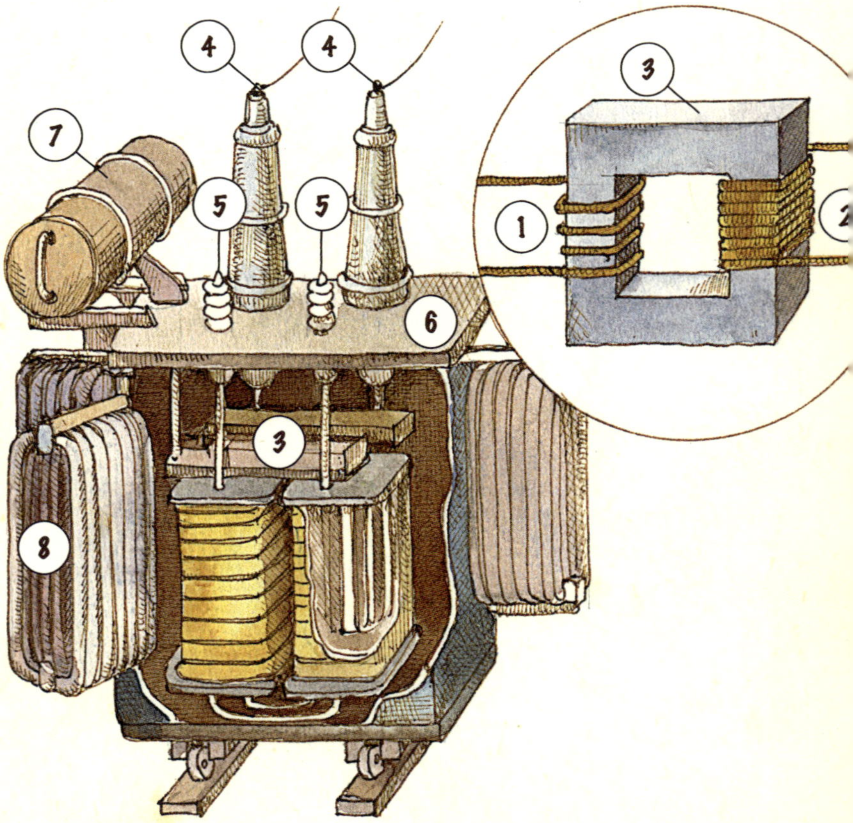

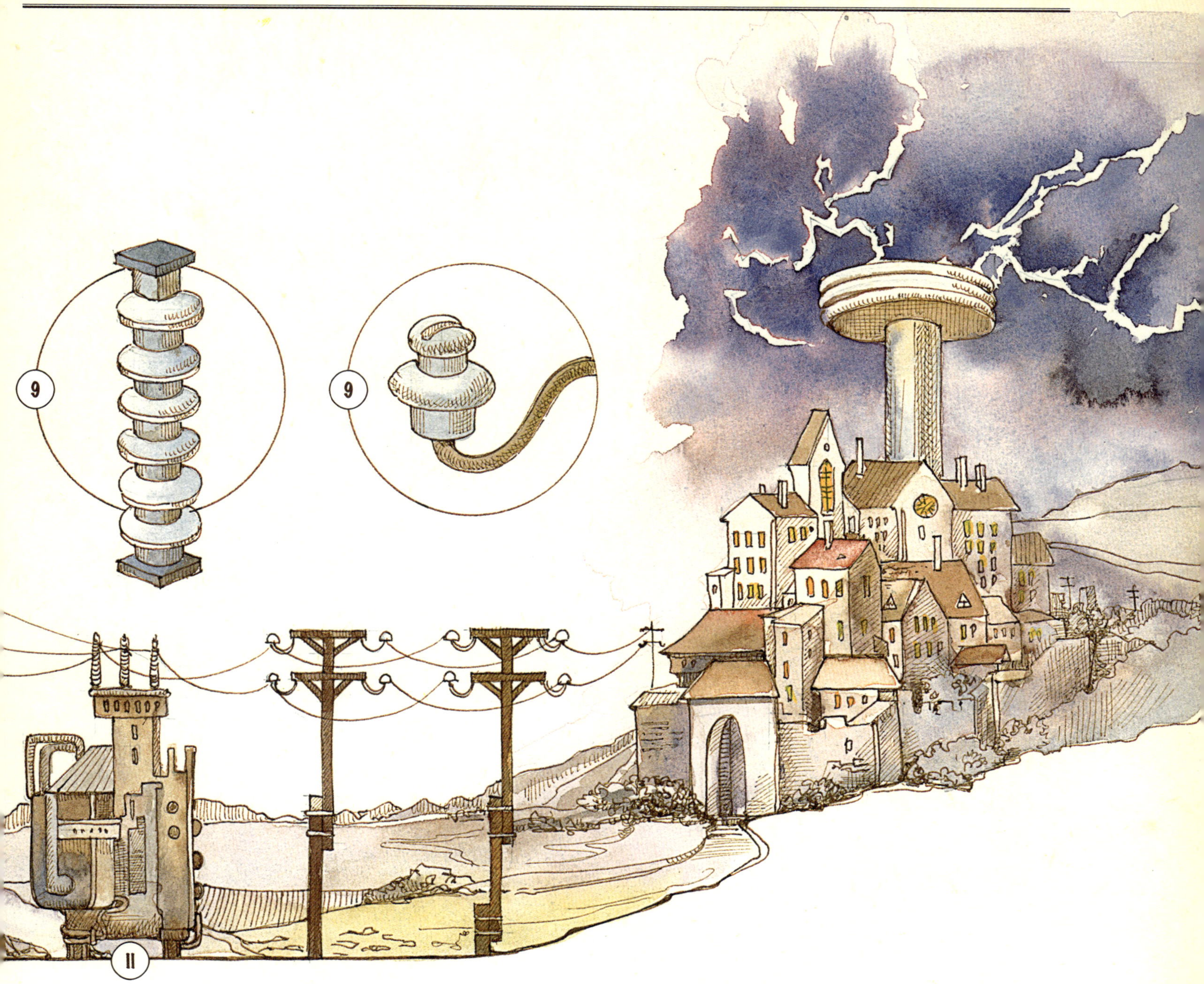

STEP-DOWN TRANSFORMER (11)

Before you can send voltage to the electrical outlets in your house, the voltage must be lowered to a value sufficient for household appliances. To reduce the voltage, the primary winding of the step-down transformer to which the current is supplied must be larger than the secondary. The lower voltage from the secondary winding is transmitted to the appliance.

WIRES

Electric current is transmitted between network elements by wires or cables that must be laid underground or raised to a significant height. You can't just lay bare wires in the ground, or you'll cause a short-circuit and many people will die. Therefore, underground cable must be covered in a layer of insulation. This can be cotton or silk threads boiled in paraffin or paper tape soaked in gum (page 200).

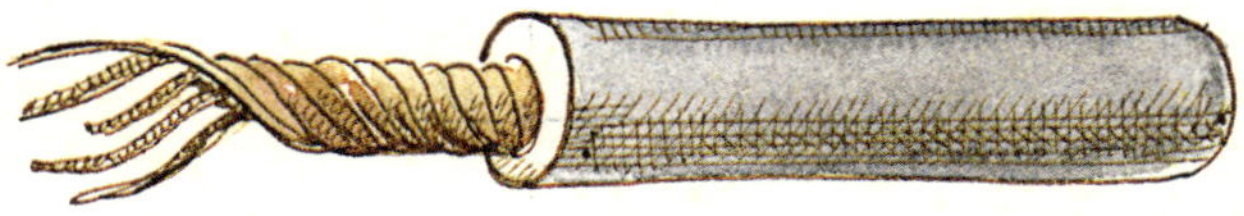

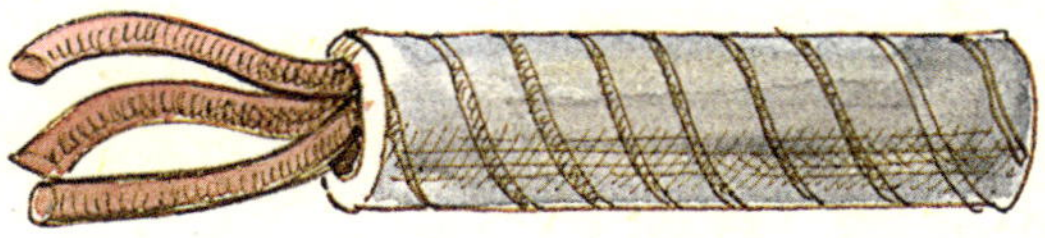

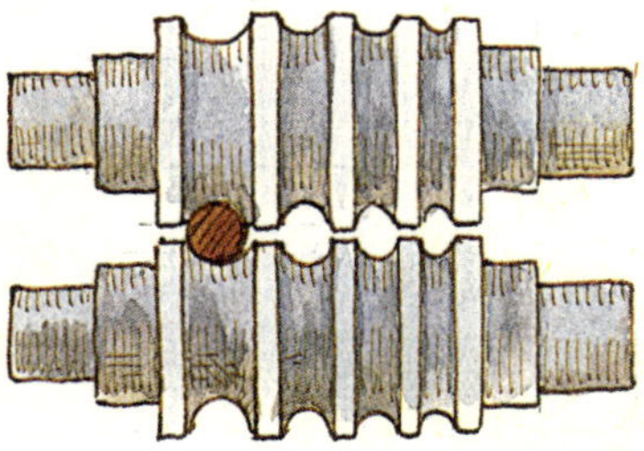

Use a combination of these materials to increase the insulating properties. Fasten the wires to metal support posts with insulators (9) made of non-conductive materials such as porcelain or glass.

To make wires, you can use section-shaped rollers similar in design to a rolling mill. Roll out a copper bar and pull it to make a long copper wire — the work horse in the field of electricity. Thin wires can be twisted and joined by a common insulation into a thick but flexible sturdy wire.

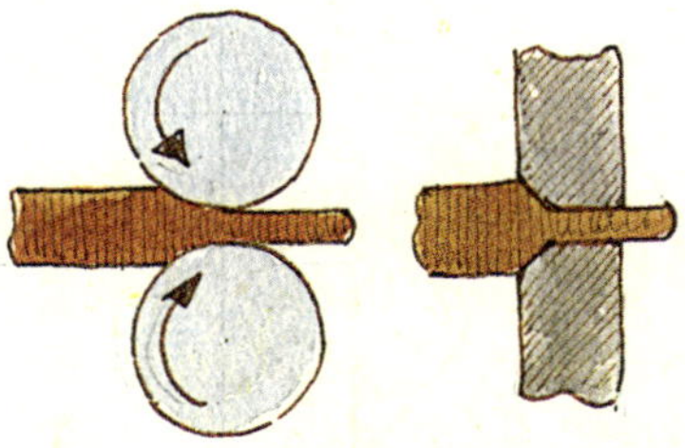

INCANDESCENT BULBS

Humans are not nocturnal, and it's difficult to forge a brighter future when you're sitting in the dark. Illuminate your path with the light bulb.

And with light bulbs flickering on in homes everywhere, you're sure to have some new ideas. They might not always be the brightest, but there will certainly be a lot of them.

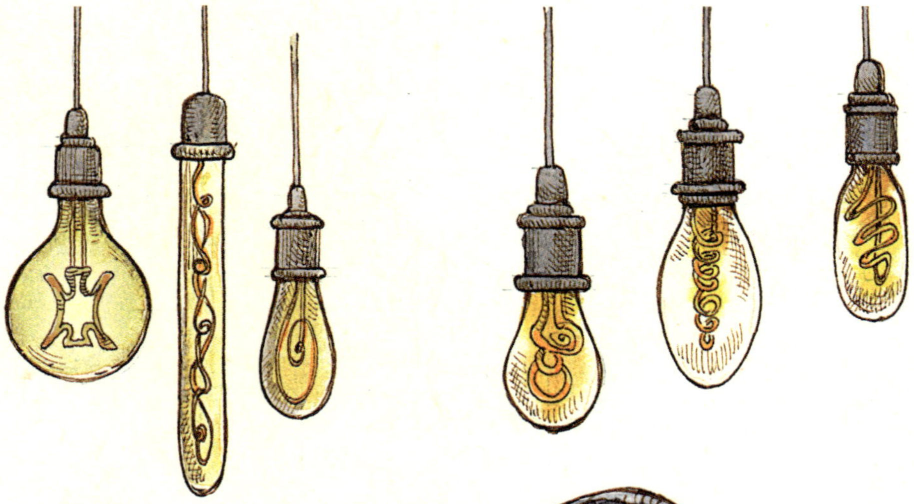

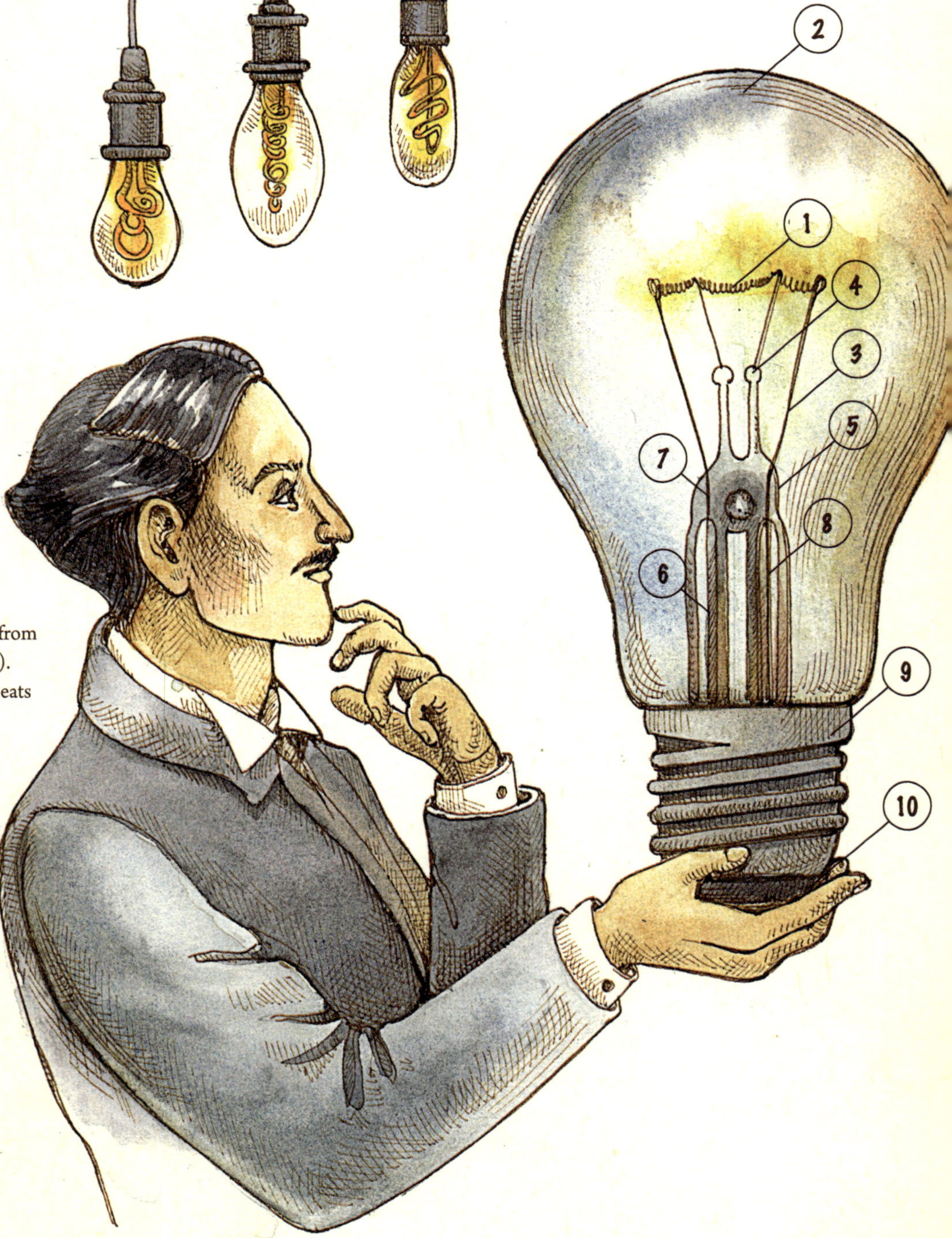

The filament that produces light can be made from a refractory metal such as tungsten (page 110). When an electric current flows through it, it heats up, and the greater the current, the higher the temperature. The current depends on the voltage. When the voltage drops, the bulb begins to glow yellow, and when the voltage increases, the light becomes whiter. The main parts are the filament (1), the glass bulb (2) and the contact wire (3). The filament can be twisted any way you like, but it is better to bend it into a curve so that the light is emitted more uniformly.

The filament should be held in place by small support wires (4) made of a refractory alloy (page 138) or ceramic (page 136). They stand on the foot of the lamp (5). Both ends of the filament are connected to the electrodes. One goes in through the base (9) into the lamp (6), and the other comes out through the fuse (7). This will protect the power circuit if the filament should suddenly break and emit an arc of electricity. The fuse wire is located in a special cavity (8). Remember to insulate the base (9) and install a contact at the bottom (10).

To protect the filament from oxidation and burnout, you must evacuate the air from the bulb or fill it with inert gas or nitrogen under low (much lower than atmospheric) pressure. Include a thin glass tube in the design that will allow you to create a partial vacuum inside. After this process is complete, you can heat the end of the tube with a torch and squeeze it off with tongs to seal it.

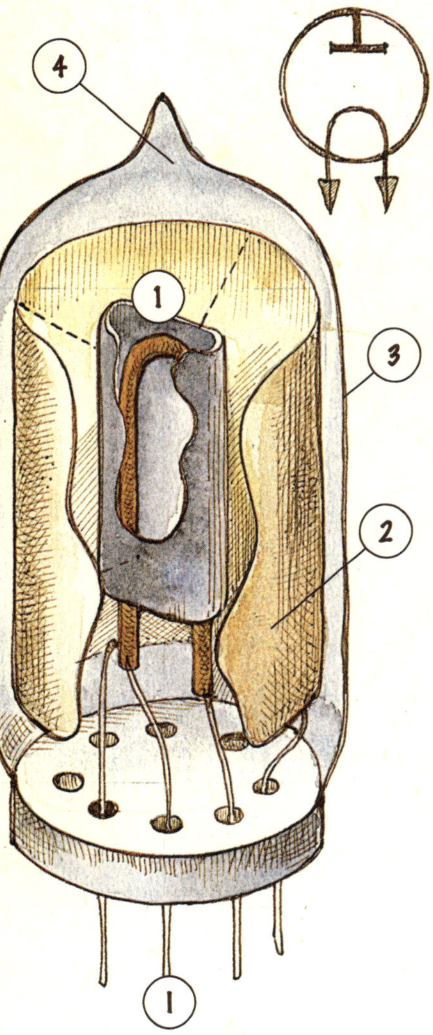

VACUUM TUBE

This is an electronic device that works by controlling the intensity of the flow of electrons moving in a vacuum. The simplest electro-vacuum tube is a diode (I). It is a sealed glass bulb with a partial vacuum inside containing two electrodes — an anode (+) and a cathode (-). When the cathode is heated, it begins to emit electrons, which carry an electric charge from the cathode to the anode. Therefore, the diode always conducts current in one direction only.

The three-electrode triode (II) is a more complicated tube. If a voltage-carrying third electrode, a fine wire grid, is placed between the cathode and the anode, it allows you to control the flow of electrons. This means that the signal can be regulated or amplified.

To build a radio transmitter with enough power to transmit a signal, you need triodes capable of carrying large currents. Such high-power transmitting triodes become very hot when in operation, so they need a good air (and in some cases, water) cooling system.

1. *Cathode*
2. *Anode*
3. *Glass bulb*
4. *Tube for evacuating air*
5. *Grid*

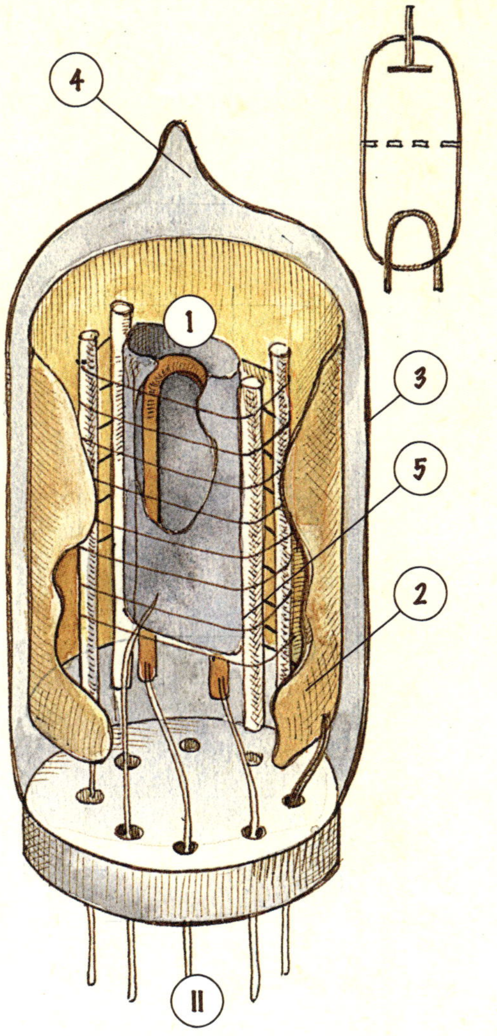

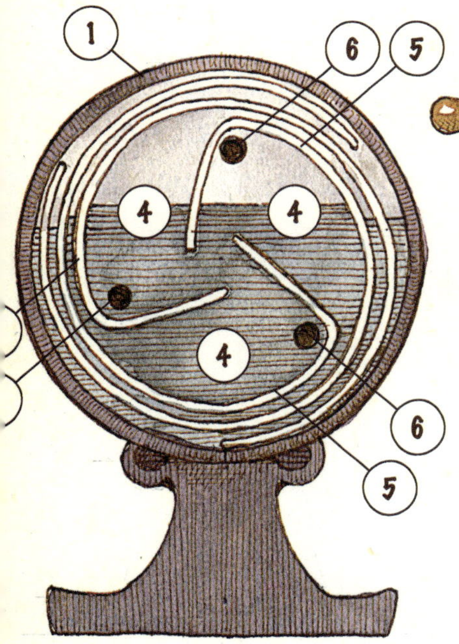

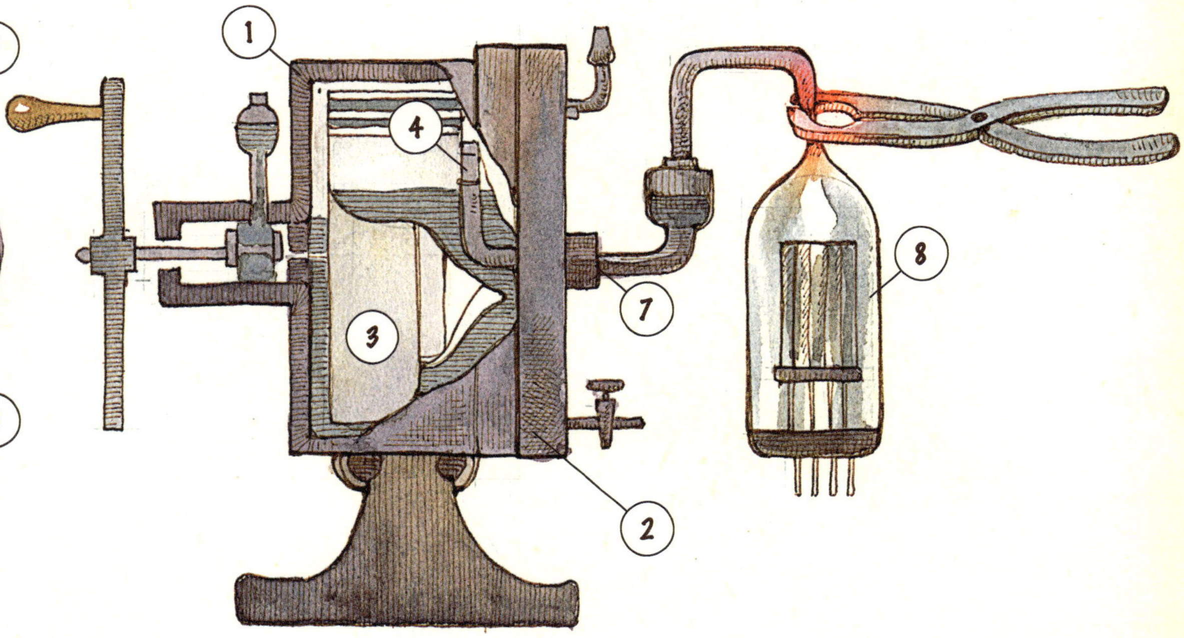

MERCURY PUMP

The pump consists of a cast-iron casing (1) that is halfway filled with mercury. The front section is covered with glass (2) so the process can be monitored. Inside the casing, a porcelain drum (3) rotates around an axis with three chambers inside (7). Each of the three chambers has a channel with an outlet to the outside (4) and an opening (5) into which pumped air is sucked from a tube (6) connected to the bulb.

As the drum rotates, air is drawn into the chambers Then the opening dips under the surface of the mercury and air is forced out through the side channels into the casing space above the mercury. The mercury pump does not work at atmospheric pressure but only with a partial vacuum inside. Therefore, an ordinary gear pump (page 162) must be used in tandem and will do the preliminary work of pumping out most of the air.

ELECTRONICS & SOLDERING

Electronics is a field of engineering that allows you to create a variety of automatic devices that control and manage electrical current. The main components of electronics are active elements, i.e., vacuum tubes. But they cannot work without their simple component parts, such as capacitors, resistors and inductors.

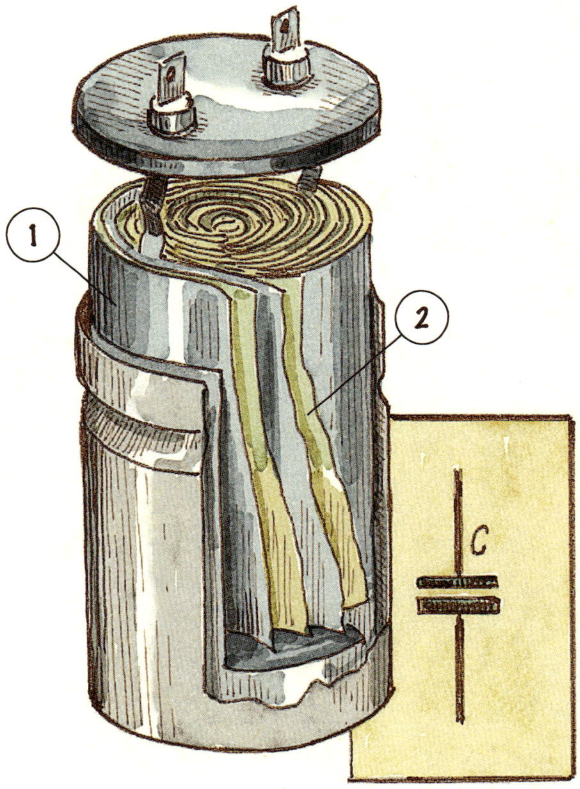

CAPACITOR

Capacitors accumulate an electrical charge. They are composed of two conductive plates (1) separated by a dielectric (2) — an insulator that does not conduct electricity (such as a thin layer of glass, mica, ceramics or even just air). When the plates are connected to a voltage source, the capacitor begins to accumulate an electrical charge. The capacitance determines the maximum charge the capacitor can hold. To release the stored charge, that is, to discharge the capacitor, you must connect a load to it. In doing so, the capacitor can give off a very short but powerful electrical impulse. The capacitor is used in electrical circuits as an energy storage unit, a filter and as part of an antiresonant circuit (in combination with inductors).

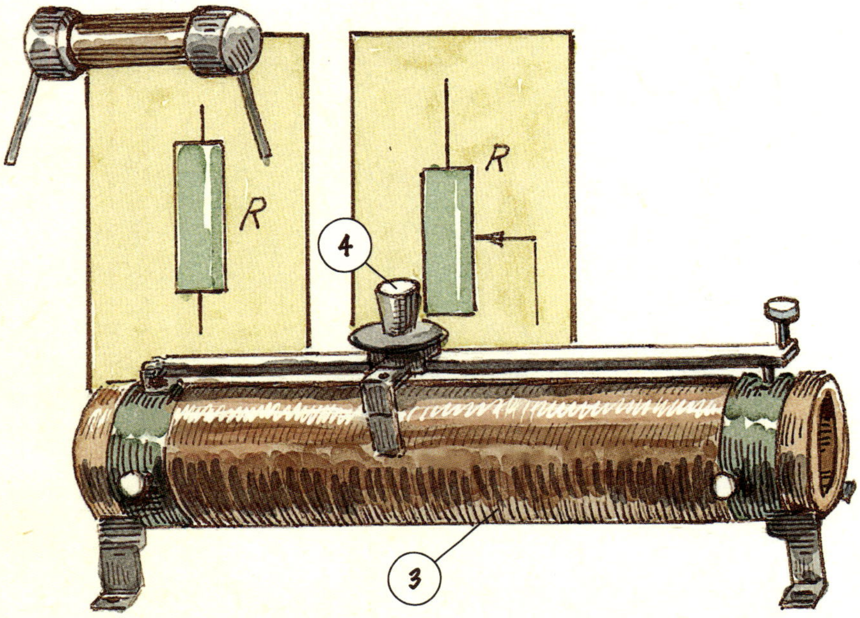

RESISTOR

Resistors create resistance to an electric current. When included in a series circuit, a resistor reduces amperage by converting electrical energy into thermal energy. A simple resistor is a short length of narrow wire surrounded by insulation (3). You can make one by winding a steel wire around a ceramic tube. Resistors can be fixed or variable. In the latter, a variable wiper-type contact (4) allows the effective length of resistor wire to be easily changed and, consequently, the strength of the current in the connected circuit. Resistors are used in electrical circuits to regulate currents and voltages.

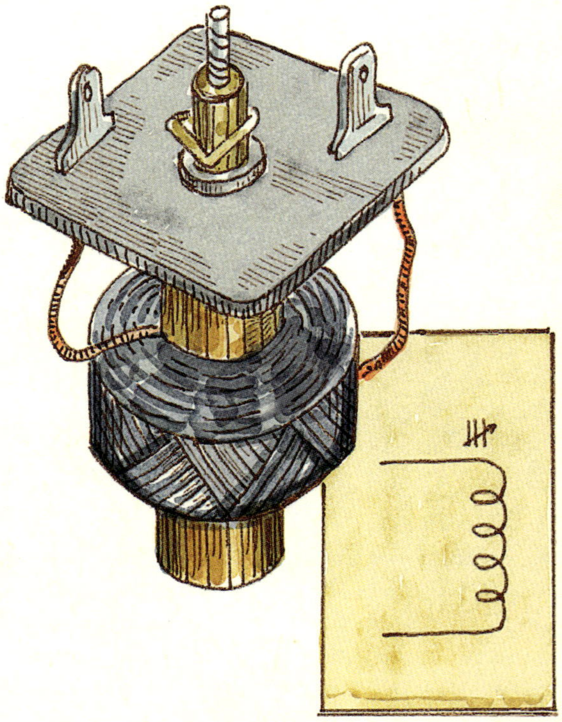

INDUCTOR

If you wind an electric wire around a metallic core or even just on a paper tube, you get an inductor. When current flows through the inductor, it stores energy — not as electrical charge, as a capacitor does, but as a magnetic field. When the power supply is switched off, it releases that energy into the circuit. An inductor has a different resistance to direct and alternating current, and the higher the frequency of the alternating current, the higher the resistance of the coil. Inductors in electrical circuits are used as energy storage units, filters, electromagnets, parts of transformers and antiresonant circuits (in combination with capacitors).

ELECTRIC SOLDERING IRON

This is a device for joining two parts together using a fusible metal alloy. The heat source can be anything — fire or electric. The main working element of an electric soldering iron is the nozzle, or soldering tip (1). This is a rod made of copper (page 110), which has a high thermal conductivity. The tip is placed in a metal tube (2) that should be wrapped with mica for electrical insulation. A steel wire should be wound over the layer of mica and clay coated on top to protect it from oxidation. This entire structure comprises the heating element (3).

The handle (4) should be made of wood to keep your hands from getting burned. As a current runs through the steel spiral, it heats the tube and the soldering tip, reaching temperatures of up to 300°C. At such high temperatures, the solder melts and can be spread over the joint of two parts so that when it cools it solidifies and connects them securely.

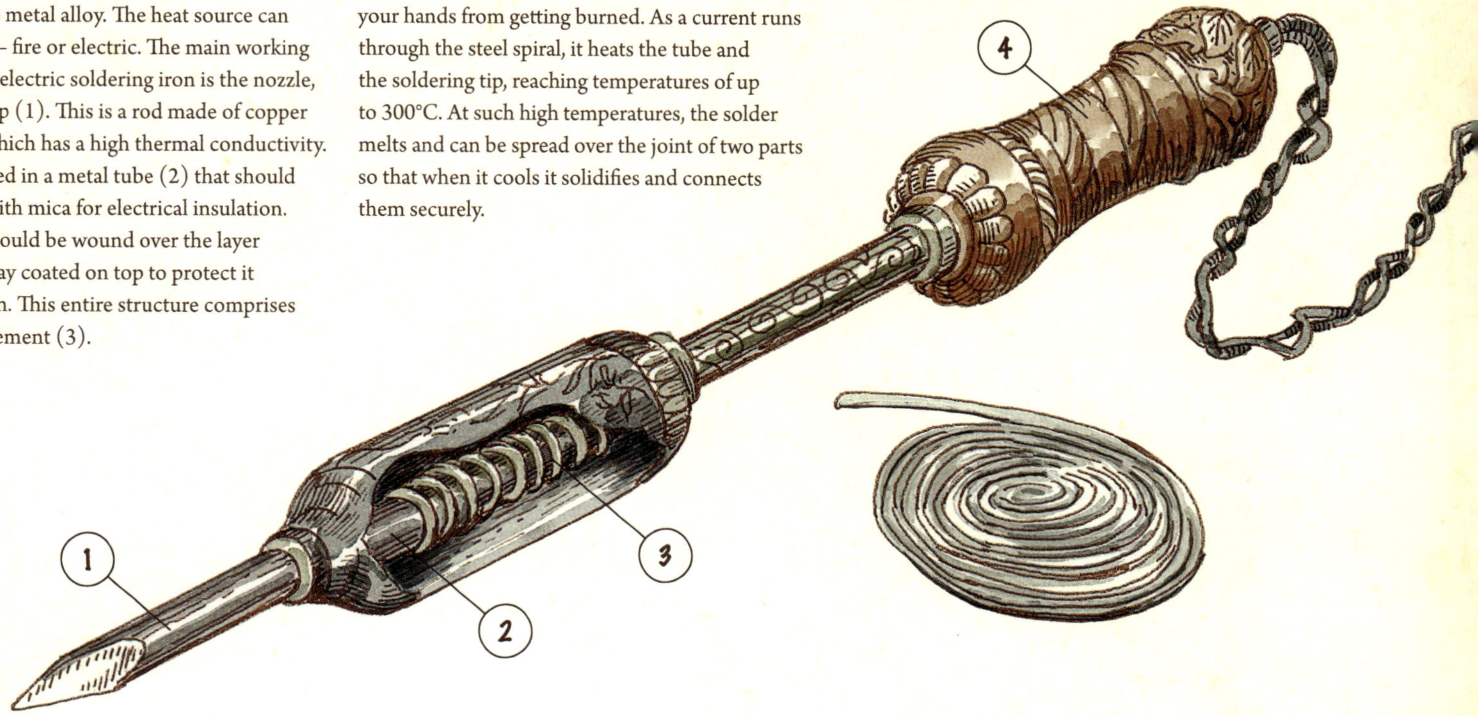

SOLDER AND FLUX

But for the soldering iron to be effective, you need a solder — a substance that melts at a relatively low temperature. Try, for instance, an alloy of tin (60%) and lead (40%). In order to make a good solder joint, the solder must bond tightly to the surface of the two parts, which must be clean and free from rust or oxidation. Use flux, a fusible mixture that coats the surface of the part in a thin layer, to clean these surfaces and protect them from oxidation when heated. The simplest option is rosin, a solid product of pine resin obtained by heating the resin to 100–160°C. The rosin can be dissolved in alcohol to improve its cleaning properties.

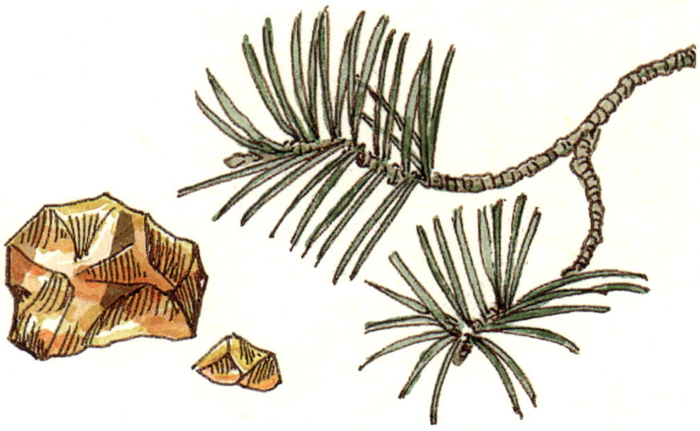

WIRED-CIRCUIT BOARDS

When you assemble any electrical device, you can use copper wire to connect the various components. But it is much more convenient to place them on a wired-circuit board — a hard surface, such as dry wood, covered in a layer of copper foil. The parts are attached to this foil by soldering, and slots in the copper layer can be used to connect the electronic parts in any way you want.

SOLDERING A RESISTOR

Press the free wire of the resistor into the contact pad with the heated tip of the soldering iron. Hold the wire solder under the tip and melt 2–3 mm onto the pad. It is very important to hold the tip on the pad for a couple seconds after adding the solder. During this time, the solder will evenly spread on the pad and the resistor wire.

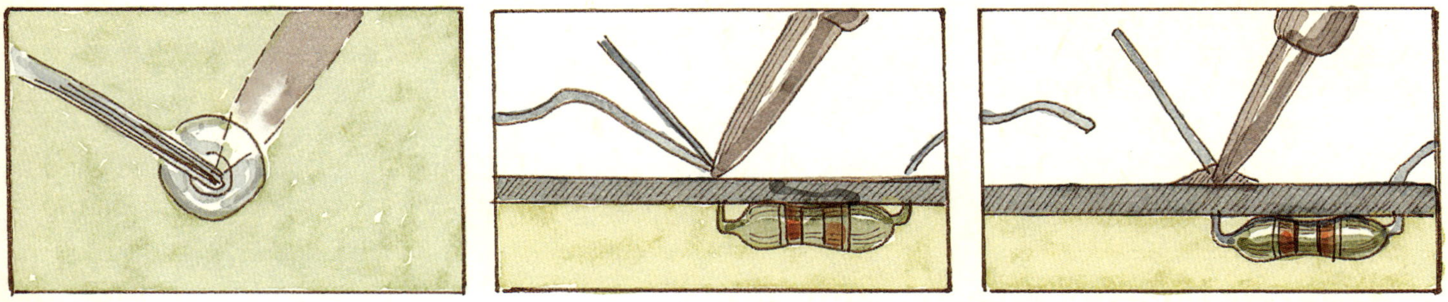

SOLDERING WIRES

Strip the oxide film off the wires with a sharp knife. Otherwise, you will get an uneven solder. Lubricate the surface of the wire with an alcoholic rosin. Pick up a decent blob of solder with the heating tip and apply a thin layer to the surface of the wire.

Twist the wires together. If you solder them overlapping without twisting, the connection will not be strong. Brush them again with a little rosin. Solder the wires once more.

POWER PLANTS

The demand for energy will only continue to rise, and at some point, you'll need to build a giant generator: a power plant. Large generators require a large amount of resources, which can be scarce, so it's better to use renewable sources that don't cause damage to the surrounding environment. That's why the ideal energy source is the sun, with power that can be harnessed even a few minutes after the sun is no longer visible.

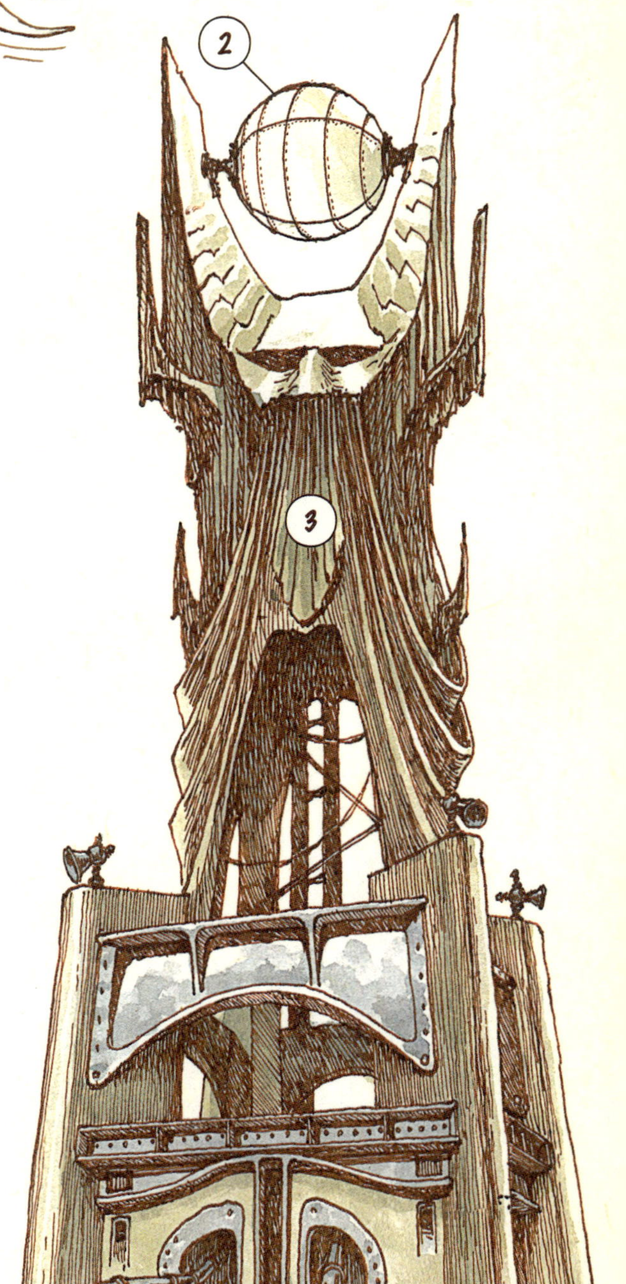

Power plants convert thermal energy into mechanical energy and mechanical energy into electrical energy. You can produce heat that turns water into steam by burning coal, oil or gas. This steam, in turn, will rotate the turbines, which are connected to the rotors of electric generators (page 194).

You can also build a solar power plant that will convert solar radiation into electrical energy. It operates on the principle of collecting concentrated solar energy using mirrors. Place the water tank (1) on top of the tower. Arrange hundreds of mirrors, called heliostats (2), around the tower so the sun's rays are directed towards the tank. The water inside will heat up and turn into steam. If the mirrors are fixed, they will be able to accurately focus the sun's rays for only a few hours a day, so make them mobile to track the sun so they can make the most of the daylight. Paint the water tank black to better absorb heat radiation. The coating should be heat-resistant but not heat-insulating, such as copper blackened over a fire.

To maximize energy efficiency, fill the tower with a mixture of sodium and potassium nitrate (page 124). This substance has a greater heat capacity and higher melting point than water, so it will retain the heat and continue producing steam long after the sun has dipped below the horizon. Circulate the molten mixture through double-walled pipes (3), forming a large furnace and minimizing heat loss. As the steam leaves the heat exchanger/steam generator (4), it goes through the pipe (5) to the steam turbine (6), a device that converts the thermal energy of steam into the mechanical energy of rotation.

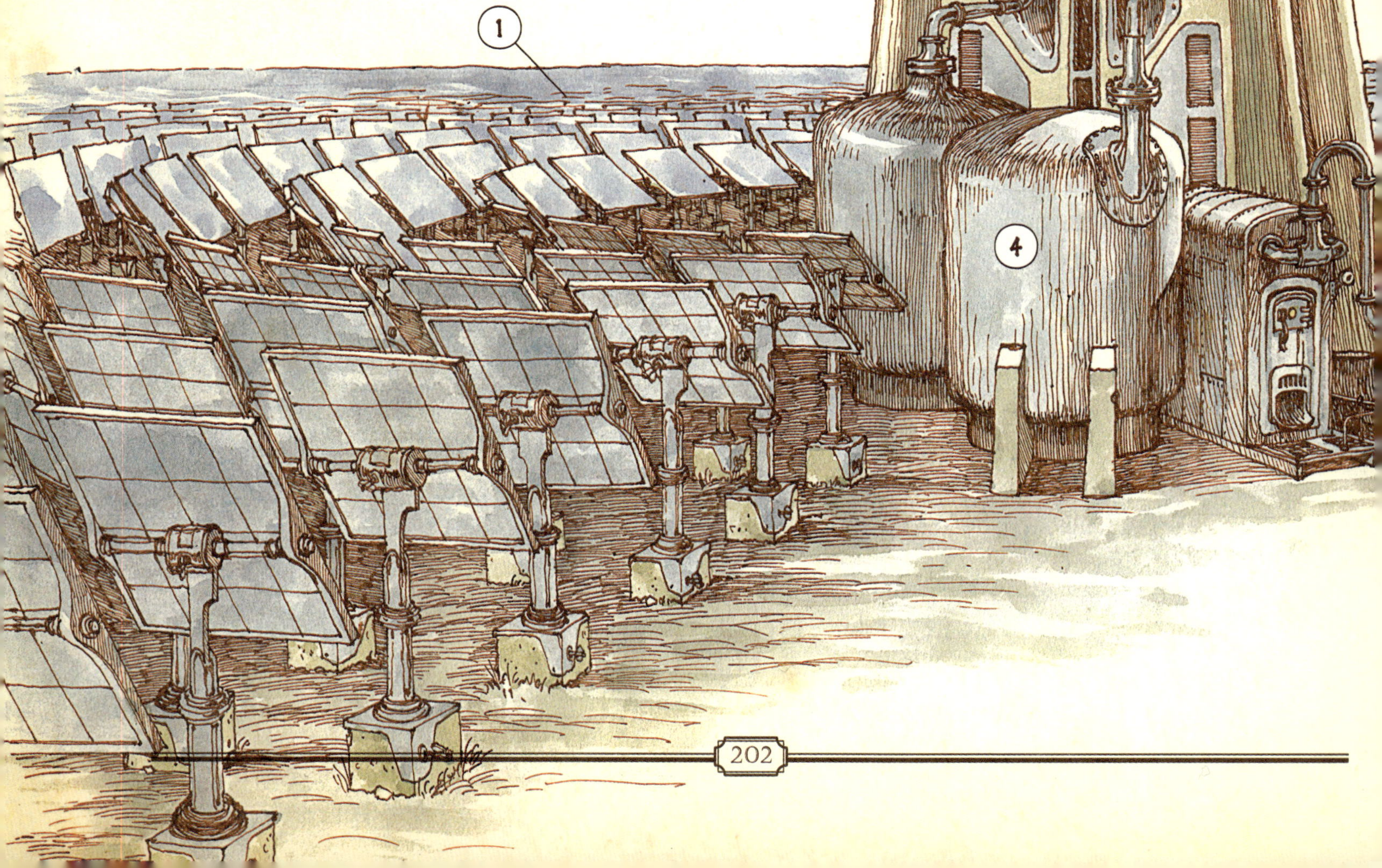

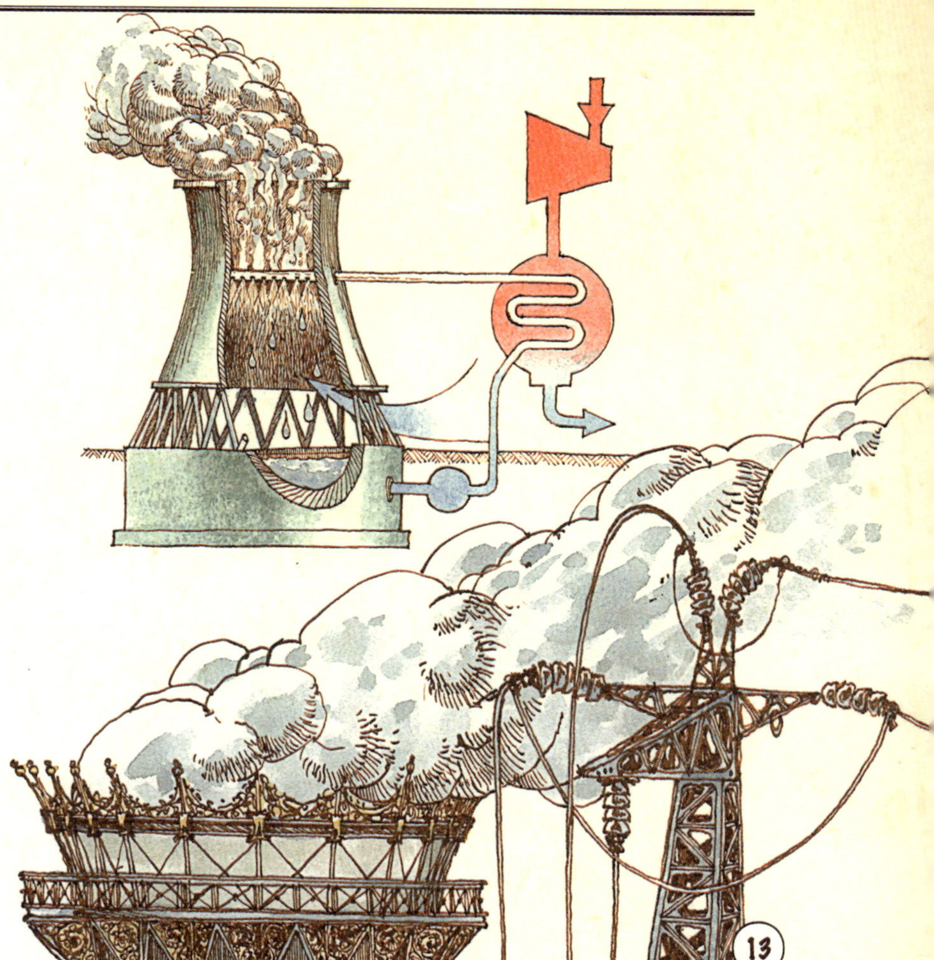

STEAM TURBINE

The main parts of the steam turbine are fixed nozzles and rotor blades (7) mounted on a movable rotor (8). Steam enters the first row of nozzles, where it expands and pushes a row of rotor blades. The rotor spins, and the steam then enters the next row of nozzles and the next row of rotor blades. This happens until the steam cools down. Then it leaves the turbine through a pipe (10) and enters a special receiving device — a steam condenser (9), where it turns back into liquid and is pumped back into the tank.

The turbine shaft is coupled with the shaft (11) of the electric generator (12) (page 194). Electricity is fed to a series of step-up transformers (page 196) and then to a high-voltage power line (13). And from there, with the help of step-down transformers and distribution substations, to people's homes.

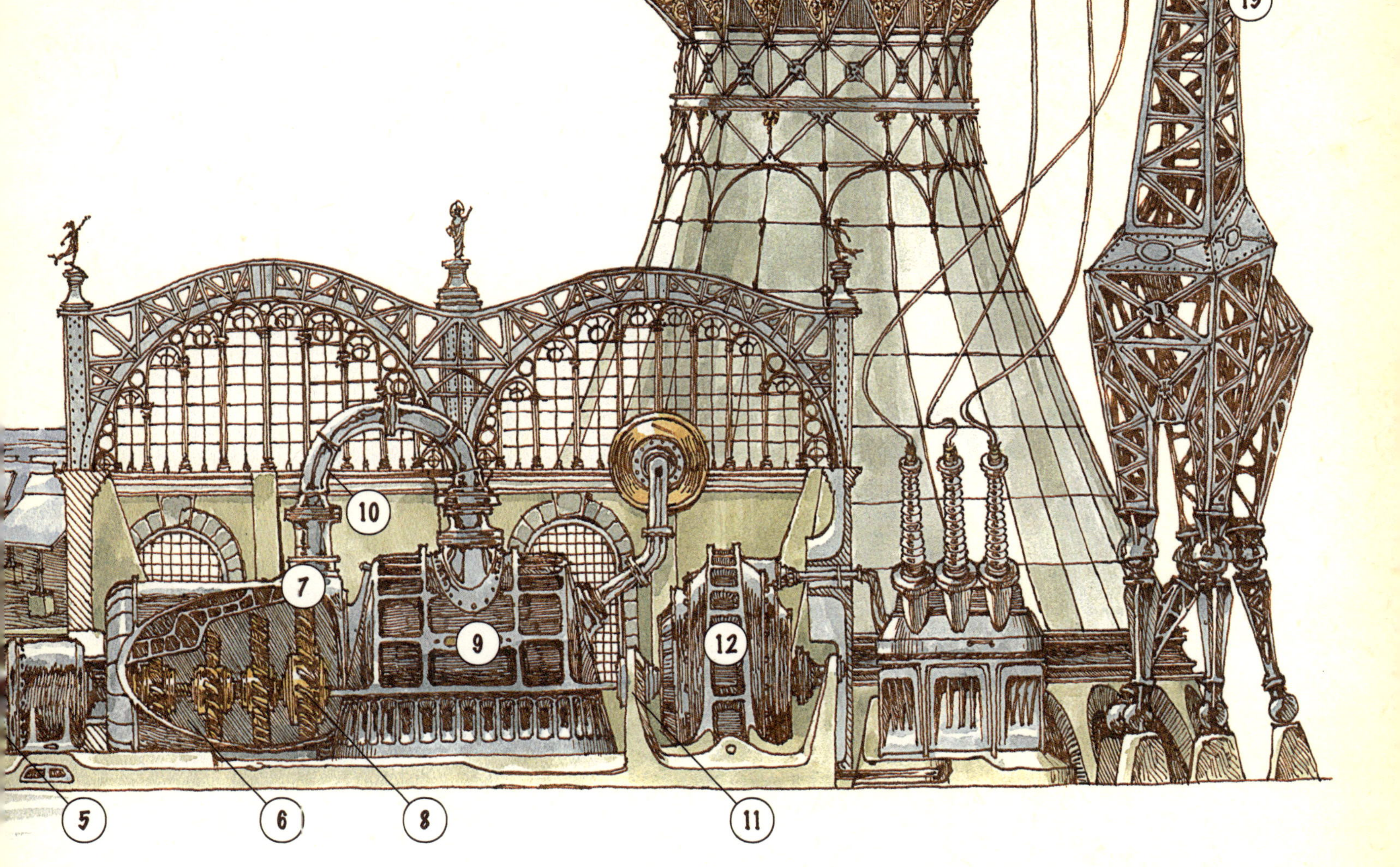

COOLING TOWERS

Not all thermal energy can be converted into mechanical energy. The steam condenser (9) must be constantly cooled; otherwise, there will be no water left for the heat from the molten salt to turn into steam. Therefore, a constant stream of cold water is supplied to the condenser, and a stream of hot water is discharged.

This water needs to be cooled, and one of the most efficient ways to do this is through cooling towers. The hot water is sprayed through nozzles at the base of the tower, and the steam rises along with the flow of cold air. Along the way, some of the steam condenses and flows down the walls of the tower into a cold water tank and is reused in the condenser cooling circuit.

SAILING

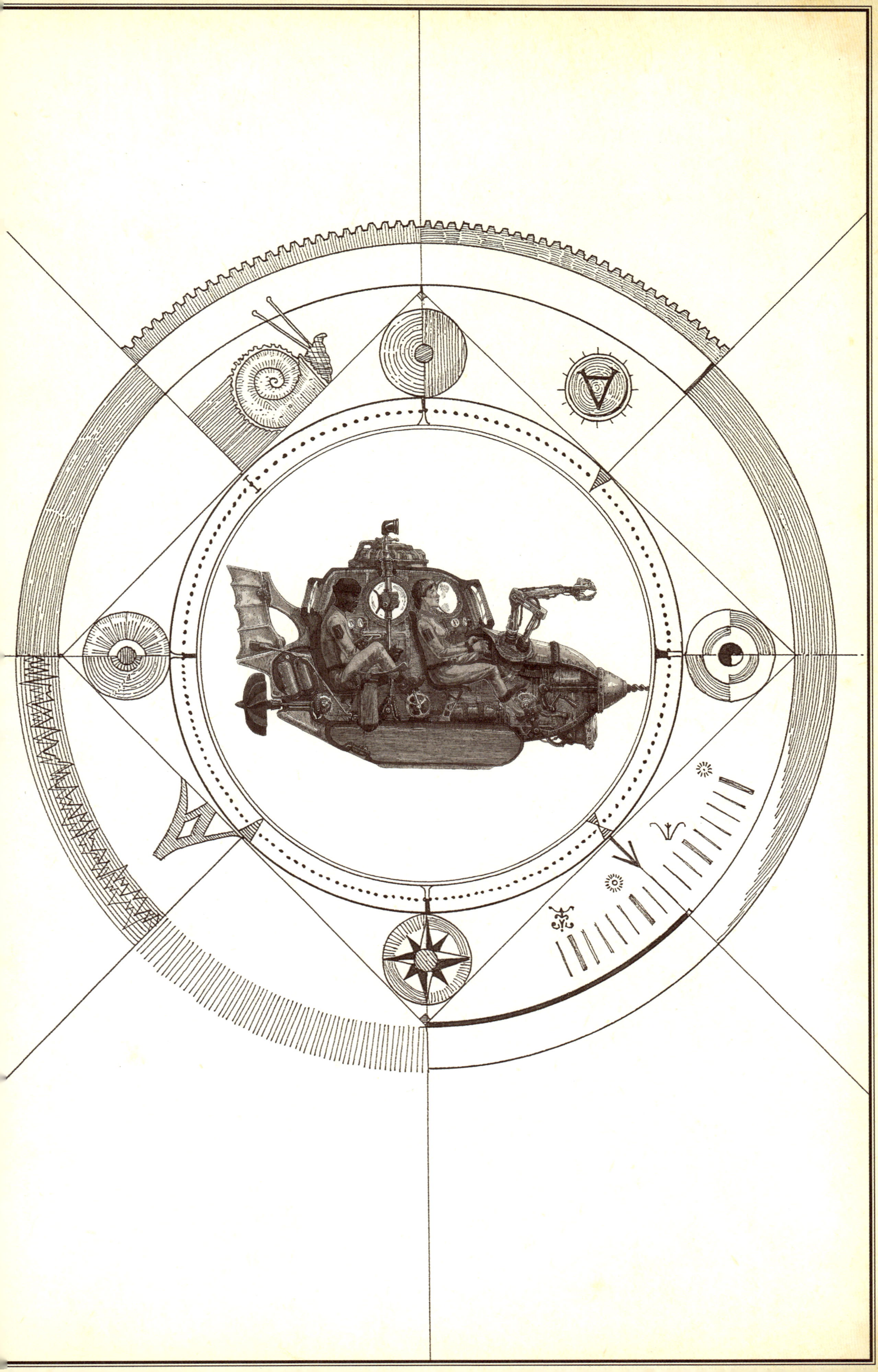

COMPASS & NAVIGATION

When you're surrounded by water on all sides and the only distinguishable landmark is the horizon, you need navigational tools to determine your position and plot a path forward. Without them, a single cloudy day that obscures the position of the sun, moon and stars is all it will take to throw you off course.

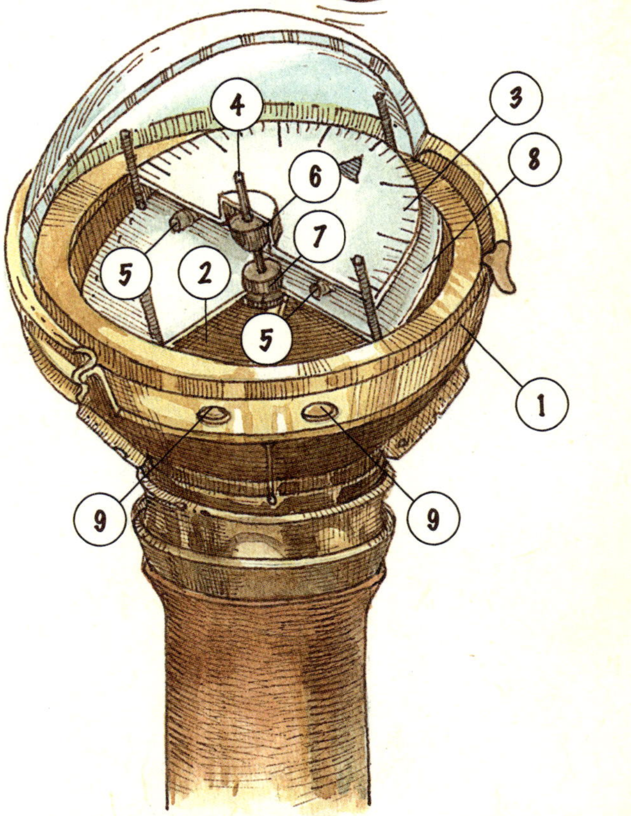

COMPASS

You can't maintain the proper heading without a compass. The arrow, a small magnet, is always aligned with the planet's magnetic field in the North-South direction. You need a liquid-filled bronze or aluminum hemisphere (but not iron, which will distort the reading) (1) filled with compass fluid (2) — petroleum oil (page 126), an ethyl alcohol solution (page 118) or glycerin with water. Floating on the surface of the liquid is the compass dial (3) — a circular scale with 360 declination marks rotating around a pivot (4). Fix permanent magnets (5) on opposite sides of the pivot and make sure they are both polarized in the same direction (page 192). The compass float (6) relieves pressure on the axle support passing through its center and is fixed on a stone footplate (7).

The thrust bearing is mounted on a stationary disc with a heading line (8), which always points towards the bow of the boat. Two holes in the lower part of the compass body allow liquid to flow into the expansion chamber (9) to compensate for changes in pressure and temperature. When the boat changes course, the compass dial remains in position thanks to the magnets. The offset of the heading line relative to the compass dial determines the direction of movement of the boat relative to magnetic north.

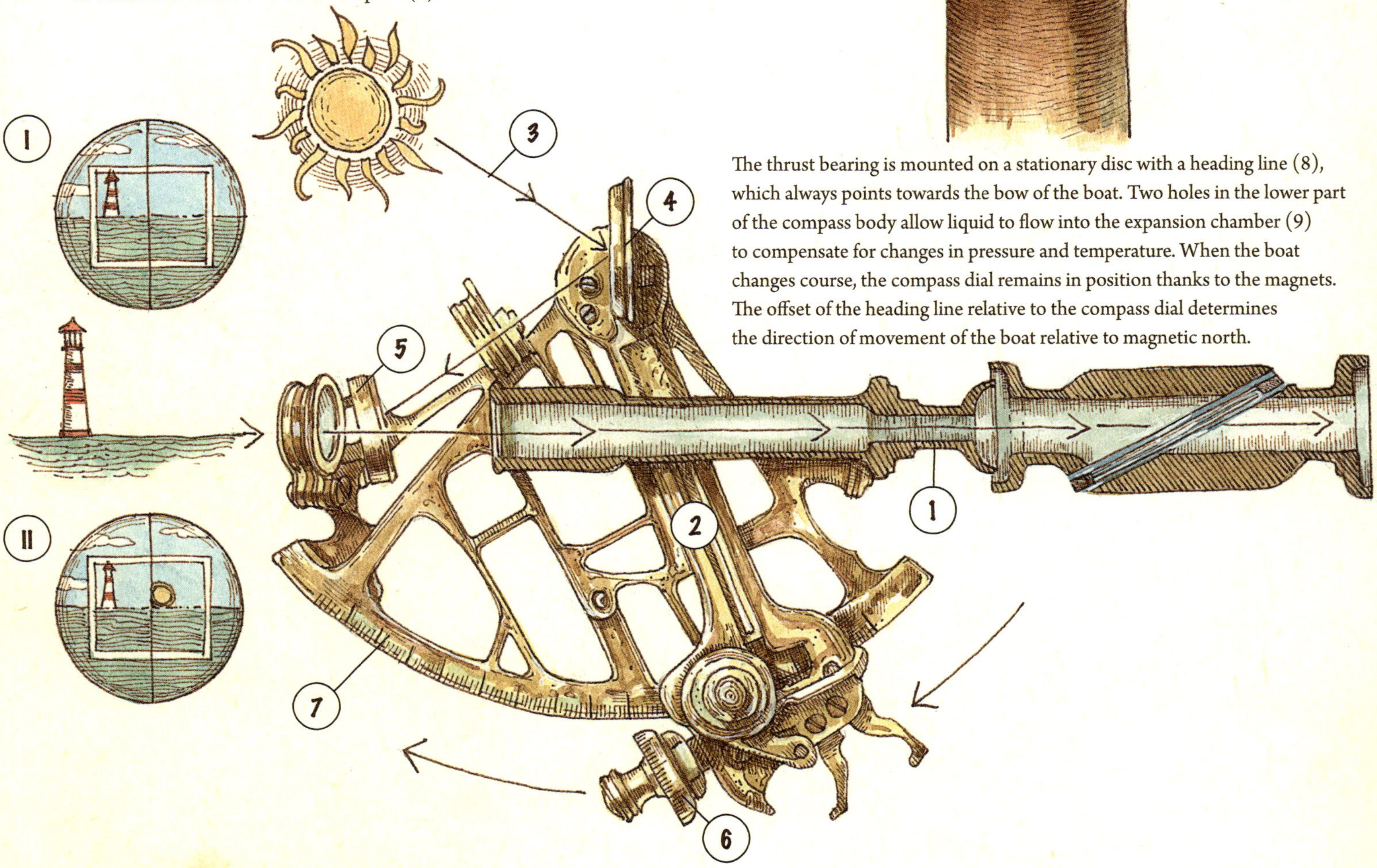

DETERMINING LATITUDE

One half of the problem of finding your location is determining your latitude, which can be found by measuring the angle of celestial objects above the horizon. Sextants measure the height of the sun or stars relative to the horizon, as well as the horizontal and vertical angles between landmarks. To keep both the astral body and the horizon in your sight, you'll need two mirrors: one fixed and one moving. The fixed mirror should be only partially silvered to allow light to pass through. Align the spyglass (1) with the horizon (I). Move the device along the horizon line and swing the rotary ruler (2) until it points directly at the astral body. Light rays (3) bounce off the first mirror (4) and are reflected in the half-transparent mirror (5), in which the horizon line is still visible.

Then bring the lower edge of the astral body to the horizon (II) by slowly twisting the screw of the micrometer drum (6). Read the degree indicated on the sextant arc (7) and record the time. The size of the angle compared to the exact time at which the measurement is taken will allow you to calculate the latitude. But before you set off on your voyage, you'll have to compile an astronomical reference book: pick one location and measure the angular height of the sun at noon several times throughout the year. The sun reaches its noontime peak at the summer solstice and the lowest point at the winter solstice. The difference in the height of the sun between these dates is equal to twice the angle of inclination of the planet's axis with its orbital plane (the degree of tilt). Measure the height of the sun at noon and correct for this calendar date to calculate the latitude of your location.

DETERMINING LONGITUDE

The second component of fixing your position is longitude. As the planet rotates to give night and day, this equates to the difference in local time between your current location and a predetermined prime meridian. You can measure local noon with a sextant, but you also need to know the time at the prime meridian, which requires an extremely accurate watch (page 166) — a marine chronometer. They are distinguished from normal watches by an internal mechanism that reduces the effect of the rolling waves on the accuracy of the movement.

The chronometer has not one but two balances that oscillate in opposite directions in the same plane. Knowing that solar noon on your meridian occurs earlier or later than at the prime meridian by X minutes and the sun passes one degree in four minutes, you need to divide X by 4 to get the desired value of the longitude of your location. Once you have a radio (page 296), you can start transmitting time signals from the prime meridian. This method is accurate, and a radio is easier to make than a chronometer.

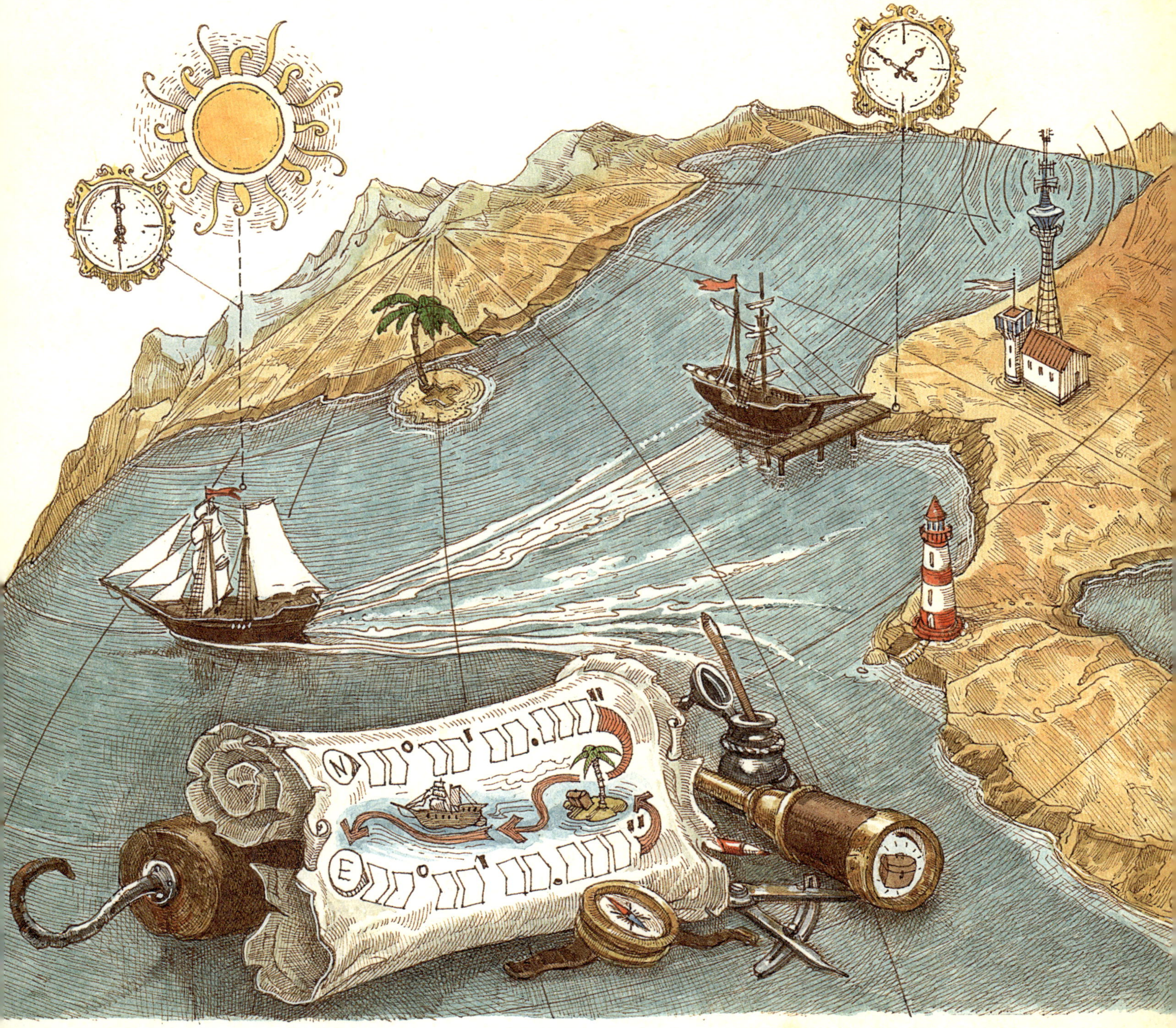

SAILS

You can put together a holistic picture of the world around you by exploring it one part at a time. But to piece together this puzzle, you'll want to move quickly and over long distances, and for that, you need a driving force. Luckily, you can create one out of thin air (literally) by harnessing the power of the wind. Sails "catch" the wind, converting its energy into forward motion that pushes the boat.

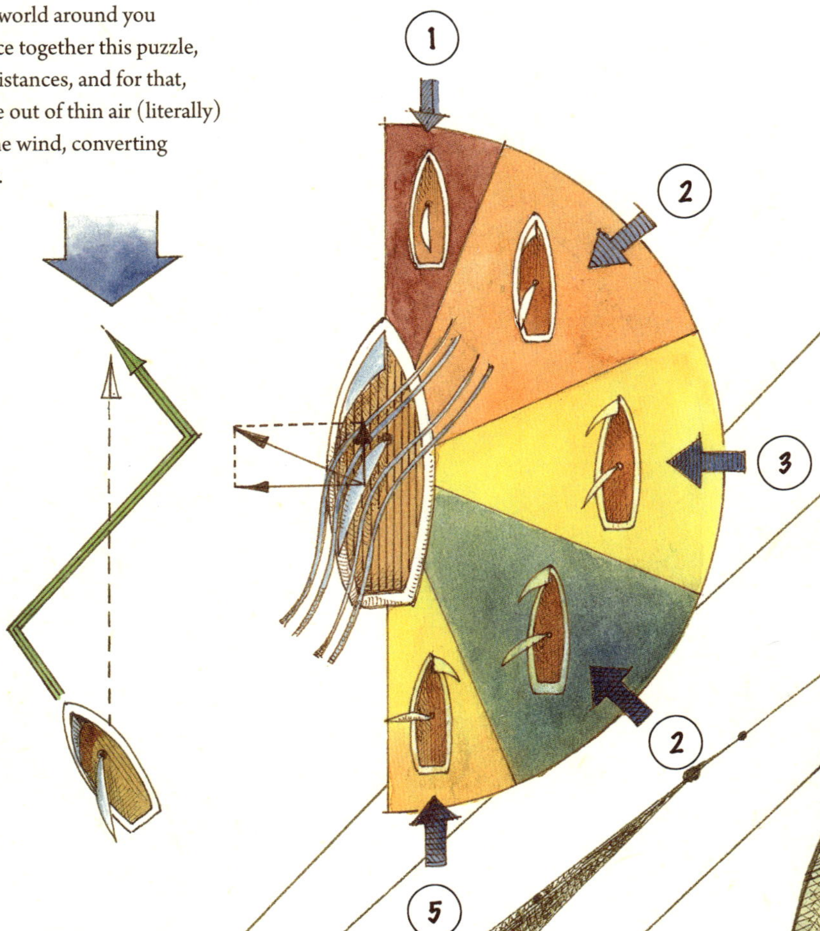

POINTS OF SAIL

The force generated by the sail is perpendicular to the direction of the wind. To move against the wind, you'll need to tack — to keep turning through the wind so that you progress upwind in a series of diagonal tracks. The direction of the wind relative to your desired course determines how you sail.

1. Sailing directly against the wind is impossible when using a sail. Turn into the wind if you want to stop the boat.
2. The wind is blowing slightly at an angle. On sharp courses, the yacht cannot go fast due to the resistance of the water.
3. The wind blows perpendicular to the direction of travel. This is the simplest course to set, suitable even for beginners out on their first independent sailing voyage.
4. The wind is blowing from the stern and from the side. This is the fastest course. Light vessels traveling along this course can exceed wind speeds.
5. The wind is blowing from the stern. This is called a "tailwind." But oddly enough, it's not the fastest way to travel: With a wind blowing from behind, the sail is unable to generate lift, and the craft cannot exceed wind speed. So don't tell sailors that you hope the wind blows their way — it will only slow them down.

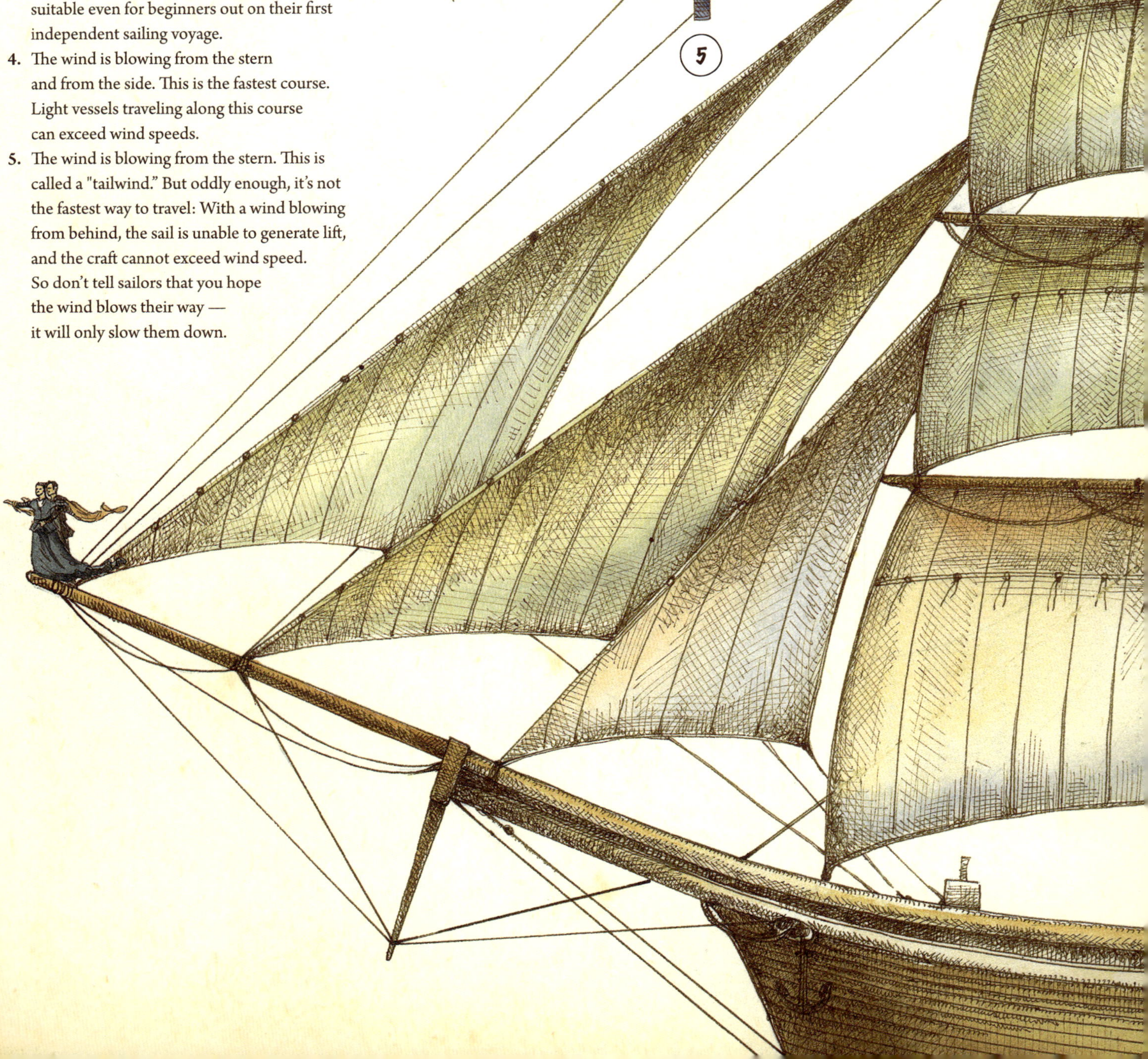

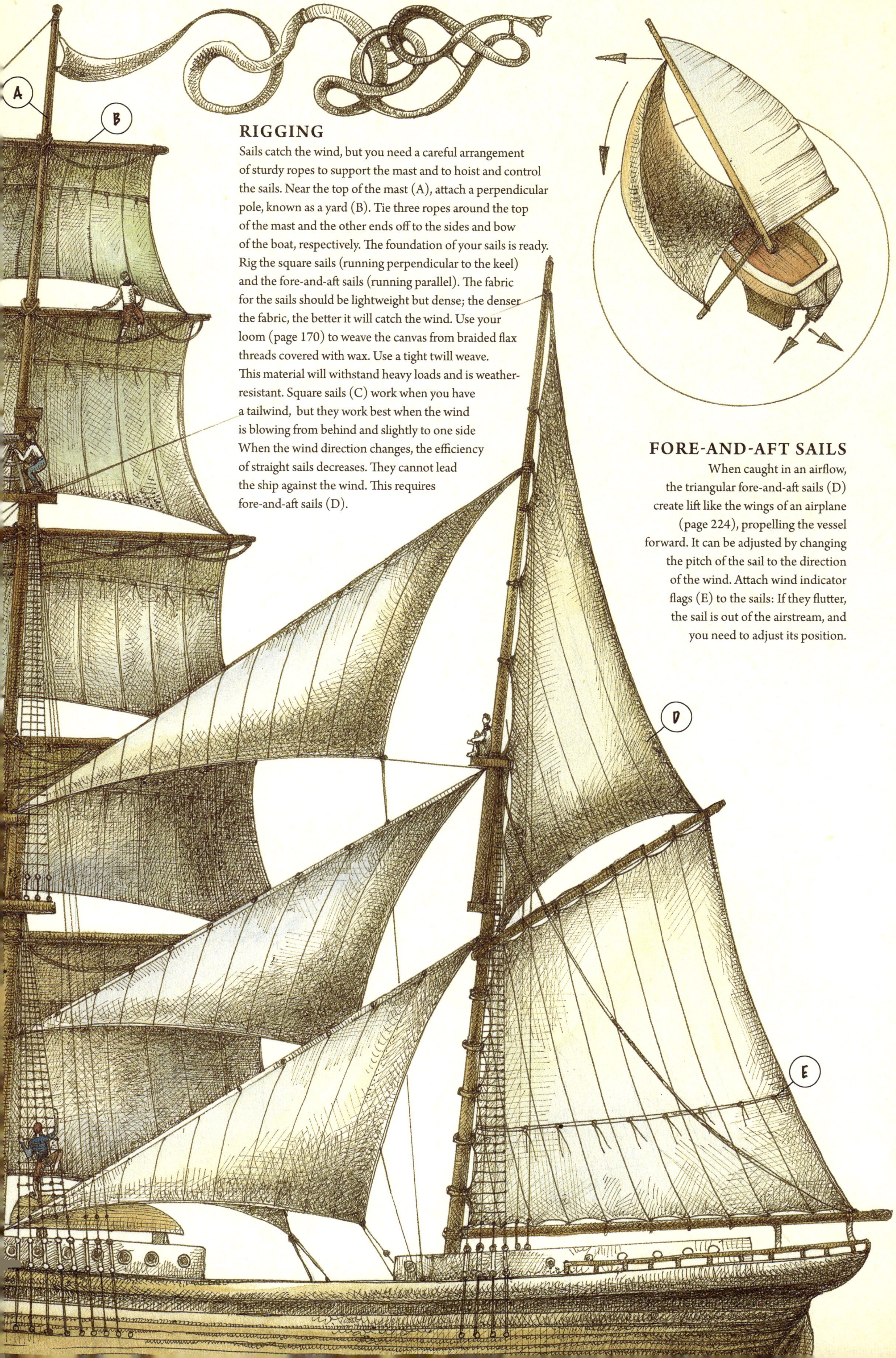

RIGGING

Sails catch the wind, but you need a careful arrangement of sturdy ropes to support the mast and to hoist and control the sails. Near the top of the mast (A), attach a perpendicular pole, known as a yard (B). Tie three ropes around the top of the mast and the other ends off to the sides and bow of the boat, respectively. The foundation of your sails is ready. Rig the square sails (running perpendicular to the keel) and the fore-and-aft sails (running parallel). The fabric for the sails should be lightweight but dense; the denser the fabric, the better it will catch the wind. Use your loom (page 170) to weave the canvas from braided flax threads covered with wax. Use a tight twill weave. This material will withstand heavy loads and is weather-resistant. Square sails (C) work when you have a tailwind, but they work best when the wind is blowing from behind and slightly to one side When the wind direction changes, the efficiency of straight sails decreases. They cannot lead the ship against the wind. This requires fore-and-aft sails (D).

FORE-AND-AFT SAILS

When caught in an airflow, the triangular fore-and-aft sails (D) create lift like the wings of an airplane (page 224), propelling the vessel forward. It can be adjusted by changing the pitch of the sail to the direction of the wind. Attach wind indicator flags (E) to the sails: If they flutter, the sail is out of the airstream, and you need to adjust its position.

BOATS & BUOYANCY

If you think you can easily learn to sail using only your intuition, hold on to your seahorses. Things aren't as obvious as they may seem. For example, sailing against the waves can give you a speed boost, and in order to prevent your ship from sinking, you'll want to load it up with cast iron.

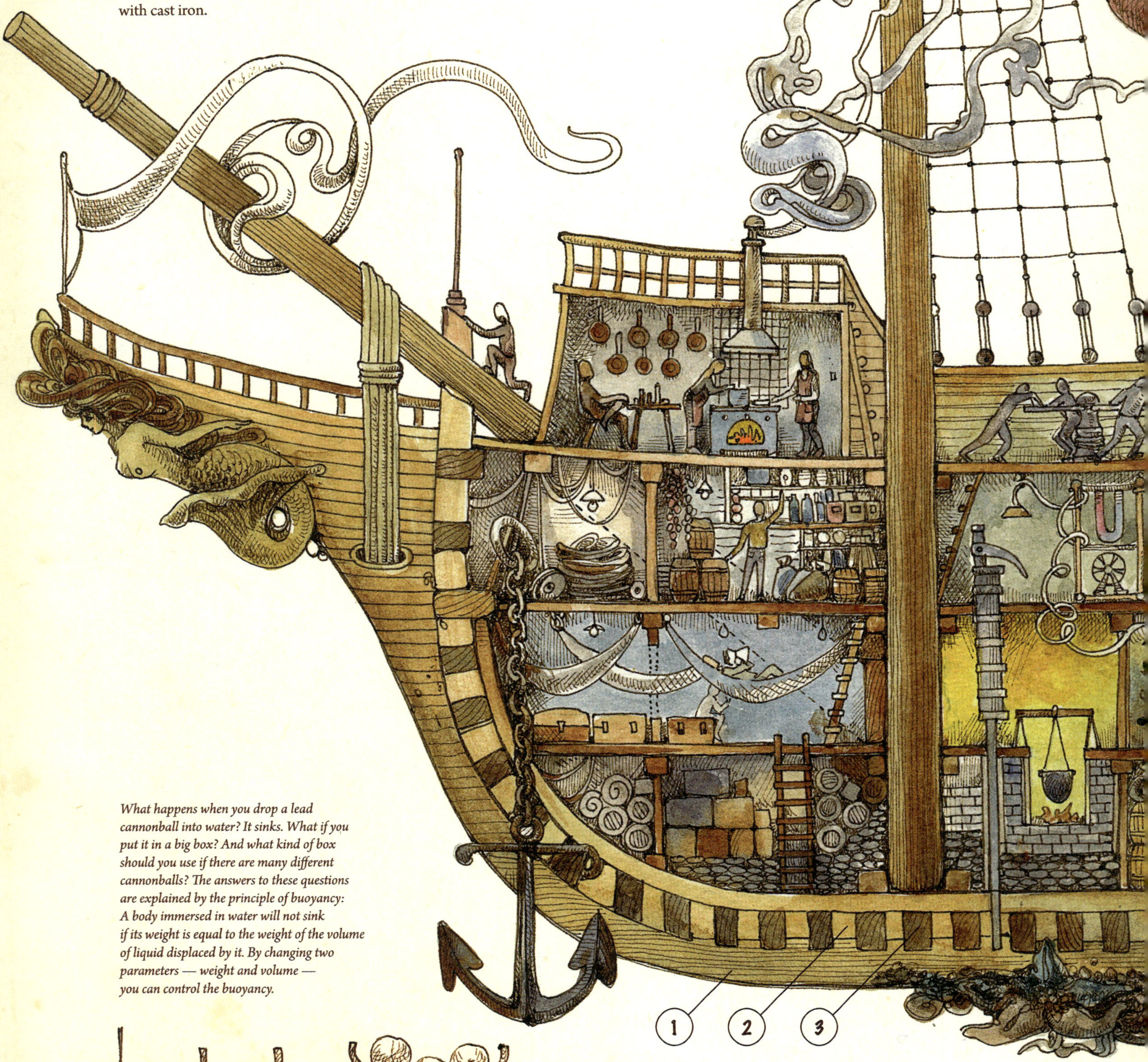

What happens when you drop a lead cannonball into water? It sinks. What if you put it in a big box? And what kind of box should you use if there are many different cannonballs? The answers to these questions are explained by the principle of buoyancy: A body immersed in water will not sink if its weight is equal to the weight of the volume of liquid displaced by it. By changing two parameters — weight and volume — you can control the buoyancy.

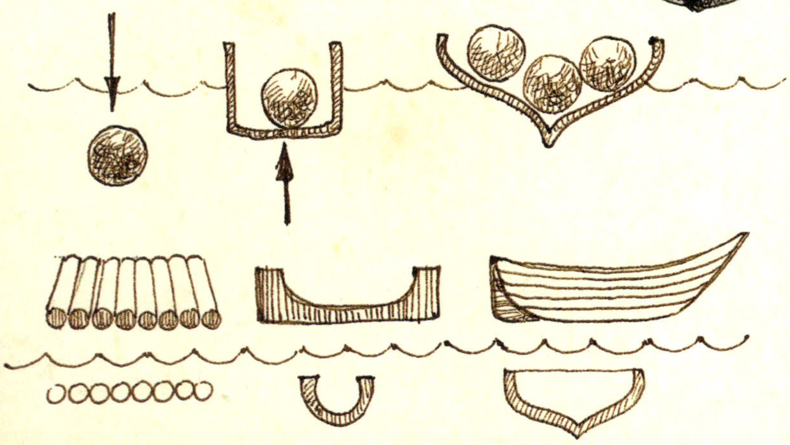

Flat-bottomed boats won't cut through rocking waves — you'll drown. To help your boat remain upright, make a hull with a keel (1) for stability. Reinforce the structure with intersecting beams running fore to aft (2) and port to starboard (3). The partitions between rooms will act like ribs, providing support as well as inner structure and insulation from the ship's hull. Use multiple layers of boards coated in a mixture of tar, sulfur (page 124) and bitumen (page 126). This substance will also protect against any bugs or mites that like to munch on wood.

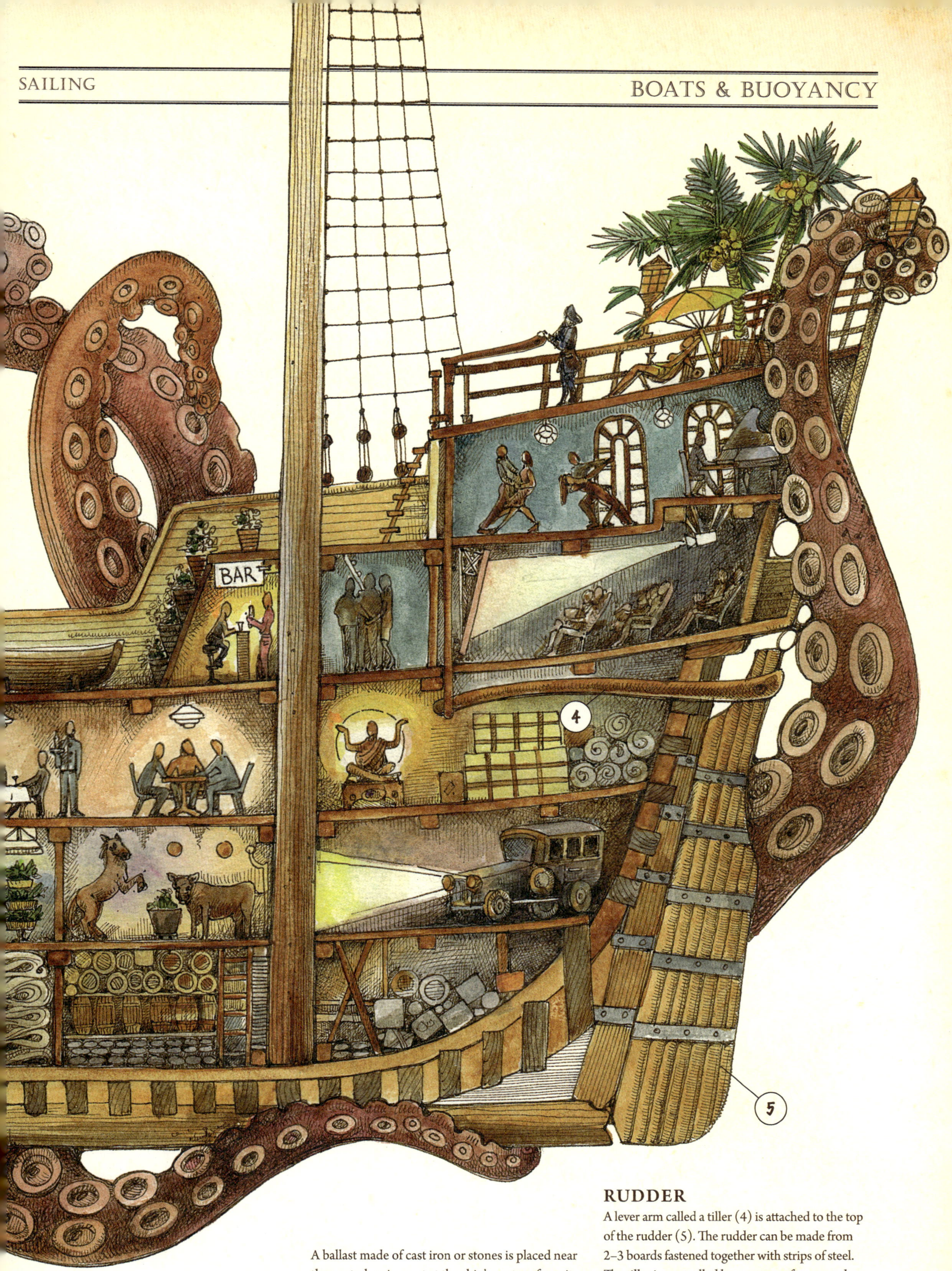

RUDDER

A lever arm called a tiller (4) is attached to the top of the rudder (5). The rudder can be made from 2–3 boards fastened together with strips of steel. The tiller is controlled by a system of ropes and pulleys, with the rope wound around a spool connected to the ship's wheel, or helm. Turning the ship's wheel pivots the tiller, which in turn forces the rudder to one side or the other. This interrupts the stream of water under the boat, changing the direction of the torque and turning the boat in the needed direction.

A ballast made of cast iron or stones is placed near the central main mast at the ship's center of gravity. Place the most weight at the center and gradually decrease it as it reaches the bow and stern. The weights can even be barrels of water. The can easily be moved to compensate for extra weight placed on the fore or aft end of the vessel. When you need to take a lot of cargo on board, just get rid of some of the ballast by draining water from the barrels.

To prevent the ship from capsizing and sinking, it must be loaded with ballast as low in the ship as possible. This will improve the ship's metacentric stability, or its ability to right itself when subjected to external forces such as waves, wind or an inept helmsman who turns the boat too sharply.

Nautical Knots

One of the most important skills any seafarer can have is the ability to tie knots. You need one knot to furl the sails, another to moor the ship and another to secure the cargo in place.

Nautical knots must be able to carry a multi-ton load while remaining easy to loosen because sailors will have to do so while many meters in the air climbing a mast, in the dark, on pitching seas and during torrential storms. There are over 500 different knots that can be used for a variety of purposes. About a dozen of them are absolutely essential for survival at sea.

Stopper knots (1, 2, 3, 7, 8) create a thicker point in the rope in order to prevent the rope from slipping through a narrow opening, such as a hole in a block.

Anchoring knots (4, 5, 6, 7,8) are used to fasten the rope to any object: for example, to moor a boat to the dock.

Bends (2, 3) join two ropes together, even those of different thicknesses.

1. Half hitch
One of the simplest knots.
Used for securing things to poles.

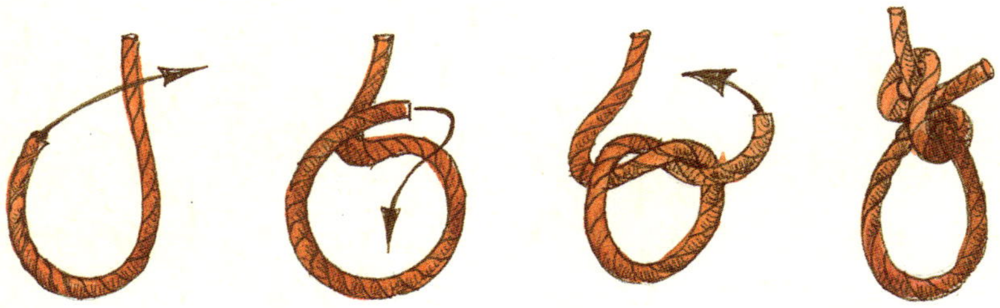

2. Bowline
Allows you to tie together cables of different thicknesses or join a thick plant fiber rope to a steel cable. It may also save a life: Bowlines are easy and secure knots to tie around people who need to be hoisted up or lowered down.

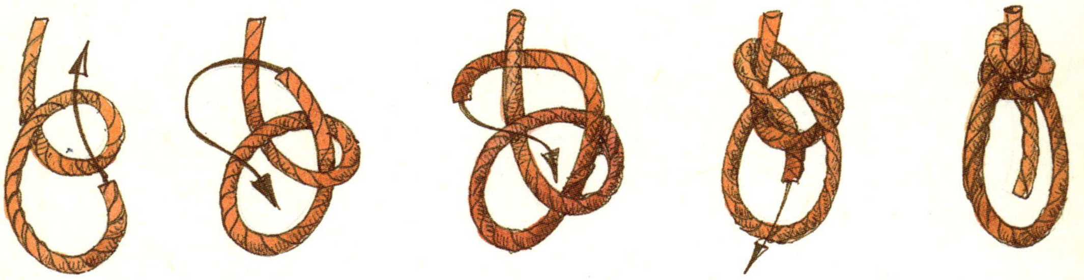

3. Figure Eight
A secure knot that won't loosen until you untie it. Can be used for belaying while descending from a height.

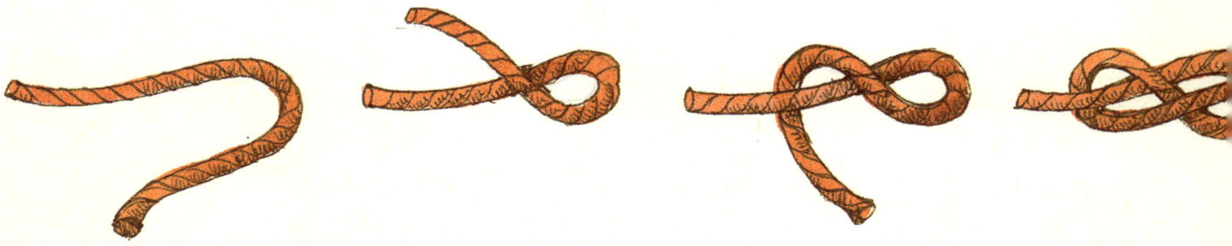

4. Clove Hitch
Used to tie lengths of thin rope, called ratlines, between a sailing ship's shrouds (rigging that holds the mast steady) to make a rope ladder. It also has non-nautical applications, such as hanging a rope between two posts for laundry, tying a bag shut or fastening a bowstring to a bow.

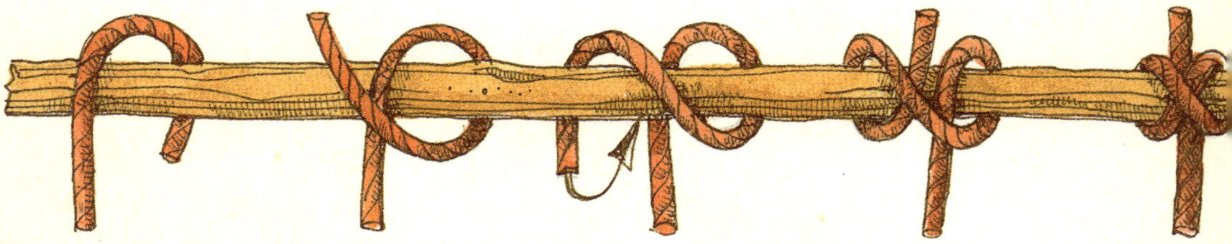

5. Cleat Hitch
A good knot for securing a rope to a cleat.

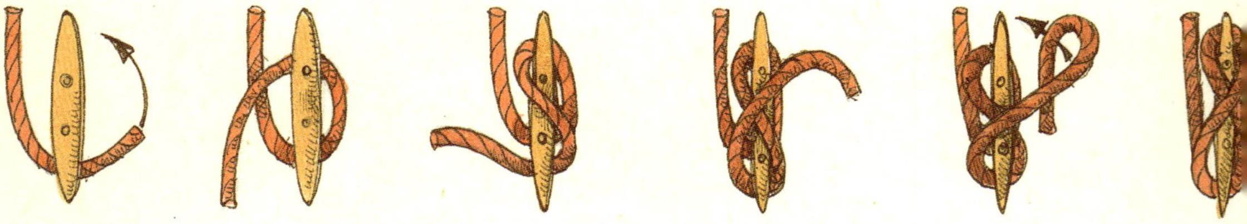

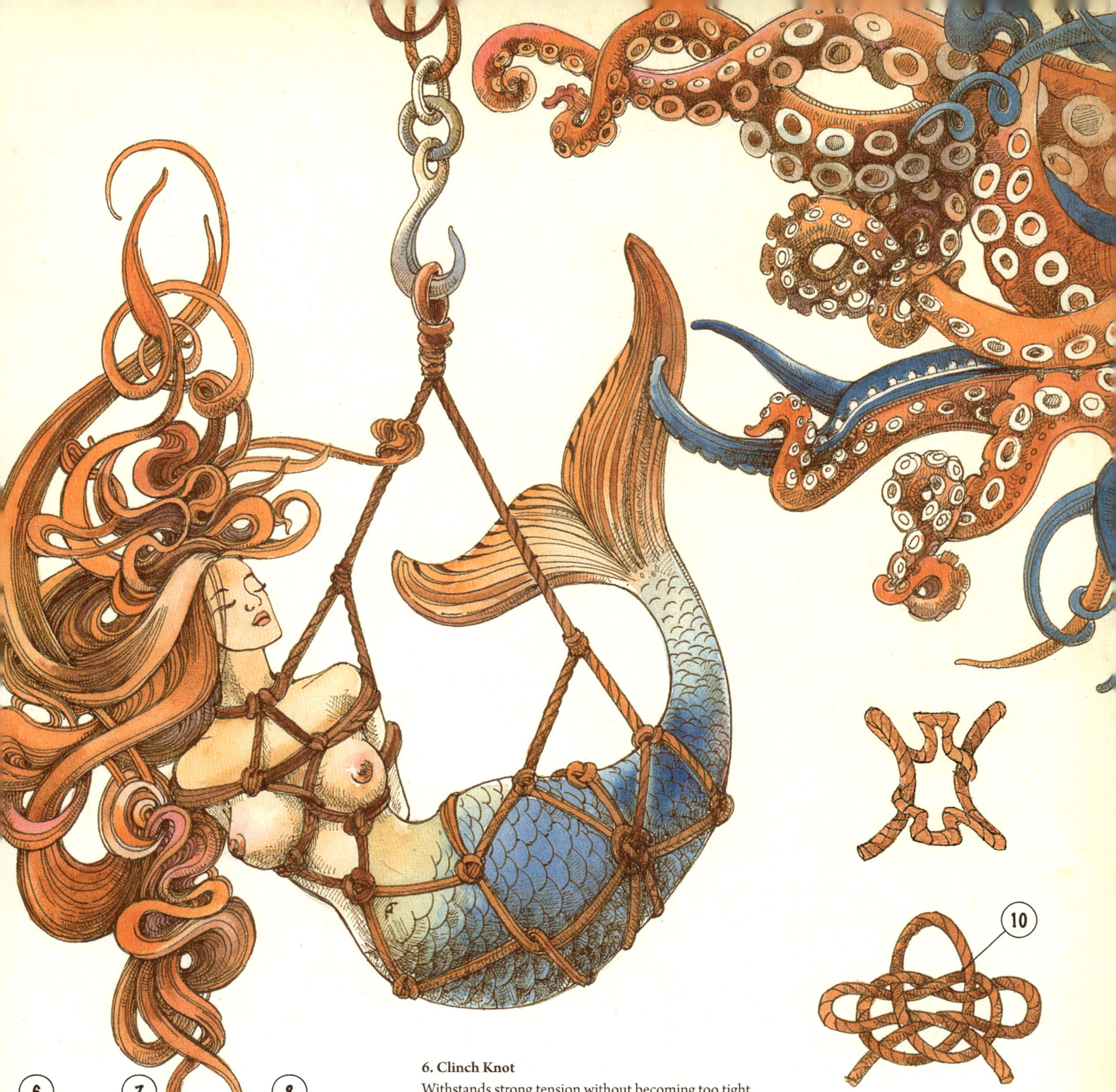

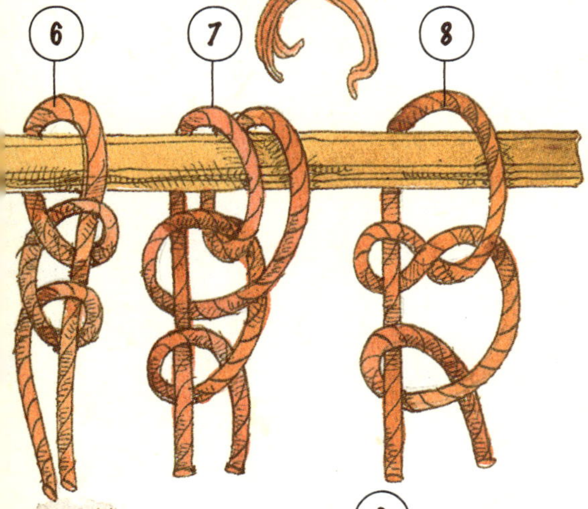

6. Clinch Knot
Withstands strong tension without becoming too tight.

7. Two Half Hitches
Used to attach a rope to an anchor.

8. Hammock knot
Easy to tie and untie, no matter how much weight it bears. Can be used to tie up mounted loads. The most suitable knot for hanging a hammock.

9. Towing Knot
Good for securing a tow line. It loosens easily under any load but won't slip or untie on its own.

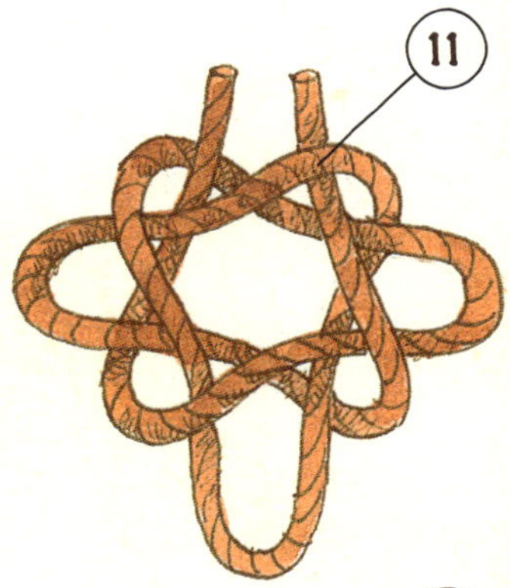

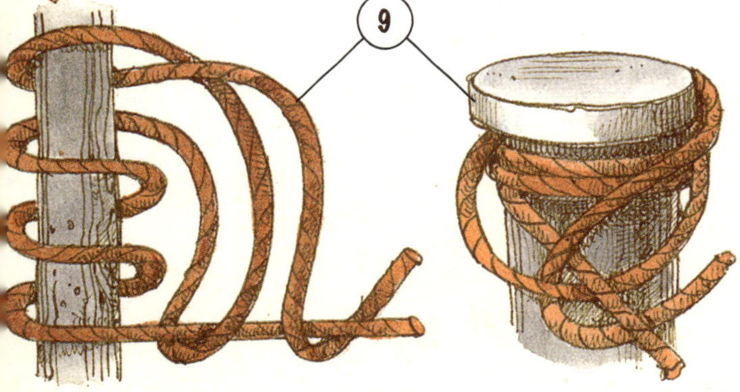

10 and 11. Masthead knot
This knot can be used to make a holster for a jug or a net for carrying objects, but make sure you have a lot of rope.

12. Running bowline
Based on a basic lasso. Can be used to catch floating logs or lift sunken objects.

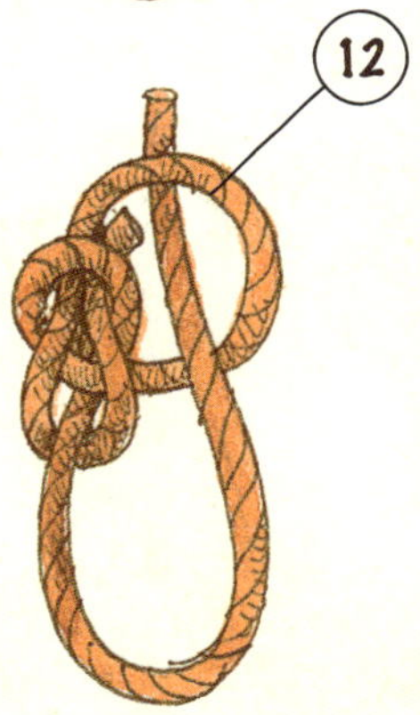

METEOROLOGY

The decision to push off from dry land and venture out into the open ocean is one that must be weighed carefully. The success of the journey and well-being of your passengers is not entirely in your hands. However, you can uncover the secrets of capricious weather patterns and choose a safer route or more suitable time to launch your vessel. To make sure you don't get caught up in the perfect storm, you need to read the signals in the sky.

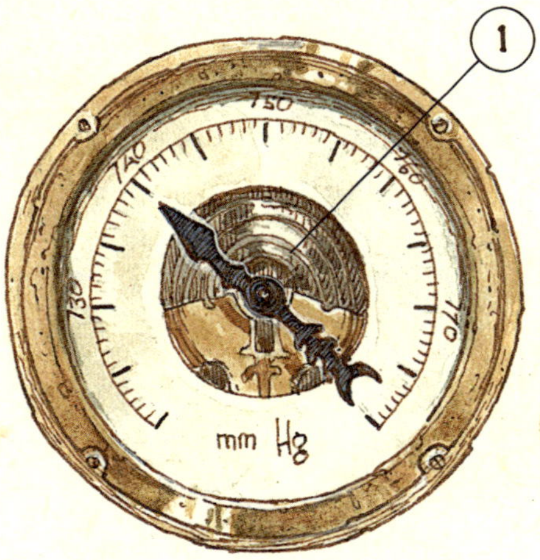

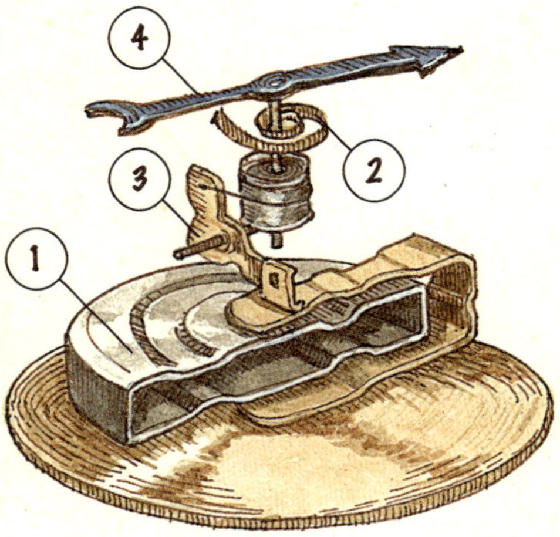

BAROMETER

This is used to forecast weather changes. Take a thin sheet of brass (an alloy of copper, zinc and a small amount of tin) and craft it into a small, air-tight box (1). Create a vacuum inside (page 198). The air column puts pressure on the box, and the brass sides of the box act as a membrane, becoming convex or concave. These changes are transmitted through the system of levers (3) to the arrow (4), which rotates along the scale to indicate the pressure. When the pressure rises, the box will compress and pull the spring (2) with the arrow attached to it; when the pressure drops, it will straighten out, pushing the spring out. If atmospheric pressure drops, expect storms and rain. If it rises, then the weather is improving — call everyone above deck! The accuracy of the barometer depends on where you store it. Keep it in the shade and avoid drafts.

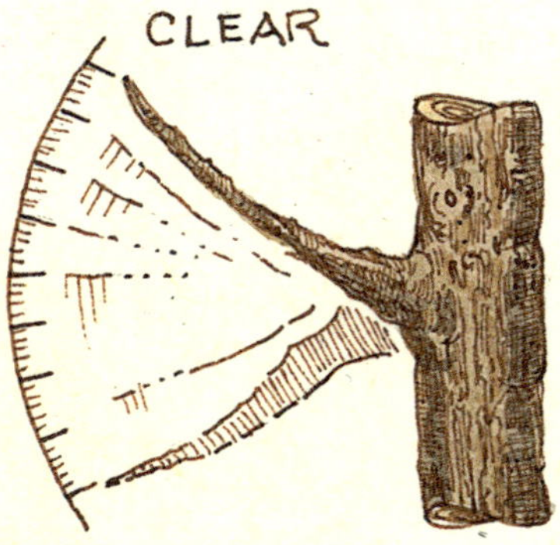

If you can't make a barometer, cut a 10–15 cm segment from the trunk of a young spruce tree. Make sure this segment includes a branch. Peel off the bark. The end of the branch will drop before rain and rise before clear weather.

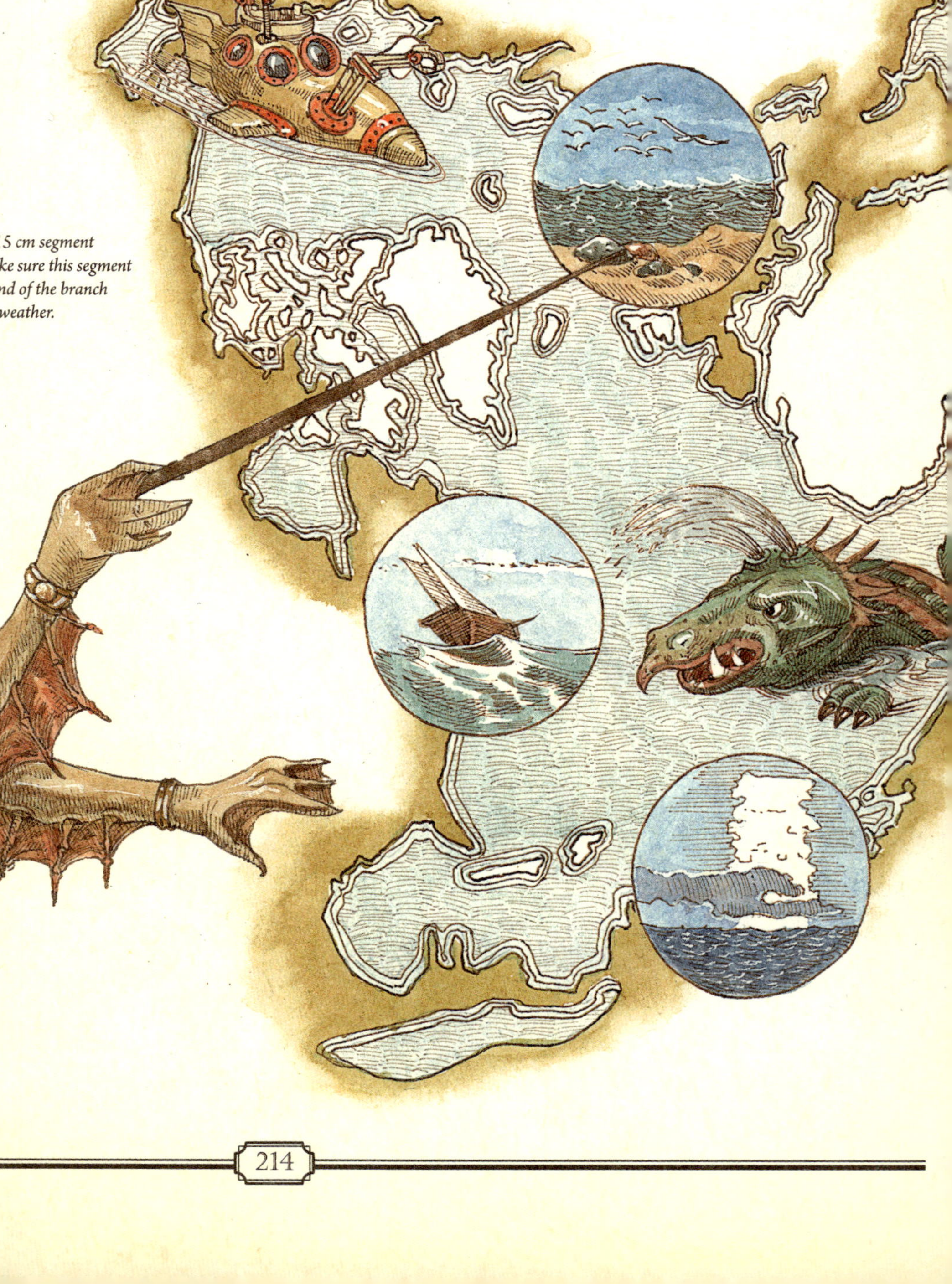

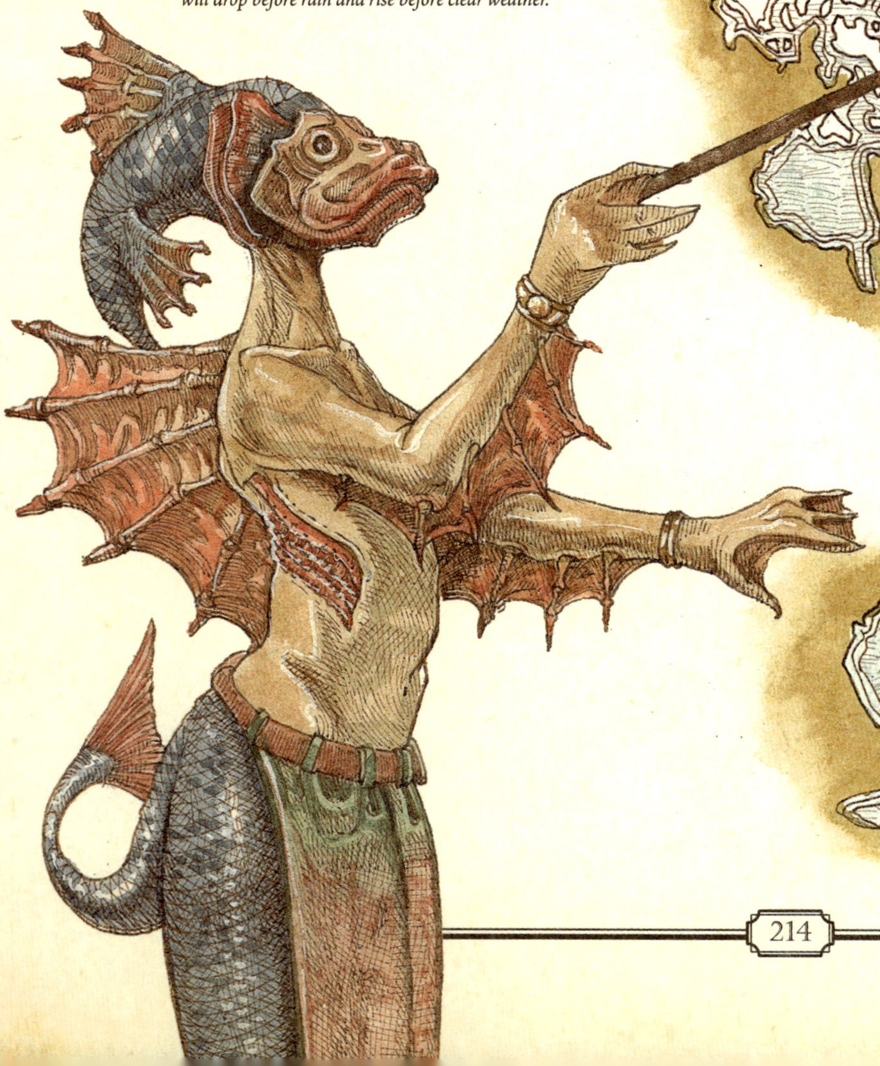

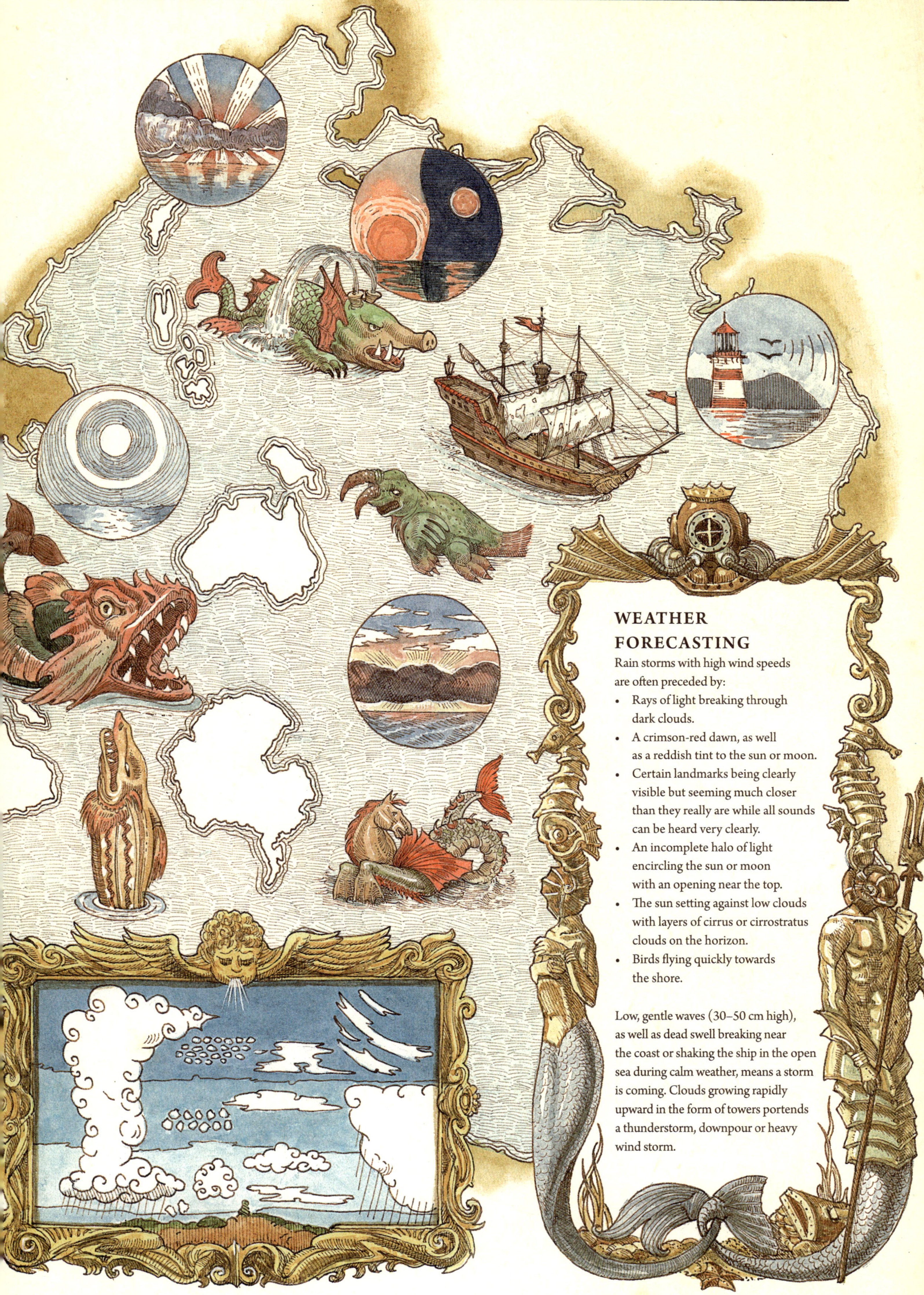

WEATHER FORECASTING

Rain storms with high wind speeds are often preceded by:

- Rays of light breaking through dark clouds.
- A crimson-red dawn, as well as a reddish tint to the sun or moon.
- Certain landmarks being clearly visible but seeming much closer than they really are while all sounds can be heard very clearly.
- An incomplete halo of light encircling the sun or moon with an opening near the top.
- The sun setting against low clouds with layers of cirrus or cirrostratus clouds on the horizon.
- Birds flying quickly towards the shore.

Low, gentle waves (30–50 cm high), as well as dead swell breaking near the coast or shaking the ship in the open sea during calm weather, means a storm is coming. Clouds growing rapidly upward in the form of towers portends a thunderstorm, downpour or heavy wind storm.

PADDLE WHEEL BOAT

Rowing downstream is a breeze, as the flow of the river carries you along. But what happens when you need to drive a loaded multi-ton vessel against the current to a channel upstream? You can still harness the safe, cheap energy generated by the river if you simply add a water wheel. After all, water wheels can be used for more than just grinding grains. The principle behind the paddle wheel boat remains the same. You can transform a water wheel into a large river-faring vessel by adding a few key elements.

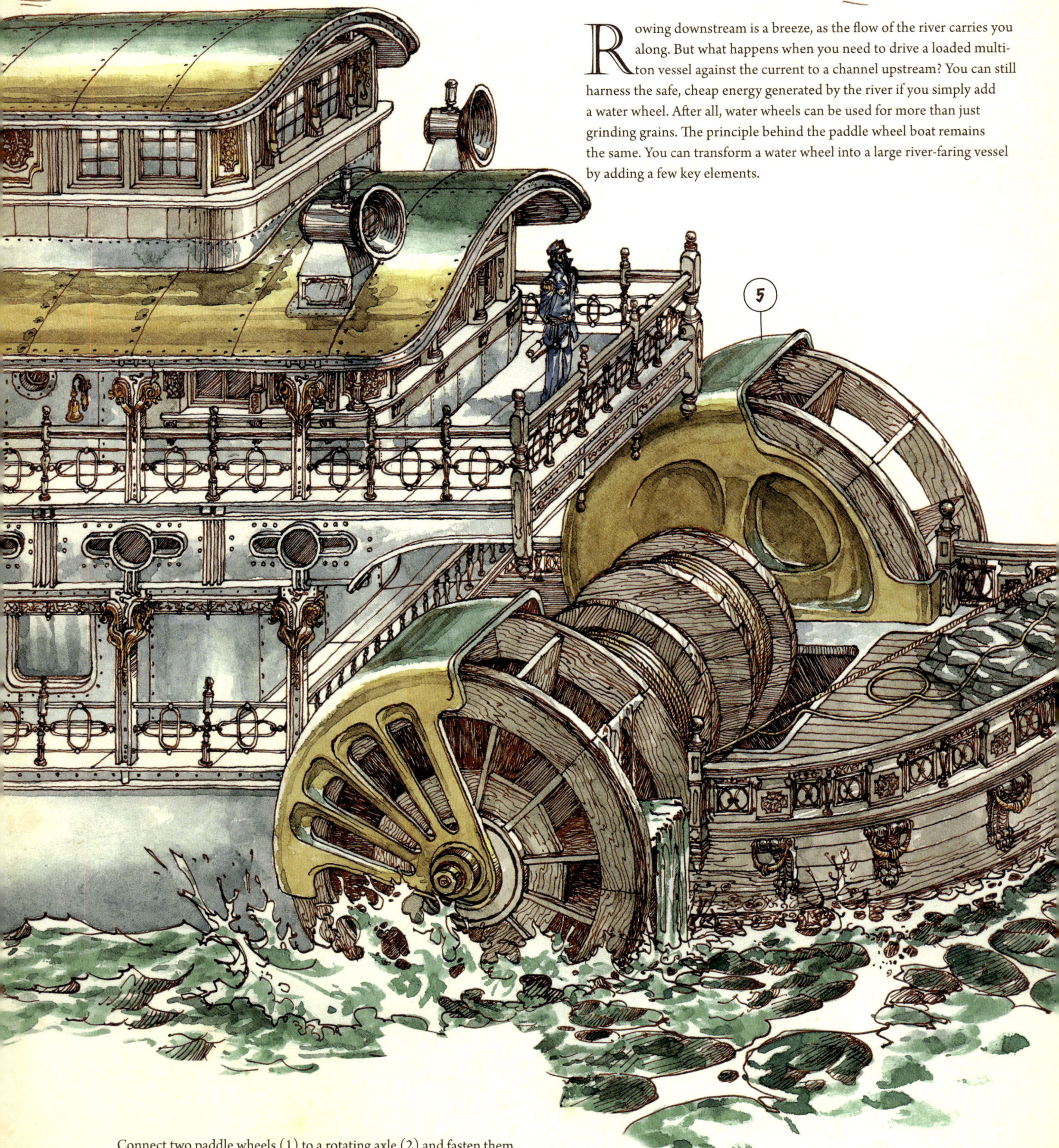

Connect two paddle wheels (1) to a rotating axle (2) and fasten them to the body of the boat. You'll need a very long, thick, sturdy rope (page 18). Attach one end of the rope to the anchor (3) and wrap the other end through the axle and around a large drum (4) so that it winds and unwinds with the movement of the paddle wheels. Carry the anchor to the front of the boat and heave it in the direction you want to go. When it's securely anchored to the bottom of the river, the current pushes against the paddles, making the wheels spin.

The rotational energy is transferred to the axle, which begins to spin, winding the rope around the drum. This allows the boat to travel upstream until it reaches the anchor, and the process starts anew. Remember: The longer the rope and the farther you throw, the farther the boat will be able to travel in one go.

The paddle wheels act as the motor of the boat, while the cable or rope wound around the drum is like a propeller. This is the same system used in mills (page 234). By the way, these wheels can be placed both on the sides of the ship's hull and behind it. The blades should be covered with a mudguard (5), which is a sheet of metal attached to the base of the wheel. You can even improve your boat model so that it moves continuously, even while you're repositioning the anchor.

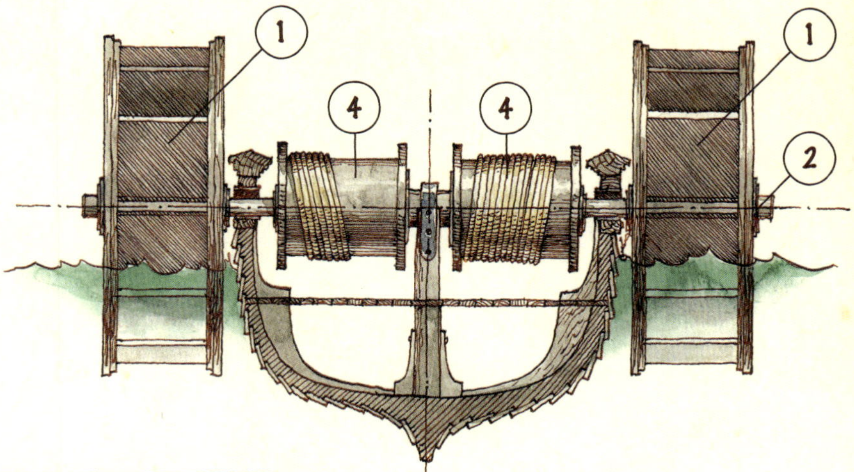

To do this, you need to fasten two ropes with anchors to the shaft and use them one after the other. While the ship is being pulled along one rope, the second is thrown further along the route. A paddle rower with two anchor ropes can carry a load of dozens of tons against the current and wind. As they turn, the wheels won't spray drops of water on the deck, and all passengers will stay dry.

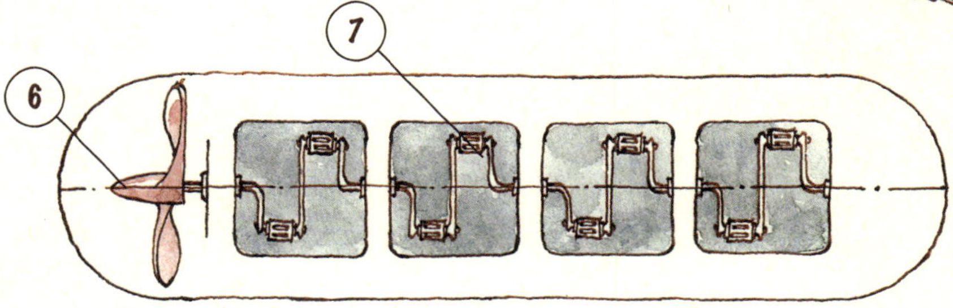

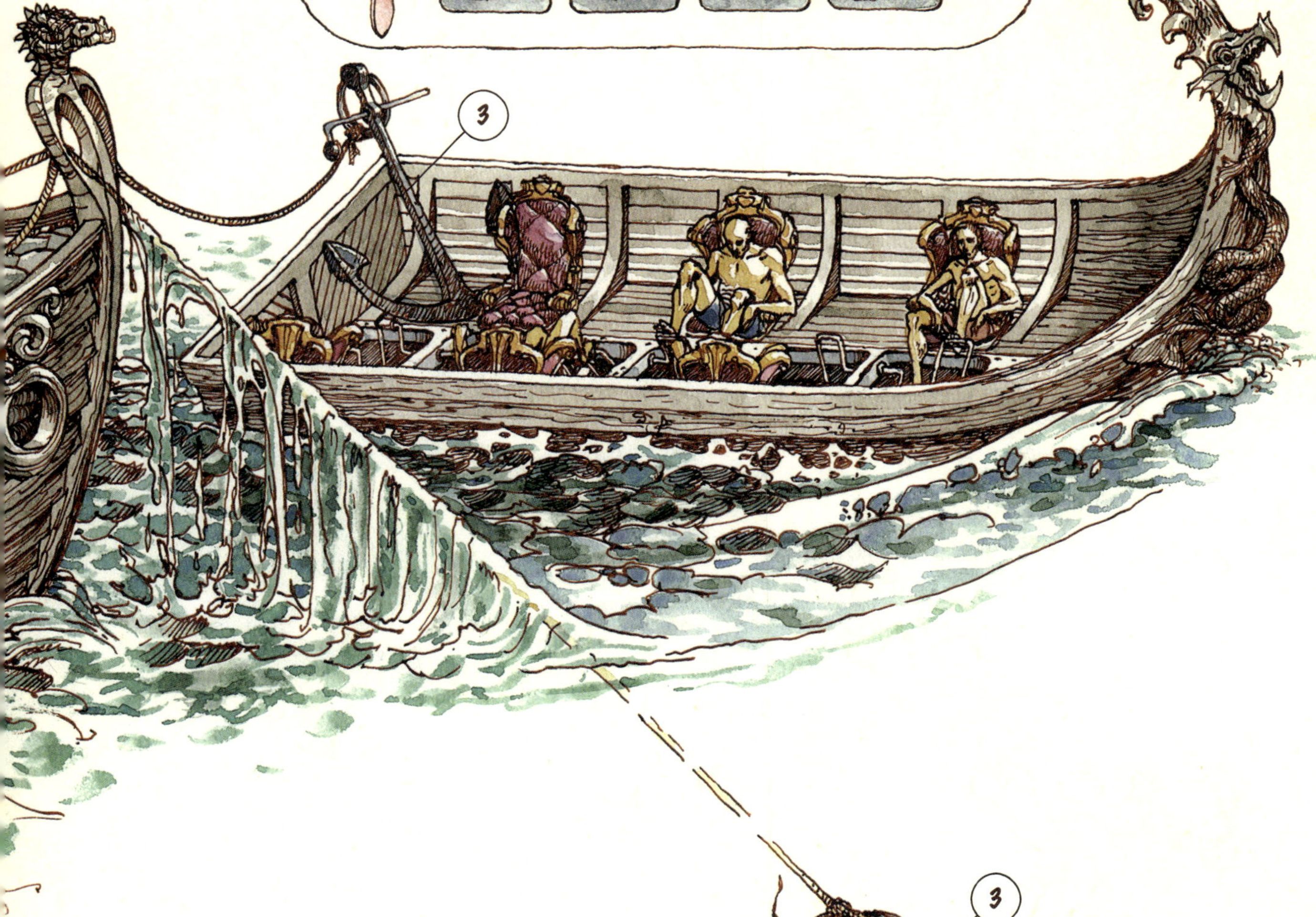

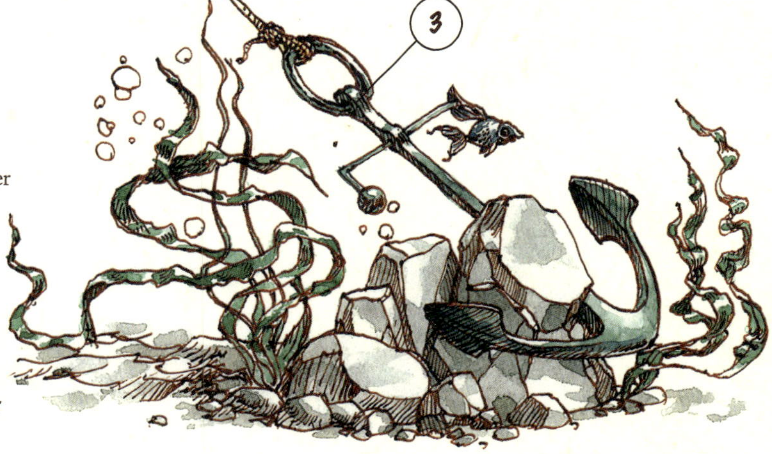

Use manpower to get the anchor closer to the intended direction of travel. Send a few of your strongest deckhands ahead in a smaller pedal-powered paddle boat (say that 5 times fast) to place the anchor. Place the paddle wheel (which can be replaced with a propeller) (6) on the same axis as the pedal drive (7).

Give your crew the order to start pedaling. The energy they generate will be transferred to the axle. Make a steering lever (8) to control your pedal boat. You can use these small boats as water taxis or have a pleasant sail around the lake. Chatting and pedal boating with a friend is a great leisure activity.

SUBMARINE

Exploring the ocean may help you uncover the mysteries of your planet's history. But human physiology has its limitations that prevent people from diving too deep or staying underwater too long. As you dive deeper, the pressure increases, compressing the air in your lungs more and more. But if you have sufficiently strong materials, you can build a sealed device capable of normalizing pressure changes, diving to great depths and staying there for a long time.

DIVING

Make the body of your vessel cylindrical. This shape distributes pressure evenly, preventing the submarine from being easily crushed. The deeper you plan to descend, the rounder your vessel should be. Include a fluid tank (1) at the bottom of the hull that will work like a fish's swim bladder. As you descend, the bladder fills with water, weighing the submarine down. When you want to surface, void the water by filling with air from a compressed air reservoir (2) located above the tank. When you dive again, the water pressure will automatically push more water into the tank through a valve (3), causing the boat to sink.

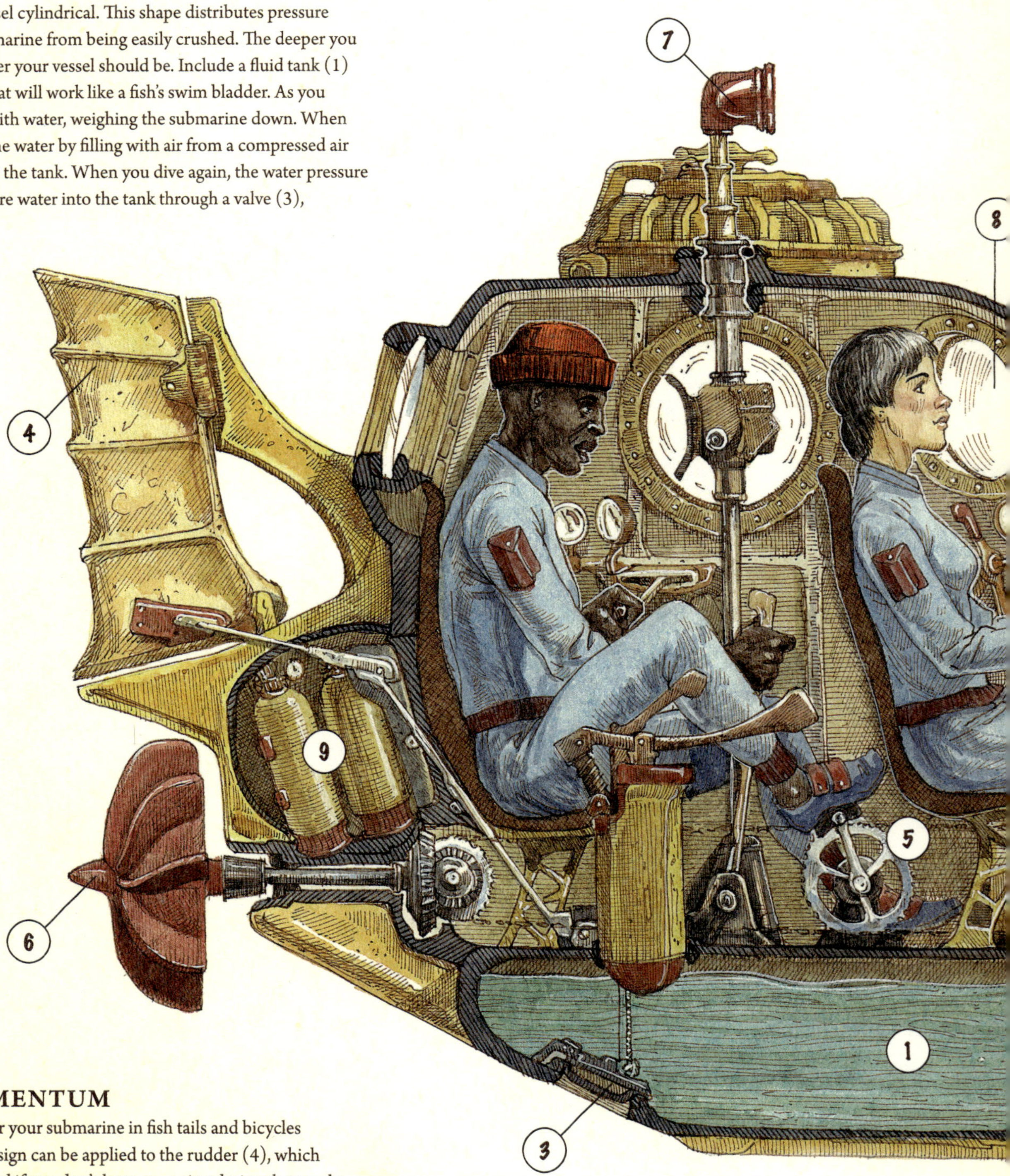

FORWARD MOMENTUM

You may find inspiration for your submarine in fish tails and bicycles (page 164). The fish tail design can be applied to the rudder (4), which is used to steer the boat. And if you don't have an engine design that works underwater, make a bicycle-powered submarine. Simply attach pedals (5) to your propeller (6) using a chain drive and bevel gears, and you're off! Of course, this only works for very small, light vessels. To make navigation simpler, install a periscope (7) using a system of mirrors (page 182). Search for evidence of ancient sunken civilizations and avoid underwater obstacles by looking through the windows (8). To ensure you can breathe normally, scrub the air of carbon dioxide by pumping it through an alkaline solution, and from time to time add fresh air from your life support cylinder (9), relieving excess pressure through the vent valve.

At shallow depths (up to 30 m) the crew can even attach hoses to the compressed air within the boat to explore the area just outside the submarine. A regulator valve supplies air from a compressed air cylinder under the same pressure as the surrounding water. Any deeper than 30 m and things get more complicated. When you breathe the compressed air, the nitrogen it contains dissolves in your blood. If the pressure drops too rapidly, this nitrogen forms air bubbles in the bloodstream, causing severe illness. That's why rapid ascents can be dangerous — your body needs time to acclimate to the pressure change.

To study the seabed, you will need a drill (10) and a movable manipulator arm (11). Give your arm ball joints (page 172) to ensure a full range of motion.

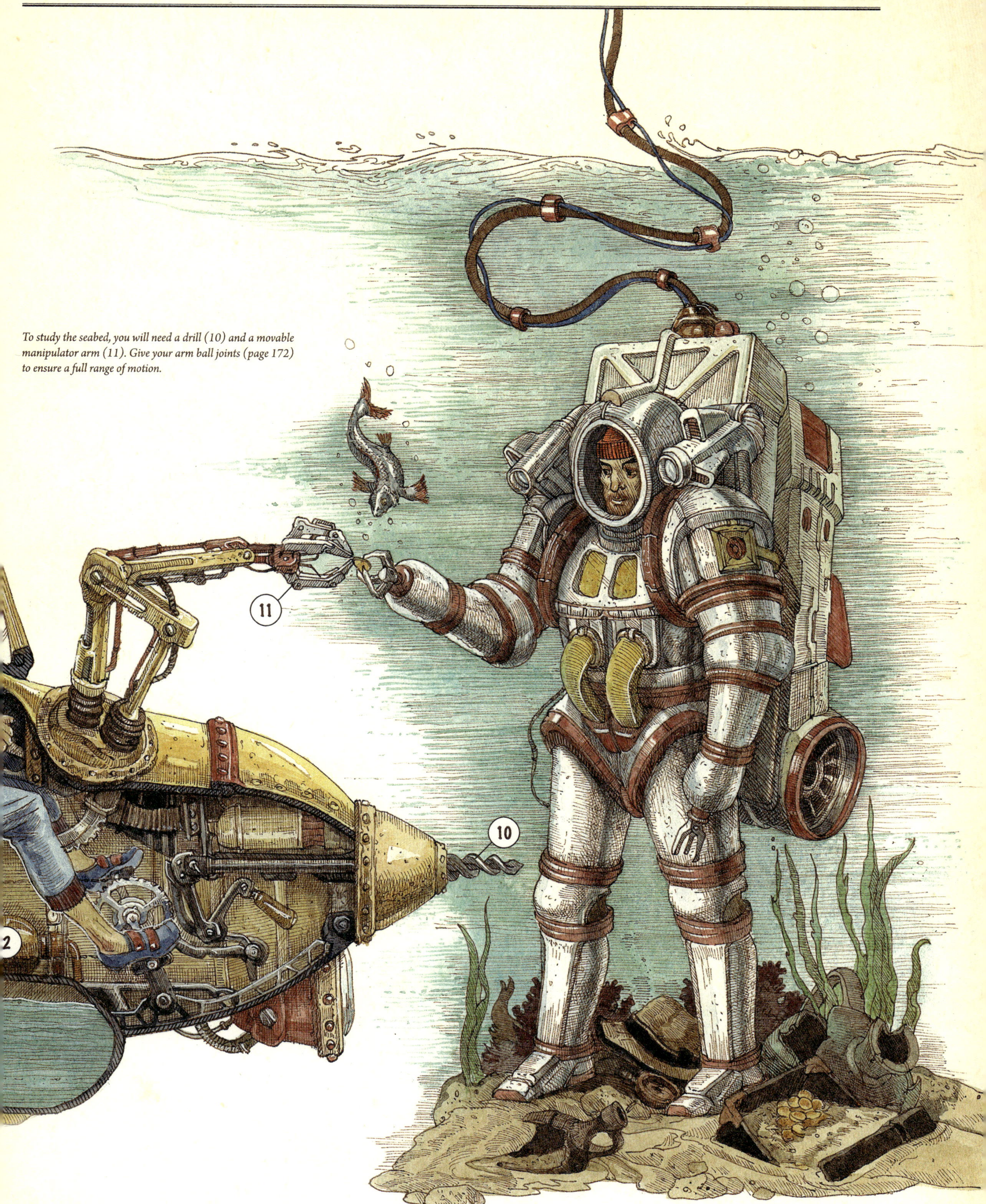

ATMOSPHERIC DIVING SUIT

At depths of 30–40 m, diving with just a compressed air tank becomes impossible because nitrogen at these pressures actually starts to have a narcotic effect on the body. Decompression time is also greatly increased. These problems can be solved by making an atmospheric diving suit, which essentially functions like a miniature submarine.

The environment inside the suit contains normal air at atmospheric pressure, so no decompression is required when returning to the surface. With a suit like this, you can work below the surface for as long as your air supply lasts. When designing your suit, make sure to use a strong material for the body plates and sealed hinge joints for the limbs.

AVIATION

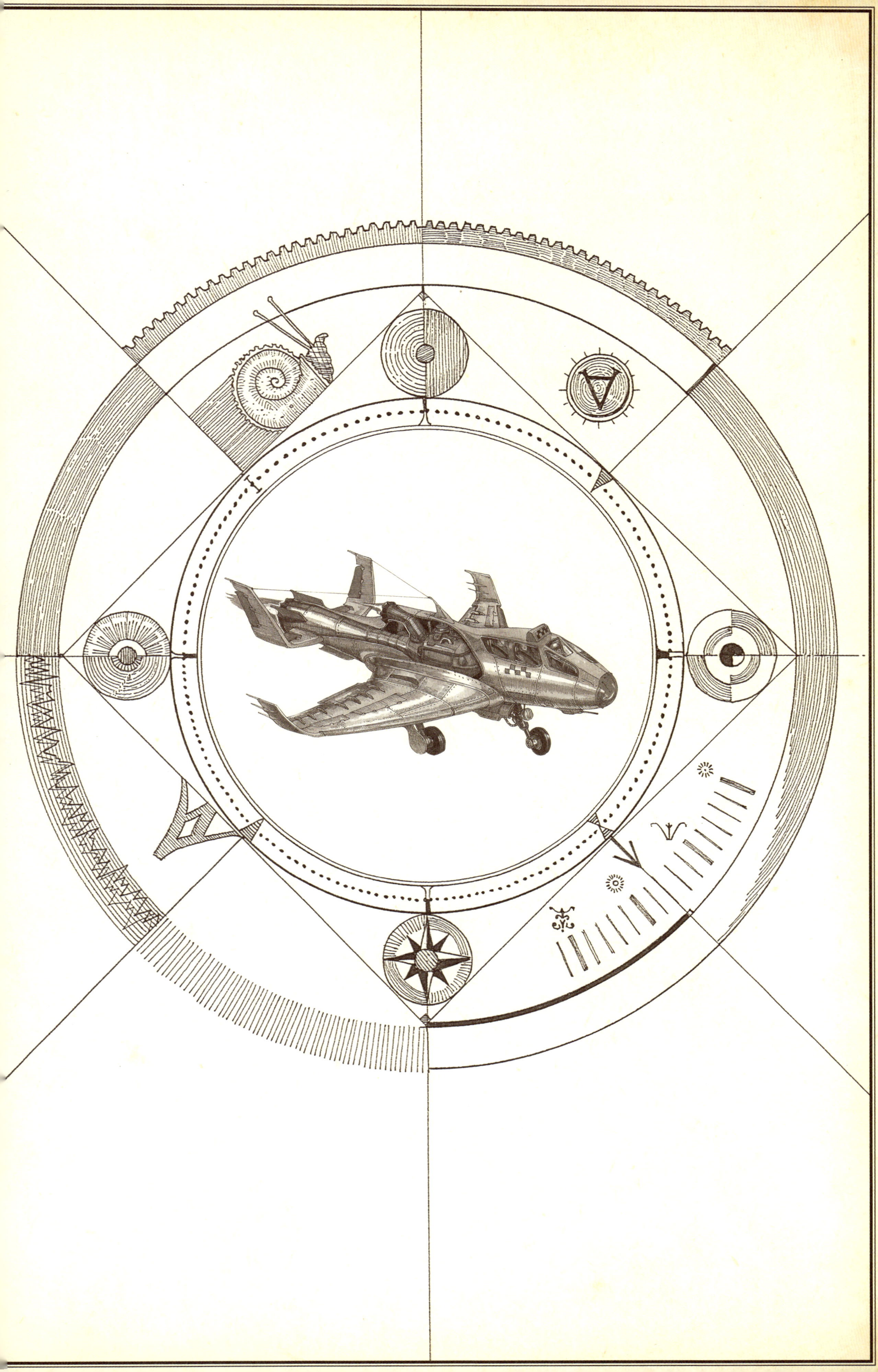

In the history of the universe, very few creatures have successfully ventured outside the bounds of their natural habitat. And those who have know doing so necessitates large-scale transformation. Fish flopped out onto dry land and became mammals; humans soared into the sky and became pilots. In the case of the latter, humanity as a whole began to experience existence on a planetary scale. Distance and geography aren't enough to hold back the tide of civilization when you're capable of flying through the air.

But how? Balloons are buffeted about by the wind, and land-lubbers like us have yet to master the capricious currents. As it turns out, the air is like a dense, transparent ocean, set in motion by a thousand tiny waves. These winds are invisible to the naked eye, though hunting them down isn't much of a challenge. You just need to look to the earth if you want to read the winds.

1. ***Heat gauge***
2. ***Parachute valve,*** *sealed while airborne and opened for descent*
3. ***Turning valves***
4. ***Ballast***
5. ***Burner***
6. ***Maneuvering vent line,*** *which allows the crew to vent air from the balloon*

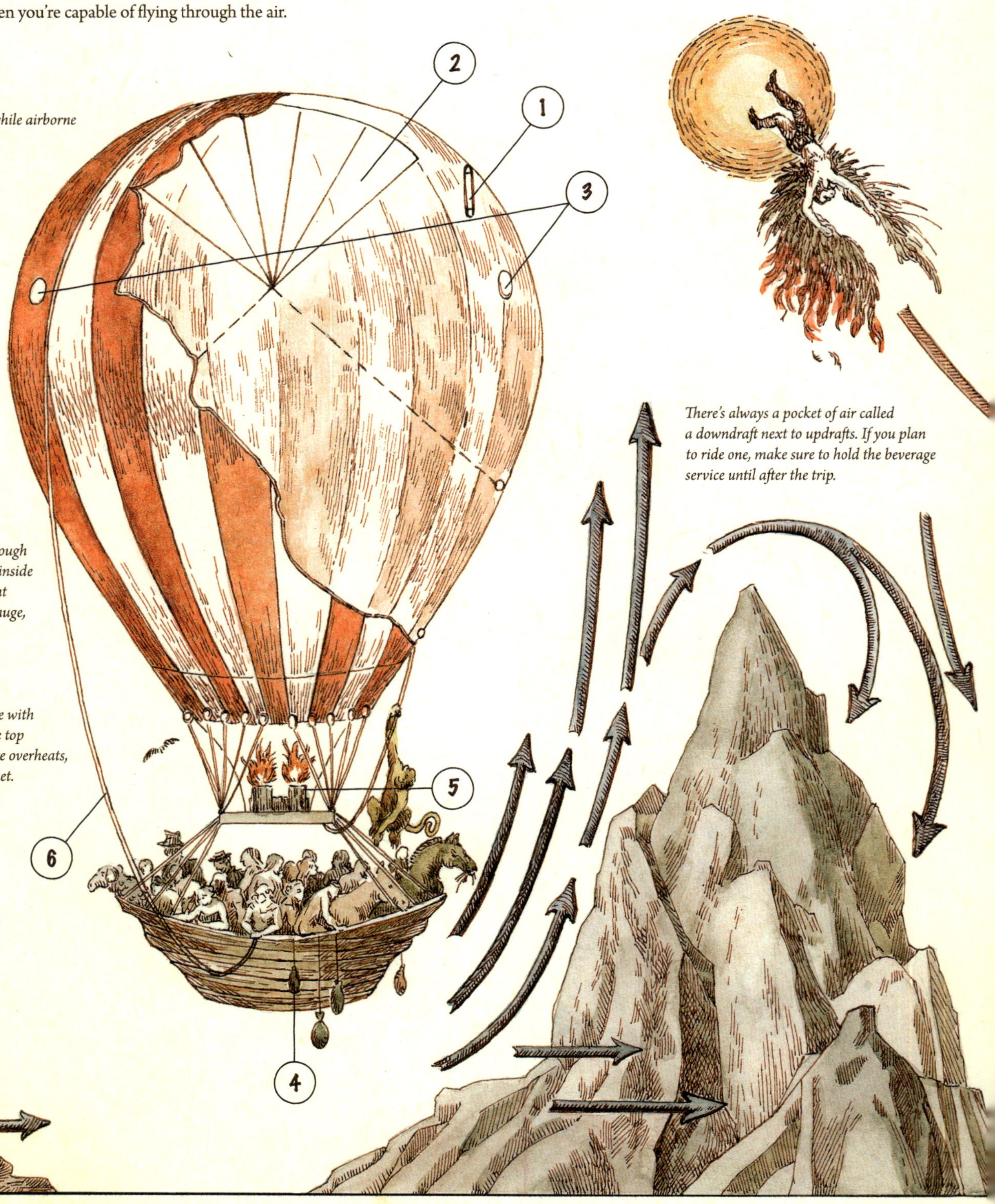

There's always a pocket of air called a downdraft next to updrafts. If you plan to ride one, make sure to hold the beverage service until after the trip.

Envelope
The balloon is made out of cloth gussets. Soak the cloth in latex, similarly to how you would a raincoat (page 116), in order to make it airtight, though you'll have to keep the hot air inside from reaching the melting point of latex. If you install a heat gauge, you can ensure you'll never fly too close to the sun.

Heat gauge
Hang a weighted flag on a wire with a low melting point close to the top of the balloon cavity. If the wire overheats, the flag will drop into the basket.

Burner
Build a fire under the opening at the bottom of the balloon cavity. Once the hot air fills the balloon, it will take off into the air. Cut off the oxygen supply to the fire if you want to lose altitude.

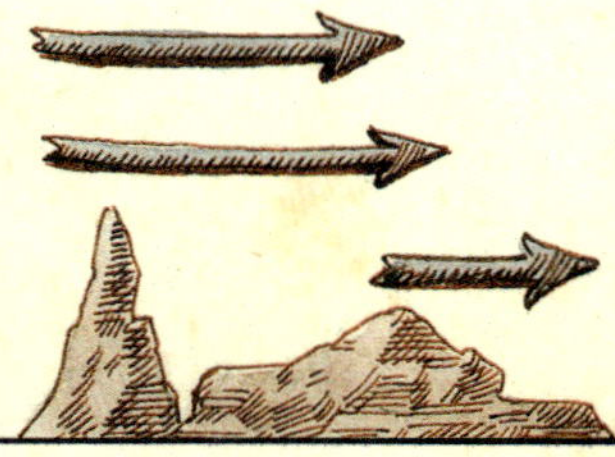

HOT-AIR BALLOONS

Flying in a hot-air balloon is simply a delight. Even if an icy jet stream is whisking you along at 300 km/h, it's still going to be warm and quiet in your basket since the balloon always moves right along with the air around it. You won't even feel the wind. And since the burner creates a pocket of warm air, it travels with you too.

THERMAL UPDRAFTS

Rays of sunlight cut right through the clear air to warm the ground. The ground, in turn, heats the air. Thin, heated air surges upward but is held in place by the thicker layer of cold air above it. Before it can break through that resistance, the warm flows gather at a single point that's easy to see. There's always an unusual phenomenon below — a patch of burnt earth in the middle of a green field, for example, or a lone hill surrounded by plains. Head in that direction, and you'll catch the updraft.

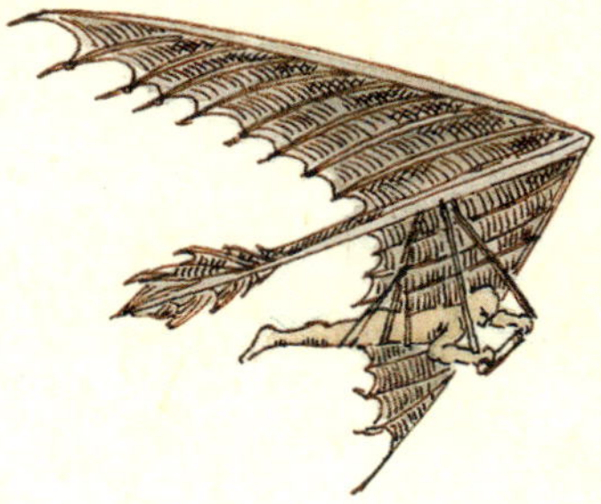

JET STREAMS

Once you're at least ten kilometers up in the air, you'll encounter powerful winds called jet streams. They can reach 300 km/h or more, and you can ride them for long distances. But even if you're not willing to risk flying this high, just remember that each altitude has its own wind. Looking to head left while you're being pulled right? Drop down a couple hundred meters, and you might find your wish granted.

The cloudy road
Thermal flows suck moisture out of the ground, which then condenses in the cold air and turns into clouds. Keep an eye on cumulus clouds before they're whisked away by the wind — there will be a thermal column underneath each of them. Hop from cloud to cloud and you'll find yourself traveling the cloudy road.

***Gliders** (page 226) can't gain altitude on their own. But if you unlock the secrets of the sky's currents, you'll still be able to stay aloft for hours.*

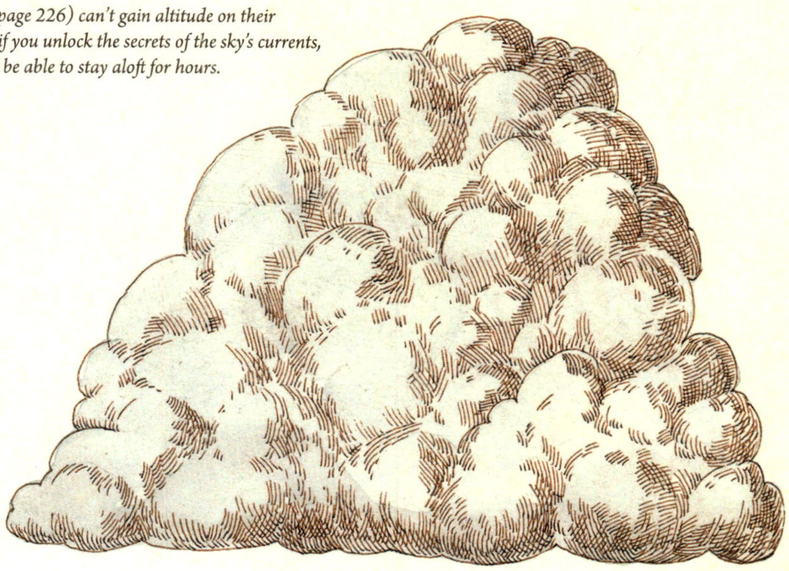

Lantern scout
Hunting air currents using trial and error isn't a great plan. Make a flying lantern out of a paper sack and a candle and launch it into the sky to see if it catches a current going in the right direction. If it does, you can send your hot-air balloon flying off right behind it.

***Careful!** When two air currents collide, you'll experience wind shear, which can be incredibly dangerous. In the blink of an eye, your balloon will head off in one direction while your gondola will be swept away in another.*

***Careful!** If you find yourself on the opposite or leeward side of a mountain, you're going to have a deceptive downslope wind blowing in your face. Flying here is highly dangerous due to the turbulence. Don't mistake a real gust of wind for its misleading cousin.*

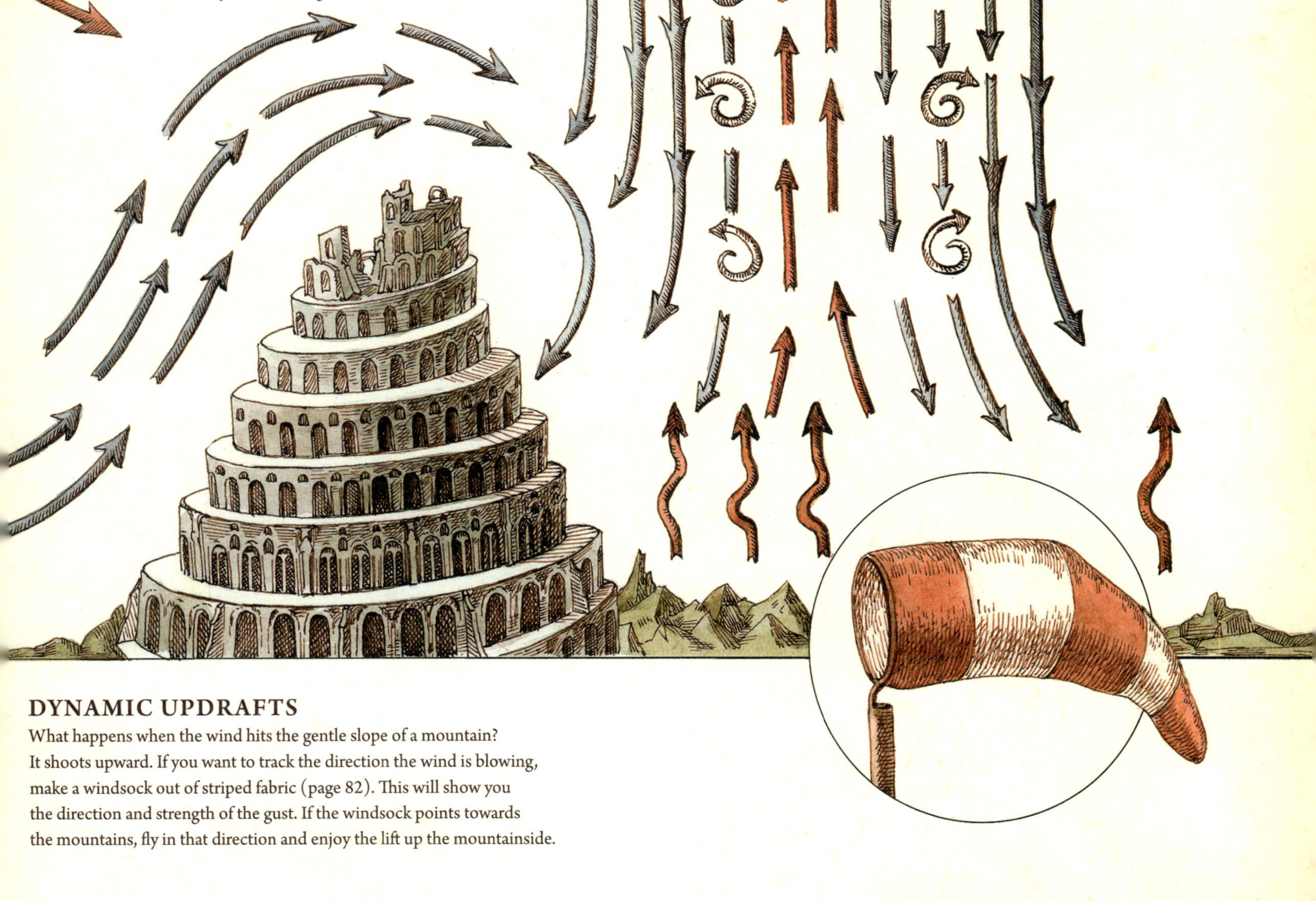

DYNAMIC UPDRAFTS

What happens when the wind hits the gentle slope of a mountain? It shoots upward. If you want to track the direction the wind is blowing, make a windsock out of striped fabric (page 82). This will show you the direction and strength of the gust. If the windsock points towards the mountains, fly in that direction and enjoy the lift up the mountainside.

AIRPLANES

If you want to travel hundreds of miles in hours instead of months, you need an airplane. For some reason, this often spurs the creation of large, crowded airports, endless check-in lines, passport controls, security checks and pointless rules about how much liquid you can take where. Try to avoid all that and remember to enjoy your flight. But the sky is far from the limit. The day you make your first journey into the great blue yonder is the day the space race begins. It is said that once upon a time, a dog was the first animal to make it to space. But you can surely do better than that.

THE WING

The main part of the airplane is the fixed wings that use airflow to create lift. The shape of the wing is asymmetrical: The upper part of the wing has a larger surface area than the lower one. The difference in airflow velocities (air moves faster above the wing than below it) creates a zone of increased pressure under the wing and a zone of decreased pressure above it. This positive pressure generated from below starts to lift the wing. The larger the area of the wing, the greater the lifting force.

During flight, the wing carries the entire weight of the vehicle, so choose a light but strong material and attach it solidly to the fuselage. Experiment with different wing shapes, angles and locations of attachment to improve aerodynamic performance. The main elements of the wing are the console, the center wing section and the aileron (a small deflectable plane at the back of the console). You could also add trailing-edge flaps that when extended down generate extra lift —for flying at low speeds during take-off and landing —but add a lot of drag. Angled wingtips help reduce the vortex that forms at the end of the wing and create extra drag.

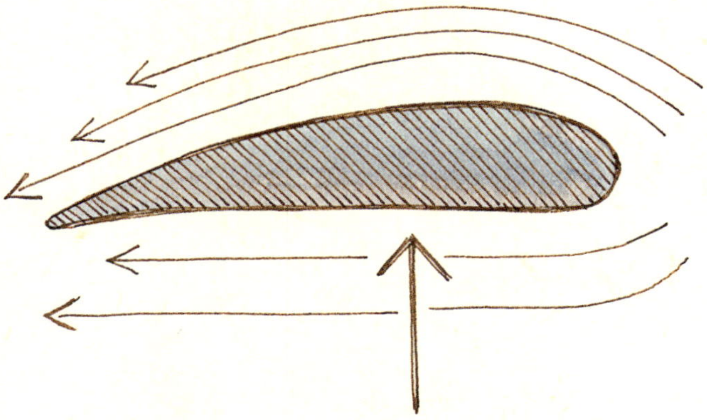

FLIGHT CONTROL

If you lower the aileron on the right wing and raise the aileron on the left wing, the right wing will have more lift and, accordingly, the airplane will roll to the left (I).

The tilted surfaces on the rear horizontal tail are elevators. They control the pitch of the aircraft. If the elevators are turned up, the tail section of the plane drops, the nose rises and the aircraft will climb to a higher altitude (III). But be careful not to pitch up too much and stall the airplane!

The airplane's fin is equipped with a vertical moving part called a rudder. Swinging the rudder to the right causes the tail of the airplane to shift to the left and the airplane itself to turn to the right (II).

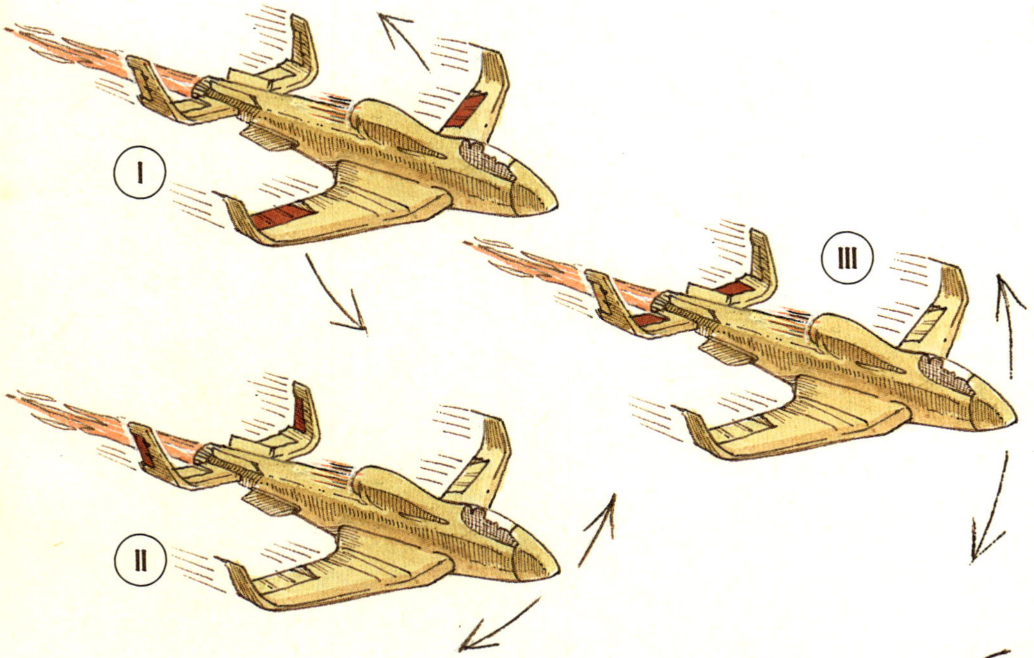

INSIDE THE COCKPIT

To control the airplane, you need to install a joystick connected to the ailerons and elevators to control the roll and pitch of the airplane and pedals for rudder control, as well as levers for the flaps, landing gear, etc.

If the airplane is small, you may have enough muscle power to change the position of the elements using cables, rods and levers, but if the airplane is more complex, you will have to add mechanical, hydraulic and electrical devices that respond to commands from the pilot.

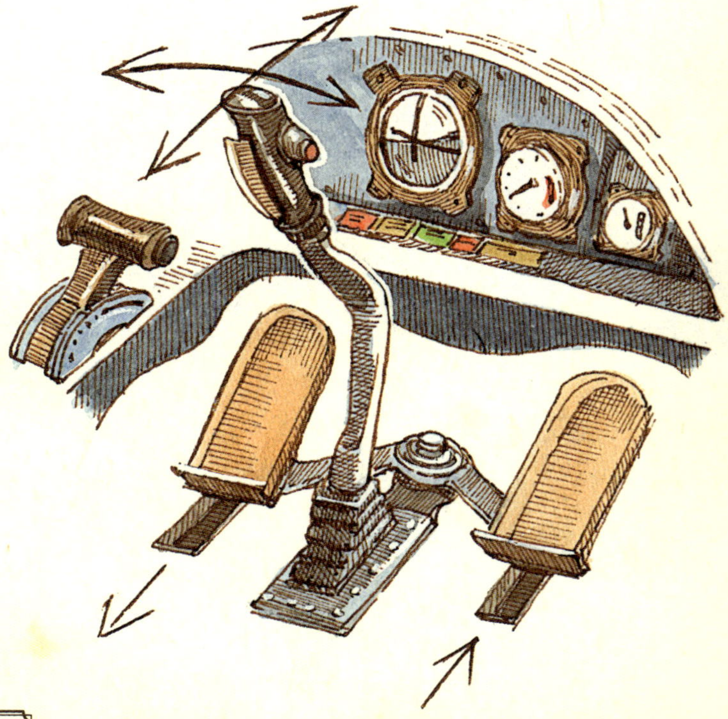

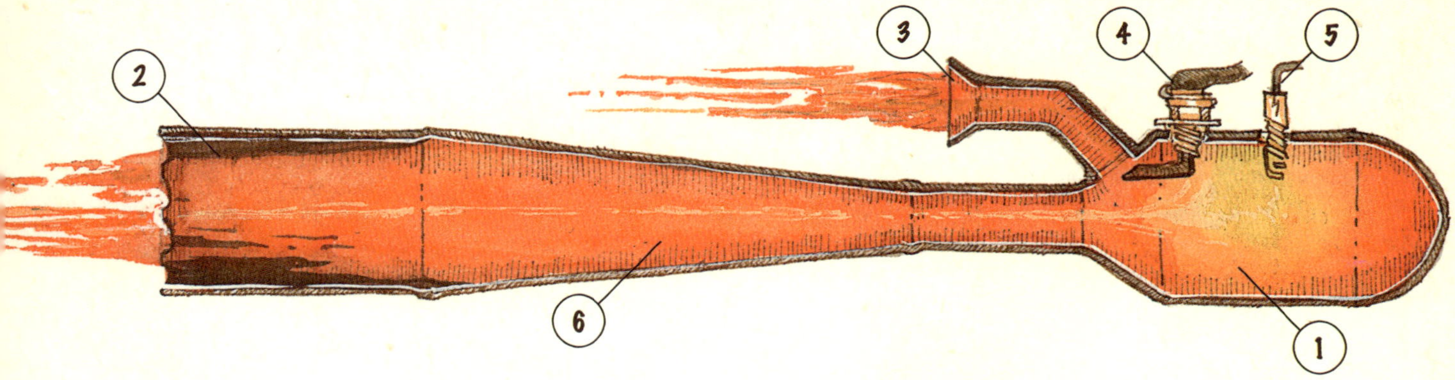

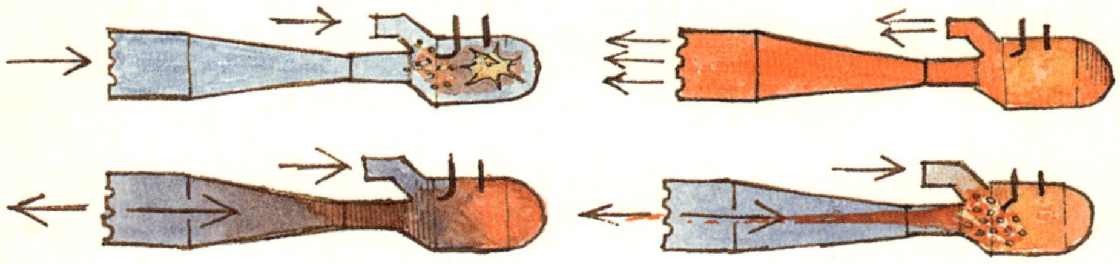

1. *Combustion chamber*
2. *Jet pipe*
3. *Air valve*
4. *Fuel valve*
5. *Spark plug*
6. *Exhaust tube*

ENGINE

In pulse jet engines, the fuel-air mixture is fed into the combustion chamber (1) in small portions at regular intervals. During flight, air and fuel are supplied to the combustion chamber through the air intake (3) and the fuel valve (4), which mix and are ignited by the spark plug (5) during operation.

Combustion byproducts escape through the nozzle (2) and the air intake, creating thrust. Due to the difference in length between the two pipes, the pressure in the air intake valve drops while combustion products are moving through the exhaust pipe (6).

This creates a partial vacuum in the combustion chamber, forcing air and part of the gases from the exhaust pipe into the chamber, which then acts as a virtual piston, compressing a new portion of the combustible mixture and igniting it. The cycle is then repeated, creating continuous thrust and forward momentum.

Because of its low power, this engine is not capable of accelerating a large airplane to take-off speed on its own. Use a catapult to make up the difference. Keep in mind that such an engine has a very high fuel consumption per unit of thrust, much higher than the turbofan or turbojet aircraft engines that you will have to build in the next stage of civilization.

1. *Console*
2. *Center wing section*
3. *Aileron*
4. *Flaps*
5. *Spar*
6. *Leading edge*
7. *Elevator*
8. *Rudder*
9. *Fin*
10. *Stabilizer*
11. *Fuselage*
12. *Nose*
13. *Cockpit*
14. *Landing gear*

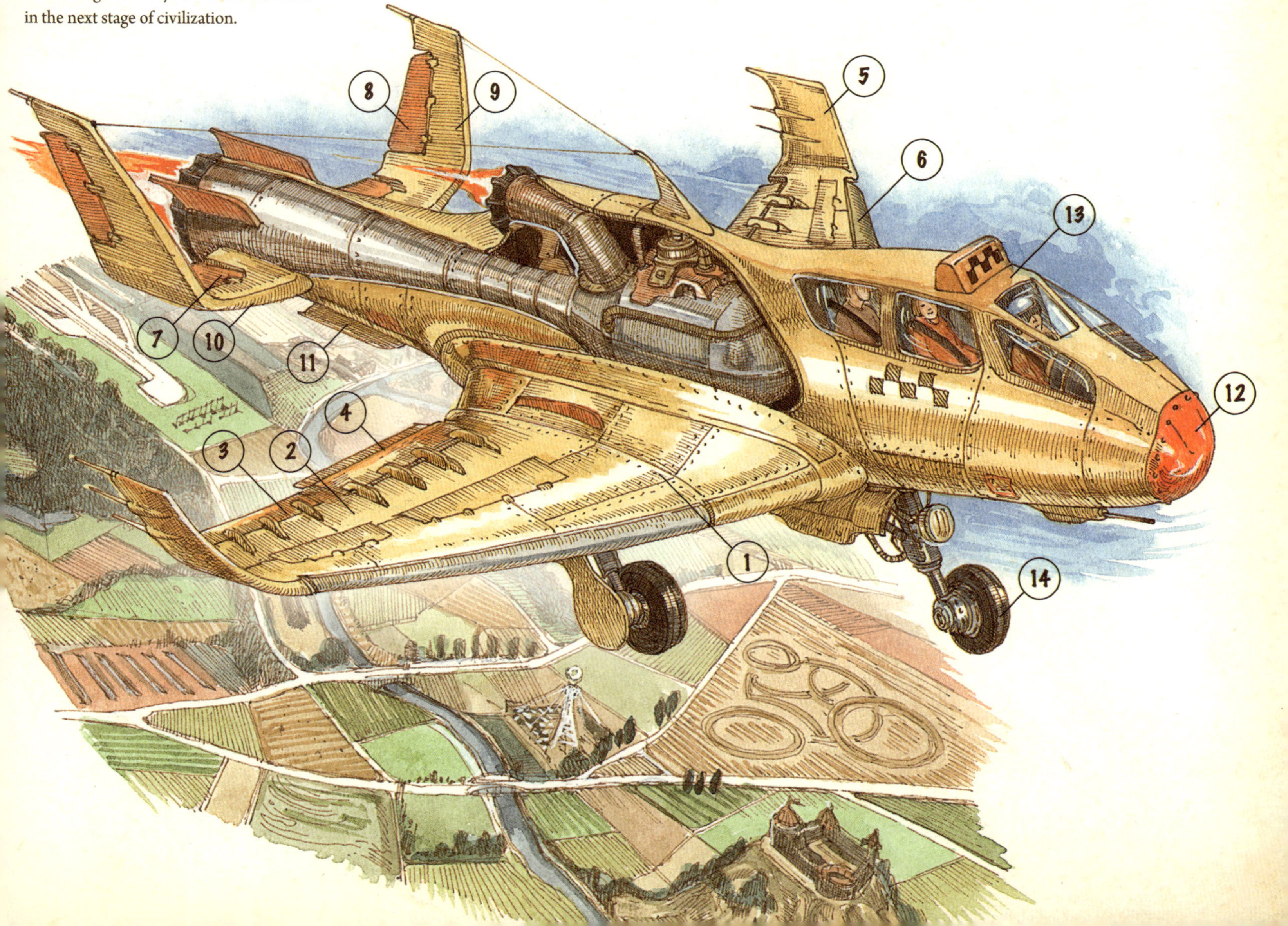

GYROPLANE

Higher and faster doesn't always mean better. Sure, planes can take you on a quick flit across the ocean, but they're ill-equipped to find someone lost in a forest or deliver a package when there's not enough room for a landing strip. But these things become possible when you invent a rotorcraft. Let's start with a simple type: a gyroplane. It's both light and maneuverable — a perfect choice for novice pilots.

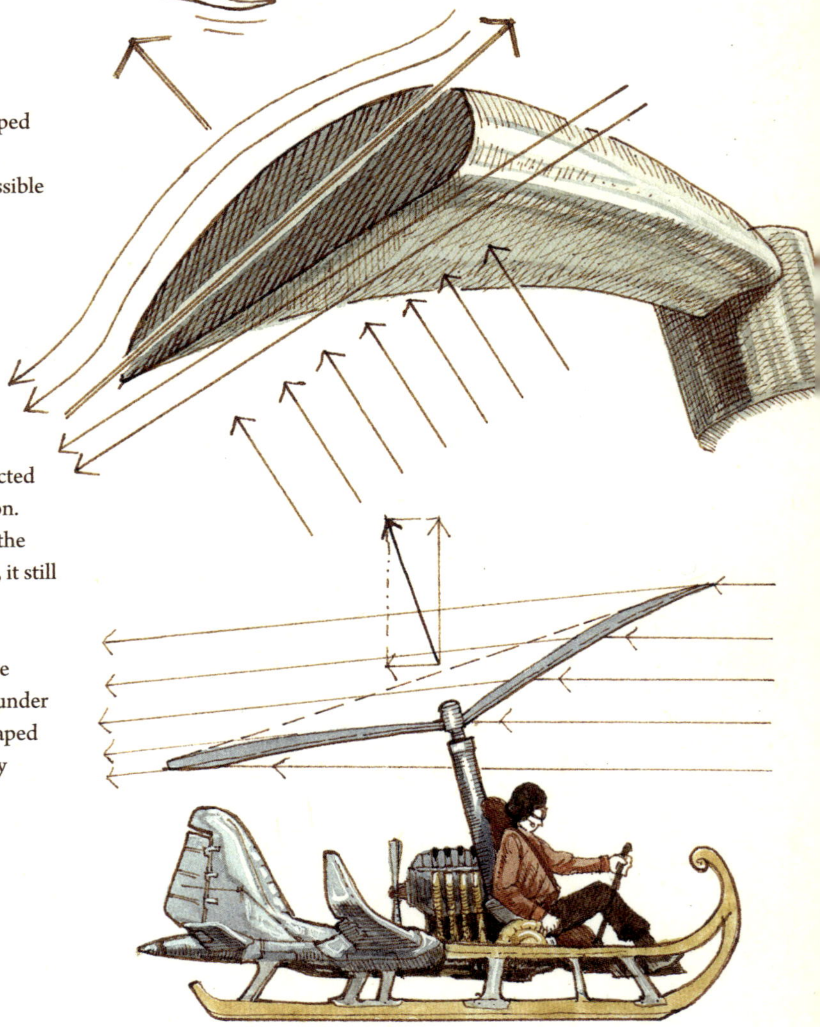

THE MAIN ROTOR

The rotor is what creates lift in gyroplanes. That being said, it isn't connected to the engine but rather spins around its axis in a state of free autorotation. So what makes it turn? As it turns out, the oncoming flow of air propels the wings. Even if you strip the engine from a gyroplane and toss it off a cliff, it still won't crash.

The key is the tilt of the rotor blades. See for yourself — the lower surface of the blade is angled against the direction it's spinning. As the air flows under the rotor, it begins to turn exactly like a windmill. The blades are also shaped like airplane wings (page 224). As they spin and cut through the air, they creates lift, an effect that's called autorotation.

You need a running start to get your gyroplane airborne, although the runway doesn't need to be as long as it does for an airplane. But for vertical takeoffs and landings, you're going to need to invent a helicopter, which is a machine with a rotor connected to an engine. The problem here is the complexity of the technology. The rotor actually changes shape several times each second. For now, perfect your craft with gyroplanes.

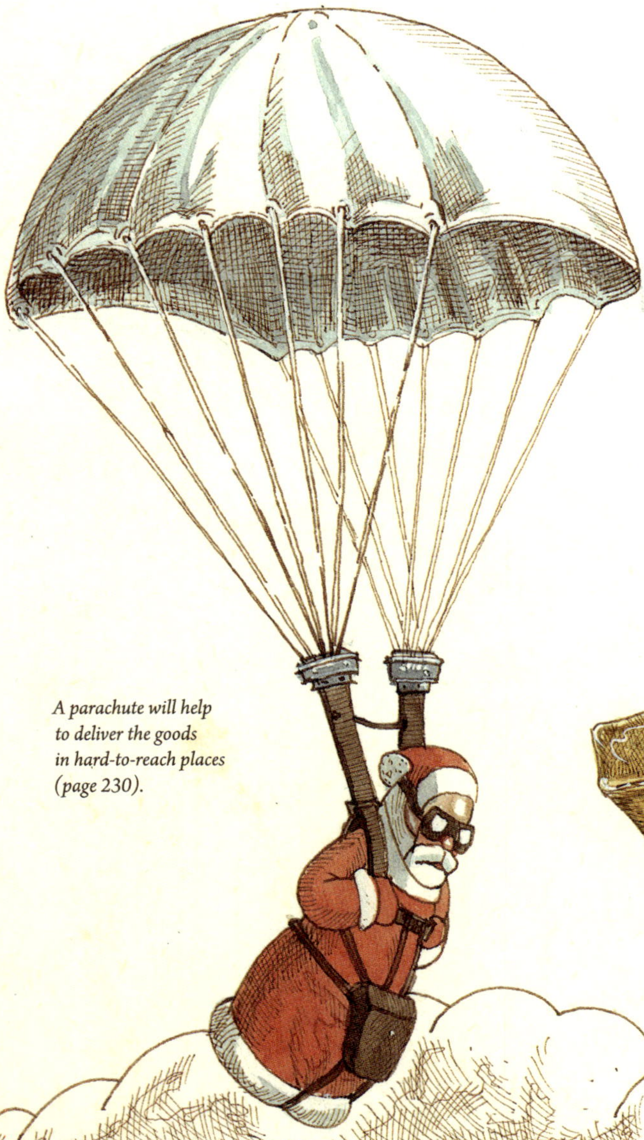

A parachute will help to deliver the goods in hard-to-reach places (page 230).

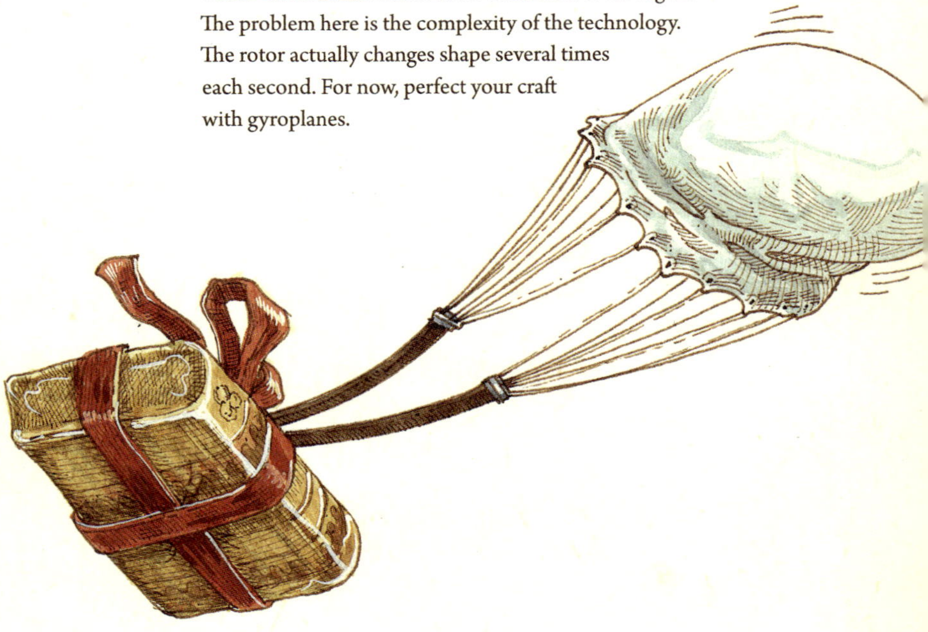

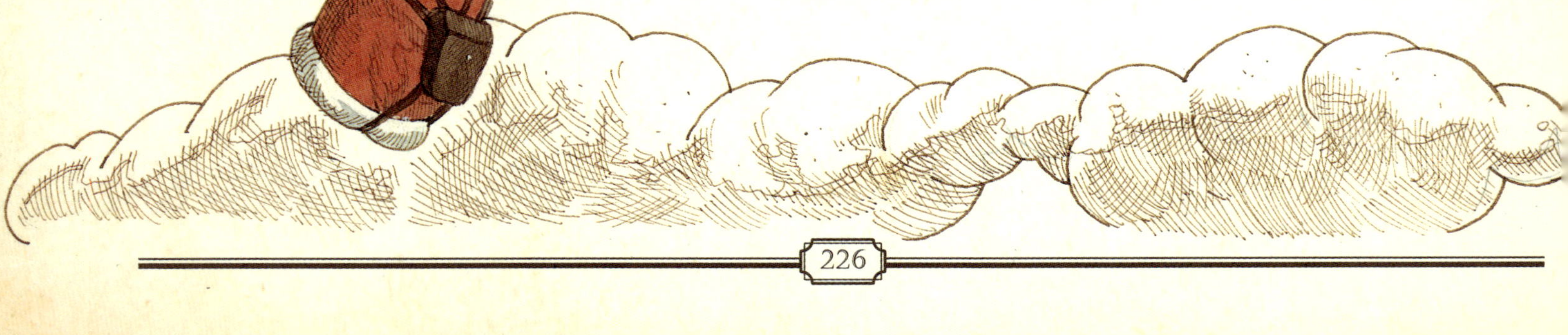

1. *Main rotor*
2. *Internal combustion engine with pusher propeller*
3. *Engine control (throttle)*
4. *Flight control*
5. *Tail fin*
6. *Rudder*
7. *Lifting surface*
8. *Ailerons (lateral control, for turning right and left)*
9. *Altitude control*
10. *Stabilizers*

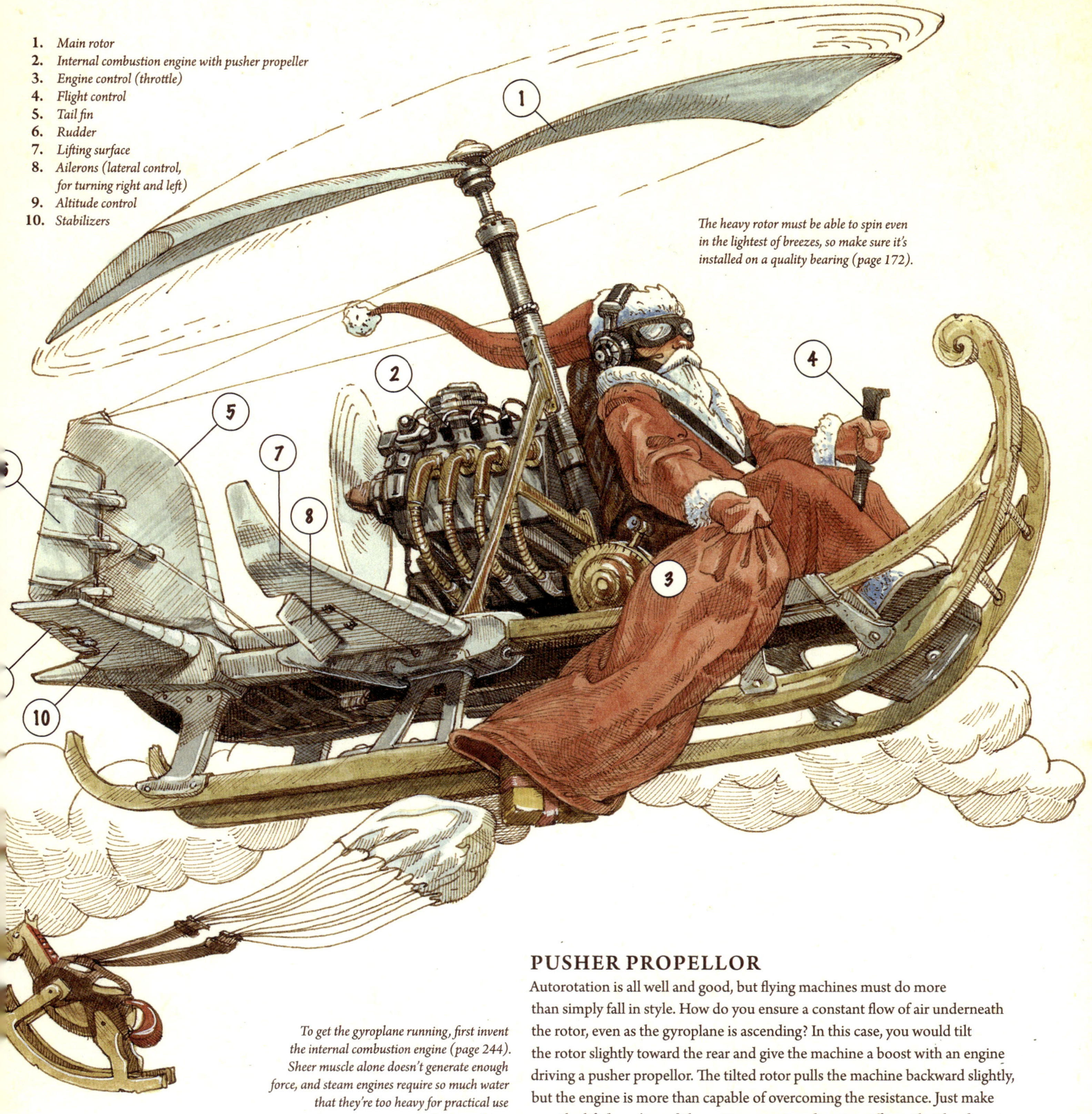

The heavy rotor must be able to spin even in the lightest of breezes, so make sure it's installed on a quality bearing (page 172).

To get the gyroplane running, first invent the internal combustion engine (page 244). Sheer muscle alone doesn't generate enough force, and steam engines require so much water that they're too heavy for practical use in flying machines.

PUSHER PROPELLOR

Autorotation is all well and good, but flying machines must do more than simply fall in style. How do you ensure a constant flow of air underneath the rotor, even as the gyroplane is ascending? In this case, you would tilt the rotor slightly toward the rear and give the machine a boost with an engine driving a pusher propellor. The tilted rotor pulls the machine backward slightly, but the engine is more than capable of overcoming the resistance. Just make sure the lift doesn't send the entire apparatus shooting off into the clouds.

STEERING

Adding a horizontal stabilizer and a fin like those seen on airplanes will make your gyroplane steerable. Controls are a piece of cake. The joystick handles roll and pitch, while the pedals are connected to the rudder and control yaw. Want to go faster? Just hit the throttle.

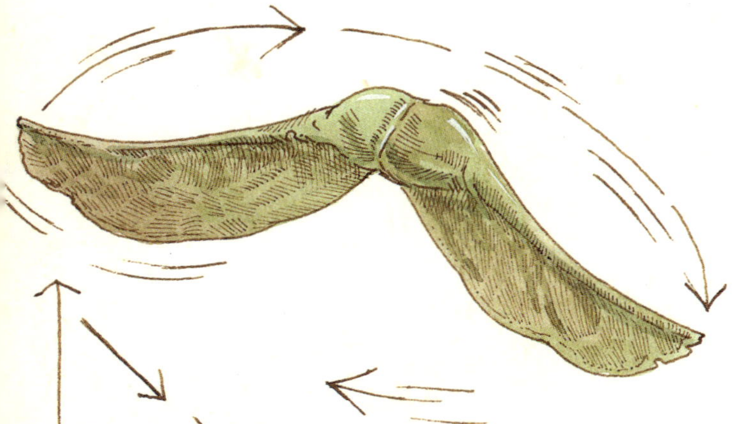

AUTOROTATION

While they may seem complex in design, there are actually gyroplanes all around you. Remember the double-winged seed pods that spin playfully down from maple trees? In childhood, you may have called them "helicopters," "whirlers" or "twisters." After dropping from the tree, they fall slowly, bearing the seeds they carry far away on the wanton wind.

DIRIGIBLE

A flying machine that's lighter than air but has a high carrying capacity? It's not a dream but the feat of engineering genius that is the dirigible. It consumes little fuel but can travel long distances and, despite its size, is very maneuverable. Although there is the issue of finding parking.

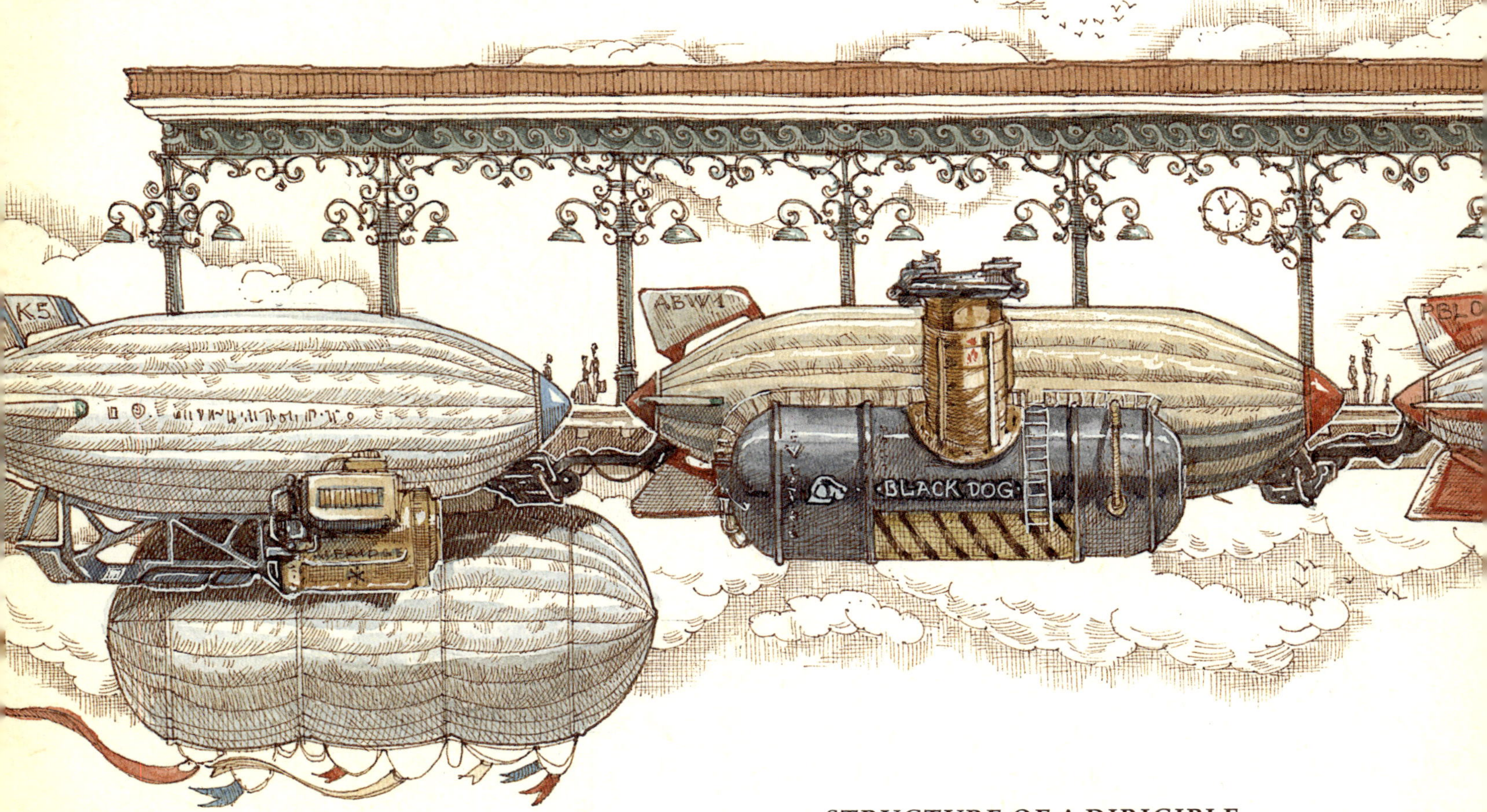

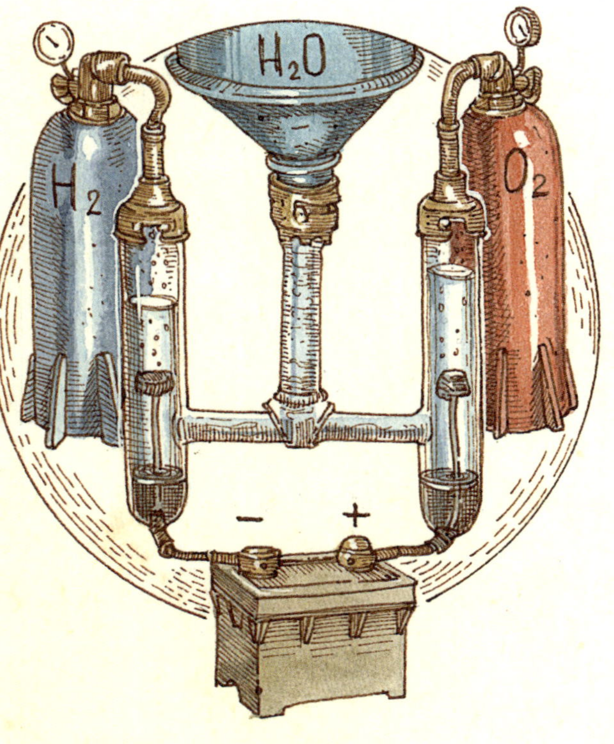

HYDROGEN PRODUCTION

Use water electrolysis. Under the influence of a constant electric current, water breaks down into oxygen and hydrogen. Apply voltage to two electrodes immersed in water. The positive side is the anode, and the negative side is the cathode. To improve conductivity, add lye to the water. Hydrogen will be released from the cathode side, and oxygen from the anode side.

STRUCTURE OF A DIRIGIBLE

Streamline the design to create extra lift and expend less fuel, and if you slightly raise the nose during flight, you can create even more aerodynamic lift, similar to the way the wings of an airplane work. You may choose to fill the body with hydrogen, which is the lightest of all gases but is extremely flammable. Saturate the fabric with latex to make it gas-tight. The envelope should be soft — the gas pressure will keep it inflated. This kind of airship is easy to assemble, disassemble and transport but cannot be made very large.

You can supplement the shell with a frame to give it rigidity. The semi-rigid airship also retains the shape of the shell due to the internal pressure of the carrier gas, but in the lower part, it has a rigid keel truss to which the habitation gondola and other elements of the airship are attached.

Rigid airships have an external load-bearing structural frame made of transverse and longitudinal load-bearing elements covered in a layer of fabric. Almost all the ship's equipment and gondola are installed inside the frame. Strike a balance between the weight of the vessel and the amount of gas: If the airship is too light, it will fly up uncontrollably. This balance must be constantly monitored. With a change in altitude, the air density and pressure change, so the ratio of the weight of the gas to the ambient air will also change. To balance the airship, use ballonets — air bags inside the outer envelope. When inflated, they reduce the volume available for the lifting gas, allowing you to compensate for the change in pressure within the envelope during ascent, descent or sudden changes in temperature: pump atmospheric air in or out of the envelope, thus controlling the total gas density and, accordingly, the lifting force of the airship. Install combustion engines (page 244) and propellers on the airship to create horizontal thrust. Place them at the back of the hull and attach the elevators to the outside to guide the boat up or down. Rudders and side propellers will come in handy during horizontal maneuvers.

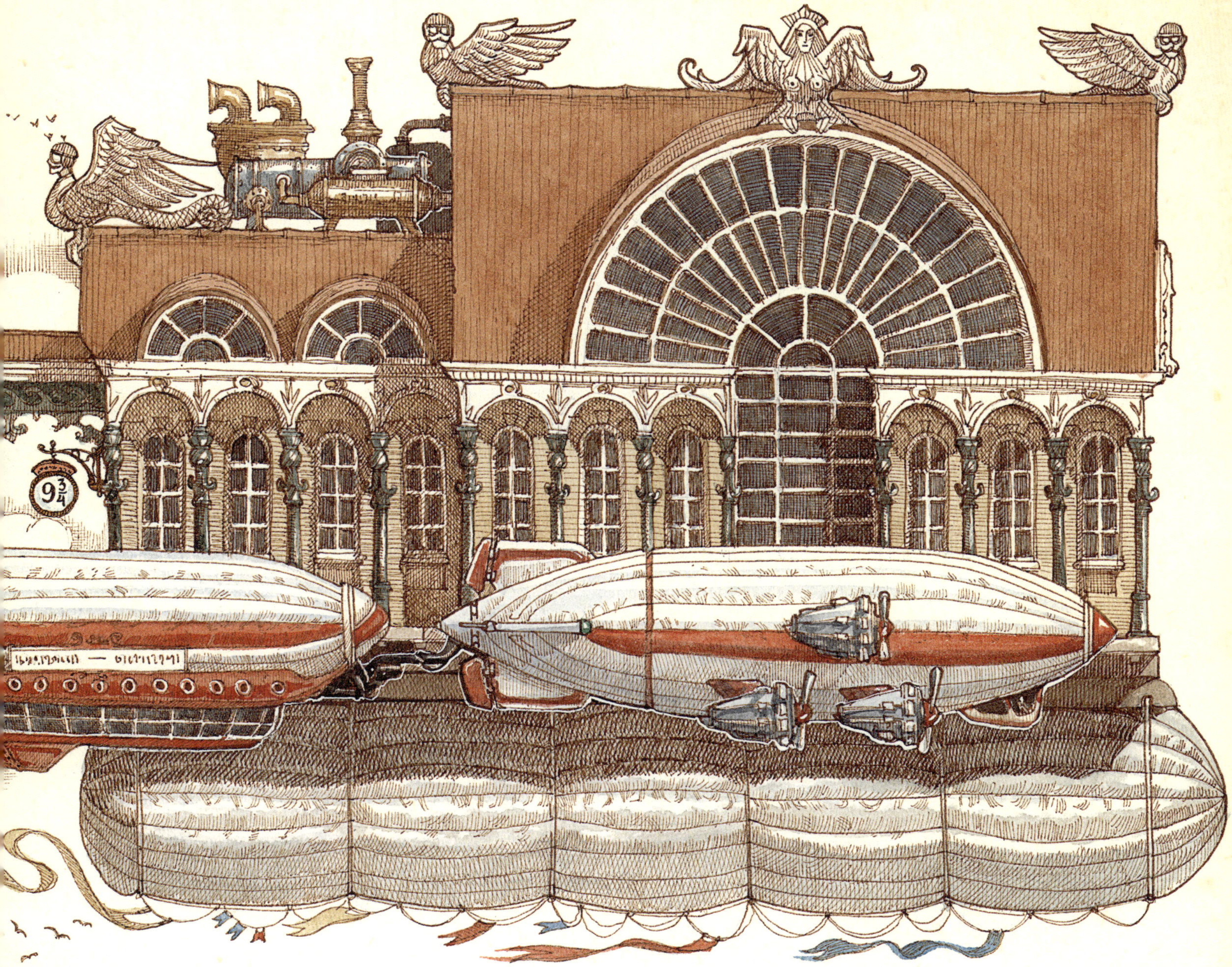

1. *Mooring device*
2. *Outer hull fabric*
3. *Main control gondola*
4. *Passenger decks*
5. *Longitudinal reinforcement ribs*
6. *Transverse reinforcement ribs*
7. *Gas balloons. To make them gastight, saturate with latex (page 116)*
8. *Internal combustion engines (page 224) and propellers to create horizontal thrust*
9. *Top and bottom stabilizers*
10. *Rudders*
11. *Side stabilizer*
12. *Elevators*

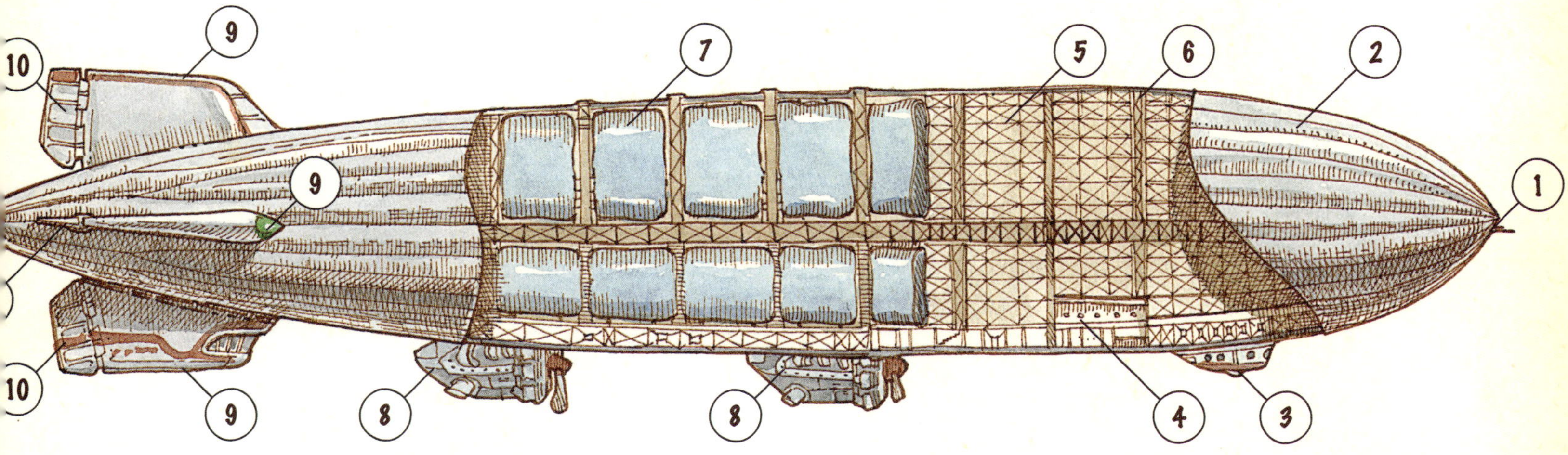

PARACHUTE

O gravity, thou art a heartless thing, forbidding man to spread his wings and fly and dooming him to plummet to the ground.

But you can slow the descent and survive the fall, even from very great heights, if you know how to pit another natural force against gravity — air resistance.

If the sails of our ships can bear us along on water waves, why not create another kind of sail to catch air waves?

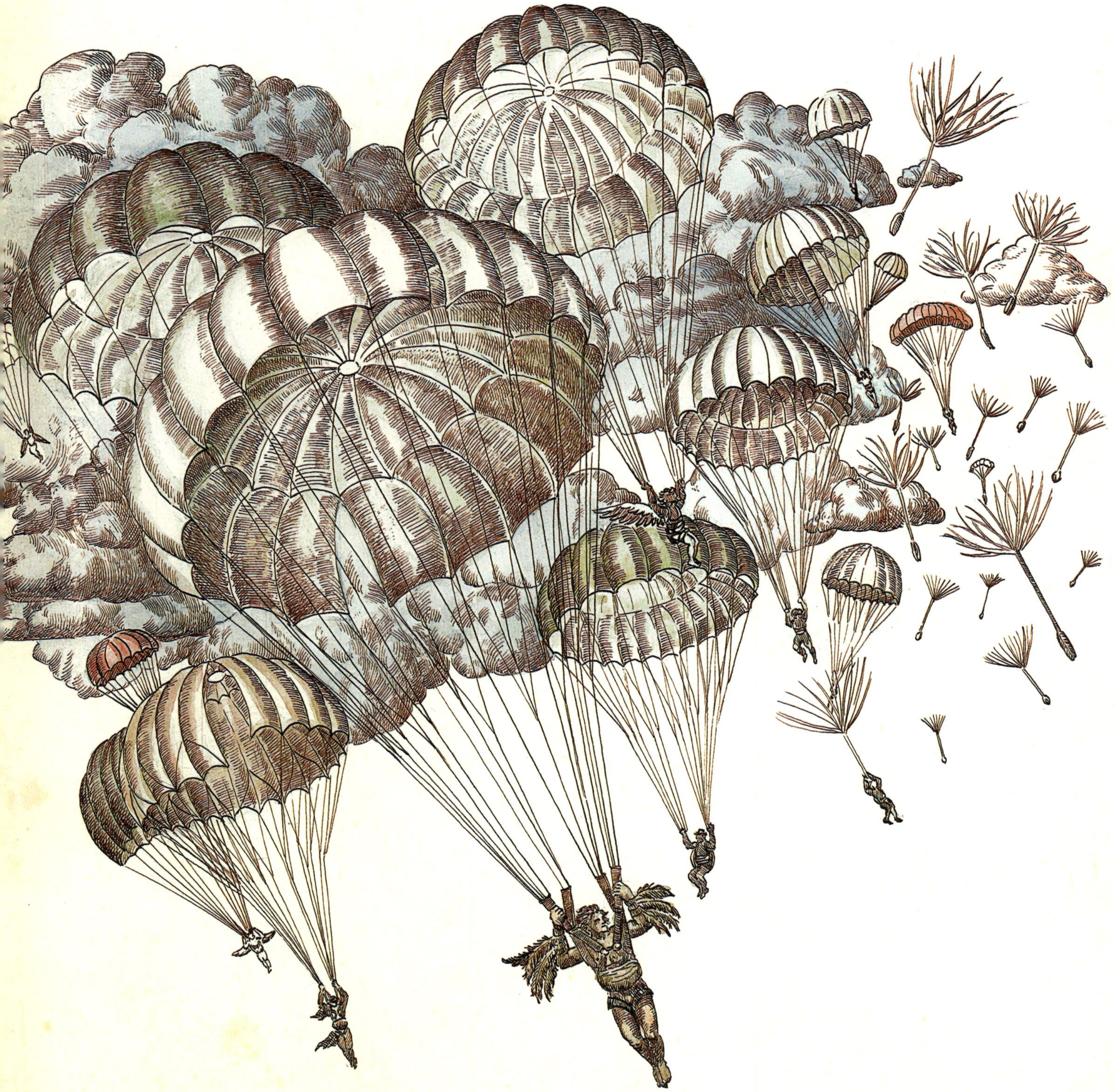

You need a large piece of airtight fabric. Ordinary canvas will not work, as it's too heavy and bulky. Use silk. If your goal is to land as safely as possible, sew a canopy parachute: cut triangular sections of fabric (1) and sew them together. Remember to reinforce the seams with wide ribbons so that the parachute does not tear at the seams under a heavy load.

Special air slots (2) should be cut in the canopy of the parachute to allow for some air flow. At first glance, this may seem to reduce the effectiveness of the parachute, but in fact, these slots release excess pressure buildup under the canopy and stabilize air flow. Fortify the parachute with a strong, wide webbing sewn into a net over the top surface of the parachute and ending in loops around the perimeter (3).

Attach suspension lines (4) — long, sturdy cords — to these loops. Make them from woven silk threads. They will slip over each other easily, which will prevent tangling when the parachute opens. Gather the suspension lines into four bundles and attach them to the parachute pack with carabiners (5). Sew a reinforcing webbing around the bottom edge of the canopy between the suspension line attachment loops.

Make the final circumference slightly smaller than the canopy itself so that it gathers at the bottom, preventing it from sagging and tangling during deployment and reducing the time it takes to fill with air.

Initially, the parachute is packed into a compact bag of complex design to await deployment. To release the parachute mid-air and make sure it catches and fully deploys in the airflow, you'll need to apply some force.

Doing this manually is difficult, but you can make the task easier with the help of a special small pilot chute (6). It will do all the work for you: As it catches the airstream, it pulls the main canopy out of the pack behind it.

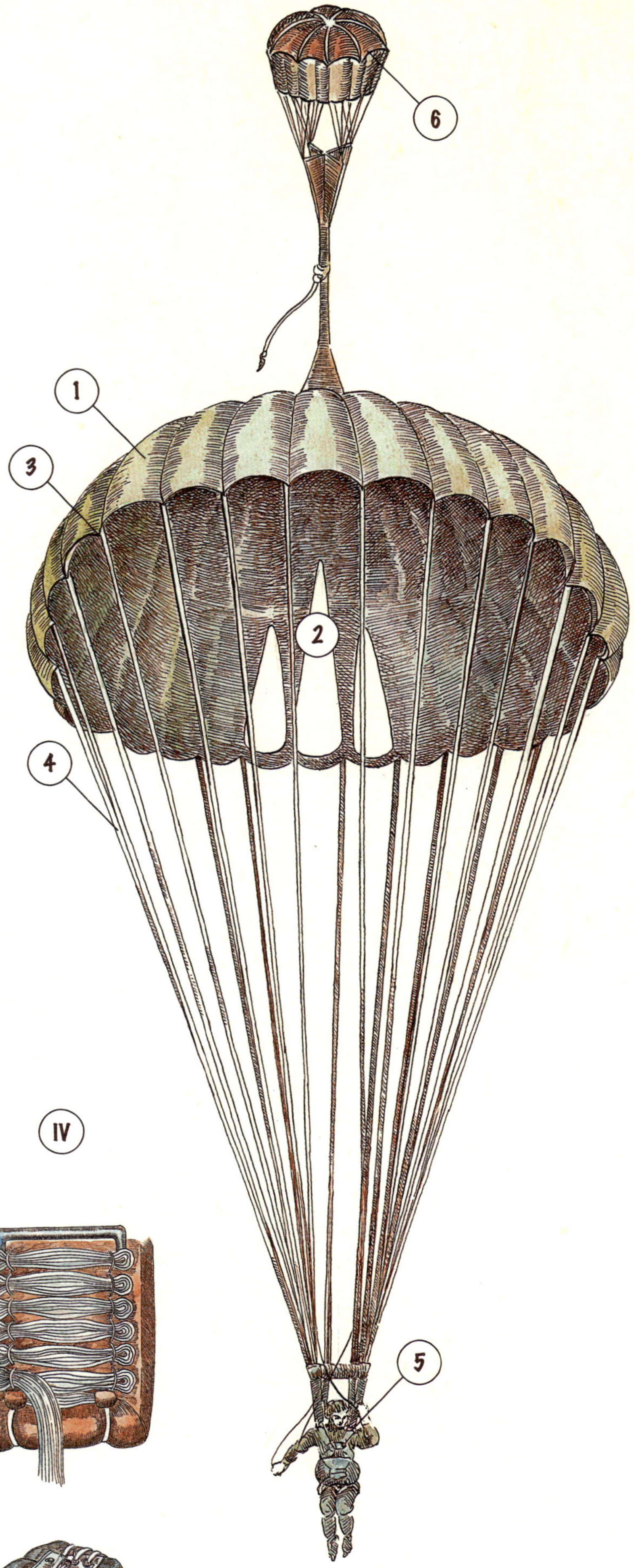

PACKING THE PARACHUTE

How the parachute is packed determines how quickly and effectively it deploys. The canopy should be folded longitudinally so that the seams remain straight. Then it is folded perpendicularly and placed in the parachute pack. The lines must also be packed in a specific way so they do not get tangled. The pilot chute fits into a special compartment separate from the main compartment of the parachute pack.

The pack consists of four flaps that open like an envelope. During the packing process, they should be held open. The different parts of the parachute are packed in the order in which they must be deployed when the parachute opens.

First, the pilot chute is folded and secured with a closing pin connected to the valve of the main parachute chamber. The suspension lines will open according to the order in which they are packed and are fastened to the canopy with shackle pins connected to tensioned elastic bands. The skydiver pulls the ring connected to a cable holding the pins. When the pins are pulled out, the tensioned elastic bands are released and quickly open the valves. The canopy of the pilot chute catches the rising air stream and unfurls, drawing the main canopy out of the bag with it.

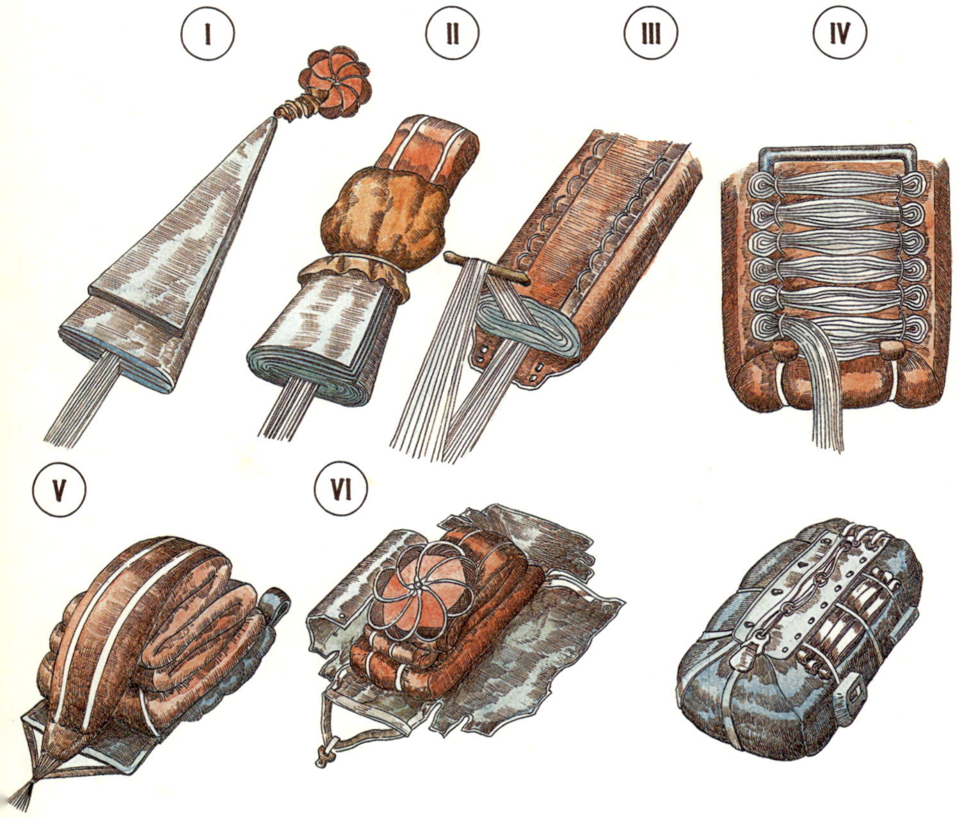

I. *Folding the canopy*
II. *Placing a protective cover*
III. *Checking the cable placement*
IV. *Bundling and packing the lines*
V. *Packing the parachute into the pack*
VI. *Placement of the pilot chute*

INDUSTRY

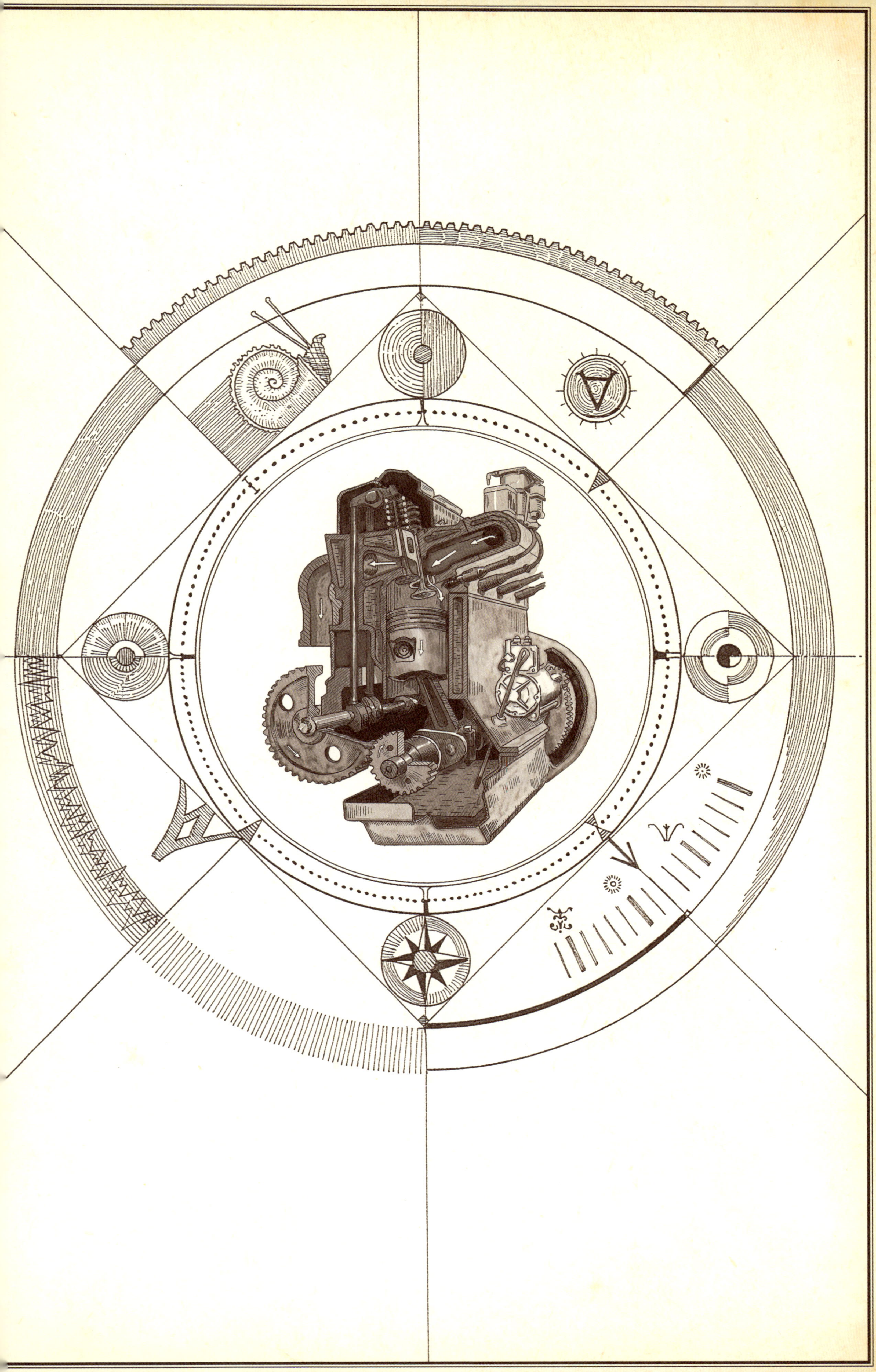

WINDMILL

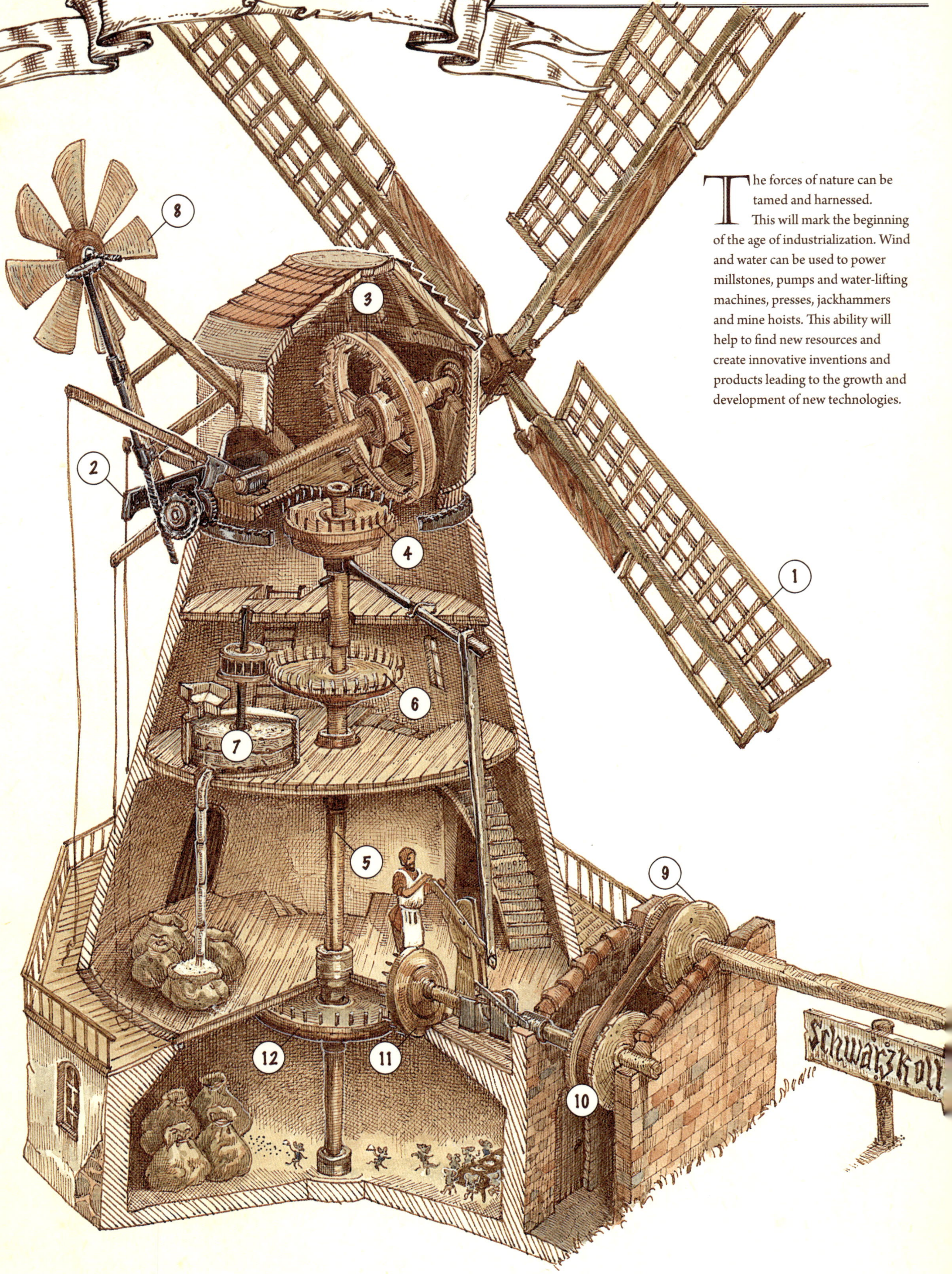

The forces of nature can be tamed and harnessed. This will mark the beginning of the age of industrialization. Wind and water can be used to power millstones, pumps and water-lifting machines, presses, jackhammers and mine hoists. This ability will help to find new resources and create innovative inventions and products leading to the growth and development of new technologies.

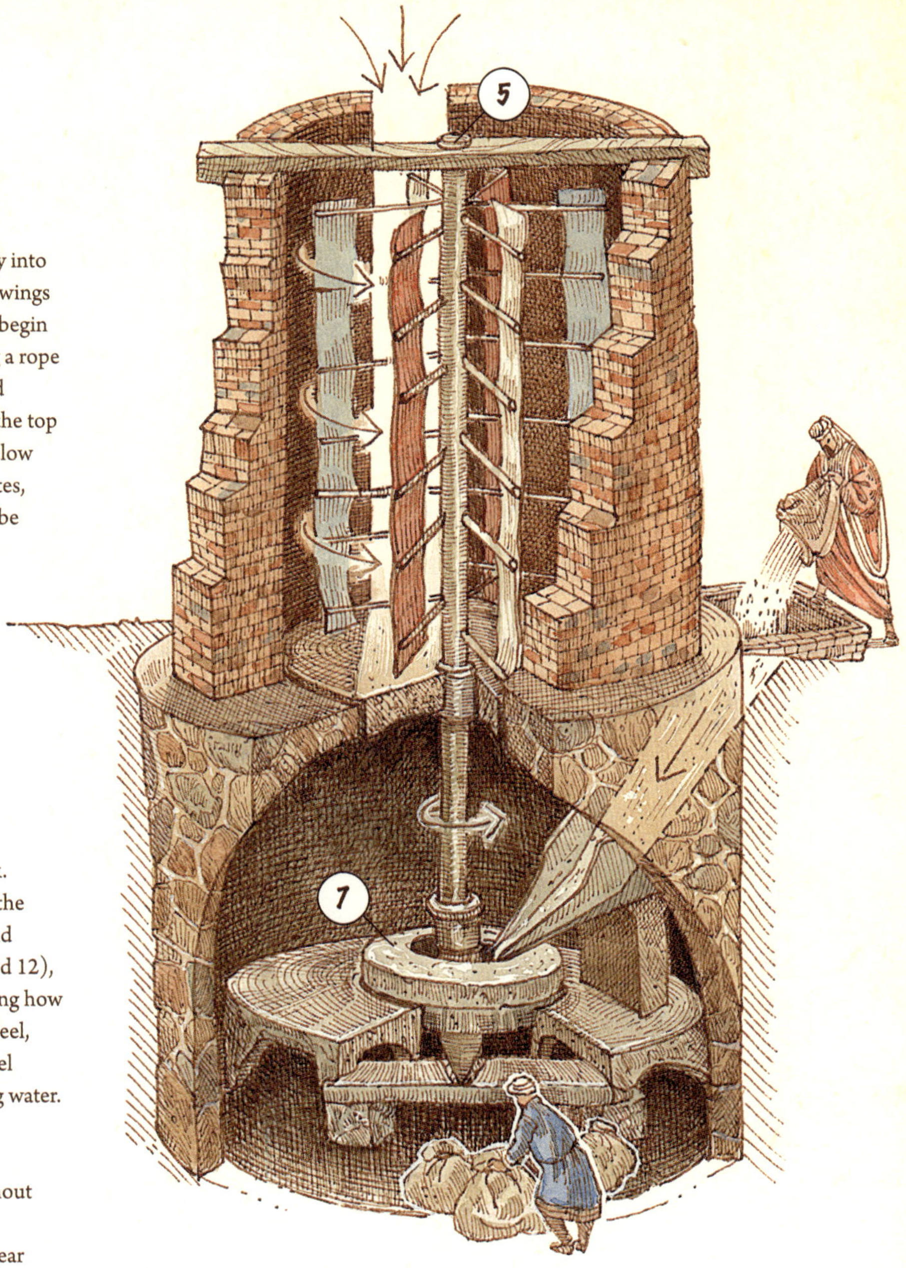

WINDMILL

Windmills are mechanical devices that convert the wind's kinetic energy into mechanical work through the aerodynamic action of the airflow on the wings of the mill. The rotor blades of the mill (1) are pushed by the wind and begin to rotate. When needed, the rotation of the blades can be blocked using a rope and chain (2) mounted on the rear of the tower. On the shaft connected to the edges, there is a large brake wheel (3) that drives a pinion (4) at the top of the central vertical shaft (5) running through the whole structure. Below is the gear (6) that drives the millstones (7). Only the upper stone rotates, while the lower remains stationary. The gap between the stones should be tiny to produce a fine grind. The finished grain flour flows through the channel into bags.

To allow the mill blades to catch the wind blowing from different directions, mount the upper turret on a rotating platform that is turned by a fantail (8) and gears.

WATER WHEEL

Convert the potential and kinetic energy of water into mechanical work. The water drives the blades of the wheel. It transmits the rotation from the water wheel (9) to the drive pulley, which uses a belt to make the second pulley (10) rotate. This is connected through a shaft to the gears (11 and 12), turning the gear wheel that rotates the millstones (7). When determining how you want to place your wheel in the river, consider that an overhead wheel, which has water poured into it from above, is more efficient than a wheel lowered into the stream, as it captures the potential energy of the falling water.

Combining a windmill and watermill will increase your efficiency — if the wind is low, use the waterwheel to continue processing grain without interruption. This requires a lever (13) capable of switching between the windmill and water wheel to power the shaft (5), which turns the gear wheel (6) driving the millstones (7). Lifting the lever engages the windmill gears through the windmill shaft (14) whilst disengaging the water wheel gears (16 and 17) through the water wheel shaft (15), and vice versa.

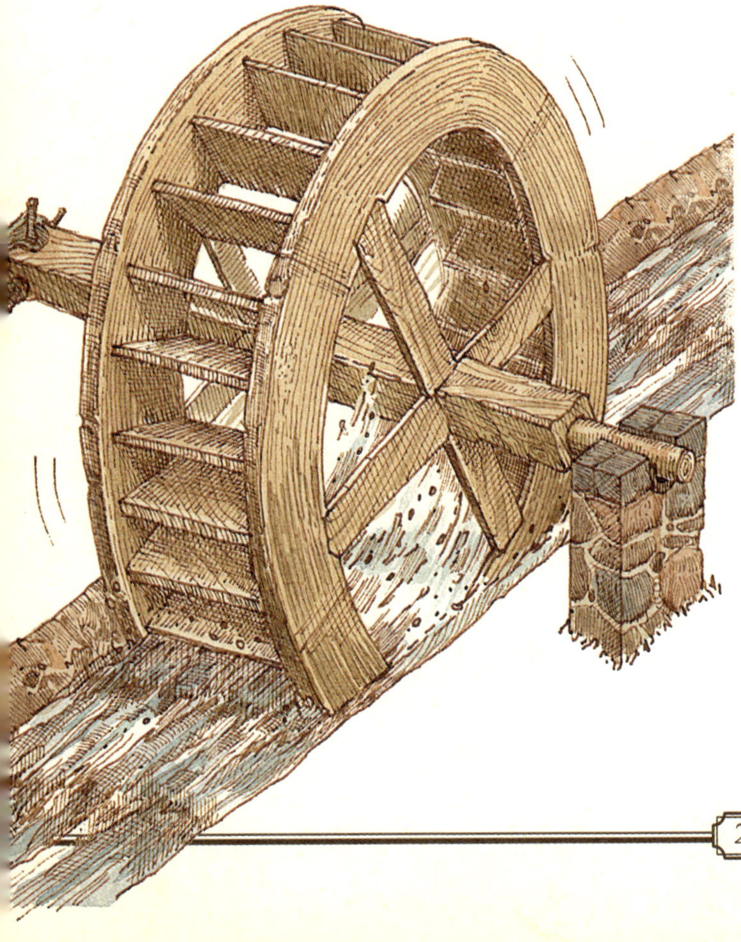

The high-speed vertical water wheel is a prototype of a more sophisticated technology: steam power (page 242) and hydroelectric power with a water turbine. This type of wheel requires a powerful and fast stream of water, such as a waterfall. You can create these technologies in the next stage of development.

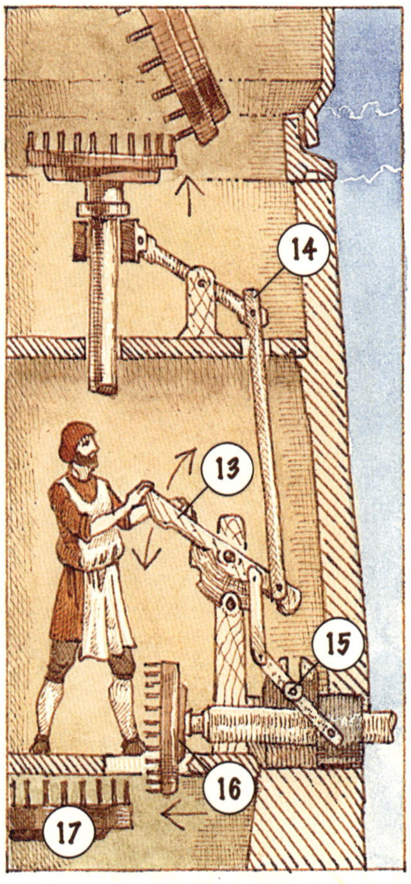

PRINTING PRESS

The printed word gives rise to the collection and distribution of knowledge. Suddenly, more people will be able to gain new knowledge and add it to their own.

Printing facilitates the spread of ideas that may form changes in your societal structure. With the help of books, flyers and pamphlets, all types of information will be available to all levels of society.

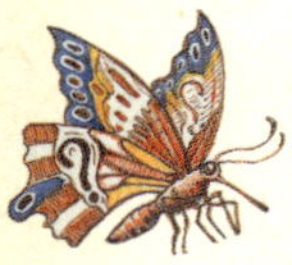

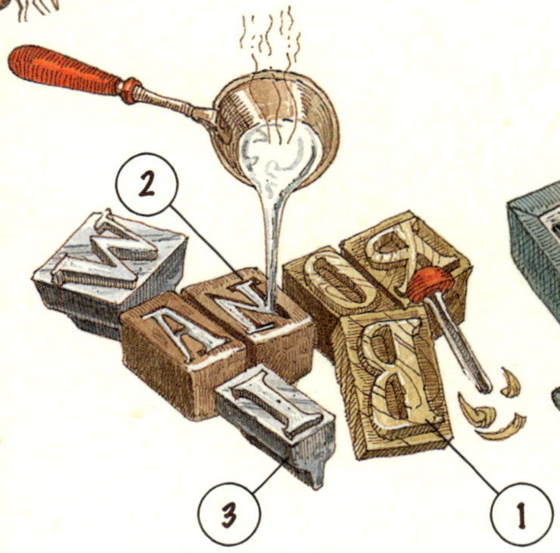

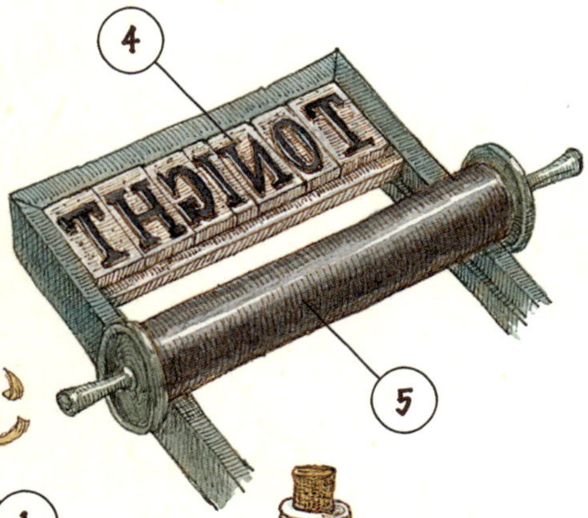

So that you're not stuck tediously transcribing texts by hand, create a printing press. You'll need individual letter stamps that you arrange to create a text, stamp onto a paper, disassemble and then rearrange to create a new text using the same type stamps. First, carve the letter stamps from wood. Press these forms into a mixture of sand and liquid glass or into a soft metal such as copper. Pour an alloy of molten lead and tin (page 110) into the resulting molds and let harden. Now you can use these stamps to print texts. Just keep in mind that you'll have to carve the wooden letters in a mirror image so that they'll end up facing the right direction on the page. The cast stamps will also be mirrored. You'll also have to get used to arranging the words backwards so that they read correctly in the printed text.

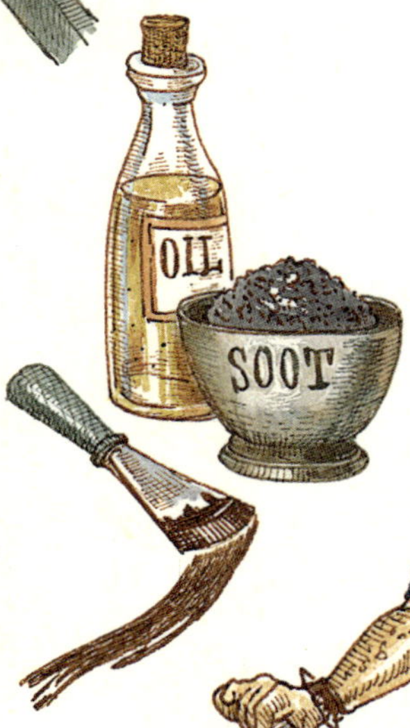

Make an oil-based ink from soot and turpentine, which can be obtained by burning pine resin. Apply the ink using a rubber roller or a ball made from goose skin and stuffed with wool. Treat the leather with urine to make it softer so that it won't wear down the typeface as quickly. Cover the roller or ball evenly with ink, and then carefully apply it to all of the letter stamps and you are ready to print.

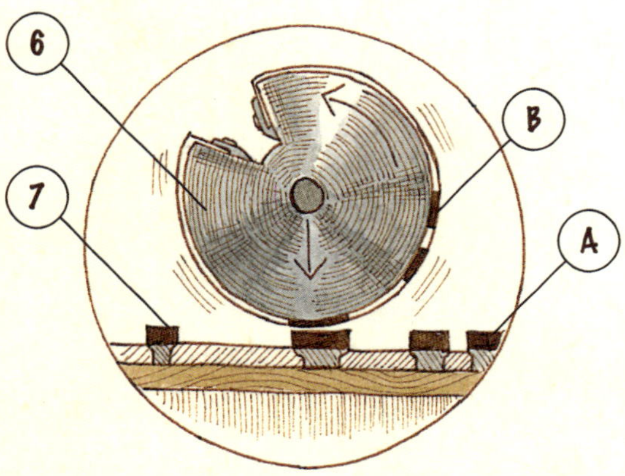

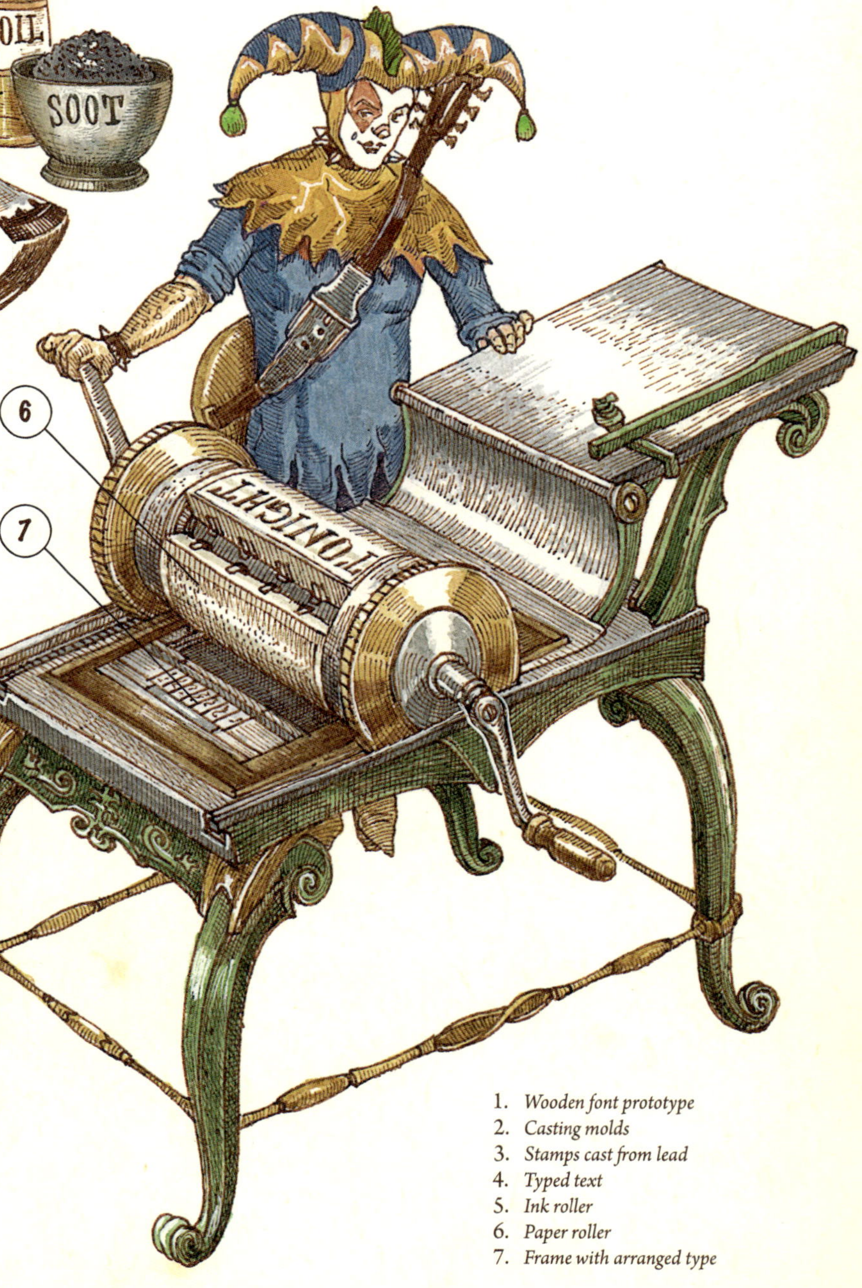

LETTERPRESS

Set the moveable metal letters in the frame (7) on the table base. Apply the ink. Attach a sheet of paper to the heavy roller (6) with a handle. To ensure the roller moves smoothly, cut guide grooves into the base of the table. Turn the roller so that the paper is pressed against the letter board. The raised letters (A) transfer the ink onto the paper (B), leaving an imprint. Make as many copies as you'd like by simply switching out the paper in the roller. Then rearrange the moveable type to make the next page and repeat the process.

1. *Wooden font prototype*
2. *Casting molds*
3. *Stamps cast from lead*
4. *Typed text*
5. *Ink roller*
6. *Paper roller*
7. *Frame with arranged type*

FLAT PRINT

Smooth down a slab of limestone using water and sand (1). Draw directly onto the slab (2) using a pencil made of soap, mutton fat wax and carbon black or ink. Make this by mixing soot with drying oil, obtained by evaporating linseed oil.

Or add soap, baking soda, carbon black and gum (resin secreted by plants when the bark is damaged) to an oil base. Rub the slab with powdered rosin (page 200) and cover with a mixture of calcined starch and sulfuric acid (3). The acidic substance will stick to the unpainted surface, making it waterproof. The painted parts will remain water absorbent.

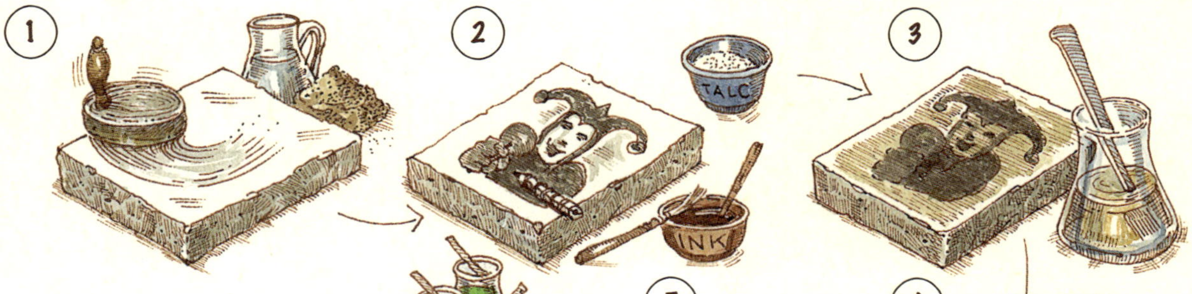

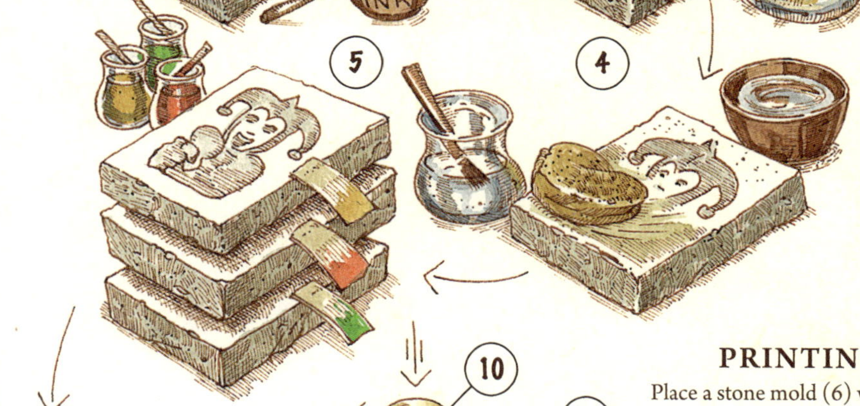

Wet the slab (4). Water and grease paint do not mix. Once applied, the pigment will stick only to parts of the stone that have been covered by wax crayon (and have remained dry). You can also make color prints. Draw a different image on the slab for each color you want to print on the paper (5) and run the sheet over several times, changing the pattern and adding colors sequentially.

PRINTING PRESS

Place a stone mold (6) with the image up on the base and lay a damp sheet of paper (7) on top. Cover with a sheet of rubber (8) and a clamp (9) on top. This will ensure that pressure is applied evenly across the surface of the stone by the roller press (10). In a printing press, it is the mold itself that moves. It is fixed on a frame (11) driven by a gear wheel (12) and is rotated with a handle (13). A huge screw (14) is connected to the pressure roller. When the wheel (15) rotates, the screw turns the rotational movement into a linear downward movement, thereby increasing the pressure and leaving a clear impression on the paper.

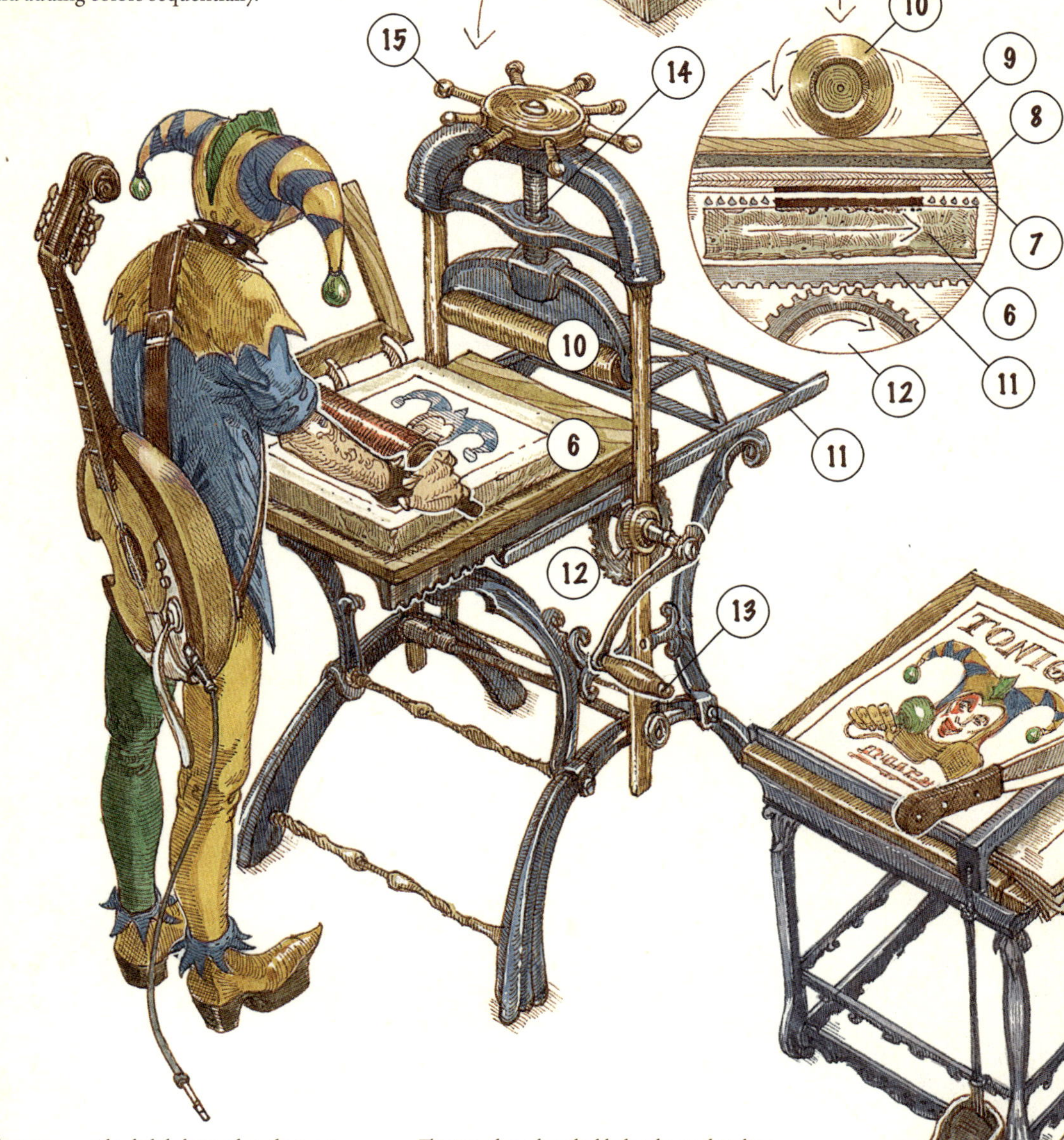

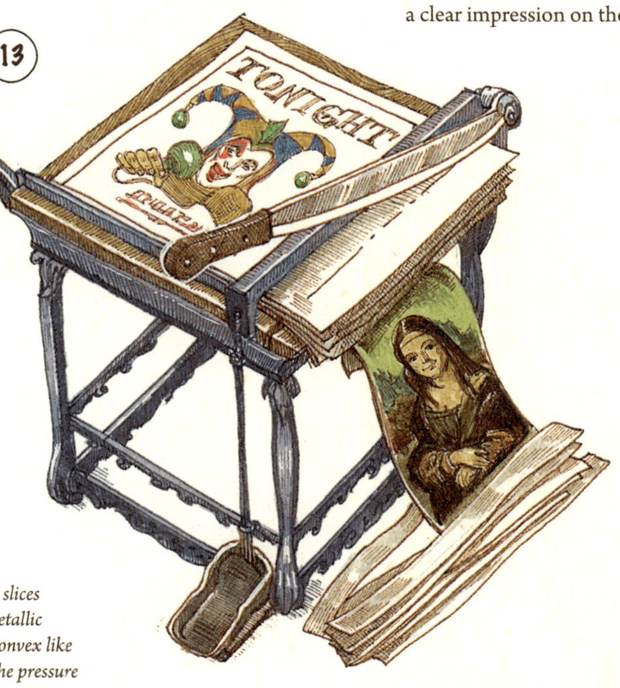

The paper must be slightly larger than the pages of the book you wish to print, leaving blank margins around the edge, which must then be trimmed. Use a guillotine-style paper cutter. Hold a stack of pages together using a press. The edge of the table should be outfitted with a metal corner for cutting.

This is so that when the blade is lowered, it slices through smoothly and slides against the metallic surface of the counter. Use a blade that is convex like a saber. This way, as you lower the blade, the pressure will be applied in a more concentrated area, reducing the force needed to cut through the sheets.

HYDRAULIC PRESS

Whoever says that brute force never solves anything is sorely mistaken. It comes in handy when you want some wine or olive oil or when you need to bend solid materials into shape. Build a hydraulic press to create a force many times greater than what you yourself can apply.

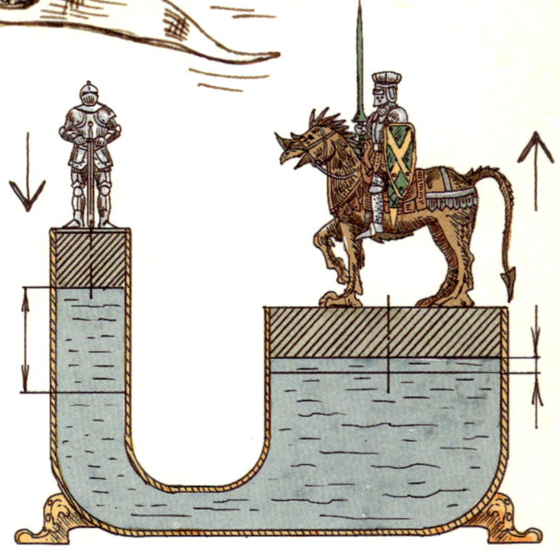

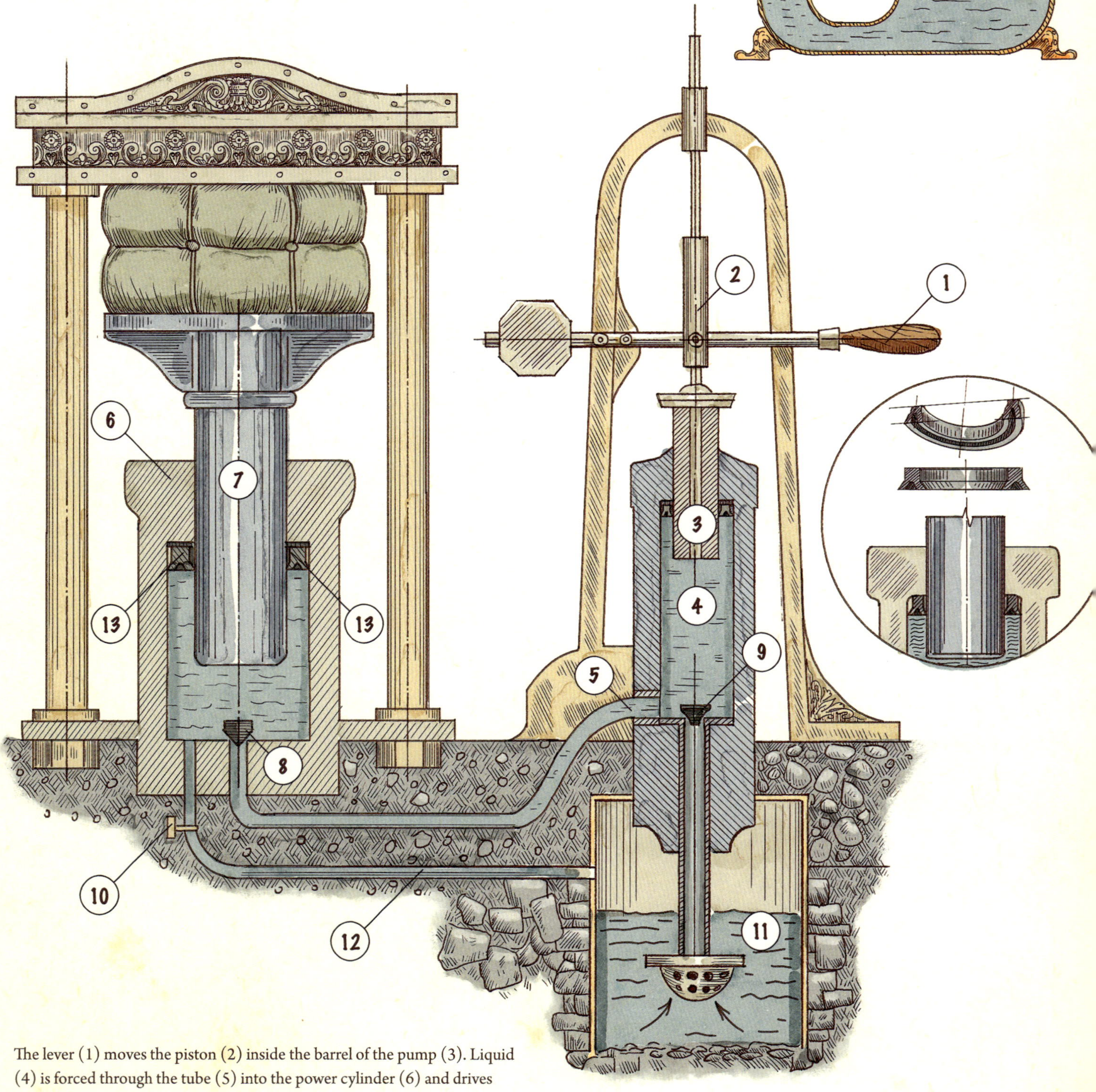

The lever (1) moves the piston (2) inside the barrel of the pump (3). Liquid (4) is forced through the tube (5) into the power cylinder (6) and drives the piston (7). When the lever is lifted, the valve (8) closes and prevents the liquid from flowing back from the cylinder, the valve (9) opens and new liquid enters the pump. When the lever is lowered, the valve (9) closes, and the fluid is sent to the working cylinder (6), raising the piston (7) even higher. The process is repeated until the work you need is done. Clamps connecting the pipe (5) with the working cylinder (6) and the pump cylinder (3) form a system of communicating vessels.

When the work is done, open the stop-gate valve (10) and the cylinder (7) will return to its original position under its own weight or with the help of a spring, and the liquid will flow back into the reservoir (11) through the return channel (12). The main element of the press is the U-shaped cuffs (13) that prevent the outflow of liquid.

MANIPULATOR ARM

Once you have practiced making simple presses and have mastered hydraulic technology, you can take on more complex tasks such as building robotic arms with hydraulically powered limbs.

Manipulator arms consist of articulated links, like the bones and joints of a human hand. Manipulators can be built with movable links that allow both translational and rotational movements. The combination and arrangement of these links will determine the mobility of the robot.

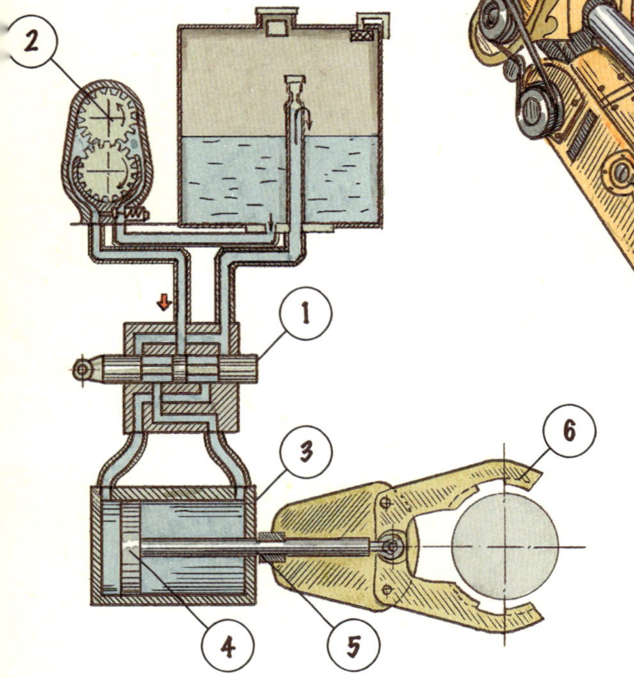

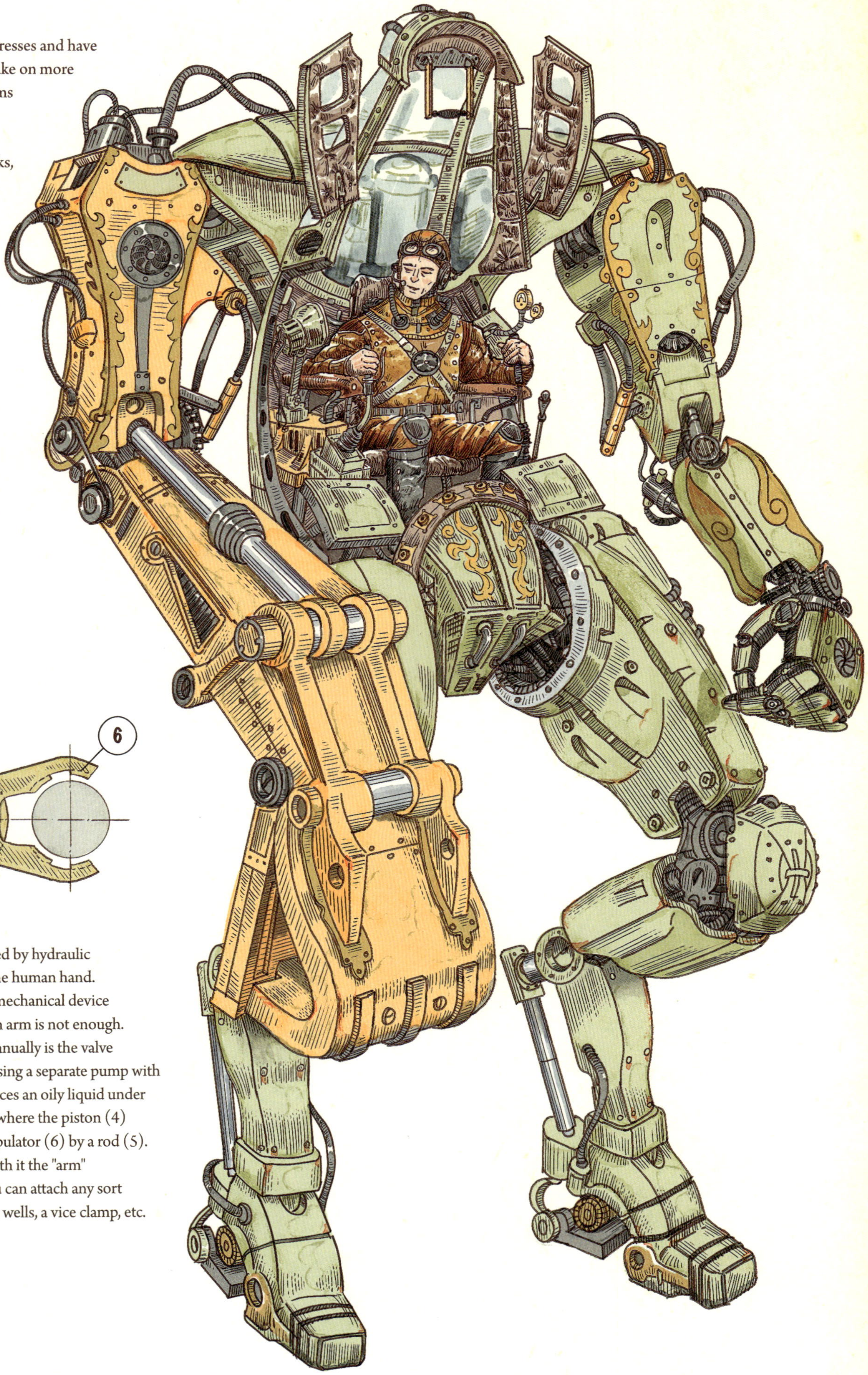

The movement of the limbs will be provided by hydraulic cylinders — analogues of the muscles in the human hand. But in order to move the heavy limbs of a mechanical device with enough force, the strength of a human arm is not enough. Therefore, the only part that is operated manually is the valve control (1), while the pressure is created using a separate pump with a steam or electric drive (2). The pump forces an oily liquid under high pressure into the power cylinder (3) where the piston (4) is located, which is connected to the manipulator (6) by a rod (5). This is what makes the piston move and with it the "arm" of the robot. In lieu of a gripping hand, you can attach any sort of device — a shovel for digging, a drill for wells, a vice clamp, etc.

If you don't install a cuff seal, the press will not work, as liquid will begin to leak out and you won't be able to create the proper amount of pressure. The seal should be made from a flexible, water-resistant material such as rubber (page 116).

One rim of the ring should be convex and the other shaped like a hollow. When liquid presses up against the U-shaped wall, the cuff, due to its flexibility, creates the necessary seal between the piston and the cylinder walls.

METAL CASTING

When you learn to use fire for more sophisticated tasks than simply roasting hunks of meat, you'll open the gateway to a whole range of useful new materials. For example, you can purify ore mined in mines to obtain metals. And since large amounts of metals, such as iron and steel, are needed to restore civilization, you'll need a smelter working round the clock.

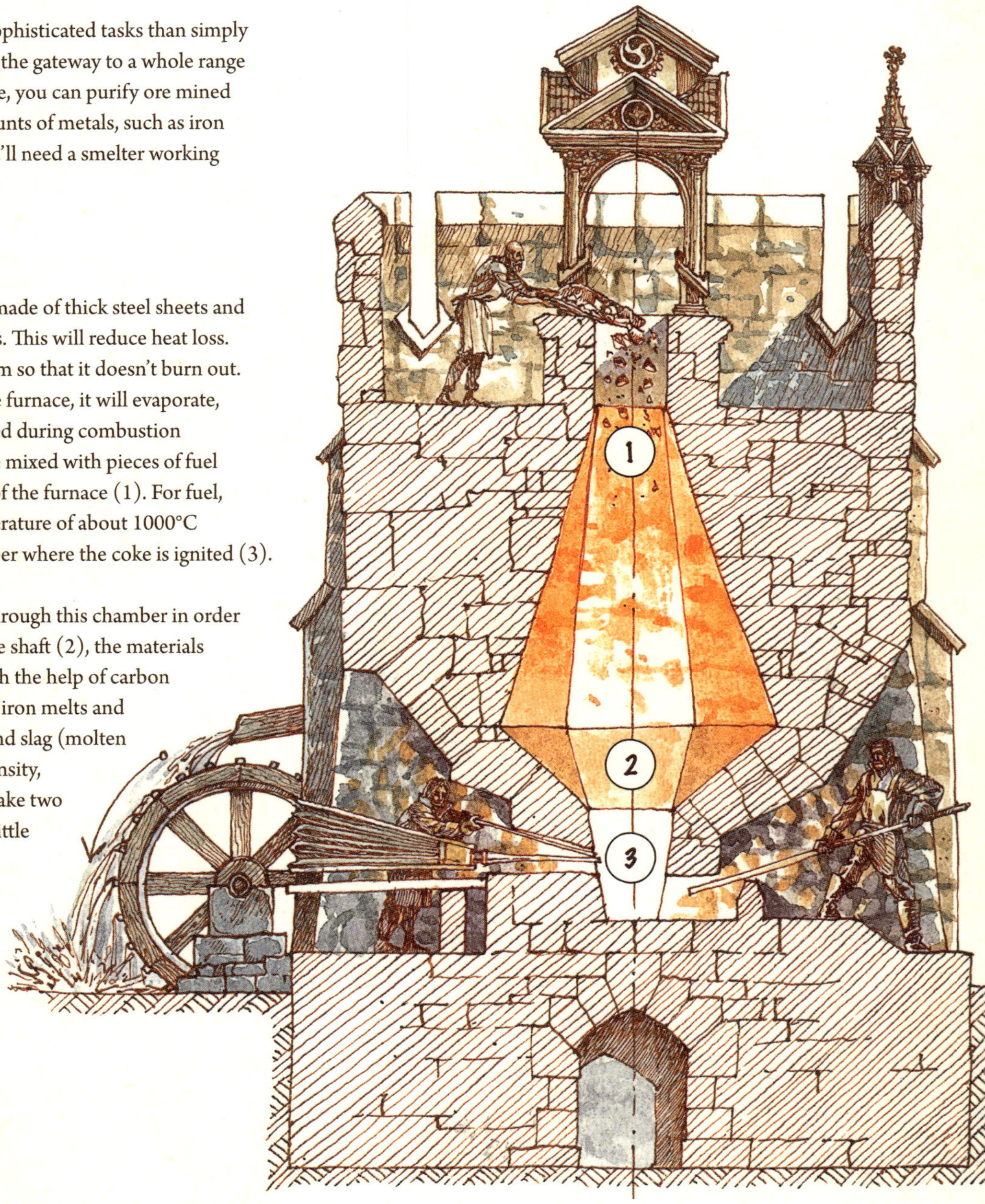

BLAST FURNACE

Cover the outside of the furnace with a casing made of thick steel sheets and make a refractory lining out of white clay bricks. This will reduce heat loss. The stove also needs some sort of cooling system so that it doesn't burn out. Use water — when it comes in contact with the furnace, it will evaporate, actively absorbing thermal energy. Gases formed during combustion are vented and raw materials (pieces of iron ore mixed with pieces of fuel and limestone) are loaded into the upper part of the furnace (1). For fuel, use coke — coal heated for 20 hours at a temperature of about 1000°C without any airflow. Below the forge is a chamber where the coke is ignited (3).

You'll need a bellows constantly pumping air through this chamber in order to stimulate combustion. In the wide part of the shaft (2), the materials are heated and iron is obtained from oxides with the help of carbon monoxide, which is formed in the furnace. The iron melts and flows down, saturated with carbon. Cast iron and slag (molten impurities) are formed. The slag has a lower density, so it floats on the surface of the molten iron. Make two channels, one for removing the slag and one a little lower for removing the cast iron. The furnace must be running constantly: If the supply of air and fuel is cut off, the temperature will drop, the materials will solidify and the furnace will stop working.

CASTING

I. Make a model out of wood. Try, for example, an angelic visage.

II. Cut the model into two pieces so that you have a flat surface for casting and place in a molding box (a box with one side missing). Pour sand mixed with refractory clay into the mold, as well as liquid glass to bind this mixture (melt the sand with soda and dissolve in water). Insert tubes into the sand to form channels for casting the metal. Pack the sand down tightly then remove the tubes and wooden model. All these details will leave impressions in the sand, cavities into which you will pour the metal.

III. Connect the top and bottom molding boxes containing the sandy imprint of your cast. Pour molten metal into the holes left by the tubes. Let it solidify. Remove the flask and break off the caked sand mold. Beneath it will be your angel head, cast in metal. Cut off the excess metal held in the tubes through which the metal was poured. Sand and polish the finished product.

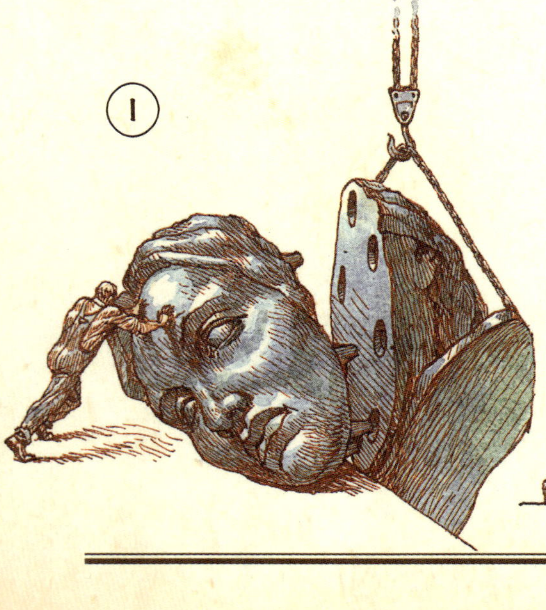

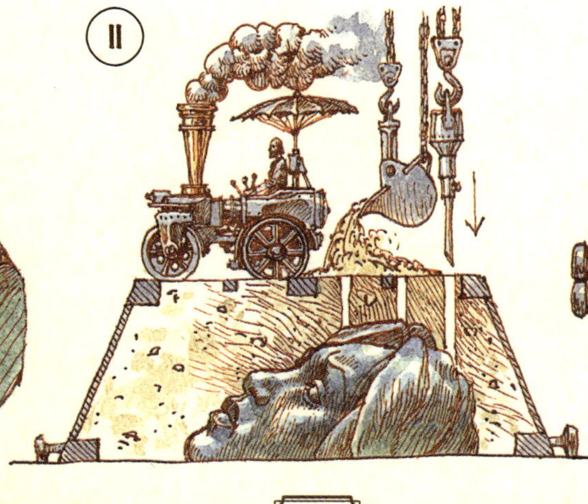

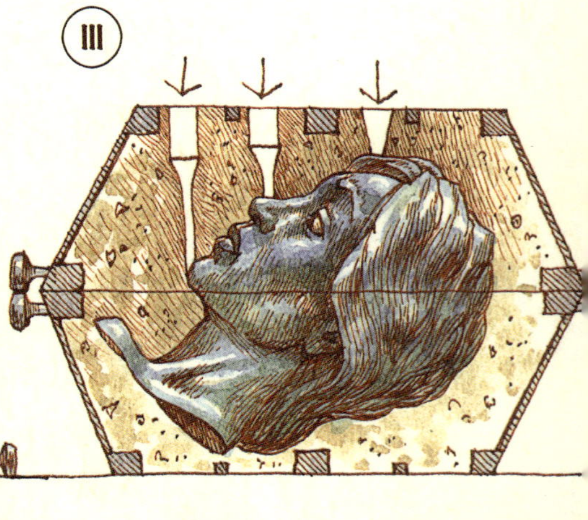

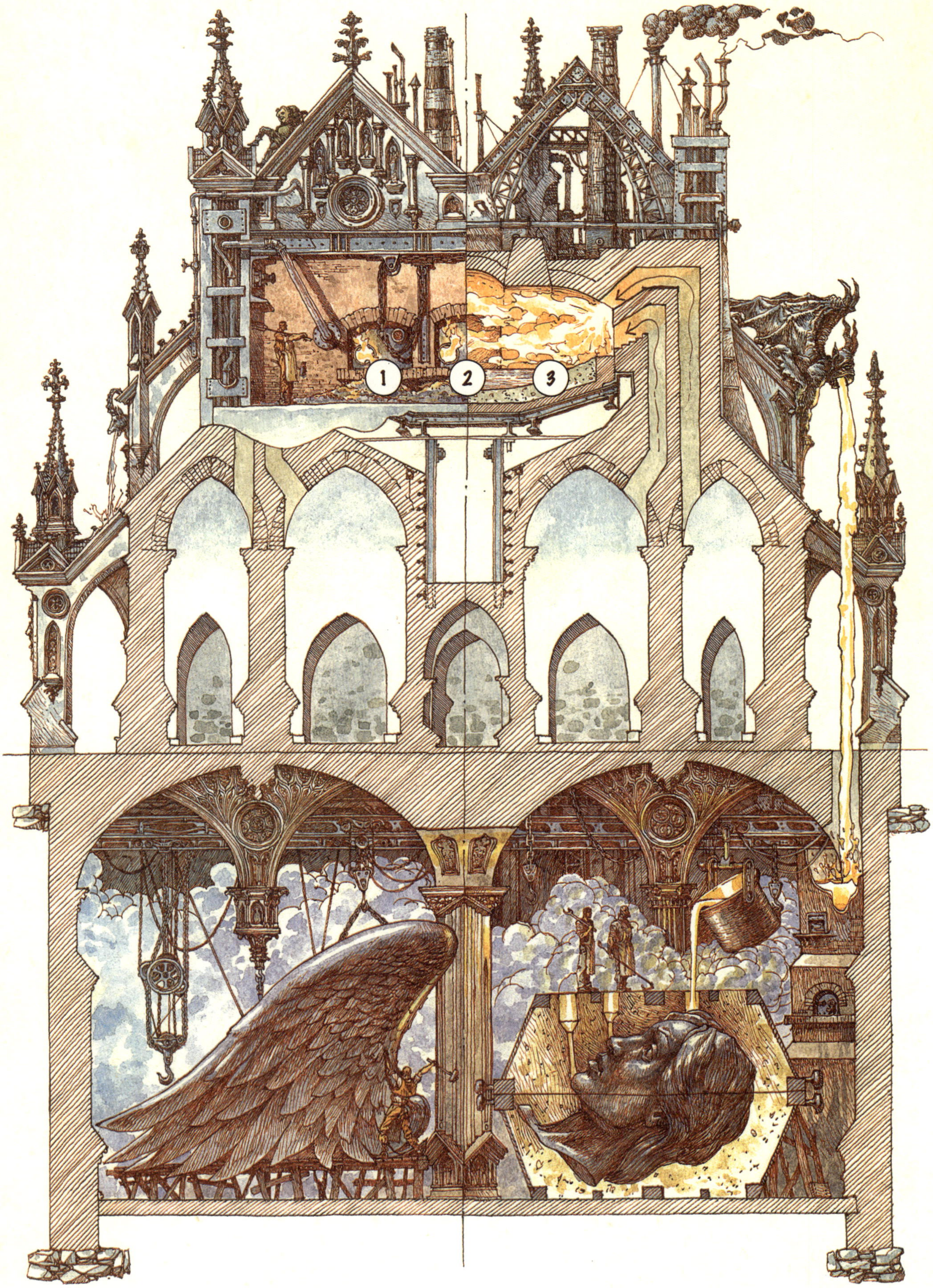

OBTAINING STEEL

Cast iron is carbon rich, which makes it hard but not ductile. It cannot be bent or rolled. But if you remove some of the carbon from the iron in an open-hearth furnace, you get steel, which can be processed more easily. Air and combustible gas are heated in one of the two regenerators (1, 2) and enter the space above the refractory brick bath (3). The heat of the flames is reflected by the low arch of the furnace and melts the metal. Iron is oxidized by atmospheric oxygen. The carbon, interacting with this oxide, burns off. Foreign impurities stick to the resulting carbon monoxide bubbles. As they rise to the surface, they form slag. Combustion products are discharged through the second regenerator, heating it. Air and combustible gas are periodically supplied through the first or second regenerator; the direction is changed by switching valves.

STEAM ENGINE

The steam in a boiling kettle makes a loose lid jump and rattle. The energy of this steam is wasted, but it could easily be put to good use. After all, why let steam dissipate into the ether when you can harness its power and use it to your advantage?

Create a steam engine. It's the first technological driver of any civilization. Steam engines deliver a level of power that even a team of horses can't match. And almost anything can serve as a heat source: firewood, coal, peat, alcohol or solar and geothermal energy.

GOVERNOR

The steam engine is not a particularly reliable mechanism. If the shaft spins too quickly, the engine can overload and blow everything up. That's why we need a governor. When the shaft rotates too quickly, the centrifugal force causes the weights to swing out, turning the valve via a system of levers that consequently reduces the flow of steam into the piston. If the shaft rotates more slowly, the weights fold under gravity and the valve opens the pipe to allow more steam to pass through. By adjusting the flow of steam in this way, the machine maintains a consistent speed.

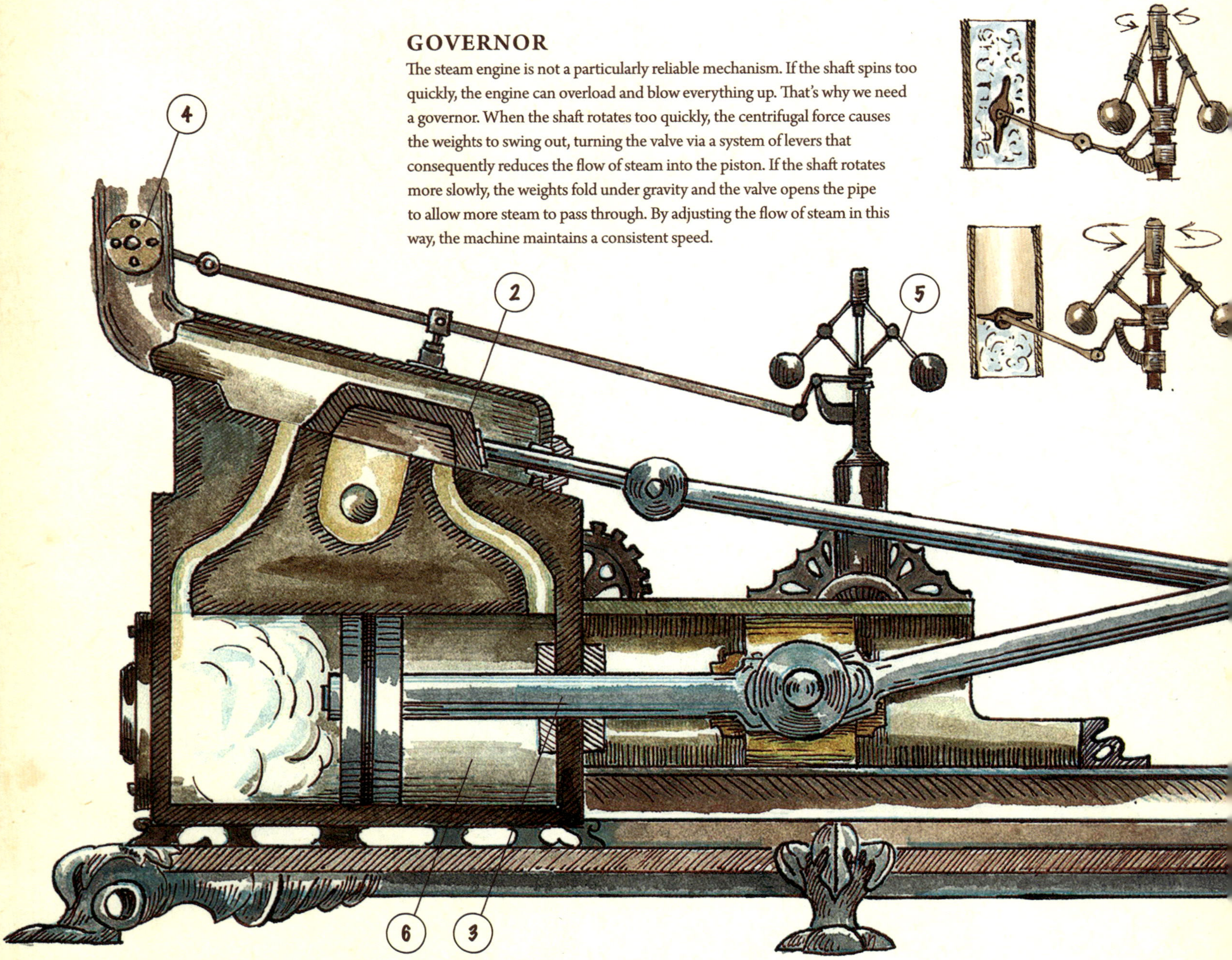

STEAM CHEST

The heart of a steam engine, the element that makes the whole huge mechanism work, is the steam chest. After steam is generated in the boiler, it flows into the steam chest. Inside are two piston-valve openings that lead to the cylinder. They serve as control valves. The left port opens, and steam rushes into the cylinder, pushing the piston forward. The flywheel makes a half-turn and pushes the piston valve, closing the left port and opening the right one. This time, steam enters through the right port, pushing the piston back. After another half-turn, the flywheel completes the circle and pushes the piston valve back into place, once again opening the left port. And so on. The flywheel makes a full revolution every two piston strokes. The machine putters forward.

The piston valve is also responsible for discharging the exhaust steam into a water-cooled condenser. Once there, the steam becomes water and is sent back to the boiler. It's a completely closed system.

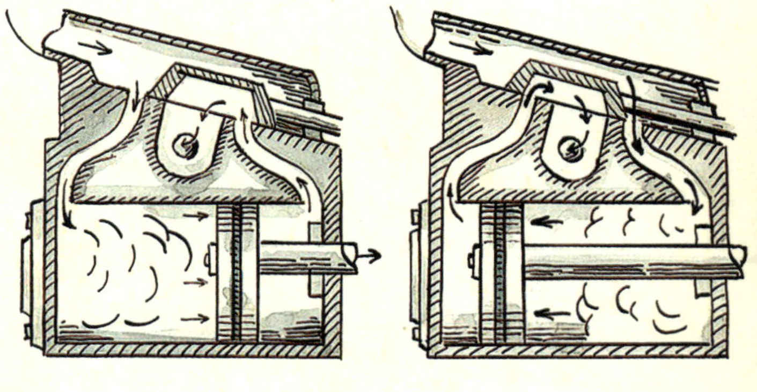

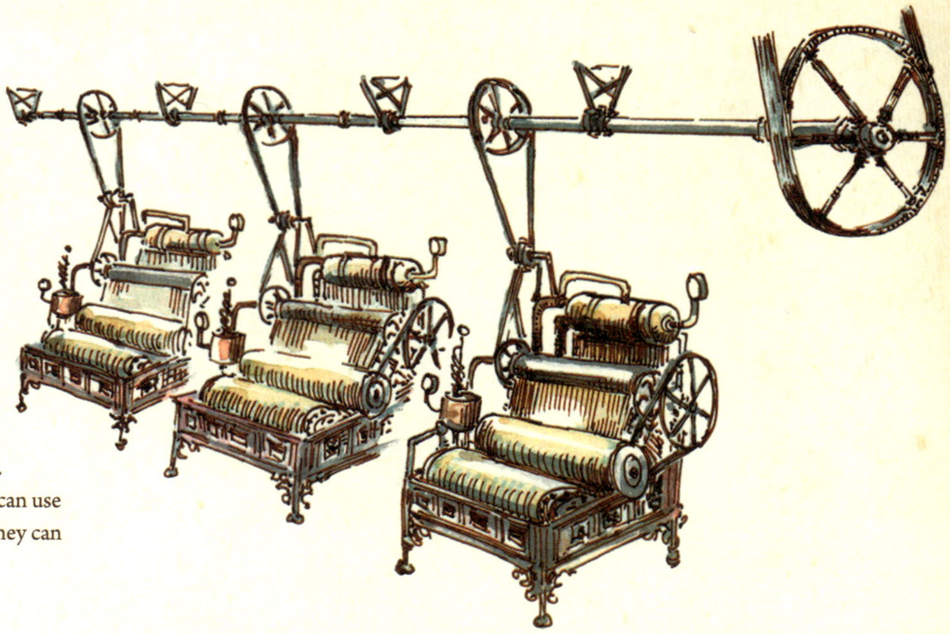

ASSEMBLY LINE

Just because you have a spinning wheel doesn't mean you have to go anywhere. With the help of a flat belt, this energy can be transferred to a drive shaft, which in turn can rotate smaller wheels to drive machinery in a factory. More importantly, this allows you to build a factory anywhere, as you aren't beholden to the fickle whims of the elemental forces of wind and water.

ROTATIONAL FORCE

Harnessing steam power to run the engines is only half the battle. What matters more is figuring out how best to use this newfound power. The first thought that comes to mind: If you have a spinning wheel, you can use it to drive somewhere. However, steam engines don't just turn wheels; they can also rotate blades and propellers, meaning you can sail away as well.

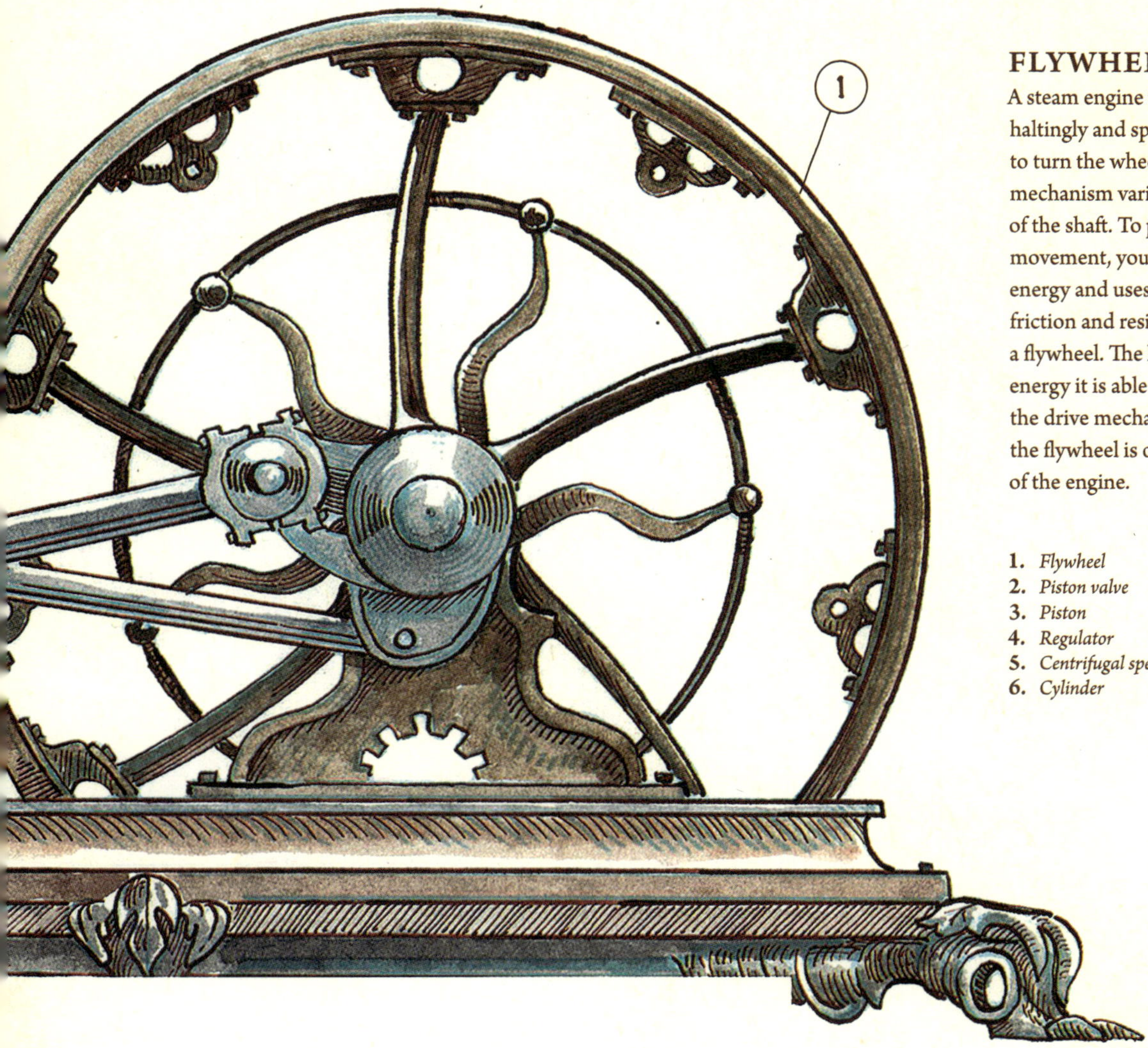

FLYWHEEL

A steam engine that drives axles tends to move haltingly and sporadically. The force needed to turn the wheel of a steam locomotive or drive mechanism varies depending on the position of the shaft. To provide a smooth, uniform movement, you need a device that stores rotational energy and uses it to compensate for uneven friction and resistance. This device is called a flywheel. The larger the flywheel, the more energy it is able to accumulate and the smoother the drive mechanism will run. That's why the flywheel is one of the largest parts of the engine.

1. *Flywheel*
2. *Piston valve*
3. *Piston*
4. *Regulator*
5. *Centrifugal speed regulator*
6. *Cylinder*

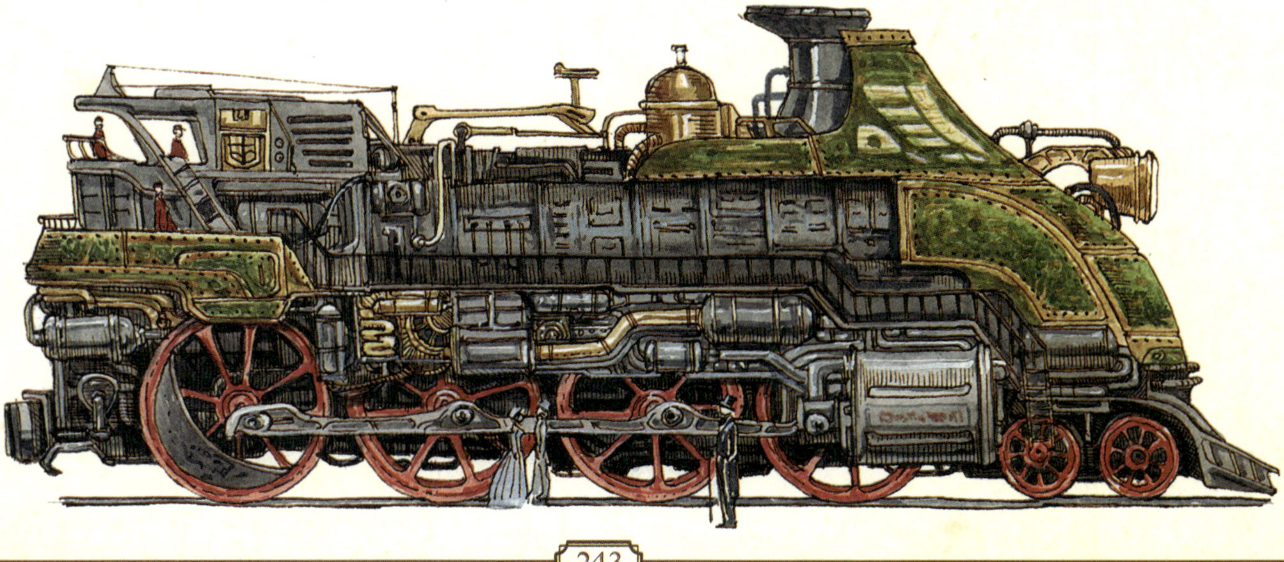

COMBUSTION ENGINE

Steam engines are very bulky and heavy, as they require a boiler and large reservoir of water. Ships and locomotives on rails can support the weight, but there's a much better design of heat engine for transport, as well as many other applications. Rather than generating steam to inject into a cylinder and drive a piston, instead use a liquid fuel that burns to produce hot gases that drive the piston — an internal combustion engine. This is more fuel efficient and can be built much smaller and lighter.

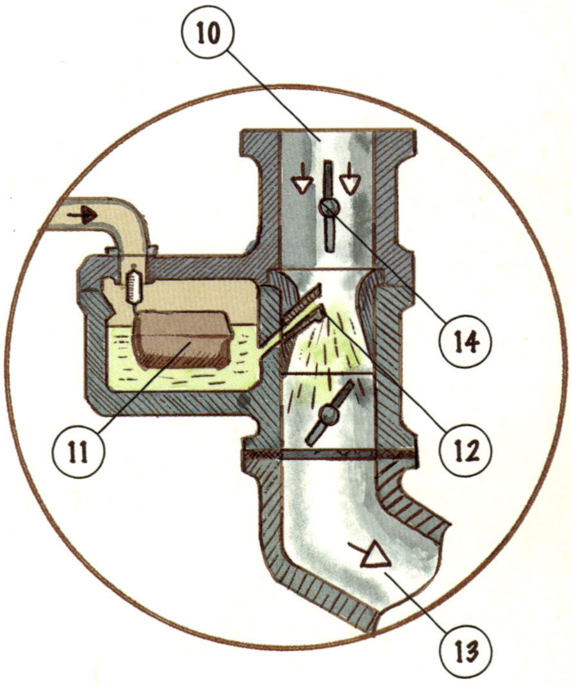

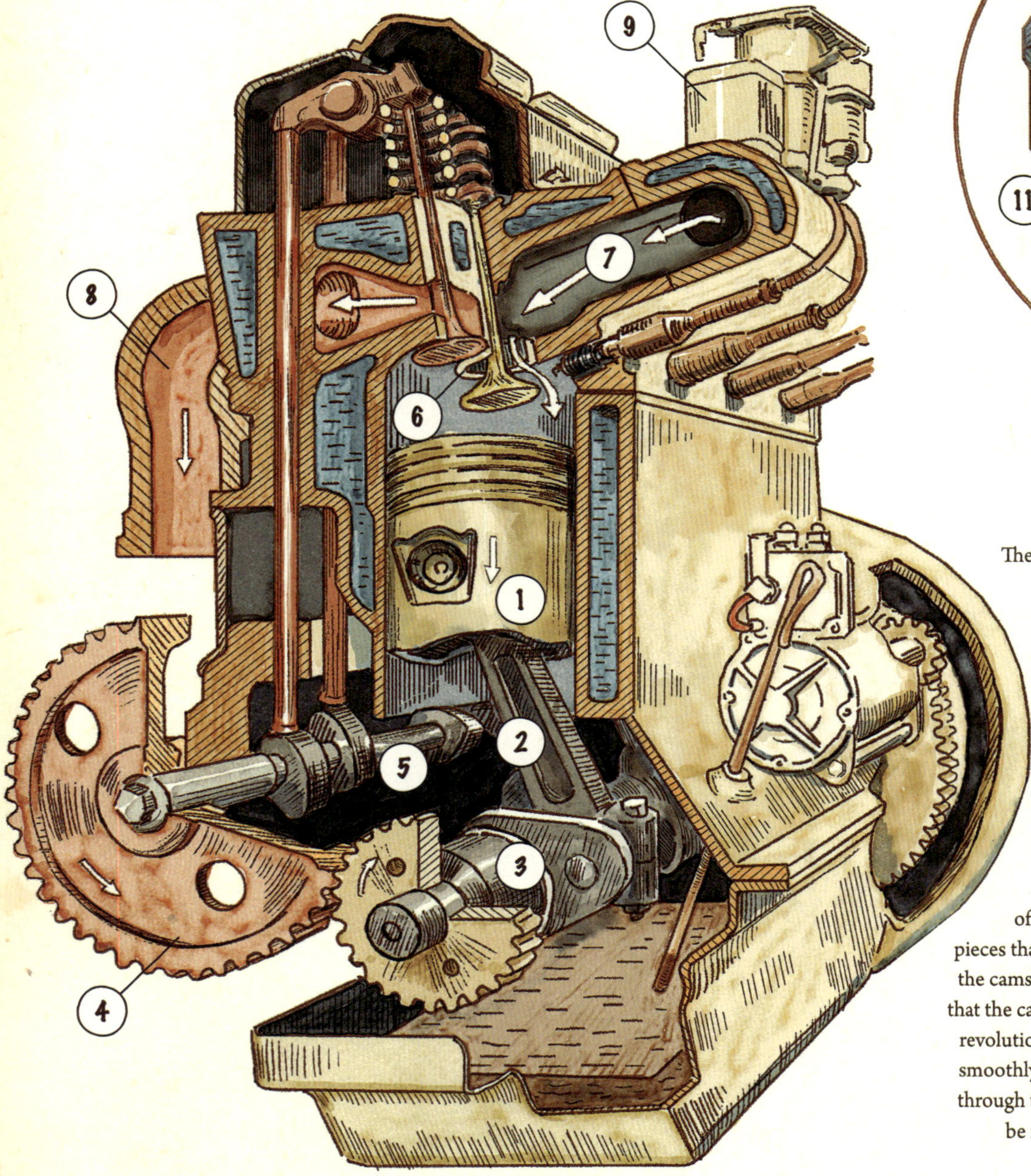

The internal combustion engine converts the energy of fuel combustion into mechanical work. Combustion takes place in the cylinder that is fitted with a piston (1). As the piston moves, it changes the volume of the cylinder. A mixture of fuel vapor and air burns inside the cylinder, increasing the pressure within the cylinder and pushing on the piston. That in turn moves the connecting rods (2), which spin the crankshaft (3). To ensure uniform rotation of the crankshaft, a massive disk known as the flywheel (4) is attached. The camshaft (5) is responsible for synchronizing the operation of the valves with the pistons. It operates cams — moving pieces that open the valves (6) when the shaft rotates. As soon as the camshaft stops pressing on the valve, it closes. It is important that the camshaft rotates half as fast as the crankshaft, making one revolution in four strokes of the cylinder. For the engine to work smoothly, new quantities of air and fuel must enter the cylinders through the intake valve (7), and the combustion products must be removed through the exhaust valve (8) at the right time.

PREPARING THE FUEL MIXTURE

Depending on the way you prepare the combustible fuel mixture, the engine can run on either gasoline or diesel. In diesel engines, the finished fuel is fed directly into the engine cylinder under high pressure at the end of the compression stroke (II), atomizing it into tiny droplets during the process. The air in the cylinder is under much higher pressure, which heats up the fuel mixture and causes it to combust without any spark. Therefore, diesel engines do not need an ignition system.

A gasoline internal combustion engine requires not a liquid fuel but a spray — a fuel-air mixture. A special device known as a carburetor (9) prepares the mixture. In the carburetor, the air flow (10) passes through a tapered tube, accelerates and sucks fuel from the float chamber (11) through a thin hole (12) and sprays it. The air damper (14) regulates the amount of fuel-air mixture (13) being supplied to the engine.

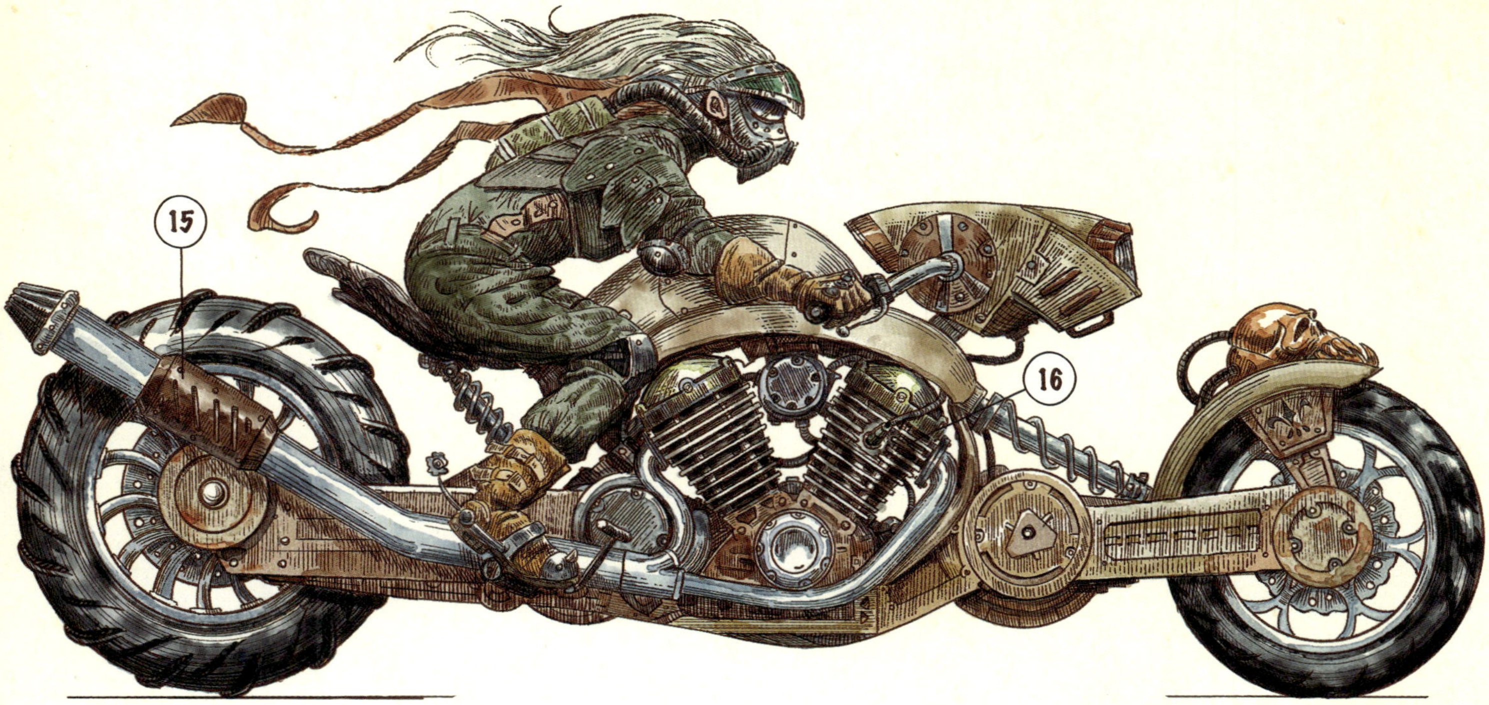

You can't just vent the exhaust gases directly from the cylinder into the atmosphere. They are scorching hot and fly out at high speeds. A muffler (15) will slow them down. It's a little box with different passages and chambers inside that functions as a sort of labyrinth for the gases. It allows them to cool down and exit almost silently through the exhaust pipe.

The immense energy released by burning fuel heats up the engine. To make sure it doesn't overheat and die, you'll need to cool it using a special liquid coolant that is pumped to the radiator (16) where it releases excess heat to the atmosphere, cooling down in the process, and then is cycled back through to absorb heat again.

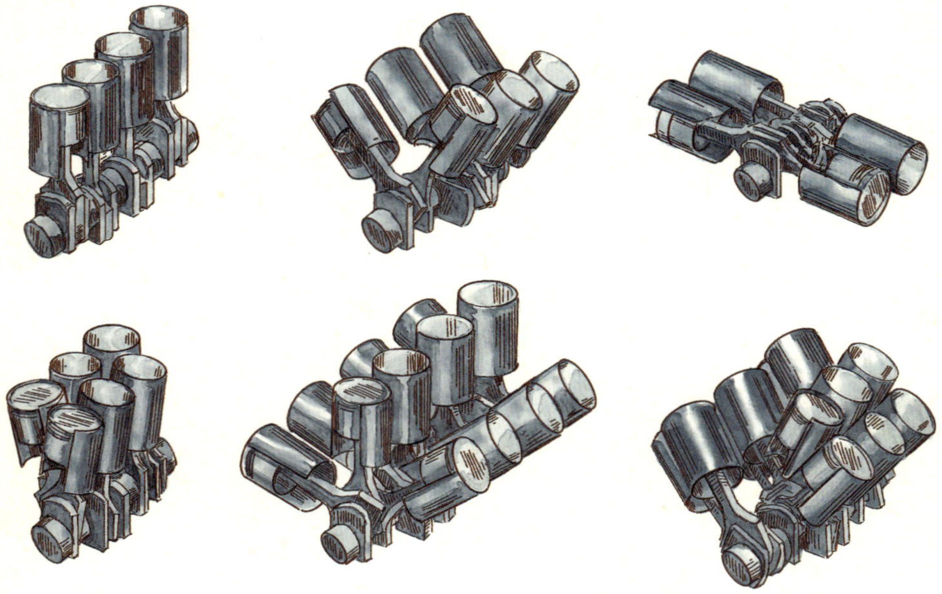

To reach high velocities, you'll need a lot of horsepower. You can increase the fuel combustion capacity of the engine by installing additional cylinders — more fuel will be burned with each revolution of the engine. The lighter you make the parts, the more efficiently the engine will work. When the piston changes directions, it expends energy to stop moving in one direction and start in the other. The lighter the piston, the less energy it needs.

FOUR STROKE ENGINE

I — fuel intake
II — compression
III — combustion
IV — exhaust
The piston makes 2 revolutions in four strokes.

A — inlet valve
B — exhaust valve
C — spark plug
D — piston
E — connecting rod
F — crankshaft
G — fuel-air mixture
H — spark
J — exhaust gases

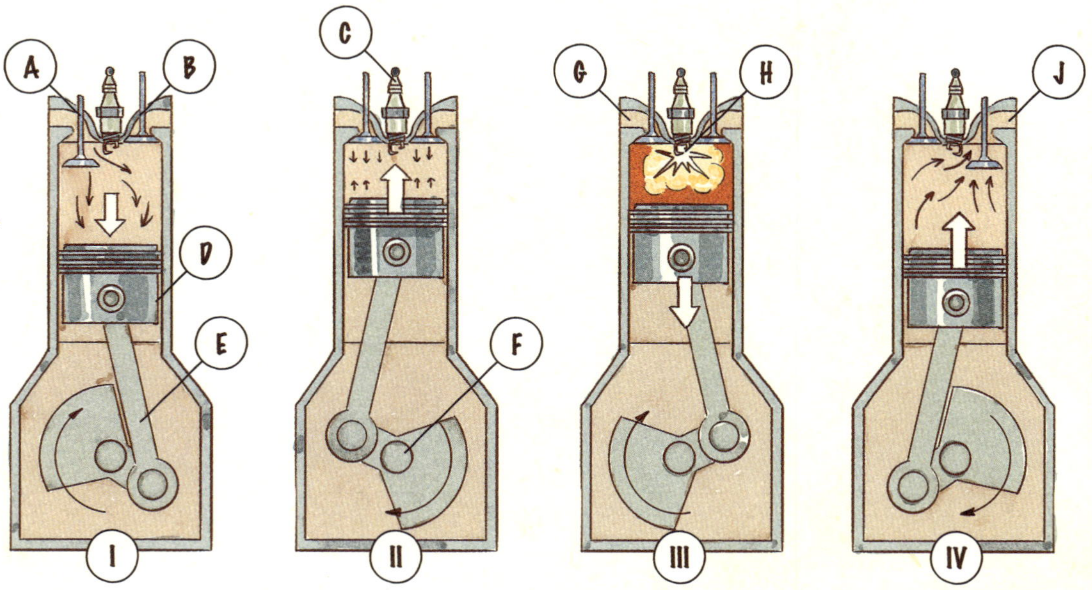

RAILROAD

With the emergence of industry comes the challenge of transporting goods over long distances. And this is essentially an economic task: You spend resources to overcome the force of friction. Your goal is to reduce costs. An asphalt road will be more efficient than a dirt road, but laying smooth steel rails and building trains to glide along them will reduce transportation costs tenfold. An even more effective solution would be reducing the friction and air resistance to nearly nil by using a vacuum tube. But along with the clatter of the wheels, all the romantic atmosphere would disappear, and then what would be the point?

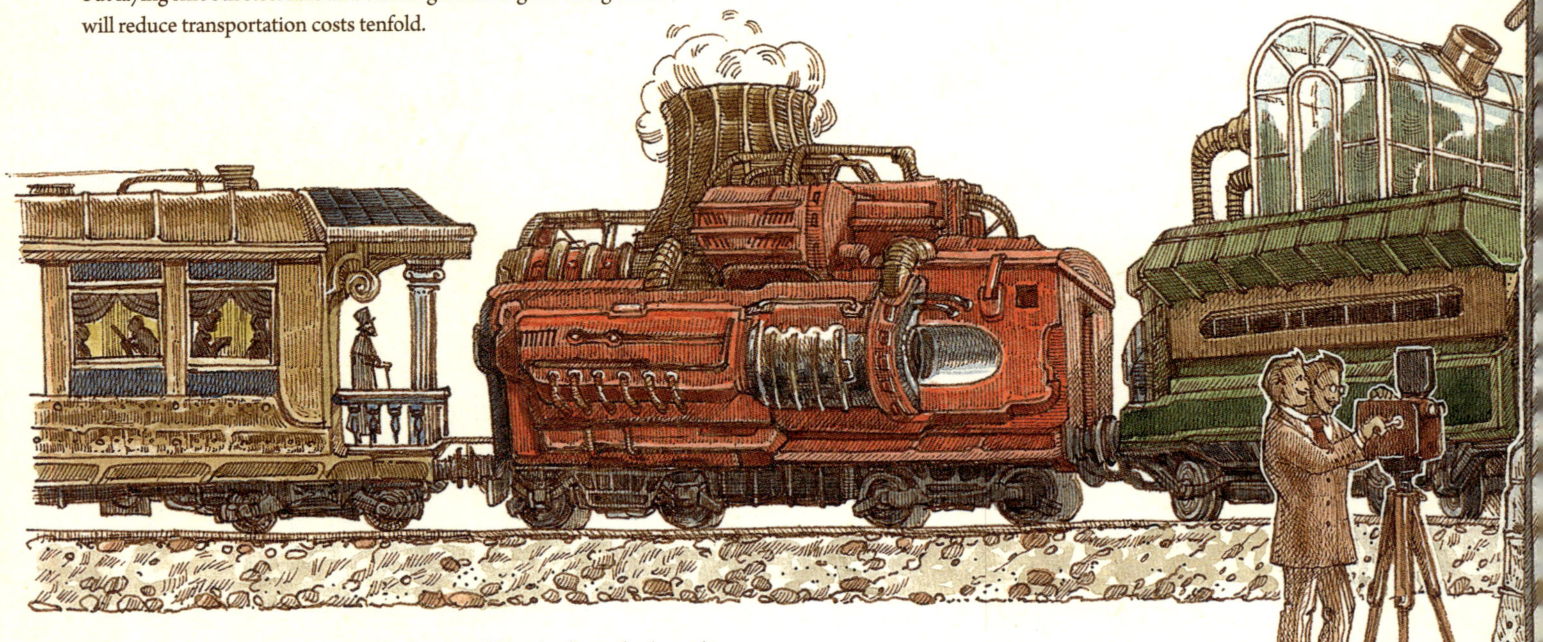

Lay a ballast layer of crushed stone and sand on top of the embankment for the road. It will help to distribute the load and protect the layer of soil underneath from cracking and erosion. Remember to lay drainage channels along the embankment; otherwise, the soil will quickly wash away.

RAILS AND RAILROAD TIES

Soak wooden ties in tar and they will last decades. Rails require steel (page 240). If you forgo a square cross-section and instead shape them like a letter "H," they will be 7 times stronger while weighing less. Try to make the upper part of the rail slightly thicker in order to compensate for the high wear it will endure as the train runs over it. The rail (1) is attached to the railroad ties (2) with clips or screws (3). You also need steel pads (4) and brackets (5) to bear some of the excess load.

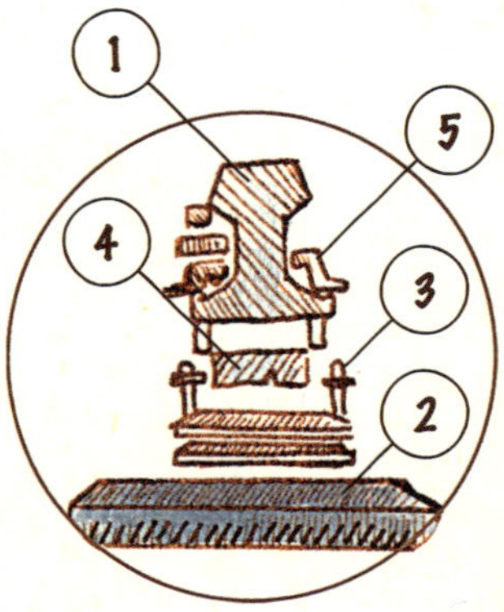

WHEELS

In order for the train to be able to turn, the wheels must be cone-shaped. The wheel is tapered so that the outer rim has a smaller diameter than the inner one. When the train is going straight, the wheels touch the track at the same point on each side and are level. But when the rail turns, one wheel touches the track at a point slightly more towards the outer rim, with a smaller diameter, so that it ends up traveling a shorter distance than the other wheel. As a result, the axle begins to shift and the train turns.

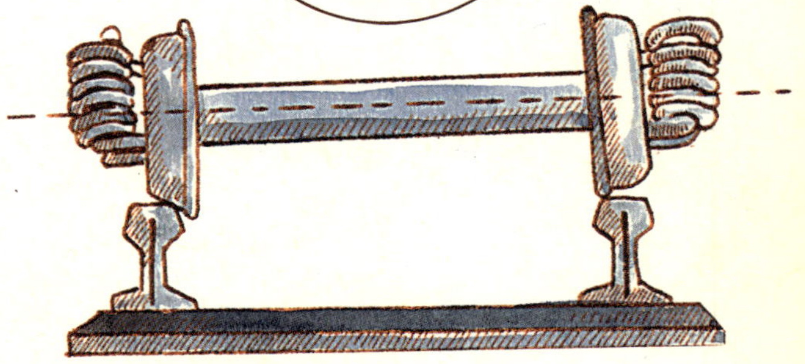

THE BRAKING SYSTEM

Accelerating a multi-ton locomotive is easier than stopping it. To stop all wheels moving at the same time, you need a braking system with an air line. A compressor (page 238) fills it with compressed air. The air enters the cylinder (1), compresses the piston (2), which moves and uses the lever mechanism (3) to push the brake pad (4) away from the wheel. When the conductor wants to brake, he opens the brake valve to release the air pressure, and the brake pads are pressed against the wheels.

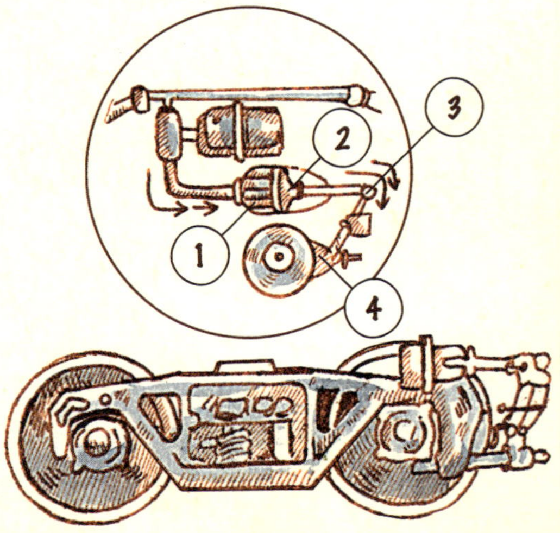

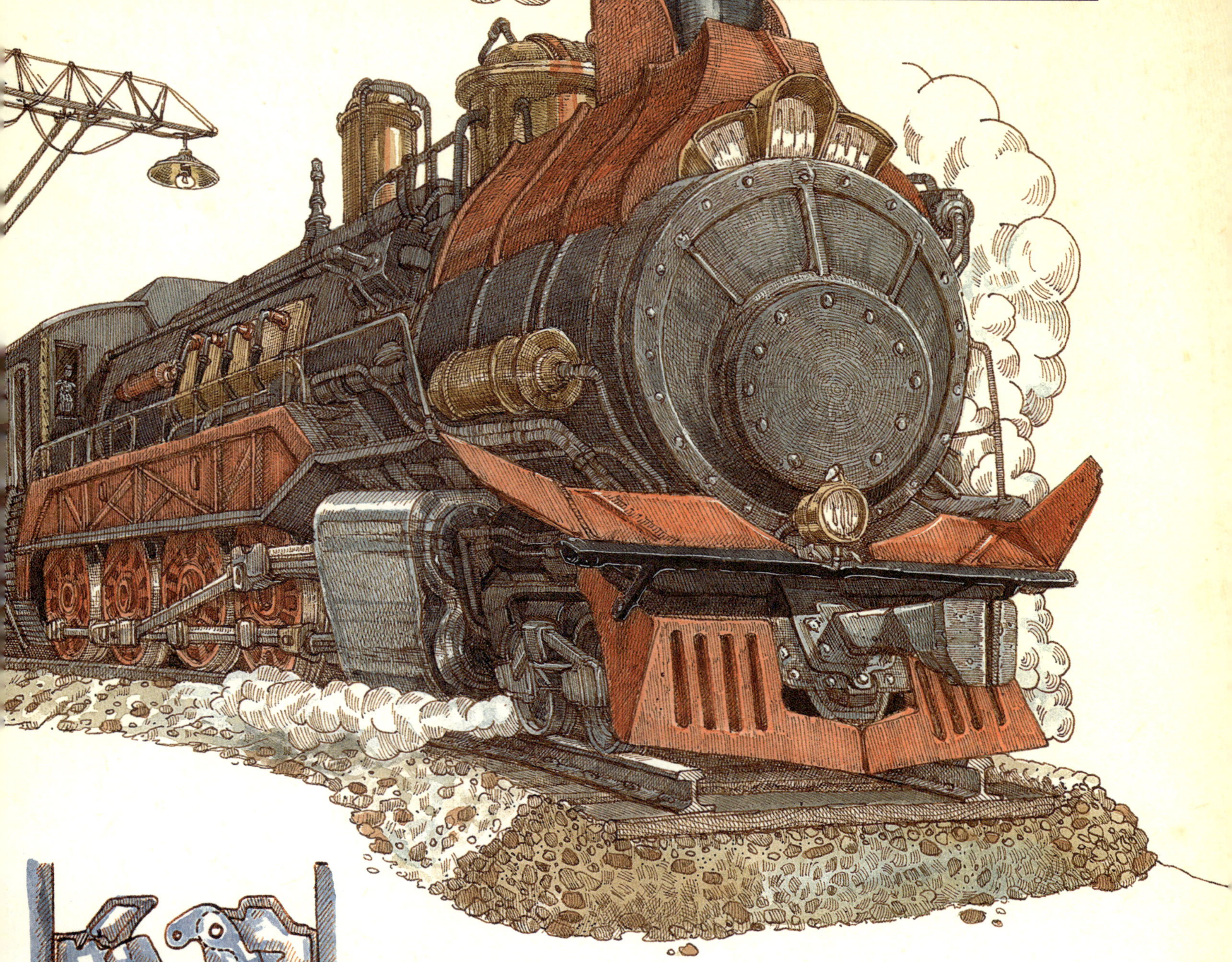

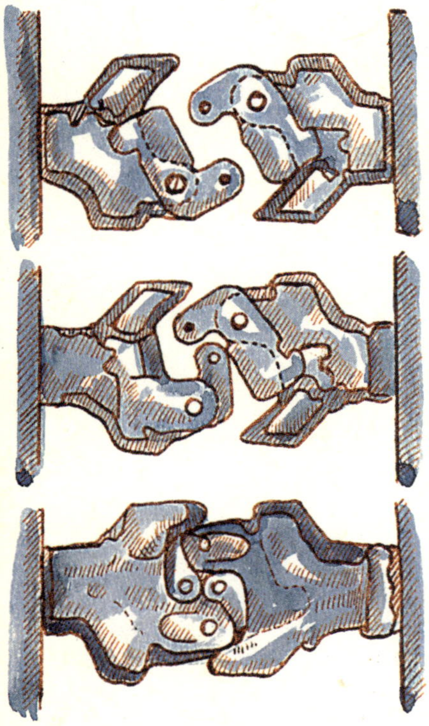

RAILWAY COUPLING

A locomotive can pull a train with dozens of cars weighing tens or even hundreds of thousands of tons. But this is only possible if the cars are securely fastened together. The simplest option is to fasten them together with bolts. But they will not withstand very high loads, and the process of coupling and uncoupling the cars will take a long time. It is better to invent an automatic coupler. It doesn't require bolts, resembles a "steel handshake" in design, operates automatically when the cars come together and withstands very high loads.

When properly fastened, the coupling locks into place with a locking mechanism. To uncouple the cars, all you need to do is raise the locking latch. The design of the couplings includes a little room for movement, allowing even a small, relatively weak locomotive to pull a heavy train. Thanks to this leeway, when the train first begins to move, it is only pulling the weight of the first railroad car. The joint inertia of the locomotive and the carriage pulls the second car, the combined inertia pulls the third and so on, all the way to the caboose.

Railroad switch

At railroad switch points, there are two fixed sections of rails, one running straight and the other branching off to the side. A moving piece at the divergence point can be moved laterally into one of two positions to direct a train towards either path.

If the moving piece remains in its initial position (I), the train continues straight. If the switch pushes the moving section to one side (II), the train wheels are redirected towards the diverging rail and it turns.

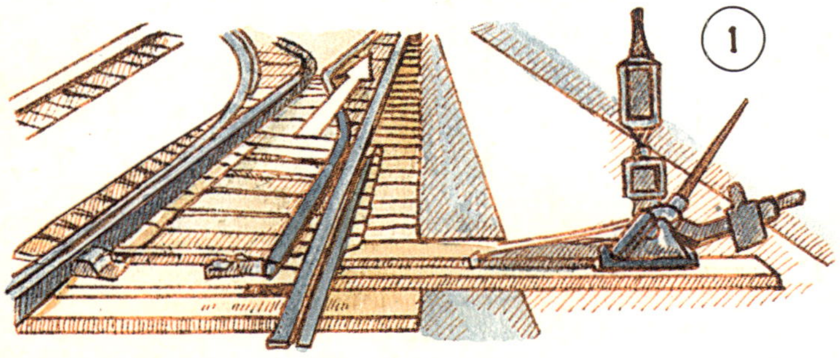

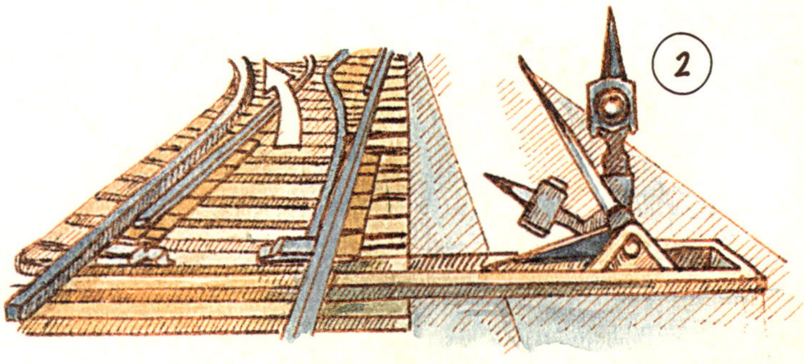

WASTE MANAGEMENT

Civilization and garbage are inseparable phenomena. Some civilizations hit a dead end when they create convenient materials that they have no way of getting rid of. So the sooner you think about how to reduce your waste to a minimum by recycling it into something new, the longer your world will survive without environmental catastrophe.

This being said, the process of recycling garbage also eats up a lot of resources. Once you figure out how to resolve this contradiction, you will become the most sustainable civilization out there! The main priority is creating a convenient system for collecting and separating trash so that most of it can be recycled and used again in other products.

First, you'll need a conveyor belt: A motor rotates the drive drum, which sets in motion a series of rollers. As they rotate, they move the belt forward, carrying the garbage through different stages of the recycling process.

Break large pieces of trash into smaller ones using powerful cutters powered by electric motors. Sort smaller waste into different size categories by sifting it through mesh sieves of various sizes. The final stage of processing is waste compaction. The finished briquettes can be taken to factories to be processed into paper, glass or other products.

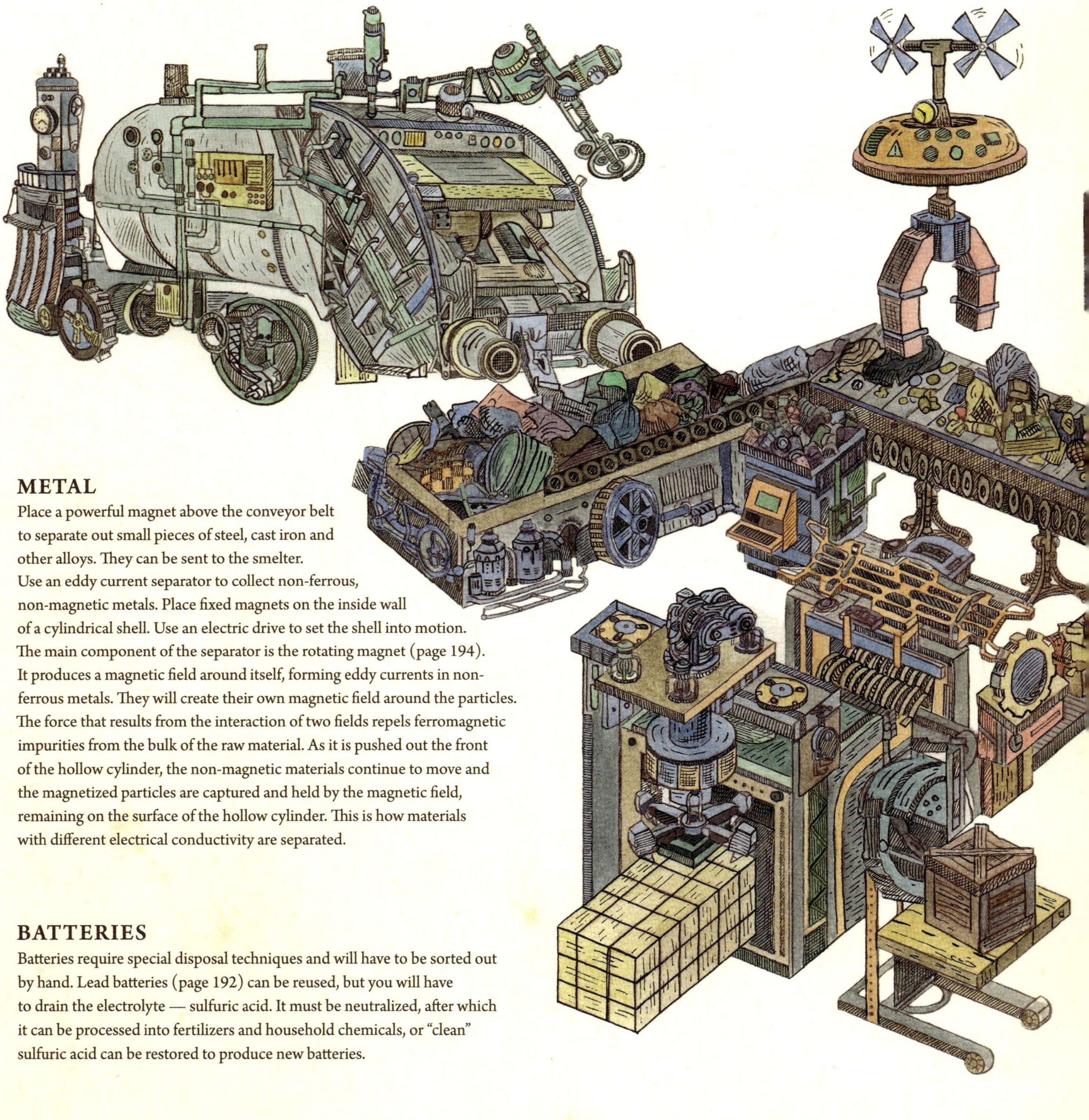

METAL

Place a powerful magnet above the conveyor belt to separate out small pieces of steel, cast iron and other alloys. They can be sent to the smelter.
Use an eddy current separator to collect non-ferrous, non-magnetic metals. Place fixed magnets on the inside wall of a cylindrical shell. Use an electric drive to set the shell into motion. The main component of the separator is the rotating magnet (page 194). It produces a magnetic field around itself, forming eddy currents in non-ferrous metals. They will create their own magnetic field around the particles. The force that results from the interaction of two fields repels ferromagnetic impurities from the bulk of the raw material. As it is pushed out the front of the hollow cylinder, the non-magnetic materials continue to move and the magnetized particles are captured and held by the magnetic field, remaining on the surface of the hollow cylinder. This is how materials with different electrical conductivity are separated.

BATTERIES

Batteries require special disposal techniques and will have to be sorted out by hand. Lead batteries (page 192) can be reused, but you will have to drain the electrolyte — sulfuric acid. It must be neutralized, after which it can be processed into fertilizers and household chemicals, or "clean" sulfuric acid can be restored to produce new batteries.

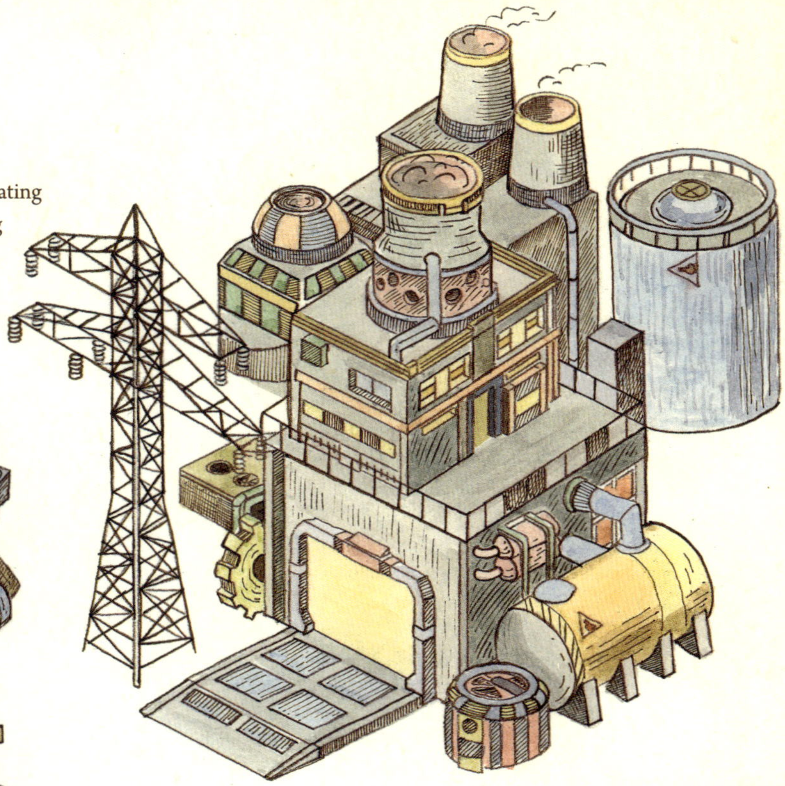

COMBUSTION AND ELECTRICITY

Unsorted waste can also be incinerated. You'll need furnaces operating at temperatures above 1000°C. The heat generated by incinerating waste can be used to generate electricity or heat water (page 156) for residential buildings. After burning, ash and slag remain. Slag is a potentially hazardous waste, but it can be used for backfilling roads and railways.

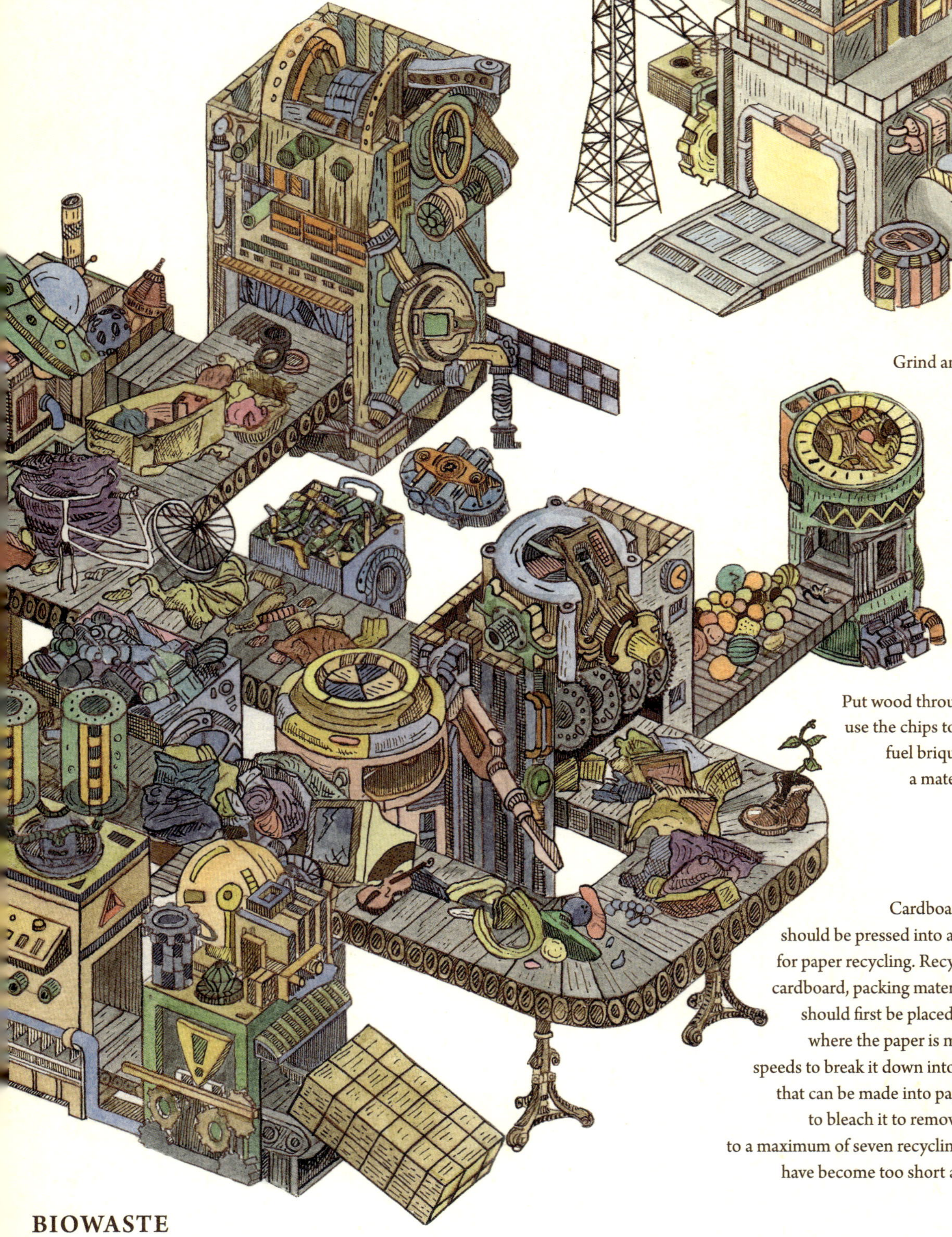

TEXTILES

Grind and turn into a fibrous mass. Make building materials out of it, such as heat and sound insulators.

GLASS

Can be recycled a practically limitless number of times. Just needs to be washed, broken and melted down.

WOOD

Put wood through a wood chipper. You can then use the chips to retain water in your fields, make fuel briquettes or mix into glue to produce a material suitable for making furniture.

PAPER

Cardboard, paper and all related materials should be pressed into a cube and sent to another factory for paper recycling. Recycled paper can be made into new cardboard, packing materials and toilet paper. Waste paper should first be placed in large drums known as pulpers where the paper is mixed with water and spun at high speeds to break it down into fibers. The end product is a pulp that can be made into paper again (page 288). You'll need to bleach it to remove the ink. Paper can be subjected to a maximum of seven recycling cycles, by which time the fibers have become too short and are unsuitable for production.

BIOWASTE

Biowaste must be separated from the rest of the garbage — organic matter gums up the works. It can be remade into biogas (page 90) and used as fuel for cars or heating. You can also ferment everything so that it decomposes faster. Make a room with metal grating for the floor and build pipes underneath through which air will blow. Aerate the crushed garbage and mix with lactic acid bacteria starter (page 104). Then heat the waste, speeding up the fermentation processes and decreasing the amount of pathogenic microflora, effectively decomposing the organic matter.

Gas is released during the fermentation process, so you'll need a ventilation system with a biofilter made out of, for example, wood chips. You must also analyze the metal content of the final product. If the biowaste is free of heavy metals, you can use it as a fertilizer saturated with nitrogen and phosphorus, and if it is not, you can use it as a non-fertile filler to use in roads and railway embankments.

MILITARY

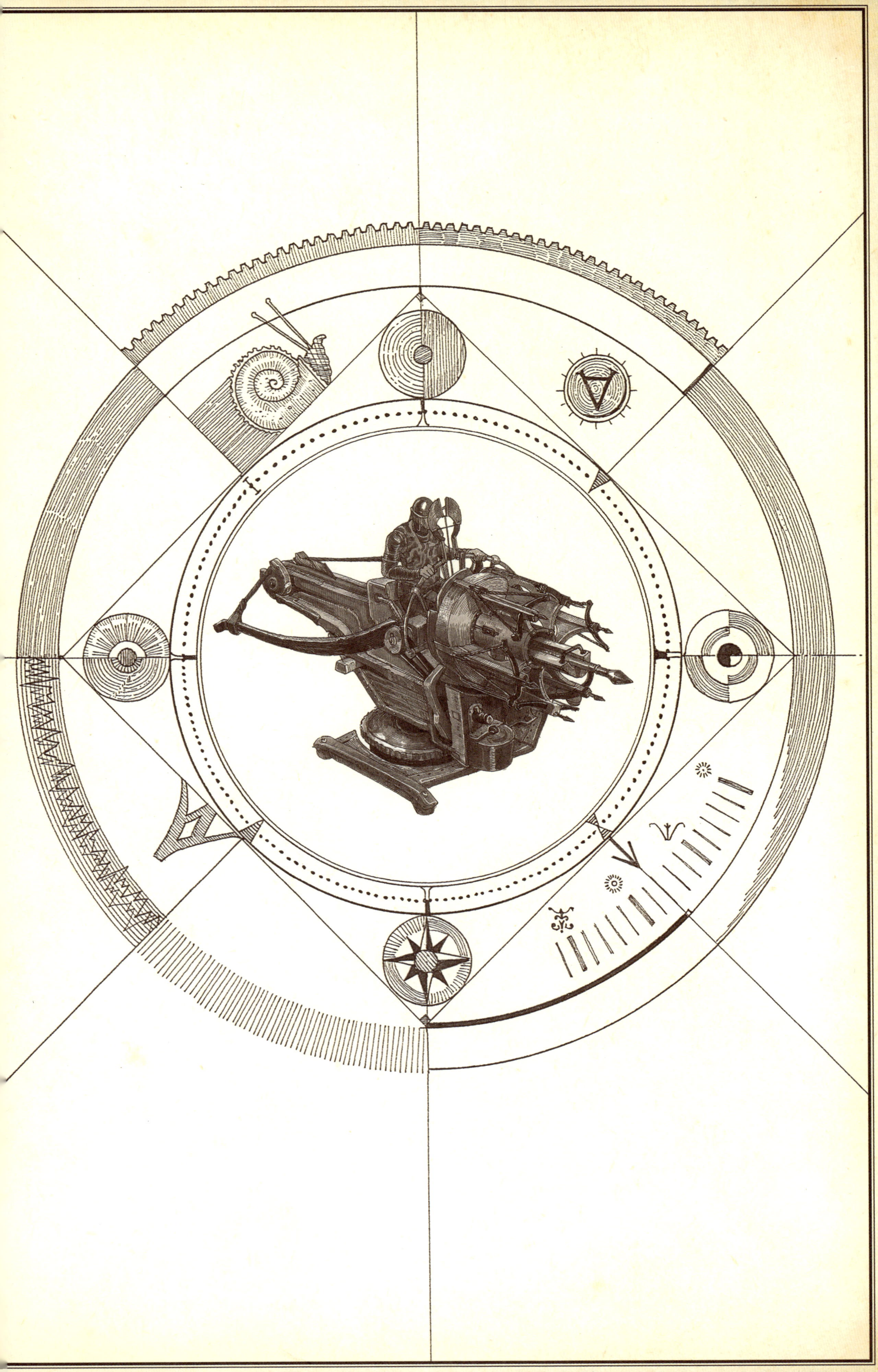

MARTIAL ARTS

Without a doubt, the best battle is the one not fought. Unfortunately, no matter how strong your desire or earnest your efforts to keep the peace and resolve everything through negotiations, there is a high probability that not all the creatures you encounter throughout your travels may be friendly and diplomatic. At some point, you'll have to accept the possibility of physical force in the fight against evil. And it's always better to be prepared.

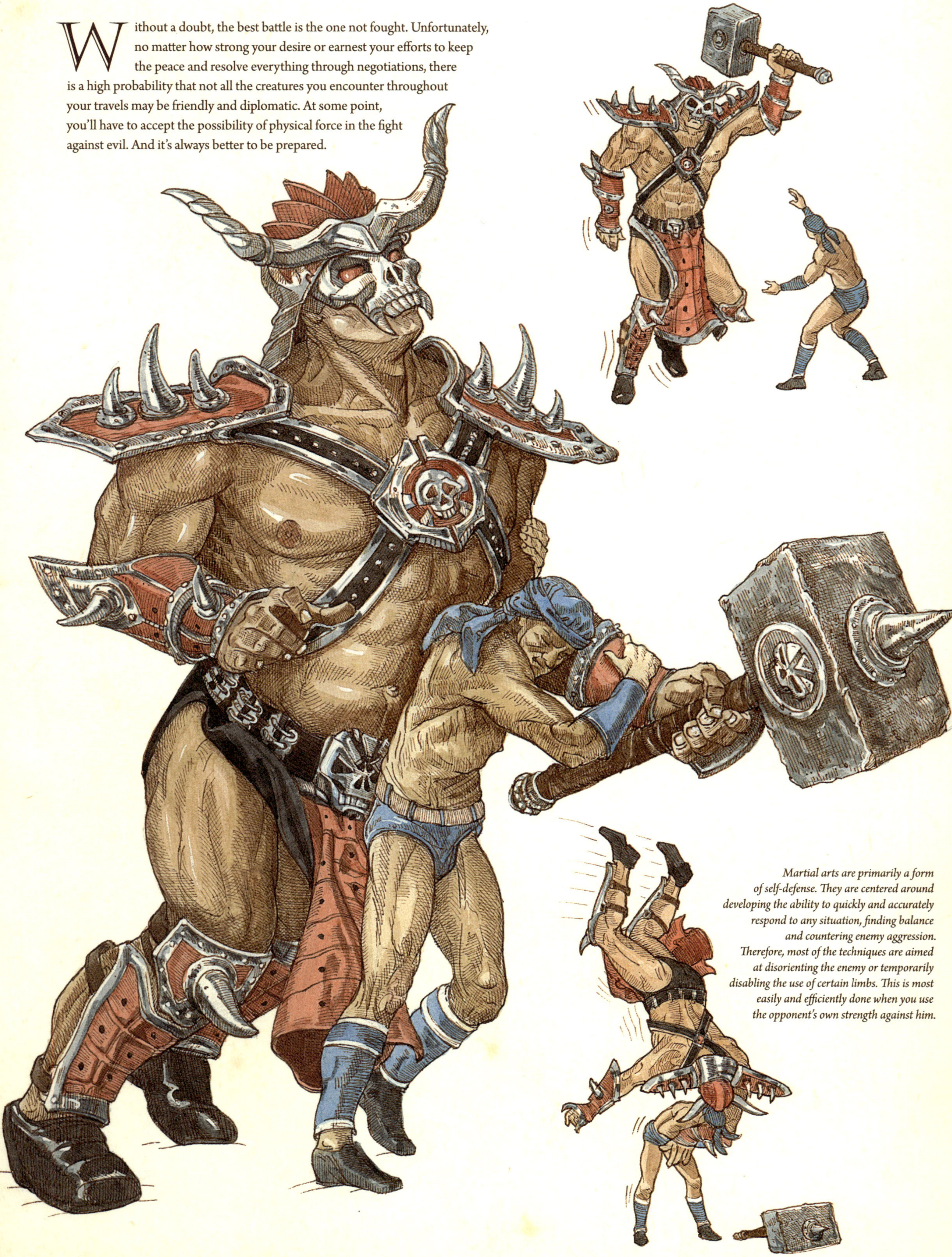

Martial arts are primarily a form of self-defense. They are centered around developing the ability to quickly and accurately respond to any situation, finding balance and countering enemy aggression. Therefore, most of the techniques are aimed at disorienting the enemy or temporarily disabling the use of certain limbs. This is most easily and efficiently done when you use the opponent's own strength against him.

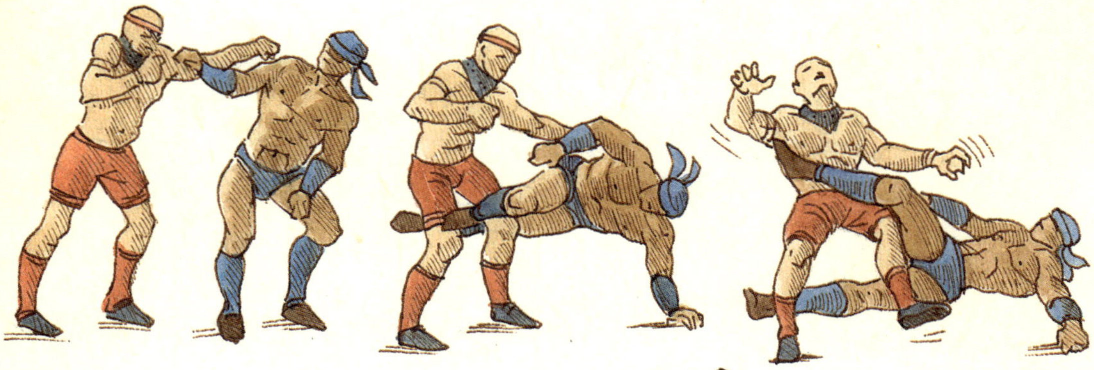

There are countless techniques used to knock an enemy off his feet, and most of them leverage the opponent's body speed and the momentum of his movement against him. Once your opponent has lost his balance, you have the clear advantage.

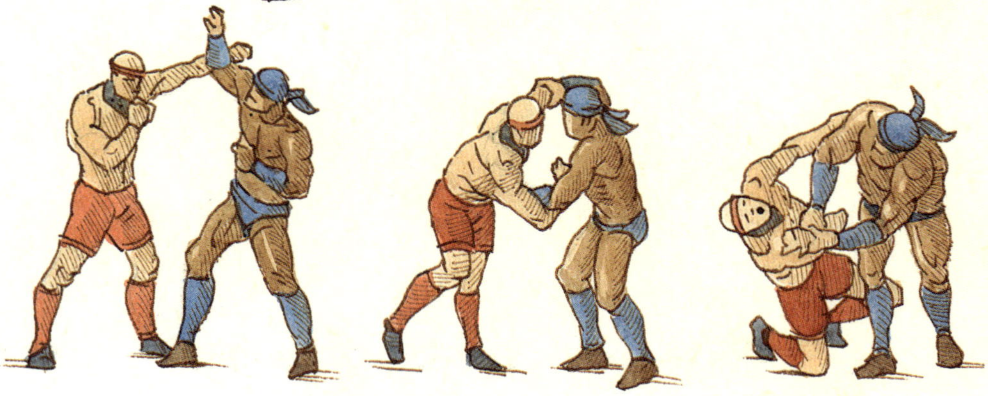

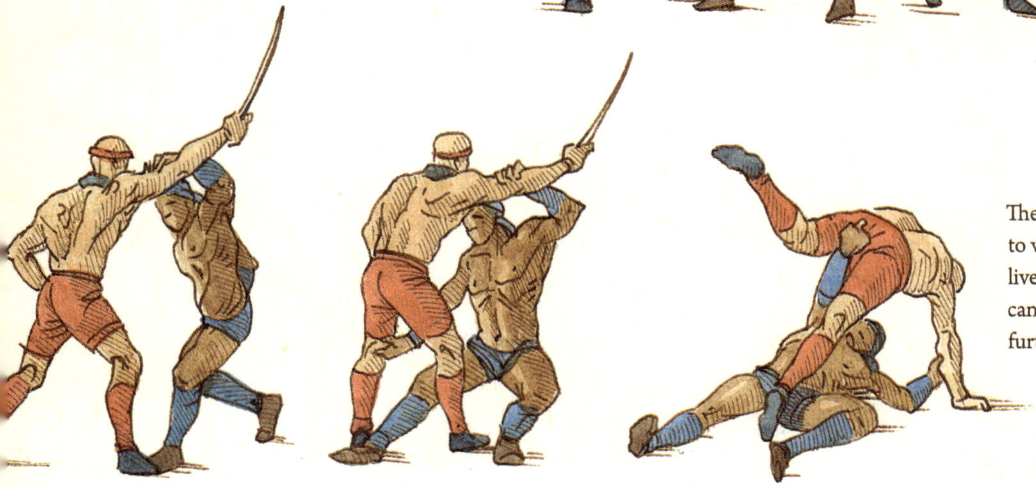

The most effective moves are disorienting jabs dealt to vital organs and nerve clusters (eyes, ears, nose, liver, kidneys, groin) and blows to the joints, which can temporarily disable an enemy and prevent further attacks.

But it is worth remembering that using improper technique will hurt you more than the enemy. Strike with the heel of your palm to avoid injury to the fingers. The best places to aim such attacks are the nose, jaw, eyes, neck and throat.

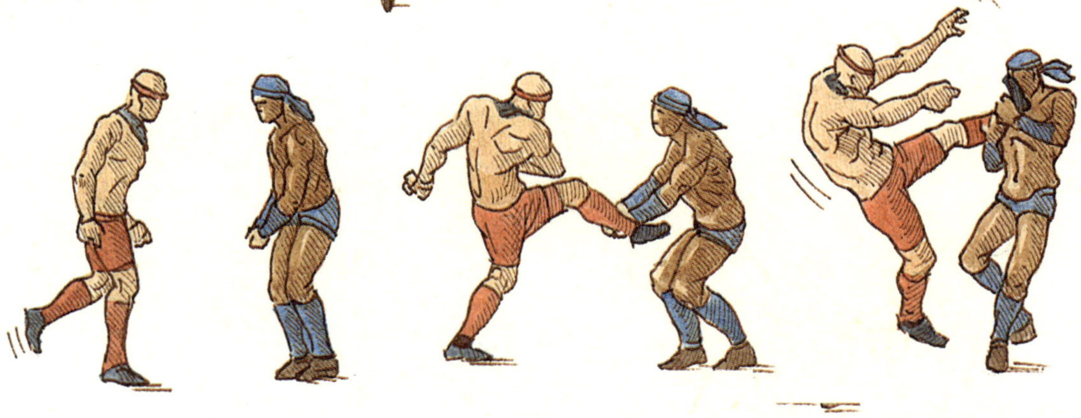

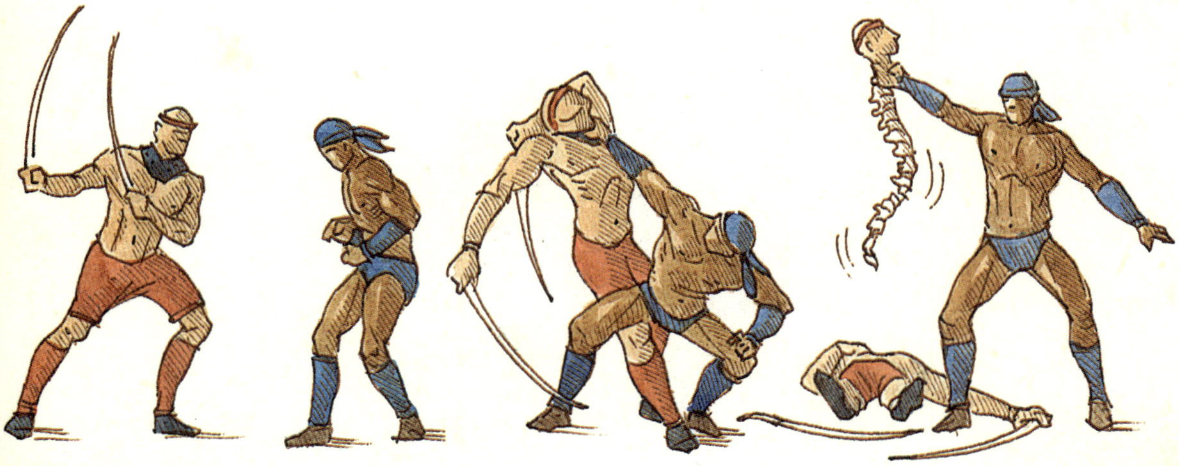

Forward, Down, Forward, Block

MELEE WEAPONS

Melee weapons are needed for close hand-to-hand combat. Crafting these kinds of weapons is a real art form. In making a single weapon, a smith may employ a whole range of woodworking and metalworking techniques: carving, forging, engraving, stamping, gilding, oxidizing. That's why you need skilled craftsmen and quality metal (page 110).

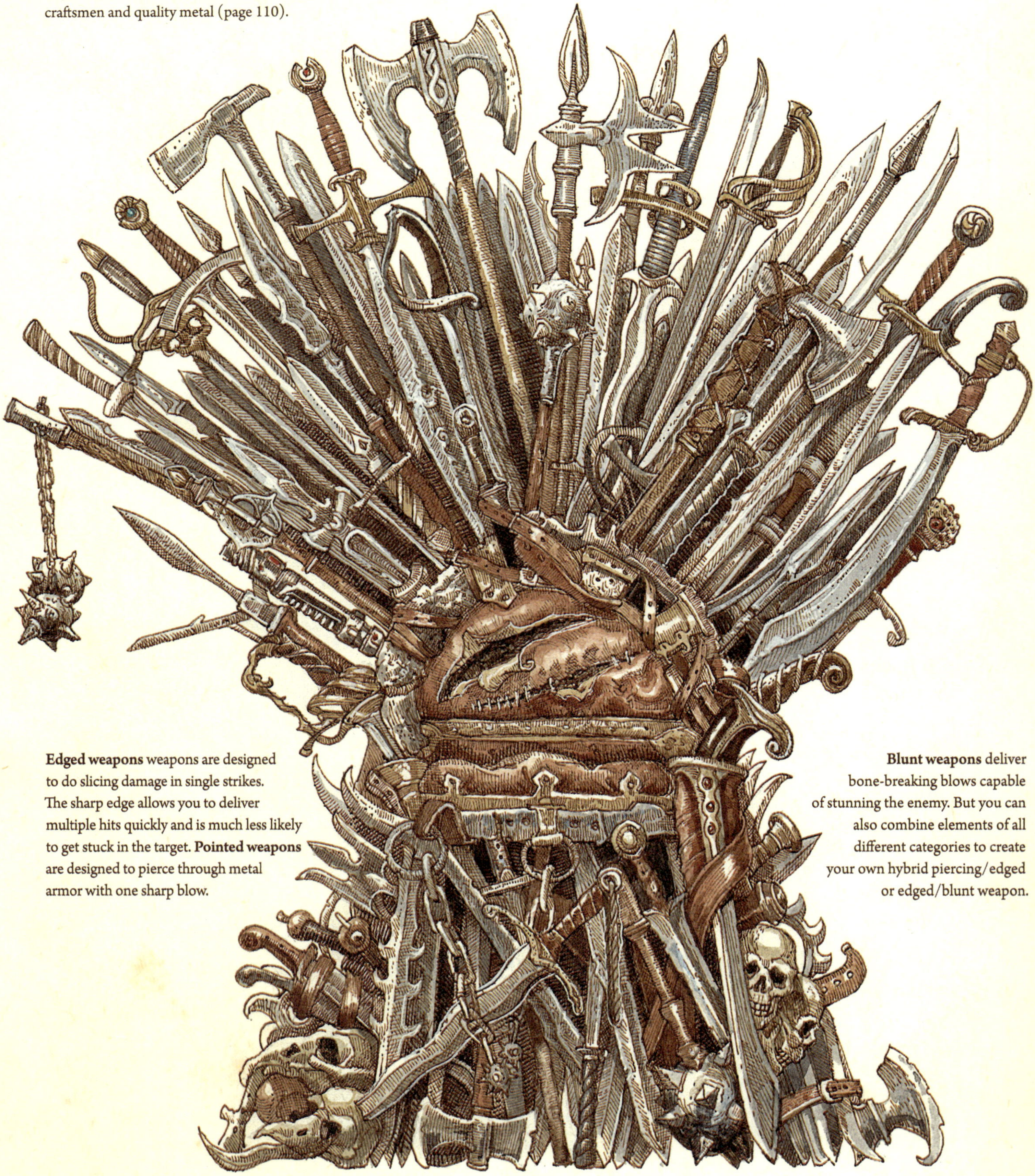

Edged weapons weapons are designed to do slicing damage in single strikes. The sharp edge allows you to deliver multiple hits quickly and is much less likely to get stuck in the target. **Pointed weapons** are designed to pierce through metal armor with one sharp blow.

Blunt weapons deliver bone-breaking blows capable of stunning the enemy. But you can also combine elements of all different categories to create your own hybrid piercing/edged or edged/blunt weapon.

Impact or crushing weapons such as maces and mallets are relatively cheap to produce and nearly indestructible. They can pierce through even heavy suits of armor (page 256) and can be wielded by both cavalry and infantry.

The striking edge of **pointed** or **edged** weapons — the tips and blades — can be made from bone, stone (such as obsidian) or metal. It's not so much the material that's important as how well you sharpen it.

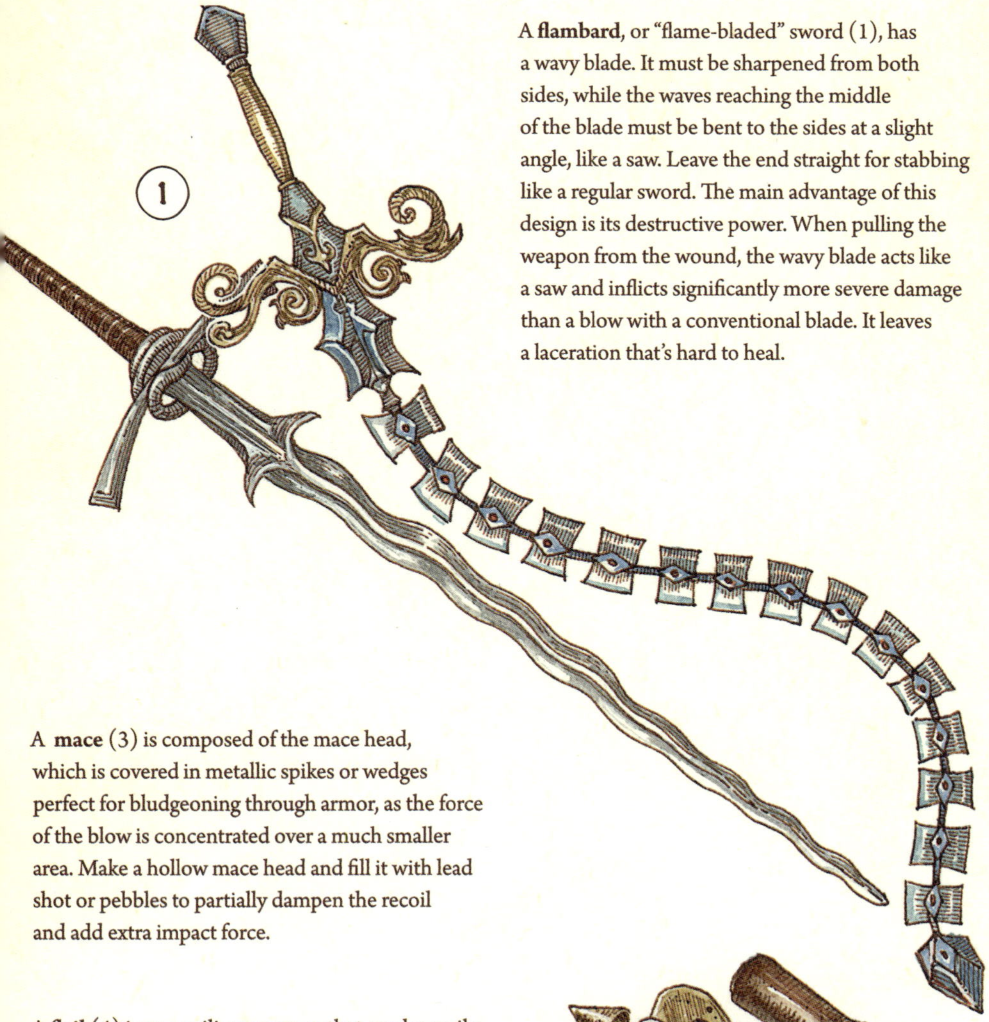

A **flambard**, or "flame-bladed" sword (1), has a wavy blade. It must be sharpened from both sides, while the waves reaching the middle of the blade must be bent to the sides at a slight angle, like a saw. Leave the end straight for stabbing like a regular sword. The main advantage of this design is its destructive power. When pulling the weapon from the wound, the wavy blade acts like a saw and inflicts significantly more severe damage than a blow with a conventional blade. It leaves a laceration that's hard to heal.

A **sledgehammer** (2) is a good weapon for fighting warriors in suits of armor (page 256). A hammer has a higher center of gravity than a sword, so the blow delivers more crushing force. In addition, all the force is concentrated into a single small area, so a warrior won't need super strength to punch through metal armor.

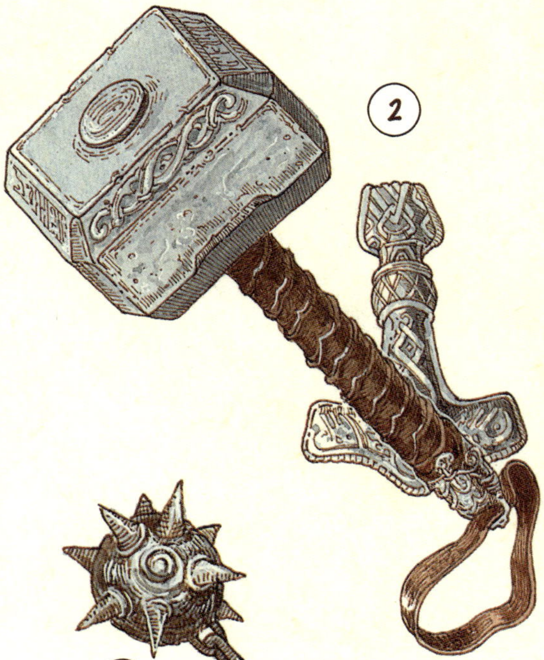

A **mace** (3) is composed of the mace head, which is covered in metallic spikes or wedges perfect for bludgeoning through armor, as the force of the blow is concentrated over a much smaller area. Make a hollow mace head and fill it with lead shot or pebbles to partially dampen the recoil and add extra impact force.

A **flail** (4) is an auxiliary weapon that can be easily grabbed at a gallop. Flail strikes are difficult to deflect even if you have a shield. The metallic head is attached to the staff by a chain, which can easily bend around shields while picking up momentum and striking the enemy with tremendous force.

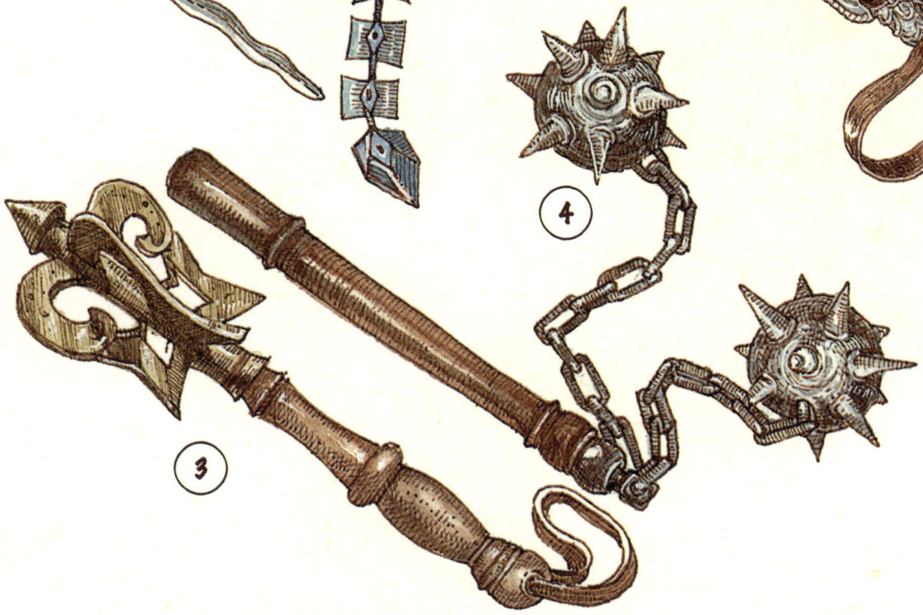

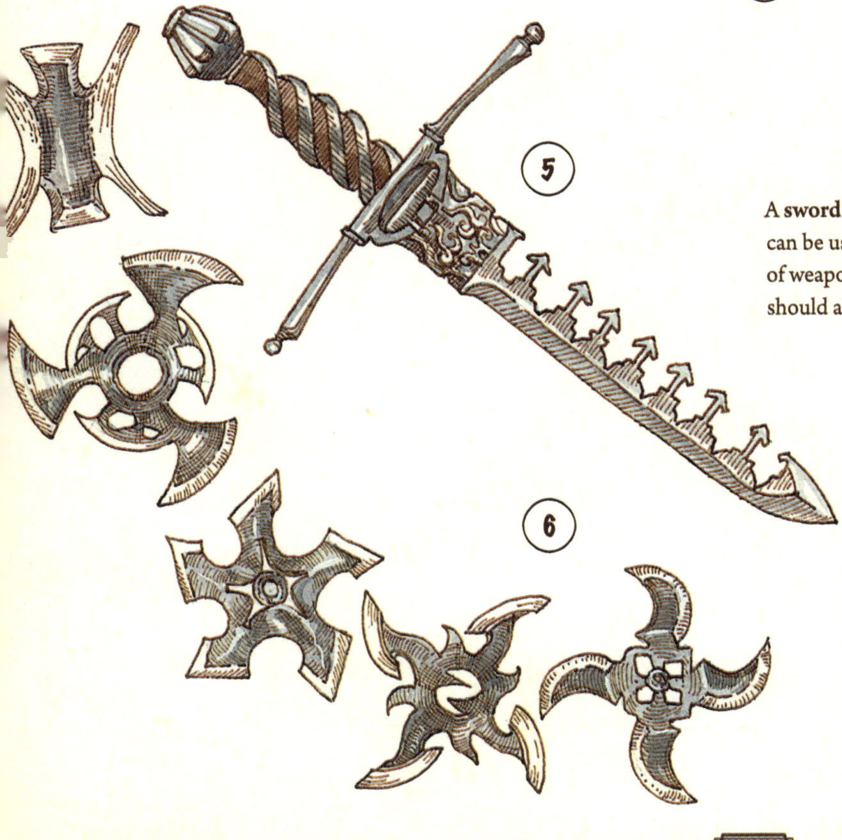

A **sword breaker** (5) has deep notches in one side of the blade. In battle, they can be used to hook an enemy's sword and pull it from his hands. But this kind of weapon isn't particularly suited for inflicting stab wounds. Therefore, you should always carry a normal, well-sharpened blade in your other hand.

Throwing stars (6) are flat discs with sharp metallic points around the edge. These points can cause devastating damage. Throwing stars are sometimes made with holes in the center so that they can be strung together while not in use. You should have a lot of them on hand, as they're essentially single-use weapons. Because of this, it makes no sense to make them from expensive, high-quality metals. Discs can also come in handy in close combat — hold them in your hands and strike any unprotected parts of the body. This won't inflict serious wounds, but it will throw the enemy off for a few seconds. And you can even use it as a sort of primitive mine by sticking one half into the dirt and leaving the top half exposed.

ARMOR & CHAIN MAIL

Many animals are born with natural armor. Humans, unfortunately, have to make it ourselves, though we do have one major advantage: we can always upgrade our equipment if an enemy comes at us with a new kind of weapon. Just remember that even the best suit of armor has its weak spots.

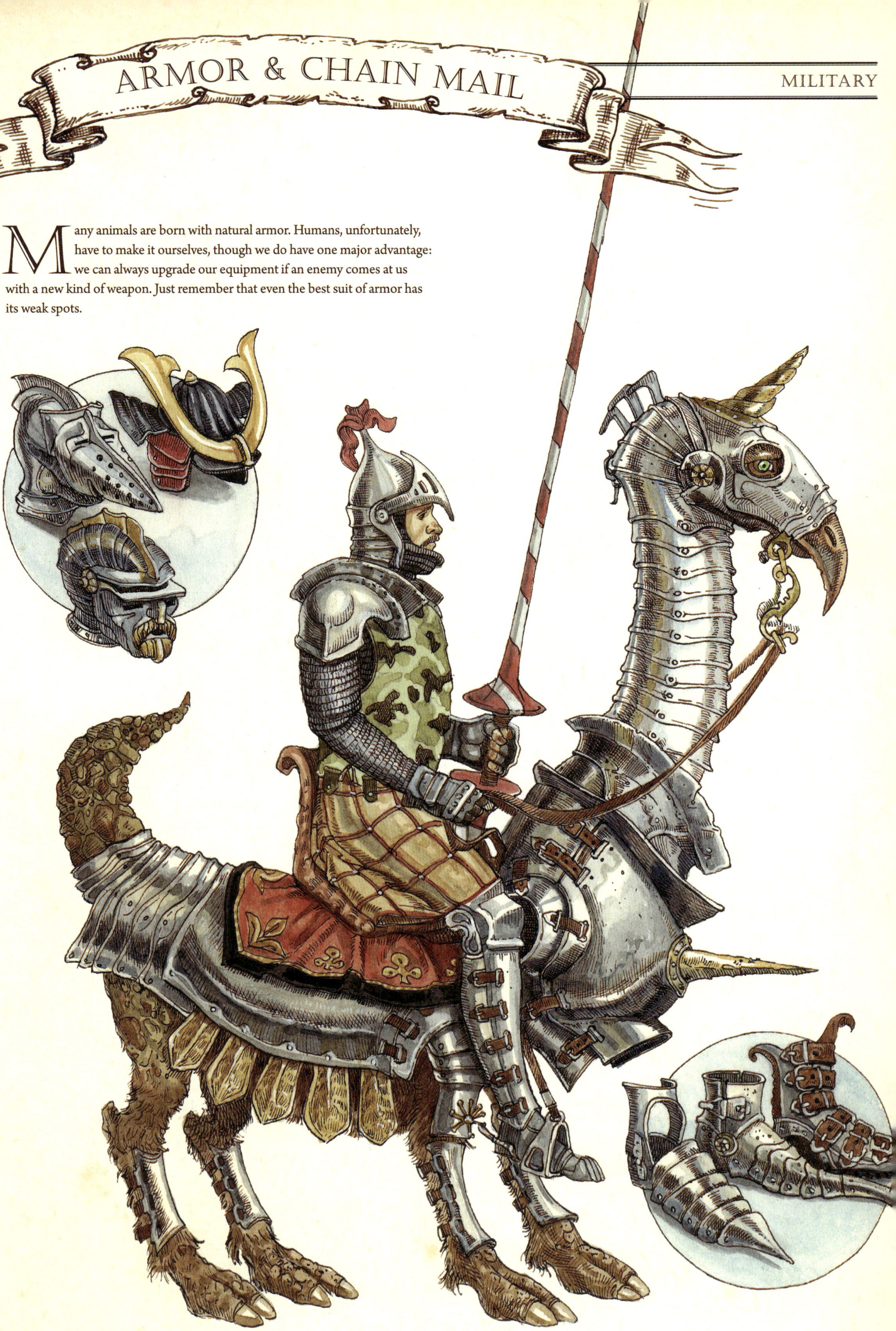

PLATES

Steel sheets molded to fit the body do wonders for fending off chopping and stabbing blows, even holding up against arrows, crossbow bolts and spears. Separate pieces are held together using straps that allow them to articulate as the user moves around.

But they're as heavy as they are expensive, and wearing them is an exhausting feat. Worn-out warriors must be wary of precise blows aimed at the joints between plates, not to mention bullets. Plated armor is nearly useless against firearms.

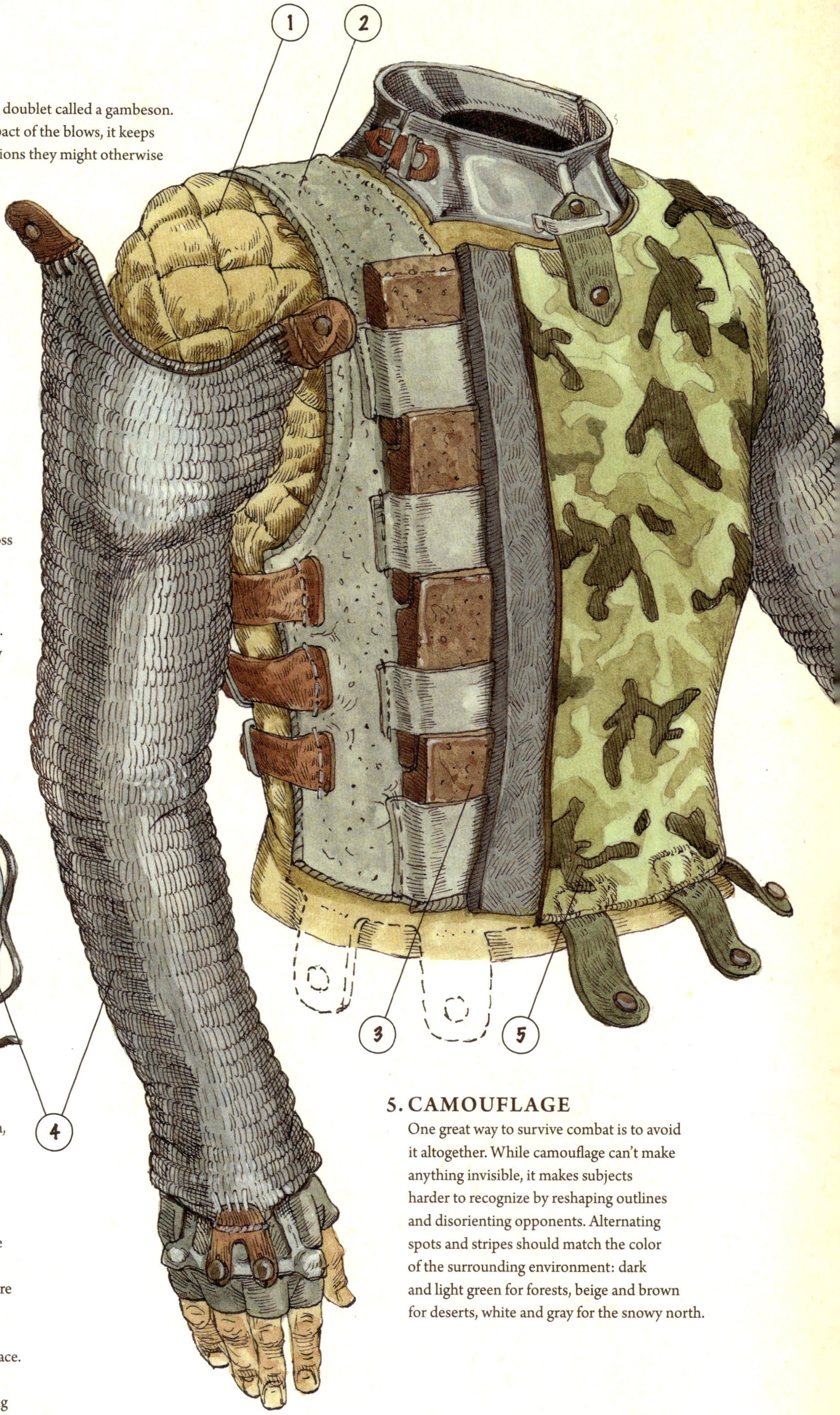

1. GAMBESON

Chain mail is best worn over a thick, padded doublet called a gambeson. While it doesn't do much to cushion the impact of the blows, it keeps the wearer safe from the scratches and infections they might otherwise sustain from their own damaged chain mail.

2. WIRE FELT

If you compress enough layers of metal wire, you'll get a dependable bulletproof garment. Not only does it dissipate the energy from bullets across a wide surface area, it absorbs some of the impact when it is compressed and the layers of wire rub against each other.

3. BALLISTIC PLATES

Bullets carry enormous amounts of energy, which means the impact must be spread across a larger area in order to avoid damage. Plate armor is no good — bullets can slice right through or deform the metal. Instead, thick blocks of steel or ceramic must be used. But while they shouldn't be so large that they weigh the wearer down, making them too small reduces the surface area needed to dissipate the energy of a blow.

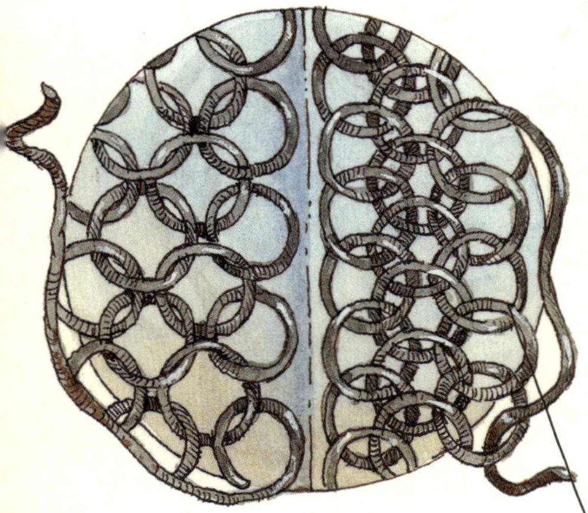

4. CHAIN MAIL

Made of metal rings linked together in a mesh, chain mail is conducive to movement and doesn't need to be fitted. To make it, start by winding a metal wire around a rod. Chop the resulting coil into pieces to get open rings, which you then chain together to make the armor. The best patterns are either 4 or 6 connections to 1 link. If you want to make sure the links don't come unclasped, rivet them together by pounding the rings flat, drilling a hole in them, and then locking 2 discs in place. Chain mail does a great job protecting the wearer from chopping blows, though stabbing blows are a different story. Arrowheads will also pierce through the rings, burying themselves in the flesh underneath.

5. CAMOUFLAGE

One great way to survive combat is to avoid it altogether. While camouflage can't make anything invisible, it makes subjects harder to recognize by reshaping outlines and disorienting opponents. Alternating spots and stripes should match the color of the surrounding environment: dark and light green for forests, beige and brown for deserts, white and gray for the snowy north.

BOW & CROSSBOW

Close quarters fighting is frequently a later phase of combat. Initially, for both offensive and defensive purposes, ranged weapons are employed in order to reduce enemy ranks from a safe distance. Catapults and trebuchets, for example, launch boulders with tremendous force. For single-warrior usage, bows and crossbows catapult arrows toward the target.

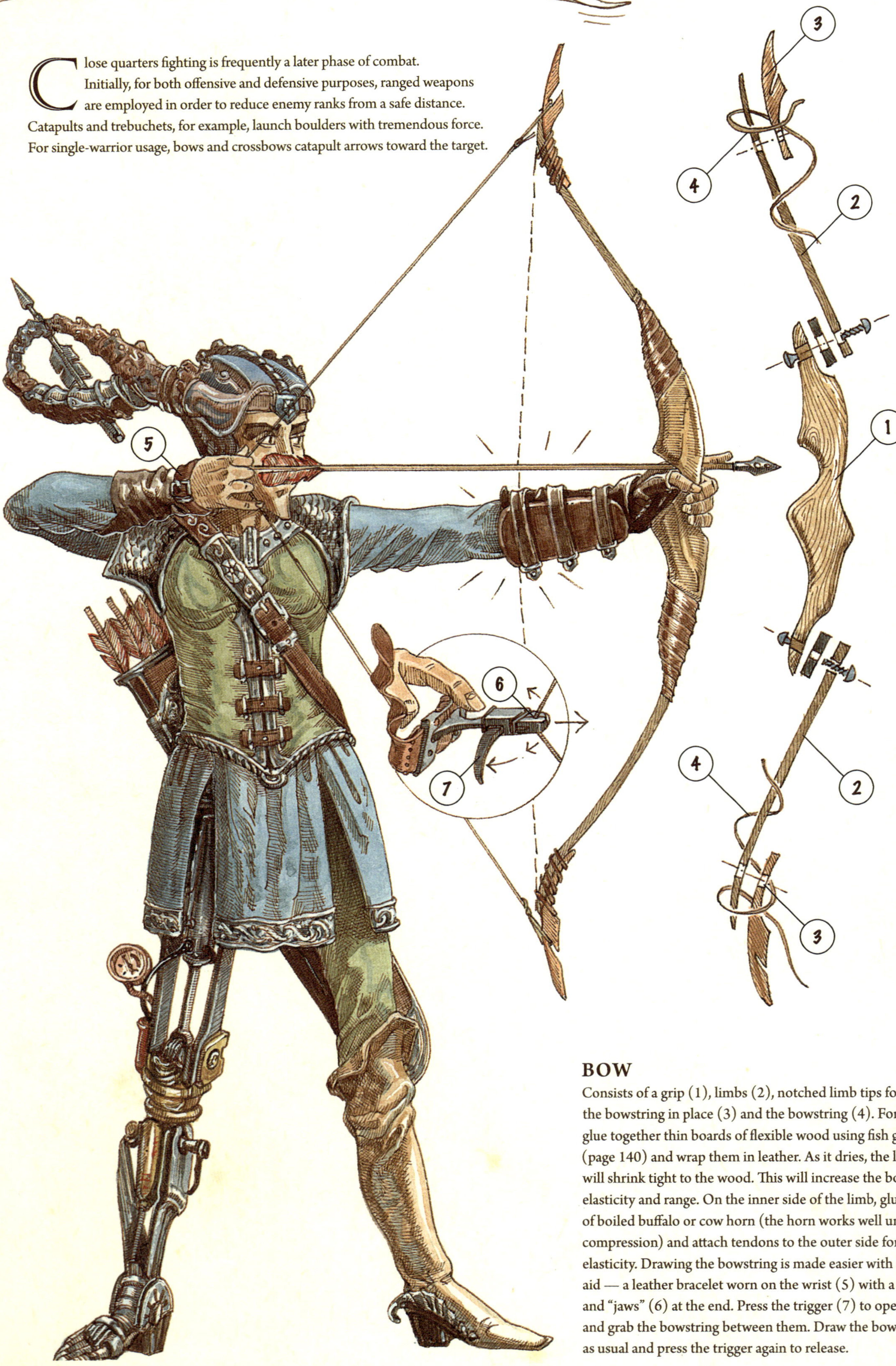

BOW

Consists of a grip (1), limbs (2), notched limb tips for holding the bowstring in place (3) and the bowstring (4). For the limbs, glue together thin boards of flexible wood using fish glue (page 140) and wrap them in leather. As it dries, the leather will shrink tight to the wood. This will increase the bow's elasticity and range. On the inner side of the limb, glue a plate of boiled buffalo or cow horn (the horn works well under compression) and attach tendons to the outer side for improved elasticity. Drawing the bowstring is made easier with a release aid — a leather bracelet worn on the wrist (5) with a metal rod and "jaws" (6) at the end. Press the trigger (7) to open the jaws and grab the bowstring between them. Draw the bowstring back as usual and press the trigger again to release.

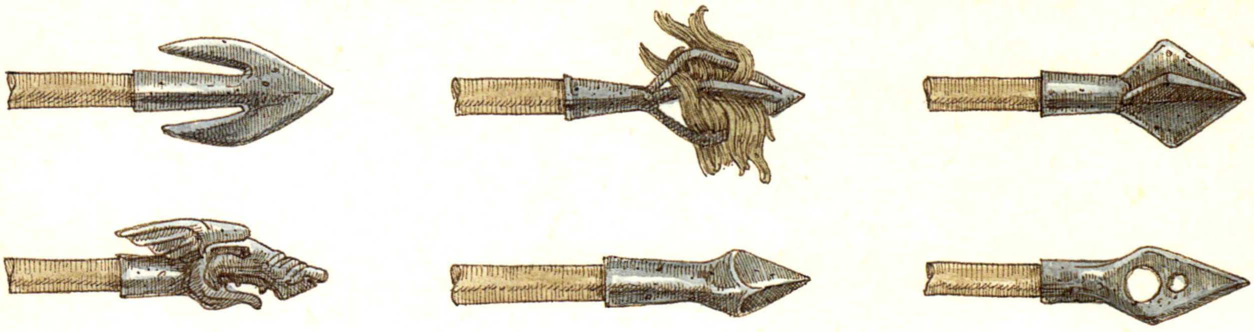

Arrowheads can be made from sharpened rocks (page 20) or animal bones. But the best material for the job is metal. The shape of the tip may vary depending on what function it serves. Blade tips are a good universal arrowhead for hunting and war. Flat tips have poor piercing power but rarely ricochet.

Cone tips have more penetration capacity and work well for hunting beasts with a thick hide. Faceted tips made from hardened steel have high impact force and are used to pierce through armor. Wrap the tip in resin-soaked cloth or other incendiary materials and ignite before shooting to set your enemy's defenses aflame.

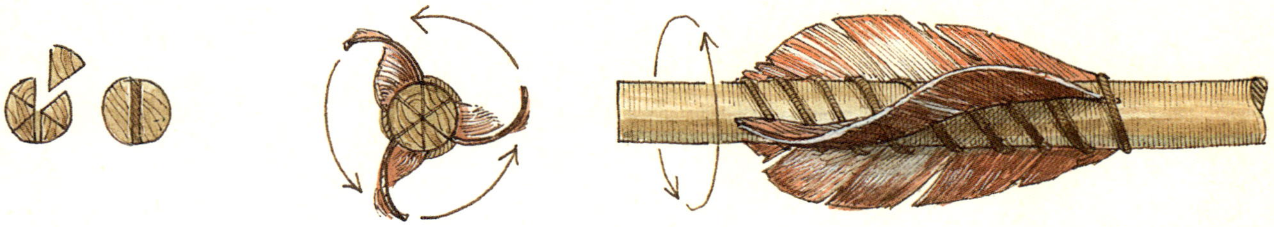

BOWSTRING & ARROWS

Glue together four thin, triangular sticks. This shaft will have optimal rigidity, which reduces wobble and deflection. Set the fletching vanes at an angle like a fan blade to stabilize the arrow during flight and improve accuracy. Make a bowstring out of animal sinew or silk (page 82).

It should be 3–5 cm shorter than the length of the bow. Tie a small loop at one end of the bowstring and a large loop at the other. Secure the small loop first. The larger loop on one end makes it easier to hook over the upper bow limb once it is under tension.

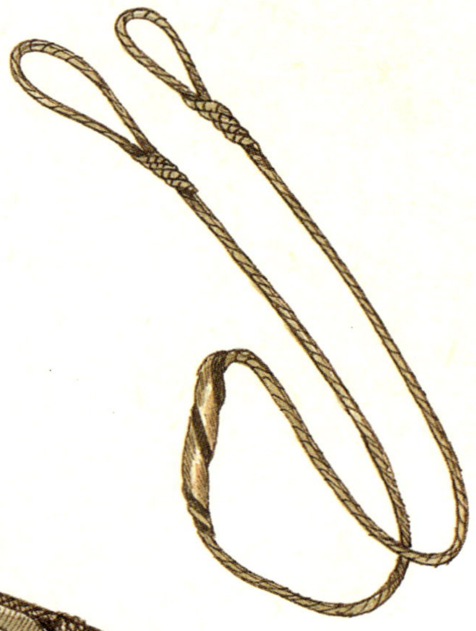

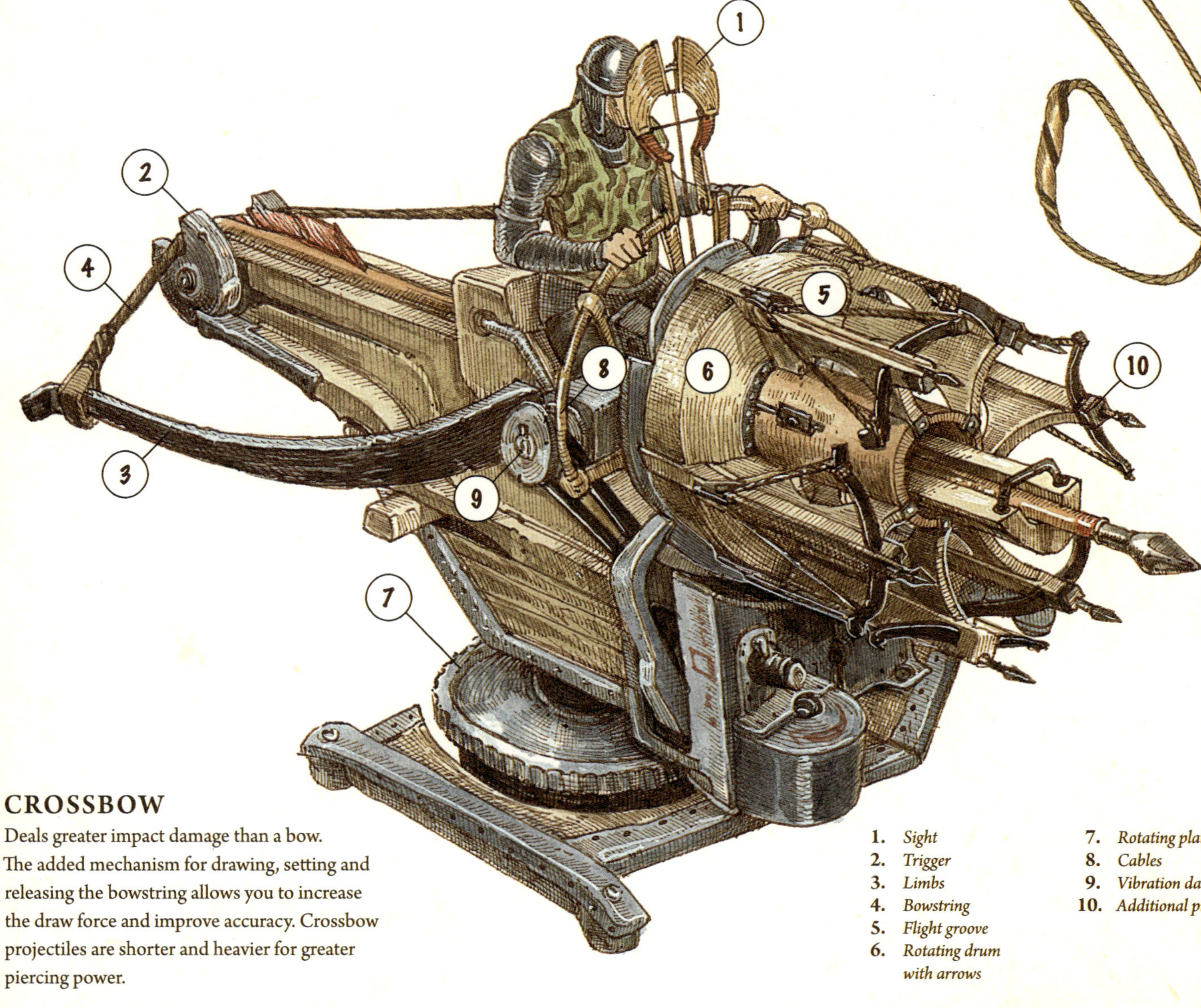

CROSSBOW

Deals greater impact damage than a bow. The added mechanism for drawing, setting and releasing the bowstring allows you to increase the draw force and improve accuracy. Crossbow projectiles are shorter and heavier for greater piercing power.

1. *Sight*
2. *Trigger*
3. *Limbs*
4. *Bowstring*
5. *Flight groove*
6. *Rotating drum with arrows*
7. *Rotating platform*
8. *Cables*
9. *Vibration damper*
10. *Additional projectiles*

SIEGE ENGINES

As soon as the first cities crop up, they'll almost immediately start putting up defensive walls. Even if you haven't made any enemies yet, you never know when they may appear. And sometimes, in order to defend your own freedom and the right to live in peace, you have to fight back.

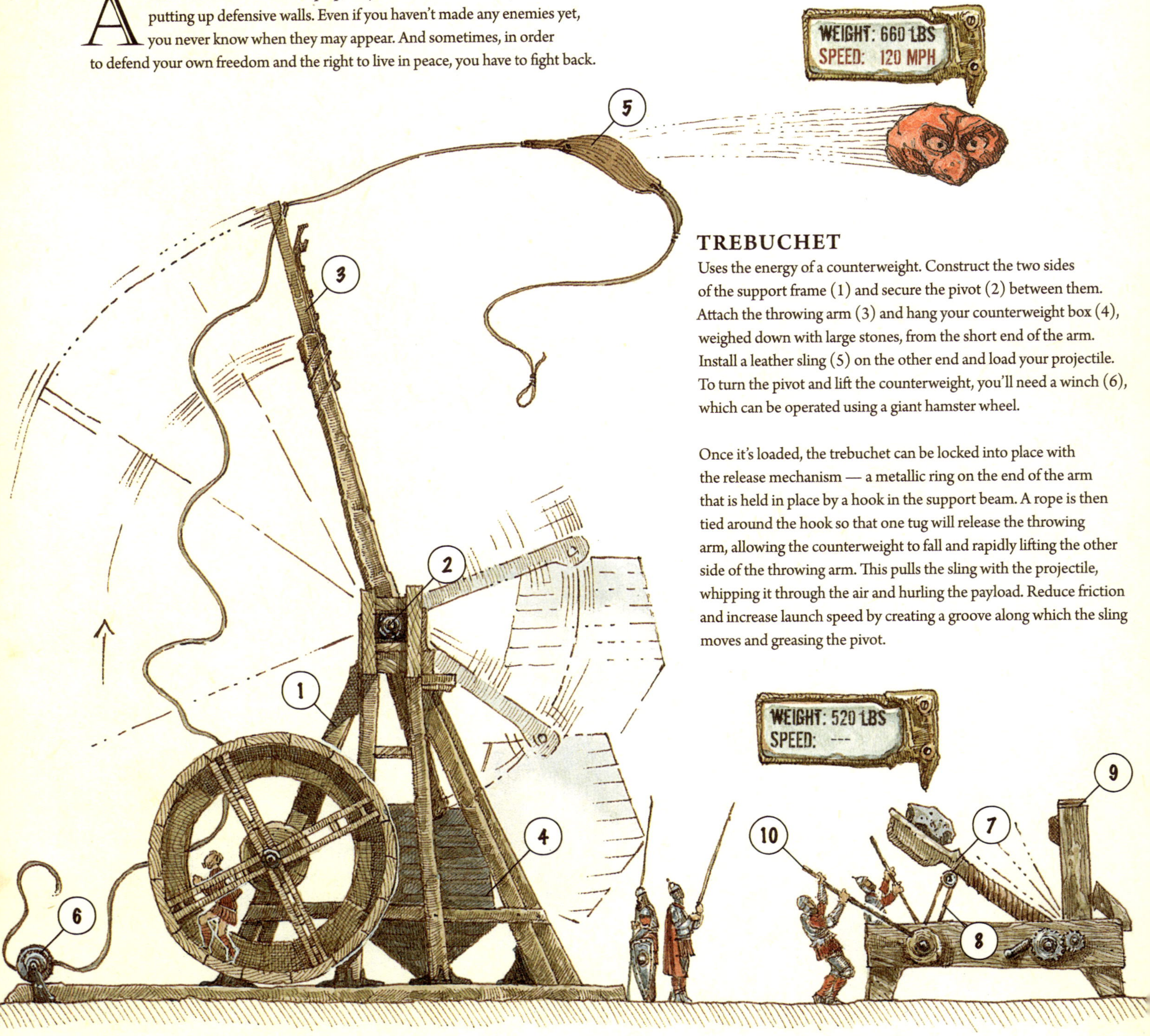

TREBUCHET

Uses the energy of a counterweight. Construct the two sides of the support frame (1) and secure the pivot (2) between them. Attach the throwing arm (3) and hang your counterweight box (4), weighed down with large stones, from the short end of the arm. Install a leather sling (5) on the other end and load your projectile. To turn the pivot and lift the counterweight, you'll need a winch (6), which can be operated using a giant hamster wheel.

Once it's loaded, the trebuchet can be locked into place with the release mechanism — a metallic ring on the end of the arm that is held in place by a hook in the support beam. A rope is then tied around the hook so that one tug will release the throwing arm, allowing the counterweight to fall and rapidly lifting the other side of the throwing arm. This pulls the sling with the projectile, whipping it through the air and hurling the payload. Reduce friction and increase launch speed by creating a groove along which the sling moves and greasing the pivot.

CATAPULT

Uses torsion energy stored in a wound rope. Attach the release mechanism to the throwing arm (7). It is held in place with a rope (8). Opposite the throwing arm is the stopping beam (9). Install a lever (10) to wind the rope and lower the throwing arm, putting it under tension. Once released, it hits the stopping beam, and the projectile is ejected.

Change the trajectory or range of the projectile by adjusting the moment of release from the sling. The earlier you release the trigger, the higher the projectile will take off, and the throwing range will decrease. Use different hooks for the sling to adjust the flight: The more the hook is bent, the further the projectile will fly, but its angle of incidence and impact force will change.

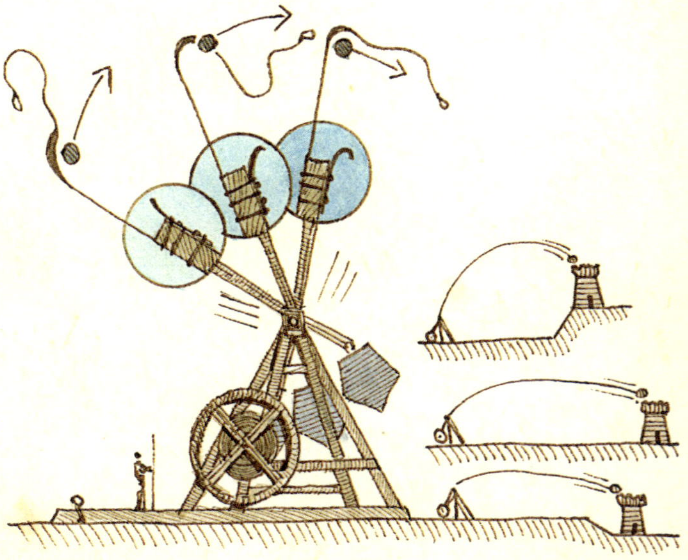

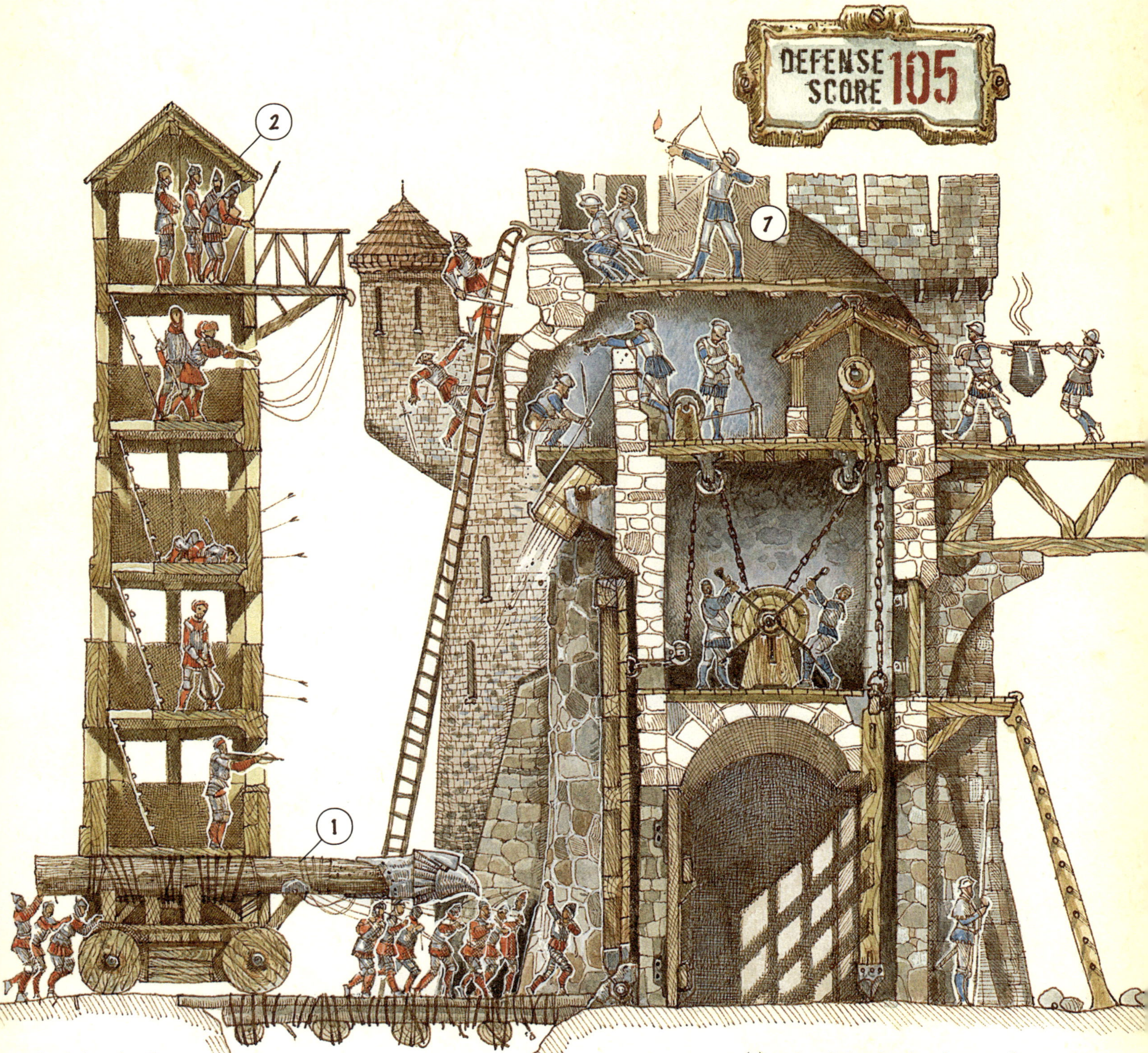

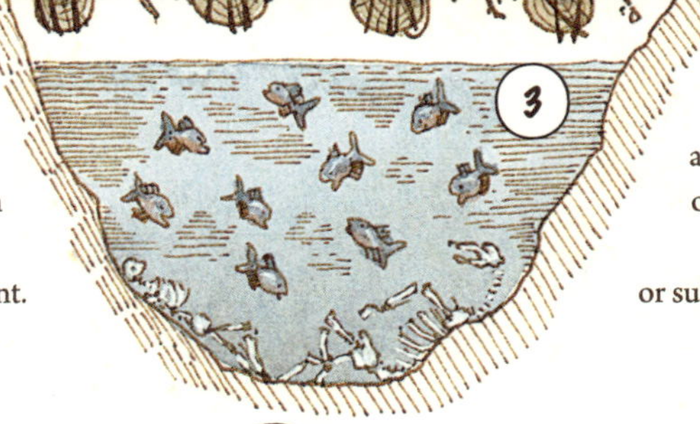

To break through walls, you need a **battering ram** (1): a frame from which a thick, heavy log is suspended. You can improve its penetrating power by adding a metal wedge or point.

A **siege tower** (2) can be rolled up directly to fortress walls, allowing warriors to climb them. If you combine a siege tower with a battering ram, the chances of breaking through will increase. The soldiers on the upper platforms will be able to provide cover fire for those breaking through the gates below. To protect your own fortress, dig a **moat** (3) or surround it with a **stake fence** (4). You can protect the walls of your fortress from attackers by pouring **boiling oil** or **tar** (5) and **dirt** (6) over them, as well as **throwing spears** and **launching arrows** (7).

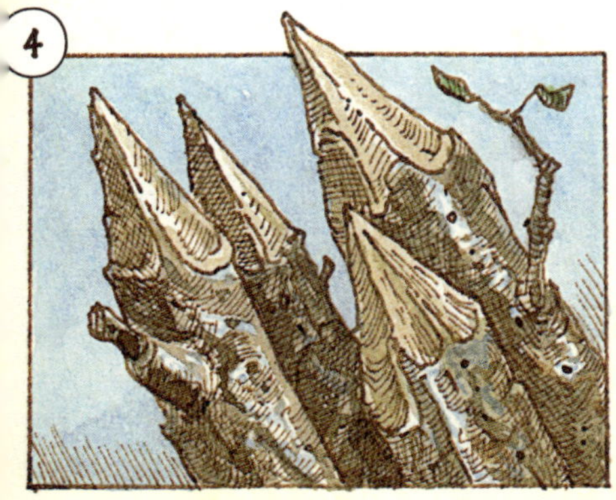

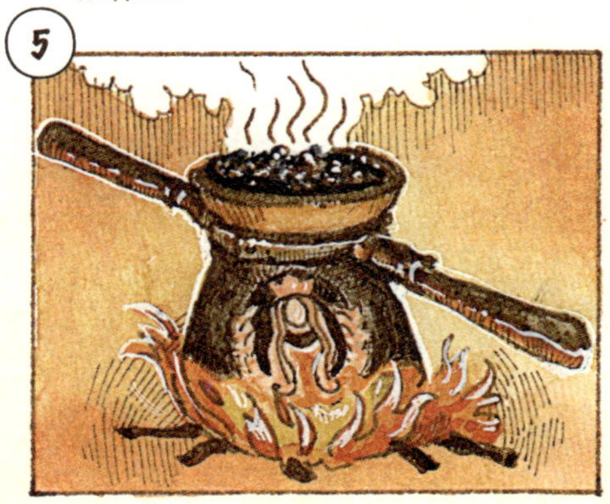

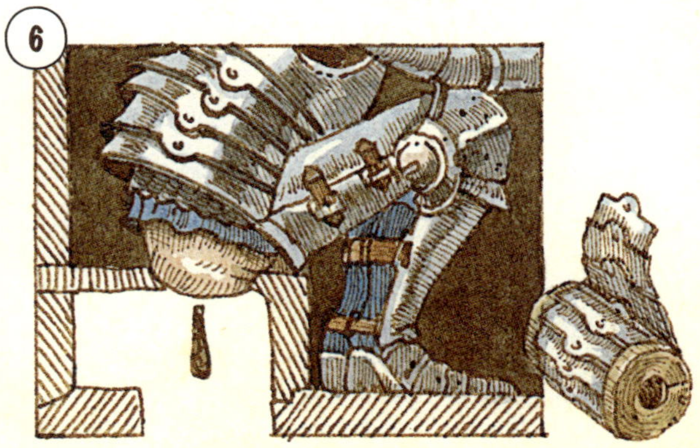

FIREARMS

You can use gunpowder for purely peaceful means, such as fireworks. But humanity has a tendency to want to weaponize everything. The pressurized gas generated during the combustion of explosives is capable of pushing a projectile out of a barrel at high speeds, giving firearms a lethal force greater than any weapon that came before them.

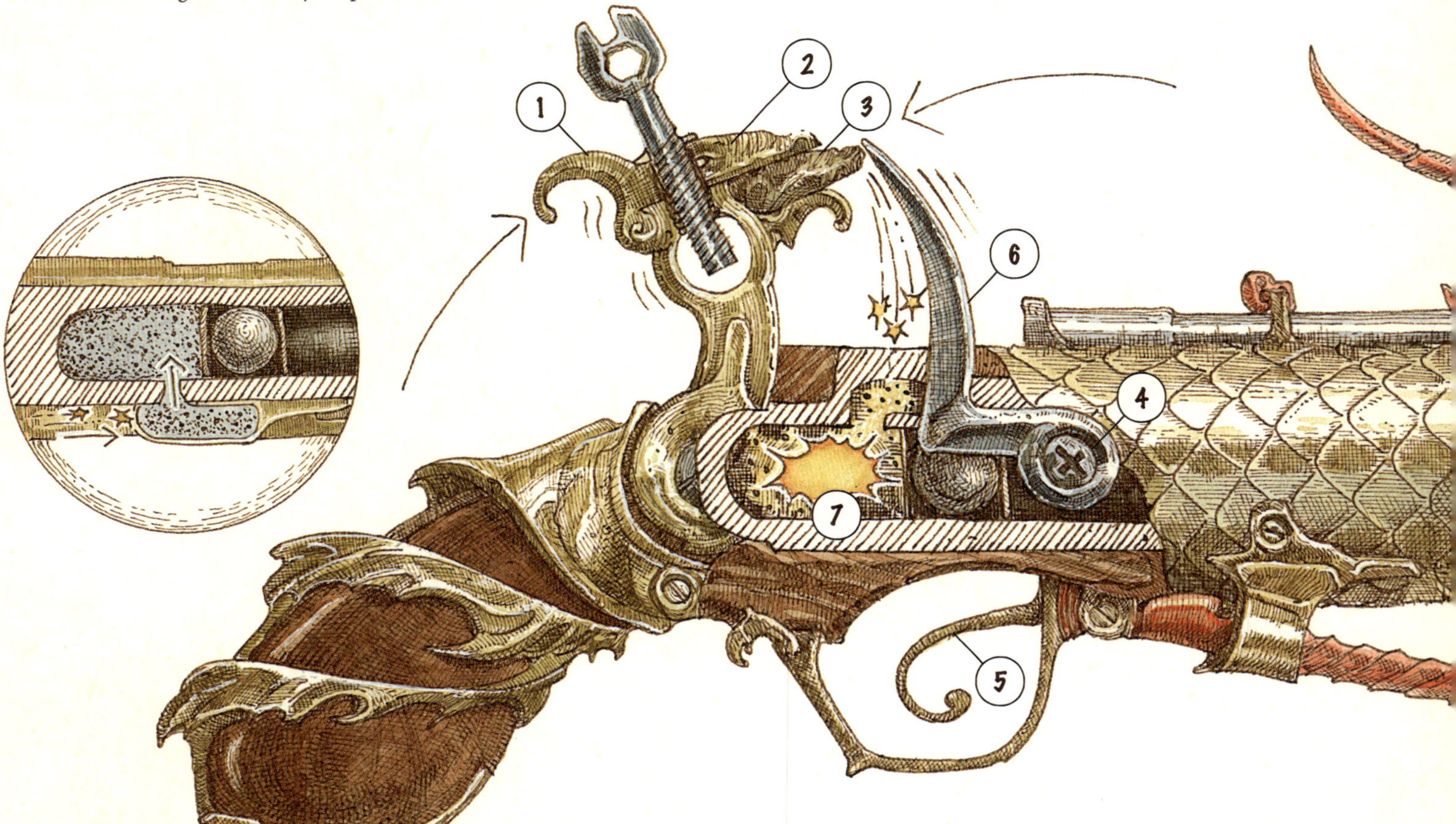

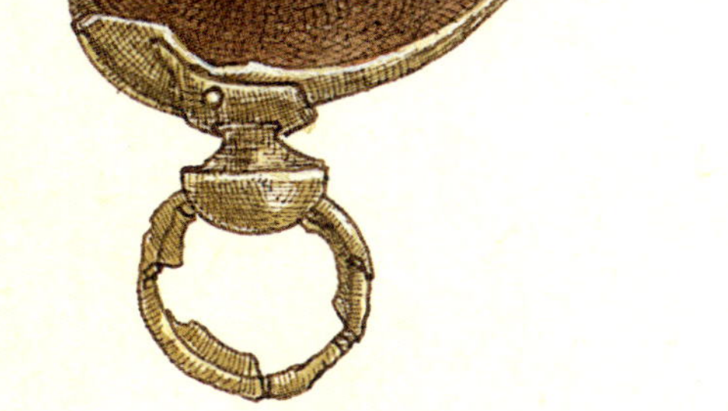

FLINTLOCK

The most complicated element of a firearm is the mechanism that ignites the explosive. The hammer (1) has a set of jaws (2), which hold a piece of sharpened flint (3) or any other material that sparks easily. When the gun is cocked, the spring (4) is highly compressed. When you press the trigger, the hammer is released and the flint strikes a steel plate (6). Simultaneously, the flash pan (7) holding the gunpowder opens. The flint striking the plate causes it to spark, igniting the gunpowder on the flash pan. The fire from the pan spreads further into the barrel and an explosion occurs, pushing the bullet.

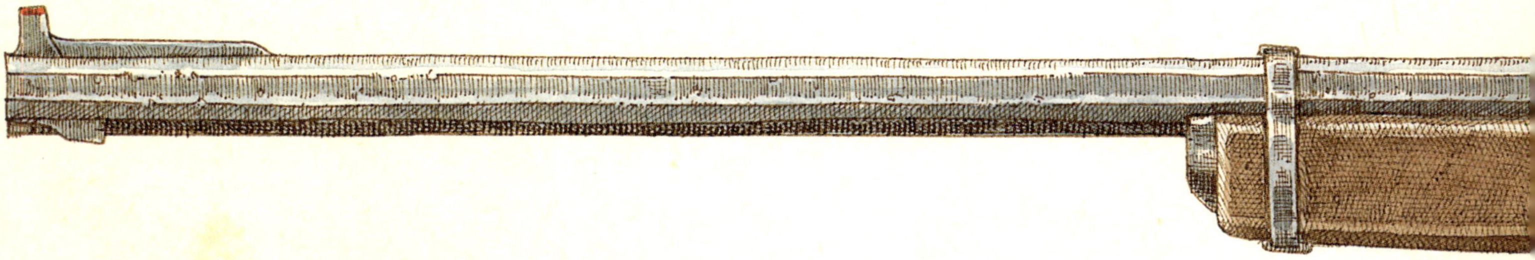

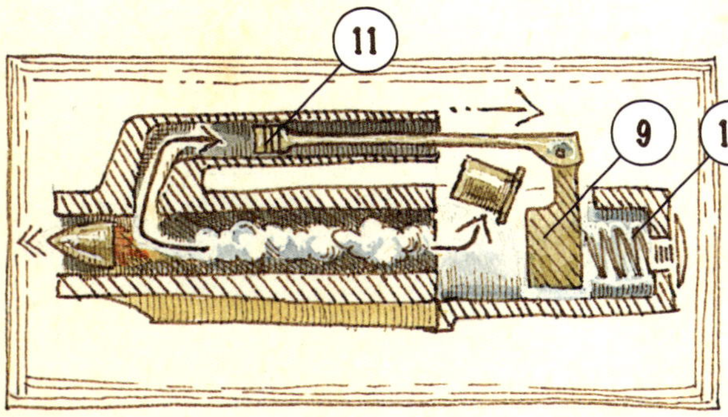

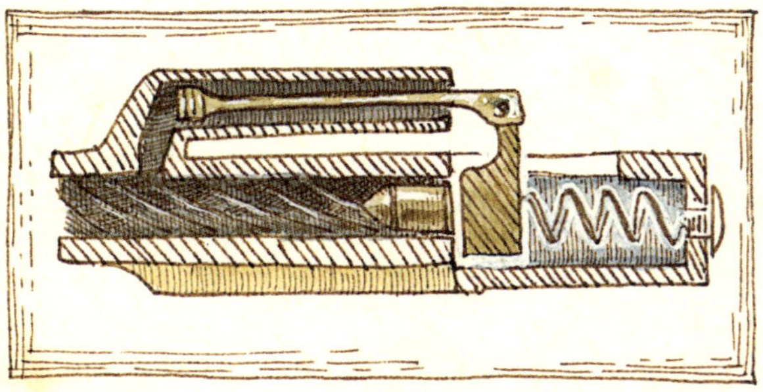

NEEDLE RIFLE

Weapons with a needle-like firing pin can shoot several times faster than a flintlock. For these weapons, you don't have to reload every shot, as with a flintlock — you can instead use a cartridge containing both the bullet and the gunpowder. Instead of flint, a firing pin (7) is used. When the trigger is pressed, the spring causes the firing pin to hit the percussion cap (8) — a copper shell covering the bottom of the cartridge — with enormous force.

The cap contains a primer — mercury fulminate. This substance explodes easily on impact and provides the spark necessary to ignite the gunpowder. The resulting gases push both the bullet and its paper cartridge casing through the rifle. The spiral grooves, or rifling, cause the bullet to spin. This ensures higher accuracy and a longer range.

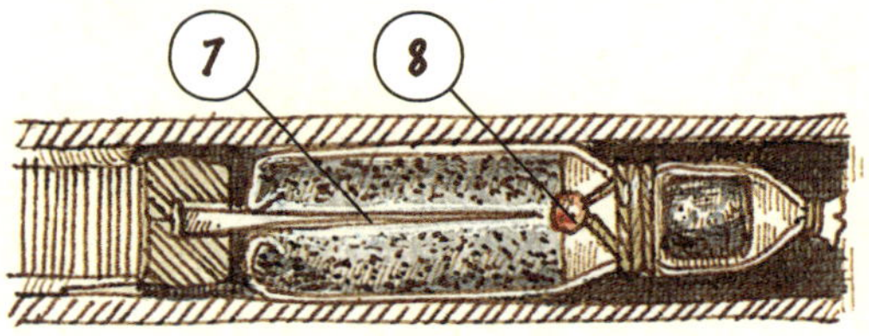

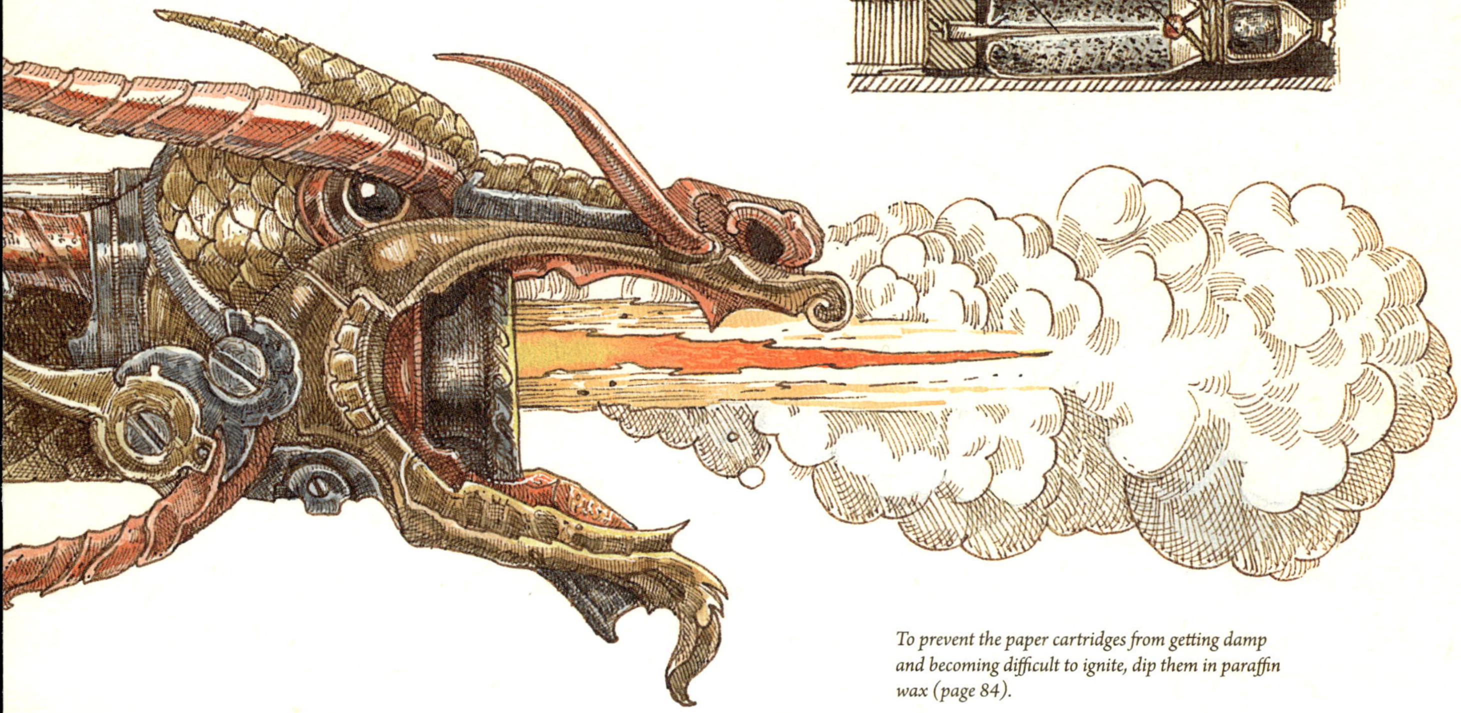

To prevent the paper cartridges from getting damp and becoming difficult to ignite, dip them in paraffin wax (page 84).

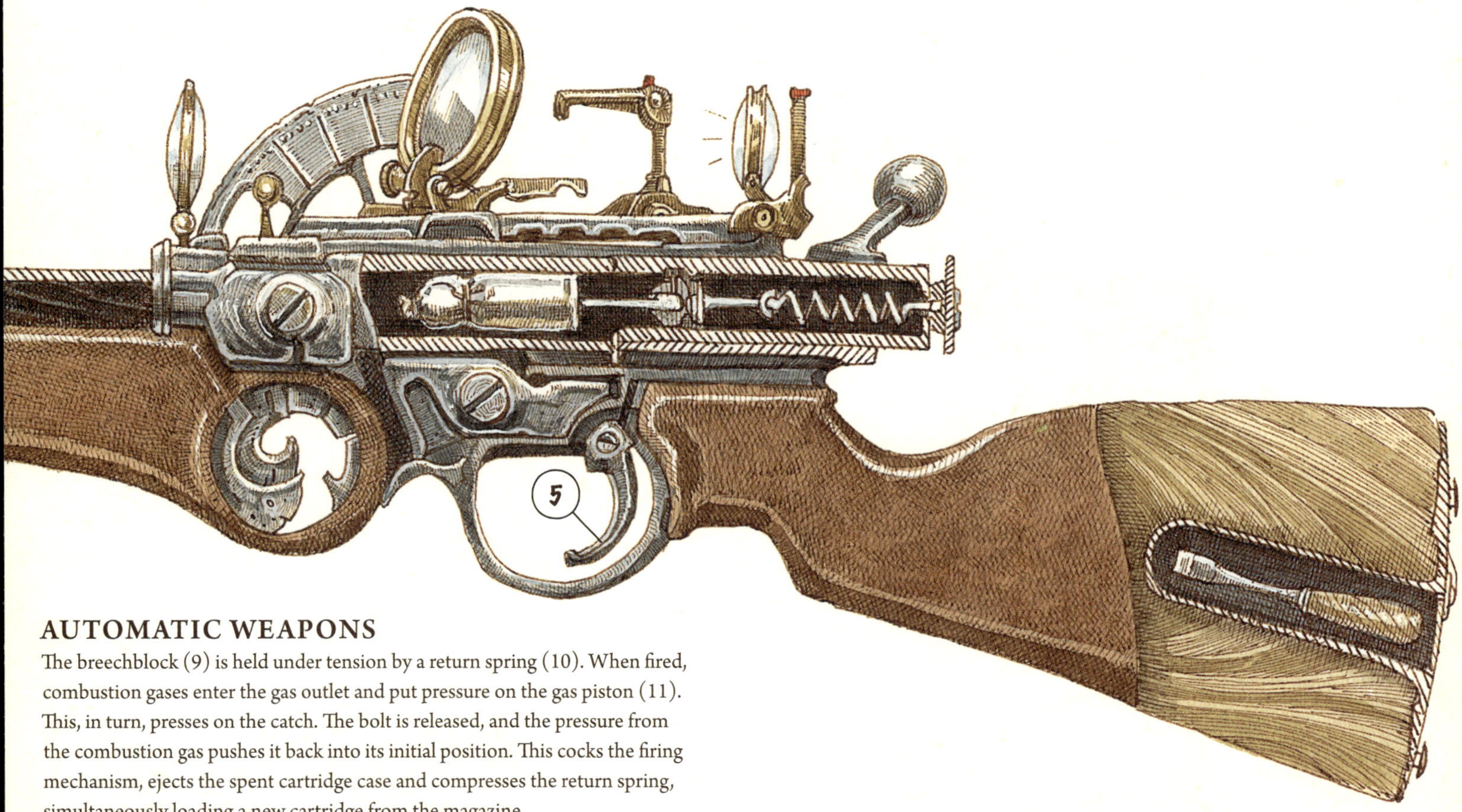

AUTOMATIC WEAPONS

The breechblock (9) is held under tension by a return spring (10). When fired, combustion gases enter the gas outlet and put pressure on the gas piston (11). This, in turn, presses on the catch. The bolt is released, and the pressure from the combustion gas pushes it back into its initial position. This cocks the firing mechanism, ejects the spent cartridge case and compresses the return spring, simultaneously loading a new cartridge from the magazine.

TANK

A tank is a mobile fortress that can traverse any terrain, overcome obstacles, ensure the safety of your personnel and also fire on enemy forces. This armored vehicle has such a menacing appearance that it may simply scare some of your enemies away.

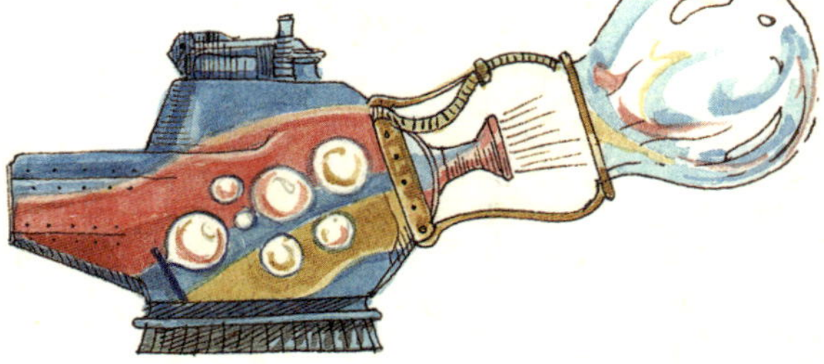

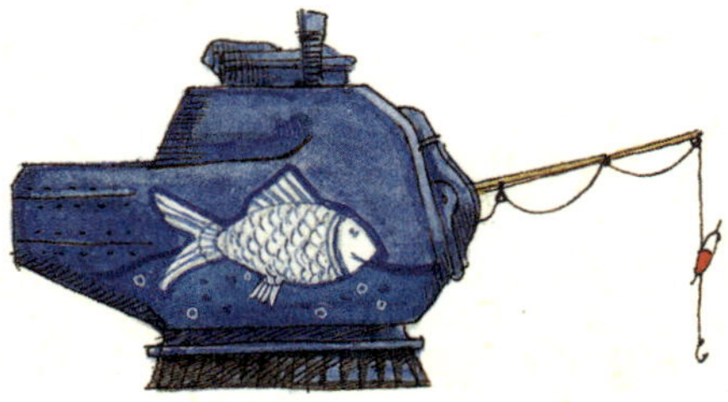

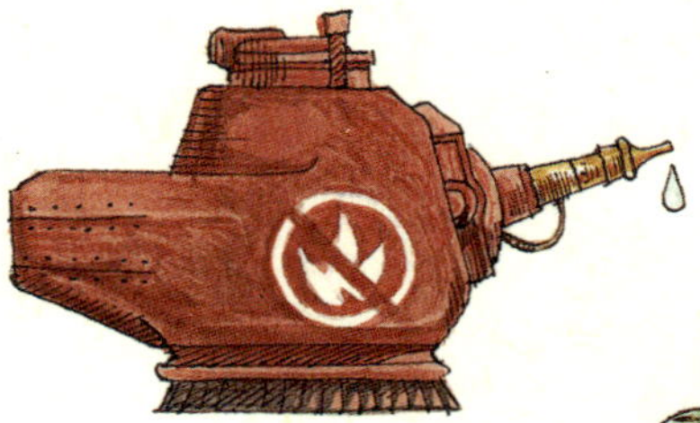

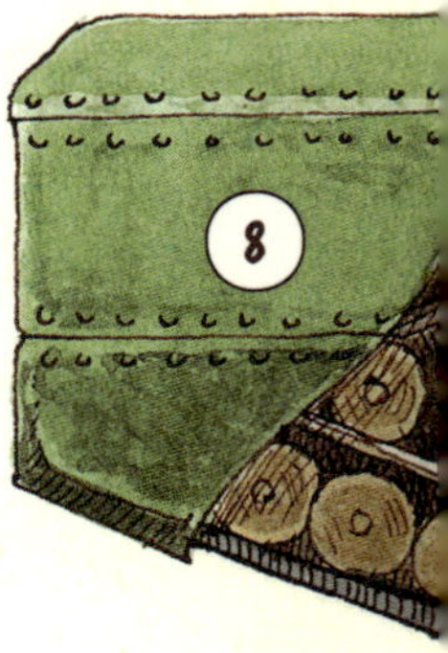

TOWER

Use a gyroscope (page 172) to maintain the gun's tilt angle and sight precision. Even as the tank rolls over rough terrain, the gyroscope will help keep your aim accurate. The turret is a removable part of the structure, so the tank can be used not only as a weapon but also for more peaceful activities.

TREADS

By using treads, tanks essentially carry their own road with them. They increase the area of contact with the ground so they don't sink into the mud and help you get over obstacles such as ditches: A long enough tread will touch the other side of the ditch before the tank starts to fall through. Treads are also perfect for diggers or other heavy vehicles on a construction site or quarry.

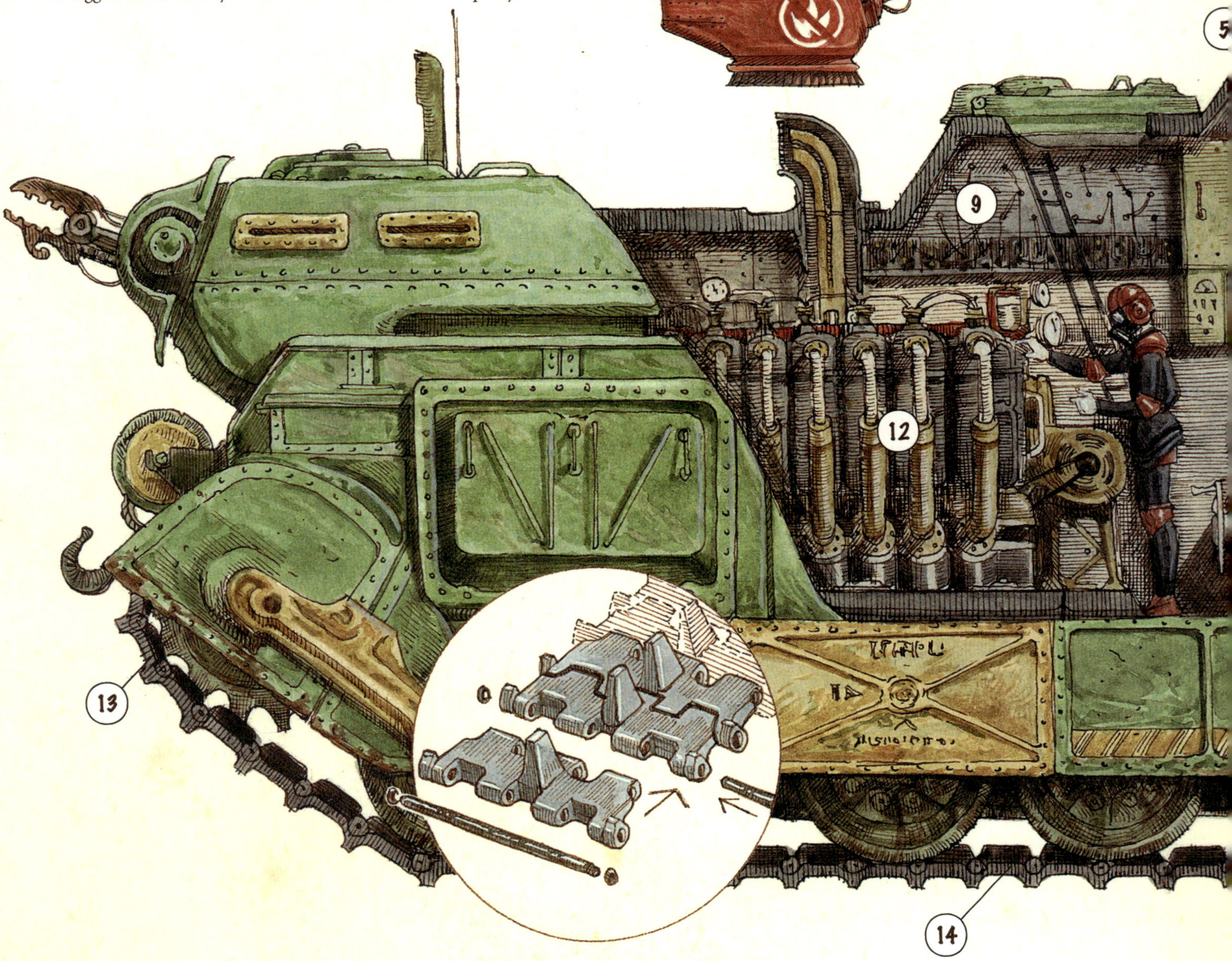

Treads are composed of many links connected at pivot points using steel pins and locking washers to form a long loop. The tracks must have protrusions at the bottom to provide traction.

The engine (12) powers the transmission and rotates the drive wheels (13), which pull the tread (14) backward, propelling the tank forward. If both treads move at the same speed, the tank moves straight. If one side is moving slower, the tank will start to turn towards the slower side.

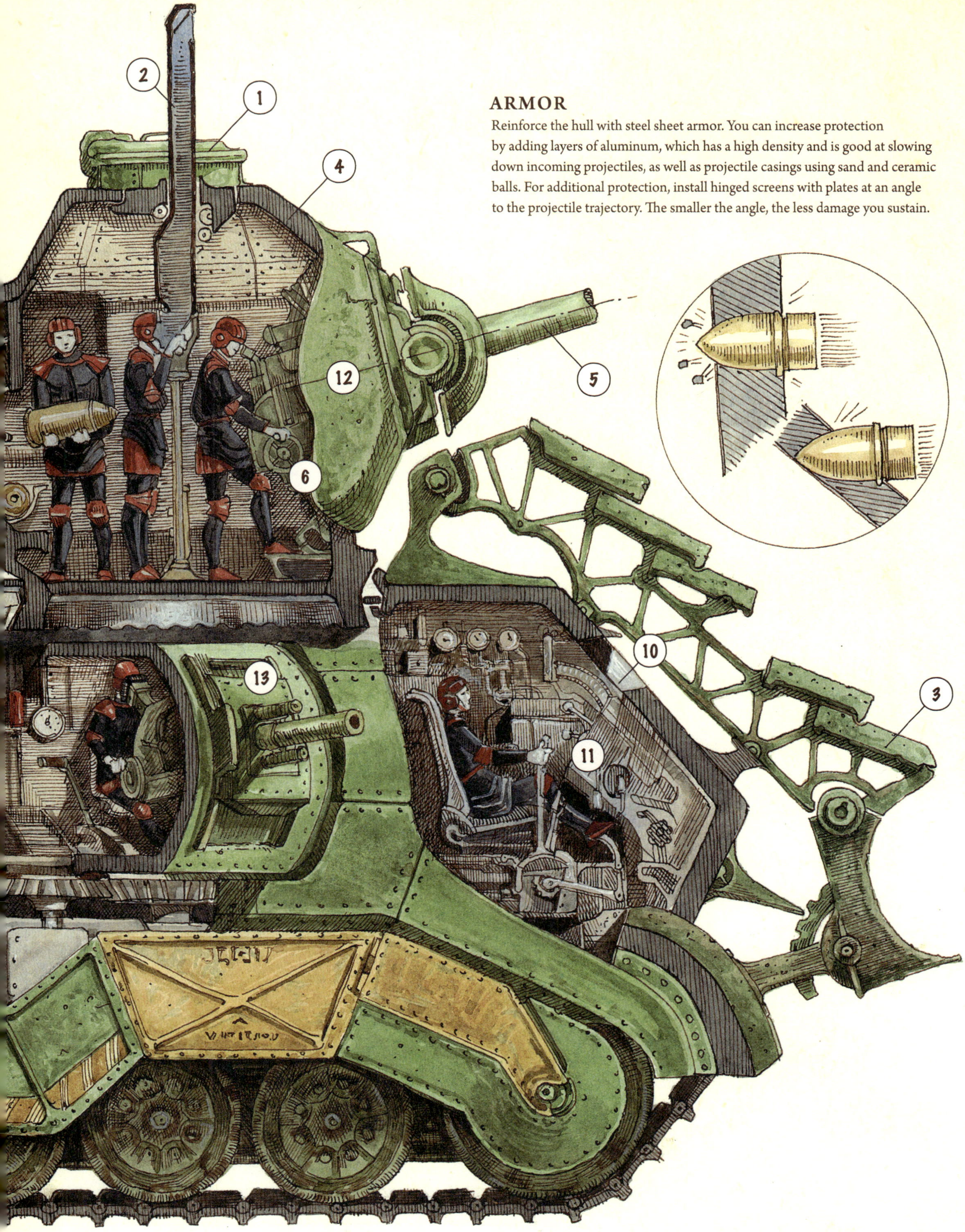

ARMOR

Reinforce the hull with steel sheet armor. You can increase protection by adding layers of aluminum, which has a high density and is good at slowing down incoming projectiles, as well as projectile casings using sand and ceramic balls. For additional protection, install hinged screens with plates at an angle to the projectile trajectory. The smaller the angle, the less damage you sustain.

1. *Entrance hatch*
2. *Periscope*
3. *Combined additional armor*
4. *Turret with 360-degree rotation*
5. *Long-range weapon*
6. *Gun elevating gear*
7. *Projectile transporter*
8. *Ammunition complement*
9. *Radio station*
10. *Surveillance devices*
11. *Gear lever*
12. *Engine*
13. *Drive wheels*
14. *Treads*

COILGUN

The force of firearms is limited by the expansion of the gases produced when they combust. Therefore, in order to lead the "artillery revolution", you're going to need a new technology. Not a more powerful explosive but a completely different form of energy. Remember that it's better to use energy for peaceful purposes, but if peace is not an option, address the situation through your coilgun.

To give your weapon the power it needs to be effective, you need to fortify the base structure. But then how do you make such a bulky machine mobile? Place it on railroad tracks and distribute the necessary pieces across several cars: the cannon on one car, the power source on another and the control station bringing up the rear.

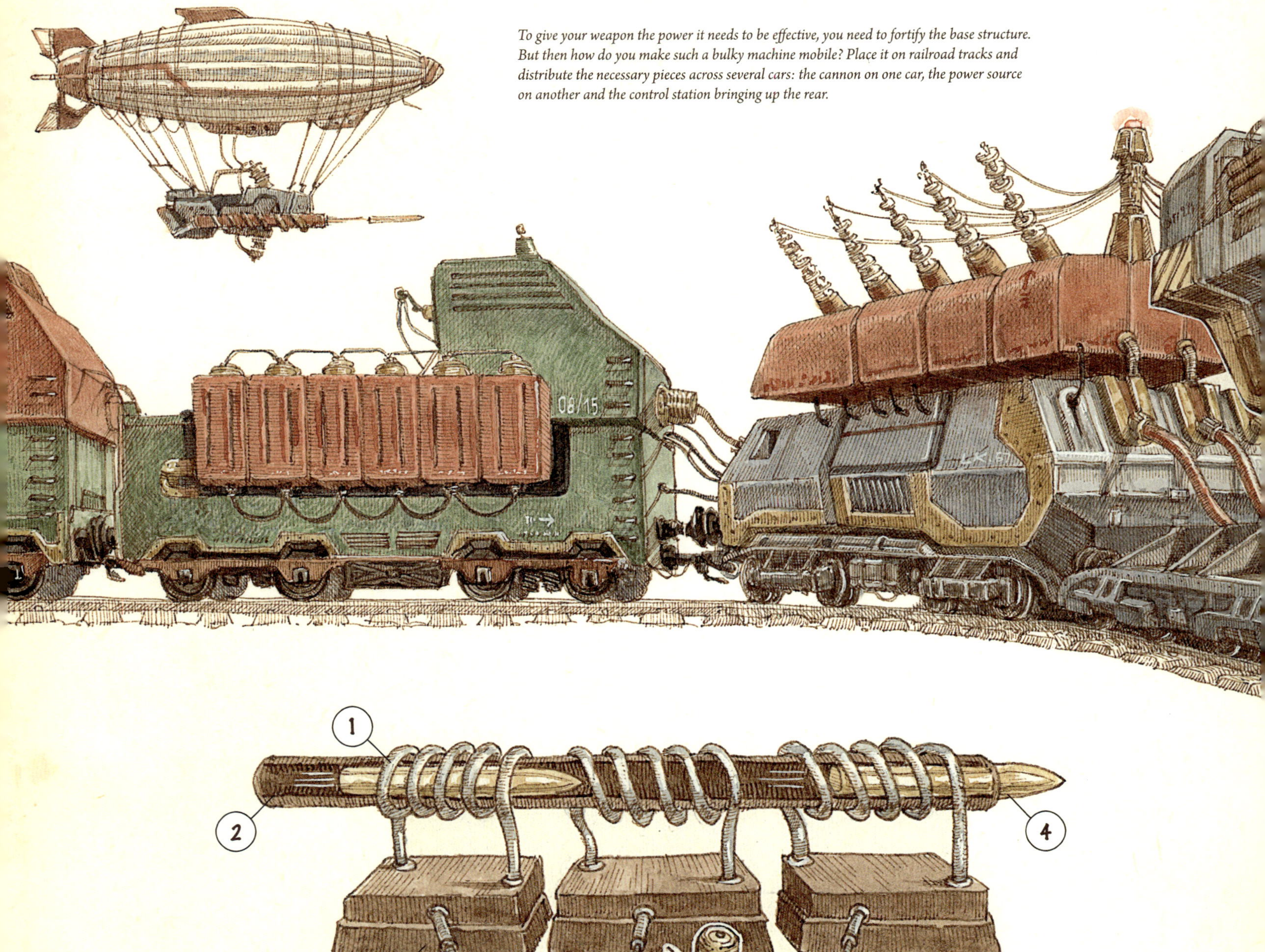

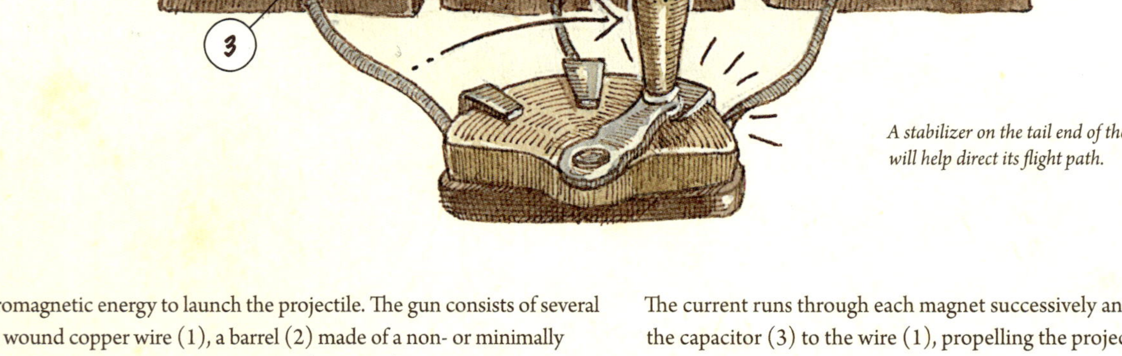

A stabilizer on the tail end of the projectile will help direct its flight path.

Use electromagnetic energy to launch the projectile. The gun consists of several coils with wound copper wire (1), a barrel (2) made of a non- or minimally conductive material — for example, ceramic (page 136) — and a robust power source (3). An electric current is run through the coil, creating a magnetic field and drawing the projectile into the barrel. To achieve the necessary launch speed, you must use a stepped acceleration system involving several electromagnets lining the length of the barrel. The current runs through each magnet successively and is dumped from the capacitor (3) to the wire (1), propelling the projectile (4). The shorter and more powerful the generated impulse, the faster it goes. The projectile must be made of a ferromagnetic material, such as steel (page 110).

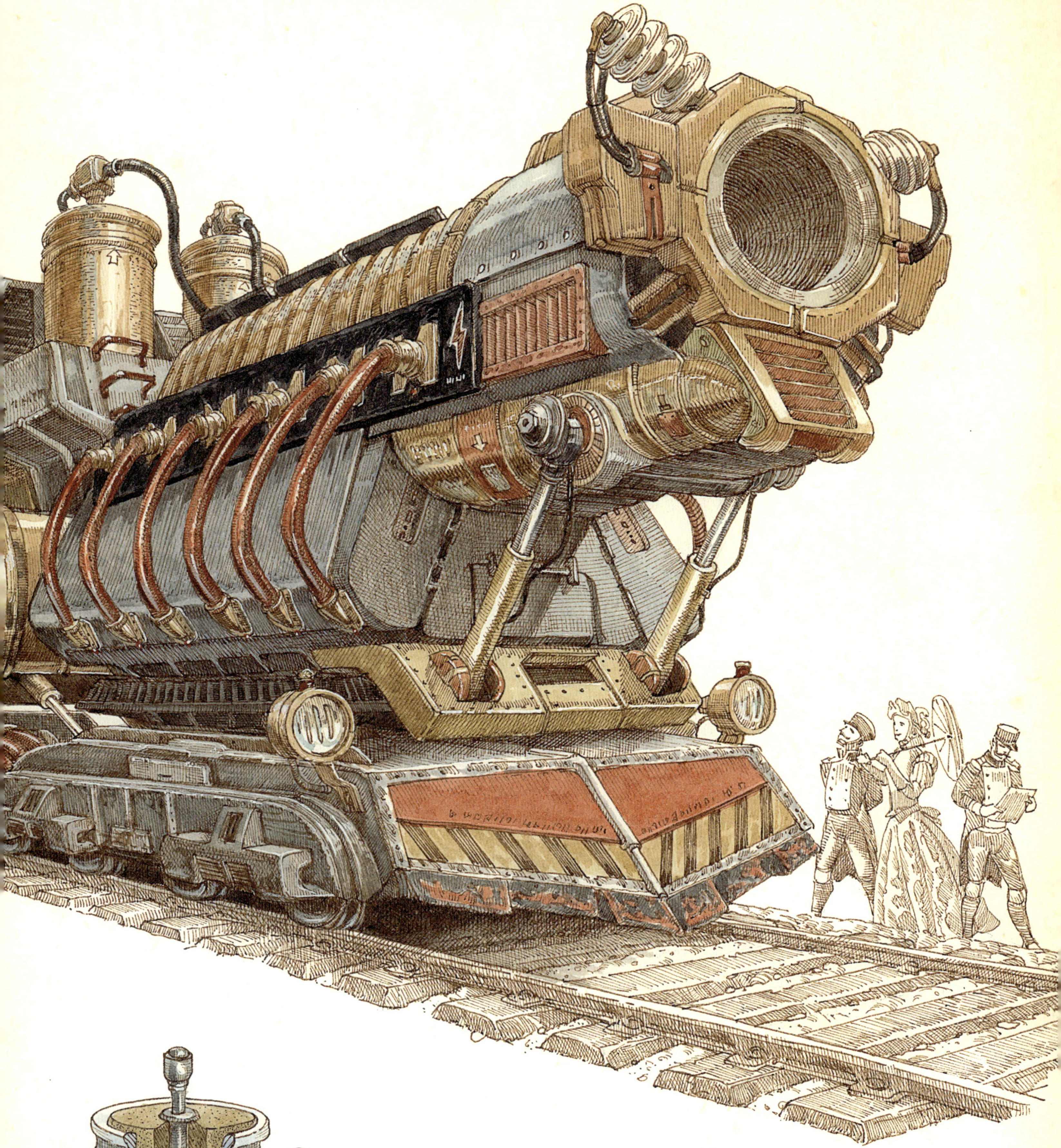

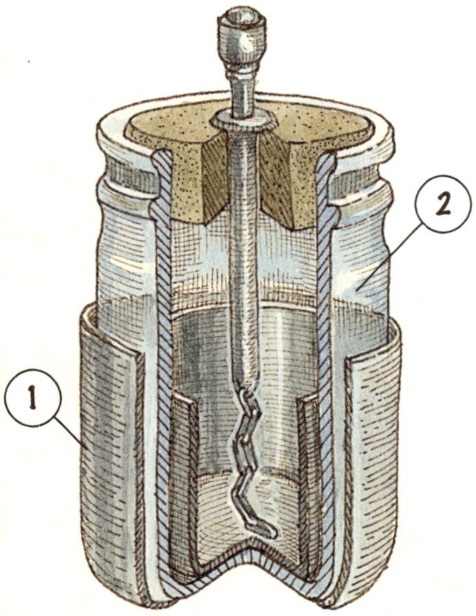

SUPERCAPACITOR

Coilguns require a power supply that is robust and rapidly-discharging — a supercapacitor. For energy storage, it is best to use high-capacity electrostatic capacitors. They are capable of accumulating a large electric charge and produce a large current when discharged.

A capacitor is a relatively simple device to manufacture. Place two electrodes consisting of metal plates inside the casing (1) and fill the space between them with a layer of dielectric material (2) as an insulator, such as rubber or resin (page 116).

EVERYDAY
LIFE

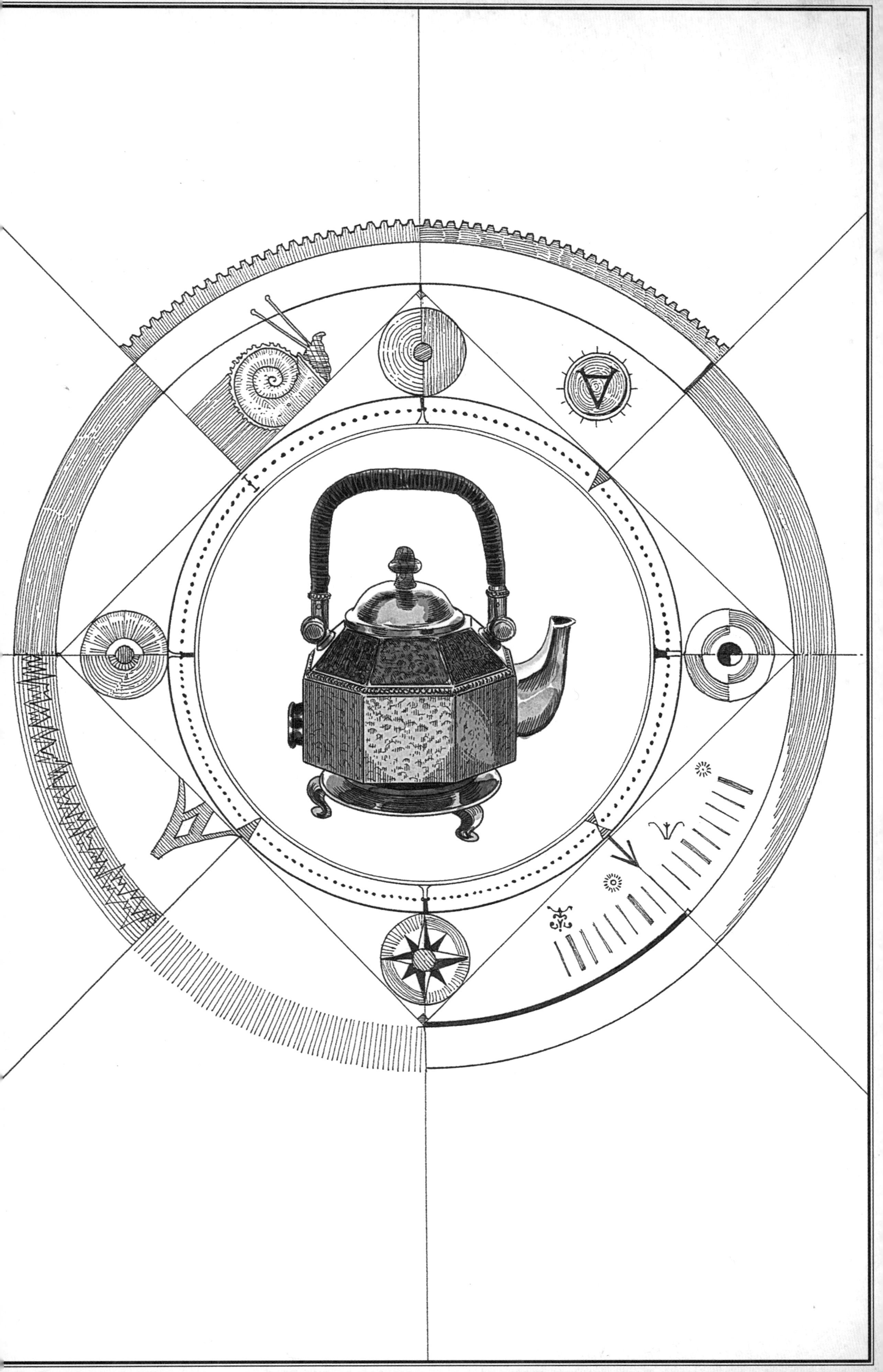

ALARM CLOCK

Evolution has given humans a rather intricate mechanism for measuring time that helps them know when to fall asleep and wake up — their circadian rhythms. Just like height or shoe size, everyone's rhythm is unique to their body. But when life gets in the way, with red-eye flights and late nights working to change the world, the system can malfunction. You have to reboot your biological clock with the help of a mechanical one.

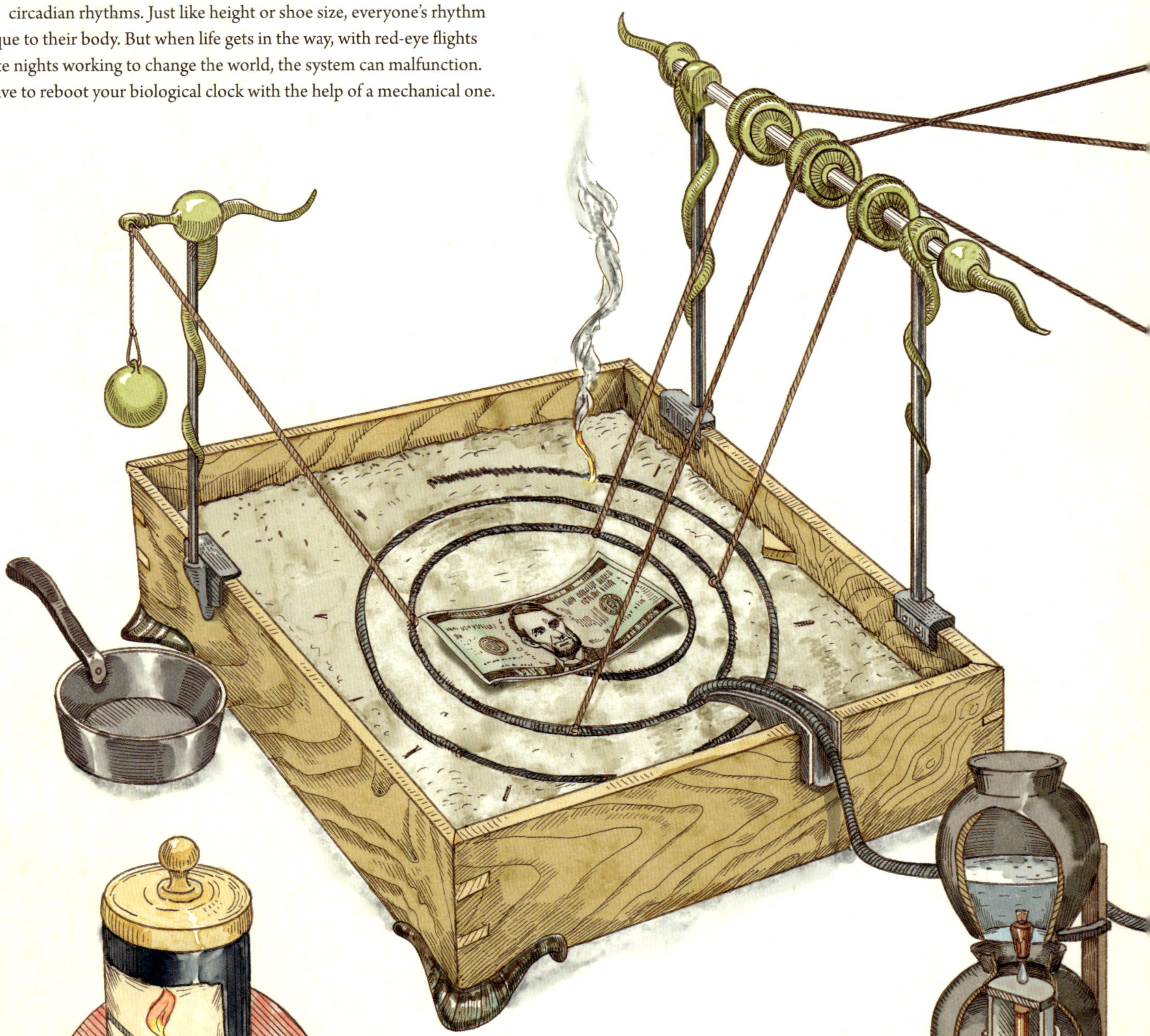

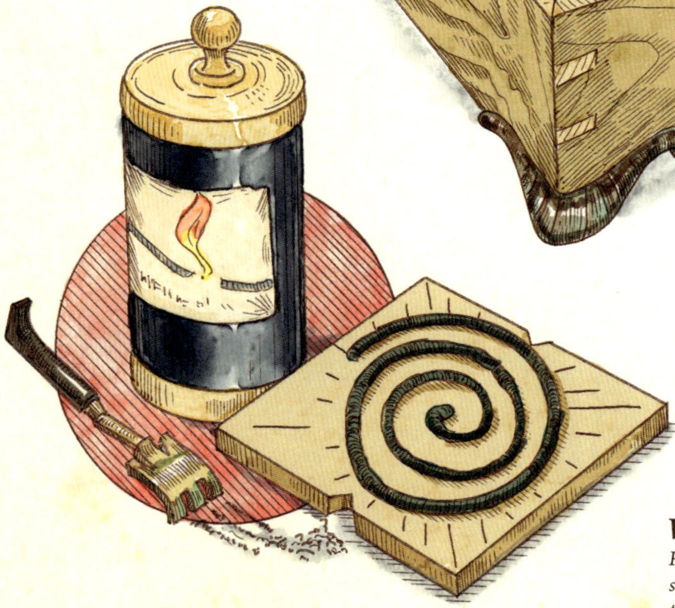

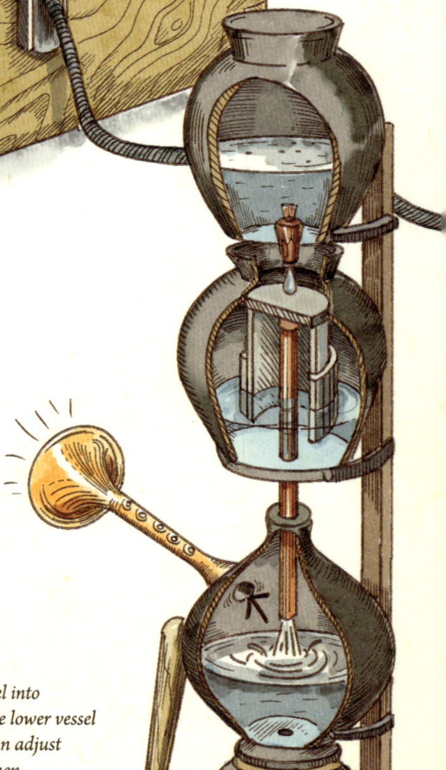

Combine shredded sandalwood or agarwood with other fragrances, such as incense, patchouli, cloves or camphor (page 200). Add water and other ingredients to regulate the burning rate: clay slows it down and rubber tree sap (page 116) speeds it up. Shape the resulting paste into a spiral shape on a flat, fireproof surface and attach a wick to the outer edge. Increase or decrease the size of the spiral so that it burns out at precisely the time you want to wake up. Once the spiral burns out completely, it will ignite the wick on the other end, triggering the alarm mechanism attached to it.

Water Alarm Clock

Find four vessels. Arrange the first two so that water flows from the upper vessel into the lower. By changing the volume of the lower vessel and the rate of flow of the liquid, you can adjust the time it takes for the vessel to fill. When, after the calculated time, the second vessel is full, the water will quickly flow through a thin tube into the third vessel, which is entirely closed except for a small hole. As water rushes in, it displaces the air, forcing it out through the small hole and producing a melodic sound. Just make sure you wake up before the water completely fills the third vessel and begins to flow into the fourth...

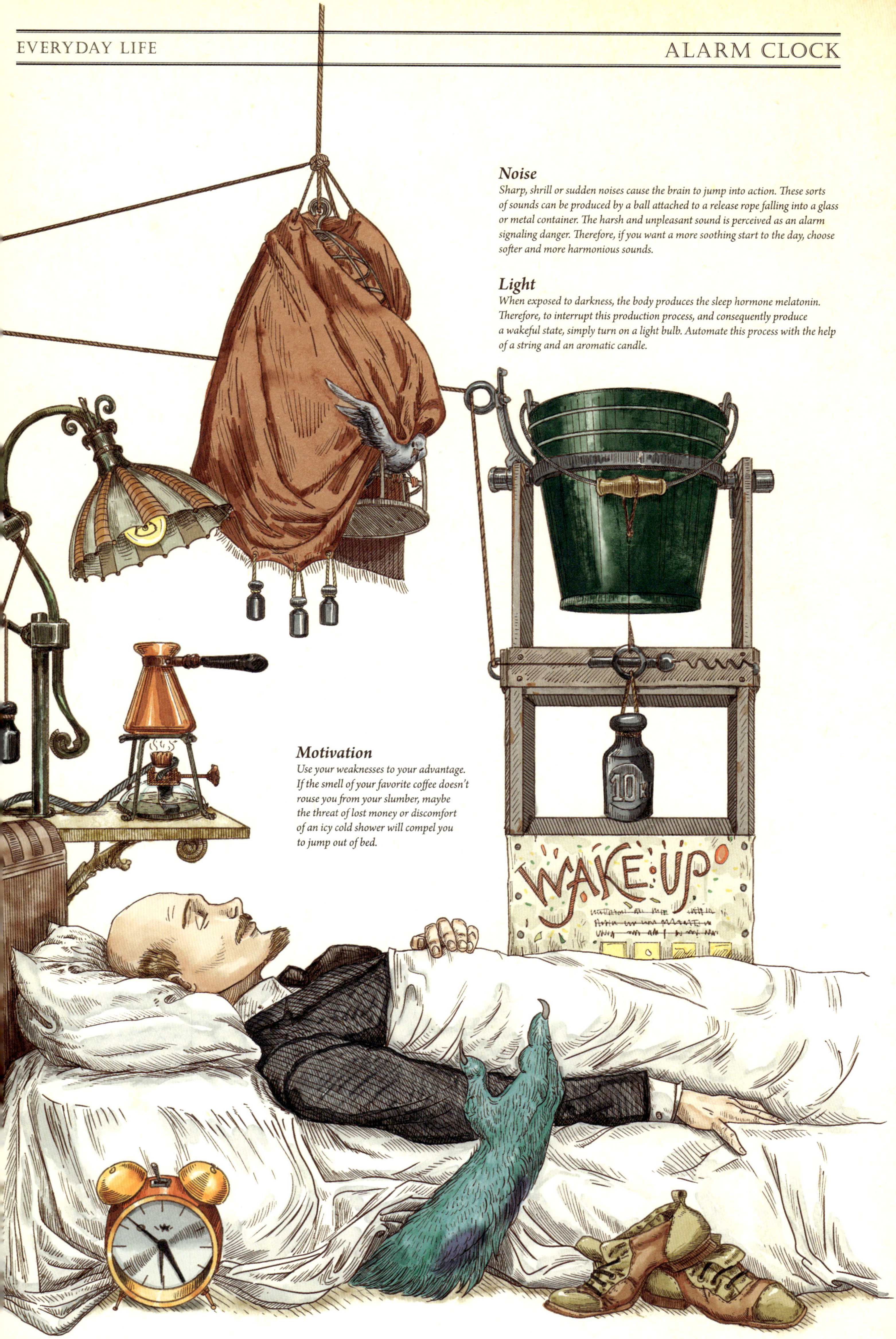

Noise

Sharp, shrill or sudden noises cause the brain to jump into action. These sorts of sounds can be produced by a ball attached to a release rope falling into a glass or metal container. The harsh and unpleasant sound is perceived as an alarm signaling danger. Therefore, if you want a more soothing start to the day, choose softer and more harmonious sounds.

Light

When exposed to darkness, the body produces the sleep hormone melatonin. Therefore, to interrupt this production process, and consequently produce a wakeful state, simply turn on a light bulb. Automate this process with the help of a string and an aromatic candle.

Motivation

Use your weaknesses to your advantage. If the smell of your favorite coffee doesn't rouse you from your slumber, maybe the threat of lost money or discomfort of an icy cold shower will compel you to jump out of bed.

TOOTHBRUSHING

There are billions of microorganisms living in human mouths. Microorganisms present in the oral cavity form a layer of bacteria on oral surfaces. Decay-causing bacteria in your mouth make acids that attack the tooth's surface, or enamel. You can lose your teeth because of it, but this is only the beginning. Over time, a knock-on effect allows these bacteria to infect other organs. Routine dental hygiene practices can eliminate these bacteria; thus, it is essential to brush teeth at least twice daily.

TOOTHPASTE

All you need to make toothpaste is a liquid and a powder. The abrasive particles of the powder scrub away stains and plaque on your teeth, while the liquid gives the toothpaste a smooth texture. You can use chalk, salt, soda or a mixture of them as a powder. Chewing on such things, however, offers a less-than-pleasant taste. You need to use some flavoring agents.

Flavoring

To brush your teeth with pleasure, use an herbal decoction instead of water. There are natural ingredients such as honey, propolis, chamomile, oak bark and aloe vera extract that have natural antimicrobial and anti-inflammatory properties. Use your favorite flavors: maybe some cocoa powder, a pinch of hot pepper or ground mint leaves?

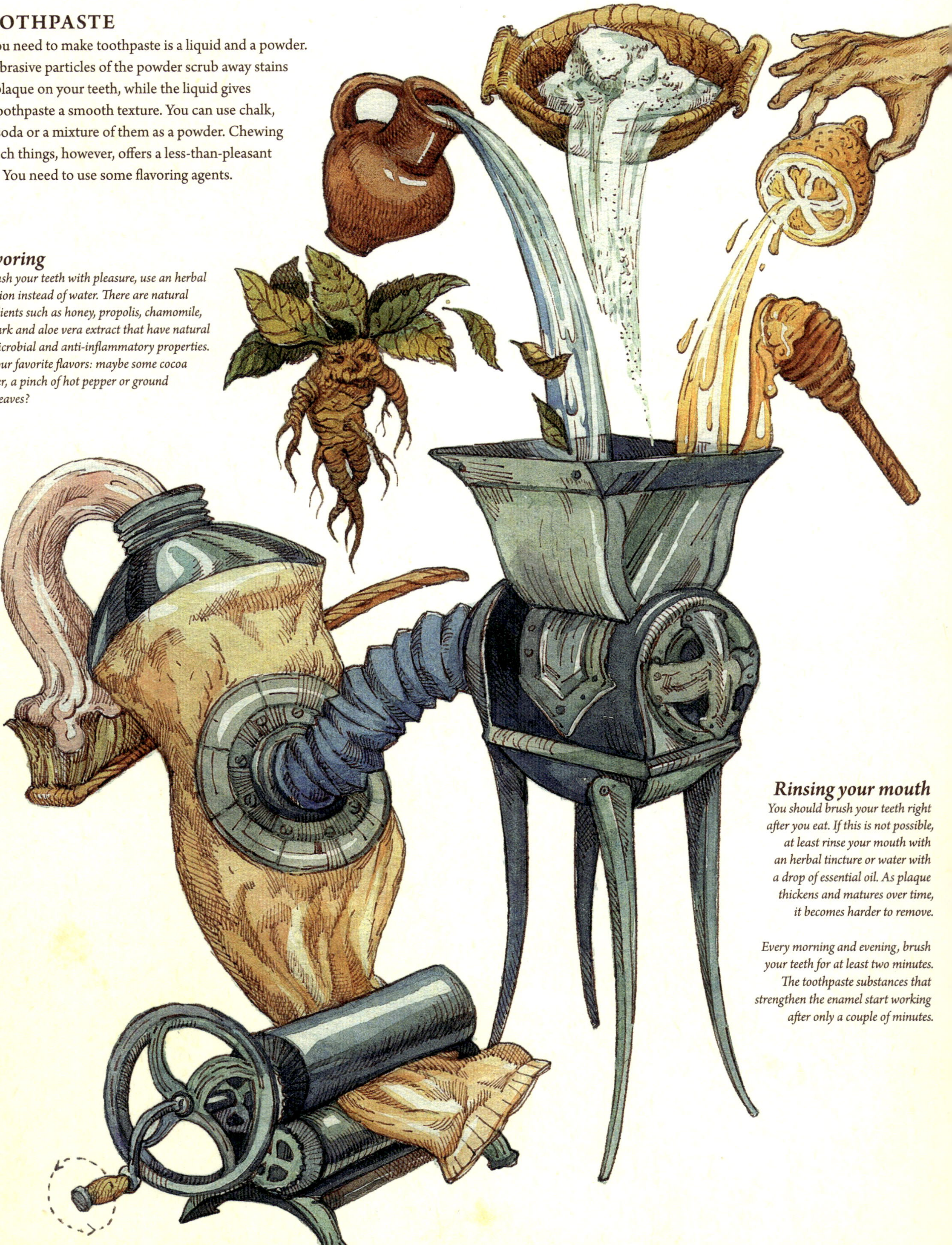

Rinsing your mouth

You should brush your teeth right after you eat. If this is not possible, at least rinse your mouth with an herbal tincture or water with a drop of essential oil. As plaque thickens and matures over time, it becomes harder to remove.

Every morning and evening, brush your teeth for at least two minutes. The toothpaste substances that strengthen the enamel start working after only a couple of minutes.

TOOTHBRUSH

A bristle toothbrush consisting of hog bristles quickly removes plaque from your teeth. That's handy but not safe; over time, these bristles can damage tooth enamel. Horse-hair bristles are softer. Marine sponges are perfectly stiff but harder to attach to a handle.

The natural bristles have a small cavity inside that holds moisture. Over time, microorganisms inhabit this cavity, and with each use, they move into the mouth. Therefore, you should change your natural-bristle toothbrush very frequently.

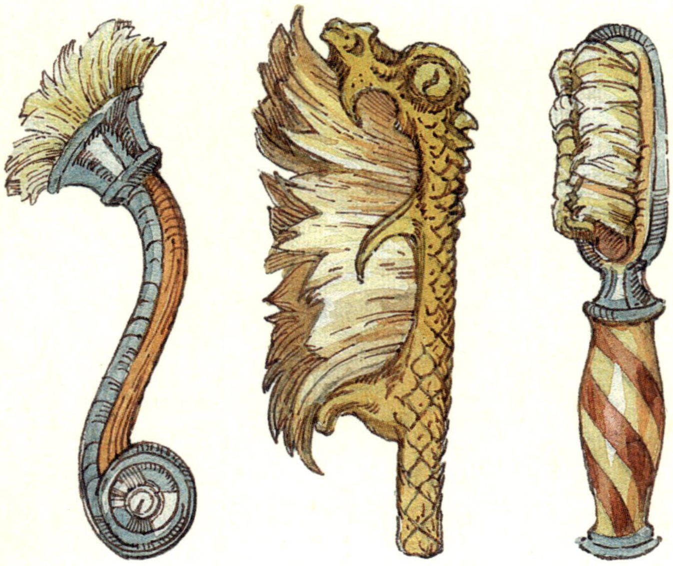

MECHANICAL BRUSH

This is a toothbrush that makes rapid, automatic brushing motions, either back-and-forth oscillation or rotation oscillation, in order to clean teeth. This means that the brush head alternates in both a clockwise and counterclockwise rotation. A winding mechanism is needed to make the movement smooth.

The coiled steel spring (page 40) is attached at one end to the brush head and at the other to the winding axle. When the key is wound, the spring will wind tighter on the axle, storing mechanical energy. When the spring unwinds, the winding axle will begin to rotate and drive the pinion. From it, the rotation is transmitted to the axle on which the bristle head is attached. When the spring is fully unwound, the brush will stop. You can adjust the length of the spring and the speed at which it springs up and down so that it spins for at least two minutes.

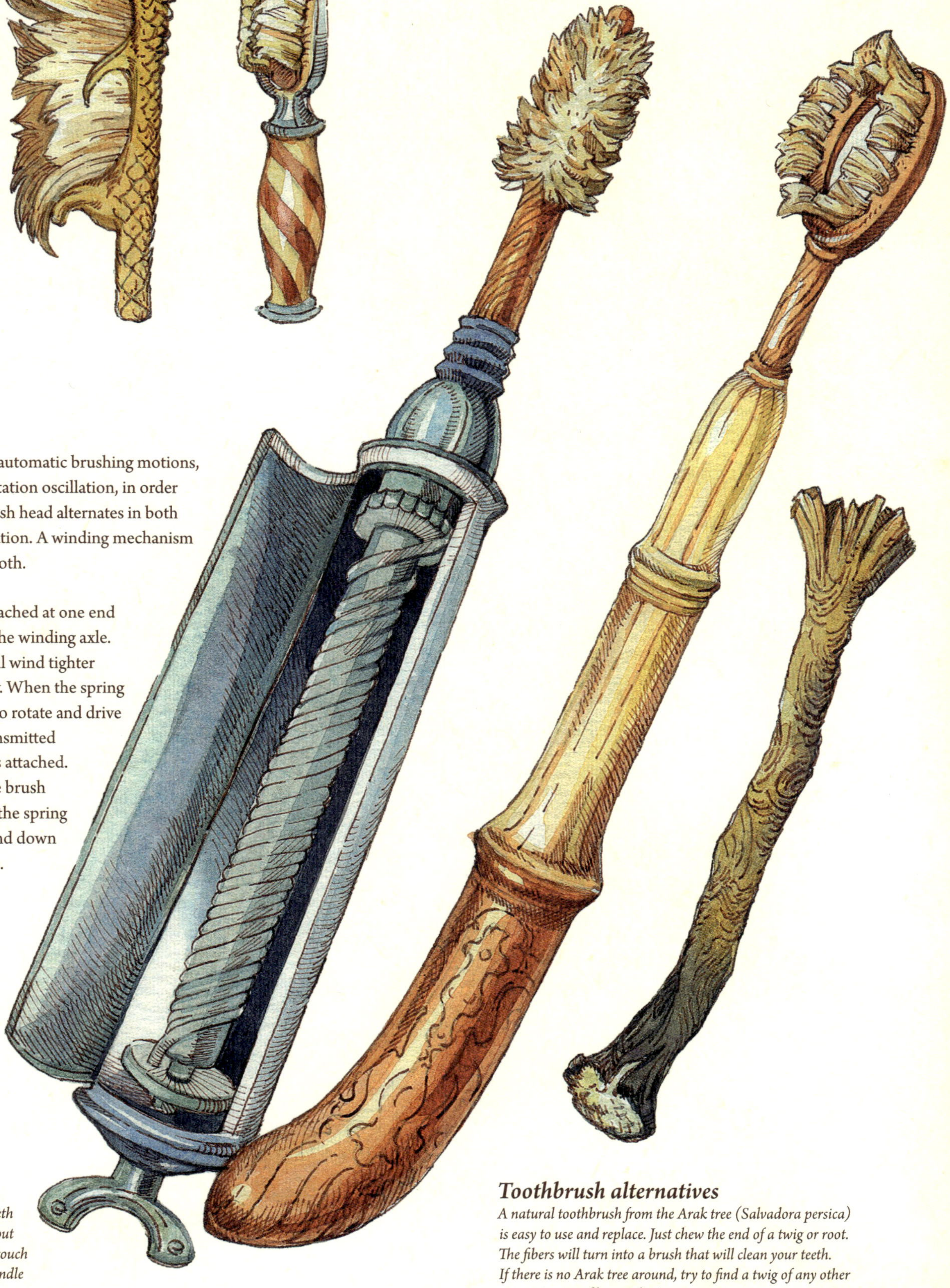

The stylish accessory

A beautiful form helps make brushing your teeth a habit you enjoy. Carve a decorative handle out of animal bone or wood. It feels so inviting to touch warm wood. You can carve patterns on the handle or embed gemstones.

Toothbrush alternatives

A natural toothbrush from the Arak tree (Salvadora persica) is easy to use and replace. Just chew the end of a twig or root. The fibers will turn into a brush that will clean your teeth. If there is no Arak tree around, try to find a twig of any other non-poisonous fibrous plant.

REFRIGERATOR

When faced with the problem of food spoilage, placing food in a box with ice seems like a logical solution. But there's an even more clever option — you can draw the heat from the food and pump it out. Invent the heat pump and you can build a refrigerator. It will keep food fresh for longer, cool your drinks and warm you with the knowledge that there's always a good meal waiting at home.

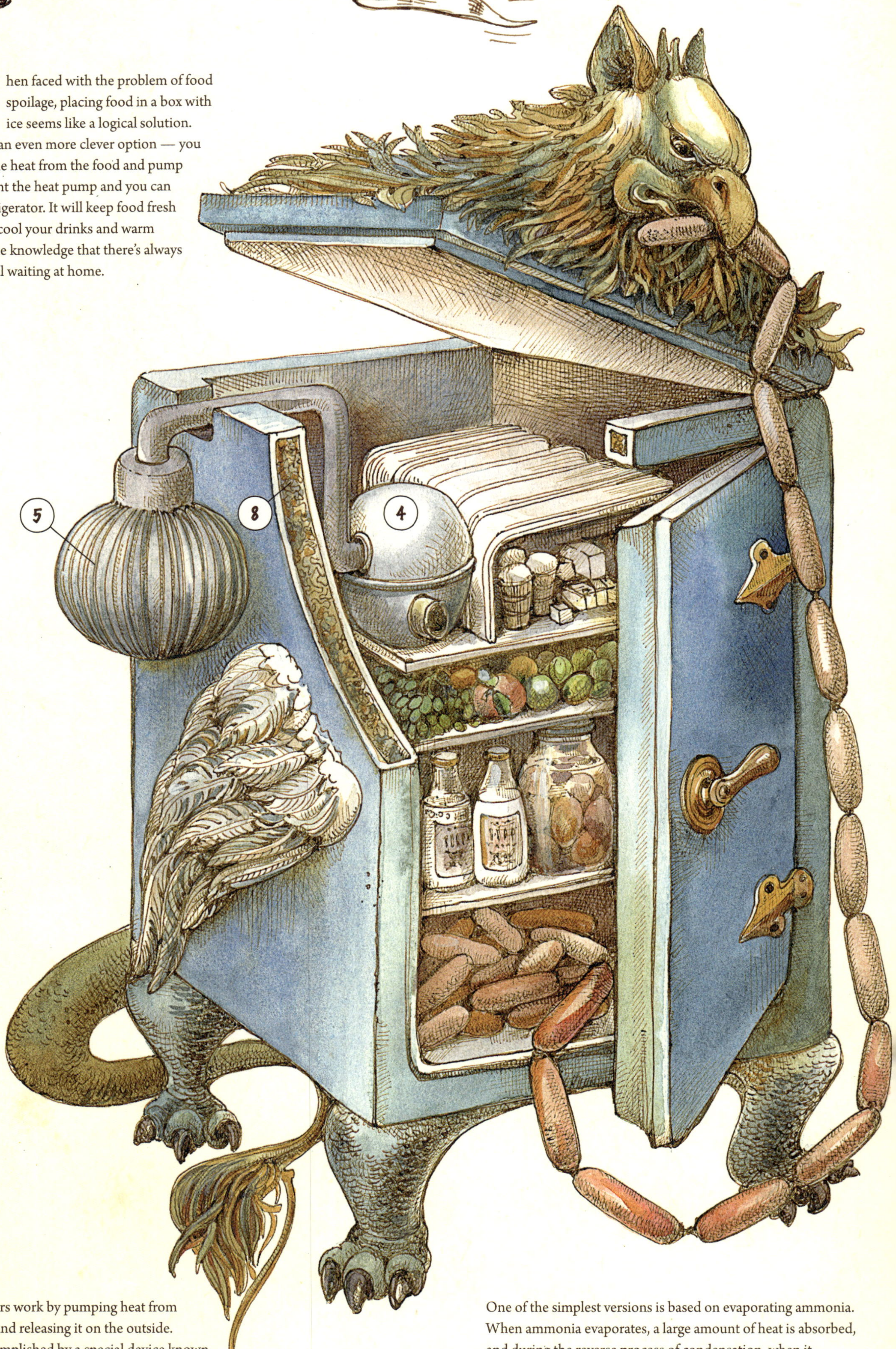

Refrigerators work by pumping heat from the inside and releasing it on the outside. This is accomplished by a special device known as a heat pump.

One of the simplest versions is based on evaporating ammonia. When ammonia evaporates, a large amount of heat is absorbed, and during the reverse process of condensation, when it is transformed back into a liquid, this heat is released.

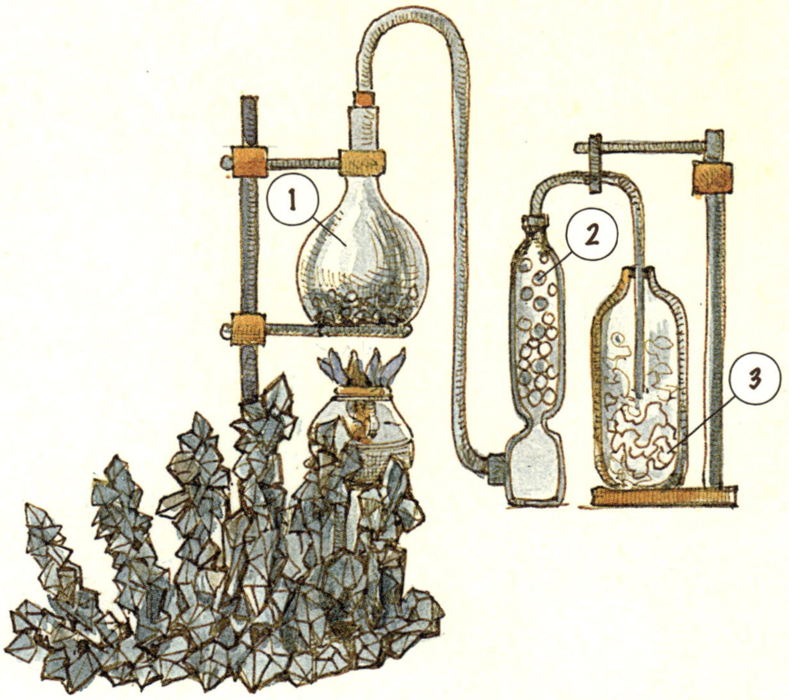

OBTAINING AMMONIA

You'll need a source of urea — urine collected from the sewage system (page 156) — and quicklime, produced by roasting limestone in a kiln. Add crushed soybeans or peeled watermelon seeds. They contain urease, a special enzyme that is a catalyst for the decomposition of urea into ammonia and carbon dioxide. Heat this mixture in a flask (1) and pass the released gas through a container with quicklime (2) to remove the water vapor and carbon dioxide.

Direct the purified ammonia into a container with distilled water (3) chilled to ice cold. (To do this, you can place this container in a larger vessel filled with ice water.) Blow the gas through the water until no more dissolves. Ammonia is highly soluble in water at low temperatures and releases a lot of heat, so be sure to add fresh ice to cool it down. Keep this solution at a low temperature or the ammonia will evaporate. Handle with care — ammonia is poisonous!

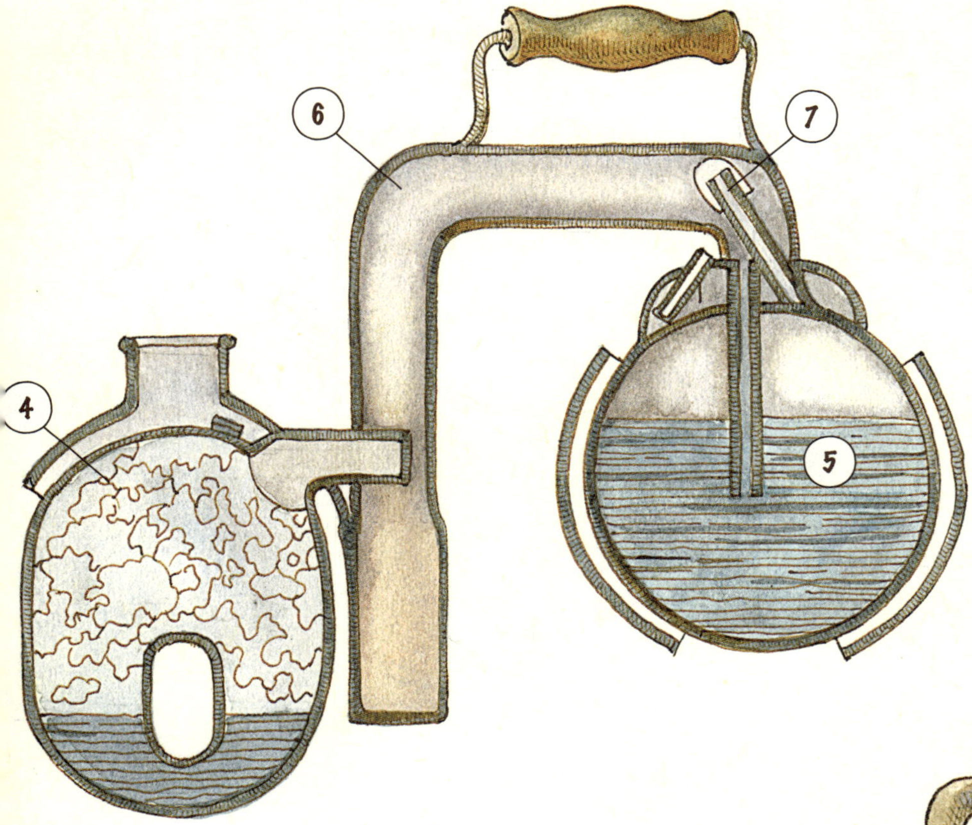

HEAT PUMP

The heat pump consists of two spherical metal containers (4, 5) connected by a strong steel pipe (6) and a siphon valve (7). Heat will be pumped between them, first in one direction during the charging step then in the other while operating. Fill one container with the previously obtained saturated solution of ammonia in water. Then seal the containers tightly.

Heat the ball containing ammonia (5) and place the second ball (4) in a container of cold water. When heated, the gas dissolved in water begins to evaporate, moves through the tube (6) into the cold ball (4) and condenses into liquid ammonia. The siphon valve (7) allows ammonia to pass through but prevents water from entering the tube. You should heat the ammonia ball over a small flame for 1.5–2 hours.

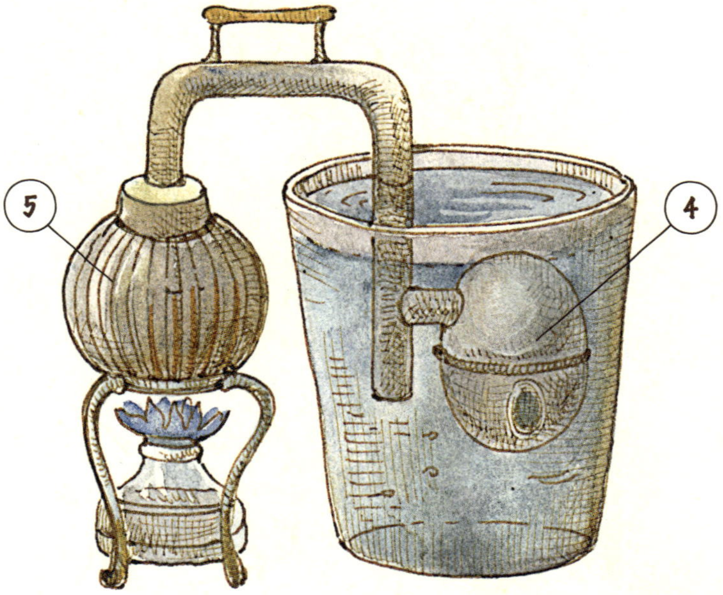

REFRIGERATION DEVICE

Cool the hot side (5) by placing it in a container of water. When it cools down to ambient temperature, the heat pump is charged and the refrigeration mechanism is ready for use. So how exactly does it work? The liquid ammonia in the cold ball (4) absorbs a lot of heat as it evaporates, effectively removing the heat from anything placed near it. The gaseous ammonia transfers this heat outside, where it condenses and moves back to the hot side (5). In turn, heat is transferred from this ball to the surrounding air.

Make a refrigerator by inserting a heat pump into an insulated box with a lid. You can use a material like sheep felt (page 120) as an insulating material. Keep in mind that the ammonia evaporation process takes up to 36 hours. During this time, the gaseous ammonia will move back into the hot side and dissolve in the water.

KITCHEN APPLIANCES

Finally, technology that does more than help you explore new lands and terrify your enemies! Now you can use it to whip up a cup of tea, a sandwich or a waffle.

Household appliances are like play sets for adults — once you've created a few prototypes, you can add new details and functions or even combine them to make multi-use tools that will simplify your life.

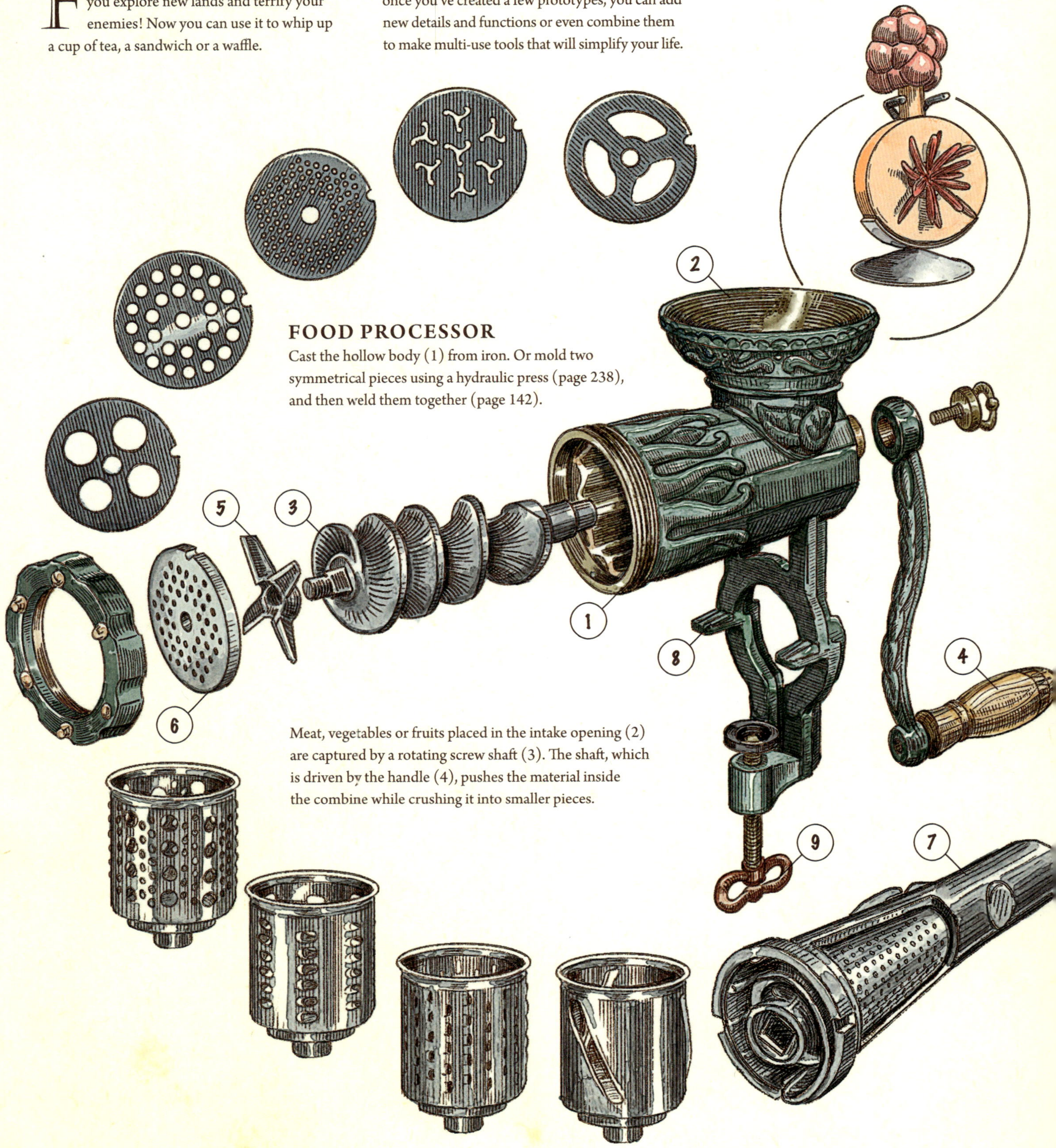

FOOD PROCESSOR

Cast the hollow body (1) from iron. Or mold two symmetrical pieces using a hydraulic press (page 238), and then weld them together (page 142).

Meat, vegetables or fruits placed in the intake opening (2) are captured by a rotating screw shaft (3). The shaft, which is driven by the handle (4), pushes the material inside the combine while crushing it into smaller pieces.

As the crushed material moves further inside the machine, it approaches the scoring knife (5), a small four-bladed piece that grinds the pieces even smaller. Then the food is forced through a grate (6), making the grind even finer. To transform the grinder into a grater, all you need to do is remove the screw shaft, cutting knife and grate from the body and fix a special metal nozzle (7).

You can adjust the thickness of the cut by changing the depth and shape of the slots in the cylinder, which can be made using a milling machine (page 144). The food processor must be securely attached to the work surface. To do this, you'll need to attach a footplate (8) to the body of the meat grinder, which will sit on the surface of the table. Attached to the footplate is a movable element with a clamp (9), which secures the food processor to the table and should be made from a durable material.

HEATING ELEMENT

To heat your food, you'll need thermal energy, which can be generated by an electric current. For your foundation, use a wire or tape made of metal alloys that has high resistance and can withstand high temperatures for a long time. An alloy of nickel and chromium (in an approximate ratio of 4:1) fortified with manganese, silicon, iron or aluminum (page 110) is the optimal choice.

Aside from having high electrical resistance, which causes the element to heat up, these alloys also form a surface layer of chromium oxide the first time they are heated, protecting the surface from further oxidation. It's best if you enclose the heating element for safety and durability.

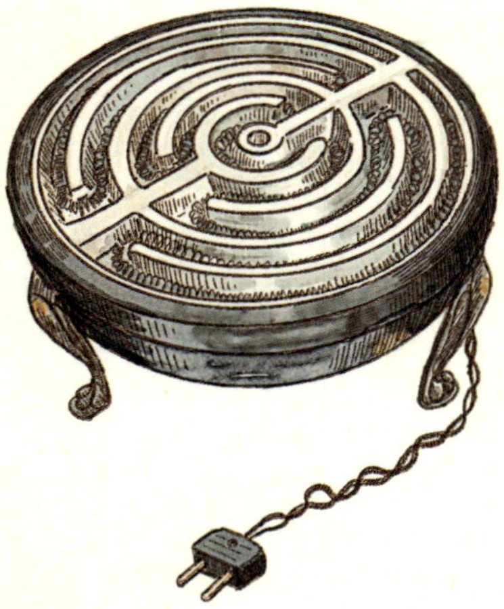

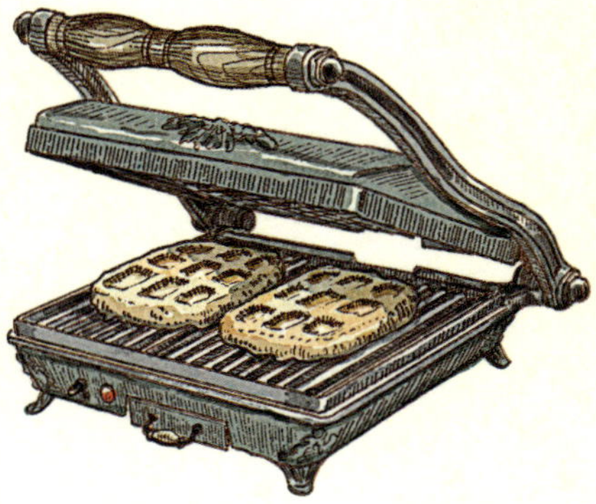

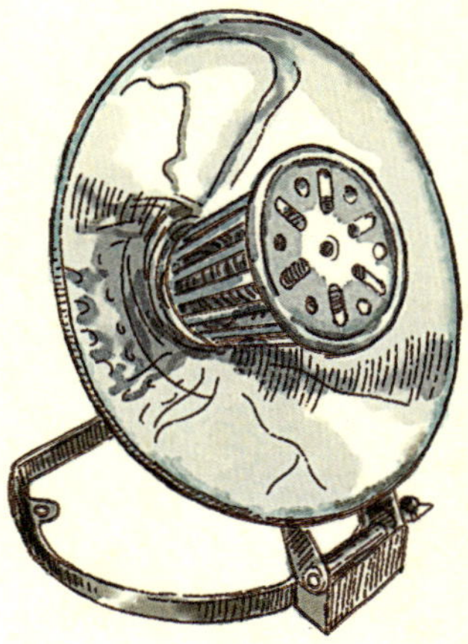

Do this by hermetically sealing and insulating the heating element. Place the coil in a brass or stainless steel tube (page 240) and fill the tube with quartz sand. Carefully insulate the ends of the tube.

Connect the heating element to an electric current using a solid brass rod as a contact pin. Now you have a unique device to convert electrical energy into heat!

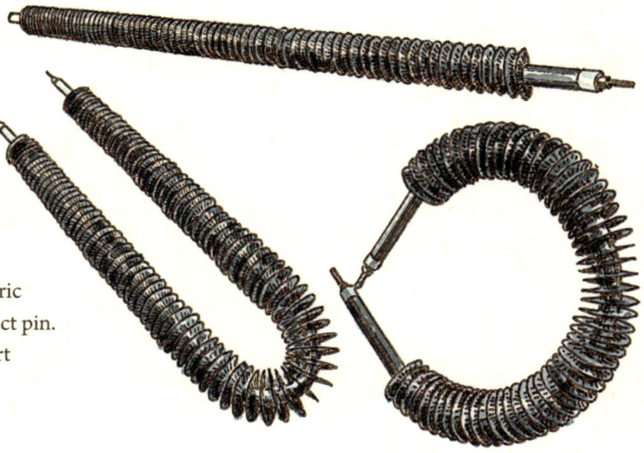

Many different devices can be made using this heating element as a base. Just make an appropriate casing and add extra details, such as a grate for a grill, a door for a toaster oven or a diffuser for a space heater. During the design process, you can come up with different devices for maintaining a constant temperature — for example, a thermal regulator that breaks the electrical circuit when the temperature gets too high.

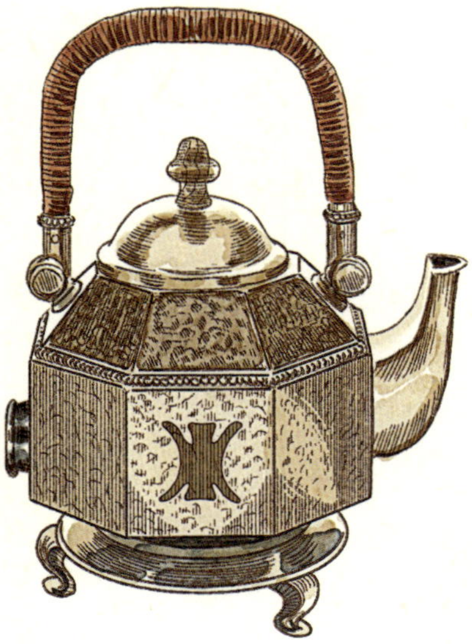

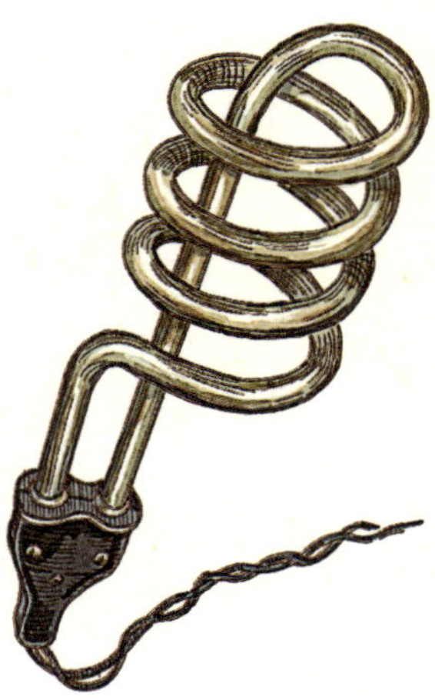

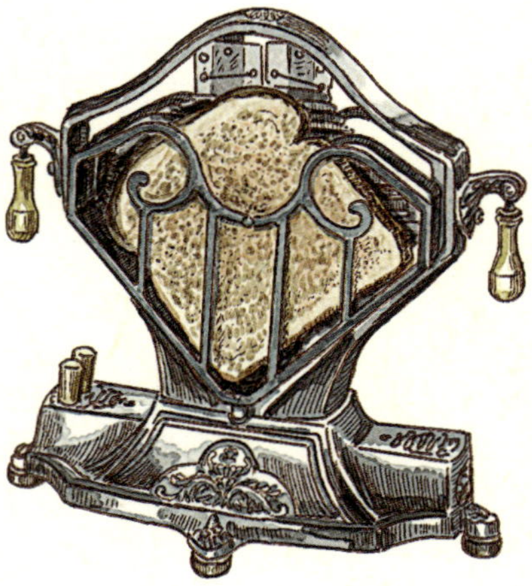

For the thermal regulator, use a bimetallic plate soldered from metals with different thermal conductivity, such as iron and copper. One end of the plate must be fixed within a holder inside the device, and the other is left free but used to close the power supply circuit.

When an electric current passes through the circuit, the plate heats up and lengthens. The copper part of the plate lengthens more than the iron part, causing the plate to bend and move away from the contact, breaking the circuit and switching the device off.

When the plate cools down, it again closes the contact, turning on the device. With this element, you can create toasters, electric stovetops or electric kettles. And with a little know-how, you can create other devices to simplify your life, such as the plumbus.

CLOTHING CARE

If you've started to feel the need to clean and press your clothing, congratulations — your civilization is advancing. But you can go even further. Lest the arduous task of hand washing and ironing clothes distract you from the more pressing work involved in rebuilding civilization, entrust the task to household appliances.

1. *Detergent drawer*
2. *Heating element*
3. *Control panel*
4. *Thermostat*
5. *Pressure sensor*
6. *Water supply hose*
7. *Spinning laundry drum*
8. *Drain hose*

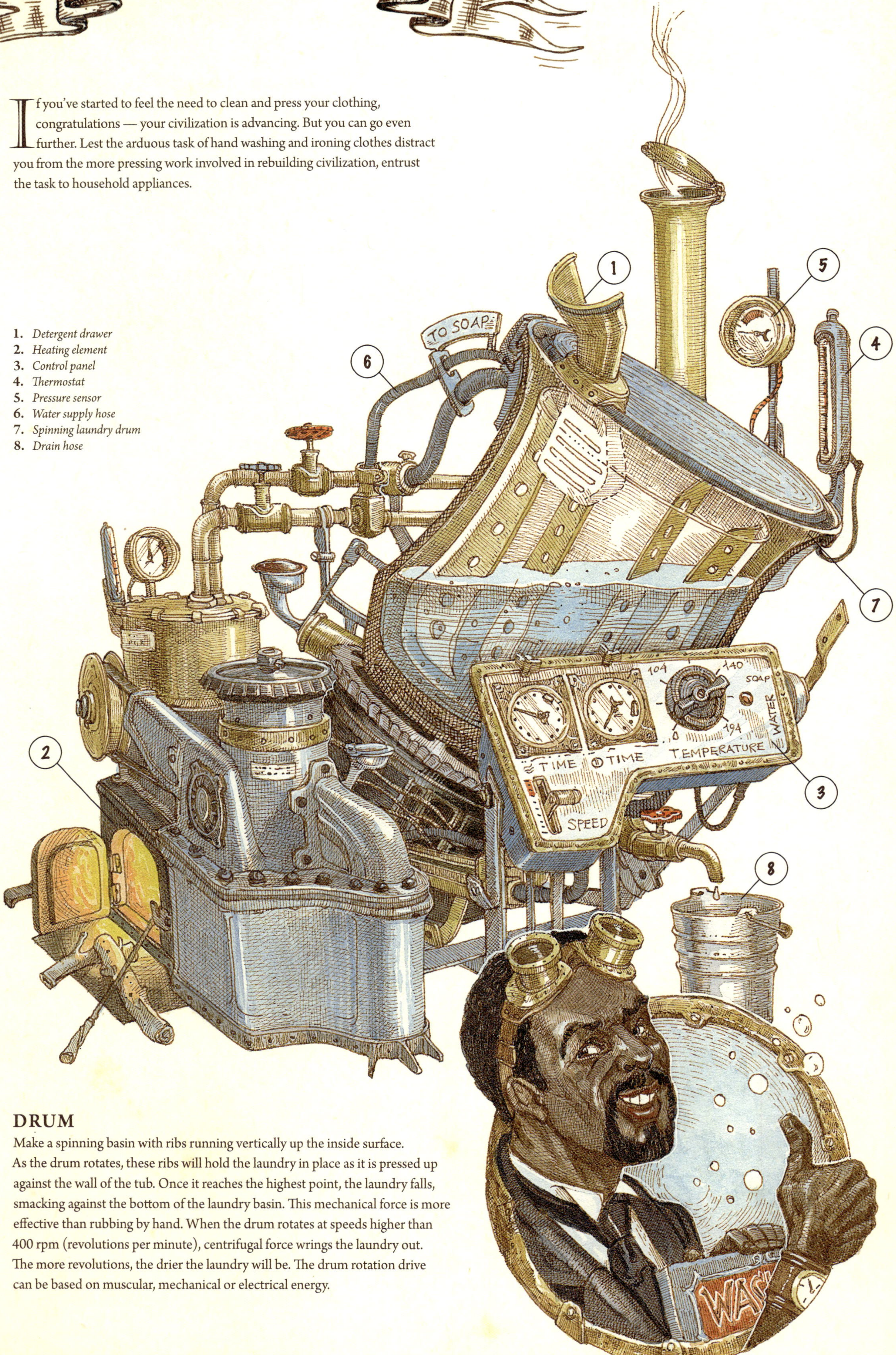

DRUM

Make a spinning basin with ribs running vertically up the inside surface. As the drum rotates, these ribs will hold the laundry in place as it is pressed up against the wall of the tub. Once it reaches the highest point, the laundry falls, smacking against the bottom of the laundry basin. This mechanical force is more effective than rubbing by hand. When the drum rotates at speeds higher than 400 rpm (revolutions per minute), centrifugal force wrings the laundry out. The more revolutions, the drier the laundry will be. The drum rotation drive can be based on muscular, mechanical or electrical energy.

STEAM GENERATOR

Water breaks the hydrogen bonds that hold together the cellulose chains in cotton or linen. Once the material dries, the bonds reform in other places. This is how wrinkles appear. A little steam will set everything right. Use a hose (2) to connect a steam generator (1) to your iron. Once the water starts boiling, the pressure will push the steam into the iron cavity.

Steam is the most important element of the iron. When you press the lever (3) located on the handle, the valve opens and a powerful jet of high-pressure steam runs from the hose into the cavity of the iron and escapes through holes in the soleplate (4). The heavier the iron, the more effective it will be. Cast iron is an ideal choice.

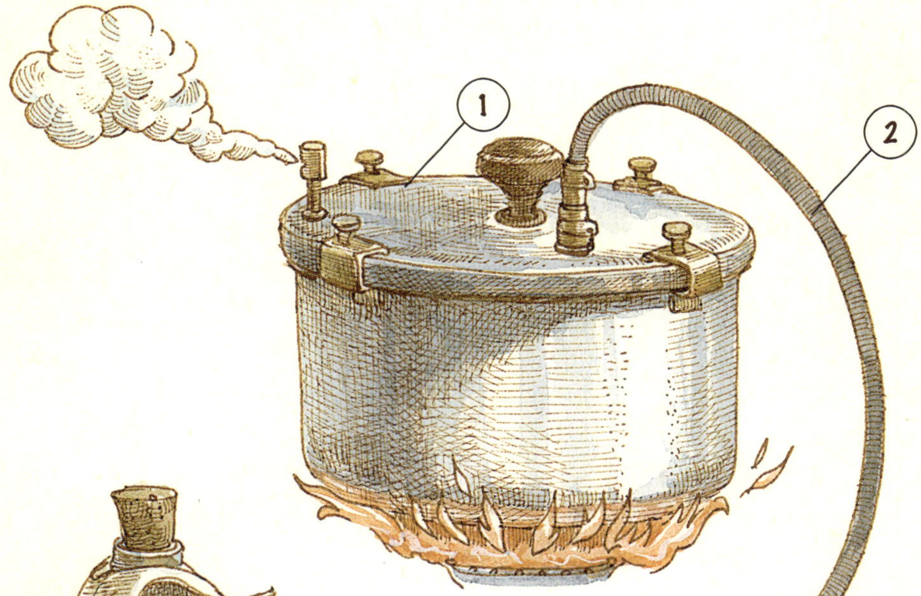

HEATING ELEMENT

The heating element (5) will heat the soleplate (4). Pour alcohol into the reservoir and ignite (6). As it burns, it will heat the coil (7) in the body, thereby gradually raising the temperature of the soleplate. The valve (8) located on the supply hose allows you to regulate the rate of flow of the alcohol to increase or decrease the temperature.

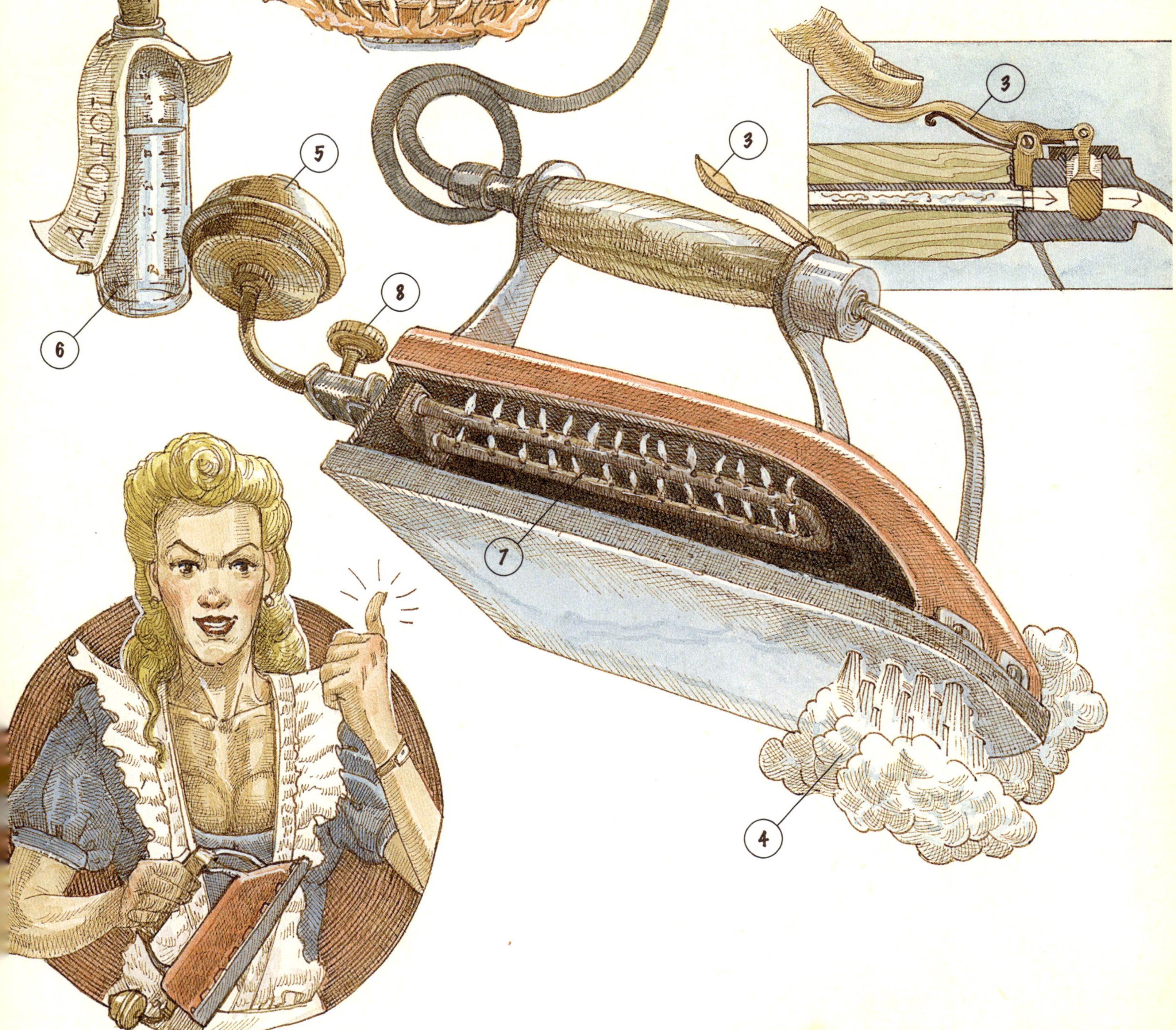

JEANS & ZIPPER

If you're now puzzling over the problem of how to provide work clothes for an entire community, there is a good solution — jeans. They can be produced quickly and can last for decades. Each stage has a secret step that improves durability.

Denim is made from cotton (page 120). Twist several threads together to increase the tensile strength. It's easier to dye individual yarns rather than the dense finished product. Dye the yarn using indigo.

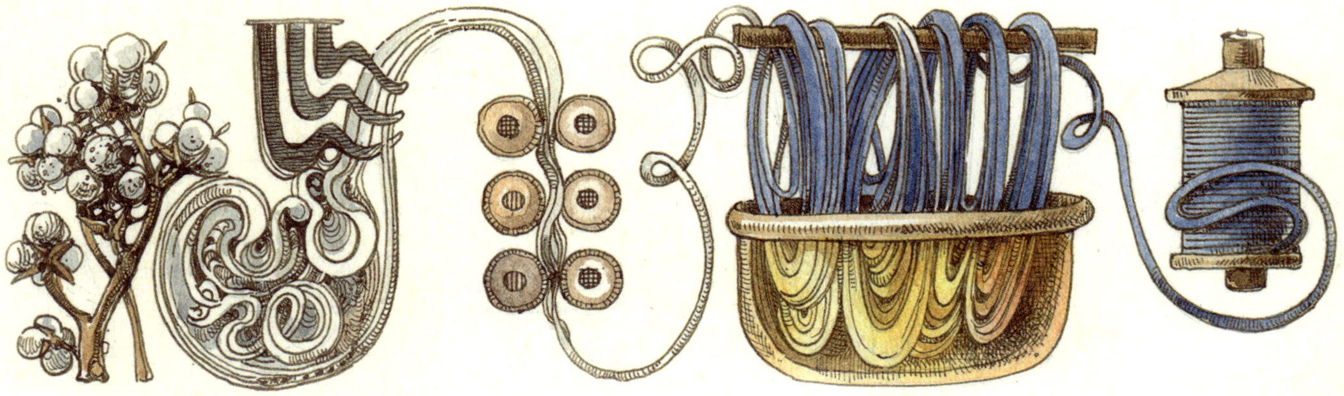

DYE

Indigo can be obtained from the leaves of *indigofera* (legume family), or from dyer's woad (crucifers family). Soak the leaves in water and let them ferment for a couple of weeks. Mix lye (page 24) into the resulting concoction, press it, dehydrate it and grind it into a powder. Dissolve it in a mix of water and sulfuric acid.

Don't be alarmed: The solution will be yellow, but the filaments will turn blue when exposed to oxygen. Dip the threads into the solution then wring them out. Repeat the cycle 7–10 times. Afterwards, treat the threads with cornstarch to make the fabric stiffer.

FABRIC

A twill weave will imbue your fabric with strength and beauty. Use 3 blue threads (longitudinal) and 1 white (transverse). This weave produces a denser material that will protect the fabric from damage and dirt.

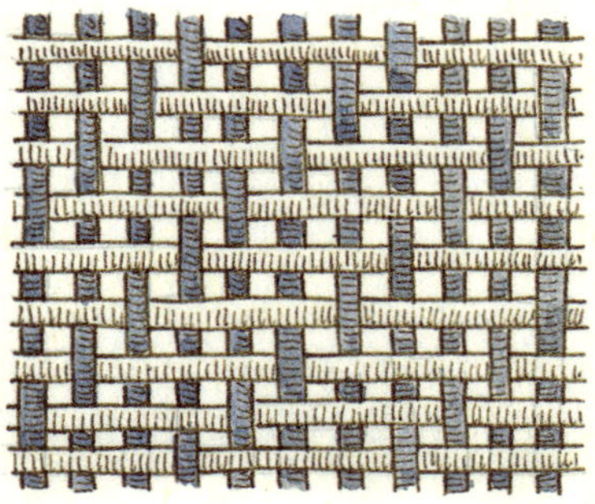

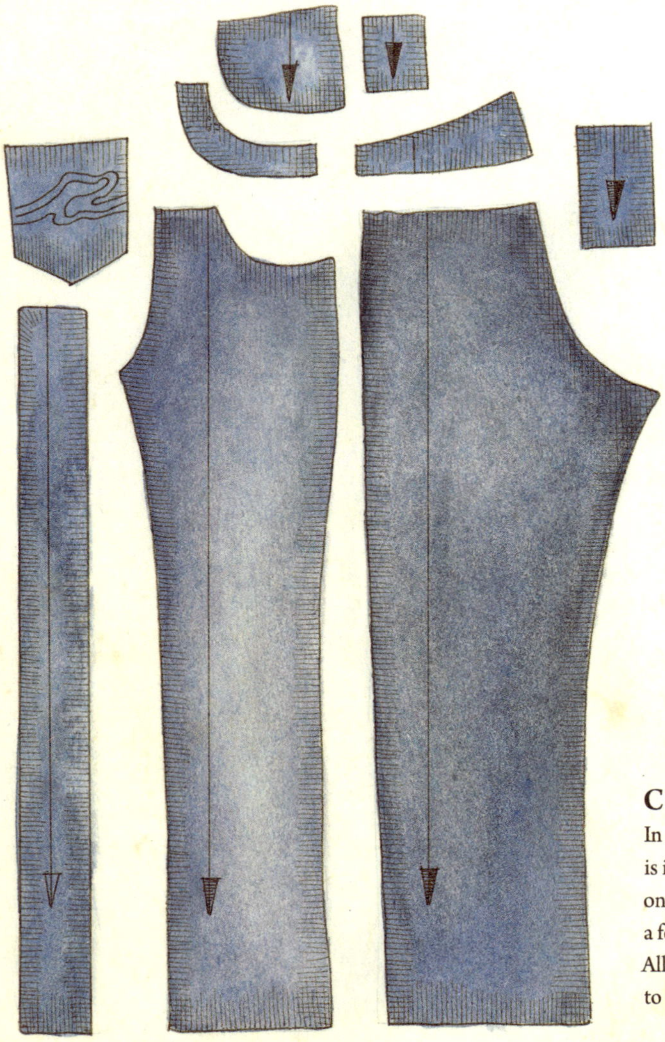

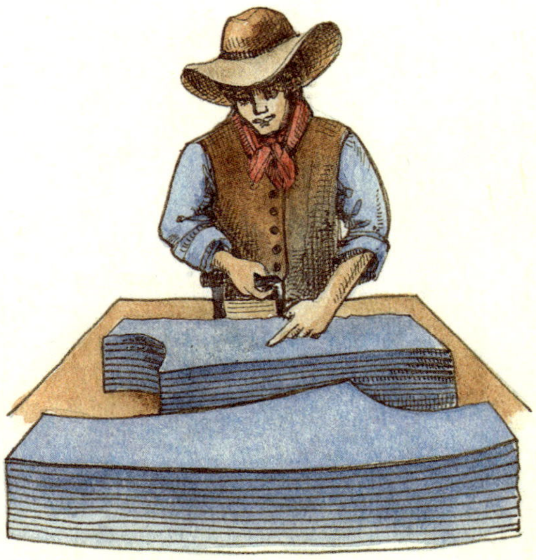

CUTTING AND SEWING

In one fell swoop, you can make pants for your entire workforce. The secret is in the cutting. Stack 100 layers of fabric together and place the paper patterns on top. A jigsaw cutter will help you slice through all the layers at once. In just a few strokes, you'll have the pieces for 100 pairs of jeans. A great time saver! All that's left is to sew the pieces together. Double up the stitches on the seams to make the pants sturdier. This protects the fabric from wear and tear.

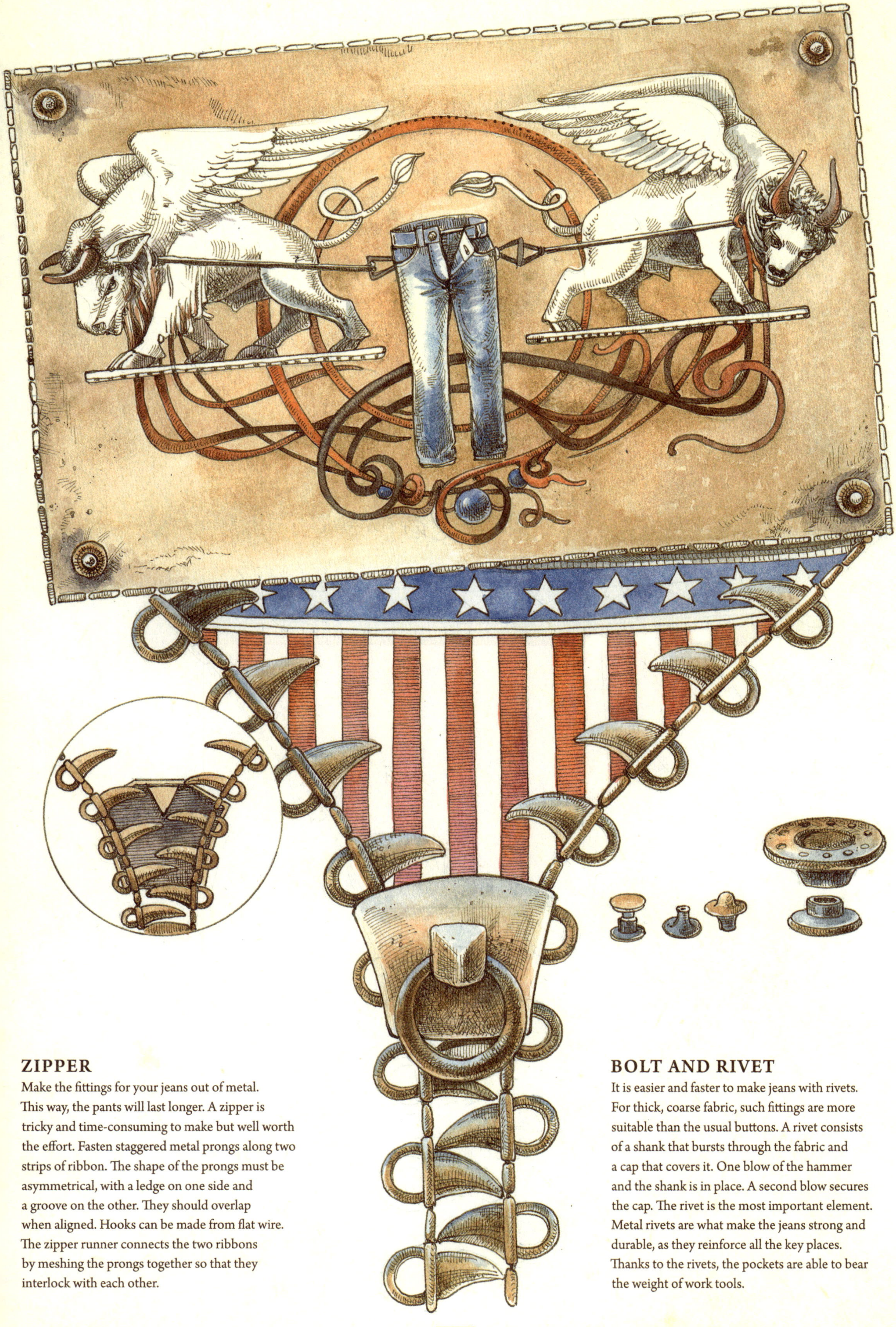

ZIPPER

Make the fittings for your jeans out of metal. This way, the pants will last longer. A zipper is tricky and time-consuming to make but well worth the effort. Fasten staggered metal prongs along two strips of ribbon. The shape of the prongs must be asymmetrical, with a ledge on one side and a groove on the other. They should overlap when aligned. Hooks can be made from flat wire. The zipper runner connects the two ribbons by meshing the prongs together so that they interlock with each other.

BOLT AND RIVET

It is easier and faster to make jeans with rivets. For thick, coarse fabric, such fittings are more suitable than the usual buttons. A rivet consists of a shank that bursts through the fabric and a cap that covers it. One blow of the hammer and the shank is in place. A second blow secures the cap. The rivet is the most important element. Metal rivets are what make the jeans strong and durable, as they reinforce all the key places. Thanks to the rivets, the pockets are able to bear the weight of work tools.

PERFUME

The olfactory system in the brain is cross-connected with areas associated with memories and emotions. The soothing scent of lavender will help you fall asleep, while just a whiff of fresh coffee in the morning can raise the dead.

Use aromas as your allies, because it's a rare person who doesn't have a sense of smell. And if you had it and recently lost it, you should probably see a doctor.

Enfleurage

Enfleurage is a process that uses fats to capture the fragrant compounds exuded by plants. Raw materials (for example, flower petals) are placed on a glass frame with clarified beef fat or on a cloth soaked in olive oil. As soon as the petals wilt, replace them with new ones. After about a month, the fat will be saturated with the fragrance. Now, you must dissolve it in alcohol and isolate the essential oil. This process requires that the container be shaken for a long period of time, but you can place the containers on vibrating platforms connected to a motor to make the work easier.

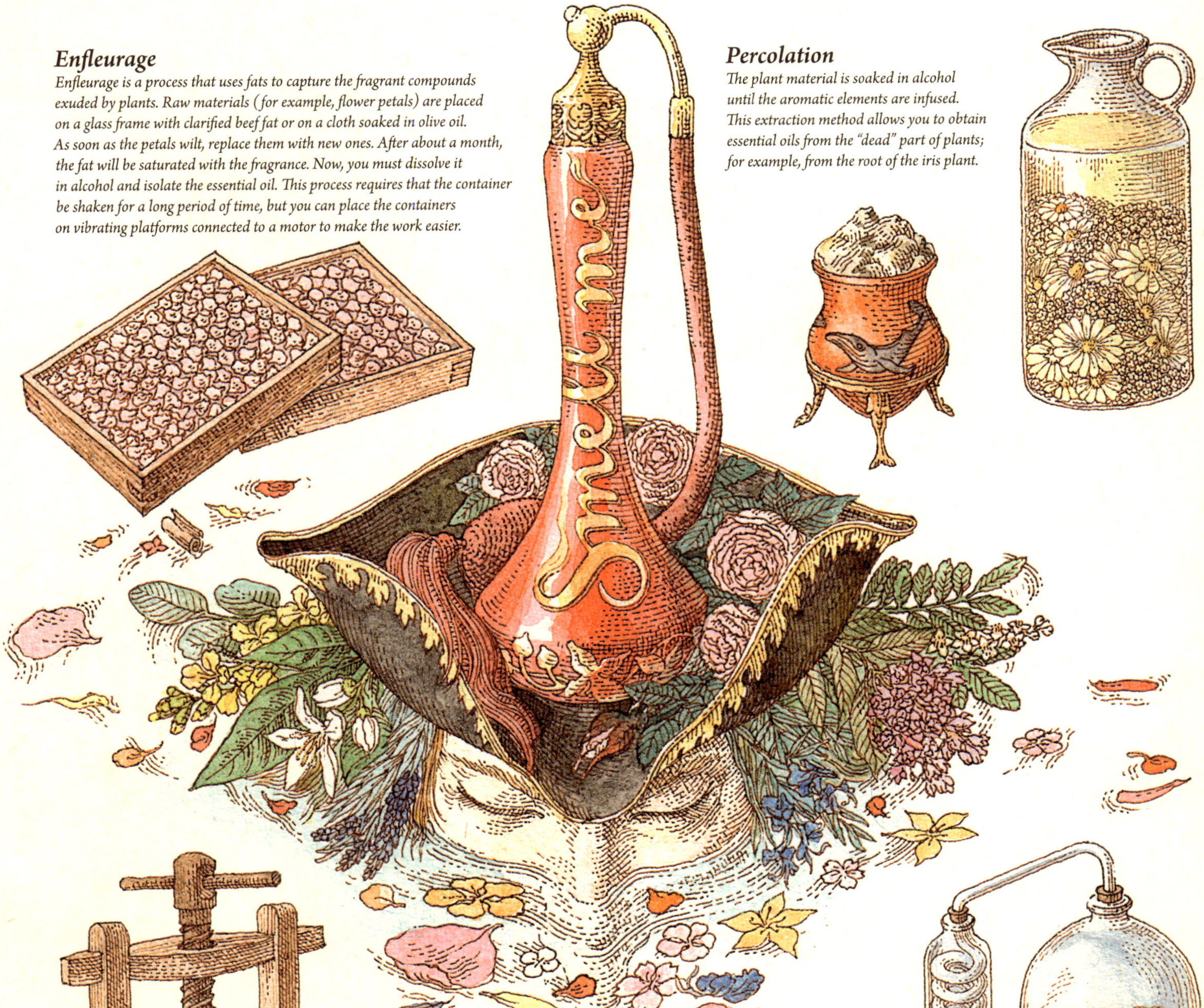

Percolation

The plant material is soaked in alcohol until the aromatic elements are infused. This extraction method allows you to obtain essential oils from the "dead" part of plants; for example, from the root of the iris plant.

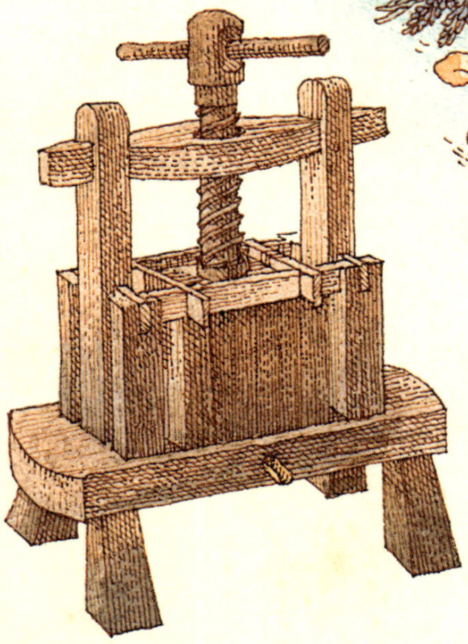

To make the aromas more saturated and long-lasting, you need ambergris — a gray wax-like substance formed in the stomach of sperm whales. After decades of sitting in the whale's stomach as it wanders the sea, the ambergris acquires a sweet, musky smell that is almost imperceptible in the final perfume.

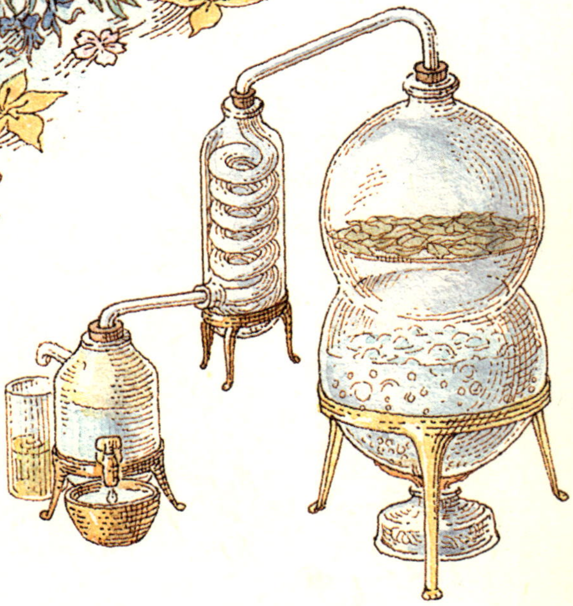

Pressing

Cold pressing is great for extracting oil from peels. Take the peel of an orange, lime or grapefruit, add a little water and place it under the press. You can also use the crushed fruit along with the pulp. Let the resulting liquid settle so that the oil rises to the surface. Skim this oil from the top and store it in a sealed glass flask.

Distillation

Distillation uses water vapor to obtain certain essential oils (for example, rose, geranium, mint or coriander oils). The exact same process is used to make moonshine (page 117). The raw material is immersed in nearly boiling water or heated with steam. Essential oil molecules mix with the steam and rise through the tube into the cooling tank. There, they once again condense into a liquid, and the water and oil separate due to their different boiling points.

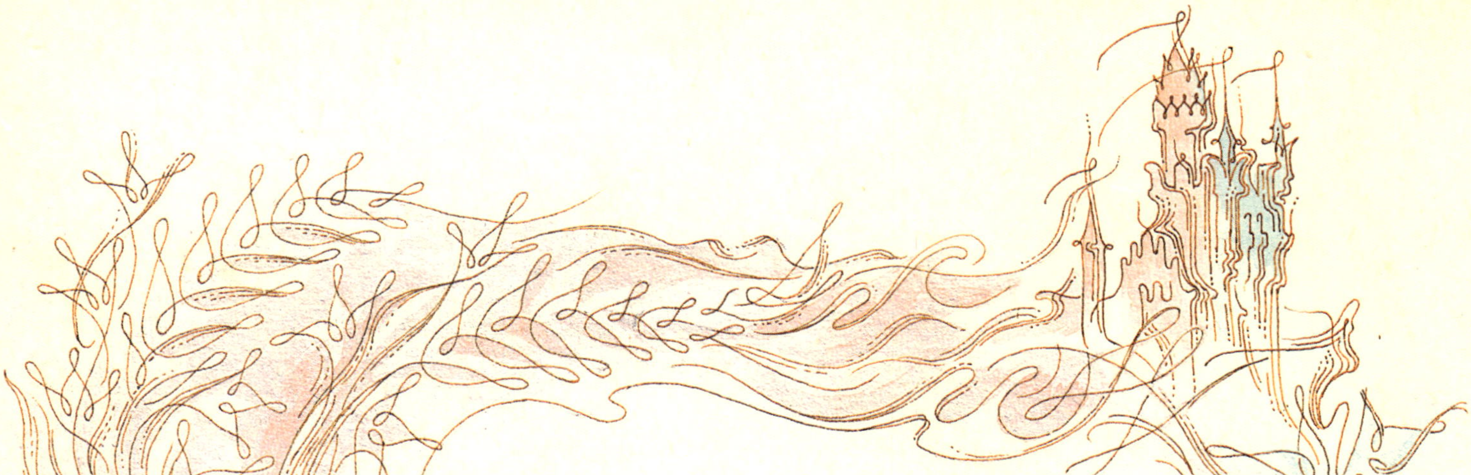

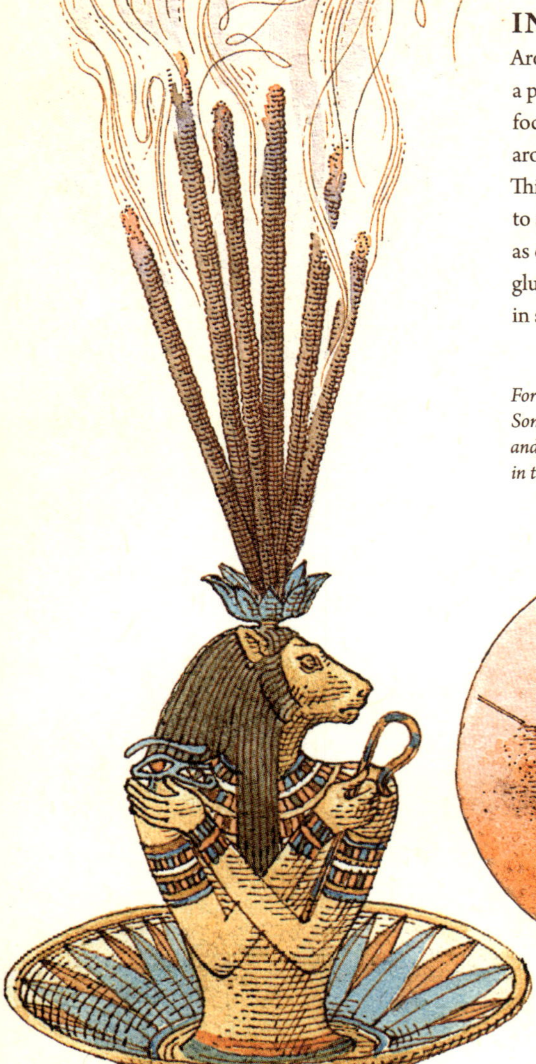

INCENSE

Aromas can be used not just on the body but in the home. Make incense — a perfume for your room. Incense creates an atmosphere and can help you focus on having a productive day or fall asleep more quickly. Grind solid aromatic compounds into a fine powder and mix with a combustible base. This will bind the aromatic ingredients together and allow the incense to smolder evenly. Ground sandalwood makes an excellent base, as well as cedar, pine and juniper. As a binding element, use a natural water-soluble glue such as gum arabic (acacia resin). Add 10% of the total weight in saltpeter (page 124).

For high-quality incense, use at least one aromatic resin in every recipe. Some good candidates are frankincense (the resin of trees in the genus Boswellia) and myrrh (the resin of trees in the genus Commiphora). Coat thin sticks in the mixture or form the paste into the shape of a cone, let it dry and ignite it!

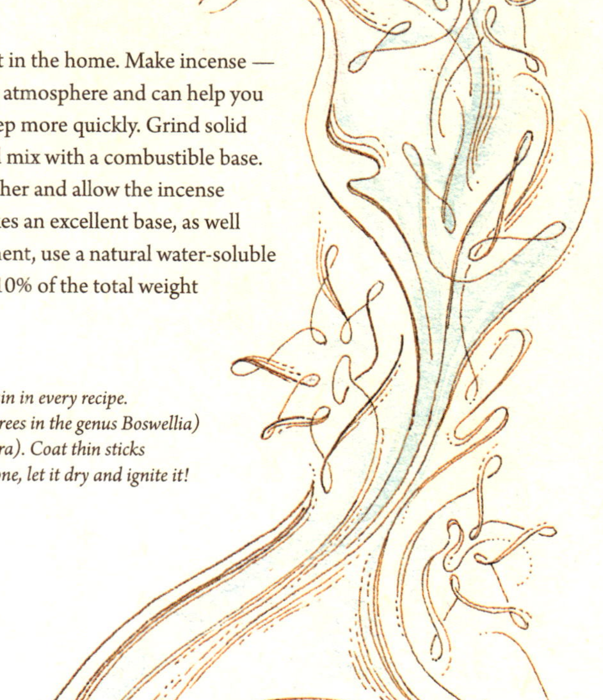

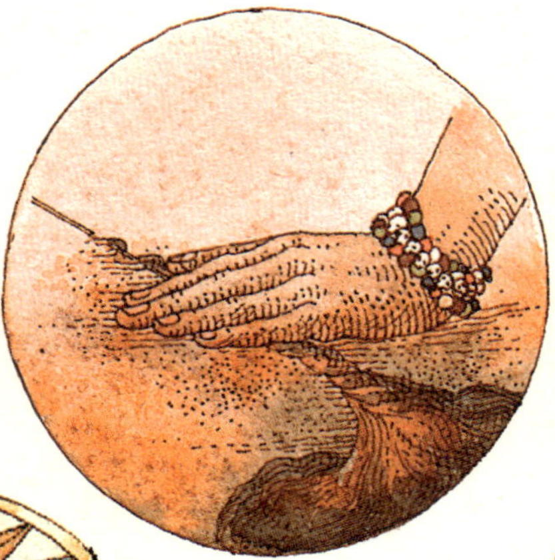

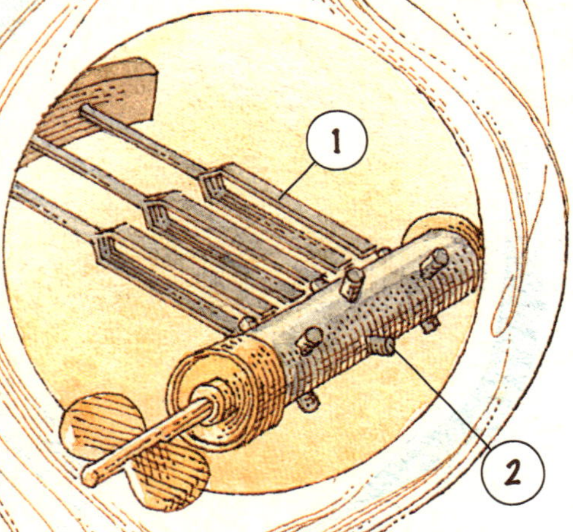

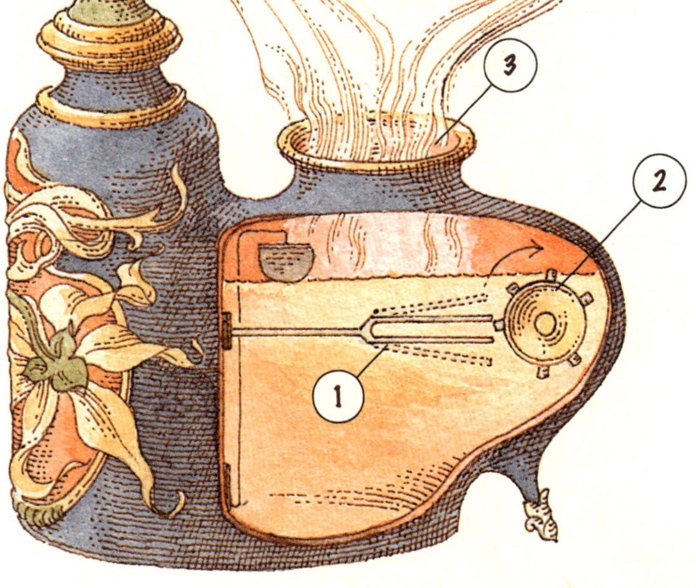

ULTRASONIC MECHANICAL HUMIDIFIER

You can fill your home with fragrance with an ultrasonic mechanical humidifier. The device will spray tiny particles of water and oil around the room. Here's how it works: Water is fed into a chamber with an ultrasonic emitter that turns it into a fine mist that is then distributed around the room. The emitter can be a curved metal plate (1) that vibrates at a very high frequency upon impact, propelling microscopic water droplets into the air. The pins (2) attached to the shaft hit the plate, setting it in motion. The intake pipe (3) draws in air. Inside the device, this air is saturated with the tiny droplets of water and oil then pumped back into the room (4). All you need is some sort of energy source — for example, a battery (page 192) connected to a motor.

The aromas of the surrounding environment have a physiological effect on people. They can increase or decrease the heartbeat, calm or excite, change moods and even increase cognitive abilities. Orange is a soothing scent, good for waiting rooms in dentist offices. And mint helps you concentrate and make fewer mistakes when completing a task.

LOCK & KEY

Inventors are generally searching for the best way to make their creations easily accessible and to optimize the production process. The simpler the structure and the fewer unnecessary details, the cheaper it will be to replicate. But with locks, the situation is somewhat different. The more clever and complicated the mechanism and the more "unnecessary" details it employs, the harder it will be for criminals to crack it.

PIN TUMBLER LOCK

Mount the lock case into the door. The secret of the locking mechanism is in the pairs of metallic pins (1, 2). The pins are spring-loaded (3). When the proper key is stuck into the lock, the teeth (4) of the key push the lower row of pins up so that the gap between the two rows of pins comes into perfect alignment, allowing the plug (5) to rotate. If the teeth of the key don't align perfectly, the pins will block the plug from turning.

You can also make a lock that seizes up when someone tries to break or pick it. For example, use glass rods to hold the springs of the pin mechanism in a compressed state. Any impact or attempt to drill or cut through the lock will shatter the glass rods, releasing the pins and permanently blocking the keyhole.

PADLOCK

A pin lock with a hinged shackle (6). When the key aligns with the pins (7), the posts lower and release the cylinder (8), which is holding the spring (9) under tension. This opens the latch, releasing the shackle (6).

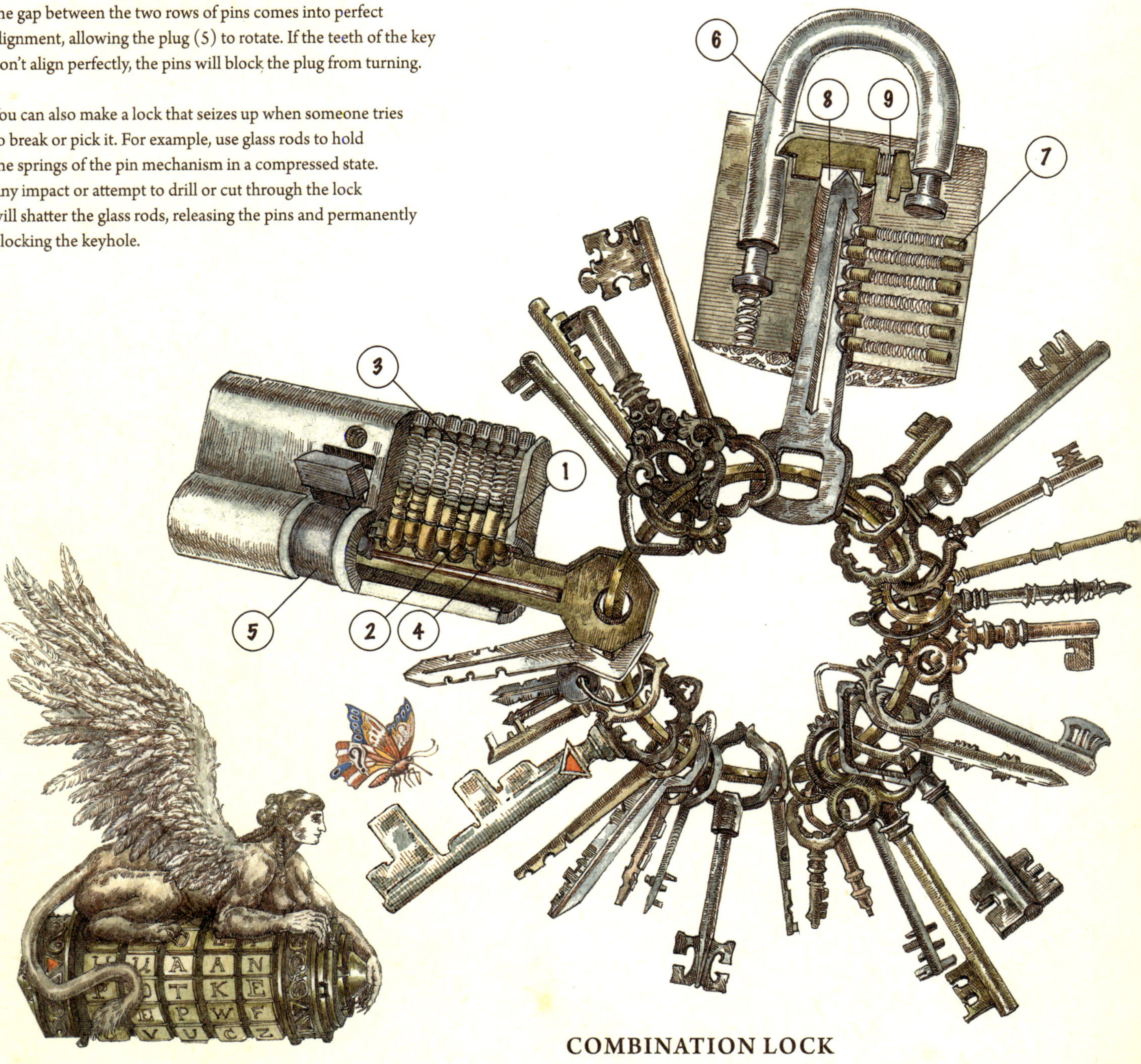

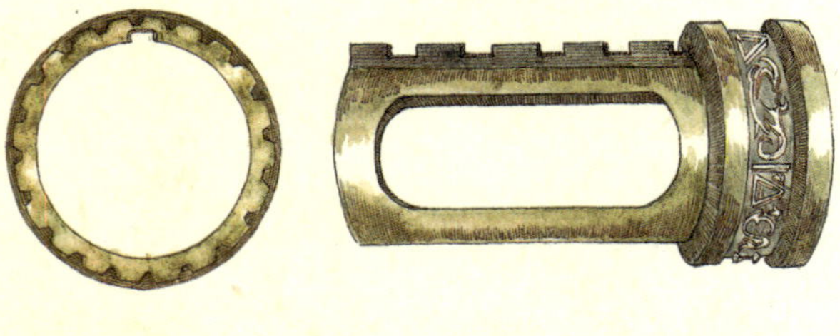

COMBINATION LOCK

You can even make locks that don't require keys at all. Instead, they use a series of rotating metal discs inscribed with symbols on the outside and notches on the inside. The cylinder with the keyhole contains spikes that hook into the rotating discs. When the notches in the discs align with the teeth on the pin, the lock can be opened. The more discs there are, the more secure the lock will be.

SAFE LOCK

The correct code is entered using a rotary dial knob with notches and numerical markings (1) around the outside. Mounted on a pin (2) inside the lock case is a piece known as the "lever" — a spring-loaded hook arm connected on one side to the bolt. Behind that are several stacked discs (4) that share a single axis of rotation (5). Each disc has a notch (6) and is constructed in such a way that when the correct three-number sequence is input, the notches align, allowing the hook of the lever (3) to slide into the groove made by all three notches. As you rotate the dial again, the lever catches on the groove, pulling the bolt to one side and unlocking the door. To open the safe, turn the dial clockwise to the first number to slide the notch on the first disc (I) into place.

Now spin the dial counterclockwise once all the way around past zero to reset, and then to the second number in the sequence (II), which then allows you to move the lever and slide the bolt back. Combine several types of locks (padlock, tumbler, combination). The more complex the combination, the more secure your possessions will be.

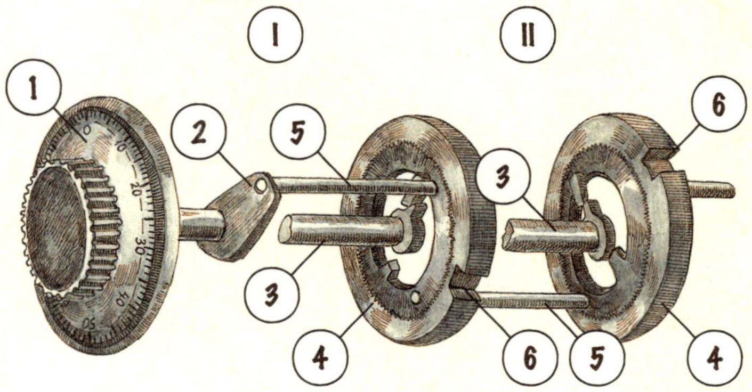

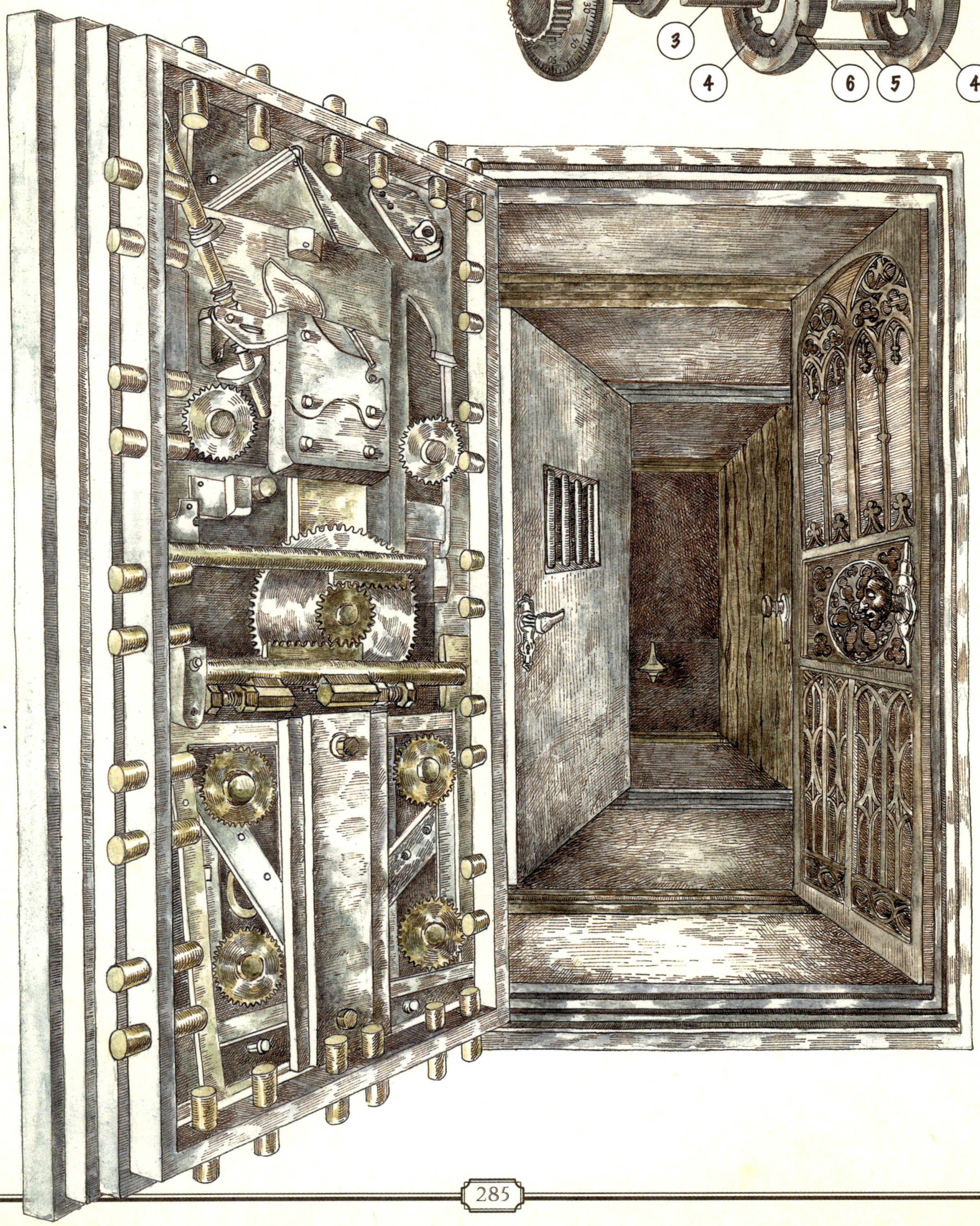

PEN & PENCIL

What is man's first impulse after inventing the spear and hunting his first mammoth? To commemorate the victory by carefully sketching a depiction of the battle on the walls of their cave. As civilization develops, writing utensils quickly follow suit.

Making a pen or pencil is relatively easy, and they'll serve you well until the first electronic keyboards hit the market. And in some more bureaucratically inclined societies, pens serve a more ritualistic purpose.

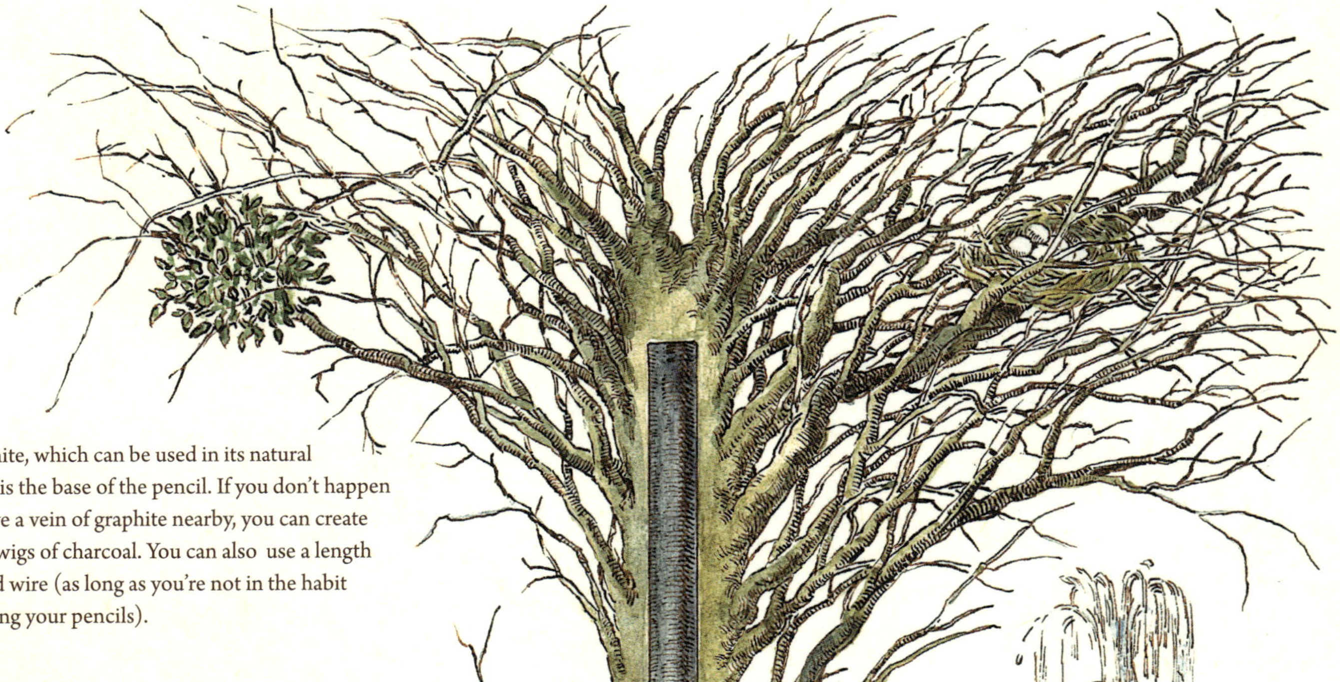

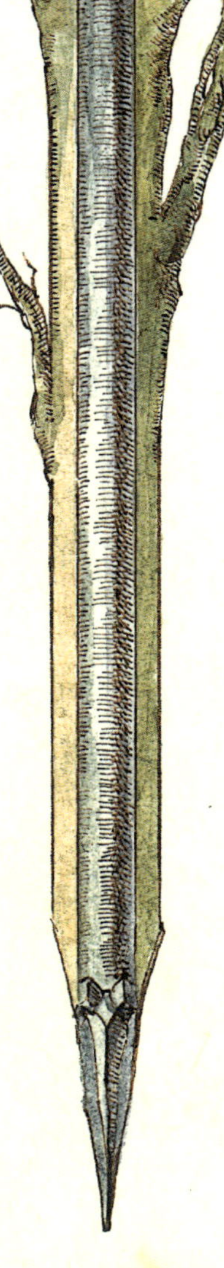

Graphite, which can be used in its natural form, is the base of the pencil. If you don't happen to have a vein of graphite nearby, you can create thin twigs of charcoal. You can also use a length of lead wire (as long as you're not in the habit of biting your pencils).

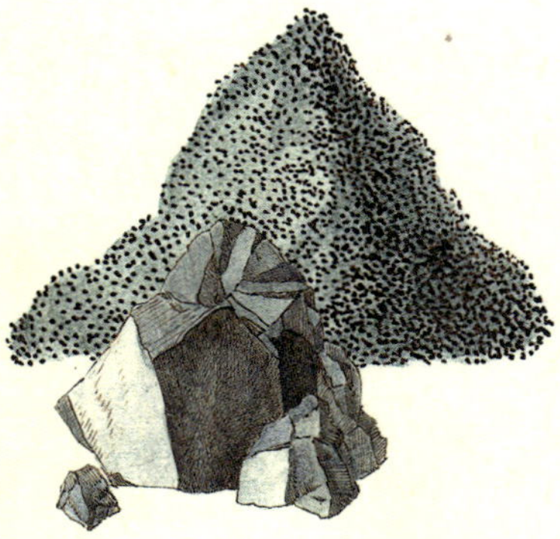

The amount of clay you add determines the degree of hardness of the pencil lead. Want to paint the world in color? Use white clay and dye for the lead.

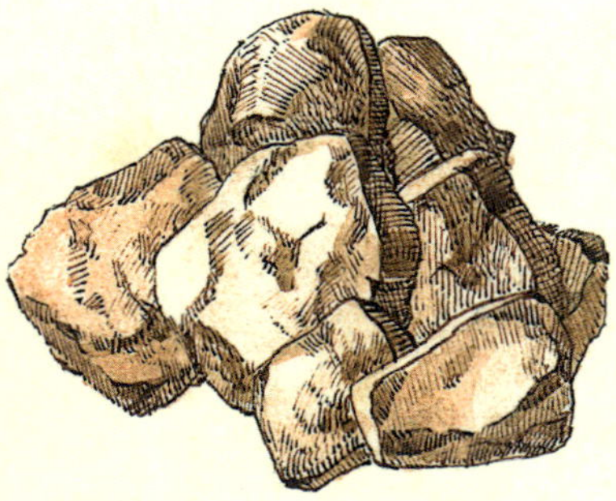

Combine your powdered graphite, clay and water. Mix until it reaches a homogeneous consistency. Add some sort of binder, for example, dextrin — carbohydrates produced by the hydrolysis of starch (page 54).

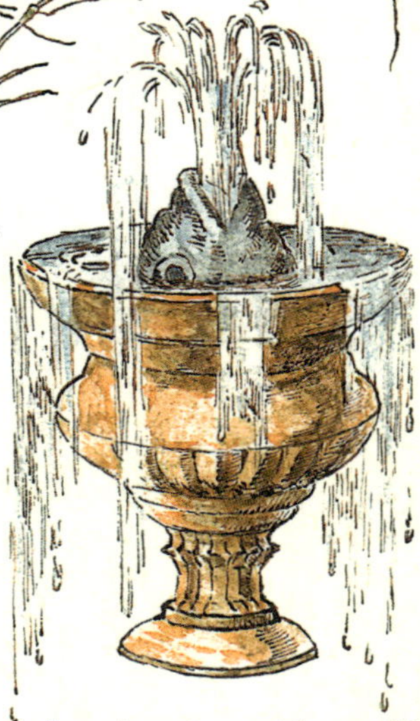

Put the resulting paste through a mincer with a small hole diameter. Now you must dry the paste and fire it in a kiln. In this step, the starch is burned out, forming pores in the lead. To make the pencil glide more smoothly, dip soft leads in hot grease and hard ones in wax.

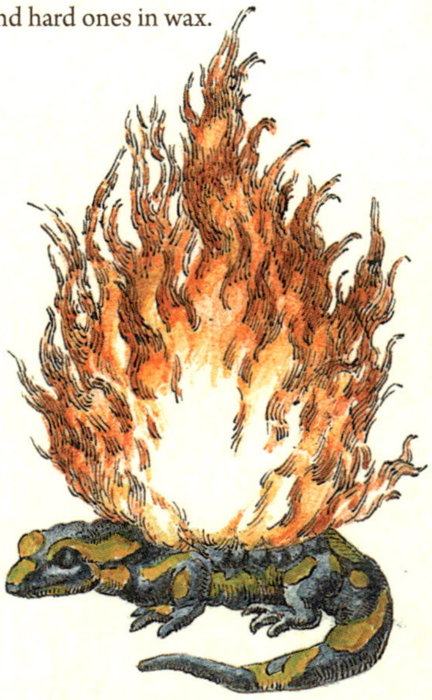

PEN

Make a paper template of your desired nib shape (experiment with different types and sizes to get the preferred line thickness) and transfer it onto a sheet of iron. Cut out the pattern, heat, and then shape around the body of the nib. Grind the tip down with emery until you're left with the desired shape. Cut a slot for the ink to flow through. The ink saturation depends on the length and width of this slot. By the way, you can solder a slotted metallic ball to the pen tip to ensure a smooth stroke.

INK

If you live by the sea, slice open a cuttlefish for an instant inkpot. If you don't have molluscs on hand, you can mix soot and vegetable oil in a 1:1.5 ratio.

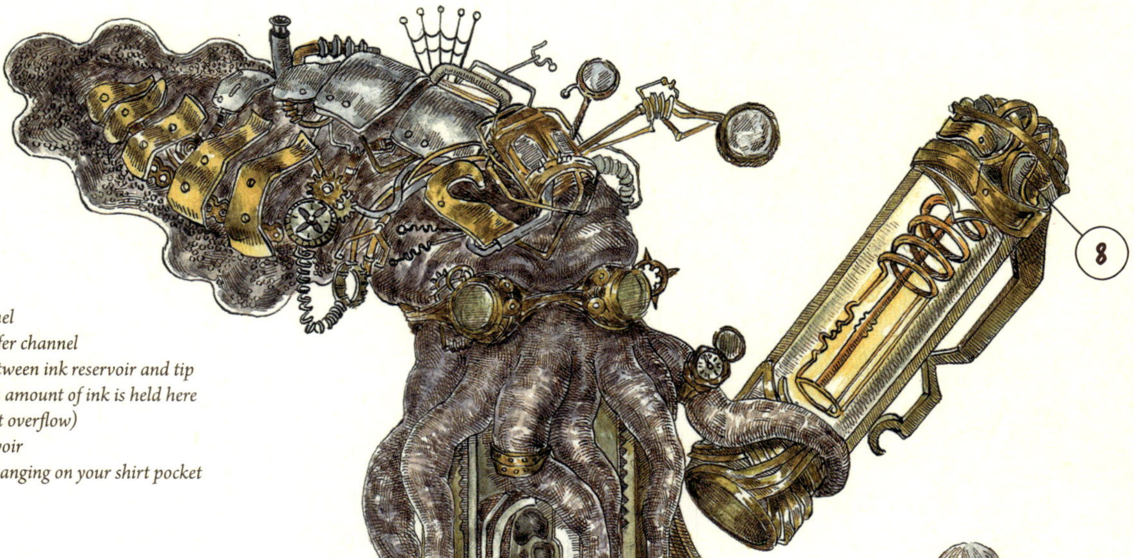

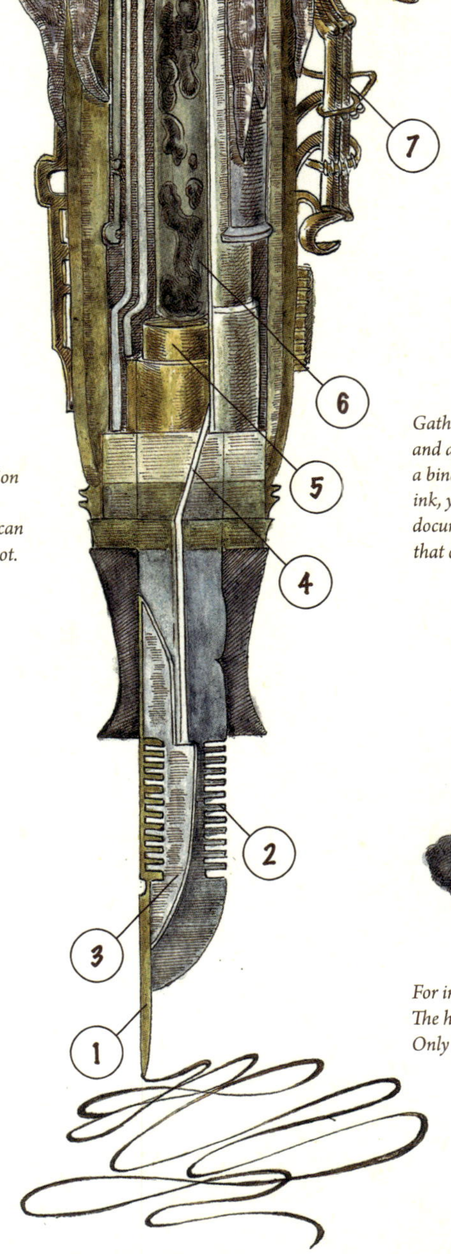

1. *Nib*
2. *Feed*
3. *Air channel*
4. *Ink transfer channel*
5. *Buffer between ink reservoir and tip (a certain amount of ink is held here to prevent overflow)*
6. *Ink reservoir*
7. *Clip for hanging on your shirt pocket*
8. *Cap*

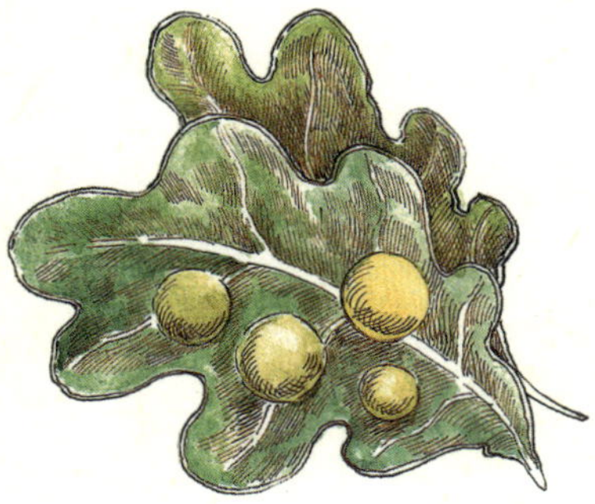

There are also plant-based alternatives: Take a gall, or "oak apple," which grows on the leaves of the oak tree. Grind it up and boil for a couple of hours or cover with water and leave to infuse for several days. Add a solution of ferrous sulfate (obtained by dipping rusty nails in vinegar) to the cooled solution. Thicken the mixture with cherry tree resin or glue (page 140). You can also use the tannins in tea leaves (page 64) or an extract of dyer's madder root. Add ginger or clove to make sure the ink keeps for several years.

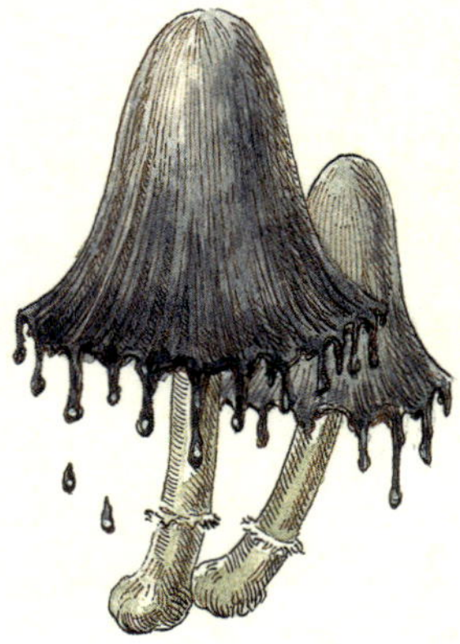

Gather some inkcap mushrooms, which grow on manure, and allow them to rot. Filter the resulting liquid then add a binder and cloves. If you mix this solution with ordinary ink, you'll be left with a means of protecting important documents: After drying, the spores form a unique pattern that can be used to prove its authenticity.

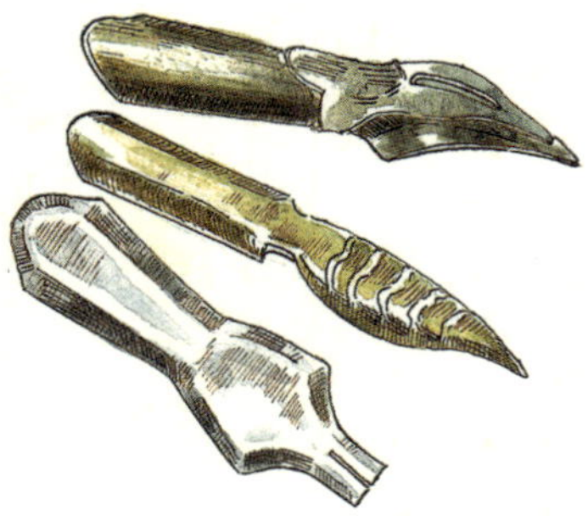

To prevent the handle from leaking, you need a feeder. This is a specially shaped sleeve hidden under the nib. On top, there are one or two capillary channels through which ink flows to the pen. Feed channels act as a sort of buffer, allowing excess ink to accumulate.

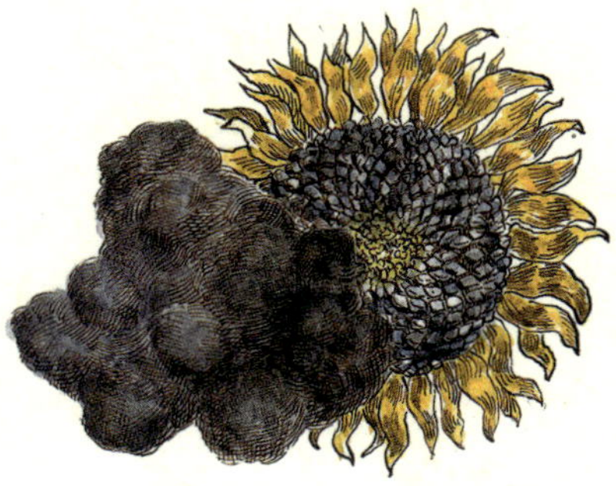

For increased secrecy, write with lemon juice or milk. The highlight of this "ink" is that it's not normally visible. Only heat will reveal the secret message.

PAPER

Paper keeps a chronicle of the past and present, as well as visions of the future — both possible and impossible. These XX pages hold the sum total of our ideas and knowledge, from harebrained to genius. Add some of your own right now — this blank sheet is for you. And, in fact, it's no longer blank.

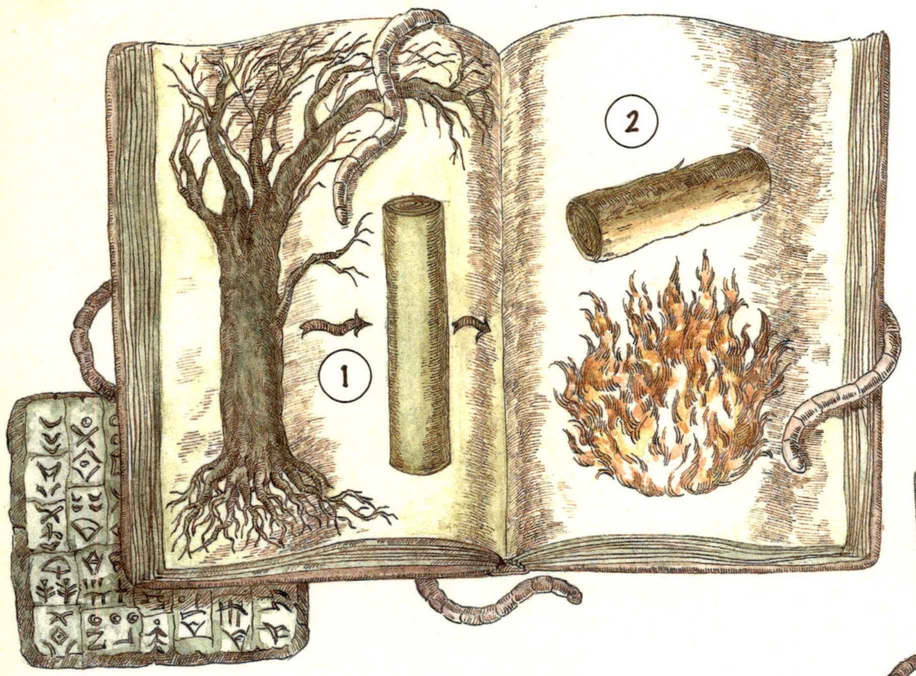

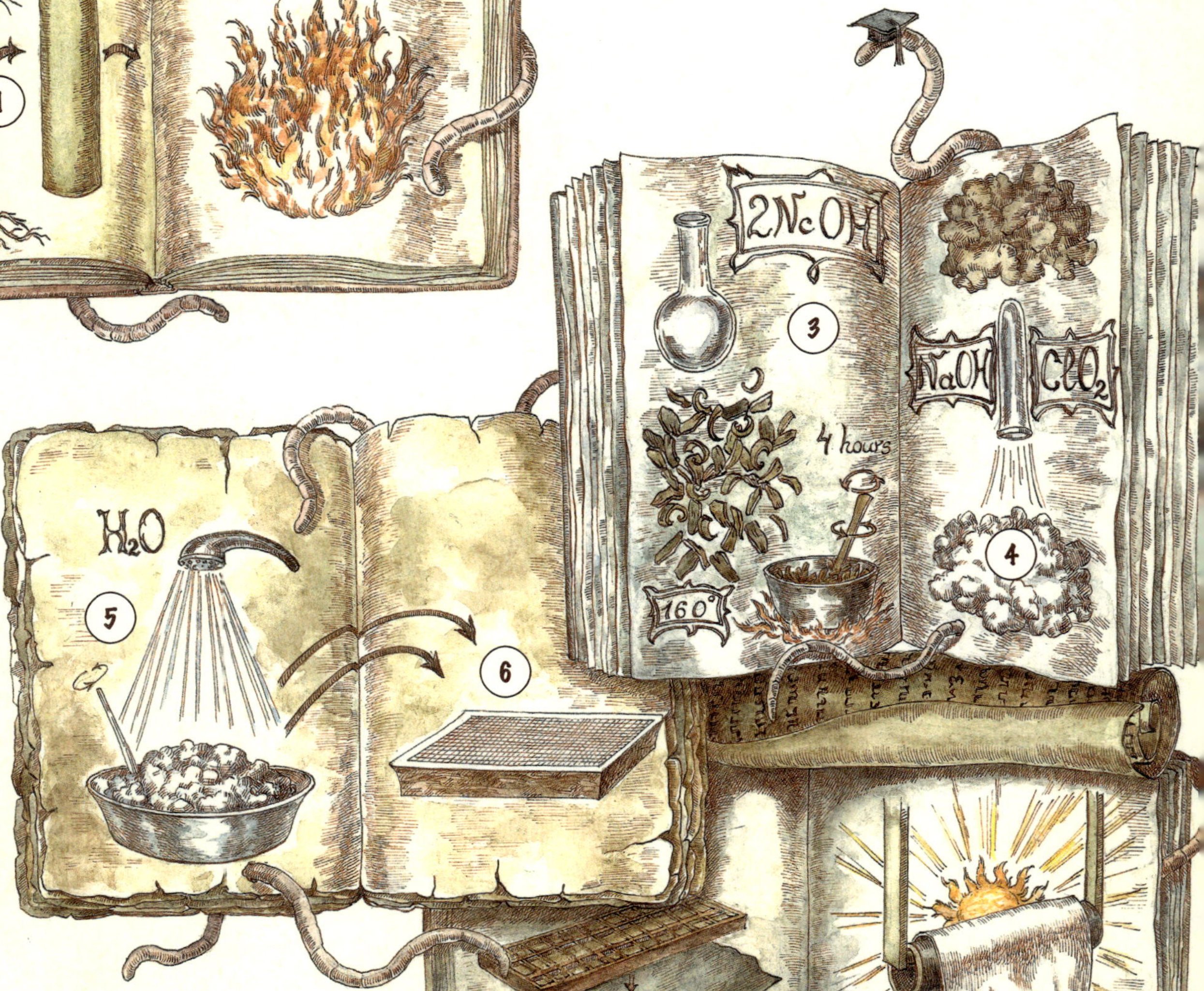

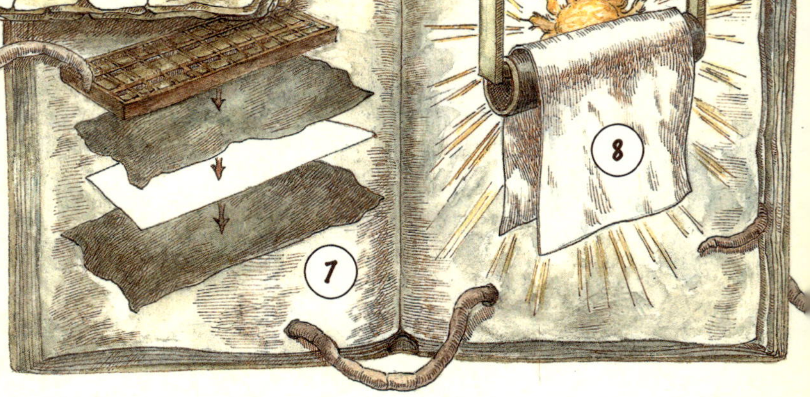

PAPER MAKING

You'll need spruce, pine or birch wood, as these trees contain the longest fibers. Remove the branches and bark from the logs (1) and use them to kindle a fire underneath a cauldron full of water. Place the prepared log on top. The steam will soften the wood (2), making it easier to pulp. Cut the wood into small chips and add an alkali solution of sodium hydroxide (page 24) to the mix. Bring to a boil and stir for at least 4 hours (3). The alkaline solution will eat away at the wood chips, transforming them into wood pulp, which can then be used to make brown paper.

If you need white paper, start by soaking it in a sodium hypochlorite solution. This can be obtained by passing an electric current through table salt using platinum electrodes. One side releases chlorine, which reacts with sodium hydroxide formed near the other electrode, synthesizing the bleaching agent sodium hypochlorite. Then rinse with a solution of sodium hydroxide, or caustic soda, and let stand (4). Repeat the process, giving the paper another bleach and caustic soda bath.

Wash any remaining chemicals out of the white wooly substance you're left with (5). Top off with more water until you reach a gruel-like consistency. Immerse a wooden frame with a fine mesh into the mixture and scoop up some paper pulp. Spread it into a thin layer and wait for the water to drain (6). Then lay the pulpy mass on a square of felt and cover with another layer of felt (7). Place in a press to squeeze out excess water and bond the fibers together. Carefully remove the sheet and let dry (8). Your paper is ready!

If you really want to hear about it

CONDOMS

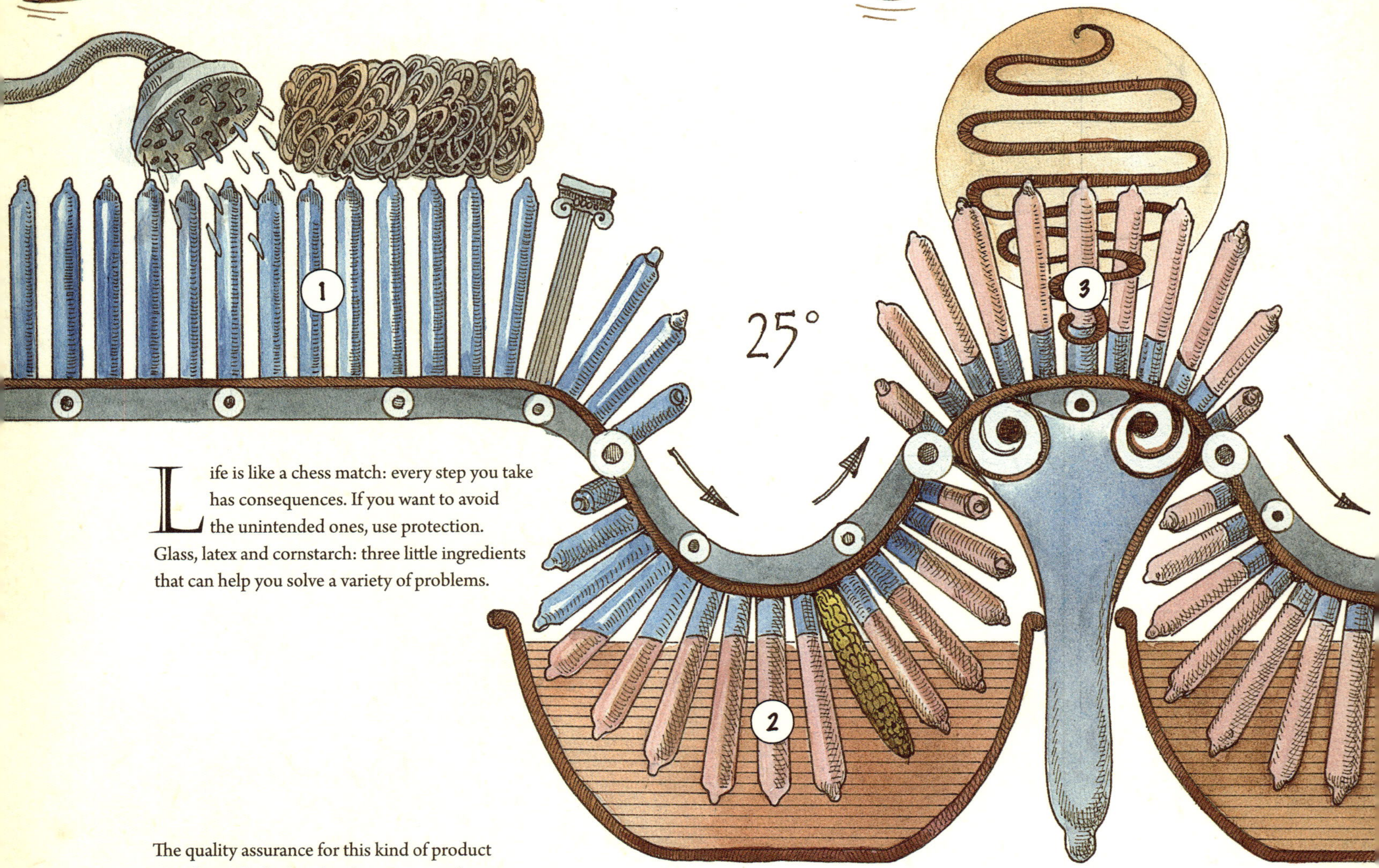

Life is like a chess match: every step you take has consequences. If you want to avoid the unintended ones, use protection. Glass, latex and cornstarch: three little ingredients that can help you solve a variety of problems.

The quality assurance for this kind of product must be at the highest level — just a single tear or puncture has the potential to change someone's life drastically.

1. Glass forms give the future condoms their shape. They move one after the other along the conveyor belt and are washed and dried using a rotating brush after each production cycle.
2. Use latex (page 116), the concentrated milky sap of the rubber tree, as your base material. This produces condoms that are impermeable, strong, thin and durable. The liquid latex is mixed in huge vats into which the glass molds are dipped. The latex must be kept at a constant temperature of 25°C so that the water doesn't evaporate, causing the material to delaminate.
3. After dipping, the latex must be well dried in a stream of cold air.
4. Once this first layer is dry, the molds are redipped and dried again. This extra layer fortifies the condom while keeping it relatively thin.
5. A rotating brush then rolls up the end of the latex, forming a rim around the opening. Later, it will be used to roll the condom into a flat disc for packaging (which can then be unpackaged at the proper moment and applied by rolling back down).
6. Now, the condom must undergo a 10-minute vulcanization process (page 116) — a heat treatment designed to give elasticity and durability to the final product.
7. You can also remove the condom from the mold using a strong stream of water.
8. The flat, rolled condom must then be rolled in a fine powder such as cornstarch. This will protect the latex from sticking to itself or your skin. But when it's being used, the condom should be slightly damp. Hence, you'll need to apply lubricant. Do not use oil-based lubricants, as they'll destroy latex. Water-based or silicone-based lubricants will work fine.

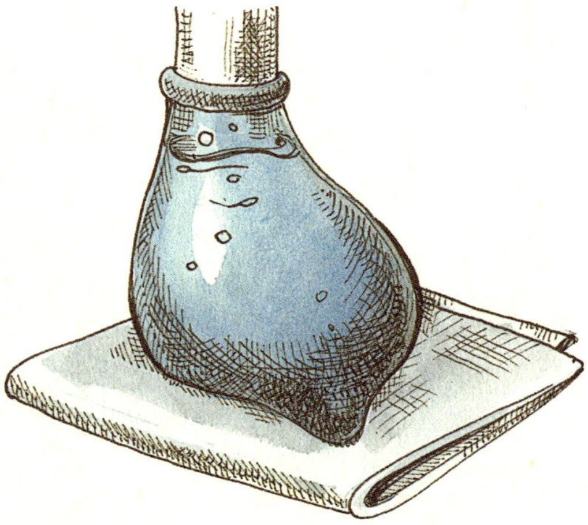

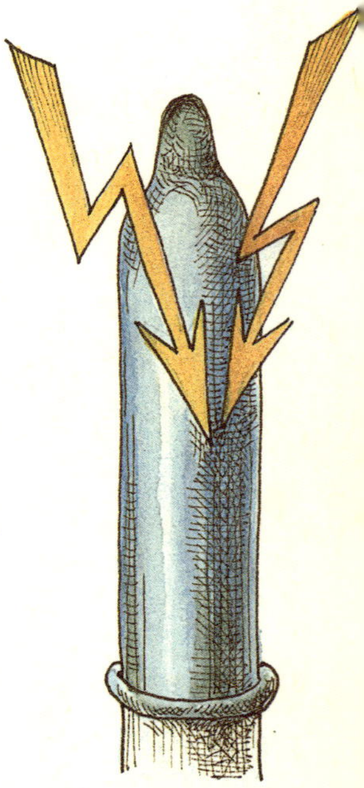

QUALITY CONTROL

Every single condom must be checked for punctures. After inflating the condom with air, its elasticity and strength are tested. Water or electricity is used to test the condom's integrity. Fill the condom with water and roll it over a piece of paper. If there are any leaks, they'll show up as water spots on the paper. To test the integrity of the product with electricity, you need to place a condom between two electrodes and run electricity through it. Since latex does not conduct electricity, even a tiny defect will allow the current to pass through, which is instantly displayed on the meter reading.

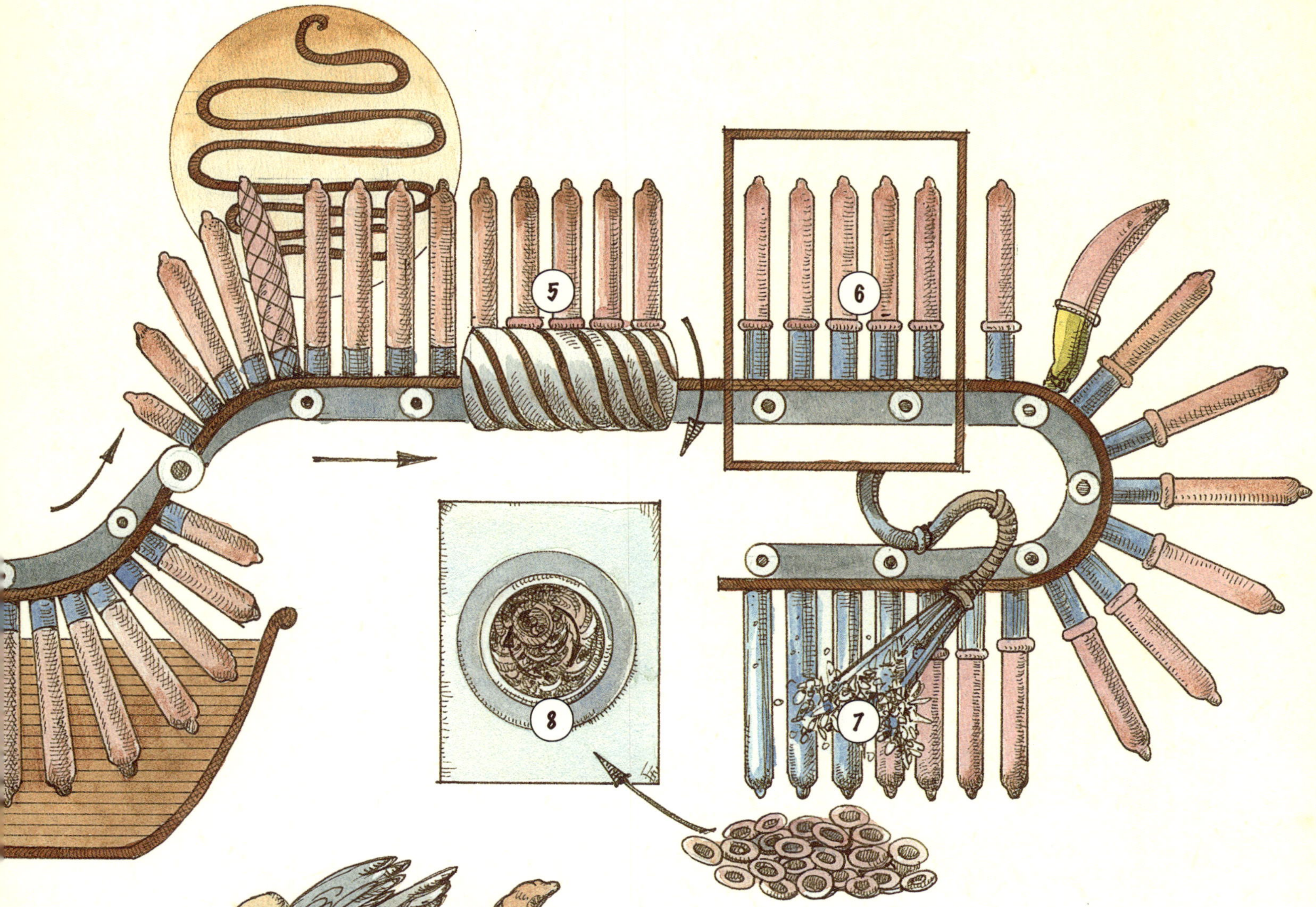

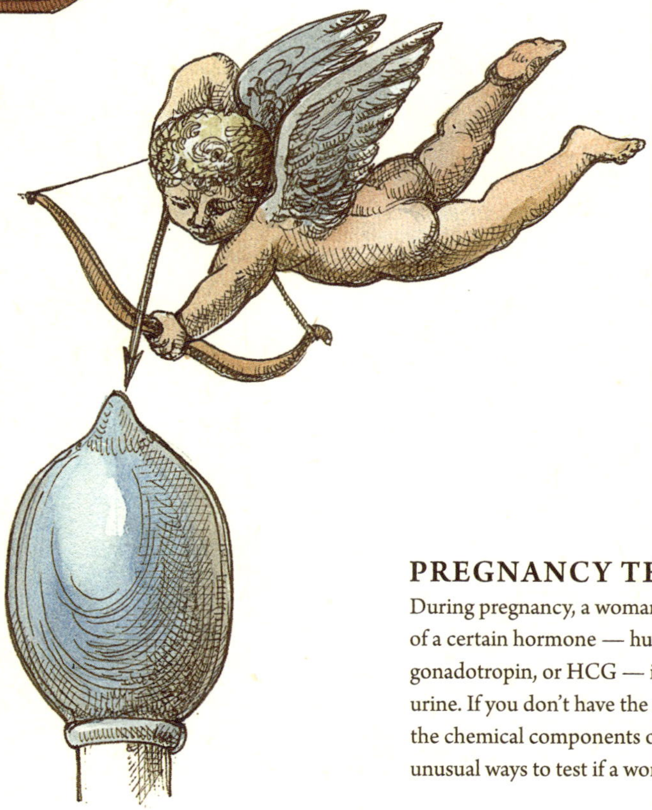

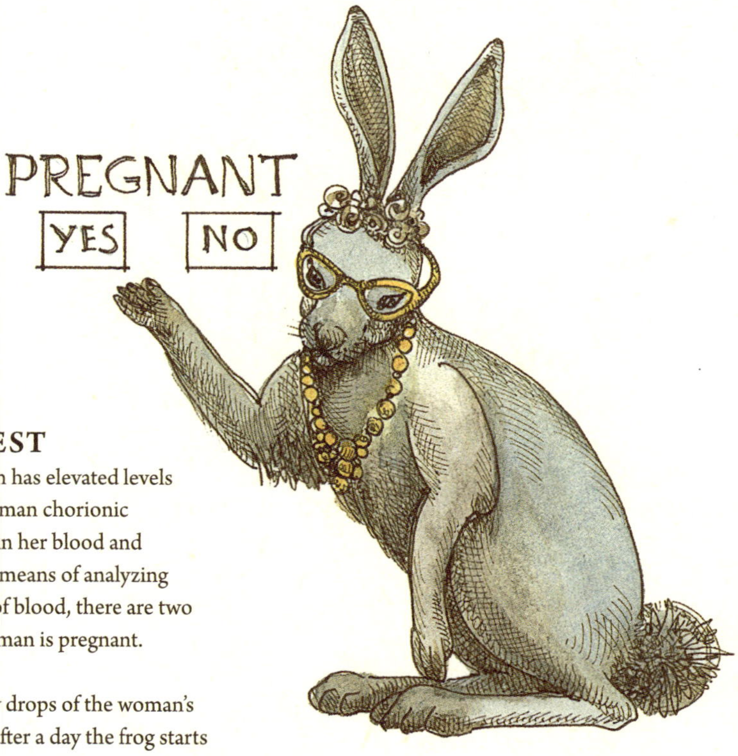

PREGNANCY TEST

During pregnancy, a woman has elevated levels of a certain hormone — human chorionic gonadotropin, or HCG — in her blood and urine. If you don't have the means of analyzing the chemical components of blood, there are two unusual ways to test if a woman is pregnant.

Use a syringe to inject a few drops of the woman's urine into a female frog. If after a day the frog starts spawning, then the woman is pregnant. The second method involves injecting urine into a rabbit then waiting 4 days before dissecting it. If the ovaries are found to be enlarged, it's highly likely the woman is pregnant.

WORD

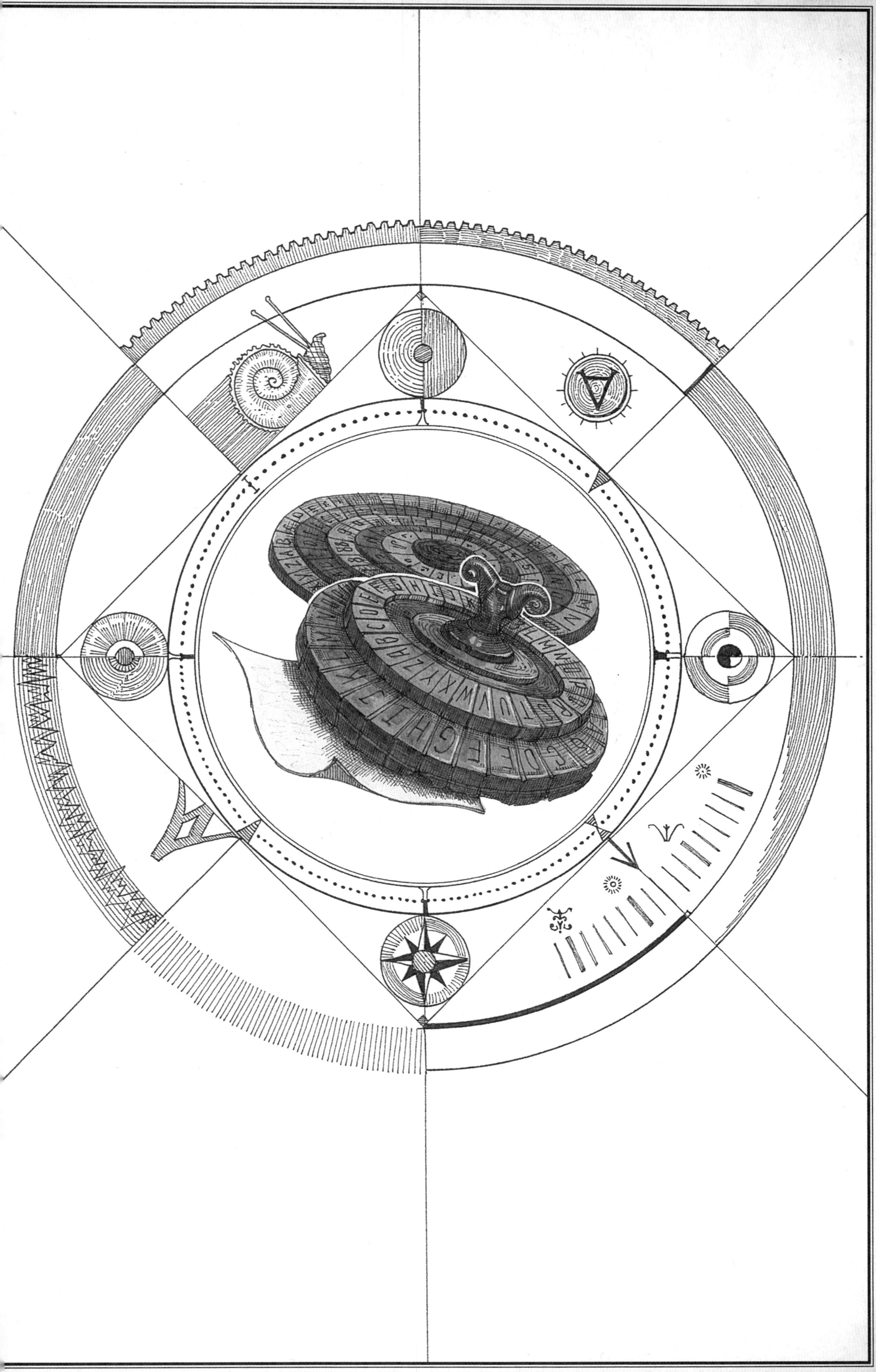

PIGEON MAIL

Human beings are social creatures. They crave constant communication even when hundreds of miles apart. If given the chance to receive messages instantly, they will send thousands a day. Fortunately, pigeons can't fly that fast. But perhaps this constraint will inspire people to be more thoughtful in their correspondence and revive the lost art of letter writing.

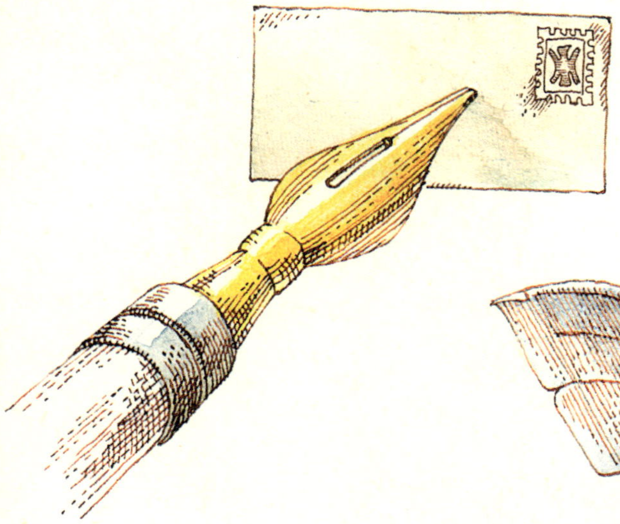

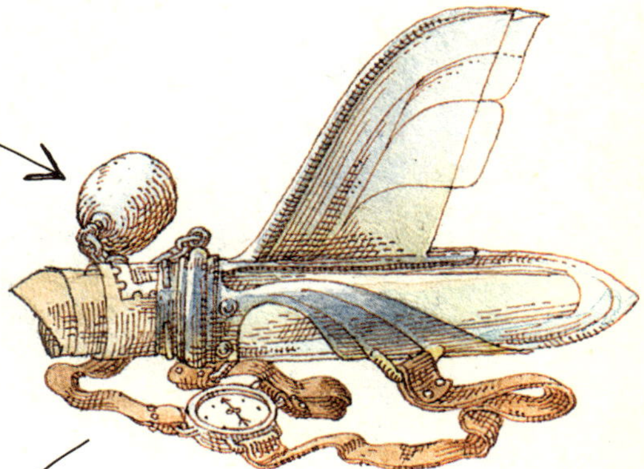

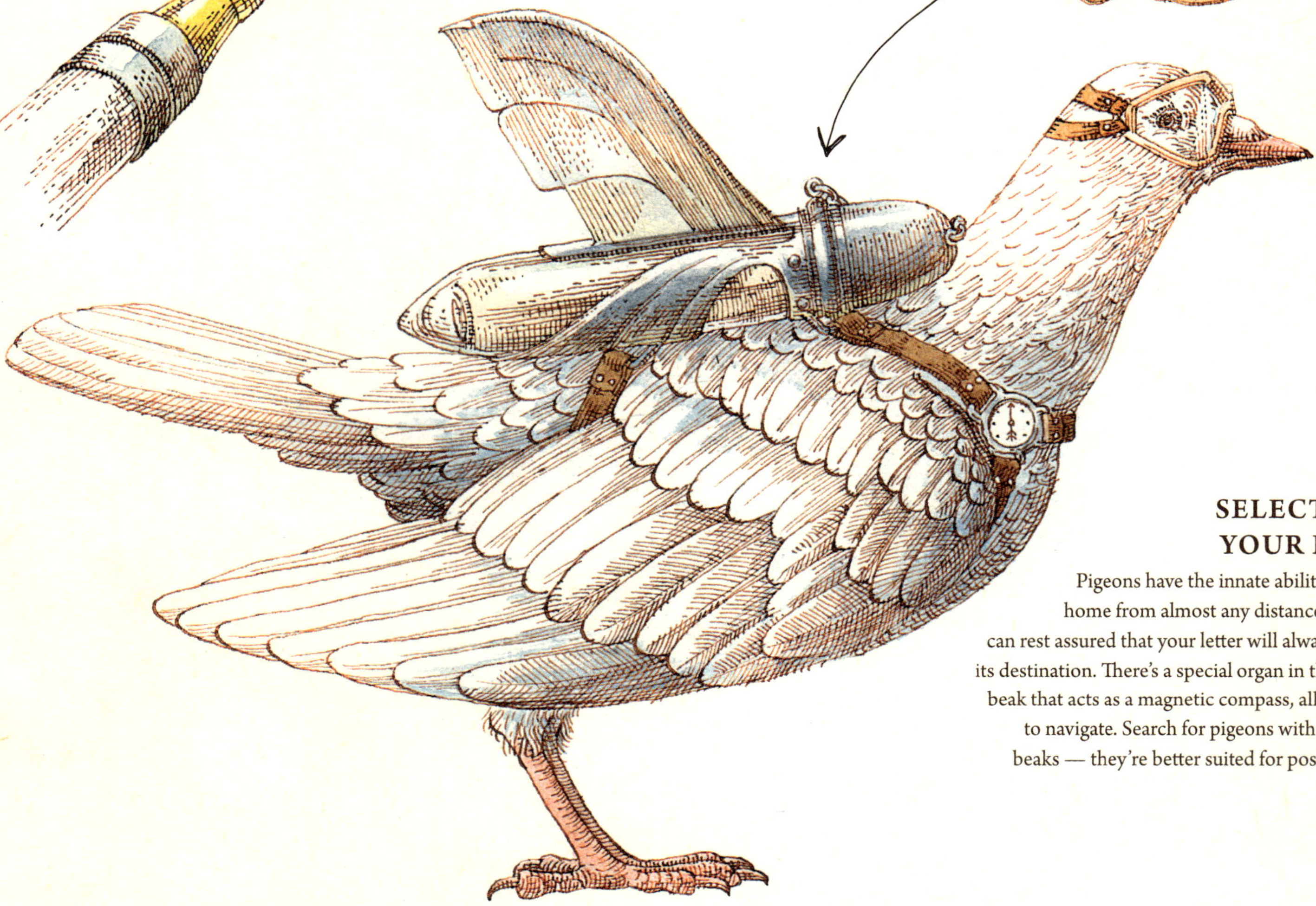

SELECTING YOUR BIRD

Pigeons have the innate ability to find home from almost any distance, so you can rest assured that your letter will always reach its destination. There's a special organ in the bird's beak that acts as a magnetic compass, allowing it to navigate. Search for pigeons with massive beaks — they're better suited for postal work.

TRAINING YOUR BIRD

Not every pigeon can be a professional postman. You've got to hand select the brightest, toughest candidates. They'll need to start learning the tools of the trade as soon as they can fly, at around three weeks old. In the first part of their training, you should release your pigeons near home and pair newbies with more experienced flyers. And feed the new trainees as soon as they return home — this will reinforce their homing instinct.

As soon as the new class graduates, it's time to play matchmaker. Pigeons are very attached to their mates, and if your postmen find love along the side of the road, they may never return. Instead, give them a honey to come home to and keep the business in the family.

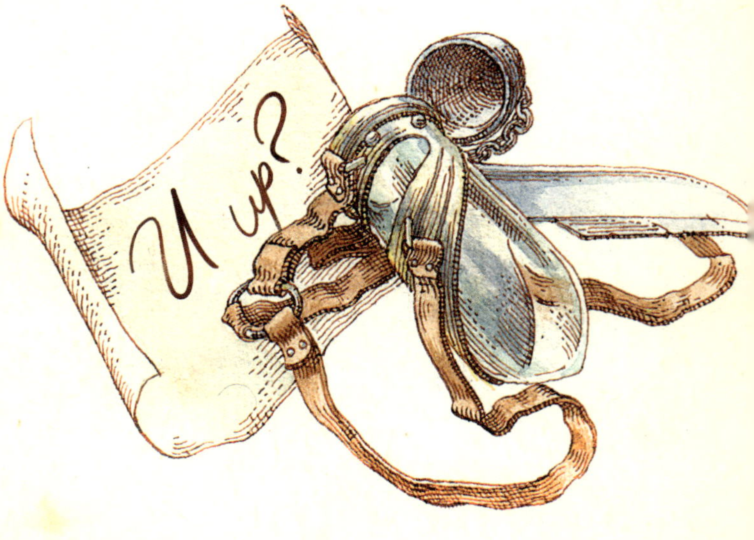

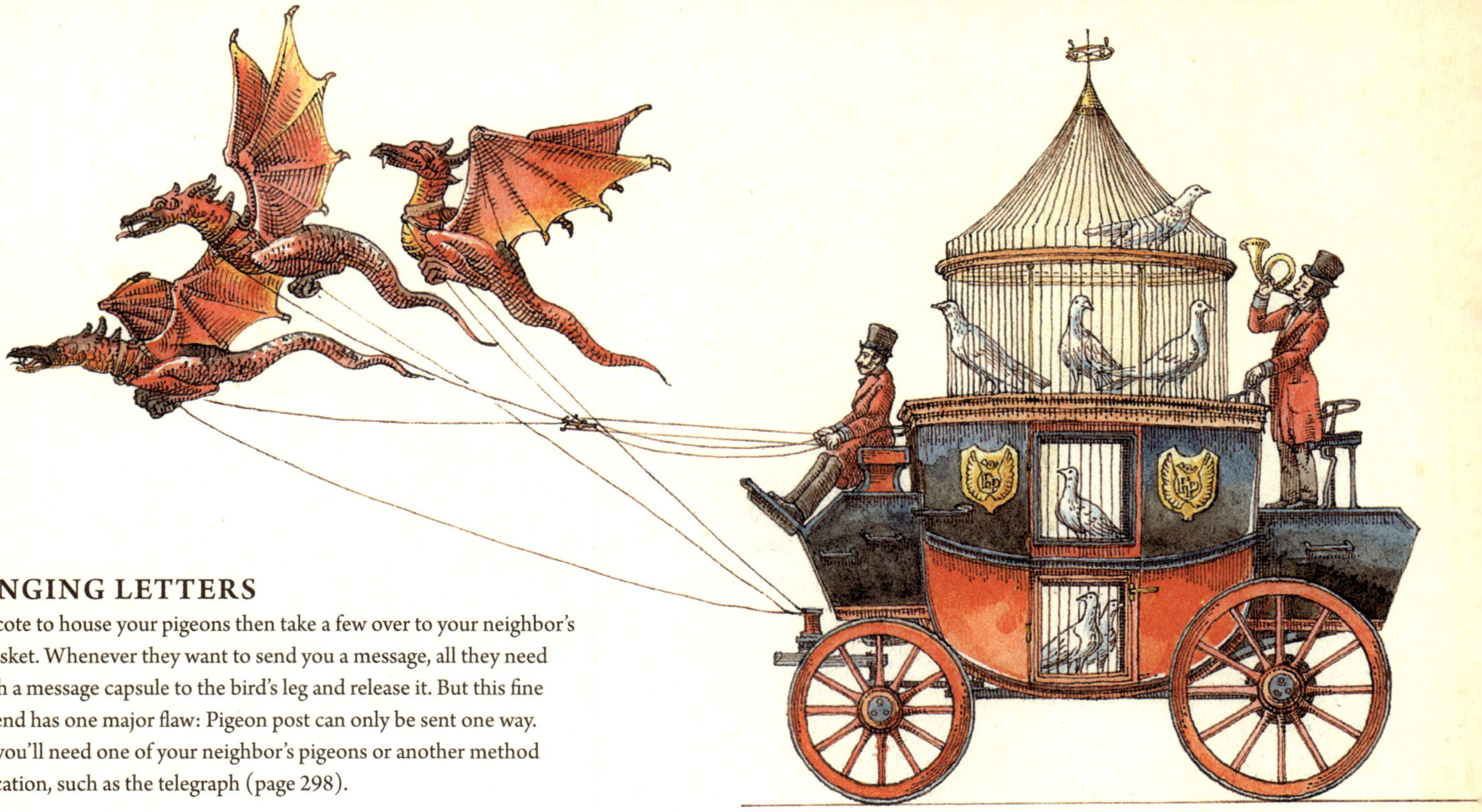

EXCHANGING LETTERS

Build a dovecote to house your pigeons then take a few over to your neighbor's house in a basket. Whenever they want to send you a message, all they need to do is attach a message capsule to the bird's leg and release it. But this fine feathered friend has one major flaw: Pigeon post can only be sent one way. To respond, you'll need one of your neighbor's pigeons or another method of communication, such as the telegraph (page 298).

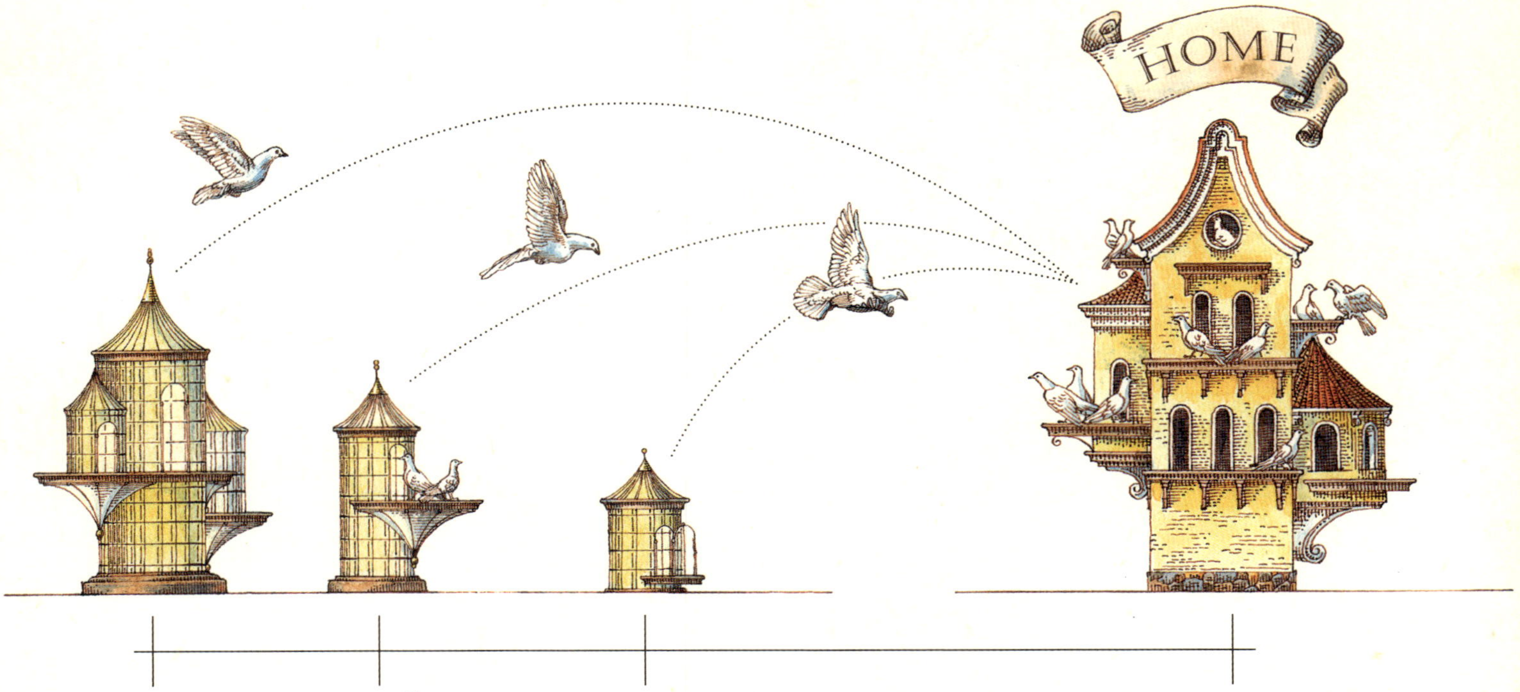

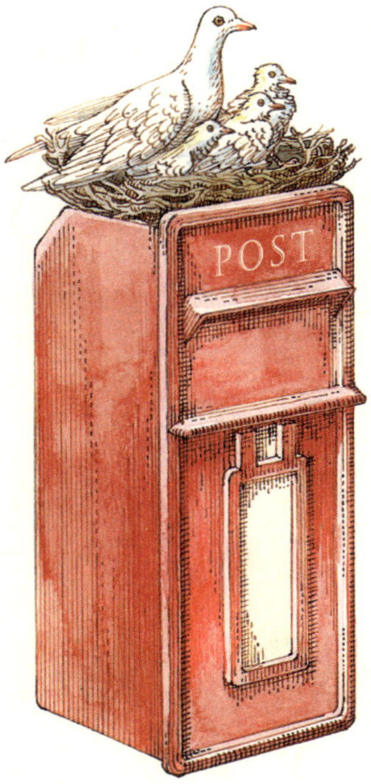

SAFETY MEASURES

Before sending your homing pigeon on its way, you need to feed and water him so that he doesn't decide to take an unauthorized lunch break en route. Find a high, open space to release your pigeon to make it easier for it to find its way.

Just to be sure, send two birds with the same message — there's always a risk that one of them will be attacked by a predatory bird. This may be a random act of fate, but if you find your pigeons are disappearing regularly, you might want to investigate to see if someone has learned how to intercept your envoys using hawks, merlins or other predatory birds.

RADIO

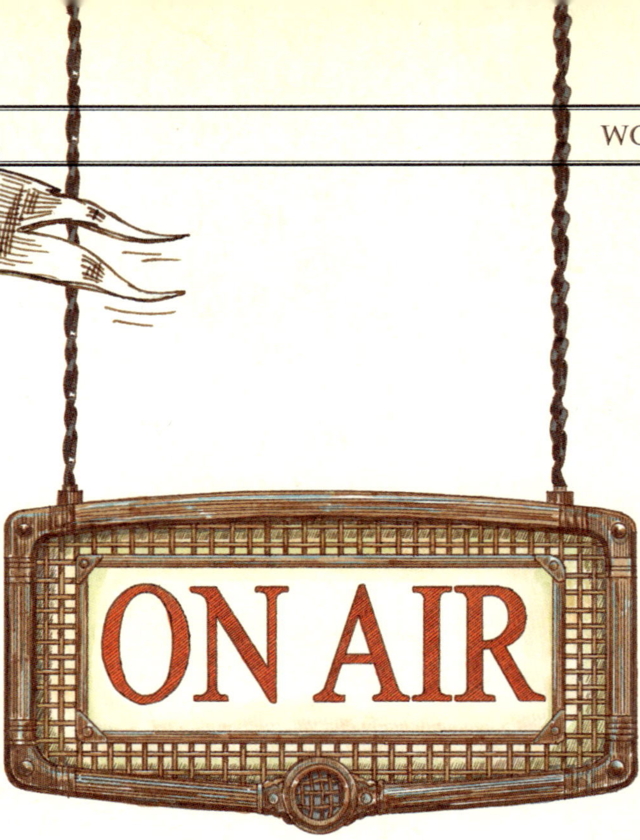

With the invention of the radio, you'll gain the opportunity to transmit your voice across vast distances without getting tangled up in wires. It's not just a way to get a message out or play your favorite song but also a powerful new tool for influencing the masses. So if you send out a fictitious emergency broadcast saying that aliens have landed and are threatening a war of the worlds, keep in mind that people just might believe you.

LONG-DISTANCE COMMUNICATION

Radio as a means of telecommunication is based on the propagation of electromagnetic waves. The distance at which they can be received depends on the power and frequency of the signal. Very low frequency radio waves (with wavelengths 10–100 km) can diffract around hills and follow the curvature of the Earth. Shortwave radio (wavelengths 10–100 m) reflects off a layer of electrically charged atoms high in the atmosphere called the ionosphere and so can also propagate over very large distances. Other wavelengths only work for line-of-sight transmissions.

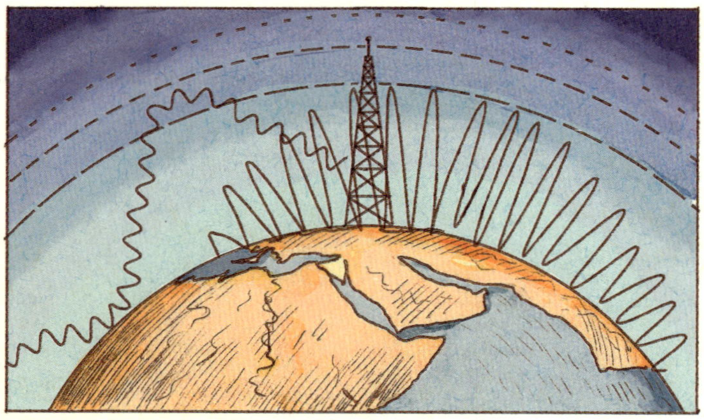

VACUUM TUBE TRANSMITTER

Radio waves can also be used to send voice messages. But this is a more complex process. You will need to assemble a transmitter using simple electron tubes (1) known as triodes (page 198) and more powerful transmitting triodes (2) that are cooled by air flow. A separate transformer (5) is needed to run the heating circuit of more powerful triodes. The microphone (3) (page 300) picks up the sound, and the circuit on one triode amplifies this signal and modulates the amplitude of high-frequency oscillations along with it. Then the overall signal is amplified and fed to the antenna (4). The transmission frequency is determined by the induction of the coils (7, 8) and the capacitance of the capacitors (9, 10). A variable inductor (8) is used to fine-tune the frequency (page 196).

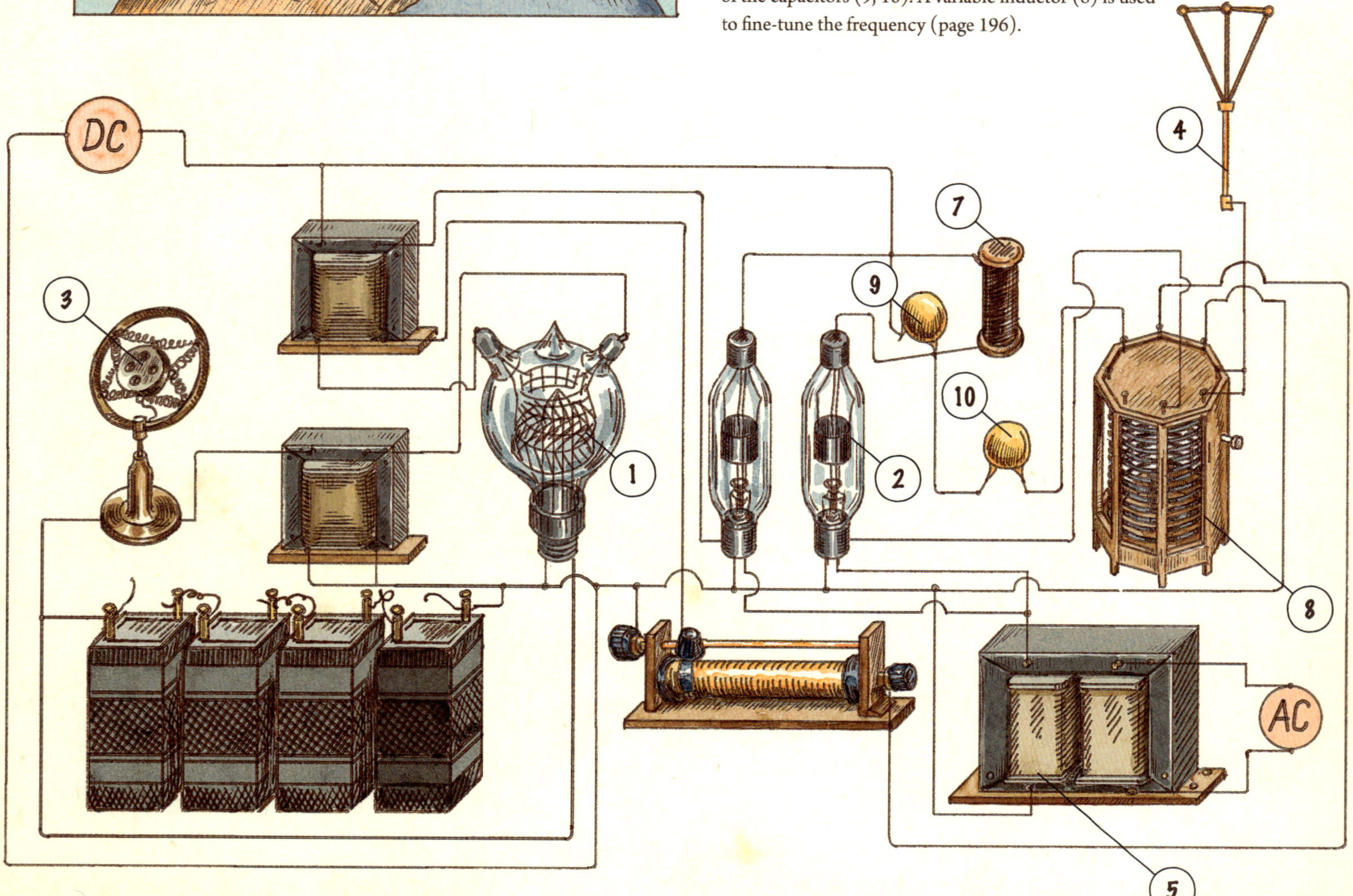

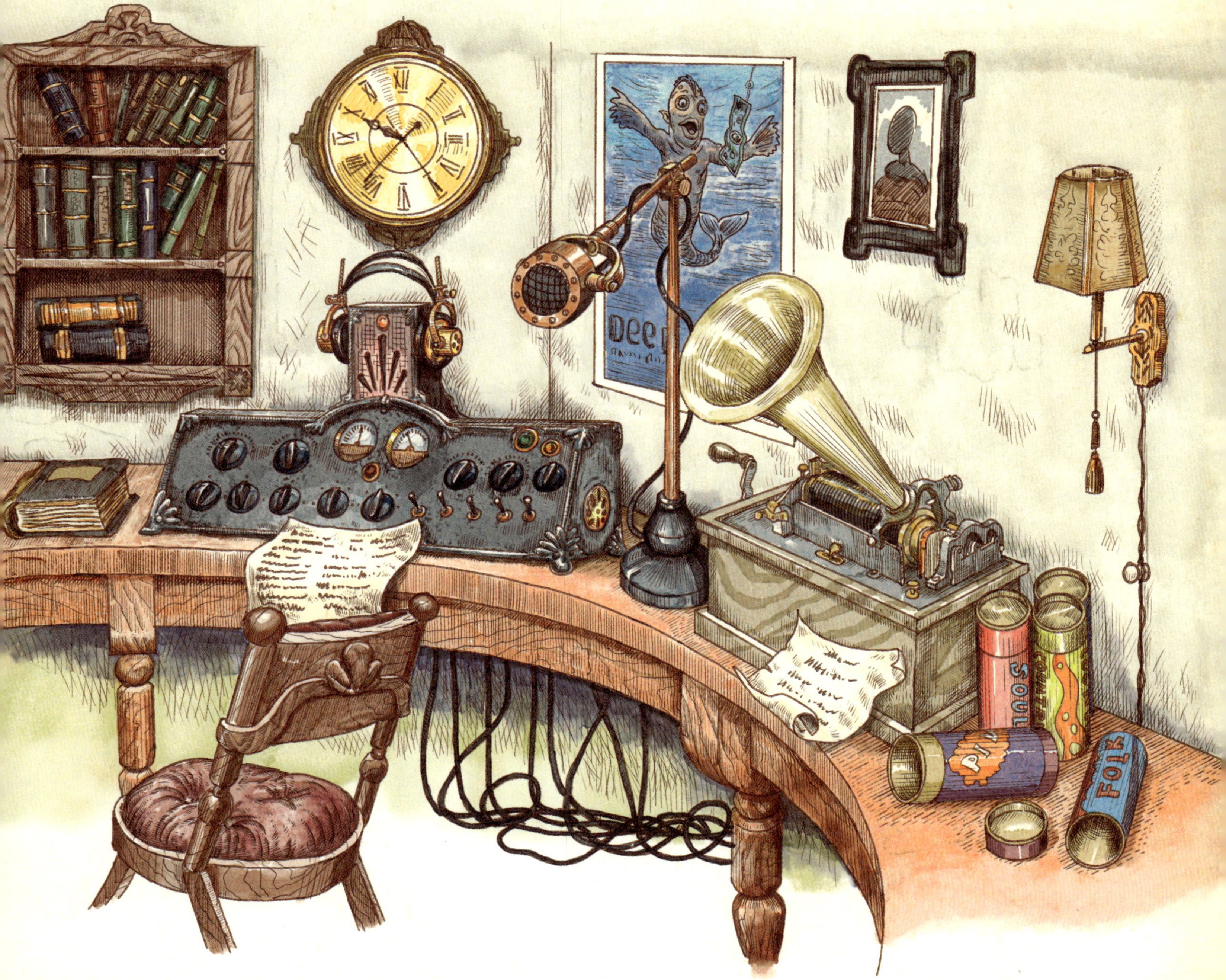

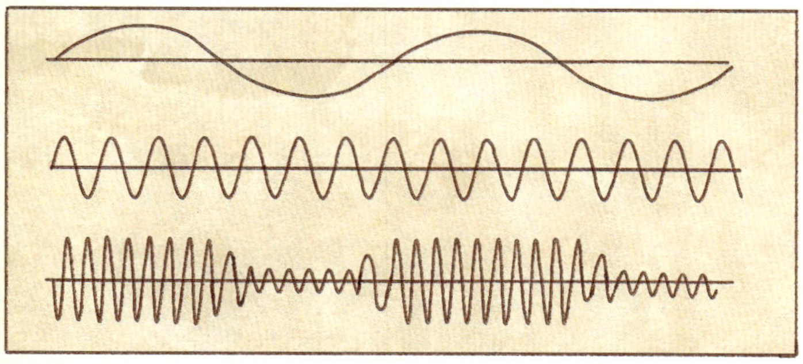

RECEIVING RADIO SIGNALS

You'll need a receiver to pick up the radio waves. The heart of the device is a simple semiconductor diode. It can be made by heating an approximately equal volume of sulfur powder and lead filings in a strong ceramic or glass container. The dark gray, sparkly mass resulting from the chemical reaction is known as galena, a crystal of lead sulfide. Attach a metal clamp connected to an electrical contact (1) and press a needle (2) connected to another contact to the surface. This is the simplest kind of detector you can make. By finding the correct position of the needle on the detector and connecting a coil (3), two capacitors (4, 5) and headphones (6) to it, you will be able to receive voice radio transmissions. But what about batteries? You don't need them — the receiver is powered by the radio waves it receives.

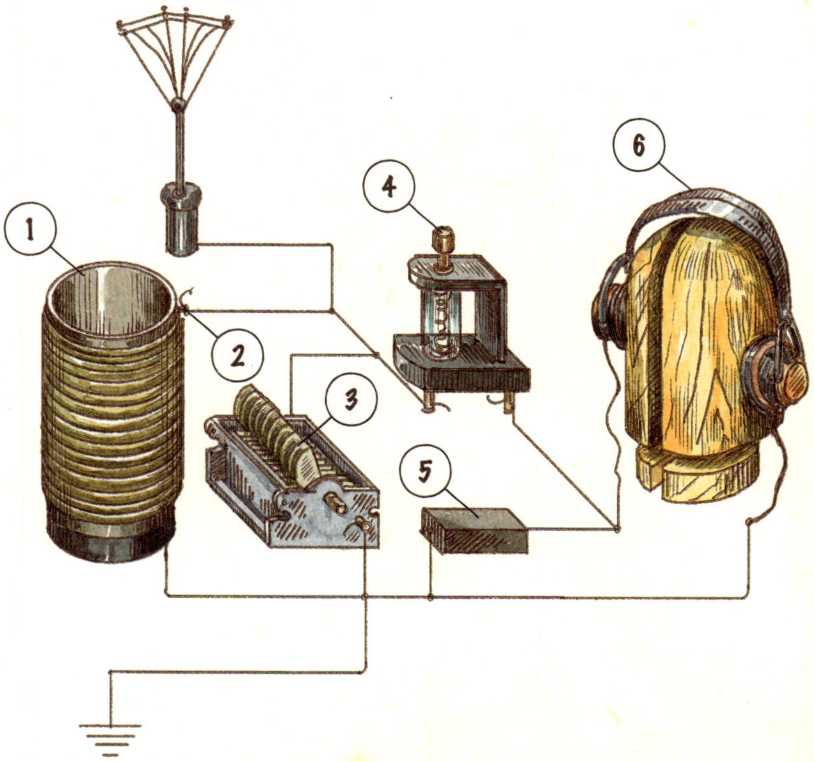

TELEGRAPH

Sending information across vast distances doesn't always require messengers. The invention of the telegraph will allow you to do away with them entirely by transmitting messages through electromagnetic waves. Without any impenetrable thickets, oceans or high walls holding you back, the only barriers to communication that remain are the interpersonal.

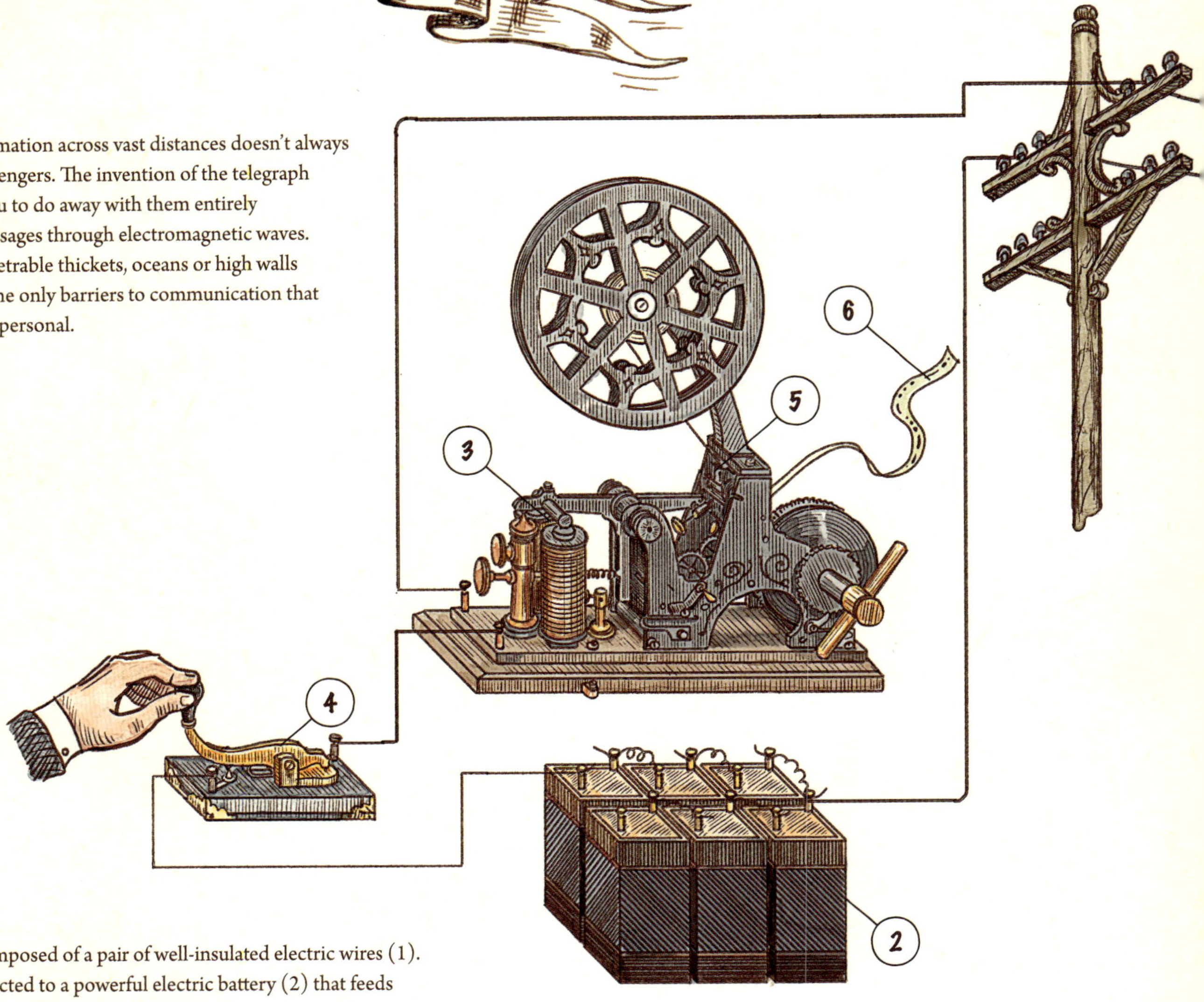

The telegraph is composed of a pair of well-insulated electric wires (1). The circuit is connected to a powerful electric battery (2) that feeds two electromagnetic coils (3) at the ends of the line. The operator at the transmitting end presses a key (4), closing the electrical circuit. When a current flows through the circuit, the coil attracts the iron plate with the pencil (5) attached, causing it to leave either a long or a short mark — a dash or a dot — on the paper roll (6). Once you encode the alphabet in dots and dashes, you can transmit any text messages over distances of hundreds of kilometers.

SPARK-GAP TRANSMITTER

Avoid any wires whatsoever by developing a radiotelegraph. The simplest way to generate a wide range of radio waves is an electric spark. The spark transmitter is a simple circuit controlled by a key switch (1). This turns on the power from the batteries (2) of the primary winding of the step-up coil (3). To make one, wind a thick varnished copper wire around an iron core. A few dozen turns should suffice. In the same circuit, install an automatic breaker — a contact that is attracted to the core when the current is activated and opens the coil power circuit. This breaker turns direct current into a series of short pulses.

Create a secondary winding (page 196) by twisting a thinner wire around the same core. This one will need to be wound several thousand times. This secondary winding increases the voltage to thousands, even tens of thousands, of volts. This high voltage creates an electrical discharge that bridges the gap (4) between two needle-like metal electrodes. Connect the grounding wire (5) to one side of the spark gap and the antenna (6) to the other.

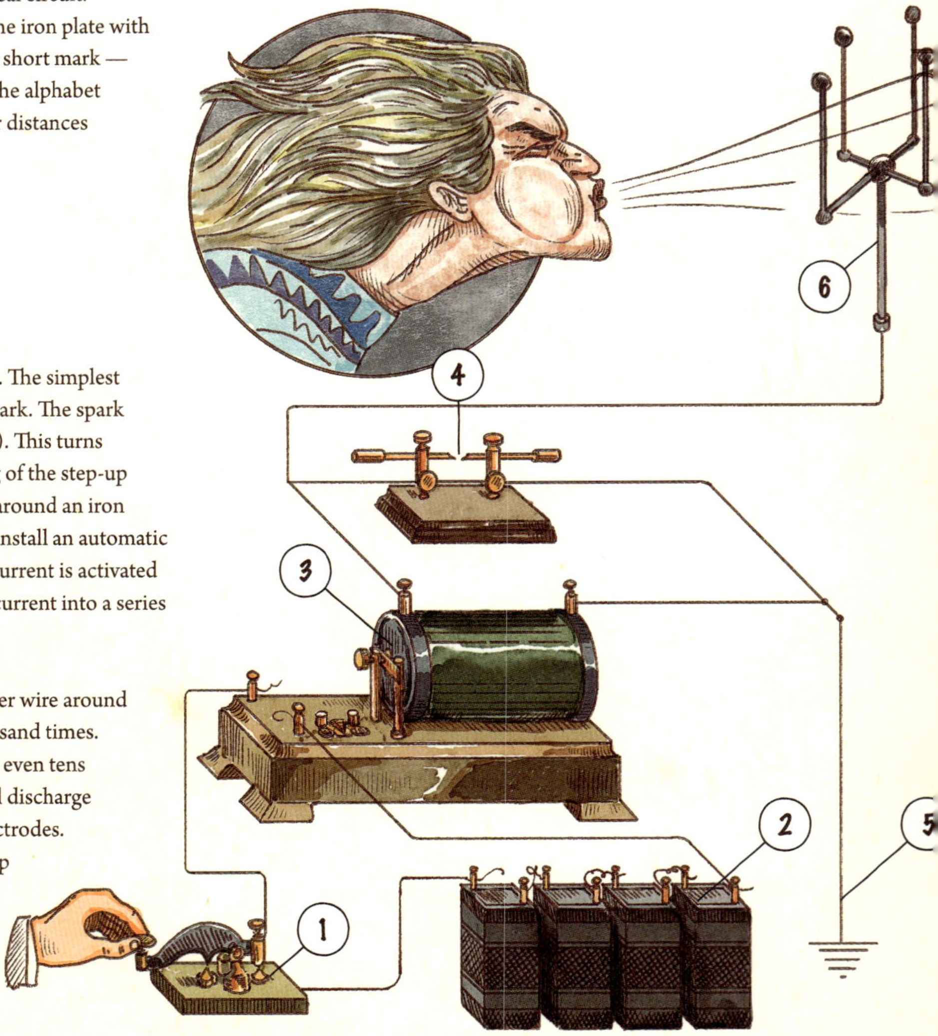

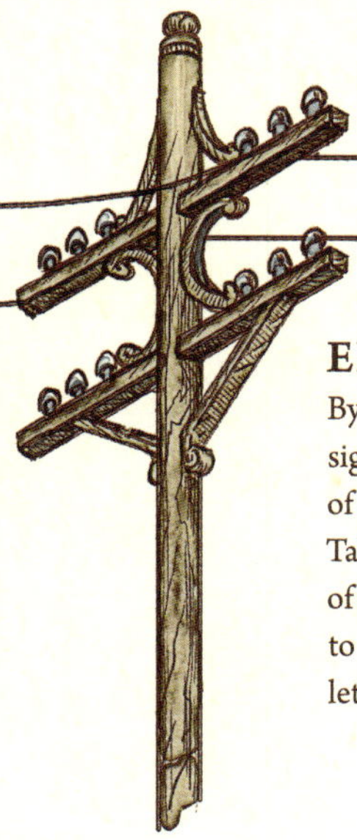

ENCODING A MESSAGE

By encoding the alphabet using a series of long (dash) and short (dot) electrical signals, any text message can be transmitted and received over distances of hundreds of kilometers, even with strong radio wave interference. Take the duration of one dot as a single unit of time. Then the duration of the dash will be equal to three dots. Take a dot-length pause to differentiate between each character, a three-dot pause between letters, and a seven-dot pause between words.

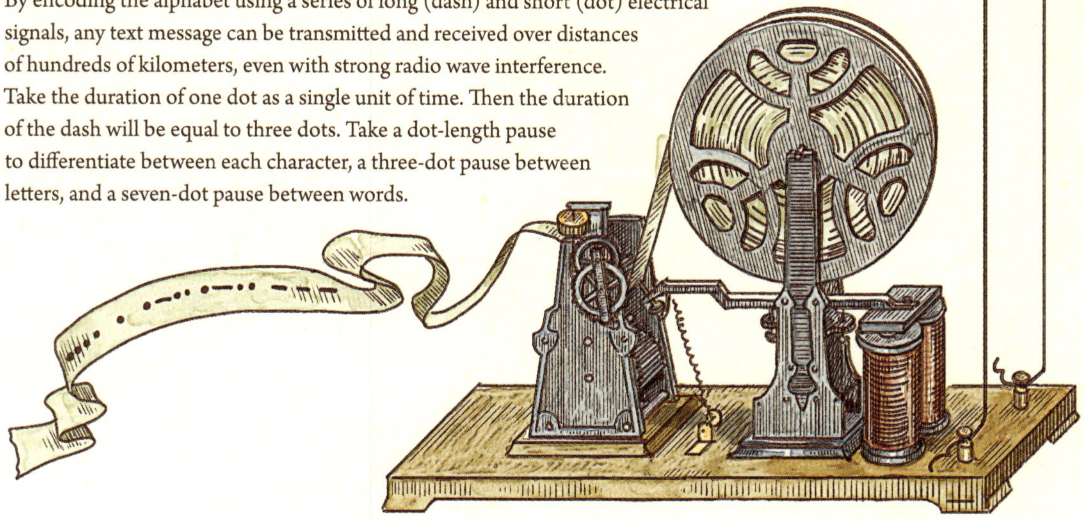

You'll need to agree on some standard convention for what series of dots and dashes will represent each letter, number and punctuation mark. Letters that are used more often should be given simpler codes. This will make the messages you send more concise. To help you memorize the alphabet and test the skills of the telegraphers — that is, the people sending and receiving messages — use pangram phrases containing all the letters of the alphabet.

For example, the pangram, "The quick brown fox jumps over the lazy dog" might look like this: - .... . / --.- ..- .. -.-. -.- / -... .-. --- .-- -. / ..-. --- -..- / .--- ..- -- .--. ... / --- ...- . .-. / - .... . / .-.. .- --.. -.-- / -.. --- --.

Urgent messages are better encoded using short phrases. For example, distress signals for ships at sea can be encoded as a short series of characters that will sound like one word, without pauses between letters: three dots, three dashes, three dots: ...---...

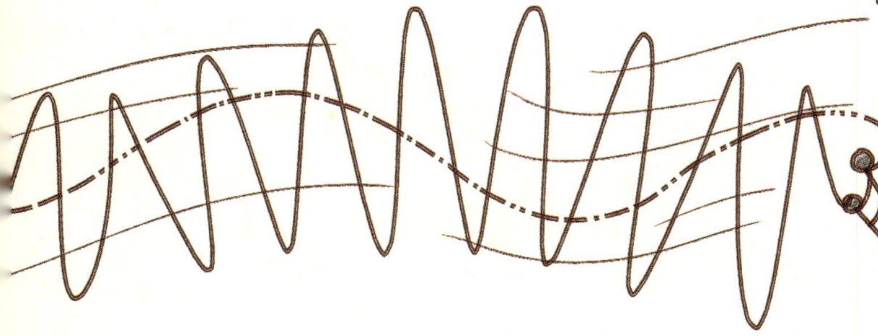

RADIOTELEGRAPH RECEIVER

The main element of the receiving end of the radiotelegraph is a glass tube filled with iron filings (1). On both ends of the tube are metal contacts connected to the ground (2) and antenna (3), respectively. When a passing radio wave induces a voltage in the antenna, the current passing through the tube causes the dust to cling together, and the electrical resistance drops sharply.

This closes the circuit that connects the batteries (4) to the relay (5). The secondary circuit of the relay turns on an electromagnetic bell (6) that signals the reception of a radio signal. The bell hammer (7) strikes the glass tube (1) during the reverse stroke, resetting it to its original state. At the same time, the bell trill repeats the sequence of signals transmitted by pressing the transmitter key — or the electrical noise of a thunderstorm raging tens of kilometers away from the receiver. So in addition to the radio transmitter, you now also have a thunderstorm predictor.

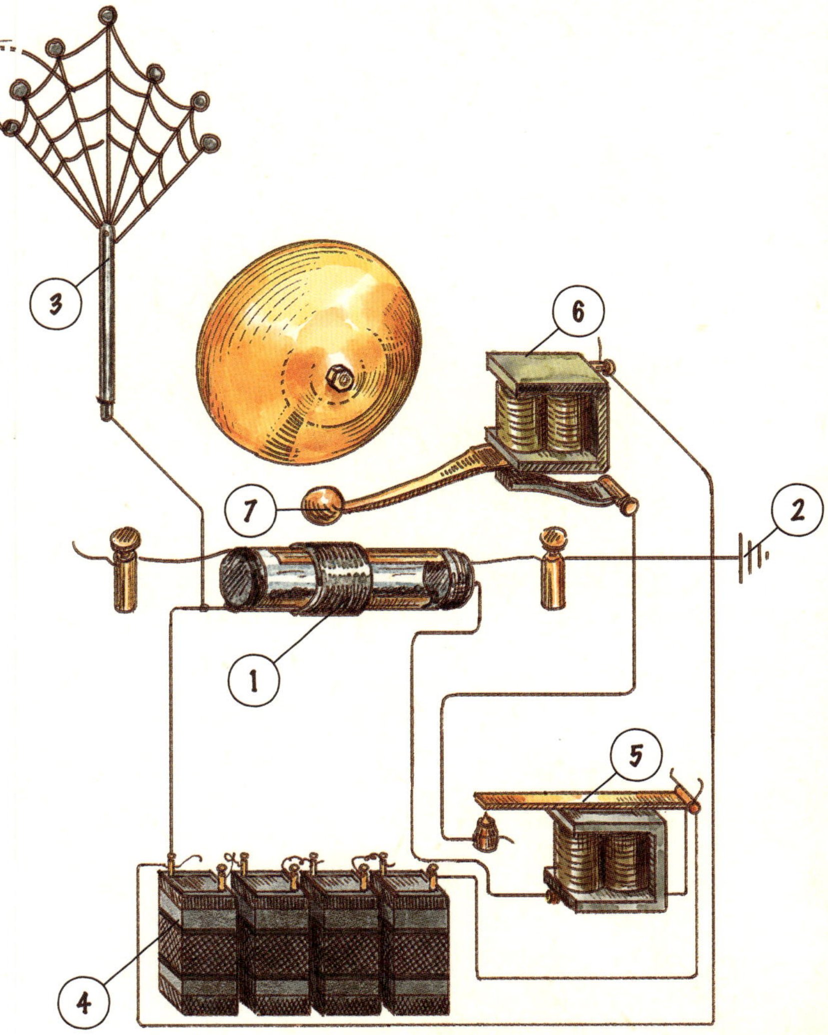

TELEPHONE

It can be hard to define the exact moment a new era dawns. But when the first telephone breaks through the silence, you'll know that your world is forever changed.

Telephone wires will wrap around the planet, connecting people through a dense network of cables and switches and freeing them from the shackles of physical space. At least as far as information exchange goes. Teleporting solid matter will take some more tinkering.

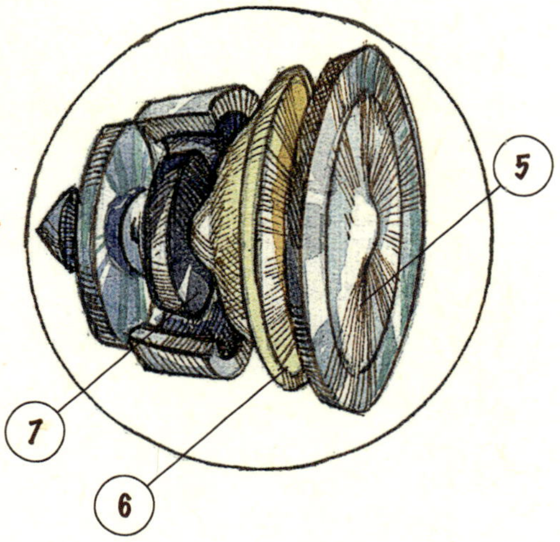

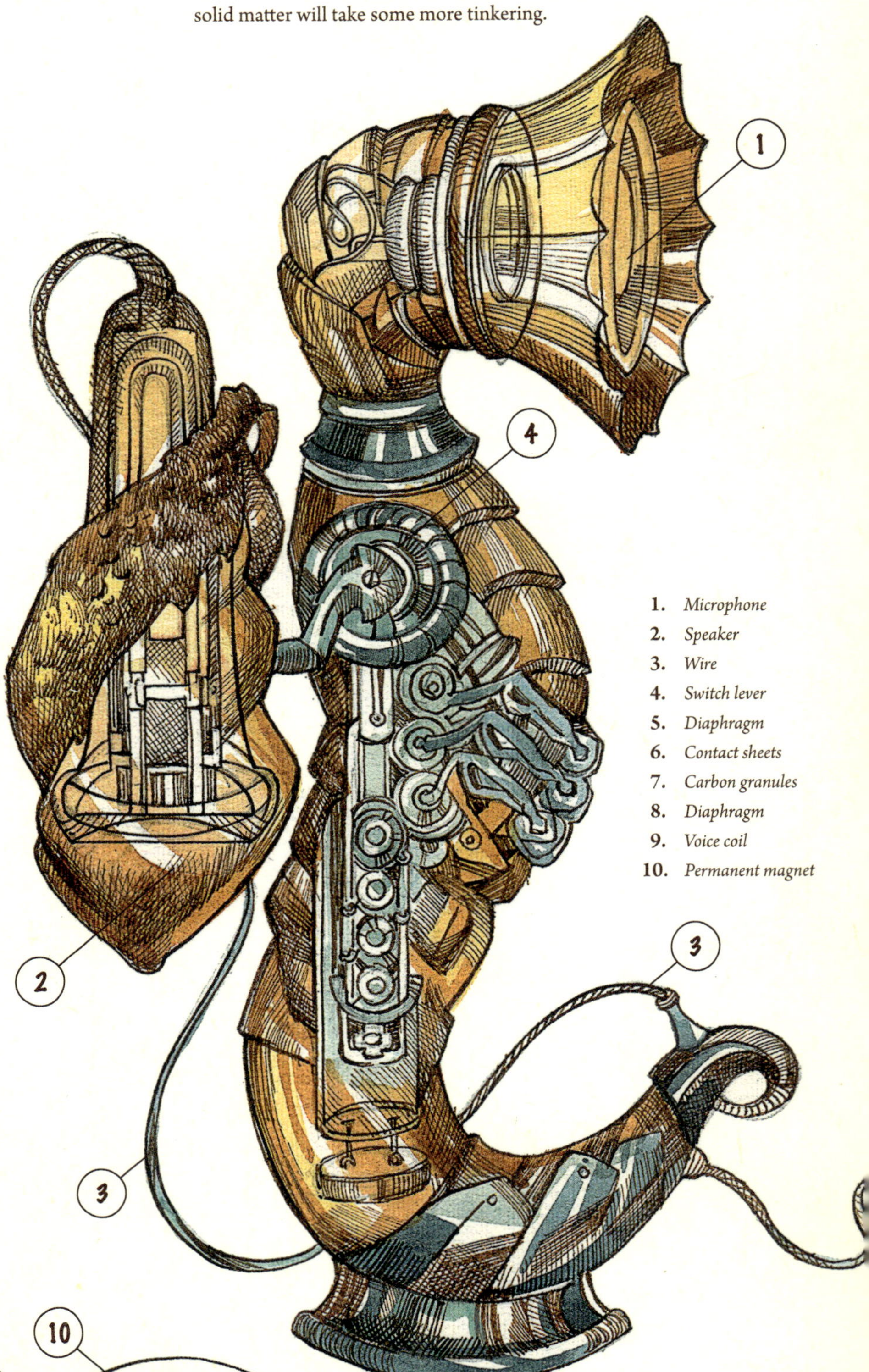

MICROPHONE

To send a sound across vast distances, it must first be converted into an electrical signal. You'll need to construct a carbon microphone. Take two sheets of metal, one very thin — around 0.05 mm thick or less. Seal them together with a small space between. Fill this space with carbon granules or graphite (page 286). The thinner plate acts as a membrane — a thin film that vibrates under the influence of sound waves. When it bends inward, the membrane pushes the carbon granules closer to one another, and when it bends outwards, the granules move farther apart.

Thus, the electrical resistance between the two plates will also fluctuate, changing the current in the circuit to which it is connected. This change in resistance is transmitted through the wires to your conversation partner, where the telephone receiver will once again convert it into audible sound waves. But in order to do this, you'll first need to construct a speaker.

1. *Microphone*
2. *Speaker*
3. *Wire*
4. *Switch lever*
5. *Diaphragm*
6. *Contact sheets*
7. *Carbon granules*
8. *Diaphragm*
9. *Voice coil*
10. *Permanent magnet*

SPEAKER

Construct an electromagnet by wrapping a length of copper wire around a hunk of iron. Connect this to a light voice coil consisting of thin copper wire (page 196) coated in an equally thin layer of rubber (page 116). Roll a piece of wax-covered paper into a cone and connect it to the voice coil. When the audio signal moves through the voice coil, the cone vibrates in the constant magnetic field produced by the electromagnet, emitting sound.

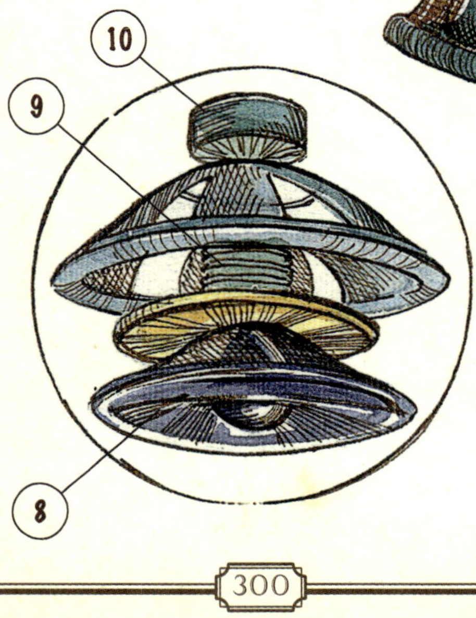

When you pick up the receiver, the hook switch (4) closes the circuit connecting you to the local telephone operator, and a tone will sound — this is how the switchboard station signals that a connection has been made. When you place the phone back on the hook, the circuit is broken and the connection is interrupted.

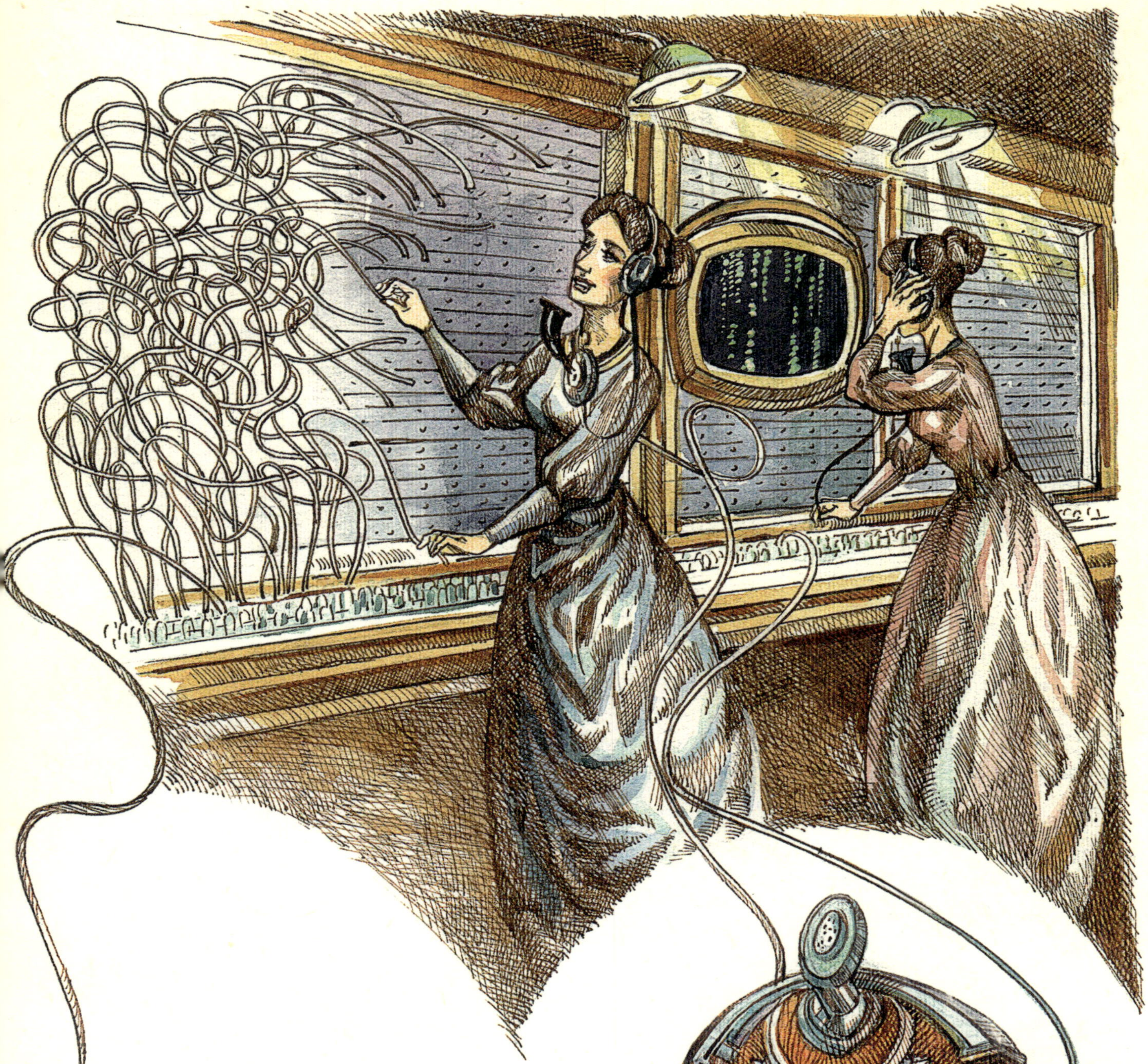

SWITCHBOARD STATIONS

But how do you connect your phone to all the other people you may ever want to call? You need an expansive network and intermediary connection points called switchboards. The telephone network begins at home with your own landline. A pair of copper wires connects the phone to a thick cable containing hundreds of wires from other local landlines. This cable then runs to the switchboard, where the cables are once again separated, and each is attached to a switch.

The switchboard is a large board with many jacks: one for each landline. Install a small lightbulb above each jack. When someone picks up the receiver on their phone, the hook switch closes the circuit and lets current flow through the wires between your home and the switchboard operator. Wire the small light bulb into the same circuit so that it is illuminated when the connection is made. The operator plugs their own microphone into the line and, after identifying who you would like to talk to, sends a "ring" signal to the receiving side. When the other end picks up the line, the operator connects the wires of the two interlocutors. If you don't feel like paying operators to whittle away their life connecting phone lines, create automatic switching stations.

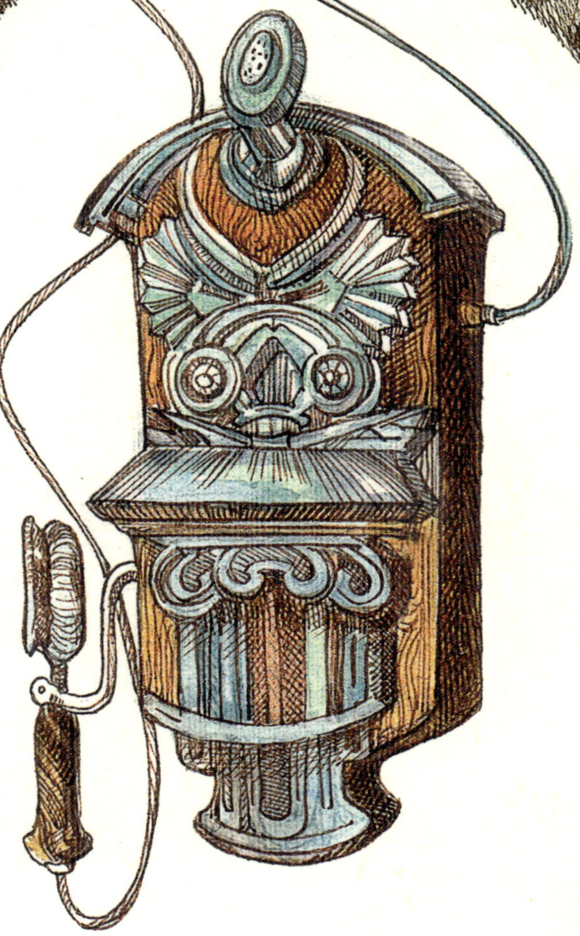

CIPHERS

The desire to know what others are doing is as old as communication itself, and people are willing to do a lot for information. The course of lives, fortunes, even the destinies of entire countries can be changed forever by a single message falling into the wrong hands. To make sure your secrets remain between you and your intended confidant, you'll need to encrypt them — record the information in some sort of secret way. The letters of each word can be altered according to an algorithm and replaced by other letters, numbers or symbols. You should learn your encryption algorithm by heart, as well as the way to decrypt messages, known as the key. There are endless options for secret codes!

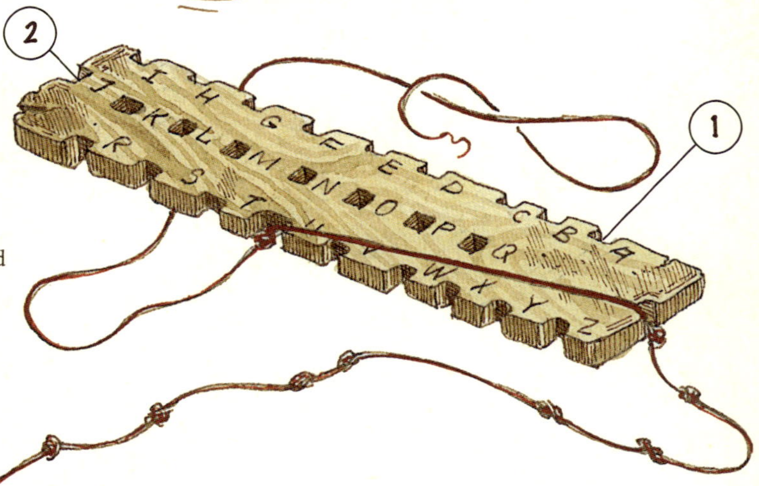

RULER

A plank and string can become a simple device for encryption. Make a notch (1) for each letter of the alphabet or symbol you wish to encrypt and make a key indicating which indent stands for which letter. Make a groove (2) in the center of one end of the plank. Now, fix your string in this groove, marking your starting point, and pull it towards the notch corresponding to the first letter of the encrypted text. Tie a knot where the thread passes over the notch. Then return the string to the central slot with this new knot as the starting point and repeat the process with the remaining letters. When you have finished encryption, remove the thread with knots from the board — this is your secret message. Whoever receives the message should have an identical copy of the original encryption board so that they can use it to "read" the knotted string.

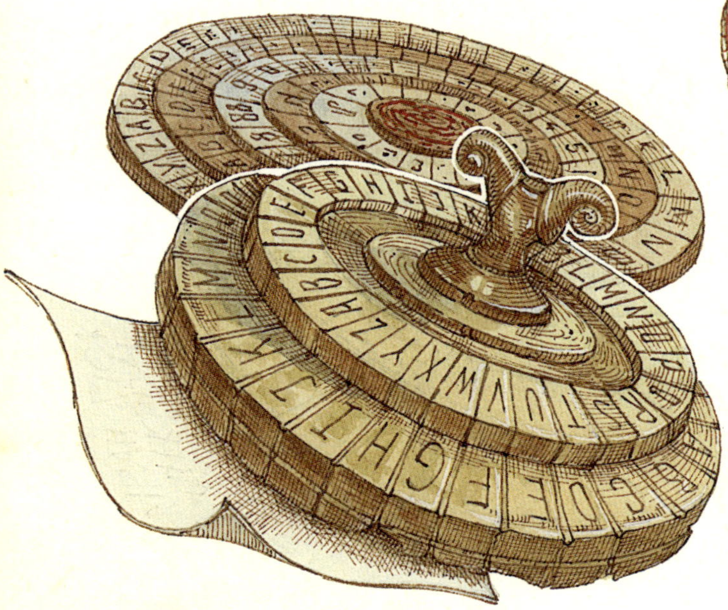

DISC

Make two discs of different diameters. Divide each into 24 sections. Write the alphabet and numbers around the outside edge of the larger disc. On the smaller disc, write the same letters and numbers but in a different order. This will be the key to the cipher. Connect the disks together in the center so that the smaller disk rotates relative to the larger one. To encrypt text, turn the wheel to a certain position and then write your message, replacing the desired letter on the outer disc with the corresponding letter on the inner disc. After that, move the inner disk and encrypt the new letter from the new position. Continue the process until you've completed the entire text. Now only those who have the same device and information about how you moved the discs during encryption will be able to read it.

SQUARES

Draw a square with 36 cells. Then divide the field into four equal sections and number each from 1 to 9. You should start by numbering the outer corners of the grid and move clockwise. Now mark the numbers from 1 to 9 so that they do not repeat in different sectors (for example, if you write a 2 in the first zone, then it can no longer be used in other zones). Cut out the squares with marked numbers — your lattice key is ready. To encrypt the text, attach the grid to a blank sheet of paper and fill in all the slots in order with the letters of your message. When you run out of holes in one sector, rotate the grate 90 degrees and continue writing. You can make three such turns. As a result, the entire sheet of paper will be filled with completely unreadable text. The message can only be read with a grid. Write down and read characters down from the top and from left to right.

BOOK CIPHER

Take a book to practice. Search through it until you find the first word of the message you want to encrypt. Record its address: the page number and the line where this word is located, as well as its numerical order on the line. Count the lines ignoring titles. You will get a code consisting of three numbers. Repeat the procedure with all the words of the encrypted message. The result will be a sequence of three-number sets, for example:

371, 17, 3 | 206, 4, 9 | 390, 12, 3 | 75, 3, 6 | 272, 25, 5 | 140, 22, 1
68, 1, 8 | 359, 4, 4 | 150, 5, 10

5	8	6	1	0	9
1	2	3	2	4	7
7	0	1	7	8	5
8	3	5	9	0	8
6	4	4	1	6	9
7	6	5	2	9	1

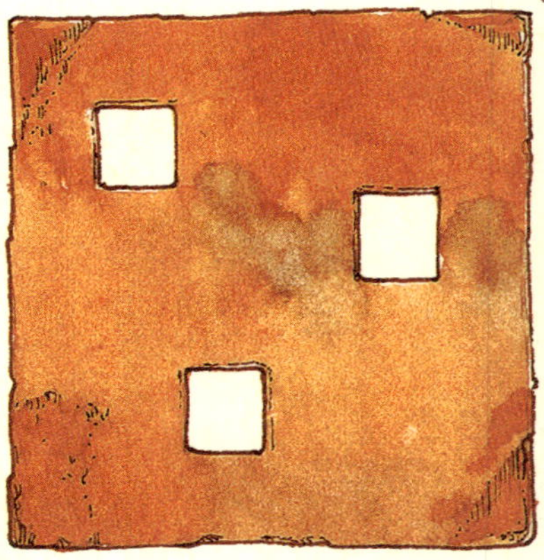

ENCODING MACHINE

There are several interchangeable rotors (1) — wheels with electrical contacts interconnected by gears. Each is divided into 26 parts, one for each letter (2). By pressing the key with the letter (3), the outer rotor moves by one gear tooth. The electric circuit connected to the battery (4) closes, and the current passes through all the rotors to the light bulb with the corresponding letter (5). This is used to encrypt the message.

Any time the rotor turns, a new chain is formed, so the same letter typed on the keyboard receives a new code each time. Once everything is encoded, you'll get a set of letter codes. They need to be transmitted by radio to their addressee. The way the letters are eventually encoded depends on the initial position of the rotors. Your addressee, who has the same machine, will put the rotors in the same position, type in the seemingly meaningless set of letters received by radio and receive your decoded message.

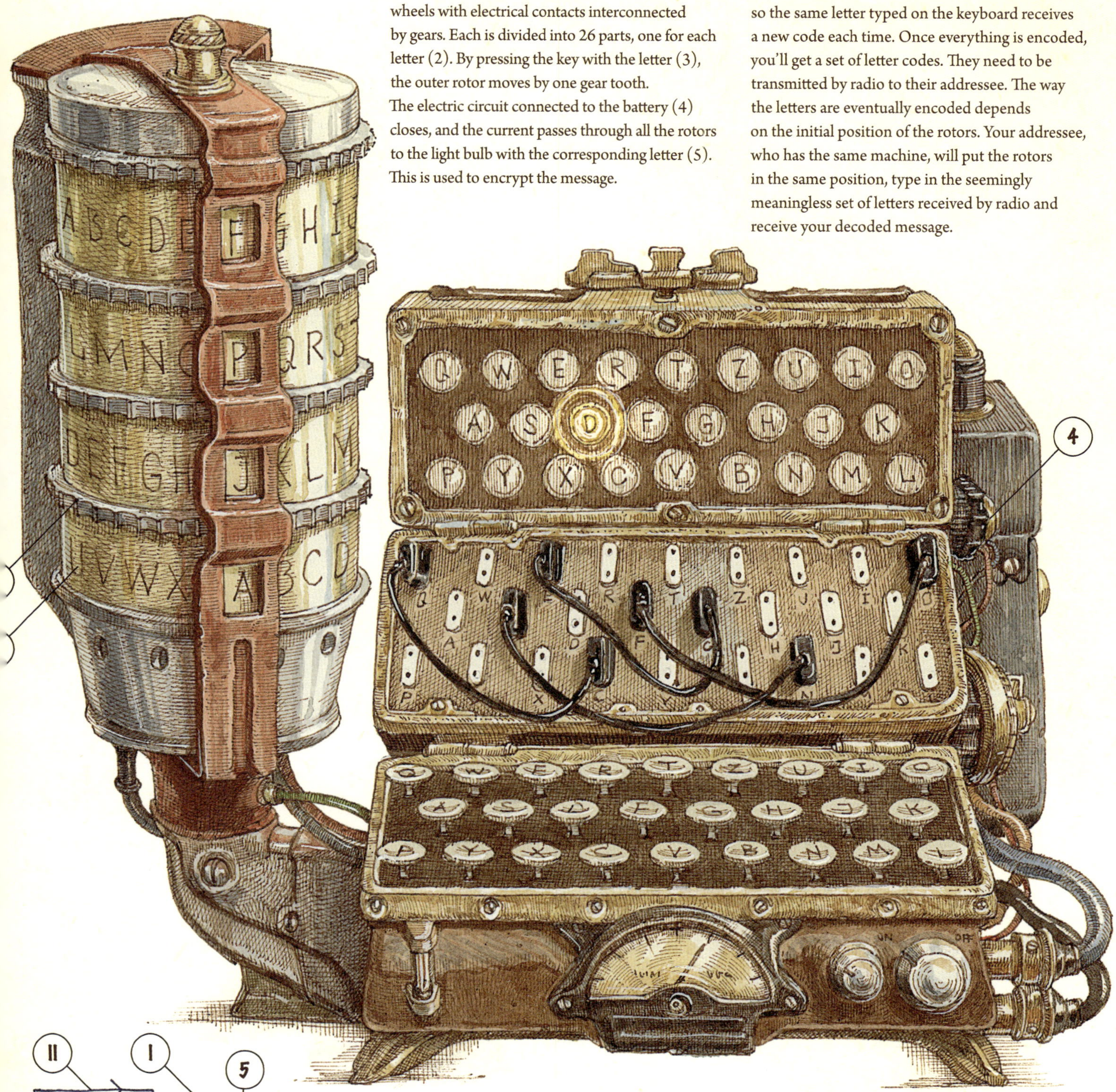

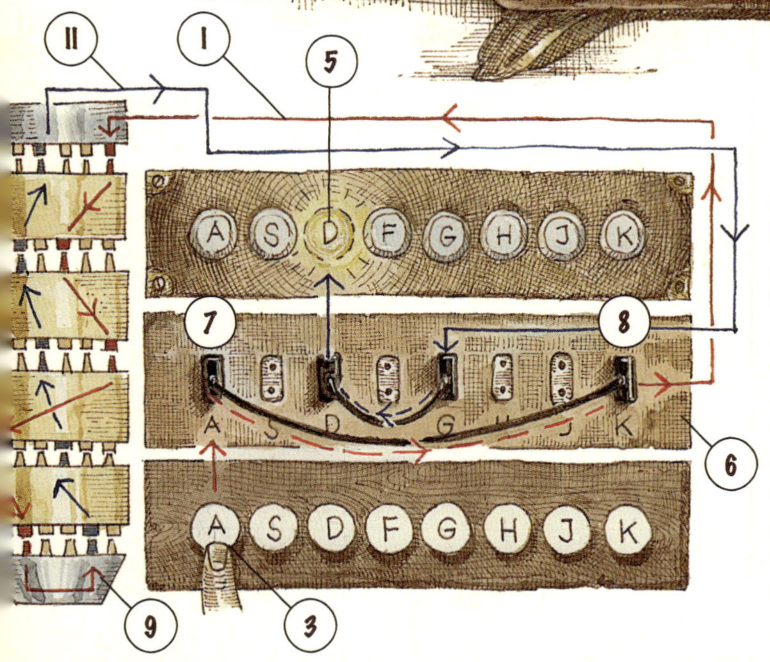

SWITCHBOARD

The switchboard (6) encodes messages by switching the input and output signals of the letters. Each letter has two sockets (7 and 8) connected by a wire. The signal coming from the switchboard panel is transmitted through the rotor, passes in turn through all four rotors (I) and enters the reflector (9). This fixed rotor, having received the signal, sends it back along a new path (II), which causes another signal transformation. Without the plugboard cables, the current would go from the keypad-controlled switches straight to the input rotor and then to the code letter light bulb. But using the panel causes the two letters to swap places before they get to the input rotor. The signal created when you press the "A" key starts at position A, enters pin K and exits pin G at position D. So the switchboard further complicates the circuit the encoded letter must travel, thereby making the encryption more complex.

TYPEWRITER

If you want to keep up correspondences, put all your paperwork in order and promote the advancement of the sciences, you'll need a faster word processing machine.

Typewriters allow you to record and proliferate information quickly without forcing readers to parse out your chicken scratch. You can produce as many identical copies of a document as you need, all in neat, readable print.

Your typewriter doesn't have to be limited to letters. You can also make machines that print musical notes, or even emojis.

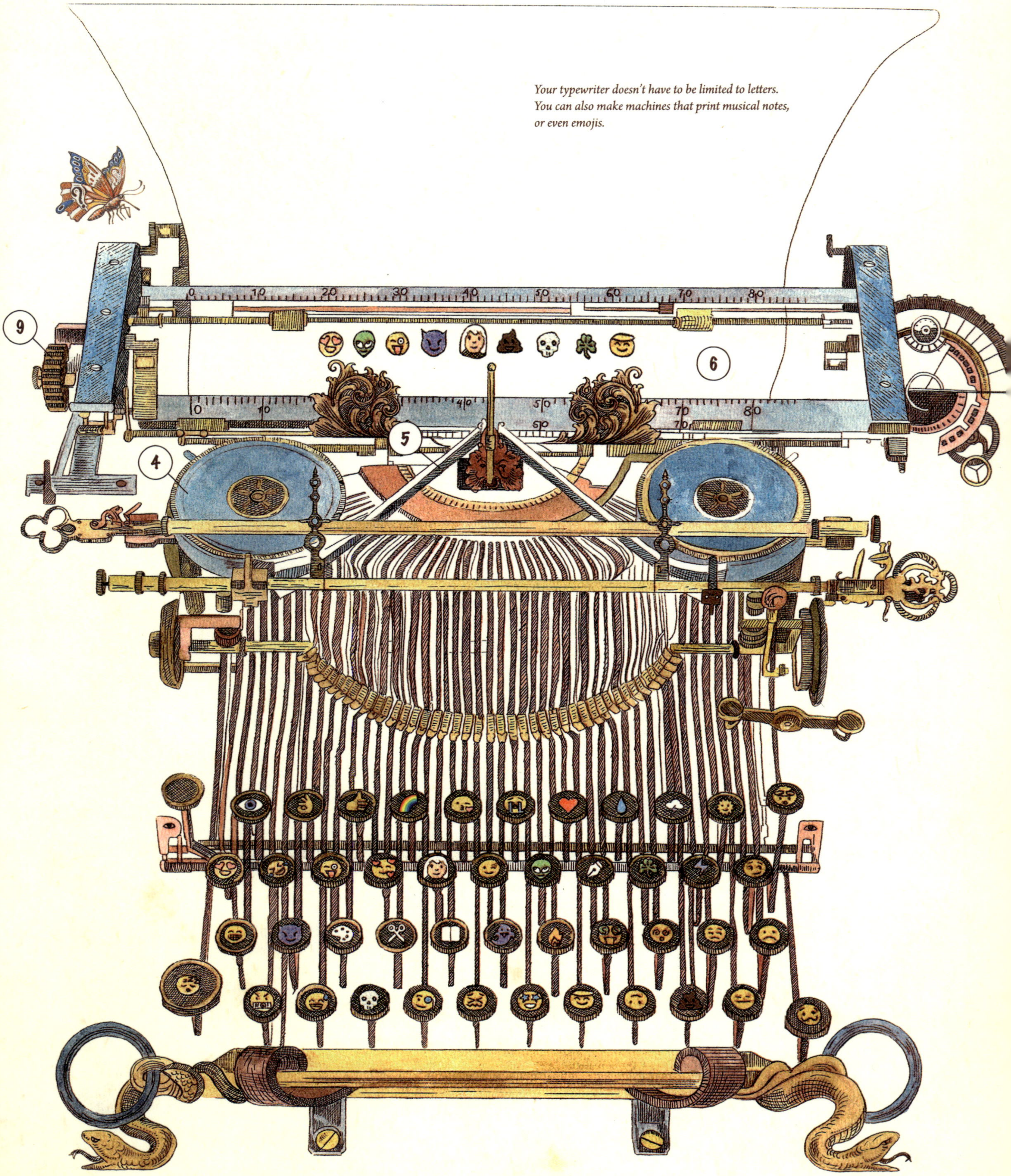

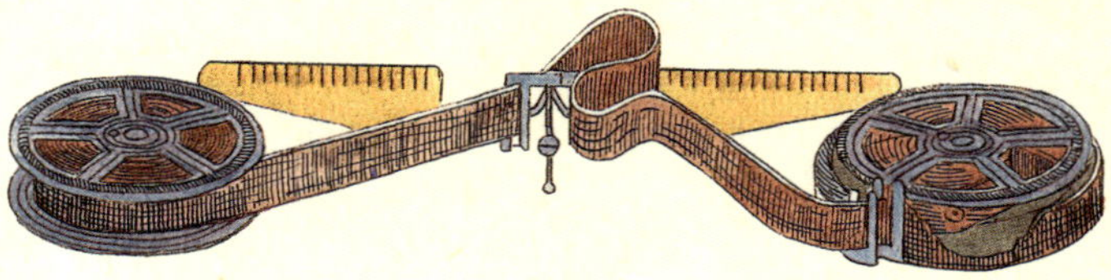

STAMP INK

To print on a typewriter, you need an ink-soaked cloth ribbon. The typewriter hammers press this ribbon against the paper, leaving an imprint of the letter behind. Use dextrin as a binder for the ink. Start by baking the starch powder at 200°C until it begins to brown. Add alcohol, pigment diluted in water and heated glycerin (it attracts moisture from the air so the tape won't dry out quickly). You can use soot obtained by burning coal as a pigment. Soot is the powder left behind on the walls of a vessel after burning wood.

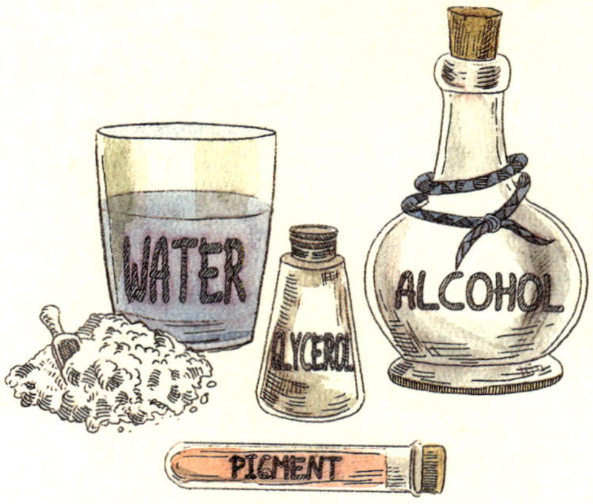

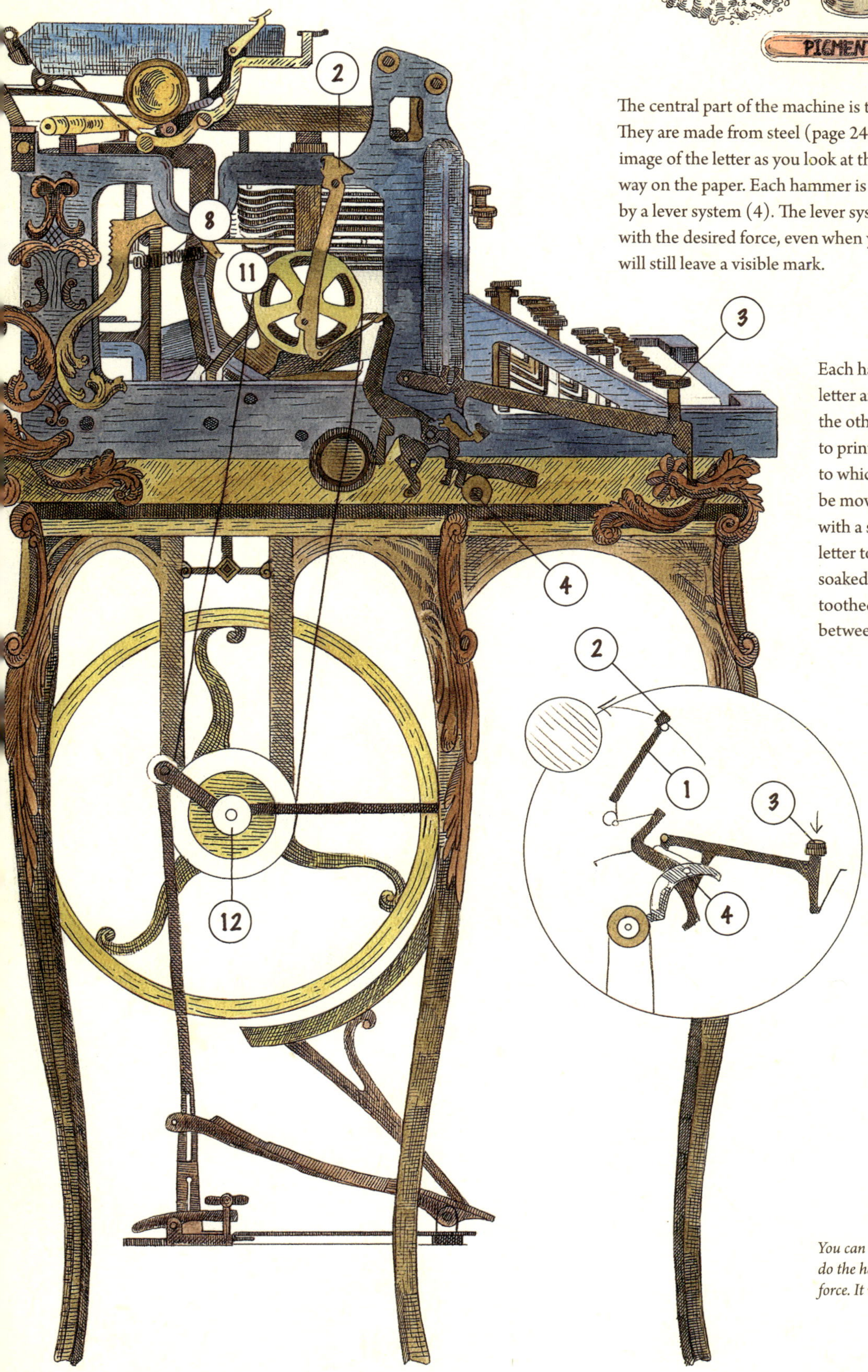

The central part of the machine is the hammers (1) with convex letters (2). They are made from steel (page 240). Note that the stamps should be a mirror image of the letter as you look at them so that they print the letter the correct way on the paper. Each hammer is connected to the corresponding key (3) by a lever system (4). The lever system allows the hammer to strike the paper with the desired force, even when you press the key very lightly, so that the ink will still leave a visible mark.

Each hammer has two letters on it: a lowercase letter and a capital letter. They are placed one below the other. You need to move the hammer up a little to print the uppercase letter. For this, the base to which all the hammer levers are attached must be movable and connected by a system of levers with a special button on the keyboard. Before the letter touches the paper, the spool (4) with the ink-soaked ribbon (5) is rotated to a specific angle using toothed cone gearing. It is lifted up and clamped between the letter and the paper (6).

The hammer strikes the paper, leaving a stamp (7). When you lift your finger from the key, the spring (8) pulls the hammer back to its original position. The carriage with the rubber rollers (9) that holds the paper in place is moved by a spring (10), a toothed wheel called an escapement (11) and two levers. The moment the hammer strikes the roller, one of the levers slips off the tooth of the wheel. At the same time, the next tooth of the stepped wheel grabs the second lever, which stops the carriage from printing the letter. The carriage shifts one space to the left and is then held in place again until the next hammer strikes.

You can add a system with a drive belt (12). The drive would do the hammering, allowing the keys to be pressed with less force. It will also increase your typing speed.

ART

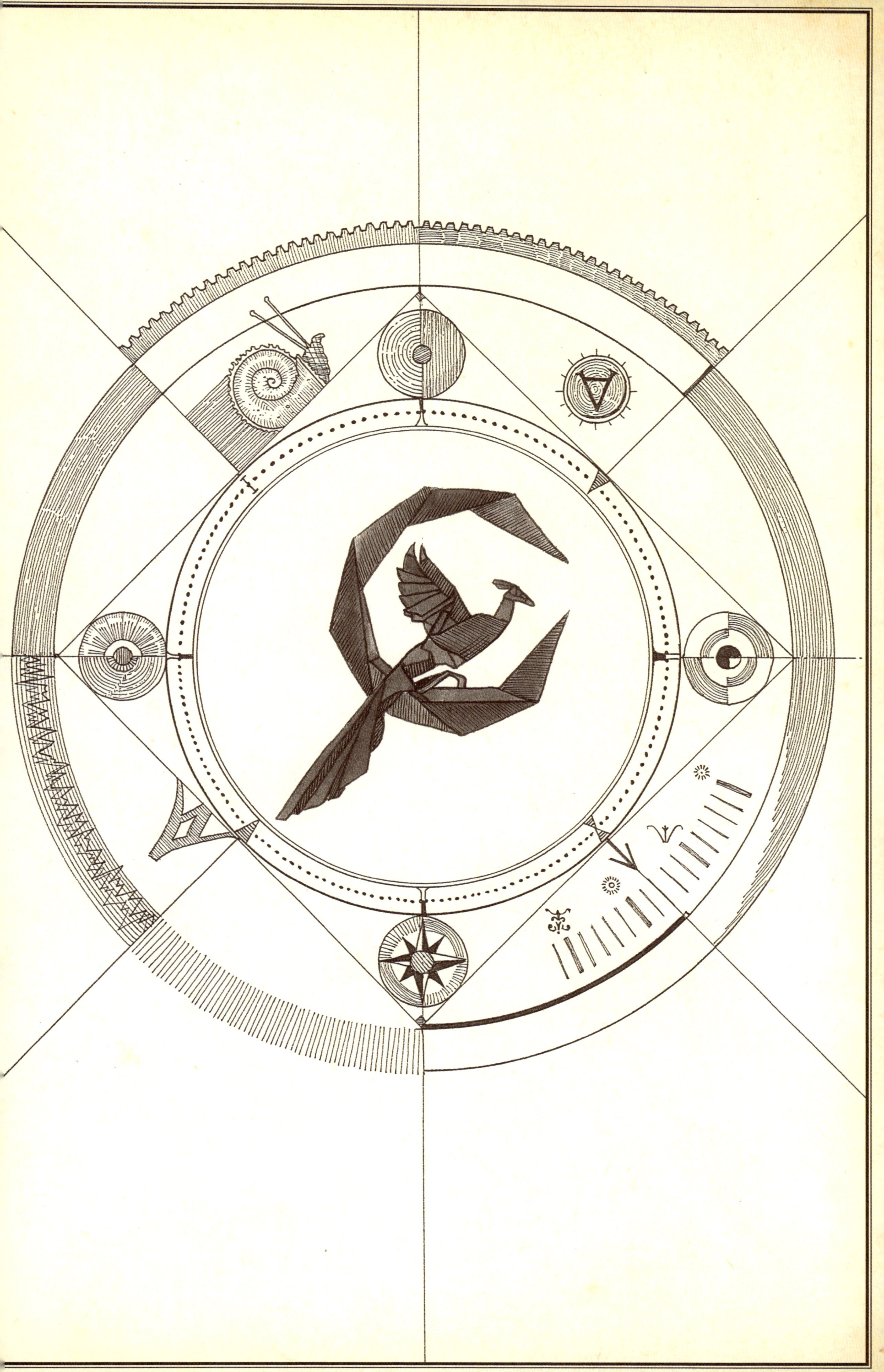

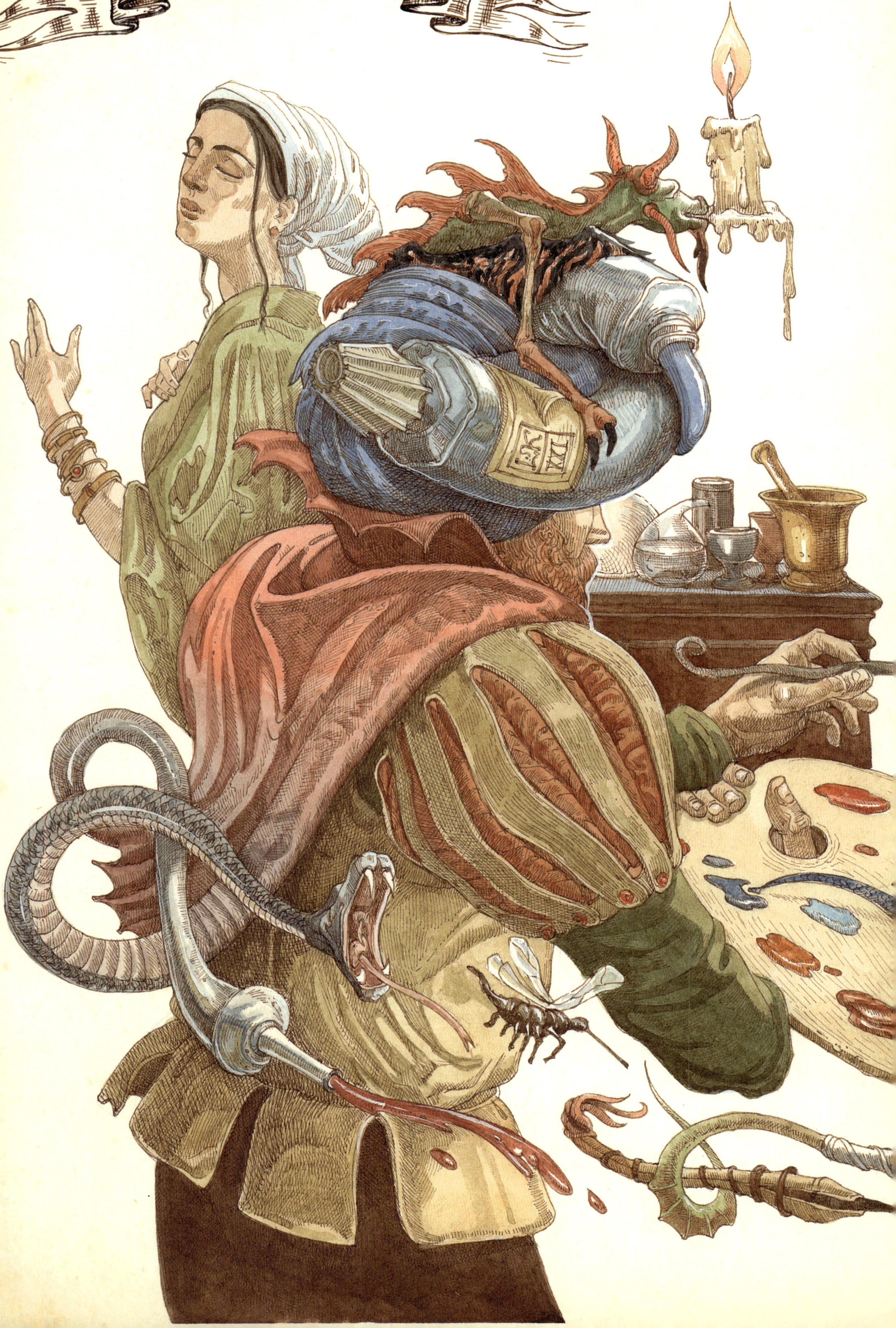

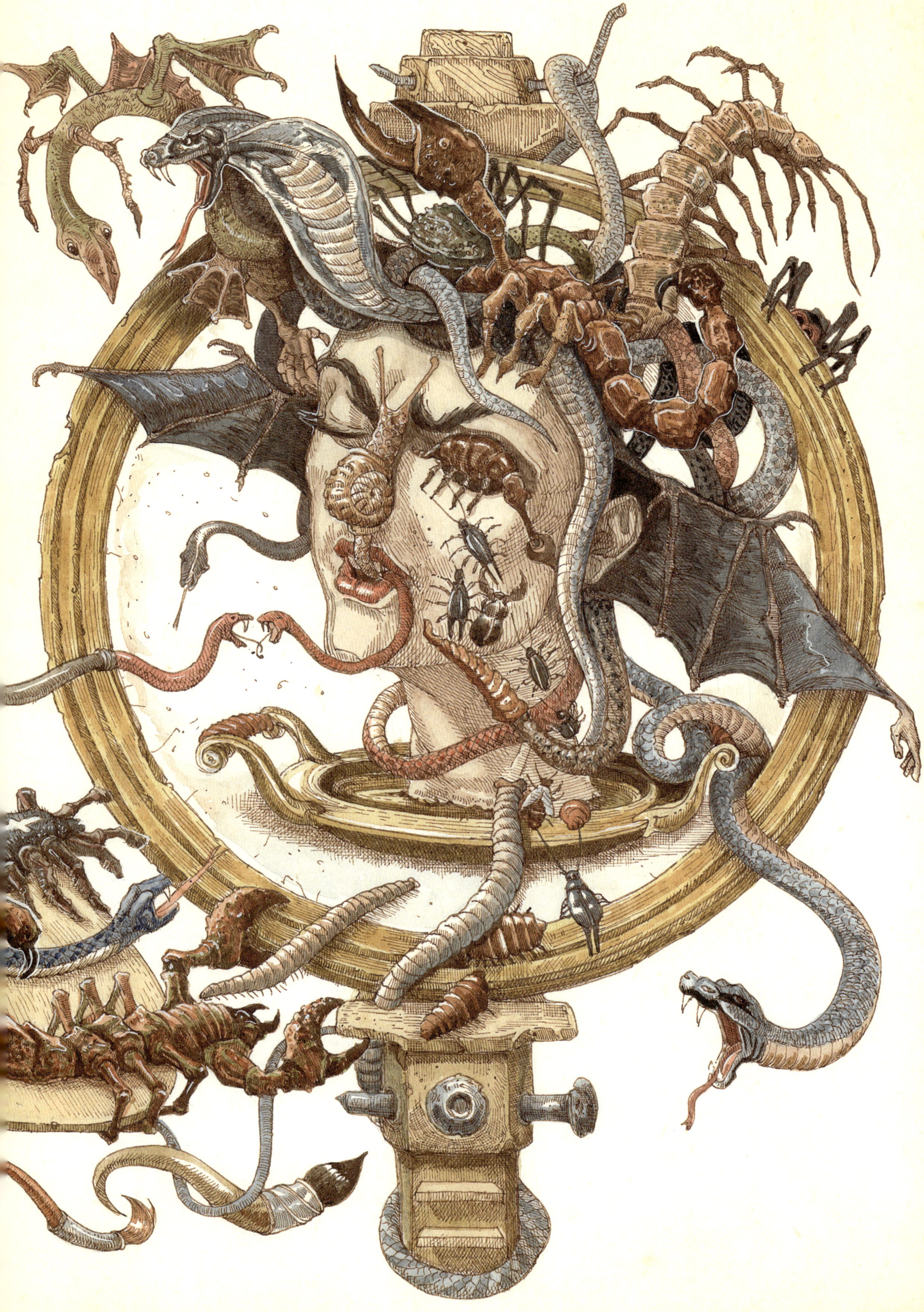

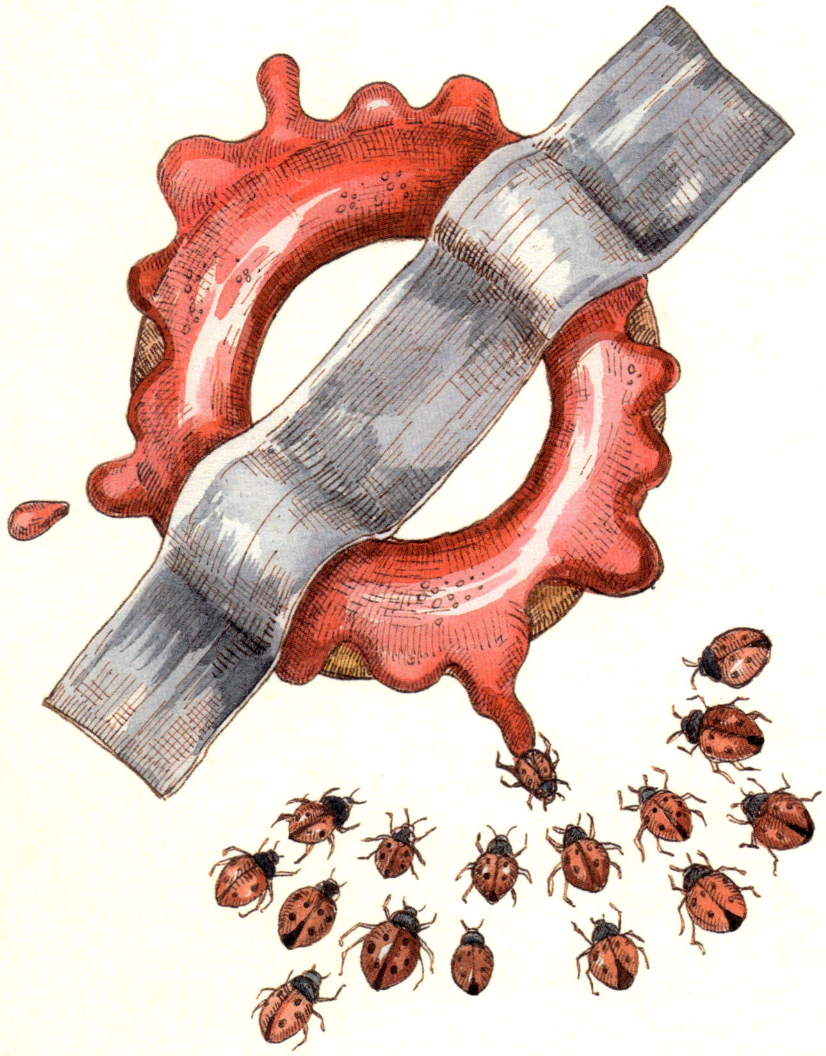

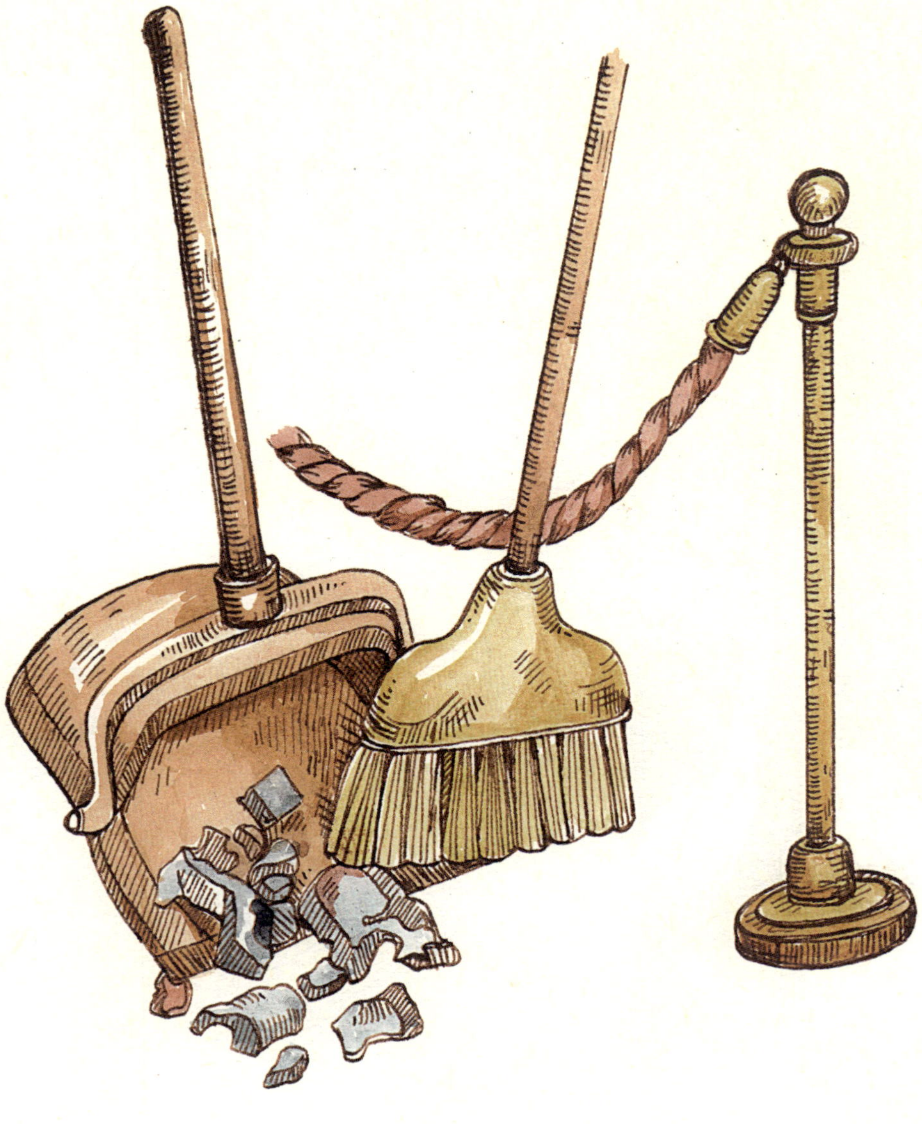

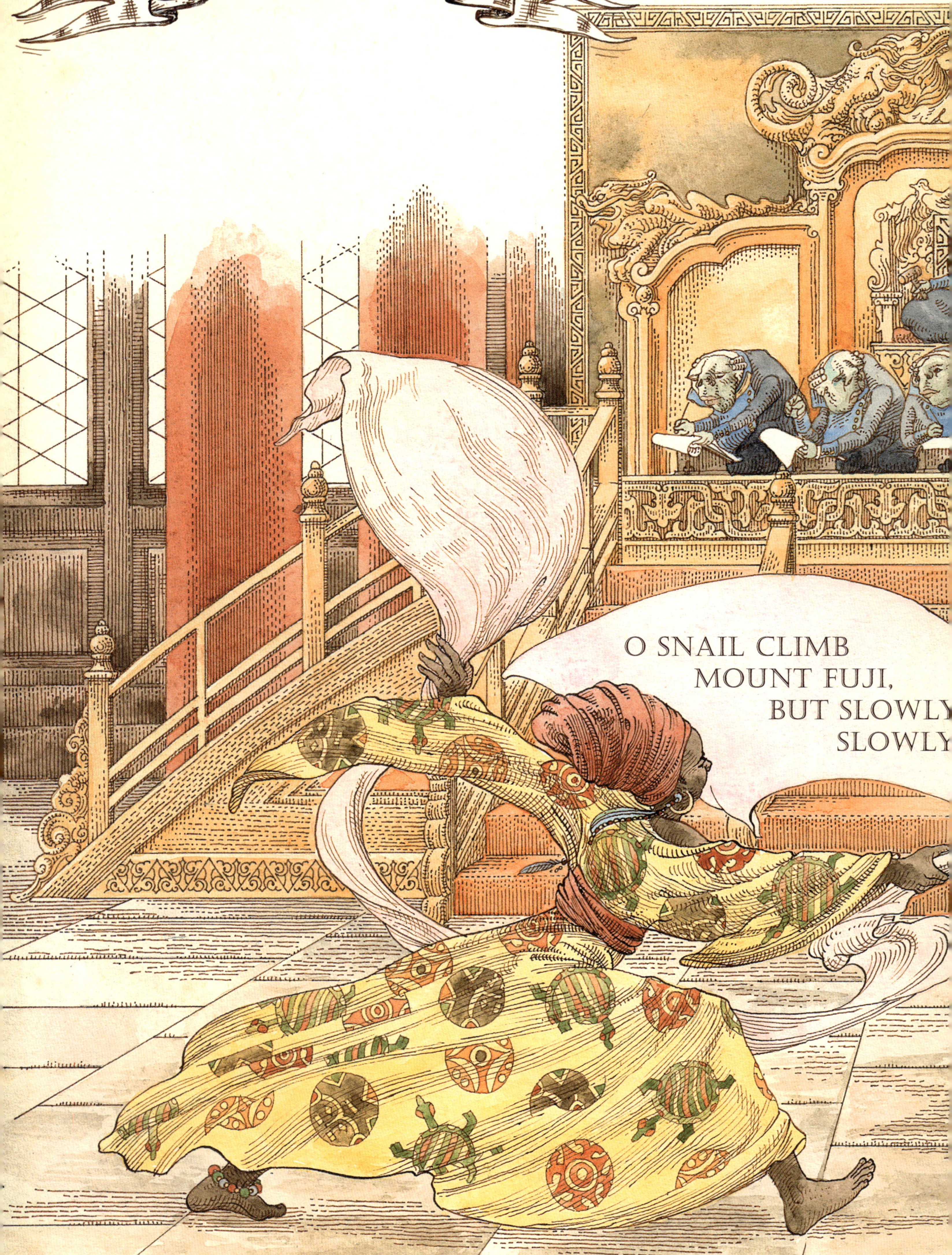
O SNAIL CLIMB
MOUNT FUJI,
BUT SLOWLY
SLOWLY

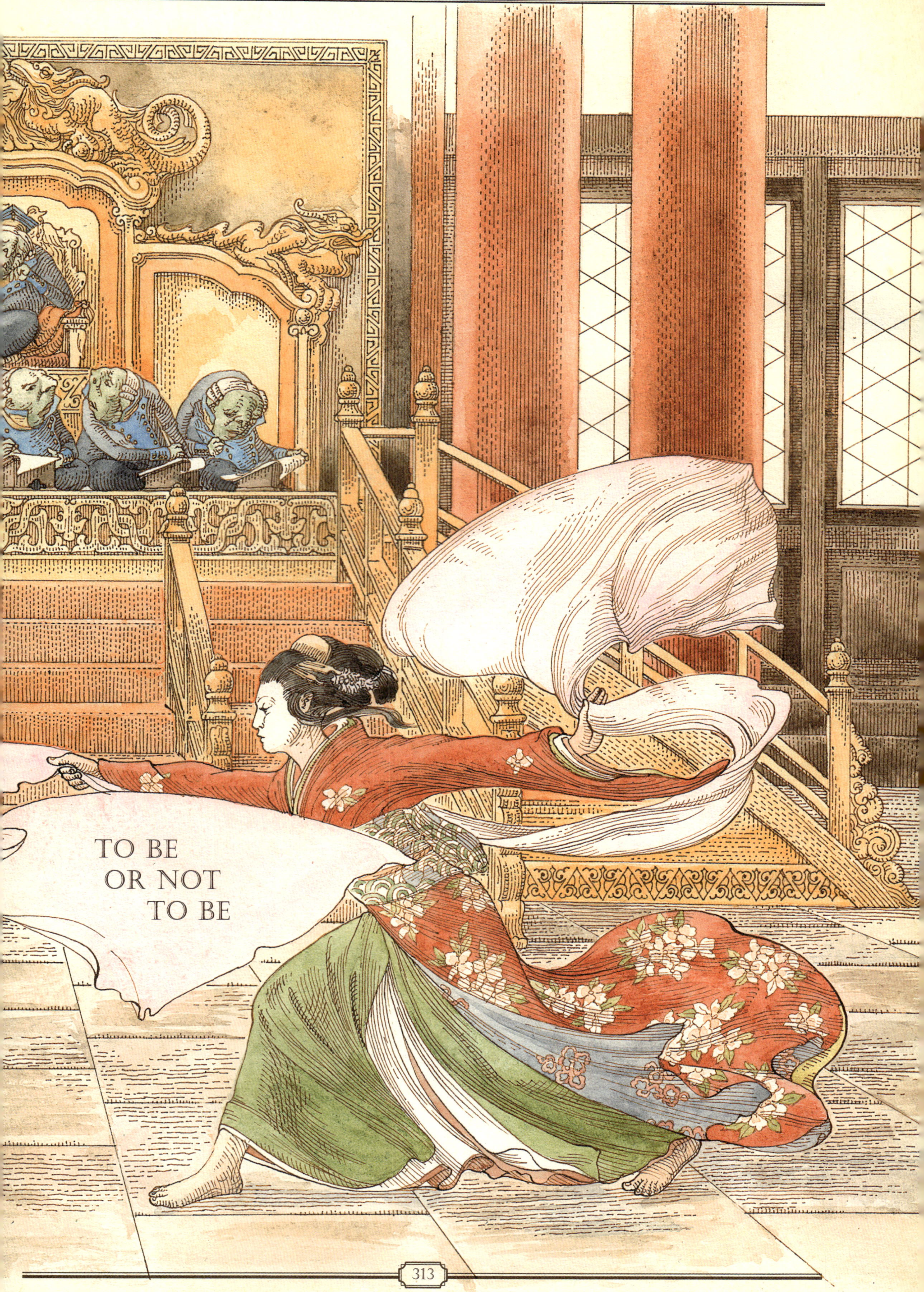
TO BE
OR NOT
TO BE

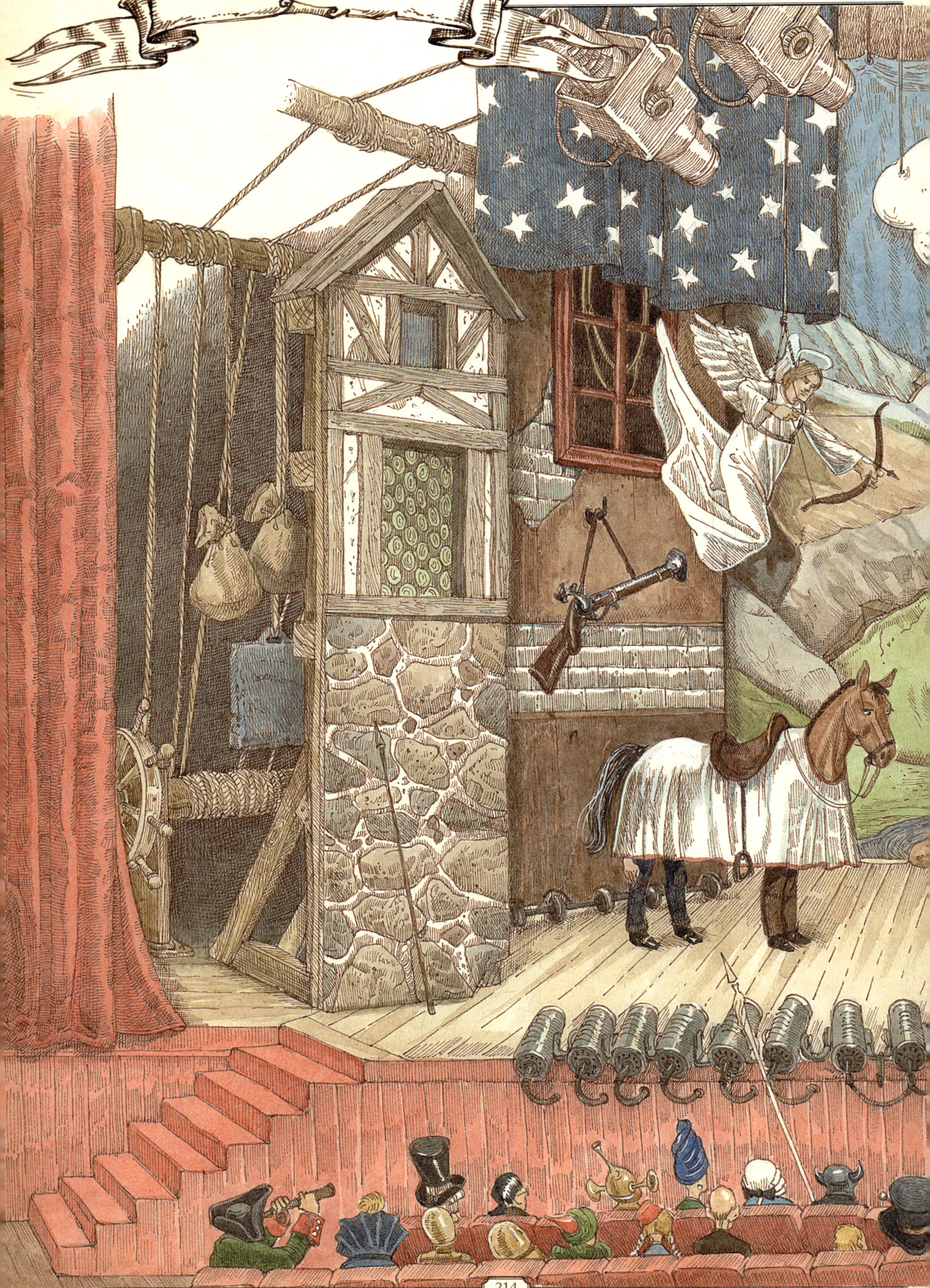

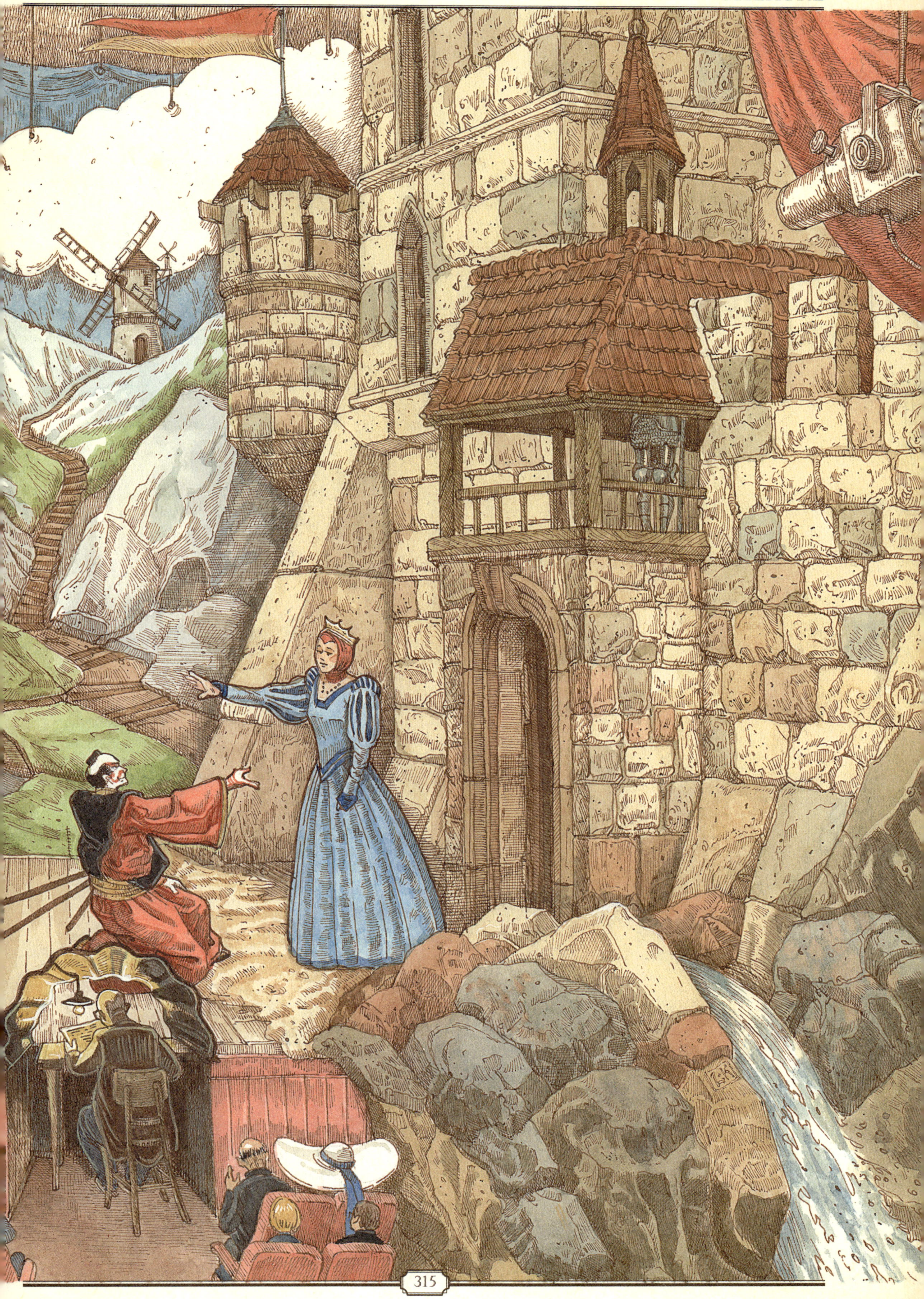

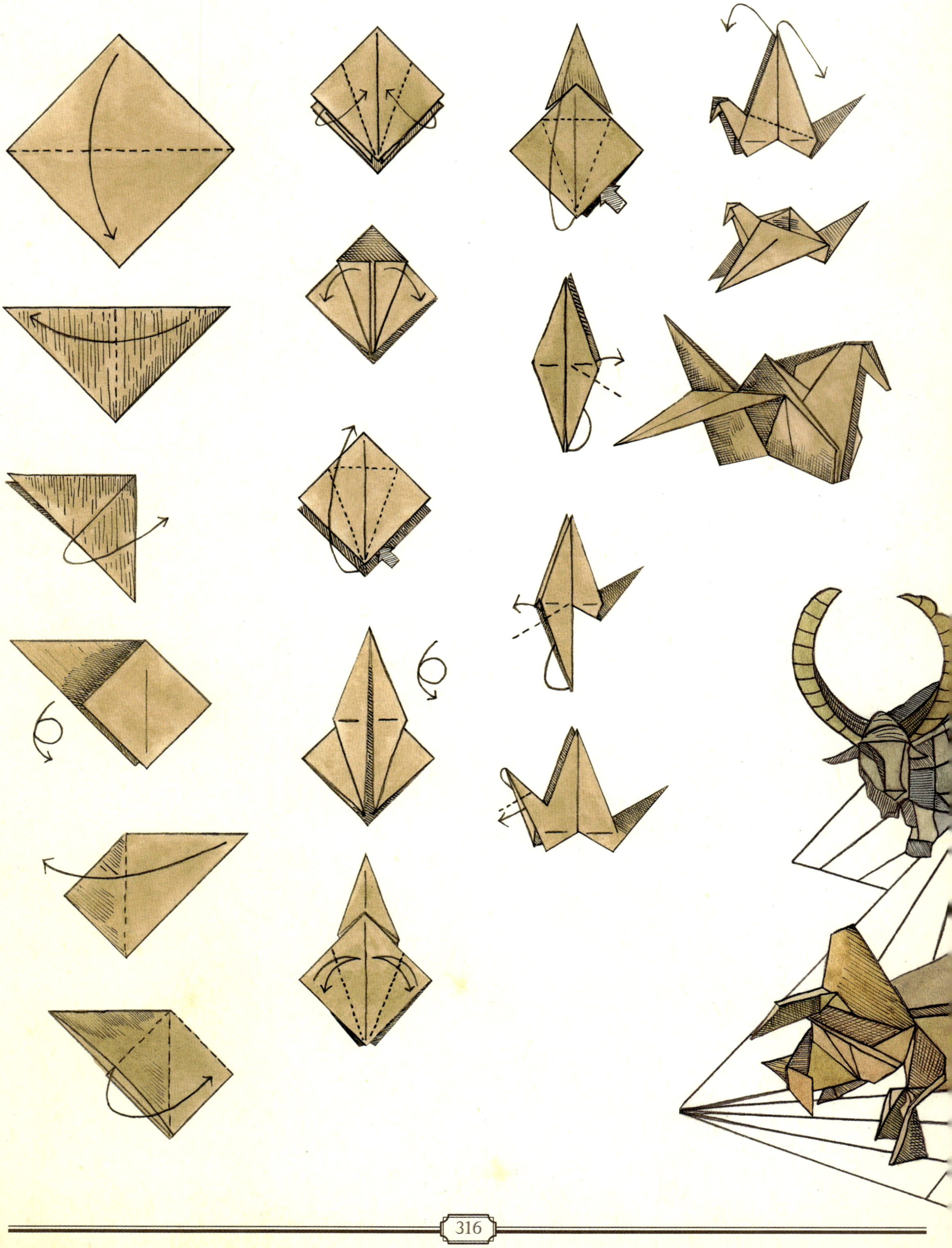

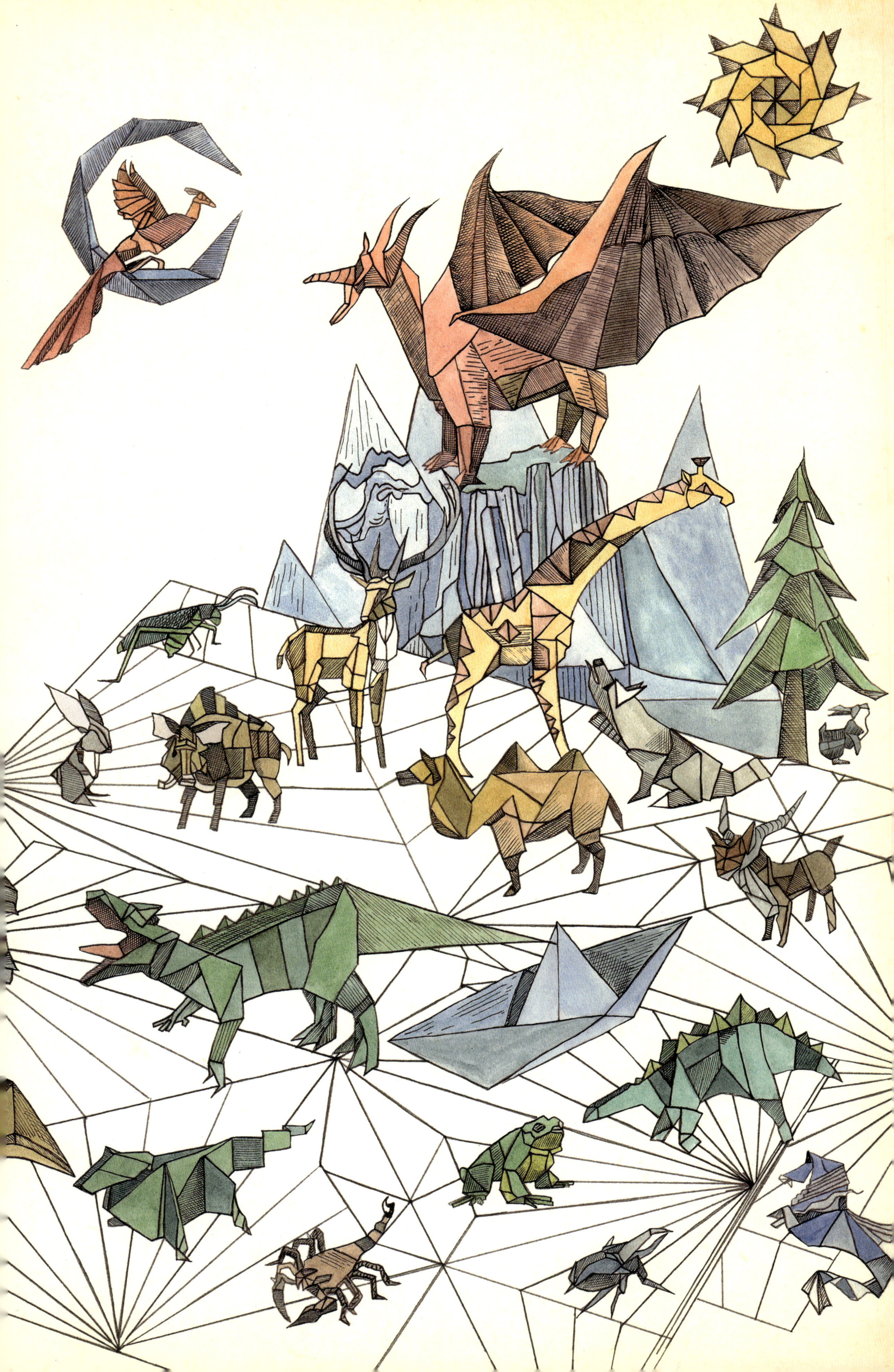

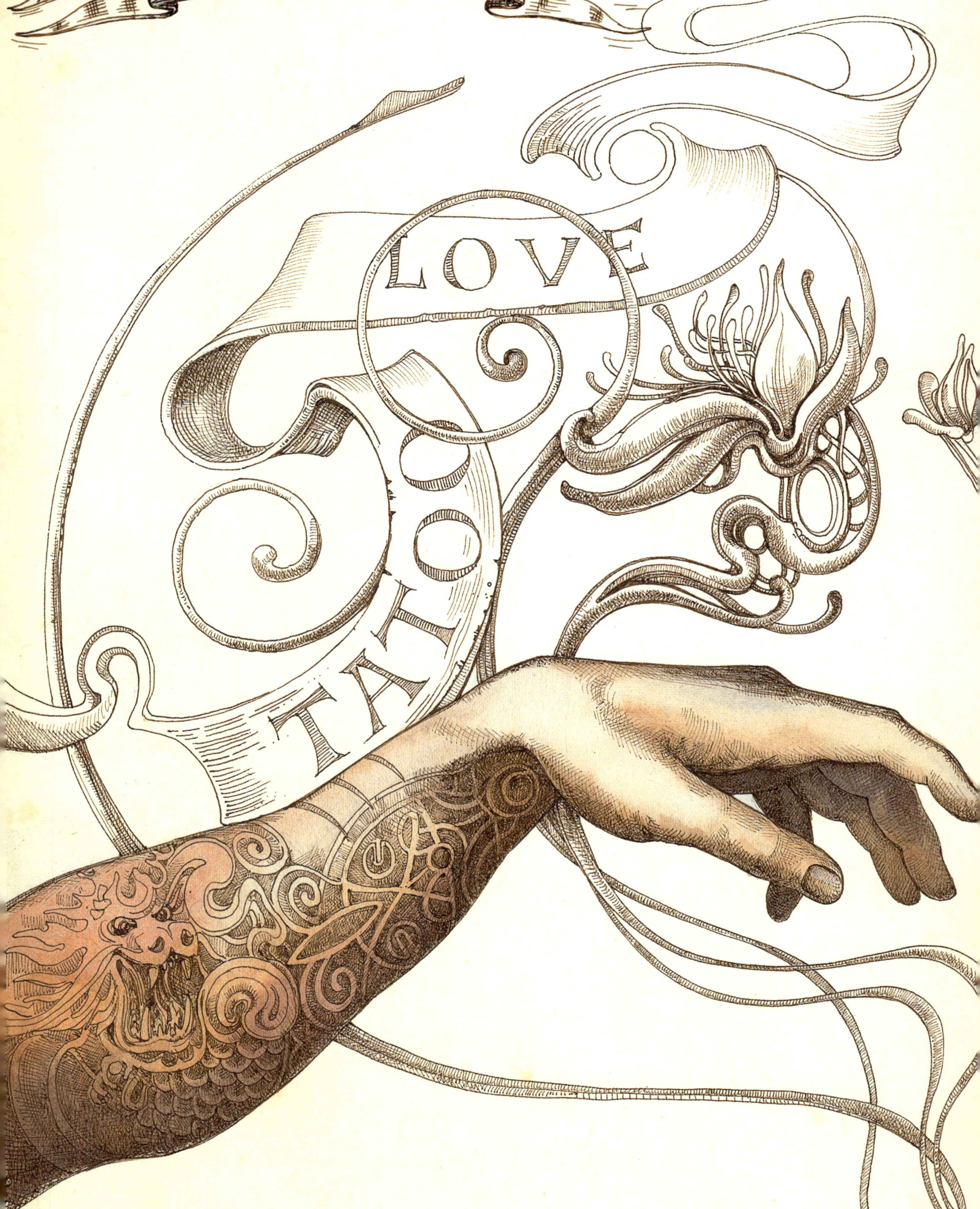
LOVE
TATTOO

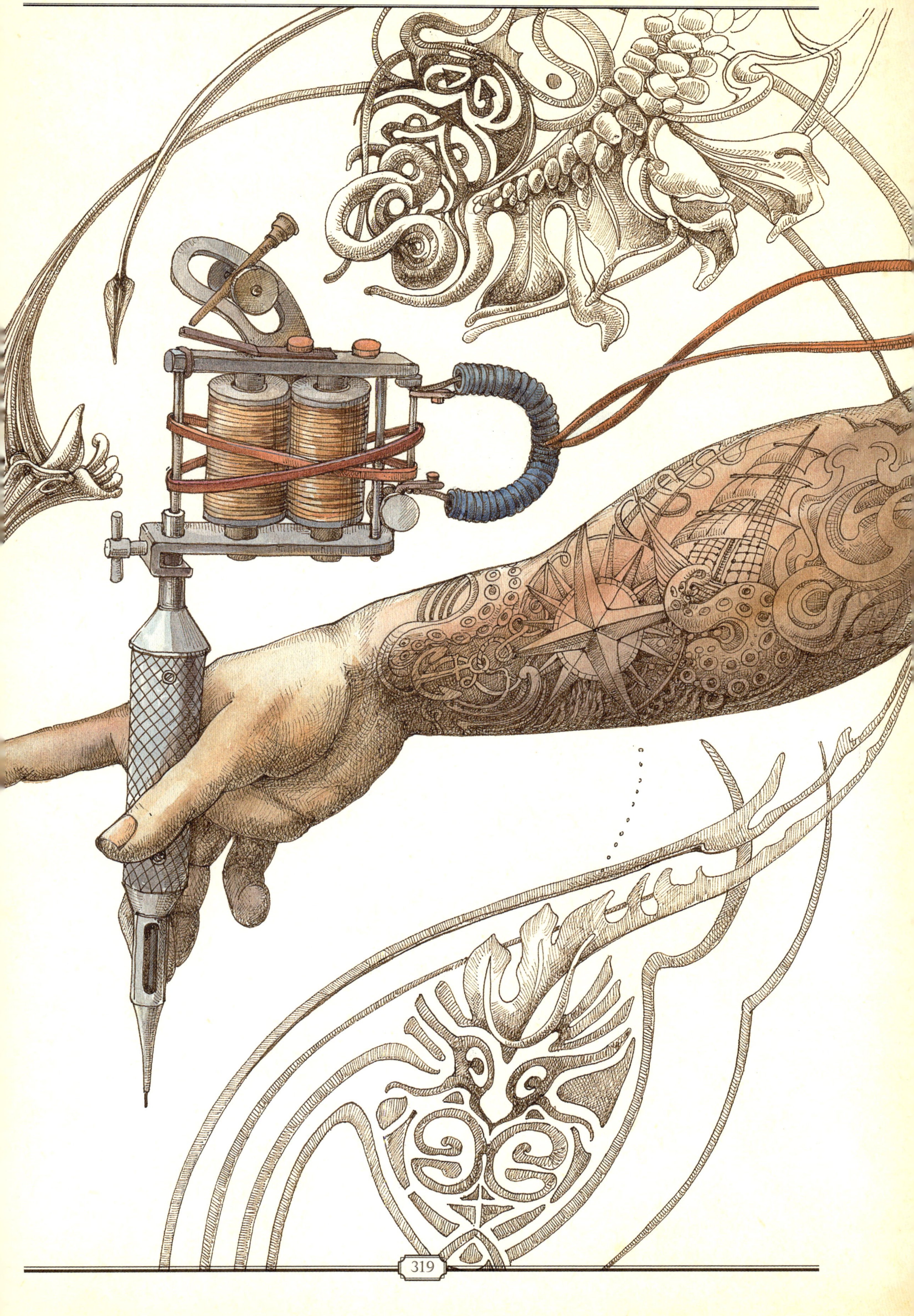

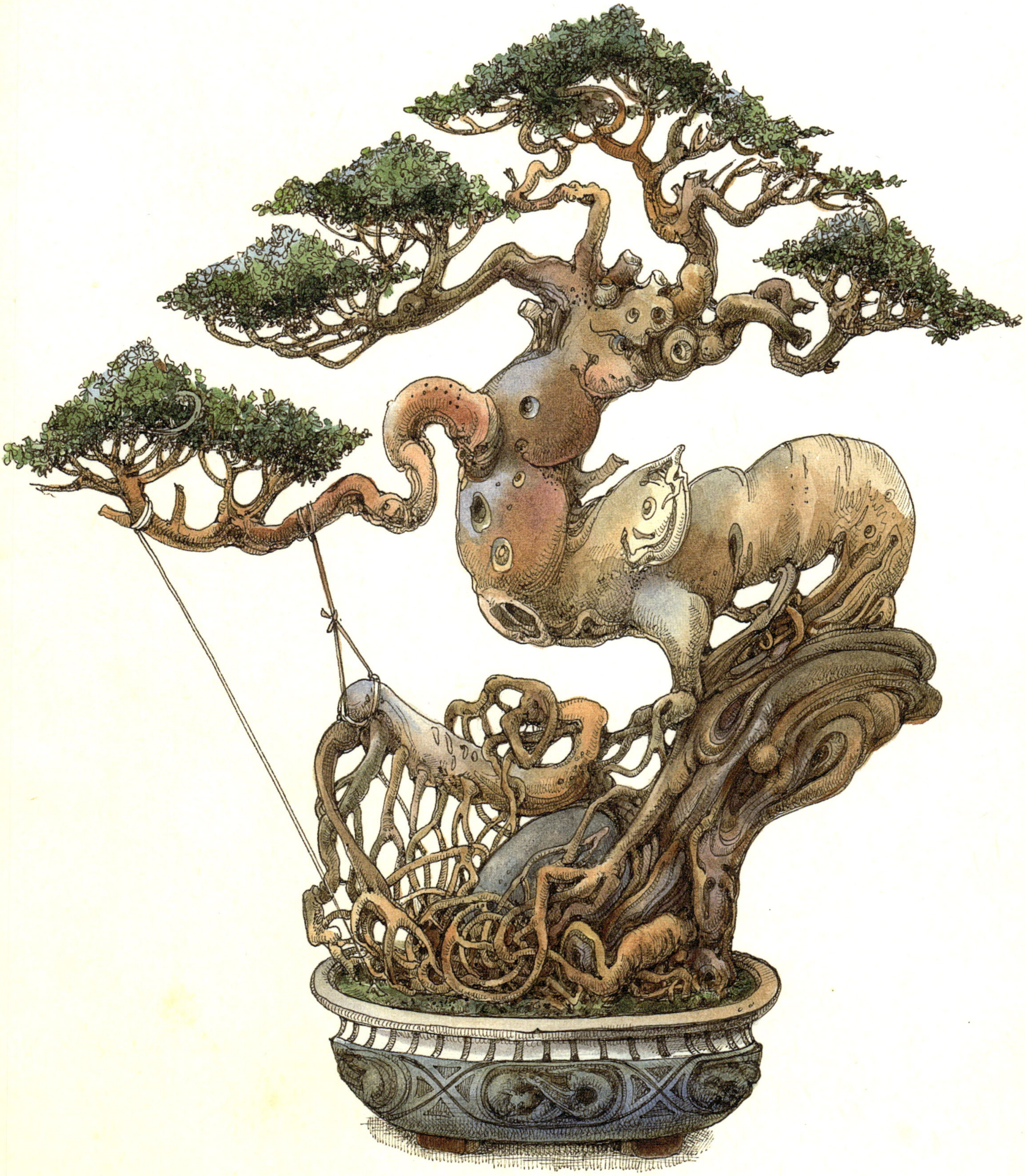

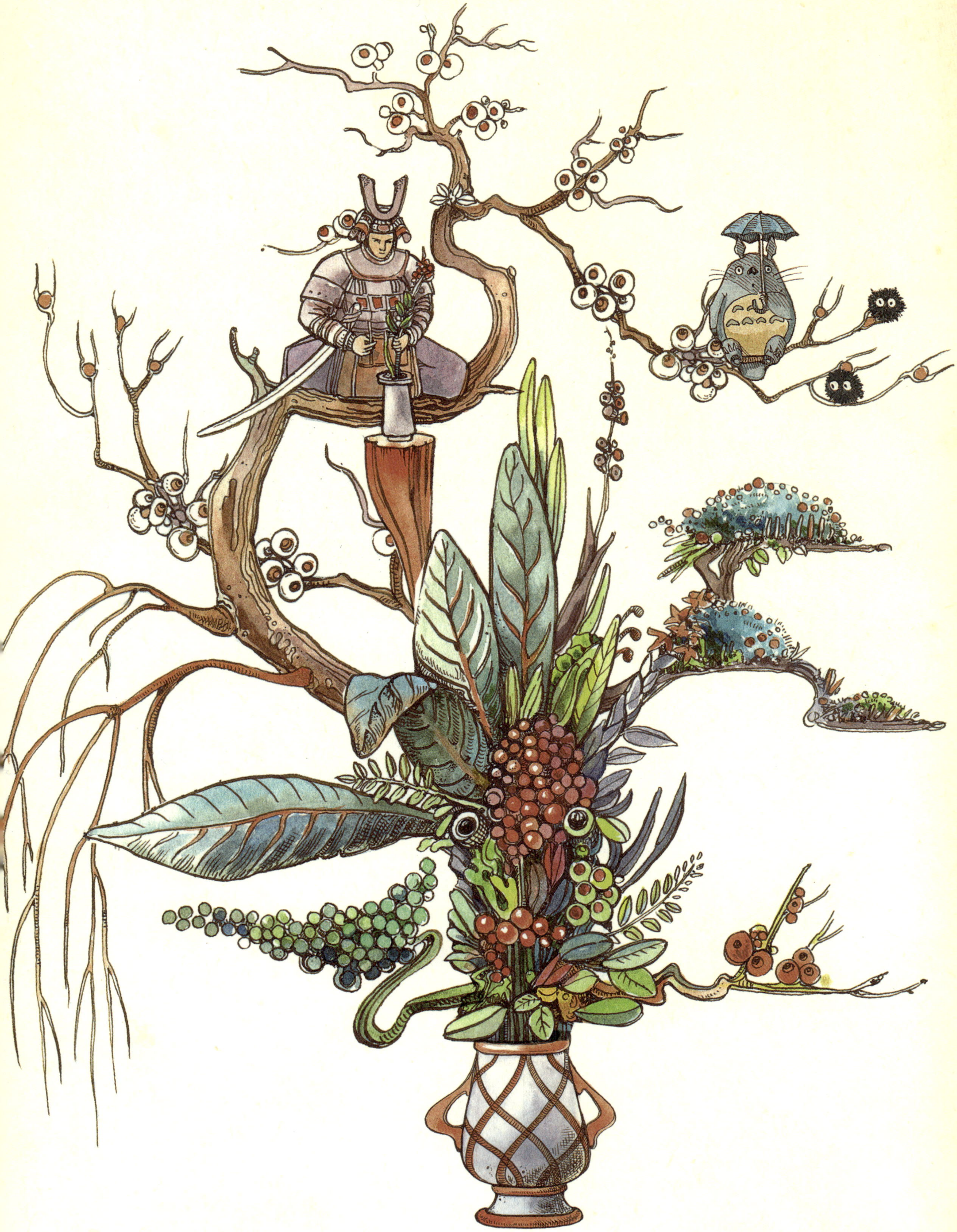

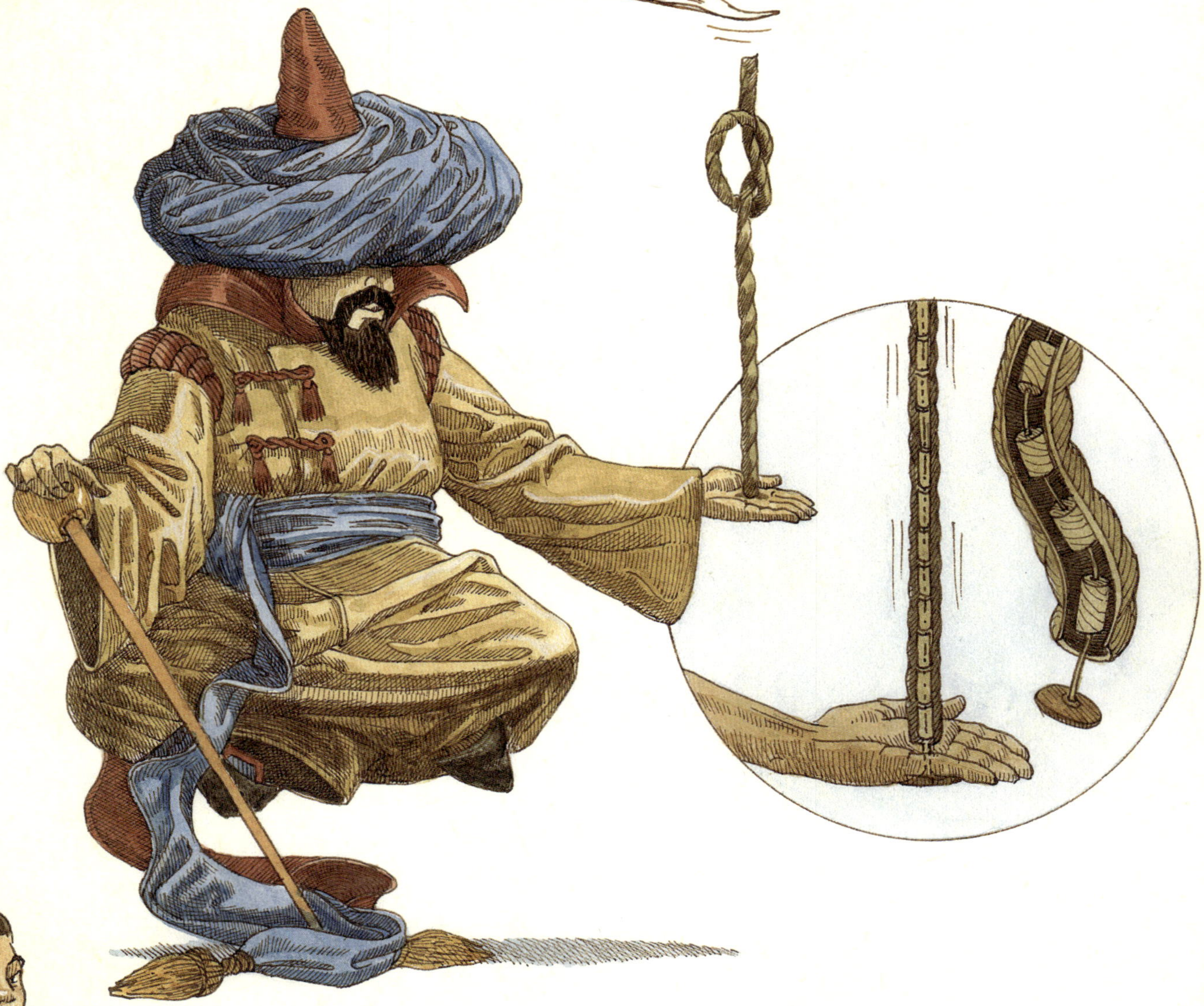

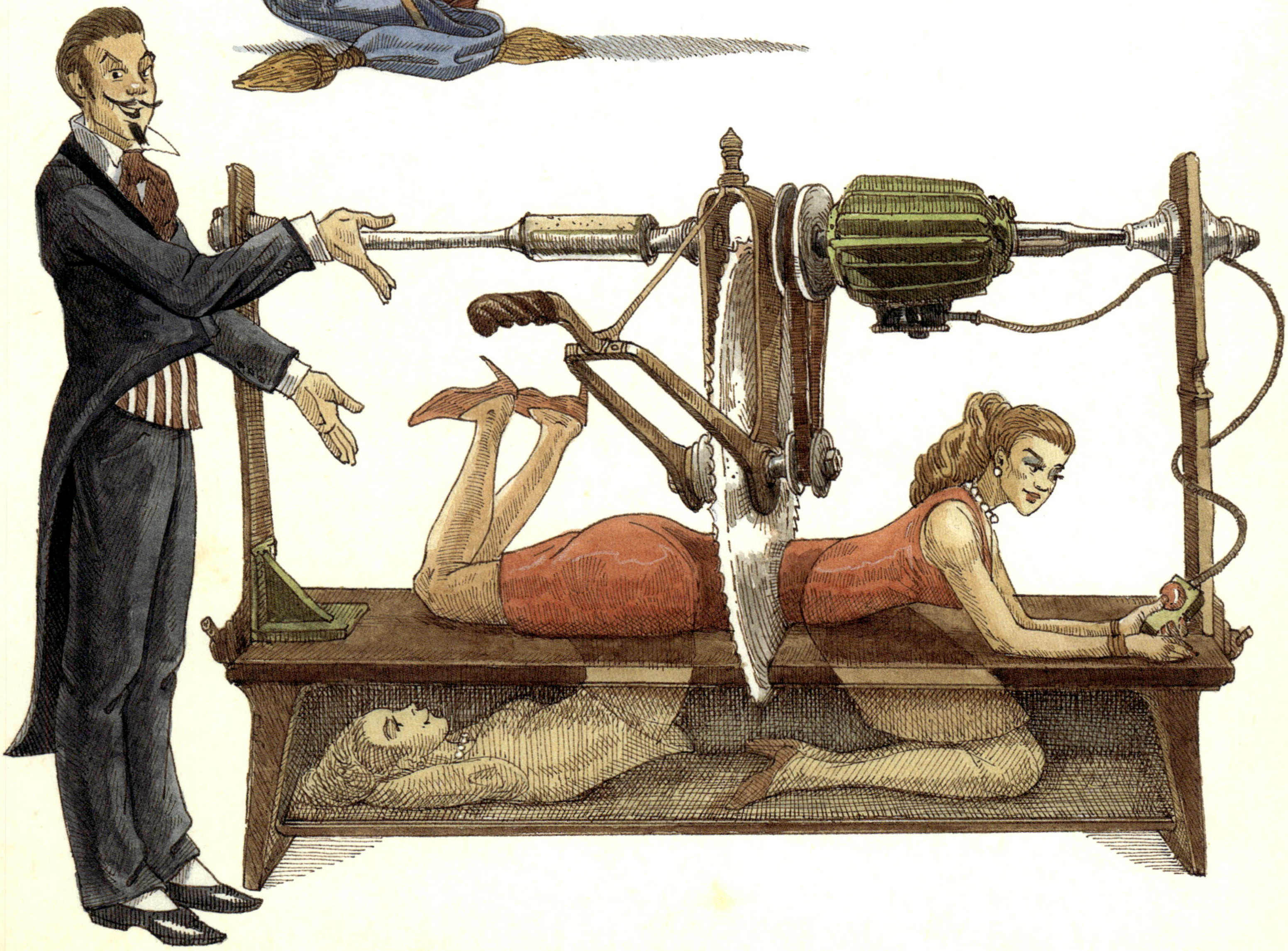

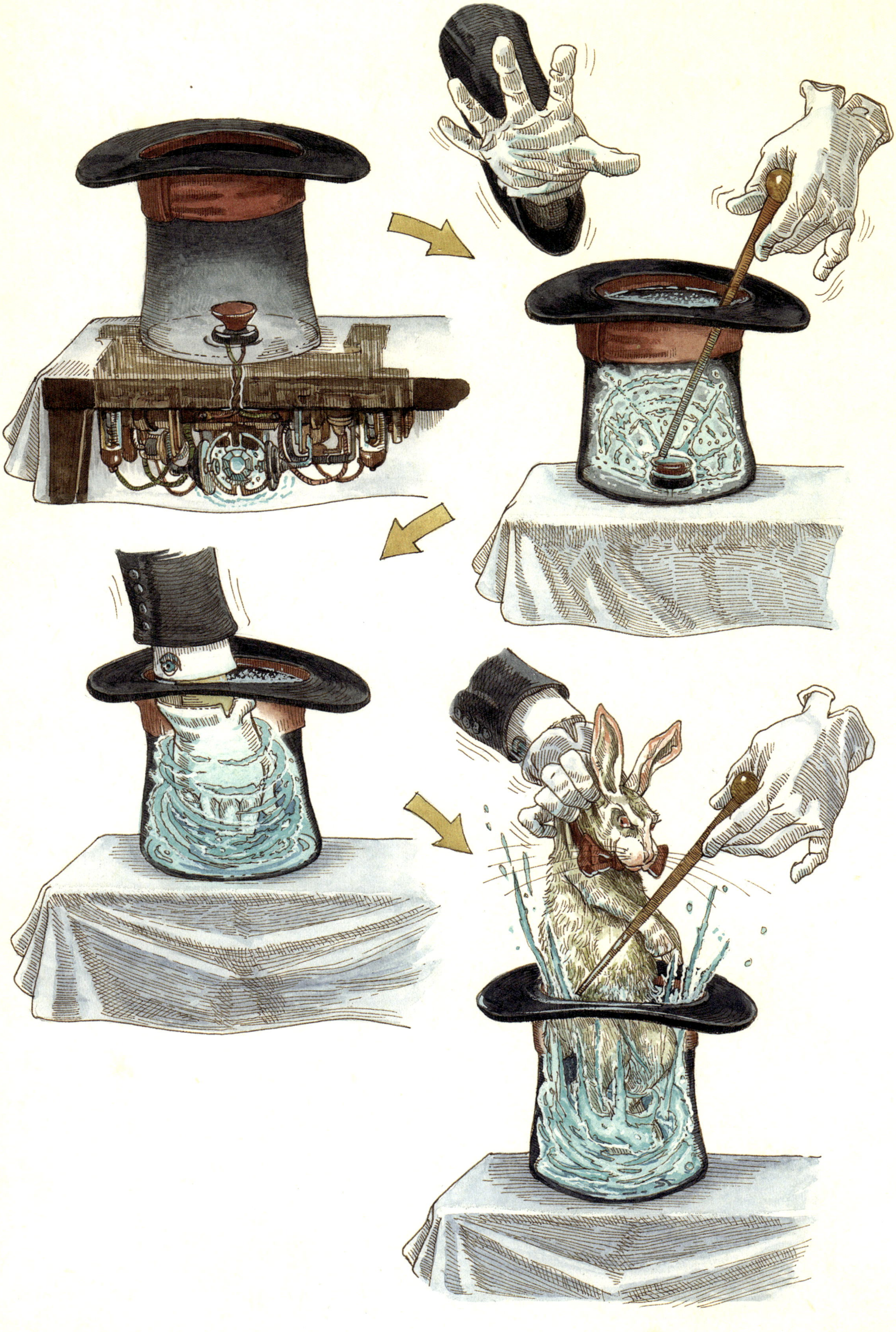

MUSIC

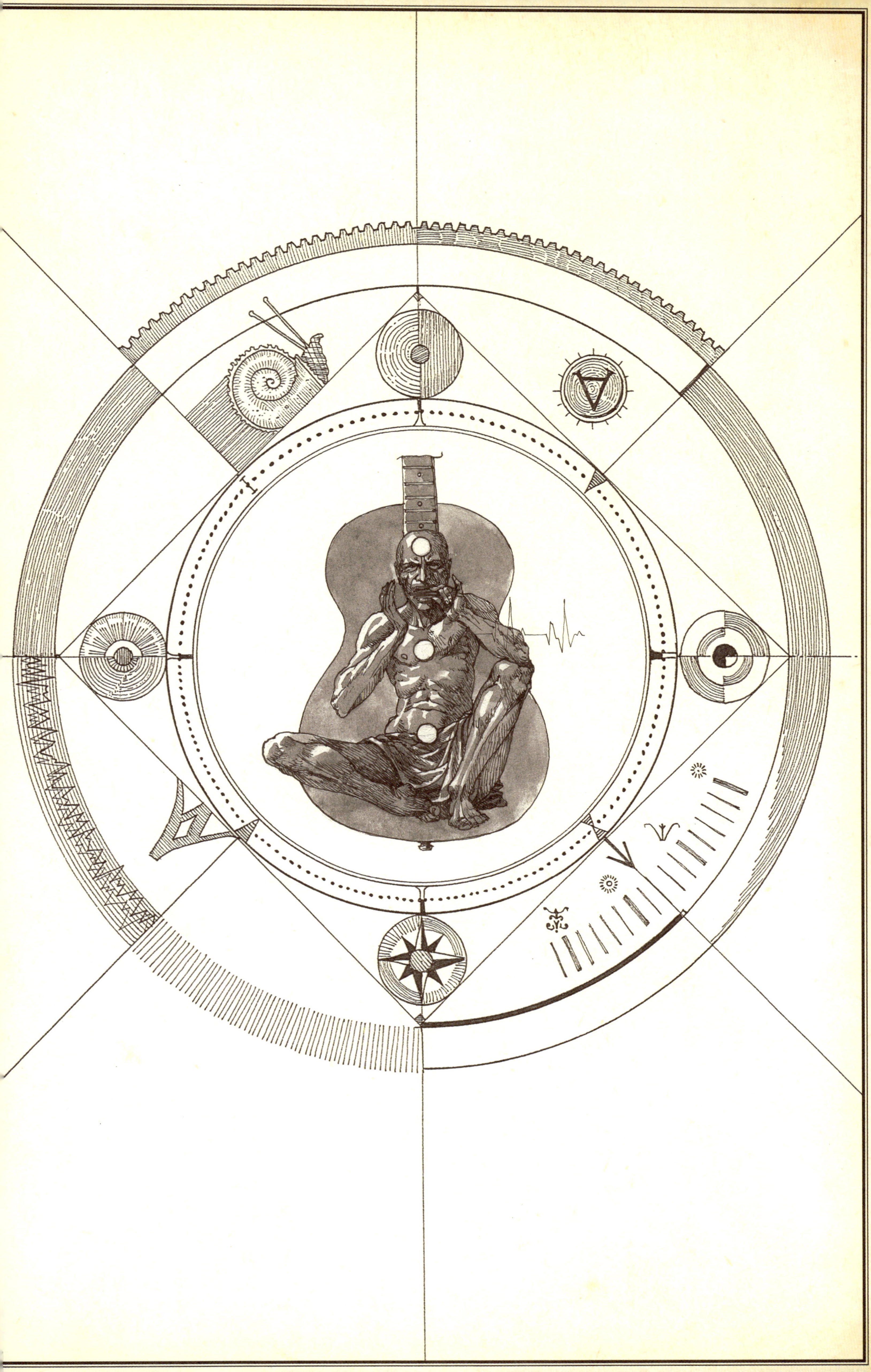

MUSIC

Music is a human phenomenon. There is no need to invent music — it arises spontaneously with humanity. Wherever you are, music will be there with you. And you already have your first musical instrument: your body. Like any other physical object in the universe, the human body is capable of producing vibrations that propagate through time and space, producing sound. Music is the modulation and manipulation of these sounds. They can be consciously created to convey a certain mood. For the listener, music can be an emotionally, psychologically and spiritually stimulating experience.

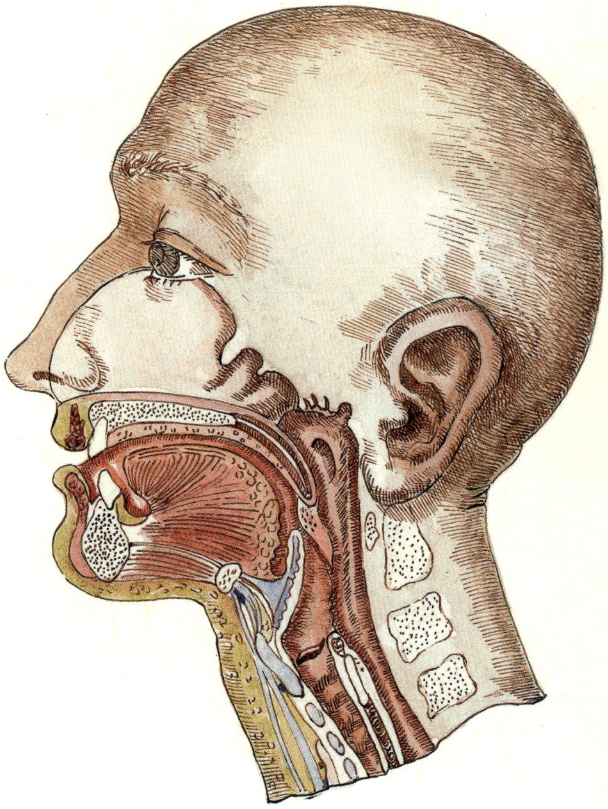

THE DIAPHRAGM AND THE SOUND "ATTACK"

The human voice is a perfect musical instrument. The powerhouse is the diaphragm, a muscular organ that draws air across your vocal chords. When you inhale, the muscles of the diaphragm contract, the volume of the chest increases and the lungs fill with air. As you exhale, you can engage your vocal chords to produce a clear sound. You can manipulate this sound by moving your tongue, lips and teeth to change the shape of the resonant cavity in your mouth or flex your vocal chords to produce different pitches.

Your body cavities amplify the sounds produced when singing and give the voice an individual color, or timbre. The upper cavities (sinuses and nasal passages) give the voice its sonorous, "buzzy" quality. The lower cavities (trachea, bronchial tubes and lungs) give the voice its soft, strong bass tones.

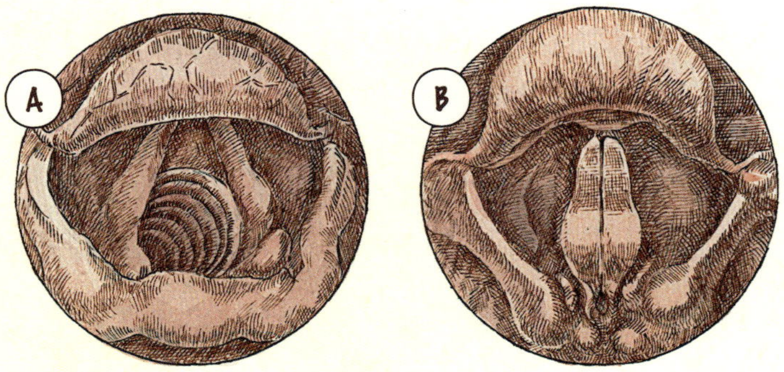

THE VOCAL CORDS

The vocal cords (also called vocal folds) are two bands of smooth muscle tissue found in the larynx. As air passes over the vocal cords from the lungs, it vibrates them and produces sound waves. The size of the cords determines the type of voice: People with low voices have longer and thicker cords, while people with high voices have shorter ones. When we breathe silently, the glottis is wide open (A), but when we sing, it narrows as the entrance to the larynx is covered by the epiglottis (B).

PITCH

The pitch of a sound is determined by its vibrational frequency. The size, length, thickness and elasticity of the resonant body influences the pitch it produces. The larger the area of the resonant body, the longer the wavelength and the fewer vibrations per second. If two strings are put under identical tension but one is shorter, the shorter string will produce a higher pitch, as it will vibrate faster. The hertz is a unit of measurement for frequency: one vibration per second equals 1 Hz. Different materials produce different characters and tones of sound, known as the timbre. Our perception of timbre is simply a feeling. It's what we're describing when we say a sound is soft or harsh, dull or ringing, etc.

Fixing the pitch of an instrument is what's known as tuning. It's important to do this to establish typical intervals between tones on a single instrument and to synchronize several instruments or voices with each other. A helpful tool is a tuning fork — an acoustic resonator in the form of a two-pronged fork with the prongs formed from a U-shaped bar of elastic metal. This constant pitch can be used as a base for an entire musical system (page 340) and to make sure all the instruments in your orchestra are in tune with each other. Otherwise, instead of heavenly harmonies, you'll hear a chaotic cacophony of sounds. You might need to tighten or loosen the tension on a string until it matches the pitch of the tuning fork.

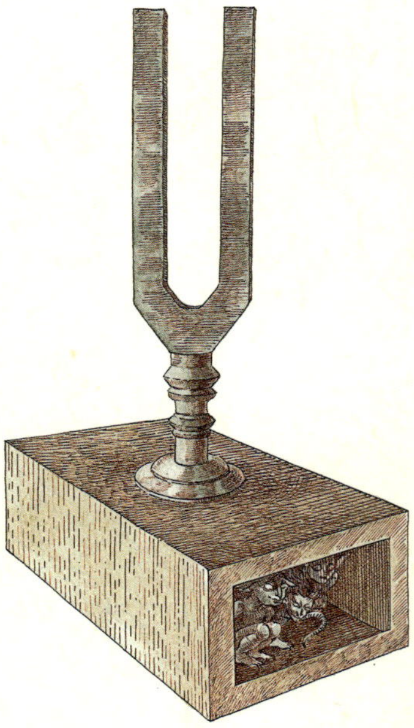

All sounds have an effect on the body. Even those outside of auditory range can still be felt as vibrations. In other words, people perceive sound with the entire body.

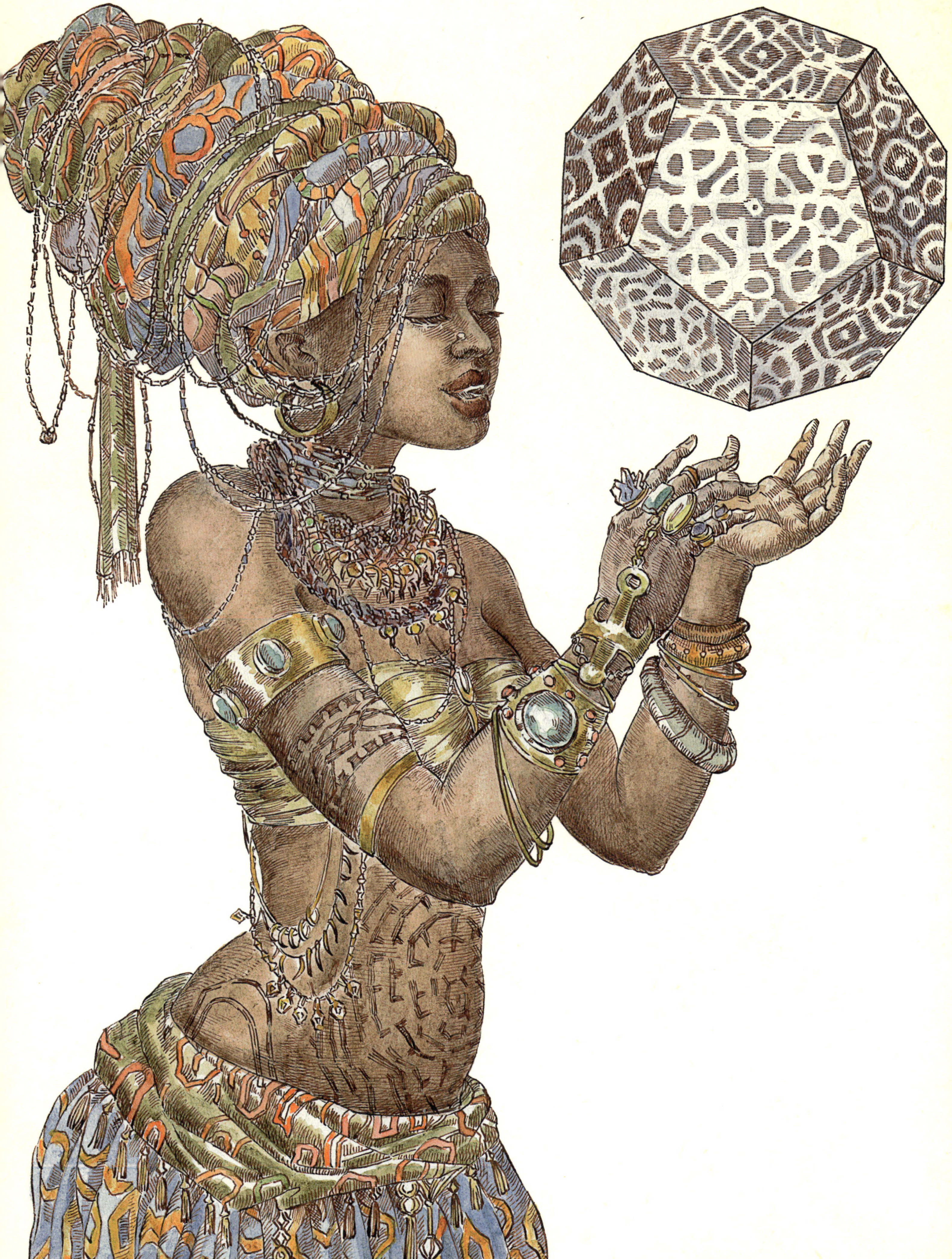

JAW HARP

Sound needs a source of vibration. And for the sound to ring out loudly and clearly, you need resonance, achieved when sound waves reflect off a surface and are amplified. The jaw harp vibrates and uses the resonance of the human body to modify the sound. You become part of the musical instrument!

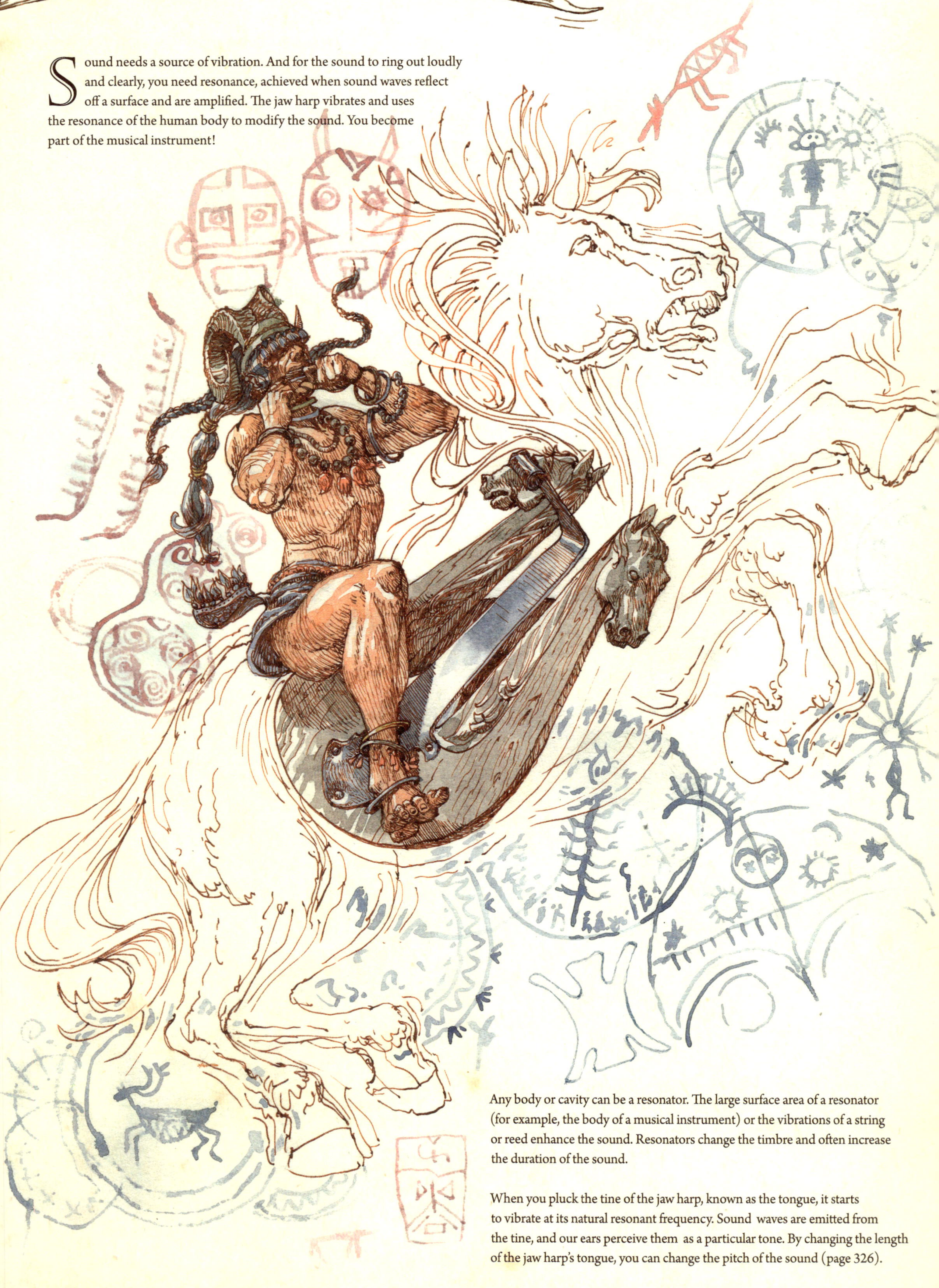

Any body or cavity can be a resonator. The large surface area of a resonator (for example, the body of a musical instrument) or the vibrations of a string or reed enhance the sound. Resonators change the timbre and often increase the duration of the sound.

When you pluck the tine of the jaw harp, known as the tongue, it starts to vibrate at its natural resonant frequency. Sound waves are emitted from the tine, and our ears perceive them as a particular tone. By changing the length of the jaw harp's tongue, you can change the pitch of the sound (page 326).

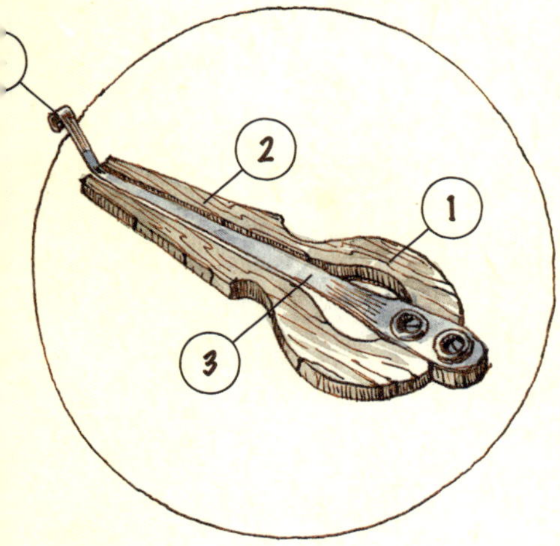

Forge the metal components from a corrosion-resistant alloy and harden them at a high temperature (page 138). The frame of the jaw harp consists of a ring (1) and two arms (2), which are pressed against the teeth. Create a notch at the base of the ring and attach the tongue (3), which can be made of any flexible material (steel, bamboo, bronze or brass). The tongue should be thin and tapered towards the plucking end.

Bend the very tip of the tongue to form the loop and trigger (4). The gap between the tongue and arms must remain even along the entire length of the inner frame — this is vital for the resonance of the jaw harp. You can weight this part with a thin plate of the same material from which the tongue is made.

Press the jaw harp against your teeth but keep your jaw slightly open to allow the instrument to move and vibrate freely. As you pluck the trigger with your fingers, you create vibrations that are transmitted to the oral cavity, which becomes a resonator. And since the vibration comes from a solid object touching your teeth, your skull and bones also begin to vibrate. Therefore, the whole body becomes a resonator.

While the fundamental pitch remains the same, by changing the shape of the oral cavity, closing and opening the throat or raising and lowering the tongue, you can produce higher or lower sounds, each rich in overtones. These occur at frequencies that are integer multiples higher than the base note (page 340).

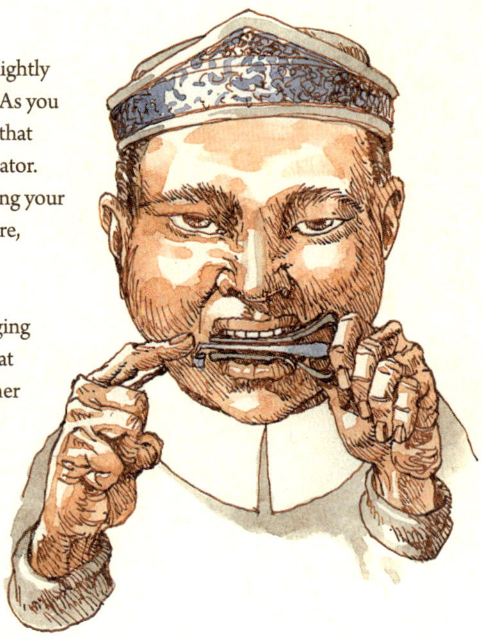

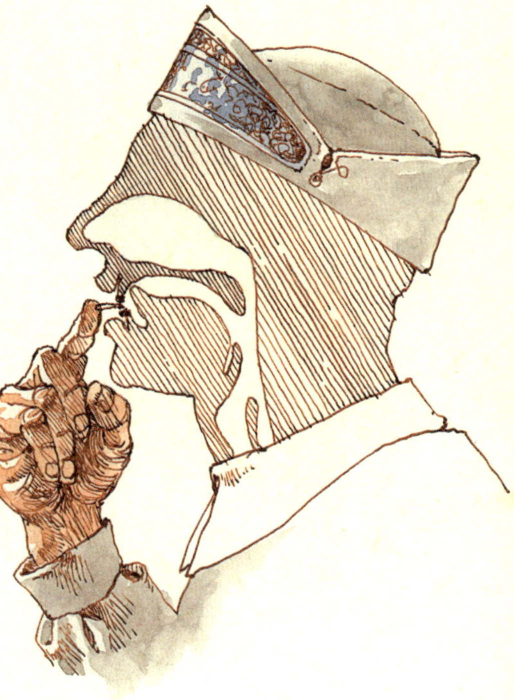

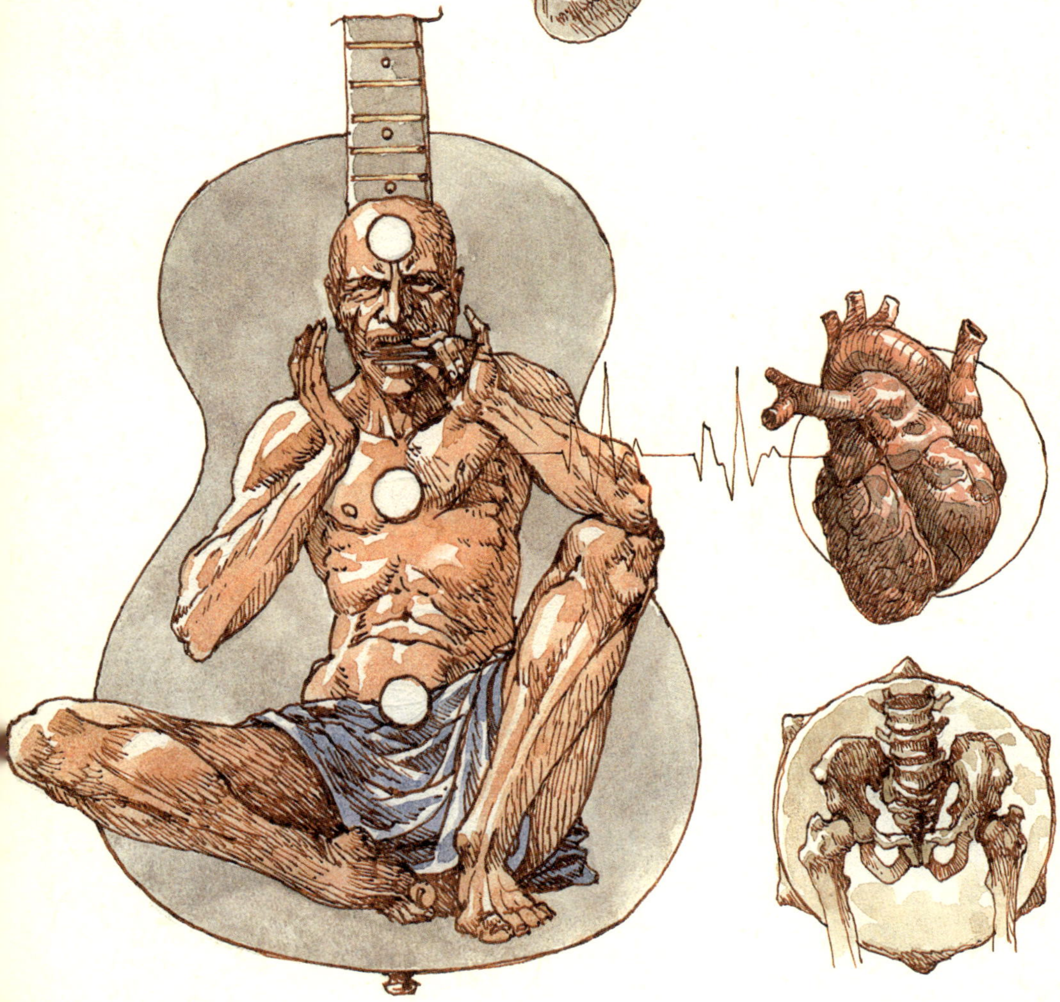

Now you are an instrument!
Use the jaw harp as a tool of self-discovery. Listen to your body and try to hear how the sound changes as it resonates through your bones. Relieve any tension you're holding from your head down. Once you've relaxed, try to groove on the vibrations and play using the natural rhythms of your body — for example, your heartbeat. When you notice internal changes, try to determine what rhythms affect them. The dulcet tones of the jaw harp are not meant to be recorded, as its magic lies in improvisation. Playing is akin to meditating or doing breath exercises (page 348).

DRUMS

Musical and biological rhythms are interconnected. Therefore, music can affect a person's mood. A calm and measured rhythm can subdue the breath and put you in a state of meditation and trance; a fast one can set the rhythm of the heartbeat, making you tremble with joy or shrink with tension or fear.

One drummer can control a mass of people: strengthen the morale and courage of warriors on the battlefield and make them act in unison or suppress the enemy's will, causing chaos in their ranks.

The tension of the drum's diaphragm determines the frequency of the oscillation. The stronger the tension of the diaphragm, the faster it vibrates and the higher the tonality of the drum. The amplitude of the vibration characterizes the energy, the force of the sound.

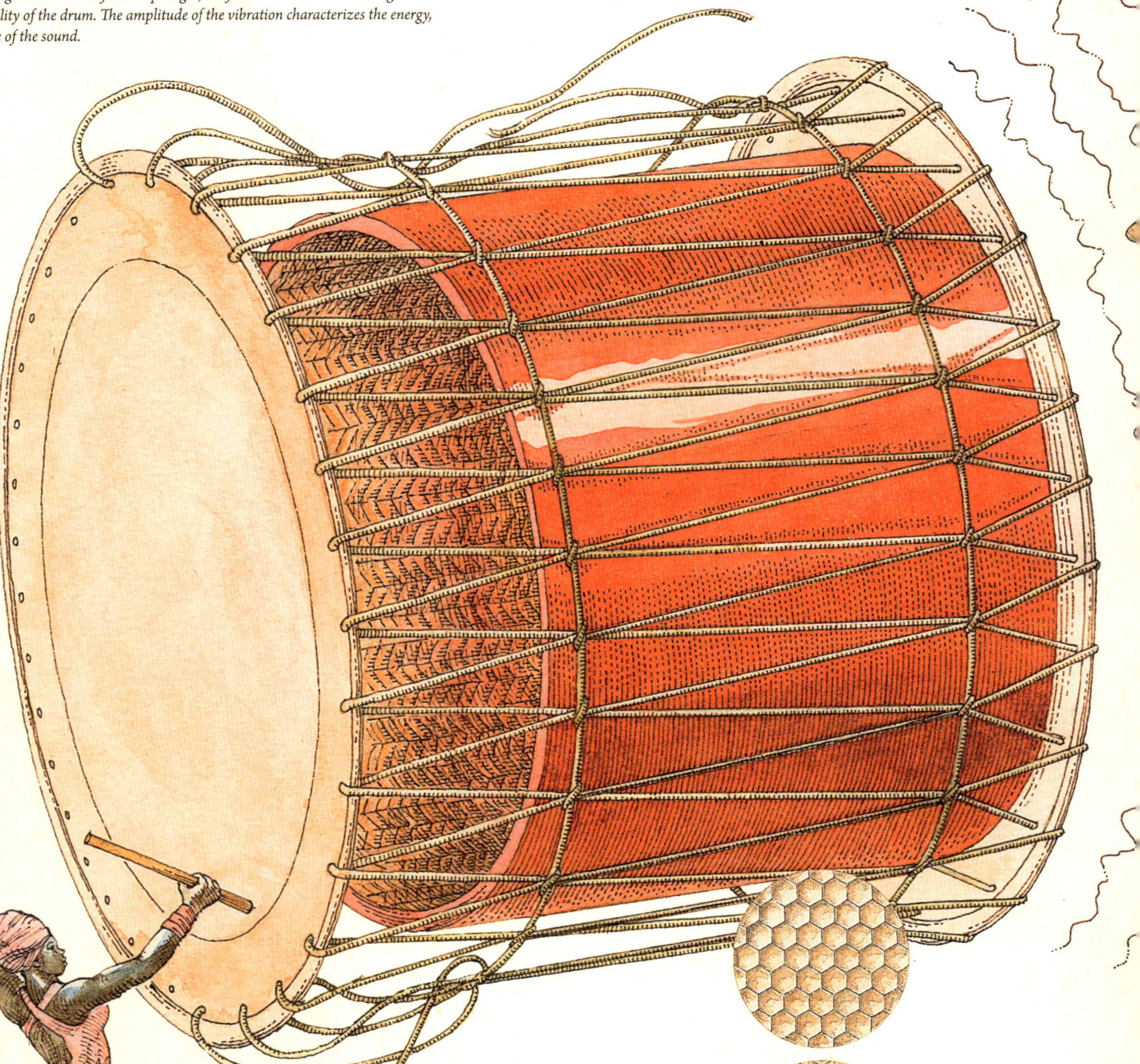

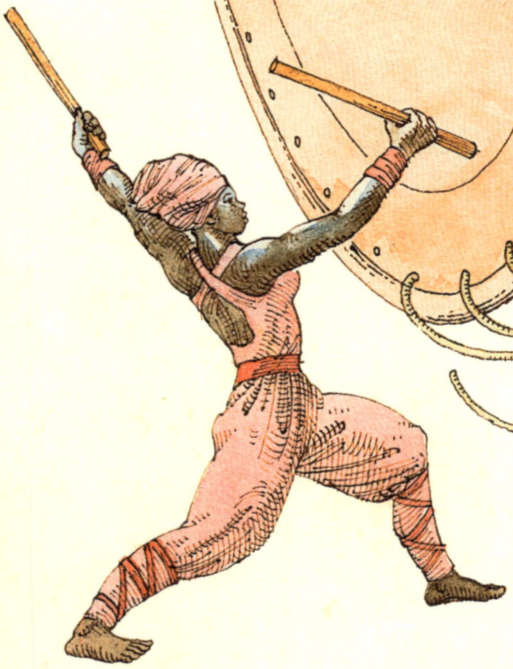

THE DRUM

Use hardwood such as elm for the drum frame. Remove the bark and the inside of the trunk to get a hollow ring. The greater the diameter, the lower the sound. Dry the wood for several years. After priming the surface, it should be smooth — roughnesses absorb sound. Make the membrane out of leather. The leather should be thicker on the side on which it is drummed, and on the opposite side of the drum, it should be thin and sensitive to the vibrations being transmitted. By adjusting the tension of the ropes pulling the diaphragm, you can change the sound.

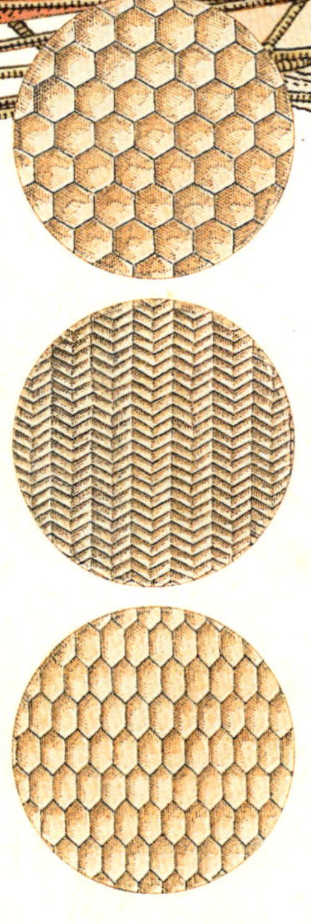

Carve a pattern on the inside of the frame. Try to experiment with the geometry of the pattern. The hexagonal cells make the sound more resonant. This kind of drum is suitable for street parties. Zigzag ones give a softer sound. Use these in drums for a small stage. Deep, elongated cells provide a powerful thunder-like sound. Use them in military drums.

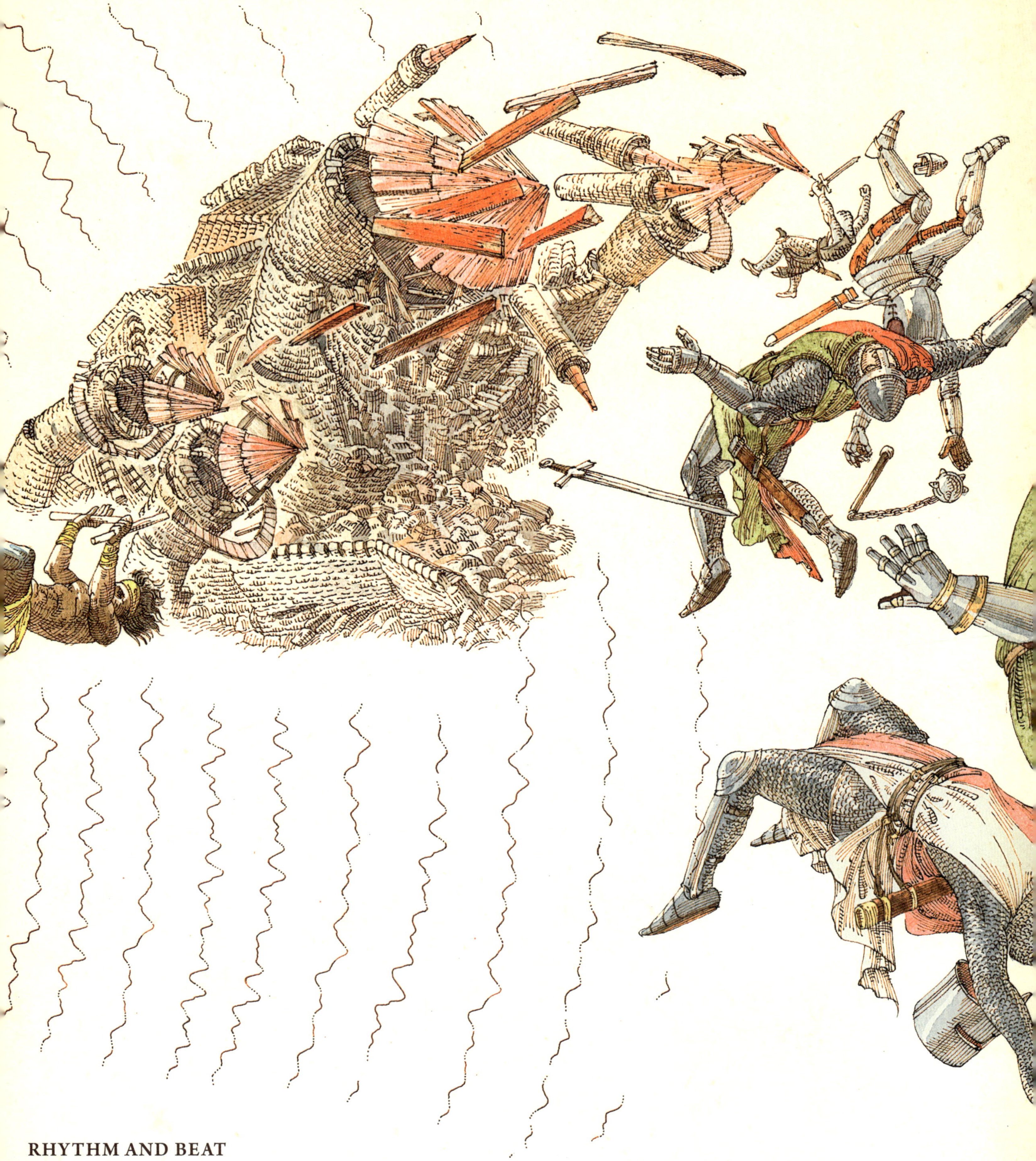

RHYTHM AND BEAT

The rhythm may be defined as the way in which one or more unaccented beats are grouped in relation to an accented one. Each note is played for its allotted period of time. It combines with other notes to form a rhythmic pattern. A musical phrase is made up of strong and weak parts. The strong is the climax, which can be highlighted, for example, by the volume of the sound. The preparation for this climax is the weak lobe. The distance (number of lobes) between the two strong lobes is the beat. The number of strong and weak bars in one beat characterizes the size of a musical phrase. Their alternation creates the "pulse" of the music, giving it the effect of constant motion.

The pattern of these sequences is mathematical. For example, in measure 3/4 there are one strong and two weak parts in one measure, each one a quarter long. The emotional perception of rhythm is related to physiology. The dominant rhythm first captures the motor center of the brain then stimulates the endocrine system. The rhythm of the music spurs the rhythm of the heart, and the increased heart rate provokes the release of hormones.

BERIMBAU

Music can transform the static into the dynamic. Musical instruments spread vibrations through the air around them. They are amplified by the body's natural resonators, allowing people to feel music with their entire beings. In response, like an echo, the body translates these soundwaves into dance. The conscious mind transforms the emotional tone of the music into movement.

The berimbau, a single-string percussion instrument, can set the rhythm (page 331) and control the dynamics, speed and vivacity of the dance movements. Its thrumming tones can make dances more organized, clear and thoughtful, as well as enhance the energy.

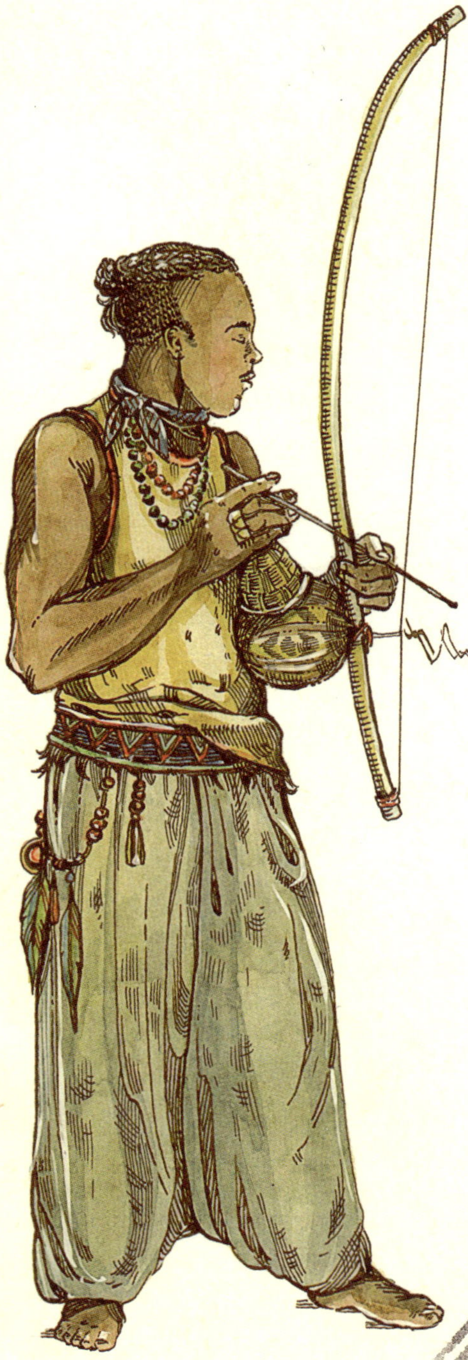

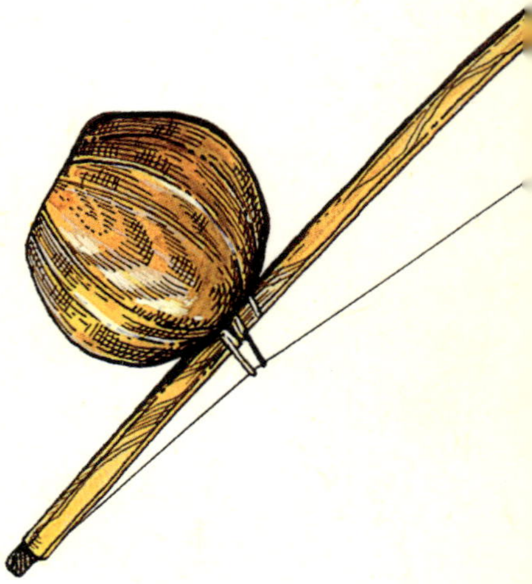

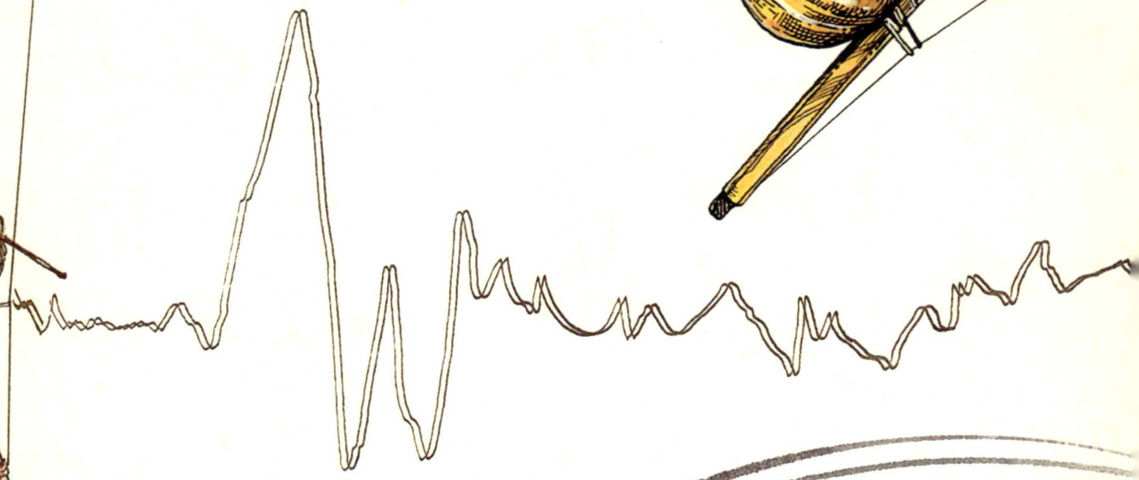

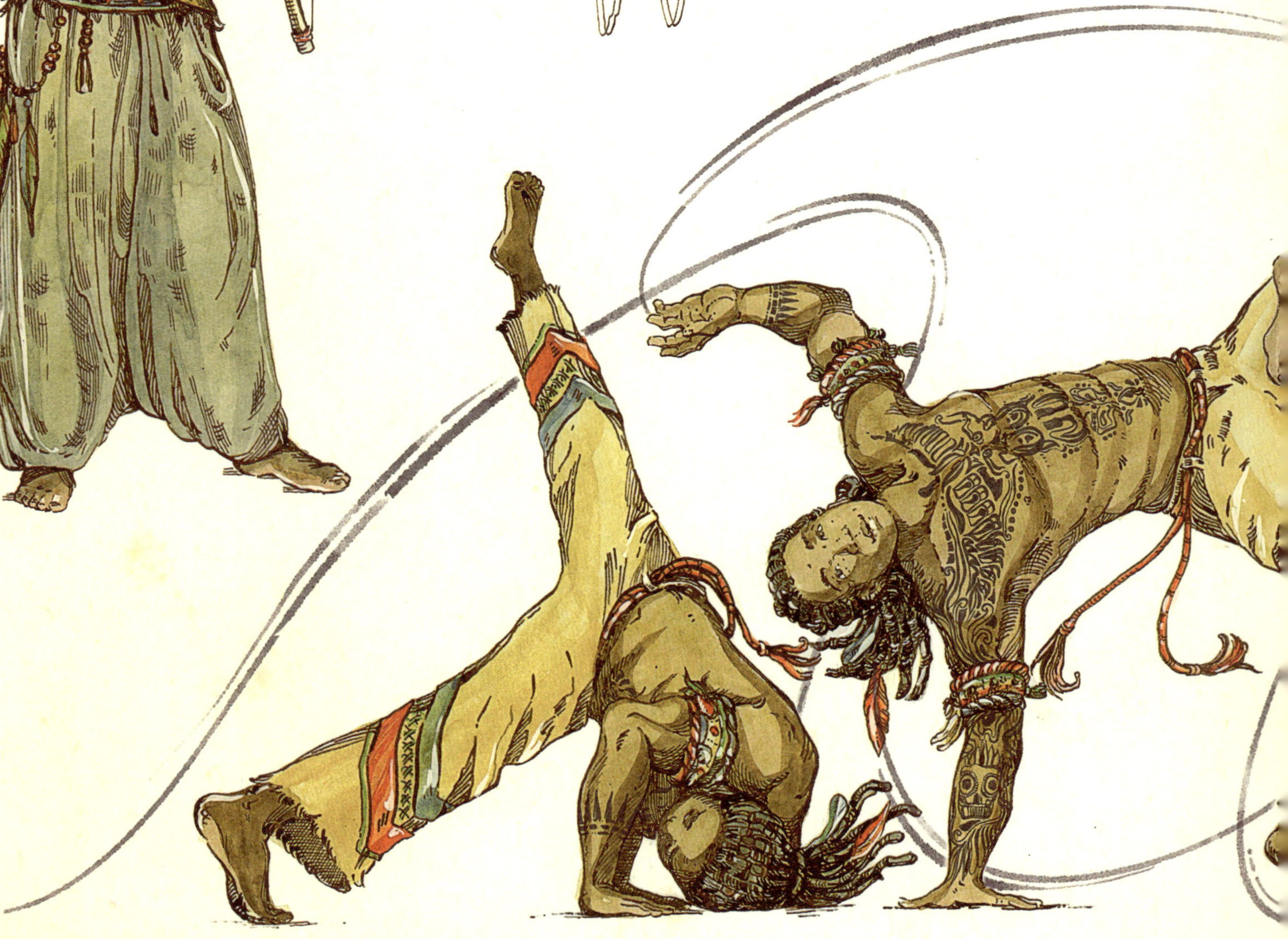

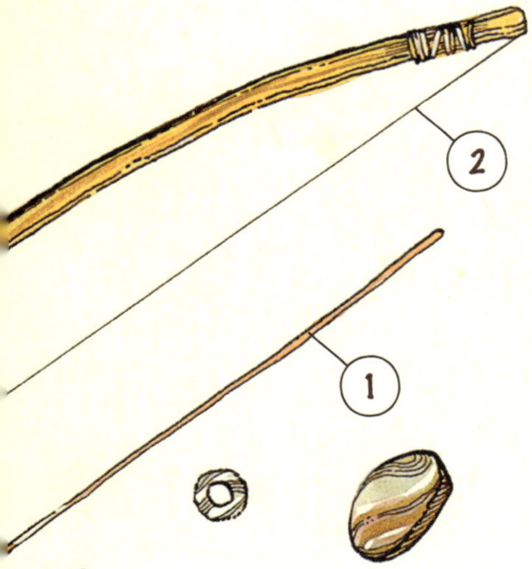

BERIMBAU

The bamboo stick (1) strikes the stretched string (2), creating a soundwave. The string can be made from animal sinew (page 78) or steel wire (page 162). Stretch it over a bent, flat branch. Soak the branch in hot water or steam it to make it more flexible. To prevent the string from slipping and the stick from splitting, wrap a thick layer of leather over the top. To amplify the sound wave, you'll need a soundboard. Use a pumpkin: cut a wide round hole in one side and two small holes in the other.

Thread a rope through the two holes in back and tie it into a loop. Pull the loop over the stick with the string stretched and tighten it. By pressing the string with a flat pebble or coin, you can change the frequency of the sound. The berimbau basically has three sounds: the open string sound, the high sound and the buzz sound.

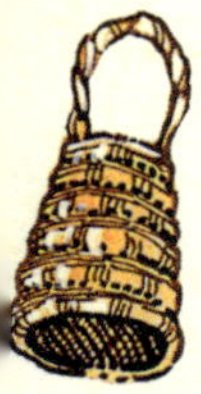

A small instrument called a caxixi is the perfect complement to the sound of the berimbau. Weave a small basket with a minimal opening, fill it with dry seeds, pebbles or shells and cork the hole with a piece of gourd. While playing the berimbau, hold the caxixi in the same hand as the bamboo stick. By alternating the different sounds of the berimbau and caxixi, you can create unique rhythms.

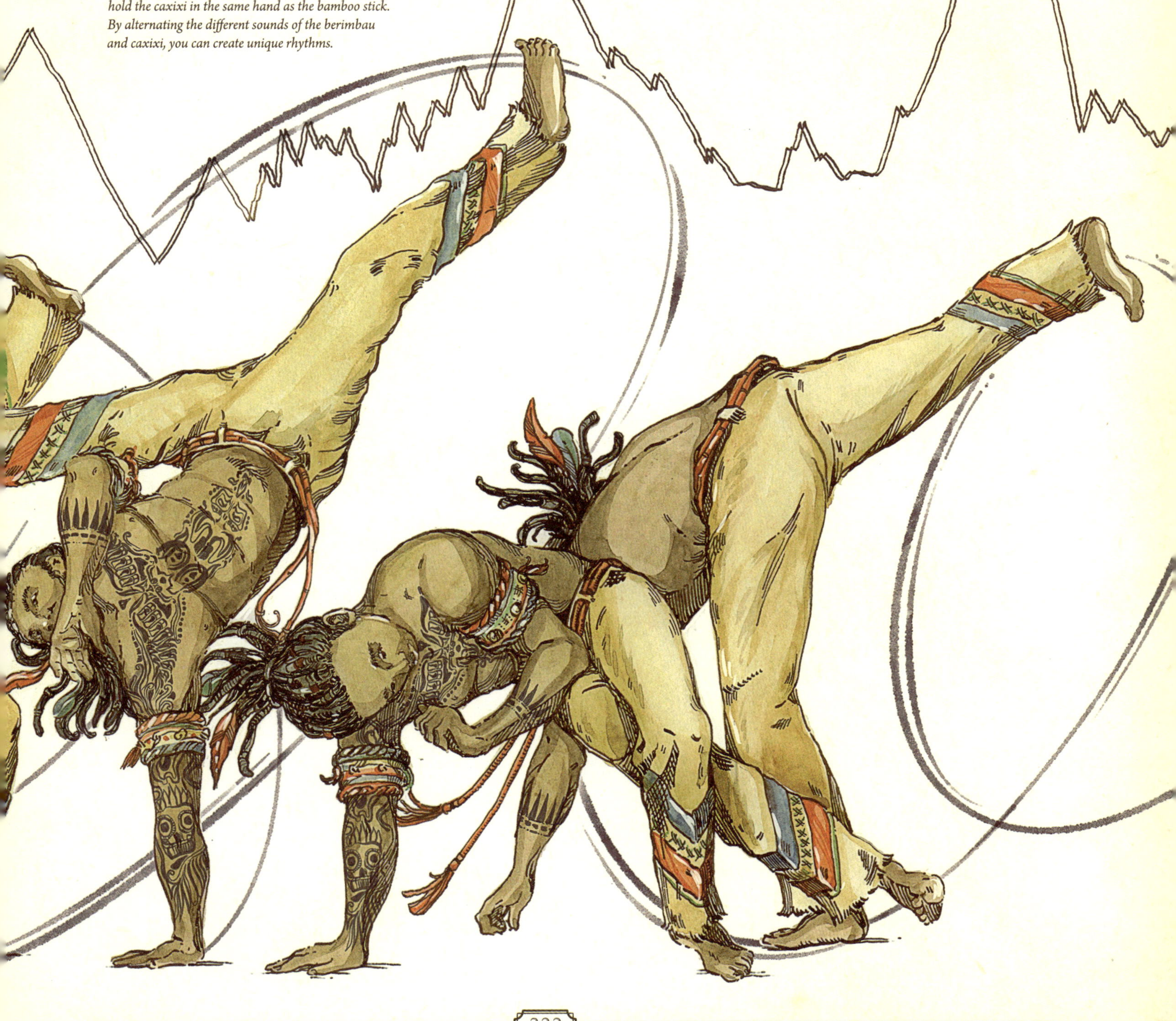

SAXOPHONE

If you put your finger gently on a loudspeaker, you will feel it vibrate. If the note is low enough, you can even see it moving. When it's pushed forward, it compresses the air in front of it, raising the pressure. Some of this air flows outwards, compressing the next layer of air. The disturbance in the air spreads outwards as a traveling sound wave. Wind instruments work by blowing into a hollow tube and altering its length to change the resonant frequency and thus the note produced.

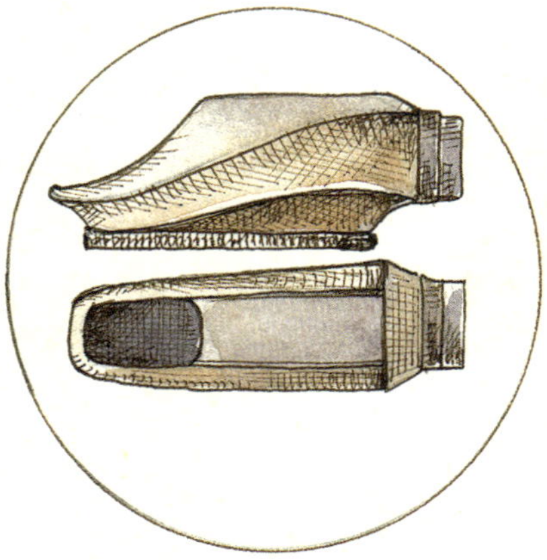

SAXOPHONE

The saxophone is characterized by a conical metal tube (1) and finger keys. The sound is produced by the reed (2) vibrating. This curved plate vibrates the air exhaled by the musician, causing the entire air column in the saxophone body to vibrate. The air exits through the resonating bell (3). By opening the valves (4) on the body, you can change the length of the air column oscillating in the tube to obtain sounds of different frequencies, or notes: Small holes produce high notes, and large ones produce low notes. To play the lowest note, all holes must be closed. There is an octave valve (5) at the top to open one of the two holes that make the note an octave higher.

REED

The main element of the saxophone is a small piece of wood — the reed (2). It performs the same function as human vocal cords when you sing (page 326) — it produces sound. The plate can be made from bamboo, rushes or reeds. The reed is attached to the mouthpiece (6) with a clamp made of metal or leather (7). The saxophone can be tuned by sliding the mouthpiece in and out. This will change the length of the instrument: the longer it is, the lower the tone.

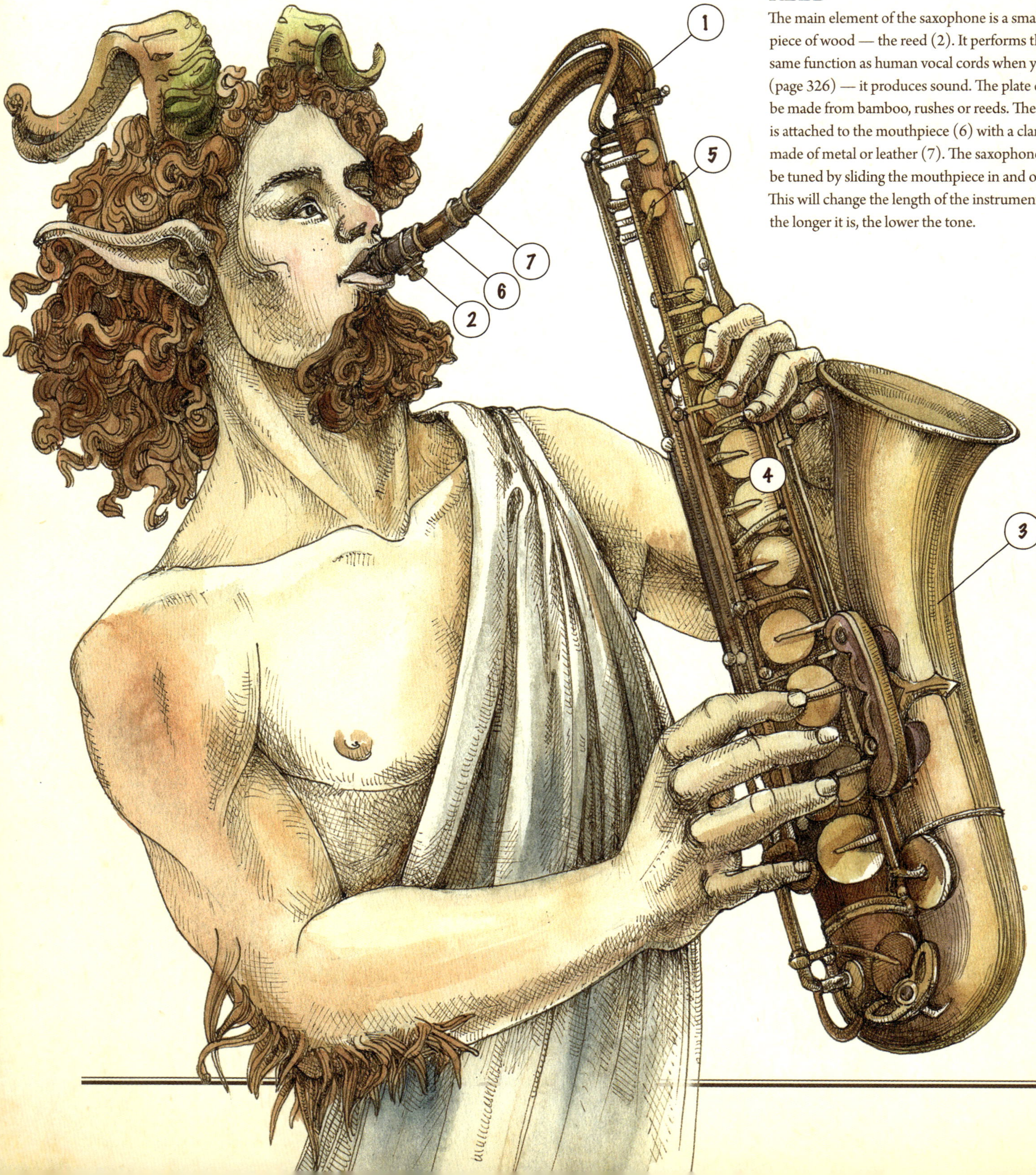

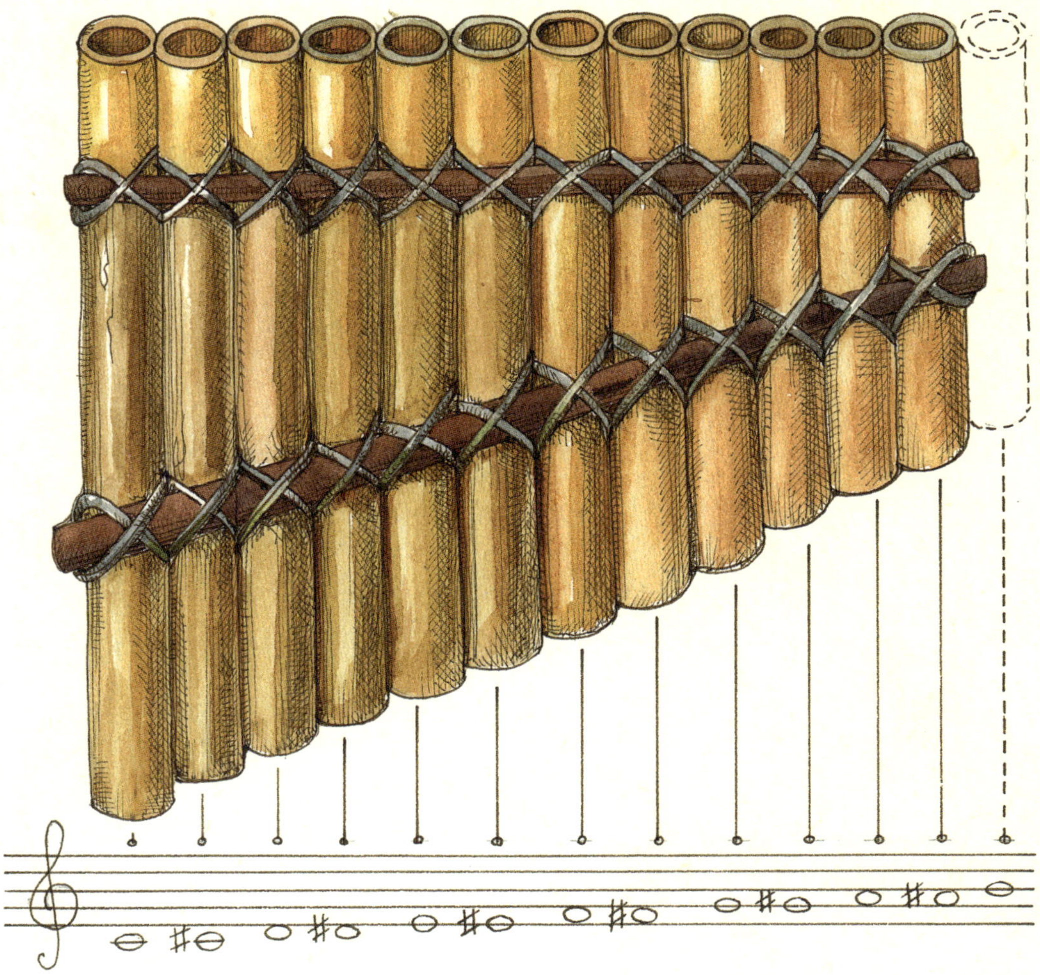

PAN FLUTE

On stringed instruments, sound waves move through the string and across the body of the instrument. In the body of reed instruments, air columns move back and forth. Connect several tubes of different lengths. In each one, the air can vibrate only at a specific frequency, meaning it produces one pitch (page 326). A tube half the size of its neighbor will produce a note twice as high. As you blow and move your lips across the tubes, you'll produce different notes with different intervals between them.

An interval is just the distance between two sounds. You can replace the several tubes with one and drill holes along the body. When all of them are open, you produce the same sound you'd get by blowing into a tube as short as the length to the first hole. If you plug all of the holes with your fingers, you'll get the same sound as blowing into a tube as long as the flute with no holes.

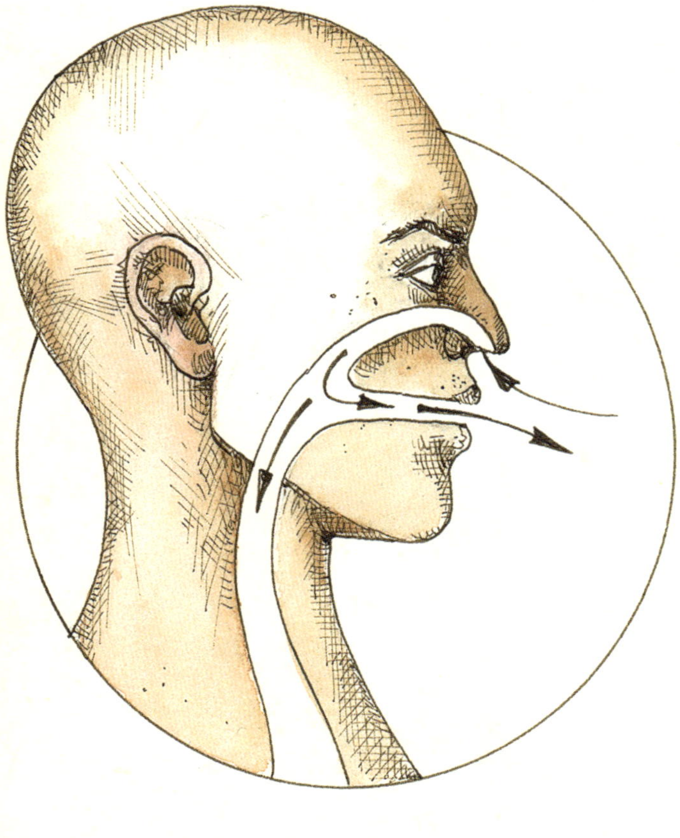

SCALES

A column of air can vibrate as a whole or divide into parts. Dividing can produce a series of sounds at specific frequencies. An unbroken column of air produces a fundamental tone. A pillar divided into two parts sounds an octave higher than the fundamental tone, and four parts sound two octaves higher. An octave is an interval in which the ratio of frequencies between sounds is one to two; that is, the frequency of sounds in each successive octave will be twice as high as in the previous one.

A smooth increase (or decrease) in the frequency of a sound is a scale. The way you choose to define intervals between notes and the octave boundaries are purely conventional. Choose, for instance, a reference frequency of 440 Hz (page 326). From this reference point, you can shift the pitch up and down by increasing or decreasing the frequency. The sequence of various intervals, tones and semitones forms a melodic pattern.

Playing certain reed instruments requires a special technique known as circular breathing. Breathe in and begin to play, gradually exhaling into the instrument. When the air in your lungs starts to run out, move the remaining air from your lungs into your mouth and squeeze it out from there with your cheek muscles while simultaneously taking another breath in through your nose. This allows you to play continuously without stopping for breath. The position of the lips, tongue and facial muscles all change to accomplish this.

ORGAN

Music is a thing removed from the material realm. It's difficult to analyze or qualify, as there is nothing tangible for us to examine. That's why when we listen to music. We rely only on our feelings, gradually switching from the rational to the emotional mind. Immersing yourself in this state can become a spiritual practice. An excellent guiding voice on this journey is a musical instrument that can produce the entire audible range, from ultra- to infra-sound, which produces a tone as rich and impactful as an entire symphony orchestra — the organ.

PIPES

Organs are made with several tiers of pipes. Every tier has its own register, meaning the pipes produce different notes of the same timbre (page 334). The more registers an organ has, the wider its range. The lowest notes are produced by wooden pipes with square cross sections (1). Metallic cylindrical pipes (2) cover the higher range. A closed pipe produces a pitch twice as low (one octave lower) than an open pipe of the same length. Organ pipes also have different constructions. In flue pipes (A), the sound is formed by an oscillating air column. In reed pipes (B), it's not the air that vibrates but a flat metal plate around which the air flows. The air pressure pushes and vibrates the plate, propagating soundwaves that are then amplified within the body of the pipe — the resonator. The shorter the opening in the reed, the higher the sound.

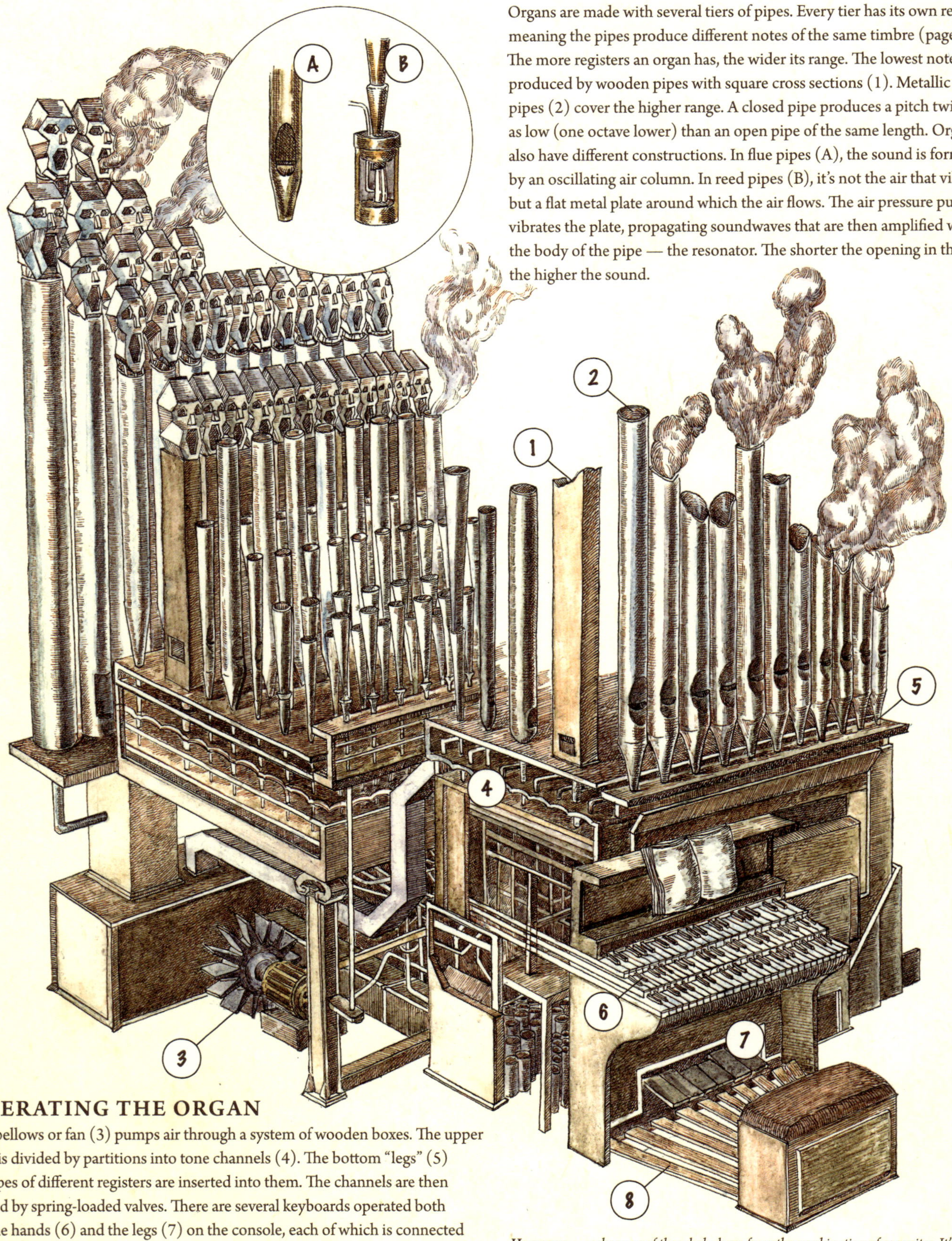

OPERATING THE ORGAN

The bellows or fan (3) pumps air through a system of wooden boxes. The upper part is divided by partitions into tone channels (4). The bottom "legs" (5) of pipes of different registers are inserted into them. The channels are then closed by spring-loaded valves. There are several keyboards operated both by the hands (6) and the legs (7) on the console, each of which is connected to several registers. When a key or pedal is pressed, the movement is transferred through wooden rods (8) to the valve (6), which then opens and allows compressed air to enter the channel.

***Harmony** — coherence of the whole, born from the combination of opposites. It's a subjective concept; everyone perceives the sound in their own way. Dissonant chords create tension, while consonant chords resolve it. The interaction between the two is one of the foundational techniques of musical expression.*

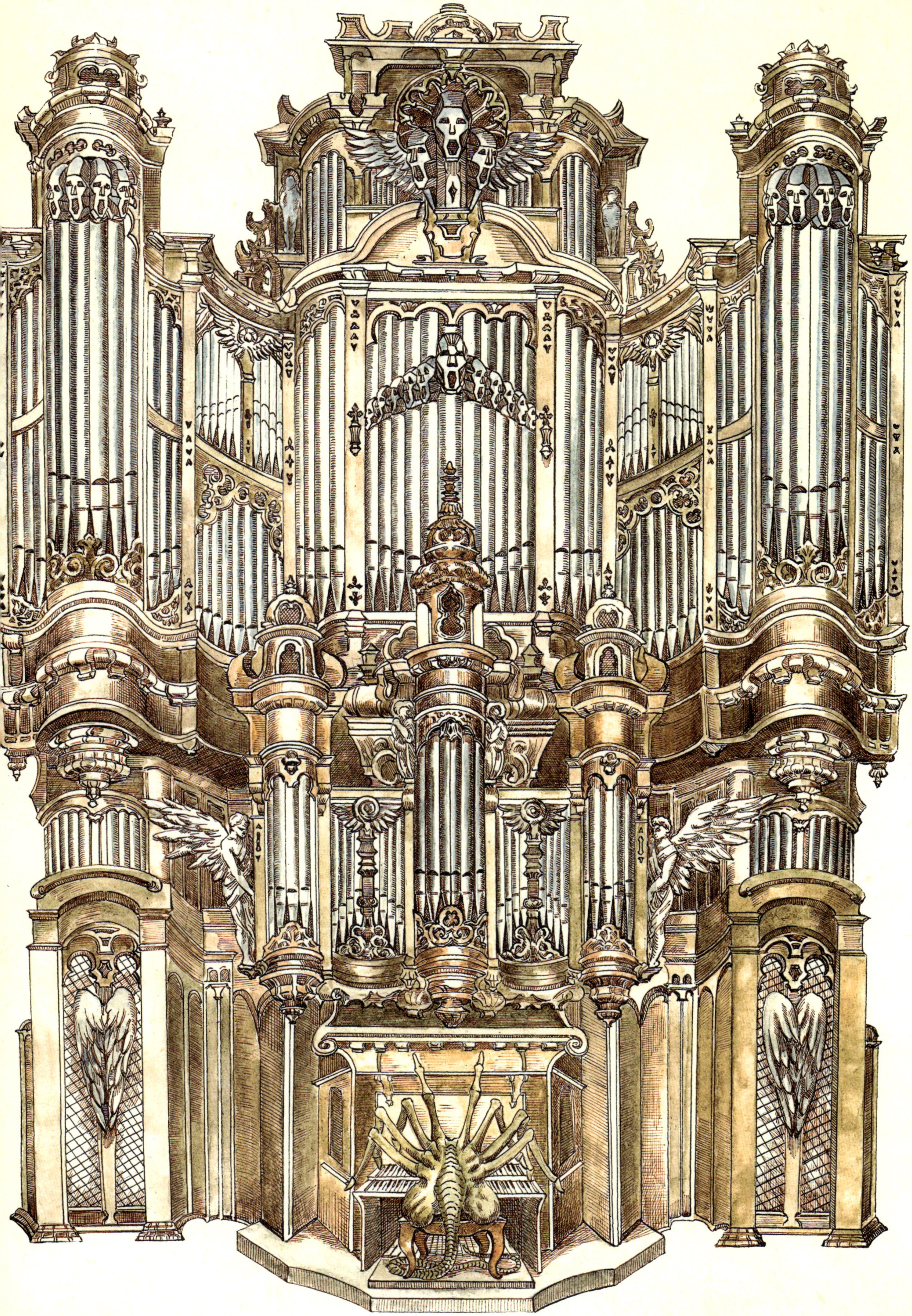

SITAR

Music creates a stream of emotions, allowing us to process and express our realities and nurture the mind and spirit. Making music is a concentration method. Both while creating and listening, the mind rises above the mundanities of everyday life, entering a state of self-observation that leads to the refinement of the soul.

The sitar can be customized and fine-tuned to your tastes. There is no single standard — anyone can construct a sitar suitable for their own preferences and skill level. It's not only the strings that sound but also all of its structural parts. Each vibrates at its own frequency and sings with its own voice. And when played, all the voices come together into a harmonious chorus.

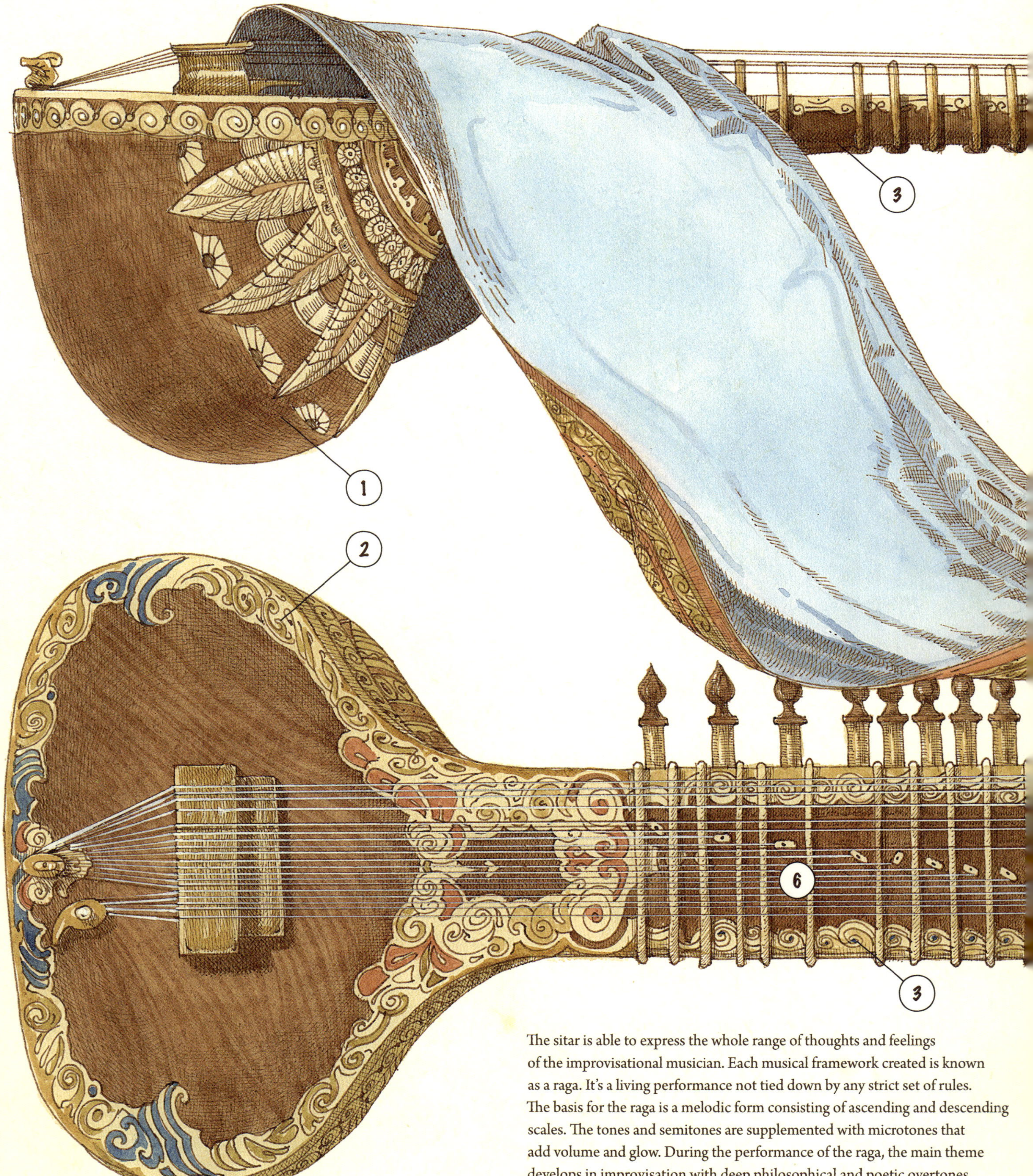

The sitar is able to express the whole range of thoughts and feelings of the improvisational musician. Each musical framework created is known as a raga. It's a living performance not tied down by any strict set of rules. The basis for the raga is a melodic form consisting of ascending and descending scales. The tones and semitones are supplemented with microtones that add volume and glow. During the performance of the raga, the main theme develops in improvisation with deep philosophical and poetic overtones. Each raga carries a certain mood idiosyncratic to that specific piece, causing the listener to experience a sense of aesthetic satisfaction.

Your civilization can develop its own set of attitudes towards sound and performance, its own ways of perceiving and processing them. And the foundation of your musical composition doesn't have to be limited to a linear melody based on a tonal sequence of sounds arranged in ascending or descending order.

You can also create music in which the sounds spiral, coil by coil, creating a trail of nuances and overtones.

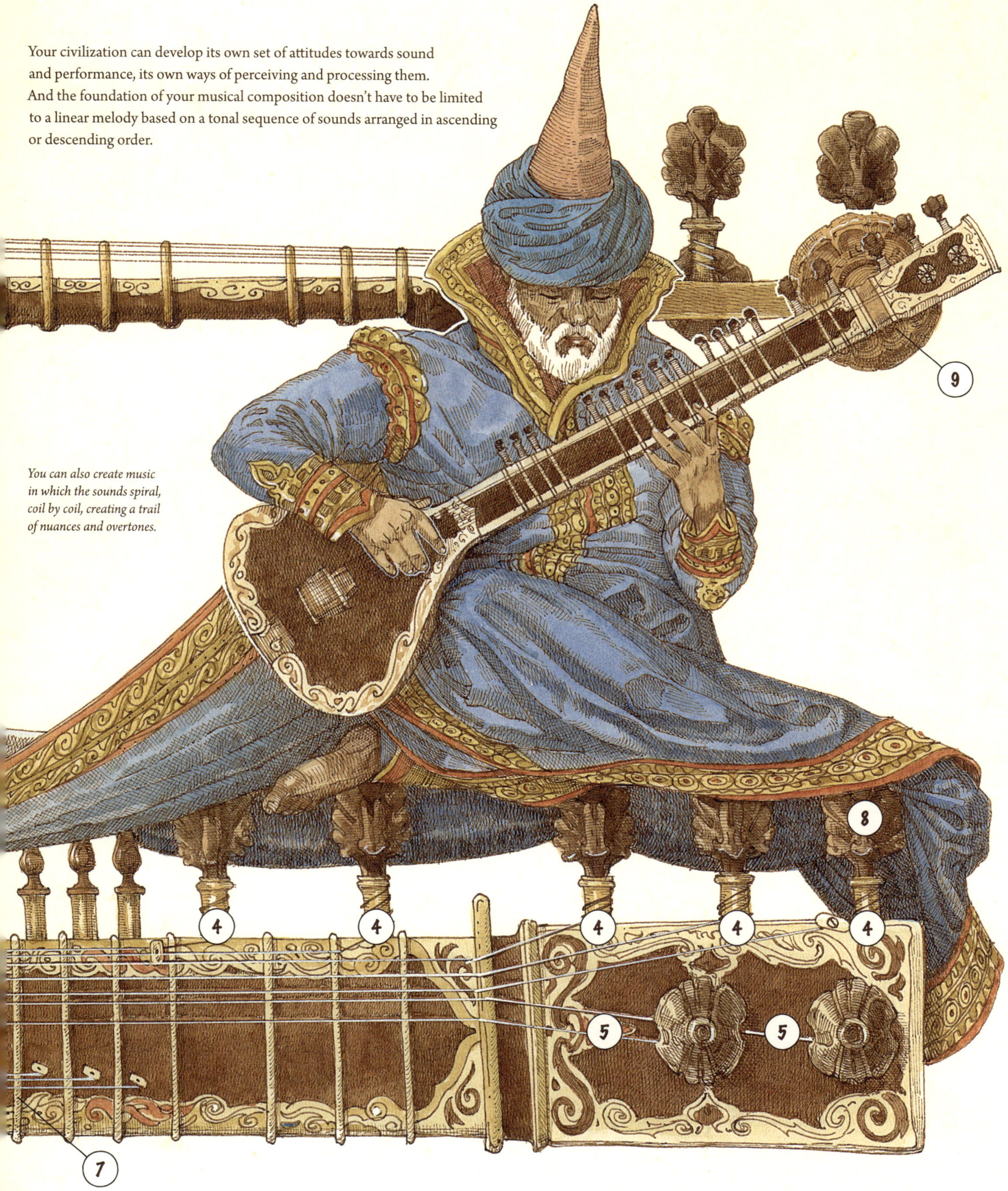

The body of the sitar is made from a pear-shaped gourd (1) that acts as the main resonator that enhances the volume of the sound. The sound board (2) acts as a second resonator that gives the sound a certain color. The neck (3), on which the strings are attached, is hollow, transmitting the vibrations of the strings. The older the wood from which it is made, the richer the sound. The vibrations are supplied by seven main strings: five of them are melodic (4), on which the main theme is played, and two are supplemental (5), continuously stretching and complementing the melody. In addition to these strings, there is also a range of smaller strings (6). These react to the vibration of the main strings and resonate, adding volume to the sound. The musician does not strum or pluck them. The resonating strings run under the frets (7), while the main set of strings lies above. The frets are made from metal and change the pitch of the sound. On a sitar, they are movable and are attached to the neck with ropes. The tuning pegs (8) stretch the strings taut. The rigidity of the material from which they are made determines the amount of energy that is transferred from the strings to the other structural elements. At the top of the neck there is an additional resonator (9) that amplifies the vibrations.

MUSIC BOX

Music is capable of uniting performers, even across language and cultural barriers. But in order to remember, record and reproduce melodies, there needs to be a standard, shared notation for writing music. You'll need to come up with a common convention.

You can share simple melodies by creating a music box. The main component is the comb (1). It is made out of metal and has tines of varying lengths. Each tine produces a different note. The shorter and thinner the tine, the higher the sound. The second element is the cylinder (2), which is covered in small pins. As the cylinder rotates, these pins displace the tines, causing them to vibrate. To make sure the music doesn't cut off abruptly in the middle of a phrase, make sure the melody is complete and looped — for example, a section of 4 or 8 measures.

To rotate the cylinder, you need a clockwork spring mechanism (page 166). When the key is inserted into the keyhole and twisted, it winds a steel band spring (4) around an axle, storing mechanical energy. As the spring unwinds, the axle rotates and sets the gear wheel (5) in motion. The rotation is transmitted to the cylinder (2). The speed of this rotation can be set by selecting the diameter of the gears. Place the mechanism inside a case (6). This will become the resonator (page 328). Add a figurine on top that will be set in motion by the same spring mechanism. Turn the key and ... *twinkle twinkle little star...*

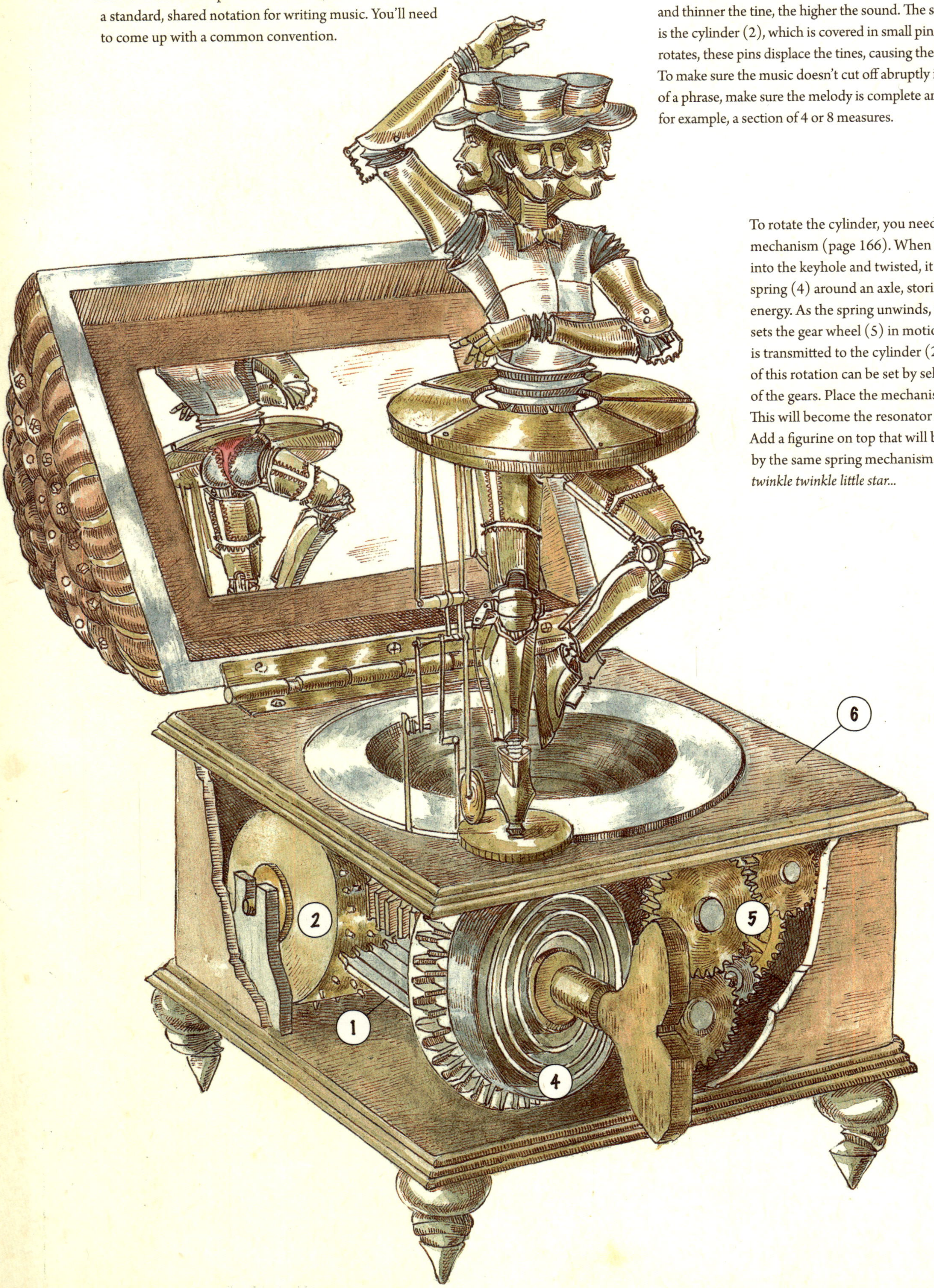

NOTES

Notes in music are used to denote sounds of a particular frequency in writing. Each note has its own frequency ranging from approximately 20 Hz to 5000 Hz. Instead of referring to these notes by their frequency, however, you can also use letters or short names to simplify things. For instance, consider organizing notes on a staff of five parallel horizontal lines. Notes can either be placed directly on one of the lines or in the space between two lines. Assign each note position a pitch. Notes located near each other on these lines, moving either up or down in ascending or descending order of pitch, form a scale. You can expand the scale by placing notes above and below the staff and adding extra "ledger lines" above, below or through the note to indicate its position.

Once you reach a frequency double that of the starting frequency, the note will sound like a higher version of the starting pitch. This interval is called an octave. Try assigning the lowest note on your scale a simple name, such as "do." Draw an extra ledger line below the lowest staff line and place this note directly on it. The next note, call it "re," goes in the blank space directly below the lowermost staff line. Move upwards, alternating line and space, for the following five notes, which could be called, say, "mi," "fa," "sol," "la" and "ti." To write music, arrange the notes on the staff in the order in which they sound. Anyone fluent in this musical notation will be able to read the music and reproduce the melody.

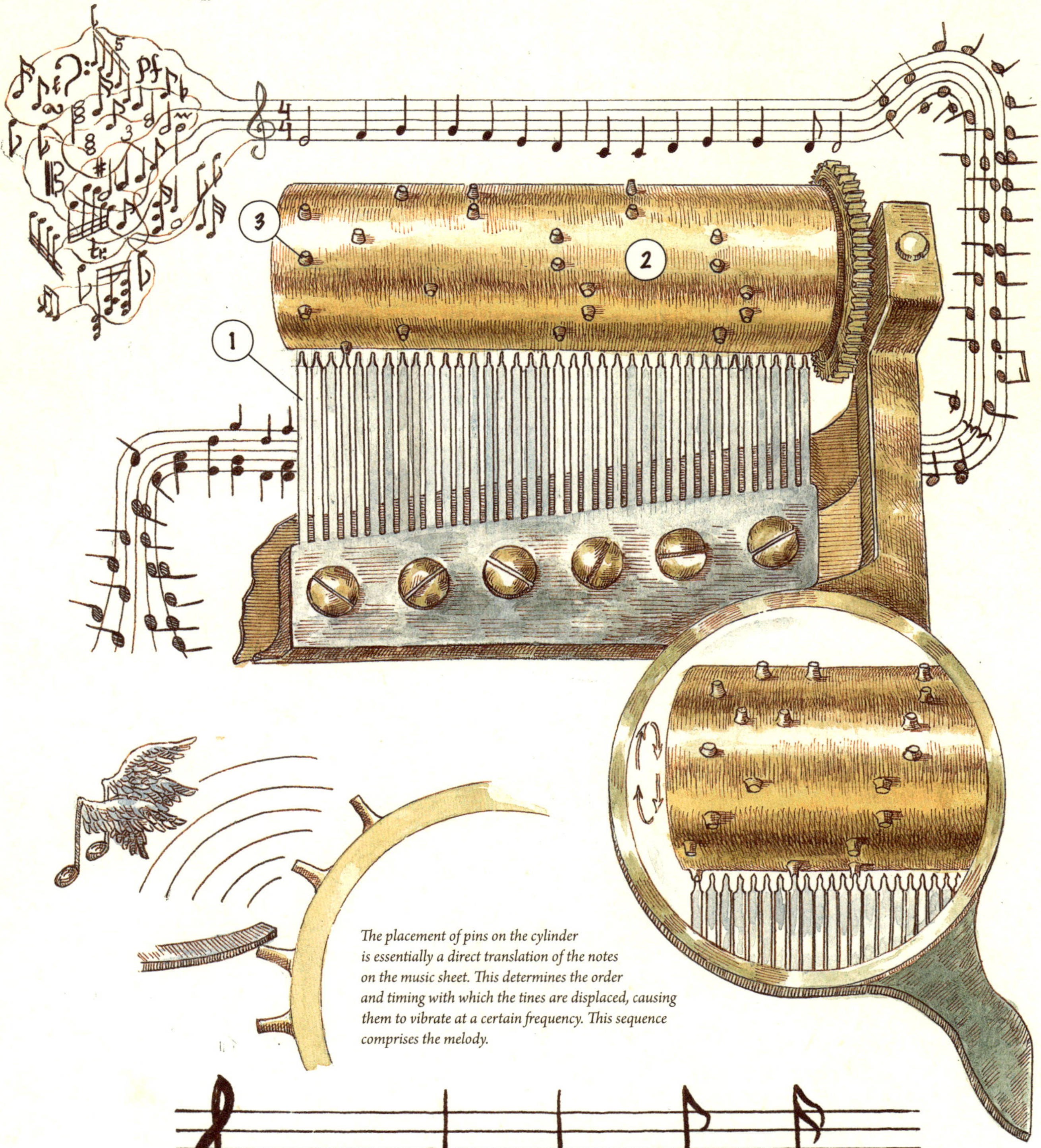

The placement of pins on the cylinder is essentially a direct translation of the notes on the music sheet. This determines the order and timing with which the tines are displaced, causing them to vibrate at a certain frequency. This sequence comprises the melody.

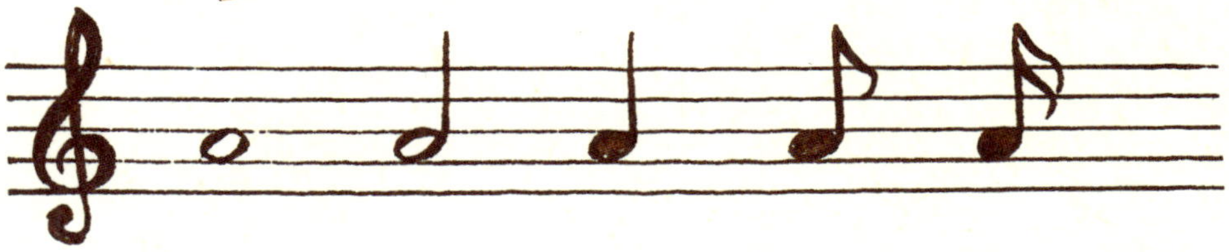

One easy way to write notes on a sheet is using ovals. You can choose to fill in the oval or keep it empty, as well as add lines to one side or flags to indicate different note lengths. An empty oval without a stick is a standard note played for four full counts. If you add a stem to one side, this "whole note" becomes a "half note," played for two counts. Fill in the oval, and it's a quarter note, played for one.

If you also add a flag to the stick, the note turns into an eighth note. As you add flags, keep decreasing the length of the note: a sixteenth note is like an eighth but with a double flag and so on. To help the notes fit on the staff better, place the stem on the right side pointing up for all notes below the middle line, and on the left side pointing down for all notes above.

PHONOGRAPH

Once you've reinvented and mastered musical instruments, you'll immediately want to find a way to record sound. There's one simple and accessible technology that will help you make a real breakthrough. Amazingly enough, all you need to record sound is a needle and a metal roller covered in an even layer of wax. The needle carves the sound into the wax, and you can use the same needle to play it back later. Being able to capture the moment and share it with others is one small step for a musician and one giant leap for the music industry.

SOUNDTRACK

Try holding your palm to your face and shouting at your hand. Feel the vibration? Sound is created by air vibrating at various speeds. The phonograph's horn collects sound waves and directs them towards a flexible diaphragm, causing it to vibrate. The diaphragm then pushes the needle, which carves a recording into the wax roll. The louder the sound, the deeper the groove.

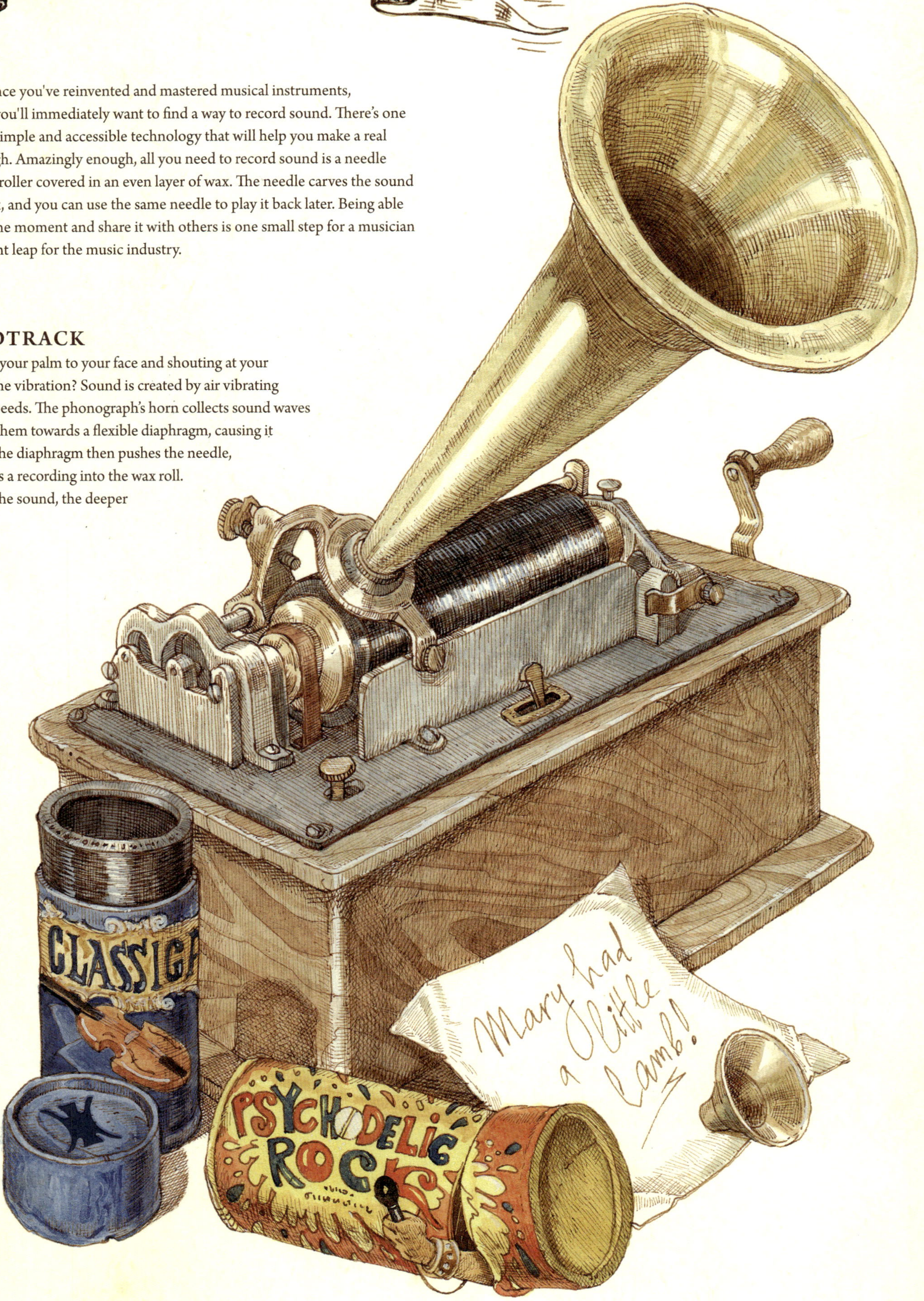

RECORDING

Slide the wax cylinder over a threaded metal cylinder. As you turn the handle, the cylinder moves slightly sideways relative to the needle. In this way, the audio recording spirals around, covering the entire wax roll from left to right. In some of the more advanced models, like the one depicted above, the cylinder itself doesn't move but rather the needle carriage and horn.

PLAYBACK

To play a recording, all you have to do is set the needle to the beginning of the track and start turning the handle. The needle pushes the diaphragm, the diaphragm creates air vibrations and the horn amplifies the sound waves. By connecting air hoses to the diaphragm instead of a horn, you can create headphones for personal playback. Headphones greatly reduce the likelihood of having unpleasant conversations with neighbors and the local authorities.

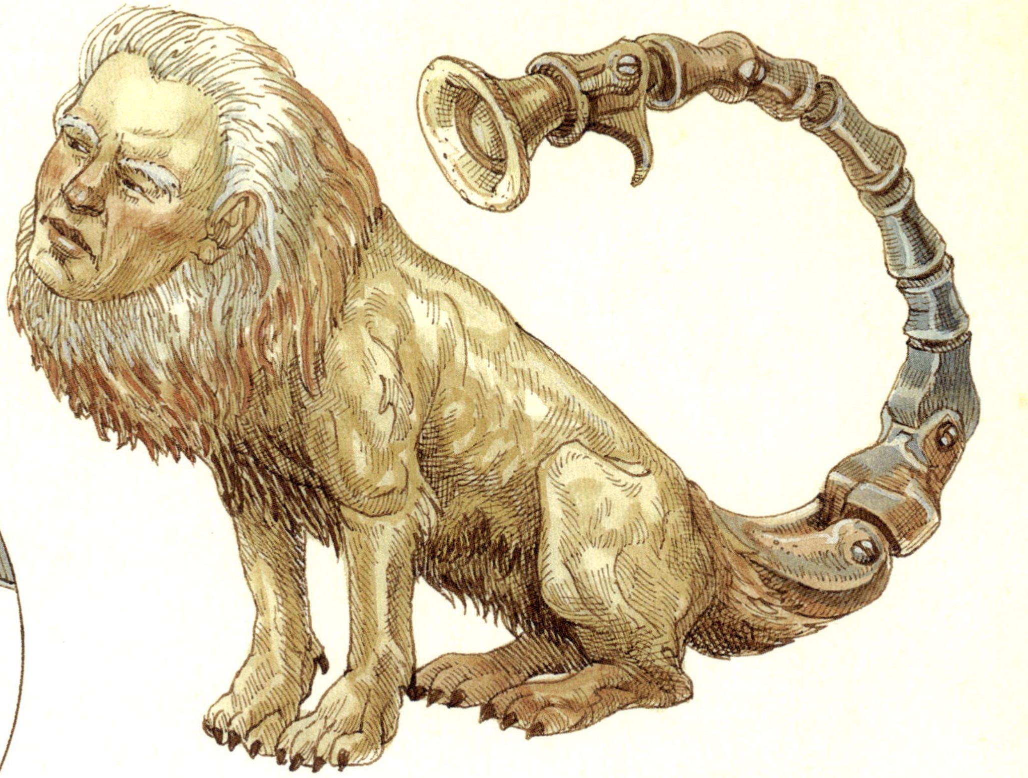

WAX ROLL

Wax is not difficult to obtain (page 84), and it's easy to form into any shape. This is also a disadvantage: The records are short-lived and deteriorate quickly in the heat. Pretty soon you'll want to invent vinyl (page 126).

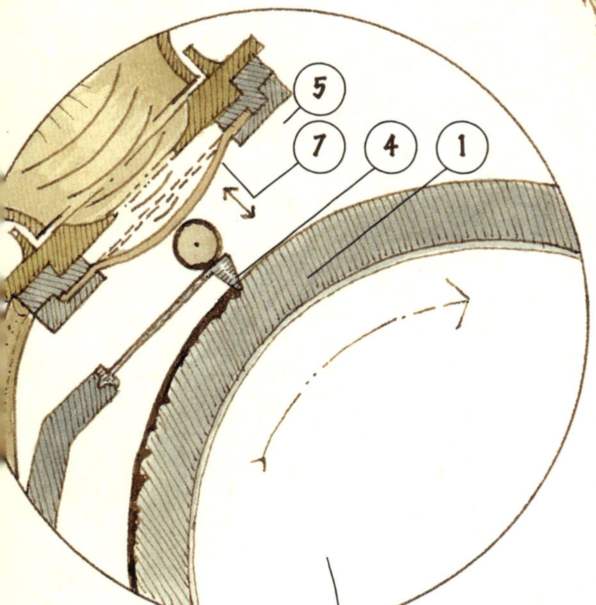

1. *Wax roll*
2. *Axis*
3. *Handle*
4. *Needle*
5. *Carriage*
6. *Horn*
7. *Diaphragm*

HANDLE

Trying to relax and enjoy the music while having to constantly turn the handle is not particularly convenient. Build a simple winding mechanism to help you unwind (page 166) or go further and connect it to a small electric motor (page 194).

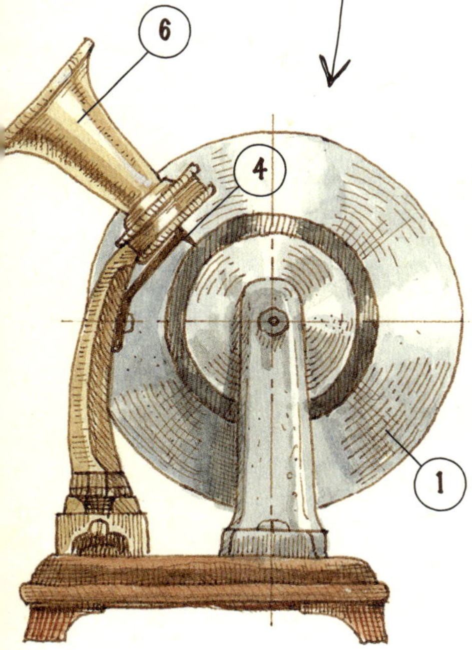

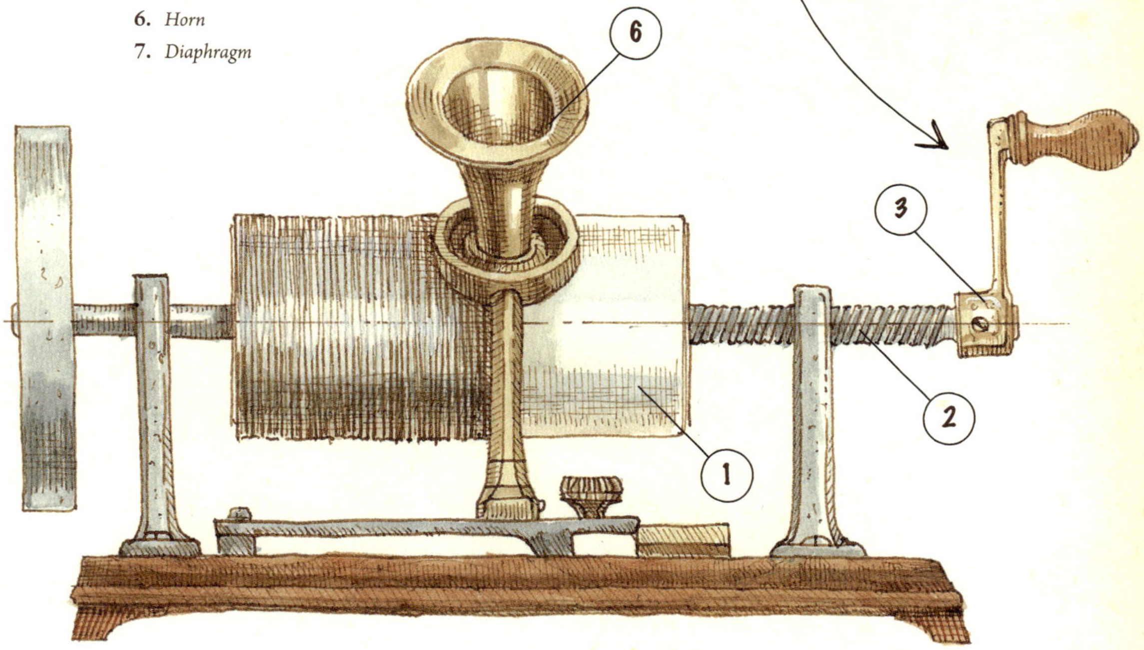

HEADPHONES

If you've already plugged into electricity (page 192), make a pair of headphones. Start with two earpieces. Attach a permanent magnet to the back side of each and make a hole in the front side. Place a flexible, slightly concave disc of thin, dense material in the middle. Attach a metal coil to the disc. Connect the two earpieces using wire.

The electricity passing through the wire magnetizes the coil, alternately attracted and repelled by the permanent magnet. This causes the disc to vibrate, creating pulsating air waves. These pass through the front part of the earpiece and vibrate your eardrum. Now you can jam to your favorite tunes with no fear of judgment from passers-by.

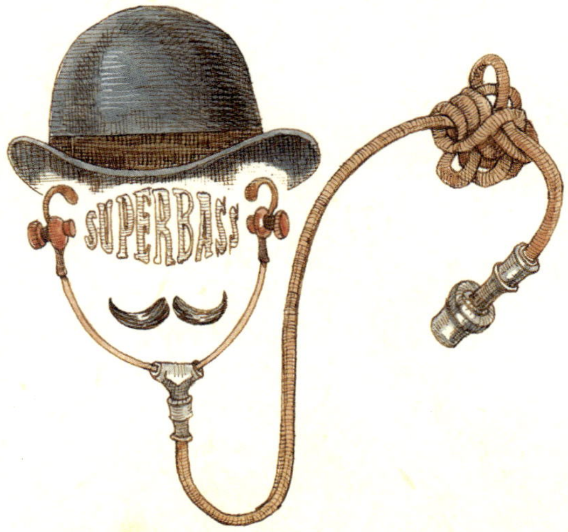

RAVE

Both music and math are among the highest abstractions of human thought, but at the same time, each has a precise definition and are, in fact, closely intertwined. Music is directly founded on numerical ratios. They define the external structure, or acoustic base, of the music: the rhythm, meter, tempo and frequency. Through music, we understand the structure of the world, which is also based on numbers, creating our own individual time flow with music moving from the past through the present and into the future.

The brain automatically connects the notes we hear with the ones that came before and creates our expectations of what will come next. When we listen to music, we don't hear individual notes but rather the unfolding of an entire musical phrase. So when composing music, instead of using individual notes as a basis, why not use a larger musical phrase — a sample?

A sample may be taken from another piece of music and developed into a whole new instrumental arrangement. You can also sample natural sounds: snippets of conversation, the patter of rain, the crashing of waves, the rustle of leaves. When creating samples, there's endless room for experimentation.

Sampling is at the heart of rave culture. There is no audience at a rave — it is a collective action. The DJ spins the turntables and gives rhythm to the movement. Ravers find themselves immersed in a sea of sound and light. This combines with the rhythmic movements to produce a hypnotic trance-like state. The rhythm and fluidity become a catalyst for a sense of community. Raves appeal to the depths of the unconscious. This is a road to your inner self, a means to throw off the shackles of everyday life that try to box in your consciousness. At the same time, the rave has the potential to free you — it allows everyone to be who they are while merging with the single breath of the mass of people.

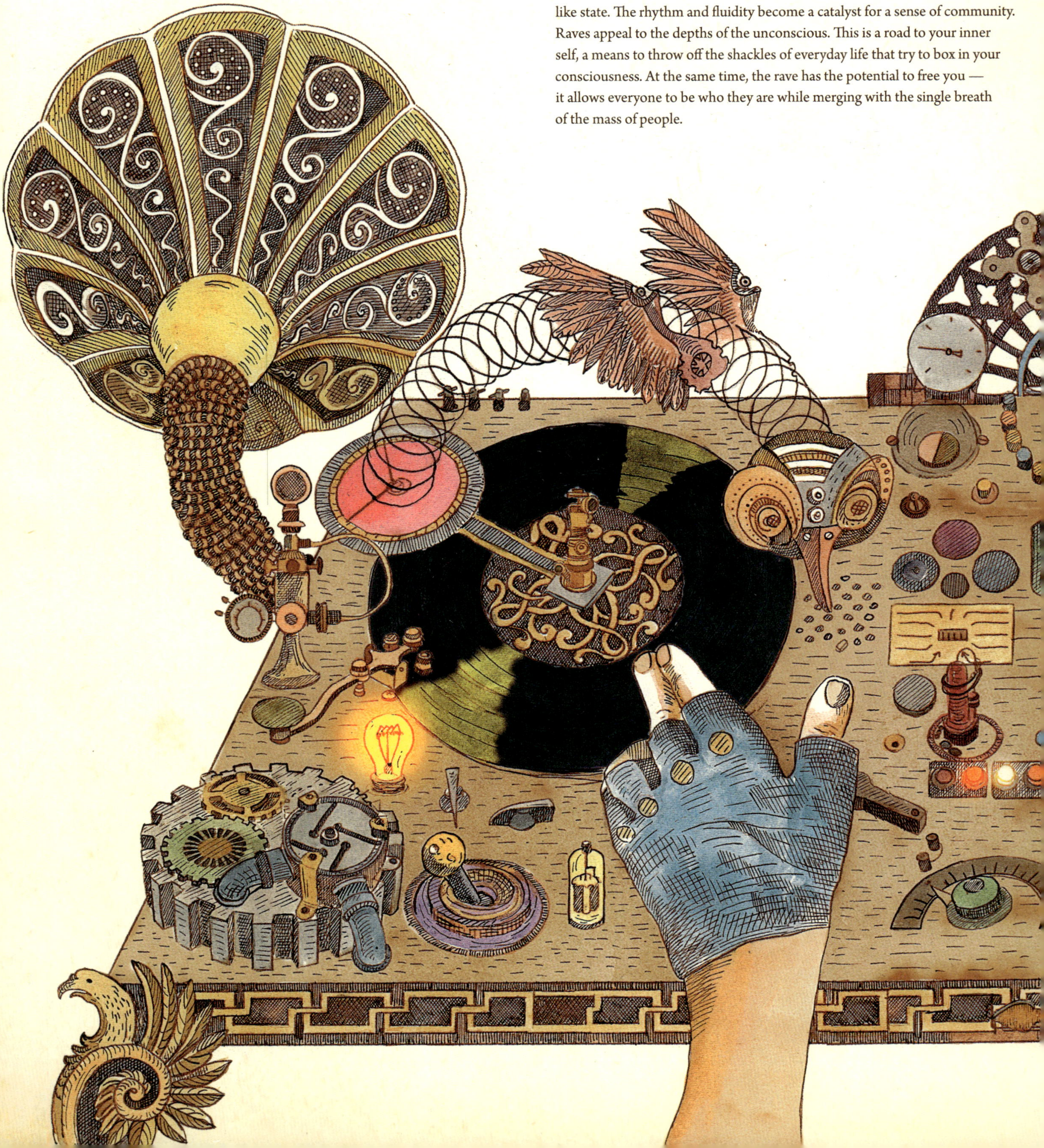

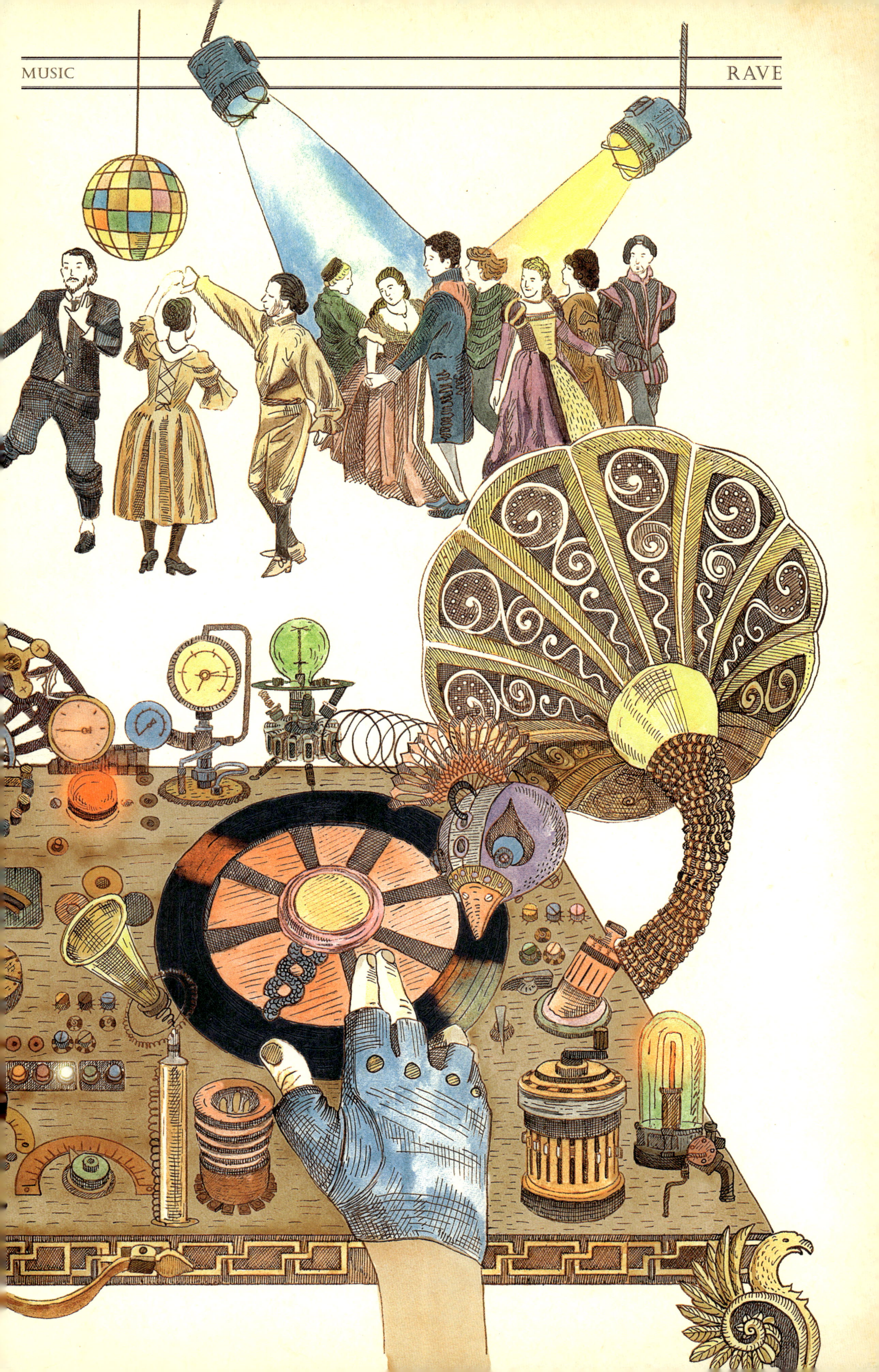

HUMAN

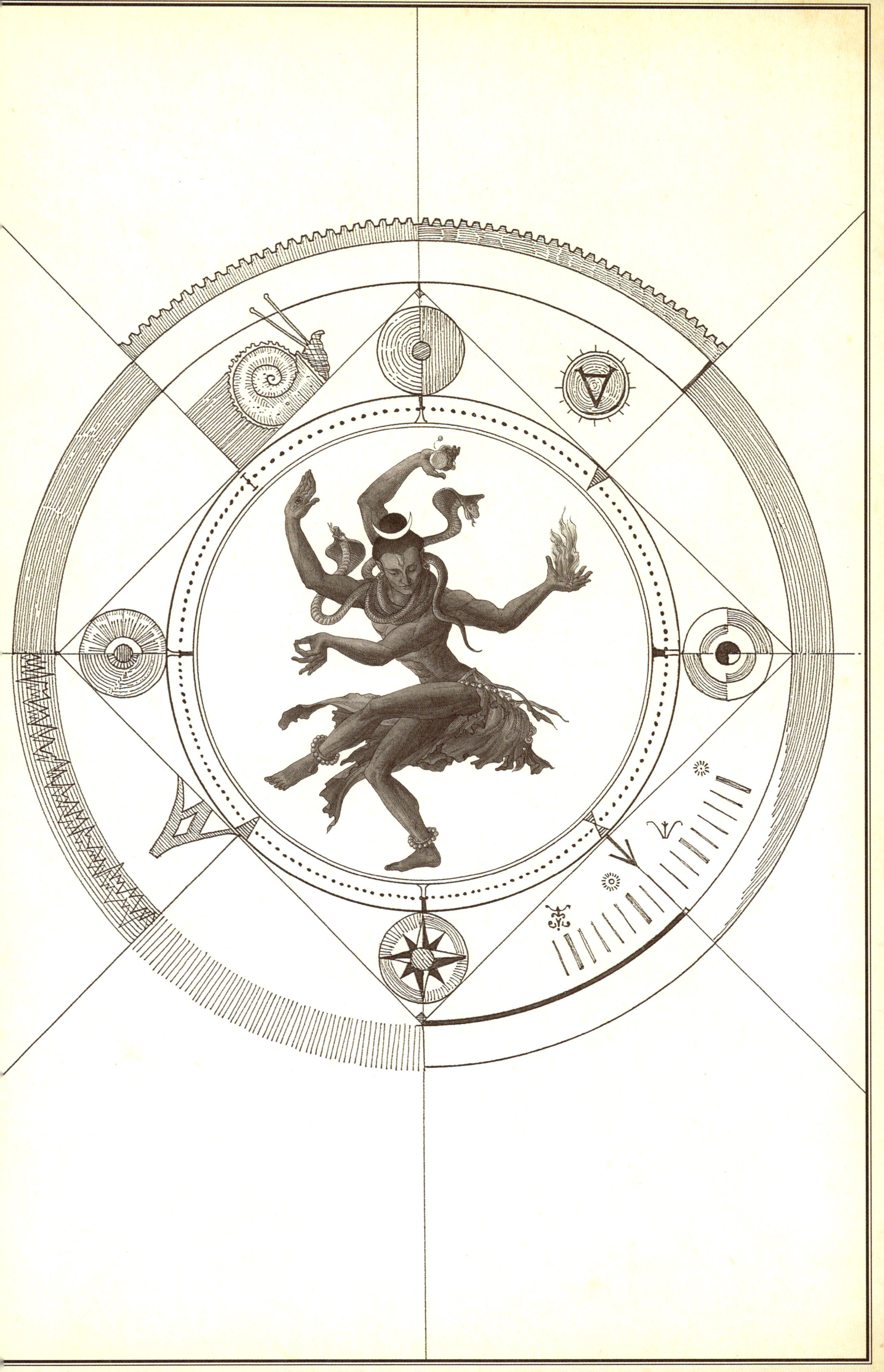

BREATHING

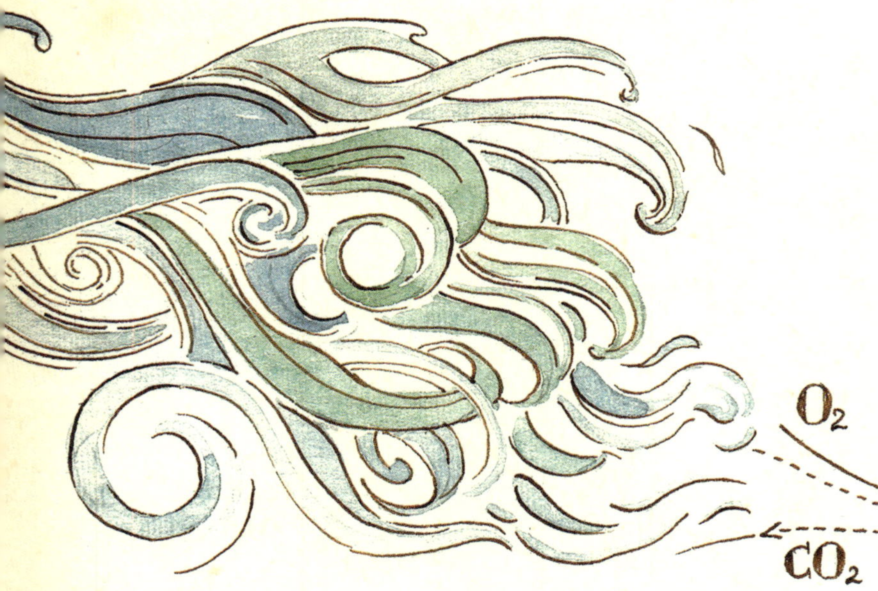

All animals, plants and many microorganisms need oxygen to survive. In humans, the process of breathing draws air into the lungs for oxygen to be absorbed into the bloodstream. The oxygen is used by all the cells of the body for chemical reactions that release the energy essential for life. By consciously controlling the frequency and depth of their inhale and exhale, people can control their emotions, reduce stress levels and even access altered states of consciousness.

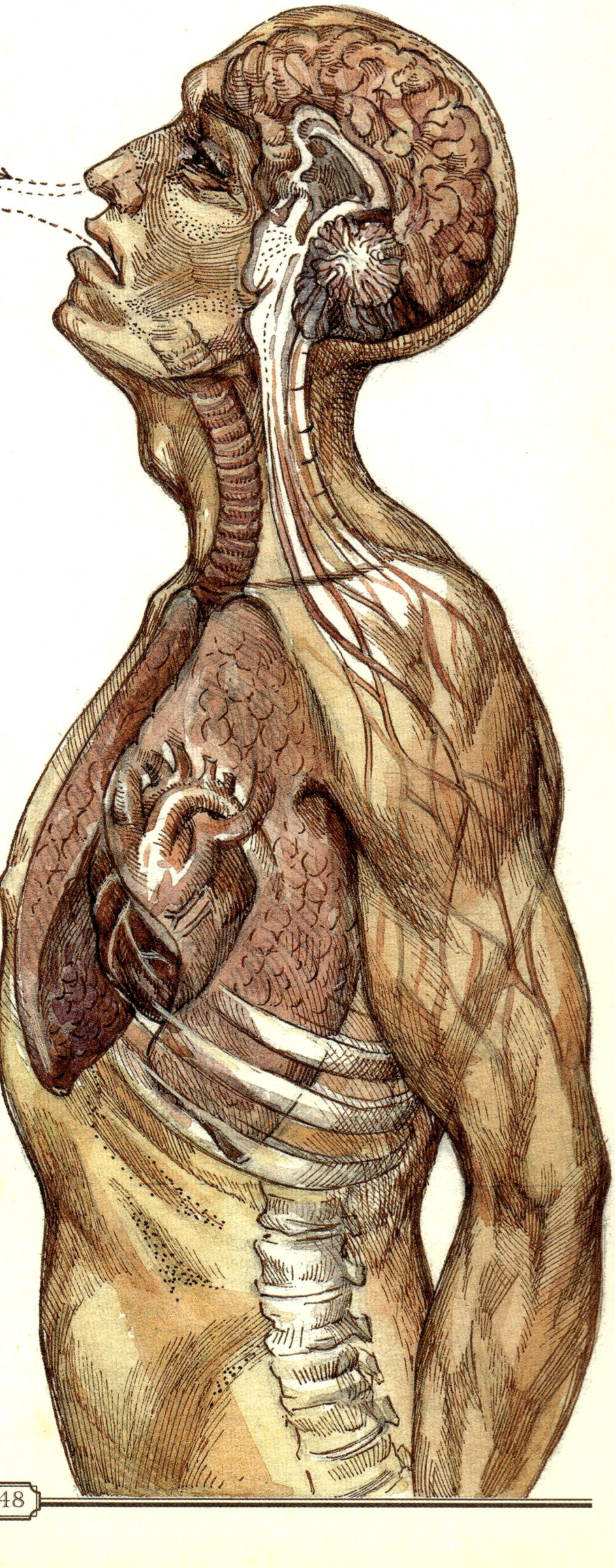

HOW DOES IT WORK?

Quick and shallow breathing activates the sympathetic branch of the nervous system — the body's "gas pedal" — and puts the body on high alert. A series of short, deep breaths brings a sense of euphoria and can put you in a sort of waking trance. Long, slow breaths and holding your breath has the opposite effect. It engages the parasympathetic branch of the nervous system (the "brake pedal"), which is responsible for rest and digestion. Exhaustion, repressed emotions and a sedentary lifestyle cause chronic muscle tension, forming something like a shell around the inner organs. This shell constricts the lung space, leading to rapid, shallow breathing and driving the body into a stress feedback loop. It usually develops in childhood due to overly tight clothing, a habit of clenching the stomach or improper posture.

If you want to slow down or get some stress relief, try the following exercise: Sit or lie down. Keep your back straight. Put one hand on your belly and concentrate on your breathing. Slowly inhale into your belly for three counts. Feel the air moving through your nose and throat, how your belly inflates. Smoothly exhale for six counts. Repeat this exercise for five minutes.

If instead you want an energy boost, use this exercise: Sit cross-legged with your back straight. Lower your chin. Close your eyes. Relax your belly and breathe into it. As you exhale, draw your belly in sharply, pushing the air out of your lungs in one swift motion. Breathe in through your nose (this exercise will also help clear your sinuses) and out through your mouth. Repeat 36 times, gradually speeding up. Do not perform this exercise if you are pregnant or have high blood pressure.

It's better to do any breathing exercises on an empty stomach. Don't try too hard to hyperventilate your lungs and hold your breath for long periods, especially when you are alone, because you might lose consciousness.

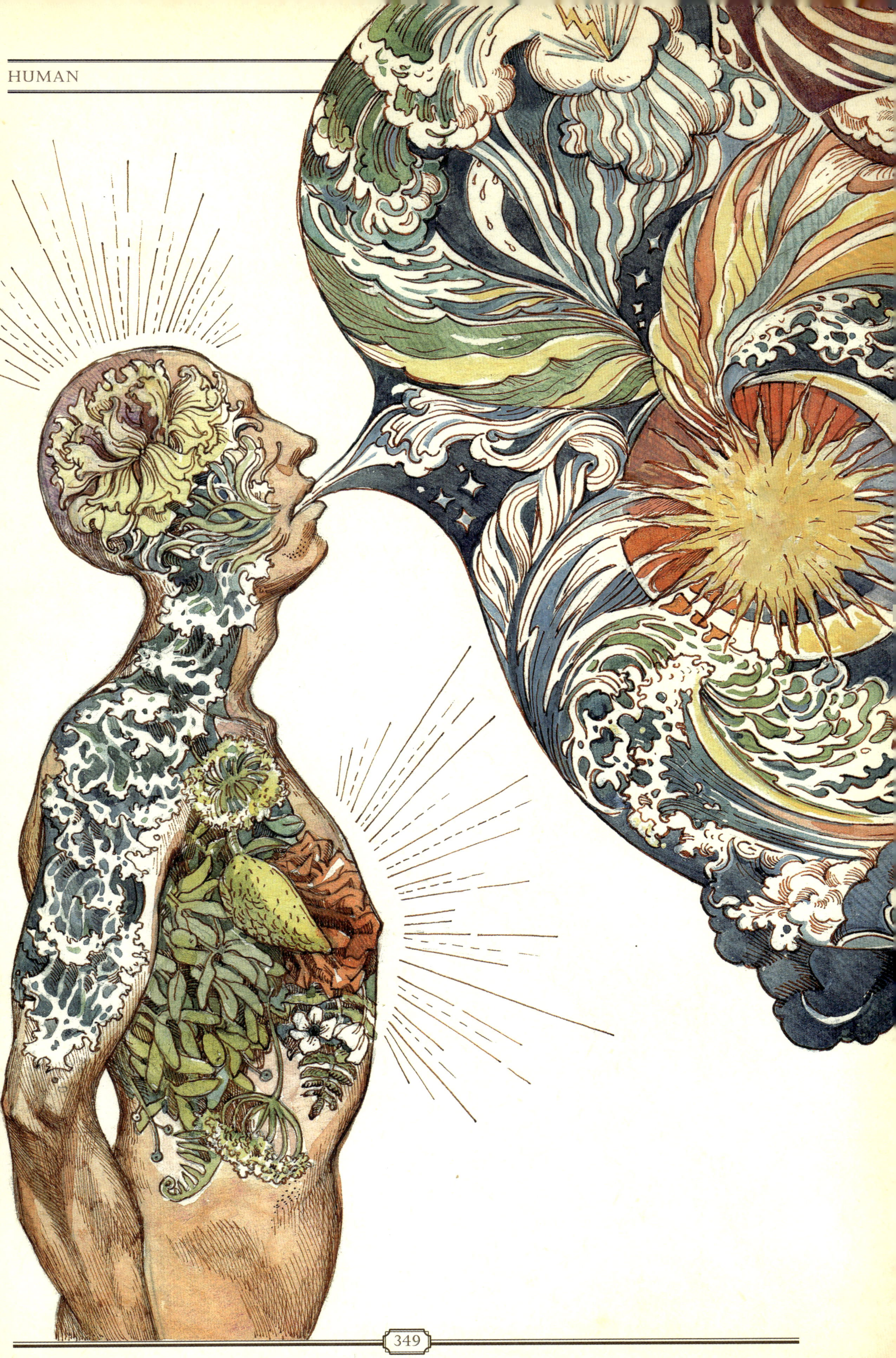

MEDITATION

Nature has given humans self-awareness, a unique ability unavailable to other animals. Humans are not only capable of feeling emotions and being consciously aware of their instincts, thoughts and actions but also of controlling them. Developing this skill, however, is impossible without the ability to carefully observe oneself and the world. Constant life distractions reduce the capacity for self-awareness — the brain goes on autopilot and begins to fall into negative patterns of thoughts and emotions.

Clear, focused engagement, by contrast, gives you access to creativity, improvisation and flow. Meditation is a powerful tool for working with the mind. It is based on relaxed concentration; concentration of attention not through an effort of will but through a sincere interest in what is happening. In meditation, the practitioner gives space to whatever is going through his mind without analyzing it or trying to change it.

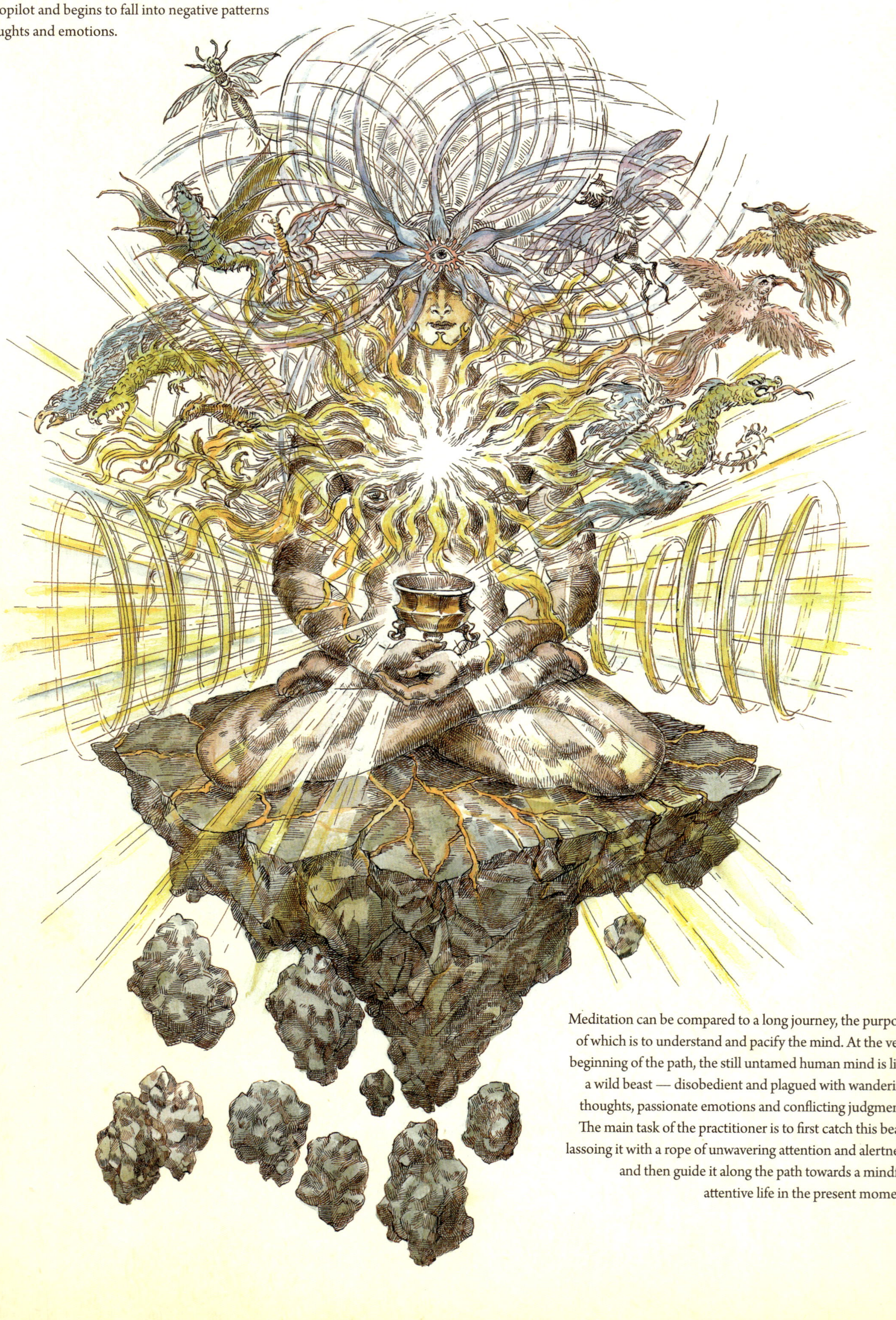

Meditation can be compared to a long journey, the purpose of which is to understand and pacify the mind. At the very beginning of the path, the still untamed human mind is like a wild beast — disobedient and plagued with wandering thoughts, passionate emotions and conflicting judgments. The main task of the practitioner is to first catch this beast, lassoing it with a rope of unwavering attention and alertness, and then guide it along the path towards a mindful, attentive life in the present moment.

Basic practice in preparation for meditation is the technique of body relaxation. To do this, set an alarm clock for 3 to 5 minutes and repeat the following steps:

1. Sit comfortably with a straight back. Close your eyes or leave them half-closed, focusing your gaze on a stationary object. Take several full, deep breaths and exhale.
2. Slowly "scan" your body from top to bottom, moving your attention from one area to another and consciously relaxing the muscles as you go: your face, stomach, groin and so on.
3. Scan your body several times until your alarm goes off.

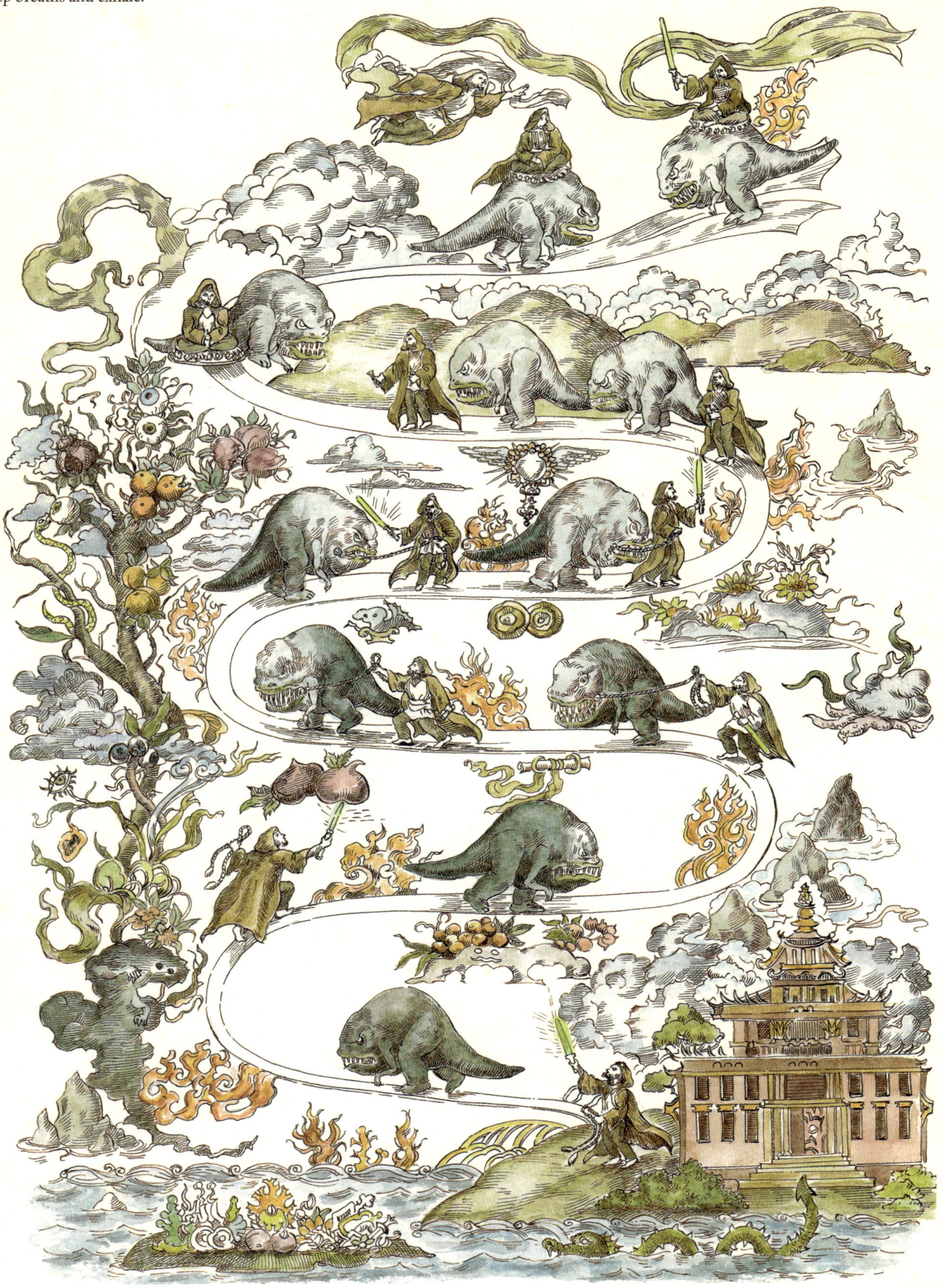

To improve your concentration skills, try observing your breath:

1. Repeat step 1 from the previous exercise.
2. Direct your attention to the feeling of your breath at the tip of your nose or in your belly. Observe your inhalations and exhalations.
3. Notice when attention slips away and patiently return to observing your breathing.
4. When the timer rings, thank yourself for practicing the exercise.

It is important to bring the experience gained in these short sessions into your daily life. This will help you transform negative habits of mind, develop empathy and embrace the world as it is. The more people in your society who know how to manage their emotions and thoughts, the more developed the civilization you will be able to create.

SELF-IMPROVEMENT

Humans have the inherent desire to constantly push the limits of their abilities. This craving for adventure is a great driving force for a developing civilization. It pushes people to explore new terrains, conquer the cosmos and populate new planets. In everyday life, it also motivates them to find ways to overcome the limitations of their bodies and minds.

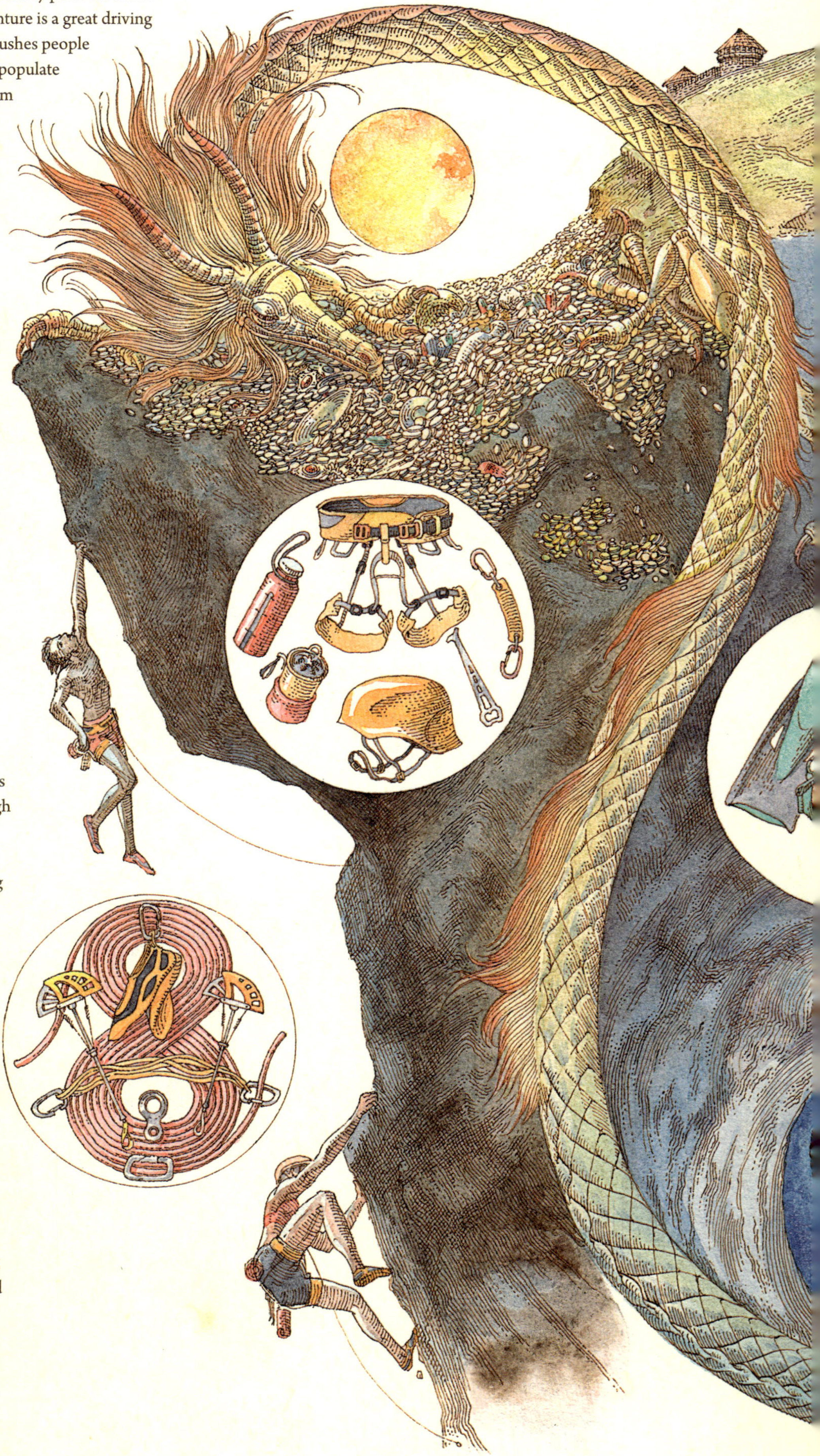

Rock climbing challenges a person's agility and endurance, as well as his ability to conquer his fears. It's a duel not only with the mountain but with yourself: your mind cries "no!" and yet you keep climbing higher and higher. The climber learns to masterfully control his body from the tips of his fingers to his toes. Every move requires total concentration and the ability to calculate actions in advance.

There are three basic principles you must learn before you can master rock climbing. The first concerns the placement of your feet: You must always climb with your toes facing forward and never turn your foot sideways. Otherwise, failure is inevitable. Your position must be extremely precise so you can transfer all the weight to your legs and pivot to the side if necessary.

The second principle is to synchronize your movements. If you're gripping a ledge with your right hand, you should lean on your left leg. In this case, the diagonal of balance passes exactly through the body's center of gravity (located in the pelvic area in front of the sacrum). This will conserve your energy. It's also important that your other leg isn't dangling in the air but is at least pressed up against the rock. This will avoid any unnecessary swaying that may throw you off balance.

The third rule is about proper body placement: Your arms should always be straight, legs bent, your center of gravity pressed to the wall. If your hips are waggling in the wind, it will put extra tension on your arms, causing them to quickly become exhausted.

You'll need special climbing equipment: shoes with a thin and flexible rubberized sole — a size or two smaller than usual to ensure a snug fit so that you can plant your feet firmly — and a bag of magnesium powder (magnesium carbonate and hydroxide bind to moisture and body oils so your hands don't slip). And, of course, your safety net: rope, a harness, carabiners and special devices for fastening stays in rock crevices with carabiners.

Climbers usually work in pairs: one climbs and the other controls the safety rope. The burden of responsibility for your own life and the life of your partner gives you the drive to power through even when your strength is waning.

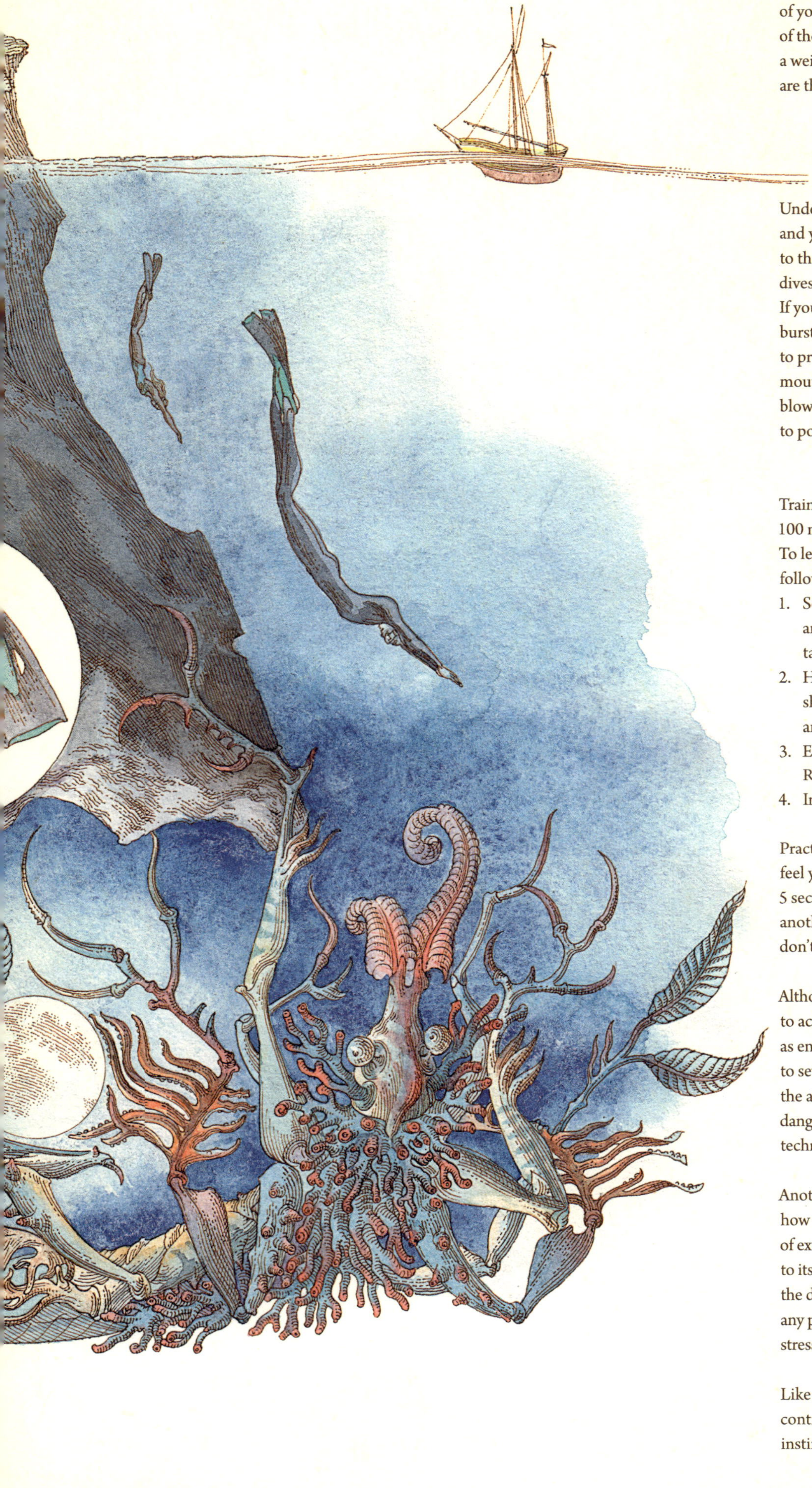

FREEDIVING

Freediving is diving into water as deep as you can using only your own held breath. Like rock climbing, it allows you to push the boundaries of your own body but this time in the depths of the ocean. Fins, a mask or goggles, a nose clip, a weight and a wetsuit, in case of cold water, are the only equipment freedivers need.

Under water, the pulse slows down significantly and your blood pressure rises as blood rushes to the heart, lungs and brain. The deeper a person dives, the more pressure is exerted on the body. If you go too far down, your eardrums can even burst. To avoid this, you need to learn how to properly equalize the pressure: close your mouth and pinch your nostrils closed then lightly blow out through your nose against this pressure to pop your ears.

Trained divers can descend to depths of more than 100 meters and hold their breath for 6–7 minutes. To lengthen your dive time, you can practice the following breath-holding exercise:

1. Seal your lips around the snorkel mouthpiece and, with the end of the tube above the water, take a deep 5-count breath.
2. Hold your breath for 20 seconds. Lower your shoulders, relax the muscles of your face and neck and hang your head.
3. Exhale through the mouth for 5 seconds. Relax your core.
4. Immediately begin the process over again.

Practice this exercise 5 minutes a day. When you feel you're starting to make progress, add another 5 seconds onto the time you hold your breath and another minute to your daily practice time but don't exceed 15 minutes.

Although holding your breath causes your body to actively produce happiness hormones known as endorphins, your psyche is still subjected to severe stress — after all, you're alone with the abyss down there. Panic in the deep can be dangerous. Freedivers are trained in deep relaxation techniques to stay clear-headed.

Another complicated aspect of diving is learning how to ascend safely — the body is in a state of extreme oxygen starvation and is being pushed to its limits. At this moment, it is important for the diver to ignore the reflex to take a breath, soothe any panic and calmly swim upward. Any excessive stress or increase in heart rate can be deadly.

Like rock climbing, freediving develops self-control and the ability to suppress one's natural instincts and move decisively towards the goal.

YOGA

Deep inside, every human being just wants to be happy. True happiness is impossible without finding a state of harmony with the world and radically transforming your mind and body. This is the aim of yoga.

Mastering the art of yoga begins with physical and breathing exercises. When combined, this cleanses the body, reduces tension and heals many diseases. This is achieved by holding certain poses, or asanas, which stretch and engage various parts of the body.

Practicing these poses improves blood circulation to the internal organs, relaxes the nervous system and relieves tension that may generate anxiety and severely distort your perception of the world.

There are various meditative techniques used for stilling the mind. By practicing them, people gain control over their thoughts and emotions, tuning into a more subtle and well-balanced view of reality.

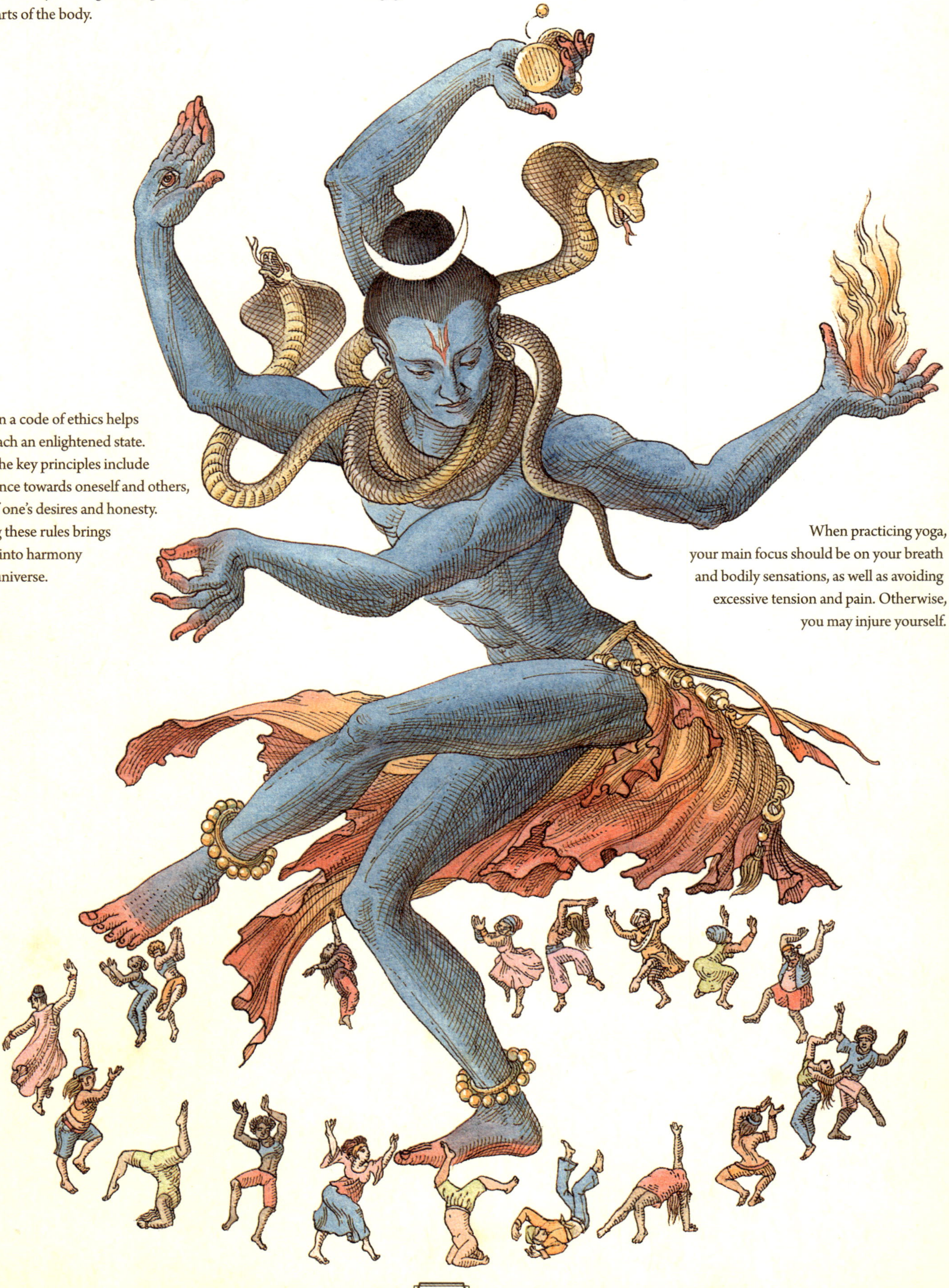

Relying on a code of ethics helps people reach an enlightened state. Some of the key principles include non-violence towards oneself and others, control of one's desires and honesty. Following these rules brings the mind into harmony with the universe.

When practicing yoga, your main focus should be on your breath and bodily sensations, as well as avoiding excessive tension and pain. Otherwise, you may injure yourself.

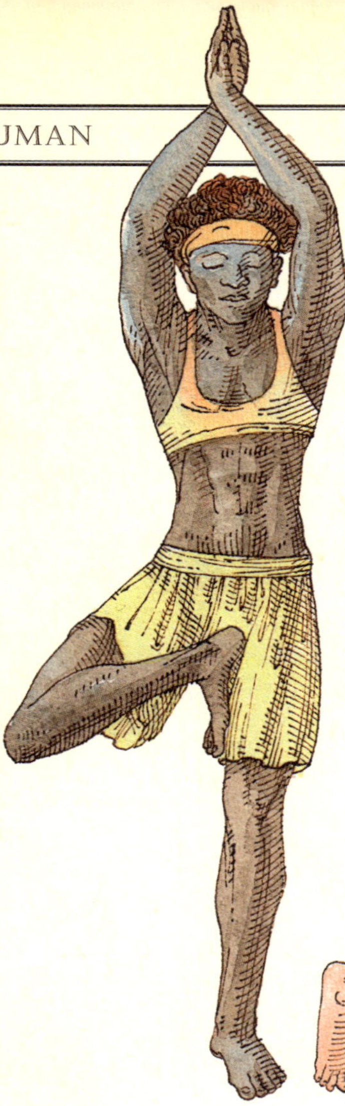

As a rule, a yoga sequence consists of a series of poses and always ends with a pose to relax the entire body. You can start your practice standing. Stand straight with heels and toes touching. Distribute your weight evenly across both feet, engage your knees, pull your stomach in and stretch your spine tall, arms by your sides. Now bend your right leg to lift it and place your heel on the inside of your left thigh, pressing into it.

Stabilize in this position and, balancing, bring your palms together and extend your arms skyward. Hold this position for as long as possible. Breathe deeply. Switch legs. This pose teaches balance and tones the leg muscles.

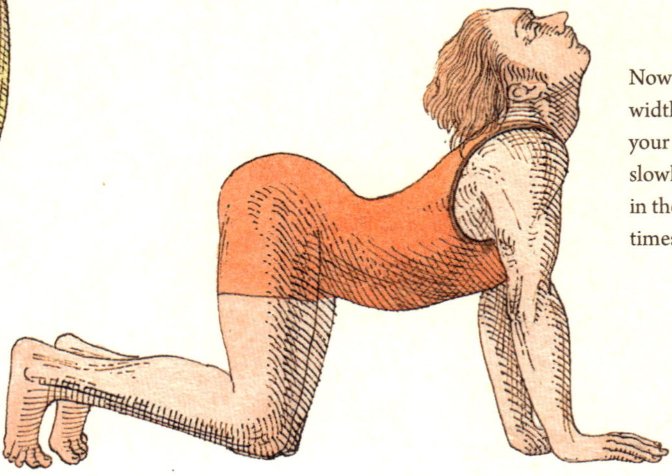

Now get down on all fours, hands placed shoulder-width apart, knees on the floor. On the inhale, arch your lower back in the “cow” pose. On the exhale, slowly stretch upward, rounding your lower back in the “cat” pose. Repeat the cycle smoothly nine times. This pose improves spine flexibility.

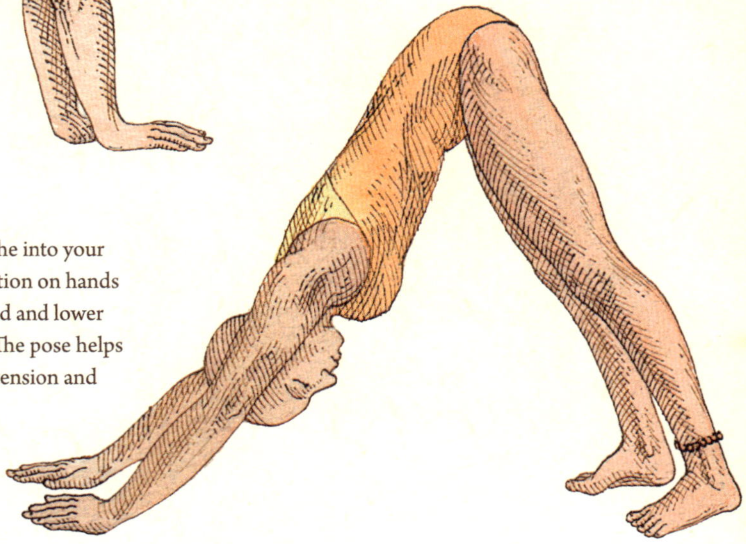

Lie on your stomach and spread your feet 30 cm wide, palms on the floor at chest level, elbows close to the body. As you exhale, lift your body off the floor, straighten your arms, put your head down between them and stretch your spine. Legs straight, knees engaged, heels pressed to the floor. Feet parallel to each other, fingers spread wide apart and directed forward.

Stand for about a minute and breathe into your belly. Start in a standard plank position on hands and toes as you exhale, lift your head and lower yourself gently to the floor. Relax. The pose helps strengthen the spine, relieve chest tension and improve digestion.

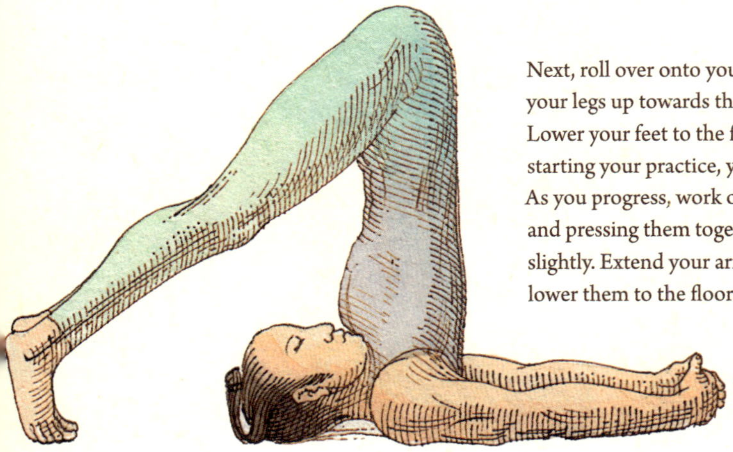

Next, roll over onto your back. As you inhale, pull your legs up towards the sky and over your head. Lower your feet to the floor. When you’re first starting your practice, you can bend your knees. As you progress, work on straightening your legs and pressing them together then engage them slightly. Extend your arms behind your head and lower them to the floor.

Your neck should be relaxed, your spine should be in one line and the weight of the body should be resting on the shoulders. Breathe calmly for a few minutes. Return to the starting position. This exercise stimulates the nervous system, massages the internal organs and has a beneficial effect on thyroid function.

The next pose is the final asana in any yoga sequence. It helps relax your mind and body as much as possible. To practice the pose, lie comfortably on your back, turn your palms towards the sky and spread your legs comfortably wide. Then close your eyes and, with calm, measured breaths, mentally scan your body starting from the head and focus on gradually relaxing each muscle. Typically, this exercise takes 5–10 minutes. This pose is considered one of the most difficult asanas in yoga, since it is very difficult for people to achieve complete relaxation.

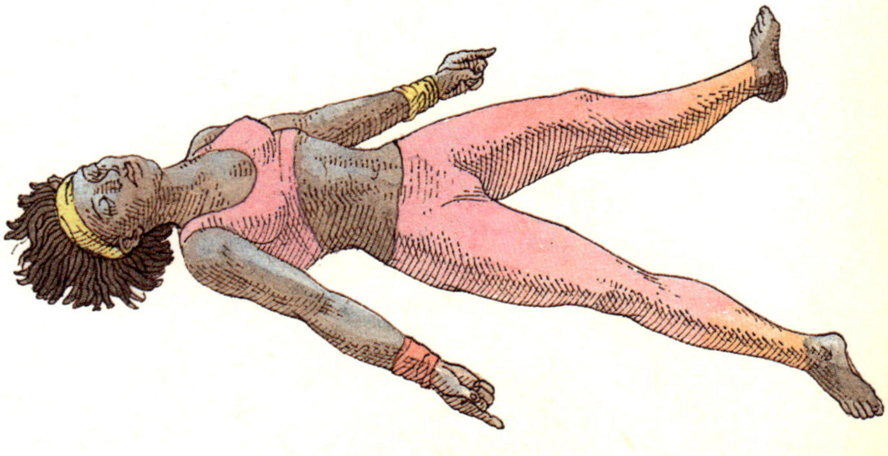

As you develop yoga practice, you acquire unique skills such as deep intuition and inner strength. Yogis attain special states of consciousness when their minds are freed from the dual perception of the world and from suffering.

QIGONG

The process of natural selection has honed the survival and self-healing mechanisms of every living being. But the further human beings progress along the path of civilization, the weaker their connection with the natural cycles becomes. They stop listening to their own bodies and lose the ability to control them.

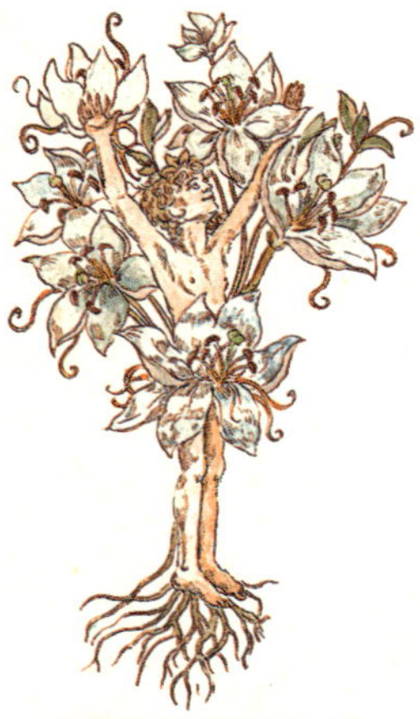

Qigong is the focused application and understanding of mind-body-spirit to improve your mental clarity and physical health through correct posture, movement, breathing, sound and focused intent. The aims of regular qigong practice are to return to the original integrity and connection with nature inherent in all living beings, free yourself from tension and return to harmony with nature.

FOLLOWING THE CYCLES OF NATURE

Qigong gives you the opportunity to build an effective activity and rest routine and adjust to the true needs of the body.

BODY POSITION CONTROL

With this skill, one avoids unnecessary stress and injury and increases the body's endurance.

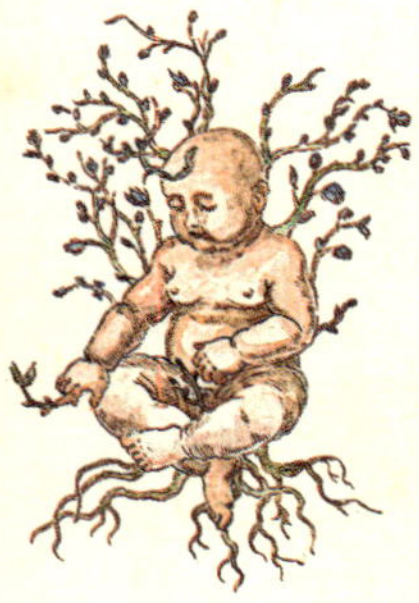

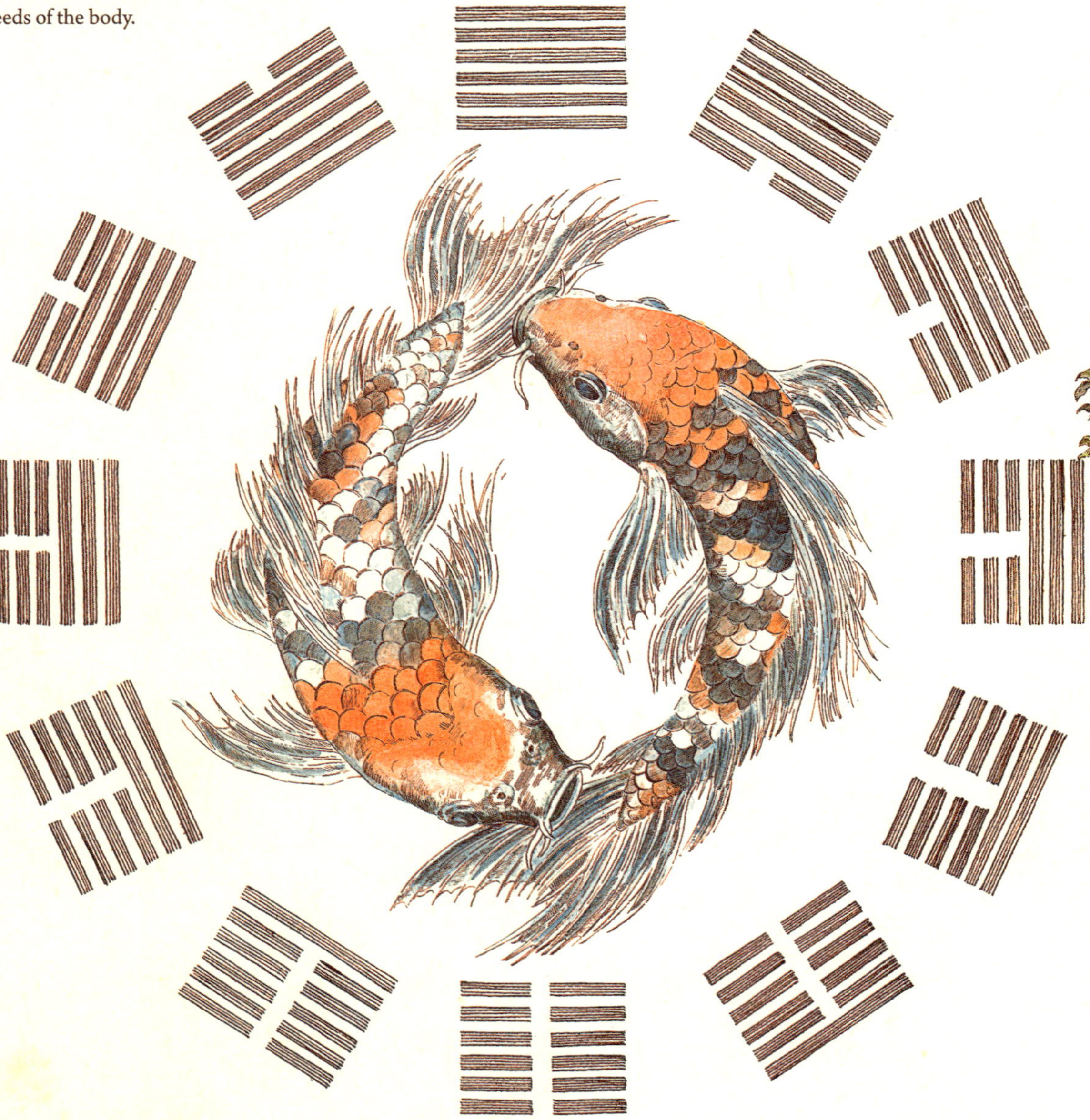

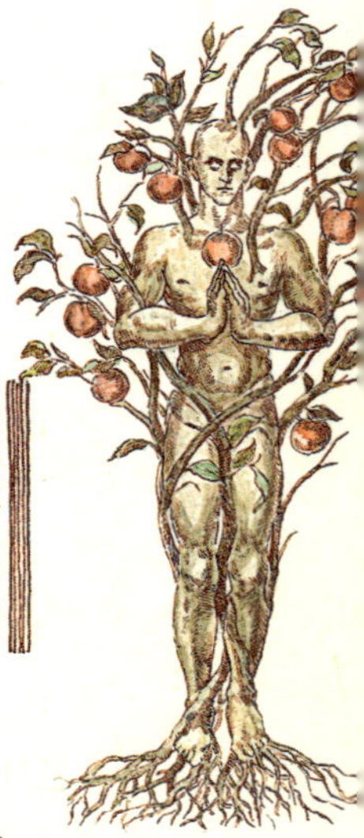

BODY RELAXATION

Move without effort, follow your inner impulses and tune your body like a musical instrument instead of controlling it forcefully. This principle makes it possible to remove muscle blocks, relax the mind and encourage self-healing.

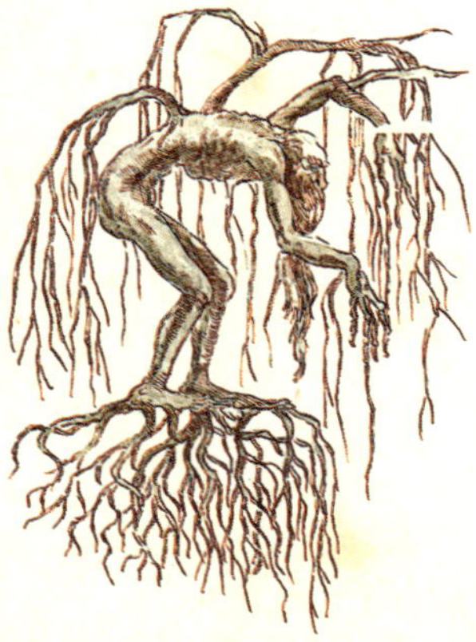

BREATH & ATTENTION CONTROL

Focusing on the depth and rhythm of the inhale/exhale cycle and body sensations helps to restore mental clarity, manage emotions and find a fuller, more holistic perception of the world.

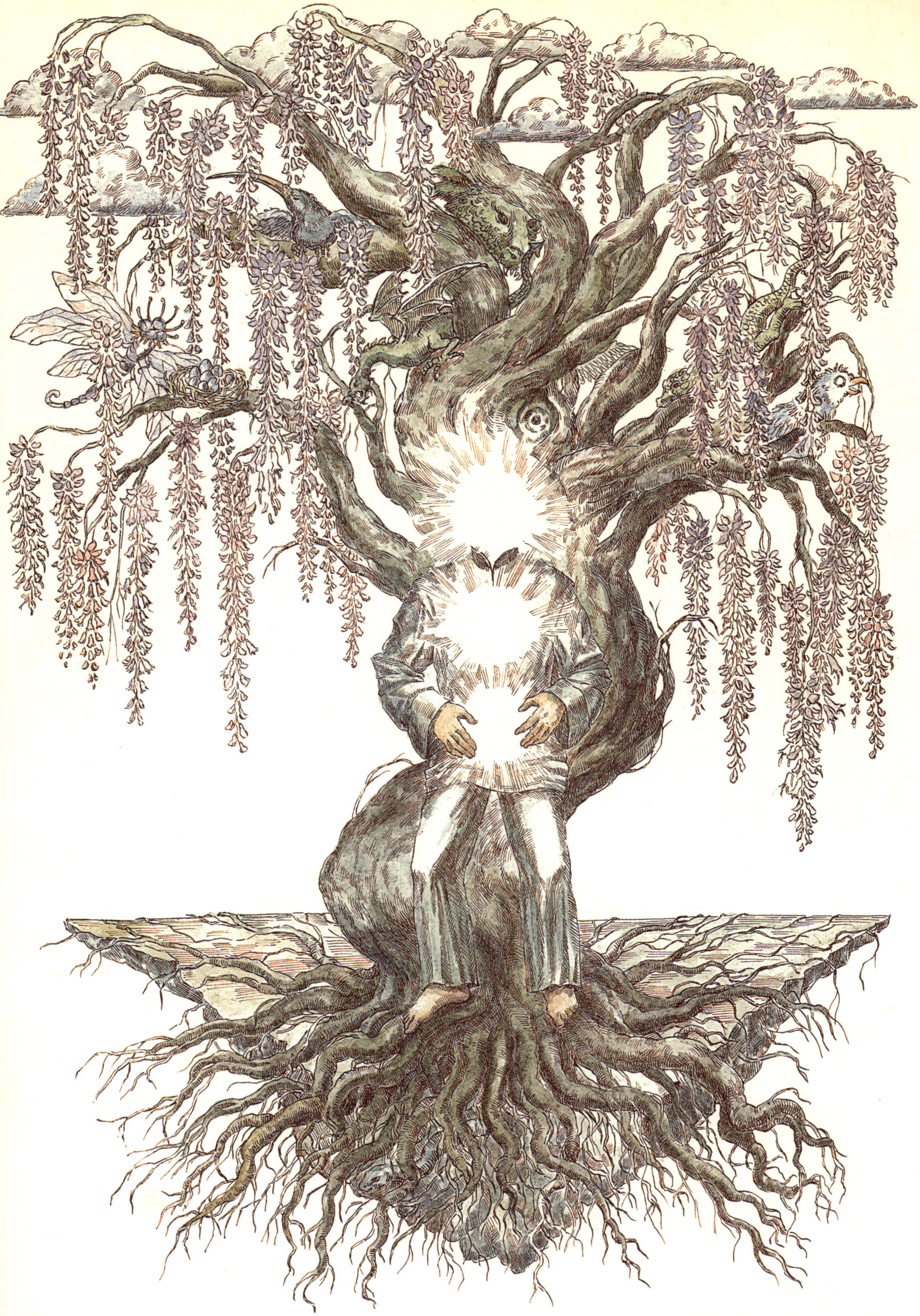

One of the basic qigong exercises is called "The Tree." To practice it, stand up straight with your feet shoulder-width apart. The tongue should lightly touch the roof of your mouth. Tailbone is tilted down. Knees are slightly bent. Shoulders are loose and open, as if you were holding an egg under your armpit. Arms are bent at the elbows and resting at your side. The top of your head points towards the sky. Eyes are partially open.

Breathing is even and measured. Stay in this position for at least 10 minutes and try to feel your body. At the end of the practice, place your hands on your stomach: women should put the right hand on the navel, the left hand on top; men, vice versa. The most important aspect of any qigong practice is reaching a calm, meditative state of mind. This is how you regain touch with your body's voice. It will guide your movement, and the healing process will begin.

DREAMS

Human understanding of the waking world is often divided into binaries—good and evil, life and death, past and present. But the universe is far vaster and more complex than the limited view of reality in which we spend our lives. Dreams unshackle our mind, giving us access to the Universal Life Source — the origin of all that is. Dreams aren't governed by logic.

The dreaming mind is subject only to the rule of feelings, sensations and images the brain has absorbed during the day and stored in either the conscious or subconscious, depending on the perceived usefulness of the information. Dream interpretation can be a real spiritual practice in meeting your true self and tapping into the creative force of the universe. It can help you develop your creativity and consciously take control of your life. It is sometimes easy to avoid unresolved conflicts, but it takes courage to face them.

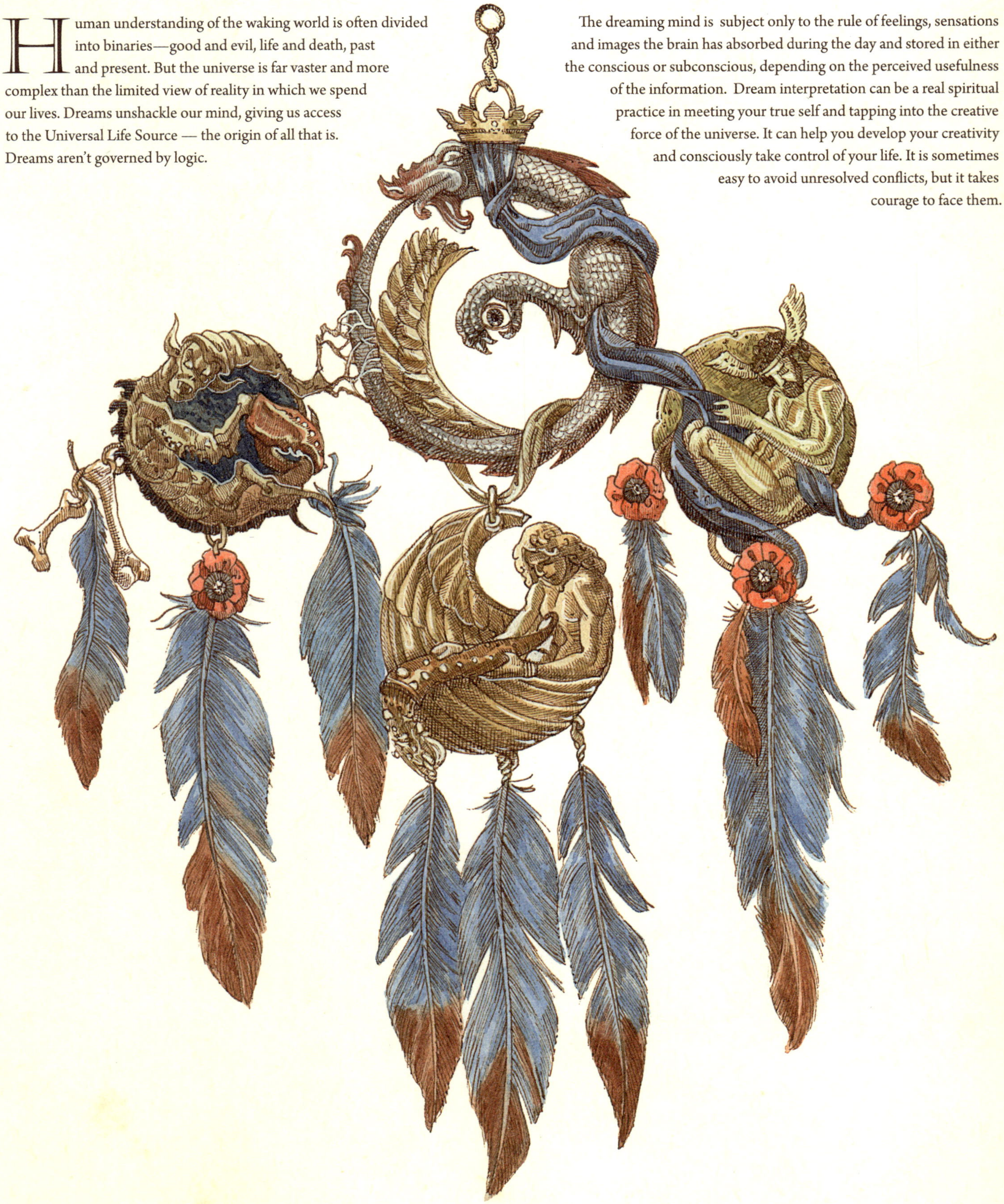

There are no moral principles in dreams. Here everyone can live their most shameful and cruel fantasies. For example, a loving, well-to-do housewife may dream of picking up a machine gun. You need to give up control and follow the natural course of the dream.

This is the structure of the psyche — only by passing through their fears can a person be healed. After waking up, give yourself 15 minutes to lie in bed in order to feel the sensations as your body recalls the details of your dream. Otherwise, the memory will be overwhelmed by your rational, conscious mind.

Following the sensations, images from sleep will begin to surface: for example, fire. What kind of fire was it? Cozy or scorching? How do you feel about the fire? Maybe you have an anger burning you from the inside out? How can you manage it?

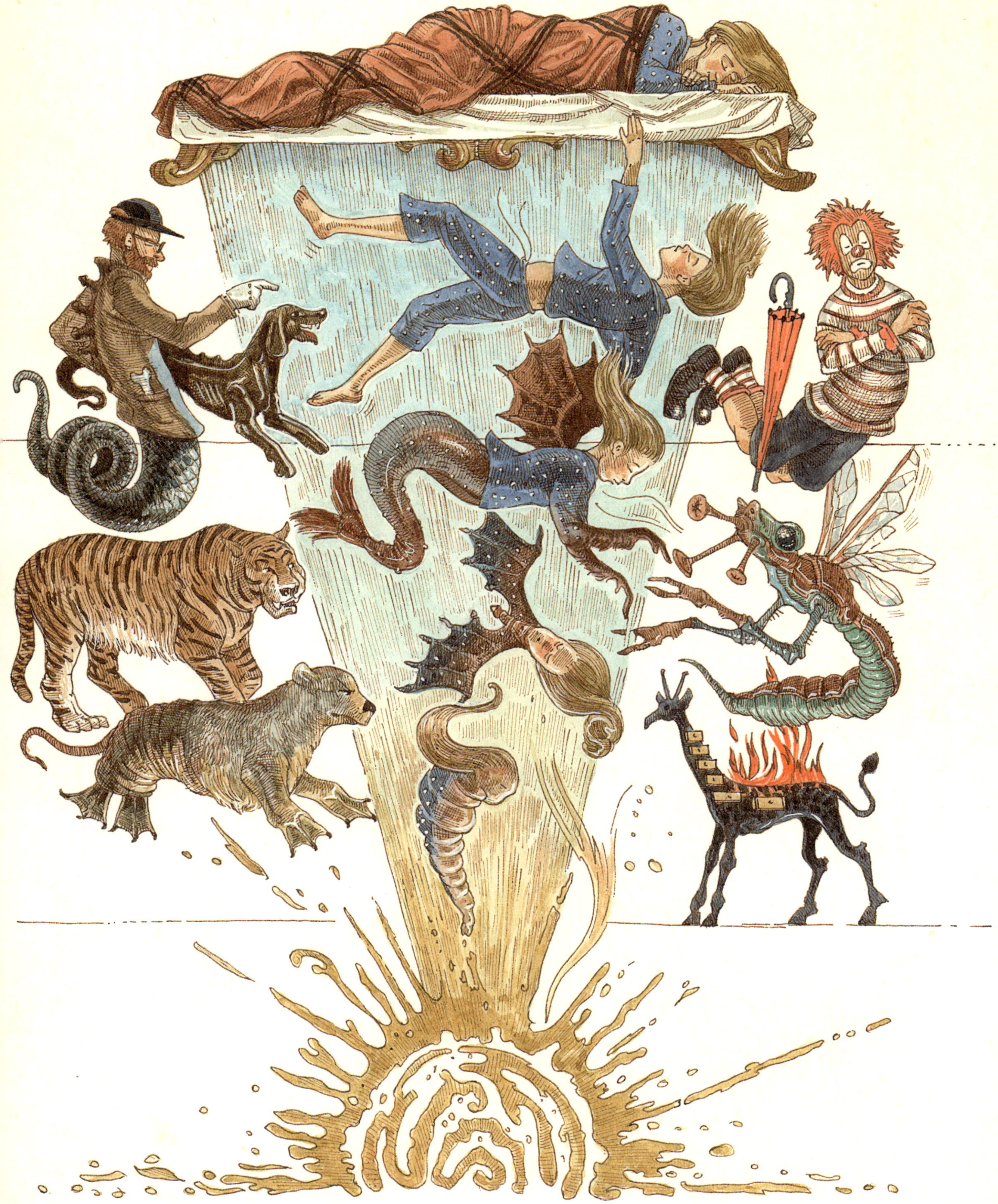

Applying logic when interpreting images from your dream is futile. Relive your dream in your memory. Disregard obvious interpretations and try to decrypt messages hidden within. For example, perhaps you were walking along the road and saw a roaring tiger. Imagine yourself as this tiger. How do you feel? Who are you growling at?

Maybe the tiger symbolizes the animal strength you are unable to recognize in yourself while awake. Dreams can portend future events or illnesses, so draw connections to your waking life. For example, let's say you dream of a kettle boiling over and spraying hot water everywhere, while in everyday life, you don't allow yourself to express your emotions and they are boiling up inside you.

Maybe your nervous system is so fried that you will experience a hypertensive emergency if you don't learn to express your emotions. Think about how to react differently. This practice allows you to turn dreams into allies on the path to a healthier, more holistic approach to life.

PSYCHOTHERAPY

Suffering is an inherent part of every sentient being's life. When the burden becomes unbearable, the mind can begin to develop coping mechanisms. These cushion the psyche from destructive experiences and help you adapt to reality.

Even if the traumatic event has been repressed from consciousness, all the feelings and sensations associated with it are imprinted on the body and nervous system. This forms a sort of protective barrier — a chronic stress memory that helps you avoid or survive similar situations — but at the same time limits personal development. These defense mechanisms are especially apparent when a person projects their emotions from past experiences onto people who had nothing whatsoever to do with them.

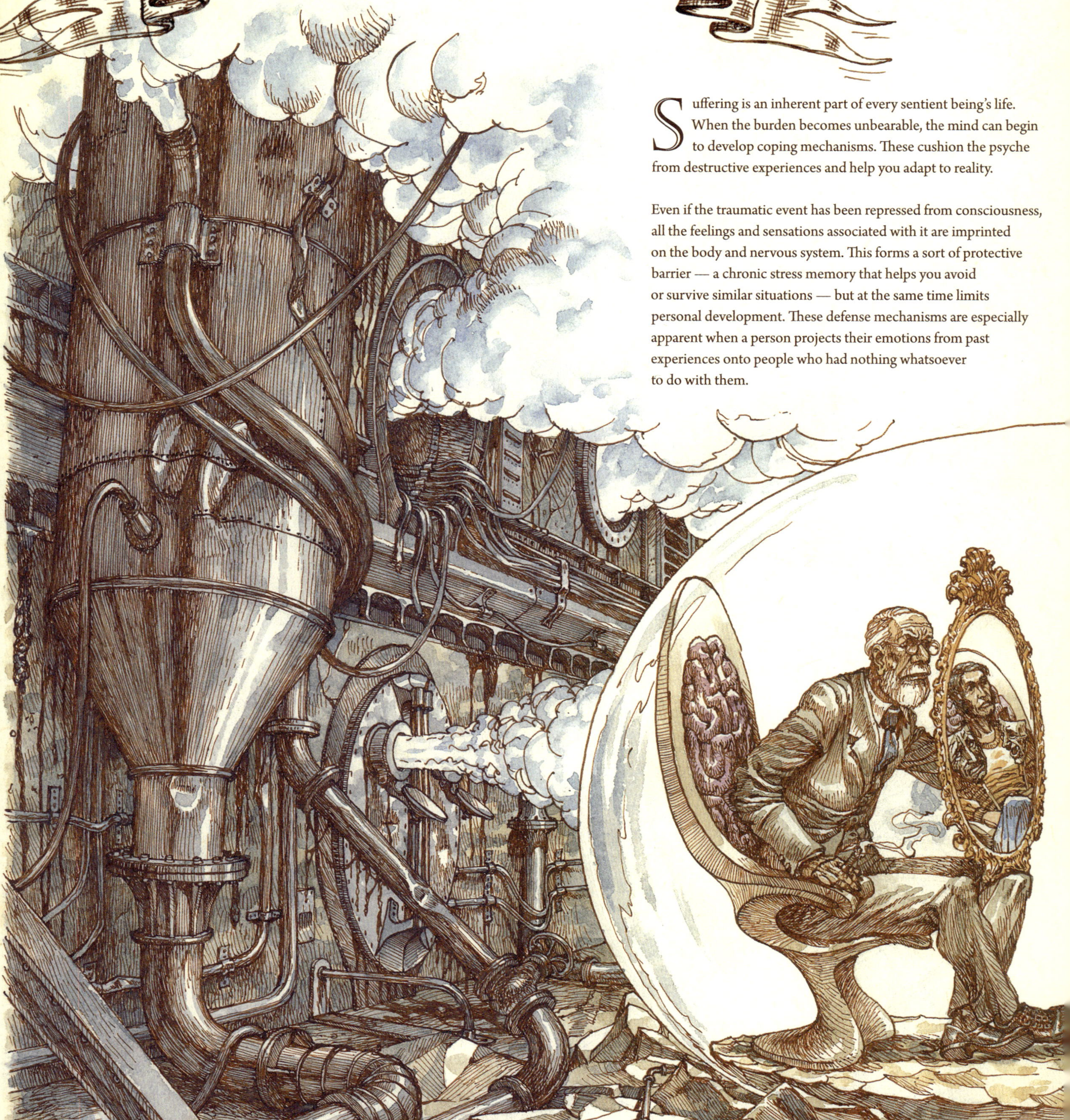

To start the healing process, you need someone who can act as a mirror to help you become aware of your traumas, projections and patterns of behavior and free yourself from their negative effects. But few are capable of such selfless listening and total engagement. Those who are become therapists. If everyone knew how to listen with interest and without projecting past experience, we wouldn't need therapists. But until we reach this utopian future, sit back in this chaise-lounge and tell me: How does that make you feel? The therapist sincerely empathizes with the person, sometimes gently nudging them towards the next step, but doesn't get emotionally involved and always remembers that the patient must travel the path of self-discovery on his own. One important skill a therapist must possess is the ability to feel another person's pain without being weighed down by their emotions. One technique is to imagine that the patient is discussing his dreams: They are illusory but at the same time very important and cause suffering.

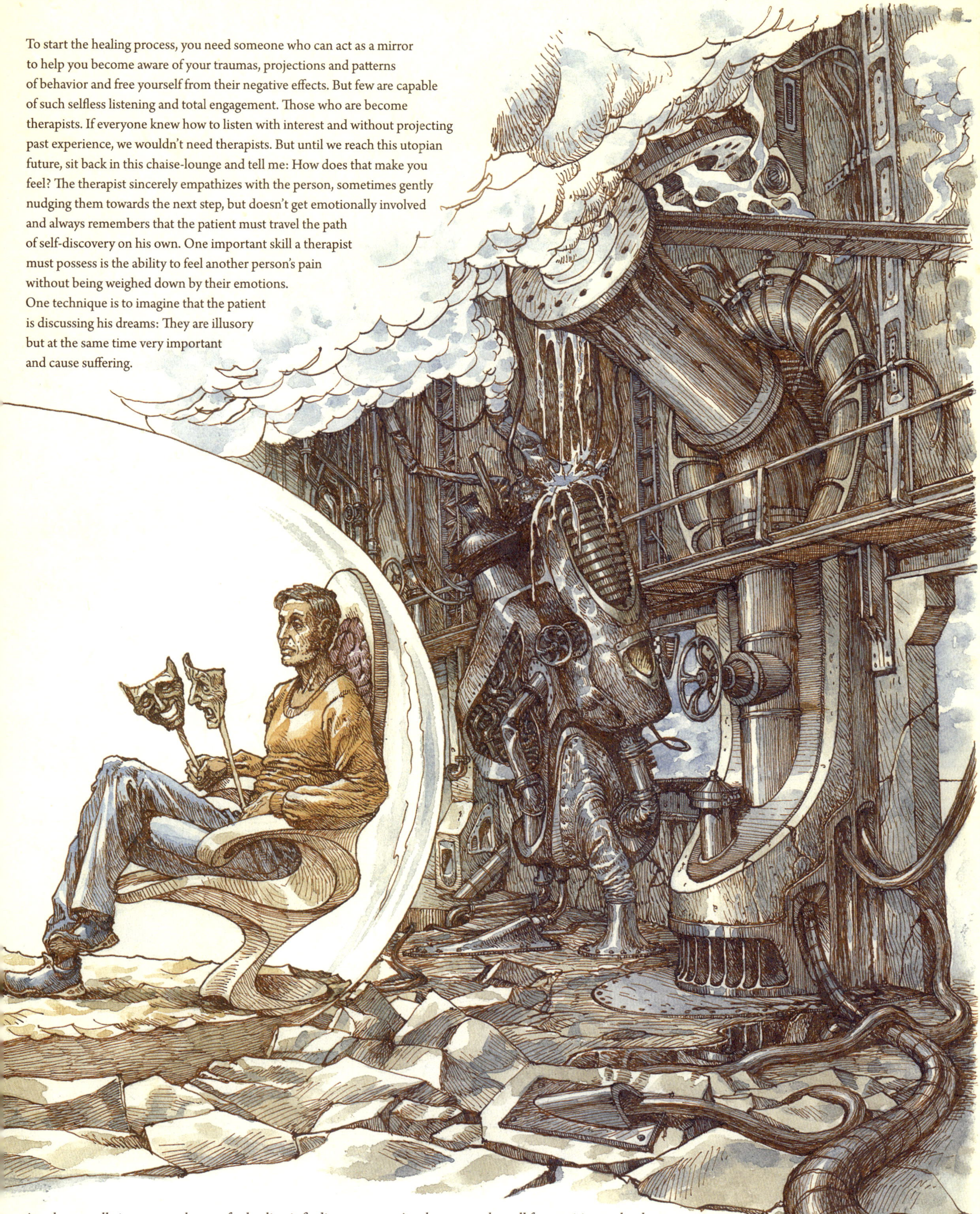

Another equally important element for healing is finding a meeting space where the patient can feel completely safe and open. The therapist may also use physical exercises, if the patient is particularly psychosomatic and experiences physical symptoms of trauma, and/or cognitive exercises, if the patient's symptoms are more cerebral.

Art therapy works well for sensitive souls whose emotions are better expressed through drawing or another art form. By sharing his pain with someone else in this kind of environment, a patient is able to escape the destructive influence of trauma-based coping mechanisms.

GAMES

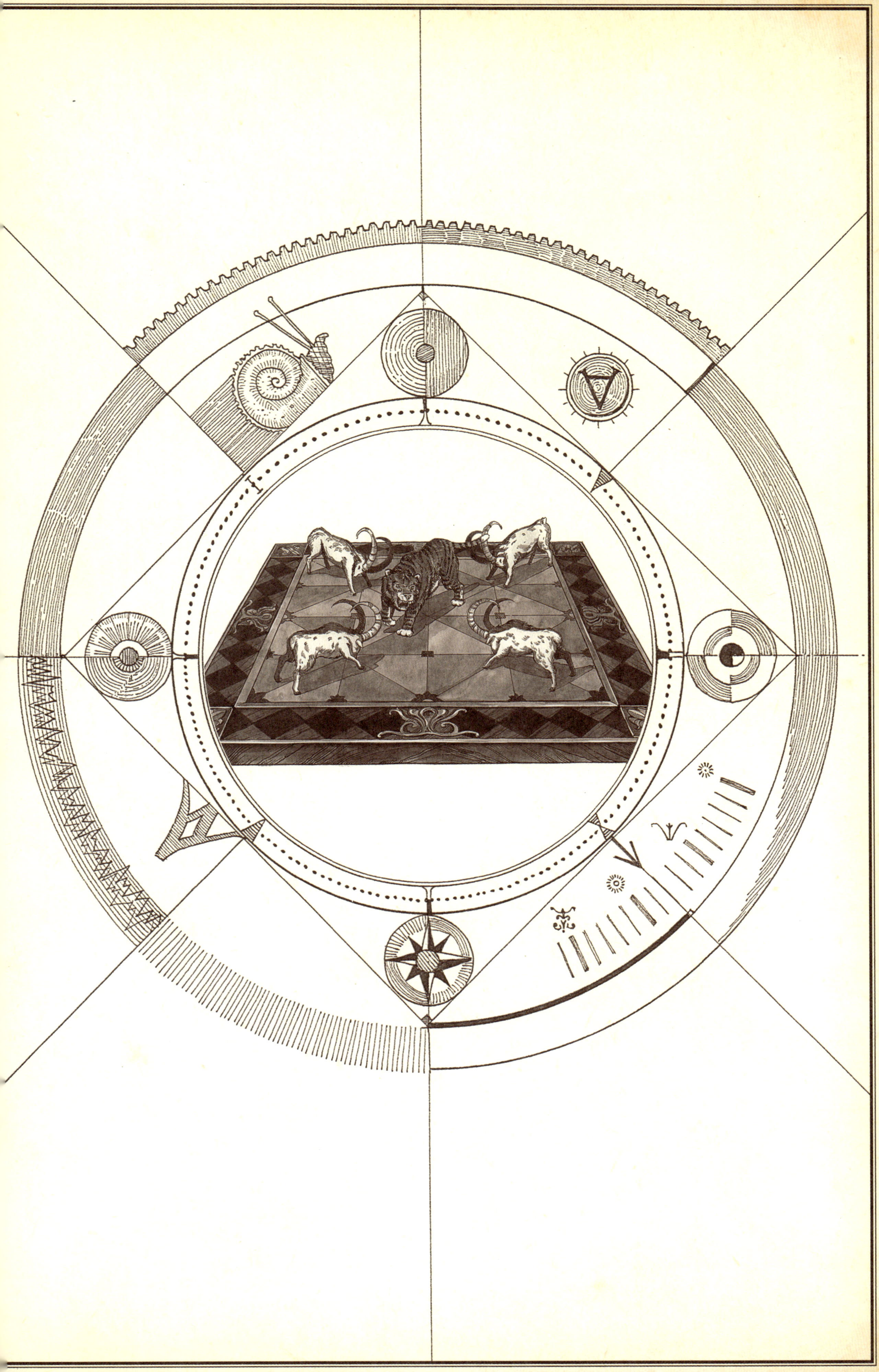

DICE

Sometimes it's nice to completely relinquish control, stop thinking, analyzing and supposing and simply say, "Let the fates decide!" If you're feeling lucky, grab a partner and throw some dice.

In this game, your luck can change in an instant — all you can do is roll and leave the rest to destiny. Spice things up and raise the stakes by making bets before each roll. The game will quickly pull you in.

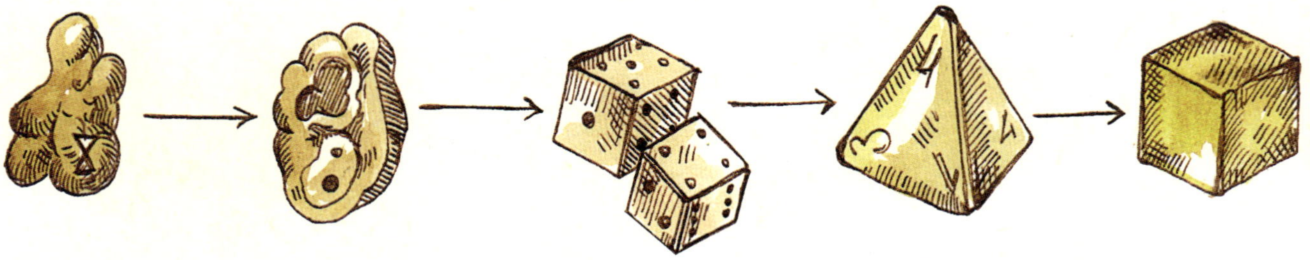

The fate in the game is decided by lots — dice with numbers printed on each side. They must be carefully crafted and balanced to ensure chance is the only factor at play. When they land on a flat surface, each side of the dice must occupy a stable position. Use small volumetric geometric shapes with equal faces, such as a pyramid or a cube.

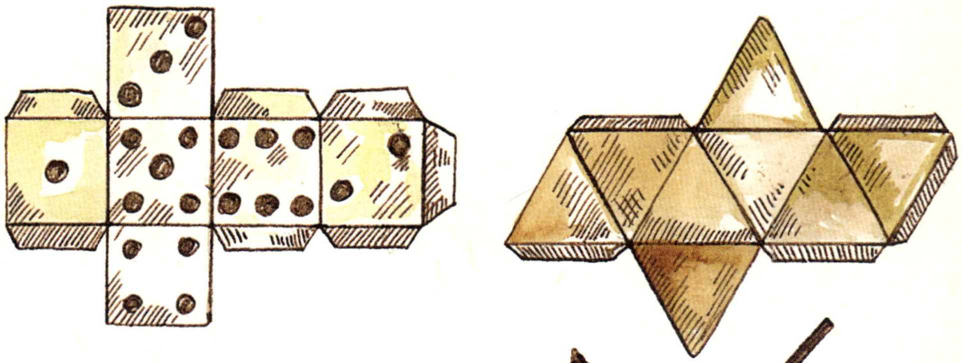

Dice can be made from any durable material: ivory, wood, stone, clay, fruit pits, agate, amber, onyx, lead — even silver or gold. Carve the material into a cube with six faces. On each of the faces, carve or paint the numbers from 1 to 6. Arrange them so that the sum of the numbers on opposite faces is 7.

To completely eliminate the possibility of players influencing the roll with a sleight of hand, use a special device that will shake and roll the dice for the players. The main objective of the game is to score the most points. The way you score depends on the game you're playing. Ready to roll?

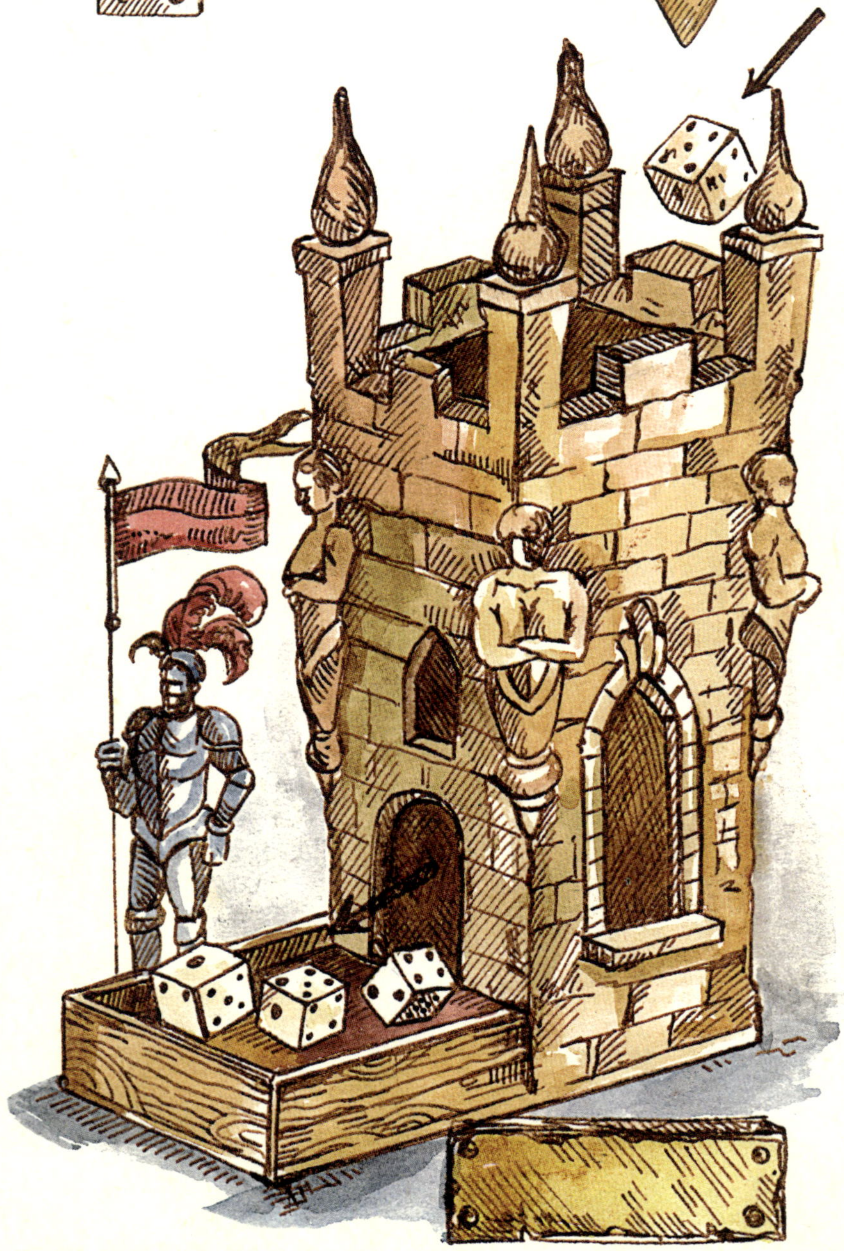

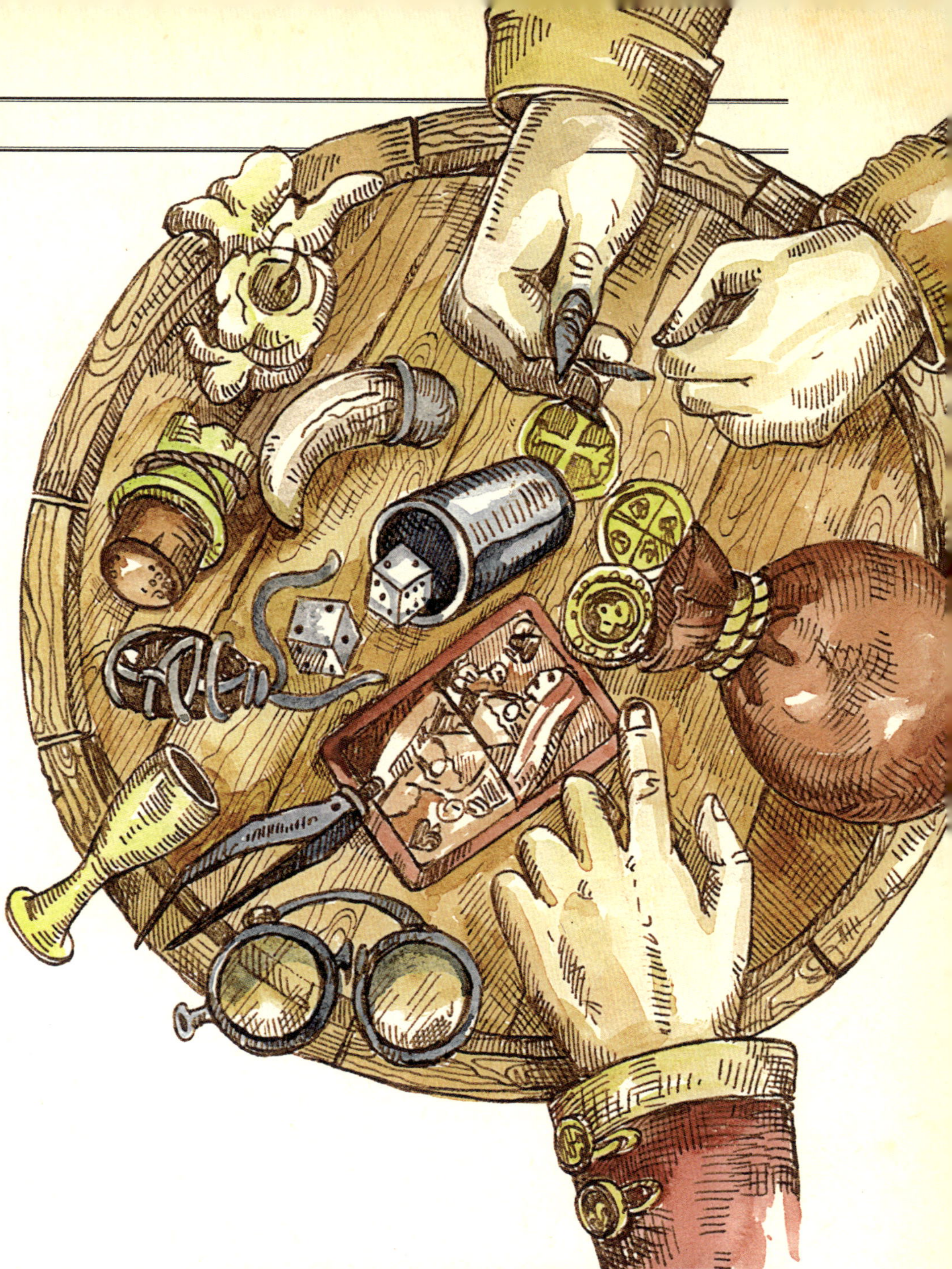

1000

This game requires 5 dice. The goal is to score exactly 1000 points. Any number of players can participate, but the sweet spot is around 4–8. Roll dice to determine who goes first. The numbers on the dice determine your score: 1s are worth 10 points, and 5s are worth 5. The rest of the numbers are considered worthless unless they occur in a three, four or five of a kind.

When you roll a three of a kind, you score the value of one of them multiplied by 10. If you roll four of a kind, multiply it by 20; and five of a kind, by 100. The best roll you can have is five of a kind 1s, which is an instant win (1 = 10 points, 10 x 100 = 1000 points).

Start a table with different columns and rows to record players and points, the stages of the game, the passing of points from one player to another and lost points. To begin, you need to roll at least 50 points to get onto the table. If you roll at least 5 points, you can set the scoring dice aside and reroll the rest for more points. But keep in mind that if you roll a hand with no scoring combinations, you lose all the points previously scored in that round. That's why you've got to know when to hold them and know when to roll them.

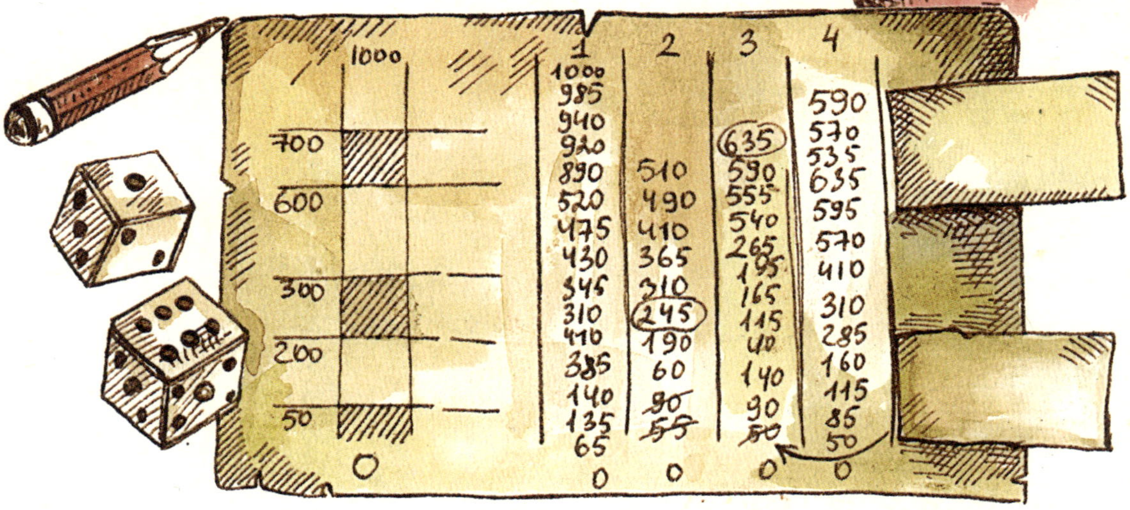

You have another opportunity to increase your score: If you start the round with fewer points than other players and end the round with more, you get to steal 50 points from any players you overtook. Another variation involves creating barrels, or point thresholds. Players in the barrel (say, scoring more than 200 but less than 300) must roll a score of 300 in one round before they are allowed to continue scoring. These barrels often occur between 200–300 and 600–700 points.

To resolve any disputes that may arise, use the triangle of numerals shown here. This pattern of numbers follows a specific principle that will help you determine each player's share. For example, before winning the entire match, player A misses two rounds, and player B misses three. How can you split the bet fairly if the game is interrupted?

Add up the number of games missing by each player: A + B = 2 + 3 = 5. Check the corresponding row in the table, i.e., the fifth one. Player A's share is equal to the sum of the first three numerals in the row (corresponding to the number of games missed by B: 1 + 4 = 5). Then the share of player A will be equal to the sum of the three (according to the number of games missing for player B) first entries in the fifth row (1 + 4 + 6 = 11), and player B's share is the sum of the remaining two numbers (1 + 4 = 5).

MANCALA, TIGERS & GOATS

The principles of conflict and conquest are at the heart of most games. But there are always exceptions to the rule. If you enjoy sharing and strategizing with others but still enjoy the excitement and skill of being cunning, play mancala. The goal is to collect as many chips as possible to fill not only your own cells but also the cells of your opponent.

It is unlikely that you will be able to win simply by accumulating chips. A different tactic is required here: take what you can and share the rest. To someone watching on the sidelines, it may appear that the players are simply sowing seeds. The gameplay itself is quite soothing.

MANCALA

When you start to get the hang of things and want to pick up the pace, the meditative activity turns into a game of chance. The playing field is a board with two rows of six pits and one larger pit on each end. It can be carved from wood, but if you don't have any on hand, that's no reason to give up. Just dig holes in the dirt or sand or even draw them on paper. Any collection of small objects can act as playing pieces: seeds, beans, small stones, etc.

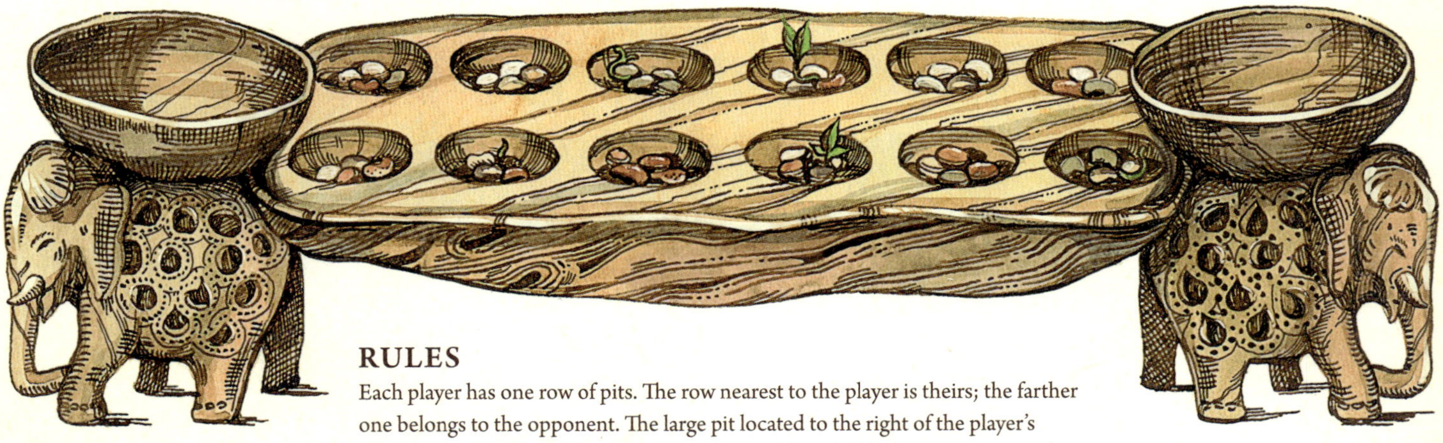

RULES

Each player has one row of pits. The row nearest to the player is theirs; the farther one belongs to the opponent. The large pit located to the right of the player's row is called a "store," and that's where your seeds are held when not in gameplay. Place 4 seeds in each small pit. You can decide who will go first by drawing lots.

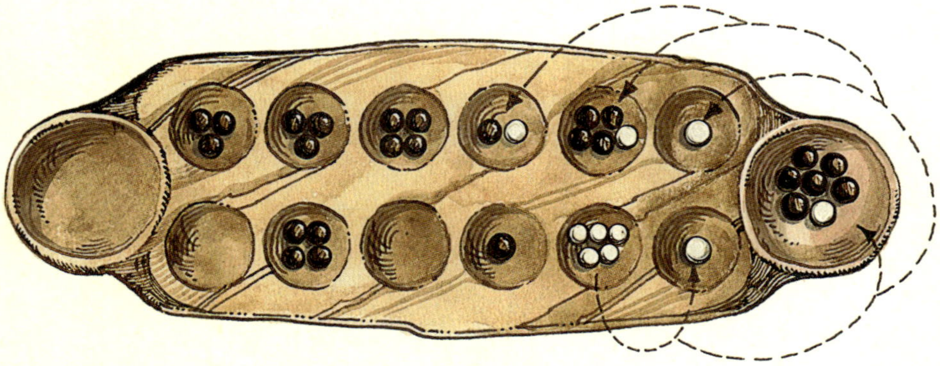

The gameplay works as follows: The starting player takes all the seeds out from any single pit on his side and drops them one-by-one into the subsequent pits, moving counterclockwise (from left to right across the player's own pits and from right to left in the pits of the opponent). If during this process you reach your store, you place a seed in it. If you reach the store of your opponent, you do not. Try to distract your opponent with captivating stories to ruin their concentration and cause them to slip up.

How to fill your store? If the last seed of your turn lands in an empty pit adjacent to an opponent's pit that contains one or more pieces, then you take all the opponent's pieces from this pit and, together with your last piece, put them in your store.

And one more clever rule: If your last seed falls in your store, you get an extra turn. If you do the calculations and sow your seeds right, you can end up taking several turns in a row!

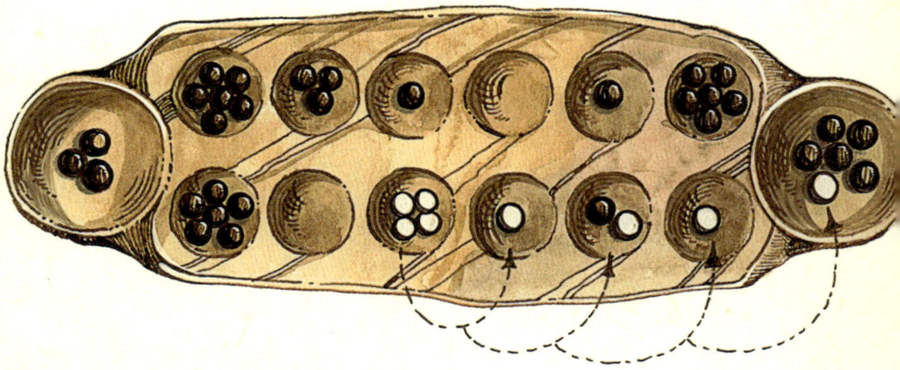

When one of the players runs out of seeds and the other does not have enough chips to replenish the opponent's pits, the game ends. The other player transfers all their remaining seeds in their pits to their store and the "harvest" takes place — counting the points.

To win, you need to collect 25 seeds in your store, and when the score is 24:24, the match is a draw. You can make the game harder by making more rows of pits, by increasing the number of seeds and adding new rules. Have fun with it! Mancala is a great way to shift and train your focus.

TIGERS AND GOATS

You may think that a goat facing a tiger is completely defenseless. For a lone goat, this may be true, but if there are several goats, then the tiger may go hungry or even end up impaled. This is a rare situation when predator becomes prey.

RULES

The game involves two players: one starts with 4 tigers, the other with 20 goats. You can use chips of different colors and sizes or carve animal figurines for more drama.

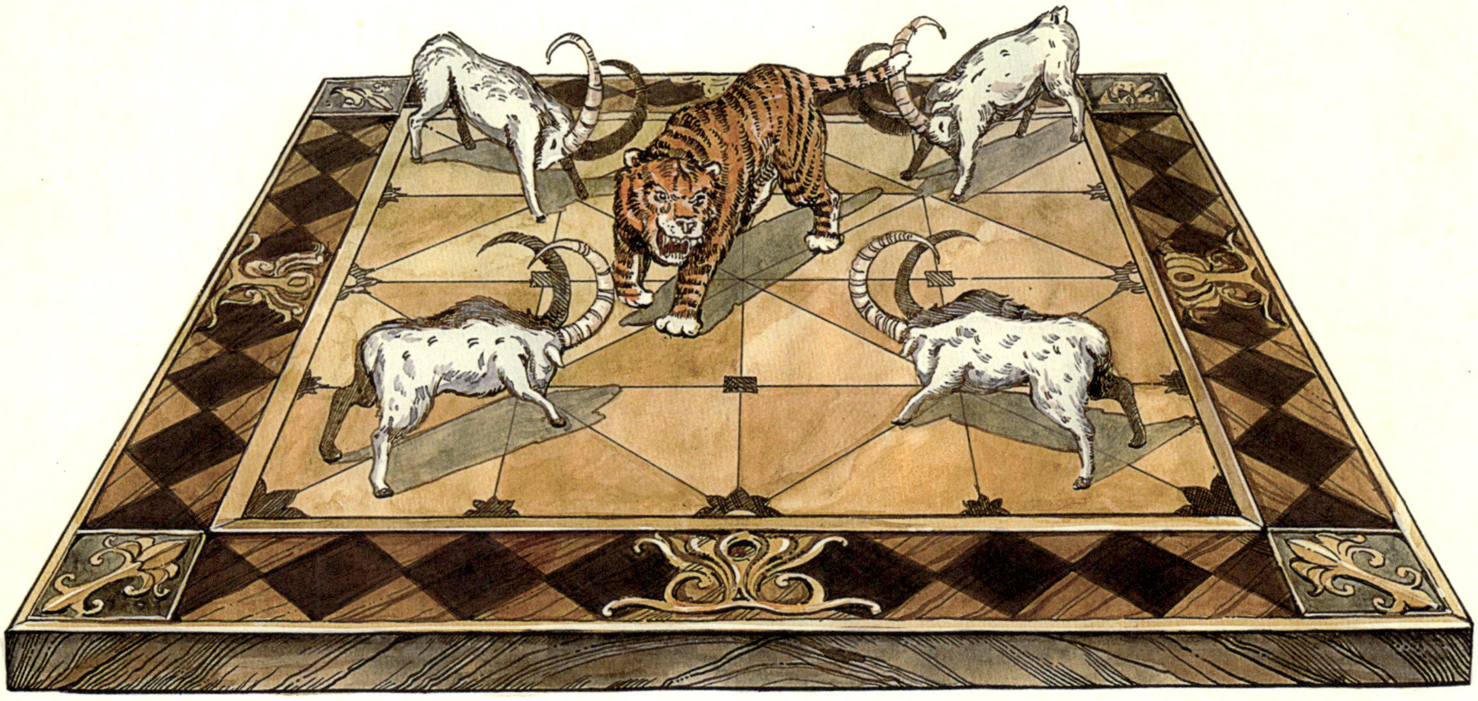

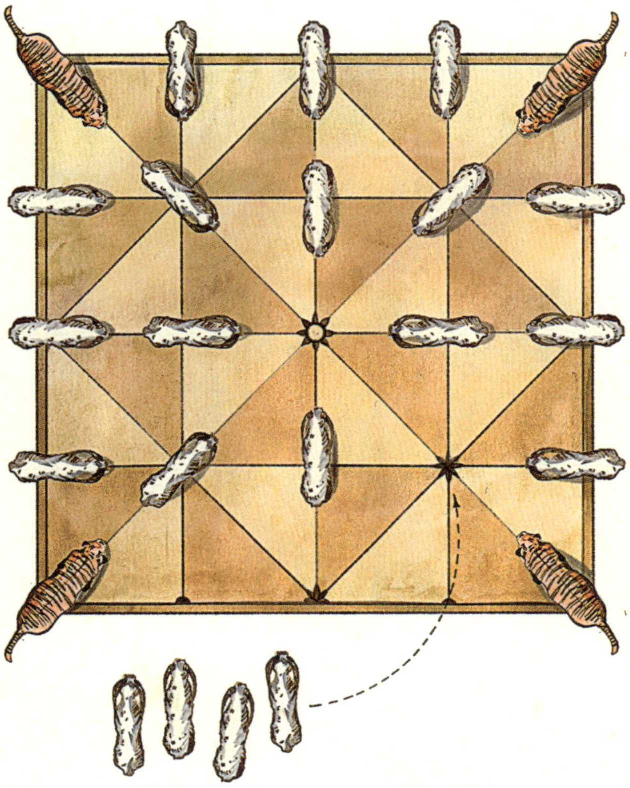

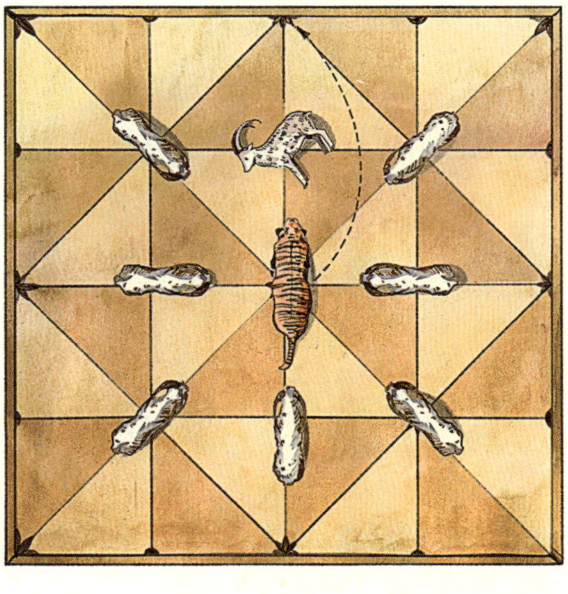

To create the playing field, start by drawing a square. Draw horizontal and vertical lines to create a 4x4 cell grid. Then draw two diagonal lines connecting opposite corners. Next, connect the midpoints of each side with diagonal lines to form a diamond. You should end up with a 25-point grid with all points connected orthogonally.

Pieces are placed on the points not on the cells. Before starting the game, place the 4 tiger pieces at the 4 corner points of the board. The goat player moves first, placing a goat on any vacant point on the playing board. With each subsequent turn, the goat player must place all of his pieces one-by-one on any remaining free point.

Until all the goats are placed on the field, the goat player cannot make any other moves. But he must place his goats carefully, for there are tigers on the prowl. A tiger captures a goat by jumping over it and landing on the adjacent point along a straight line. To win, the tigers must capture 5 goats, or the goats must hem in the tigers until they are unable to move.

CHESS

Chess is much more than just a game. It is the realization of an individual's full potential while locked in fierce battle and fighting for social recognition. It is the advancement of creative ideas and the beauty in seeing a plan unfold.

There's something for everyone: the search for truth, the metaphor of a military battle, the intellectual duel, mental entertainment and aesthetic appreciation when analyzing a game between two masters or solving puzzles in artificially created scenarios. Chess develops intuition, logical thinking, concentration and strategy.

Chess is a two-player game that uses a square gameboard of 8x8, or 64, cells, which alternate dark and light in a checkerboard pattern. Label the cells in both the horizontal and vertical directions — for example, use letters for the horizontal axis and numbers for the vertical.

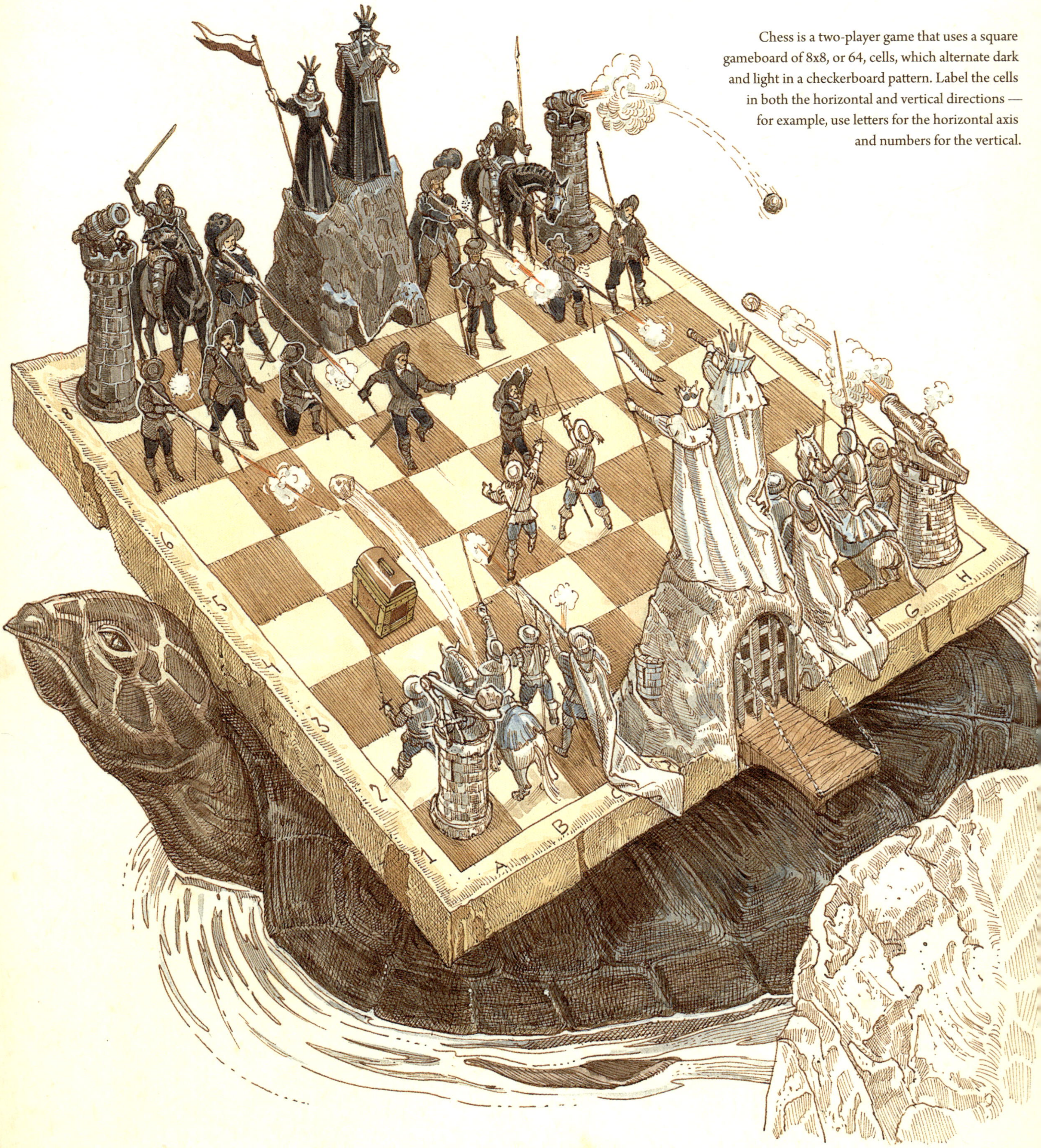

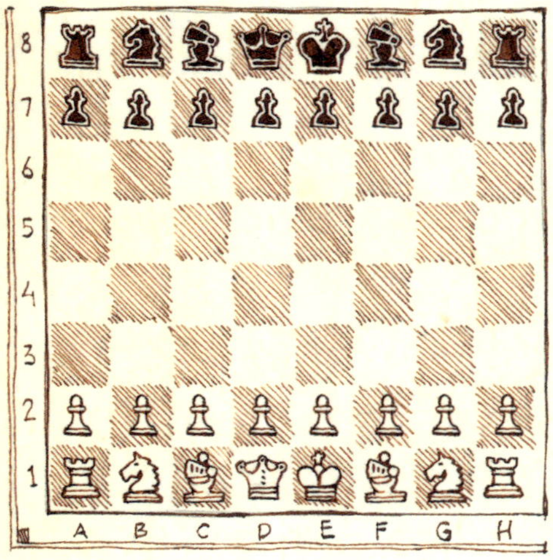

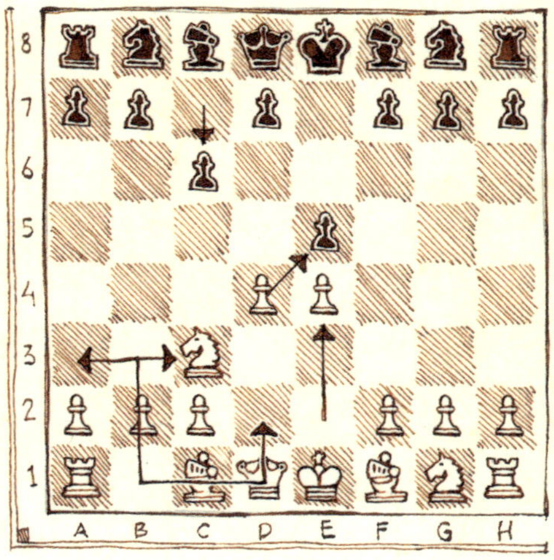

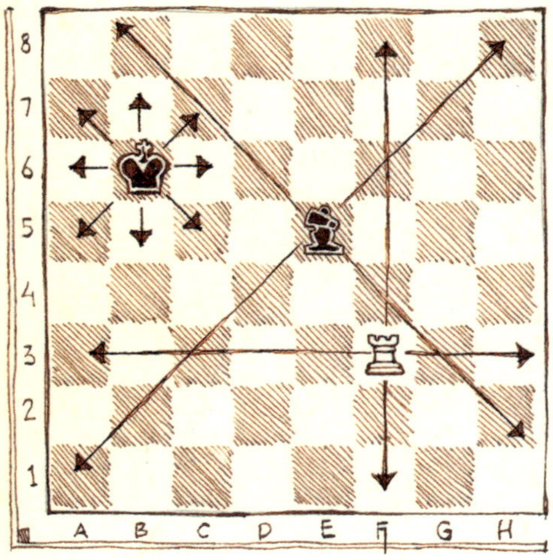

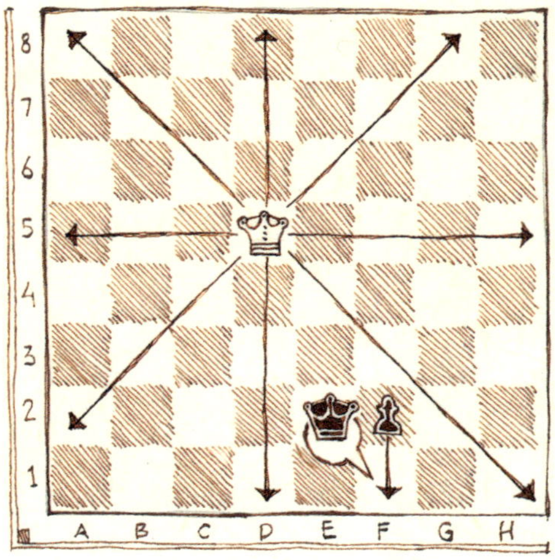

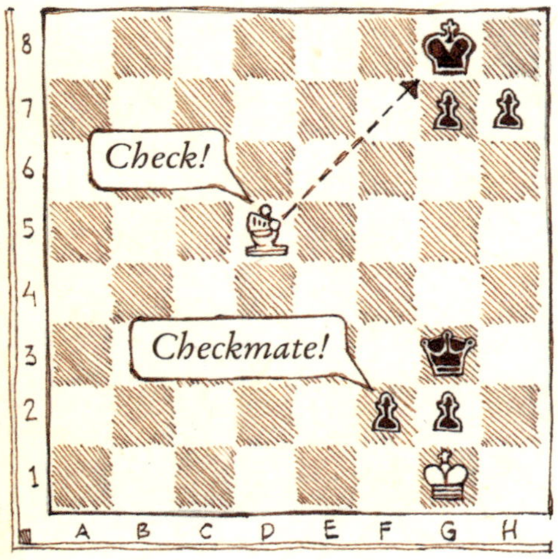

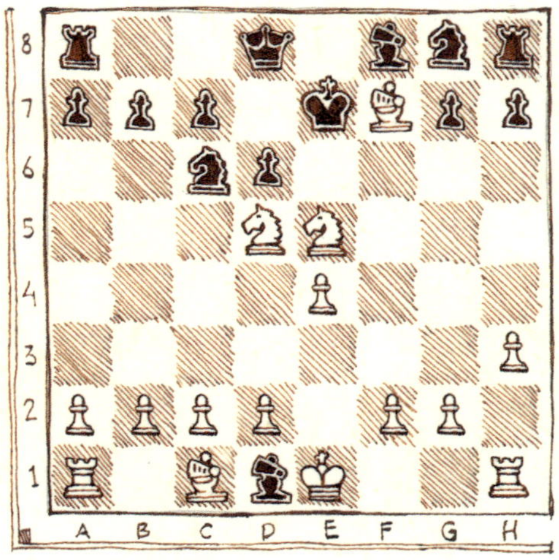

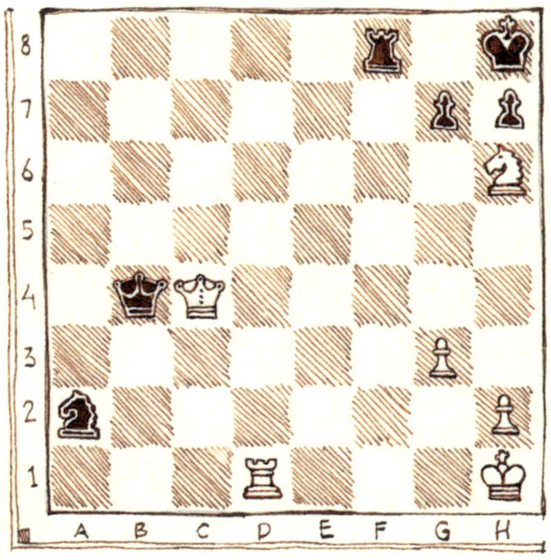

Each player has a set of 16 pieces of his own color: 8 pawns, 2 rooks, 2 bishops, 2 knights, 1 queen and 1 king. You can name the pieces whatever you like as long as their abilities are clearly defined. Line the pieces up in two horizontal rows on each side of the board. The first row should be entirely pawns. The second should have rooks at the edges and, moving towards the center, knights, then bishops. The center squares are occupied by the king and queen, with the queen on the square of her color.

The **pawn** can only move one forward one space at a time, except for its first move, in which it can jump two spaces at once as long as the spaces are unoccupied. A pawn can attack and capture opponents pieces that stand on a diagonal to the pawn.

The **knight** moves two spaces in any non-diagonal direction and then one more space in any non-diagonal direction.

The **king** is the most important and valuable figure. He can walk and attack one space in any direction, including diagonals, but cannot move to or remain on a space that is under direct threat of capture by an opponent's piece. Opponent kings must always remain at least one space away from each other.

The **bishop** moves and attacks diagonally any number of spaces, provided that there are no other pieces blocking the path. The bishops remain on the same color space as they started, so each player has a black space bishop and a white space bishop.

The **rook** moves any number of spaces vertically and horizontally, provided that there are no other pieces blocking the path.

The **queen** is the strongest piece on the field. Combining the abilities of the rook and the bishop, she can move any number of spaces in any direction. Even a pawn has a chance to be promoted to a queen (or any other piece except the king) by moving across the entire field and reaching the back row of the opponent's side of the board.

Record moves by using algebraic notation. It is based on the system of coordinates created by the intersection of the letters and numbers used to label the horizontal and vertical vertices. Each space has an alpha-numeric code: for example: a1, g5.

The name of each piece is abbreviated and written with a capital letter: King = K, Queen = Q, Bishop = B, Knight = N, Rook = R. The Pawn has no notation.

This notation describes both the chess piece moved with the new square it has moved to on the chessboard. Play this short game to practice and get a feel for each piece: ***1. e4 e5; 2. Bc4 d6; 3. Kf3 Kc6; 4. Kc3 Cg4; 5. Ke5 Cd1; 6. Bf7 Ke7; 7. Kd5.***

In this game, the black King is checkmated in just seven moves. White creates a trap for black by sacrificing his most powerful piece — the Queen. Black takes White Queen and loses sight of the threat to his King.

The goal of the game is to find the weak spots in the opponent's defense and "checkmate" the king by putting it under direct threat of capture in such a way that the opponent cannot move their king out of danger or capture the attacking piece. White moves first. When the king is under direct threat of capture but can still escape, it's known as a "check." The player whose king is in check must make a move to escape or evade capture. When no such legal moves exist, a "checkmate" is declared and the game ends. Some chess matches are particularly bloody, with heavy casualties on both sides. These often end in a stalemate, when the player whose turn it is to move is not in check but has no legal move. At this point, nobody can win, so you declare a draw.

GO

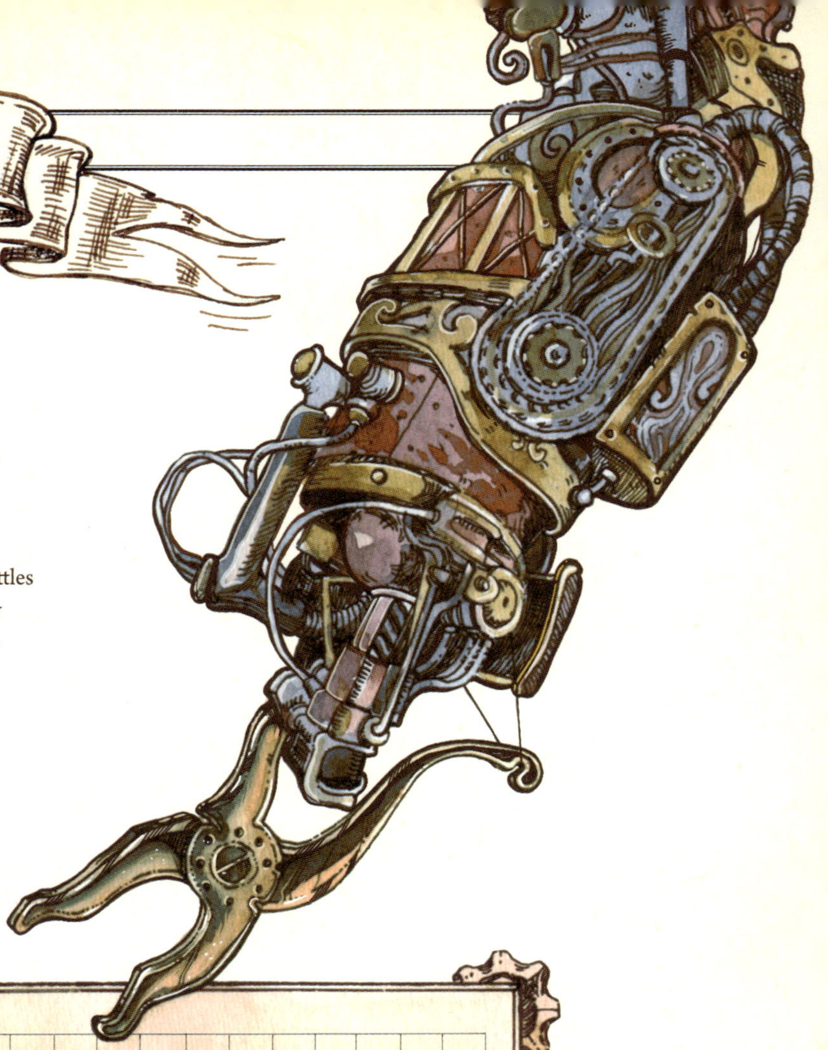

Imagine you are a ruler and you have the opportunity to take over the whole world. But there is someone else with the exact same opportunity as you. What would you do? What steps and actions do you take? Could you make your own state bigger and stronger? All of these questions can be answered with a game of Go.

Go tests your abilities to conquer and fortify territories. There are no battles or decisive attacks, and you need to be a keen strategist to win, gradually implementing your plan one step at a time and thoughtfully building up your position.

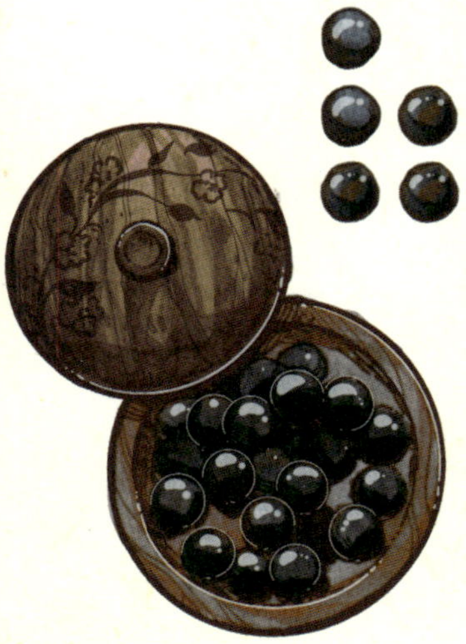

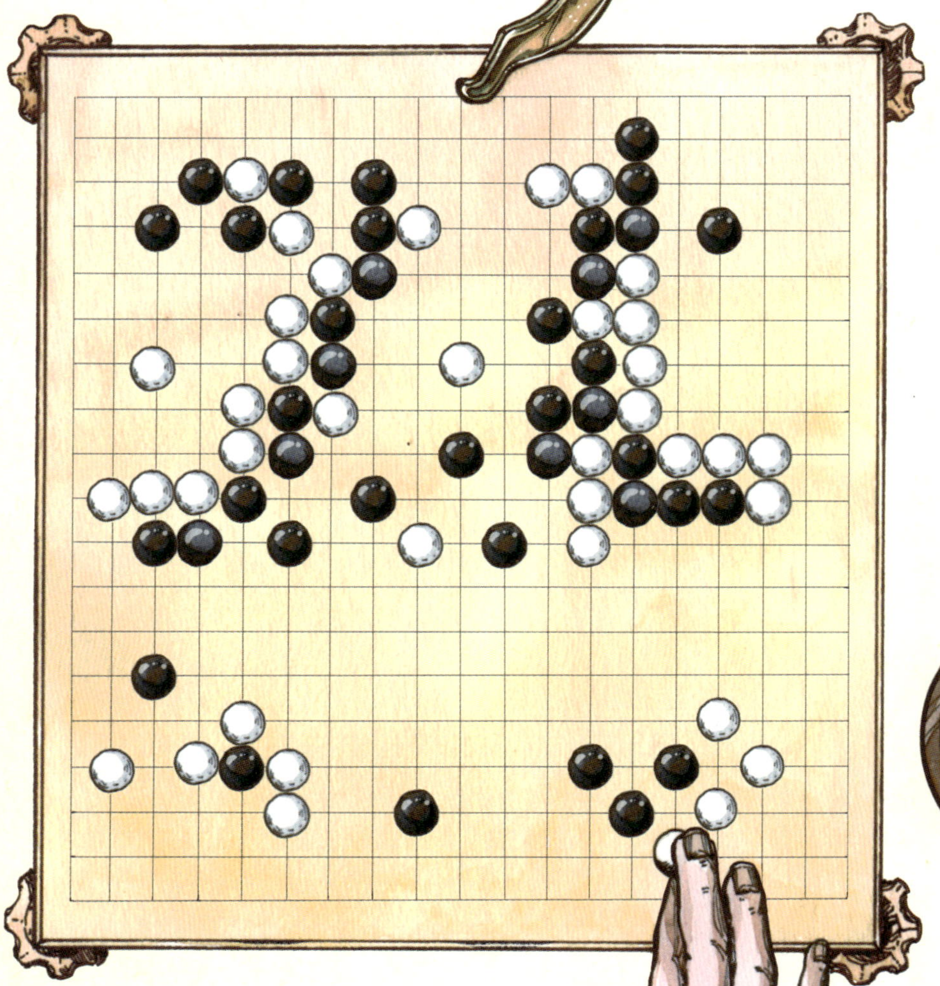

Excessive risk-taking and aggressive strategies can result in losses, while staying constantly on the defensive can give the enemy an advantage. Try to find a balance: if you have a lot of territory, don't be afraid to surrender some of it; if you don't, it may be time to stir up the pot a little.

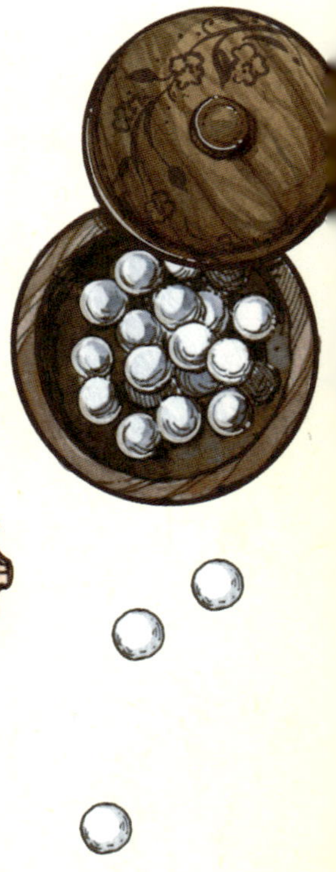

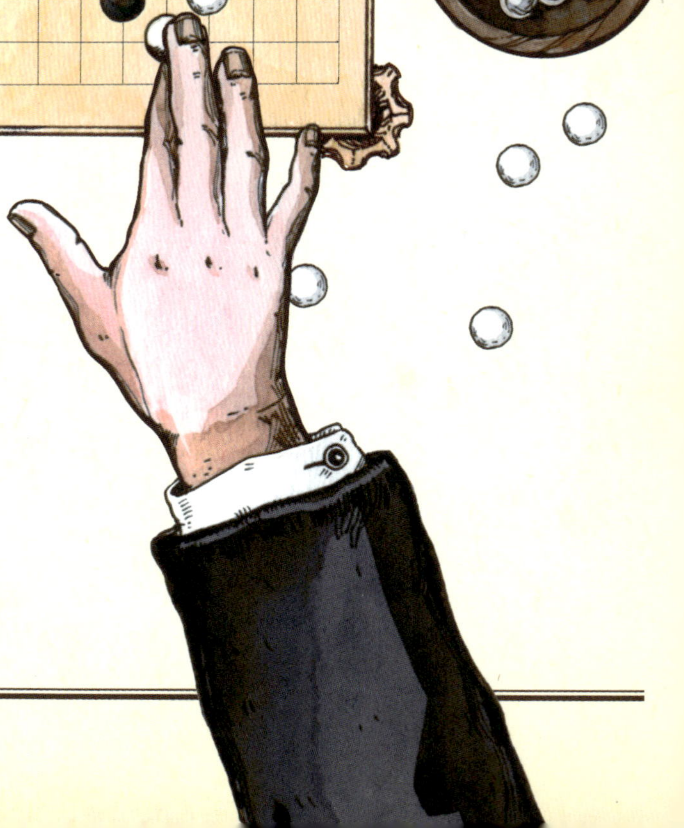

The gameboard can be made of wood. Divide the playing surface into a 19x19 grid. While still learning or teaching, you can start with smaller boards: 9×9 or 13×13. It is better to make two sides of the board slightly shorter, with a ratio of 15:14, as this will create the ideal perspective for both players.

The stones (usually black and white) represent your army and the enemy's army. They can be made from glass, ceramics, shells or real stones: ordinary, semi-precious, precious. A 19x19 board has 361 points. This means that you need 180 and 181 stones, respectively, to play. Craft two holding cups: one for your stones, the other for your opponent's stones.

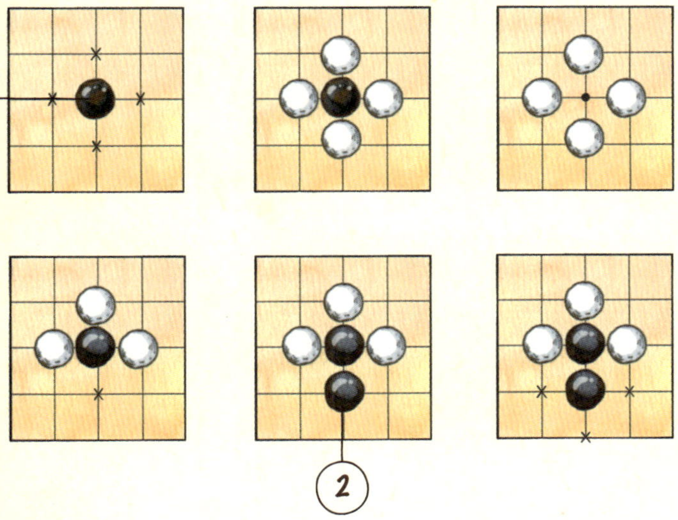

At the start of the game, you're a commander with an army at your disposal, and in front of you is free territory that you need to conquer. Your task is to capture more territory than the enemy. There are only six basic rules and an unlimited number of ways to win.

Empty board: The game starts with an empty playing field. The stones are placed not on the empty cells but at the intersection points between lines.

Turn taking: Black makes the first move. Placing one stone constitutes one move. Try to first take territory in the corners of the board, then on the sides and, finally, move on to the action in the center.

No take-backs. Once you've placed a stone on the board and removed your hand from it, your turn is over. The stone placed on the field can no longer be moved; it becomes part of the boundaries of your territory.

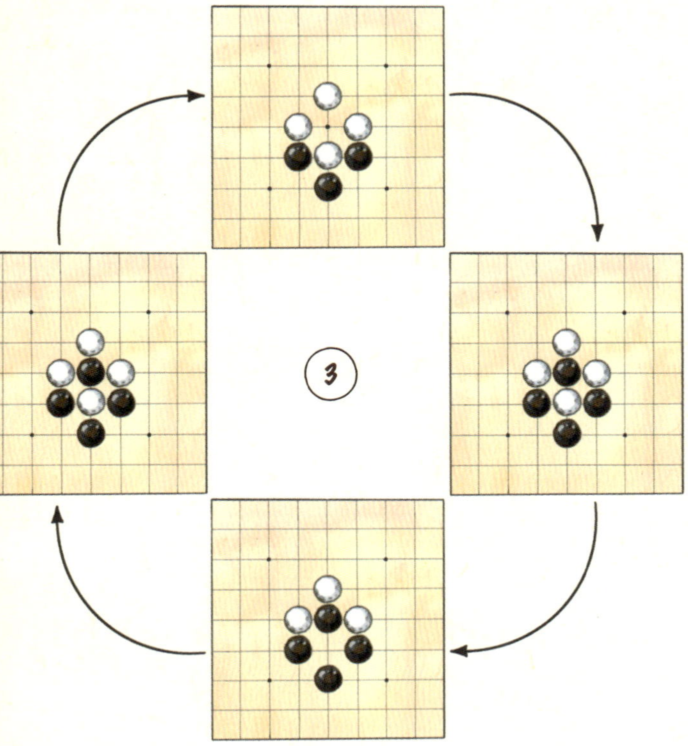

Life and Death: Every stone placed on the field starts out as "alive." The life force of any stone or group of same-colored stones is determined by the number of neighboring free spaces, or "liberties," it has. Groups of same-colored stones share the liberties around the boundary of the group. Liberties closed within a group are called "eyes." At the very beginning of the game (1), each stone has four liberties. If an enemy blocks off all four liberties, the stone "dies," meaning it is taken prisoner and removed from the field. If you notice you are in danger of losing your last liberty, you can place a second stone (2) next to the first. Thus, one stone saves the other and they become a group.

Combining stones into groups significantly increases the chances of capturing a large territory. Each new stone enlarges the group, expanding over more space. If you form at least two closed eyes within the group, you create a fortress. This group of stones obtains eternal life because the enemy cannot close both eyes in one move.

In Go, "suicidal" moves are forbidden, meaning plays that result in that player's own stones being removed from the board or placing a stone in a position with no remaining liberties. One exception is when the step is a strategic maneuver forcing the opponent to sacrifice their entire group.

4

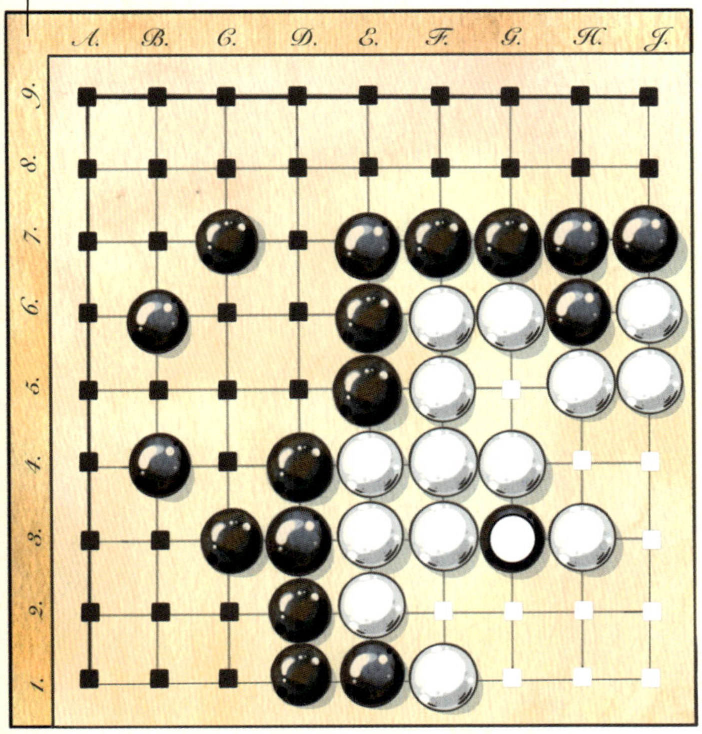

Repetition. In Go, it is forbidden to make a move that repeats a position that was already on the board in this game. The simplest example of this can be seen in Figure (3): White makes a move by removing a piece with no liberties left. Black can place a stone in the formed place, thereby blocking white's liberty and also removing it from the board. This returns the board to its initial state from a few moves prior. In order to comply with the "no repetition" rule, Black cannot make a move similar to White's. They must make any other move, and, if they wish, can repeat this move after White responds and changes the field. Unless, of course, White chooses to occupy this space with their next move.

Completion: Eventually, the players reach a point where there are no viable moves left; it's impossible to expand your territory or attack your enemy's territory by placing a stone. When one of the opponents can't find (or doesn't have) any such moves left, he says, "Pass" and skips a move. After three passes, the game is over.

Figure (4) shows a completed game board. As you can see, both players still have stones on the board. The territory is divided. Who has won? This is determined by comparing the number of points. Each eye left on the board counts as a point, as does each prisoner taken by either side. It's important to take into account White's handicap due to the fact that Black made the first move. This is usually calculated by giving White a 6.5 point head start.

PLAYING CARDS

While life sometimes forces you to rely on chance, cards are a game of cold calculation. Although the luck of the draw is, of course, up to fate, the game itself is not. The player's main trump cards are pure reason and self-control.

The ability to gain the upper hand in a situation with a high degree of uncertainty depends only on the player's ability to qualitatively evaluate the opponent's cards and make the best decision. Luck is just an idle spectator watching the mind games from the sidelines.

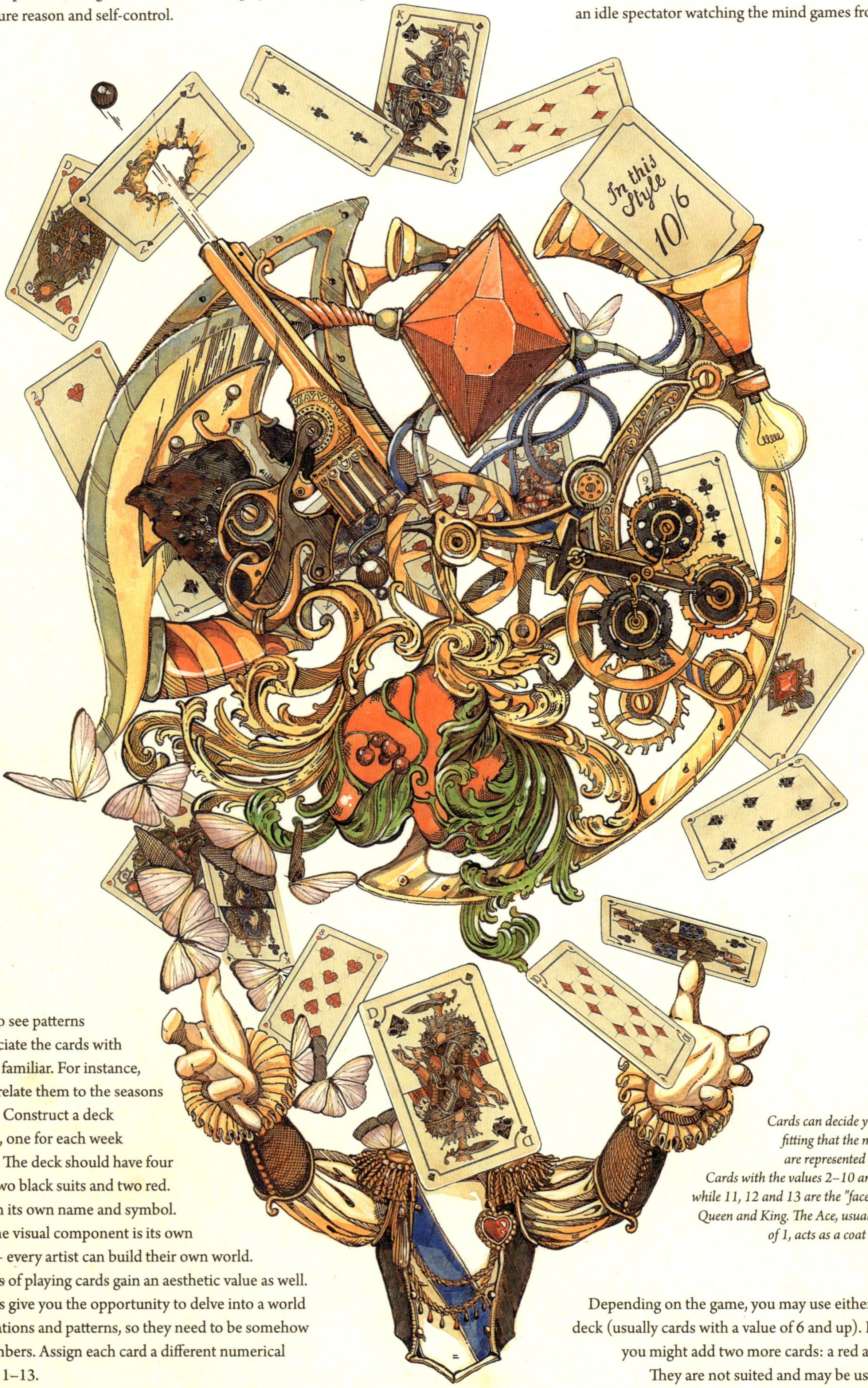

SUITS

It's easier to see patterns if you associate the cards with something familiar. For instance, you could relate them to the seasons of the year. Construct a deck of 52 cards, one for each week of the year. The deck should have four "seasons:" two black suits and two red. Assign each its own name and symbol. Creating the visual component is its own art form — every artist can build their own world. These kinds of playing cards gain an aesthetic value as well. Card games give you the opportunity to delve into a world of combinations and patterns, so they need to be somehow tied to numbers. Assign each card a different numerical value from 1–13.

Cards can decide your fate, so it's only fitting that the most powerful cards are represented by powerful figures. Cards with the values 2–10 are simply numbered, while 11, 12 and 13 are the "face cards" — the Jack, Queen and King. The Ace, usually assigned a value of 1, acts as a coat of arms for the suit.

JOKERS

Depending on the game, you may use either a full or partial deck (usually cards with a value of 6 and up). For some games, you might add two more cards: a red and a black joker. They are not suited and may be used as wild cards.

POKER

Poker is one of the most exciting and dynamic card games out there. But there has to be something important on the line. Playing with stakes makes everything juicier. Everyone throws a little into the communal pot when they make a bet. Poker usually uses a full deck of 52 cards and can be played by 2 to 10 people. At the beginning of the game, the dealer hands out two cards, face down, to every player. The two players to the left make the first mandatory bets. Now begins the acting, mind reading, psychological games and, most importantly, the betting! Players take turns in a circle, starting with the person to the left of the dealer. Everyone can:

- **Make a bet** (something of value)
- **Call** by betting something of equal value to the highest bet
- **Raise** by betting something of a higher value
- **Fold** by handing in your cards and forfeiting.
- **Check** and bet nothing if your bet is already the highest or if everyone else has checked. The betting ends when everyone has either called the highest bet or folded. If everyone folds but you, you win that hand!

After the first round of betting, the dealer places the first round of three "community cards" face up on the table. Players use these cards along with the cards in their hand to create certain combinations that are assigned different values.

After seeing this first round of community cards, players take this new information into account and the next round of betting begins. Once this is over, another community card is placed on the table.

Another round of betting follows, and the last community card is placed (there should be 5 in total). This is followed by a final round of betting, and if there are more than two players left at the end (i.e., they didn't fold), then all players still in the game reveal their cards. Whoever has the best hand wins. If there's a tie, then friendship wins — the pot is split.

Remember, you don't always need a good hand to win. Sometimes you just need to know how to play a bad one and have a good poker face. What matters is not the hand you actually have but the hand your opponent thinks you have. Count cards and analyze what cards the other players could be holding.

You can bluff and pretend that you have very good chances of winning, put psychological pressure on your opponent by raising the stakes or fold and bow out before you lose all your chips. But you must never let your opponent know what's going on in your head. This is the art of the game and the only chance of winning.

Poker Hand Rankings (from highest to lowest score)

1. ***Royal flush** — the five highest cards of any one suit*
2. ***Straight flush** — five cards in a sequence, all in the same suit*
3. ***Four of a Kind** — 4 cards of the same rank, one of each suit*
4. ***Full house** — 3 of a kind with one pair*
5. ***Flush** — any 5 cards of the same suit but not in a sequence*
6. ***Straight** — 5 cards in a sequence but not of the same suit*
7. ***Three of a kind** — 3 cards of the same rank*
8. ***Two pair** — 2 different pairs*
9. ***Pair** — 2 cards of the same rank*
10. ***High card** — when you can't make any other hands, the highest card wins*

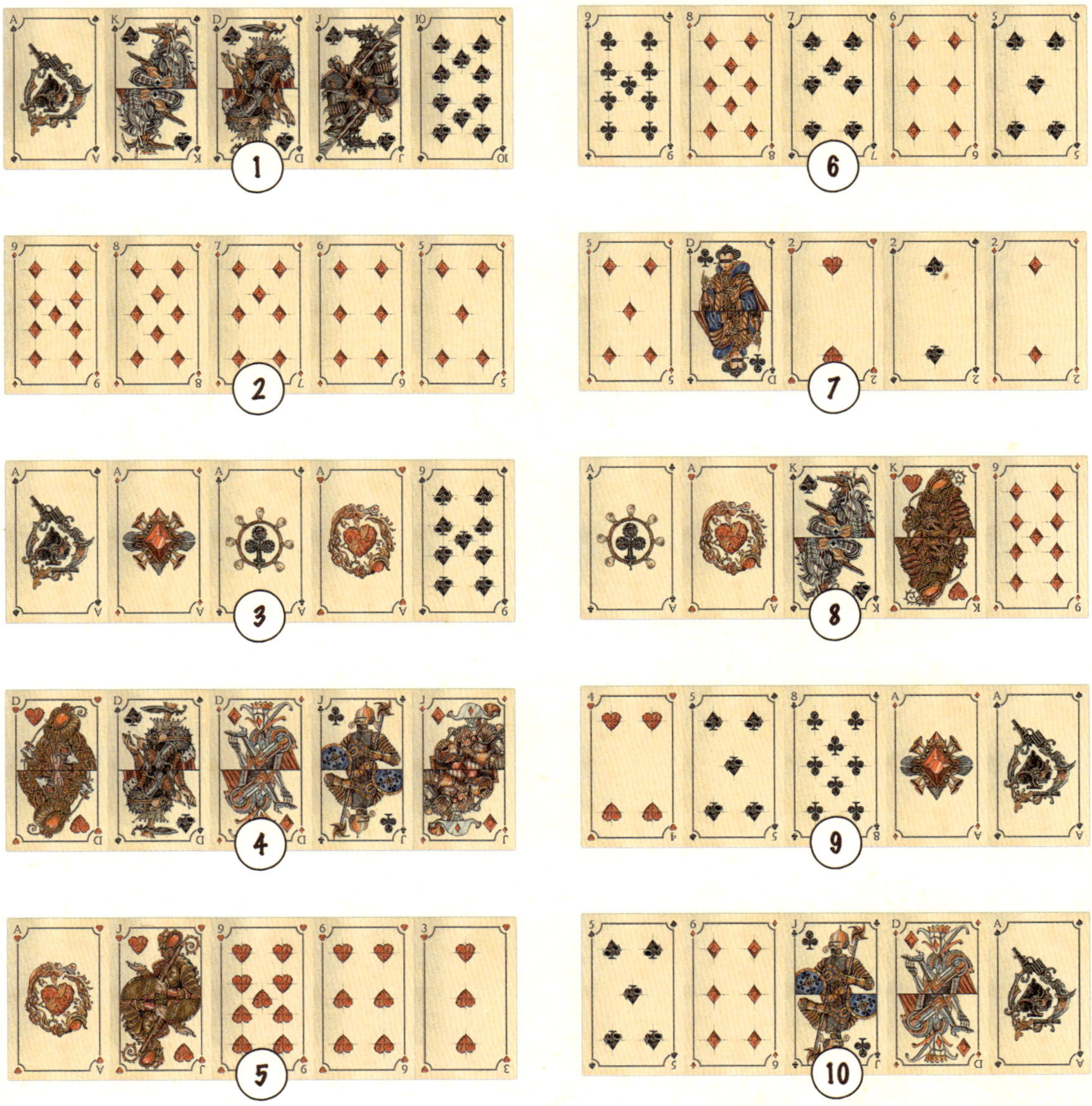

THE MILL

All the world's a stage, and we are merely players. And the rules of the game are intricate and complicated. Some follow them unquestioningly, some try to cheat and some toe the line between the two. Determining the winner is a difficult task. There are infinite variables, and fortune and fate have a hand in things. There are no unbiased judges.

Perhaps that's why people invent games: They're simulations of real life that follow strict patterns of behavior and interaction with the enemy in the struggle for victory. But there are also those who play only against themselves, and there are no winners or losers — only spectators.

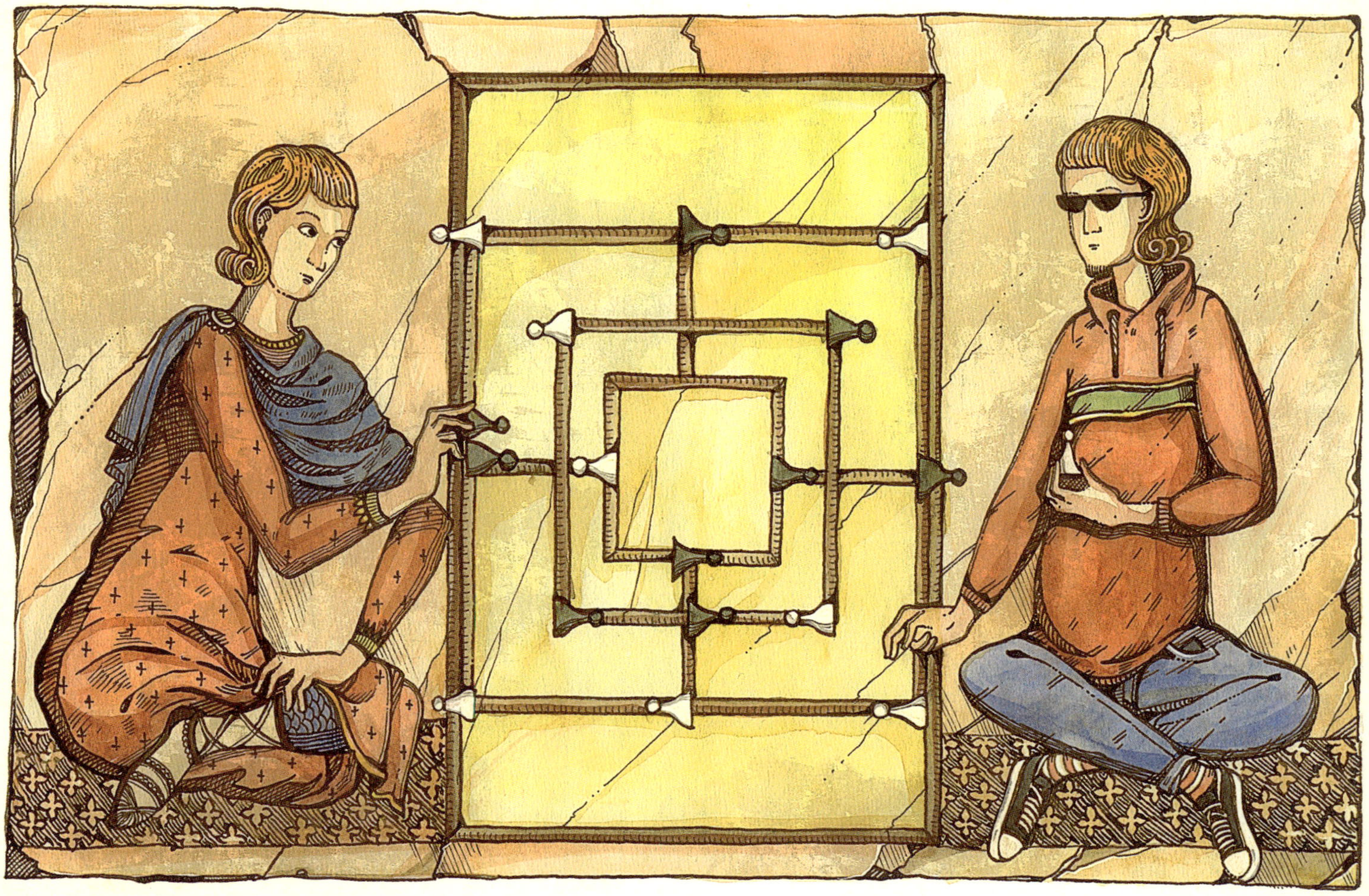

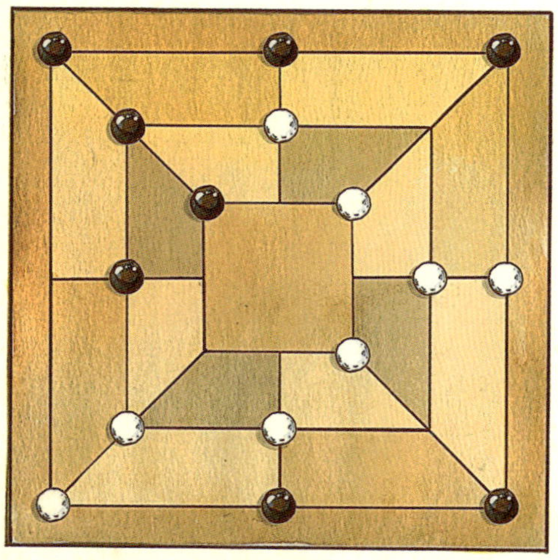

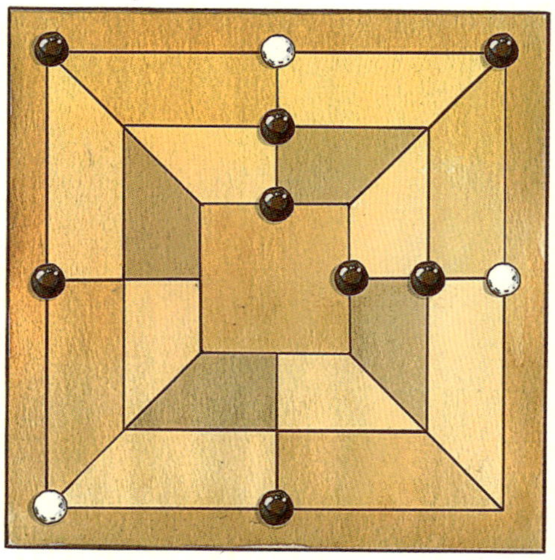

THE MILL

To play The Mill, you will need a board marked as shown and 9 chips of 2 colors. Use lots to determine who plays which color and who starts first. The playing field contains 24 points. Players start phase 1 by taking turns placing their chips on any free point on the board. The objective is to build a "mill," or a row of three same-colored chips. Once a player has succeeded, they can remove an opponent's chip from the field. Chips can only be removed from mills if no other chips remain to be removed. When all the pieces are on the board, start playing: take turns moving the chips to any adjacent free space while trying to build a mill.

If you manage to build two in one turn, then you remove two of your opponent's chips. A mill can be formed in the same place several times, but the player can only remove an opponent's chip after the first one. When one of the players is left with only 3 chips, they get an advantage: During their turn, they can start rearranging their chips freely, without heeding the "one adjacent point per move" rule, while the other player continues to play by the old rules until they, too, have only 3 chips remaining. A player who can no longer make a move or has fewer than 3 chips left loses the game.

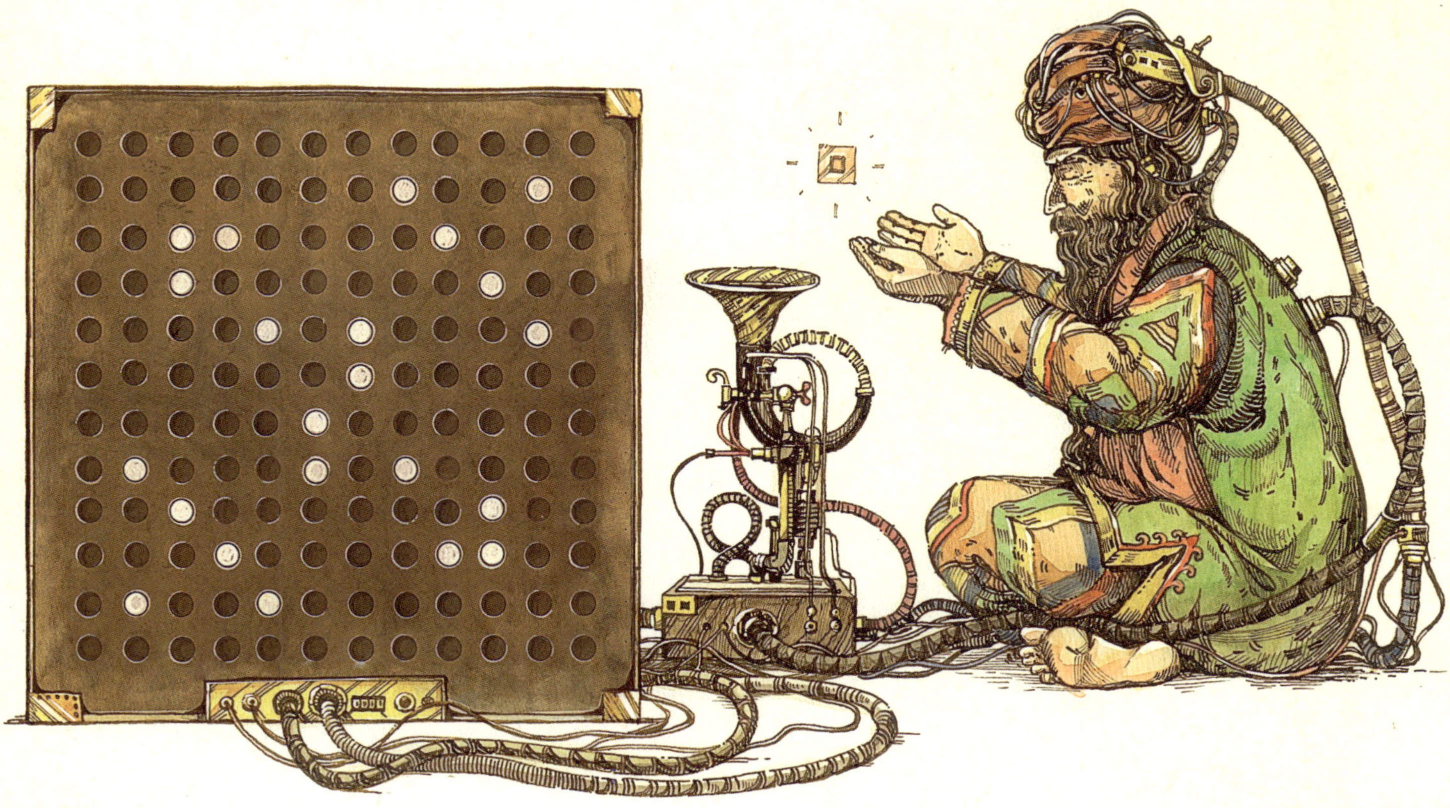

THE GAME OF LIFE

"Life" can hardly be called a game. It is, rather, a scientific abstraction, capable of imitating anything from the development of civilizations to the behavior of social groups. You will not have an opponent. The patterns have a life of their own, giving you the role of a spectator who monitors compliance with the "genetic laws" that govern the movement of the pieces. Just like our own, the universe of the game is constantly expanding, so the playing field is a theoretically infinite grid. Each cell is bordered by eight others, and these neighbors have a direct effect on the cell. While it may not be within your capabilities to make a truly infinite playing field, the bigger it is, the longer and more captivating the game will be. In the future, you can even make boxes with small lights instead of playing pieces to make gameplay even more spectacular!

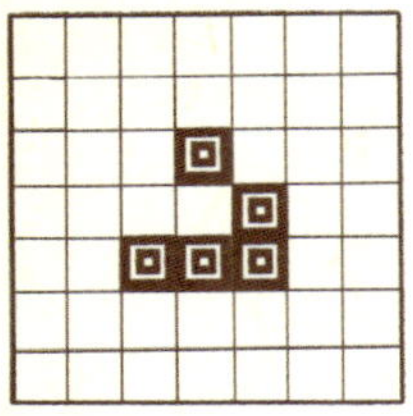

You must be very careful: the slightest inaccuracy can disrupt the development of the whole system because all transformations occur simultaneously.

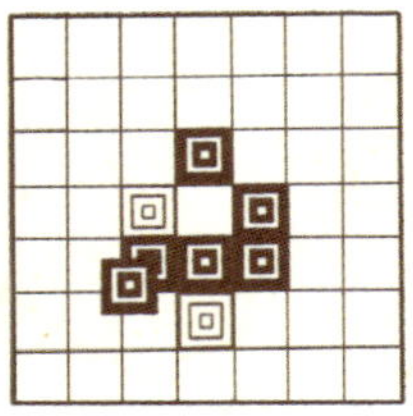

Place a second black checker on the checkers that should die. Put white checkers in places where new shapes will appear.

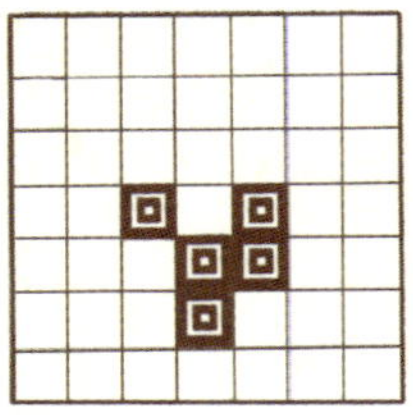

Remove any dying checkers and replace the white newborn checkers with black ones.

To start, build an arbitrary figure of 5–8 chips on the field. This is your organism. Then arrange pieces according to the rules of the "genetic laws":

- **Existence:** A piece with 2 or 3 free spaces next to it is alive.
- **Extinction:** A piece with 4 or more neighbors next to it dies due to overpopulation. A chip with 1 or no neighbors dies of loneliness.
- **Birth:** A new piece is born on each empty cell with exactly 3 chips adjacent to it.

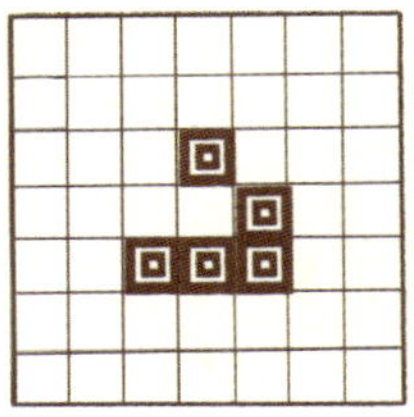

"Ships" can travel indefinitely within the space of the universe. They are important because they form new configurations when they collide and can be used to transmit information over long distances.

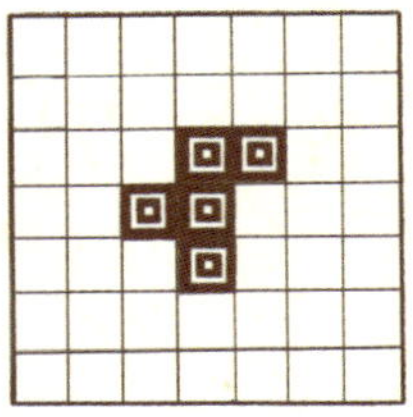

R-pentominoes live for a very long time. Such figures stabilize only after 1,103 generations.

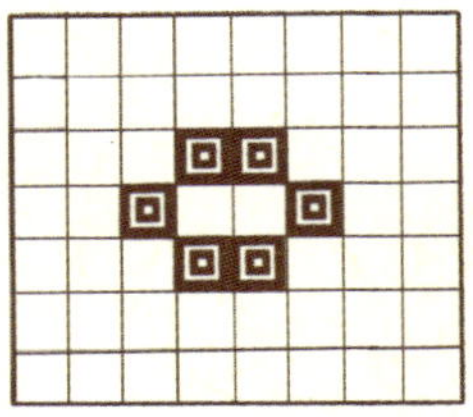

Stable patterns that don't change over the generations are known as "still life," such as the beehive shown here.

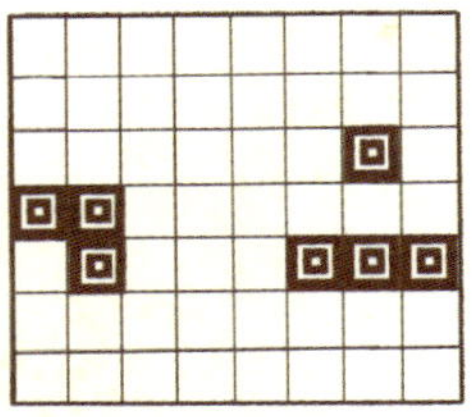

This configuration, the "hard nut," suddenly disappears after 130 turns.

The ultimate goal of the game is to find new organisms with interesting properties. Shapes can behave in different ways. Some die as soon as they appear. Others grow to fill the whole space, and still others are constantly transforming.

Try creating "glider guns" that shoot out new shapes, "puffer trains" that drive across the field and leave trails of exhaust behind them and so on.

The game ends if there are no living pieces left on the field, the configuration of the gameboard is an exact replication of a previous state or the system has stabilized (none of the cells are able to change states).

BULQUACK

To play is to be free. Play is one of the ultimate forms of free expression — it's impossible to determine how exactly a game will develop or to anticipate the final score. At the same time, games usually impose a set of rules and conditions that aren't present in the real world. The main purpose of the game is simply to play it. When we do, we solve problems that teach us new concepts and allow us to acquire new skills. Playing is one of the main ways we communicate with each other and with our own inner worlds, both real and imaginary. Games teach us that if we are unsatisfied with our own reality, we can always change it.

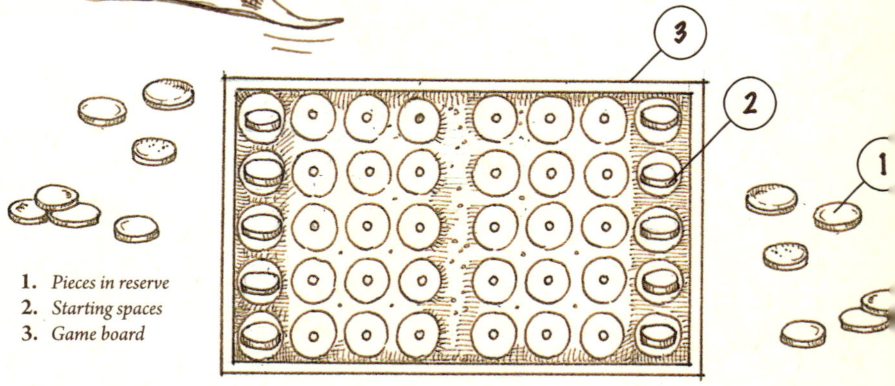

1. *Pieces in reserve*
2. *Starting spaces*
3. *Game board*

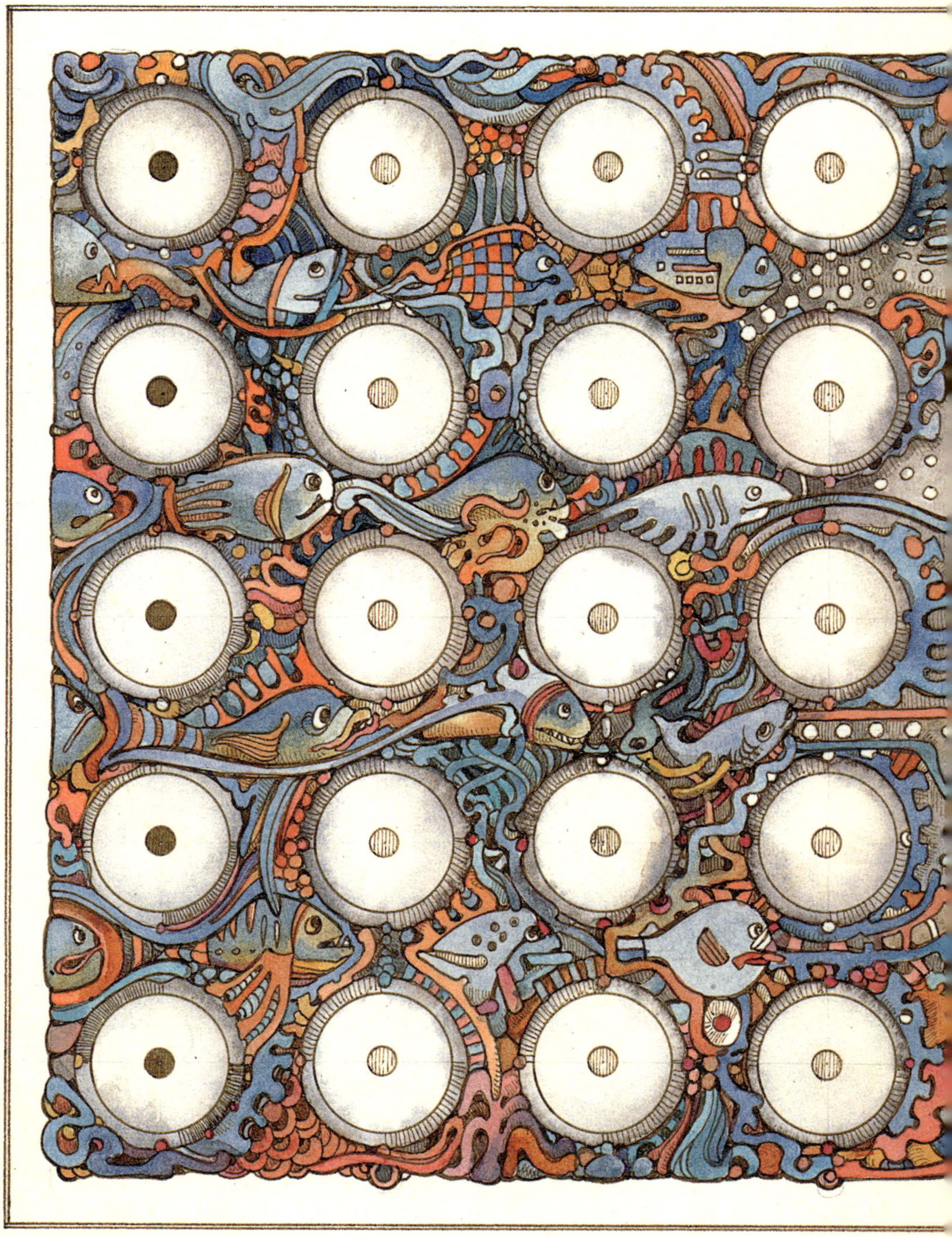

GAME SETUP

1. Find 20 playing pieces (coins, rocks, buttons, etc.).
2. Place the game board between the two players.
3. Each player takes 10 playing pieces and places them in front of themselves.
4. Each player takes 5 of their pieces and places them on each of their starting spaces.
5. Choose the first player in any way you want.

HOW TO PLAY

Players take turns. On your turn, you must perform one of the following actions: **Place a New Piece** or **Move and Attack**. Let's look at the action in more detail.

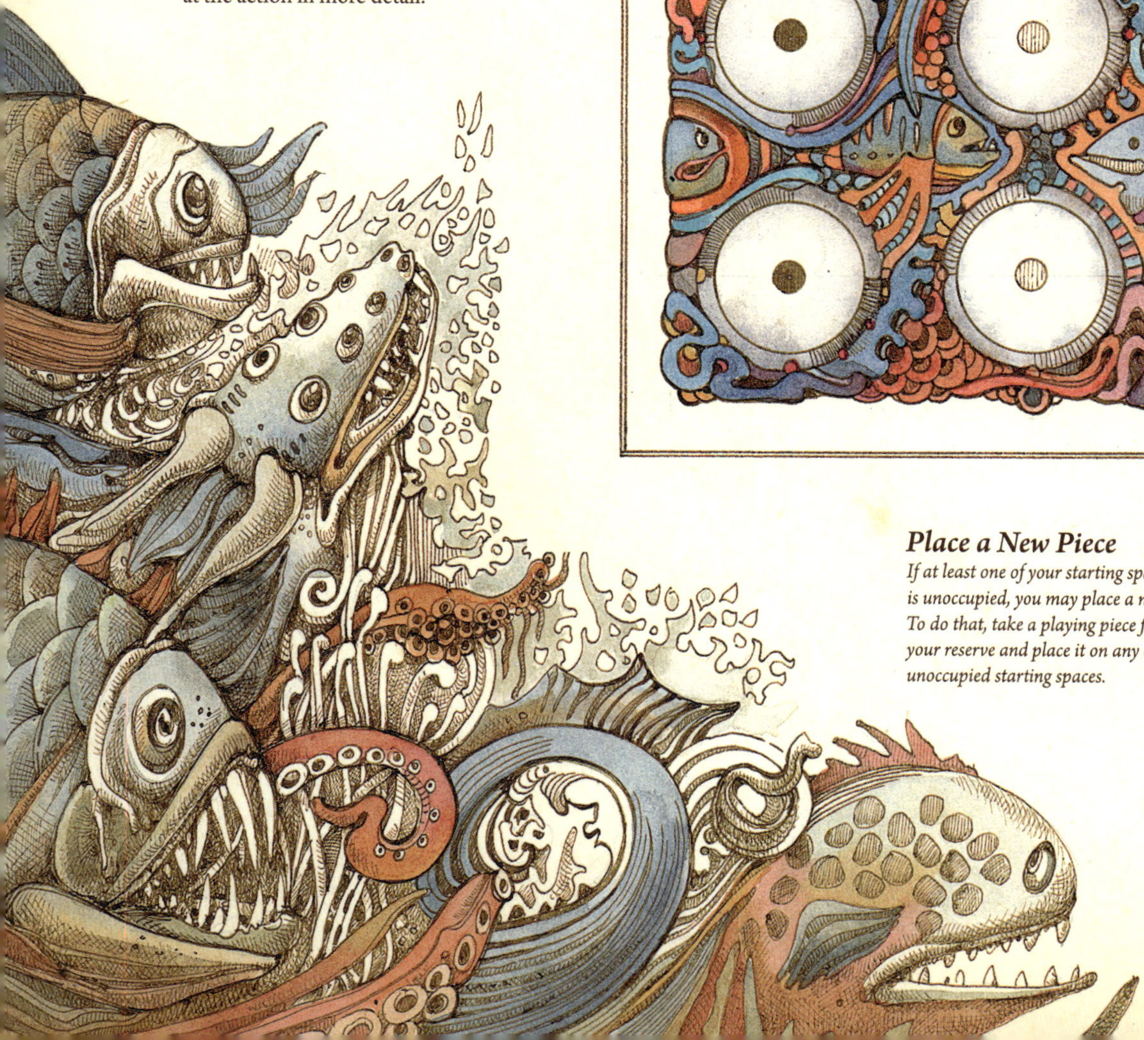

Place a New Piece

If at least one of your starting spaces is unoccupied, you may place a new piece. To do that, take a playing piece from your reserve and place it on any of your unoccupied starting spaces.

Repeating moves

The current player may declare a draw if the opponent has repeated a series of moves three or more times that results in the same arrangement of pieces on the game board on the opponent's side.

End of the Game and Victory

The game ends immediately when one of the players destroys five opponent's pieces. That player is declared a winner.

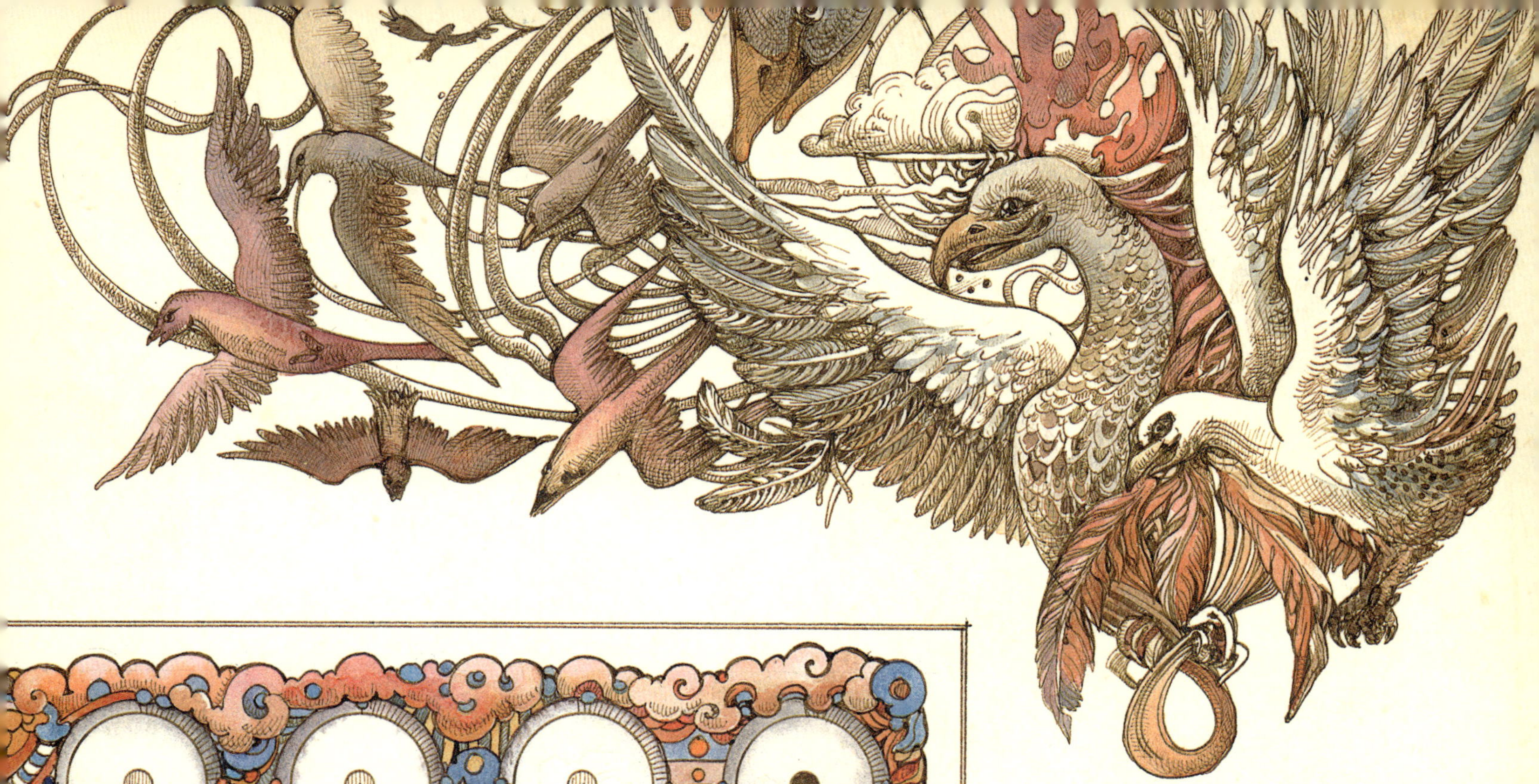

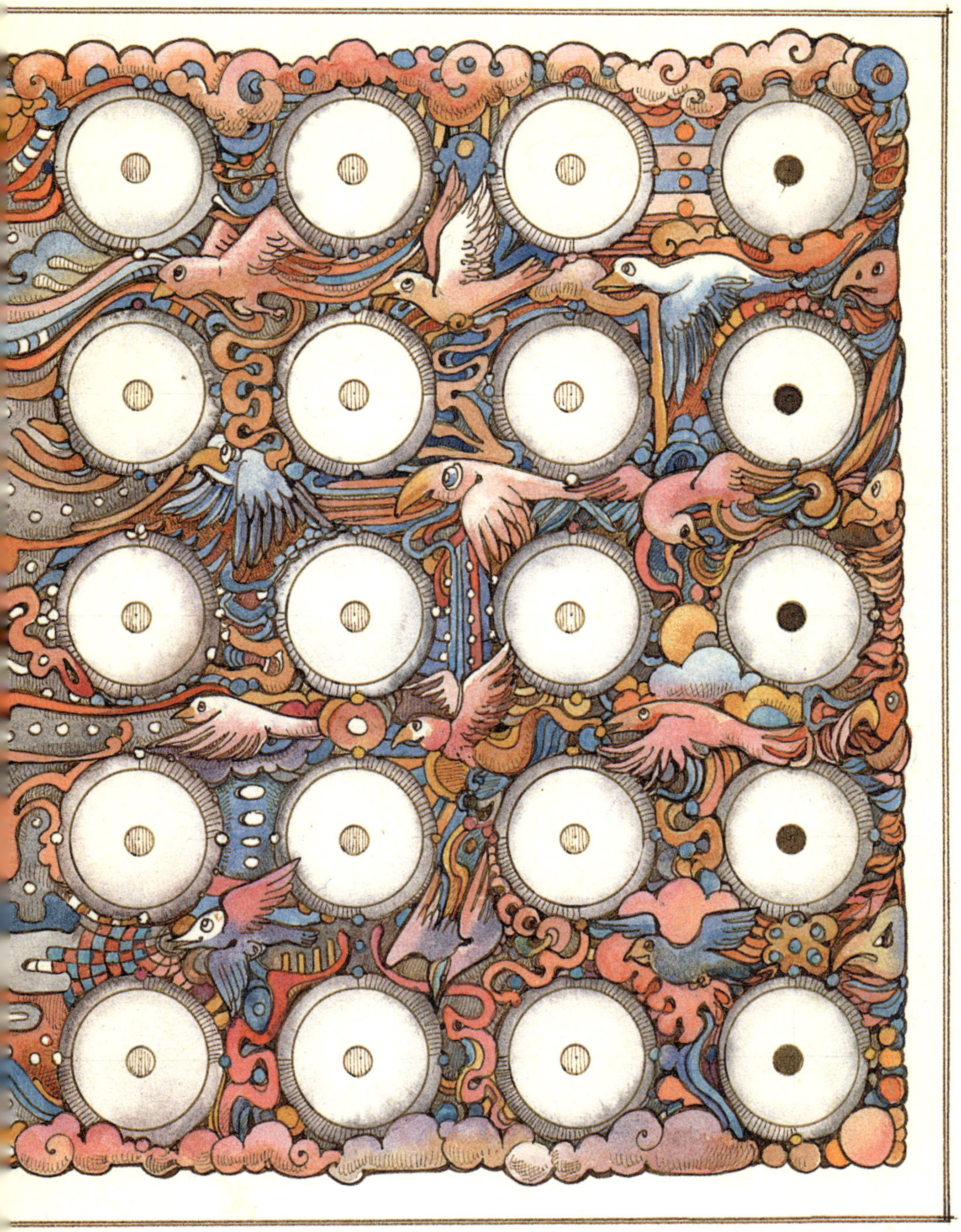

Attack Rules

After you move the playing piece, it "shoots" toward the opponent. The range of attack is equal to the number of pieces behind the active piece plus 1.

Example: *You moved the piece 1 space forward. There are 2 more pieces standing behind it. Therefore, the piece attacks the 3rd space (marked with a lightning bolt).*

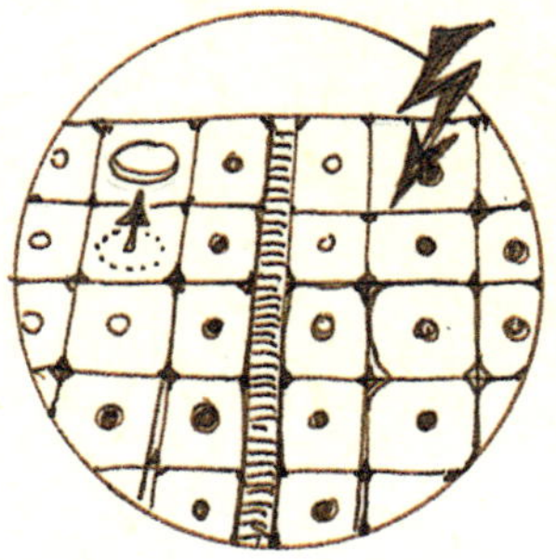

Failed Attack

If the attacked space is empty or contains your own playing piece, nothing happens.

Successful Attack

If the attacked space contains an opponent's piece, it is destroyed and removed from the game. Take the attacked piece off the board and keep it as a trophy separate from your reserve. After that, return all your playing pieces that participated in the attack back to your reserve.

Example: *The player on the left has successfully attacked the opponent's piece. At the end of the turn they take the opponent's piece as a trophy and return their own pieces that participated in the attack. Specifically, the piece that led to the attack and the 2 pieces behind it. The piece standing at the edge of the game board did not participate in the attack, so it remains on the board.*

Move and Attack

Choose any piece on the game board and move it to an adjacent space. Movement rules:

- *Pieces can move forward, backward, left and right but not diagonally.*
- *A space can contain up to 1 piece at a time.*
- *If a space is occupied by another piece, you can jump over that space.*
- *If there are several occupied spaces in a row, you can jump over all of them.*

Exception: *The playing piece is not allowed to jump over the dividing line in the middle or the boundaries of the game board.*

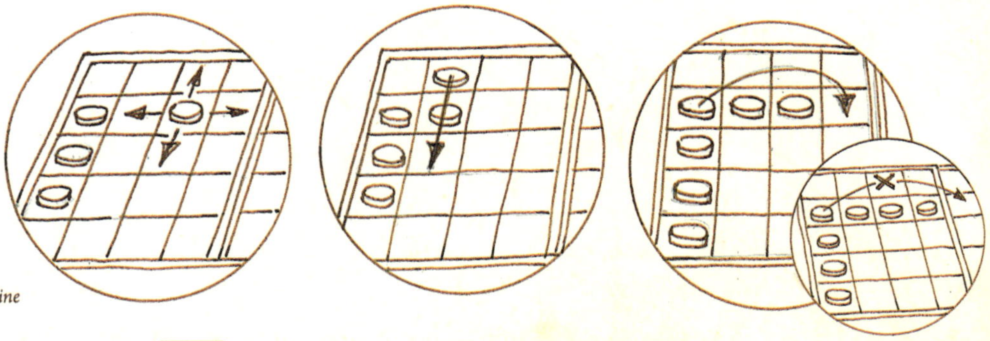

AUTOMATONS

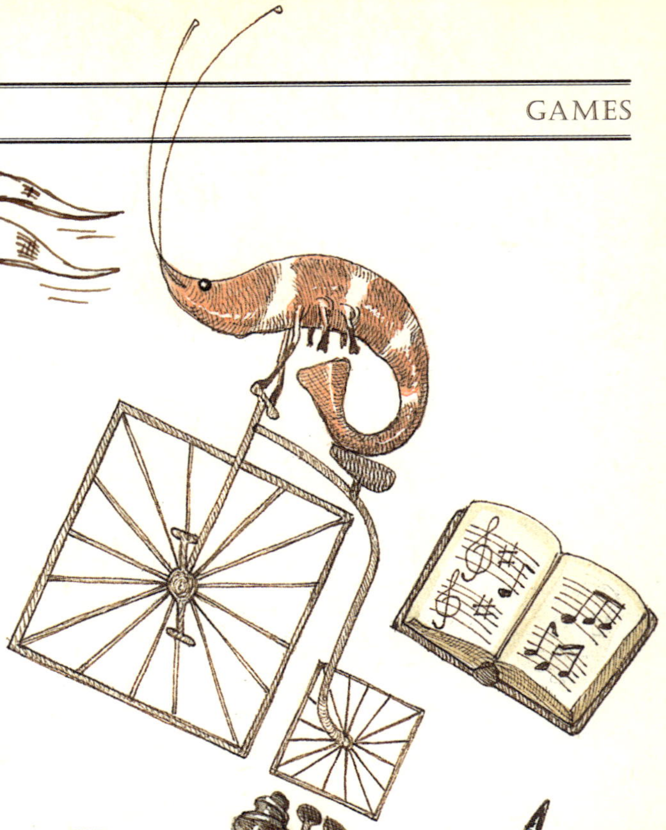

The world through a child's eyes is always a bit different. A child can invent a whole world just by playing with pebbles. They come up with characters and stories for their toys, inserting their own world into the one that surrounds them. Crickets become musicians, fish learn to talk, and mice dance ballet. Mechanical toys called "automatons" can add their own life to the world of the child, broadening that teeming universe even further.

CHARACTER

It all starts with a character, but giving a toy character is not an easy task. Everything matters here: facial expressions, posture, abilities. Whether it's a little mouse, a huge spider, or even a shrimp—with your imagination, characters can acquire personalities, interests, or even jobs. An automaton can be everyone or anyone!

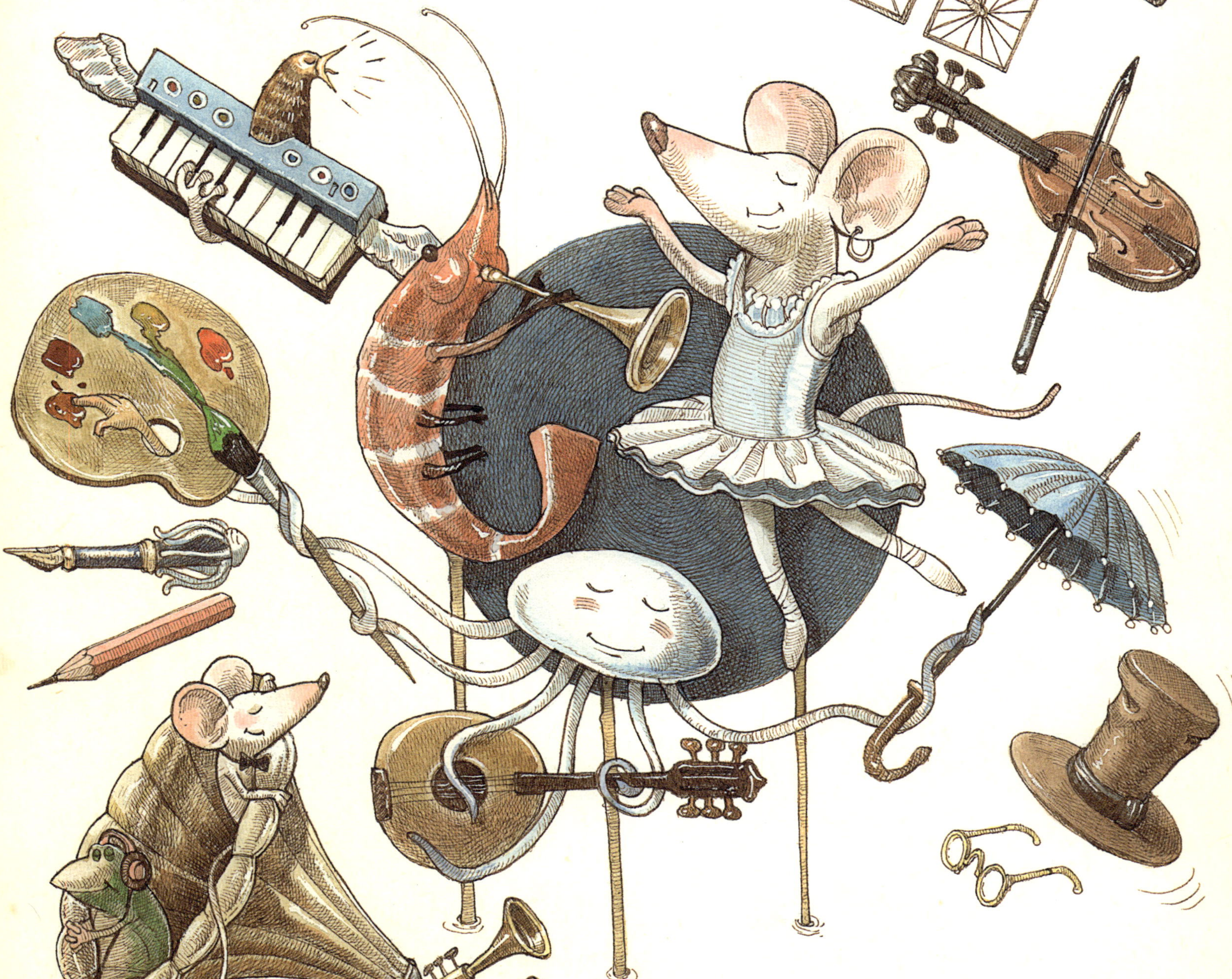

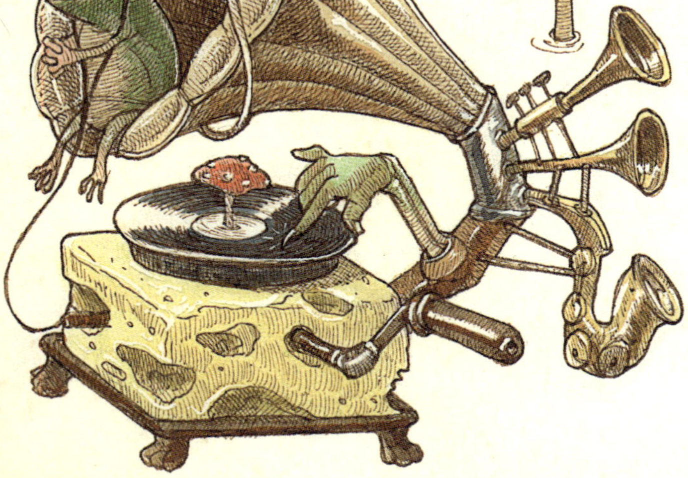

ACCESSORIES

As soon as you decide on a character, it's time to pick accessories. Give the mouse an umbrella if it's raining, or put it on a bicycle. Give your shrimp a violin and trombone. Frogs can have spear toothpick-weapons – and don't forget about armor. This way, you'll create a whole world with its own rules. Then it's just a matter of making it move and dance.

MECHANICAL NODES

Humanity has conquered the energy of motion and learned to transform it. There are a huge number of mechanisms serving different purposes. Some of them can help you bring the world you've created to life.

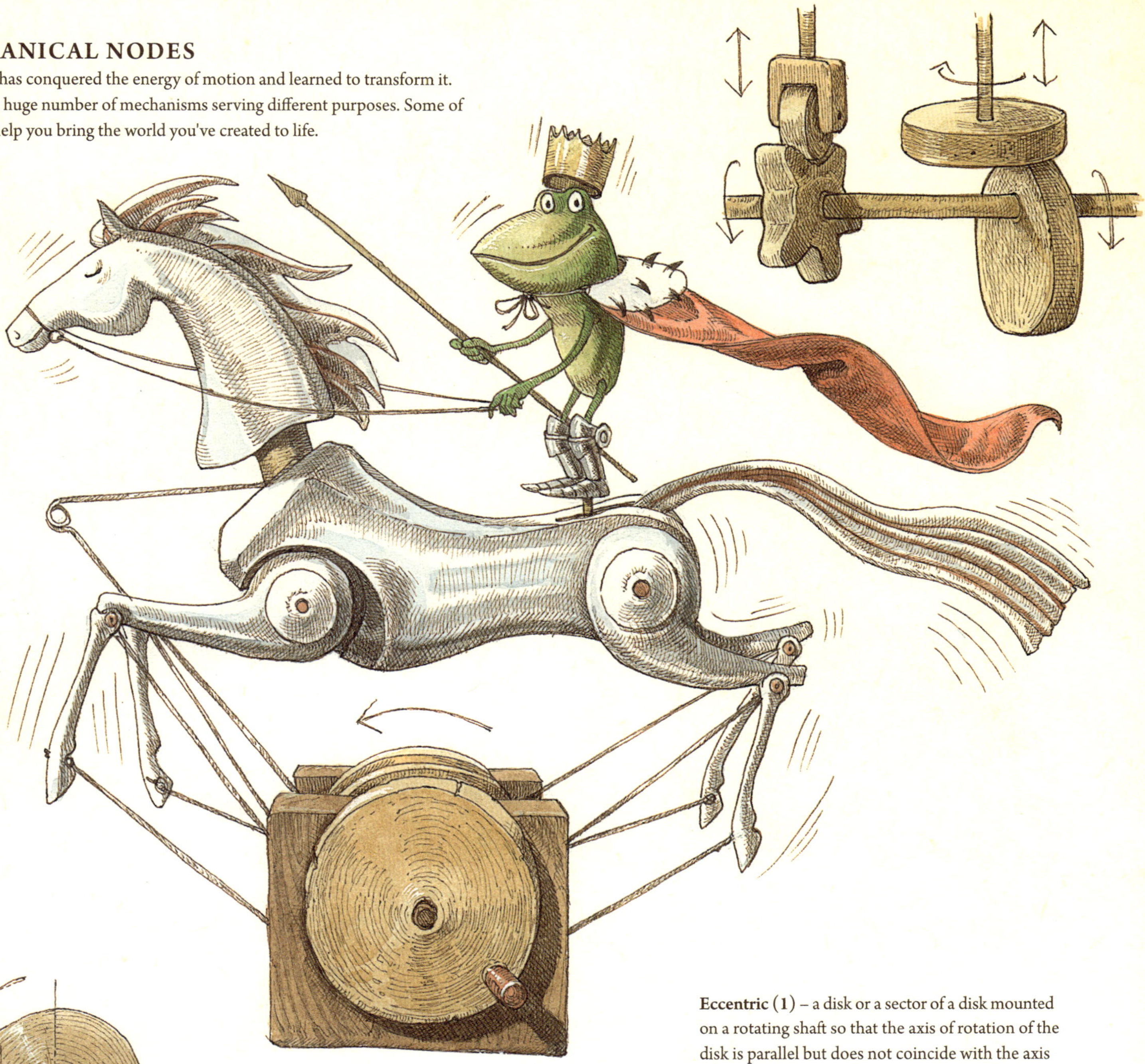

1

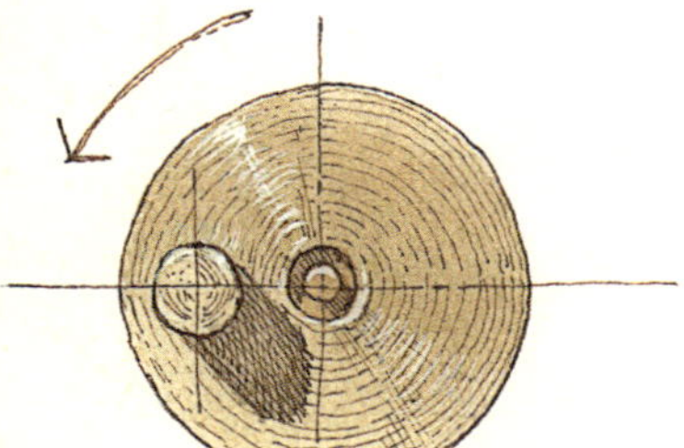

2

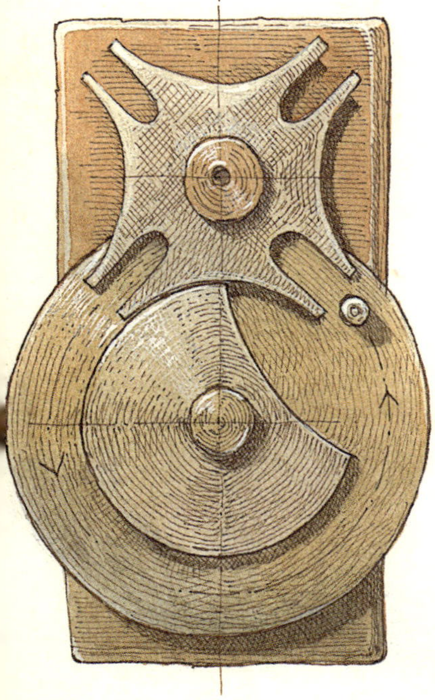

3

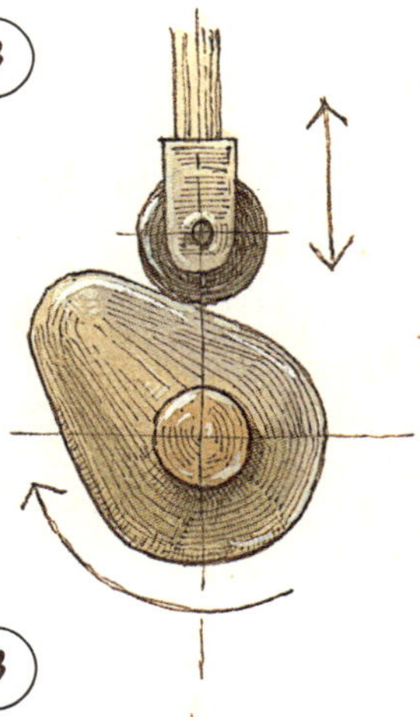

3

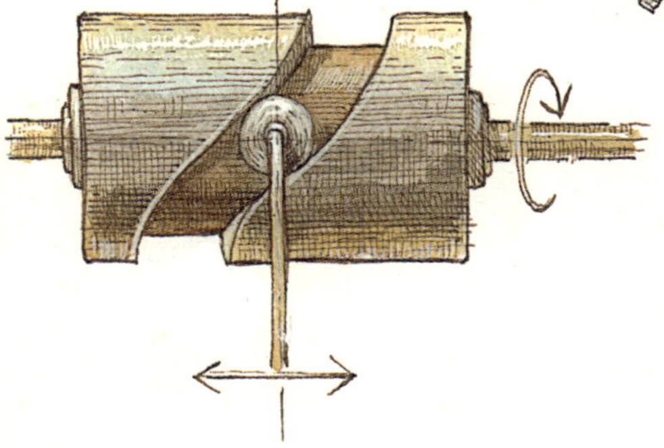

4

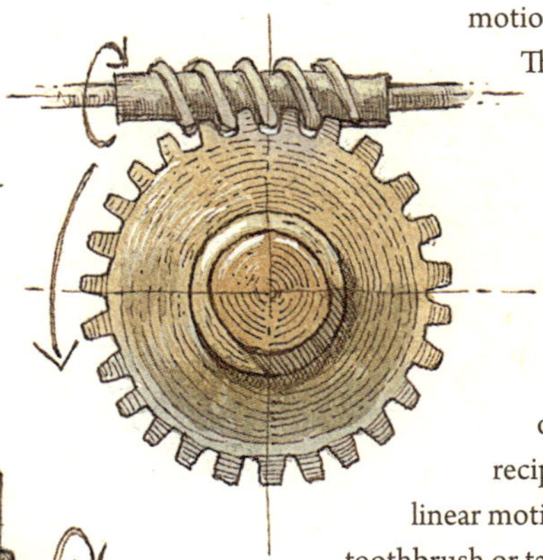

Eccentric (1) – a disk or a sector of a disk mounted on a rotating shaft so that the axis of rotation of the disk is parallel but does not coincide with the axis of rotation of the shaft, to convert rotary motion into linear motion, like half a pulley mechanism.

Maltese Mechanism (2) – a mechanism of intermittent motion that converts uniform rotary motion into intermittent rotary motion. This mechanism is used in clocks and film projectors to make the turning of one big gear power different movements of smaller ones.

Cam Mechanisms (3) are designed to convert the rotary or linear motion of a cam into reciprocating-rotary or reciprocating-linear motion of a pusher, like in an electric toothbrush or tattoo machine.

Endless screw or worm gear (4) – a mechanical transmission accomplished by the engagement of a worm and its mating worm wheel, to convert angular velocity and torque.

DELICATESSEN

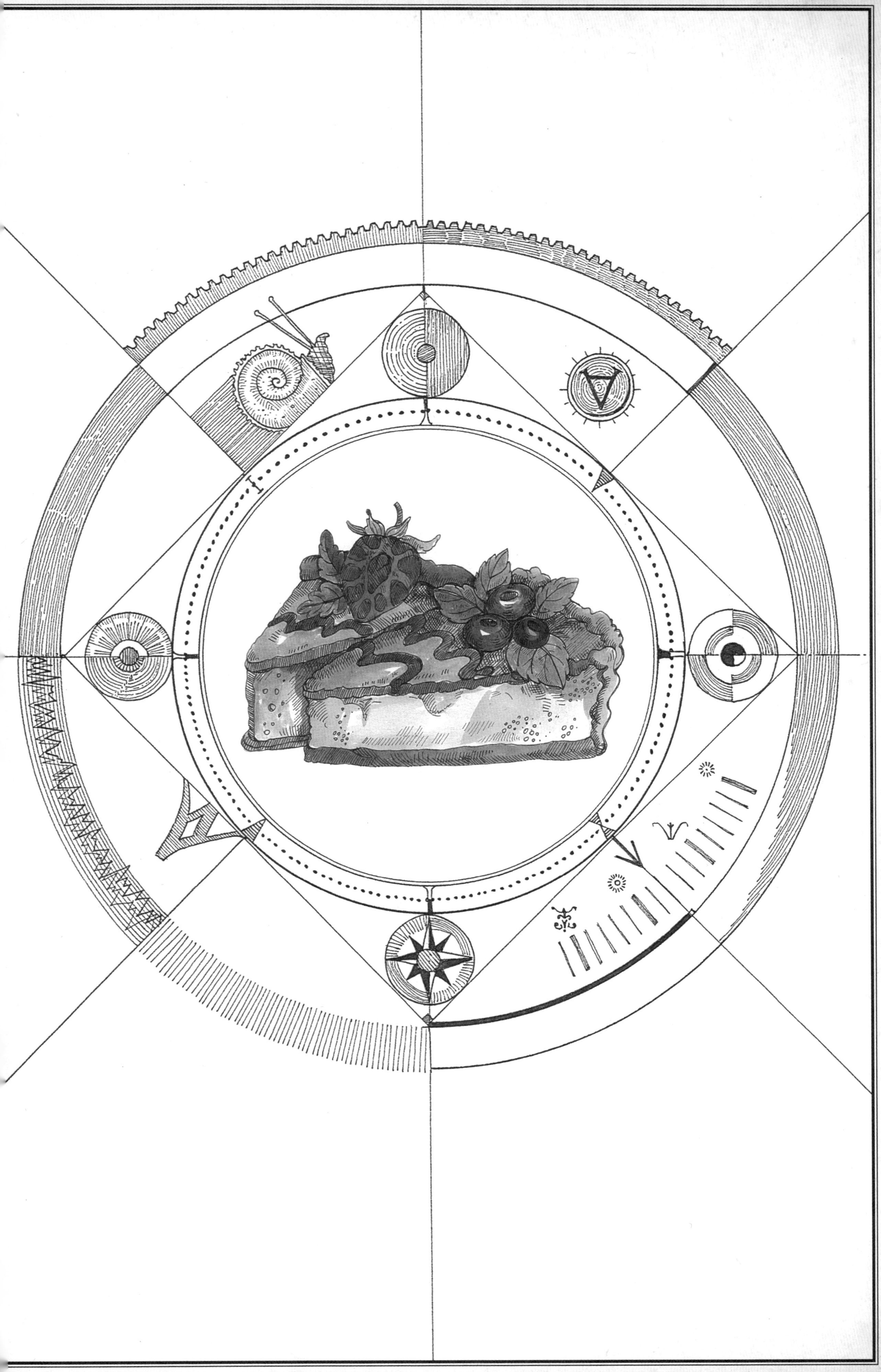

SUSHI

Food is, of course, important for its caloric and nutritional value. But it's also so much more than that! Food is an opportunity for personal growth and self-expression. New flavors and sensations cause new connections to form in your brain, and a good meal can heal more than just your body. You know what they say — you are what you eat. So why not create the best version of yourself by preparing a well-balanced meal? It's time to learn how to make sushi. The only thing you'll have to cook is the rice. This is the main secret of sushi: do not complicate what can be done simply.

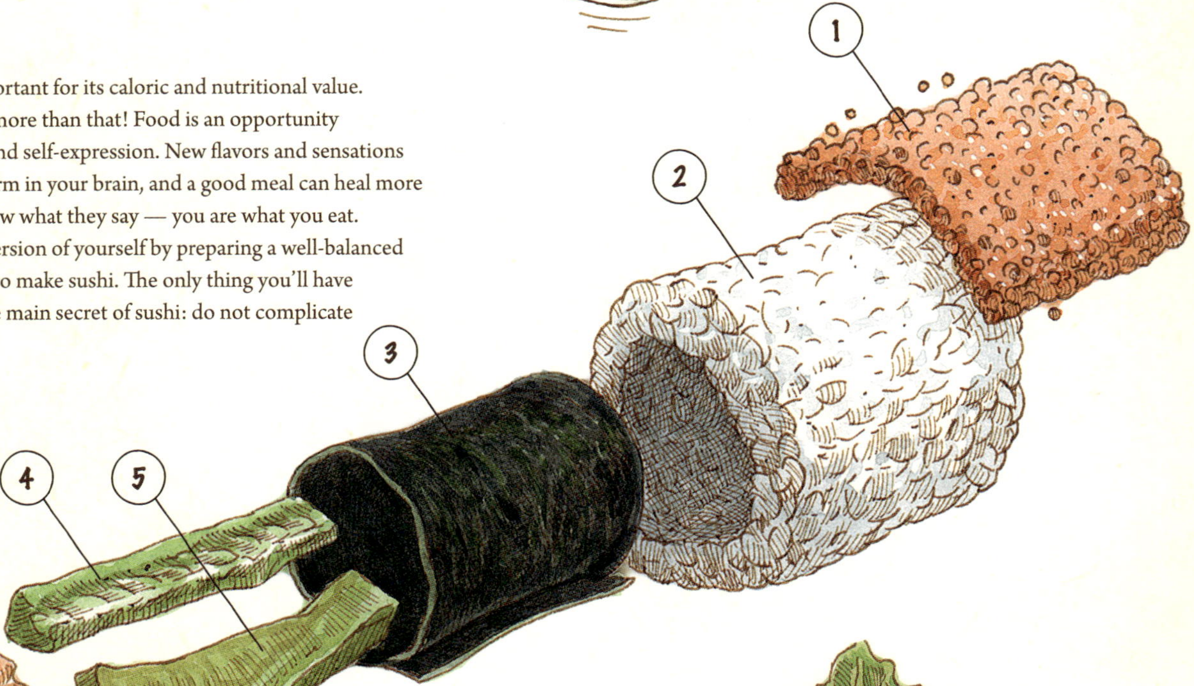

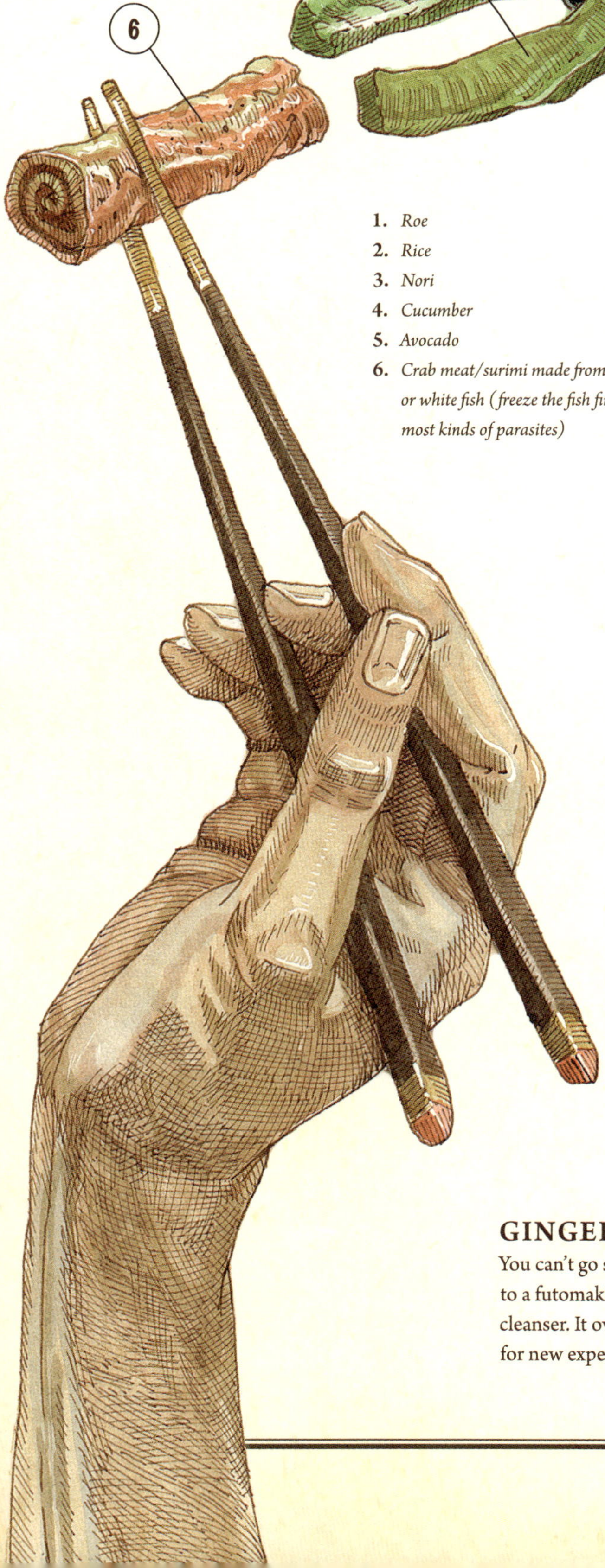

1. *Roe*
2. *Rice*
3. *Nori*
4. *Cucumber*
5. *Avocado*
6. *Crab meat/surimi made from crab or white fish (freeze the fish first to kill most kinds of parasites)*

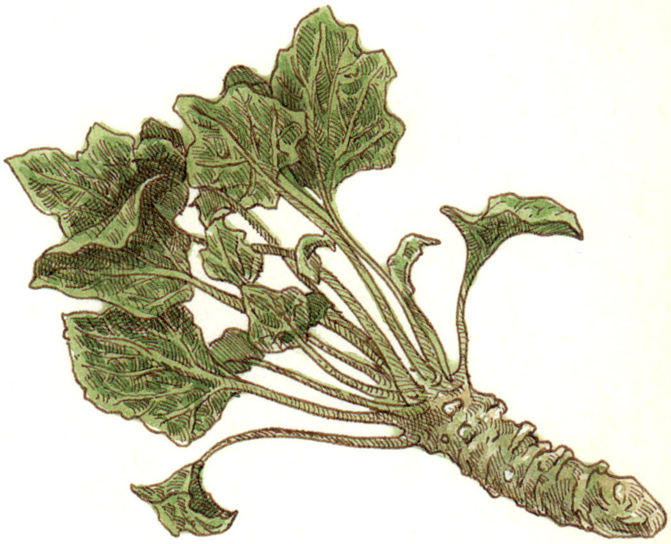

WASABI

There's not just a method to preparing sushi — there's also a method to eating it. Add wasabi, the grated root of a special kind of horseradish. Mix it with soy sauce, a fermented product of soybeans. This creates a combination of all five flavors: sweet, bitter, salty, sour and umami. Dip the sushi in fish-side first, and do not allow the rice to soak in the sauce or it will absorb too much. Better yet, use a piece of ginger as a "brush." Learn to use chopsticks instead of a fork — you need to eat the sushi whole, as biting into it or breaking it with a fork will ruin its structural integrity.

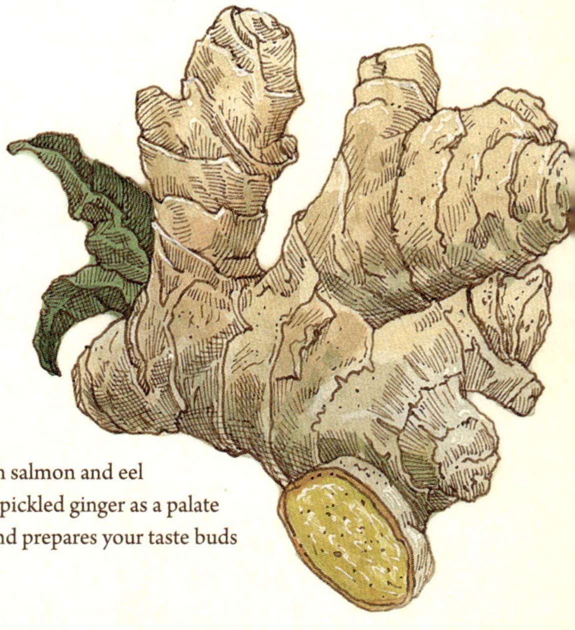

GINGER

You can't go straight from a piece of nigiri with salmon and eel to a futomaki roll — the tastes will clash. Use pickled ginger as a palate cleanser. It overpowers any lingering flavors and prepares your taste buds for new experiences.

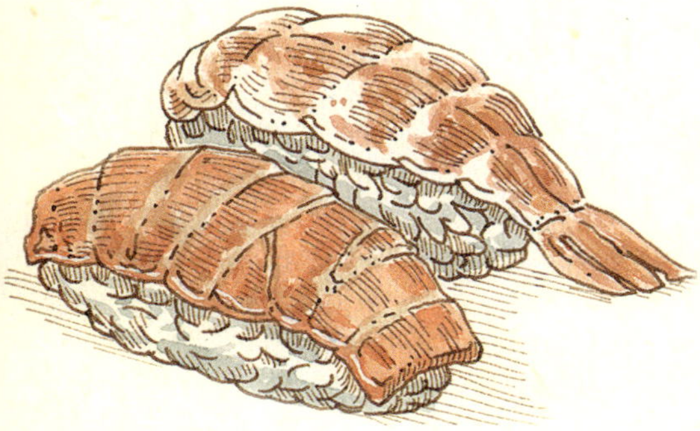

Nigiri
A rectangular mound of rice topped with a thin slice of fish, squid or other seafood.

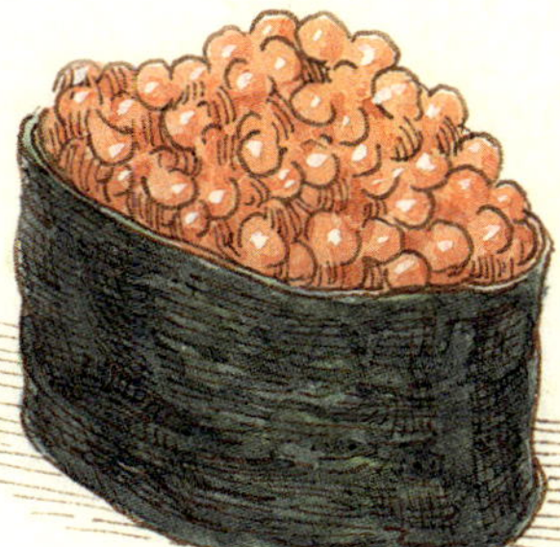

Gunkan Maki
Named after the battleship it resembles, gunkan maki is a rectangular mound of rice wrapped in dried nori (find this seaweed growing on the bottom of seafaring boats). Load the "deck" of the boat with roe, seaweed, finely chopped fish marinated in sauce, etc.

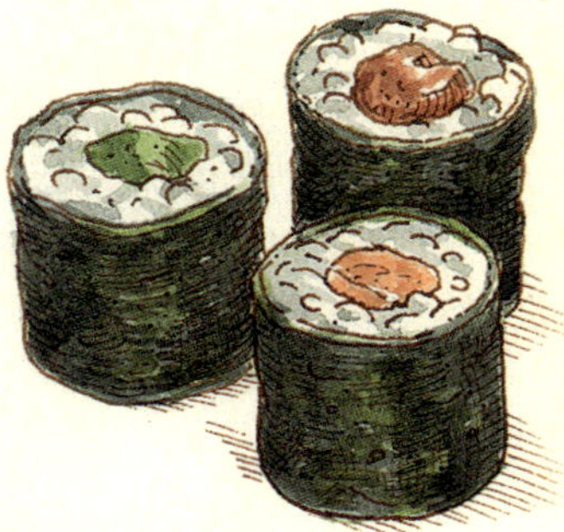

Maki (sushi roll)
Rice and fillings rolled in a sheet of seaweed. If there is a single filling, it is a hosomaki roll. Maki is made using a bamboo mat. Lay down a sheet of nori and spread rice on top, making sure to leave a lip at one end to seal the roll together. Place fillings on one side and roll everything up. Cut into pieces with a large knife soaked in cold water.

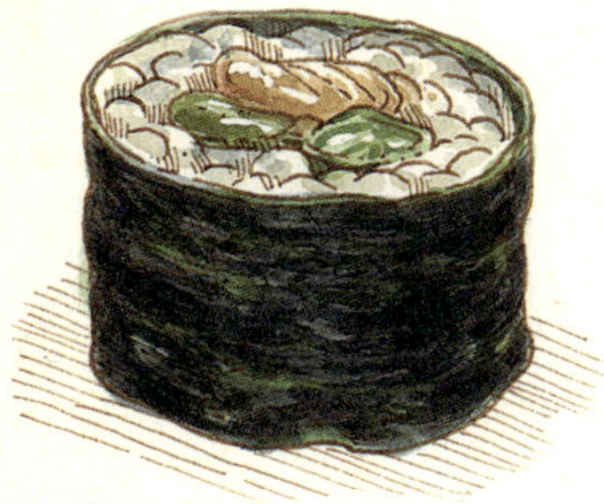

Futomaki
Large (3–4 cm thick and 4–5 cm wide) maki with several fillings.

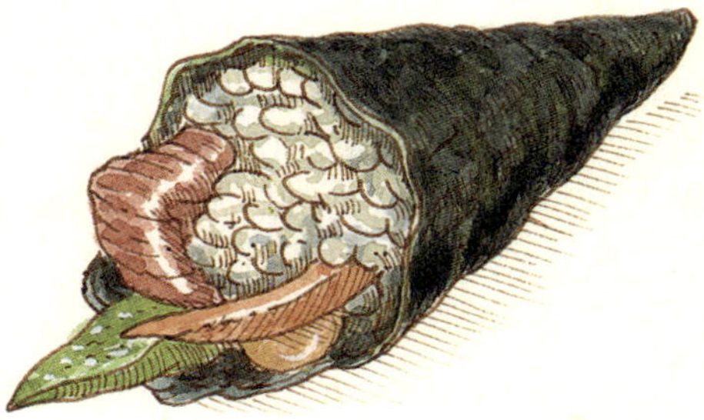

Temaki (hand roll)
Large, cone-shaped sushi roll. Usually eaten with the hands, as it is too heavy to be lifted with chopsticks.

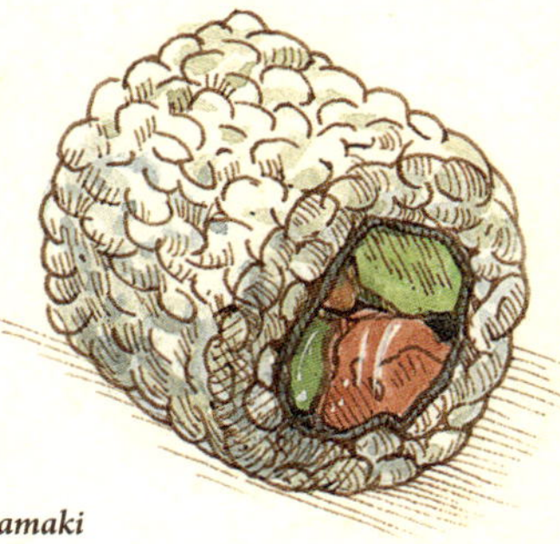

Uramaki
Outside: rice sprinkled with caviar or toasted sesame seeds. Inside: a layer of nori and filling.

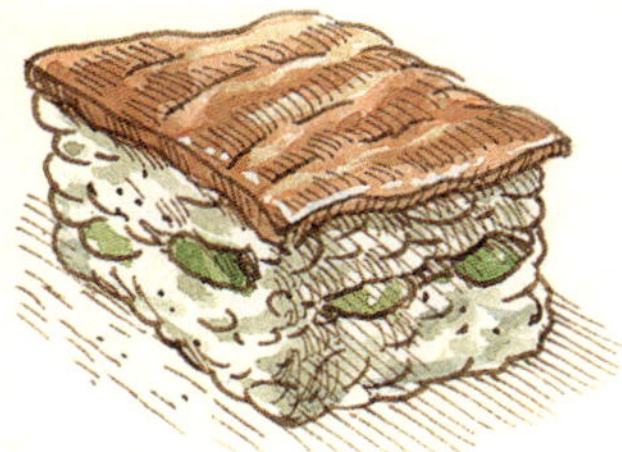

Oshi (pressed sushi)
Sushi in the form of dense rectangular bars consisting of layers of rice and fillings.

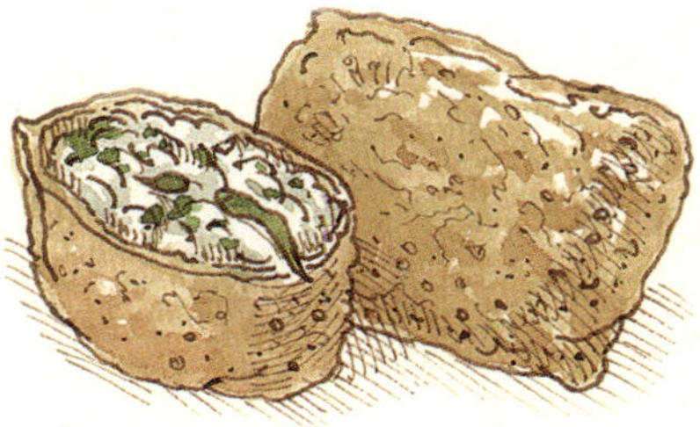

Inari
A bag of fried tofu or omelet stuffed with rice.

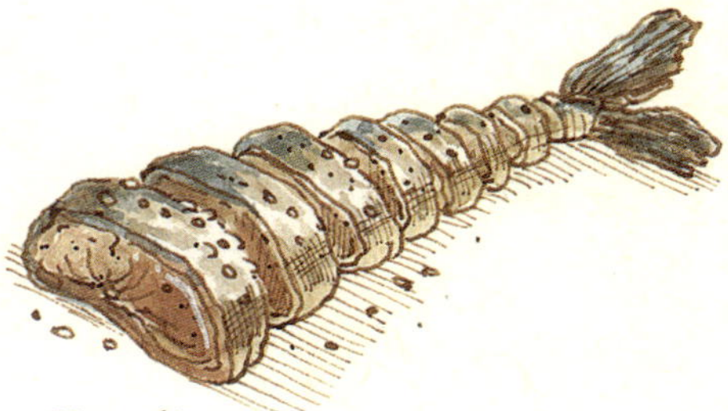

Narezushi
This is actually a way of preserving fish. The fish is salted in barrels, mixed with raw rice and placed under a press. After a period of six months to three years, the dish is ready. This method allows you to preserve the fish over long periods of time.

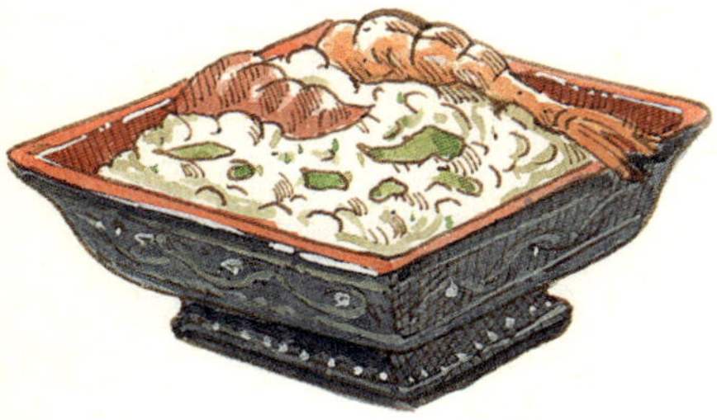

Chirashi
Sushi for the lazy: a plate of rice with fish and other toppings laid on top.

RICE

The most important element of sushi is properly cooking the rice. It should be sticky while maintaining its structure. Round white rice works best. Rinse 500 g of rice with cold water 5 times, cover with clean water and leave to soak for 15 minutes. Place in a heavy-bottomed saucepan and cover with water in a 1:1 ratio. For flavor, add a piece of dried nori seaweed (but remove it just before water starts to boil). Bring to a boil over high heat and wait for the excess water to evaporate. Then reduce heat and cook for another 30 minutes. Let the rice sit.

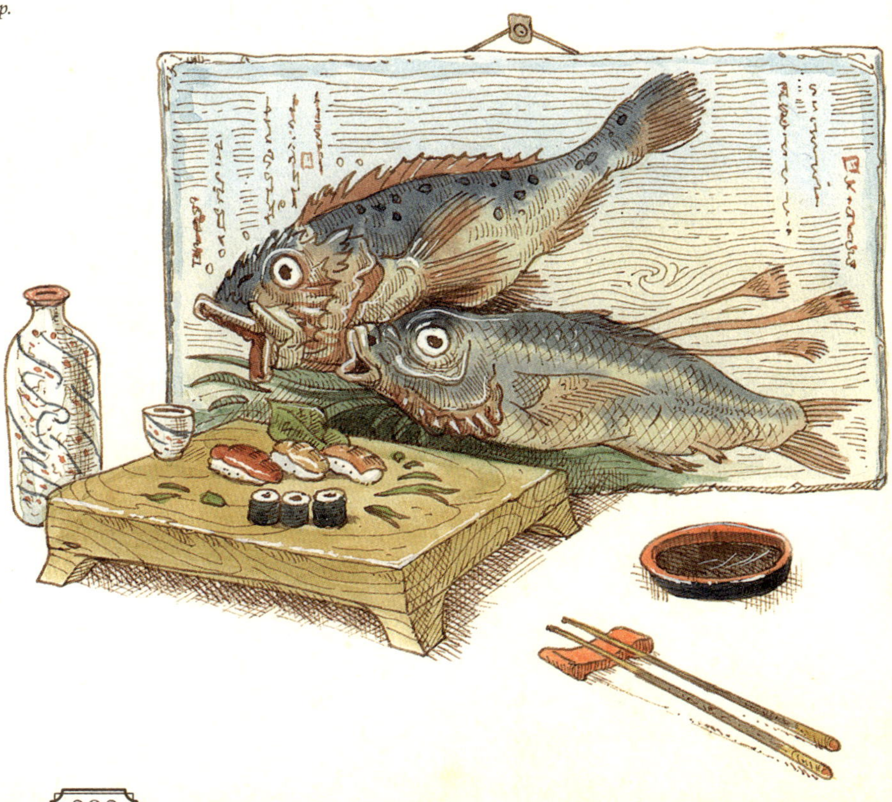

Add seasonings while rice is still warm:

- *Mix 125 ml of rice vinegar (mirin) and 20 grams each of salt and sugar.*
- *Heat the mixture over a fire without bringing it to a boil (about 5 minutes).*
- *Add 15 g of kombu seaweed and let simmer for about an hour (This is an optional ingredient. Without it, the rice will still be sticky and tasty, but kombu adds a complexity of flavor).*
- *Mix into rice and allow it to sit for an hour.*

RAMEN NOODLES

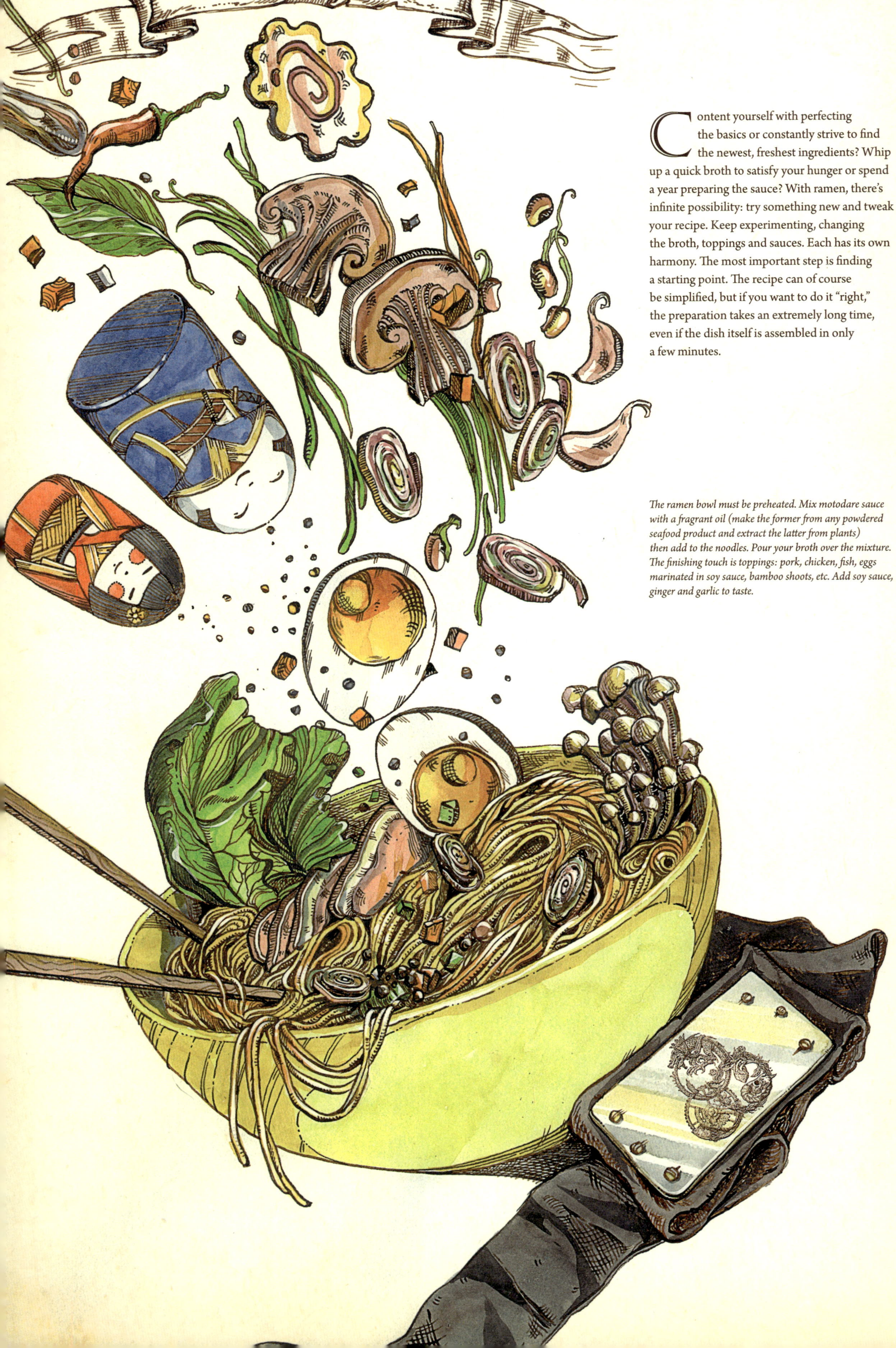

Content yourself with perfecting the basics or constantly strive to find the newest, freshest ingredients? Whip up a quick broth to satisfy your hunger or spend a year preparing the sauce? With ramen, there's infinite possibility: try something new and tweak your recipe. Keep experimenting, changing the broth, toppings and sauces. Each has its own harmony. The most important step is finding a starting point. The recipe can of course be simplified, but if you want to do it "right," the preparation takes an extremely long time, even if the dish itself is assembled in only a few minutes.

The ramen bowl must be preheated. Mix motodare sauce with a fragrant oil (make the former from any powdered seafood product and extract the latter from plants) then add to the noodles. Pour your broth over the mixture. The finishing touch is toppings: pork, chicken, fish, eggs marinated in soy sauce, bamboo shoots, etc. Add soy sauce, ginger and garlic to taste.

NOODLES

Made from four main ingredients: wheat flour, salt, water and kansui, which is essentially alkaline water (a mixture of potassium carbonate and sodium carbonate in varying proportions). Kansui gives the noodles elasticity and acts as a preservative. You can substitute kansui with roasted baking soda: pour on a baking sheet and roast at 170–200°C until the baking soda loses 1/3 of its mass (this may take a couple of hours).

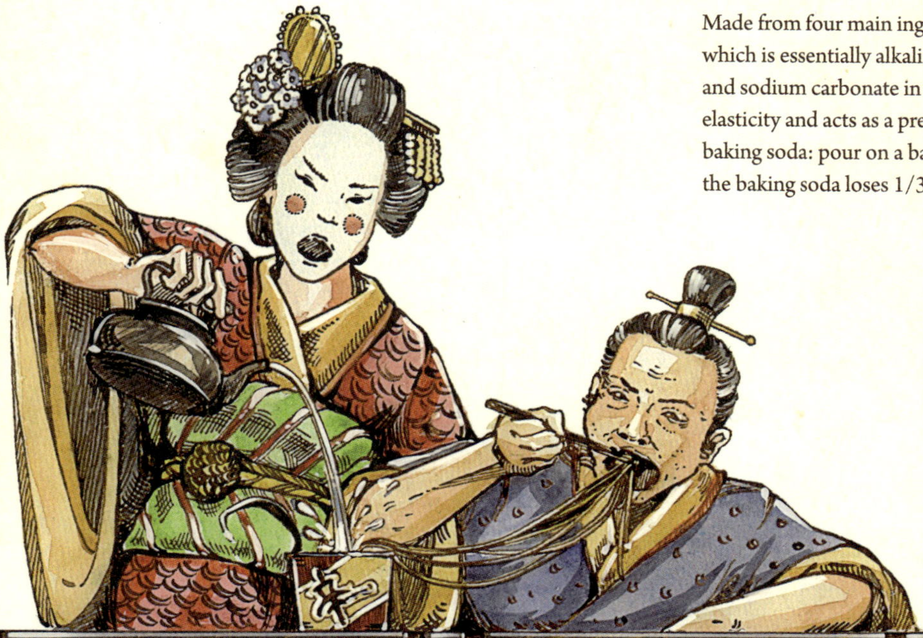

INSTANT NOODLES

A very practical recipe — it keeps for a long time and cooks up quickly. Boil the noodles for 1.5–2 minutes. Rinse in lightly salted water to remove excess starch. Separate into portions and form into blocks. Fry into shape in boiling vegetable oil.

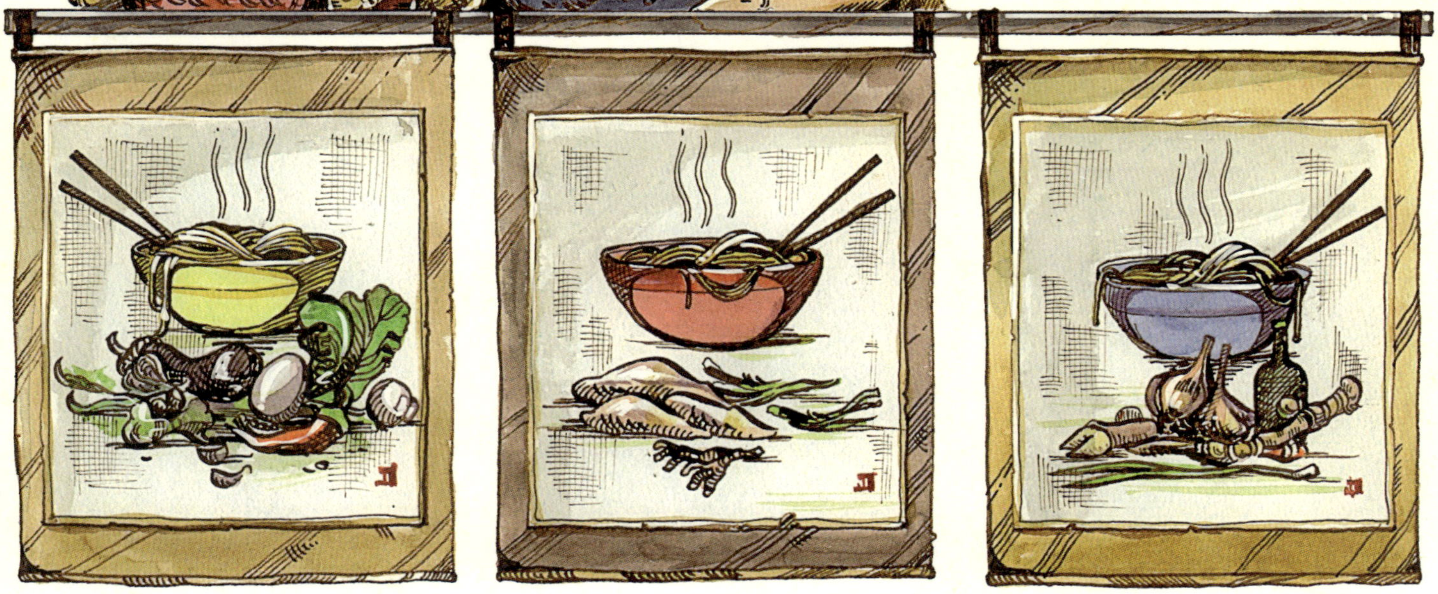

Pork broth—Tonkatsu

- *1.5 kg pork bones with fat (add pork hooves and tails for richness)*
- *Sesame oil (to taste)*
- *1 large onion*
- *1 head garlic*
- *1 small piece ginger*
- *2 leeks*

1. *Cover pork bones, fat and hooves with cold water until completely submerged.*
2. *Put on high heat and bring to a boil.*
3. *Coarsely chop the onion, garlic and ginger. Fry in hot sesame oil until charred. All the ingredients should turn black.*
4. *After the broth comes to a boil, pour it out and rinse the bones with cold water.*
5. *Take the cleaned bones, charred vegetables and remnants of the oil in which they were fried and place them in a saucepan, cover with cold water and bring to a boil.*
6. *Skim off the foam, reduce heat and cover.*
7. *Leave the broth to simmer for at least 24 hours. Open the lid periodically and add water. The bones should remain completely submerged in the liquid.*

Motodare sauce

This gives the ramen a special, rich taste.
Mix the following ingredients:

- *Anchovies marinated in soy sauce for a week*
- *Dried algae marinated in saline solution for a week*
- *Dashi broth. Make by placing a piece of dried kombu seaweed in a saucepan, cover with a liter of water and let sit for 20 minutes. Then put on medium heat. Before boiling, take out the kombu, add bonito tuna shavings (cooked tuna which is then smoked, dried and cut into thin slices). After 3 minutes, strain the broth through a fine sieve.*
- *Sake or rice wine*
- *Rice vinegar*

Miso broth

- *500 g soybeans*
- *500 g Koji rice (a grain grown with Aspergillus oryzae mold). Enzymes produced during koji fermentation break down the proteins and starches found in soybeans into amino acids and sugars, which give the dish its umami flavor (page 100) and sweetness.*
- *215 g sea salt*
- *3 tsp soy sauce*
- *1 tsp sugar*
- *1 star anise pod*

1. *Rinse the beans and soak in cold water for at least 18 hours.*
2. *Rinse again and cook until soft.*
3. *Pour half a glass of warm water into the rice to partially rehydrate, add salt and stir.*
4. *Mash the beans into a paste.*
5. *Add rice and stir.*
6. *Roll the resulting dough into balls, place them in a container and press them down slightly.*
7. *Sprinkle with salt, cover with cling wrap and place a weight on top.*
8. *Leave the miso paste to ferment at room temperature for a year.*
9. *Combine your miso paste (2 tablespoons), soy sauce and sugar. Bring 750 ml of water to a boil, add the mixture and star anise. Bring the broth to a boil again.*

FAST FOOD

Modern life moves fast, constantly striving to build up industries and produce new goods and technologies. Soon the food industry will follow suit. But fast doesn't always mean good.

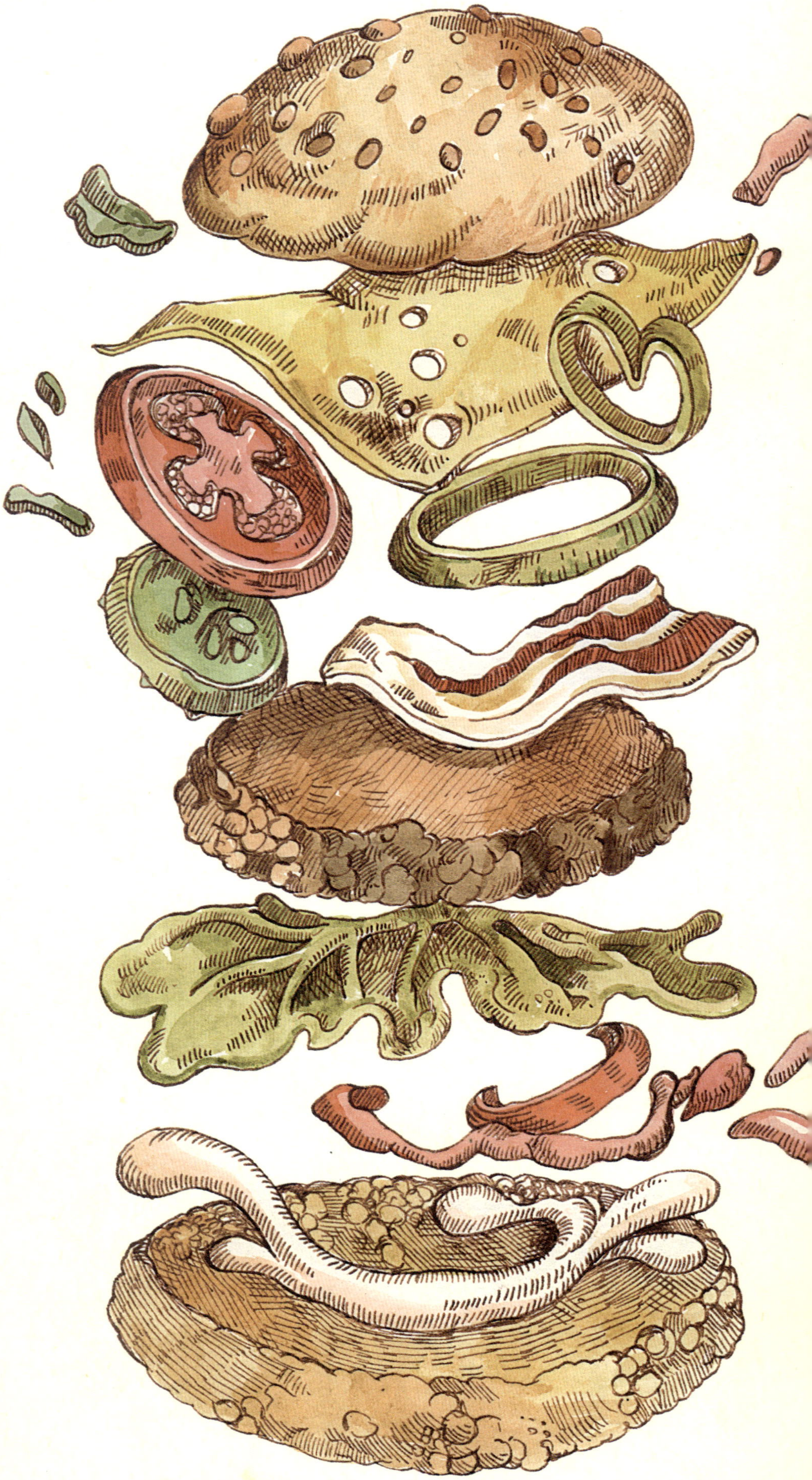

BURGERS

Fast food, by definition, must be calorically dense in order to satisfy hunger quickly. But the quality of calories varies greatly. Choose the right ingredients to make sure you get enough of everything you need: proteins — poultry, nuts, meat, fish; healthy fats — olive oil, avocado, oily ocean fish; and carbohydrates — grains, sugar, honey, cereals, fruits, vegetables. Cut the bun into two halves and place the filling in between. Topping possibilities are limited only by your imagination: pile veggies, herbs, cheese, tofu, bacon and/or egg on top of your protein (meat or fish). And don't forget — sauces are key.

MAYONNAISE

Separate the yolks of two room-temperature eggs. Whisk together with ½ teaspoon of mustard, 1 teaspoon sugar, ½ teaspoon lemon juice (or apple cider vinegar). Pour olive oil over the mixture in a thin stream, whisking constantly until it reaches the desired consistency. Add another ½ teaspoon of lemon juice. Whisk. The mass will thicken considerably.

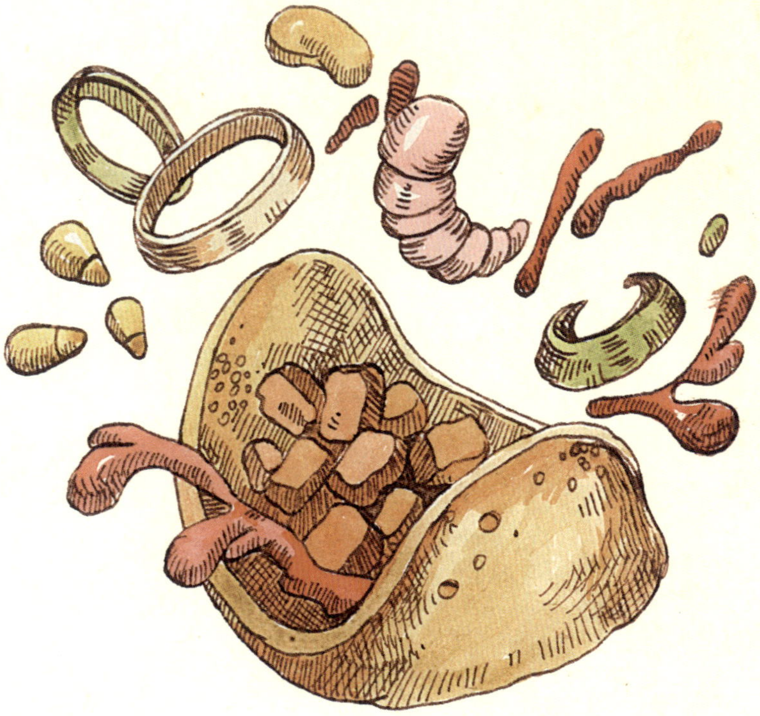

TACO

Place the filling — beef, pork, chicken, seafood, refried beans and/or vegetables — into a thin corn or wheat flour tortilla. Even stewed cactus pulp can be a good filling! Then pile high with cheese, cilantro, onions, salsa and guacamole. To make the latter, cream an avocado and add tomatoes, cilantro, lime juice and spices. Salsa is just finely chopped tomatoes with onions, celery, chili and lime juice.

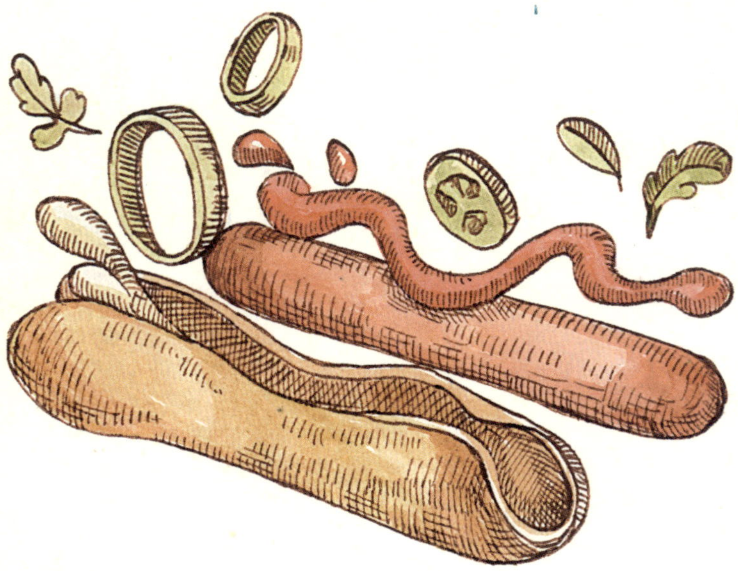

HOT DOG

Grind your meat of choice and mix in egg, milk, butter, salt and spices to taste. Minced onions and garlic also make good additions. Hand-roll your meat mixture into sausage shapes or pipe it into the intestinal lining of a cow or other animal. Whenever someone gets a hankering for hot dogs, just fry or boil them directly in the skin. Place your hot dog in a premade bun (page 94), season with sauces and add fresh, pickled or fried veggies, herbs, cheese or any other toppings you like.

FRENCH FRIES

Deep-frying is a cooking method using large quantities of oil heated to 130–180°C. This allows you to quickly cook dense foods such as potatoes, as well as soft cheese balls, pieces of meat, etc. Put the food in a sieve, wire tray or any other mesh container, and then immerse it fully in boiling oil for a couple of minutes. The oil must completely cover the food, so make sure you have a big enough pot before you start.

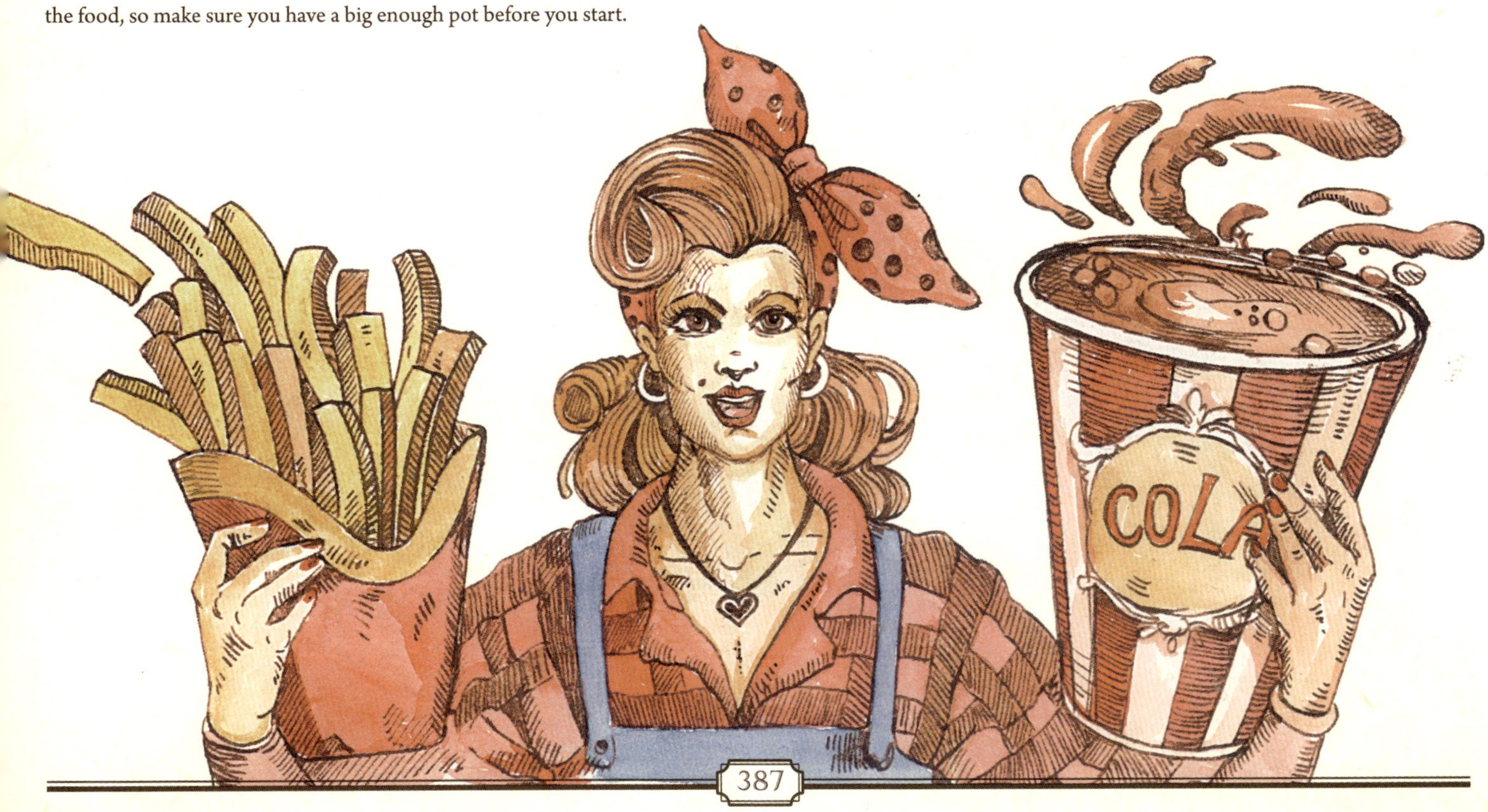

SOFT DRINKS

In a developed civilization, you can get bored consuming ordinary liquid that's nothing more than just necessary for life. The soda making machine can be a perfect intersection of fun and functional as it will add tickling bubbles, sweetness and many different flavors to the water. At the same time, fizzy drinks can be stored longer because carbon dioxide preserves and suppresses the development of pathogenic bacteria.

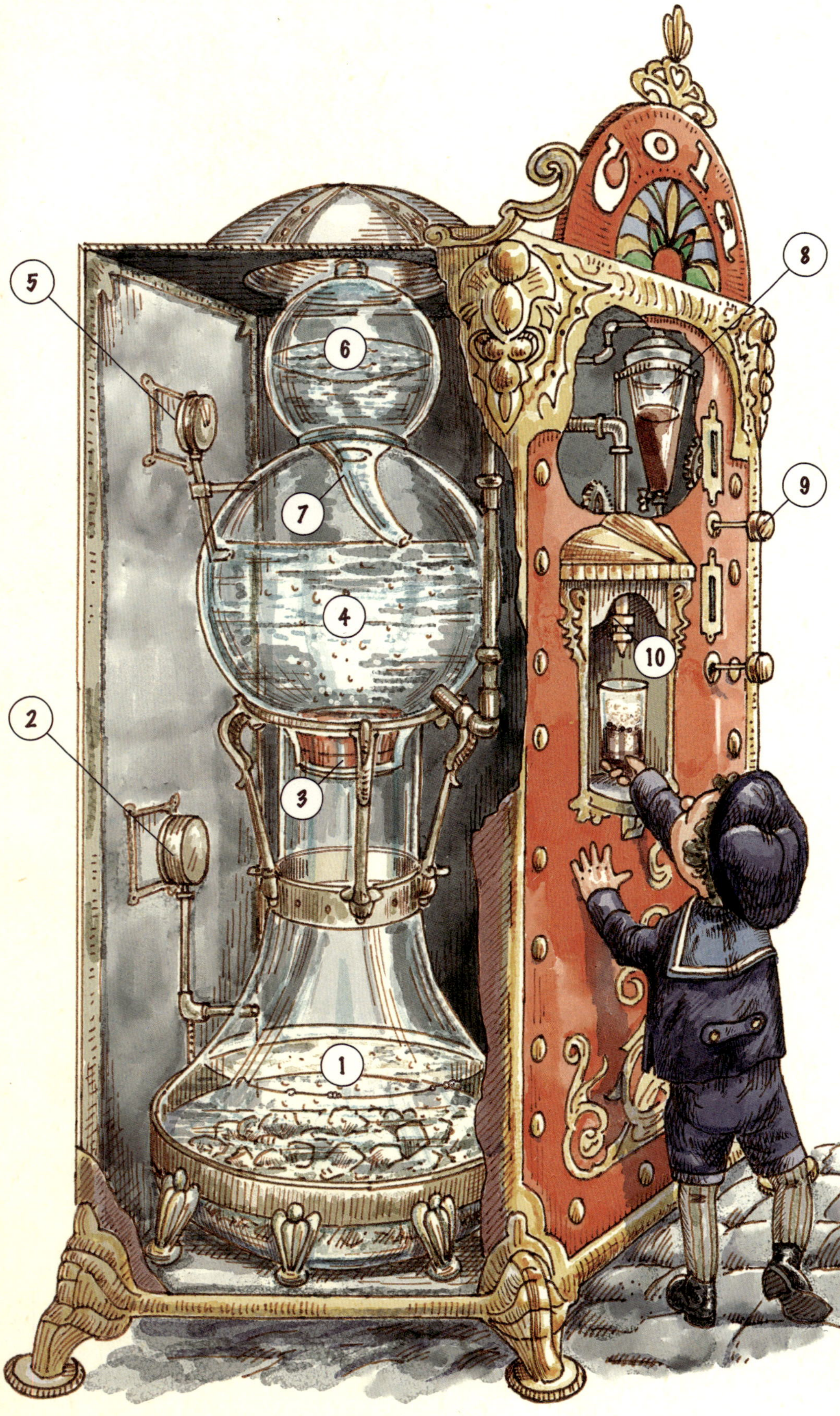

Construct an apparatus that will carbonate beverages at the press of a button. Your participation is limited to installing the necessary components and periodically maintaining them.

The first and only step of carbonation is infusing water with carbon dioxide. The simplest way to do this is through chemical reactions between natural carbonates — for example, marble, limestone or chalk — and some sort of strong acid, such as sulphuric or hydrochloric. Unstable carbonates such as soda or potash (page 24) decay in even the weakest organic acids, such as the citric acid contained in lemon juice.

To dissolve gas in water, you'll need several separate vessels that seal tightly together:

- In the lower vessel (1) place the carbonate minerals and acid for generating the gas. Install a separator valve (3) that will allow gas to rise into the middle chamber while preventing the water from escaping.
- Fill the middle vessel (4) with the water (5) you want to carbonate. It's better if it's pre-chilled — gas dissolves better at low temperatures. Fit a tap to the bottom of this vessel so you can drain the prepared soda water (10).
- The upper vessel (6) serves to receive the water from the middle vessel that is displaced by the bubbles — and pushed up the curved tube (7) — while maintaining an air-tight seal.

1. *Chamber with natural carbonates*
2. *Acid input spigot*
3. *Separator valve*
4. *Saturator (where the water is infused with gas)*
5. *Water input*
6. *Expansion tank*
7. *Curved tube*
8. *Syrup mixer*
9. *Syrup distributing handle*
10. *Drink dispenser*

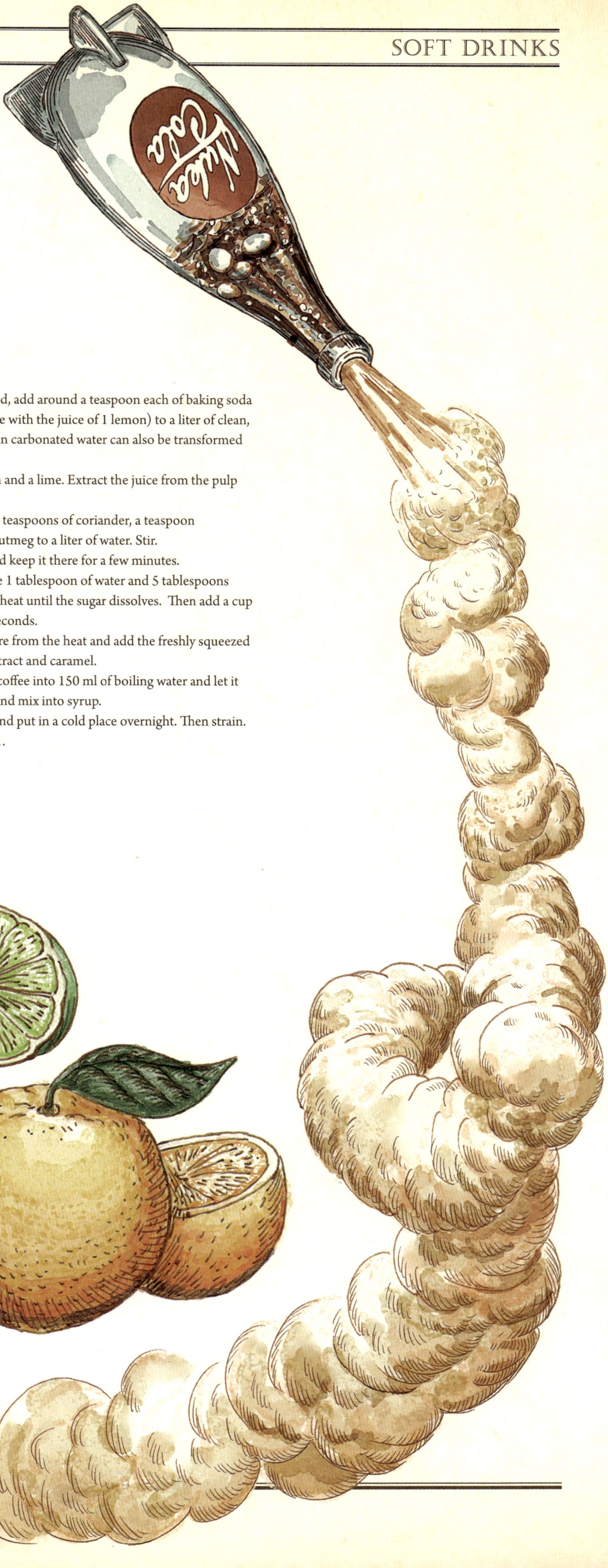

For a simpler carbonation method, add around a teaspoon each of baking soda and citric acid (you can substitute with the juice of 1 lemon) to a liter of clean, cold water, mix — and voila! Plain carbonated water can also be transformed into a light energy drink.

1. Finely zest 2 oranges, a lemon and a lime. Extract the juice from the pulp of the fruit.
2. Add the zest, 300 g of sugar, 2 teaspoons of coriander, a teaspoon of cinnamon and a pinch of nutmeg to a liter of water. Stir.
3. Bring the mixture to a boil and keep it there for a few minutes.
4. Prepare the caramel: combine 1 tablespoon of water and 5 tablespoons of sugar in a saucepan on low heat until the sugar dissolves. Then add a cup of hot water and boil for 30 seconds.
5. Remove the citrus zest mixture from the heat and add the freshly squeezed juice, a teaspoon of vanilla extract and caramel.
6. Stir 2 tablespoons of ground coffee into 150 ml of boiling water and let it steep for 10 minutes. Strain and mix into syrup.
7. Wait for the mixture to cool and put in a cold place overnight. Then strain.
8. Mix with soda in a ratio of 1:1.

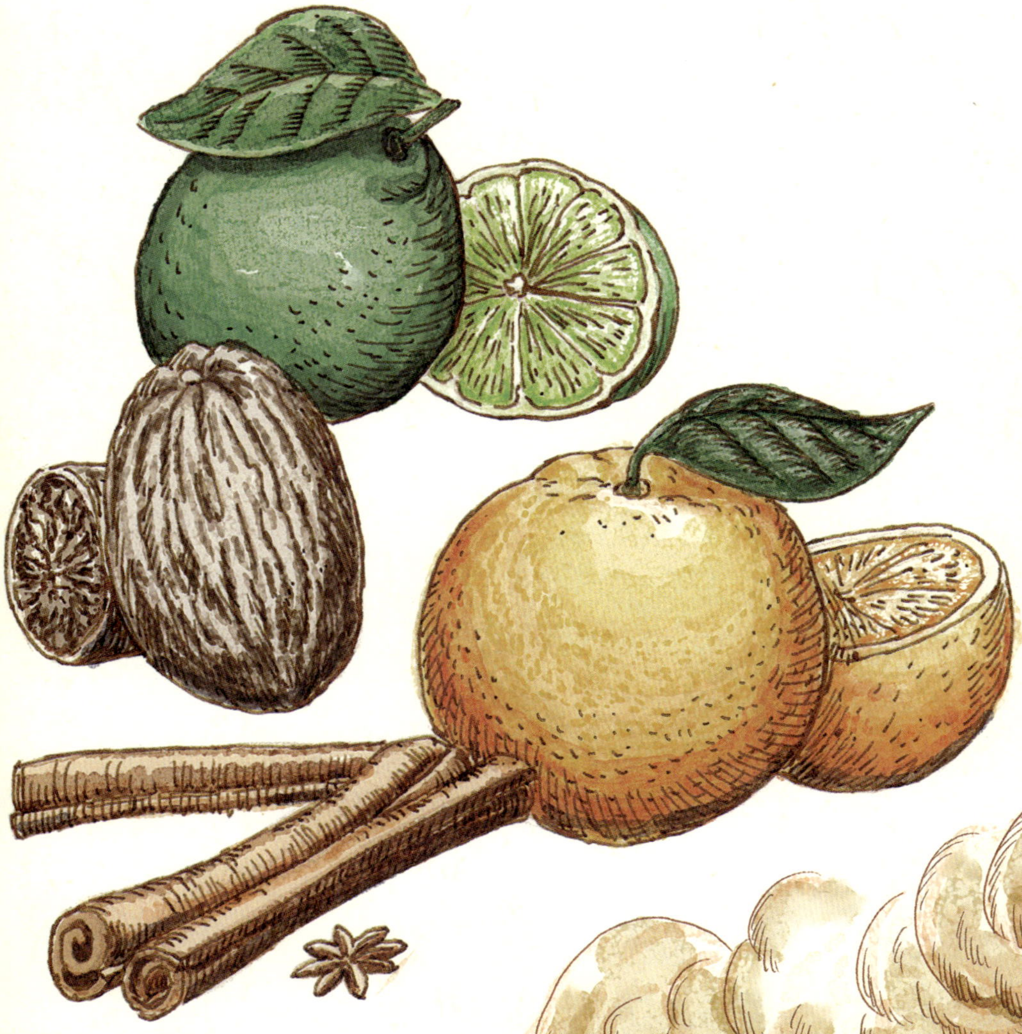

ALCOHOL

In low spirits? Concentrate the best moments in life by distilling your own alcohol. Distillation is a process that purifies and increases the alcohol content of your fermented beverages.

Any sweet or starchy liquid will do: juice, pomace, crushed grains mixed with water. Experiment with different raw materials, fermentation methods and flavorings to create a wide variety of drinks. Here are just a few ideas.

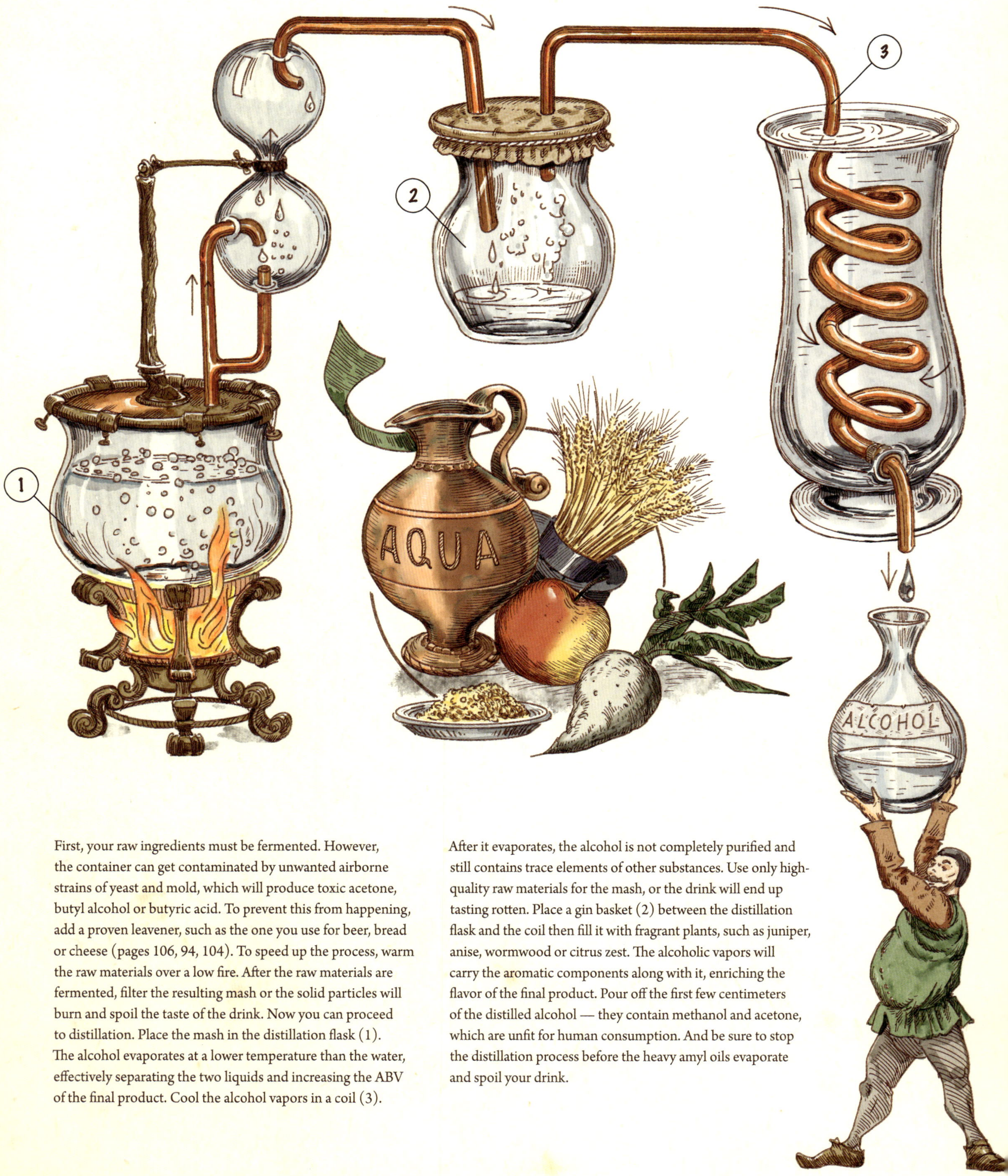

First, your raw ingredients must be fermented. However, the container can get contaminated by unwanted airborne strains of yeast and mold, which will produce toxic acetone, butyl alcohol or butyric acid. To prevent this from happening, add a proven leavener, such as the one you use for beer, bread or cheese (pages 106, 94, 104). To speed up the process, warm the raw materials over a low fire. After the raw materials are fermented, filter the resulting mash or the solid particles will burn and spoil the taste of the drink. Now you can proceed to distillation. Place the mash in the distillation flask (1). The alcohol evaporates at a lower temperature than the water, effectively separating the two liquids and increasing the ABV of the final product. Cool the alcohol vapors in a coil (3).

After it evaporates, the alcohol is not completely purified and still contains trace elements of other substances. Use only high-quality raw materials for the mash, or the drink will end up tasting rotten. Place a gin basket (2) between the distillation flask and the coil then fill it with fragrant plants, such as juniper, anise, wormwood or citrus zest. The alcoholic vapors will carry the aromatic components along with it, enriching the flavor of the final product. Pour off the first few centimeters of the distilled alcohol — they contain methanol and acetone, which are unfit for human consumption. And be sure to stop the distillation process before the heavy amyl oils evaporate and spoil your drink.

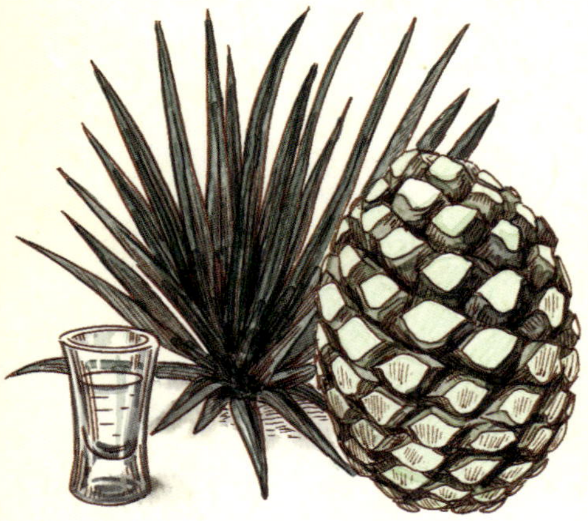

Tequila

Use blue agave as your base. Bake the fruit of the cactus to break down the complex carbohydrates into simple ones then grind into a pulp. The resulting mash must be fermented and then distilled. Dilute the resulting alcohol with water until it reaches the desired concentration and age in barrels for several months.

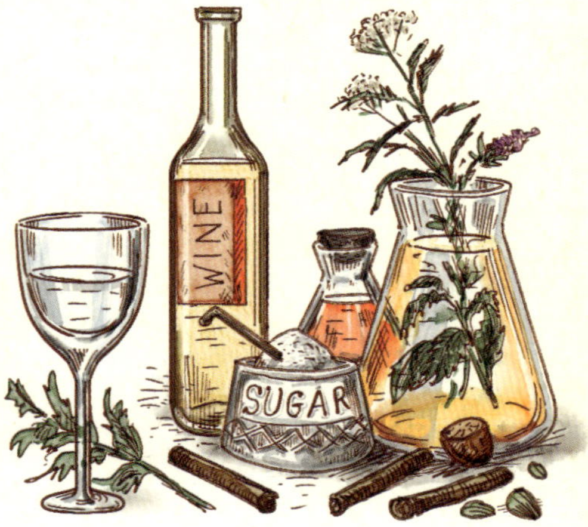

Vermouth

Wine with added herbal notes. Allow the herbs to steep in the wine for several weeks. Cinnamon, citrus zest and wormwood are all good flavoring options. Distill the infusion. Pour the resulting alcohol into a new batch of wine to dilute it, allow it to age and bottle.

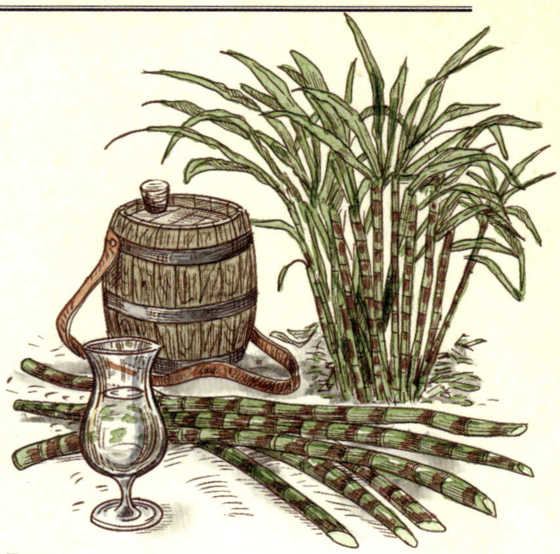

Rum

Use sugarcane juice — or more precisely, sugarcane byproducts (page 102) — as your base. After fermenting and distilling, pour the rum into barrels and set in the cellar to age.

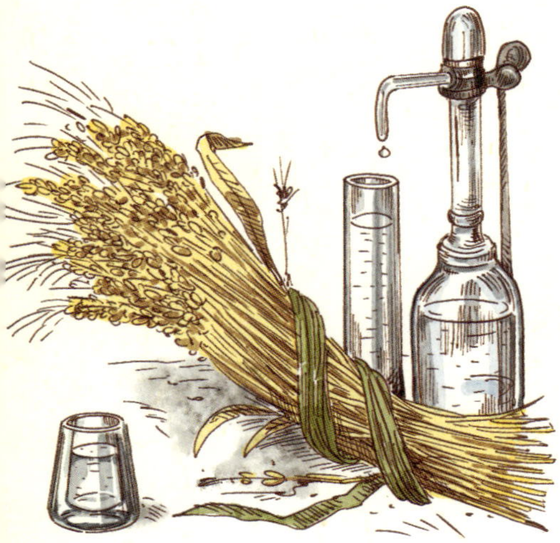

Vodka

The first step is pouring boiling water over wheat or any other grain (page 54). After fermentation and distillation, the alcohol must be purified even more in a process called rectification (page 118). Then run it through a charcoal filter. Dilute the resulting 96% alcohol with water to 40% ABV then bottle.

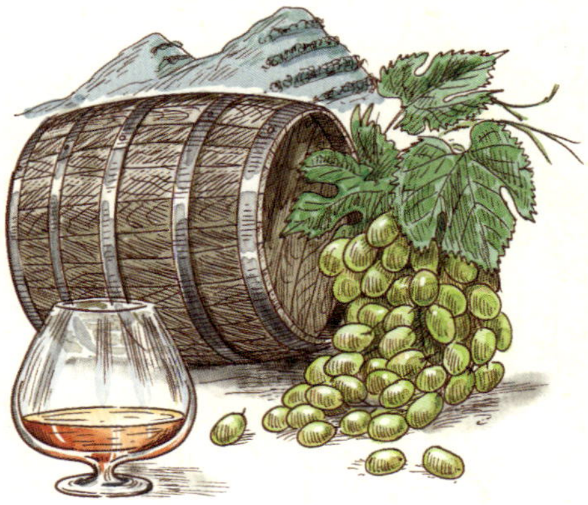

Brandy

Use grapes grown in humus-carbonate soils (page 62). Such varieties will give the distilled wine a unique taste and aroma. Finally, achieve the desired flavor by aging the wine in wooden barrels for a period of 3–15 years — and sometimes even longer! Good things come to those who wait: The longer it ages, the deeper and more complex the flavor.

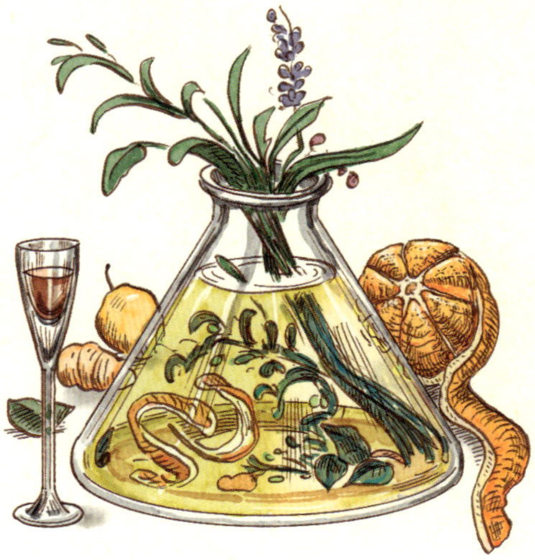

Liqueurs

Infuse vodka or brandy with berries and/or fruits and let it brew. Again, the quality of the drink depends on the aging period: from several months to several years. Once aged, filter the tincture or distill once again. Can also be mixed with fruit syrups.

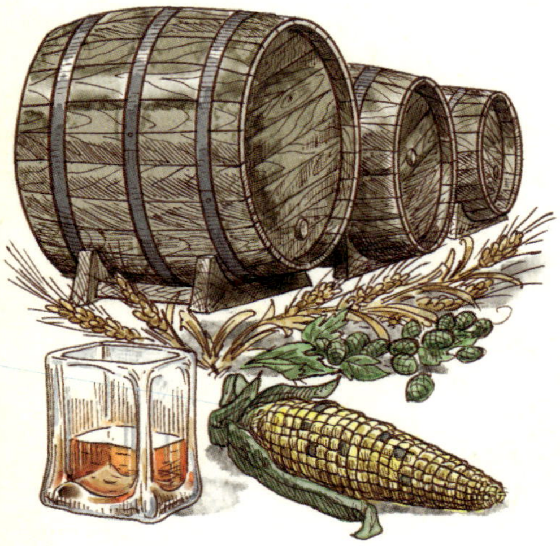

Whiskey

Take malt (page 106) from sprouted barley kernels (you can also use wheat, rye or even corn). Mix the ground grains with water and heat to obtain wort. Distill the fermented wort, pour into oak barrels and let rest — ideally, for about 10–15 years. Your patience will be rewarded when you take your first sip of this earthy, full-bodied beverage.

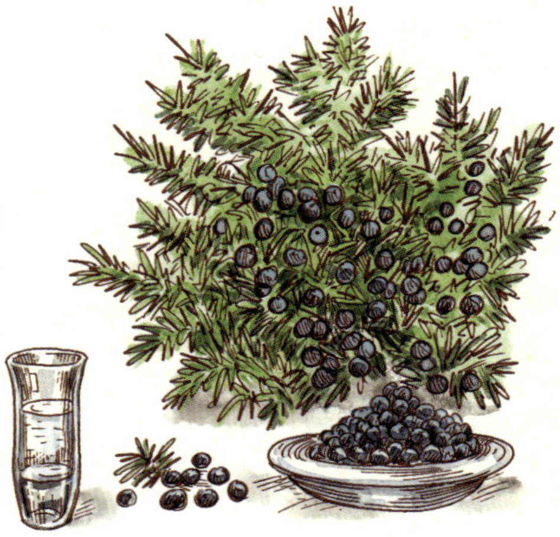

Gin

Distill grain alcohol. Add juniper berries, a little lemon or orange peel and other herbs such as anise, fennel, cinnamon and coriander. Then distill again. A well-prepared gin is sharp, dry and has a distinct juniper flavor.

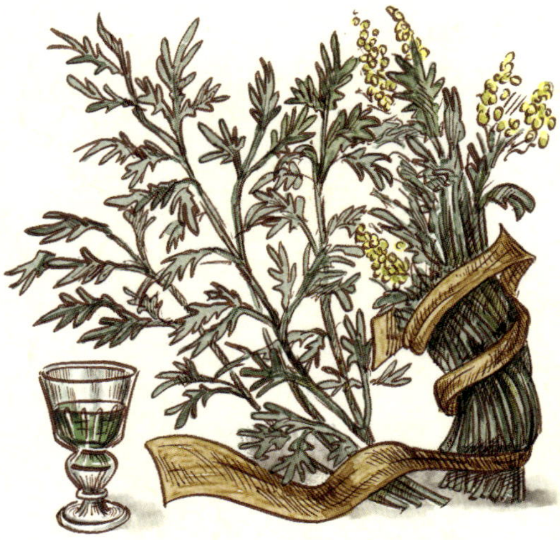

Absinthe

Make an alcoholic tincture from a variety of herbs — anise, fennel, angelica, lemon balm, chamomile and, most importantly, bitter wormwood, which contains an essential oil that imbues the drink with its unique taste.

COCKTAILS

Not everyone enjoys life straight, no chaser. Those who need a spoonful of sugar with their medicine should try their hand at cocktails. These drinks come in a variety of flavors, from complex, unfamiliar, boundary-pushing beverages to familiar favorites. Finding the right ingredients is the most important step to soften heavy drinks and make them easier to enjoy.

Ingredients may include liqueurs, juices or even cream. All elements, both alcoholic and otherwise, should enhance and highlight each other. The secret lies in the balance between light and rich, strong and weak, sour and sweet. Experiment and have fun! Try a couple of time-proven classics to get started. But even here, there's always room for improvisation

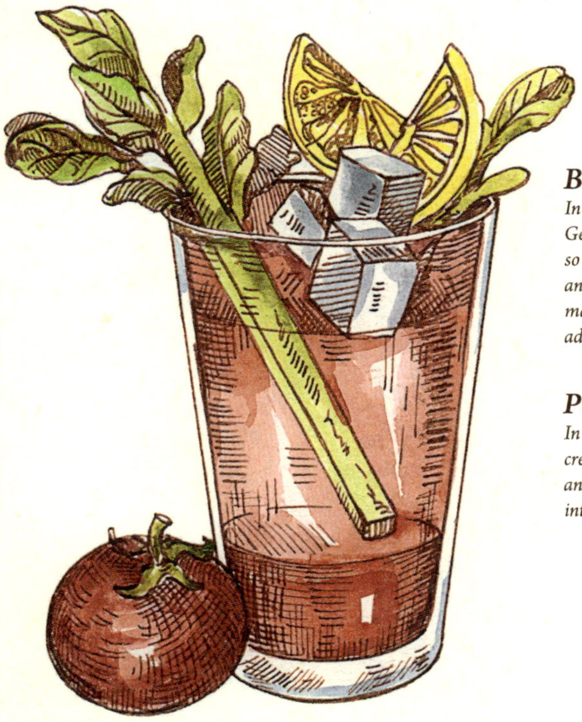

Bloody Mary

In a chilled highball glass, pour 150 ml tomato juice. Gently add 40 ml of vodka by pouring it over a bar spoon (2) so it doesn't mix with the juice. Add salt and pepper to taste and a few drops each of hot sauce and sour fermented sauce made with vinegar, sugar and fish. Ice and lemon juice can be added to taste. Garnish with a celery stalk.

Pina colada

In a blender, pour 60 ml of light rum, 30 ml each of coconut cream or milk and regular cream, 180 ml of pineapple juice and crushed ice. Blend for 15 seconds then pour the contents into a glass and garnish with a slice of pineapple and a cherry.

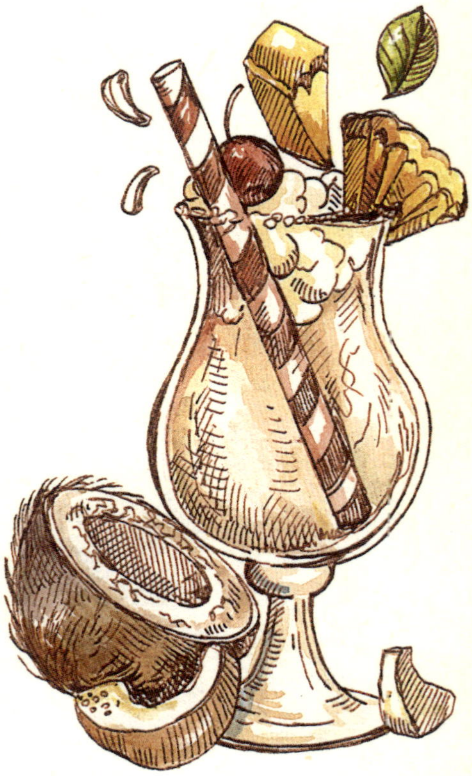

It's best if you avoid mixing more than four or five non-alcoholic ingredients and two alcoholic ones (one for the base, the other to add flavor). The only shared ingredient in 99% of all cocktails is ice. It's important to pay attention to proportions and mixing techniques.

To accomplish this, use a metallic vessel with a lid, known as a shaker (1), to thoroughly combine all of your ingredients. Fill with ice first then add your alcohols and ingredients of choice — from lowest to highest ABV. There are two main mixing techniques:

Long shake — As the name suggests, this involves vigorous shaking over a longer period of time and is used for drinks that contain pieces of fruit or berries, spices and herbs.

Dry shake — This is used for thick, smooth, homogenous cocktails. No ice is required here unless the drink contains eggs, milk or cream. Stick a large metal coil in the bottom of the shaker to speed up the process and integrate the ingredients more effectively. Shake then strain to remove any small pieces of fruit or ice that may remain.

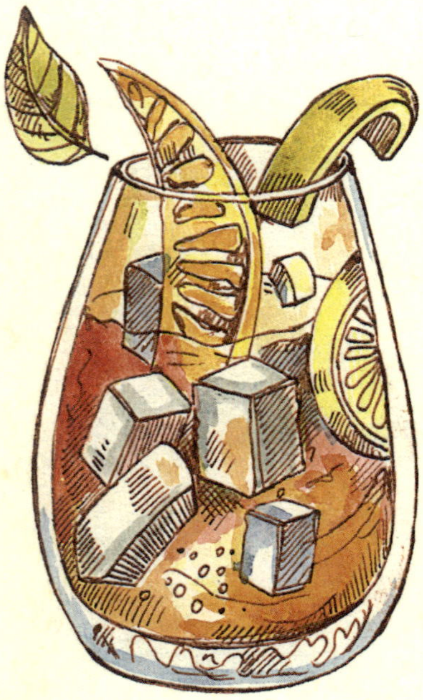

Old fashioned

Place a lump of sugar in a lowball glass. Add 2–3 drops of water and a bitter tincture made of orange, ginger, nutmeg, cloves and cardamom. Crush the sugar and bitters mixture into a kind of syrup then fill the glass halfway with ice and add 25 ml of bourbon corn whiskey. Mix thoroughly — this allows time for the glass to cool and the ingredients to start interacting with each other. Add more ice and another 25 ml of bourbon. Stir again then garnish with orange peel. The taste should be light and slightly tart. A cherry on top adds a pop of color and flavor.

Mojito

Place 3–4 sprigs of mint leaves in a tall glass, then add 2 teaspoons of sugar syrup (ideally cane sugar [page 102]) and lime juice. Muddle with a bartender's pestle (3) — but not too hard or you may release the bitter components in the mint. Fill a glass to the top with crushed ice. Pour in 40 ml of light rum and 150 ml of soda or soda water (page 390). Stir with a bar spoon to reincorporate the mint leaves. Garnish with a fresh sprig of mint and a wedge of lime.

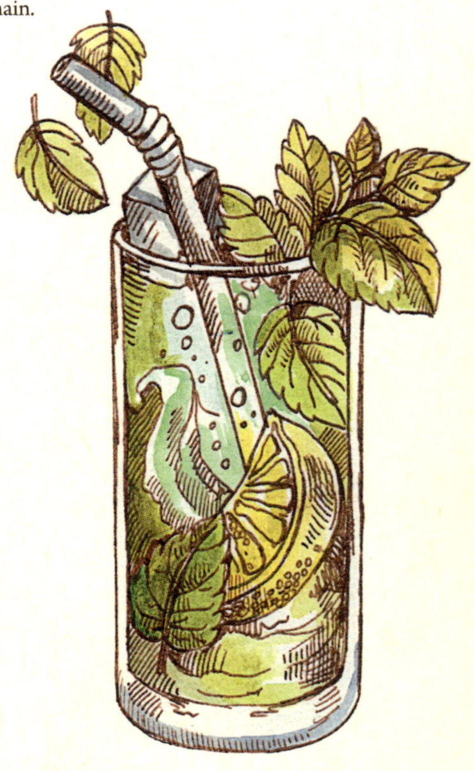

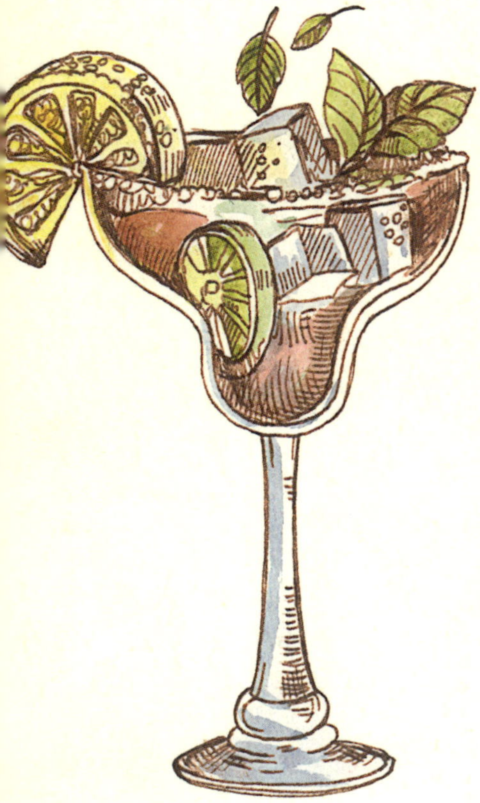

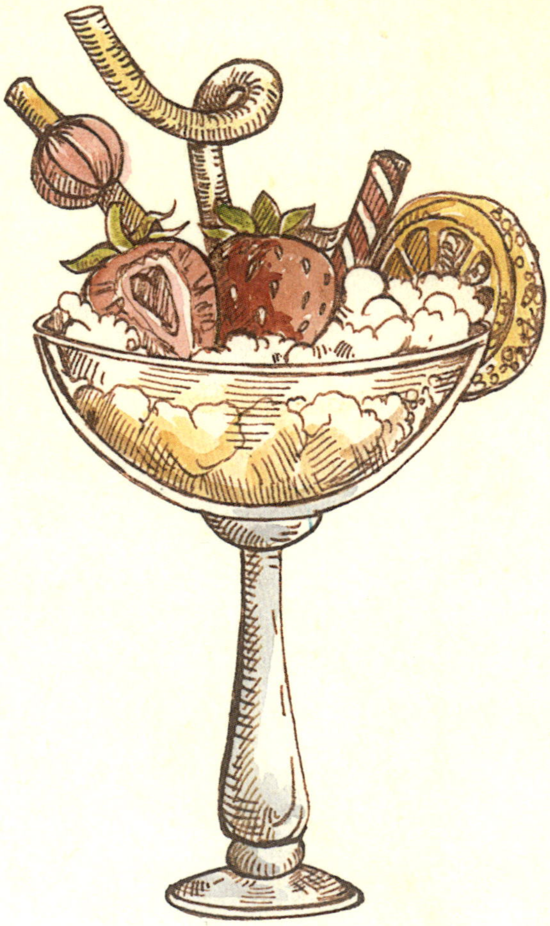

Margarita

Moisten the rim of a glass with a slice of lime or orange, and then dip into a saucer of coarse salt to add flavor and counter the harsh taste of the tequila (page 390). Mix 30 ml of tequila, 20 ml of orange liqueur and 30 ml of freshly squeezed lime juice in a shaker. If it tastes too bitter, add sugar syrup. Put ice in a glass and pour the resulting mixture on top.

Tequila Sunrise

Freeze water in an ice tray (4) and fill a highball glass with cubes. Pour 50 ml tequila and 10 ml grenadine (a thick, sweet syrup made from pomegranate seeds) over the ice. To obtain pomegranate juice, put the seeds through a press (5) to remove the pulp. Top up with orange juice and stir gently with a cocktail spoon. While stirring, press the spoon against the sides of the glass so that the back of the spoon faces out and you don't break the ice cubes. Garnish with an orange wedge.

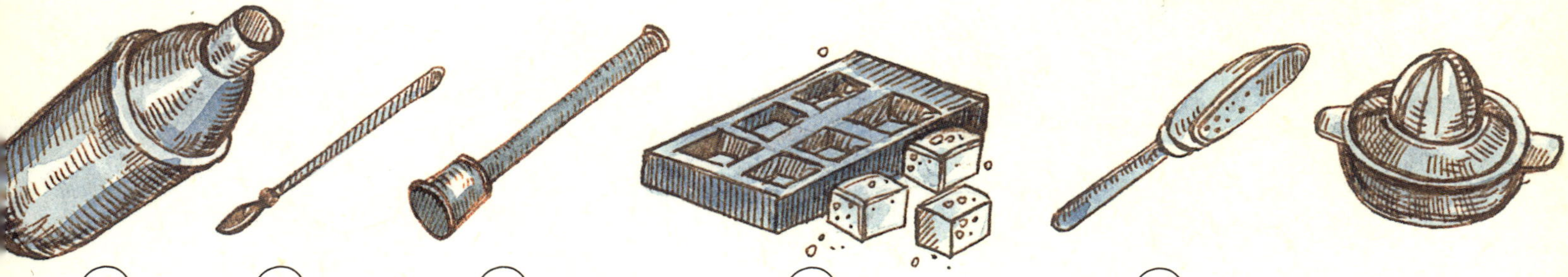

1 2 3 4 5

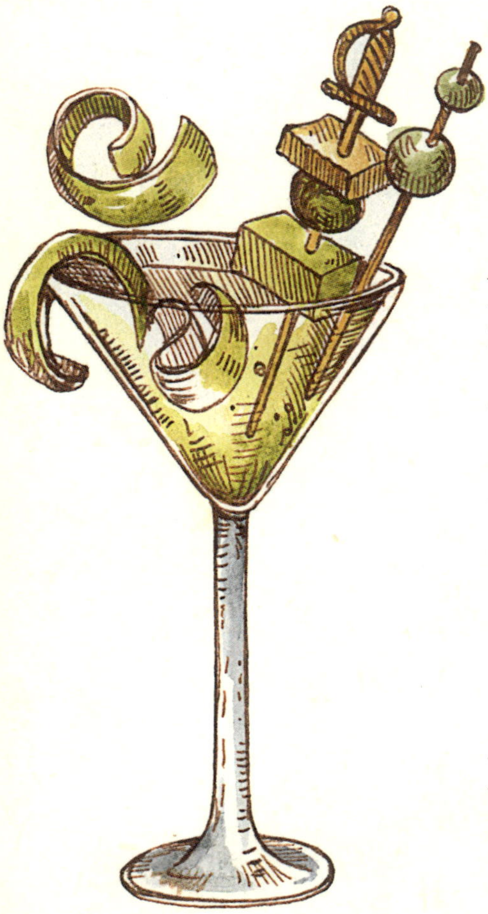

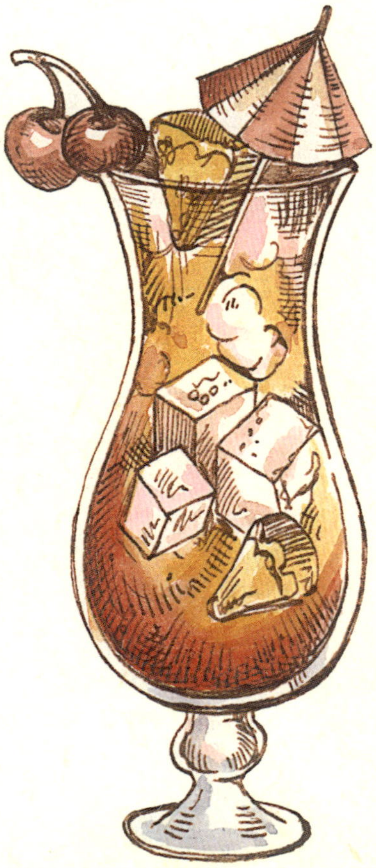

Martini

In a shaker filled with crushed ice, mix 50 ml gin and a dash of vermouth (page 391) then strain and pour into a glass. The drink will be cold, but the ice won't change or dilute the flavor as it melts. Add an olive and garnish with a lemon wedge.

Cosmopolitan

Fill the shaker with ice, 40 ml vodka, 15 ml Cointreau (a strong orange peel liqueur), 30 ml of fruit juice and 15 ml of lime juice. Whisk thoroughly and strain into a chilled glass. Garnish with a twist of lime peel.

By the way, a bartender's spoon (2) is a handy tool. Add an additional tool to the other end, such as a pestle, fork or flat disc that can be used to layer drinks. If the handle is spiral shaped, it can be used to reduce the flow rate of a liquid as you add it into your drink.

DESSERTS

Some foods fill our stomachs and help our bodies stay fit and healthy. Balanced meals with the proper proportions of complex carbohydrates, proteins and fats give us the strength and energy we need to face our day. But what a bore! Despite what you may think, the essence of human happiness is actually quite prosaic: hormones. Add a dessert at the end of a meal to feed both your belly and your soul, liven up your taste buds and give yourself a quick dose of happy hormones. A little something sweet can really go a long way.

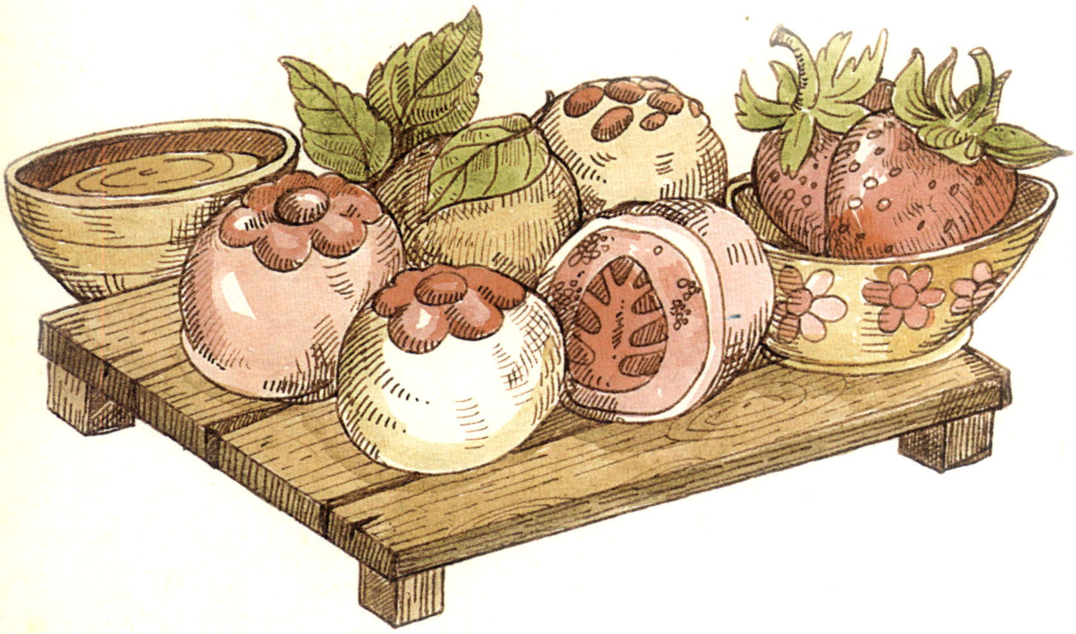

MOCHI

Unsweetened rice (page 70) makes for great desserts. Use a starchy, round grain, matte rice. Soak it overnight, boil it and grind it in a mortar. Add a little water and use a wooden mallet to beat and knead the rice until it becomes a homogenous mass.

Roll this dough into balls then make a dimple in the center with your thumb and press in fillings. Anything can make a good filling: fruits, berries, boiled beans, cream. Bake or pan fry the finished mochi. Savor this dish slowly — the viscous rice balls are easy to choke on.

TURKISH DELIGHT

Combine sugar, cold water and fruit juice in a saucepan over low heat. As soon as it boils, add cornstarch diluted with warm water and cook for 15 minutes, stirring constantly. You should get a thick, gelatinous mass.

Add nuts, place in a high-walled baking sheet and cool at room temperature. Then set aside in a cooler place for 8–12 hours. When the sugar has hardened, cut into smaller squares and roll in coconut flakes, powdered sugar or cinnamon.

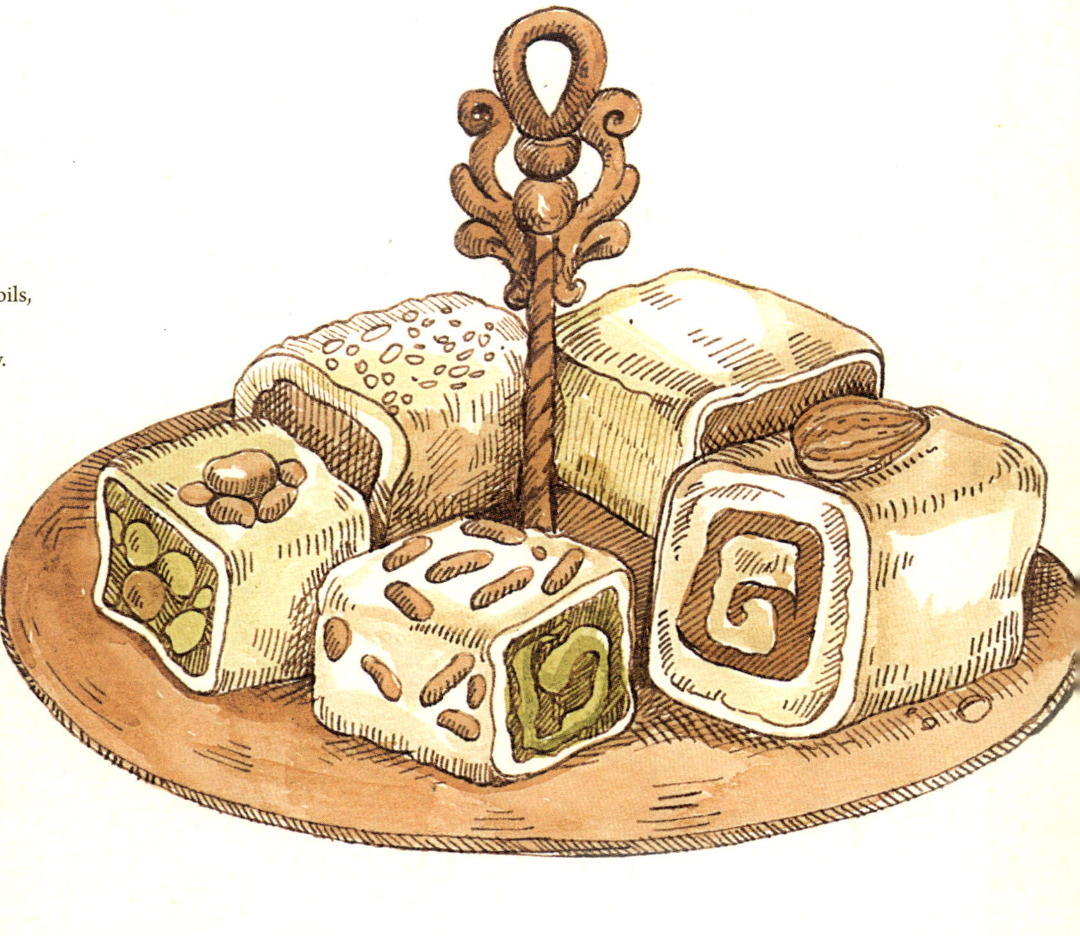

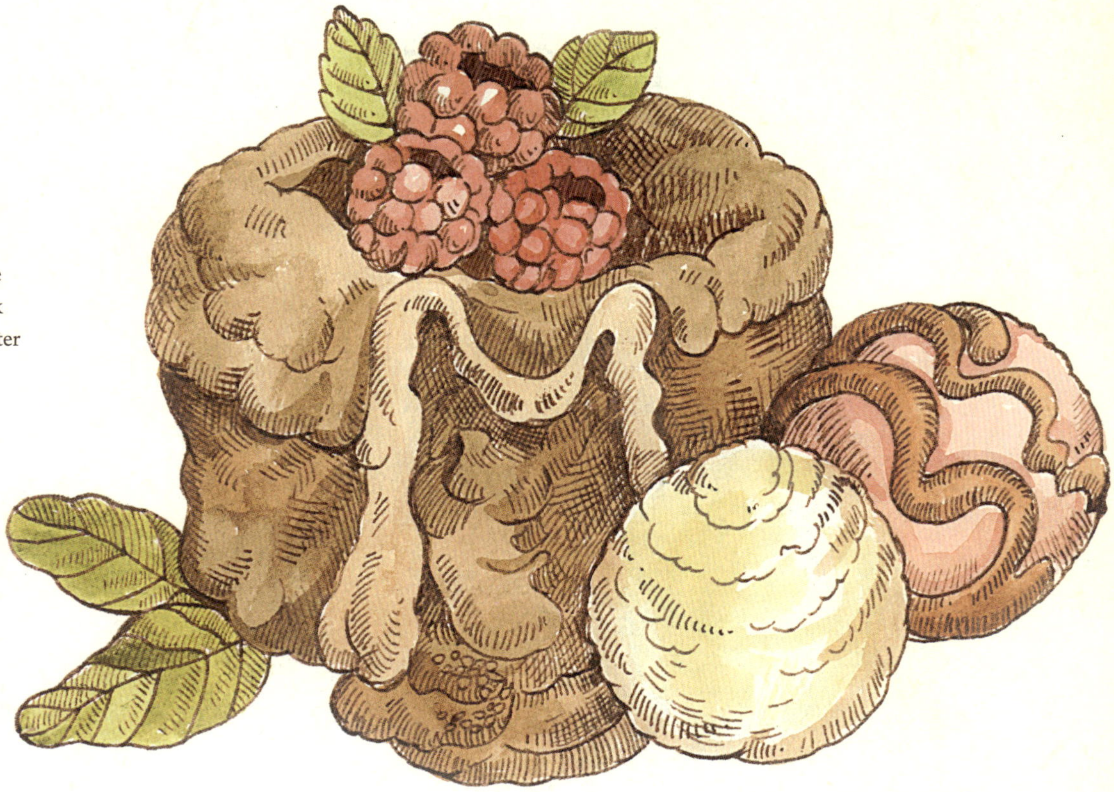

CHOCOLATE LAVA CAKE

A childhood favorite of many, the lava cake is a chocolate souffle cake with a liquid chocolate center. To make "lava" you need eggs, butter, dark chocolate, flour, sugar and cocoa. Melt warm butter and chocolate, stirring regularly. Beat eggs and sugar to stiff peaks and mix flour with cocoa. Then combine and mix thoroughly.

Butter small cake pans and sprinkle with cocoa powder then fill three quarters of the way up with your dough and bake them for 7–8 minutes at a temperature of 180°C. Remove the fondants from the oven when an oily film starts to form on their surface. Transfer the prepared muffins to a plate, garnish with powdered sugar, chocolate chips or berries. Serve immediately; otherwise, the molten core will harden.

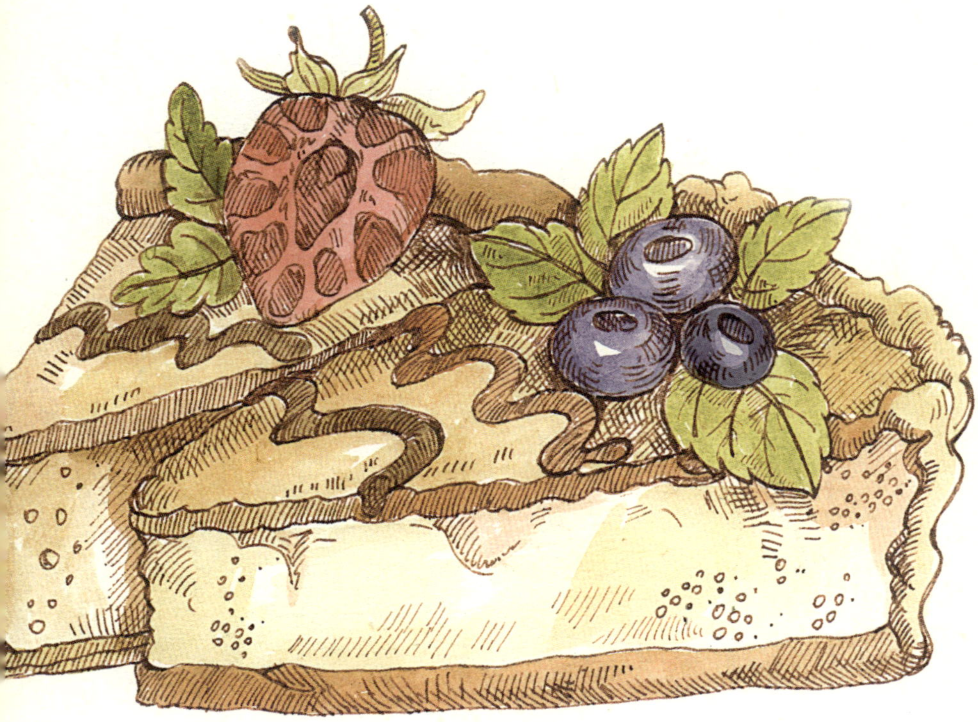

CHEESECAKE

Cheesecake doesn't need to be baked, making it both delicious and convenient. For the crust, you need shortbread dough or cookies. Crush them into crumbs and mix with melted butter then press into the bottom of a round cake mold. Now for the secret ingredient: gelatin.

Mix your gelatin with lemon juice, water and sugar. Place the mixing bowl in a warm water bath and stir until completely dissolved. Whisk together cream and cream cheese then combine with the gelatin mixture. Pour the resulting creamy mass onto the biscuit base and smooth. Store the cheesecake pan in a cool place overnight. Once completely solidified, decorate with berries and fruits.

The gelatin must be prepared in advance. This takes time. Simmer cow bones, horns, cartilage and joints in water for 10 hours. Collagen will form on the surface of the water. Strain the broth and cook for a few more hours until a thick mass is formed. This jelly-like mass can then be dehydrated to form gelatin.

MOLECULAR GASTRONOMY

Food is one of life's most accessible pleasures, but as with any earthly delight, you can have too much of a good thing. Eating the same meal day in and day out quickly becomes a chore. But food can be deconstructed and restructured in new and exciting ways using science. The secret of molecular gastronomy is in cooking methods. All food products, like any other substances, are composed of chemical elements. This means that if you understand the chemical composition, you can experiment endlessly: highlight the main flavors, try new combinations and create unusual textures. Molecular gastronomy gives you the opportunity to elevate ordinary foods into extraordinary dishes and the permission to play with your food. You'll come out of the experience with a dish that won't break your diet and a fresh new perspective on life.

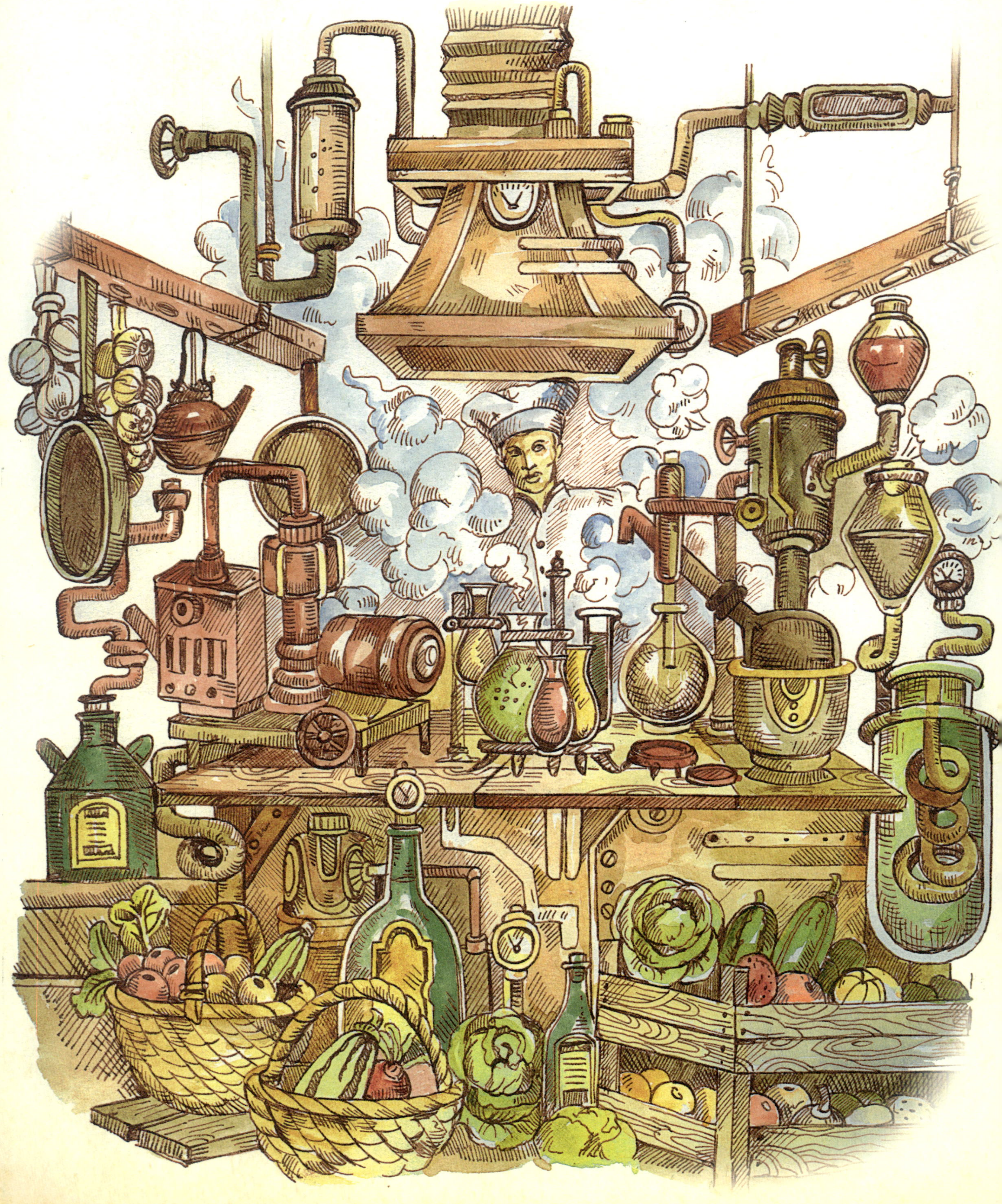

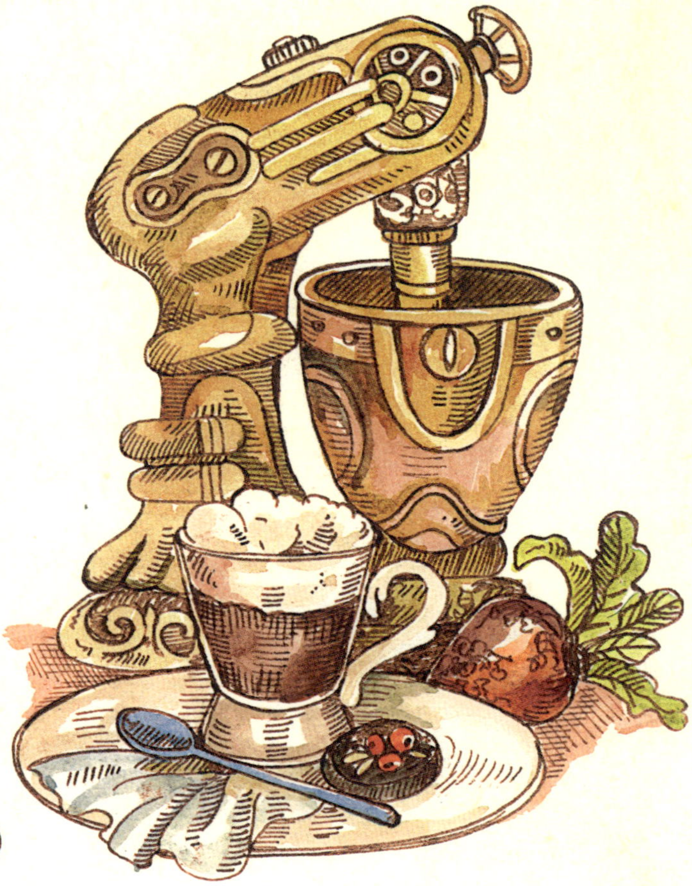

BORSCHT CAPPUCCINO

You're probably used to thinking of cappuccino as a coffee drink and borscht as a main course. But what if we threw the rules out the window? To make a borscht cappuccino, first chop an onion, grate a beet and a carrot and simmer them all together in a pot with some oil. Add a tablespoon of tomato paste, let simmer for another minute, and then add a liter of vegetable broth. Keep the mixture at a low boil for 30 minutes. So far, looks like regular borscht, right? Time to mix it up.

Process the borscht in a blender (page 276) and strain through a thick sieve. Put the strained mixture back in the blender and add 0.1% of the total volume of guar or locust bean gum. Obtain this by grinding guar or carob seeds into a powder, which acts as a thickener and texture stabilizer. Pour the resulting mixture into another bowl. Next, blend together half a spoonful of cream with sauerkraut and strain. Add 0.7% of the volume in agar. This substance is obtained from kelp algae (page 100). The agar mixture must be brought to a boil, poured into another bowl and, after thickening, blended once again. Now you need to turn the liquid mixture into foam. This can be done using a soda maker (page 388). Pressurized gas will saturate the mixture with bubbles, whipping it into a foam. And the added guar gum will help the foam hold its structure longer. Pour the borscht into a glass and add foam on top. Your borscht cappuccino is ready.

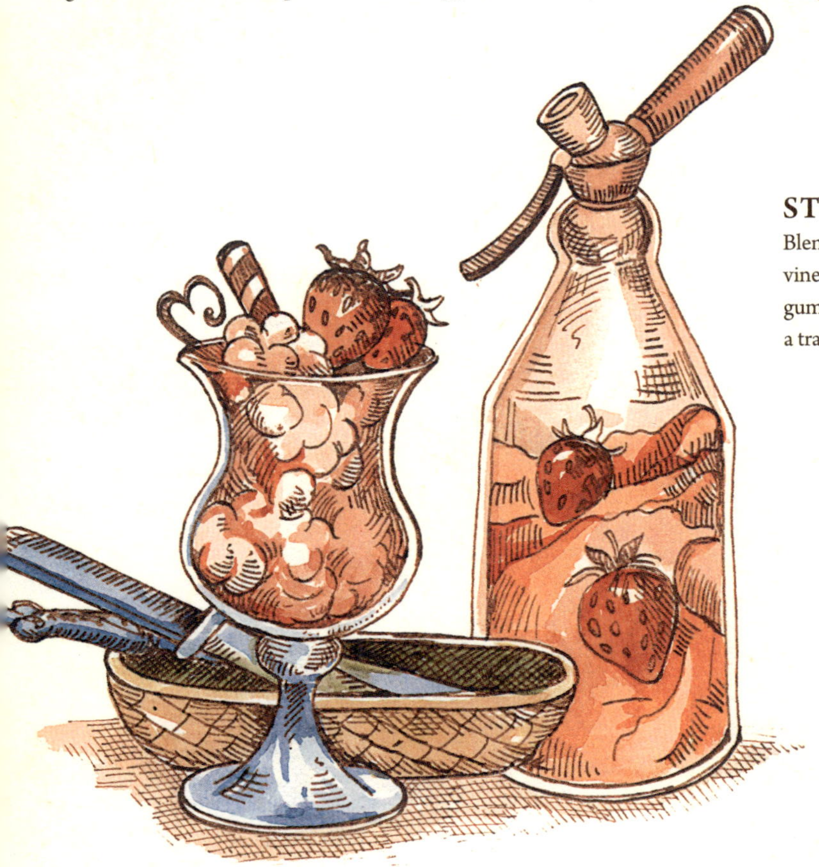

STRAWBERRY FOAM

Blend together 200 g of strawberries, a few cilantro leaves, 14 g of balsamic vinegar, 30 g of sugar and 150 g of water. Strain through a sieve. Add 1 g of guar gum and pour into your soda maker. Your foam is complete! Just spray it into a transparent glass to enjoy the full aesthetic effect.

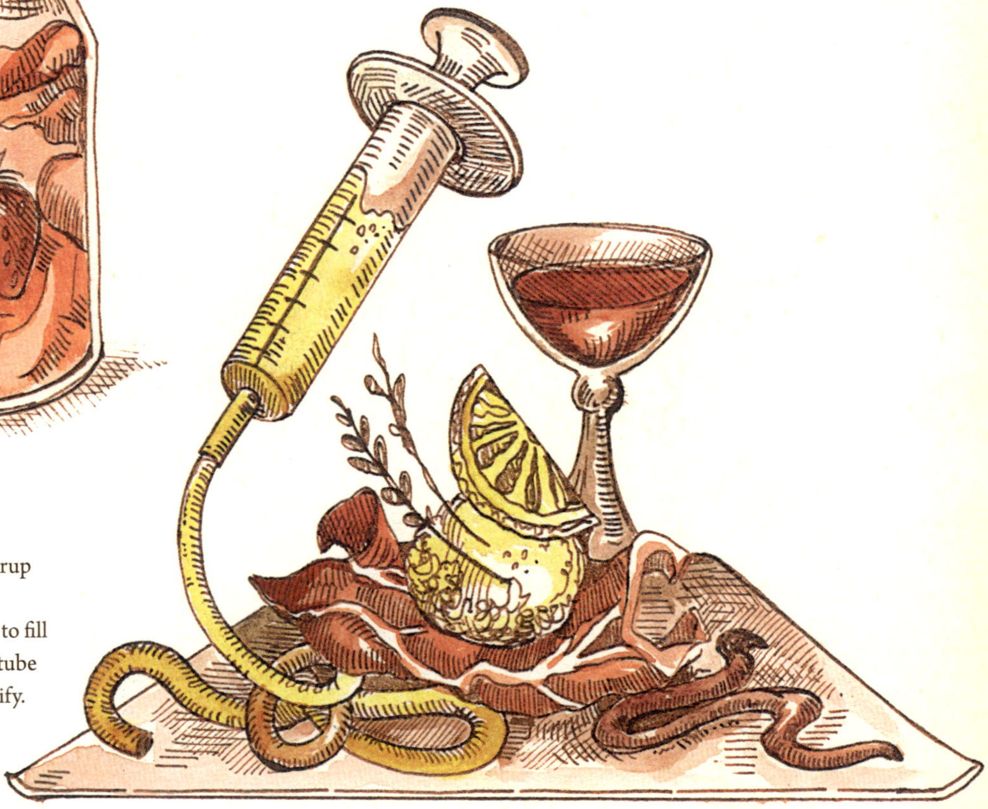

CITRUS SPAGHETTI

Mix 400 ml orange juice, 25 ml thick orange syrup, 75 ml sugar syrup and 25 g agar. Heat the mixture in a saucepan without bringing it to a boil. Suck the resulting liquid into a syringe (page 36). Use it to fill a long, flexible rubber tube with liquid (page 116). Immerse this tube in cold water for a couple of minutes to allow the mixture to solidify. Then reconnect the syringe and tube and use the pressurized air to push the orange spaghetti from the tube. Garnish with an orange wedge.

It's not imperative that you use oranges — this method can be used to make spaghetti out of anything. The only requirement is that it can first be liquified.

Perhaps the only rule in molecular cuisine is that eyeballing measurements won't work. Every gram counts. Get the proportions wrong and your orange spaghetti will become orange jelly. But even that is an exciting new texture, so by the standards of molecular gastronomy, it would be a success!

SOCIETY

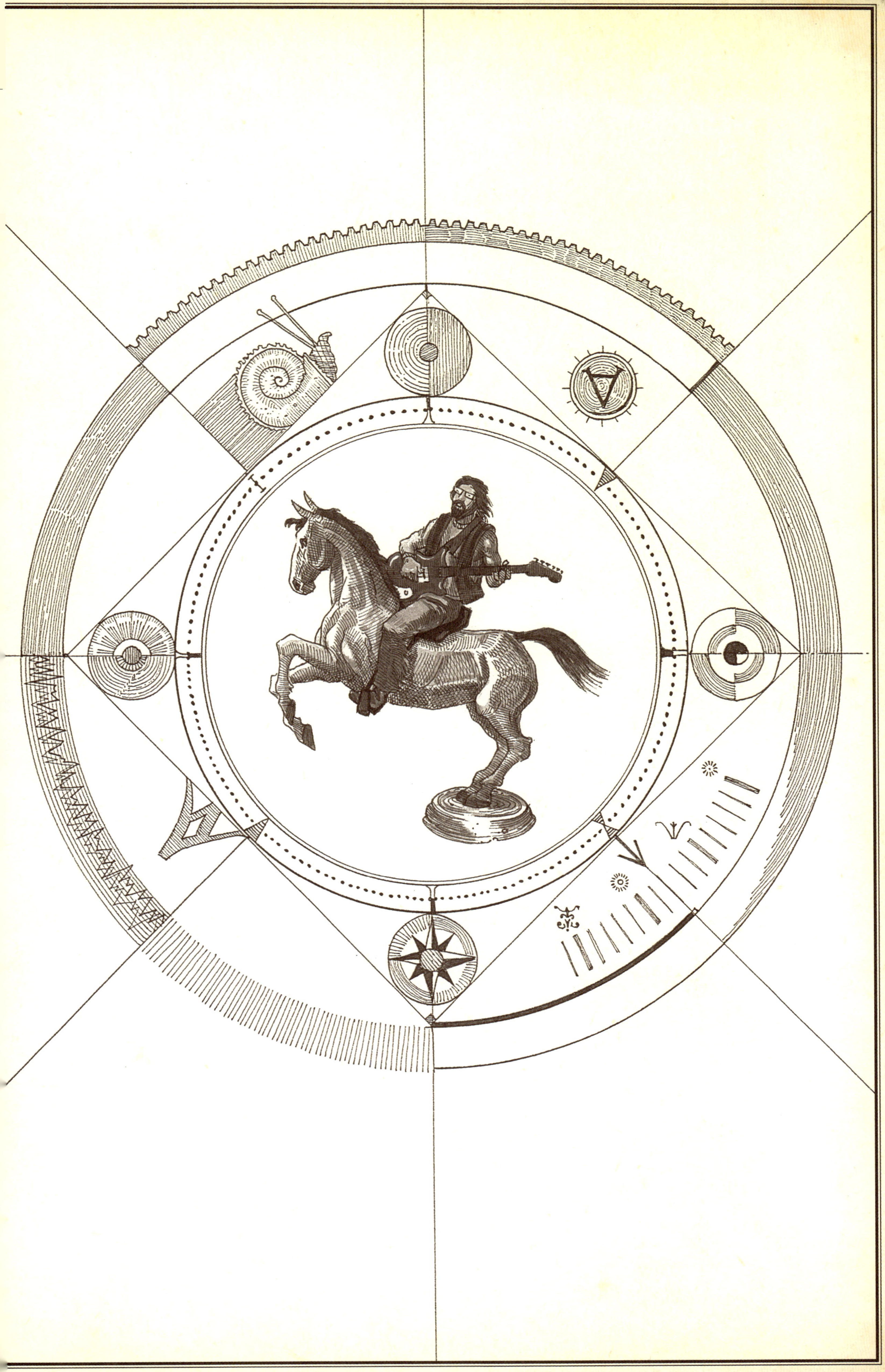

RITE OF PASSAGE

Human society is like a living organism, with cells constantly changing form to fulfill specific roles within the body. The formation and survival of a society is connected to the variety of the unique social roles or models of behavior followed by all members of the community. These roles are associated with the stages of an individual's personal development — physical, psychological or spiritual — and with specific events throughout their life, such as a girl becoming a woman, a woman becoming a wife, and so on. If a person gets stuck at a certain stage and is unable to naturally pass into the next, it affects the evolution of the entire society, since each role implies the performance of unique functions necessary for sustaining society.

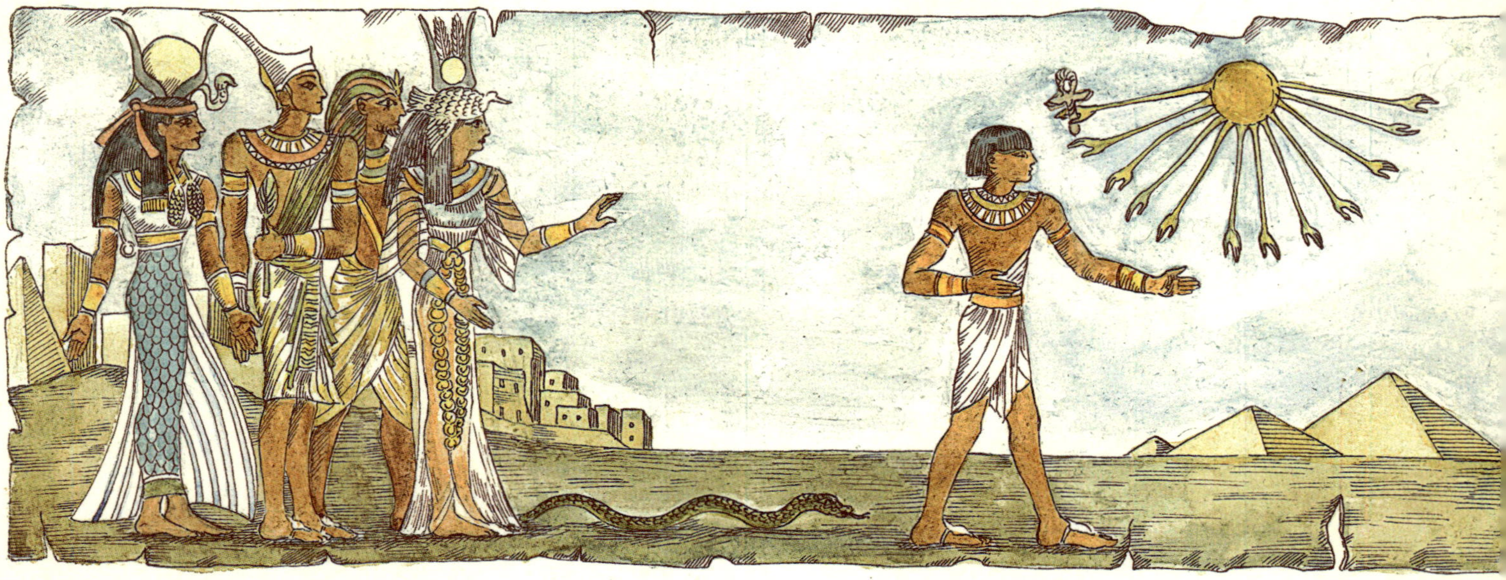

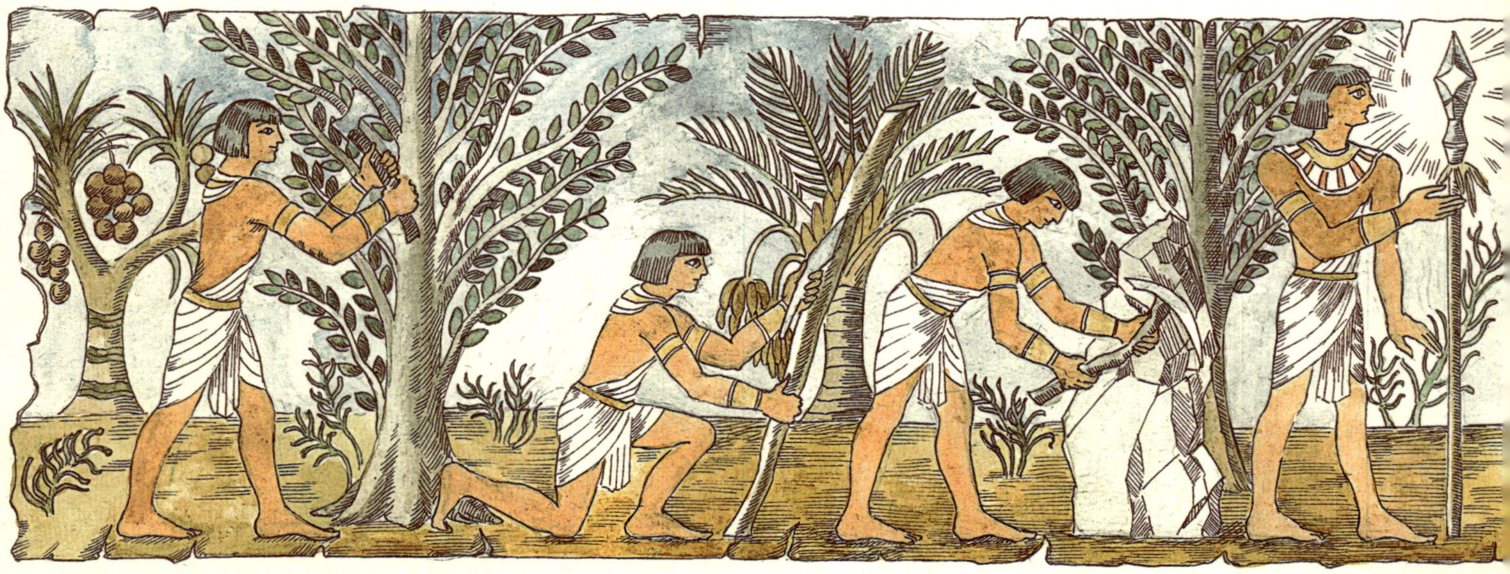

HOW TO CREATE YOUR OWN RITE OF PASSAGE

1. Determine which social groups and roles exist within your society. How do people move among groups? What functions do they fulfill? What skills do they have? How do these groups change over time?
2. Observe what exactly dies and what is reborn during the process of moving from one role to another. It's better if the rite is created by those who have already undergone this transition, as they have a better understanding of what the initiates are going through. This work is usually best performed by people who have deep, long-standing spiritual practices (such as meditation), as well as experienced shamans.
3. Find a symbol that reflects this transition — the ritual will be centered around this object. There must be three phases in the rite: life before death (the old role), death and rebirth (the new role). Remember that the death in the ritual is symbolic — don't mutilate your initiates.
4. During especially important rituals, such as those associated with growing up, the initiate may be asked to undergo certain physical and psychological tests. For example, young men may be sent into the forest to learn how to survive, manage their fears and aggression, feel confident in their abilities and finally take responsibility for their actions and lives.
5. Instruct all members of the community on how to conduct the ceremony. If the ritual itself is not a secret, think about how to disseminate this information to the public.

The process of changing roles is something that can be guided and celebrated using a rite of passage. During the ceremony, the initiate experiences the symbolic death of the former role and the birth of a new one, becoming a member of a new community with its own special set of rules. Because of this, both identity and responsibilities change drastically.

For example, the ceremony of knighthood commemorates a boy reaching manhood and makes him a member of the military aristocracy, and a wedding reinforces the spouses' promises to remain faithful to each other while simultaneously establishing them as "family people" and moving them into a new stratum of society. The ceremony can carry both a sacred meaning understood only to those who have passed through and a more practical one, creating a high level of uniformity within a group and making it easier to manage.

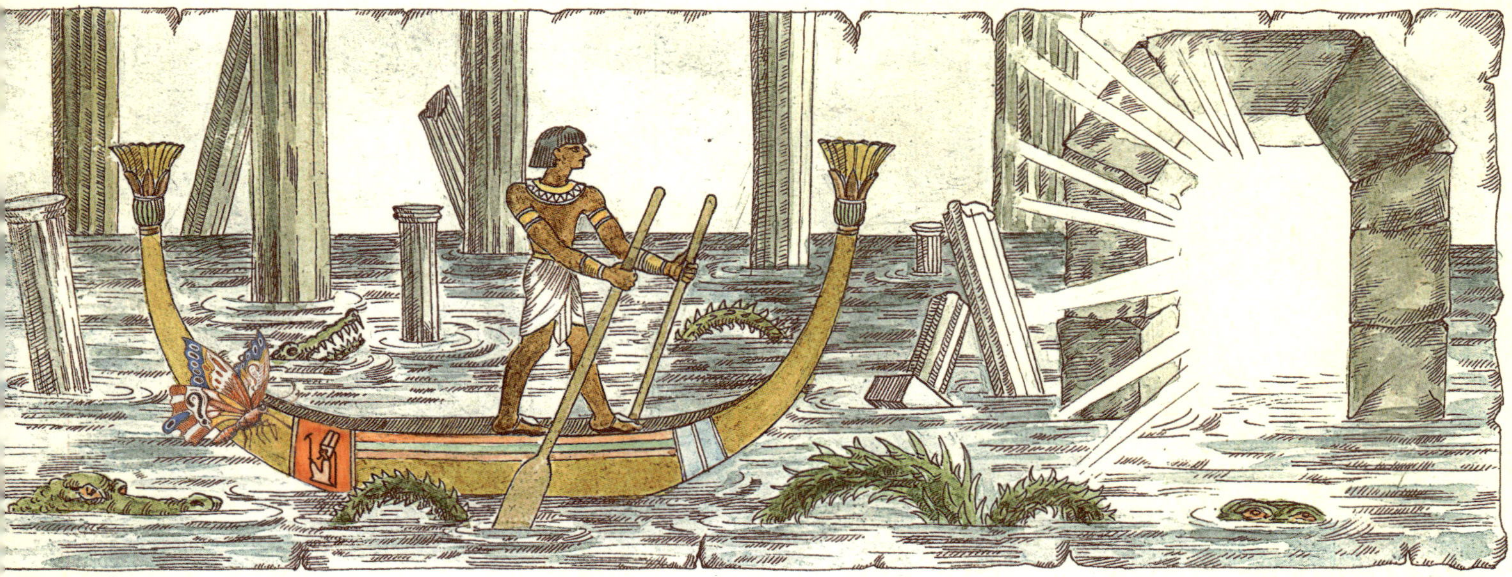

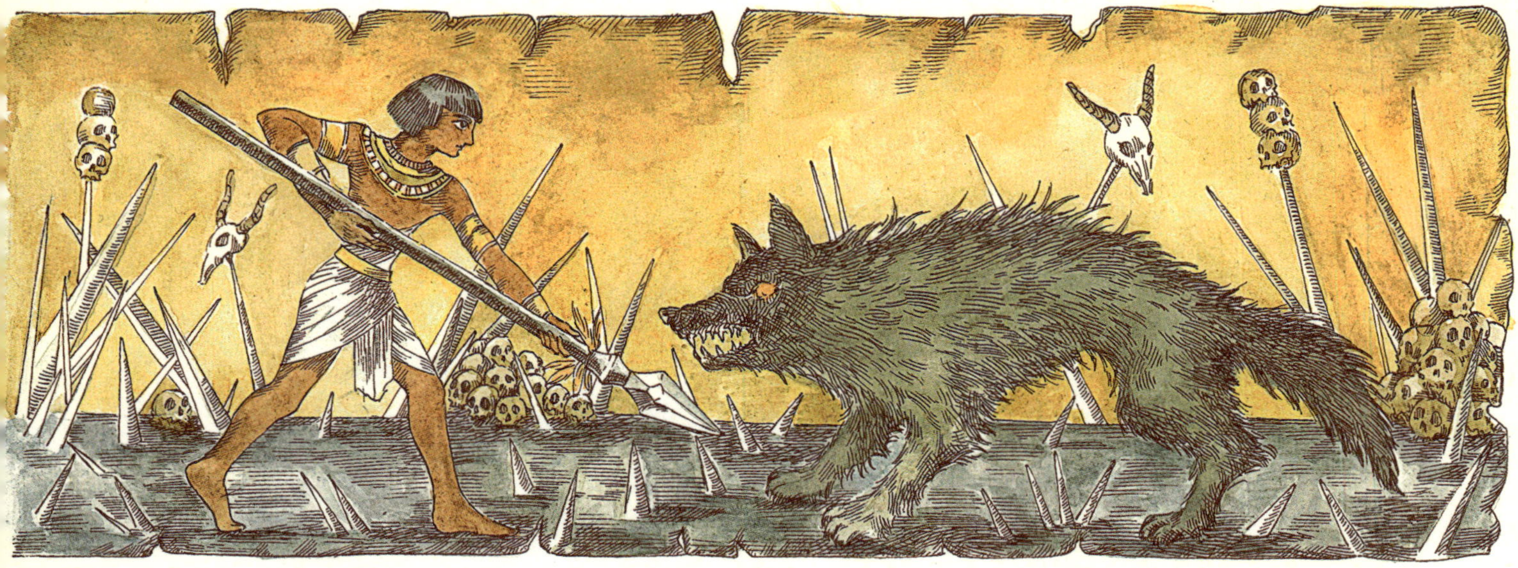

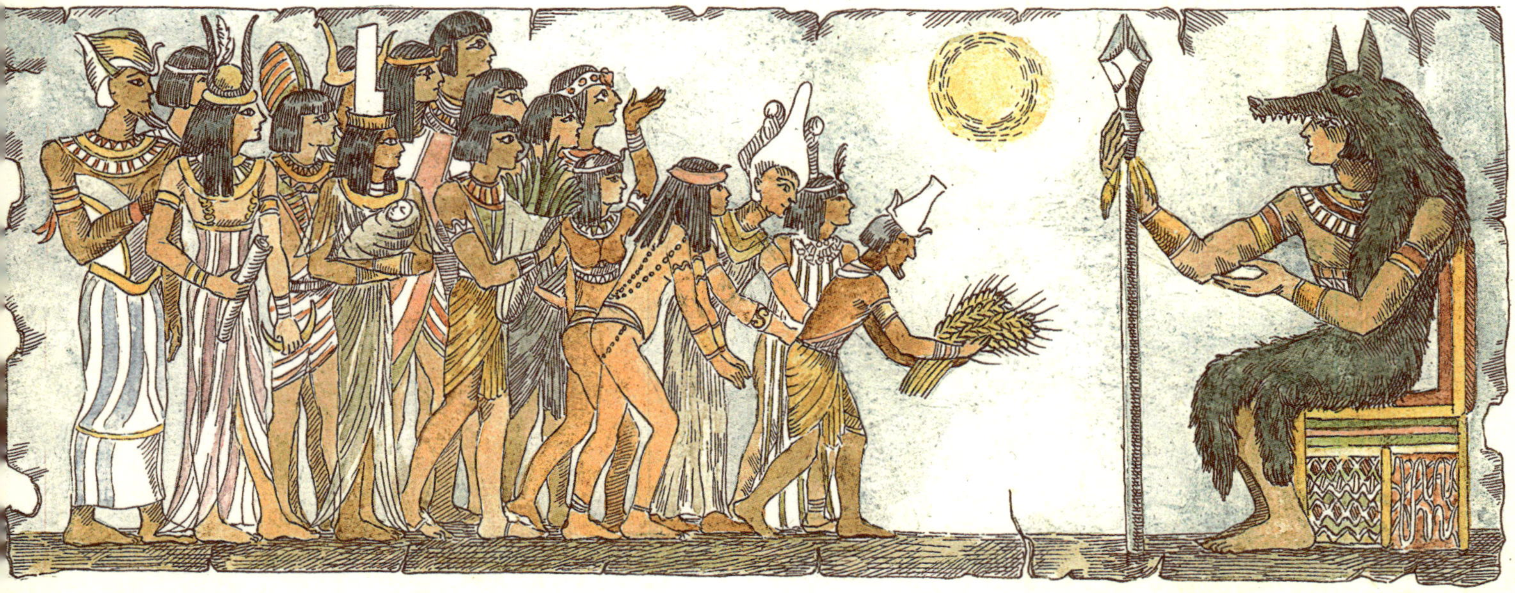

CHANNELING AGGRESSION

By nature, sentient creatures are aggressive creatures. From an evolutionary standpoint, this trait was necessary to ensure survival: satisfying needs, defending borders, dominating other species and conquering new territories. If you want to create a highly-developed and sustainable civilization, you need to learn how to channel this aggressive energy.

One good tool for sublimating aggression is football. This team sport allows you to assert your superiority over your enemies not by shedding blood but by scoring goals. Instead of immediately waging war on a neighboring village or city, you can first sort out your differences and relieve tension with a quick game before sitting down at the negotiation table with a cooler head.

To play a football match, you will need a leather ball, two goalposts with nets, a mowed field or a city square and two opposing teams. The simplest version of the game is to send any number of players onto the field and establish just one rule: "Don't kill anyone." In this case, the main goal of relieving tension will be achieved, but the game itself will be little more than a giant brawl.

If you want the game to be entertaining for outside observers, you need to come up with a strict set of rules. The players will have less freedom — for example, they may be prohibited from touching the ball with their hands — but the game will become more exciting to watch.

You must decide how many players can be on the field at one time and which actions are legal and which are not, such as tripping an opponent, and then provide penalties in the event these rules are violated. It's worth considering the procedure for determining the winner if the teams are tied when the timer runs out; otherwise, the game may end in a scuffle. A referee will monitor to make sure everyone is playing by the rules.

Assign each player the role of defender, attacker or goalkeeper. Each role comes with a special strategy and particular patterns of behavior. Because of this, the scene unfolding on the field is almost like a theatrical drama, and crowds of spectators will flock to the stadiums to watch.

As they watch their team try to score goals against the opponent, the fans go through a rollercoaster of emotions: joy, anger, sorrow. Thanks to the human capacity for empathy, this joint pastime strengthens bonds between people, bringing even complete strangers closer together. They feel unity and involvement in a common cause, as if they, along with the football players, are defending their city from the invaders.

Football can also be used to maintain morale and discipline in the military and as a freetime activity for youth.

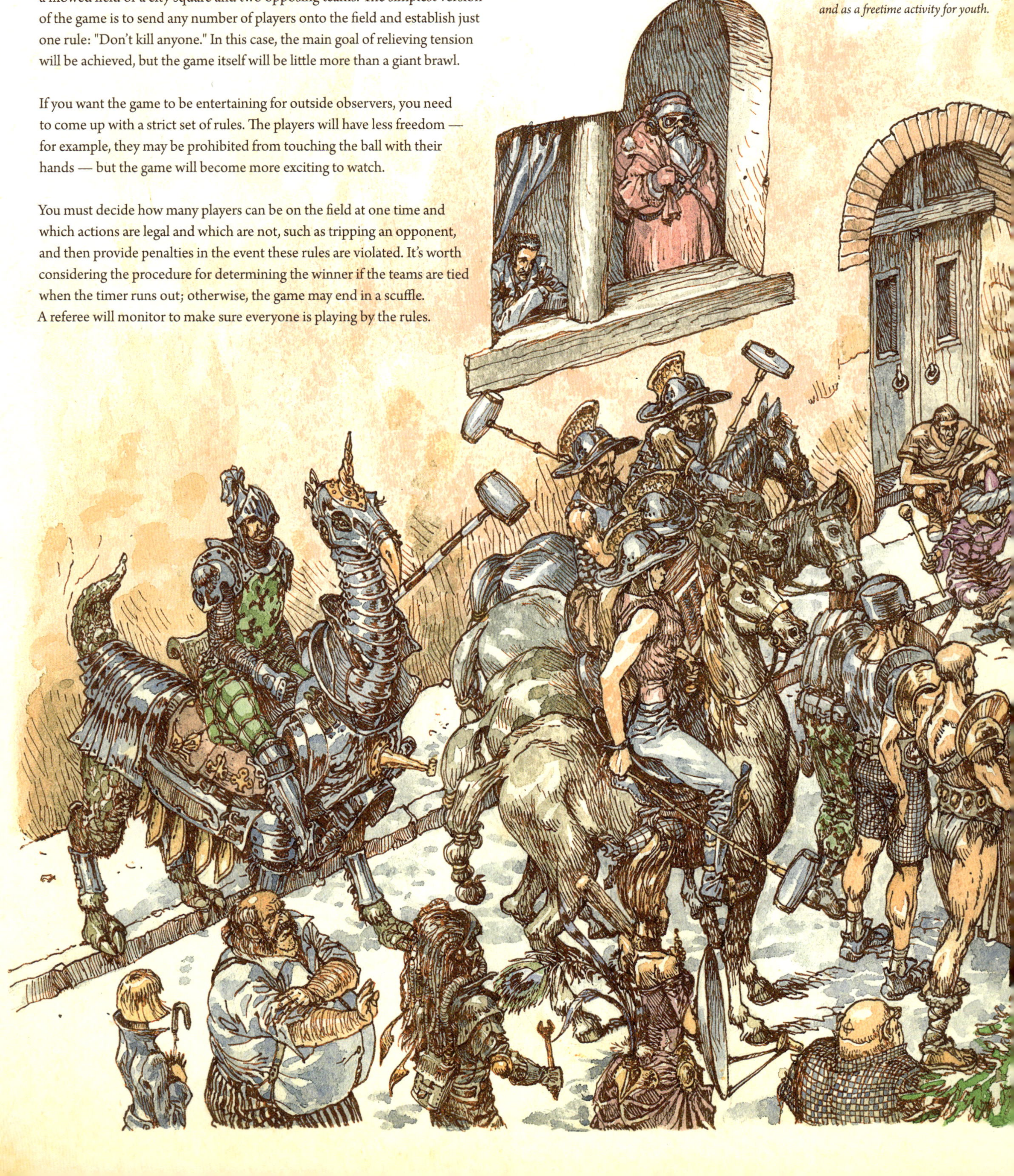

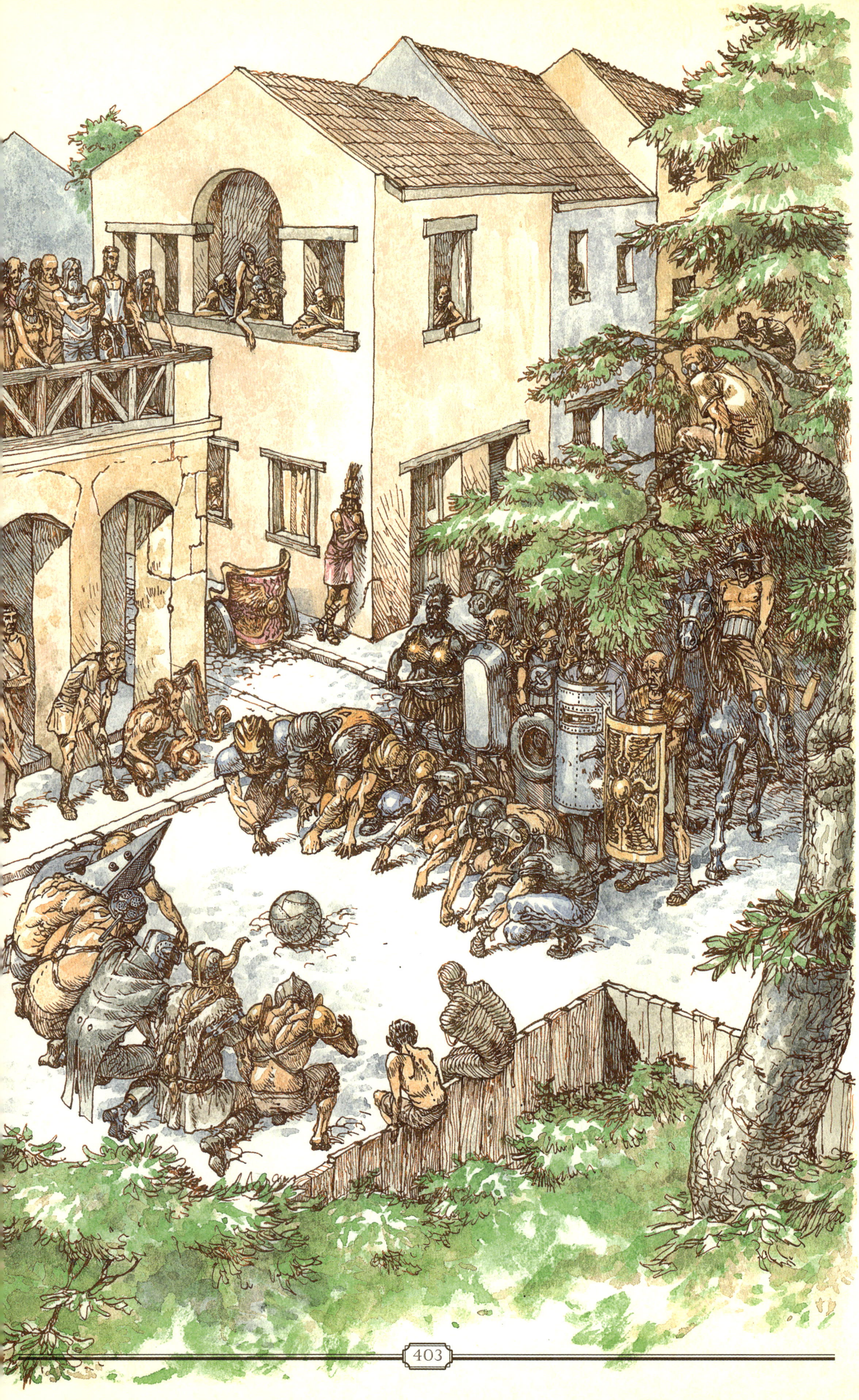

STORYTELLING

Humans have the unique ability to think in abstract terms. They create and believe in constructs that exist exclusively in their imaginations — money, gods, human rights, laws, social hierarchies, freedom. These constructs or myths are passed down through generations, forming common social conceptions, which can sometimes be false: for example, that the world they live on is flat.

But the value of these concepts is not in their truth or falsehood but rather in the fact that they help solve the problem of survival by creating a large group of like-minded thinkers. Often, adherence to certain ideas becomes the basis of serious ideological conflicts — even wars. The best instrument for passing down shared beliefs is storytelling. Listeners identify with the characters in the story and live through the twists and turns of the plot with them. At this moment, the shield of critical thinking is down, and the storyteller gains access to the deeper parts of the human psyche.

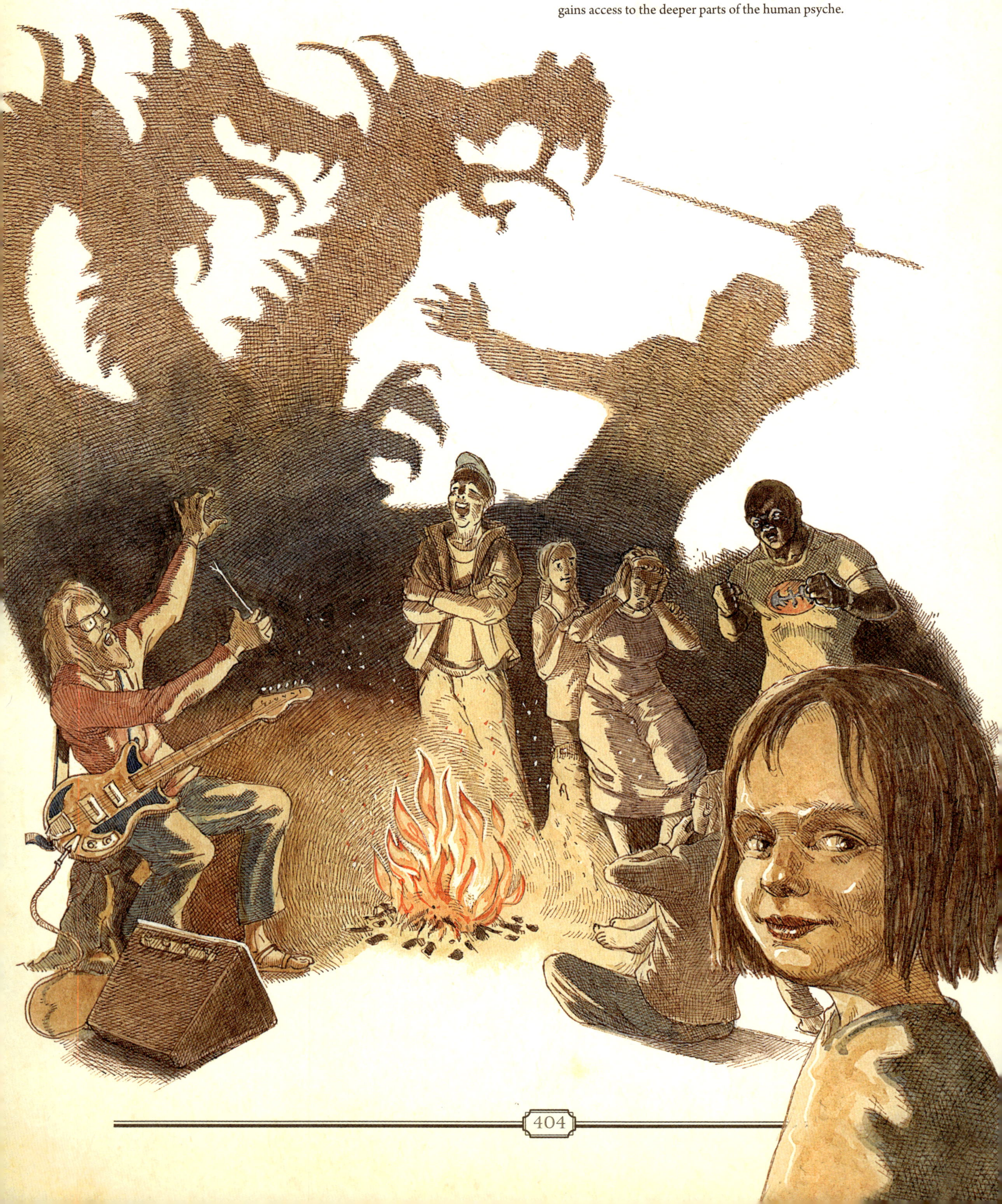

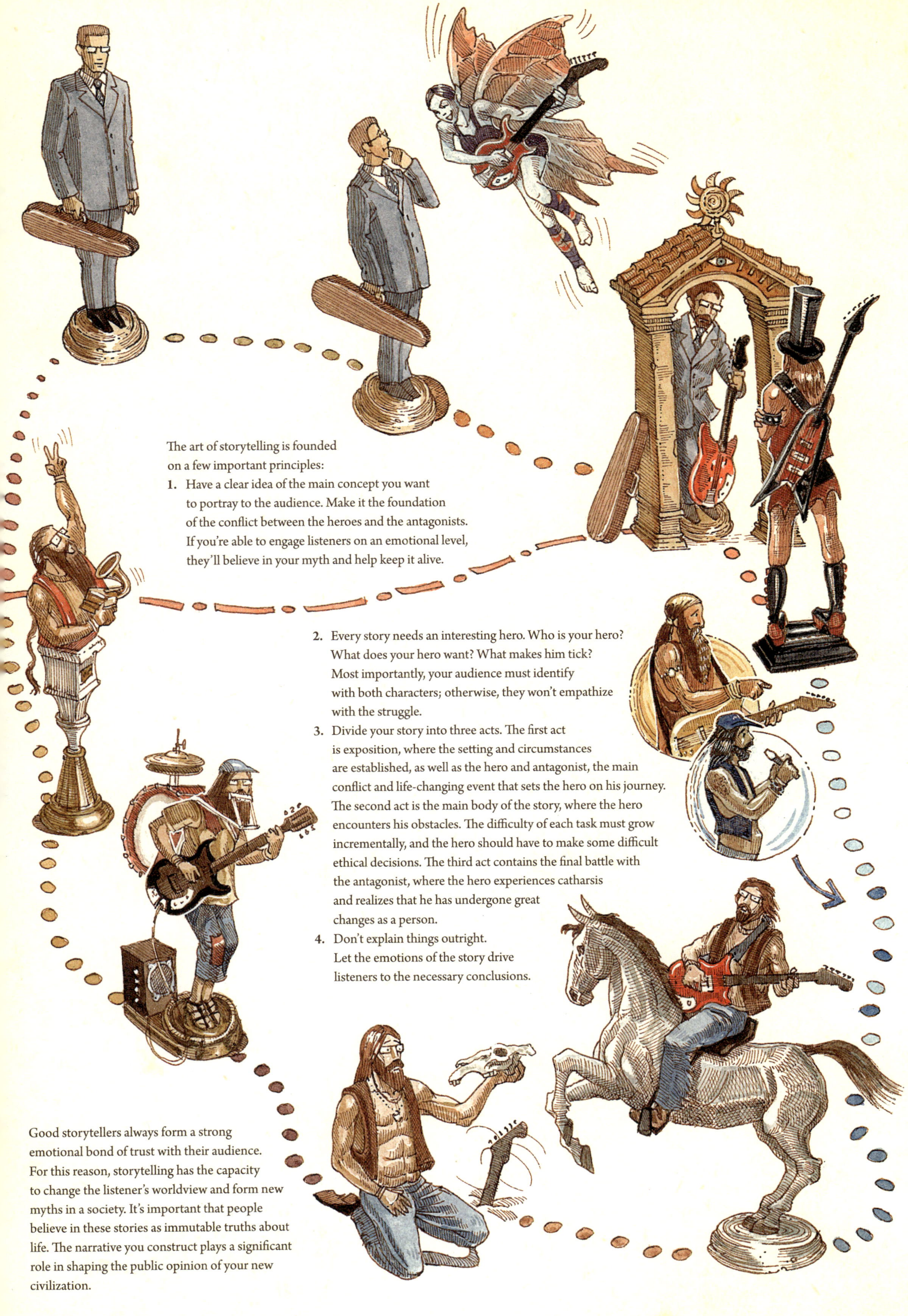

The art of storytelling is founded on a few important principles:

1. Have a clear idea of the main concept you want to portray to the audience. Make it the foundation of the conflict between the heroes and the antagonists. If you're able to engage listeners on an emotional level, they'll believe in your myth and help keep it alive.
2. Every story needs an interesting hero. Who is your hero? What does your hero want? What makes him tick? Most importantly, your audience must identify with both characters; otherwise, they won't empathize with the struggle.
3. Divide your story into three acts. The first act is exposition, where the setting and circumstances are established, as well as the hero and antagonist, the main conflict and life-changing event that sets the hero on his journey. The second act is the main body of the story, where the hero encounters his obstacles. The difficulty of each task must grow incrementally, and the hero should have to make some difficult ethical decisions. The third act contains the final battle with the antagonist, where the hero experiences catharsis and realizes that he has undergone great changes as a person.
4. Don't explain things outright. Let the emotions of the story drive listeners to the necessary conclusions.

Good storytellers always form a strong emotional bond of trust with their audience. For this reason, storytelling has the capacity to change the listener's worldview and form new myths in a society. It's important that people believe in these stories as immutable truths about life. The narrative you construct plays a significant role in shaping the public opinion of your new civilization.

CITIES

If you want your civilization to flourish, build cities. The concentrated population naturally spurs the formation of professional communities: merchants, mercenaries, artisans, artists and so on. This increases labor productivity, allowing you to accumulate more resources and creating a vertical power structure for a more effectively run society. Citizens enjoy a relatively safe life, and thanks to the division of labor, they'll be able to find work, exchange information and goods, enjoy an active social life and keep up-to-date on the latest gossip. You must also determine what your city will specialize in — this will give you a competitive advantage and determine the direction of development. If you lack points of attraction, residents will start to leave, and soon your city will look more like a ghost town.

Sacred spaces are a magnet for new residents. In some places, they are religious buildings, and in others, temples of science or art. Everyone needs entertainment, regardless of your civilization's stage of development and location in the universe, so open theaters and galleries and support the development of the creative intelligentsia. Promote scientific advancement by building universities. In turn, this will lead to economic growth and the overall advancement of society. Ultimately, the interaction among large, successful cities will lead to the creation of states.

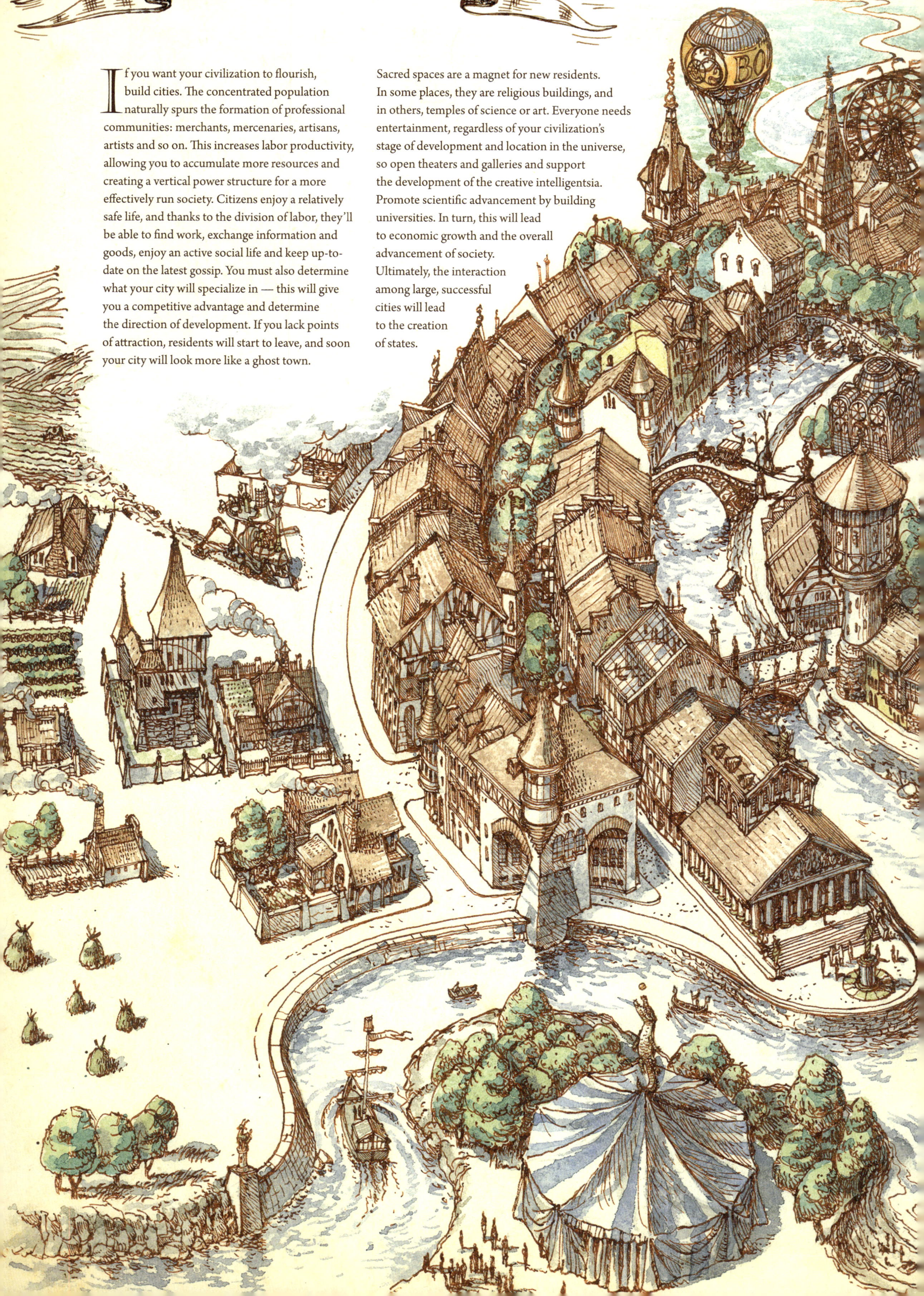

Location is key. As a rule, successful cities usually crop up at intersection points of trade routes or around agricultural hubs. It's good if you have some natural barriers nearby, such as mountains or rivers, that can act as extra protection. Remember that the city is a living and constantly changing organism. All of its systems, sewers and roads, need to be designed with potential population growth in mind.

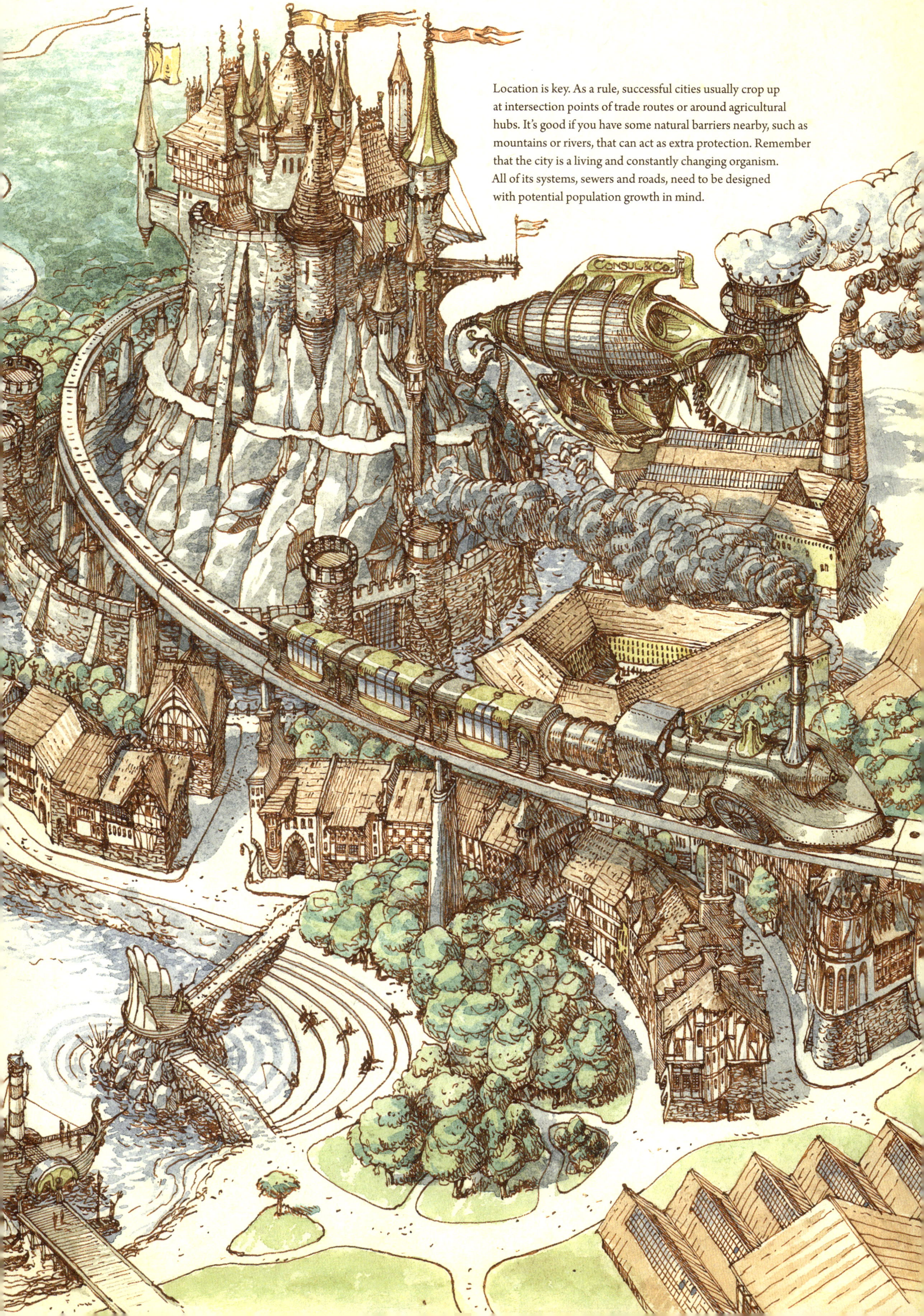

FESTIVALS

For humans, taking breaks from the daily routine and the fight for survival is vital. Otherwise, they are unable to create. Negative thoughts start to accumulate in their minds, they become more prone to conformism and society enters a period of stagnation. Festivals and carnivals help relieve the tension and reboot the creative mind.

Festival culture is a living contradiction to the hierarchies, dogmas and norms meant as societal safeguards. These kinds of celebrations bestow a sense of freedom, allowing people to leave their duties and responsibilities behind for a while and immerse themselves in the festive atmosphere, becoming truly spontaneous and authentic.

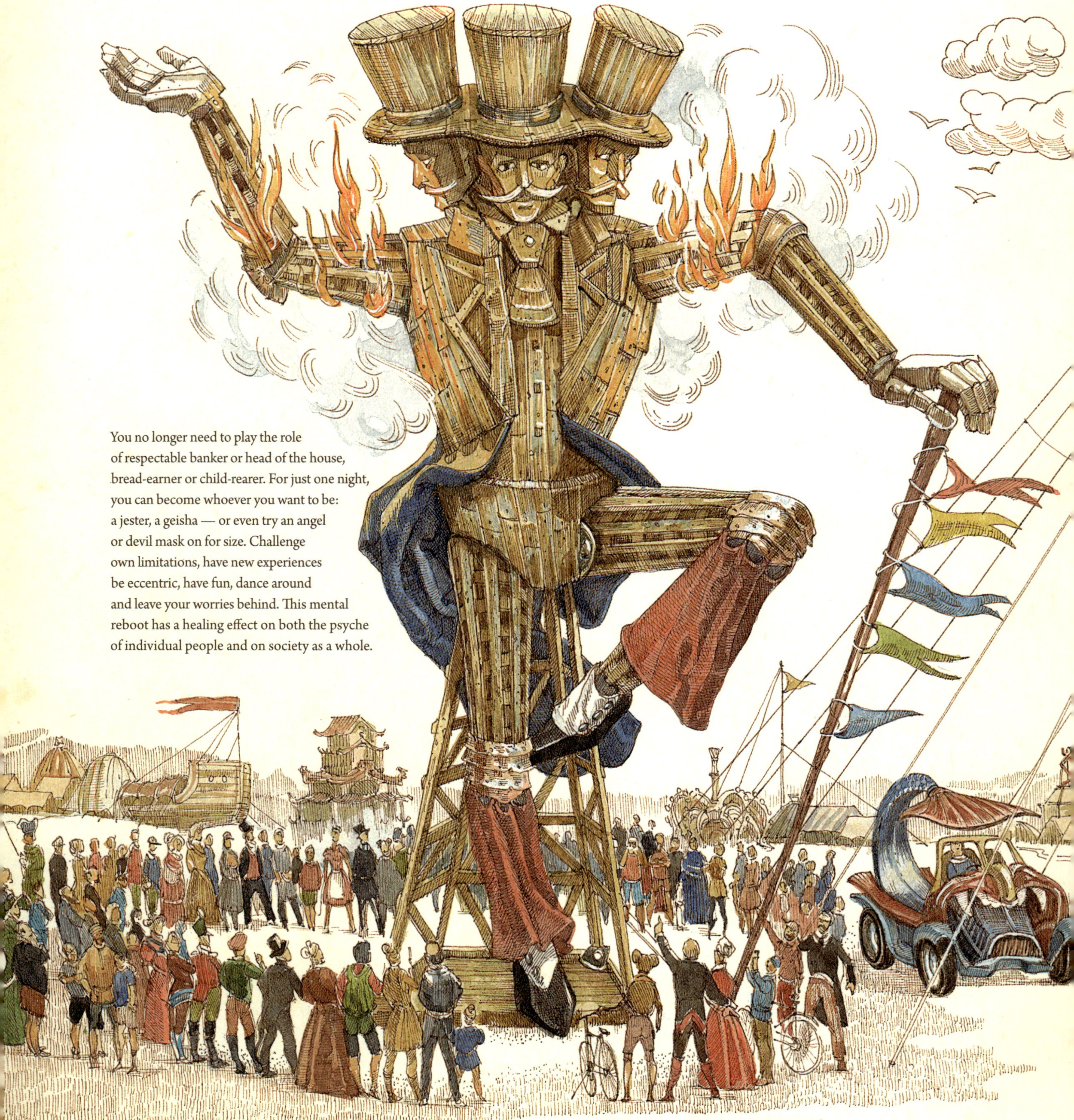

You no longer need to play the role of respectable banker or head of the house, bread-earner or child-rearer. For just one night, you can become whoever you want to be: a jester, a geisha — or even try an angel or devil mask on for size. Challenge own limitations, have new experiences be eccentric, have fun, dance around and leave your worries behind. This mental reboot has a healing effect on both the psyche of individual people and on society as a whole.

Experiencing joy and happiness together strengthens social bonds. People begin to synchronize with each other, creating a powerful environment for manifesting creative energies.

HOW TO ORGANIZE A FESTIVAL

The best site for a festival is one that is extraordinary in some way or made extraordinary through decorations, art pieces and lighting. This will give the guests the impression that they've been transported to some wondrous world governed by an entirely different set of laws, making it easier to cast off their normal social roles, discard their inhibitions, tune into a new wavelength and open themselves up to new experiences.

It's important to organize the decor and events around a central theme, which is best expressed through some sort of symbol endowed with sacred meaning. This will create a unifying conceptual focal point, bringing the participants in the festival even closer together. Come up with a mission statement for your new community. In this way, your festival can be transformed from a mere celebration to a social experiment. For example, you can ban the use of money so that all exchanges will be made on the basis of giving and gratitude.

People are what make festivals. Therefore, you should form a community of like-minded people who will collaborate to build decorations and equip the space — working together always brings people closer. However, do not rush to expand your audience, or the event may lose its unique spirit.

May your festival be a source of creative inspiration for people. May it lead to the development of visionary ideas and the creation of a happier, more sustainable society. Perhaps this way, your descendants won't have to build a new civilization from the ruins of the last one.

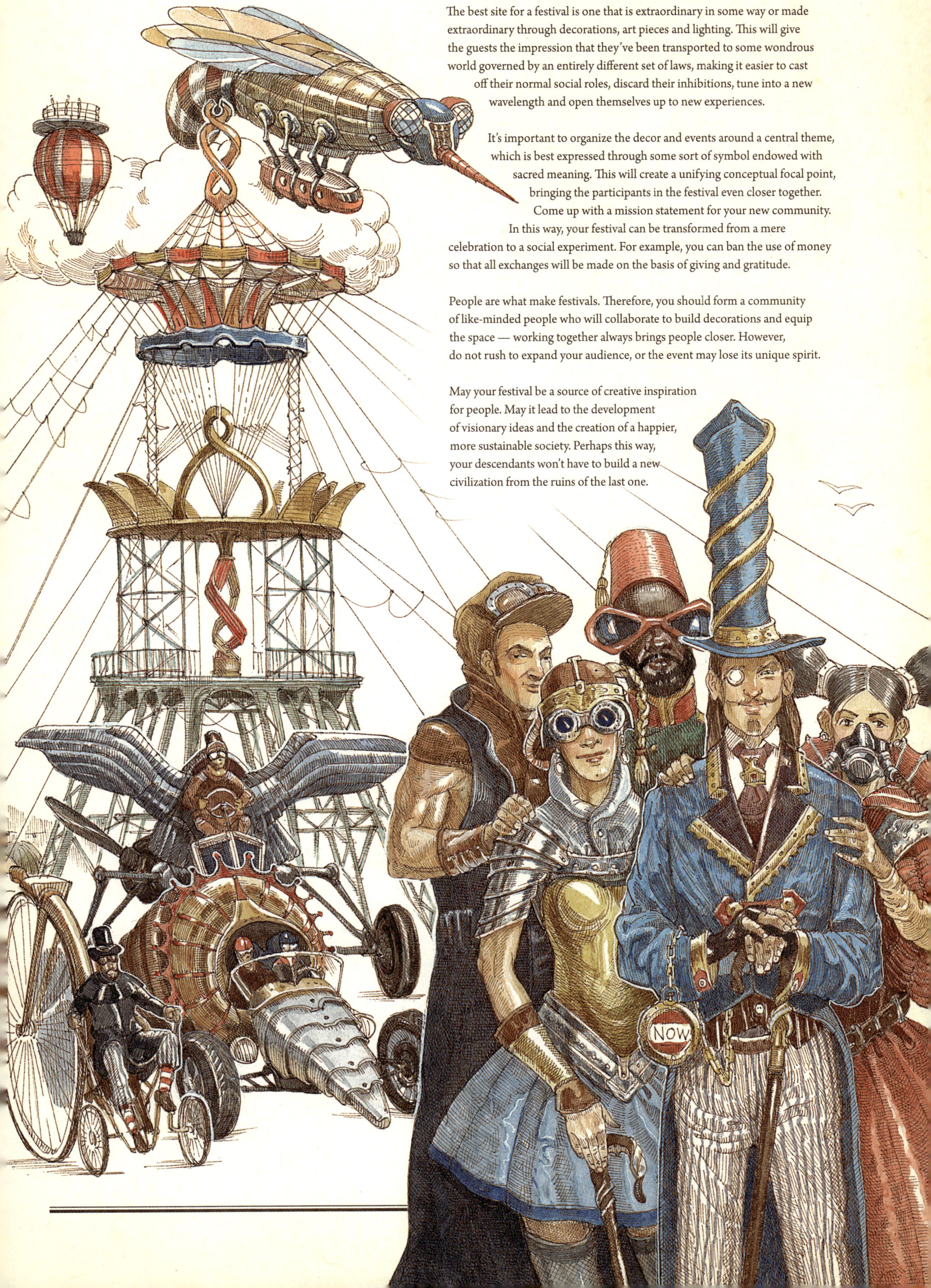